Legal Research, Analysis, and Writing

Kathryn L. Myers

Saint Mary-of-the-Woods College

PEARSON

Boston   Columbus   Indianapolis   New York   San Francisco   Upper Saddle River
Amsterdam   Cape Town   Dubai   London   Madrid   Milan   Munich   Paris   Montréal   Toronto
Delhi   Mexico City   São Paulo   Sydney   Hong Kong   Seoul   Singapore   Taipei   Tokyo

Editorial Director: Vernon R. Anthony
Executive Editor: Gary Bauer
Editorial Project Manager: Linda Cupp
Editorial Assistant: Tanika Henderson
Director of Marketing: David Gessell
Senior Marketing Manager: Mary Salzman
Senior Marketing Coordinator: Alicia Wozniak
Marketing Assistant: Les Roberts
Senior Managing Editor: JoEllen Gohr
Senior Project Manager: Steve Robb

Creative Director: Jayne Conte
Cover Designer: Suzanne Behnke
Cover Image: © Kim Karpeles / Alamy
Media Project Manager: April Cleland
Full Service Project Management: Nancy Kincade,
    PreMediaGlobal USA, Inc.
Composition: PreMediaGlobal USA, Inc.
Printer/Binder: Edwards Brothers Malloy State Street
Cover Printer: Lehigh-Phoenix Color/Hagerstown
Text Font: Minion Pro 11/13

Credits and acknowledgments for material borrowed from other sources and reproduced, with permission, in this textbook appear on the appropriate page within the text.

Copyright © 2014 by Pearson Education, Inc. All rights reserved. Manufactured in the United States of America. This publication is protected by Copyright, and permission should be obtained from the publisher prior to any prohibited reproduction, storage in a retrieval system, or transmission in any form or by any means, electronic, mechanical, photocopying, recording, or likewise. To obtain permission(s) to use material from this work, please submit a written request to Pearson Education, Inc., Permissions Department, One Lake Street, Upper Saddle River, New Jersey 07458, or you may fax your request to 201-236-3290.

Many of the designations by manufacturers and sellers to distinguish their products are claimed as trademarks. Where those designations appear in this book, and the publisher was aware of a trademark claim, the designations have been printed in initial caps or all caps.

Library of Congress Cataloging-in-Publication Data
Myers, Kathryn L.
  Legal research, analysis, and writing / Kathryn L. Myers.
    pages cm
  ISBN 978-0-13-507713-9 (pbk.)
  1. Legal research—United States.   2. Legal composition.   3. Legal assistants—United States—Handbooks, manuals, etc. I. Title.
  KF240.M945 2014
  340.042'073—dc23
                                                              2013014756

10 9 8 7 6 5 4 3 2 1

ISBN 10:   0-13-507713-3
ISBN 13: 978-0-13-507713-9

Brief Contents

Preface xvii

CHAPTER 1 Introduction to Legal Research 1

CHAPTER 2 The Structure of Government and the Court System 24

CHAPTER 3 Understanding the Origins and Organization of the Law 47

CHAPTER 4 Types of Law 81

CHAPTER 5 Legal Citation Form 110

CHAPTER 6 Citing Sources: *The Bluebook* and *ALWD* 131

CHAPTER 7 Tools for Manual and Online Research 162

CHAPTER 8 Main Secondary Authorities 194

CHAPTER 9 Finding Aids, Drafting Aids, and Miscellaneous Secondary Authorities 236

CHAPTER 10 Researching Enacted Law and Related Materials 269

CHAPTER 11 Researching the Common Law (Case Law) 313

CHAPTER 12 The Administrative Agencies and Special Laws 349

CHAPTER 13 Updating and Validating Research 393

CHAPTER 14 The Foundation of Writing 443

CHAPTER 15 The Case Brief 479

CHAPTER 16 Writing an Internal Memorandum of Law 511

CHAPTER 17 Writing External Briefs 537

CHAPTER 18 Correspondence 574

CHAPTER 19 Drafting Pleadings and Other Litigation Documents 606

Appendix I Form Documents, Briefs, Memoranda 636
Appendix II Non Legal Citations 667
Appendix III Internet Sources 673
Glossary 685
Index 701

Contents

Preface   xvii

CHAPTER 1   Introduction to Legal Research   1

Introduction to Research   2
The Role of Legal Research in General   2
The Role of the Paralegal in Research   3
The Terminology of Legal Research   5
Introduction to Legal Publications   5

  Primary Law   5
  Secondary Law   6
  Citations   7

Law Library Options   10

  Physical Libraries   10
  Online Libraries   11

Performing Legal Research   13

  Federalism and the Supremacy Clause   14
  Primary Sources: Constitution   15
  Primary Sources: Statutes   15
  Primary Sources: Case Law   15
  Primary Sources: Administrative   16
  Research Results: Putting It in Writing   17

Ethics in Legal Research   18

  Unauthorized Practice of Law   18
  Confidentiality   18
  Ethical Dilemmas   19

The Joys and Sorrows of Legal Research   20

Summary   20 • Review Questions   20 • Application Exercises   20
Citation Exercises   21 • Quick Check   21 • Research   22 • Internet Research   22
Media Resources   23 • Internet Resources   23

CHAPTER 2   The Structure of Government and the Court System   24

Levels and Branches of American Government   25

  Federal Government   25

    Federalism and the Supremacy Clause   25 • Separation of Powers   26
    The Executive Branch   26 • Legislative Branch   26 • Judicial Branch   27
    Administrative Agencies   28

  State Governments   28

    Executive Branch   28 • Legislative Branch   28 • Judicial Branch   28
    Administrative Branch   29

The Hierarchy of the Courts   29

  Federal   29

    United States District Courts   30 • United States Courts of Appeals   31
    United States Supreme Court   32 • Specialized Courts   34

State Courts   35 • Trial Courts   35 • Intermediate Courts of Appeal   39
Highest Court   40

Jurisdiction   40

Venue   43

Summary   43 • Review Questions   43 • Citation Exercises   44 • Quick Check   44
Multiple Choice   44 • Research   45 • Internet Research   45
Media Resources   45 • Internet Resources   46

CHAPTER 3   Understanding the Origins and Organization of the Law   47

Categories of the Law   48

Case Law   48

The Origins of the Common Law System   48 • Equitable Law   50
Judicial Remedies   51

Enacted Law   59

Constitutions   59 • Statutes   60

Hierarchy of Law   64

Federal Law   64

U.S. Constitution   64 • Statutes   64 • Common Law   66
Administrative Regulations   67 • Administrative Decisions   72

State and Local Law   72

State Constitutions   72 • Statutes   73 • Common Law   74
Administrative Regulations   74 • Administrative Decisions   74
Charters   75 • Ordinances   77

Summary   78 • Review Questions   78 • Application Exercises   78
Citation Exercises   79 • Quick Check   79 • Research   79 • Internet Research   79
Media Resources   80 • Internet Resources   80

CHAPTER 4   Types of Law   81

Ten Types of Law   82

Constitutions   83

Statutes   84

Cases   86

Federal   86 • State   87

Administrative Regulations   88

Administrative Decisions   91

Rules of Court   91

Charters   92

Ordinances   92

Executive Orders   93

Treaties   93

Case Analysis and the Research Process   93

Case Analysis   93

The Research Process   96

Primary Authority   97

Secondary Authority   100

Mandatory Authority   101

Mandatory Enacted Law   101

Mandatory Common Law   102

    Lower Court Decisions   102 • Higher Court Decisions   102 • Precedent   102
    Diversity Cases   103 • Courts in Other States   104

Persuasive Authority   104

  Persuasive Common Law   104

Summary   107 • Review Questions   107 • Application Exercises   108
Citation Exercises   108 • Quick Check   108 • Research   109
Internet Research   109 • Media Resources   109 • Internet Resources   109

CHAPTER 5   Legal Citation Form   110

Citations   111

Legal Citation Manuals   111

    The Bluebook   112 • *The Divisions of* The Bluebook   113
    The Bluebook Online   114

  ALWD   115

    Differences between *The Bluebook* and *ALWD*   115

When to Cite   116

Placement of Citations   117

Quotations   119

  Altering Quotations   120

String Citations   121

    Order of Citations in a String   122 • Signals in Citations   123

Non-Legal Citation Formats   124

  MLA   125

  APA   126

Ethics in Writing   128

Summary   128 • Review Questions   128 • Application Exercises   129
Citation Exercises   129 • Quick Check   129 • Research   129
Internet Research   130 • Media Resources   130 • Internet Resources   130

CHAPTER 6   Citing Sources: *The Bluebook* and *ALWD*   131

The Bluebook and *ALWD*   132

Using *The Bluebook* and *ALWD*–Typeface Issues   132

Using *The Bluebook* and *ALWD*–Primary Authorities   132

  Cases in General   133

    Names of Parties   133

  Reporters   137

    Pinpoint Citations: Court and Jurisdiction   138

  Federal Courts   138

  State Courts   139

  Cases on the Internet   140

Short Citation Forms   141

  Short Forms for Cases   141

  Constitutions   142

  Statutes and Legislative Materials   143

    Formatting   144

Title of the Code   144

Sections and Subsections   145

Publisher, Supplements, and Date   146

Multiple Sections and Subsections   146

Session Laws   147 • Statutes on the Internet   148
Short Forms for Statutes   148

Rules   149

Federal Rules   149 • State and Local Rules   150
Administrative Materials   150

Using *The Bluebook* and *ALWD* with Secondary Authorities   151

Encyclopedias   151

Treatises and Books   152

Annotations   154

Restatements   154

Periodicals   155

Legal Dictionaries   156

Attorney General Opinions   157

Looseleaf Services   157

Secondary Authorities on the Internet   158

Summary   159 • Review Questions   159 • Application Exercises   159
Citation Exercises   160 • Quick Check   160 • Research   160
Internet Research   161 • Media Resources   161 • Internet Resources   161

CHAPTER 7   Tools for Manual and Online Research   162

Ethics in Research   163

Unauthorized Practice of Law   163

Confidentiality   164

Candor   165

The Tools of Research   166

The Library   166

Organization   166 • Permanence   166 • Assistance   167
Quality or Quantity   167

The Internet   167

Using the Internet   169 • Organization   169 • Permanence   169
Quantity or Quality   169

The Library and the Internet   169

Manual Research   170 • Updating the Research   172

Internet Research   172

Non-subscription   172

General Tips on Using Search Engines   174 • Other Methods of Searching
for Non-Subscription Materials   174 • Weighing the Material   175

Subscription Services   179

Westlaw   179 • LexisNexis®   182

The Research Process   186

What Needs to Be Found?   186

How Much is Known about the Problem Being Researched?   186

How In-depth Should the Research Be?   186

Do the Findings Need to Be Updated?   187

What Is The Final Product to Be Produced?   187

Analyze the Client's Facts   187 • Recognize the Law   187
Find the Law   188 • Make a Research Trail   188 • Update the Search   189
Report the Research and Comment on the Adversary's Position   189
Other Services   189

Summary   190 • Review Questions   190 • Application Exercises   191
Quick Check   191 • Research   192 • Media Resources   192
Internet Resources   192

CHAPTER 8   Main Secondary Authorities   194

Understanding Secondary Authority   194

Encyclopedias   199

General or National Encyclopedias   199

Corpus Juris Secundum (C.J.S.)   200
American Jurisprudence 2d (Am. Jur. 2d)   200
Specialized Encyclopedias   203

State Encyclopedias   204

Researching with Legal Encyclopedias   204

Annotations   209

Researching in A.L.R.s   213

Restatements   216

Researching in Restatements   217

Treatises, *Hornbooks*, and Books   221

Researching in Treatises   223

Periodicals: Law Reviews, Law Journals, and Other Periodicals   224

Law Reviews and Law Journals   225

Bar Associations and Paralegal Associations   227
Special Interest Publications   228 • Legal Newspapers and Newsletters   228

Researching in Periodicals   228

Ethical Considerations when Using Secondary Sources   231

Summary   231 • Review Questions   231 • Application Exercises   232
Citation Exercises   233 • Quick Check   233 • Research   234
Internet Research   235 • Media Resources   235 • Internet Resources   235

CHAPTER 9   Finding Aids, Drafting Tools, and Miscellaneous Secondary
Authorities   236

Digests   237

The History of Digests   237

American Digest System   237 • Specialized Digests   240

Researching in Digests   240

Words and Phrases   245

Background   245

Researching in *Words and Phrases*   245

Attorney General Opinions 246
    Background 246
    Researching with AG Opinions 248
Looseleaf Services 249
    Foundation of Looseleaf Services 249
    Researching in Looseleaf Services 253
Jury Instructions 253
    Basics of Jury Instructions 253
    Researching with Jury Instructions 256
Form Books 256
    Background 256
    Researching with Form Books 258
Legal Dictionaries and Thesauri 260
    The Value of Dictionaries and Thesauri 260
    Researching with Dictionaries and Thesauri 261
Directories 262
    The Use of Directories 262
    Researching in Directories 263
        Statement of Practice Summary 264
Summary 265 • Review Questions 265 • Application Exercises 265
Citation Exercises 266 • Quick Check 266 • Research 267
Internet Research 267 • Media Resources 268 • Internet Resources 268

CHAPTER 10 Researching Enacted Law and Related Materials 269

What is Enacted Law? 270
Constitutions 271
    The U.S. Constitution 271
    State Constitutions 273
    Researching Constitutional Law 273
Statutes 276
    The Making of Statutes 276
    Federal Statutes 276
    State Statutes 280
    The Elements of Statutes 281
    Uniform Laws 282
    Researching Statutes 286
Legislative History 291
    Foundational Principles for Using Legislative History 291
    Researching Legislative History 294
Municipal Law 301
    Charters 301
    Ordinances 303
    Researching in Municipal Law 303
Rules of Procedure and Court Rules 304
    Federal Rules 304
    State Rules 305
    Researching Rules of Court 306

Summary   307 • Review Questions   307 • Application Exercises   308
Citation Exercises   308 • Quick Check   309 • Research   309
Internet Research   310 • Media Resources   310 • Internet Resources   311

CHAPTER 11   Researching the Common Law (Case Law)   313

The Foundation of the Common Law   314

General Information   314

Court Opinions   314

Finding Case Law   317

Federal Reporters   317

United States Supreme Court   318 • United States Courts of Appeals   323
United States District Courts   326 • Federal Rules   327
Other Federal Materials   327 • Researching Federal Case Law   327
The National Reporter System   328 • Digests   329
Internet and Fee-Based Services   329

State Materials   331

Finding Parallel Cites   332 • Regional Reporters   333 • Digests   333

Parts of a Case   335

Parties or Case Name   339

Party v. Party   339
State v. Party or United States v. Party or Commonwealth v. Party   340
In re Party   340 • Ex rel. Party (Ex rel. Bonner).   341
Ex parte Party Name (Ex parte Franklin).   341

Docket Number   342

Date of Decision   342

Syllabus or Synopsis (Summary)   342

Topic and Key Number   342

Headnote   342

Attorneys of Record   343

Writing Judge   343

Opinion   343

Majority   344 • *Per curiam*   344 • Concurring   344 • Dissenting   344
Plurality   344 • Memorandum   344 • In-chambers   344 • En banc   344

Decision   345

Other Judges/Justices   345

Concurring and Dissenting Opinions   345

Summary   345 • Review Questions   345 • Application Exercises   346
Quick Check   346 • Research   347 • Internet Research   347
Media Resources   347 • Internet Resources   347

CHAPTER 12   The Administrative Agencies and Special Laws   349

Administrative Agencies   349

General Information   349

Making Federal Administrative Law   354

Publishing Federal Administrative Law   355

Federal Register   355 • Code of Federal Regulations   359

Administrative Decisions   360
  Researching Federal Administrative Law   362
    Regulations   362
  Indexes and Tables of Contents   363
GPO Access   363
  Computer-Assisted Legal Research   364
    Administrative Decisions   365
  State and Local Administrative Agencies   369
    State Administrative Agencies   371
Executive Materials   374
  Executive Orders   377
  State Executive Orders   379
Proclamations   379
Presidential Memoranda   382
International Law   383
  Overview   383
  Researching International Law   384
Summary   390 · Review Questions   390 · Citation Exercises   390
Quick Check   390 · Research   391 · Internet Research   391
Media Resources   392

CHAPTER 13   Updating and Validating Research   393
Validating Research and the Appeals Process   394
  Ethics and Validating Research   395
  Basics of the Validation Process   395
  Shepard's Citators   397
  The History of *Shepard's*   398
  Validating Cases with *Shepard's*   398
  Validating Statutes with *Shepard's*   400
  Validation Using the State Editions of *Shepard's*   400
Closer Look at Sheparding Cases and Enacted Law in the Print Version   402
  Sheparding Cases in the Print Version   402
  Enacted Law in Print Version of *Shepard's*   407
  Sheparding in the Topical Citators in Print   410
Validating Cases and Enacted Law Using Electronic Services   411
  Shepard's Online   411
  Auto-Cite   413
  Lexcite   413
A Closer Look at the Process of Validating Research with *Shepard's*   414
  The Process of Validating Cases in the Print Version of *Shepard's*   414
  The Process of Validating Enacted Law in the Print Version of *Shepard's*   414
  The Process of Sheparding Research Electronically   415
    Shepard's Online—Cases   415 · *Shepard's* Online—Enacted Law   418

Westlaw and KeyCite 419
  Overview of KeyCite 419
  KeyCiting Cases 419
  KeyCiting Statutes 425
  Other West Products 430
  Demonstration Using KeyCite to Perform Research 431
Comparison between *Shepard's* and KeyCite 434
Other Citator Services 434
Summary 440 • Review Questions 441 • Application Exercises 441
Quick Check 441 • Internet Research 442 • Media Resources 442
Internet Resources 442

CHAPTER 14 The Foundation of Writing 443

General Overview of Legal Writing 444
Writing Basics 444
The Writing Process 445
  The Prewriting Stage 446
    Understanding the Assignment 446 • Organization 447
    Placement of Information 448
  The Drafting Phase 449
    Tone 449 • Voice 449 • Using Legal Language and Vocabulary 449
    Using Headings 450 • Writing Paragraphs 450
Grammar 452
  The Parts of Sentences 452
  Subject–Verb Agreement 453
    Compound Subject 454 • Indefinite Pronouns 454
    Collective Nouns 454 • Additional Problems 454
  Noun-Pronoun Agreement 455
    Personal Pronouns 455 • Reflexive Pronouns 456 • Relative Pronouns 456
    Gender Pronouns 457
  Verb Tense 457
  Modifiers 458
    Adverbs 458 • Other Common Modifier Problems 458
Punctuation 459
  The Period 459
  Commas 460
  Semicolons 462
  Colons 463
  Apostrophes 464
  Ellipses 465
  Question Marks 465
  Quotation Marks 465
  Parentheses 467
  Brackets 467
Word Usage 468
Wordiness 469

The Editing and Proofreading Stage   470
    Editing   470
    Using a Spell Checker   471
    Proofreading   472
Writing in Other Forms of Communication   474
    Telephones and Voicemail   474
    Email   474
    Faxes   475
    Text Messaging   475
Summary   476 • Review Questions   476 • Application Exercises   476
Internet Research   478 • Media Resources   478 • Internet Resources   478

CHAPTER 15   The Case Brief   479
The Case Brief Process   480
The 11-Part Brief   480
    Citation or Caption   485
        Parties   485
    Objectives and Theories of the Parties   486
    Procedural History   487
    Facts   489
    Issues   490
    Holding   494
    Reasoning   495
    Disposition   497
    Commentary   498
    Updating   499
IRAC   499
    Issue Section   500
    Rule Section   500
    Application Section   501
    Conclusion Section   502
IFRAC (also called FIRAC)   503
CRRACC   505
Ethical Considerations When Preparing Case Briefs   507
Summary   507 • Review Questions   507 • Application Exercises   508
Citation Exercises   509 • Quick Check   509 • Research   509
Media Resources   510 • Internet Resources   510

CHAPTER 16   Writing an Internal Memorandum of Law   511
The Purpose of the Internal Memorandum   512
Preparing to Write the Internal Memorandum   513
    Understand the Assignment   513
    Note Any Constraints on the Assignment   513
Outlining   514

Drafting the Memorandum   516

    Heading   517

    Issues   517

    Facts   520

    Analysis   521

    Conclusion   529

    Recommendations   530

    The Complex Internal Memorandum   531

    Table of Contents   531

    Table of Authorities   532

    Summary of Issues and Conclusions   533

    Appendix   533

Proofreading and Editing   533

Summary   533 • Review Questions   533 • Application Exercises   534
Citation Exercises   534 • Quick Check   534 • Research   535
Internet Research   535 • Media Resources   536 • Internet Resources   536

CHAPTER 17   Writing External Briefs   537

Advocacy Documents in General   538

    Case Caption   538

    Table of Contents   539

    Table of Authorities   541

    Introduction or Preliminary Statement   543

    Statement of Facts   544

    Statement of Issues or Questions Presented   547

    Summary of the Argument   549

    Argument   549

    Conclusion   551

    Signature and Date   552

    Certificate of Service   553

    The Appendix: Exhibits   554

    Rules of Court   554

Trial Briefs   554

Appellate Briefs   556

    Components of an Appellate Brief   563

        Jurisdiction Statement   564

    Word Count Certificate   565

    Amicus Curiae Briefs   566

Writing Effective Briefs   567

Oral Argument   568

Converting an Internal Memorandum of Law into an Appellate Brief   569

Ethical Considerations When Preparing Court Documents   570

Summary   570 • Review Questions   570 • Application Exercises   571
Citation Exercises   571 • Quick Check   571 • Research   572
Internet Research   572 • Media Resources   573 • Internet Resources   573

CHAPTER 18   Correspondence   574

General Features of Legal Correspondence   575

Formatting Legal Correspondence   575

Ethical Considerations in Correspondence   576

Audience   578

Content   578

Basic Components of Letters   578

Heading   578 • Date   579 • Special Mailing or Delivery Instructions   580
Inside Address   580 • Reference (Subject) Line   581
The Salutation (Greeting)   582 • The Body   582
The Closing   585 • The Signature Block   585
Notations of Enclosures, Initials of Preparer, and Copies Sent   585
Second Page Headings   587

Types of Correspondence   587

Informational Letters   587

Transmittal Letter   587 • Confirming Letters   588
Appointment Letters   589 • Information Letters   589
Invoice Letters or Billing Statements   590

Demand Letter   591

Opening   592 • Fact Statement   592 • Analysis   592
Damages and Injuries   593 • The Settlement Offer or Demand   594
Consequences   594 • Date of Compliance   594

Opinion Letter   594

Statement of the Issue   595 • Fact Statement   596 • Analysis   596
Conclusion   596

Emails and Faxes   599

Emails   599

Faxes   600

Confidentiality   600

Email and Faxing Etiquette   600

Summary   603 • Review Questions   603 • Application Exercises   603
Citation Exercises   603 • Quick Check   604 • Research   604
Media Resources   605 • Internet Resources   605

CHAPTER 19   Drafting Pleadings and Other Litigation Documents   606

Pleadings   607

Formatting Pleadings   608

Complaint   611

Statutes of Limitations   611 • Gathering Facts   612
Elements of the Complaint   613

Responsive Pleadings   618

Amended Pleadings   620

Motions   621

Discovery   624

Depositions   625

Interrogatories   626

Requests for Production and Entry on Land   630

Requests for Admissions 631

Requests for Physical and Mental Examination 632

Authorizations 633

Summary 634 • Review Questions 634 • Application Exercises 634
Quick Check 634 • Research 635 • Internet Resources 635
Media Resources 635 • Internet Resources 635

Appendix I   Form Documents, Briefs, Memoranda 636

Appendix II   Non Legal Citations 667

Appendix III   Internet Resources 673

Glossary 685

Index 701

PREFACE

A good paralegal with excellent legal research and writing skills can be invaluable to attorneys and clients alike. This book was developed to provide students with a guide to the intricacies of legal research and writing. The goal of legal research is to locate pertinent laws that govern the client's situation. It is critical for a researcher to understand how the laws are made, how the lawmaking bodies interact, how to decide which law is applicable at which point, how to read the law, and how to integrate applicable laws with a client's situation. This book emphasizes these items, provides lessons on how to avoid obstacles during the process, and gives extensive examples, exercises, figures, and checklists for reference.

The processes used in legal research change constantly because new sources emerge, some are redefined, and some sources are discontinued. How one does research is also constantly changing. The greatest challenge of writing a legal research and writing book is to write one that remains current so that the users learn how to resolve legal issues in the most efficient way.

While the organization of the text was intentional, the text is organized to allow an instructor to begin with any of the sources examined in the book. There is always a question as to whether a researcher should begin with secondary sources or primary sources, but the research section of the textbook presents secondary sources first. The reasoning behind this choice is that new paralegal students do not have a wealth of background information on subject areas. Therefore, learning to use the secondary sources as background references and starting points for research seems reasonable.

The book provides an overview of the legal system and all of the legal authorities that paralegals need to understand. It covers the structure of the government and the court system, how law is organized, and what will consistently be referred to as the ten types of law.

Next the text provides information on citing legal as well as non-legal sources. *The Bluebook* and *ALWD* are the primary citing tools used. In addition, students will be introduced to both Modern Language Association (MLA) and American Psychological Association (APA) citations.

The research section provides tools for manual and computer-assisted or online legal research, using paid subscription services as well as free online services. Even though this is a computer age, there are many firms and other entities that still rely on printed books for research. With this in mind, the section on manual research is extensive and does come first. Learning to research manually will provide a solid foundation on which students will become much better researchers when using the computer. This section begins with a discussion of the main secondary authorities that researchers use when the problem is not completely understood. From there, discussion focuses on tools such as finding aids, drafting aids, and other available secondary authorities.

The discussion of researching enacted law is followed by a discussion of researching common law (case law). Then the next level in the legal authority hierarchy, administrative agencies, is discussed. The final element in research is updating and validating authority.

The next part focuses on legal writing. Paralegals who write well will have abundant opportunities in their employment areas. By delegating research and writing tasks to the paralegal, the attorney or other supervisor makes the office cost-effective for the client, thereby saving the client money.

Students will be introduced to techniques for writing case briefs, interoffice memoranda of law, external briefs, correspondence, and pleadings. Some of the most important steps in writing case briefs, memoranda, and other legal documents are the identification of legal issues and the organization and presentation of research findings in the written document.

One problem with writing any book that provides electronic sources is that the sources change—often rapidly. That is also true for legal materials, as the major publishing companies constantly improve their products and there is seemingly more information each day from free sources. So, the exhibits in the book illustrate what was found on a particular day, and readers should understand that the author's exhibits may differ somewhat from the source content that readers will see at later times. Another thing to remember is that while the surface features of the sources may change, the underlying structure will not. For example, creating a terms and connectors query, or Boolean search, on LexisNexis and Westlaw is substantially the same process no matter how the screen may appear.

CHAPTER FEATURES

The chapters are designed to provide students with various ways to comprehend the concepts that are presented in the chapter. Chapters include the following features:

- Beginning—Each chapter will begin with learning objectives, an overview, and an opening scenario that will set the stage for the chapter material.
- Examples—Every major principle or concept is followed by an example to illustrate it. Students have commented over the years that there aren't enough examples in the textbooks they use. Therefore, this text has abundant examples not only to help the instructor teach but also to help the students learn the principles and concepts presented.
- Tables—Various tables show the relationship between concepts in the chapter. For example, Table 8-1 provides the source of secondary law and gives the purpose of that source, whereas Table 8-2 provides the common features of secondary materials.
- Figures—Various figures present a visual representation of the text and are included when that visual helps readers further identify the content of the chapter section. These figures may include tools, such as a screenshot from Westlaw or LexisNexis, a page from a legal encyclopedia, or a diagram of the hierarchy of law.
- Checklists—These checklists provide a logical progression of activity, such as researching case law for understanding how to use a legal encyclopedia.
- Margin notes—Margin notes contain tips that help provide another reference for the information preceding the tip, such as a website to find additional reading or a different way to state the material that was presented. In addition, some practices and procedures are pointed out, such as creating a database of web addresses for state government sites or for sites that will frequently be used.
- Citing the Law—This tool provides students with reinforcement of the proper way to cite whichever material is being discussed in the content of the chapter.
- Ethics Alerts—Ethics alerts periodically will provide the students with a reminder that they have certain obligations to their supervisors to maintain an ethical and professional relationship.

- Key Terms—Key terms used in each chapter are defined at the end of that chapter. A glossary at the end of the text provides all key terms in one location.
- Review Questions—Review questions take the student back to the primary concepts within the chapter material.
- Application Exercises—These exercises provide the student with a connection between the theory presented in the textbook and the reality of actually performing the activity.
- Citation Exercises—Exercises to reinforce use of proper citation format are available in nearly every chapter of the textbook.
- Quick Check—A short quiz can be found in each chapter.
- Research—Nearly every chapter has some type of research problem that requires students to find the answer to a legal question. The research may be in statutes or administrative regulations, in case law, or in other areas. Ideally, students will complete this section of exercises through manual research.
- Internet Research—This research can be conducted using paid subscription sources or free websites.
- Media Resources—This section provides useful videos or demonstrations related to the primary topics within the chapter.
- Internet Resources—These resources include websites that support the content of the chapter. In addition, all Internet resources have been gathered in Appendix III at the end of the text.

Pedagogy

In consideration of the different learning styles of students, several features have been included to assist in their learning:

- Learning objectives provided at the beginning of each chapter
- Key terms are bold within the chapter and defined both at the end of the chapter in which the terms appear and in a glossary
- Various visual aids that provide a different view of critical points
- End-of-chapter material in various formats to hone and reinforce the student's knowledge
- Numerous websites useful to understanding chapter content follow each chapter and are also collected in Appendix III.

Supplements

Legal Research, Analysis, and Writing is supported by an array of instructor and student resources.

Instructor's Supplements   To access this and other supplementary materials online, instructors need to request an instructor access code at **www.pearsonhighered.com/ irc**. Within 48 hours after registering, you will receive a confirmation e-mail that includes an instructor access code. When you receive your code, go to the site and log on for full instructions on downloading materials you wish to use.

- ***Instructor's Resource Manual.*** Instructors have access to an extensive *Instructor's Resource Manual* that accompanies the text. This online manual provides resources and other ancillary materials including sample syllabi, lesson plans, additional exercises, PowerPoint presentations (as applicable), answers to exercises, and additional documents to support learning.

- *MyTest Test Bank.* This program can create custom tests and print scrambled versions of a test at one time, as well as build tests randomly by chapter, level of difficulty, or question type. The software also allows online testing and record-keeping and the ability to add questions to the database.

- *Online PowerPoint™ Lecture Presentation Package.* Lecture Presentation screens for each chapter are available.

This textbook is also available split into two separate books:
Legal Research (ISBN: 0-13-281837-X)
Legal Analysis and Writing (ISBN: 0-13-281836-1)

Student Supplements

- *Legal Research, Analysis, and Writing* is available in two eBook formats, *CourseSmart* and Adobe Reader. *CourseSmart* is an exciting new choice for students looking to save money. As an alternative to purchasing the printed textbook, students can purchase an electronic version of the same content. With a *CourseSmart* eTextbook, students can search the text, make notes online, print out reading assignments that incorporate lecture notes, and bookmark important passages for later review. For more information, or to purchase access to the *CourseSmart* eTextbook, visit **www.coursesmart.com**.

Finally, students, you should remember that excellent researchers are curious, persistent, and flexible people who enjoy finding that needle in a haystack. Enjoy research and writing.

ACKNOWLEDGMENTS

Writing the first book is not an easy task. I look back and realize that I could have said to myself what I say to the students all the time: "You don't know what you don't know." Because I didn't know what I didn't know, many people gave a lot of time to help me see this project through to the end.

I would like to acknowledge all the people at Pearson Higher Education who helped me create this text and who have shaped its contents. Gary Bauer, Executive Editor; Linda Cupp, Editorial Project Manager; and Tanika Henderson, Editorial Assistant, stuck with me and had the faith that this project would be completed. A special thanks goes to Evan Voboril for his copyediting of this edition.

No textbook is really good without reviewers. I would like to thank the reviewers listed below. Their insights into this first manuscript provided many valuable comments and suggestions that I liberally borrowed. Thanks to the following:

Laura Alfano, *Virginia College Online*
Carina Aquirre, *Platt College, Ontario*
Hannah Barnhon, *National College*
Christine R. Bork, *Gloucester County College*
Carol Brady, *Milwaukee Area Technical College*
Brian Craig, *Minnesota School of Business*
Steven Dayton, *Fullerton College*
Robert Donley, *Central Pennsylvania State University*
Lisa Duncan Robinson, *Central Carolina Community College*

Teri Fields, *Clayton University*
Heidi Getchell-Bastien, *Northern Essex Community College*
Patty Greer, *Berkeley College*
Deborah Hoffman, *Columbus State Community College*
Kent Kauffman, *Indiana University-Purdue University, Ft. Wayne*
Steven Kempisty, *Bryant & Stratton College, Liverpool, New York*
Heidi Koeneman, *Ivy Tech Community College, Ft. Wayne*
David Michael Morfin, *Platt College, Texas*
Carole Olson, *El Centro College*
Beth Pless, *Northeast Wisconsin Technical College*
Dena Sukol, *Community College of Philadelphia*
Cathy Underwood, *Pulaski Technical College*
Deborah Vinecour, *SUNY, Rockland*
Bobby (Buzz) Wheeler, *Highline Community College*
Laurie Wicker, *Brookline College*

I am indebted to my peers in the American Association for Paralegal Education who, unknowingly over the years, provided me with inspiration as well as exercises and teaching tips. I especially want to thank Thomas F. Goldman for his belief in and support of me during this endeavor. He made an excellent role model as an author who strives to give the best materials to the students and instructors.

I thank the students who, over the years, have helped me become a better professor. The lessons I have learned from them have helped to hone this text and to create the exercises within. One of my students who deserves special thanks is Andrea D. Thompson for pulling together and double-checking all of the Internet sites that we used herein. Also, I extend a special thank you to one of my students, Sabrina Kramer, for her invaluable assistance.

I thank in advance all of the paralegal students and instructors who read and use this text. I hope it becomes a very dog-eared member of your personal library.

Last but not least, I want to thank my family, who gave up many hours with me because I had a book to work on. My mother never lived to see the book finished, but she was proud that I started writing it. I appreciate all of the support that Michael gave by learning to recognize the big white thing in the kitchen was a refrigerator and housed food that he could actually cook. The book would not have been possible without the support and encouragement of my biggest fan–my daughter, Jami. Even though Jami is an adult, she still reminds me of the things that I missed while I was drafting chapters. Luckily for me, she took the research course and she offered some valuable insight into things that needed to be included in the book from a student's perspective. So, Jami Myers Selzer, this is for you.

ABOUT THE AUTHOR

Kathryn L. Krocza Myers is Associate Professor and Coordinator of Paralegal Studies at Saint Mary-of-the-Woods College (SMWC), a small, Catholic, liberal arts college for women in Saint Mary-of-the-Woods, Indiana. She has been involved in paralegal education since 1982 when she helped create the college's paralegal program.

She has been active in the American Association for Paralegal Educators (AAfPE) since 1989. She has served on numerous committees, was editor of *The Paralegal Educator,* and served as President of AAFPE in 2001–2002. She has chaired and served on the national conference committee since 2002. She has been a frequent speaker at regional and annual AAfPE conferences, often covering research and writing.

She is actively involved in paralegal organizations and frequently creates continuing education sessions on legal research and writing, as well as other topics, for programs sponsored by the Indiana State Bar Association, the Indianapolis Bar Association, and Indiana Paralegal Association. She has been a speaker for the National Association of Legal Assistants (NALA), the National Federation of Paralegal Associations (NFPA), Illinois Paralegal Association, American Alliance of Paralegals, Inc. (AAPI), Navy Legalmen, and others. She has served NALA on its certifying board, served on NFPA's Board of Directors, and is on the credentialing board for AAPI. She reviews, publishes, and lectures on various areas of paralegal education such as research and writing, grant writing, litigation, career development, communication, internships, and substantive law topics.

In 2010, Indiana Governor Mitchell Daniels named her an Outstanding Hoosier. The award, presented during the AAfPE conference, was presented by her long-time friend and supporter, The Honorable John G. Baker, Chief Judge of the Indiana Court of Appeals. After several visits to the SMWC Law Day, a program she organized at the Woods that brings the Indiana Court of Appeals to campus to present an actual case to area middle and high school students, Judge Baker decided that they should "take the show on the road," and today the Indiana Court of Appeals travels to various cities in Indiana meeting with students at the high school and college levels. The SMWC Law Day program was named the ABA "Outstanding Law Day Program for 1998."

Locally, she has been Vice President in Children's Theatre of Terre Haute and a Girl Scout leader. She is a Court Appointed Special Advocate (CASA), on the CASAKids board after serving two years as its president, and is a Mother's March of Dimes volunteer. She also holds a black belt in Tae Kwon Do.

chapter **one**

INTRODUCTION TO LEGAL RESEARCH

Sean Nel/Shutterstock

LEARNING OBJECTIVES

After completing this chapter, students should be able to:

1. Describe the research process.
2. Describe the research responsibilities of a paralegal.
3. Describe the products of legal research.

CHAPTER OVERVIEW

Most of the duties of paralegals involve some type of research, analysis, or writing. A valued paralegal will have keen research and writing skills. Unlike other forms of research and writing, legal research seems mysterious and complicated because the language and terms used are unique to the legal field.

Legal research is the foundation of any good law practice. Before a lawyer can enter a courtroom and successfully argue the client's case, the legal team must research the applicable law. Research culminates in a written legal document, such as a pleading, brief, or internal memorandum. This is true whether the case is a criminal case, civil case, or administrative matter. This chapter will provide a basic understanding of legal terminology, the role of the paralegal, and the ethical duties that accompany the research process.

OPENING SCENARIO

John had just graduated with a degree in paralegal studies from a prestigious paralegal program at a local college. He secured a job at Allworthy Law Firm through his paralegal internship, which his advisor had set up during his last semester of school. What a stroke of genius! But now it was his fateful first day as a real employee!

After John was acclimated to his new office, his supervising attorney, Jami, came in with several file folders. "Now that you are a full-time employee, you need a few client files to work on. You can finish up any projects that you covered in the internship, and then I have a few legal issues for you to research. Are you ready?"

John was excited to start working, but he was a little hesitant. Although research had been an important course during his studies, he had never done any major research projects during his internship. However, John had a great professor for his research and writing course who gave her students plenty of practice problems. It was the hardest course in the curriculum, but he would later use what he learned again and again during his career. One of the most important lessons he learned from his professor was to "start with the basics."

INTRODUCTION TO RESEARCH

A large part of a paralegal's duties involve research, analysis, and writing. Therefore, it is important to develop keen research and writing skills in order to become a valued player on the legal team.

Legal research and writing require specialized skills and knowledge, and many of the terms used in legal writing are unique to the legal field. Many paralegals find it helpful to own and use a *legal dictionary* or a combination of a legal dictionary and *thesaurus*.

Legal research is a very "hands-on" process. To begin to get an idea of how legal research works, it may be helpful to explore the aisles of a law library and examine the inside of some of the books. Of course, legal research can also be accomplished with a computer. But the most effective research often will be a combination of book and computer research. Finding the right information may require opening dusty old books in addition to exploring websites.

This chapter will introduce the basics of legal research, and will describe the process, the available resources, and the types of research that will be expected of a paralegal. Some attention is also given to the ethical aspects of research, such as avoiding the unauthorized practice of law.

THE ROLE OF LEGAL RESEARCH IN GENERAL

Legal research is the foundation of any successful law practice. Before entering a courtroom and making an argument on behalf of a client, the lawyer and his or her trusted paralegal must first research the client's case. This may involve multiple tasks such as finding applicable law and legal *precedent*.

Even if a case is similar to cases the lawyer has handled before, the law applicable to the current case may be different due to the *venue* or *jurisdiction*, recent updates in the law, or differences in the facts. Each case requires fresh legal research to ensure that the legal team is using the most current and correct law. This research usually culminates in a piece of legal writing such as a pleading, brief, or

---

Legal dictionary

A dictionary that is similar to a standard English dictionary, but primarily contains definitions of legal terms.

Thesaurus

A book that provides synonyms and antonyms.

TIP

A good way for students to increase their vocabulary is to continually look for new words to learn. Challenge classmates to learn a new word each day. Make flashcards of unfamiliar terms and set up a quiz.

TIP

Legal research and writing are two of the most important skills in the quest to be a paralegal.

Precedent

Prior decisions of the same or a higher court, which a judge must follow in deciding a subsequent case that has the same or similar facts and issues.

Venue

The specific geographical area over which the court has the authority to litigate and determine a case. Venue must not be confused with jurisdiction, which implies the inherent right of the court to legally decide a particular type of case.

Jurisdiction

The authority and power to apply specific types of law (federal, state, or local; criminal, quasi-criminal, administrative, or civil) in a specific geographic area.

internal memorandum. This is true whether the case is a *criminal case*, *civil case*, or *administrative matter*.

Most lawyers find they need assistance in performing all of the legal research their caseload requires. However, lawyers are often reluctant to assign research projects to paralegals because they are not convinced that paralegals are adept at the research process. Therefore, it is incumbent on a paralegal student to take this area of education very seriously. Doing research well means researching economically and presenting the findings from legal research with accuracy, brevity, and clarity.

> ## Ethics Alert 1-1
>
> Researching economically is important because the time spent researching will generally be billed to the client. Working on a client's case means considering what will best serve the client's needs. One way to insure that the client is being served best on a research project is to make a research plan before beginning a search. Remember to keep track of the time spent researching so that the client can properly be billed for the work.

The findings from legal research are often presented in a *memorandum of law* (or *legal memorandum*). This type of document is usually written for the attorney supervisor, and will remain within the office rather than be filed with the court or sent to the opposing side. A legal memorandum is only used internally, by the attorney or others involved in the case. The attorney will often use the research to prepare other documents he or she will submit to a court. Details about the legal memorandum will be presented later.

[handwritten note: should still be put in client's file]

Legal research and writing are so important to the practice of law that the American Association for Paralegal Education (AAfPE) identifies legal research as one of the core competencies that a successful paralegal needs to possess. Nearly every paralegal program has at least one research, or research and writing, course within its curriculum. It may be interesting and useful to visit the AAfPE website to review its discussion of core competencies or other useful information (www.aafpe.org).

THE ROLE OF THE PARALEGAL IN RESEARCH

Traditionally, a paralegal is a "team player" and provides support to a lawyer or team of lawyers. Although paralegals generally work independently, they are under the supervision of a lawyer. Once the client's issue has been thoroughly researched and analyzed by the paralegal, the findings are submitted to the supervising attorney for review. That attorney then will further analyze the research and provide legal advice to the client.

A research assignment might begin with the client coming to the office to hire the firm. The attorney talks with the client and then introduces the paralegal to the client. The paralegal may do the following:

1. *Interview the client or review client documents to identify the factual question raised by the client's problem:* Fred came to the office because he was in an automobile accident where Annie, the other driver, passed another car on a two-lane road and hit Fred's car head-on. Now, Annie's insurance company will not reimburse Fred for his losses to his car and the injuries he sustained from the

---

Criminal case
A case in which the state or federal government brings an action against someone accused of violating a criminal law.

Civil case
A case involving a person, corporation, or other entity suing a person, corporation, or entity in which the damages generally are monetary.

Administrative matter
A hearing before a panel or administrative law judge of an administrative agency.

Memorandum of law
An internal document in a law firm in which a paralegal or an attorney analyzes a client's legal position without arguing for a specific interpretation of the law.

wreck because the company claims that its insured was not at fault. Fred wants to know what he can do.

2. *Conduct research to find law that applies to the client's factual question:* What law will apply—federal or state? What is the first type of law to check—statutes or case law? What is the law in Fred's state regarding recovery for losses sustained in an automobile accident?

3. *Analyze the law in relationship to the client's factual question:* Determine what evidence is necessary to prove that when Annie passed the other vehicle unsafely, she failed to meet her responsibility to maintain control of her vehicle and obey the rules of the road.

4. *Communicate the findings to the supervising lawyer or other supervisor:* Quite often a memorandum of law must be prepared to present the findings to the supervisor.

When the process is completed, the memorandum is delivered to the attorney or other supervisor. The detailed, and sometimes lengthy, memorandum is not submitted to the court itself, although it may become the basis for documents the attorney submits to a court. Because the memorandum is used only internally by the attorney, it should be written in a neutral tone, meaning that it presents both sides, so the attorney can plan an appropriate strategy. In some ways, research is like chess—it is important to plan for the moves that might be made in the long term, not just the next immediate move.

The above scenario is an example of only one type of task a paralegal may perform. Paralegals provide a variety of legal functions depending on the type of law office. The information in Table 1-1 details just a few of the interesting roles of a paralegal, and examples of responsibilities the paralegal may have within each of these roles. This is only a sampling of the many duties a paralegal may have.

TABLE 1-1   Roles of the Paralegal

Role	Sample Responsibilities
Interviewing	• Interviewing witnesses in the office or in the field • Conducting client intake interviews
Gathering legal facts	• Locating evidence that may be important to the client's case • Reviewing documents produced in discovery • Interviewing clients and witnesses to develop the case
Summarizing legal facts	• Drafting pretrial memoranda • Drafting office memoranda for supervisors • Summarizing testimony from depositions
Conducting legal research	• Locating applicable constitutional provision, statutes, case law, regulations, or other law to support the client's position • Examining legal authority that may be adverse to the client's position
Summarizing legal findings	• Drafting interoffice memoranda of law • Drafting briefs for the court
Drafting legal documents	• Drafting memoranda for supervisors • Drafting letters to clients • Drafting pleadings for the court
Reviewing legal documents	• Checking research submitted by opposing counsel • Reviewing motions and pleadings received from other parties
Updating research	• Shepardizing® cited cases • Reviewing new slip opinions • Shepardizing or using other services to update cited cases.

THE TERMINOLOGY OF LEGAL RESEARCH

Knowing and understanding the terminology of the legal profession is essential to success as a paralegal. In the legal world, words are power. Using legal terms correctly can bolster a message and strongly advocate a position. A paralegal should become a "wordsmith" by learning new terms or expanding knowledge about terms that are already known. Many new vocabulary words may be acquired by paying close attention to the terms used within this text.

INTRODUCTION TO LEGAL PUBLICATIONS

Paralegals should be familiar with the various types of legal publications and their locations. A new paralegal should first locate these resources in a law library and learn how to use them. It is also important to become familiar with electronic research tools, such as online subscription services and Internet resources.

Primary Law

Legal publications are either ***primary sources of law*** or ***secondary sources of law***. Primary sources are the law itself, and are outlined in Table 1-2.

TIP

Students can increase their vocabularies in a number of ways, such as by searching for new words to add to their vocabulary or subscribing to an Internet service that provides a word of the day. Two sources are www.merriam-webster.com and www.dictionary.reference.com. In the alternative, students can buy a legal dictionary or thesaurus and start with "A." Just imagine how many new words could be learned by the time students finish their educational program!

Primary source
The law itself, such as constitutions, statutes, case law, administrative rules, and other sources.

Secondary source
Materials that purport to explain the meaning or applicability of the actual law or primary authorities.

TABLE 1-2   Primary Sources of Law

Source of Law	Purpose
Constitutions	The United States Constitution is the supreme law of the land. No law can contravene the Constitution. It also establishes the structure of the federal government. For example, art. III, § 1 establishes the U.S. Supreme Court. Each state also has its own constitution.
Statutes	Statutes are enacted by legislatures to proscribe conduct, define crimes, create inferior government bodies, appropriate public monies, and in general promote the public welfare. Federal statutes are enacted by the United States Congress. The legislatures in each of the states enact statutes, too. Statutes may be either ***procedural*** or ***substantive***. For example, the federal statute 26 U.S.C. § 2501 imposes a tax on gifts. The Indiana statute I.C. 35-34-1-1 describes the procedure for starting a criminal case.
Cases, court opinions, court decisions	Court opinions and decisions are law written by judges rather than legislatures. In an opinion, the judge either will interpret statutory law or apply the common law. These cases establish precedent for deciding similar cases in the future. *Marbury v. Madison,* 5 U.S. 137 (1803), is an important decision establishing the authority of the U.S. Supreme Court to interpret the law.
Administrative regulations	Administrative regulations are rules established by a government agency. They frequently relate to providing benefits to people. For example, 20 C.F.R. 404 relates to employee benefits.
Administrative decisions	Administrative decisions are decisions handed down by administrative law judges. For example, *A & W Smelters & Refiners, Inc.* (CERCLA 106(b) 94-14) was a decision in a hearing before the Environmental Protection Agency.
Rules of court	Rules of court are procedural laws governing the mechanics of litigation in a particular court. For example, Fed.R.Civ.P. 26 requires parties to disclose certain information before litigation begins in federal court.
Charters	A charter is the fundamental law of a local unit of government that allows the entity to function.
Ordinances	Ordinances are laws of a local legislative branch, such as a county or city council.
Executive orders	Executive orders are issued by a government's chief executive officer, such as the president or a state governor. An example is Executive Order 13508, which sets up a plan to protect the Chesapeake Bay.
Treaties	Treaties are international agreements between two or more countries. For example, the North American Free Trade Agreement (NAFTA) is a treaty among the United States, Canada, and Mexico.

TIP

Students should memorize and understand these ten types of law. It will make their work much easier later on!

Case reporters

Books containing cases that have been decided by courts of law. They are grouped according to designations set either by the courts themselves (official reporters) or by publishing companies such as West (unofficial reporters).

Code books

Books that house the statutes passed by state and federal legislatures.

Case reporters and *code books* are examples of primary sources.

> The *United States Reports, Supreme Court Reporter,* and *Supreme Court Reporter, Lawyer's Edition,* house the opinions of the U.S. Supreme Court. *United States Reports* (U.S.) is the official reporter, while the unofficial reporters are the *Supreme Court Reporter* (S.Ct.) from West, and *United States Supreme Court Reports, Lawyers' Edition* (L.Ed.), now published by LexisNexis.
>
> The *Federal Reporter* collects the opinions of the federal Courts of Appeals (the federal circuit courts). The current series is F.3d.
>
> Each state has at least one set of statutes.

Secondary Law

Secondary law consists of anything that describes or explains primary law. Legal encyclopedias, journals, law reviews, and treatises are examples of secondary sources of law. Table 1-3 describes different types of secondary materials that are available at most law libraries and online research services.

Corpus Juris Secundum (C.J.S.) and *American Jurisprudence* 2d (Am.Jur.2d) are legal encyclopedias. Legal encyclopedias can be a good starting place to find out how the law addresses a certain point, and are useful for getting ideas for further research. They present overviews of the law, organized by topic, with references to controlling authority.

The ultimate goal in research is to find the primary law that supports the client's position. Secondary authority should never take precedence over primary authority. The sources of primary and secondary authority will be discussed in more detail in later chapters.

TABLE 1-3   Secondary Sources of Law

Source of Law	Purpose
Legal encyclopedias	Legal encyclopedias are multivolume sets that explain the law on both the national and state levels. For example, *Corpus Juris Secundum* is an encyclopedia describing law drawn from all reported cases in the United States.
Digests	Digests are multivolume sets of books that act as an index to the case reporters and contain short summaries of cases. One example is the *Federal Practice Digest 4th*, which helps researchers locate cases reported in the federal court system.
Treatise	A treatise is a thorough analysis of one legal subject. Examples include *Wharton's Criminal Procedure, 14th* (Thomson Reuters)
Form books	Form books contain forms that lawyers can use as guides when they are preparing documents. Examples include *Current Legal Forms with Tax Analysis* and Vaughan's (complete) *Alabama Form Book*.
Law reviews	A law review is a scholarly legal journal published by a bar association or an organization of students at a law school. The *Harvard Law Review* is one of the preeminent legal periodicals.
Journals	Journals are similar to law reviews, but often focus on a specific subject or region, such as the *New York Law Journal* and the *Computer Law Review and Technology Journal*, respectively.
Legal periodicals	There are many other law-related magazines, journals, and newspapers in addition to law reviews, such as the *ABA Journal* and the *Banking Law Journal*.
Loose-leaf publications	Loose-leaf services provide continually updated materials that are meant to be kept in a binder. Major publishers of loose-leaf services are the Bureau of National Affairs (BNA), Commerce Clearing House (CCH), Lexis Legal Publishing/Matthew Bender, and the Research Institute of America (RIA).
Legal dictionaries and thesauri	Legal dictionaries are similar to standard English dictionaries, but focus only on legal terms. The most frequently used legal dictionary is *Black's Law Dictionary*. Thesauri (the plural of *thesaurus*) provide synonyms and antonyms or alternate terms to the word being researched.

Citations

Most primary and secondary legal authorities are identified by a ***citation***. The citation is much like the address of the material—it gives the reader the location so it can be found easily. Understanding how citations are written will not only help locate the materials, but will also enable a writer to provide the proper citations according to the rules of each jurisdiction. Most jurisdictions will require either the format found in *The Bluebook: A Uniform System of Citation* (*The Bluebook*) or the *ALWD Citation Manual* (*ALWD*). Some jurisdictions may have their own rules. The basic elements of citation format are simple and have some degree of consistency. Example 1-1 provides samples of some of the most frequently used citation formats.

In the early days of the United States, legal materials were very limited in scope. Each state collected the laws that it passed, there was no single system for the entire country, and it was almost impossible for one person to research cases nation-wide. As the country grew, it became apparent that researchers needed a system to access the cases from all state and federal jurisdictions in order to find cases discussing similar points of law. Since 1879, West's National Reporter System has compiled cases from state and federal courts and organized them into various reporter sets.

Volumes in a set are numbered consecutively. A new series starting with volume 1 is begun when one series becomes too unwieldy. For example, in the *Atlantic Reporter*, after reaching 300, a new series called Atlantic Second Series begins; it starts with the volume 1 *A.2d.* The numbering system is the same whether the reporter is in physical books or located on the Internet.

Citation
Information that helps the researcher locate material in a law library or online. A citation is also called a *cite*.

EXAMPLE 1-1   CITATION FORMATS

Statutes: 26 U.S.C. § 2501 (West 1998) is the citation of a federal statute. The number 26 is the title within the federal code. The § symbol means the section number. (Holding the ALT key and typing 21 on your keypad at the same time make the § in MS Word. If you use Microsoft Word®, go to *Insert*, and then *Symbol*; find the section mark by choosing *More Symbols* and then *Special Characters*. The directions may vary by application.) The number 2501 indicates the section number of the statute. The parenthetical material is the publisher and the year of publication.

Cases: A citation for a case will usually have the names of the parties and then the reporter location. Parties may be persons, governmental entities, or business organizations. In a case citation, only the last name of the first party on each side of the dispute is listed. For example, for the case *Roe v. Wade*, 314 F. Supp. 1217 (N.D. Tex. 1970), the plaintiff was Roe, the defendant was Wade, and the case is found in volume 314 of the *Federal Supplement*. The case starts on page 1217. It was a federal case filed originally in the northern federal district court in Texas in 1970. *Roe v. Wade,* 410 U.S. 113 (1973) is the citation to the same case on appeal to the U.S. Supreme Court. The parties are the same, but the case is found at volume 410 of the *United States Reports,* starting on page 113.

Pinpoint Citations: These citations tell exactly where in the document specific quoted or referenced language can be found. In the citation for *Abele v. Markle*, 452 F.2d 1121, 1125 (2nd Cir. 1971), the case is found in volume 452 of the *Federal Reporter,* second series, and it begins on page 1121. The comma followed by 1125 means that a specific point of law or quoted language appears on page 1125 of the *Abele* case. The case was decided by the Second Circuit Court of Appeals in 1971.

Statutes
Law enacted by either the federal or state legislatures. Federal statutes are sometimes referred to as Acts of Congress.

Pinpoint citation
A citation that takes the reader to the exact page where a quotation can be found.

CITING THE LAW 1-1: STATUTES

Citations to state statutes are similar in some states and quite different in others. It is important to check *The Bluebook, ALWD,* or local rules for the jurisdiction in which the case is pending. Here are some examples of citations to state statutes:

New Hampshire – N.H. Rev. Stat. Ann. § 208:1-b (2003) (N.H. is New Hampshire, Rev. means "revised," Stat. means "statute," Ann. means "annotated" and 208:1-b is the title and section number.)
California – Cal. Civil Code §1793.22 (West 2008)
Connecticut – Conn. Gen. Stat. Ann. §4-166 (West [year])
Indiana – Ind. Code §35-1-1-1 (2008) or Ind. Code. Ann. §35-1-1-1 (West 2008)
Pennsylvania – [Title number] Pa. Consol. Stat. §[section number] (year)
Texas – Tex. Rev. Civ. Stat. Ann. [article number] (West [year])

Some abbreviations or terms commonly found in citations are short for *statute* (Stat.), *code, code annotated* (ann.), and *revised* (Rev.).

Official

Describes reporters or sources of law that are published by the source itself, such as *United States Code* and *United States Reports.*

Unofficial

The text of law published by a publishing company and not by the governmental entity from which the law originates.

Legal materials are categorized as **official** and **unofficial**. It is important to understand that official citations are not necessarily superior to or more authoritative than unofficial ones. *Official* means that the governmental body that issued the statute or case has published the document. *Unofficial* means that the governmental body has supplied a commercial publishing company with the text of the case or statute. The publishing company may then add some enhancements to help the reader understand the material. For example, the official publication of the statutes enacted by the U.S. Congress is the *United States Code* (U.S.C.). That means that in this set of books, the only information provided is the law and anything that Congress chooses to include. The unofficial publication of the statutes is published by Thomson-Reuters (formerly West, and referred to herein as West) in the *United States Code Annotated* (U.S.C.A.). This set of books contains the law as enacted by Congress, and adds enhancements such as cross-references to related information, references to forms, and brief references to cases where the law was discussed.

Some sources have suspended their official publications; notably, some states no longer publish their own case reporters. For example, Indiana no longer publishes the *Indiana Reports* (Ind.) or the *Indiana Appellate Reports* (Ind.App. or Ind. Ct.App., depending on the date). Legal professionals in Indiana now rely on the cases that are published in the *North Eastern Reporter* (N.E., N.E.2d). Table 1-4 provides a sample of citation formats.

This is not an exhaustive list. However, the materials listed here are commonly used in many research projects and are often used in research training.

When one is writing a citation, the punctuation and spelling in the abbreviations is important, and the periods and commas must be correctly placed in the accepted citation format. *The Bluebook* or *ALWD*, as well as local rules for formatting, should be checked for proper citation formats.

TABLE 1-4 Citation Formats

Tool	Abbreviation	Coverage
United States Reports	U.S.	Official source of cases from the U.S. Supreme Court.
Supreme Court Reporter	S.Ct.	Unofficial source for U.S. Supreme Court cases published by West (Thomson-Reuters).
United States Supreme Court Reports, Lawyer's Edition	L.Ed., L.Ed.2d (2d means the series, not the edition)	Unofficial source for U.S. Supreme Court cases originally published by Lawyer's Cooperative (LexisNexis).
United States Law Week	U.S.L.W.	Unofficial source for U.S. Supreme Court cases, originally published by the Bureau of National Affairs (BNA).
Federal Reporter	F., F.2d, F.3d	Unofficial source for the opinions of the United States courts of appeals, published by West.
Federal Supplement	F.Supp., F.Supp.2d	Unofficial source for the opinions of the United States district courts, published by West.
Atlantic Reporter	A., A.2d	Unofficial source for the state appellate courts of Connecticut, Delaware, District of Columbia, Maine, Maryland, New Hampshire, New Jersey, Pennsylvania, Rhode Island, and Vermont; published by West.
North Eastern Reporter	N.E., N.E.2d	Unofficial source for the state appellate courts of Illinois, Indiana, Massachusetts, New York, and Ohio; published by West.
North Western Reporter	N.W., N.W.2d	Unofficial source for the state appellate courts of Iowa, Michigan, Minnesota, Nebraska, North Dakota, South Dakota, and Wisconsin; published by West.
Pacific Reporter	P., P.2d, P.3d	Unofficial source for the state appellate courts of Arizona, California, Colorado, Hawaii, Idaho, Kansas, Montana, Nevada, New Mexico, Oklahoma, Oregon, Utah, Washington, and Wyoming; published by West.
South Eastern Reporter	S.E., S.E.2d	Unofficial source for the state appellate courts of Georgia, North Carolina, South Carolina, Virginia, and West Virginia; published by West.
South Western Reporter	S.W., S.W.2d, S.W.3d	Unofficial source for the state appellate courts of Arkansas, Kentucky, Missouri, Tennessee, and Texas; published by West.
Southern Reporter	So., So.2d, So.3d	Unofficial source for the state appellate courts of Alabama, Florida, Louisiana, and Mississippi; published by West.
United States Code	U.S.C.	Official source for the statutes passed by the U.S. Congress.
United States Code Annotated	U.S.C.A.	Unofficial source for the statutes passed by the U.S. Congress; published by West.
Corpus Juris Secundum	C.J.S.	National legal encyclopedia; published by West.
Federal Register	Fed. Reg.	The official source of the daily publication of rules, proposed rules, and notices of federal agencies, organizations, and presidential documents.
Code of Federal Regulations	C.F.R.	An unofficial publication of federal agency rules recorded in the Federal Register.
American Jurisprudence	Am.Jur., Am.Jur.2d	National legal encyclopedia, originally published by Lawyer's Cooperative (West).
American Law Reports	A.L.R., A.L.R.2d, A.L.R.3d, A.L.R.4th, A.L.R.Fed.	Annotation of selected cases to provide valuable guidance and understanding in different areas of law.

NM also has N.M. which is New Mexico Reports

CASE EXCERPTS 1-1: *Nicholson v. State*

In rare cases, court decisions have been adversely affected by improper citations. For example, in *Nicholson v. State*, 48A02-0108-CR-533 (Ind.Ct.App., 2002), the court held:

> We direct counsel for Nicholson and Baker to Appellate Rule 22, which states that *citations to cases in briefs are to follow the format put forth in the current edition of a Uniform System of Citation (Bluebook)*. When referring to specific material within a source, a citation should include both the page on which the source begins and the page on which the specific material appears. Uniform System of Citation Rule 3.3 (17th ed. 2000). As we noted in *Barth v. Barth*, 693 N.E.2d 954, 956 (Ind. Ct. App. 1998), *trans. denied* 706 N.E.2d 169 (Ind. 1998) we will not, on review, search through the authorities cited by a party in order to try to find legal support for its position. *We will consider assertions of error to be waived where an appellant's non-compliance with our rules is so substantial that it impedes our consideration of them. Id.* at 957. We further direct counsel to our recent statement in *Howell v. Hawk*, 750 N.E.2d 452, 460 n.3 (Ind. Ct. App. 2001): "We ask Appellants' counsel to re-new his acquaintance with the Bluebook and our Rules governing citation to cases. Appellants' brief almost completely lacks pinpoint citations within the relevant cases cited, and includes numerous blank (wholly superfluous) citations to the Indiana Appellate Court Reports (Ind.App.), which ceased to exist after 1979. We prefer to resolve cases on the merits; nevertheless, we remind counsel that *improper citation could amount to failure to make a cogent argument and result in waiver of our consideration of an issue, and such citation does not facilitate our review of the merits.*" (Citation omitted.) (Emphasis added.)

This case serves as a reminder that the importance of correct citations cannot be underestimated. Citations are discussed in detail in later chapters.

LAW LIBRARY OPTIONS

Physical Libraries

Law library
A library that houses a collection of legal materials.

Various types of *law libraries* are available for research, such as county, bar association, and law school facilities. Law school libraries are usually the largest, and generally have all major legal publications, such as national reporters, federal statutes, and state materials. Students in paralegal programs are sometimes granted access to the collections in these libraries, and it may be worthwhile to check.

Counties and cities also maintain law libraries, which often are located in or near a courthouse. The courthouse may have its own law library. Permission to use these libraries should be obtained from the staff at these facilities. Larger law firms or bar associations also may maintain libraries of some kind. While the use of these libraries is limited to members, paralegal students may have access. In large cities such as Washington D.C., law libraries may be found in various governmental agencies and offices.

A good researcher also should be familiar with the enhancements provided in unofficial sources. Enhancements may include annotations to other resources (such as cases) that help interpret statutes, and pocket parts that include citations to the newest case law. Some sources also include *key topics and numbers*, which organize law by subject matter and point of law for easier searching.

Key topics and numbers
An enhancement from West Publishing Company that organizes the law by topics and then assigns a key number to each point of law.

A researcher using a well-stocked law library, such as one at a large law firm or at a law school, may have access to a law librarian who is familiar with the library's resources and can provide guidance. Often, the librarian will give a tour of the primary and secondary sources and terminals available for online research. If Internet research services are available, the librarian may provide the passwords needed.

Online Libraries

Like other types of research, much of today's legal research can be performed on-line using ***computer-assisted legal research (CALR)***. There are two main online legal databases: LexisNexis® and Westlaw™. These services maintain virtual law libraries where a researcher can find both primary and secondary sources. Both require a password and charge a fee for their use, so it is important to have proper training on how to use these systems before logging on and starting any research.

Computer-assisted legal research or CALR

Research using subscription-based services such as Westlaw® or Lexis/Nexis®, among others.

Some college programs offer training in one or both services. Both providers also have representatives who will come to the office or meet with users at a local law library to demonstrate how to use the system. If an office has a subscription to one of these services, the law librarian or supervisor can assist with getting properly trained on how to use it. However, in order to become truly skilled at CALR, a user must develop experience by actually using the service. Figure 1-1 shows a screen shot of a retrieved case, *Aktiebolaget Electrolux v. Armatron Intern., Inc.,* 999 F.2d 1 (1st Cir. 1993), as it would appear on Westlaw.

The right side appears much the same as the case would appear in a reporter. The caption of the case is followed by the synopsis or syllabus that summarizes what the case is about, as well as its history. On the left side are various enhancements from the publisher such as KeyCite® (for updating), a case outline, and links to related C.J.S. materials.

Figure 1-2 is a screen shot of LexisNexis that shows how to perform a search.

This search is being done in law reviews, as indicated on the dark grey bar. Natural language is used for the search, meaning that search terms—whether words, phrases, or sentences—are entered as they are spoken. A search may also be accomplished using "terms and connectors"—single search terms or phrases that are linked by designated connecting words. On the right, the publisher provides other databases that can be accessed, such as federal and state cases. The methods and techniques used for searching are often similar across different services. Once one system is learned, using the others will be easier.

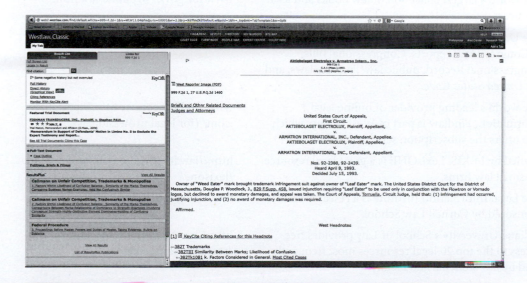

FIGURE 1-1 Westlaw

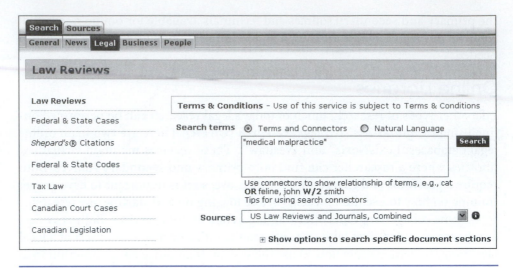

FIGURE 1-2   LexisNexis

Other subscription services, such as Casemaker® and FastCase®, are available to lawyers and law firms, sometimes by virtue of their bar association dues. Besides the subscription legal database services, there are also several Internet legal research sites that are free. These sites are more limited in their content than LexisNexis and Westlaw, but they can be quite helpful, especially when the subscription sites are not available. Researchers should be cautious when using free Internet sites, however. It is important to check a site's credibility to ensure that it contains updated and reliable legal information. It is best to use only reputable websites that can be authenticated, such as those provided by law schools and federal and state governments.

Table 1-5 shows some suggested free legal research websites that provide access to the same primary sources of the law. This is in no way an exhaustive list. Some sites require registration at no charge, but users should avoid providing personal information when registering.

TABLE 1-5   Suggested Free Legal Research Online Resources

Source	Content	Citation
Library of Congress	The world's largest collection of law books and legal resources.	www.loc.gov/law/public/law.html
U.S. Government Printing Office	The U.S. Government Printing Office supplies links to Congressional reports, Congressional bills, Congressional Record, public laws, private laws, and the *United States Code.*	http://www.gpoaccess.gov/
Findlaw, which is sponsored by Westlaw	The world's leading provider of online legal information, Findlaw is part of West Group, which also offers the subscription service Westlaw.	www.findlaw.com or http://lp.findlaw.com/ (for legal professionals)
LexisONE, which is sponsored by LEXIS	Owned by LEXIS, LexisONE is a great legal resource for small law firms.	http://law.lexisnexis.com/webcenters/lexisone/
Cornell University Law School	The Legal Information Institute is a research service sponsored by Cornell Law School.	www.law.cornell.edu
Indiana University School of Law	Indiana University's School of Law provides free access to the top 20 legal resources most frequently used by law students and faculty.	http://law.indiana.edu/lawlibrary/research/resources/
Washburn University School of Law	Washburn University's School of Law offers free access to ATLAS, its law library search engine.	http://washburnlaw.edu/library/

PERFORMING LEGAL RESEARCH

When a paralegal receives a project, he or she must first decide whether or not legal research is necessary, and if so, must apply the research process using the appropriate resources. Checklist 1-1 provides an overview of that process.

Checklist 1-1   FIVE STEPS OF LEGAL RESEARCH

I. Analyze the facts.
   A. Know the factual situation completely and know the client's objective.
   B. Identify the legal questions to be researched. Be sure to consider not only the client's position but also the opposing side. This will become the counteranalysis portion of the memorandum.
   C. Identify the parties involved and their special standing under the law, if any (such as the tenant in a lease or the purchaser in a contract).
   D. Determine the subject matter (such as real or personal property, contracts, or torts).
   E. Determine the basis of the action (such as negligence, breach of contract, or strict liability).
   F. Determine the defenses to the claim (such as self-defense or contributory negligence).

II. Recognize the law.
   A. Determine what court or agency has primary jurisdiction.
   B. Decide whether statutes, codes, or administrative rules or regulations are involved.
   C. Determine whether it is a substantive or procedural problem.

III. Find the law.
   A. Keep a record of page numbers or sections that are relevant. Briefly summarize any law that is "on point."
   B. If the problem is an unfamiliar area of law, read some secondary authority to become familiar with the nature of the law. The secondary authority generally provides a starting point for the research.
   C. Identify the leading case on an issue. It often provides a key to many other cases.
   D. Use the TAPP rule: Focus on the **T**hing involved, the **A**ct or activity creating the problem, the **P**ersons involved, and the **P**lace to which problem is related.
   E. Try the "topic approach":
      1. Start with a summary of the contents.
      2. Select what appears to be the appropriate fact topic.
      3. Select the volume that includes coverage of that topic and turn to the beginning of the topic. Read the scope note to see if the topic is relevant.
      4. Run through the summary of contents to identify relevant subtopics.

IV. Update the research.
   A. Use *Shepard's Citations* or some other updating service to locate cases that cite or are cited in appellate court level decisions.
   B. Make sure updating is thorough. The updating process includes both finding the case and reading it to distinguish or compare it to the case at hand.
   C. Review pocket parts and advance sheets for more current information.

(Continued)

question
↓
federal or state?
↓
which law applies?
↓
read & understand the law

V. Report the research.
   A. Always discuss problems with a supervisor. Do not waste time if you don't understand the problem.
   B. Report concisely but completely both sides of the question. Check the adversary's citations. Citations that are taken out of context may have a different meaning in the text from which they were taken.
   C. Provide the lawyer enough information about the law to enable him or her to reach a final determination.

Federalism and the Supremacy Clause

Federalism
The theory or method of dividing powers between the federal and state governments.

Legal research is easier if one understands the organization and structure of our government. One essential concept in our government is *federalism*. Understanding this concept will help one know what books and other tools to use.

The people of the United States are governed by two separate sets of laws: the laws of the 50 states, and the laws of the federal government. When researching a legal issue, the researcher must first determine which set of laws applies to the factual question. Once a researcher determines the appropriate set of laws is determined, the researcher will know which set of books to look in for the applicable case law or statutes. For example, if a client wishes to obtain a divorce from his wife, state law will govern the action. If both parties are residents of New Mexico, then the state law of New Mexico will apply. On the other hand, if a client believes she was fired due to a speech impairment, that action is governed by the Americans with Disabilities Act (ADA), which is a federal law.

There are some instances when both federal and state laws apply to a factual question. In these situations the U.S. Constitution's *Supremacy Clause* dictates that federal law supersedes state law if the two laws are conflicting. A portion of that clause reads as follows:

Supremacy Clause
Article VI of the U.S. Constitution states, "This Constitution, and the Laws of the United States which shall be made in Pursuance thereof . . . shall be the supreme Law of the Land; and the Judges in every State shall be bound thereby, any Thing in the Constitution or Laws of any State to the Contrary notwithstanding."

This Constitution, and the Laws of the United States which shall be made in Pursuance thereof . . . shall be the supreme Law of the Land; and the Judges in every State shall be bound thereby, any Thing in the Constitution or Laws of any State to the Contrary notwithstanding.[1]

States often adopt their own versions of federal laws, and both state and federal law may govern a particular factual question. Often, a state will adopt a version of the federal law that is more favorable to the citizens of the state than the original federal version. In such a case, the legal team will likely suggest that the client sue under the state version of the law. For example, the Fair Labor Standards Act (FLSA) is a federal law governing an employee's right to unpaid overtime. Most states have adopted some version of this law. If a client were owed unpaid overtime, the attorney would need to decide if a client would be better off suing under the federal law or his or her state law. (The text of the FLSA may be found at http://www.dol.gov/whd/. That site also sets forth the state FLSA law at http://www.dol.gov/whd/state/state.htm.)

After determining whether state or federal law should apply, a researcher should determine which source of law would be most applicable to the problem. There are four main primary sources of law you are most likely to use at both state and federal levels. These are constitutions, statutes, cases, and administrative rules and regulations. Each of these four types have been outlined, but an overview is given here.

[1]United States Constitution. Article VI. http://www.archives.gov/exhibits/charters/constitution_transcript.html

Primary Sources: Constitution

The U.S. government was established through the **U.S. Constitution**, adopted on September 17, 1787. The Constitution is often referred to as the "supreme law of the land" and no U.S. state or federal law may contravene the laws within this document. The substance of the U.S. Constitution is summed up in the Preamble:

> We the people of the United States, in order to form a more perfect union, establish justice, insure domestic tranquility, provide for the common defense, promote the general welfare, and secure the blessings of liberty to ourselves and our posterity, do ordain and establish this Constitution for the United States of America.

Each of the 50 states also has a constitution, which can be found in statute or code books. Constitutional law can therefore be state law, federal law, or both. Both the U.S. and state constitutions contain laws that establish the government, define the government's functions, and describe the government's obligations to its citizens. They also may include protections of certain rights.

Some law firms do a lot of work in constitutional law, and their cases are often based on alleged violations of the rights protected by the amendments to the U.S. Constitution. Many other firms do not handle many cases with constitutional issues. However, even if one is working in a practice that does not encounter many constitutional cases, the first question when beginning research should always be whether a constitutional issue is involved, since constitutional law is the highest law in the hierarchy of laws.

Primary Sources: Statutes

When most laypeople talk about laws, they are usually thinking of statutes. Both federal statutes and state statutes exist. While there is only one set of federal statutes, each state has its own unique set of statutes, and thus state laws may vary from state to state. This is one reason lawyers must be licensed to practice law in a particular state. Statutes cover a wide variety of topics, from how to properly incorporate a business to what constitutes a murder.

We often refer to statutes as being **procedural** or **substantive**. Procedural statutes set forth the rules of procedure, such as how to serve a subpoena, or how to file a complaint. Substantive statutes regulate rights or duties. For example, substantive statutes may govern driving an automobile, inheriting from a decedent, or buying property.

Civil statutes govern personal rights and remedies, and include laws concerned with businesses, insurance, and education. Criminal statutes are designed to prevent harm to society by punishing certain conduct, such as murder, assault, burglary, and identity theft.

Federal statutes are found in a set of books called the *United States Code* (U.S.C.). State statutes are found in separate state code books such as *The Texas Penal Code,* containing all Texas state criminal laws, and *Minnesota Statutes,* containing all civil and criminal statutes of the State of Minnesota. Each state will have a unique name for its set of statutes. Both *The Bluebook* and the *ALWD Citation Manual* give the citation rules for statutes, including the names and abbreviations to use.

Primary Sources: Case Law

Researchers usually will spend the bulk of their research time looking at **case law**. Even if a researcher knows what statutes apply to a factual question, he or she still needs to understand how those statutes are applied to that question. Researching

U.S. Constitution
The fundamental document that the people of the United States, through their representatives, adopted at the Constitutional Convention in 1787. It is the supreme law of the land.

Procedural
A type of law governing the manner in which rights are enforced or the law prescribing the procedure to be followed in a case. Example: Rule 4 of the Federal Rules of Civil Procedure governs how pleadings can be served on a party.

Substantive
Law that defines the conduct expected of citizens in general. For example, traffic laws that govern the operation of motor vehicles are substantive laws.

Case
The word *case* has different meanings depending on the context. In legal research, a case is a dispute before a court of law, or a lawsuit. It also refers to a written opinion of a judge or court that decides or comments on a lawsuit. A "case on point" is a case that may serve as precedent for a current matter. The phrase "case law" refers to the law laid down in the decisions of the courts in similar cases that have been previously decided. The phrase "case of first impression" means that the court has not previously decided a particular issue arising in the case, and the court is therefore hearing the issue for the first time, without any precedent to guide it. A casebook is a book containing court decisions and other materials in a specific field of law. Generally, it is used for teaching students.

case law is often the third step in the legal research process, when the law is analyzed in relationship to the client's factual question.

Case law is judge-made law. When an appellate judge decides a case, the ruling becomes law that lower courts must follow. The appellate judge's ruling is called **precedent**, and is treated as law. The legal doctrine of *stare decisis* means that a court must follow precedent if the precedent applies to the case before it.

Our common law system is based on the old English *common law* system, which existed before most laws were enacted through legislation. Common law is based on decisions of the courts or similar entities. In common law, the decision of the pending case depends on the similar cases that have gone before. If there is no previous law, the judges are faced with a novel situation or a "case of first impression," and that decision becomes new law.

Case law is made at both federal and state levels. Federal case law is published for three different types of court. Federal district courts are at the trial level of the federal system, and their cases are published primarily in the *Federal Supplement* (F.Supp.). Cases from the U.S. Courts of Appeals, or the intermediate level of appeal, are found generally in the *Federal Reporter* (F., F.2d, F.3d). U.S. Supreme Court cases are located in the *United States Reports* (U.S.) and unofficial reporters such as the *Supreme Court Reporter* (S.Ct.), *Supreme Court Reports, Lawyers' Edition* (L.Ed.), and *United States Law Week* (U.S.L.W.).

At the state level, trial court decisions generally are not published. Appellate case law, including both intermediate and final appeals, is published in reporters once the case is decided. For instance, all published Missouri state appellate court cases can be found in the *South Western Reporter* (S.W., S.W.2d, S.W.3d). The oldest cases appear in the S.W. series, and the newest cases appear in the S.W.3d series.

Primary Sources: Administrative

Administrative rules and regulations are made by special ***administrative agencies*** that are given the power to implement statutes enacted by the legislature. If the agency is a state agency, it is given the power to make rules and regulations by its state legislature. If the agency is a federal one, it is given the power to make rules and regulations by the federal government. These proposed rules and regulations are published in the *Federal Register*. Once finalized, the rules and regulations are published in the *Code of Federal Regulations* (C.F.R.), which is similar to the state and federal statute books.

Administrative agencies handle specialized areas of regulation. An agency created to handle aviation issues will not have the authority to regulate housing for the homeless. Likewise, an agency with regulatory authority in Arizona holds no legal authority in New Hampshire. Some examples of federal administrative agencies are the Food and Drug Administration (FDA), the Occupational Safety and Health Administration (OSHA), and the Federal Communications Commission (FCC). States have similar agencies that govern matters within the state, such as the Indiana Occupational Safety and Health Administration (IOSHA) and the Missouri Public Service Commission (PSC).

Agencies vary in the way they hear and make decisions regarding regulatory violations. Many federal and state agencies use ***administrative law judges (ALJs)*** within their agencies. These judges are required to be impartial, and an ALJ usually only hears cases before a single agency. Some state agencies use ALJs that sit on panels that hear cases originating from many different agencies. In either system, parties must generally exhaust appeals before the administrative judges before suing the regulatory agency in a state or federal court.

Stare decisis

A doctrine from Latin that means "let the decision stand." Judicial decisions stand as precedent for cases that arise in the future as long as they involve similar issues or facts. In other words, if the same or similar legal issues are presented, even though by different parties, the decision of the previous court should be used as precedent.

Common law

Law that is found in the decisions of courts rather than in the statutes made by legislatures. It is also called "judge-made law." The roots of our common law come from the English law adopted by the early American colonies.

Administrative rules and regulations

Rules that are made by an administrative agency, and have the force of law.

Administrative agencies

Agencies set up to handle issues that arise within the administrative area of law.

Administrative law judges (ALJs)

Also referred to as a hearing officer or hearing examiner, the ALJ is the person who conducts hearings before an administrative agency. The ALJ generally has expertise in the subject matter of the agency.

Research Results: Putting It in Writing

Once a paralegal's research is complete, it usually is reduced to some form of document. The most common research document is the internal legal memorandum. Research may also be used to write a *pleading* or a *trial brief*. Later in this course, several chapters will provide information on how to create a legal memorandum as well as other legal documents. Some of the basics of legal writing are shown in Checklist 1-2.

Pleadings
Formal statements by the parties to an action setting forth their claims and defenses, such as a complaint, answer, or counterclaim.

Trial brief
A type of legal writing that is presented to the court to argue in favor of a client's position or against the opposing position. The purpose of this document is advocacy.

Checklist 1-2   BASICS OF LEGAL WRITING

1. Tell the reader everything in the first two sentences.

2. Avoid adjectives. An adjective equals an assertion, which equals an opinion, which equals doubt.

3. When in doubt, quote. One should not paraphrase unless he or she is totally certain that the legal significance of every word of the paraphrased material is comprehended.

4. All sources should be cited. Let the reader know where to find the authority for each point that is made.

5. If a statute or a contract is central to the problem, quote it immediately.

6. Identify every document by preparer, addressee (if any), and date.

7. Give the full name of an entity the first time you mention it, before resorting to an abbreviation.

8. Avoid confusion between the ordinary meaning of a certain phrase and its specialized meaning in a certain legal context by using phrases such as "within the meaning of."

EXERCISE 1-1

Look at this sample of a client situation, and answer the questions that follow.

Alice, a new client, comes to the office, and explains that she had an accident after purchasing a new car. She left the dealer's car lot immediately after the purchase, pulled onto 9th Street (a north/south street), approached a stop light at 9th and Main, and stopped. When the light changed to green, Alice proceeded into the intersection, where she was hit by Kyle, who was traveling east on Main Street. He failed to stop at the traffic light. Kyle claims that his light was green.

1. Alice wants to know if she can sue Kyle for the damages to her new car and for the injuries she sustained. What research should be done first?

2. What laws would govern in this case? Is it governed by state law or federal law? Why?

3. Where can the researcher find the laws governing the damage to Alice's car and the injuries to herself? Where would be the first place to look?

4. Do the laws referenced in question 3 apply to Alice's case? Where is the next place to look?

ETHICS IN LEGAL RESEARCH

American Bar Association (ABA)
The country's largest voluntary professional association of attorneys. The goals of the ABA are to promote professionalism and advance the administration of justice. The ABA approves paralegal programs that voluntarily submit their materials for approval.

Unauthorized practice of law (UPL)
The practice of law without holding a license to practice law in that state or jurisdiction.

Confidentiality
An ethical duty requiring that private communications not be disclosed to others.

While paralegals assist lawyers in day-to-day activities, they must know the difference between legal research and legal advice. A licensed attorney may legally and ethically offer legal advice, but a paralegal may not. The model ethical rules of the *American Bar Association* (*ABA*), called the Model Rules of Professional Conduct, can be found at http://www.abanet.org/cpr/mrpc/mrpc_toc.html. While these rules are generally addressed to attorneys, paralegals also are expected to adhere to them. One rule specifically mentioning paralegals and legal assistants is set out in full in Figure 1-3.

Unauthorized Practice of Law

Unauthorized practice of law (*UPL*) is practicing law without a license. It is prohibited in all 50 states and is considered a crime in most. It is easy to commit UPL unintentionally. Therefore, it is important to be conscious of how paralegal responsibilities are handled. The danger frequently arises when a paralegal is asked to interview a client to obtain information, and thus it is important for the paralegal to be careful when speaking to clients. Any words that could be perceived as legal advice might be interpreted as UPL. Paralegals also should refrain from inserting personal opinions about the facts of a client's case in any writing. The writing should be limited to the legal research and any analysis of that research.

Confidentiality

Another ethical consideration for paralegals is that of *confidentiality*. Attorneys and paralegals alike owe a duty of confidentiality to the client. This duty becomes effective at the time of the first client meeting, and the paralegal may be the first person to meet with the client to obtain information. Thus, it is important to

FIGURE 1-3 Model Rules of Professional Conduct

A. Rule 5.3 Responsibilities Regarding Nonlawyer Assistants

With respect to a nonlawyer employed or retained by or associated with a lawyer:

(a) a partner, and a lawyer who individually or together with other lawyers possesses comparable managerial authority in a law firm shall make reasonable efforts to ensure that the firm has in effect measures giving reasonable assurance that the person's conduct is compatible with the professional obligations of the lawyer;

(b) a lawyer having direct supervisory authority over the nonlawyer shall make reasonable efforts to ensure that the person's conduct is compatible with the professional obligations of the lawyer; and

(c) a lawyer shall be responsible for conduct of such a person that would be a violation of the Rules of Professional Conduct if engaged in by a lawyer if:

(1) the lawyer orders or, with the knowledge of the specific conduct, ratifies the conduct involved; or

(2) the lawyer is a partner or has comparable managerial authority in the law firm in which the person is employed, or has direct supervisory authority over the person, and knows of the conduct at a time when its consequences can be avoided or mitigated but fails to take reasonable remedial action.

remember that whatever the client discloses (whether verbally or in the form of documents) is *privileged* and must be kept confidential.

Ethics Alert 1-2

Generally, under the attorney-client privilege (a rule of evidence that varies from state to state), whatever a client discloses to his or her attorney regarding the client's case cannot be used as evidence against the client. If a paralegal accidentally discloses this material, it might be used as evidence by the opposing legal team. Thus, it is very important to maintain confidentiality at all times, even during casual conversations.

The attorney-client relationship is based on loyalty and honesty. The client must feel secure that anything said to any member of the team will be kept confidential. This ensures that the client can share information freely so that the legal team can best represent the client. No one in the office can discuss a client matter with anyone other than those members of the team who are working on the client's case.

Generally, the same rule applies to paralegals: any information regarding a client's case should not be disclosed to any party outside the law office. Telling a spouse or best friend what happened at the office that day is not acceptable, even if the names of the parties are not disclosed. Any disclosures, if required, are best left to the attorney. When in doubt, a supervisor should be consulted first.

Ethical Dilemmas

Many other ethical dilemmas may arise when a paralegal is performing legal research. Some of the problems that might arise in the legal research process are shown in Table 1-6.

Privilege

A rule of evidence that protects from disclosure certain information given within a particular relationship. Under the attorney-client privilege, whatever a client discloses to his or her attorney cannot be used as evidence against the client. If a paralegal accidentally discloses this material, it might be used as evidence by the opposing legal team. It is very important to remember to maintain confidentiality at all times, even during casual conversations.

TABLE 1-6 Ethical Dilemmas

Ethical Rule	Problem	Solution
Candor (Model Rules of Professional Conduct, Rule 3.3)	You are unable to find the legal answer the client or your attorney supervisor hoped for.	You owe an ethical duty to be honest in your research. Always present truthful legal research so that your attorney supervisor will be well informed when offering legal advice to the client or making arguments in court.
Conflict of Interest (Rule 1.7, Current Clients, and Rule 1.8, Former Clients)	You begin researching an issue on a client's case and you realize that you worked on a matter against that client at a previous law firm.	Be sure to inform your attorney supervisor immediately that you had previously worked on the case so that an ethical wall can be built to insulate you from the case. Also inform the attorney if you have an interest in the outcome of any legal dispute your office handles, or if you know of anyone on the legal team that might.
Unauthorized Practice of Law (Rule 5.5)	The client called and the attorney is not in the office. The client asks you to explain how the case is progressing.	You need to explain to the client that as a paralegal you cannot give any advice. Telling the client "how the case is progressing" may be giving legal advice. Tell the client you will have the attorney contact him or her.
Confidentiality (Rule 1.6)	You are having lunch with a friend who works at another law firm in town. She wanted your opinion about a question she had about researching an issue. Suddenly, your friend begins telling you about the details of a case she is researching.	You need to explain to your friend that you cannot hear about the details of her client's situation and excuse yourself from your luncheon. You need to report your luncheon to your supervisor.

The bottom line is that if there is any question about whether something is ethically right or wrong, the supervising attorney should be consulted.

THE JOYS AND SORROWS OF LEGAL RESEARCH

Legal research may be the hardest course the student paralegal may take, but it also may be the most rewarding. Legal research is sometimes similar to looking for the proverbial "needle in a haystack," but it can make or break a case. For someone who likes puzzles, enjoys reading cases or mysteries, or understands how finding an answer can help the client, legal research will be fun and rewarding.

If one invests in this class and takes in all the tips and tricks offered, legal research will be a valuable course. The successful student will engage with the material and enjoy the journey.

SUMMARY

One of the main roles of a paralegal is performing legal research. The legal research process, which includes identifying a client's factual question, finding law that applies to that question, analyzing law, and communicating the findings to the supervisor, is the foundation of paralegal work.

Success in legal research depends on knowing the main primary and secondary sources of U.S. law, and where they may be found. Understanding the use of a law library and online subscription services or free Internet services is also essential.

Ethics are critical to remember while performing research. It is imperative that paralegals not insert opinions or advice, especially when meeting with a client or communicating research findings. Attorneys must supervise paralegals, and only licensed attorneys may ethically and legally provide legal advice.

REVIEW **QUESTIONS**

1. What is the value of learning the terminology associated with legal research?
2. What is the difference between venue and jurisdiction?
3. How do the concepts of precedent and stare decisis relate to one another?
4. What is the difference between primary authority and secondary authority?
5. What is meant by "exhaustion of administrative remedies"?
6. Why is it important for paralegals to be familiar with, and to abide by, the Model Code of Professional Responsibility of the American Bar Association?
7. Give two purposes or unique characteristics of each of the following: constitutions, statutes, cases, and administrative law.
8. What is a memorandum of law?
9. Why do paralegals work under the supervision of attorneys?
10. What are four general duties that might be performed by a paralegal?

APPLICATION **EXERCISES**

1. John is a paralegal for a small family practice. He is asked to do the following activities by his supervisor, Jami. Which of the following are ethical, appropriate activities for a paralegal, and which are unethical activities that may be the unauthorized practice of law (UPL)? Identify which of the following activities could be construed as UPL:
   a. John is asked to interview Sam, a new client.
   b. John is asked to look over Sam's custody agreement and summarize it.

c. Sam asks John if he will regain full custody of his kids and John responds.

d. John is asked to find the latest law applicable to Sam's case.

e. John tells Sam that he should seek more money for child support.

2. With respect to each of the activities in question 1, what steps may John take to assist Jami in the representation of this client without engaging in UPL? Explain each step chosen and tell why that step was chosen.

3. Identify the abbreviations for the following sources, and state whether each is official or unofficial, if applicable:

a. *United States Code Annotated*

b. *United States Reports*

c. *North Western Reporter*

d. *Corpus Juris Secundum*

e. *Federal Register*

f. *Pacific Reporter*

g. *Southern Reporter*

h. *Code of Federal Regulations*

i. *United States Law Week*

CITATION **EXERCISES**

1. What is the official source of federal statutes?

2. What is the value of unofficial sources? Explain why you would consult an unofficial source of a case or statute.

3. What is the codified version of the administrative regulations made by agencies at the federal level?

4. For each of the following items, create the appropriate citation.

a. Smith is the plaintiff and Jones is the defendant. Jones lost at trial, and appealed the case to the Tennessee Court of Appeals. The case was reported on page 294 in volume 200 of the *South Western Reporter,* second series, and was decided in Tennessee in 2005.

b. American Underwriters Insurance was sued by Camilla Edwards. American Underwriters Insurance appealed to the U.S. Supreme Court. The Court heard and decided the case in 2009.

It was subsequently reported in the official reporter, volume 493, on page 1112.

c. The State of Missouri prosecuted Jonathan Horowitz for murder. Horowitz appealed to the state supreme court and the case was reported in volume 398 of *South Western Reporter,* second series, in 2007, on page 398.

d. Freddie Faker was sued by Tammy Tucker, and the case was decided in 2008. The case was filed in the U.S. District Court for the Northern District of Indiana and reported on page 999 of *Federal Supplement* in volume 498.

e. The appellant is Ashley Jones, the appellee is Paul Smith, and the case begins on page 644 in volume 289 of the *Federal Reporter,* second series. It was a Seventh Circuit case decided in 2005.

f. What does the cite 50 U.S.C.A. §1752 (West 1987) mean? Identify the meaning of each part of this citation.

QUICK **CHECK**

1. What is the first stage of the legal research process in which an attorney or paralegal might meet with the client?
   a. Interviewing
   b. Conducting research
   c. Analysis
   d. Communicating

2. In what stage of the legal research process is the law applied to the facts of the client's case?
   a. Interviewing
   b. Conducting research
   c. Analysis
   d. Communicating

3. In what stage of the legal research process are the findings reported to the supervisor?
   a. Interviewing
   b. Conducting research
   c. Analysis
   d. Communicating

4. In what stage of the legal research process does a paralegal find law that applies to the client's case?
   a. Interviewing
   b. Conducting research
   c. Analysis
   d. Communicating

5. What are large sets of books that contain written case decisions or opinions from state and federal courts?
   a. Case reporters
   b. Code books
   c. Digests
   d. Form books

6. What are sets of books that contain short summaries of points of law in cases?
   a. Case reporters
   b. Code books
   c. Digests
   d. Form books

7. What books, sometimes called *practice books,* contain sample documents?
   a. Case reporters
   b. Code books
   c. Digests
   d. Form books

8. What are books containing either federal or state statutory law called?
   a. Case reporters
   b. Code books
   c. Digests
   d. Form books

9. The two most thorough legal research databases require a subscription.
   a. True
   b. False

10. If you know how to conduct online legal research, there is no need to familiarize yourself with book-based research.
    a. True
    b. False

11. What term refers to the relationship between the states and the federal government?
    a. Federalism
    b. Supremacy Clause

12. What term refers to the article of the U.S. Constitution that declares all federal laws superior over any conflicting state laws?
    a. Federal Clause
    b. Supremacy Clause

    c. Commerce Clause
    d. State Law Clause

13. Which type of law is used to define a government's functions?
    a. Statute
    b. Constitution
    c. Case
    d. Administrative regulation

14. Which type of law results from legislative action?
    a. Statute
    b. Constitution
    c. Case
    d. Administrative regulation

15. Which type of law is made by judges?
    a. Statute
    b. Constitution
    c. Case
    d. Administrative regulation

16. Which type of law is created by an agency rather than a court or legislature?
    a. Statute
    b. Constitution
    c. Case
    d. Administrative regulation

RESEARCH

It is suggested that these exercises be performed in books in a physical library, if possible. **Each case should be found in the library or on the Internet.** Then, the *Bluebook, ALWD,* or an Internet site should be consulted for the correct format when citing the case in the answer.

1. To see what factual situation 11 U.S.C.A. § 330 (West 1991) addresses, examine the statute using the TAPP technique for analyzing facts: things, acts, persons, and places.
   a. What things are involved in the statute?
   b. What acts are involved in the statute?

   c. What persons are involved in the statute?
   d. What places are involved in the statute?

2. State the full citation for 400 U.S. 379.
3. State the full citation for 359 N.E.2d 1151, assuming that this case is cited in a document to be filed in an Illinois court.
4. Find 5 U.S. 137 (1803). What is the proper citation for this case? Identify each part of the caption.

INTERNET **RESEARCH**

1. Access your state's ethical rules. Find the rule, if any, that identifies the attorney's responsibility toward paralegals. (If your state does not have such a rule, find a state that does.) Cite your source.

2. Select another state's ethical rules and find the rule, if any, that identifies the attorney's responsibility toward paralegals. Compare it to the rule in your state. Is the

language the same? If not, identify the differences and explain what you think may be the impact of those differences.

3. Find three secondary sources of legal information that contain definitions of legal terms. Search in each for a definition of *fiduciary.* Compare and contrast the definitions. Cite the sources.

4. Find the website for your highest state court. Cite the address. Find three services that the website provides, such as oral arguments, full-text case retrieval, or information about the justices. Summarize these services.

5. Start a database or card file with the citations to valuable Internet resources that you learn about during this course. It is suggested that you include, at a minimum, the name of the source, the web address, the last date the source was updated, the last date the source was visited.

MEDIA **RESOURCES**

Your instructor may have access to the following videos, or they may be found on the ancillary website for this textbook.

"Confidentiality Issue: Need to Know Circle" (Paralegal Practice and Ethics-Related Video Segment from *The Paralegal Professional Classroom Video Series* DVD)

"Conflict of Interest Issue: Relationships with Clients" (Paralegal Practice and Ethics-Related Video Segment

from *The Paralegal Professional Classroom Video Series* DVD)

"Legal Research: Are Books Obsolete?" (Paralegal Practice and Ethics-Related Video Segment from *The Paralegal Professional Classroom Video Series* DVD)

"UPL Issue: Helping the Client without Practicing Law" (Paralegal Practice and Ethics-Related Video Segment from *The Paralegal Professional Classroom Video Series* DVD)

INTERNET **RESOURCES**

These resources are the beginning of a series of websites for your use. It is suggested that you create a database of these websites in accordance with the Internet Research exercises.

Be sure to continue referencing each chapter, as the sites will not be repeated.

ABA:	www.abanet.org
AAfPE:	www.aafpe.org
Cornell University Law School:	www.law.cornell.edu
Indiana University School of Law:	http://law.indiana.edu/lawlibrary/research/resources/
Internet Legal Research Group:	http://www.ilrg.com
'Lectric Library:	http://www.lectlaw.com
Legal documents:	http://www.docstoc.com/search/memorandum-of-law-in-support-of-motion-for-summary-disposition-or-judgment/
LexisNexis:	http://www.lexis.com/
LexisOne (Free):	www.lexisone.com
Library of Congress:	http://www.loc.gov/index.html
Purpose of Legal Research	http://topics.law.cornell.edu/wex/legal_research
The Legal Memorandum	http://sparkcharts.sparknotes.com/legal/legalwriting/section2.php
The Supremacy Clause and Federal Preemption:	http://www.law.umkc.edu/faculty/projects/ftrials/conlaw/preemption.htm
The Unauthorized Practice of Law, A Paralegal's Duty and Responsibility:	http://webster.utahbar.org/barjournal/2006/01/the_unauthorized_practice_of_l.html
Thomson Reuters (West):	http://www.westpub.com or www.thomson.com
Unauthorized Practice of Law by a Paralegal: What It is and How to Avoid It:	http://www.dcba.org/brief/mayissue/2002/art40502.htm
U.S. Government Printing Office:	http://www.gpoaccess.gov/
Washburn University School of Law:	http://washburnlaw.edu/library/
Westlaw:	http://web2.westlaw.com/signon/default.wl?fn=_top&rs=WLW8.08&vr=2.0&bhcp=1
Westlaw (Free):	www.findlaw.com

VanHart/Shutterstock

chapter **two**

THE STRUCTURE OF GOVERNMENT AND THE COURT SYSTEM

LEARNING OBJECTIVES

After completing this chapter, students should be able to:

1. Describe the basic structure of American government.

2. Locate print and non-print information about the duties and powers of the United States Supreme Court.

3. Explain the two- and three-tiered structure of the court system.

4. Outline the organization of the federal and state court systems.

5. Identify the roles of jurisdiction and venue in a court system.

CHAPTER OVERVIEW

All citizens are affected by the American legal system, although most know very little about the system unless they become personally involved in it. All paralegals should have a working knowledge of the major concepts and processes of our legal system. Chapter 1 introduced the basic concepts of federalism, the supremacy clause, jurisdiction, venue, state courts, and federal courts. In this chapter, each of these concepts will be discussed.

OPENING SCENARIO

Heather Dobbs, a new client, came into the office today. Heather lives in Indiana but works in Illinois. On her way home from work last week, she was stopped at a stop sign at a four-way intersection. She looked both ways and proceeded into the intersection. She had seen a truck coming from the west on the cross street, but knew that both streets were controlled by stop signs. Unfortunately for Heather, the truck driver failed to stop at his stop sign and struck Heather's car. The damage to her car was extensive and Heather was taken to a local hospital. Paul Roberts, the truck driver, lives in Illinois. Heather wants to retain the Allworthy Law Firm to represent her and help her recover the losses she sustained in the collision.

LEVELS AND BRANCHES OF AMERICAN GOVERNMENT

The Constitution organizes the federal government into three main branches: executive, legislative, and judicial. In addition to the three branches, there is a "fourth branch" of government, consisting of the administrative agencies. Although not described explicitly in the Constitution, this branch is significant, and is included in most discussions of the government.

Federal Government

The federal government is a good starting point for discussing the structure of American government, because it is the "umbrella" under which everything else falls within our system.

Federalism and the Supremacy Clause In a government based on *federalism*, there is a division of power between a central body of government and many sub-bodies. In the United States, the federal government holds the primary powers, but certain other powers are left to the states. This concept originated with the framing of the Constitution.

The founding fathers believed there was a definite need for a centralized government, but recognized that freeing the colonies from a powerful central government (England) was the basis for the Revolutionary War. Therefore, a compromise was struck. This compromise was achieved through the ***Supremacy Clause***, the ***Necessary and Proper Clause***, the ***Commerce Clause***, and the ***Tenth Amendment***.

The Supremacy Clause, in Article VI of the Constitution, basically states that the Constitution and any laws that Congress makes are the "Supreme Law of the Land."[1] The Necessary and Proper Clause, Article 1, Section 8, gives the federal government the right to make whatever laws are necessary to carry out the powers granted to it in the Constitution.[2] The Commerce Clause, Article VI, Section 8, gives the federal government the right "[t]o regulate Commerce with foreign Nations, and among the several States, and with the Indian Tribes."[3] Although this provision uses the term "commerce," many laws that do not obviously seem to relate to commerce have been held to fall within the power granted by this clause.

It is the Tenth Amendment that grants powers to the individual states. It says that "The powers not delegated to the United States by the Constitution, nor prohibited by it to the States, are reserved to the States respectively, or to the people."[4]

---

[1]United States Senate. *Constitution of the United States, Art. VI.* S.PUB.103-21. Prepared by the Office of the Secretary of the Senate. http://www.senate.gov/civics/constitution_item/constitution.htm#a6

[2]United States Senate. *Constitution of the United States, Art. I, §8.* S.PUB.103-21. Prepared by the Office of the Secretary of the Senate. http://www.senate.gov/civics/constitution_item/constitution.htm#a1_sec8

[3]*Id.*

[4]*Id. Amend. X.* http://www.senate.gov/civics/constitution_item/constitution.htm#amdt_10_(1791)

Federalism
A form of government in which there is a division of power between a central body and sub-bodies. In the United States, that means that the federal government holds the primary power, but certain powers are reserved to the states.

Supremacy Clause
The clause of the U.S. Constitution that makes it the supreme law of the land: "This Constitution, and the Laws of the United States which shall be made in Pursuance thereof; and all Treaties made, or which shall be made, under the Authority of the United States, shall be the supreme Law of the Land." (U.S. Const. art. 6)

Necessary and Proper Clause
A clause in the Constitution giving Congress the authority to make laws: "To make all Laws which shall be necessary and proper for carrying into Execution the foregoing Powers, and all other Powers vested by this Constitution in the Government of the United States, or in any Department or Officer thereof." (U.S. Const. art. I, § 8)

Commerce Clause
The clause in the U.S. Constitution that gives Congress the power to regulate commerce between the states and between the United States and foreign countries.

Tenth Amendment
An amendment to the U.S. Constitution that reserves to the states any powers not delegated to the federal government: "The powers not delegated to the United States by the Constitution, nor prohibited by it to the States, are reserved to the States respectively, or to the people." (U.S. Const. amend X)

FIGURE 2-1 The Three
Branches of Government[5]

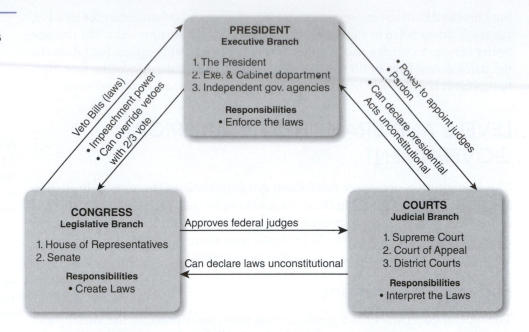

Separation of Powers The division of the federal government is based on a concept called the ***separation of powers***. This means the government is divided into three distinct branches: executive, legislative, and judicial. Figure 2-1 shows this division.

Each branch has its own unique functions. The powers of each also are limited through a system of ***checks and balances*** on one another. This system provides an additional assurance that no one entity will become all-powerful. For example, as shown in Figure 2-1, Congress has the power to approve federal judges, but the judicial branch has the power to decide whether laws made by Congress are valid under the Constitution.

This concept of checks and balances is important when updating legal research, because it is essential to confirm that a law created by one branch is not superseded by a superior law or decision made by another branch. For example, a decision made by the United States Supreme Court may have declared a law made by Congress to be invalid.

The Executive Branch The ***executive branch*** is headed by the president of the United States, and includes the president's staff, presidential appointees, and the various administrative agencies that the president oversees. It is responsible for enforcing the laws made by the legislative branch. The U.S. Constitution not only gives the executive branch authority, but also limits that authority. For example, the president appoints the justices of the United States Supreme Court, but Congress must approve an appointment by a vote of two-thirds of the Senate.

The president has a cabinet comprising the heads of 15 departments, such as the departments of commerce, defense, education, homeland security, state, transportation, treasury, and others. The cabinet's role is to advise the president on any subject relating to the duties of each department. These heads also oversee the agency or agencies under them.

Legislative Branch The main function of the U.S. Congress is to create laws, which are called ***statutes***, or the United States ***Code***. Congress is a ***bicameral*** legislature, meaning it is divided into two chambers: the Senate and the House of Representatives. Figure 2-2 shows how a bill moves through these chambers to become a law.

Separation of powers
The division of the power of the federal government into three separate branches: the executive, legislative, and judicial.

Checks and balances
A system that guarantees no one branch of government will become all-powerful.

Executive branch
One of the three divisions of government set forth in the Constitution. The branch of government that is primarily responsible for enforcing the laws.

Statutes
Laws created by state and federal legislatures.

Code
A set of statutes that are codified into topics, called "titles." For example, all of a jurisdiction's automobile statutes will be in the same title of the code books.

Bicameral
Having two chambers or divisions, such as the two houses of Congress.

---

[5]About Politics. 2011. http://aboutpolitics.com/easy_politics/gov_branches.html

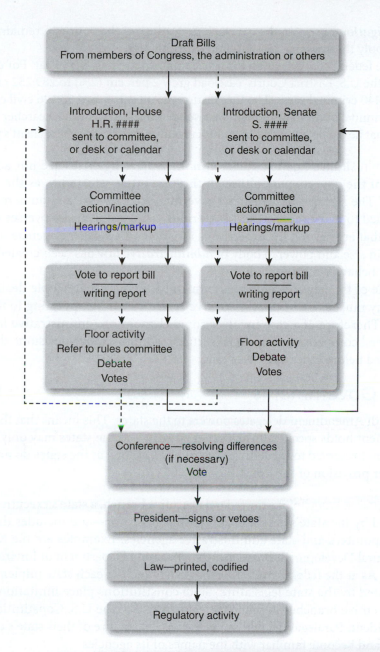

FIGURE 2-2 How a Bill Becomes Law[6]

Judicial Branch The judicial branch is charged with administering justice through the courts. The federal courts were created in Article III, § 1 of the Constitution, which states in part:

> The judicial Power of the United States, shall be vested in one supreme Court, and in such inferior Courts as the Congress may from time to time ordain and establish. The Judges, both of the supreme and inferior Courts, shall hold their Offices during good Behavior, and shall, at stated Times, receive for their Services a Compensation which shall not be diminished during their Continuance in Office.[7]

[6]How a Bill Becomes Law. Reed Elsevier. LexisNexis. 2007. http://www.lexisnexis.com/help/cu/The_Legislative_Process/How_a_Bill_Becomes_Law.htm

[7]United States Senate. *Constitution of the United States, Art. III,* §1. S.PUB.103-21 Prepared by the Office of the Secretary of the Senate. http://www.senate.gov/civics/constitution_item/constitution.htm#a3

Litigation
The process by which one contests an issue in a legal proceeding.

Administrative agencies
Organizations created by the executive branch of state or federal government that implement laws made by the legislative branch. Examples are the Environmental Protection Agency and the Occupational Safety and Health Administration.

Administrative law
Law that defines the powers, limitations, and procedures of administrative agencies, as well as the rights of individuals who deal with these agencies.

> **TIP**
> For a useful reference, bookmark http://www.usa.gov/Agencies /Federal/All_Agencies/index.shtml.

Exhaust administrative remedies
In dealing with administrative agencies, an individual must pursue all remedies available at the agency level before appealing to the appropriate state or federal court.

> **TIP**
> Each state government has a website. It would be useful to find the website for one's state of residence or employment and bookmark it. These websites provide useful information on each branch of state government and state agencies.

> **TIP**
> Create a database of web addresses for the state government sites that could prove useful later.

> **TIP**
> Paralegals should become familiar with their state legislature's organization. Locate the home page of the state legislature and bookmark it.

Litigation occurs in the courts. It is the duty of the courts to remain neutral and to apply the laws in a fair and impartial manner.

The federal courts hear an extensive number of cases every year. For example, in 2011, the U.S. District Courts' caseload grew 2 percent (2%) to 289,252 civil cases and 788,440 criminal cases. The U.S. Courts of Appeals heard 55,126 civil cases and 12,198 criminal cases.[8] This growth in cases demonstrates why a researcher needs to be sure that he or she has found the most current cases to support the client's position.

Administrative Agencies   The ***administrative agencies*** are not actually a branch of the government, although they are often referred to as the "Fourth Branch." The agencies of the federal government are diverse and numerous. Each was created to manage crises, address serious social problems, or oversee complex matters that are beyond the expertise of legislators. Because the agencies continue to grow in size and power, a body of ***administrative law*** has been created to govern their behavior and functions.

One of the key concepts in administrative law is that people dealing with an agency must ***exhaust administrative remedies*** before appealing to the court system. Therefore, if a case involves some element of administrative law, such as workers' compensation or social security, administrative decisions should be researched before other sources of law.

State Governments

The Tenth Amendment delegates powers to the states. This means that the federal government holds specifically delegated powers, and the states may only legislate in areas not reserved to the federal government, as long as the states do not violate any other provision of the Constitution.

Executive Branch   Like the federal executive branch, a state's executive branch is headed by the state's chief executive—the governor—and includes the governor's appointees and state administrative agencies. Examples are the Kentucky Agricultural Development Board and the Wyoming Department of Environmental Quality. As at the federal level, the executive branch of each state implements the law created by the state legislature. State constitutions place limitations on the state executive branches in much the same way that the U.S. Constitution limits the president. Paralegals should know the basic structure of their state's executive branch, and become familiar with the names of its agencies.

Legislative Branch   All states have a bicameral legislature like the U.S. Congress, except for Nebraska, which has a unicameral legislature. Most states name their legislative bodies the "House of Representatives" and the "Senate," but some use different terminology to describe the chambers. For example, California has an Assembly and a Senate, and Maryland has a Senate and a House of Delegates.

Judicial Branch   Just like the federal judiciary, state judiciaries are charged with the administration of justice. State courts may have two or three "tiers," or levels. If a system is two tiered, there will be a trial-level court and one level of appeal. The three-tiered systems mimic the federal system in that there is a trial level, an intermediate level of appeal, and a final level of appeal. The trial-level courts have various

[8]United States Courts. *Federal District Court Workload Increases in Fiscal Year 2011.* 2012. http:// www.uscourts.gov/News/NewsView/12-03-13/Federal_District_Court_Workload_Increases_in _Fiscal_Year_2011.aspx

names in different states, such as "trial," "county," "superior," "circuit," "supreme," or "district." Some states may use the designation "supreme" as the name of the trial-level court, while other states use "supreme" as the name of the highest-level court. It is critical that a researcher ensure that the proper name is used for the proper court.

It is often important for paralegals to understand how judges are chosen. Knowing how judges think, how they rule, and how they are influenced can be a great advantage when working on a case. Although the federal judges are appointed for life, many state judges are required to run for office. Around 85 percent of the nation's state judges face some kind of election. For example, Indiana trial court judges must run for office, while judges at both the appellate and supreme court levels must run for retention during the first general election after they have served 2 years, and then every 10 years thereafter.

Opponents of using elections to choose judges argue that the election process results in politics unduly influencing judicial decisions. As an alternative, some states, such as Colorado, use a merit-based system for appointing judges. In Colorado, nominating commissions interview candidates and submit panels of up to three finalists to the governor, who must make an appointment from that list.[9]

Administrative Branch Working with administrative agencies on the state level is different from working with the federal agencies. The procedures vary among state agencies, and the agencies are identified by different names, such as "board," "commission," "department," "committee," or "council." Knowing how state agencies work will help a paralegal understand cases that originated at the administrative level before they reached the court system.

THE HIERARCHY OF THE COURTS

A majority of paralegal jobs are found in *litigation* firms. It is therefore important to become familiar with court systems, including each court's function, procedures, rules, and place in the hierarchy of courts.

In the United States, there are essentially 52 different legal systems–that of the federal government, the District of Columbia, and each of the 50 states. Each system has its own set of statutes and cases. Paralegals do not need to know all of these laws, but it is important to know how to find the laws, and understand the processes and functions within each system.

Federal

The Constitution sets up the federal court system under Article III, § 1.[10] This section explicitly names only the U.S. Supreme Court, but it allows Congress to create other federal courts. Congress passed the Judiciary Act of 1789, which set up the original 13 district courts and 3 circuit courts of appeal. Although the Judiciary Act has been amended several times, the basic structure remains the same. The federal system is a three-tier system because it has three levels, or tiers, as shown by Figure 2-3.

Each level has a special function. The **United States District Courts** are the federal trial courts, which sit at the lowest level in the federal system. In the middle level are the **United States Circuit Courts of Appeal**, which are the first level of appeal.

> **TIP**
>
> It is beneficial for researchers to learn the name and abbreviation of every court in the jurisdiction in which they work, as well as the federal courts. Knowing this information without having to look it up helps researchers find and understand the material quicker.

United States District Courts
The trial courts in the federal court system.

United States Circuit Courts of Appeals
Courts of intermediate appeal in the federal court system.

[9]Larry C. Berkson, updated by Rachel Caufield and Malia Reddick. *Judicial Selection in the United States: a Special Report.* 2010. http://www.judicialselection.us/uploads/documents/Berkson_1196091951709.pdf

[10]United States Senate. *Constitution of the United States, Art. III, §1.* S.PUB.103-21 Prepared by the Office of the Secretary of the Senate http://www.senate.gov/civics/constitution_item/constitution.htm#a3

FIGURE 2-3 Hierarchy of the Federal Courts[11]

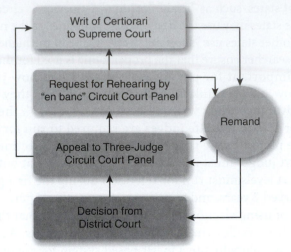

United States Supreme Court
The highest court in the federal court system.

Case or Controversy
A requirement that courts will decide cases only when some actual disagreement is the reason for bringing the lawsuit.

Moot
No real controversy exists.

Standing to sue
Having an interest in the case; arises because the party was injured or has an interest that was adversely affected.

United States Bankruptcy Courts
Courts of exclusive jurisdiction that hear only bankruptcy matters.

Exclusive jurisdiction
Power given to a court to hear a certain type of matter that no other court has the authority to hear.

Court of International Trade
A court that reviews civil actions arising out of import and export transactions and federal statutes affecting international trade.

United States Court of Federal Claims
A court that decides private claims against the United States where individuals seek monetary compensation.

Judge
A person, either elected by the people or appointed by an executive of the government, who presides over legal matters and renders a decision.

The highest level is the **United States Supreme Court**, which is the final court of appeal. There are also several specialized courts.

In order for a court to hear a matter, there must be a **case or controversy**, as stated in Article III of the Constitution. The courts generally will not hear "**moot**" cases, meaning those that are already resolved.

In addition, a court will only hear cases filed by plaintiffs who have **standing to sue**. This means the plaintiff has suffered an actual or threatened loss or has a significant connection to the incident that is the subject of the lawsuit. In other words, if Paul Campbell did some injustice to Emma Radcliff, John Swartz cannot file a lawsuit against Paul, because the injustice did not happen to John.

United States District Courts At the bottom level in the federal system are the 94 U.S. District Courts, which are trial courts. Each state, as well as the District of Columbia and Puerto Rico, has at least one federal district court. In addition, three territories—the Virgin Islands, Guam, and the Northern Mariana Islands–have district courts that hear federal cases. The district courts have the authority to hear nearly all categories of federal cases, including both civil and criminal matters.

The **United States Bankruptcy Courts** are specialized courts that are separate units of the district courts. Federal courts have **exclusive jurisdiction** over bankruptcy cases. This means that a bankruptcy case can be filed only in a U.S. Bankruptcy Court.

There are two special trial courts that have nationwide jurisdiction over certain types of cases. The **Court of International Trade** addresses cases involving international trade and customs issues. The **United States Court of Federal Claims** has jurisdiction over most claims for money damages against the United States, including federal contracts, unlawful "takings" of private property by the federal government, and a variety of other claims against the United States.

With the exception of the territorial courts (Guam, the Northern Mariana Islands, and the Virgin Islands), each federal district **judge** is appointed for life after nomination by the president and confirmation by the U.S. Senate. The federal district judges can be removed involuntarily only when they violate the standard of "good behavior," and then only when they are impeached by the United States House of Representatives, followed by a trial in the United States Senate and a conviction by a two-thirds vote.

[11]Curtis Edmonds, J.D. Federal Court Concepts. *Explaining the Structure.* Georgia Institute of Technology. 2003. http://www.catea.gatech.edu/grade/legal/structure.html

> ### CITING THE LAW 2-1: U.S. DISTRICT COURT CASES
>
> The judicial decisions of U.S. District Courts are reported in a publication called the *Federal Supplement*. They are cited using the abbreviation for the district in which the case appears. These abbreviations vary among the various jurisdictions. Paralegals should become familiar with the court names and abbreviations within the jurisdiction where they are working.
>
> The citation to the U.S. District Court case *Plute v. Roadway Package System, Inc.*, 141 F. Supp. 2d 1005 (N.D. Cal. 2001) tells the reader that this case was filed in the United States District Court, Northern Division of California (N.D. Cal.), reported in the *Federal Supplement, Second Series* Reporter (F. Supp. 2d), and decided in 2001. The "141" is the volume number of the *Federal Supplement* in which the case appears, and the case starts on page 1005. The parties are *Plute* and *Roadway Package Systems, Inc.*

Federal district court judges generally function much like state court trial judges. The trials can be jury trials or bench trials (without a jury). Witnesses are heard, evidence is presented, and judgments are rendered. A majority of all federal cases that are filed are resolved at the federal district court level.

United States Courts of Appeals   In the middle level of the federal system are the United States Courts of Appeals, created by the Judiciary Act of 1789. The primary function of the judges in these courts is to review cases that have been appealed from U.S. district courts. The judges examine what occurred in the district court and make sure the parties received a fair trial. In civil matters, either party may appeal the decision of the trial court. In criminal matters, generally only the accused may appeal a guilty verdict, and the government does not have the right to appeal if the accused is found not guilty. However, either side in a criminal matter may appeal a sentence.

The justices, sitting in a panel, review the **record** of the trial and the **appellate briefs** filed by the parties. The panel generally consists of three judges. The attorneys may present an oral argument. The court's role is to decide whether any legal errors occurred in the lower court. The appellate review is limited to the following:

- the record in the proceedings below (the transcript, pleadings, and orders);
- the issues of law raised below (if not raised in the lower court, an issue is **waived**, meaning lost);
- material errors (errors that affected the decision, such as allowing inadmissible evidence that influenced the jury's verdict), and
- final orders (with some exception, the review is from a completed proceeding).

The appellate court does not consider issues of fact. It does not hear evidence, and does not listen to testimony from witnesses or receive exhibits.

The U.S. Courts of Appeals also have the duty of reviewing and enforcing decisions appealed from federal administrative agencies, such as the Environmental Protection Agency (EPA), the U.S. Fish and Wildlife Service, and the National Labor Relations Board (NLRB). When a United States Court of Appeals renders a decision, the parties *may* have one more appeal—to the United States Supreme Court.

Record
The official materials of the pretrial and trial proceedings, including pleadings, orders, exhibits, and a transcript of the testimony.

Appellate briefs
Written arguments submitted to a court of appeals to support a party's position. The briefs argue for or against the lower court's decision and request that the decision be affirmed, modified, or reversed.

Waived
Refers to a right or alternative that has been given up.

FIGURE 2-4 Table of the United States Courts of Appeals

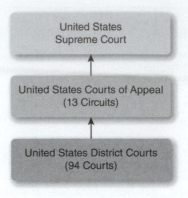

The United States has divided the courts of appeals into 13 circuits—12 regional circuits, and an additional court for the Federal Circuit. Each court sits in one location. For example, the U.S. Court of Appeals for the Seventh Circuit sits in Chicago. Each court of appeals hears appeals from every district court within its region. To illustrate, if a client worked in Colorado and a case from the United States District Court for the District of Colorado was being appealed, it would be heard by the U.S. Court of Appeals for the 10th Circuit. The Court of Appeals for the Federal Circuit hears appeals in specialized cases such as those from the Court of International Trade, the Court of Federal Claims, and patent law cases. Figure 2-4 shows how the circuits are divided.

United States Supreme Court There is only one Supreme Court in the federal court system. It has one **Chief Justice** and eight **Associate Justices**. A quorum is met by the presence of any six justices, and the vote of the Chief Justice counts equally with that of the other Justices. Figure 2-5 shows the Justices who sat on the Supreme Court in 2012.

The U.S. Supreme Court Justices take office in the same manner as all federal judges–after nomination by the president and approval by the Senate. The terms "justice" and "judge" technically mean the same thing; however, "justice" is generally reserved for those sitting on the U.S. Supreme Court or a state's highest court. Individuals sitting on lower courts are referred to as "judges."

Each of the Justices is assigned to one of the federal judicial circuits. This assignment allows a Justice to be responsible for handling special or emergency matters within the assigned circuit, such as injunctions and stays of execution.

Chief Justice
The Justice on the U.S. Supreme Court with the administrative authority to assign cases and preside over the Court.

Associate Justices
The eight Justices who, along with the Chief Justice, make up the U.S. Supreme Court.

CITING THE LAW 2-2: U.S. COURTS OF APPEALS

The decisions of the United States Courts of Appeals are cited in the Federal Reporter series. In the case *Robinson v. Golder,* 443 F.3d 718 (10th Cir. 2006), the opinion appears in volume 443 of the *Federal Reporter, Third Series.* The case begins on page 718. It was decided by the 10th Circuit Court of Appeals in 2006. The parties are Robinson and Golder. Note that the party names are written in italics. Party names are always italicized or underlined when written as part of a citation in a memorandum, brief, or other document.

FIGURE 2-5 The U.S.
Supreme Court Justices[12]

The current U.S. Supreme Court,
from left, is made up of Justices
Sonia Sotomayor (top left), Stephen
G. Breyer, Samuel A. Alito Jr., Elena
Kagan, Clarence Thomas (bottom
left), Antonin Scalia, John G. Roberts
Jr., Anthony M. Kennedy, and Ruth
Bader Ginsburg.[13]

The U.S. Supreme Court is located in Washington, D.C., and holds session
from October through June. Its appellate review in most cases is discretionary, meaning that the court hears only the cases it wishes to hear. The Court
often looks at cases that will affect society as a whole rather than those that are
more limited in scope. The Supreme Court reviews cases originally tried in state
courts, provided there is some federal or constitutional issue at stake. In certain
instances, such as when states, ambassadors, or public ministers are parties, the
U.S. Supreme Court has original jurisdiction, as authorized under Article III, § 2
of the Constitution.

In order to appear before the Supreme Court, a party must file a petition for
a ***writ of certiorari,*** explaining why the case should be heard by the Court. The
Justices review each petition and then vote whether to grant the review. At least
four must vote in favor for the review to be granted. If the petition is not granted,
the decision of the court of appeals stands as issued. If the petition is granted,
it does not mean that the party wins the case. It merely means that the case will
receive a review by the Supreme Court.

Writ of certiorari
A formal written request to have
the U.S. Supreme Court review
a case; the decision to review the
case is at the Court's discretion.

There is no magic formula that determines which cases the Justices
deem worthy of being heard. Often the Justices look for cases that relate to an
important social issue. In some instances, the Justices will take a case involving an issue that lower courts across the nation have disagreed on, or where a
state court made a final decision on a federal question that was contrary to other
courts. Realistically, with over 8,000 filings a year, the Court simply cannot
accommodate every case.

[12]*The Washington Post.* 2010. http://voices.washingtonpost.com/reliable-source/2010/10
/rs-_supreme_court.html

[13]Barnes, Robert. *The Washington Post.* Washington Politics. The High Court. 2012. http://www.
washingtonpost.com/politics/how-is-the-roberts-court-unusual-a-law-professor-counts-the-
ways/2012/03/02/gIQAk1nKrR_story.html

Ethics Alert

Paralegals and attorneys must comply with the rules of the U.S. Supreme Court, or any court, when submitting documents. For example, U.S. Sup. Ct. R. 33 sets forth detailed rules on the form of documents, such as the size and type of font, page length, margins, and even the color of the cover. If the rules are not followed, several sanctions could be imposed ranging from the court not accepting the documents, to reprimands for the attorney, to a civil suit for malpractice.

Concurring opinion
An opinion in which a judge agrees with the decision of the majority, but has different reasons for the decision.

Dissenting opinion
A written opinion of a judge who disagrees with the decision of the majority of judges in a case.

TIP

When a case that has a concurring or dissenting opinion is used as authority, particularly if it is a dissenting opinion, a researcher should always continue to monitor that case during the time preceding the client's trial or settlement.

TIP

Visit the Tax Court website (http://www.ustaxcourt.gov) and view the video *"An Introduction to the United States Tax Court"* to gain a better understanding of what functions this court performs. This website also provides a set of the rules of practice of the Tax Court.

In order to reach the U.S. Supreme Court, one must petition or request that the Court hear the case through a writ of certiorari. Once a writ of certiorari has been granted, the case proceeds, in many ways, like a case at the appellate level. The Justices review the record and the legal briefs from the parties and may hear oral arguments. To prevail, there must be a majority vote of the Justices who have heard the case. An opinion is rendered by the Court, and is published. If a Justice agrees with the decision but not with the reasoning of the other Justices, and feels compelled to give his or her own reasoning, the Justice might issue a ***concurring opinion***. If a Justice disagrees with the majority decision, the Justice may issue a ***dissenting opinion***. Neither concurring nor dissenting opinions are law. Only the majority opinions constitute law. The concurring and dissenting opinions do have a purpose, however. Often these opinions may signal some change that eventually may occur within the legal system.

Specialized Courts The U.S. District Courts, the U.S. Courts of Appeals, and the U.S. Supreme Court are referred to as "constitutional courts" because they derive their power and authority from Article III of the U.S. Constitution. But there are several other courts within the federal system that deal with special issues. These specialized courts are often referred to as legislative courts because they are created under Article I of the U.S. Constitution. Most paralegals may never work within any of these courts. Nevertheless, every paralegal should be familiar with what these courts do. One of the most recognizable courts is the U.S. Tax Court. This court issues decisions about income, estate, and gift tax matters.

The U.S. Court of Federal Claims, once called the U.S. Claims Court, hears claims other than tort claims in which the plaintiff seeks monetary damages from the U.S. government. Examples of such lawsuits are tax refund suits and contractors' claims arising from work on federally funded projects.

CITING THE LAW 2-3: U.S. SUPREME COURT CASES

The decisions of the U.S. Supreme Court are published by multiple services. The official reporter is the *U.S. Reports* (U.S.). The unofficial reporters are the *Supreme Court Reporter* (S.Ct.), *United States Supreme Court Reports, Lawyers' Edition* (L.Ed.), and *United States Law Week* (U.S.L.W.). In the case of *Diamond v. Diehr*, 450 U. S. 175 (1981), the parties are Diamond and Diehr. This 1981 case can be found in volume 450 of the *U.S. Reports* beginning on page 175. Unlike the cases reported in other reporters of lower court opinions, a researcher cannot tell from the citation from what court this case originated. Since the U.S. Supreme Court can hear cases from anywhere in the United States, one has to read the case to make the determination of where else this case has been heard.

Formerly known as the U.S. Court of Military Appeals, the U.S. Court of Appeals for the Armed Forces is the final appellate court to review court-martial determinations within the various military branches. Decisions by this court are directly reviewable by the U.S. Supreme Court.

The U.S. Court of International Trade, once called the Customs Court, handles trade and customs disputes from anywhere in the nation. This court can hold sessions in foreign countries. The president appoints nine judges for a lifetime term, just as Article III judges are appointed.

Another specialized court is the U.S. Court of Appeals for Veterans Claims, which hears matters surrounding veterans' issues. It is an appellate-level court that reviews decisions from the Board of Veterans Appeals. [Note: The citations for specialized courts vary by the court and will be discussed in chapters 5 and 6.]

State Courts The courts in the federal system are separate from those courts in the state system. Each state, and the District of Columbia, has its own court system that is established by the laws of that particular state.

Many states have a three-tiered system similar to the federal system, with a trial court, an intermediate appellate court, and a final appellate court (the court of last resort), often called a supreme court. There are some states, however, which have a two-tiered system, with a trial court and an appellate court. It should be noted that the names of the courts differ from state to state. Therefore, it is incumbent upon the trusted paralegal to check the name of the court before the client's documents are filed.

Figure 2-6 shows an example of the three-tiered court system in Illinois. Note that the Illinois trial courts are called "circuit courts." In comparison, Figure 2-7 shows the two-tiered system used in Montana. Trial courts in Montana are called district courts, and there is no intermediate appellate level. This comparison demonstrates why good paralegals should check the court names and rules of the state in which they work before filing any documents.

Trial Courts Trial courts are generally the courts where a case is first heard. In these courts, attorneys present arguments, often to a jury; witnesses are examined and cross-examined; evidence is introduced; and a verdict is rendered.

Trial courts may be referred to by many names, so paralegals must become familiar with the names of the courts in the jurisdictions where their firms practice. Trial courts may be referred to as circuit courts, district courts, courts of common pleas, courts of chancery, or superior courts. In New York, the designations are particularly confusing to someone from outside the state because the trial court is called a supreme court, which is usually the name of most states' courts of final appeal!

Many states also create specialized, limited jurisdiction courts, such as probate, criminal, and family courts.

In addition to the standard trial and appellate courts, many state court systems have small claims courts where an individual or organization may bring a suit to recover money within a certain limit, such as $10,000. The small claims court rules vary by state, and one should check them before using this type of court.

Considering how many cases are reported, it may be surprising to learn that most disputes are settled without going to trial. Of those cases that are

TIP

Puerto Rico has a court system as well, but this discussion concentrates on the 50 states and the D.C. system.

TIP

The National Center for State Courts provides the state court structure for every state. One should visit and bookmark http://www.courtstatistics.org/Other-Pages/State_Court_Structure_Charts.aspx.

TIP

The National Center for State Courts has a website (http://www.ncsc.org/Topics/Civil/Small-Claims-Courts/Resource-Guide.aspx) with links to every state's small claims rules as well as to information on all state-level courts.

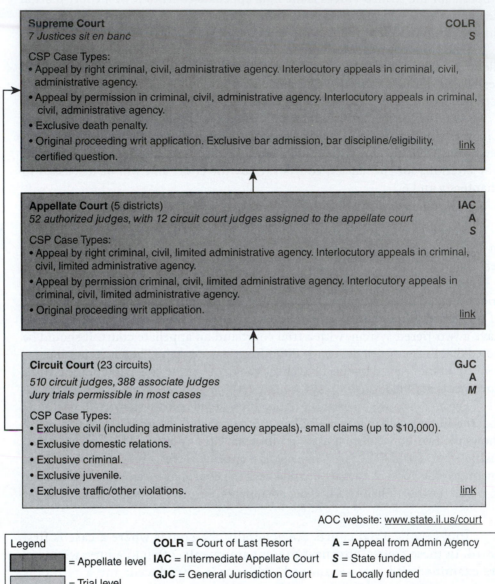

Illinois
(Court structure as of Calendar year 2008)

Supreme Court   COLR S
7 Justices sit en banc

CSP Case Types:
• Appeal by right criminal, civil, administrative agency. Interlocutory appeals in criminal, civil, administrative agency.
• Appeal by permission in criminal, civil, administrative agency. Interlocutory appeals in criminal, civil, administrative agency.
• Exclusive death penalty.
• Original proceeding writ application. Exclusive bar admission, bar discipline/eligibility, certified question.   link

Appellate Court (5 districts)   IAC A S
52 authorized judges, with 12 circuit court judges assigned to the appellate court

CSP Case Types:
• Appeal by right criminal, civil, limited administrative agency. Interlocutory appeals in criminal, civil, limited administrative agency.
• Appeal by permission criminal, civil, limited administrative agency. Interlocutory appeals in criminal, civil, limited administrative agency.
• Original proceeding writ application.   link

Circuit Court (23 circuits)   GJC A M
510 circuit judges, 388 associate judges
Jury trials permissible in most cases

CSP Case Types:
• Exclusive civil (including administrative agency appeals), small claims (up to $10,000).
• Exclusive domestic relations.
• Exclusive criminal.
• Exclusive juvenile.
• Exclusive traffic/other violations.   link

AOC website: www.state.il.us/court

Legend		COLR = Court of Last Resort	A = Appeal from Admin Agency
▇ = Appellate level	IAC = Intermediate Appellate Court	S = State funded
▨ = Trial level	GJC = General Jurisdiction Court	L = Locally funded
	LJC = Limited Jurisdiction Court	M = Mixed state and locally funded
	↑ = Route of appeal	

FIGURE 2-6 State Court Structure for Illinois[14]

Civil case
A lawsuit to enforce a right or to obtain compensation for a wrong (other than a criminal offense) done by a party to another party. These cases usually request money damages or equitable relief (such as an injunction or specific performance).

Suit
A case brought in court.

Plaintiff
The person or entity that files a complaint and commences a lawsuit.

actually filed in the trial courts, 75 percent are civil matters. A ***civil case*** involves conflicts between people or organizations, and begins when one or more of these persons or entities brings ***suit*** by filing a complaint in court. Filing a lawsuit is the first step of **litigation**, or seeking resolution of a legal dispute by judicial process. The most common types of actions are personal injury, family law, and contracts. In a civil case, the person who files the lawsuit, or ***plaintiff***, is seeking

[14]National Center for State Courts. 2009. http://www.courtstatistics.org/Other-Pages/State_Court _Structure_Charts/Illinois.aspx

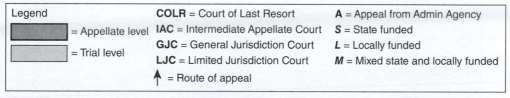

Montana
(Court structure as of Calendar year 2008)

Supreme Court   **COLR**
7 *Justices sit en banc and in panels*   **S**

CSP Case Types:
- Exclusive appeal by right criminal, civil, administrative agency. Interlocutory appeals in criminal, civil administrative agency.
- Exclusive death penalty.
- Exclusive original proceeding application for writ, certified question, advisory option.   link

---

Water Court   **GJC**
(4 divisions)   **S**
1 *chief judge*, 4 *water judges, water masters as needed*
No jury trials

CSP Case Types:
- Real property, limited to adjudication of existing water rights.

link

District Court (56 counties)   **GJC**
43 *judges*   **A**
Jury trials   **M**

CSP Case Types:
- Tort, contract, real property rights. Exclusive mental health, estate, civil appeals, miscellaneous civil.
- Exclusive domestic relations.
- Misdemeanor. Exclusive felony, criminal appeals.
- Juvenile.   link

Workers'   **GJC**
Compensation Court   **S**
1 *judge*
No jury trials

CSP Case Types:
- Limited to workers' compensation disputes.

link

Justice's Court   **LJC**
(66 courts)   **L**
25 *justices of the peace plus 39 judges who serve both justice's Court and City Court*
Jury trial expect in small claims

CSP Case Types:
- Tort, contract, real property rights ($0–$7,000), small claims ($3,000).
- Preliminary hearings, misdemeanor.
- Traffic infractions, parking.

City Court   **LJC**
(81 courts)   **L**
32 *judges plus 39 judges who serve both City Court and Justice's Court*
Jury trials in some cases

CSP Case Types:
- Tort, contract, real property rights ($0–$7,000).
- Preliminary hearings, misdemeanor.
- Traffic infractions. Exclusive ordinance violations.

Municipal Court   **LJC**
(5 courts)   **L**
7 *judges*
Jury trials

CSP Case Types:
- Tort, contract, real property rights ($0–$7,000).
- Preliminary hearings, misdemeanor.
- Traffic infractions, parking.

AOC website: www.courts.mt.gov

Legend
■ = Appellate level
□ = Trial level

COLR = Court of Last Resort
IAC = Intermediate Appellate Court
GJC = General Jurisdiction Court
LJC = Limited Jurisdiction Court
↑ = Route of appeal

A = Appeal from Admin Agency
S = State funded
L = Locally funded
M = Mixed state and locally funded

FIGURE 2-7 Two-Tiered System in Montana[15]

damages in the form of money to compensate the plaintiff for losses alleged to have been caused by some other person or entity, who is the *defendant*.

In a *criminal case*, the government enforces the law by bringing charges against a person accused of committing a crime, such as robbery, murder, or drunk driving. The government is seeking punishment for a crime committed against a victim, but is acting for the benefit of the entire state. The government wants the

Defendant

The person or entity against whom an action is filed.

Criminal case

A Cases brought by the government against a person accused of violating criminal law.

[15]*Id.* at http://www.courtstatistics.org/Other-Pages/State_Court_Structure_Charts/Montana.aspx

Caption
The heading of the complaint; appears on all subsequent pleadings in a lawsuit.

CITING THE LAW 2-4: STATE TRIAL COURTS

Because trial court decisions are not published in the reporter system, the information by which we reference them is found in the *caption* of the pleadings. The court name is generally the first piece of information on the page. If Allworthy Law Firm filed the complaint in the opening scenario, the caption might look something like this:

Firm's or Attorney's Information

Firm Name

Address

State of Indiana)

Vigo Circuit Court

)   SS:

County of Vigo)   Terre Haute, Indiana

Heather Dobbs,

        Plaintiff,   Case No.: No. 12-3-456789-1

    vs.   Complaint

Paul Roberts,

        Defendant

_____

Comes now the Plaintiff ... .

1. [Claim for Relief]

2. [Claim for Relief]

3. [Claim for Relief]

WHEREFORE, the Plaintiff prays that ... .

Dated this 29th day of May 2013

                        Firm Name

                        Address

                        Firm's or Attorney's

                        Information

    Verification

    When citing the law, the last names of the party names in the caption become the party names in the citation.

---

court to order the person who committed the crime to be punished, either by going to prison, paying a fine, or receiving some other penalty.

Trial courts are on the bottom tier of the court hierarchy. That means that no other court is required to follow the trial court's decisions. The decisions are only binding on the parties who are named in the lawsuit.

Intermediate Courts of Appeal   If a state has a three-tier system, it will have an intermediate level of appellate courts that reviews decisions made by lower courts and administrative agencies. The appellate courts look to correct errors of law. Generally, a panel of three to seven judges hears an appeal. Like the U.S. Courts of Appeal, these courts may hear an oral argument and the judges may write concurring and dissenting opinions.

State intermediate appellate courts are called by different names in different states. They may be referred to as Courts of Appeals, Circuit Courts of Appeals, Intermediate Courts of Appeals, Supreme Court Appellate Term, District Superior Courts, or other designations.

> **TIP**
>
> Researchers can find the courts of every state at http://www.statemaster.com/graph/gov_sta_cou_nom_int_app_cou-state-court-nomenclature-intermediate-appellate.

CITING THE LAW 2-5: INTERMEDIATE COURTS OF APPEAL

State cases at the appellate level are published in the national reporter system in the regional reporters. Many states no longer publish the official versions of the cases, and regional reporters or unofficial reporters must be relied on. Each regional reporter contains cases from a group of states, as shown in Table 2-1.

TABLE 2-1   Division of West's Regional Reporters

Source	Abbreviation	Coverage
Atlantic Reporter	A., A.2d	Unofficial source for the state appellate courts of Connecticut, Delaware, District of Columbia, Maine, Maryland, New Hampshire, New Jersey, Pennsylvania, Rhode Island, and Vermont; published by West
North Eastern Reporter	N.E., N.E.2d	Unofficial source of the state appellate courts of Illinois, Indiana, Massachusetts, New York, and Ohio; published by West.
North Western Reporter	N.W., N.W.2d	Unofficial source of the state appellate courts of Iowa, Michigan, Minnesota, Nebraska, North Dakota, South Dakota, and Wisconsin; published by West.
Pacific Reporter	P., P.2d, P.3d	Unofficial source of the state appellate courts of Arizona, California, Colorado, Hawaii, Idaho, Kansas, Montana, Nevada, New Mexico, Oklahoma, Oregon, Utah, Washington, and Wyoming; published by West.
South Eastern Reporter	S.E., S.E.2d	Unofficial source of the state appellate courts of Georgia, North Carolina, South Carolina, Virginia, and West Virginia; published by West.
South Western Reporter	S.W., S.W.2d, S.W.3d	Unofficial source of the state appellate courts of Arkansas, Kentucky, Missouri, Tennessee, and Texas; published by West.
Southern Reporter	So., So.2d, So.3d	Unofficial source of the state appellate courts of Alabama, Florida, Louisiana, and Mississippi; published by West.

Each state has its own citation format, so paralegals should always check *The Bluebook, ALWD,* or another citation manual.

(Continued)

TIP

Remember that one purpose of a citation is to give the reader all the information he or she needs to find the case or other authority that has been cited. Properly citing a case, with complete and correct information, is the way to accomplish that task. It is often the responsibility of a paralegal to cite-check authorities in documents created by individuals in the firm.

In the opening scenario, if Heather Dobbs lost at trial and chose to appeal the decision, the appellate court's opinion would be published in the national reporter system. In Indiana, there is no longer an official reporter, so it would be published only in the regional reporter for her state. The citation to her case might be *Dobbs v. Roberts*, 500 N.E.2d 111 (Ind.Ct.App. 2009). The abbreviation "Ind.Ct.App" tells the reader that the case is before the Indiana Court of Appeals.

In the case of *State v. Ordway*, 261 Kan App. 2d 776, 934 P.2d 94 (1997), the official reporter does exist, so both the official (Kan. App. 2d) and the unofficial (P.2d) citations are given, with the official reporter listed first in most states. The reader then has the option of locating the case in either source. Cases also can be found on state government Internet sites, such as that of Arkansas, where one can find citations like this: *Smith v. Jones*, 2012 Ark. 37, 378 S.W.3d 437. The citation contains no year, as the Arkansas Supreme Court has stated that it is unnecessary.

Highest Court   The decisions appealed to the state supreme court or highest state court are heard by a panel of an odd number of judges so that a tie vote is not possible. A state's highest court functions much like the U.S. Supreme Court. Attorneys file briefs, the justices review the record from the lower court, the attorneys may engage in oral argument, and the judges confer to reach a decision.

In most states, the highest state court is called the "supreme court," but there are exceptions. The District of Columbia has the District of Columbia Court of Appeals. Maryland's Court of Appeals is that state's highest court. The same is true for New York. Maine and Massachusetts have a Supreme Judicial Court, and West Virginia has the Supreme Court of Appeals. A good paralegal will check the names of the courts in the state in which a case is filed.

Like state appellate court opinions, state supreme court opinions are found in the regional reporters. Many states no longer publish the official versions of their supreme court cases, so the unofficial reporters are relied upon. Each state has its own required citation format, so *The Bluebook* or *ALWD* should always be checked.

JURISDICTION

Jurisdiction
The power and authority of a court to hear and decide a case.

Each court, whether in the federal or state system, has a designated *jurisdiction*, or the power and authority to hear and decide certain cases. Each court has jurisdiction to hear cases from within a certain geographic area. For example, the federal district court in the Eastern District of Kentucky can hear cases from counties within that region of Kentucky. The U.S. Courts of Appeals can hear cases from the district courts within their regional circuits. That means that the U.S. Court

CITING THE LAW 2-6: STATE SUPREME COURT CASES

In the opening scenario, assume that Heather Dobbs lost at the appellate level and chose to appeal the decision to the state's supreme court. When that decision is final, the opinion will be published in the regional reporter that covers her state. This case will appear in the *North Eastern Reporter*, since Indiana no longer publishes the official version. So, the citation to her case would be as follows: *Dobbs v. Roberts*, 538 N.E.2d 765 (Ind. 2009). In this citation, "Ind." is the abbreviation for the Indiana Supreme Court.

of Appeals for the Third Circuit cannot hear cases from district courts within the Eighth Circuit. The same holds true for state cases. The court system of one state cannot hear cases from another state. If a state's trial courts are organized by county, the trial courts in one county cannot hear cases from another county.

The goal in research is to find authority that applies to the client's situation, so it is important to understand the geographical jurisdiction of the courts. For example, if a client lives in Maricopa County, Arizona, and the client is involved in a dispute over the sale of property in that county, the goal in research is to find Arizona statutes and case law that are binding on the courts of that jurisdiction.

Another element of jurisdiction is the authority of a court to decide, or **adjudicate**, a dispute involving a particular defendant. For the court to have that power over a defendant, the court must have **personal jurisdiction** (also called **in personam jurisdiction**) over the defendant. This concept is critical in litigation, because without personal jurisdiction, the defendant may have a reason to have the case dismissed.

The court can obtain personal jurisdiction over the defendant by giving the defendant notice of the action against him or her. This can be accomplished by **service of process**, which usually involves delivering a copy of the **complaint** along with a **summons**. If the court cannot obtain service over the person of the defendant, the court may still be able to hear the case if the court can establish **in rem** or **quasi in rem** jurisdiction. *In rem* jurisdiction means that the property that is the subject of the lawsuit is located within the court's geographic area. *Quasi in rem* jurisdiction exists if the defendant owns property located within the state, even though the property itself is not the subject of the lawsuit.

A third element of jurisdiction is the power of the court over the subject matter of the dispute. The rules of procedure dictate that certain kinds of cases must be brought in certain courts. For example, the federal courts have jurisdiction if a federal law, such as a federal statute or constitutional provision, is at issue in the lawsuit. If so, it is called a "federal question" case. Thus, if a lawsuit alleges that someone's freedom of speech rights were violated when that person was physically removed from a political rally, the case arises under the First Amendment and therefore is a federal question that can be heard in a federal district court.

A federal court may also have jurisdiction over a case based on diversity of citizenship (28 U.S.C. §1332). Diversity jurisdiction has two elements: the **domicile** of the parties and the value of the case. If the case involves residents of different states on opposite sides of the litigation, and if the amount in controversy exceeds $75,000, the case can be filed either in state court where either party lives, or in federal court. A federal court will apply federal procedural law but will apply the substantive law of the state in which the court sits, including the state's law of conflict of laws.

To understand diversity jurisdiction, it may be useful to review how it applies to the opening scenario. Heather, the plaintiff, is from Indiana, and Paul, the defendant, is from Illinois. Assume that Heather was driving a luxury SUV that was totaled in the crash. The market value of the SUV at the time of the crash was $53,000. In addition to the loss of her car, Heather had a broken leg and other physical injuries from the broken glass. Her medical bills to date are $103,565.07. To determine if this case may be filed in federal court, the following factors must be considered:

- The parties are from different states, since the plaintiff is from Indiana and the defendant is from Illinois;
- The amount in controversy exceeds $75,000, because the plaintiff's car is valued at $53,000, and her medical bills so far are $103,565.07.

Adjudicate
The process that a court or administrative agency undertakes to resolve a dispute.

Personal jurisdiction
The power of a court over the parties, particularly the defendant, in litigation. Also known as *in personam* jurisdiction.

In personam jurisdiction
Jurisdiction over the person.

Service of process
A method of giving notice to the defendant that a lawsuit has been filed against him or her.

Complaint
The document that initiates a civil lawsuit; it is where the plaintiff states a cause of action against the defendant.

Summons
The process by which the defendant is brought within the jurisdiction of the court. A summons generally accompanies a complaint.

In rem
Jurisdiction that arises because the property that is the subject of the lawsuit is located within the court's geographic area of coverage.

Quasi in rem
Jurisdiction over a person's interest in property.

Domicile
A person's permanent home; the place to which he or she intends to return. Each person can have only one domicile, but can have many residences.

TIP

Although a person can have many residences, a person can have only one domicile—or the place to which the person intends to return and to which the person has a permanent connection.

The facts above establish a basis for diversity jurisdiction in federal court. However, which court to file in is a strategic question for the attorney. The attorney would look at the laws on both the federal and the state level and decide which laws best serve the client. If the attorney chose to file in federal court, it could be in either Indiana or Illinois. If the attorney filed in the U.S. District Court for the Southern District of Indiana, the court would apply Indiana substantive law. The attorney might also consider which courts would be more likely to be sympathetic to the client, and which location would be most convenient.

Ethics Alert

The paralegal would never determine in what court the client's lawsuit would be filed. That amounts to giving legal advice, which is the unauthorized practice of law.

Generally, in criminal cases, federal courts have jurisdiction if the alleged activities are a crime under federal law. For example, a robbery of a bank that is insured by the Federal Deposit Insurance Corporation (FDIC) is a federal crime, and will be tried in federal court.

There are several categories of subject-matter jurisdiction, which must also be considered when determining where a lawsuit may be filed. These are the classifications of subject-matter jurisdiction:

- Exclusive
- Concurrent
- General
- Limited
- Original
- Appellate

If a court has exclusive jurisdiction over a certain type of matter, it is the only court that can hear that type of matter. For example, the federal district courts have exclusive jurisdiction to hear bankruptcy cases pursuant to 28 U.S.C. §1334 (2007). Other types of cases handled exclusively by the federal district courts are suits against the U.S. government, federal crimes, claims of copyright or patent infringement, and some admiralty cases. Some state courts also have exclusive jurisdiction over certain cases. For example, in Indiana, only the county circuit courts may hear adoption cases.

Concurrent jurisdiction means that two or more courts have jurisdiction to hear a case. An example would be a ***cause of action*** that alleges a violation of both state and federal law, such as an age discrimination case. Another example might be a child custody action in a state where a court of general jurisdiction and a family law court both have the authority to hear it.

General jurisdiction means that a court can hear any kind of case. State courts of general jurisdiction can handle any cases that raise issues under state law, such as state constitutions and statutes. Federal courts of general jurisdiction can handle any cases that raise federal questions, such as issues based on the Constitution, federal statutes, or other federal laws.

Limited jurisdiction gives a court the power to hear only certain kinds of cases. For example, a family law court cannot hear criminal matters. A small claims court cannot hear personal injury actions where the damages exceed a certain dollar amount. A probate court, which handles wills and the administration of estates, would not be able to hear non-probate matters.

Concurrent jurisdiction
Exists when two or more courts have jurisdiction over the same lawsuit.

Cause of action
The plaintiff's reason for bringing suit. The cause of action must allege enough facts to support a claim, and provide a basis for the court to grant some kind of relief.

General jurisdiction
Jurisdiction to hear and decide any type of case.

Limited jurisdiction
A type of jurisdiction in which a court has the power to hear only certain types of cases. For example, family law courts cannot hear criminal matters.

Original jurisdiction means that the court is the first court to hear a case. The court of original jurisdiction is usually a trial court. It may have exclusive, general, concurrent, or limited jurisdiction, depending on the court.

    Appellate jurisdiction means that the court has the power to review the decisions of lower courts to determine whether an error of law was committed. In some matters, a party has a right to appeal, while at other times, the court has discretion as to whether an individual case will be reviewed.

    Jurisdictional issues are often very complex, and the rules of jurisdiction often give a party a choice among more than one court. When such a choice exists, the decision of where to file is based on the strategy planned by the attorney, and a paralegal will not be making the choice as to which court to file the case in. However, jurisdictional questions often require substantial research, and it is incumbent upon paralegals to have a basic understanding of these issues.

Original jurisdiction
The power of a court that is the first to hear a case.

Appellate jurisdiction
The authority of a court to review a lower tribunal's decision.

VENUE

Venue is often confused with jurisdiction, but they are very different concepts. Venue is the location, such as the county or judicial district, in which the case is to be tried, and becomes an issue only if jurisdiction already exists. If more than one court has jurisdiction to hear a case, the question becomes which venue the case will be tried in. Venue may be changed by agreement of the parties or through a motion. The choice of venue in civil cases may be determined by where a person is domiciled, where the person works, or where the incident giving rise to the cause of action occurred. In criminal matters, venue is usually determined by where the crime took place.

Venue
The location where the case will be tried. Venue may be based on factors such as where the parties are domiciled, where the action took place, or where the crime was committed.

SUMMARY

It is essential for every paralegal to understand the basic structure of government, especially that of the court system. Part of that understanding must include knowledge of the hierarchy of government and the courts on both the federal and state levels.

REVIEW QUESTIONS

1. Describe the basic hierarchy of the federal court system.
2. Explain how appointments are made to the federal courts.
3. In what types of matters does the U.S. Supreme Court have original jurisdiction?
4. Explain the difference between a three-tiered and a two-tiered system of courts.
5. Compare and contrast the different forms of jurisdiction.
6. How does venue differ from jurisdiction? When does venue come into play?
7. Explain the roles that the different branches of government play in administrative law.
8. What is mean by the term "federalism"? How does this concept impact government in the United States?
9. Explain how one can exhaust administrative remedies. How does it affect the right to bring a lawsuit?
10. What is the concept of "case or controversy"? Why is it important when filing a lawsuit?

CITATION **EXERCISES**

Use *The Bluebook: A Uniform System of Citation* or *ALWD* to answer these questions. Properly cite each resource. Include the cited rule with the answer.

1. A case located at page 690 of the *North Western Reporter*, volume 480 where Betsy Ross was sued by George Washington. The case was decided by the Indiana Supreme Court in 2005.

2. Article 2, Section 3, clause 1 of the U.S. Constitution.

3. Fifth amendment to the U.S. Constitution.

4. Preamble of the Oklahoma constitution.

5. Sections 848 and 853 of title 21 of the *United States Code*, published in 1988.

6. Disciplinary rule 5-106(c) of the Model Code of Professional Responsibility, published in 1980.

7. The federal statute that is §1956 of title 50 of the *United States Code*, published in 2006.

8. Section 21 of *Corpus Juris Secundum*, volume 11, discussing bonds, which was published in 1995.

9. Title 31 of the *Code of Federal Regulations* published in 1999, covering section 515.329.

10. Volume 351 of the *Federal Reporter*, second series, page number 193, where American General Insurance appealed a decision to the second circuit court of appeals against Jennifer Aniston in 2007.

QUICK **CHECK**

Matching: Match the Source in column A with the correct item or description in column B

Source

1. Trial courts

2. Statutory law

3. Administrative law

4. Two-tier system

5. Three-tier system

6. Common law

7. The Bill of Rights

8. U.S. Supreme Court

9. Tenth Amendment

10. Constitutional law

Item or Description

a. A court system that does not have an intermediate level of appellate review.

b. Freedom of speech

c. *Roe v. Wade*

d. Reserves rights to the states.

e. The first 10 amendments to the U.S. Constitution

f. Hear witness testimony, view exhibits, and render decisions

g. A court system that has a trial court, an intermediate level of appeals, and a final level of appeal.

h. The Civil Rights Act

i. Tax code

j. Highest court in the system

Determine which court would hear each type of case listed below: state, federal, or both.

1. Criminal cases

2. Diversity cases involving less than $75,000

3. Patent and trademark cases

4. Bankruptcy cases

5. Contract disputes

6. Criminal cases involving a local law

7. Violations of Environmental Protection Agency regulations

8. Violations of Indiana Occupational Safety and Health Administration regulations

9. Divorces

10. Diversity cases involving $75,000 or more

MULTIPLE **CHOICE**

1. American law has its origins in the laws of which country?
   a. France
   b. Spain
   c. England
   d. Japan

2. A senator is part of which branch of government?
   a. executive
   b. legislative
   c. judicial
   d. administrative
3. In the system of checks and balances, judges have the ability to do which of the following?
   a. Enter into treaties with other countries.
   b. Determine their own jurisdiction over legal matters.
   c. Enact statutes based on their court's decisions.
   d. Determine whether current statutes are constitutional.

4. Enumerated powers include which of the following?
   a. The right of state governments to govern local issues
   b. The right of city governments to create municipal ordinances
   c. The right of the federal government to deal with international issues
   d. The right of state courts to decide bankruptcy cases

RESEARCH

1. Find a regulation that governs the use of ladders in swimming pools.
   - Properly cite the source.
   - Summarize the source.
2. Research your state's law on obtaining a driver's license.
   - What is the age at which you can get a permit?
   - What is the age at which you can get a license?
   - Are there any special parameters associated with obtaining your license?

   - Compare your findings with the laws in another state.
   - Properly cite to the laws referenced.
3. Find a case in your jurisdiction where the accused was sentenced for kidnapping, and appealed the decision of the trial court. (Hint: Use search terms in an Internet search engine, or go to a law library and use the indexes of a digest.)
4. Find the case *Robinson v. Golder*, 443 F.3d 718 (10th Cir. 2006). Summarize the facts of the case. What was the main question being decided? What was the result?

INTERNET **RESEARCH**

Note: Remember to cite your sources.

1. Locate the home pages of the state senators and other legislators for your area.
2. Locate the website for U.S. Courts and find the location and contact information of the district court for your area.
3. Find the website for the U.S. Supreme Court. Within that website, find the discussion of traditions of the court. Select three traditions and summarize them.

4. Find the website for the courts of your state. Locate the information that discusses how your judges are selected. Is it by popular vote? Must they run on a party ticket? Are they appointed? Briefly describe the process.
5. Find 28 U.S.C. §41 (2003). What is the purpose of this statute? What does it do?

MEDIA **RESOURCES**

Your instructor may have access to the following videos:

Paralegal Practice and Ethics-Related Video Segment from *The Paralegal Professional Classroom Video Series* DVD. Other videos are available on the Internet.

An Introduction to the United States Tax Court: http://www.ustaxcourt.gov/

Checks and balances: http://videos.howstuffworks.com /hsw/12971-our-constitution-a-system-of-checks-and -balances-video.htm#

The Difference Between Civil and Criminal Cases: Paralegal Practice and Ethics-Related Video Segment from *The Paralegal Professional Classroom Video Series* DVD

INTERNET **RESOURCES**

These resources are the beginning of a series of websites for your use. It is suggested that you create a database of these websites in accordance with the Internet Research exercises.

Be sure to continue referencing each chapter, as the sites will not be repeated.

Courts of Appeals:	http://www.uscourts.gov/courtsofappeals.html
Federal Judicial Center, Impeachments of Federal Judges:	http://www.fjc.gov/public/home.nsf/hisj
Findlaw:	www.findlaw.com
Findlaw for Legal Professionals:	http://lp.findlaw.com/
The National Center for State Courts (Court Structure):	http://www.courtstatistics.org/Other-Pages/State_Court _Structure_Charts.aspx
The National Center for State Courts (Small Claims):	http://www.ncsc.org/Topics/Civil/Small-Claims-Courts /Resource-Guide.aspx
Presidential Executive Orders:	http://www.whitehouse.gov/briefing-room /presidential-actions/executive-orders
Supreme Court:	http://www.supremecourtus.gov/about/about.html
Upcoming Supreme Court cases:	http://www.onthedocket.org/
U.S. Courts:	http://www.uscourts.gov/outreach/resources /comparefedstate.html
U.S. Court of Appeals for the Armed Forces:	http://www.armfor.uscourts.gov/
U.S. Court of Federal Claims:	http://www.uscfc.uscourts.gov/
U.S. Customs Court:	http://www.cit.uscourts.gov/

chapter **three**

UNDERSTANDING THE ORIGINS AND ORGANIZATION OF THE LAW

Mariusz Szczygiel/Shutterstock

LEARNING OBJECTIVES

After completing this chapter, students should be able to:

1. Identify the sources of federal and state law.

2. Understand the concepts of binding authority, persuasive authority, and *stare decisis*.

3. Understand the development of the common law.

4. Explain the hierarchy of law on both the federal and state levels.

CHAPTER OVERVIEW

Understanding how the courts came to be and the remedies they provide for litigants is important in research. In addition, it is necessary to understand the hierarchy of the law in order to know what law should be applied to a particular case. This understanding is important not only in legal research but in all law-related matters.

OPENING SCENARIO

It was a very busy week for John, a paralegal at a general practice firm. First, Heather Dobbs came in with a personal injury claim for compensatory damages. Later that week, Jack Hammer came in to see about ejecting his tenant from his apartment building because the tenant had not paid rent for three months. While Jack felt badly for the tenant because the tenant lost his job, Jack needed to make money, too. Then, Nancy Smith came to the firm to file a complaint against her neighbor, Norman Pardee. He has parties every night until 3 or 4 A.M. and Nancy goes to work at 6 A.M. She wanted an injunction to make Norman stop having parties, or at least to stop making noise after 1:30 A.M. And then there was Craig Douglass, who entered a contract with Jason Big. Craig thought he agreed to supply Jason with 100 widgets at 75 dollars per widget. But Jason thought he was buying 50 widgets at 100 dollars per widget. Craig wants the court to reform the contract according to reflect his responsibility to supply 100 widgets at 25 dollars per widget, which is what he thought he had agreed to.

What laws do these scenarios involve, and what are the different remedies for these claims?

CATEGORIES OF THE LAW

A paralegal will often perform research to find the law that can be used to make an argument to the court for or against a particular position. The first step is to determine if the issue involves federal or state law, and the second step is to determine the types of laws that are applicable.

There are two general types of *primary authority* used in research: case law and enacted law. *Case law* is made when an appellate court decides a legal issue in a dispute before it. When the court decides a case, it issues a written opinion stating its decision and its reasoning for the decision. Unlike case law, enacted law is not created to resolve a dispute. Enacted law is created by legislatures in order to set guidelines in place for future behavior.

Case Law

After laws are enacted by legislatures, judicial opinions issued by courts affect how those laws are applied. Judicial opinions have the effect of interpreting and modifying existing laws, or applying them to new situations. In addition, the judiciary can find that certain laws are unconstitutional, which renders those laws invalid. This body of case law handed down by the courts is sometimes referred to as the *common law*.

The Origins of the Common Law System   Understanding the "why" behind a subject sometimes makes the subject easier to understand and apply. To understand the function of common law, it is helpful to know how common law came to be.

The American legal system is derived to a large extent from the English system of common law. During the Revolutionary War, the American colonists sought to win their independence from British rule. But there were some elements of the British system of government that the founding fathers kept in place, such as the English common law system. This system was distinct from the French *civil law* system, which was based entirely on an established civil code, rather than judge-made case law. Had the French beaten the British in the French and Indian War and asserted control over the American colonies, our system might be based on the French civil code system.

Primary authority
The law itself. Types of primary authority include constitutions, statutes, and case law.

Case law
Judicial opinions issued by courts that affect how other laws are interpreted or applied. Judicial opinions in cases have the effect of modifying existing laws. In addition, the judiciary can find that certain laws are unconstitutional, which renders them invalid.

Common law
Law based on principles enunciated in decisions handed down by judges, which provide precedent for subsequent cases, as distinguished from statutory law enacted by legislatures.

Civil law
1) Any law that is not criminal in nature or 2) A legal system originating in continental Europe that emphasizes codified law, rather than case law.

TIP

The French influence is still seen in Louisiana, which is the only state with a basis in civil law. So, if a researcher is in Louisiana reading this material, he or she should remember that the Louisiana system is somewhat different!

The common law system began when the Anglo-Saxon kings ruled England. The realm was organized into communal units called "hundreds," each headed by an official called a "reeve." The hundred served a judicial function by holding court monthly, and dealing with both civil and criminal matters.[1]

The hundreds combined to form shires, which were roughly the equivalent of counties. The sheriff (derived from the term "shire reeve") was the principal officer of the shire. He collected taxes, administered justice, and performed some judicial functions through the shire court, which convened two times a year. There was no right of appeal to the highest authority (the king).[2]

In 1066, William the Conqueror invaded England and defeated the Anglo-Saxons. William came from Normandy, a region on the coast of France. He decreed that all of the land in the country belonged to the French king, but allowed most of the customary Anglo-Saxon laws to remain in place. William did make one dramatic change: He separated church and state and removed the bishops from the communal courts. William declared that the church must decide its matters under its own **canon law** (church law) instead of by customary law.[3]

Canon law
Law governing the Catholic Church during medieval times.

William and his Norman followers brought with them many aspects of French law and culture. The French legacy exists in various legal terms in use today, such as *acquit, en banc, voir dire,* and *demurrer.* Court documents were issued in Latin, and today those remnants of Latin are in words such as *mandamus, mens rea, actus reus, res judicata, in rem,* and *certiorari.*[4]

Later, William's great-grandson, Henry II, implemented many reforms that still have an impact on the British and American legal systems. He strengthened the judiciary by appointing judges who traveled throughout the country as "circuit riders" and decided disputes in the name of the king. These were the predecessors of the circuit judges of today. Henry also created a central judiciary (a court of common pleas) that applied the same law in each jurisdiction, deciding cases in a consistent and predictable manner by following how previous cases with similar situations had been decided. This was the origin of the doctrine of *stare decisis,* or following precedent.[5] In the royal courts, Henry also implemented a jury system in criminal cases, similar to today's grand juries.[6]

In 1215, King John signed the well-known *Magna Carta Libertatum* (the "charter of freedom"), one of the most important documents in the history of English law. The Magna Carta was created in response to an uprising of barons who demanded guarantees of their rights and privileges. In the charter, the king acknowledged that his rule was not arbitrary, and that both he and the barons were subject to the rule of law. For example, the Magna Carta decreed that the king's subjects could not be punished "except by the lawful judgment of his peers and by the law of the land."

When the colonists came to the New World and established the first colonial governments, they brought with them the basic principles of the Magna Carta, which were incorporated into their colonial **charters**. For example, the 1622

---

[1]Matthew Hale. *The History of the Common Law.* http://www.constitution.org/cmt/hale/history _common_law.htm

[2]Matthew Hale. *The History of the Common Law.* http://www.constitution.org/cmt/hale/history _common_law.htm

[3]*Id.*

[4]Adil Bouharaoui. *Some lexical features of English legal language.* 2003–2011. http://www .translationdirectory.com/articles/article1763.php

[5]Matthew Hale. *The History of the Common Law.* http://www.constitution.org/cmt/hale/history _common_law.htm

[6]*Id.*

EXHIBIT 3-1 THE MAGNA CARTA AND ITS EFFECT TODAY

When representatives of the young republic of the United States gathered to draft a constitution, they turned to the legal system they knew and admired—English common law as it had evolved from the Magna Carta. The U.S. Constitution is "the Supreme Law of the Land," just as the rights granted by Magna Carta were considered a supreme law that could not be arbitrarily canceled by the will of the king.

This heritage is also apparent in the Bill of Rights. The Fifth Amendment guarantees:

> *No person shall . . . be deprived of life, liberty, or property, without due process of law*

Written 575 years earlier, the Magna Carta declares:

> *No freeman shall be taken, imprisoned . . . or in any other way destroyed . . . except by the lawful judgment of his peers, or by the law of the land. To no one will we sell, to none will we deny or delay, right or justice.*

In 1957, the American Bar Association acknowledged the debt American law and constitutionalism owed to the Magna Carta by erecting a monument at Runnymede, the site of its original signing. Yet, despite the connection between the Magna Carta and American concepts of liberty, they are very distinct in purpose. Magna Carta is a charter of ancient liberties guaranteed by a king to his subjects within the feudal system; the Constitution of the United States is the establishment of a democratic government by and for "the People."[7]

Charter

The fundamental law of a municipality or local governmental unit that authorizes the entity to perform designated governmental functions.

Charter of Connecticut guaranteed the colonists the "liberties and immunities of free and natural subjects." Later, when the colonists united against the tyranny of British rule, they fought to preserve the liberties that had their beginnings in 13th-century England.

The system of law reporters for publishing cases also has its origins in the 13th century. An English lawyer named Henry de Bracton compiled a collection of legal cases and commentaries called *De Legibus et Consuetudinibus Angliae* (loosely translated, "On the laws and customs of England"). In this work, he incorporated principles from Roman (civil) law and canon (church) law.[8] Lawyers continued to collect cases from the most important courts in a series of "Year Books" similar to today's case reporters. These were replaced around 1535 by a series of official reports collected by various authors, who were often important jurists. Of these authors, two of the most well known are Chief Justice Edward Coke and Sir William Blackstone. Blackstone's famous work, *Commentaries on the Laws of England* (1766), is well known in America and is still referenced in many modern legal textbooks.

Equitable Law Although in the 13th century Henry II had done much to reform the English legal system, by the 15th century the judges in English courts were spending much of their time dealing with technicalities rather than promoting justice. A system had evolved in which most common law claims were reduced to a rigid set of technical forms, or "writs." Each type of claim had a specific writ with a precise set of technical requirements. If a claim did not meet the

[7]U.S. National Archives & Records Administration. Featured Documents. *The Magna Carta.* http://www.archives.gov/exhibits/featured_documents/magna_carta/

[8]New Advent. Henry de Bracton. 2009. http://www.newadvent.org/cathen/02726c.htm

requirements of any existing writ, no remedy was available. Parties who could not find a remedy in the common law courts could petition the king as a last resort, and appeals to the king occurred with increasing regularity. To reduce the backlog, the king referred cases to the Lord Chancellor, who decided them on the basis of *equity*, rather than strict rules of law.[9]

At first, the chancellor was similar to an administrator, who was often a member of the clergy. He therefore had not been educated in the common law as lawyers at that time usually were. Instead, chancellors were more familiar with canon law (the law of the Catholic Church), and some were also well versed in the ancient Roman concepts of justice and equity. The chancellors therefore responded to arguments on the basis of fairness or morality rather than legal technicalities.

As the king increased the use of chancellors as avenues of appeal, the courts of chancery, or *courts of equity*, arose. No jury was used in the chancery court, and the decisions were based on the circumstances of each case and principles of justice and fairness, rather than on rigid rules of law. Whereas at common law, monetary awards were typical outcomes, the courts of equity used *injunctions* and *specific performance* as the primary remedies in civil disputes. Two innovations in these courts were the writ of *subpoena*, used in an effort to speed the hearings, and the writ of *summons*, to require people to appear.[10]

For a long time, the English courts administered the common law and equitable law in separate courts with separate rules and remedies. Eventually, the boundaries of each court were set, and equity took over when common law was not adequate for the situation. The chancellors began to collect and publish their decisions around 1650 to establish equitable precedents similar to common law precedent.

In America, common law and equitable law were not combined into one court until around 1900.[11] Now, a plaintiff may sue for both common law damages (money) and equitable remedies (injunctions or specific performance or other relief) in the same lawsuit. The jury decides the common law issues and the judge decides the equitable issues.

Judicial Remedies   The courts have a wide array of remedies that can be applied to a given case. The ability to understand these remedies, identify when a remedy is appropriate, and support the client's position with appropriate research will make the paralegal a valuable member of the legal team.

When a party prevails, the court is presented with a request for remedies based on common law or equitable law. Common law remedies, in most instances,

Equity
Justice handed down by chancery courts based on principles of fairness, rather than on rigid rules of common law.

Courts of equity
Courts that determine cases when a loss cannot be measured in money damages.

Injunction
A court order that commands someone to act, or prohibits an act or conduct; usually imposed in courts of equity.

Specific performance
An equitable remedy in which a party is compelled to perform its obligations under a contract.

Subpoena
A court order requiring someone to appear before the court.

Summons
The document that informs the defendant that he or she has been sued and advises the defendant of a date when a response is due.

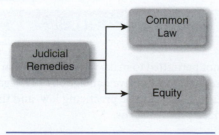

FIGURE 3-1

[9]Matthew Hale. *The History of the Common Law.* http://www.constitution.org/cmt/hale/history_common_law.htm

[10]Matthew Hale. *The History of the Common Law.* http://www.constitution.org/cmt/hale/history_common_law.htm

[11]Chancery, Court of Equity. The 'Lectric Law Library. 1995–2012. http://www.lectlaw.com/def/c225.htm Id

FIGURE 3-2 Remedies at
Common Law

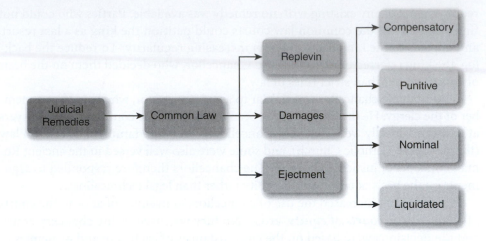

are limited to the court's determination of some legal right and the award of monetary damages. When monetary damages are not sufficient to resolve the litigants' disputes, concepts of equity are applied.

Common Law Remedies Each type of case at common law has several options for remedies depending on the nature of the case. Figure 3-2 shows a breakdown of the common law remedies.

The most common type of common law remedy is **damages**. The most common form of damages is **compensatory damages**, so called because they *compensate* the person for his or her losses. The case of Heather Dobbs is an example. She was injured and her car was wrecked when it was struck by another vehicle. The damages she hopes to recover are compensatory—she wants to receive money for the loss of her car and for the medical bills, pain and suffering, and lost wages resulting from her injuries.

If the defendant had intentionally hit her car to deliberately injure her, Heather would ask for **punitive damages** in addition to compensatory damages. Punitive damages are also called **exemplary damages**, and are awarded to punish a wrongdoer. They are awarded if it is proven that a defendant engaged in conduct that was willful, wanton, malicious, aggravated, or performed with an evil disposition. Punitive damages are intended to dissuade other people from engaging in the same type of conduct.

Damages
The loss a person incurs as a result of injury, whether from a negligent or intentional act, or from some other unlawful act or omission by another.

Compensatory damages
Damages that compensate the injured party for some type of loss, such as the cost of repairing or replacing an automobile, lost wages from work, hospital and doctor bills, or property damage.

Punitive damages
A monetary award that is over and above compensatory damages; imposed to discourage a wrongdoer and others from engaging in the same activity. Usually awarded when it can be shown that the person committed the act with malice or evil intent.

Exemplary damages
A monetary award over and above compensatory damages, granted to discourage a wrongdoer and others from engaging in the same activity. Usually awarded when it is shown that an act was committed with malice or evil intent. Also called punitive damages.

Ethics Alert 3-1

As a paralegal, one is not permitted to make the determination of whether a cause of action will include a request for punitive damages. A paralegal cannot suggest this to the client, because to do so would be practicing law, and the paralegal would be committing unauthorized practice of law.

However, the courts do not allow plaintiffs to recover unlimited punitive damages. Case Excerpt 3-1 is a punitive damage case involving a bad faith claim against an insurance company.

Insurers are expected to be fair in the treatment of their insured and when dealing with claims against the insured. When the insurance company treats its insured unfairly, the insured may have a claim against the insurance company for "bad faith," and can seek punitive or exemplary damages in addition to the amount of the underlying insurance claim. An example of such a claim is presented in *State Farm Insurance v. Campbell*. In its opinion, the Supreme Court established a set of principles for awarding punitive damages, which must be applied on the particular facts and circumstances of each case.

CASE **EXCERPT 3-1:** *State Farm Insurance v. Campbell, 538 U.S. 408 (2003)*

FACTS OF THE CASE

Curtis Campbell caused an accident in which one person was killed and another permanently disabled. His insurer, State Farm Mutual Automobile Insurance Company, refused to settle with the injured parties, and took the case to trial. State Farm assured Campbell and his wife that it would represent their interests. However, State Farm lost the case at trial, and a judgment was entered against Campbell for the damages sustained in the accident. The Campbells then sued State Farm for bad faith, fraud, and intentional infliction of emotional distress. The jury found that State Farm's decision not to settle was unreasonable and awarded the Campbells $2.6 million in compensatory damages and $145 million in punitive damages, which the trial court reduced to $1 million and $25 million respectively. The Utah Supreme Court reinstated the $145 million punitive damages award.

QUESTION

Is an award of $145 million in punitive damages, when full compensatory damages are $1 million, excessive and in violation of the Due Process Clause of the Fourteenth Amendment?

CONCLUSION

The Court held that the punitive award of $145 million was neither reasonable nor proportionate to the wrong committed, and it was thus an irrational, arbitrary, and unconstitutional deprivation of the property of the insurer.

Justices Antonin Scalia, Clarence Thomas, and Ruth Bader Ginsburg *dissented*. Justices Scalia and Thomas argued that the Due Process Clause provides no substantive protections against excessive or unreasonable awards of punitive damages. Justice Ginsburg noted that the decision overstepped states' traditional territory to regulate punitive damages.[12]

The *Campbell* court set out three guideposts regarding the assessment of appropriate punitive damages: a case must have 1) the degree of reprehensibility of the defendant's misconduct; 2) the disparity between the actual or potential harm suffered by the plaintiff and the punitive damages award; and 3) the difference between the punitive damages awarded by the jury and the civil penalties authorized or imposed in comparable cases. 538 U.S. 408, 418.

However, the *Campbell* court added three additional principles for courts to follow, namely:

> "[A] defendant should be punished for the conduct that harmed the plaintiff, not for being an unsavory individual or business." (538 U.S. 408, 423)

[12]*State Farm Mutual Auto Ins. Co. v. Campbell,* 538 U.S. 408 (2003) at http://www.oyez.org /cases/2000-2009/2002/2002_01_1289

(Continued)

Dissent
A judicial opinion that disagrees with the majority decision.

Defendants should not be subjected to excessive fines just because they have deep pockets. (538 U.S. 408, 427–28)

The Court declared that few awards that exceed 'a single-digit ratio between punitive and compensatory damages' will pass constitutional scrutiny. The only possible exception is where a particularly egregious act has resulted in relatively meager economic damages. On the other hand, where compensatory damages are substantial, the Court suggests it is possible that a punitive damages award of only equal value may be enough to reach the outermost limits of the due process guarantee. (538 U.S. 408, 428)[13]

[13]*State Farm Mutual Auto Ins. Co. v. Campbell,* 538 U.S. 408 (2003) at http://supreme.justia.com/us/538/408/index.html

Nominal damages
A small or token amount of money that is awarded when no actual loss resulted, but a wrong was committed.

Liquidated damages
Money awarded based on a prior agreement signed by the parties. In a contract, it is a stated amount that parties agree will be paid should a party default on the terms of the contract.

Replevin
An action to recover possession of chattels (personal property) that was wrongfully taken.

Chattels
Personal property, as distinguished from real property (land).

Ejectment
An action for possession of land.

Nominal damages are awarded in cases where a party has been wronged, but the amount of loss is not measurable or the specific harm is not documented. Example 3-1 illustrates a situation where nominal damages might be awarded.

Liquidated damages are often awarded in breach of contract actions. Contracts often include provisions that stipulate an amount that will be due should one party fail to complete the terms of the contract. Courts will uphold these clauses if the actual damages are uncertain or difficult to calculate, if the parties have agreed in advance to stipulate to the damages, or when it appears that the amount agreed upon is reasonable and does not appear to have been coerced. As discussed in *Braswell v. City Of El Dorado, Arkansas*, courts view liquidated damage clauses based on the individual facts surrounding the contract.

Some remedies at common law, such as replevin and ejectment, are not awards of money. *Replevin* is used in lawsuits to recover the possession of *chattels*, or personal property, that were unlawfully taken. When the plaintiff brings a lawsuit for replevin, the personal property is taken from the defendant and returned to the defendant after sufficient notice has been given. *Ejectment* is awarded where a plaintiff seeks to recover possession of land, in addition to damages. It is frequently used in landlord-tenant cases.

Equitable Remedies   Equitable remedies are awarded when common law remedies are inadequate. Although common law remedies and equitable remedies were once handled by separate courts, they now occur simultaneously within the same court. However, if there is a case where both remedies are requested and a jury is hearing the case, the judge will decide the equitable portion while the jury

---

EXAMPLE 3-1   NOMINAL DAMAGES

Neighbor A was constantly walking over a track in Neighbor B's yard. Neighbor B asked Neighbor A to refrain from walking on his yard (he is a perfectionist and spends hours manicuring his lawn). Neighbor A persists, causing a small worn spot in Neighbor B's yard, and Neighbor B wants satisfaction. Neighbor B does not have any identifiable damage or loss except that he is out of pocket for a bag of grass seed, some topsoil, and a little water. However, Neighbor B has the right to keep Neighbor A off his property. Neighbor B is entitled to a trivial amount as a token of his rights.

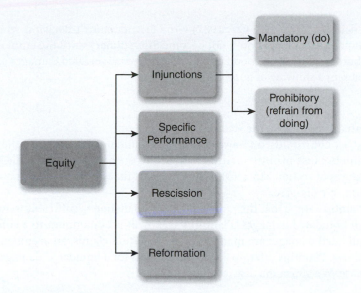

FIGURE 3-3 Remedies under Equity

decides the common law portion. Figure 3-3 identifies the types of remedies available under equitable law.

CASE EXCERPT 3-2: *Braswell v. City of El Dorado, Arkansas, 187 F.3d 954 (8th Cir. 1999)*

(Note: In the following case, the court found that liquidated damages were upheld in one instance while disallowing them in another.)

This is an action under the Fair Labor Standards Act, 29 U.S.C. 201-219 (FLSA), in which plaintiffs, twenty-five members of the fire department of defendant City of El Dorado, alleged that defendant failed to pay plaintiffs overtime wages and retaliated against plaintiffs for their pursuit of their FLSA rights. Plaintiffs prevailed at trial but appealed the district court's award of partial liquidated damages on the overtime claim and its failure to award liquidated damages on the retaliation claim. We affirm the award on the retaliation claim but reverse and remand the award on the overtime claim.

DISCUSSION

Overtime Claim

Statutory Scheme and Standard of Review

Any employer who violates the overtime provisions of the FLSA "shall be liable to the employee or employees affected in the amount of their unpaid . . . overtime compensation . . . and an additional equal amount as liquidated damages." 29 U.S.C. 216(b) (emphasis added). An award of liquidated damages is "intended in part to compensate employees for the delay in payment of wages owed under the FLSA[.]" *Hultgren v. County of Lancaster*, 913 F.2d 498, 508-09 (8th Cir. 1990).

An award of liquidated damages under section 216(b) is mandatory unless the employer can show good faith and reasonable grounds for believing that it was not in violation of the FLSA. Id. at 509; see also *Joiner v. City of Macon*,

(Continued)

814 F.2d 1537, 1539 (11th Cir. 1987) ("the district court's decision whether to award liquidated damages does not become discretionary until the employer carries its burden of proving good faith. In other words, liquidated damages are mandatory absent a showing of good faith.").

* * *

Liquidated Damages on the Retaliation Claim
The district court refused to award plaintiffs liquidated damages on the retaliation claim because plaintiffs failed to show how such an award would effectuate the purposes of section 215(a)(3). Plaintiffs assert that the district court abused its discretion. We disagree.

Plaintiffs argue that the jury's finding of retaliation is sufficient to justify an award of liquidated damages. Plaintiff's argument is tantamount to a conclusion that liquidated damages are mandatory in retaliation claims, an argument we rejected above. Plaintiffs offer no additional reasons for a liquidated damages award in this case. We affirm the district court.

CONCLUSION

We reverse the district court's liquidated damages award on the overtime claim. We affirm the district court's determination on the request for liquidated damages on the retaliation claim.[14]

[14]*Braswell v. City of El Dorado Ark.*, 187 F.3d 954 (8th Cir. 1999). http://openjurist.org/187/f3d/954/bobby-braswell-v-city-of-el-dorado-arkansas

Injunctions are probably the most common form of equitable remedy. This type of court order can make the defendant act, or refrain from acting, in a way that injures the defendant. If the defendant chooses to ignore the injunction, the court can order the defendant to pay a fine, go to jail, or lose the right to litigate an action.

Injunctions can be permanent, preliminary (interlocutory), or temporary. A temporary restraining order (TRO) is common in a domestic relations case where abuse by a spouse is alleged. The preliminary injunction and TRO are generally used to protect the rights of a party until a full hearing occurs.

A permanent injunction is issued after a hearing where all of the parties involved have received notice and have been given an opportunity to present evidence. As illustrated in the *eBay* case here, injunctions are often ordered when a judge needs to balance the plaintiff's harm against the due process rights of the defendant.

Reformation is awarded when the written agreement of the parties does not accurately or adequately express the actual or intended agreement of the parties. As the name implies, the court reforms the written agreement to express the true intention of the parties or to rectify the injustice caused by it. Reformation is usually ordered in cases of fraud, mistake, or ambiguous language in the agreement.

Rescission is a remedy in which the court cancels the contract or agreement. It is awarded where the court has found that duress, fraud, undue influence, innocent misrepresentation, or mistake induced one of the parties to consent to

---

TIP

During the economic crisis of 2009, one issue before the U.S. Supreme Court was on the sale of Chrysler's assets to Fiat. Justice Ruth Bader Ginsburg ordered a preliminary injunction on a Monday but late on Tuesday, the U.S. Supreme Court refused to revisit the issue after two lower courts approved the sale. This removed the uncertainty posed by a decision by Justice Ginsburg on Monday to temporarily halt the deal pending further review.[15]

Rescission
The cancellation of a contract because it was based on fraud or unilateral error.

---

[15]Michael J. de la Merced. Supreme Court Delays Sale of Chrysler to Fiat. *New York Times*. June 8, 2009. http://www.nytimes.com/2009/06/09/business/09chrysler.html

CASE **EXCERPT 3-3:** *eBay v. Merc-Exchange,* 547 U. S. 388 (2006)

(Court Summary)

Petitioners operate popular Internet Web sites that allow private sellers to list goods they wish to sell. Respondent sought to license its business method patent to petitioners, but no agreement was reached. In respondent's subsequent patent infringement suit, a jury found that its patent was valid, that petitioners had infringed the patent, and that damages were appropriate. However, the District Court denied respondent's motion for permanent injunctive relief. In reversing, the Federal Circuit applied its "general rule that courts will issue permanent injunctions against patent infringement absent exceptional circumstances." 401 F. 3d 1323, 1339.

Held: The traditional four-factor test applied by courts of equity when considering whether to award permanent injunctive relief to a prevailing plaintiff applies to disputes arising under the Patent Act. That test requires a plaintiff to demonstrate: (1) that it has suffered an irreparable injury; (2) that remedies available at law are inadequate to compensate for that injury; (3) that considering the balance of hardships between the plaintiff and defendant, a remedy in equity is warranted; and (4) that the public interest would not be disserved by a permanent injunction. The decision to grant or deny such relief is an act of equitable discretion by the district court, reviewable on appeal for abuse of discretion. These principles apply with equal force to Patent Act disputes. "[A] major departure from the long tradition of equity practice should not be lightly implied." *Weinberger v. Romero-Barcelo*, 456 U. S. 305, 320. Nothing in the Act indicates such a departure. pp. 2–6.

401 F. 3d 1323, vacated and remanded.[16]

[16]*eBay v. Merc-Exchange*, 547 U.S. 388 (2006). http://www.supremecourtus.gov/opinions/05pdf/05-130.pdf

the contract. Generally, each party then returns any money or property received from the other party in performance of the terms of the agreement. The case of *H. Prang Trucking Co., Inc.* illustrates how rescission operates where monetary damages are not an adequate remedy.

CASE **EXCERPT 3-4:** *H. Prang Trucking Co., Inc., v. Local Union No. 469,* 613 F.2d 1235 (3d Cir. 1980)

On appeal Prang argues (1) that the district court erred in concluding that there was an agreement to arbitrate the issue in dispute, (2) that if there was an agreement to arbitrate, the court erred in failing to find the Union's demand for arbitration barred by the statute of limitations, estoppel, laches, or waiver, and (3) that the court erred in failing to reform the contract to exclude the provisions giving rise to this dispute or, alternatively, in failing to rescind the agreement because of a mutual mistake of fact. Because it is unclear from the record if the district court considered the issues of reformation and rescission that were presented to it, and because the district court failed to make adequate findings to support its decision on those issues if it did consider them, we vacate the

(Continued)

judgment and order of the district court and remand for further proceedings. In view of our disposition of this appeal, it is unnecessary for us to address Prang's first two contentions at this time.

At the conclusion of the testimony before the district court, Prang requested the court "to either reform or rescind the agreement on the basis of mutual mistake of fact and/or law." App. 262a. Treating Prang's request as a motion to amend the pleadings, the district court granted the motion to amend but declined to state whether it would consider Prang's new theory of relief.

In its findings of fact and conclusions of law, the district court did not directly address the issues of reformation or rescission. The court did state, however, that "(Prang's) argument that there was an 'understanding' to continue the contract on the basis of an expired Article deleting the payment of owner-operators' pension and welfare benefits, is without merit." App. 45a. To the extent that this conclusion addresses Prang's most recent theory of relief, there are no findings of fact in the record to provide a basis for review.

Both reformation and rescission are equitable remedies that are sparingly granted. Reformation presupposes that a valid contract between the parties was created but, for some reason, was not properly reflected in the instrument that memorializes the agreement. *American Casualty Co. v. Memorial Hosp. Ass'n,* 223 F.Supp. 539 (E.D.Wis.1963). Rescission, on the other hand, may be an appropriate remedy where the contracting parties made a mutual mistake of fact. *Beecher v. Able,* 441 F.Supp. 426 (S.D.N.Y.1977), *Aff'd,* 575 F.2d 1010 (2d Cir. 1978). Although both concepts arise more frequently in the area of traditional contract law, their applicability is not unknown in the field of labor contracts. *See, e. g., Food Handlers Local 425 v. Valmac Industries, Inc.,* 528 F.2d 217 (8th Cir. 1975); *West Coast Telephone Co. v. Local Union No. 77, IBEW,* 431 F.2d 1219 (9th Cir. 1970). A determination of their applicability or inapplicability in a particular case, however, turns on the precise facts surrounding the transaction in question. See *Calhoun v. Bernard,* 333 F.2d 739 (9th Cir. 1964). In this case adequate findings to support a determination of the doctrines' applicability or inapplicability were not made.

In addition to factual findings, a determination of whether reformation or rescission may be appropriate in this case involves complex legal questions. Specifically, the effect, if any, of the arbitration clause introduces an element of uncertainty not present in many contract cases. *See, e. g., West Coast Telephone Co. v. Local Union No. 77, IBEW, supra* (reformation issue not arbitrable under terms of arbitration clause); *Cf. Prima Paint Corp. v. Flood & Conklin Mfg. Co.,* 388 U.S. 395, 87 S.Ct. 1801, 18 L.Ed.2d 1270 (1967) (claim of fraud in inducement of entire contract in an action under Arbitration Act of 1925, 9 U.S.C. §§ 1-14, is for arbitrator). These issues have not been briefed on appeal, and it does not appear from the record that the parties thoroughly developed these topics below. We believe that the trial court should have an opportunity to pass on these important questions in the first instance.[17] (emphasis added)

[17]*H. Prang Trucking Co., Inc., V. Local Union No. 469,* 613 F.2d 1235 (3d Cir. 1980). http://bulk.resource.org/courts.gov/c/F2/613/613.F2d.1235.78-2057.html

The equitable remedy **specific performance** is used in cases where the plaintiff asks the court to order the defendant to fulfill his or her duties under a contract. For this remedy to be awarded, there must be a valid contract. It is also limited to situations where there is no adequate remedy at common law or where money damages are not sufficient to make the plaintiff whole. Examples 3-2 and 3-3 provide some insight into how specific performance operates.

EXAMPLE 3-2   SPECIFIC PERFORMANCE

Kaitlyn Sizemore contracted with a highly regarded painter, Henri Mopay, to create a portrait of her family. After completing half of the painting, Mopay stopped work in breach of the contract. Kaitlyn was outraged and found an attorney to file a lawsuit for specific performance. The court found in her favor and issued an order forcing Mopay to finish the portrait. If the painter still fails to finish the portrait, the court may hold Mopay in contempt. Here, money damages would not be sufficient if Kaitlyn wanted the portrait done by this specific painter. She could hire another painter, but that painter may not have the same prestige or style as Mopay.

EXAMPLE 3-3   SPECIFIC PERFORMANCE

John agreed to work on a horse ranch during the summer. Before John arrived, he signed a contract for $150 per week plus room and board. In return, he agreed to work daily except Sundays. When John arrived, the owner of the ranch changed the terms of the contract to $125 per week plus room and board plus a young pony. John could stable the pony on the grounds while he worked and take the pony with him when summer was over.

At first, John did not want to change the terms, but he ultimately agreed. During the summer, John spent every free minute he had working with the pony. By summer's end, this pony was on its way to becoming a fantastic barrel-racing horse. The owner had second thoughts and gave John the originally agreed-upon salary but told John he would not let him keep the pony.

John wanted the horse, and filed a lawsuit for specific performance. Money would not adequately compensate John for the horse because the particular horse and the time John committed to training the horse made the horse unique. In other words, the money would not allow John to buy the same horse with the same qualities elsewhere. Hence, specific performance would be appropriate.

Enacted Law

Enacted law is the body of law that is passed by a designated group, such as a legislature, rather than handed down by the courts through judicial precedent.

Constitutions A constitution is a set of fundamental laws or principles upon which a state or nation's government is organized. The U.S. Constitution, the supreme law of the land, is the fundamental law for our nation, just as each state's constitution is the fundamental law for that state.

The first constitution of the United States was the Articles of Confederation, which attempted to create a unified government at end of the Revolution. However, the government established under the Articles was too weak, and the confederation of states lacked unity. And yet, while the people wanted a strong government, they did not want one that controlled their every move. They wanted a government that shared power with the people.

> **EXHIBIT 3-2 PREAMBLE TO THE U.S. CONSTITUTION**
>
> We the People of the United States, in Order to form a more perfect Union, establish Justice, insure domestic Tranquility, provide for the common defense, promote the general Welfare, and secure the Blessings of Liberty to ourselves and our Posterity, do ordain and establish this Constitution for the United States of America.

Before resigning his commission as commander-in-chief, Washington wrote a letter to the states in June of 1783 in which he recommended the creation of "a supreme power to regulate and govern the general concerns of the confederated republic."[18] The new Constitution, framed in 1787, responded to the need for a strong central government. It granted Congress the authority to raise revenue, regulate trade, pay off its debts, and deal effectively in international affairs.[19]

The U.S. Constitution describes the federal government's powers and sets limits on those powers. The U.S. Constitution has three main parts: the preamble, the articles, and the amendments.

The Preamble begins with the inclusive language "we the people," which indicates a contract has been established between the government and the people, and expresses the will of the people. Exhibit 3-2 provides the 52 words of the Preamble.

Even as the Constitution was drafted, it was soon recognized that additional protections were needed for individual rights and liberties. The framers responded by drafting the Bill of Rights, which added 10 amendments to the new Constitution.[20] These amendments provide guarantees of certain personal rights and liberties, and limit the power of the government in many ways.

The Tenth Amendment addresses states' rights. The Constitution grants certain powers to the federal government in Article I, and what powers it does not specifically retain for itself, it grants to the states through the Tenth Amendment.

Statutes Statutes are laws created by legislatures. Congress is the legislative branch where statutes are created at the federal level. Each state government also has a legislature where state laws are created. A bill is a proposed statute that has not yet been voted on by the legislature. The bill follows a procedure for passage in which it is discussed in committees, and then heard and voted on by both houses of the legislature (except for Nebraska that has a unicameral legislature). It is then signed into law by the executive branch (the state governor or the president).

Statutes are categorized as procedural or substantive. ***Procedural law*** pertains to the processes by which courts operate, or the means for enforcing rights in the courts. For example, Federal Rule of Civil Procedure 4 (Fed.R.Civ.P. 4) establishes the procedure for service of a summons and complaint on a party. ***Substantive law*** is an area of law that governs the conduct expected of citizens in general. Examples of substantive laws are the laws defining criminal offenses, and traffic laws that establish the rules of the road.

> **TIP**
>
> A researcher should cite to the U.S. Constitution when using it as a source. An example is U.S. Const. art. IV, § 5(b). For a law that has been repealed, the citation would be U.S. Const. amend. XXI (repealed 1933 by U.S. Const. amend. XVII). State constitutions will vary by state, so check the *Bluebook, ALWD,* or other source for the proper format. Here are some examples: S.C. Const. art. IV, § 4, Art. V, § 3(b)(3); Fla. Const. (year of adoption).

Procedural law

Law governing the manner in which rights are enforced or procedures are followed by courts.

Substantive law

The law that defines duties, rights, responsibilities, and the conduct expected of citizens in general.

---

[18]*The Founder's Constitution.* http://press-pubs.uchicago.edu/founders/

[19]*Id.*

[20]Revolutionary War and Beyond. *The First Ten Amendments or The Bill or Rights.* 2008–2011. http://www.revolutionary-war-and-beyond.com/first-ten-amendments.html

CITING THE LAW 3-1: STATUTES

Statutes begin life as *session laws*. The citations of all session laws have several parts in common: the legislature identifier, the ordinal contraction for the legislature number, and the session designation. In addition, enrolled acts sometimes are given public law numbers. For example, in Indiana, Senate Enacted Act (SEA) 10 became Public Law (P.L.) 81-2008. "81" is the chronological number given when the bill is passed, and "2008" designates the year of the session. When the session laws are compiled, they become the Acts of Indiana and the citation becomes "2008 Ind. Acts [page number]." Each state has its own designation, so researchers need to consult the *Bluebook*, *ALWD*, or other citation manual for exact information. Here are some examples of how session laws may appear:

- Iowa H. File 790, 88th Gen. Assembly, 1st Sess. (April 27, 2009)
- Session Laws of Kansas: 2008 Kan. Sess. Laws [page number]
- Acts of Alabama: 2008 Ala. Acts [act number]
- Session Laws of Arizona: Ariz. Sess. L. ch. [chapter number] (2008) or Ariz. Sess. L. § [section number] (2008)

Once the bills are passed and the session ends, the public laws are codified into the code of the state or the federal government. The statute then takes on a different format. A federal statute has title number (1–51), code identifier for the *United States Code* (U.S.C.), section symbol (§), section number, and a year of passage (year). For example, 42 U.S.C. § 2601 (2003) is Title 42, Section 2601, and passed in 2003. States will vary, but here are some examples:

- Code of Iowa: Iowa Code § section number (year) (official) or
- Iowa Code Annotated: Iowa Code Ann. § section number (West year) (unofficial)
- Kansas Statutes Annotated: Kan. Stat. Ann. § section number (year) (unofficial) or
- Vernon's Kansas Statutes Annotated: Kan. Stat. Ann. § section number (West year) (unofficial)
- Alabama Code: Ala. Code § section number (year) (official)
- Arizona Revised Statutes: Ariz. Rev. Stat. § section number (year) (official) or
- Arizona Revised Statutes Annotated: Ariz. Rev. State. Ann. § section number (West year) (unofficial)

Session laws
The collected statutes that are enacted during a session of a legislature, whether state or federal.

Ethics Alert 3-2

Candor to the court means that a lawyer cannot "fail to disclose to the tribunal legal authority in the controlling jurisdiction known to the lawyer to be directly adverse to the position of the client and not disclosed by opposing counsel" (Model Rules of Professional Conduct, Rule 3.3). This means that the paralegal has a duty to advise the attorney when legal authority is adverse to the client.

Sometimes enacted law may be given a "popular name," by which the statute may be commonly known, such as *Megan's Law* or the *Amber Alert*. *Megan's Law*, the informal name given to all laws that provide the public with access to the records of sex offenders, was named for Megan Kanka, who was a victim of a sexual offender. Amber Alert is a universal child abduction alert. Similarly, AMBER stands for "America's Missing: Broadcasting Emergency Response" but

---

EXHIBIT 3-3 RESOURCES WITH INFORMATION ON LEGISLATIVE HISTORY

- *U.S. Code Congressional & Administrative News (U.S.C.C.A.N.)*
- *House and Senate Journals*
- *Congressional Monitor*
- *Congressional Quarterly (CQ)*
- *CCH Congressional Index*
- *Congressional Information Service Annual (CIS)*
- *Digest of Public General Bills and Resolutions*

---

was originally named for a nine-year-old child who was abducted and murdered. The federal statutes have a Popular Name Table to help researchers locate statutes when only the popular name is known.

Occasionally it is necessary to research the ***legislative history***, which is the record of certain events in the history of a bill before it was signed into law. This history can be used to obtain information to help interpret the language of a statute. A researcher may search in the *Congressional Record*, hearing transcripts, or committee reports to uncover discussions of the bill before it was passed. Since its inaugural session, the United States Senate has kept a journal of its proceedings in accordance with Article I, Section 5 of the Constitution. State legislatures maintain similar records of their proceedings as well.

Materials on the legislative history of statutes may be found in numerous resources. Exhibit 3-3 provides some examples.

The presentation of legislative history varies depending on the legislature being covered. An example is shown in Figure 3-4.

Legislative history
The record of everything that happened in the legislature pertaining to a statute prior to its being enacted.

FIGURE 3-4 Page from Uncorrected Proofs of the Journals of the Massachusetts House

Journal of the House

Tuesday, January 20, 2009.

Met according to adjournment at eleven o'clock A.M., in an Informal Session, with Mr. Donato of Medford in the Chair (having been appointed by the Speaker, under authority of Rule 5, to perform the duties of the Chair).

Prayer was offered by the Reverend Robert F. Quinn, C.S.P., Chaplain of the House, as follows:

> Eternal God, at the beginning of today's legislative session we pause for a moment to focus our attention on You, and the role of spiritual values in our lives. In our decision making process, may we be guided by Your values, principles and precepts which gives meaning and direction to us in our own daily lives. Today we celebrate the inauguration of our 44th president. We pray that he and his administration will be successful and will advance peace, justice, prosperity and stability in our country and in our communities.
>
> Inspire us, as a nation, to make our communities safe and cooperative in promoting jobs, education and housing opportunities for all people. May the enthusiasm and happiness of today remain with us as we together build a strong, civil and ethical society. When we disagree on sensitive or controversial issues, let our disappointment be honest,

respectful, based on sound reasoning and principles and on the meaning of the common good.

Grant Your blessings on the Speaker, the members and employees of this House and their families. Amen.

At the request of the Chair (Mr. Donato), the members, guests and employees joined with him in reciting the pledge of allegiance to the flag.

Appointments of the Minority Leader.

The Minority Leader announced that he had made the following appointments:

That Representative Polito of Shrewsbury had been appointed to the special commission established (under Section 87 of Chapter 169 of the Acts of 2008) for the purpose of making an investigation and study relative to the burning of construction and demolition waste as it relates to the renewable energy portfolio standard program established by section 11F of chapter 25A of the General Laws;

That Representative Smola of Palmer had been appointed to the special commission established (under Section 88 of Chapter 169 of the Acts of 2008) to examine the environmental and economic impact of establishing a green building plan for the Commonwealth;

That Representative deMacedo of Plymouth had been appointed to the Creative Economy Council established (under Chapter 354 of the Acts of 2008) to develop a statewide strategy for the enhancement, encouragement, and growth of the creative economy in the Commonwealth and to promote through public and private means responsive public policies and innovative private sector practices; and

That Representative Ross of Wrentham had been appointed to the special commission established (under Section 3 of Chapter 509 of the Acts of 2008) to study the transferability of tax credits under subsection (p) of section 6 of chapter 62 of the General Laws and section 38AA of chapter 63 of the General Laws.

Order.

On motion of Mr. DiMasi of Boston,—

Ordered, That when the House adjourns today, it adjourn to meet on Thursday next at eleven o'clock A.M.

At thirteen minutes after eleven o'clock A.M., on motion of Mr. Peterson of Grafton (Mr. Donato of Medford being in the Chair), the House adjourned, to meet on Thursday next at eleven o'clock A.M., in an Informal Session.[21]

FIGURE 3-4 Page from Uncorrected Proofs of the Journals of the Massachusetts House (*Continued*)

TIP

Legislative history is not the law. It can give insight into the thinking of the legislature if, and only if, the records have a clear-cut statement to that effect. Legislators may vote for statutes for different reasons. There will be no line of text in the history that says, "Senator Hoskins voted for S.B. 101 because . . . ." There is also the possibility that a legislator will add documents or information about a statute in an effort to influence how the statute is viewed later. All of these factors need to be weighed when researching legislative history.

Within the journal of legislative proceedings, a researcher may find statements as to why a bill was introduced, what prompted the legislature to enact the statute, or what problem the legislators were trying to solve by enacting the statute. Quotations from this material may provide powerful support when arguing a particular interpretation of a statute on behalf of a client. However, this legislative history is not the law. It can only be used as persuasive authority for a particular interpretation.

[21]State of Massachusetts. Journal of the House. 2009. http://www.mass.gov/legis/journal/hj012009.pdf

Ordinance

A law created by legislatures of local governments, such as county councils, county commissioners, or city councils.

City councils, county boards of supervisors, county commissioners, and other entities of local government are local legislatures that pass laws called ***ordinances***. For example, a city may have a health code that, among other things, ensures that food served in restaurants is safe to eat. The city may also have a health inspector that inspects the local restaurants for compliance with the health code.

HIERARCHY OF LAW

Just as the courts have a hierarchy, so too does the law. The hierarchy of law means that certain laws are more important than, or take precedence over, others. Generally, federal law controls federal matters and state law controls state matters (with some exceptions). No law can contravene the U.S. Constitution.

Federal Law

Primary federal law consists of the Constitution, statutes, common law, administrative regulations, and administrative decisions.

U.S. Constitution More often than not, constitutional questions arise from a claim that a person's rights (under the Bill of Rights) were violated. For example, the scenario at the beginning of this chapter presents a constitutional issue.

When preparing to research, one of the first questions to ask is, "What is the highest authority that is likely to govern the client's situation?" Being familiar with the basics of the Constitution will make it easier to decide whether a constitutional issue is involved.

Annotated

A notation or comment that explains or enhances the understanding of the material.

The text of the U.S. Constitution is published in many sources. Two most frequently used sources are the *United States Code Annotated* (published by West) and the *United States Code Service* (published by LexisNexis). Annotated versions of the U.S. Constitution are also available using Westlaw and LexisNexis, and on the Internet through the U.S. Government Printing Office. ***Annotated*** means that notes follow each section of the law. These notes summarize relevant court decisions, law review articles, and other legal authorities on the section of law.

Statutory law

Laws enacted by federal and state legislatures.

Statutes Statutes are next in the federal hierarchy. A deeper discussion of statutes will follow later in this text. When researching statutes, it is important to know in what areas Congress exclusively creates laws. For example, the scenario at the beginning of the chapter might have potential federal claims, and knowing which of these areas are within the purview of congressional authority can be a helpful starting point.

Private laws

The rules of conduct that govern activities that occur among or between persons.

It is not necessary to memorize the federal statutes, but it may be useful to become familiar with some of the 51 titles, or at least the areas that a law firm deals with most. Table 3-1 provides a listing of the titles.

Public law

Law dealing with the relationship between the people and their government, the relationship between the agencies and the branches of government, and the relationship between governments themselves.

Statutes are often referred to as ***statutory law***. Local governments, states, and the federal government can make statutes. Statutes cover all sorts of topics, including criminal and civil liability. Each body has a process for the passing and publishing of laws.

Slip law

Official publication of a statute shortly after it has been passed by the legislature. It is admissible in court as evidence of the statute's passage.

The U.S. Congress passes ***private laws,*** which govern relations between people, and ***public laws,*** which govern relations between people and their government, or between different parts of government. When federal statutes are first passed and published, they are called ***slip laws***. At the end of the congressional session, all newly passed federal laws are published chronologically in *Statutes at Large*. The statutes are later codified, or organized into the ***code*** of the federal law, under the appropriate title pertaining to its subject.

Code

The published statutes of a jurisdiction that are arranged in a systematic form.

TABLE 3-1   *United States Code* Titles

- Title 1   General Provisions
- Title 2   The Congress
- Title 3   The President
- Title 4   Flag and Seal, Seat of Government, and the States
- Title 5   Government Organization and Employees
- Title 5   Government Organization and Employees—Appendix
- Title 6   Domestic Security
- Title 7   Agriculture
- Title 8   Aliens and Nationality
- Title 9   Arbitration
- Title 10   Armed Forces
- Title 11   Bankruptcy
- Title 11   Bankruptcy—Appendix
- Title 12   Banks and Banking
- Title 13   Census
- Title 14   Coast Guard
- Title 15   Commerce and Trade
- Title 16   Conservation
- Title 17   Copyrights
- Title 18   Crimes and Criminal Procedure
- Title 18   Crimes and Criminal Procedure—Appendix
- Title 19   Customs Duties
- Title 20   Education
- Title 21   Food and Drugs
- Title 22   Foreign Relations and Intercourse
- Title 23   Highways
- Title 24   Hospitals and Asylums
- Title 25   Indians
- Title 26   Internal Revenue Code
- Title 27   Intoxicating Liquors
- Title 28   Judiciary and Judicial Procedure
- Title 28   Judiciary and Judicial Procedure—Appendix
- Title 29   Labor
- Title 30   Mineral Lands and Mining
- Title 31   Money and Finance
- Title 32   National Guard
- Title 33   Navigation and Navigable Waters
- Title 34   Navy (Repealed)
- Title 35   Patents
- Title 36   Patriotic Societies and Observances
- Title 37   Pay and Allowances of the Uniformed Services
- Title 38   Veterans' Benefits
- Title 39   Postal Service
- Title 40   Public Buildings, Property, and Works
- Title 41   Public Contracts
- Title 42   The Public Health and Welfare
- Title 43   Public Lands
- Title 44   Public Printing and Documents
- Title 45   Railroads
- Title 46   Shipping

TABLE 3-1   (*Continued*)

- Title 46   Shipping—Appendix
- Title 47   Telegraphs, Telephones, and Radiotelegraphs
- Title 48   Territories and Insular Possessions
- Title 49   Transportation
- Title 50   War and National Defense
- Title 50   Appendix—War and National Defense
- Title 51   National and Commercial Space Programs[22]

TIP

When using general Internet sites, a researcher should be sure that the sites are reliable by finding a site that has been recommended by an instructor or in textbooks, and trying to find the official site of the topic being searched. For example, the official site for the *United States Code* is http://www.gpoaccess.gov /uscode/index.html.

Slip opinion

A single judicial decision published shortly after it has been issued by the court and before it is collected and printed in a reporter.

The *United States Code* (U.S.C.) is the government's official publication of all the federal statutes, arranged by subject matter. The outside binding of each volume is printed with the code sections contained in that volume. For example, to find 18 U.S.C. §121, a researcher would look for the volume containing Title 18, and then look within it for section 121.

The annotated versions of code books can be very helpful in statutory research. They provide references to cases and other materials that apply or interpret the statutes. The *United States Code Annotated* (West) and *United States Code Service* (LexisNexis) are annotated federal statutes available both in hard copy and through subscription legal databases such as Westlaw and LexisNexis.

Common Law   The third level in the hierarchy of law is common law. In the common law, judges interpret and apply existing law to the circumstances of the cases before them.

When a federal case is first decided, the decision is issued as a ***slip opinion***, which is a single judicial decision published shortly after it has been issued by the court and before it is collected and printed in a reporter. Cases from the federal district courts are reported in the *Federal Supplement*. The researcher must know which cases are mandatory authority for the client's situation.

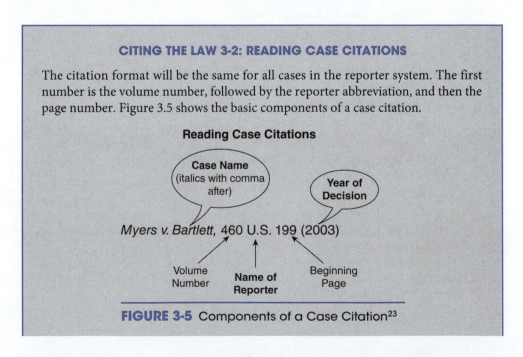

CITING THE LAW 3-2: READING CASE CITATIONS

The citation format will be the same for all cases in the reporter system. The first number is the volume number, followed by the reporter abbreviation, and then the page number. Figure 3.5 shows the basic components of a case citation.

Reading Case Citations

Case Name
(italics with comma after)

Year of Decision

Myers v. Bartlett, 460 U.S. 199 (2003)

Volume Number

Name of Reporter

Beginning Page

FIGURE 3-5 Components of a Case Citation[23]

[22]GPO Access. *Browse the U.S. Code by Title.* 2012. http://www.gpoaccess.gov/uscode/browse.html

[23]Criminal Justice Education. *How to Read a Case Citation.* 2012. http://www.cjed.com/citations.htm

The diagram below shows the basic components of a case citation.

1. **Case Name**–Present in italics (or underlined) followed by a comma. The last name of the first party on each side is used. The "v." means versus and is followed by a period.
2. **Volume Number**–The volume number of the reporter in which the case appears.
3. **Reporter Abbreviation**–Each reporter has an abbreviation that is used in citations.
4. **Page Number**–This number represents the first page upon which the case appears.
5. **Date of Decision**–This date is when the court decided the case.

Table 3.2 shows examples of federal case citations properly formatted.

TABLE 3.2   Proper Citation Formats for Federal Cases

Court	Citation (Rule 10 of the *Bluebook*)
U.S. Supreme Court	*Brown v. Helvering*, 291 U.S. 193 (1934).
Courts of Appeals	*Antonov v. County of Los Angeles Dep't of Pub. Soc. Servs.*, 103 F.3d 137 (9th Cir. 1996).
	Natural Res. Def. Council v. NRC, 216 F.3d 1180 (D.C. Cir. 2000).
	Oregon Steel Mills, Inc. v. United States, 862 F.2d 1541 (Fed. Cir. 1988).
U.S. District Courts	*Huangyan Imp. & Exp. Corp. v. Nature's Farm Prods.*, 99 Civ. 9404 (SHS), 2000 U.S. Dist. LEXIS 12335 (S.D.N.Y. 2000). Note: A citation to LexisNexis is used when a case is unpublished or if there is no other citation option.
	Glinsey v. Baltimore & O.R.R., 356 F. Supp. 984 (N.D. Ohio 1973), rev'd, 495 F.2d 565 (6th Cir. 1974).
	Chatoff v. West Publ'g Co., 948 F. Supp. 176 (E.D.N.Y. 1996).
	Allen v. Hunter, 65 F. Supp. 365 (D. Kan. 1946).
Court of Claims	*Ex'r of Estate of Wicker v. United States*, 43 Fed. Cl. 172 (1999).
	Express Foods, Inc. v. United States, 229 Ct. Cl. 733 (Cl. Ct. 1981).*
	*Note: The parenthetical reference "Cl. Ct." must be included in pre-1982 cites to the Ct. Cl. reporter but is unnecessary in cases cited to the Cl. Ct. reporter.
Bankruptcy Court	*Weiner v. Perry, Settles & Lawson, Inc.*, 208 B.R. 69 (B.A.P. 1st Cir. 1997).
Tax Court	*Allied Equip. Leasing II v. Comm'r*, 97 T.C. 575 (1991).
Military Court	*United States v. Zamberlan*, 45 M.J. 491 (C.A.A.F. 1997).

Reading cases is an important skill in researching. A case has identifiable parts, as shown in Figure 3-6. Identifying each of these parts will aid in researching and understanding cases.

Administrative Regulations   Administrative regulations and decisions, the bottom of the hierarchy and often referred to as the "fourth branch" of government, apply to people and entities that have issues with administrative

Pelman ex rel. Pelman v. McDonald's Corp.
396 F.3d 508
C.A.2 (N.Y.), 2005.
January 25, 2005 (Approx. 5 pages)

United States Court of Appeals,
Second Circuit.

Ashley PELMAN, a child under the age of 18 years, by her mother and natural guardian, Roberta PELMAN, Roberta Pelman, Individually, Jazlen Bradley, a child under the age of 18 years, by her father and natural guardian, Isreal Bradley, and Isreal Bradley, Individually, Plaintiffs-Appellants,

v.

MCDONALD'S CORPORATION, McDonald's Restaurants of New York, Inc., McDonald's, 1865 Bruckner Boulevard, Bronx, New York and McDonald's, 2630 Jerome Avenue, Bronx, New York, Defendants-Appellees.

No. 03-9010.

Argued: Oct. 13, 2004.
Decided: Jan. 25, 2005.

Background: Two minor customers of fast food restaurant chain sued chain claiming consumption of chain's food caused obesity and related serious health problems, and that chain violated false advertising and deceptive trade practices provisions of the New York Consumer Protection Act. The District Court, Sweet, J., 237 F.Supp.2d 512, dismissed complaint with leave to amend. Following amendment, restaurant chain moved to dismiss. The United States District Court for the Southern District of New York, Robert W. Sweet, J., 2003 WL 22052778, again dismissed. Customers appealed.

Holding: The Court of Appeals, Rakoff, District Judge, sitting by designation, held that allegations stated claim against chain for violation of deceptive trade practices provision of New York Consumer Protection Act.

Vacated and remanded.
West Headnotes

[1] ☑KeyCite Citing References for this Headnote

←170B Federal Courts

←170BVIII Courts of Appeals

←170BVIII(K) Scope, Standards, and Extent

←170BVIII(K)7 Waiver of Error in Appellate Court

←170Bk915 k. In General. Most Cited Cases

Minor customers of fast food restaurant chain abandoned their claims on appeal that chain engaged in false advertising in violation of the New York Consumer Protection Act, following District Court's dismissal, where their appellate brief contained no argument as to why the dismissal of such claims was incorrect. F.R.A.P. Rule 28, 28 U.S.C.A.; N.Y. McKinney's General Business Law § 350.

. . .

*509 Samuel Hirsch, Samuel Hirsch & Associates, P.C., New York, New York, for Plaintiffs-Appellants.

Bradley E. Lerman, Winston & Strawn LLP, New York, New York (Thomas J. Quigley, Bruce R. Braun, Scott P. Glauberman, on the brief), Anne G. Kimball and Sarah L. Olson, Wildman, Harrold, Allen & Dixon, Chicago, Illinois, of counsel, for Defendants-Appellees.

Before: KEARSE and CALABRESI, Circuit Judges, and RAKOFF, District Judge.[FN*]

[FN*] The Honorable Jed S. Rakoff, United States District Judge for the Southern District of New York, sitting by designation.

FIGURE 3-6 Parts of a Case

RAKOFF, District Judge.

In this diversity action, plaintiffs Ashley Pelman and Jazlen Bradley, by their respective parents, Roberta Pelman and Isreal Bradley, appeal from the dismissal, pursuant to Rule 12(b)(6), Fed.R.Civ.P., of Counts I–III of their amended complaint. See *Pelman v. McDonald's Corp.*, 2003 WL 22052778 (S.D.N.Y. Sept. 3, 2003), 2003 U.S. Dist. LEXIS 15202 ("*Pelman II*").[FN1]

Each of the these counts purports to*510 allege, on behalf of a putative class of consumers, that defendant McDonald's Corporation violated both § 349 and § 350 of the New York General Business Law, commonly known as the New York Consumer Protection Act, during the years 1987 through 2002.

. . .

Accordingly, the district court's dismissal of those portions of Counts I–III of the amended complaint as alleged violations of § 349 is VACATED, and the case is REMANDED for further proceedings consistent with this opinion.

C.A.2 (N.Y.), 2005.
Pelman ex rel. Pelman v. McDonald's Corp.
396 F.3d 508
© 2011 Thomson Reuters. No Claim to Orig. US Gov. Works.[24]

[FN1] The district court (Robert W. Sweet, Judge) had previously dismissed the original complaint without prejudice to re-plead. See *Pelman v. McDonald's Corp.*, 237 F.Supp. 2d 512, 543 (S.D.N.Y.2003) ("*Pelman I*"). Plaintiffs then filed a four-count amended complaint, but thereafter voluntarily dismissed Count IV. See *Pelman II*, 2003 U.S. Dist. LEXIS 15202, at *5. In addition, in *Pelman II*, the district court dismissed as time-barred the individual claims of the parent co-plaintiffs, see id., at * 18, and plaintiffs have not challenged this determination on appeal.

FIGURE 3-6 Parts of a Case   (*Continued*)

agencies, such as when someone files a claim for unemployment compensation. Administrative regulations are the substantive and procedural rules that carry out the purposes of the statutes. The statutes are the framework that sets out basic law and the regulations are the more detailed laws that provide day-to-day rules for the implementation of the statutes. Regulations have the force of law. Administrative decisions are handed down by administrative law judges (ALJs), and are binding upon the parties of a particular agency dispute.

Regulatory agencies create regulations according to rules and processes defined by the Administrative Procedures Act (APA), 5 U.S.C. § 551 *et. seq.* Under the APA, before a regulation goes into effect, an agency must provide a way for interested parties to comment, offer amendments, or object to the regulation.

For some regulations to become effective, the requirement is only publication and an opportunity for comments. Other regulations require publication and one or more formal public hearings. The agency's enabling legislation states which process is to be used in creating the regulations. Regulations requiring hearings can take several months to become final.

When a regulation is passed, it is published in the *Federal Register* (Fed.Reg.), which is the official daily publication for rules, proposed rules, and notices of federal agencies and organizations, as well as executive orders and other presidential documents. It is updated daily by 6 A.M. and is published Monday through Friday, except federal holidays (http://www.gpoaccess.gov/fr/index.html).

[24]*Pelman ex rel. Pelman v. McDonald's Corp.*, 396 F.3d 508 (2d Cir. 2005). http://web2.westlaw.com/find/default.wl?rs=WLW11.10&rp=%2ffind%2fdefault.wl&vr=2.0&fn=_top&mt=Westlaw&cite=396+F.3d+508+(2005)&sv=Split

Searching in the *Federal Register* is a little different than searching in U.S.C.A. or U.S.C. To search by page, the page number ("page XXX", in quotes) is entered in the search terms box on the access page of the Internet. The *Federal Register* citation 60 FR 12345 refers to page 12345. *Federal Register* pages start with page 1 of the first issue and continue sequentially until the end of the calendar year. To search for a *Code of Federal Regulations* (C.F.R.) citation, the title is entered (in quotes), followed by the words *CFR* and *part*, followed by the part number. For example, 40 CFR part 55 is the citation for part 55 of Title 40 of the Code of Federal Regulations.

The listserv service can be joined to receive updates automatically. The updates may be received by visiting http://listserv.access.gpo.gov; selecting the *Federal Register* Table of Contents LISTSERV electronic mailing list; accessing and selecting the online mailing list archives, FEDREGTOC-L; joining the list; and then following the instructions.

An administrative regulation in a *Federal Register* may look very different than the statute in the code book. Exhibit 3-4 shows a page of a regulation in the *Federal Register*.

EXHIBIT 3-4 PAGE FROM FEDERAL REGISTER

[Federal Register: April 9, 2009 (Volume 74, Number 67)]

[Proposed Rules]

[Page 16162–16169]

From the Federal Register Online via GPO Access [wais.access.gpo.gov]

[DOCID:fr09ap09-21]

ENVIRONMENTAL PROTECTION AGENCY

40 CFR Part 300

[EPA-HQ-SFUND-2009-0062, EPA-HQ-SFUND-2009-0063, EPA-HQ-SFUND-2009-0064, EPA-HQ-SFUND-2009-0065, EPA-HQ-SFUND-2009-0066, EPA-HQ-SFUND-2009-0067, EPA-HQ-SFUND-2009-0068, EPA-HQ-SFUND-2009-0069, EPA-HQ-FUND-2009-0071, EPA-HQ-SFUND-2009-0072, EPA-HQ-SFUND-2009-0073, EPA-HQ-SFUND-2009-0074, EPA-HQ-SFUND-2009-0075; FRL-8790-2]

RIN 2050-AD75

National Priorities List, Proposed Rule No. 50

AGENCY: Environmental Protection Agency.

ACTION: Proposed rule.

SUMMARY: The Comprehensive Environmental Response, Compensation, and Liability Act ("CERCLA" or "the Act"), as amended, requires that the National Oil and Hazardous Substances Pollution Contingency Plan ("NCP") include a list of national priorities among the known releases or threatened releases of hazardous substances, pollutants, or contaminants throughout the United States.

The *Code of Federal Regulations* (C.F.R.) is the codification of the general and permanent rules published in the *Federal Register*. The C.F.R. is the finalized version of the regulation after it is first posted in the *Federal Register,* and is arranged by subject matter. It is divided into 50 titles that represent broad areas subject to federal regulation. Each volume of the C.F.R. is updated once each calendar year and is issued on a quarterly basis, as follows:

- Titles 1–16 are updated as of January 1st.
- Titles 17–27 are updated as of April 1st.
- Titles 28–41 are updated as of July 1st.
- Titles 42–50 are updated as of October 1st.

Each title is divided into chapters, which usually bear the name of the issuing agency. Each chapter is further subdivided into parts that cover specific regulatory areas. Large parts may be subdivided into subparts. All parts are organized in sections, and most citations in the C.F.R. are provided at the section level. A list of agencies and where they appear in the C.F.R. may be found in Appendix C of the U.S. Government Manual (http://www.gpoaccess.gov/CFR/).

The citation contains the title number, the C.F.R. abbreviation, the part number, section number (after the decimal), and the year. A unique aspect of the C.F.R. is that each volume is listed by year. So, 21 C.F.R. 1603.1 (2010) is a different regulation from 21 C.F.R. 1603.1 (2011). They are not updated by pocket parts. Exhibit 3-5 shows a page from a C.F.R. volume.

EXHIBIT 3-5   PAGE FROM C.F.R.

[Code of Federal Regulations]

[Title 20, Volume 2]

[Revised as of April 1, 2008]

From the U.S. Government Printing Office via GPO Access

[CITE: 20CFR404.140]

[Page 69–70]

TITLE 20—EMPLOYEES' BENEFITS

CHAPTER III—SOCIAL SECURITY ADMINISTRATION

PART 404_FEDERAL OLD-AGE, SURVIVORS AND DISABILITY INSURANCE (1950)—Table of Contents

Subpart B Insured Status and Quarters of Coverage

Sec. 404.140 What is a quarter of coverage.

(a) General. A quarter of coverage (QC) is the basic unit of social security coverage used in determining a worker's insured status. We credit you with QCs based on your earnings covered under social security.

(b) How we credit QCs based on earnings before 1978 (General).

Before 1978, wages were generally reported on a quarterly basis and self-employment income was reported on an annual basis. For the most part, we credit QCs for calendar years before 1978 based on your quarterly earnings. For these years, as explained in Sec. 404.141, we generally credit you with a QC for each calendar quarter in which you were paid at least $50 in wages or were credited with at least $100 of self-employment income. Section 404.142 tells how self-employment income derived in a taxable year beginning before 1978 is credited to specific calendar quarters for purposes of Sec. 404.141.

(c) How we credit QCs based on earnings after 1977 (General). After 1977, both wages and self-employment income are generally reported on an annual basis. For calendar years after 1977, as explained in Sec. 404.143, we generally credit you with a QC for each part of your total covered earnings in a calendar year that equals the amount required for a QC in that year. Section 404.143 also tells how the amount required for a QC will be increased in the future as average wages increase. Section 404.144 tells how self-employment income derived in a taxable year beginning after 1977 is credited to specific calendar years for purposes of Sec. 404.143.

(d) When a QC is acquired and when a calendar quarter is not a QC (general). Section 404.145 tells when a QC is acquired and Sec. 404.146 tells when a calendar quarter cannot be a QC. These rules apply when we credit QCs under Sec. 404.141 or Sec. 404.143.

Administrative Decisions When parties who are subject to regulation by an agency dispute, an agency action, or regulation, the issue is brought before the administrative tribunal, and the result of the dispute is reported as an administrative decision. These decisions are often available online. For example, to find decisions from the Environmental Protection Agency, a researcher can go to the EPA website at http://www.epa.gov/ and follow the drop-down menu for "law and regulations."

State and Local Law

Each state is basically self-governing, meaning that it has its own set of laws, including its own constitution. Under the Tenth Amendment, states are free to make laws to govern their own citizens on any matters not granted to the federal government, or prohibited by the U.S. Constitution.

State Constitutions Researchers should have some familiarity with their own state's constitution. States have used the U.S. Constitution as a model for their own constitutions, setting the constitutions up in the same fashion with similar articles and sections. For example, Indiana's preamble is very similar to that of the U.S. Constitution:

> **TO THE END**, that justice be established, public order maintained, and liberty perpetuated; WE, the People of the State of Indiana, grateful to ALMIGHTY GOD for the free exercise of the right to choose our own form of government, do ordain this Constitution.[25]

Constitutional law issues are very often federal issues. However, when researching a constitutional law issue, it is also important to research the law regarding the state's constitution. A state constitution may give the citizens of the state broader rights than those rights guaranteed by the U.S. Constitution.

TIP

For citation format, check with the *Bluebook, ALWD,* or other citation manual.

[25]Indiana State Constitution. Preamble. http://www.in.gov/legislative/ic/code/const/art1.html

A state's constitution is usually published in code books, along with the statutes for that state. The constitution can also normally be found online through the state's official home page. Since all parts of constitutions are labeled, finding a particular cited provision in a constitution is a straightforward process.

Statutes   Each state's legislature or assembly creates its own statutes. Some states still publish official statutory compilations, while other states rely on unofficial compilations.

The process of enacting laws at the state level is similar to that at the federal level. State statutes are first published as slip laws. At the end of each legislative session, they are published chronologically and are usually referred to as session laws. Later they are codified and organized by subject matter in state code books. These laws may be referred to as public laws, statutes at large, codes, bills, chaptered bills, or by other monikers.

Annotated versions of state code books are usually available. State code books are generally updated by pocket parts. State statutes can also be accessed through Westlaw and LexisNexis, as well as other online resources such as the state legislature's official homepage.

> **TIP**
>
> A researcher should always cite to the official source if one is available.

CITING THE LAW 3-3: STATE STATUTES

The citation format will vary depending on the state. Researchers should become familiar with the different citation formats so that a statute can be easily recognized when seen. Most statutes will follow a similar format of four elements. To cite a state statute, the following four elements are usually listed in this order:

1. The state abbreviation;
2. The code's abbreviation;
3. The section number of the statute; and
4. The year on the spine of the code volume (*not* the year the statute became effective).

For example, the following Massachusetts statute is cited Mass. Gen. Laws Ann. ch. 265 § 29 (1958):

Element	Citation Form
State	Mass.
Code abbreviation	Gen. Laws Ann.
Chapter and section numbers	ch. 265 § 120.16
Year on volume spine	(1958)

If this statute had been updated in the pocket part (hard copy), the format would be Mass. Gen. Laws Ann. ch. 265 § 29 (Supp. 2002):

Element	Citation Form
State	Mass.
Code abbreviation	Gen. Laws Ann.
Chapter and section number	ch. 265 § 120.16
Supplement year	(Supp. 2002)

The pocket parts of the statutes should be checked every time a statute is found in the hard copy. If the statute is found in an electronic research service, the updated version will appear automatically.

> ### CITING THE LAW 3-4: STATE CASES
>
> If the state maintains an official reporter, that reporter should be cited in addition to and preceding the unofficial reporter, which in most states is part of the West Reporter System. However, many states have discontinued the publishing of official reporters, and only the unofficial reporter is cited. If no official reporter exists, the court designation will appear in the parentheses with the date. The case citation will look similar to the federal case citations shown previously. Each West Reporter presents the cases in exactly the same way with exactly the same enhancements.

Common Law   Cases within the common law create precedent, which is binding on other courts. This case law also affects the interpretation of statutes and constitutional provisions. In a typical project, a researcher will spend a great deal of time reading and analyzing cases, whether on the federal or state level. The published decisions of state courts at the appellate level are found in official or unofficial reporters. Sometimes decisions are unpublished or unreported, but sometimes these opinions may be found on Westlaw, LexisNexis, or the Internet.

Reading cases is one of the most significant parts of the research process. Researchers should spend some time reading cases to gain a familiarity with the language of the courts, the different areas of law, how the courts write, and the types of information courts use for support in reaching their decisions.

Administrative Regulations   Like federal agencies, state agencies issue regulations that govern their day-to-day operation. The state regulations also provide the means to enforce the law that the agency is responsible for. Each state has a state administrative procedures act similar to the federal Administrative Procedures Act (APA). The state's APA defines the obligations and procedures of the state agencies as they develop rules and regulations, as well as the procedures to be followed in the hearings and proceedings before each agency.

Many states have adopted the Model State Administrative Procedures Act (MSAPA), which was developed by the National Conference of Commissioners on Uniform State Laws (NCCUSL). The NCCUSL develops uniform laws states can use as models for their state statutes. The latest version of the MSAPA, developed in 2010 with the participation of the American Bar Association (ABA), addresses significant developments such as the emergence of the Internet as an efficient and low-cost method for communicating with the public. The latest revision also addresses changes in agency rulemaking and legislative oversight, as well as the large number of judicial decisions on federal and state administrative procedure.

Administrative Decisions   Like federal administrative agencies, state and local agencies also hold hearings conducted by an ALJs. Compared to trial and appellate judges, ALJs consider a much narrower range of matters, depending on the agency's area of responsibility. ALJs require technical expertise in that area in order to interpret and enforce the law and regulations governing that field. With their narrow range of cases, ALJs have the opportunity to become experts, unlike most trial and appellate judges.

When each state agency hears and decides an issue brought before it, the agency delivers an administrative decision and reports the decisions on a state,

> **EXHIBIT 3-6 WISCONSIN EMPLOYMENT RELATIONS COMMISSION**
>
> STATE OF WISCONSIN
>
> BEFORE THE WISCONSIN EMPLOYMENT RELATIONS COMMISSION
>
> In the Matter of the Petition of
>
> **AFSCME, COUNCIL 40, AFL-CIO**
>
> Involving Certain Employees of
>
> **RICHLAND SCHOOL DISTRICT**
>
> Case 56
>
> No. 68080
>
> ME-1246
>
> **Decision No. 24683-C**
>
> **Appearances:**
>
> **Kirk D. Strang** and **Edward J. Williams**, Davis & Kuelthau, S.C., Ten East Doty Street, Suite 600, Madison, Wisconsin 53703, appearing on behalf of Richland School District.
>
> **Michael J. Wilson** and **Thor Backus**, 8033 Excelsior Drive, Suite "B", Madison, Wisconsin 53717-2900, appearing on behalf of the Richland School District Employees, Local 2085-B, AFSCME, AFL-CIO.
>
> **FINDINGS OF FACT, CONCLUSIONS OF LAW AND ORDER CLARIFYING BARGAINING UNIT**
>
> On June 13, 2008, AFSCME, Council 40, AFL-CIO, filed a petition with the Wisconsin Employment Relations Commission on behalf of the Richland School District Employees, Local 2085-B, AFSCME, AFL-CIO to clarify an existing Local 2085-B bargaining unit of Richland School District employees by inclusion of three positions: the District Receptionist/Secretary Maintenance & Transportation, the Business Secretary—Budgetary and Bookkeeping, and the Secretary—Special Education/Pupil Services.
>
> A hearing on the petition was held on September 12, 2008 and continued on October 3, 2008 before Examiner Michael O'Callaghan and Commissioner Paul Gordon. The District, contrary to AFSCME, asserted that the positions are properly excluded from the bargaining unit by way of mutual agreement with the AFSCME prior to the representation election in . . . .

agency, or bar association website. An agency decision will appear in a format different from that of a court case. Even though a paralegal may not work for a firm that deals with agency matters, a paralegal should become familiar with the rulings available in administrative decisions. An example of an agency decision from Wisconsin is shown in Exhibit 3-6.

Charters A **charter** is the grant of authority or rights by a superior authority to a lesser or inferior entity. A typical example is a charter granted by a state authorizing a municipality or corporation to exist. The charter states that the grantor formally recognizes that the recipient has the rights specified within the charter. Some of the earliest charters in American history are the documents giving royal permission to start a colony.[26]

Charters are most often researched by those working for a governmental entity. Many charters have certain elements in common. A typical charter is shown in Exhibit 3-7, the charter for the town of Winthrop, Massachusetts.

EXHIBIT 3-7   CHARTER

Winthrop Town Hall   1 Metcalf Square, Winthrop, MA 02152
                                      mkaras@town.winthrop.ma.us

Winthrop Town Charter

TOWN OF WINTHROP CHARTER

ARTICLE 1

INCORPORATION; SHORT TITLE; DEFINITIONS

SECTION 1-1: INCORPORATION

The inhabitants of the Town of Winthrop, within the territorial limits established by law, shall continue to be a municipal corporation, a body corporate and politic, under the name "Town of Winthrop."

SECTION 1-2: SHORT TITLE

This instrument shall be known and may be cited as the Winthrop Home Rule Charter, 2005.

SECTION 1-3: DIVISION OF POWERS

The administration of the fiscal, prudential and municipal affairs of Winthrop, with the government thereof, shall be vested in an executive branch consisting of a council president, a legislative branch consisting of a town council and an administrative service headed by a town manager. Except as otherwise provided in this charter, the legislative branch shall not exercise any executive or administrative function, the executive branch shall not exercise any legislative or administrative function and the administrative service shall not exercise any legislative or executive function.

SECTION 1-4: POWERS OF THE TOWN

Subject only to express limitations on the exercise of any power or function by a municipal government in the constitution or in the general laws of the Commonwealth, it is the intention and the purpose of the voters of Winthrop through the adoption of this charter to secure for themselves and for their government all of the powers it is possible to secure as fully and as completely as though each such power were specifically and individually enumerated herein . . . .[27]

---

[27]Town of Winthrop Charter. Winthrop, MA. 2012. http://www.town.winthrop.ma.us /pages/WinthropMA_Bylaws/towncharter?textPage=1

---

[26]Yale Law School. Colonial Charters, Grants, and Related Documents. 2008. http://avalon.law.yale .edu/subject_menus/statech.asp#ge

Ordinances   An **ordinance** is a law made by government on the local level, such as a city or county council. Ordinances set standards or govern daily functions of the municipality, such as trash pickup, lawn maintenance, or dog licensing. Exhibit 3-8 provides a sample of an ordinance from Warwick, Rhode Island.

Ordinances can vary depending on the needs of the municipality. Paralegals working in local government or in a firm with clients who interact with the local government will find themselves sorting through the ordinances that apply to the situation.

EXHIBIT 3-8   SEWER AUTHORITY ORDINANCE FROM WARWICK, RI

CHAPTER 2.

SEWERS AND SEWERAGE*

ARTICLE I.

SEWER AUTHORITY

---

* Editor's Note: The Warwick Sewer Authority was created by P.L. 1962, ch. 254. Subsequent amendments which are substantive in nature are reflected in the history notes following each section, as well as in the Charter Comparative Table.

Sec. 2.1. Authority to plan, etc., sewage works; definitions; bonding authorized; sewer charge, assessment authorized.

The city of Warwick is authorized and empowered, in accordance with the provisions of this act, to plan, lay out, construct, finance, operate and maintain sewage works for a part or the whole of its territory and for such purposes to take by eminent domain or otherwise any lands, water rights, rights-of-way, or easements, public or private, in said city necessary for accomplishing any purpose mentioned in this act. Such sewage works may include sewers and sewer service connections, pumping stations, sewage treatment works, sewage disposal works, and other works essential to the proper collection and disposal of the sewage of said city.

As used in this act, unless the context otherwise requires:

"Authority" means the sewer authority authorized by this act.

"City" means the City of Warwick.

"City Council" means the city council of the City of Warwick.

"Common sewer" means a sewer in which all abutters have equal rights of entrance and use.

"Cooling water" shall include the clean waste water from air conditioning, industrial cooling, condensing and similar apparatus and from hydraulically powered equipment. In general, cooling water will include only water which is sufficiently clean and unpolluted to admit of being . . . .

SUMMARY

Effective research requires the researcher to understand the basic organization of our legal system: how law is divided, where the law comes from, and the hierarchy of the different types of law. It is also vital to understand the types of remedies afforded by the broader categories of law.

REVIEW **QUESTIONS**

1. What is the difference between common law and civil law?
2. What is the significance of the Magna Carta? What is its effect on the legal system today?
3. What are the origins of England's reporter system, and how does it compare to our current case reporter system?
4. Why do both common-law and equitable remedies exist? What are the differences between the two?
5. What is the most frequently used type of common law damages? What is its purpose?
6. What is specific performance, and when is it awarded? Give an example.
7. Why would reformation be ordered in a contracts case? Explain.
8. What is the purpose of nominal damages? Should they be awarded? Why or why not?
9. What is the order of hierarchy of enacted law?
10. What is the difference between substantive and procedural law? Give an example of each.

APPLICATION **EXERCISES**

1. In many awards of punitive damages, the state statutes require that punitive damages be awarded when there is something more than gross negligence, which often is characterized as an "evil mind" motivated by spite, malice, or the intent to defraud.

   In *Jacques v. Steenberg Homes, Inc.,* 563 N.W.2d 154 (Wis. 1997), the defendant sold a mobile home to the plaintiff's neighbor. The defendant asked the plaintiff for permission to move the trailer across plaintiff's land and the plaintiff refused. The defendant ultimately moved the trailer across the land, the plaintiff called the sheriff, and the defendant was cited. The plaintiff sued the defendant for trespass. Were the defendant's actions sufficient to warrant an award of punitive damages? Explain and justify your answer.

2. What policy would prevent a court from enforcing a liquidated damage clause? Find two articles that support your position. Explain why the articles you chose should be relied on. Look at the website, the author (if any), and the sources cited in the article. How recently has the website been updated?

3. In a case involving a claim against an insurance company based on bad faith, the plaintiffs were awarded $600,000 in compensatory damages, but no award for punitive damages. The lower court granted the insurer's motion to prevent the jury from being instructed that they may consider punitive damages. On appeal, the plaintiff argued that the jury should have been instructed that it could consider punitive damages.

   Is an instruction for punitive damages required in every insurance bad faith case, or is the New Mexico Court of Appeals correct that there should be a finding of mental state beyond "bad faith" for imposition of punitive damages in insurance bad faith cases? *Sloan v. State Farm Mutual Automobile Insurance Co.,* 320 F3d 1073 (10th Cir. 2003). http://openjurist.org/320 /f3d/1073/sloan-v-state-farm-mutual-automobile -insurance-company

4. State the term or concept of which each statement is an example.

Laws created by the Environmental Protection Agency.		Governor Napolitano has the power to create these orders.	
Laws created by Congress.		The type of law created in court decisions.	
The supreme legal document of the United States, and of each state.		The doctrine that states that federal law takes priority when state laws conflict with federal laws.	

CITATION **EXERCISES**

1. What is the correct abbreviation of the United States Court of Appeals for the 2d Circuit?

2. Give the correct citation for article I, section 9, clause 2 of the U.S. Constitution.

3. What is the official source of federal statutes?

4. What is the difference between a session law and a codified law? Cite one of each.

5. Cite a case. The appellee is George Michels. The appellant is Michelle Fredricks. The Seventh Circuit decided the case on July 15, 2012, and it was reported on page 1013 of *Federal Reporter*, third series, in volume 606.

6. Cite a statute from your jurisdiction that deals with divorce.

QUICK **CHECK**

1. The first 10 amendments to the U.S. Constitution are known as the _____.

2. _____ are notes that follow each section of the law. These notes summarize relevant court decisions, law review articles, and other legal authorities on the section.

3. In the United States, when our legislative bodies first make a law, it is called _____ or _____.

4. When federal statutes are first passed and published, they are called _____.

5. _____ are agencies created by the legislative or the executive branches.

6. As regulations are passed, they are published in the _____, which is organized chronologically.

However, the rules and regulations are later codified and arranged by subject matter in the _____.

7. Our system of courts originated in _____ and was called a _____.

8. In the hierarchy of law, _____ or _____ have more authority than cases.

9. _____, which are laws that govern local activities such as noise, are generally enacted by local governmental bodies.

10. A _____ is a grant from a governmental entity, generally to form a community.

RESEARCH

1. Find and cite a case that discusses the awarding of injunctions. What was the issue(s)? What was decided?

2. Locate this case: *Safeway Stores, Inc. v. Broach*, 654 S.W.2d 811 (Tex.App. 14 Dist., 1983). Provide the citation of the site used. Next, summarize the facts, identify the issue, identify the court's decision, and explain why the court decided the way it did.

INTERNET **RESEARCH**

1. Locate a website with the ethical rules or professional conduct rules for your state. Provide the citation for the site. Find the rule that discusses candor to the court. Cite the rule. Summarize the rule and provide two examples of how the duty could be applicable in research.

2. Find the homepage for the U.S. senators and representatives that represent you and your state. Provide contact information. (This information may be used when creating a practice portfolio.)

3. Find an article that discusses our common law system. Be sure that the site is a valid site. Do not use Wikipedia—the material on Wikipedia can be posted by anyone and is not authenticated. Summarize the contents of the article and specifically identify three major points. Trade your article site with a classmate and repeat the process. Then compare your findings. Did you both agree on three major points? Why or why not? If possible, discuss your selections and try to compromise on three major points. Report on the results.

MEDIA **RESOURCES**

Your instructor may have access to the videos identified as the Paralegal Practice and Ethics-Related Video Segment from *The Paralegal Professional Classroom Video Series* DVD by Pearson. One example is "The Difference between Civil and Criminal Cases."

About.com. U.S. Government Info. *The US Federal Court System.* 2012. http://video.about.com/usgovinfo/The-US -Federal-Court-System.htmn

Howcast. *How to Understand the American Judicial System.* n.d. http://www.howcast.com/videos/425723-How-to -Understand-the-American-Judicial-System

Kaye, Judith S. *A Court System for the 21st Century.* PBS Video. 2009–2012. http://video.pbs.org/video/1972297584/

INTERNET **RESOURCES**

Congressional Monitor:	http://www.thecongressionalmonitor.com/?m=20090225
Congressional Quarterly:	http://corporate.cq.com/wmspage.cfm?parm1=12
Congressional Records Index:	http://www.gpo.gov/customers/cri.htm
Guide to the House of Representatives:	http://www.house.gov/
Guide to the Legislative Archives:	http://www.archives.gov/legislative/index.html
Senate Journal:	http://memory.loc.gov/ammem/amlaw/lwsj.html
State Constitutions:	http://www.constitution.org/cons/usstcons.htm
State primary authority:	http://www.whpgs.org/f.htm
State statutes:	http://www.law.cornell.edu/statutes.html
U.S. Constitution:	http://www.usconstitution.net/const.html or http://www.archives.gov/exhibits/charters/constitution .html

chapter **four**

TYPES OF LAW

ijphotos/Shutterstock

LEARNING OBJECTIVES

After completing this chapter, students should be able to:

1. Differentiate between primary and secondary sources.

2. Identify appropriate uses of primary and secondary sources.

3. Locate known relevant authority using its proper citation.

4. Categorize authority as to its weight and value.

5. Perform computer-assisted legal research.

CHAPTER OVERVIEW

Law in general may be broadly divided into 10 types, and understanding these types of law will aid in the research process. It is also vital to understand what constitute primary and secondary authorities. The paralegal must also understand the distinction between mandatory and persuasive authority. These basic categories will aid the paralegal in the development of a research plan that can be tailored to almost any research project.

OPENING SCENARIO

This is a big research week for our paralegal, John. Heather Dobbs came into the office today because she is sure, after her initial consultation with John and his boss, Jami, that she wants to file a complaint. A truck, driven by Paul Roberts, failed to stop at the four-way stop sign and struck Heather's car in the passenger door. Heather lives in Indiana but works in Illinois. Paul lives in Illinois. The damage to the car was extensive and Heather was taken to the local hospital. She has been released from the hospital with a broken right leg, a dislocated shoulder, and two cracked ribs. Paul's insurance company is balking at covering the hospital bills because the company is adamant that Heather did not stop at the stop sign and therefore caused the collision. Heather is facing additional bills from physical therapy and renting a car, and also incurred lost wages and pain and suffering. She does not want to pay for these items and does not believe her insurance company should, either. She is ready to file a complaint.

TEN TYPES OF LAW

Understanding *how* to find the answers to legal questions begins with understanding the types of primary authority. Having a firm grasp of what constitutes "law" will make the remainder of the course easier to understand and absorb. Most primary authority comes from 10 different sources, as shown in Table 4-1. These different types of law should be kept in mind as the research process unfolds.

TABLE 4-1   Primary Sources of Law

Source of Law	Purpose
Constitutions	The U.S. Constitution is the supreme law of the land. No law can contravene the Constitution. For example, Art. III, sec. 1 sets forth the creation of the U.S. Supreme Court. The First Amendment gives us the right to have free speech, religion, press, and assembly, and the right to petition our grievances. Each state also has its own constitution.
Statutes (also referred to as "codes")	These laws are enacted by the U.S. Congress and the legislatures in each of the 50 states. Statutes are enacted to regulate conduct, define crimes, create inferior government bodies, appropriate public monies, and in general promote the public welfare. Statutes are both *procedural* and *substantive*. For example, I.C. 35-34-1-1 is a procedural statute regarding the commencement of criminal prosecutions. 26 U.S.C. § 2501 is a substantive statute that determines what transfers are taxable.
Cases (also referred to as court opinions and court decisions)	Cases are legal precedent, created by judges rather than legislatures. Judges can interpret and apply either statutory law or common law from other cases. For example, *Marbury v. Madison,* 5 U.S. 137 (1803) established precedent that provides the basis for judicial review. In *Commonwealth v. Jones,* 880 S.W.2d 544 (Ky. 1994), the court ruled that it would not substitute its decision for that of a jury regarding the occurrence of facts.
Administrative regulations	Regulations are similar to statutes but are created on an administrative level. They often pertain to providing benefits to someone, such as 20 C.F.R. 404 regarding the Social Security Act. They may also regulate a profession, such as 18 VAC 60-20 (2008), which regulates the practice of dentistry and dental hygiene.
Administrative decisions	Administrative decisions are handed down by administrative law judges (ALJs). For example, *A & W Smelters & Refiners, Inc.* (CERCLA 106(b) 94-14) is an ALJ order regarding environmental cleanup. *IDEM v. Hungler,* 2008 OEA 1 is an ALJ decision regarding the Clean Water Act.
Rules of court	Rules of court are procedural laws governing the mechanics of litigation in a particular court. For example, Fed.R.Civ.p. 26 (FRCP 26) involves the duty to disclose in discovery. Alaska Sup. Ct. R. 11(a)(1) is a court rule establishing the proper citation format.
Charters	A charter is a fundamental law of a local unit of government that allows the entity to function, such as the charter for the town of Windsor Locks, CT.
Ordinances	An ordinance is the law from a local legislative branch such as a county or city council. For example, OH 337.20 "muffler; muffler cutout; excessive smoke, gas or noise" is an ordinance that restricts noise and pollution within the city of Hubbard, Ohio.
Executive orders	An executive order is issued by a jurisdiction's chief executive officer, such as the president of the United States or a state governor. For example, Executive Order 13508 is an order by President Obama regarding the protection and restoration of the Chesapeake Bay.
Treaties	Treaties are international agreements between two or more countries, such as the North American Free Trade Agreement (NAFTA), which is a trade agreement among the United States, Mexico, and Canada.

TABLE 4-2 Hierarchy of Law

Federal Law	State Law
U.S. Constitution	U.S. Constitution
U.S. Code (Federal Statutes)	State Constitution
U.S. Supreme Court Cases	State Statutes
U.S. Courts of Appeals Cases	State Supreme Court Cases
U.S. District Court Cases	State Appellate Court Cases
Administrative Regulations	Administrative Regulations
Administrative Decisions	Administrative Decisions
	Ordinances

Each of these 10 types of law may be referred to by a number of terms or phrases. For example, court opinions are referred to as "rules of law" or legal doctrine. Legal doctrine comes from the judicial opinions of the courts and is therefore the currency of the law.[1]

Not every research project will use every type of law. However, a researcher who knows the different types of laws can identify what law is more likely to be used in a given situation so that a lot of time is not wasted searching every source. Some of the laws will be used frequently, some less frequently, and some not at all, depending on the type of case to which the authority is applied.

It is also essential to understand that there is a hierarchy to the 10 types of law. Within this hierarchy, some types of law generally supersede (are superior to) others. See Table 4-2 for a quick explanation of the hierarchy of those types most frequently used.

Constitutions

A constitution is the founding document of a state or nation, setting forth the basic structure and principles by which it is governed. The principles contained in a constitution are generally very broad, and will have few details or explanations. When beginning a research project, the state and federal constitutions are often the first source to check, since they are superior to all other laws.

The U.S. Constitution is referred to as "the supreme law of the land," and nothing can contravene it. The Constitution consists of articles that provide the basic rights of citizens and the structure for the operation of government. They are based on broad principles that cover things such as the organization of the three branches of government, the relationship between federal and state governments, the relationships between the states, and how the Constitution may be amended.

Most of the 27 Amendments to the Constitution concern the rights of individuals and the states. The first 10 amendments are known as the Bill of Rights. Other amendments address topics such as the electoral college, voting, income tax, and rights and liabilities of states.

Reading a treatise on constitutional law may provide a good background for those who will be working in that field. Legal encyclopedias will also provide solid background information, since they focus on the rulings of the U.S. Supreme Court. The decisions of the Supreme Court are crucial in interpreting the Constitution.

The Tenth Amendment to the U.S. Constitution gives powers not retained by the federal government to the 50 states, each of which has its own constitution.

---

[1]Tiller, Emerson H. & Cross, Frank B. *What is Legal Doctrine?* 100 N.W. L. Rev. 517 (2006)

Although each state is independent, most of the states have fashioned their constitutions after the U.S. Constitution. State constitutions are more frequently amended than is the U.S. Constitution. For example, there have been almost 150 state constitutions that have been amended approximately 12,000 times.[2]

State constitutions typically provide the same rights given in the U.S. Constitution, but often grant additional rights. The states are permitted to do this as long as those additional rights do not contravene the U.S. Constitution.

Statutes

Statutes, also referred to as codes, legislation, acts, or session laws, are enacted by the U.S. Congress and the legislatures in each of the 50 states. Statutory law is the heart of most research problems. All statutes can be found online in free or subscription services. The researcher should check for statutory authority after determining that there is no constitutional question, since statutory authority is the next highest authority.

Statutes are enacted to regulate conduct, define crimes, create inferior government bodies, appropriate public monies, and in general promote the public welfare. Statutes are either *procedural* or *substantive*. The basic provisions of a statute include the following:

- the opening provisions that give the statute's name, definition, and scope;
- the operative provisions that give the general rule, exceptions, enforcements provisions, and consequences of violation; and
- the closing provisions that provide the effective date, severability, and sunset provisions, which require periodic review of the statute.

As the legislative session progresses, proposed bills are submitted and given a chronological number indicating the order in which they were presented. After the president or governor signs the bill and the legislative session ends, the bills are collected into acts or session laws and published, often as slip laws. These slip or session laws are not used for most statutory research because they are presented chronologically. However, if research on legislative intent is performed, slip laws will become an important part of the research process. Once the session ends, the slip or session laws are **codified**, meaning that like statutes are organized together under "titles." For example, all federal statutes regarding taxes are found in Title 26, while all statutes pertaining to war are found under Title 50. In Indiana, all the property laws are in Title 32, automobile statutes in Title 9, and family law matters in Title 31. Figure 4-1 shows the difference between a public law and a codified statute.

State statutes are given a variety of names, depending on the custom of the state. Table 4-3 shows the titles some states have given to their statutory compilations.

Paralegals should become familiar with the names designated for the statutes of the jurisdictions in which they work. This information can be found in local libraries, on the state government website, and in the citation manual used in the jurisdiction.

Both the annotated and official versions of statutes are arranged by topic and include all statutes currently in force. Most research is best done in the annotated versions, because the annotations provide additional information such as citations to cases where the statute was applied, cross-references to secondary sources that can be used for further understanding, and other sources that have applied the statute.

Codified

Collecting and arranging the laws in a systematic order with like materials (such as by subject or topic) in the same location within the statute books. The laws inform the public of acceptable and unacceptable behavior.

[2]John Joseph Wallis, NBER/University of Maryland State Constitution Project, www.stateconstitutions.umd.edu

First column shows public law; second column shows codified statute. A researcher should note that the titles, sections, and subsections in the public law change when the statute is codified, even though the language stays the same.

Americans with Disabilities Act of 1990, Pub. L. No. 101-336, 104 Stat. 327	Americans with Disabilities Act of 1990, 42 U.S.C. §§ 12101–12213
SEC. 2. FINDINGS AND PURPOSES. (a) Findings—Congress finds that— (2) in enacting the ADA, Congress recognized that physical and mental disabilities in no way diminish a person's right to fully participate in all aspects of society, but that people with physical or mental disabilities are frequently precluded from doing so because of prejudice, antiquated attitudes, or the failure to remove societal and institutional barriers;	Sec. 12101. Findings and purpose (a) Findings The Congress finds that (1) physical or mental disabilities in no way diminish a person's right to fully participate in all aspects of society, yet many people with physical or mental disabilities have been precluded from doing so because of discrimination; others who have a record of a disability or are regarded as having a disability also have been subjected to discrimination;
SEC. 3. DEFINITION OF DISABILITY. As used in this Act: (1) DISABILITY – The term 'disability' means, with respect to an individual— (A) a physical or mental impairment that substantially limits one or more major life activities of such individual; (B) a record of such an impairment; or (C) being regarded as having such an impairment (as described in paragraph (3)). (2) MAJOR LIFE ACTIVITIES – (A) IN GENERAL – For purposes of paragraph (1), major life activities include, but are not limited to, caring for oneself, performing manual tasks, seeing, hearing, eating, sleeping, walking, standing, lifting, bending, speaking, breathing, learning, reading, concentrating, thinking, communicating, and working.[3]	Sec. 12102. Definition of disability (1) Disability – The term "disability" means, with respect to an individual (A) a physical or mental impairment that substantially limits one or more major life activities of such individual; (B) a record of such an impairment; or (C) being regarded as having such an impairment (as described in paragraph (3)). (2) Major Life Activities (A) In general – For purposes of paragraph (1), major life activities include, but are not limited to, caring for oneself, performing manual tasks, seeing, hearing, eating, sleeping, walking, standing, lifting, bending, speaking, breathing, learning, reading, concentrating, thinking, communicating, and working.[4]

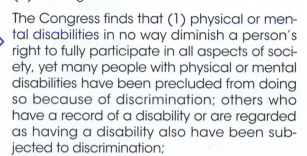

FIGURE 4-1 Public Law and Codified Statutes

One approach to researching statutes is to look at the assignment given or issue in question and then identify key words contained in it. Those key words are then used to find the statutes that relate to the client's issue in the index of the statutes, just as key words are used in the index of a general book. The key words will lead to applicable statutes. If it is determined that a statute may apply to the issue

[3]https://www.civilrights.dot.gov/sites/default/files/uploads/documents/110-325_law.pdf

[4]http://www.gpo.gov/fdsys/pkg/USCODE-2010-title42/pdf/USCODE-2010-title42-chap126.pdf

TABLE 4-3 Statute Identification

State	Statutory Compilation
California	California Commercial Code
Connecticut	Connecticut General Statutes
Illinois	Illinois Compiled Statutes
Kentucky	Kentucky Revised Statutes Annotated
Louisiana	Louisiana Revised Statute Annotated or Louisiana Code Civil Procedure Annotated (or other subject matter codes)
Maryland	Maryland Code Annotated (subject abbreviation), such as Md. Code Ann. Pub. Safety
Massachusetts	Massachusetts General Laws Annotated
North Dakota	North Dakota Century Code
Pennsylvania	Pennsylvania Consolidated Statutes
Texas	Texas Business and Commercial Code (or other subject matter division)
Washington	Washington Revised Code

being researched, it should be located in the appropriate volume and read, as well as any annotations (if the volume is annotated). If the statute applies to the research question, the next step is to find cases that support the statutory language. Researchers read the language of each provision that might apply to the research issue and then look at the next level of law for support: cases that interpret the statutes.

Cases

Case law is also referred to as common law, judge-made law, court opinions, or cases. Case law is created when a judge is presented with a case or controversy that he or she is asked to decide. In reaching its decision, the court interprets statutes or applies common law. When the decision in a case is published, it becomes *precedent* for other cases that have similar issues and facts.

Precedent
A prior opinion involving facts, issues, and rules of law sufficiently similar to the facts, issues, and rules of law under current consideration; can be used to guide the court's decision in the current case.

Federal Three levels of courts exist on the federal level. At the trial level are the U.S. District Courts, which have general jurisdiction over civil and criminal cases. There are 94 federal district courts with at least one court in every state, as well as in the District of Columbia and Puerto Rico. Territorial courts similar to district courts exist in U.S. territories. Bankruptcy courts are separate courts from the district courts; these federal courts have exclusive jurisdiction over bankruptcy cases.

The intermediate level is the U.S. Courts of Appeals, which in many instances are the last level of appeal in the federal court system. The district courts are assigned into 12 regional circuit courts; in addition, there is a nationwide Federal Circuit Court that hears specialized cases, such as patent cases. The courts of appeals do not hear evidence. Generally, the assigned judges read briefs and discuss the case with the panel of judges assigned to the case. On occasion, attorneys present oral arguments.

The final level of appeal in the federal system is the U.S. Supreme Court. No official reports of Supreme Court cases were published until the late 19th century. The first reporters were named after individuals who compiled and published them, such as Dallas, Cranch, and Wallace.

TIP
It is helpful to hear an oral argument to gain an understanding of what an oral argument is like. Some oral arguments are available online.[5]

---

[5]One such location, this one for the U.S. Court of Appeals for the Federal Circuit, is http://www.cafc.uscourts.gov/oral-argument-recordings/search/audio.html. 2012.

From U.S. District Court to U.S. Supreme Court

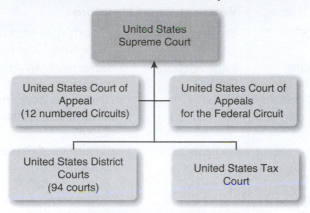

From U.S. Specialized Courts to U.S. Supreme Court

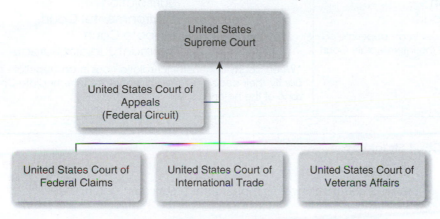

From United States Military Court to U.S. Supreme Court

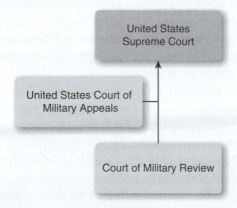

FIGURE 4-2 The Federal Court System

State Most paralegals work in the state system rather than the federal system. Most state trial courts do not publish opinions; however, exceptions do exist, such as the trial courts in New York. When a trial court decision is appealed, the state appellate court will render a decision, which may be published in a state reporter. Some states have a two-tier system with only one level of appeal, while others have a three-tier system with two levels of appeal. The names given to the state appellate-level courts vary depending on the state.

TIP

Researchers should check with the local rules to confirm the court names.

Colorado Court Structure		Vermont Court Structure	
State High Court	Court(s) of Last Resort Supreme Court	State High Court	Court(s) of Last Resort Supreme Court
Intermediate Court	Intermediate Appellate Court(s) Court of Appeals	Intermediate Court	Intermediate Appellate Court(s) This state does not have an Intermediate Appellate Court
Trial Court	Court(s) of General Jurisdiction* District Court Water Court Denver District Court Denver Juvenile Court Denver Probate Court Court(s) of Limited Jurisdiction County Court	Trial Court	Court(s) of General Jurisdiction* Family Court Superior Court District Court Court(s) of Limited Jurisdiction Environmental Court Probate Court Vermont Judicial Bureau

*When courts of general jurisdiction act in an appellate capacity, their decisions may appear in the Intermediate Court zone of the history display.

*When courts of general jurisdiction act in an appellate capacity, their decisions may appear in the Intermediate Court zone of the history display.

FIGURE 4-3 Comparison of State Court Structures[6]

Figure 4-3 compares two examples of the state court systems.

Administrative Regulations

The executive branch and its agencies exercise government authority through administrative law. The source from which the agency derives its power determines the agency's right to issue and enforce the regulations. For example, Congress creates an agency by passing an "enabling act" and giving the agency authority to create regulations that have the force of statutes.

Agency regulations are generally referred to as "codes," which sometimes causes new researchers confusion since statutes sometimes are also referred to as "codes." The key is to know what service the research is covering.

Administrative regulations provide the details for outlining and enforcing the administrative policy. Regulations are critical in administrative agencies because they are the operating rules and detailed directions for the agencies' operation. Regulations set forth specific requirements that an agency must follow, such as the things an agency can and cannot do. Regulations may include specific procedures and assign specific responsibility.

On the federal level, regulations are proposed in the executive departments and agencies. Once proposed, the regulations are published in the *Federal Register* (Fed.Reg.) so that the public can comment on the proposed rules. Once permanent, the rules are codified and published in the *Code of Federal Regulations* (*C.F.R.*), which is divided into 50 titles that represent broad areas that are subject to Federal regulation. All *C.F.R.* titles are updated yearly.[7] Unlike other research materials, they are not cumulative. Each year stands on its own. Figure 4-4 shows a page from 32 C.F.R. Ch. VI, §§ 720.14–720.19 (2002).

> **TIP**
>
> The U.S. Government Manual (http://www.gpoaccess.gov/gmanual/) and the Federal Regulatory Directory (current edition) are two sources for research.

[6]State Court Organizational Chart. http://wlwatch.westlaw.com/aca/west/statecrtorg.htm#CO

[7]GPO Access. *Code of Federal Regulations* (CFR): Main Page. 2010. http://www.gpoaccess.gov/cfr/

naval legal service office or the Marine Corps staff judge advocate, shall prepare a written request for temporary custody of the member addressed to the State official charged with administration of the State penal system. The request shall designate the person(s) to whom the member is to be delivered and shall be transmitted via the military judge to whom the member's case has been assigned. If the request is properly prepared, the military judge shall approve, record, and transmit the request to the addressee official. The Act provides the State with a 30-day period after receipt of the request before the request is to be honored. Within that period of time, the governor of the State may disapprove the request, either unilaterally or upon the prisoner's request. If the governor disapproves the request, the command should coordinate any further action with the Judge Advocate General.

(3) *Responsibilities.* The cognizant command shall ensure that the responsibilities of a receiving jurisdiction, delineated in section 2. Article IV of the Act, are discharged. In particular, the Act requires that the receiving jurisdiction:

(i) Commence the prisoner's trial within 120 days of the prisoner's arrival, unless the court, for good cause shown during an Article 39(a), UCMJ, session, grants a continuance necessary or reasonable to promote the ends of justice;

(ii) Hold the prisoner in a suitable jail or other facility regularly used for persons awaiting prosecution, except for periods during which the prisoner attends court or to any place at which his presence may be required;

(iii) Return the prisoner to the sending jurisdiction at the earliest practical time, but not before the charges that underlie the request have been resolved (prematurely returning the prisoner will result in dismissal of the); and

(iv) Pay all costs of transporting, caring for, keeping, and returning the prisoner to the sending jurisdiction, unless the command and the State agree on some of other allocation of the costs or responsibilities.

§§720.14–720.19   [Reserved]

Subpart B—Service of Process and Subpoenas Upon Personnel

Source: 57 FR 5232, Feb. 13, 1992, unless otherwise noted.

§720.20 Service of process upon personnel.

(a) *General.* Commanding officers afloat and ashore may permit service of process of Federal or State courts upon members, civilian employee, dependents, or contractors residing at or located on a naval installation, if located within their commands. Service will not be made within the command without the commanding officer's consent. The intent of this provision is to protect against interference with mission accomplishment and to preserve good order and discipline, while not unnecessarily impeding the court's work. Where practical, the commanding officer shall require that the process be served in his presence, or in the presence of a designated officer. In all cases, individuals will be advised to seek legal counsel, either from a legal assistance attorney or from personal counsel for service in personal matters, and from Government counsel for service in official matters. The commanding officer is not required to act as a process server. The action required depends in part on the status of the individual requested and which State issues the process.

(1) *In-State process.* When a process server from a State or Federal court from the jurisdiction where the naval station is located requests permission to serve process aboard an installation, the command ordinarily should not prevent service of process so long as delivery is made in accordance with reasonable command regulations and is consistent with good order and discipline. Withholding service may be justified only in the rare case when the individual sought is located in an area under exclusive Federal jurisdiction not subject to any reservation by the State of the right to serve process. Questions on the extent of jurisdiction should be referred to the staff judge advocate, command counsel, or local naval legal service office. If service is

---

FIGURE 4-4 *Code of Federal Regulations*[8]

[8]AmicusVeritas.org. American Military Poverty Law Project. Hallinan's Violation of Nary's Rights. http://amicusveritas.org/AMPLP/laws.htm

States create regulations for state agencies, commissions, or boards. For example, Figure 4-5 shows a portion of the index for the Indiana Administrative Code.

FIGURE 4-5 Indiana Administrative Code Index (excerpts)

Indiana Administrative Code

Latest Update: January 4, 2012
(Certificate of Authenticity)

TITLE 10   OFFICE OF ATTORNEY GENERAL FOR THE STATE
TITLE 11   CONSUMER PROTECTION DIVISION OF THE OFFICE OF THE ATTORNEY GENERAL
TITLE 15   STATE ELECTION BOARD
TITLE 16   OFFICE OF THE LIEUTENANT GOVERNOR
TITLE 17   OFFICE OF COMMUNITY AND RURAL AFFAIRS

* * *

TITLE 33   STATE EMPLOYEES' APPEALS COMMISSION
TITLE 35   BOARD OF TRUSTEES OF THE INDIANA PUBLIC RETIREMENT SYSTEM
TITLE 40   STATE ETHICS COMMISSION
TITLE 42   OFFICE OF THE INSPECTOR GENERAL
TITLE 45   DEPARTMENT OF STATE REVENUE

* * *

TITLE 120   DEPARTMENT OF HIGHWAYS
TITLE 130   PORTS OF INDIANA
TITLE 135   INDIANA FINANCE AUTHORITY
TITLE 140   BUREAU OF MOTOR VEHICLES
TITLE 145   RECIPROCITY COMMISSION OF INDIANA

* * *

TITLE 290   DEPARTMENT OF HOMELAND SECURITY

* * *

TITLE 310   DEPARTMENT OF NATURAL RESOURCES
TITLE 311   STATE SOIL AND WATER CONSERVATION COMMITTEE
TITLE 312   NATURAL RESOURCES COMMISSION
TITLE 327   WATER POLLUTION CONTROL BOARD
TITLE 328   UNDERGROUND STORAGE TANK FINANCIAL ASSURANCE BOARD
TITLE 329   SOLID WASTE MANAGEMENT BOARD
TITLE 330   STREAM POLLUTION CONTROL BOARD OF THE STATE OF INDIANA
TITLE 330.1 WATER POLLUTION CONTROL BOARD

* * *

TITLE 610   DEPARTMENT OF LABOR
TITLE 615   BOARD OF SAFETY REVIEW
TITLE 620   OCCUPATIONAL SAFETY STANDARDS COMMISSION
TITLE 630   INDUSTRIAL BOARD OF INDIANA
TITLE 631   WORKER'S COMPENSATION BOARD OF INDIANA
TITLE 635   WAGE ADJUSTMENT BOARD
TITLE 640   INDIANA UNEMPLOYMENT INSURANCE BOARD[9]

[9]Indiana General Assembly. Indiana Administrative Code. 2012. http://www.in.gov/legislative/iac/

References in the first section are to various board and commissions, while in the second section, there is a similarity to the federal agency listings, such as the Department of Highways (similar to the Department of Transportation), and the Department of Homeland Security (similar to the Homeland Security Department).

Administrative Decisions

Similar to the court systems, the administrative agencies act in a judicial capacity when administrative law judges (ALJs) hear and decide particular matters. An ***administrative hearing*** occurs when there is a dispute before an administrative agency, board, or commission.

Administrative hearing
A hearing before an ALJ.

The decisions made at administrative hearings are broadly classified as advisory opinions, informal adjudications, and formal adjudications. Advisory opinions are not binding, but instead are interpretations of statutes and regulations that provide guidance on agency policy and expectations. Informal adjudication decisions are discretionary and generally not reviewable by a court. In making these decisions, ALJs are governed by special statutory requirements or the agency's regulations.

Formal agency decisions are also called quasi-judicial decisions. An independent ALJ or agency commissioner takes on a role much like a court. These proceedings have the following characteristics:

- They adjudicate disputes arising out of the interpretation or violation of enabling statutes or regulations.
- They report decisions similarly to case law.
- The decisions are usually reported in writing.
- The proceedings are used as fact-finding inquiries into how regulations apply to a particular situation.

They are not strictly bound by prior decisions, but the decisions have precedential value, so attorneys who practice before an agency can use the decisions as an important primary source of the law.

Rules of Court

All courts have rules to govern their procedures for conducting business. Court rules are referred to in a variety of ways, such as "rules of court" or "rules of procedure." The rules may determine what pleadings can be filed, the time limits for the filing of pleadings, how a defendant can be served, and what matters are appealable. Court rules may be created by a combination of court and legislative actions.

In general, both federal and state courts are first governed by statutory law that gives the courts their powers and jurisdiction, and often sets some procedural rules. If the legislature adopts rules, those rules likewise have the power of statutory law. Statutes also give the courts some authority to adopt their own rules for their processes and procedures. Some rules apply generally to all courts, some apply only to certain types of courts, and some are local rules that apply only to a particular court. In addition, courts promulgate rules for their own internal operating procedures.

At the federal level, the U.S. Supreme Court creates the rules for all federal courts under authority from 28 U.S.C. § 2072. Although the rules are made under the authority of the Supreme Court, in actuality they are drafted and approved by committees of the Judicial Conference of the United States. Rules of the federal district courts are referred to as the *Federal Rules of Civil Procedure* (Fed.R.Civ.P.) and the *Federal Rules of Criminal Procedure* (Fed.R.Crim.P.). The circuit courts have their own appellate practice rules called the *Federal Rules of Appellate Procedure* (Fed.R.App.P.).

State courts operate in a similar way, and most states model their court rules on the federal rules. The rules may be variously named, with titles such as the following:

- Rules of Civil Procedure
- Rules of Criminal Procedure
- Rules of Evidence
- Rules of Civil Appellate Procedure
- Rules of the Supreme Court
- Rules of Juvenile Procedure
- Local Court Procedural and Administrative Rules
- Rules of Family Procedure
- Rules of Probate Procedure
- Uniform Rules for Courts Exercising Criminal Jurisdiction
- Uniform Rules for the District Courts

Researchers must check the applicable rules of the jurisdictions in which they work.

Charters

Charters

The fundamental law of a municipality or local governmental unit which authorizes the entity to perform designated governmental functions. It is a city's basic source of law.

A *charter* serves as the founding document of an organization, such as a city or municipal corporation. It is different from a constitution in that it is granted to the organization by a superior sovereign power rather than established by the people themselves. The American colonies originated when the British government gave charters to groups to settle in America, such as Charter of the Dutch West India Company (New York). Since that time, charters have evolved to fit the needs of society. Congressional charters, for example, established the First Bank of the United States in 1791 and the Tennessee Valley Authority in 1933. Today, municipal charters establish cities, towns, and villages, for example.

Ordinances

Ordinances are laws promulgated by counties, cities, and towns. Many of these local governments make some or all of their local laws available online, but sometimes physically appearing at appropriate designated offices may be necessary. Typically, the most commonly referenced universal ordinances, such as those governing zoning and waste burning, are published online. For example, Ortonville, Minnesota, provides its entire code of ordinances online, while the City of Long Prairie makes only its most requested ordinances available through the Internet.[10] Larger cities, such as Chicago, use publishing companies to publish all their ordinances online and keep them current.[11]

---

[10]Minnesota State Law Library. http://www.lawlibrary.state.mn.us/ordinance.html

[11]Municipal Code of Chicago, Illinois. American Legal Publishing Company. 2011. http://www.amlegal.com/library/il/chicago.shtml

Executive Orders

Executive orders are issued by the president, the governor of a state, or the mayor of a town. When issued by the president, these orders are legally binding documents generally used to give direction to a federal agency and department officials in executing policies or laws established by Congress. Executive orders directed at those outside of the U.S. government are referred to as presidential proclamations.

One of the most well-known executive orders is President Lincoln's Emancipation Proclamation, which declared the freedom of all enslaved persons within the Confederacy. In more recent times, President Clinton fought a war with Yugoslavia pursuant to an executive order, and President Obama signed an executive order stopping the deportation of certain immigrants brought into the United States at a young age. A problem with executive orders is that they do not require congressional approval to take effect, but they have the weight of statutes.

State governors issue executive orders in much the same manner as the president does. Executive orders issued by a governor can freeze regulations, create commissions, and proclaim a state of emergency. Many executive orders issued by governors can be found on state websites.

Treaties

A treaty is an agreement between two or more independent nations. The president holds the power to make treaties with other countries, but must have the consent of two-thirds of the senators present. Since the 97th Congress, treaties have been identified by a hyphenated number, similar to public laws, with the first number referring to the congressional session during which the treaty was submitted and the second number being a chronological sequence number. For example, Treaty 112-5 is the fifth treaty sent to the 112th Congress.

CASE ANALYSIS AND THE RESEARCH PROCESS

Case Analysis

There are a number of laws that may be applicable to a given research issue. For example, the case of Heather Dobbs's car accident does not appear to have any constitutional issues involved, so it likely is not a constitutional question. It could be a statutory question, because it involves a statute that establishes a standard of conduct for driving. A paralegal researching this set of facts would also look at case law involving facts that are similar to Heather's facts to see how the courts interpret the statute. This process of applying the law to the client's facts is a form of *case analysis*.

Cases originate from a civil or criminal dispute that the courts are asked to decide. A *civil dispute* involves one of several possibilities:

1. a person suing a person;
2. a person suing a corporation;
3. a person suing the government;
4. a corporation suing a corporation;
5. a corporation suing the government;
6. the government suing a person;
7. the government suing a corporation; or
8. a government agency suing another government agency.

Case analysis
The study of law based upon analyzing opinions written by judges and justices in actual cases. Also called "case method."

Civil dispute
A legal dispute over any matter other than a criminal matter, and involving issues that are not criminal in nature.

Criminal action

An action brought by some governmental entity (prosecutor, district attorney, state's attorney, U.S. Attorney, U.S. Attorney General) involving an allegation that a crime has been committed.

Judgment

In a civil matter, the court decision as to the rights of the parties based on the pleadings filed and the evidence presented; in a criminal matter, the determination, or lack thereof, of guilt.

Facts

Any information about an actual person, place, or thing.

Rules of law

Legal doctrines that govern conduct.

Holding

The judicial decision based on applying the law to the facts.

Opinion

The written explanation of how the court reached its holding.

The basis of the civil dispute can be any issue that not does not involve the violation of a criminal statute. A ***criminal action*** is brought by some governmental entity (a prosecutor, district attorney, state's attorney, or U.S. Attorney General) alleging that a crime has been committed. The court renders its decision by issuing a ***judgment***, which sets forth the rights and duties of the parties involved in a civil matter and the guilt or lack thereof in a criminal matter.

Generally, a court bases its judgment on two factors: 1) the ***facts*** of the dispute before it and 2) the ***rules of law*** that must be applied to those facts. A fact is any information about a person, place, or thing. The rule of law is any of the 10 types of law outlined in Table 4-1. The court looks at the facts and the rule of law and applies its interpretation of the law to the facts of the case before the court. The application is called the ***holding*** of the court. There is a holding for each issue before the court. For example, if a case has two issues to be resolved, the court will deliver two holdings. The written explanation of how the court reached its holdings that appears in the body of the ***opinion*** is called the reasoning or rationale.

Researchers should be aware that the same set of facts may give rise to three types of cases: a civil action, a criminal action, or an administrative hearing, as illustrated in Simulation 4-1.

Before the court can make a decision, there must be a case or controversy brought before it. A dispute may come to a law firm through a client, such as Heather Dobbs in the opening scenario, or Katie in Simulation 4-1. A dispute can also come to a firm when an agency sues a company or when a government sues an alleged criminal, for example.

The legal research process starts by identifying the important facts of the client's case and the legal questions presented by those facts. A court undertakes a similar process when deciding a case. For many paralegals, the fact analysis

---

SIMULATION 4-1   CASE ANALYSIS

Katie was taking her grandfather to the doctor's appointment that had been scheduled three weeks ago. She was running a little late and she was not sure where she was going. She was proceeding north on Water Street and was driving a little faster than she should have been driving. Suddenly, a moving truck owned by Magnificent Movers, traveling east on Fire Street, ran a stoplight at the intersection of Water Street and Fire Street and collided with Katie's car on the driver's side. The impact was so severe that Katie's grandfather died at the scene. Katie was rushed to the hospital because she was unconscious and severely bleeding from a wound to her head. The driver of the moving truck suffered a broken leg.

At the scene, the police searched the moving van because one of the officers smelled a strange odor and believed it to be marijuana. The smell, coupled with the fact that the passenger was not very coherent, gave the officers probable cause to search the vehicle. The owner of the moving van was called to the scene. The passenger was a friend of the driver's whom the driver had picked up as a favor. This was in violation of company policy.

With respect to the scenario, answer the following:

1. How many possible lawsuits might there be?
2. What type of cases would you have?
3. Who are the possible parties in each lawsuit?
4. What courts would hear each case?
5. What should be done first?

will begin with reviewing a client file, and in some cases, interviewing the client. In either case, the paralegal should be diligent in fact gathering. The client does not always recognize what facts are important, and yet facts that seem unimportant to the client may point to a significant legal issue. The first caveat in fact gathering is that whenever there is any uncertainty as to a fact or legal issue, the paralegal should always ask questions to clarify the problem.

Once all of the facts in a client's case have been identified, they should be categorized. This process is fluid, and categorizing the facts continues throughout the legal research process. For the purposes in legal research, there are three basic types of facts to explore:

1. Key or relevant facts
2. Explanatory or context facts
3. Legally unimportant facts

Key facts are facts that, if different or nonexistent, would change the outcome of the case. Key facts are also referred to as **relevant facts**. What is key, or relevant, will depend on the circumstances of each case. Examples of relevant facts are those that have some type of direct effect on the decision of the case or explain the relationship between the parties.

The client's case may also have **explanatory facts**, which are sometimes referred to as **context facts**. These facts are important because they help explain, clarify, or flesh out the relevant facts. When a researcher applies a statute to the client's case, it should be applied to that specific set of facts, including those that describe the context of those facts. **Legally unimportant facts** are those that, while sometimes interesting, have no bearing on the client's legal case. In order to separate this group of facts from those that are relevant, a researcher can do one of the following:

- Remove the fact and then determine whether removing the fact would significantly affect the outcome of the case.
- Check whether changing the fact would significantly affect the outcome of the case.

The researcher must also keep in mind that different people may use different words to describe the same thing. It is always important to think of alternate terms for the facts presented. Finding alternate terms will expand research opportunities, aid in investigation, and connect witnesses and different pieces of evidence. For example, a "motor vehicle" may also be referred to as a car, an automobile, a truck, an SUV, or a van. Alternate terms for a particular subject can be thought of as a "cartwheel of facts" with a main or center word with spokes for the alternate terms, as shown in Figure 4-6.

As the research proceeds, the researcher should continually ask questions about the client's facts. Doing so will help the researcher learn more about the legal concepts and issues involved in the case. Sometimes it is difficult to determine which client facts are most relevant until more information is presented. Facts that seemed legally unimportant in the beginning may need to be recategorized as relevant.

The next step is to determine the questions of fact or factual issues. Factual questions need to be determined before determining the legal questions. One way to distinguish between questions of fact and questions of law is to ask what sources are consulted. If the researcher consults the law only, it is a question of law. Factual questions are resolved by gathering information and interpreting the factual situations.

Key facts

Facts that, if different or non-existent, would change the outcome of the case; may be referred to as "relevant facts."

Relevant facts

Facts that are legally and factually important to the client's case; also referred to as "key facts."

> **TIP**
>
> Memorize the definition of key facts as these facts will be critical in research.

Context or explanatory facts

Facts that add additional information to the key facts; also called explanatory facts.

Legally unimportant facts

Facts that exist in a client's situation or a case but are not key to the outcome of the case.

> **TIP**
>
> Researchers should remember these categories of facts as they work through the research process.

> **TIP**
>
> The term "motor vehicle" in Figure 4-6 is in quotation marks. Quotation marks play an important role in computer-assisted legal research. Quotation marks indicate that the term is a phrase search; it tells the computer that those two words are to be searched together and in that order.

> **TIP**
>
> A researcher might ask himself or herself: Does removing or changing this fact significantly change the client's situation? If so, it is a legally relevant fact. Does this fact supplement or explain a legally relevant fact? If so, it is an explanatory fact. Does removing or changing this fact significantly change the client's situation? If not, it is likely a legally unimportant fact.

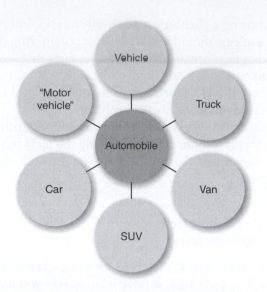

FIGURE 4-6 The cartwheel is actually for the term "automobile"

TIP

Questions of law also exist, but this is a discussion of facts.

TIP

The plural of memorandum is memoranda.

Legal interoffice memorandum
A written explanation of how the law applies to a given set of facts, usually from a client's situation. Also called a "memorandum of law."

Persuasive authority
Any source of authority that the court relies upon, but is not required to rely upon.

The following are examples of questions of fact:

- Is the amount of spousal support reasonable?
- Did the truck run a red light before the collision occurred?

A researcher cannot conclude whether spousal support is reasonable without comparing the amount of support to facts such as total income and expenses. The researcher cannot conclude whether the truck ran a red light without examining certain facts or opinions such as statements of witnesses and the timing of the traffic signals.

Once the factual questions raised by the client's problem are identified, the law that applies to the factual question must be found. When a case that seems to apply to the client's case is located, the facts and law in the client's case and the facts and law in the published case must be compared to see if there are significant similarities (discussed in greater detail in Chapter 14). Once legal authority supporting or affecting the client's position has been found and updated, the results are communicated to the attorney, usually by writing a ***legal interoffice memorandum*** (also called a legal memorandum, or memo). Figure 4-7 shows a basic format for an interoffice memorandum.

The Research Process

The legal research process begins when the client brings a set of facts and a question or questions of law to the firm for resolution. The attorney determines the questions to be researched and gives the assignment to the paralegal. The paralegal then analyzes the law as it applies to the client's facts and writes an interoffice legal memorandum to the attorney explaining how the law applies. The legal research process is shown in Table 4-4.

One of the many responsibilities of a paralegal is to find the law that applies to the client's case. However, finding the law is not sufficient; the paralegal must also determine what law applies. Legal authority may be categorized as primary, secondary, mandatory, or ***persuasive authority***, as shown in Table 4-5.

FIGURE 4-7 Format of Interoffice Memorandum

TIP

While this is a basic format for an interoffice memorandum, researchers should use the format preferred by the employer. One of the first things to do before writing a memorandum is to ask for a sample or ask if there is a preferred format that should be used. It is much better to ask a question than to spend time re-doing something that was done the wrong way!

Interoffice Memorandum of Law

To: Jami Supervisor

From: John Paralegal
Date: August 15, 2012

RE: Heather Dobbs v. Paul Roberts
Office File Number: Civ 09-209

(Note: The section headings may be on the margin or centered.)

Assignment:	(Briefly explain what was to be done and what has been done in the memo.)
Legal Issue(s):	(Sometimes called "Questions Presented." Each issue is written separately and researched separately. This is the most important step in the process. Without a good issue statement, the research easily can stray far afield.)
Facts:	(Put in the key facts and the context facts that are needed to provide a clear understanding of the client's situation.)
Analysis:	(Sometimes called the "discussion." Here the law is applied to the facts, and each issue is individually and completely discussed.)
Conclusion:	(What does the law say is the answer?)
Recommendations:	(What else should be done? What additional information is needed?)

TABLE 4-4 The Legal Research Process

Identify factual question raised by client's problem

Find law that applies to factual question

Analyze law that applies to client's factual question

Communicate findings to attorney supervisor

PRIMARY AUTHORITY

Primary authority is the law itself. A court could rely on any of the 10 types of law or primary types of authority, such as constitutions, statutes, and case law, to reach its decision. Primary authority is also referred to as rules of law, and constitutes any pronouncement from the government that is enforceable and that in some fashion creates a standard of conduct by which all citizens must abide. When researching an issue, the ultimate goal is to find the mandatory, primary authority, because it is this authority that determines the outcome.

It is not enough to find the mandatory and primary authority; a researcher must also make sure that the law is still valid, meaning that it has not had material added or subtracted, been overruled or been otherwise compromised. In order to confirm that the authority is still valid, the authority must be *updated*. Primary authority can be updated in different ways, so a researcher should make sure that

Primary authority
The law itself. The court may rely on any of the primary types of authority, such as constitutions, statutes, and case law.

Update
To confirm that a source is still valid or still good law.

TABLE 4-5   Research Authority

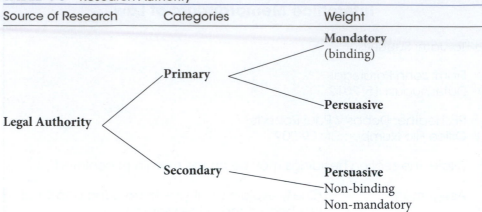

Source of Research	Categories	Weight
Legal Authority	Primary	Mandatory (binding)
		Persuasive
	Secondary	Persuasive Non-binding Non-mandatory

Pocket parts

A method of updating legal material; generally a paperback or softcover supplement or pamphlet located in the back of the main text.

Shepardize

The Shepard's™ service provides information such as parallel citations, subsequent history, validity of the source, and additional leads to other law.

the most current version of the law is reviewed and used. Some basic considerations for updating authorities are as set out in Table 4-6.

TABLE 4-6   Updating Primary Sources of Law

Source of Law	How Updated
• **Constitutions**	• The U.S. Constitution maybe amended in two ways. The first method, the Constitutional Convention, has never been used. The other is to have a bill pass both houses by a two-thirds majority, and then be ratified by three fourths of the states within a certain time frame. While the actual Constitution does not often change, the interpretation of the Constitution can change through the opinions of the judiciary. This is why reading and understanding cases is so important in constitutional law. • State constitutions are ratified by the people of the state during a general election. They are interpreted by the appellate courts of that state.
Statutes	• Statutes on both the federal and state levels are updated through ***pocket parts.*** For online updating, researchers must check the national or state government websites, as well as research services such as Westlaw and LexisNexis.
Cases, court opinions, court decisions	• Cases are not updated per se. They are reported in the reporter system or are issued by the court itself. However, to make sure that the case is still good law, researchers must ***Shepardize*™** or otherwise check each citation to be sure that the case has not been reversed or otherwise negatively impacted by other cases. (Shepardizing and other methods of updating are discussed in Chapter 12.)

Administrative regulations	• Each volume of the *Code of Federal Regulations* (in print and in the official online version) is updated only once a year, so researchers must consult other sources to find new developments. Two useful updating methods are the following:
	• **eCFR Approach**
	• The website www.ecfr.gov is an *unofficial* tool for updating a CFR section. This information should be double-checked by looking up the *Federal Register* references at the end of the eCFR version. Researchers should note especially the *Federal Register* citations from the past year.
	• **List of Sections Affected Approach**
	• The List of Sections Affected (LSA) shows which CFR sections have been affected by final or proposed regulations. It is organized by title and section of the CFR. It is further updated by the *Federal Register.* Sources for the LSA include the following:
	  • *Code of Federal Regulations, List of Sections Affected,* available at law libraries.
	  • List of Sections Affected via GPO Access (http://www.gpoaccess.gov/lsa/browse.html)
	• State regulations are updated in a similar fashion, and researchers should check the authorities for the jurisdiction in which they work.

TABLE 4-6   *(Continued)*

Source of Law	How Updated
• **Administrative decisions**	• Locating agency decisions is not easy. These decisions are not all reported in one reporter, nor are they regularly reported. If researchers are dealing with a major agency, the decisions may be covered by one of the following sources: • *Shepard's U.S. Administrative Citations*, available in print or via LexisNexis, covers major agencies such as the Federal Trade Commission and Securities and Exchange Commission. For a complete list of agencies covered, see the print edition (Law Indexes). • Specialized *Shepard's,* such as *Shepard's Federal Tax Citator,* in print or via LexisNexis. • KeyCite via Westlaw, covering selected agencies. See the KeyCite scope for a full list. • Like regulations, agency decisions are reviewable by the federal courts. Therefore, if the agency is not covered by one of the sources listed above, researchers should use case law research techniques to locate any federal court decisions that may affect the agency decision being used.
Rules of court	• Each court, whether federal or state, has its own updates. To update federal court rules, researchers can: • (a) Look in the recent issues of *Federal Rules Decisions*, which reprints new rules for all federal courts. The new rules are published in the front of the F.R.D. just before they go into effect. • (b) Check the relevant court website. For Civil Procedure, Criminal Procedure, and Evidence rules, check the Federal Judiciary Home page (www.uscourts.gov/rules/index.html). • (c) On Westlaw, search for updates in the US-ORDERS precedential database. Alternatively, rules that have been amended have an "UPDATE" link one can click on to jump to the relevant update page. • State court rules are part of the statutes and therefore are updated with pocket parts. Often one of the best places to find updated rules of court is on state ethics or bar association pages.
• **Charters**	• To update town charters, researchers can search in the city or town records, either manually or on the city or town website.
• **Ordinances**	• As with charters, researchers will usually find updates to ordinances by manually searching the city or town records or by visiting the city or town website.
• **Executive order**	• Presidential executive orders can be found on the Freedom of Information Act website or in paper format, as well as in the *Federal Register* and on the website for the various agencies affected. • Executive orders of state governors are often provided on the state website.
• **Treaties**	• The best way to update treaties is through a paid service such as Westlaw or LexisNexis, although the search can also be performed manually through the various treaty publications issued by the government.

Ethics Alert 4-1

Failure to review the pocket parts or other supplements to the law is a breach of the ethical duty to research accurately and thoroughly. Researchers should be familiar with the Model Rules of Professional Conduct, and in this instance, Rule 3.3, which states in part,

> [4] *Legal argument based on a knowingly false representation of law constitutes dishonesty toward the tribunal. A lawyer is not required to make a disinterested exposition of the law, but must recognize the existence of pertinent legal authorities. Furthermore, as stated in paragraph (a)(2), an advocate has a duty to disclose directly adverse authority in the controlling jurisdiction that has not been disclosed by the opposing party. The underlying concept is that legal argument is a discussion seeking to determine the legal premises properly applicable to the case.*

While this is directed at the attorney, the paralegal working for the attorney also has the obligation to thoroughly and completely perform that research.

SECONDARY AUTHORITY

Secondary authority is not the law itself and is written by an entity other than a court, legislature, agency, or other government entity. Although finding primary law is the ultimate goal of research, secondary authority can explain primary authority or assist in locating it. However, it is not the law. Table 4-7 shows the major types of secondary authority.

TABLE 4-7 Secondary Sources of Law

Source of Secondary Authority	Purpose
Legal encyclopedias	These multivolume sets of books, published for both the national and state levels, explain the law and are organized much like a general encyclopedia. Researchers should use the index with keywords to locate the information needed. Examples are *Corpus Juris Secundum* [sample cite: 11 C.J.S. *Bonds* § 21 (1995)] and *West's Indiana Legal Encyclopedia* [sample cite: 11 I.L.E. *Bonds* § 23 (1995)].
American Law Reports **(Annotations)**	This multivolume-series of books provides articles that present cases, dissect them point by point, and provide commentary as to how other courts in multiple jurisdictions resolved the same issues. The ALRs often look at cases that deal with unsettled areas of law and provide leading judicial opinions. Each is updated and has an index.
Treatises, hornbooks, and nutshells	These books, often in single volumes, are published on one legal subject and provide an expert view on that subject. Some examples are *Prosser on Torts* or *Wharton's Criminal Procedure*, 15th (Thomson Reuters).
Words and phrases	This multivolume set is similar to a legal dictionary but includes multiple entries on how terms or words in statutes, court rules, administrative regulations, or contracts have been defined by the courts. Research is generally accomplished through the index.
Restatements	A treatise set covering 15 areas, written by the editors at the American Law Institute (ALI), which organizes and summarizes the common law of the United States. Restatements are divided broadly into chapters, divided into narrow titles, and then subdivided into sections. Each section begins with a restatement of the law in boldface, followed by comments, hypothetical illustrations, and background information on the rule's development, including case, statute, treatise, and journal citations. Restatements often influence court decisions. Although they are only persuasive authority, they are often cited by the courts. Research is generally done using keywords and the index. An example of a restatement is *Restatement of Contracts, Second*.
Law reviews	Published by law schools and usually edited by law students, these scholarly publications focus on in-depth research and writing on legal issues. Many law schools have a main law review and other area-specific law reviews, such as *Duke Law and Technology Review*.
Law journals	Similar in many instances to a law review but often considered secondary to law reviews, they typically focus on one area of law. Examples are *Duke Journal of Gender Law & Policy, Hamline Journal of Public Law and Policy*, and *Computer Law Review and Technology Journal*.
Legal periodicals	Legal periodicals include a wide range of law-related magazines, journals, and newspapers, including law school resources as well as resources from other legal entities. Examples are the *ABA Journal* and *Banking Law Journal*.
Loose-leaf publications	Services that provide continually updated material meant to be kept in a binder. The major publishers of loose-leaf services are the Bureau of National Affairs (BNA), Commerce Clearing House (CCH), Lexis Legal Publishing/Matthew Bender, and Research Institute of America (RIA).
Legal dictionary	These dictionaries are similar to a standard English dictionary, but cover only legal terms. *Black's Law Dictionary* is the most widely used law dictionary. Courts will cite *Black's* to support their definition of a legal word or phrase. Other examples are *Ballentine's Law Dictionary*, Merriam-Webster's *Dictionary of Law*, and *Oran's Dictionary of the Law*.
Uniform model laws	Uniform laws are carefully drafted model laws for potential enactment by state legislatures. State legislatures can reject them, enact them in entirety, or enact them with modifications. Uniform laws are authored by the National Conference of Commissioners on Uniform State Laws (NCCUSL), a group that aims to promote uniformity of state law. Since its founding in 1892, NCCUSL has drafted over 200 uniform laws such as the *Uniform Commercial Code,* the *Model Business Corporation Act*, and the *Model Penal Code*.

Secondary authority is particularly useful for research in two instances. First, if the area is new to the researcher, he or she can use secondary materials to gain some background on the topic. In addition, secondary authority often leads to additional resources, such as more detailed information about the topic, and citations to other authorities that discuss the issue being researched.

Since secondary authority is not the law, it should not be used in a memorandum (except in certain circumstances, which will be discussed in Chapter 8). Secondary authorities may quote from the law itself. If the secondary authority is quoting *from the law,* then the best option for the researcher when writing a memorandum is to quote directly from the law rather than from the secondary authority. The primary authority should be quoted as the law, and the secondary authority used to bolster arguments on the interpretation of the primary authority.

MANDATORY AUTHORITY

Mandatory authority is anything that the court *must* rely upon in deciding the case before it. Only primary authority, such as the Constitution or one of the other 10 types of law, can be mandatory authority. The first rule of thumb is that a court is never required to rely on secondary authority such as an encyclopedia, treatise, or law review article. Secondary authority can never be mandatory authority.

Mandatory authority
Any law that the court must rely upon in making its determination or reaching its decision.

If the statute governs the conduct, situation, or issue at hand, it is mandatory. A statute from the state of Illinois is primary authority because it is enacted by the legislature and is the law itself. It is mandatory in the state of Illinois if it applies to the situation under review. In Heather Dobbs's situation, she pulled up to a stop sign and stopped, but Paul Roberts did not stop at his stop sign. An Illinois statute on failure to stop would be primary since it is a statute applying to drivers in that state. It would be mandatory because an Illinois court would be required to follow it.

However, not all primary authority is mandatory authority. In Illinois, there is a statute regarding the sequence in which vehicles must stop when there is no controlling stop sign. It is primary authority because it is a statute and a statute is the law. But it would not be mandatory in Heather's situation, and the court would not be required to follow it. Even though it is primary authority, this statute regarding the order of movement when there is no controlling stop sign has nothing to do with failing to stop at a stop sign.

Similarly, a Kansas statute on stop signs is primary authority, but it is not mandatory for the Illinois court that is hearing Heather's case. Illinois courts are not required to follow the laws of any other state. So, a statute from Kansas would have no more authority in the situation in Illinois than would a statute from Hawaii or Alaska.

Mandatory Enacted Law

There are three tests to consider in determining when enacted law is mandatory:

1. The appropriate law must be applied to the appropriate jurisdiction. For example, an applicable Illinois statute would control in an incident in Illinois, but not in Kansas.
2. The body enacting the law intended it to apply to the particular incident; thus, it should apply to the client's facts and issue.
3. The particular law does not violate the hierarchy of law or some higher law. For example, a statute cannot violate a constitutional provision.

If an agency promulgates a regulation that violates a statutory provision, the regulation will not be mandatory even though it applies to the factual situation. Similarly, if a state passes a statute that is found to be in violation of the U. S. Constitution, it will not be mandatory for cases it was intended to cover. State enacted law is generally mandatory only in the state where the law was promulgated.

Federal enacted law may be mandatory authority in state courts in certain situations. A common example is when the U.S. Constitution applies to a given situation. Since the U.S. Constitution is the highest authority in the United States, it supersedes any state law that contradicts it. Federal statutes and federal regulations also may be superior to state laws in situations where the federal government maintains control and authority, such as issues involving interstate commerce, bankruptcy, patents, or foreign matters. For example, if a matter filed in state court involved interstate commerce, the federal statutes or regulations would be mandatory authority in that court.

Mandatory Common Law

Mandatory common law is often referred to as "binding authority." Just like enacted law, there are times when a court is required to follow common law. However, two tests must be met before the case can be used. First, the facts and the law considered in the opinion must be sufficiently similar to the facts and law at issue in the client's case. Sometimes this is referred to as being **on point, analogous**, or **on all fours**. Heather Dobbs had a stop sign and Paul Roberts had a stop sign. She stopped. Paul did not. A case that is on all fours would be a prior opinion where the plaintiff was struck by a vehicle whose driver ran a stop sign. The facts are similar, albeit abbreviated here, and the law would be the statute that governs the rights and responsibilities of driving when an intersection is controlled by a stop sign. A case that is not on point would be a personal injury accident that occurred when a car crossed the median on an interstate highway and collided with an oncoming vehicle.

The second prong of the test concerns the court hearing the case. For common law to be mandatory and binding, the opinion must be written by a court that is higher or superior in the hierarchy than the court deciding the present case. To know whether the opinion is mandatory, it is important to understand the hierarchy. Even if this test is met, the opinion must also be on point, or the facts and issues and law must be sufficiently similar to warrant the application of the opinion to the present case.

Lower Court Decisions   A court is not required to rely on an opinion written by a lower court, even if it is on point. The court may use the opinion as persuasive authority. For example, the U.S. Supreme Court would not be required to rely on an opinion from a U.S. district court or a U.S. court of appeals, because these courts are lower in the hierarchy.

Higher Court Decisions   A state trial court hearing a case may rely on the decision of the state's highest court. The decisions of the highest court would be mandatory authority because of the hierarchy of courts. The same is true in the federal system. In a U.S. District Court case, the decisions of the U.S. Supreme Court case would be mandatory. Decisions from the U.S. court of appeals for a particular circuit are binding on the district courts within that federal circuit.

Precedent   Courts in the common law system follow the principle that courts must decide cases with similar facts and issues in the same way, unless there

On point

The facts of the case and the facts of the client's situation are sufficiently similar; also referred to as "analogous" or "on all fours."

Analogous

Sufficiently similar. Usually refers to a comparison of the facts and issues of a case with the facts and issues of a client's situation. Also referred to as "on point" or "on all fours."

On all fours

A prior opinion is "on all fours" when the facts and issues are substantially the same as the facts and issues currently before the court (or in the client's case). Also referred to as "on point" or "analogous."

is good reason not to do so. This principle is embodied in the concept of ***stare decisis***, which literally means, "to let the decision stand." If a prior case involves a set of law and facts that are similar to the case currently under consideration, the prior opinion is precedent for the current case. If the prior opinion and the current case are similar, and no new law has intervened to affect the current case, then the prior opinion should guide the court in making a decision. It is important to note, however, that any court can reject the precedent or ***overrule*** its own decision as long as a higher authority has not issued a mandatory opinion covering the facts and rules of law.

Diversity Cases   Generally, federal courts only handle questions of federal law, pursuant to their subject matter jurisdiction. However, in cases of ***diversity of citizenship***, a federal district court may be required to apply state law. Diversity of citizenship is decided based on a two-prong test. First, there must be *complete* diversity—all of the parties on each side of the controversy must be from different states than the parties on the opposite side. For example, if three plaintiffs are from New Mexico, and two defendants are from South Carolina, diversity exists. However, if there is a plaintiff from New Mexico, a plaintiff from South Carolina, and two defendants from South Carolina, diversity does not exist. Second, the value of the claims must exceed $75,000. Even if the plaintiff is not ultimately awarded $75,000, the requirement is met if that amount is alleged and is provable at the time the complaint is filed.[12] Table 4-8 illustrates how diversity jurisdiction operates.

In a diversity case, the federal court applies the common law of the state in which the court sits. In the Heather Dobbs case, if Heather lived in Missouri and Paul lived in Illinois, *and* the matter in controversy exceeded $75,000, Heather could choose to file the lawsuit in Missouri or in Illinois. If she filed the lawsuit in a U.S. District Court in Illinois, the court would apply the Federal Rules of Civil Procedure in its management of the case, but would apply the substantive laws of the state of Illinois in deciding the case. If she chose to file suit in U.S. District Court in Missouri, the court would apply the substantive laws of Missouri in reaching a decision. The federal courts would apply the state law of the state in which the court sits to decide the controversy, and therefore state court opinions would be mandatory authority in the federal court.

Stare decisis
Literally means "let the decision stand." The doctrine that courts should decide cases with similar facts, issues, and rules of law in the same way unless there is good reason not to do so.

Overrule
A court's refusal to follow its own previous ruling even though the precedent is similar in facts and rule of law.

Diversity of citizenship
Jurisdictional basis when parties to the lawsuit are from different states and the amount in controversy exceeds $75,000. If those factors exist, a plaintiff may file the lawsuit in either state court where the parties live or where the incident occurred, or may file in the federal court in the state in which one of the parties lives.

TABLE 4-8   Diversity of Citizenship

Plaintiff	Defendant	Diversity
From Wisconsin	From Wisconsin	No
From Wisconsin	From North Dakota	Yes
One from Wisconsin One from North Dakota	From Wisconsin	No
One from Wisconsin One from North Dakota	From California	Yes
One from Wisconsin One from North Dakota	One from Wisconsin One from Illinois	No
One from Wisconsin One from North Dakota	One from Indiana One from Illinois	Yes

[12]28 U.S.C. § 1332 (2011)

TIP

There are very few absolutes in law. Researchers should always expect, and look for, an exception.

Full Faith and Credit Clause
Art. IV, § 1 of the U.S. Constitution. This clause states, "Full Faith and Credit shall be given in each State to the public Acts, Records, and judicial Proceedings of every other state."

TIP

The area of conflicts of laws is very complex, and choice of law will not be the decision of the paralegal. However, paralegals should recognize the terms and understand the basic substance. For more understanding of this issue, researchers may want to view the yearly survey of cases Choice of Law in the American Courts in 2010: Twenty-Fourth Annual Survey, [13] in which the author reported on more than 3,000 cases that discussed the conflicts of law issue.

Conflicts of law
Situations in which the laws of more than one jurisdiction may be applied to the case, and each choice of law will yield a different outcome. The decision of the court depends on the jurisdictional laws that the court applies to the case.

Subject matter jurisdiction
The power of a court to resolve a particular type of matter.

Personal jurisdiction
The power over a defendant to render a decision and bind the defendant to the court's judgment.

Case of first impression
A novel case with an issue that has not been decided by the courts in the jurisdiction.

Courts in Other States   The general rule is that one state court is not required to follow the decisions issued by another state court, regardless of whether another state's cases are on point. However, in some limited situations, a state court must apply the law from another state.

In some cases, the ***Full Faith and Credit Clause*** of the U.S. Constitution applies. Article IV, § 1 states, "Full Faith and Credit shall be given in each State to the public Acts, Records, and judicial Proceedings of every other state." This provision ensures that people cannot go from state to state to resolve conflicts. Once a matter has been adjudicated, the opinion of the court rendering the decision must be afforded full faith and credit in every other state. If Heather Dobbs loses at the trial level in the Illinois court, her next option is to file an appeal with the next level of Illinois courts. If she re-files the lawsuit against Paul Roberts in Michigan, the Michigan court could dismiss the case based on the Illinois judgment. Without the Full Faith and Credit Clause, Heather Dobbs could take her case to all 50 states. While that might be a plaintiff's lawyer's dream, it would be a nightmare for everyone else, including the defendant, the witnesses, the courts, the insurance companies, and others.

The other exception is based on the concept of ***conflicts of law***. Under certain circumstances where the law of more than one state applies, the court of one state may be required to apply the law of another state. Courts faced with a choice of law issue generally have two alternatives. In cases where the choice of law is *procedural*, they can apply the law of the forum (*lex fori*). Where the choice of law is *substantive*, the court can apply the law of the site of the transaction or occurrence that gave rise to the litigation in the first place (*lex loci*).

Heather Dobbs's accident also may present a conflicts of law problem. The accident occurred in Illinois, but the negligence lawsuit was brought in Missouri state court. The Missouri state court has ***subject matter jurisdiction*** (it has jurisdiction to hear negligence cases), and ***personal jurisdiction*** (jurisdiction over the parties). The laws of both Missouri and Illinois would come into play, but it is quite possible that the major elements of each state's negligence law will be quite different. Under conflicts of law doctrine, a court of Missouri may be required to apply the law of Illinois. Therefore, if the wreck and subsequent injury happened in Illinois, and that state is the center of the dispute, the Missouri court may apply Illinois negligence law. So, any opinions from Illinois with analogous facts, issues, and rules of law will be mandatory on the Missouri court.

PERSUASIVE AUTHORITY

Persuasive authority can be any source the court may choose to rely on, but is not required to rely on. Generally, persuasive authority falls into categories. The first is a prior court opinion that the court finds persuasive, even though the court is not required to follow that prior opinion. The second type is any secondary authority that the court finds persuasive, even though the court is not mandated to follow that authority.

Persuasive Common Law

In a ***case of first impression***, a court is deciding a legal question that no court within the jurisdiction has decided before. In these cases, there is no mandatory authority on that question within the jurisdiction. The court will therefore rely

---

[13]Symeon C. Symeonides. *Choice of Law in the American Courts in 2010: Twenty-Fourth Annual Survey.* 57 *American Journal of Comparative Law* 269 (2009). American Society of Comparative Law.

on persuasive authority from other jurisdictions. If there is an analogous opinion from a court in another jurisdiction that has decided the same question, that opinion may be used to guide the court in its decision. For example, if the case of first impression is from Arizona, cases in California or Maine that are on point may be used as persuasive authority by the court in Arizona.

It is sometimes difficult to comprehend how a court in a busy legal system could be faced with many new questions. However, it is exactly because of the changing society that new situations arise all the time. For example, new legal questions frequently arise because of changes in technology that have come about in the last few years. Twenty years ago, society would not have anticipated the legal issues related to electronic identity theft, digital music piracy, or adoptions by single or same-sex parents, and yet today these are common subjects.

The Heather Dobbs example illustrates how persuasive authority may come into play. Heather Dobbs's accident occurred in Illinois, Paul Roberts lives in Illinois, but the negligence lawsuit was brought in Indiana state court, because that is where the plaintiff lives. The cases that the Indiana trial court must rely on are cases on point from the Indiana Court of Appeals and the Indiana Supreme Court. Figure 4-8 shows how cases can be distinguished as mandatory or persuasive.

For an opinion to be utilized as mandatory authority, it must be analogous *and* be written by a higher court than the court considering the opinion. If the opinion does not meet both of these criteria, it might be used as persuasive authority. However, even if an opinion written by the higher court is not exactly on point, it might be used as persuasive authority if the court's reasoning has some merit. For example, the higher court's opinion may not be factually on point, but may enunciate some general legal principle or doctrine that is applicable.

In some instances, the court may wish to consider a decision from a court that is lower in the hierarchy. Again, the court does not have to follow the opinion from the lower court because, since it comes from a lower court in the hierarchy, that opinion is not mandatory. However, if Heather's case was on appeal to the state Supreme Court and the paralegal found a case from a lower court that was analogous, there is no harm in the paralegal providing the information. The state Supreme Court *can* and *may* choose to consider the lower court opinion.

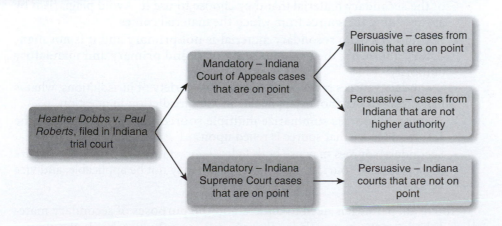

FIGURE 4-8 Mandatory and Persuasive Authority

There are many criteria that a court may weigh in its consideration of whether to adopt an opinion from another jurisdiction. A judge may be persuaded to consider a certain position if there are a number of jurisdictions that have adopted the same position. A court might also be persuaded by an opinion based on the soundness of its reasoning. Generally, the following factors typically considered:

- There appears to be a majority of jurisdictions with a consensus.
- A great deal of literature has developed in one direction.
- The opinion has been cited frequently and in a positive manner.
- The opinion is well reasoned.

After examining these factors, it is up to the judge or justices to decide whether to use the proffered opinion from another jurisdiction.

A paralegal should always give careful consideration as to whether to rely on persuasive authority in a research document. All available sources within the court's jurisdiction should be thoroughly searched for mandatory authority before searching in other jurisdictions for persuasive authority. If paralegals and their supervisors can be assured that no mandatory authority exists, they can do a systematic search in other jurisdictions for analogous cases. The paralegal need not cite all available persuasive authority, buy only those cases that are the most compelling and on point.

Persuasive Secondary Authority Secondary authorities, such as treatises, encyclopedias, legal periodicals, law reviews, and annotations, are valuable research tools, but are not the law. Secondary authority can *never* be mandatory authority, but it does serve important purposes.

Those new to research have a tendency to quote from secondary authorities because these authorities often quote the law itself, and may sound very "official." If a secondary authority has provided an important quote from a primary authority, the primary authority should be quoted directly. Researchers should also find the primary source and read it to make sure that the quote in context says what it appears to say in the secondary authority.

In addition to paraphrasing the primary authority, the authors of secondary authorities often provide an analysis of the material that paralegals may be tempted to use. Researchers should be aware of some pitfalls in using these summaries:

Plagiarism
Using someone else's material without giving proper acknowledgement or citing the source.

- *Plagiarism* occurs when researchers are so enthralled by the language of the secondary material that they choose to use it. Avoid plagiarism by always citing the source from which the material comes.
- A summary from secondary material is not primary and it is not mandatory authority; the goal of writing is to find primary and mandatory authority.
- Secondary sources review materials from a variety of jurisdictions; what is being viewed may not be applicable in the jurisdiction in question.
- Secondary sources summarize multiple sources; each source should be reviewed before that source is relied upon.
- Secondary sources may use both federal and state materials; if the client's issue is in state court, the federal materials may not be applicable, and vice versa.

Above all, paralegals need to understand the purposes of secondary materials and then use the materials for those purposes only. Paralegals should use the secondary sources to find and understand primary sources of law and to bolster, not restate, the interpretation of the primary authority. The value of secondary sources is that they aid in the understanding of legal concepts and in finding additional authority, either in footnotes or in the main body of the text. The paralegal should be cognizant of the fact that supervisors and the courts are often leery of relying on secondary materials because cases are ultimately decided based on primary and mandatory authority. Therefore, researchers should read and use the primary authority as the source when the primary authority is available.

There are times when using the secondary authority may be useful in persuading the court to adopt a position. In order to do so, researchers should consider the following guidelines:

- The ultimate goal is to provide primary authority. Secondary authority is not a substitute for primary authority.
- Secondary authority should be presented only after the primary authority has been presented.
- The secondary authority should not merely repeat the primary authority.
- The secondary authority should help the court or a supervisor to interpret the primary authority. This is particularly appropriate when there is not an abundance of primary authority or when it is a case of first impression.
- Most importantly, whenever secondary authority is used, it must be made very clear that the material is, in fact, secondary authority.

SUMMARY

There are essentially 10 types of law that every paralegal should know by name and by purpose. It is primary authority that the court first looks to rely upon when deciding a case. It is a paralegal's job to find the primary authority that controls the client's situation and to present the findings to the supervisor in a well-constructed and well-analyzed memorandum of law.

Primary authority is the law itself. Secondary authorities are basically used to understand and to find primary authority. It is rare that secondary authorities are used as support for the client's position, although there are certain rules for when that can occur.

Mandatory authority is that authority upon which a court must rely. Persuasive is any type of authority that the court chooses to rely upon when it is not required to do so. The goal is to find mandatory authority. If mandatory authority does not exist or if there is a dearth of mandatory authority, one can present persuasive authority.

REVIEW **QUESTIONS**

1. Give an example of each of the 10 types of law.
2. Explain the difference between a holding and a judgment.
3. Describe a factual situation in which you would use administrative regulations in research.
4. Explain how primary authority differs from secondary authority.
5. Explain the tests used to determine whether a case is mandatory authority.
6. What are key facts?
7. What are legally insignificant facts?
8. In the hierarchy of courts, some courts are required to follow the rulings of other courts. Identify three scenarios in which one court is required to follow the decisions of another court. (For example, a state court of appeals is considering a trial court's decision. Is the trial court's decision mandatory authority?)
9. Identify when a researcher would use secondary authority in research.
10. What ethical concerns can arise in the research process?

APPLICATION **EXERCISES**

Questions 1–8 are based on this scenario:

Jennifer Garrett was crossing a street in Indianapolis, Indiana. She was crossing within a crosswalk when she was hit by a red station wagon driven by 16-year-old Jonathan Banks, who was talking on a cell phone at the time. Jonathan lives in Muncie, Indiana. Jennifer says she crossed when the crosswalk light gave her the right of way. Jonathan jumped out of the car and apologized to Jennifer, telling her he did not see her. Jennifer suffered a broken leg. She sues Jonathan in a trial court in Marion County where Indianapolis is located.

For questions 1–5, identify the type of fact described. Select from the following options:

A. Relevant fact
B. An explanatory fact
C. A legally unimportant fact

1. The driver was driving a red station wagon.
2. Jennifer was walking in the crosswalk.
3. The driver was a 16-year-old boy.
4. The driver apologized to Jennifer.
5. Jennifer suffered a broken leg.

For questions 6–8, select from the following options:

D. A case in the Indiana Supreme Court
E. A case in a Kansas trial court
F. An excerpt from an Indiana law review article that discusses injuries to pedestrians
G. An excerpt from *Corpus Juris Secundum* discussing injury to a pedestrian in a crosswalk

6. What authority is mandatory for the trial court in Indiana?
7. What authority is primary?
8. What authority is persuasive?

CITATION **EXERCISES**

Find the following either manually in a law library or on the Internet. Be sure to cite the source properly.

1. Find 984 F.2d 182. Provide the proper citation for this document.
2. Find the following U.S. Supreme Court case from 1961 based on the title of the case: *Mapp v. Ohio*. What is the full citation of the case, including the parallel citations from the United States Reports (U.S.), Supreme Court Reporter (S.Ct.) and Supreme Court Lawyers Edition (L.Ed.)?
3. What are the United States Public Law (Pub. L.) and the United States Statutes at Large (Stat.) citations for the federal Speedy Trial Act of 1974?

QUICK **CHECK**

Classify each of the following as primary or secondary, mandatory or persuasive. Each type of authority will have at least two classifications.

1. The decision of the highest state court in your state on modification of child support when researching a modification issue.
2. The decision of a Tennessee federal district court when the client's issue is a violation of freedom of speech and the client is from Memphis.
3. A C.J.S. section on modification of child support.
4. A law review article on the modification of child support.
5. The decision of a trial court in your state on modification of child support when you are researching a modification of child support issue.

6. A statute from a neighboring state on modification of child support when you are researching a modification of child support issue.
7. A federal regulation on welfare recipients when you are researching a modification of child support issue.

Identify each statement as true or false. If the statement is false, rewrite the statement so it is true:

1. All primary authority is mandatory authority.
2. An opinion from the U.S. District Court for Indiana can be mandatory for the U.S. Supreme Court.
3. A federal regulation is mandatory in a state court.
4. An opinion in one state can be mandatory for a court in another state.

Fill in the blank for the following questions (1–3) using the following word choices:

Legal analysis   Factually   Case law   Legally

1. A legal researcher should look for cases that are both [_____] and [_____] similar to the client's case.

2. [_____] is the process of comparing and contrasting facts and legal issues.

3. A legal researcher should look at [_____] to find factual situations similar to the client's case.

RESEARCH

1. Find the Full Faith and Credit Clause of the United States Constitution. Summarize the law, identify when it might be primary, secondary, mandatory, or persuasive, and provide the proper citation form.

2. Access the site for your state's rules of court. When may an unpublished opinion be cited or relied upon?

3. Find 984 F.2d 182. Who are the parties? What is the case about? Summarize key facts. What are the issues?

4. When was the Antiterrorism and Effective Death Penalty Act of 1996 (PL. 104–132) signed by President Clinton?

5. Using KeyCite, Shepard's, or another citation service, verify the citation for the following decision: *State v. Rodewald*, 372 N.W.2d 824 (Minn. App. 1985). Is this case still good law? If the case has been reversed or is no longer good law, what is the citation for the case that reversed or overruled the decision?

6. Browse the table of contents of the United States Code (U.S.C.). Which title deals with crimes and criminal procedure?

INTERNET RESEARCH

1. Access the Shepard's site on LexisNexis (www.lexisnexis.com) or another reliable website that presents information on Shepard's. Write a summary paper on at least three features of Shepard's and include a report on the process of Shepardizing. If you have the ability, bookmark the home screen or add the address to your Internet resources.

2. Access West services at www.west.thomson.com. At the bottom of the screen, look for "product support" and click "User Guides." Select four user guides, one of which must relate to KeyCite. Write a summary paper on the three features and include a report on the process of KeyCiting. If you have the ability, bookmark the home screen or add the address to your Internet resources.

3. Take a tutorial on either of the systems described in questions 1 and 2.

4. Find the definition of collateral estoppel in two online dictionaries. Is there any difference in the two definitions? Is one better than the other? Why? Cite the sources used.

5. Give the URL for a website on the Internet where you can search cases from the United States Court of Appeals for the Eighth Circuit. Find a case, cite it, and identify the "law" used in the case.

MEDIA RESOURCES

"UPL Issue: Interviewing a Client" (Paralegal Practice and Ethics-Related Video Segment from *The Paralegal Professional Classroom Video Series* DVD)

INTERNET RESOURCES

Cases and codes: http://www.findlaw.com/casecode/
eCFR: www.ecfr.gov
U.S. Constitution: http://www.gpoaccess.gov/constitution
Federal Judiciary Home page: http://www.uscourts.gov/Home.aspx
LexisNexis: www.lexisnexis.com
List of Sections Affected via GPO Access: http://www.gpoaccess.gov/lsa/browse.html
State Constitutions: http://www.constitution.org/cons/usstcons.htm
West: www.west.thomson.com

Stephen Coburn/Shutterstock

chapter **five**

LEGAL CITATION FORM

LEARNING OBJECTIVES

After completing this chapter, students should be able to:

1. Understand and use standard legal citation formats.

2. Locate and access information effectively in various formats.

3. Critically evaluate information.

4. Understand the legal and ethical issues associated with using information.

5. Understand non-legal citation formats.

CHAPTER OVERVIEW

Paralegals often are given the task of cite checking, which means confirming that the citations in a document are accurate and correctly formatted according to the rules of proper English and legal writing. This chapter will provide an overview of the basic rules and requirements of proper citation form. Some background is also provided on the basics of legal citation according to standards established by the Modern Language Association, the American Psychological Association, *A Uniform System of Citation: The Bluebook,* and *ALWD Citation Manual,* as well as other citators.

OPENING SCENARIO

John was not pleased with the way this week was starting off. He had several briefs that he needed to verify to be sure that the cases had proper citation format and that the cases cited were still good law. He was to be the "last set of eyes" on these documents before they were filed with the court. In addition, he was continuing his research on the Heather Dobbs and Norman Pardee cases, and had to prepare interoffice memoranda for them. Of course, that meant more cite checking! He was glad that his paralegal instructors had been adamant that he learn the rules of proper citation. His copies of *The Bluebook: A Uniform System of Citation*, 19th Ed., and *ALWD* were dog-eared and stained from all the late nights of cite checking during school. He also had been to a couple of seminars on cite checking since graduating from his paralegal program. Now that he was working in a firm, he understood why cite checking is really important after all!

CITATIONS

At first, citation and cite checking may seem to be a complex process. For most students, legal citation will be something entirely new, and they will have nothing to compare it to in other learning experiences. It may seem like learning chemistry formulas or the rules of a foreign language. However, through practice and experience, the rules of citation will eventually become second nature.

It must be remembered that citations do not exist for their own sake, and are not mere technicalities. The citations that generally appear in a memorandum, brief, or other court document are as important as any other element of the document. The citations will usually appear in the narrative text, and not only must they give accurate information, but also they must be punctuated correctly.

At first, *citations* are often difficult for students to understand because they seem to be a jumble of numbers, words, or acronyms. However, citations are important because they provide the reader with the ability to locate the sources that are relied on in the writing. Citations are also an acknowledgement to the author of the source. They are used within the text, in footnotes, or in endnotes.

Citation
Letters and number combinations, or other identifying information, that helps the reader find the source of the materials being used.

There are three primary reasons why citations, whether legal or non-legal in format, are of paramount importance. First, the author of the source deserves to receive credit for the ideas presented. Second, if a writer fails to cite a source, the rights of the originator of the material are violated. Third, it is important to identify the way ideas developed, as well as the time at which they developed, to prove the value of the ideas being presented.

LEGAL CITATION MANUALS

The rules for legal citations are found in various legal *citation manuals*. There are several legal citation manuals on the market; however, there are two primary ones. The first is *The Bluebook: A Uniform System of Citation*, 19th Ed. (*The Bluebook*). This citation manual was originally produced by Harvard Law School, and since 1934 has been compiled by the editors of the Columbia Law Review, the Harvard Law Review, the University of Pennsylvania Law Review, and The Yale Law Journal.[1] The online version of *The Bluebook* was launched in 2008. The other primary citation manual is *ALWD Citation Manual: A Professional System of Citation*, 4th Ed., (*ALWD*) by Darby Dickerson.[2]

Citation manual
A manual providing a standard for legal citations, and acting as a depository or warehouse of accepted citation practices. The two primary resources are *Bluebook: A Uniform System of Citation*, 19th Ed., and *ALWD Citation Manual: A Professional System of Citation*, ALWD 4th Ed.

The ultimate goal of citations is to give the reader information. Researchers should consider this purpose while working through the maze of citation rules. Following the citation manual will ensure that the reader is given accurate information about a writer's sources. The elements of citations specified in a legal

TIP

Paralegals should be familiar with the citation manual required by the jurisdictions in which they work. Many state courts have their own citation rules that take precedence over *The Bluebook* or *ALWD* for documents filed with those courts.

[1] Christine Hurt. *The Bluebook at Eighteen: Reflecting and Ratifying Current Trends in Legal Scholarship*. 82 Ind. L. J. 49 (*2007*).

[2] *See* A. Darby Dickerson, *An Un-Uniform System of Citation: Surviving with the New Bluebook* (*Including Compendia of State and Federal Court Rules Concerning Citation Form*), 26 Stetson L.Rev. 53, 57–58 (1996).

TIP

Other legal citation manuals for U.S. jurisdictions are *Legal Citation Style Guide* at http://www.legalcitation.net/; *International Citation Manual* at http://law.wustl.edu/wugslr/index.asp?id=5512; *Introduction to Basic Legal Citation* at http://www.law.cornell.edu/citation/; *Universal Citation Guide*, by the Citation Formats Committee of the American Association of Law Libraries, at http://www.aallnet.org/Archived/Publications/AALL-Publications/universal-citation-guide.pdf; and *The University of Chicago Manual of Legal Citation (The Maroonbook)* at http://lawreview.uchicago.edu/resources/docs/stylesheet.1009.pdf

citation manual are meant to give the reader information to answer four principal questions:

1. What is the authority being relied upon?
2. Where can the authority be found?
3. What body created the authority?
4. When was the authority created?

First and foremost, a citation identifies the authority that the writer relied upon. Experienced readers will immediately know the value of the source by reading the citation. For example, they will know a government website has more validity than Wikipedia. The citation tells the reader exactly where the source can be found so the reader can locate it, and also tells when the authority was created so the reader can determine whether it is current.

A citation manual provides a standard for legal citations and acts as a depository or warehouse of accepted citation rules and practices. The writer consults this depository to determine if the legal citations in a document conform to the standard practice required by the industry. Conforming to standard practice ensures that readers who are familiar with those practices will understand the citations. Failure to conform to the required practice may also signal a lack of knowledge or attention to detail on the part of the writer, and undermine the writer's credibility.[3]

Knowing how to use the citation manuals is also an important skill that prospective employers will consider. Using correct citation form is similar to using correct grammar. Correct grammar distinguishes someone with a certain level of education from someone without. Similarly, using correct legal citation form distinguishes those who have legal education from those who do not. In the legal profession, attention to detail is important, and sloppiness in citation form may affect perceptions of one's competence and credibility.

Both *The Bluebook* and *ALWD* are similar, even sharing some rules; however, there are some major citation differences that are worth noting.

The Bluebook   *The Bluebook* is the best-known set of rules for citation form. There is a rule for every aspect of citation, such as spacing, punctuation, italics, ordering, abbreviations, and quoting. The downside of using *The Bluebook* as a reference is that it is not user-friendly and is not a useful teaching tool.

The Bluebook was created around 1926 to provide a system for legal professionals to convey the authenticity of the materials relied upon in their daily work. The first edition of *The Bluebook* was only 26 pages long and covered little more than the rules about footnote formatting.[4] Today's text exceeds 500 pages. The manual has been known as the "Blue Book" since 1939, when it was first given a blue cover. However, *The Bluebook* did not become the official title until the 15th edition in 1991.[5]

In several states, *The Bluebook* is the only recognized authority on citations, and its use is required in those jurisdictions. Other states either require a different citation manual or do not specify a citation manual at all.

TIP

The following states require use of *The Bluebook*: CA, DE, FL, IN, NC, SC, TX, WA, WI. Some states allow for the use of either *The Bluebook* or the state citation manual, as does California.

---

[3] Darby Dickerson & the Association of Legal Writing Directors, *ALWD Citation Manual* 3–4 (Aspen L. & Bus. 2000).

[4] *The Bluebook : A Uniform System of Citations*. 2010. https://www.legalbluebook.com/Public/Introduction.aspx

[5] *See* James W. Paulsen, *An Uninformed System of Citation*, 105 Harv. L. Rev. 1780, 1782–83 & n.6 (1992) (book review).

The Divisions of The Bluebook The researcher is not expected to read and memorize the entire text of *The Bluebook*. However, it is helpful to mark, in some fashion, the rules and materials that are used the most.

The current edition of *The Bluebook,* as well as its Internet site (http://www.legalbluebook.com/), are organized in very specific sections that are divided into three primary parts. The text begins with a quick reference section that gives examples of commonly used citation forms. These examples are presented in two typeface styles: one for law reviews on the inside front cover, and one for practitioners on the inside back cover. Specific topics and rules are provided, along with various examples pertaining to the subdivisions within each rule. The same examples are given for both styles, so that the researcher can identify the differences. The style shown on the back cover is the one that paralegals will be most concerned with when citing sources.

The preface describes the changes to the current edition from previous editions, indicates new material, and presents some useful hints for using the material. For example, the preface to the 19th edition describes changes to the Bluepages, more than 30 changes or modifications to the rules, and three table updates and expansions. Noting these changes immediately will ensure that the researcher does not make mistakes through relying on the formatting from a previous edition.[6]

The **Bluepages** is probably the most often-referenced section. The material on these pages provides a simplified view of the rules that are used most frequently. Each rule is given with examples to enhance the explanation.[7] These common rules are followed by the Bluepages tables, which provide an easy reference for the practitioner. For example, Bluepages table BT1 provides suggested abbreviations. BT2 gives the jurisdiction-specific citation rules and style guides for local citation practices. This table has been greatly expanded, since local rules of a particular court take precedence over *The Bluebook.*[8] The Bluepages provide grounding in the basic citation rules for drafting and proofing legal documents. For example, B5 is a section on sources and authorities, with a focus on cases. Another value of the Bluepages is that they show how to adapt information presented in the law review format to the format used by practitioners.

The main body of *The Bluebook,* printed on white paper with a blue top edge, contains the detailed rules and stylistic elements. This section is subdivided into two parts: rules 1 through 9, which are general rules, and rules 10 through 21, which are rules pertaining to specific types of authority.[9] Rules for both primary and secondary materials and are indicated with an "R." For example, R11, discusses citation forms for constitutions.[10]

The material in the white pages must be adapted to the formats for the documents and legal memoranda on which the paralegal will be working. All of the examples in the body of *The Bluebook* are written as if the writer were writing a law review article. Paralegals will not be writing in this style, so it is important to understand that the examples within the text must be converted to the format for practitioners, as shown in the inside back cover and in the Bluepages.

Bluepages
The section of *The Bluebook* that contains the major rules that legal practitioners use in daily work, such as in legal memoranda and court documents.

---

[6]*The Bluebook*. 2010. https://www.legalbluebook.com/Public/Introduction.aspx

[7]*Id.*

[8]*The Bluebook: A Uniform System of Citation*. (Columbia Law Review Ass'n et al. eds., 19th ed. 2010)

[9]*Id.*

[10]*The Bluebook: A Uniform System of Citation*. (Columbia Law Review Ass'n et al. eds., 19th ed. 2010)

TIP

Researchers, particularly those who are not wordsmiths, should consider having a thesaurus available.

TIP

To create the section (§) symbol in Word, hold the ALT key while entering 21 on the numeric keypad. It also may be inserted by selecting the Insert pull-down menu, clicking on "symbols" (and perhaps clicking on "more symbols"), and then choosing the section symbol. One can create a hot key by using Insert > Symbol > More Symbols > Special Characters > choose § > Shortcut Key. Then make up a key combination you can remember. (e.g., use ctrl-8.) > Assign > Close. In Word-Perfect, click on Insert >Symbol > in Set section of Symbol choose Typographic Symbols > click on "section" symbol>click on Insert > Close. For Mac OS, U.S. Keyboard layout: Opt + 5 U.S. Extended Keyboard layout: Opt + 6. The exact sequencing for this insert will vary among versions of Word.

Blue Tips

The online reference section in *The Bluebook* for frequently asked questions about citation format.

The next section, which is identified by pages with blue edges on the side, provides various tables of information. It may be helpful to mark or tab the most frequently used pages for quick reference. Table 1 (T1) provides the citation format and abbreviations for every state and federal entity and legal authority. In the current edition, this table has been subdivided into four parts for easier access: T1.1 Federal Judicial and Legislative Materials; T1.2 Federal Administrative and Executive Materials; T1.3 States and District of Columbia; and T1.4 Other U.S. Jurisdictions.[11] Table 6 provides abbreviated case names while Table 7 gives the abbreviated court names. Table 13 provides information on periodicals, and Table 15 provides abbreviations for the services.

The last section is the index. This index is used just like any other index: one takes the key words from the problem, identifies alternate words for the key words, and searches for matches in the index. However, using the index in *The Bluebook* requires a researcher to think like the editors who created it, and to understand that the answer one is searching for may be in more than one place.

Simulation 5-1 is an example of how to find information in the index for *The Bluebook.*

The Bluebook Online   The Internet site for *The Bluebook* (http://www .legalbluebook.com/) is useful in a number of ways. Users can obtain a subscription to the online service, thereby eliminating the need for a paper copy. For those who prefer the paper version of *The Bluebook,* one of the most helpful features on the Internet site is the update section. Major changes are issued only when a new edition is printed. For example, the 17th edition was first printed in 2000, and the 19th edition was printed in 2010. Any changes from the printing in 2000 were added to subsequent printings. Before another printing of the 19th edition or a new edition occurs, additional changes will be posted on the Update section of *The Bluebook* site (http://www.legalbluebook.com/Public/Updates.aspx).

The editors created ***Blue Tips*** (http://www.legalbluebook.com/Public /BlueTips.aspx) to provide answers to frequently asked questions about citation format. They gathered the most useful answers and grouped them by subject. The answers are connected to the appropriate rule, and hyperlinked to the location of the authority. The tips can be searched and provide excellent examples for a better understanding of the material.

SIMULATION 5-1   FINDING A CITATION FORMAT IN *THE BLUEBOOK*

John's supervisor, Jami, asked him to look for the proper way to cite a statute passed in 1973 that is found at Section 2001(c) in Title 42 of the United States Code. The key words might be "statute," "code," "law," "act," "canon," "ordinance," "enactment," or "session law." "Statute" is probably the main word that he will use. If he looked in the index under "statute," the index would also tell him to consider "codes" and "session laws." The index does not always provide an alternate location, but if it does, that would be another feature of the index he could use.

To begin, John looks under the term "statute." The index directs him to *Rule 12 (see also name of jurisdiction)* or Table T.1. The rule and T.1 provide examples of proper citation format. If John looked under "codes," the index would lead him to *codes, statutory, R 12.3.* The resulting format for the citation above would be 42 U.S.C. § 2001(c) (1973).

---

[11]*Id.*

In the first entry, the question revolved around whether to include information about state trial courts. On the first line, the subject is given and references the rule from which the authority comes. It is followed by an explanation and an example. The second tip provides information on citations to an Internet source.

The foregoing information is only an overview of the value of *The Bluebook*. Nothing replaces actually checking the manual or using the full online version of *The Bluebook* for the proper citation format and any updates.

ALWD

The Bluebook's biggest competitor among citation manuals is Darby Dickerson's *ALWD Citation Manual: A Professional System of Citation,* 4th ed., affectionately referred to as *ALWD* (pronounced "all wood" or "all wid"). This manual was first proposed to the Association of Legal Writing Directors (ALWD) in 1997 as a tool to help students and professionals better understand the rules and requirements outlined in *The Bluebook*. Three years later, ALWD released its citation manual for legal professionals. A great deal of research went into the development of the book, including a review of the available legal citation manuals and actual legal documents, and comments by professors, librarians, and other professionals.[12]

The purposes of the new manual were to create a system that did not change with each edition, to provide a teaching tool, and to make the citation system sensible and consistent with the usage of actual practitioners. ALWD selected Darby Dickerson, director of legal writing at Stetson University and a noted expert on legal citation, to draft the manual. It first appeared in May 2000 and is now in its fourth edition. The manual has been adopted by approximately 100 law schools, 50 paralegal programs, several law journals, and a few courts. However, most state courts still require *The Bluebook*.[13]

The fourth edition of ALWD provides conversion charts for comparison to the 19th edition of *The Bluebook,* as well as charts, updated examples, and new rules on citing live performances.[14] More information is available at www.alwd .org (the group) and ALWD Citation Manual Resources at http://www.alwd.org /publications/citation_manual.html.

Differences between *The Bluebook* and *ALWD*

While there are more similarities than there are differences between *ALWD* and *The Bluebook,* it is important for those who adopt *ALWD* instead of *The Bluebook* to be aware of some of the major differences.

Table 5-1 provides some basic differences between *The Bluebook's* and *ALWD's* most-cited rules, such as those for cases, typeface, and the Internet.

Even if a paralegal education program uses *ALWD*, the local rules in the jurisdiction where a paralegal ultimately works should be checked to see what manual is required by the courts. It may well be *The Bluebook*.

Note

A new edition of ALWD is due for publication in 2013.

TIP

Students can find a PowerPoint presentation of the major differences at http://www.alwd.org/publications /third_edition_resources.html. No similar PowerPoint presentation is available for the fourth edition.

[12]ALWD Association of Legal Writing Directors. 2007–2012. *ALWD Citation Manual Resources*. http://www.alwd.org/publications/citation_manual.html

[13]Steven D. Jamar. The ALWD Citation Manual: A Professional Citation System for the Law. 2000. http://iipsj.com/SDJ/scholarship/alwdciterev.htm

[14]*The ALWD Citation Manual: A Professional System of Citation*. About the Book. 2012. CCH. http://www.alwdmanual.com/books/dickerson_alwd/default.asp

TABLE 5-1   Differences between *The Bluebook* and *ALWD*[15]

Topic	The Bluebook	ALWD
Purpose	Presents the rules and is primarily for reference	Created as a teaching and learning tool
Typeface	Rule 2 (law review footnotes); B 13	Rule 1
Cases	Rule 10 and B5	Rule 12
U.S. Supreme Court cases	Allows only official citation and no abbreviation of United States in the title	Allows *parallel citations* and abbreviation of United States (U.S.) in the title
Page carry-overs	Rule 3.2 requires that repetitive numbers be dropped. For example, pages 1233–34.	Rule 5 makes page carry-over style optional. For example, either 1233–34 or 1233–1234 is acceptable.
Books and treatises	Rule 14.2 and B6 requires "et al." for more than two authors and includes no publisher information. For example, Eugene F. Scoles & Peter Hay, *Conflict of Laws* § 13.20, n. 10 (5th ed. 2010).	Rule 22 requires "et al." for three or more authors, and publisher information is included. For example, Symeon Symeonides, Wendy Collins Perdue, Arthur Taylor Von Mehren] would be: Symeon Symeonides, et.al., *Conflict of Laws: American, Comparative, International* (West Group, 1998).
A.L.R. annotations	Rule 16.6.6 requires the author, the word "Annotation," the title of the annotation, and the location.	Rule 24 leaves out the "Annotation" reference in the citation.
Internet	Rule 18 has different rules depending on whether the source can be accessed only in print or both in print and on the Internet.	Rule 40 provides for abbreviations of names to save space and uses "accessed" rather than "visited."

Parallel citations
Citations reported in more than one location or source. Example: a case from the Iowa Court of Appeals that is also reported in the North Western Reporter.

WHEN TO CITE

In most documents prepared by paralegals, sources must be cited in order to give credence to the law or source being used. The source must be cited at the point of reference. Three simple conventions govern when a reference must be provided:

1. If someone else's ideas are used, cite the source.
2. If the source is used in such a way that its identity is unclear, make it clear.
3. If someone helped write the document, acknowledge the help.

If any information is taken from any source, for any reason, the authority should be cited. Failure to cite an authority tells the reader that there is no authority for that source and the summary is just the writer's opinion. When using another source as an authority, the writer must read the piece of authority, write an analysis of what was read, and then cite the authority.

Plagiarism
The use of someone else's material without giving credit to the source or obtaining the author's permission to use the material.

Plagiarism is using someone else's material without giving credit to the source or obtaining the author's permission to use the material. Adopting the vocabulary and phrases of an author, using them throughout a paper, and not using quotation marks around each phrase or key word will result in plagiarism. To avoid potential plagiarism, a researcher should rephrase the material by thinking about what is being read, outlining an argument that reflects the conclusions drawn, adding quotations where they are necessary to acknowledge someone else's thoughts, and presenting evidence to support the argument. This process will make the difference between actually analyzing and interpreting information, and merely using an answer or idea created by someone else. Obviously, in situations where a professional is working at the last minute, he or she will not have time to analyze and interpret. However, it does not matter if a paralegal is using *Corpus Juris Secundum* (C.J.S.) or looking at an associate's paper—if it is not one's own work, it must be cited.

[15]http://www.alwdmanual.com/books/dickerson_alwd/authorUpdates.asp

Paraphrasing is something that we all do, all the time. To paraphrase is to state someone else's ideas in your own words. The ideas of others are often paraphrased in legal documents. The writer should continually view the document from the reader's perspective. If the reader might say, "What was the source of that idea?", cite the source, even if the material was rewritten or paraphrased.

Another related issue has arisen as researchers have become more dependent on the Internet. It is often very easy and tempting to copy and paste text found on web pages and other online sources. Researchers should not cut and paste from various documents unless each passage is credited to the original author and properly cited. The temptation to cut and paste may also be avoided by printing the web material and referring to it as one would a book, so that cutting and pasting is not as convenient. One should insert the citation at the time of writing instead of waiting until the end to prepare the citations.[16]

When using material from another source, a researcher should give whatever citation information is necessary for the reader to track the citation, read the entire original document, and evaluate the material. The following is the basic information that should be included when citing books and Internet sources of books not in print:

Books:

- the author's name,
- the name of the book, the publisher,
- the date and place of publication, and
- the page number of the quotation.

Internet sources of electronic books not readily available in print:

- the author,
- the date if available or (n.d.) if no date is available,
- the title, and
- the URL of the page (its location on the web), not just the home page.

Just listing the top-level web address is far from sufficient for tracking the source, and could lead to a charge of plagiarism.

PLACEMENT OF CITATIONS

After determining whether a citation is needed, the researcher must determine where it should be placed in the text. A citation is not needed if the citation has already been given and a reference to that authority is incorporated at a later point. An example would be the following:

> In *Kassel v. Consolidated Freightways Corp.*, 450 U.S. 662 (1981), the court was faced with the question of whether a state law prohibiting the use of 65-foot double trailer trucks was unduly burdensome on interstate commerce. After a discussion about the power of the state to regulate commerce, the *Consolidated* court held that "65-foot double-trailer trucks were as safe as the shorter truck units . . . state law impermissibly burdened interstate commerce."

The *Consolidated* case was cited in the first sentence. The reference to the "*Consolidated* court" in the second sentence tells the reader that the discussion

Paraphrase
To state someone else's ideas in your own words.

---

[16]Purdue Online Writing Lab. *Paraphrase: Write it in Your Own Words.* 2010. http://www .luminafoundation.org/publications/The_Degree_Qualifications_Profile.pdf?f22064

of the previously cited case is continuing. There is no reason to repeat the citation unless it becomes unclear what *Consolidated* is referring to.

Once it is decided that a citation is needed, the next question to determine is where the citation should be placed. There are three ways a citation may be placed within text:

Citation sentence
Placement of a citation in a separate sentence following the textual sentence and containing only the citation.

Embedded citation
A citation placed within a textual sentence that forms a key part of the sentence but is not set off by commas.

Citation clause
Placement of a citation within the textual sentence when it is not a key part of the sentence.

1. The citation is in a separate ***citation sentence*** that follows the textual sentence.
2. The citation is ***embedded*** within and is a key part of the textual sentence itself.
3. The ***citation clause*** is placed within the textual sentence but is not a key part of the sentence.

When the citation is in a separate citation sentence, the reader knows that the citation supports the entire point made in the preceding sentence. The citation begins with a capital letter and ends with a period. For example:

> The Constitution provides for three distinct branches of government. U.S. Const. arts. I–III.

While this is a citation to a provision of the U.S. Constitution, the concept would be the same whether the citation was to a statute, a case, or any other material.

If the citation is embedded into the textual sentence, it forms a key part of the sentence. The citation can be supplied within the sentence without setting it off using commas, unless normal punctuation rules would demand that it be set off by punctuation. However, embedding the citation often makes the sentence weaker and reduces the impact of the cited statement. The best option is to rewrite the sentence so that the citation can be used in a separate sentence. Example 5-1 shows the difference between placing the citation in the middle of the sentence and at the end.

Citation clauses are needed when the citation supports only part of the textual sentence and the authority is not the key to the entire sentence. A citation clause is set off by commas and most often occurs when a sentence has two or more authorities. For example:

> In the *Colyer* case Judge Anderson determined that mere membership in the communist party was not a threat to the country. *Colyer v. Skeffington*, 265 F. 17 (1920). Judge Anderson was later overruled on the communist

---

EXAMPLE 5-1   GOOD AND BETTER CITATION PLACEMENT

Good: The court in *City of Chicago v. Village of Elk Grove Village*, 820 N.E. 2d 1158 (Ill. App. 1 Dist. 2004), held that the trial court was correct in determining that disconnection is not a matter pertaining to the government and therefore the Village does not have the power to enact an ordinance concerning disconnection.

Better: The court held that the trial court was correct in determining that disconnection is not a matter pertaining to the government and therefore the Village does not have the power to enact an ordinance concerning disconnection. *City of Chicago v. Village of Elk Grove Village*, 820 N.E. 2d 1158 (Ill. App. 1 Dist. 2004).

issue, *Skeffington v. Katzeff,* 277 F. 129 (1922), but his decision and reasoning was often later cited. *Galvan v. Press,* 347 U.S. 522 (1954); *Bovinas v. Savoretti,* 146 F. Supp. 274 (1956).

In the above example, the first mention of *Colyer* is a textual reference. The reference to *Skeffington* is a citation clause. The last case citation is a citation sentence.[17]

If a section from a case was summarized and compared to the client's situation in the same sentence, the citation would apply only to the summary of the case and not to the comparison being made to the client's situation.

Another example of an embedded citation occurs where there is language from one statute and one case cited in the same sentence:

> Special legislation is prohibited under Ind. Const. Art. IV, § 22 and the constitutional debates make clear that the lack of a uniform assessment practice was one of the main concerns underlying section 22, *State v. Myers,* 146 Ind. 36, 38, 44 N.E.2d 801, 801–02 (1896).

QUOTATIONS

Quotations must be presented properly so that the reader can distinguish between material from a cited source and the writer's personal information. The words of the quoted text must be exact unless any omissions or alterations are properly identified. All the words must be spelled as they are written, even if the spelling is incorrect in the source. The typeface, capitalization, and punctuation must be identical.

If the passage is relatively short (less than 50 words or no longer than three or four lines), the quoted passage is placed in quotation marks and embedded within the sentence, as shown in Example 5-2.

If the passage is longer than 50 words or more than three or four lines of text, the quoted text should be set off from the rest of the text as a "block quotation," started on a new line, indented on both sides, and single-spaced. No quotation marks are used for a block quotation. This method is shown in Example 5-3.

Writers also need to punctuate correctly within quoted material. Periods and commas are always placed within the closing quotation marks. Punctuation from the original quote, such as exclamation marks or question marks, should be placed inside the quotation marks, as shown here:

> The court asked the central question, "Should such conduct be severely limited?"

EXAMPLE 5-2   SAMPLE QUOTATION FORMAT LESS THAN 50 WORDS

The *Zan* court found that rather than using the money paid by Lawrence for educational purposes, Joyce used the money to live on, which was not the purpose of the clause in the agreement. "In our view, such was not the intent and spirit of the Agreement." *Id. at* 1289.

---

[17]Suffolk University Law School. Frequently Asked Questions. 2012. http://www.law.suffolk.edu/library/research/bluebook/faq.cfm#Difference

> **EXAMPLE 5-3   QUOTATIONS OF MORE THAN 50 WORDS**
>
> The defendant contends that the plaintiff failed to utilize her rehabilitative main-
> tenance. This issue was discussed in another Indiana case, *Zan v. Zan,* 820 N.E.2d
> 1284 (Ind.Ct.App. 2005). The trial court found for Lawrence and Joyce appealed.
> The court found that rather than using the money paid by Lawrence for educa-
> tional purposes, Joyce used the money to live on, which was not the purpose of the
> clause in the agreement. The court held:
>
>> Although our supreme court has not squarely decided the issue presented to-
>> day, it is our view that the trial court may modify the Agreement under these
>> circumstances. To hold otherwise may circumvent the parties' ability or desire
>> to bargain independently without court intervention. Put another way, a party
>> may be loath to enter into an agreement such as the one here, knowing that a
>> court could not intervene in the event of changed circumstances.
>
> *Id.* at 1288.

Punctuation of material that the writer adds is placed outside the quotation marks:

> Is it clear from the contract that the actions were "reasonable and necessary"?

For a quotation within a quotation, indicate the internal quotation with single quotation marks, not double:

> "In our view, such was not the 'intent and spirit' of the Agreement."

"Intent and spirit" is an internal quotation, so only single quotation marks are used.

Altering Quotations

Often it may be necessary or preferred to quote a passage without starting at the beginning of the sentence of the quoted material. The first letter of the first word to be used is placed in brackets. For example, here is a sentence from a case:

> "The Appellant was entitled to ownership in the land by virtue of his inherit-
> ance, which was properly documented in the will."

For some reason, the entire sentence is not going to be used. If the quote is used within a sentence, it would appear as follows:

> The court held that "[t]he Appellant was entitled to ownership in the land by virtue of his inheritance, which was properly documented in the will."

Here the letter *T* in the word *the* no longer begins the sentence, so the *t* is set in brackets and changed to lowercase: "[t]he."

Any words that are left out of a quote are indicated by using ***ellipsis points***, which consist of three periods (. . .) separated by spaces before, after, and between the periods. Ellipsis points are generally available as a symbol in most word processing applications. Had the information in the middle been eliminated, the sentence would have looked like Example 5-4.

To emphasize something in a quotation, italicize the emphasized element and at the end of the quotation and place the words "emphasis added" in a bracket. The resulting sentence might look like Example 5-5.

Ellipsis points
A method of indicating to a reader that material from a quota-tion has been omitted. Ellipsis points are a series of three periods with spaces before, between, and after the periods. If the omission comes at the end of a sentence, a fourth period (the sentence period) is added.

EXAMPLE 5-4   OMISSIONS IN QUOTATIONS

"The Appellant was entitled to ownership . . . by virtue of his inheritance, which was properly documented in the will."

The omission of words at the end of the sentence is indicated by three ellipsis points plus a period:

"The Appellant was entitled to ownership of the land by virtue of his inheritance . . . ."

The omission of one or more paragraphs in a quoted piece is indicated by placing four periods in paragraph formation.

"The Appellant was entitled to ownership in the land by virtue of his inheritance, which was properly documented in the will."

. . . .

"The Appellant was also entitled to the bequest as stated in the second codicil to the will."

EXAMPLE 5-5   EMPHASIS ADDED

"The Appellant was entitled to ownership in the land *by virtue of his inheritance,* which was properly documented in the will." (emphasis added).

EXAMPLE 5-6   *SIC*

"The court held that Appellant was entitled to ownership in the land by virture [*sic*] of his inheritance, which was properly documented in the will."

If the quoted material has an error in it, the text should be presented exactly as it appears in the source. The writer may indicate that the error originated in the source by adding **sic** in italics surrounded by brackets at the point of the error. If it contained an error, the sentence might look like Example 5-6.

There are numerous rules that cover plagiarism and the use of quotations, and those summarized above are only a few of the rules that are encountered frequently. A good writer will always check citation manuals, grammar textbooks, or reliable Internet sites before submitting a document.

Sic
A note indicating to the reader that an error originated in the source material. *Sic* is placed in brackets immediately after the word that contains the mistake.

STRING CITATIONS

String citations are multiple citations that support one proposition and that are written one after another. Each citation should be separated from the next by a semicolon so that the reader can easily distinguish the elements of one citation from those of another. All that is presented is the citation. Example 5-7 shows string citations.

In the first example, the reader gets a brief explanation of *Hanon v. Dataproducts Corp.,* but if he or she were interested in the rest of the cases, the

String citations
Groups of citations that together support a proposition.

EXAMPLE 5-7   STRING CITATIONS

Sailors' argument is grounded in his view that the rate case was only nominally public. Sailors argues that NSP had a duty to disclose many of the developments in the rate proceeding because the information did not adequately enter the market. *See, e.g., Hanon v. Dataproducts Corp.*, 976 F.2d 497, 503 (9th Cir. 1992) (stating that "brief mention in a few poorly circulated or lightly regarded publications" does not relieve a corporation of the duty to disclose material information); *In re Convergent Technologies Sec. Litig.*, 948 F.2d 507, 513 (9th Cir. 1991); *In re Apple Computer Sec. Litig.*, 886 F.2d 1109, 1116 (9th Cir.), cert. denied, 496 U.S. 943, 110 S.Ct. 3229, 110 L.Ed.2d 676 (1989); *Siebert v. Sperry Rand Corp.*, 586 F.2d 949, 952 (5th Cir.1978); *Powell v. American Bank & Trust Co.*, 640 F.Supp. 1568, 1578–81 (N.D. Ind. 1986).

B. L. *Sailors v. Northern States Power Co.*, 4 F. 3d 610 (8th Cir. 1993).

Here is another example:

The Creasons failed to allege sufficient facts supporting either element of a substantive due process claim. First, the Creasons do not allege or argue their monetary interest in being free from a special assessment is a liberty interest "deeply rooted in this Nation's history and tradition" so as to be protected by the Fourteenth Amendment. *Washington v. Glucksberg*, 521 U.S. 702, 721, 117 S.Ct. 2258, 138 L.Ed.2d 772 (1997) (quotation omitted). Second, the City's imposition of the special assessment was not so "arbitrary" or "conscience-shocking" as to violate due process. *See Lingle v. Chevron U.S.A. Inc.*, ___ U.S. ___, ___, 125 S.Ct. 2074, 2084, 161 L.Ed.2d 876 (2005); *Lewis*, 523 U.S. at 846, 118 S.Ct. 1708; *Bonebrake v. Norris*, 417 F.3d 938, 942 (8th Cir.2005).

Creason *v. City of Washington*, 435 F. 3d 820 (8th Cir. 2006).

reader would have to access those cases and read them. In the second example there is no hint as to what any of the cases are about.

When preparing an interoffice memorandum, string citations are not the best choice for citation format. While string citations are used in many reported cases, an interoffice memorandum is aimed at explaining a position to the reader. In order to explain a position as clearly as possible, it is critical to discuss each of the authorities cited. Usually only the leading cases need to be cited and discussed. The other citations in the String citations do not help explain the position, and are not necessary.

There are two exceptions in which a string citation may be appropriate in an interoffice memorandum. The writer may want to show the true breadth of support for a position, and listing additional cases in a string citation will show the extent of that support. Listing the authorities that support a view is acceptable as long as it is done *after* sufficiently discussing and supporting a position.

The other exception is based on the preferences or goals of the supervisor who assigned the research problem. The supervisor may want the citations presented without discussion of any except those most on point or most current. The supervisor's wishes control, so it is important to always check those expectations.

Order of Citations in a String   If multiple citations are placed into a string of citations, they must be placed in the correct order based on the hierarchy of the authority and whether one authority is more helpful or on point than the other authorities. The most helpful authority should be cited first, according to *The Bluebook* Rule 1.4 and B 4.5. *ALWD* has no such consideration, but does provide the order in rule 45.

Basically, after the most helpful authority is cited, the citations are placed in the following hierarchy:

1. constitutions
2. statutes
3. treaties
4. cases
5. legislative materials
6. administrative and executive materials
7. resolutions, decisions, and regulations of intergovernmental organizations
8. records, briefs, and petitions
9. secondary authorities

Within federal cases, citations are ordered with the U.S. Supreme Court first, followed by U.S. Courts of Appeal (by circuit), and then U.S. District Courts (by state and then by district). The cases are then listed by date if there are several cases in each subgroup. State authority is likewise listed hierarchically: supreme court, followed by intermediate appeals courts, followed by trial courts, if their cases are reported. Within the state authorities, the rule is to place the state information alphabetically, so that Indiana material comes after Colorado material and before North Carolina material. There are some unique rules for listings within each group, so checking the citation manual is important.

Secondary authorities pose a slightly different problem since there is no real hierarchy. The order is set by the rules, which generally state that the work is alphabetized by the author's last name, or by the first word in the title if there is no author. Next, as stated in *ALWD* Rule 46 and Rule 1.4 in *The Bluebook,* the order is as follows:

1. uniform codes, model codes, and restatements
2. books, pamphlets and like items
3. journals by author
4. book reviews (not by students)
5. student-written law review materials
6. annotations
7. magazine and newspaper articles
8. working papers
9. unpublished materials
10. electronic sources

Signals in Citations   **Signals** are used to indicate to the reader how the authority cited plays a role in the narrative. The signal appears before the citation and may or may not be capitalized depending on where in the sentence the signal appears. If it is at the beginning of a citation sentence, it is capitalized. If the signal appears in a citation clause, it is not capitalized. The signals are always italicized or underlined unless they are verbs in a sentence structure, such as in a footnote. If the signal has two words, such as "*see also,*" and underlining instead of italicizing is the preferred form, the underlining is a solid line under both words, such as "see also". Punctuation is not placed after the signal. The order of the signals is governed by Rule 44.8 in *ALWD* and Rule 1.2 and B4 in *The Bluebook.*

Both *ALWD* and *The Bluebook* use signals in similar ways, but there are some subtle differences. Both agree that a writer does not use a signal if the

Signals

Markers that indicate important information is to follow.

Group	Signals
Showing support	*Accord* (law of one jurisdiction similar to law of another jurisdiction)
	see (implicit support or dicta)
	see also (addition, but less direct, support), *cf.* (support by analogy)
	no signal (if the citation directly supports the narrative)
Showing comparison	*Compare, compare . . . with* (compare authorities that reach different results)
Showing contradiction	*But see* (cited authority contradicts proposition implicitly or contains dicta)
	but cf. (authority contradicts proposition by analogy)
	contra (authority contradicts proposition)
Showing background information	*See generally* (cites helpful background information)

FIGURE 5-1 Signals

citation directly supports the proposition stated in the document or when the citation identifies the quotation's source. Both manuals classify the signals into four main groups: signals that show support, signals that show comparison, signals that show contradiction, and signals that indicate background material. See Figure 5-1 for the signal groups and the types of signals that typically fall into each group.

Another common signal is *e.g.*, which is used quite often to show an example, particularly a representative example instead of all the authority found. *ALWD* uses *e.g.* without a comma; however, *The Bluebook* requires that a comma follow the signal.

Both manuals agree that signals should include a parenthetical explanation about the meaning and value of the authority. The parenthetical is placed after the source. Both manuals, however, provide very detailed requirements on how to use these signals. A writer should check rules 1.3 in *The Bluebook* and 44.8 in *ALWD* to ensure that the appropriate information is used.

NON-LEGAL CITATION FORMATS

Students may have some familiarity with citation formats in standard bibliographies for research papers written in non-legal courses. There are two primary citation formats for writing formal, non-legal papers: **Modern Language Association (MLA)** and **American Psychological Association (APA)**. Other formats are found in the *Chicago Manual of Style* (CMS), the *American Medical Association Manual of Style* (AMA), and Kate L. Turabian's *Manual for Writers of Research Papers, Theses, and Dissertations* (referred to as *Turabian*).

It is worthwhile to become familiar with the style manuals of the Modern Language Association (MLA) and the American Psychological Association (APA). Writing papers in the legal world may require the use of these manuals. In addition, having an understanding of general, non-legal citation formatting may assist the researcher in understanding legal citation formatting. Proper formatting

Modern Language Association (MLA)

A writing format that is generally associated with writing in the liberal arts and humanities areas, such as in English, philosophy, theater, music, modern languages, religion, and history.

American Psychological Association (APA)

The writing format most often used in the social sciences, such as psychology and sociology; also used in the hard sciences (chemistry and biology).

TIP

CMS, AMA, and Turabian are not discussed here.

will also make students better writers in other classes and in various other writing tasks throughout life. Students need to understand the two formatting styles because they may be required to write an article for a law-related magazine or other publication that does not rely on legal formatting as set forth in *The Bluebook* or *ALWD*.

As with legal citation formats, the goal of non-legal formats is to give the reader enough information to find the sources used. This allows the reader to verify the information presented in the document.

MLA

One of the two major formatting styles is that of the Modern Language Association (MLA). MLA provides a citation format that is generally associated with writing in the liberal arts and humanities areas, such as English, philosophy, theater, music, modern languages, religion, and history. The MLA publishes two authoritative explanations of MLA style: the *MLA Handbook for Writers of Research Papers* (currently in its seventh edition) for high school and undergraduate research papers, and the *MLA Style Manual and Guide to Scholarly Publishing* (currently in its third edition) for graduate students, professional writers, and scholars.[18]

MLA uses a two-pronged approach to citations: the signal phrases and parenthetical citations in text, and the ***Works Cited page*** listing. The combination of the two reference points provide the writer with a way to credit the sources used in a paper and gives the reader a way to retrieve the materials cited. A ***signal phrase*** indicates that a quotation, summary, or other material is taken from a source and used. The citation in text provides information to lead the reader to the Works Cited page, so the signal phrase information for a book (highlighted in blue), for example, generally would provide the author and the page:

> Kathryn Myers states that "failure to cite the authority from which information is borrowed is plagiarism and subjects a student to various forms of punishment" (93).

If the signal phrase does not identify the author, the author's name is given in the parenthetical reference following the cited material. Note that there is no punctuation between the author's name and the page reference. For example:

> "If you fail to cite the authority from which you borrow information, you are plagiarizing the material and you can be subject to various forms of punishment" (Myers 93).

Writers will often cite a reference that is a whole page long, but divided into paragraphs. It is a good practice to provide a reference at the end of each paragraph so that the reader will know with certainty that none of the information within the paper comes from anyplace except the source. It also prevents the reader from assuming that no source is cited at all.

Writers then provide the complete reference, including the author, title, place of publication, publisher, and date, on the Works Cited page. The Works Cited page always begins on a new page at the end of the paper, and lists the works cited in alphabetical order by author, or by work if an author is not noted. Each work is presented in three main parts, each followed by a period: 1) the author's

TIP

If writers are unfamiliar with MLA or APA citation rules, an excellent source to bookmark is *The Owl* at Purdue, http://owl.english.purdue.edu.

Works Cited page
In MLA format, the page that lists the sources cited within the paper.

Signal phrases
Signals consisting of multiple words that direct the reader to additional information.

---

[18]Modern Language Association. *MLA Handbook for Writers of Research Papers* and the *MLA Style Manual and Guide to Scholarly Publishing*. 2010. http://www.mla.org/style_faq1

TABLE 5-2   MLA Citations

Type of Authority/ Source	Citation in Text	Works Cited Page
Book	(Myers, 111)	Myers, Kathryn. Legal Research, Analysis, and Writing. New Jersey: Pearson/Prentice Hall, 2014.
Journal Article	(Castledine, 75)	Castledine, Jacqueline. "In a Solid Bond of Unity: Anticolonial Feminism in the Cold War Era." Journal of Women's History 20.2 (2008): 57–81.
Newspaper Article	(Johnson, A4)	Johnson, Reed. "Michael Jackson's Legacy Won't Be Decided in Court." Los Angeles Times 2 July 2009: A4.
Newspaper on the Web	(Johnson, 2009)	Johnson, Reed. "Michael Jackson's Legacy Won't Be Decided in Court." Los Angeles Times 2 July 2009. 7 July 2009 <http://www.latimes.com /entertainment/news/la-et-michael-legacy7 -2009jul07,0,7501191.story>

TIP

There are various sources on the Internet that are useful for checking MLA format. Earlier, *The Owl* at Purdue was mentioned. Other sites are Long Island University's Citation Style for Research Papers at http:// www2.liu.edu/cwis/cwp/library /workshop/citation.htm, *MLA Citation Style* at Cornell University's Citation Management: MLA Citation Style at http://www.library.cornell.edu /newhelp/res_strategy/citing/mla .html, and *Using MLA Style to Cite and Document Sources* at http://bcs.bedfordstmartins.com /resdoc5e/RES5e_ch08_s1-0011 .html. Websites may come and go, so if the site does not exist, one might go to the home page of a source and use any search mechanism that the website provides.

In-text citations

Citations within the body of a paper that refer the reader to a list of references.

Reference list

In APA format, the listing at the end of the paper that provides complete information on the sources referenced within the paper.

or editor's name (with last name first); 2) the title of the work underlined; and 3) the publishing data, which includes the place of publication, the publisher, and the date of publication. For example:

> Myers, Kathryn. Legal Research, Analysis, and Writing. New Jersey: Pearson/Prentice Hall, 2014.

While there are numerous formats depending on the type of source being used, Table 5-2 provides a few examples of some common MLA citation formatting.

APA

The American Psychological Association (APA) style is most often used in the social sciences, such as psychology and sociology, and is also used as the "hard" sciences, such as chemistry and biology. It is presented in the Publication Manual of the American Psychological Association (*Publication Manual*).

APA recommends that a writer use ***in-text citations*** that refer the reader to a list of references. An in-text citation gives the author of the source, the date of publication, and sometimes a page number in parentheses. For example:

> Myers (2010) states that "failure to cite the authority from which you borrow information is plagiarism and subjects a student to various forms of punishment" (p. 93).

A ***reference list*** is placed at the end of the paper. The entries are double-spaced and listed alphabetically by author's last name, or alphabetically by title if there is no author. Each entry in the reference list begins with the author's last name, followed by the author's first and middle initials. If there are multiple authors, the authors are separated by an ampersand (&):

> Myers, J., & Myers, K.

The publication year is placed in parentheses: (2010). The book title is italicized, and only the first word and the word after a colon are capitalized, followed by a period:

> Legal research, analysis, and writing.

If the work has an editor, the name is abbreviated and placed after the title, followed by the note "Ed." in parentheses:

Myers, K. (Ed.)

The final element is the two-letter state code; however, omit the state for well-known cities such as London, New York, or San Francisco. Provide the publisher's name but omit "Inc.," "Books," "Publ.," or "Co." in the publisher's name.

Upper Saddle River, NJ: Pearson/Prentice Hall.[19]

The entire entry in the reference list would be as follows:

Myers, K. L. (2010). Legal research, analysis, and writing. Upper Saddle River, NJ: Pearson/Prentice Hall.

For an article, the basic format is the author's last name, then initials for first and middle names, a comma and ampersand (&) before the last author in the list, and a period:

Myers, K., & Myers, J.

The authors are followed by the year of the publication in parentheses, followed by a period: (2010). The third element is the article title, which is not italicized. Only the first word is capitalized and the first word after a colon, along with all proper nouns. The title is followed by a period:

In a solid bond of unity: Anticolonial feminism in the Cold War Era.

Next is the journal name with the volume, issue, and page numbers. All important words are capitalized and the title and volume number are italicized:

Journal of Women's History 20(2) 57–81.[20]

Use the abbreviation for page (p.) or pages (pp.) to provide the page numbers from the sources being used. The first line of each reference entry is flush to the left margin and any subsequent lines of the single entry are indented five to seven spaces to form what is called a **hanging indent**.[21] The questions of when to underline and when to italicize are vital, too. APA seems to prefer italicizing for books or comparable titles.

See the Appendix for more information on MLA and APA formatting.

> **TIP**
>
> Just as for MLA formatting, there are several sites that provide useful information on APA formatting. Those sites comparable to the MLA sites are *The Owl* at Purdue, http://owl.english.purdue.edu/owl/resource/560/01/; *APA Citation Style* at Cornell University at http://www.library.cornell.edu/resrch/citmanage/apa; and *Using Principles of APA Style to Cite and Document Sources* at http://bcs.bedfordstmartins.com/resdoc5e/RES5e_ch09_o.html.

Hanging indent
The second and subsequent lines of a single entry, indented five to seven spaces from the margin.

TABLE 5-3   APA Citations

Type of Authority/Source	Citation in Text	References
Book	(Myers, 2010)	Myers, K. L. (2010). *Legal research, analysis, and writing.* Upper Saddle Rock, NJ: Pearson/Prentice Hall.
Journal article	(Castledine, 2008, p. 75)	Castledine, J. (2008). In a solid bond of unity: Anticolonial feminism in the Cold War Era. *Journal of Women's History 20*(2) 57–81.
Newspaper article	(Johnson, 2009, p. A4)	Johnson, R. (2009, July 2). Michael Jackson's legacy won't be decided in court. *Los Angeles Times* p. A4.
Newspaper on the Web	(Johnson, 2009)	Johnson, R. (2009, July 2). Michael Jackson's legacy won't be decided in court. *Los Angeles Times.* Retrieved from http://www.latimes.com/entertainment/news/la-et-michael-legacy7-2009jul07,0,7501191.story

[19]American Psychological Association. *The Basics of APA Style.* 2012. http://www.apastyle.org/learn/tutorials/basics-tutorial.aspx

[20]*Id.*

[21]Bedford St. Martin's. Research and Documentation Online, 5th Ed. *Social Sciences: APA manuscript format.* http://bcs.bedfordstmartins.com/resdoc5e/RES5e_ch09_s1-0008.html#RES5e_ch09_s2-0008

ETHICS IN WRITING

Ethics are a vital part of the paralegal profession, and must be considered in every aspect of a paralegal's personal and professional life. Ethics are the minimum standards of conduct that a particular industry or profession sets for its practitioners. The Model Rules of Professional Conduct (MRPC), created by the American Bar Association (ABA), set the standards of ethics for the legal profession. Many professions, such as doctors and psychologists, have analogous codes of ethics. There is also an unwritten code of ethics for the Internet, which helps to foster continued growth and preserve the reliability of the information provided on the Internet.

While paralegals are not directly governed by the MRPC, paralegals are expected to abide by those rules as part of the legal team. Paralegals often perform a large amount of research, which can involve several ethical considerations such as competence. Rule 1.1 requires that attorneys be competent and specifically requires that lawyers possess "the legal knowledge, skill, thoroughness and preparation reasonably necessary for the representation."[22] When the paralegal engages in research, the paralegal is an extension of the attorney; therefore, the skill, thoroughness, and preparation that the paralegal uses when researching are governed by this ethical rule.

Rule 3.3, Candor to the Court, is the ethical rule stating that the attorney must disclose "legal authority in the controlling jurisdiction known to the lawyer to be directly adverse to the position of the client and not disclosed by opposing counsel."[23] When researching, it is incumbent upon the paralegal to provide the attorney with all relevant authority, whether for or against the client's position.

SUMMARY

Citing sources correctly is important for many reasons, but two of these are paramount. First, the reader must be given enough information on the sources used to be able to verify the credibility and validity of the material. Second, ideas of others must be properly credited to avoid plagiarism.

This chapter has presented only an introduction to citations used in research and writing. The rules of *The Bluebook* and *ALWD* will be presented in greater detail in the next chapter. For now, it is important to understand the basics of citing sources, and the differences between *The Bluebook* and *ALWD*. Generally, the best solution is to ask the professor or supervisor which format is preferred.

REVIEW **QUESTIONS**

1. Identify three differences between *The Bluebook* and *ALWD*.
2. What is a signal in citation formatting? What is its purpose?
3. When would you use *id.* in citation formatting?
4. Explain why plagiarism is an ethical concern.
5. List three steps that you can take to avoid plagiarizing a document.
6. What is the main difference between the Bluepages and the white pages in *The Bluebook*?
7. Explain how to present quotes of 50 words or more.
8. When is it appropriate to use string citations? Why is it not the best practice? Explain.
9. When should material be cited? Explain why.

---

[22]American Bar Association. Model Code of Professional Responsibility. Rule 1.1. 2011. http://www
.americanbar.org/groups/professional_responsibility/publications/model_rules_of_professional
_conduct/rule_1_1_competence.html

[23]*Id.* Rule 3.3

APPLICATION **EXERCISES**

1. Take a topic of interest that relates to law or the legal profession. For example, consider the ethics of legal practice or the paralegal profession as a viable option for employment. Find two sources. Write a one- to two-page paper using the two sources. Properly cite the sources within the document and in the appropriate reference area. Add another page where you identify which citation format was used and why.

2. Look at the Bluepages of *The Bluebook*. Identify two rules that might be used most often in the remainder of this class. Summarize the rules and provide two examples (not in this text) that illustrate these rules.

3. The following text is a quotation from a case. The material comes from pages 168 and 169 of the case. The defendant was James Madison, the plaintiff was William Marbury, and the case is found on page 137 of volume 5 of the U.S. Supreme Court Reports (Cranch). It was decided in 1803. Properly present the quotation in the form it should appear, and properly cite the source.

   It is then the opinion of the Court, 1. That by signing the commission of Mr. Marbury, the president of the United States appointed him a justice of peace . . . and that the seal of the United States, affixed thereto by the secretary of state, is conclusive testimony of the verity of the signature, and of the completion of the appointment; and that the appointment conferred on him a legal right to the office for the space of five years. 2. That, having this legal title to the office, he has a consequent right to the commission; a refusal to deliver which is a plain violation of that right, for which the laws of his country afford him a remedy.

CITATION **EXERCISES**

The following string citations were found in a case. Place the citations in the proper order.

Texas Rev. Crim. Stat., Arts. 1071–1076 (1911); Texas Penal Code of 1857, c. 7, Arts. 531–536; Texas Laws 1854, c. 49, § 1, set forth in 3 H. Gammel, Laws of Texas 1502 (1898). See G. Paschal, Laws of Texas, Arts. 2192-2197 (1866); Texas Rev. Stat., c. 8, Arts. 536–541 (1879).

QUICK **CHECK**

Write the correct citation for each example according to the current edition of *The Bluebook: A Uniform System of Citation* (the "Bluebook") or the current edition of *ALWD*. State the rules that apply for each correction. Use the citation rules applicable to court documents and legal memoranda, rather than those used for law review footnotes.

1. *ALWD* allows parallel citations for U.S. Supreme Court cases.

2. Ellipsis points can be used to indicate that individual words have merely been altered to begin a quotation.

3. A quotation of fewer than 50 words or three lines should be indented on both sides and single spaced.

4. Adding string citations after your explanation of a point is a good idea, because you should show the reader every source that agrees with what you have written.

5. There is a hierarchy in the order of citing cases within a string of cases that starts with the Constitution.

6. The best way to avoid plagiarizing material is to put quotes around everything.

7. A citation clause occurs when the citation is placed within the textual sentence but is not a key part of the textual sentence.

8. If you wish to emphasize something within a quotation, you can change the word without making any additional notation.

9. If you wish to quote material but you want to leave out words in the middle of the quote, ellipsis points may be inserted to indicate the missing information.

10. Signals are important to tell the reader at least four things: support, clarification, supplemental material, and contradiction.

RESEARCH

1. Find a treatise on torts or contracts. Prepare a summary of a point of law in 250 words or less in one of the sources. Properly cite the reference in both formats.

2. Find a statute governing child support in your state. Paraphrase the statute and cite the reference.

INTERNET **RESEARCH**

1. Locate an article in a law review that is of interest to you. Properly cite the source, considering that the material is consecutively paginated.
2. Select a website, preferably one that is not popular. Evaluate the site based on the following:
   a. Sponsorship
   b. Author
   c. Currency
   d. Links
   e. Purpose
   f. Permanency
   g. Objectivity

MEDIA **RESOURCES**

1. Video: **MLA Citation Format, Part 1—Put Your Papers & Essays in Perfect MLA Style** http://www.youtube.com/watch?v=EK0CH6ePGgI

2. **APA Citation Style & Format-Fifth (5th) Edition** http://www.youtube.com/watch?v=w_-RB93hB10

INTERNET **RESOURCES**

All Law.com:	http://www.alllaw.com
APA style:	http://www.apastyle.org/learn/tutorials/basics-tutorial.aspx
Copyright law:	http://www.copyright.gov/title17/circ92.pdf
Findlaw:	http://www.findlaw.com
Georgetown Law Library:	http://www.ll.georgetown.edu
Hieros Gamos:	http://www.hg.org
International Citation Manual:	http://law.wustl.edu/wugslr/index.asp?id=5512
Introduction to Basic Legal Citation:	http://www.law.cornell.edu/citation/
Jurist:	http://www.jurist.law.pitt.edu
Law.com:	http://www.law.com
Lawsource.com:	http://www.lawsource.com
Legal Citation Style Guide:	http://www.legalcitation.net/
LLRX.com:	http://www.llrx.com
MLA Citation Style at Cornell University:	http://www.library.cornell.edu/newhelp/res_strategy/citing/mla.html
MLA style:	http://www.mla.org/style
"NoodleTools":	http://www.noodletools.com/
"Son of Citation Machine":	http://citationmachine.net/
The Bluebook:	http://www.legalbluebook.com
The Bluebook online:	http://www.legalbluebook.com/Public/Tour.aspx
The Owl at Purdue:	http://owl.english.purdue.edu
The University of Chicago Manual of Legal Citation (The Maroonbook):	http://lawreview.uchicago.edu/resources/docs/stylesheet.1009.pdf
Thomas:	http://thomas.loc.gov
Virtual Chase:	http://virtualchase.justia.com/

chapter **six**

CITING SOURCES: *THE BLUEBOOK* AND *ALWD*

Junial Enterprises/Shutterstock

LEARNING OBJECTIVES

After studying this chapter, students should be able to:

1. Understand and apply the basics of legal citation formatting.

2. Demonstrate how to cite-check references.

3. Correctly cite legal authorities.

4. Identify the information necessary to solve a problem or answer a question.

5. Understand the legal and ethical issues associated with using information.

CHAPTER OVERVIEW

Paralegals are often given the task of cite-checking. This process involves making sure that citations are accurate and correctly formatted according to the rules. This chapter will focus on *The Bluebook, ALWD,* and the rules required by many jurisdictions. It is not possible to cover every possible rule. However, knowing the basic rules of citation for the most commonly used materials will provide a strong foundation for the new paralegal.

OPENING SCENARIO

Jami called John into her office at about 5 P.M. on Wednesday. She told him that an **appellate brief** was due to be filed on Friday, and that it was up to him to confirm every **citation** within the brief and to make sure that the **table of authorities** was correctly presented. She would have the brief ready for him by noon on Thursday, and it had to be filed in the Court of Appeals by 4 P.M. on Friday.

Appellate brief
A brief filed with the appellate court asking the court to review a decision of the lower court for errors of law.

Citation
A combination of words, letters, and numbers that helps the user find the source of the information being quoted or referenced.

Table of authorities
A list of references, such as cases, statutes, and rules, in a legal document, along with the numbers of the pages on which the references appear.

John knew that he would have a busy afternoon on Thursday and was glad that he had some of Friday morning to finish up if necessary. However, he knew that there would be numerous citations because this was a case with many issues. It had been quite some time since he had prepared a table of authorities. He was glad he kept his textbook from his Legal Research class. It was going to come in handy!

THE BLUEBOOK AND *ALWD*

In the last chapter the two primary citation manuals currently in use were introduced: *The Bluebook: A Uniform System of Citation*, 19th Ed., and *ALWD Citation Manual: A Professional System of Citation,* 4th Ed. *The Bluebook* has been widely accepted by law schools, attorneys, judges, and now paralegals. In 2000, *ALWD* became available, and its simpler rules made it quite popular. This chapter provides comparison of *The Bluebook* and *ALWD* in the major citation formats.

Many states also supplement the citation rules in the manuals with local citation rules. These local court rules take precedence over any manual. It is therefore essential to check local authorities to see exactly what is required.

Students will not have to memorize every rule, but they should be able to identify when a citation is needed, what information to include, the format it should appear in, and when a rule needs to be checked. As students use citations more regularly, applying the rules will become second nature.

USING *THE BLUEBOOK* AND *ALWD*–TYPEFACE ISSUES

TIP

The rules allow for case names and other sources to be either underlined or italicized. When one is working as a paralegal, one's office or local jurisdiction will determine which is preferred. For now, the course instructor should determine the preference. Typeface conventions such as underlining or italicizing must be consistent throughout each document.

In order to use *The Bluebook*, students need to observe the difference between the typeface convention for law review footnotes and the typeface convention for documents and legal memoranda. *ALWD* does not make this distinction.

The bulk of the rules set forth in the white pages of *The Bluebook* show how the material would appear in law reviews or journals. However, paralegals will need to use the typeface convention for practitioners, as shown on the back cover and in the Bluepages of *The Bluebook*. Essentially, law review footnotes require the case name to appear in regular typeface, while court documents and legal memoranda require the case name to be set in italics. Students need to remember this going forward. The examples given here reflect the format for court documents and other legal writings and not that for footnotes in law reviews. Therefore, students will have the citation format needed for class and can make comparisons to *ALWD*.

Another major difference in typeface convention is in the *Bluebook's* formatting of citations to constitutions and books. The law review footnote format shows titles in large and small capital letters, while the format for legal memoranda and court documents does not. *ALWD* does not require separate formatting for law reviews and court documents.

USING *THE BLUEBOOK* AND *ALWD*–PRIMARY AUTHORITIES

The citations used most frequently are those for cases, constitutions, statutes, rules, and secondary material.

Cases in General

The citation rules for cases are found in *The Bluebook* Rules 10 and B5, and Rule 12 in *ALWD*. The citation rules begin with an overview of the basic citation form with reference to the key sections of the rule and complete citations for some cases, as well as the **short form** for a citation, as discussed in *The Bluebook* Rule 10.9 and *ALWD* Rule 12.20. The section also supplies examples of cases for various purposes such as cases that are filed but not decided, unpublished decisions, and published decisions. Standard case citations are generally made up of the elements shown in Exhibit 6-1.

Short form
A citation form that is used if the case has been completely identified, so that the reader can easily find the full citation.

EXHIBIT 6-1 ELEMENTS OF CASE CITATIONS

Example:

> *Jones v. White,* 352 Ill.App.3d 316, 816 N.E.2d 1106, 1108 (Ill. App. 4th Dist. 2004).

1. The *name* of the case (usually the last name [or company name] of the first litigant on each side) in italics or underlined; nothing else in the citation is italicized or underlined
2. The *volume number* of the official reporter containing the case (if there is an official reporter)
3. The abbreviation for the official reporter
4. The page number in that official reporter on which the case begins
5. The volume number of the unofficial reporter containing the case (at a minimum)
6. The abbreviation for that unofficial reporter
7. The page number in that unofficial reporter on which the case begins
8. The "pinpoint" page for specific information in that case (if there is a quote)
9. The abbreviation for the court that decided the case (if no official citation is available)
10. The year the case was decided

Although the basic rules may seem straightforward, there are many key elements to remember and numerous intricacies that must be considered in the citation of cases. In each citation, there is a rule for every word, punctuation, space, typeface, and number. For example, if Matthew Mitchell were suing Alaina Mitchell for divorce in a Massachusetts court, the case citation, along with the applicable rules, would be as shown in Example 6-1.

The rules described in this chapter are only a few of the most important elements that paralegals should become familiar with immediately. Paralegals also have the responsibility to check *The Bluebook* or *ALWD* or another appropriate citation manual, as well as local rules, to confirm the proper citation format.

TIP
Researchers may notice that when writing the abbreviation for the second or third series or more, 2d is used rather than 2nd and 3d instead of 3rd. This is a departure from the way one might write these terms in non-legal writings.

Names of Parties If there is more than one party on either side of the case, only the first party's name on each side is listed. So, if the case were *Niece v. McKee* and *Flinn, Flinn* would not be listed.

Correct: *Niece v. McKee*
Incorrect: *Niece v. McKee and Flinn*

EXAMPLE 6-1   RULES FOR A CASE

Mitchell v. Mitchell, 62 Mass. App. Ct. 769, 821 N.E.2d 79 (2005).

The full citation of the case is dictated by *The Bluebook* Rule 10 and B5 and Rule 12 in *ALWD*.

The parties' given names are omitted; hence, the case is *Mitchell v. Mitchell*. *The Bluebook* Rule 10.2.1(g); *ALWD* Rule 12.2(c).

The typeface for case names is always underlined or italicized. *The Bluebook* B5.1.1, B2, and Rule 10.2; *ALWD* Rule 12.2(a)

The "v." means versus; it is always lowercase and followed by a period. *The Bluebook* R.6.1(b); *ALWD* Rule 12.2(a).

Court, jurisdiction, and reporter for Massachusetts are stated according to *The Bluebook* Rule 10.4(b) and T.10; *ALWD* Rule 12.4 and Appendix 1

For spacing of abbreviations, refer to *The Bluebook* Rule 6.1 and T.1 (Massachusetts); *ALWD Rule* 12.4.

The year of the decision is required. *The Bluebook* Rule 10.5; ALWD Rule 12.7.

If the case is on the Internet, the citation must be written as stated in *The Bluebook* Rule 18 and *ALWD* Rule 12.15.

If there has been a consolidation of cases, only the first case is referenced. For example, if the cases of *Alaina Niece v. Abby McKee* and *Thia Flinn v. Ellen Ochsenbein* were consolidated, the reference would be only to *Niece v. McKee*. (*The Bluebook* Rule 10.2.1(a); *ALWD* Rule 12.2(b)(1)).

> **Correct:** *Niece v. McKee*
>
> **Incorrect:** *Niece v. McKee, Flinn v. Ochsenbein*

Terms that indicate additional parties are also omitted, such as "et al." (*ALWD* Rule 12.2(c)(2)) or "d/b/a" (*ALWD* Rule 12.2(e)), as well as other names for a party on either side.

> **Correct:** *Niece v. McKee*
>
> **Incorrect:** *Niece et al. v. McKee d/b/a Pretty Lady Boutique*

The legal status of the parties, as well as other types of descriptive terms, are not listed.

> **Correct:** *Niece v. McKee*
>
> **Incorrect:** *Niece, plaintiff v. McKee, defendant*

If dealing with *in rem* jurisdiction cases (ALWD Rule 12.2(p)), a writer omits everything except the first-listed item or group.

> **Correct:** *In re Golf Course A*
>
> **Incorrect:** *In re Golf Course A, Golf Course B, and Golf Course C*

The Bluebook Rule 10.2.1(b) covers how to cite procedural phrases, such as "on the relation of," "on behalf of," and "in the matter of." All such phrases should be shortened to "*In re*" (*ALWD* Rule 12.2(b)(p)) unless adverse parties are named, in which case "*ex rel*" is used (*ALWD* Rule 12.2(o)(p)).

> **Correct:** *Smith v. Indiana ex rel. Jones*
>
> **Incorrect:** *Smith v. Indiana on the relation of Jones*

EXHIBIT 6-2 ABBREVIATIONS IN CASE NAMES

Word	Abbreviation
And	&
Association	Ass'n
Brothers	Bros.
Company	Co.
Corporation	Corp.
Incorporated	Inc.
Limited	Ltd.
Number	No.

Other examples of correct formats:

In re Lafayette

Estate of Jones v. Smith

Ex parte Friedman

In re Will of Myers

Rule 10.2.1 (c) and Table 6 at *ALWD* Rule 12.2(e)(8) discuss how to abbreviate words within a case name. The key is to abbreviate any well-known acronyms, such as National Labor Relations Board (N.L.R.B.). Exhibit 6-2 shows eight of the most common abbreviations used in cases. Notice that all of the abbreviations include periods, except "&" and "ass'n."

One question that often arises is when to use the word "the" in a case citation. "The" is omitted if it is the first word of a party's name, but is included if the case is an *in rem* action or if it identifies the highest royalty (*The Bluebook* Rule 10.2.1(d); *ALWD* Rule 12.2(q)).

- **Correct:** *Indianapolis Power & Light Co. v. Simmons*
- **Incorrect:** *The IPaLCo v. Simmons*
- **Correct:** *Chicago Tribune v. Wrigley*
- **Incorrect:** *The Chicago Tribune v. Wrigley*
- **Correct:** *Prince v. The King*
- **Incorrect:** *The Prince v. The King*

It is particularly important to know when to use part of the party's name or omit descriptive terms such as titles. In some cases, a certain word may be essential, and in some names, it should be omitted (*The Bluebook* Rule 10.2.1(e); *ALWD* Rule 12.2(e)(p)).

Correct: *Smithfield v. Canfield*

Incorrect: *Smithfield v. Canfield, Executor*

Correct: *Trustees of Harvard v. Johnson*

Incorrect: *Board of Trustees of Harvard v. Johnson*

When a title includes geographic terms, such as "State of," "People of," or "Commonwealth of," the term is included when the decision being cited is from that state (*The Bluebook* Rule 10.2.1(f); *ALWD* Rule 12.2(l)). For example, Massachusetts is a commonwealth, so in cases decided in that state, the state name would appear as follows:

Correct: *Commonwealth v. Spadoni*, 126 Mass. 198, 298 N.E.2d 100 (1999).

Incorrect: *Commonwealth of Massachusetts v. Spadoni*

However, if the case were not being cited within the geographic region, the citation would be *Massachusetts v. Spadoni*, 487 U.S. 199 (2001). In this citation, the case is before the U.S. Supreme Court, so it is outside the jurisdiction of Massachusetts. Geographic designations that are *not preceded* by a preposition are retained. Thus, *Tyson v. Indiana Department of Corrections* is the correct format, while *Smith v. Board of Public Works of Cincinnati* is not.

One of the easy ways to initially determine that a case is a criminal matter instead of a civil matter is to look at the parties. If one of the parties is a state, it is probably a criminal matter. Some states are technically "commonwealths" rather than states. There are only four states that are designated as "commonwealths": Kentucky, Massachusetts, Pennsylvania, and Virginia. In these cases, only the word "State" or "Commonwealth" is used, and the name of the state or commonwealth is omitted.

Correct: *State v. Tyson*, 334 N.E.2d 176 (Ind. 1999).

Incorrect: *State of Indiana v. Tyson*, 334 N.E.2d 176 (Ind. 1999).

Correct: *Commonwealth v. Smith*, 268 S.E.2d 119 (Va. 2001).

Incorrect: *Commonwealth of Virginia v. Smith*, 268 S.E.2d 119 (Va. 2001).

This guideline usually holds true unless the case was not decided by a court in the state. An example would be a criminal case that is appealed to the U.S. Supreme Court:

Correct: *Indiana v. Tyson*, 419 U.S. 327 (2001).

Incorrect: *State of Indiana v. Tyson*, 419 U.S. 327 (2001).

Correct: *Virginia v. Smith*, 399 U.S. 284 (2000).

Incorrect: *Commonwealth of Virginia v. Smith*, 399 U.S. 284 (2000).

The parties' first names and initials are omitted unless the names or initials are of businesses (*The Bluebook* Rule 10.2.1(g)(h); *ALWD* Rule 12.2(c)(d)(e)).

Correct: *Mitchell v. Mitchell*

Incorrect: *Michael Mitchell v. Margaret Mitchell*

Correct: *H.H. Gregg v. Facemeyer*

Incorrect: *Gregg v. Facemeyer (because H.H. Gregg is a business)*

When dealing with foreign names the surname is included, along with all following names, such as del Carmen Galbis Díez. Chinese and other Asian names present special situations, since the given name follows the surname, such as Yao Ming of the Houston Rockets. The citation would be *Yao Ming v. Perry*.

When businesses are parties, some abbreviations are omitted when the second abbreviation restates a similar term such as "Ltd.," "Inc.," or "L.L.C." and follows a term such as "Co.," "Corp.," or "Ass'n" (*The Bluebook* Rule 10.2.1(h); *ALWD* Rule 12.2(e)(5)(8))

Correct: *Southern Expectations Co. v. Shendell*

Incorrect: *Southern Expectations Co., Inc. v. Shendell*

Working in employment and labor law means frequently working with cases involving unions. The union name should be cited using the simplest terminology. The United Auto Workers is UAW, and Local 51, International Brotherhood of Teamsters, Chauffeurs, Warehousemen & Helpers, is Local 51, Int'l Brotherhood of Teamsters. These and other abbreviations are found in *The Bluebook* Rule 10.2.1(i) and *ALWD* Rule 12.2(f).

Reporters

The names of early American reporters may seem peculiar because they were often named after the editors rather than the courts from which the cases were reported. For example, in Indiana the early Supreme Court reports dating back to 1830 were called *Blackford's Reports*, after Isaac Blackford who was not only an Indiana Supreme Court justice but also its editor and publisher.

Today, however, these reporters are cited by the official series name, and the name of the editor is omitted.

The early *United States Reports* are similar to the early state reporters in that from 1790 to 1874, they were named for the editors—Wallace, Black, Howard, Peters, Wheaton, Cranch, and Dallas. An early *U.S. Reports* citation would appear as *Green v. White,* 1 Wall.100 (1863). Today, the citation is written as *Green v. White,* 68 U.S. (1 Wall.) 125 (1863). These rules are found in *The Bluebook* R. 10.3.2 and Table 1 and in *ALWD* Sidebar 12.4.

Cases today may be published in both "official" and "unofficial" reporters. The official versions are published by the government, and contain only the case as written by the court. The unofficial version is provided by a publishing company, under the direction of the court, and has additional information and features written by the company. These added features include a ***synopsis or syllabus***, ***headnotes***, ***key topics***, and ***key numbers***. A researcher should always check the availability of both official and unofficial case reporters in their jurisdiction.

The names of reporters and other sources are governed by *The Bluebook* Rule 10.3, table 1 (T.1) and Appendix 1, 1A and 1B and *ALWD* Rule 12.4. If a state has both official and unofficial citations, these are referred to as ***parallel citations*** (*The Bluebook* Rule 10.3.1; *ALWD* Rule 12.4(d)). For example, if a case is reported from the Iowa Supreme Court, it will be reported in the Iowa reports and also in the *North Western Reporter*.

Some states no longer publish official reporters, and in those jurisdictions, the writer should cite the unofficial version, and include the jurisdiction (the court) in the parentheses with the date. However, local court rules ultimately dictate the proper format and should be checked.

Where no preference or rule is given as to which reporter to cite, a writer should cite to the appropriate regional reporter and then indicate the court and its geographical jurisdiction within the parentheses with the date of the decision. However, if the case is from the state's highest court, the name of the court should not be included. For example, the highest court in the state of Indiana is the Indiana Supreme Court. The proper information would be (Ind. 2009), not (Ind. Sup. Ct. 2009). However, the middle court of appeals in Indiana would appear in a citation as (Ind. Ct. App.).

A full citation should include both the official and unofficial reporters if both are available. A writer provides these parallel citations as a courtesy to the reader because the writer never knows which service the reader may have access to. This fulfills the purpose of citations—providing the reader with access to the material. Citing both official and unofficial versions has an additional purpose within the law office. Internal memoranda often become trial briefs that are submitted to the court, and the court may require parallel citations. If the citations already exist within the memorandum, work is not duplicated by reviewing each source to find the parallel citation for the trial brief.

TIP

He also happened to be a territorial judge and first speaker of the Indiana House.

Syllabus or synopsis

A one-paragraph summary of a court opinion, usually identifying how the case arrived at the current point within the legal system. It is usually found only in an unofficial reporter.

Headnotes

Paragraphs of information that summarize points of law.

Key topics

A set of 400 legal topics developed by the West Publishing Company to organize key numbers and help researchers find legal authorities.

Key numbers

A series of more than 80,000 numbers assigned by West Publishing Company to summaries of points of law. All topics and key numbers are the same in every state and in the federal system.

Parallel citations

Citations reported in more than one location or source. Example: a case from the Nevada Supreme Court that is reported in *Nevada Reports* and the *Pacific 2d* reporter.

The Bluebook Rule 10.3.2 and *ALWD* Rules 12.3 and 12.4 discuss how to cite to a reporter. There are four basic components: 1) volume number, 2) the reporter designation, 3) the page upon which the case begins, and 4) the date in parentheses for all bound print cases and annotations.

> **Correct:** *Wemple ex rel. Dang v. Dahman*, 103 Haw. 385, 83 P.3d 100 (2004).

> **Incorrect:** *Wemple ex rel. Dang v. Dahman*, 103 Hawai'i 385, 83 Pacific 3d 100 (2004).

Citations for federal cases normally will be to the *Federal Reporter* (F., F.2d, F.3d), but may also be found in specialized reporters such as the *Bankruptcy Reporter* (B.R.) for the bankruptcy appellate panel. The U.S. Court of Federal Claims, U.S. Court of International Trade, U.S. Tax Court, and other specialized courts have individual reporters. Thomson/West publishes a reporter of "unreported" U.S. Court of Appeals decisions, called the *Federal Appendix* (Fed. Appx.), because of the online availability of unpublished U.S. Court of Appeals' cases.

Pinpoint Citations: Court and Jurisdiction A common error among students and practitioners alike is the failure to make a citation complete when there is no official reporter. Citations are sometimes written with only the unofficial reporter and the date. A vital piece of the citation format is missing: the jurisdiction. The jurisdiction is necessary to show where the case originated. For example, the citation *Wemple ex rel. Dang v. Dahman,* 103 Haw. 385, 83 P.3d 100 (2004) makes it easy to determine that the case comes from the Hawai'i Supreme Court because it is in the official citation form for Hawai'i Supreme Court cases (103 Haw. 385). However, if the Hawai'i Supreme Court no longer published the official reporter, the unofficial regional reporter (P.3d) would be used. In that event, the jurisdiction needs to be specified:

> **Correct:** *Wemple ex rel. Dang v. Dahman*, 83 P.3d 100 (Haw. 2004).

> **Incorrect:** *Wemple ex rel. Dang v. Dahman*, 83 P.3d 100 (2004).

In the incorrect example, all that is known is that the case is found in the Pacific regional reporter. This jurisdiction cannot be identified as any specific one of the 14 states reported in the *Pacific Reporter*. The reader would not know the jurisdiction and, consequently, how much authority to give this source. If the reader is in Arizona, this Hawaiian case is only persuasive authority, not mandatory authority. However, if the correct citation is presented, the reader knows immediately that it is a case from Hawaii. (*The Bluebook* R. 10.4, T.1 or T.2, T.7, and T.10; *ALWD* Rule 12.4(c)(d), Sidebar 12.5, Appendix 1).

Federal Courts

Citations to the federal courts are governed by *The Bluebook* Rule 10.4(a) and *ALWD* Rule 12.4(c), Sidebar 12.4, App. 1. U.S. Supreme Court cases are generally cited to the *United States Reports* (U.S.). Since only Supreme Court decisions are reported in those books, no other identifying information is needed, unless a case was decided prior to 1875. A proper citation would be *Roe v. Wade*, 410 U.S. 113 (1973). However, if there is no access to the *United States Reports* (U.S.), citations can be made to the *Supreme Court Reporter* (S.Ct.), *United States Supreme Court*

Reports, Lawyers' Edition and *Lawyers' Edition 2d* (L.Ed.2d), or *United States Law Week* (U.S.L.W.), in that order of preference.

When citing cases from U.S. circuit courts, the circuits are identified numerically, with two exceptions: the Federal Circuit and the United States Court of Appeals for the District of Columbia. Example 6-2 shows proper citation format for the United States Courts of Appeals.

- **Correct:** 7th Cir. (United States Court of Appeals for the Seventh Circuit)
- **Incorrect:** C.C.A.7th
- **Incorrect:** CA7
- **Correct:** D.C. Cir. (United States Court of Appeals for the District of Columbia)
- **Correct:** Fed. Cir. (United States Court of Appeals for the Federal Circuit)
- **Correct:** *Brown v. Hot, Sexy and Safer Productions,* 68 F.3d 525 (1st Cir. 1995). (indicating the First Circuit)

United States District Court case citations include the district but not the division. These cases can be found primarily in the *Federal Supplement* (F. Supp., F. Supp.2d). Other reporters include the *Federal Rules Decisions* (F.R.D.), West's *Bankruptcy Reporter* (B.R.), *Federal Rules Service* (Fed. R. Serv., Fed. R. Serv. 2d,, Fed. R. Serv.3d), *Federal Cases* (F. Cases.), and a few specialty reporters.

A researcher should check the tables of *The Bluebook* or the appendices of *ALWD* to make sure that the appropriate designation is included, since district courts in some states use Eastern and Western, some use Northern, Southern and Central, and others simply use District. Example 6-3 provides citation formats for some district court cases.

State Courts

When citing to a state case, a researcher should first determine whether the state has an official reporter and what the local court rules require. For most states, if an official reporter exists, and the local court rules require it, the official reporter should be cited, followed by the unofficial reporter and the date in parentheses. If there is no official reporter, the court designation is placed in parentheses with the date of the decision. Researchers should consult *The Bluebook* T.1 and BT 2, *ALWD* Appendices 1 and 2, and local rules for the individual state to confirm the proper format. Generally, for the highest court, the state abbreviation is used, and for the lower court, state and court abbreviations are used, as shown in Example 6-4.

EXAMPLE 6-3   U.S. DISTRICT COURT CASE CITATIONS

- **Correct:** S.D.N.Y. (Southern District of New York)
- **Incorrect:** S.D.N.Y.C.D. (Southern District of New York, Central Division)
- **Correct:** *Doe v. Bolton,* 319 F. Supp. 1048 (N.D. Ga. 1970). (For the Northern District Court in Georgia)
- **Incorrect:** *Doe v. Bolton,* 319 F. Supp. 1048 (N.D. Ga. C.D. 1970).

EXAMPLE 6-4   STATE COURT CITATIONS

- **Correct:** *Wind v. Willows,* 238 S.W.2d 193 (Ark. 2000).
- **Incorrect:** *Wind v. Willows,* 238 S.W.2d 193 (Ark. Sup. Ct. 2000).
- **Correct:** *Ramone v. Lydon,* 112 SW.2d 389 (Ark. Ct. App. 2000).
- **Incorrect:** *Ramone v. Lydon,* 112 S.W.2d 389 (Ark. App. 2000).

Cases on the Internet

Although nearly any case may be found using computer-assisted legal research (CALR), combining online research with traditional library techniques is often the best way to thoroughly research most legal issues, according to many researchers. However, as the cost of books and library space continues to sky-rocket, firms are maintaining smaller print libraries and relying more on the Internet, either through free sites or paid subscription services such as Westlaw and LexisNexis. The cases available on these services are more up-to-date, and there are some opinions that are available on the Internet but are not published in the printed volumes.

Some additional rules specifically apply to Internet citations, as set forth in *The Bluebook* R. 18 and *ALWD* Rules 38, 40. In general, a full citation to a work from the Internet must include the following components:

- The author's full name, or the name of the site owner if the author cannot be determined. (If the author or site owner cannot be determined, the citation must begin with the title.)
- The main title plus the title from a particular page in italics.
- A pinpoint citation such as a paragraph or section number.
- The date and time as appearing on the site, or if none, the note "last updated" or "last modified.[1]
- The URL (primary if there are multiple URLs) containing the protocol (http:), domain name, directory, and file:

  http://www.domain.edu/directory/file

TIP

See The *Bluebook* R. 10.3.3 (public domain format), R. 10.8.1 (pending or unreported cases), and R. 18 (electronic media) or *ALWD* Rules 12.4, 12.12. and 12.15 (case citation), 39 (Westlaw and LexisNexis), 40.1 (full citation format), and 38 (online citations).

For opinions found at one of the law school sites or on Findlaw.com, the proper format must include the parties, pagination and publication date, and the Internet URL appended at the end of the citation:

Marbury v. Madison, 5 U.S. 137 (1803), available at http://www.law.cornell.edu/supct/html/historics/USSC_CR_0005_0137_ZS.html

If the Internet is the only location, *"available at"* should not be used.

Cases found on Westlaw and LexisNexis have unique citation formats, but each service is slightly different.

Example 6-5 shows examples of Internet citation formatting.

The purpose of Westlaw and LexisNexis citations, like any citations, is to allow the reader to find the cases cited. However, a case should only be cited to Westlaw or LexisNexis if it is not available in a traditional reporter. If both are available, the citation should be only to the printed volume.

---

[1]*The Bluebook,* Rule 18.2.2(c)

EXAMPLE 6-5   UNREPORTED CASES ON WESTLAW AND LEXISNEXIS

> *Washington v. Werner*, No. 96-8-00197-6, 1998 WL 283537 (Wash. Ct. App. June 2, 1998).
>
> *Albrecht v. Stanczek*, No. 87-C9535, 1991 U.S. Dist. LEXIS 5088 (N.D. Ill. Apr. 18, 1991).

1. Washington v. Werner and Albrecht v. Stanczek are parties' names.

2. No. 96-8-00197-6 and No. 87-C9535 are docket numbers.

3. 1998 WL 283537: 1998 indicates that it was decided in 1998; WL means Westlaw, so this is a case published on Westlaw; 283537 is the internal number on Westlaw.

   1991 U.S. Dist. LEXIS 5088: 1991 indicates the decision date; U.S. Dist. Lexis indicates it was a U.S. District Court case; 5088 is the internal number on LexisNexis.

4. Wash. Ct. App. June 2, 1998 and N.D. Ill. Apr. 18, 1991 show the court and date of decision.

SHORT CITATION FORMS

Short citation forms are used once a case has been completely cited and subsequent references to the citation are needed. There are two basic forms that must be used: *Id.,* or the case name in ***short form***. These two forms are not interchangeable, and each has a specific purpose.[2] The most important, overarching rule regarding the citation of cases is to avoid confusing the reader.

Short Forms for Cases

Id. is an abbreviation of the Latin for *idem,* meaning "the same." The main purpose of the *id.* notation is to save space while providing the reader with the information necessary to understand the cited material. When *id.* is used, there can be no additional citations between the full citation and *id. Id.* is italicized or underlined, is followed by a period, and is capitalized only if it begins a citation sentence. If the cite is to the same page as was previously cited, only *id* is written, without the page number. If the cite is to a different page of the same case, *id.* is written with "at" followed by the page number upon which the information appears. For example, if a citation is made to a specific page of a (fictional) case, the first reference would read like this:

> *Wind v. Willows*, 238 S.E.2d 193, 195 (Ark. 2000).

If the analysis of that case continues, it may be necessary to reference another point on the same page of the case:

- **Correct:** *Id.*
- **Incorrect:** *Id.* at 195.

However, if the next point referenced is on page 196, the notation would change:

- **Correct:** *Id.* at 196.
- **Incorrect:** *Id.* 196.
- **Incorrect:** Id. at 193, 196.

Id.
A note referring the reader to the full citation that immediately precedes the reference in the document. Its main purpose is to save space while still providing the reader with the information necessary to understand the material presented.

Short form
A citation form that is used if the case has been completely identified, so that the reader can easily find the full citation.

---

[2]*The Bluebook* Rule 10.9, 18.8; *ALWD* 12.2, 40.2

If the preceding citation is a string of citations, *id* is not used. In that instance, the short form is used.

The short form of case citations is used to cite to a previously cited case when other authority has intervened between the original citation and the second reference. Rules for the short form are found at B5.2 and R. 10.9 in *The Bluebook* and Rule 44.2 in *ALWD*. The short form must include 1) the shortened case name; 2) the volume number of reporter; 3) the abbreviation of the reporter name; 4) "at"; and 5) the **pinpoint** page number.[3]

Pinpoint

The exact page in a case on which the referenced information is found.

- **Correct:** *Wind,* 238 S.E.2d at 195.
- **Correct:** 238 S.E.2d at 195.
- **Incorrect:** *Wind v. Willows,* 238 S.E.2d 193 at 195 (Ark. 2000).
- **Incorrect:** *Wind,* 238 S.E.2d 193 at 195.
- **Incorrect:** *Willows,* 238 S.E.2d at 195.

In some cases, the name of the second party may be used if using the name of the first party will confuse the reader. For example, if multiple cases are found where *Wind* was a party, using the name of the second party might avoid confusion. Or, if the research resulted in several criminal cases in California, it would be confusing if each case were referenced as "*State.*" In that instance, a writer would choose the second party for one or more of the cases to avoid confusion.

In the short form, names are also shortened, particularly those of businesses, as long as the result is not confusing to the reader. For example, if a cited case were *Goodyear Tire & Rubber Co.,* a writer could shorten the case name to *Goodyear* as long as the reader would not be confused.

If a parallel citation is required, the short form is slightly different. For the parallel citation of the fictional case *Wind v. Willows,* 198 Ark. 304, 238 S.W.2d 193 (2000), the short form would include both the official and unofficial reporters, so that it would appear as follows:

- **Correct:** *Wind,* 198 Ark. at 306, 238 S.W.2d at 195.
- **Correct:** 198 Ark. at 306, 238 S.W.2d at 195.
- **Incorrect:** *Wind v. Willows,* 198 Ark. 304 at 306, 238 S.W.2d 193 at 195 (Ark. 2000).
- **Incorrect:** *Wind,* 198 Ark. 304 at 306, 238 S.W.2d 193 at 195.

These are just a few of the most frequently used rules for citing cases. When faced with a new or different type of citation, check *The Bluebook, ALWD,* or some other appropriate citing source before submitting any document. All sources should be double-checked to make sure that the authorities are properly cited in the document.

Constitutions

A citation for a constitutional provision is specified in *The Bluebook* Rules 11 and B6 and *ALWD* Rule 13. The citation must include these elements:

1. the abbreviation of the constitution
2. the abbreviation for the word "amendment" or "article"
3. amendment number or article number
4. section symbol (§)
5. section number
6. abbreviation for clause
7. clause number

[3]*The Bluebook* R. B5.2, R. 10.9, and R. 18.8; *ALWD* 11.2, 12.20, and 40.2

TABLE 6-1   Citing the Constitution

Correct	Incorrect
U.S. Const. art. III, §2.	United States Const. Art. III, section 2.
N.J. Const. art. II, §2, cl. 1.	N.J. const. article II, section 2, clause 1.
U.S. Const. amend. XVIII (repealed 1933).	United States Const. amendment XVIII (*repealed by* amend. XXI).
U.S. Const. amend. XVIII, *repealed by* U.S. Const. amend. XXI.	U.S. Const. Amend. XVIII, (*repealed by* U.S. Const. amend. XXI 1933).

One major difference between this citation format and those previously discussed is that there is no date. A date would be used only if one were citing to a provision that has been amended, superseded, or repealed, as shown in Table 6-1.

When parts of the U.S. Constitution are discussed in textual sentences, *The Bluebook* R.8 requires that those parts be capitalized. A constitution is capitalized when naming it in full or anytime the U.S. Constitution is discussed (*The Bluebook* R. 8; *ALWD* Sidebar 13.1). Example 6-6 illustrates these rules in practice.

Id. is the only short form used for constitutions. If the constitutional citation appears later in a document, the full citation must be used.

Statutes and Legislative Materials

Statutes passed by legislatures are initially presented as **session laws**. Once the session concludes, the session laws are **codified**, usually by subject matter. For example, in the *United States Code*, all statutes regarding bankruptcy are found in Title 11. All statutes regarding copyright are in Title 17. This holds true for state statutes, too. In Indiana, all statutes for motor vehicles are in Title 9 and all statutes for probate are in Title 29.

Both official and unofficial versions of the statutes are available, just as there are official and unofficial versions of the cases. The official version is the preferred source. For example, the official version of the federal code is the *United States Code* (U.S.C.).

Multiple unofficial versions are also available, most notably the *United States Code Annotated* (U.S.C.A.), published by Thomson Reuters (West), and the *United States Code Service* (U.S.C.S.), distributed by LexisNexis. While the official code gives only the statute as it comes from the legislature, the unofficial versions provide additional help such as notes to decisions, cross-references to forms and secondary material, and other helpful information.

Session laws
Laws that are passed during a session of the legislature. The laws are presented chronologically as passed and then, at the end of the session, are codified into the statutory scheme of the state or federal systems.

Codified
The process of taking session laws from the legislatures and organizing them, usually by subject matter.

TIP

The United States Code is codified only once every six years. If a statute is being read online in Westlaw or LexisNexis and a year appears next to the code provision, it indicates the most current unofficial code.

TIP

A statute is printed in regular type with no underlining or italicizing of any part of the statute.

EXAMPLE 6-6   CAPITALIZATION AND THE CONSTITUTION

Correct: "The equal protection clause in the California Constitution is similar to the Equal Protection Clause in the U.S. Constitution."

Correct: The U.S. Const. art. IV, §1 (as a citation).

Correct: The court relied on search and seizure as found in the U.S. Constitution Article IV, Section 1 (in textual sentences).

Correct: Ca. Const. art. 1, §7 (as a citation).

Correct: The California court relied on article I, section 7, or the equal protection clause (in textual sentences).

Some states, however, have ceased publishing the official versions of the statutes, just as they have ceased publishing the official versions of cases. While some states continue to publish the official statutes, others use only the legal publishers. Further, some of the states publish on either Westlaw or LexisNexis, some publish on both, and some states (such as California and Kansas) use other online publishers. If the state has an official code, that source should be cited. Because of the multiple versions of codes, it is a good practice to refer to the citator (such as *The Bluebook* Rules 12 and B5 and *ALWD* Rule 14) and local rules to find out exactly what each jurisdiction requires with regard to published statutes.

Formatting   Statute citations are generally made up of the following parts:

1. the title of the code (often included in the section numbering),
2. the abbreviation for the name of the code,
3. the section symbol and section number being cited, and
4. the year of the current code volume.

A citation to a federal statute would appear in one of two ways:

42 U.S.C. § 1983 (2000).

42 U.S.C.A. § 1983 (West 2000).

Sometimes federal statutes are known by common names. In those instances, the writer would provide the official name of the act along with all the information for the statute. Here is an example:

Richard B. Russell National School Lunch Act, 42 U.S.C. § 1751 (1946).

State statutes may appear differently both stylistically and by typeface. For example, this is a citation to the Indiana Code:

Correct: typeface for law review—IND. CODE § 31-1-2-3 (2003) or IND. CODE ANN. § 31-1-2-3 (West 2003) or IND. CODE ANN. § 31-1-2-3 (LexisNexis 2003).

Correct: typeface for court documents and legal memoranda—Ind. Code § 31-1-2-3 (2003) or Ind. Code Ann. § 31-1-2-3 (West 2003) or Ind. Code Ann. § 31-1-2-3 (LexisNexis 2003).

Incorrect: I.C. § 31-1-2-3 or I.C.A. § 31-1-2-3.

In Indiana, "31" is the title, "1" is the article, "2" is the chapter, and "3" is the section. Other states may have a different format, such as Iowa:

Iowa Code § 185.4 (2005) or Iowa Code Ann. § 185.4 (West 2005).

Iowa's statutory form does not resemble that used in the federal system or in Indiana's system. Each state's statutory citation format may appear differently, and it is important to check local rules and cross-reference that format with the appropriate citation manual. Exhibit 6-3 provides tips to find the proper citation form for a state.

Title of the Code

The title of the code, or the code name, should always be included, and should be checked for the preferred format of the state in question. If there is no preference in that jurisdiction, any of the options available may be used. For example, there are three Indiana citation formats. However, the stated preference is

EXHIBIT 6-3 FINDING A STATE'S STATUTORY CITATION FORMAT

1. Locate the appropriate state information (*The Bluebook* T.1 and *ALWD* Appendix 1). For example, Indiana appears on page 240 T.1 of *The Bluebook* and 419 Appendix 1 of *ALWD*.

2. Look in the Indiana information for "statutory compilations."

3. Under the heading are two columns of information in *The Bluebook*; on the left are references to the various sources and on the right is the appropriate format. For example, the following appears for Indiana where each "x" represents a portion of the citation, such as 31-1-2-3:

Indiana Code: Ind. Code § x-x-x-x (year).

West's Annotated Indiana Code: Ind. Code Ann. § x-x-x-x (West year).

Burn's Indiana Statutes Annotated: Ind. Code Ann. § x-x-x-x (LexisNexis year).

New Jersey citations would look like this:

New Jersey Statutes Annotated N.J. Stat. Ann. § x:x (West year).
New Jersey Revised Statutes (1937) N.J. Rev. Stat. § x:x (year).

ALWD information is basically the same as the information in *The Bluebook*, but instead of using "x", *ALWD* shows "Ind. Code § 34-1-1-1 (Year), Ind. Code Ann. § section number (LexisNexis year)," "Ind. Code Ann. §34-1-1-1 (West year)."

In any state's citation format, "x" or the words "section number" will represent some reference number to fill that slot. The citation form should be used by substituting the proper numerical references and making sure that the correct code year is in parentheses. This format should be copied exactly, but one should use regular type rather than the law review and footnote typeface when using *The Bluebook*. This is the same as the federal statutes, where T.1 shows "x U.S.C. § x" (year). A citation to the *United States Code* would be 42 U.S.C. § 2001 (2000).

to cite to Ind. Code, if therein. In Louisiana, one may cite from one of six listed codes. In Kentucky, two options are given. The title should be properly abbreviated in citations but not in textual sentences.

Some states have separate codes for specific subject matter. Among Louisiana's six options for codes are "subject matter codes." New York and Texas are two other states that rely on codes designated for certain subject matters. When a state code is organized this way, the subject matter is included as part of the code name. For example, Vernon's Texas Business Corporation Act Annotated is formatted as "Tex. Bus. Corp. Act Ann. Art. X (Vernon year)."

Sections and Subsections

In citations to specific sections of a statute, the code name or title is followed by a section symbol (§). (Simulation 6-1 explains how to make a section or paragraph symbol.) In textual sentences, however, the word *section* is spelled out.

The format for the section number will vary by state, and may include dashes, colons, periods, words, or any combination with the section number, so the appropriate format should always be confirmed. A space is always included

> ### SIMULATION 6-1   CREATING § AND ¶ SYMBOLS
>
> For PCs: Hold the "ALT" key while typing "21" on the keypad. To make a paragraph symbol, hold the "ALT" key while typing "20." Note: This will not work with the numbers at the top of the keyboard, only with the keypad numbers. Thus, this will work only if "NumLock" is turned on.
>
> The second option is to go to the "Insert" dropdown menu, select "symbol," and look through the various symbols for the § or ¶ symbol. Insert the symbol and close the box. Creating a keyboard shortcut or "hotkey" might be a timesaving idea, since these symbols are used frequently in legal writing.
>
> - For Macs: Hold the "Option" key and type 6 for a section symbol or 7 for a paragraph symbol. The numbers at the top of the keyboard will work for this application.

between the section symbol and the section number. When citing a specific subsection of a statute, the entire section number, followed by the subsection number, should be provided; these are often separated by dashes or parentheses. The subsections are generally used as pinpoint citations to identify the specific portion of the statute being cited.

Publisher, Supplements, and Date

The name of the publisher may be necessary depending on the code and the applicable rules. If using the official code, the publisher is not included. However, if using an unofficial code, the name of the publisher is placed in the parentheses with the date of the code.

Unless an online service such as Westlaw or LexisNexis is being used, it is necessary to check the **pocket parts** for the most recent updates to a statute. If a statute has been updated through a supplement, the citation format must include "Supp." with the date in parentheses. If using an unofficial code, the publisher is included before "Supp." For example, citing a supplement to an unofficial version of a New Jersey statute would appear as follows: N.J. Stat. Ann § 3:17-1 (West Supp. 2004).

The code year must also be included in the citation, which may be found on the book spine or on the title page. The order of preference is to use the date on the book spine first, and if none is on the spine, to use the date on the title page. If no date appears in either place, the copyright date is used. The code year is not the year the statute was enacted—it is the year of the latest printing of the code. The date of the supplement may be found on the title page of the supplement. If there is no year on the title page of the supplement, then the copyright year of the supplement is used. For example, a citation to a New Jersey statute last printed in 2003, and supplemented in 2006, would read N.J. Stat. Ann § 3:17-1 (2003 & Supp. 2006). Table 6-2 shows a variety of examples found in different states.

Multiple Sections and Subsections

If multiple statutory sections are cited, the section numbers should be separated by a hyphen with two section symbols (§§) to indicate multiple sections. For example: 42 U.S.C. §§ 2001–2011 (2000). On the other hand, if citing a statute that spans more than one subsection within a section, one section symbol is

Pocket parts
Paperback inserts that update authorities until a new bound volume is created, usually located in the back of the volume or in a separate paperback volume.

TIP

Confusion may be encountered when citing supplements or even publishers. In recent years, publishing companies have consolidated. Lawyers' Cooperative became part of LexisNexis, and West became part of Thomson Reuters. Some states may have print copies of codes or supplements (pocket parts) that identify one publisher, while *The Bluebook* or *ALWD* shows a different publisher. In general, one should follow the examples in T.1 of *The Bluebook* and Appendix 1 in *ALWD* for the citation formation and then insert the correct publisher's name as needed.

TABLE 6-2 State Statute Samples

Appearance in *The Bluebook*	Appearance in *ALWD*	Appearance in Usage
N.J. STAT. ANN. § x:x (West year)	N.J. Stat. Ann. § [section number] (West Year)	N.J. Stat. Ann § 3:17-1 (West 2004)
Ohio Rev. Code Ann. § x.x (Lexis/Nexis year)	Ohio Rev. Code Ann. § [section number] (Lexis year)	Ohio Rev. Code Ann. § 3313.6012 (LexisNexis 2003) or Ohio Rev. Code Ann. § 3313.6012 (Lexis 2003)
[Chapter number] Ill. Comp. Stat. [no./sec. no.] (year)	[Chapter number] Ill. Comp. Stat. [article number/section number] (Year)	110 Ill. Comp. Stat. 305/8a (2003)
N.C. Gen. Stat. § x–x (year) (LexisNexis)	N.C. Gen. Stat. § [section number] (Lexis Year)	N.C. Gen. Stat. § 116-11(10a) (LexisNexis 2003) or (Lexis 2003) respectively
Okla. Stat. tit. x, § x (year)	Okla. Stat. tit. Title number, § [section number] (Year)	Okla. Stat. tit. 70, § 1210.531(C) (2003)
Tex. [subject] Code Ann. § x (West year)	Tex. [Subject Abbreviation] Code Ann. § [section number] (Vernon Year)	Tex. Educ. Code Ann. § 51.403(e) (West 2003) or (Vernon 2003) respectively

used (§), and subsections are separated with a hyphen. An example is N.C. Gen. Stat. § 116-11(10a)-(10d) (West 2003). Digits that repeat should be dropped if those digits precede a punctuation mark, unless the reader is confused. If there is a possibility of confusion, the repeated digits are retained, or the word *to* is added to separate the sections or subsections. For example: Ind. Code Ann. § 31-1-2-3 to -5. If Ind. Code Ann. § 31-1-2-3-5 were written, a reader would be very confused!

Session Laws Session laws are not encountered often by most researchers. However, the basic citation form should be learned.

Session laws can be either "public" or "private." Public laws affect the public generally. Examples are tax and bankruptcy law. Private laws affect individuals or small groups rather than the public at large. An example of a private law would be an immigration law addressing the entry of a person or family after the quota of the home country has been met. Private laws are few in comparison to public laws, which are passed each session.

Session laws may also be permanent or temporary. If a law is temporary, it will have an expiration date, while a permanent law will continue until another law is passed to repeal it.

When each law is passed by the federal legislature, it is published by the United States Government Printing Office (GPO) and referred to as a "*slip law*." When the legislative session ends, the individual laws are bound in chronological order in *United States Statutes at Large*. It takes an extended period of time for the *United States Statutes at Large* to be published.

States' session laws are generally published within a shorter period of time. The bound volumes may be called Acts of [State], session laws, or some other name. Each state's session law names are listed in *The Bluebook* T.1 and *ALWD* Appendix 1.

In the citation of a session law, the first element is the name of the statute, which should accompany the public law or chapter number. The official name, popular name, or both, are used, but if the word *the* is the first word of the law's name, it is not included in the citation. If the statute does not have a popular or official name, the act

Slip law

A single law passed by Congress or state legislature; so called shortly after it has been issued and before it is codified.

EXAMPLE 6-7   SESSION LAW CITATION

- Joint Resolution of Nov. 23, 1993, Pub. L. No. 103-150, 107 Stat. 1510 (Lexis through 1996 legislation).
- White-Slave Traffic (Mann) Act, ch. 395, 36 Stat. 825 (1910) (codified as amended at 18 U.S.C. §§ 2421-2424 (2000)).[4]

These citations can be identified as follows:

1. Titles or descriptive information: Joint Resolution of Nov. 23, 1993 and White-Slave Traffic (Mann) Act

2. Session of legislature and chronological bill number: Pub. L. No. 103-150: Public Law Number 103–150

3. Volume and page numbers: 107 Stat. 1510. 107 is volume number of *Statutes at Large* and 1510 is the page on which the text of the law begins; 36 is the volume number and 825 is the page number

4. Chapter number: Ch. 395

5. Date

[4]*The Bluebook* Rule 12.4

---

is identified by a full date with the expression "Act of [date]" or "Act effective [date]." Next, the volume number of the session laws is given, or the year if no volume number exists, followed by the abbreviation for the name of the session laws.

The *Statutes at Large* are the official session laws, and the abbreviation for this service is "Stat." Example 6-7 shows how its citation would appear.

If the statute has been or will be codified, the code information should be cited parenthetically, if it is known.

Statutes on the Internet   Internet resources for statutes have particular concerns and considerations. When citing to material on the Internet, the Uniform Resource Locator (URL) should be stated precisely so that the reader will be taken directly to the source cited. The home page of a site is not sufficient. If the URL is simple and understandable, the entire address, as it appears in the browser's address bar, should be used. There are times, however, when the source used has a very long, unwieldy URL that is full of textual and non-textual characters. In those instances, it is sufficient to use the root URL of the site followed by a parenthetical that explains how to access the information.[5]

A parallel citation to an Internet source with the same content as a print source may be provided if it improves access to the source cited, according to *The Bluebook* Rule 18.2.2 and *ALWD* Rule 38. The Internet citation should be introduced with the explanatory phrase "*available at*." An example is the following: Santa Monica, Cal., Mun. Code ch. 4.04.040 (2009) *available at* http://www.qcode.us/codes/santamonica/.

Short Forms for Statutes   There are two methods for citing a statute in short form.[6] *Id.* may be used when the same statute is cited immediately before the reference. It is used alone if citing to the same section, or written with a new section or subsection number if there is a change.

---

[5]*Id.* rule 12.4
[6]*Id.* rules 12.10 and B5.2 and *ALWD* 14.13.

EXHIBIT 6-4 SHORT FORM OF STATUTORY CITATIONS

Explanation	Example
To present a complete citation	42 U.S.C. § 1971 (2003)
If there is a subsequent citation with no intervening statutes	*Id.*
Citing the same statute but different subsection	*Id.* § 1971(a)
Citing the same title with a new section	*Id.* § 1973
Citing a different title	50 U.S.C. § 1601 (2000)

Named Act, Full Citation	Short Forms
Carl D. Perkins Career and Technical Education Act of 2006 10 U.S.C. § 2301 (2006)	10 U.S.C. § 2301 or Carl D. Perkins Career and Technical Education Act § 2301 or § 2301

State Statute	Short Form
Okla. Stat. tit. 70, § 1210.531(C) (2003)	tit. 70, § 1210.531(c) or § 1210.531(c)

The second option is to repeat the statute's number. This is used particularly when a second statute is cited. Repeating the first statute's number eliminates confusion for the reader. Exhibit 6-4 is a sampling of the proper use of both *id.* and repeating the statute's number; however, one should always check the rules carefully to make sure that the statute is cited properly.

Rules

Citations for procedural and court rules are specified at *The Bluebook* Rules 12.8.3 and BT.2, and *ALWD* Rule 17 and Appendix 2. Since each court has a different format for its own rules, it is important to confirm with local jurisdictions. *The Bluebook* and *ALWD* will provide the general format; however, if the local court has rules, use that form instead of *The Bluebook* or *ALWD* form.

Federal Rules Citations to federal rules generally have three parts:

- The abbreviation "Fed. R." (with a space between Fed. and R.)
- The abbreviated reference to the specific type of rule (with spaces)
- The specific rule number

Examples:

Federal Rules of Civil Procedure 26: Fed. R. Civ. P. 26

Federal Rules of Appellate Procedure 11: Fed. R. App. P. 11

Federal Rules of Criminal Procedure 14(a): Fed. R. Crim. P. 14(a)

Federal Rules of Evidence 804: Fed. R. Evid. 804

The federal courts issue local rules, as well. Generally, a writer would provide the name of the court that is issuing the rule:

Seventh Circuit Court of Appeals rule 4(b): 7th Cir. R. 4(b)

Local Rules of the United States District Court for the Northern District of Indiana1.1: N.D. Ind. L. R. 1.1

TIP

In addition to the court website, another useful location for local court rules is a free site, www.llrx .com/courtrules/.

State and Local Rules   Most courts have rules for citation formatting, and a court's website should be checked for specific rules of citation. If the court has a specific format, it should be used instead of anything listed in *The Bluebook* or *ALWD*. *The Bluebook* Table 1 and Appendix 2 in ALWD provide the website for every state and federal entity.

Generally, the following elements are included:

- Court issuing the rule (Crim. Ct., Fam. Ct., Prob. Ct., JV or Juv. Ct.)
- Abbreviation indicating the court rule (Ct. R., L.R., Civ. P., Crim. P.)
- Rule number

Examples:

Washington Supreme Court Rule 4.2: Wash. Sup. Ct. R. 4.2.

Marion County, Indiana Local Rule 49, Administrative Rule 00-1: Marion Co. LR49-AR00-1.

For court rules, the only option for a short form is *id.* If *id.* cannot be used because other sources have intervened between the original citation and *id.,* the full citation should be repeated. *Supra* cannot be used with court rules.

Administrative regulations
The rules of the administrative agencies, similar to the statutes created by the federal and state legislative bodies, which govern how the agency operates.

Administrative Materials   Administrative regulations and decisions follow a similar pattern to statutes and cases. Federal ***administrative regulations*** are first presented in the *Federal Register* (Fed. Reg.) and are later codified in the *Code of Federal Regulations* (C.F.R.). The *Federal Register* is cited with the common name of the rule, volume number, Fed. Reg., initial page, pinpoint page, and date. A citation to a regulation would look like this:

> ***The Bluebook:*** Nutrition Standards in the National School Lunch and School Breakfast Programs, 76 Fed. Reg. 2543 (Jan. 13, 2011) (to be codified at 7 C.F.R. parts 210). (Only *The Bluebook* requires the common name of the rule.)

> ***ALWD:*** 76 Fed. Reg. 2543, 2346 (Jan. 13, 2011)

Final federal administrative regulations in the C.F.R. include the C.F.R. title number, the abbreviation "C.F.R.," the section symbol and specific section, and the date of the code edition. An example would be: 40 C.F.R. pt. 52 (2010), or 40 C.F.R. § 63.6585 (2010). Regulations from the C.F.R. are found on electronic databases and, when cited there, must include the name of the database provider, such as Westlaw, LexisNexis, or GPOAccess, and the exact date through which the C.F.R. is current on that database. The *Code of Federal Regulations* is a yearly publication, meaning that if one is looking for a citation for the 2010 version of 40 C.F.R. § 63.6585, it would be necessary to look in the 2010 volumes, not in the current version.

Administrative decisions
Cases decided on the administrative agency level to settle disputes revolving around an agency issue.

Administrative decisions are decisions of agencies, similar to cases decided by courts. Administrative citations are similar to those for cases, with one added component (the agency abbreviation):

- Case name in italics or underlined
- Volume number
- Reporter abbreviation
- Page upon which the decision begins
- Agency abbreviation
- Date

Many agency abbreviations are listed in the citators (*The Bluebook* T1.2; *ALWD* Appendix 8). Here is an example of a citation to an agency decision:

Trojan Transp., Inc., 249 N.L.R.B. 642 (1980).

Trojan Transp., Inc., is the party involved, 249 is the volume number, N.L.R.B. is the abbreviation for the National Labor Relations Board, 642 is the page upon which the decision begins, and 1980 is the date of the decision.[7]

USING *THE BLUEBOOK* AND *ALWD* WITH SECONDARY AUTHORITIES

The Bluebook Rules 15-19 and B8-B10 and *ALWD* Rules 22 and 23 provide the rules for most secondary materials. The following secondary authorities are addressed in the discussion:

- Encyclopedias
- Treatises
- Annotations
- Restatements
- Periodicals
- Dictionaries
- Attorney General Opinions
- Looseleaf Services

Encyclopedias

Legal encyclopedias, like academic encyclopedias, are sources of general information that provide background information and citations to primary authorities. Encyclopedias should not be cited unless there is no primary authority available. If the courts are faced with a novel situation, providing a discussion of these secondary authorities can help the reader to understand a concept. If a sufficient foundation is provided for using an encyclopedia, the citation must contain these elements:

- Volume number
- Name of the encyclopedia, properly abbreviated
- Title of the article or information (underlined or italicized)
- Section symbol (§) and section number
- Year of publication

There are two primary national legal encyclopedias: *Corpus Juris Secundum* (C.J.S.) and *American Jurisprudence 2d* (Am. Jur. 2d). Many states also have encyclopedias such as *Indiana Law Encyclopedia* (I.L.E.) or those from West's "Jurisprudence" series, such as *New York Jurisprudence* and *South Carolina Jurisprudence*.

Volumes of encyclopedias generally have multiple topics within one volume. For this reason, the citation must include the topic. Otherwise, the reader will not know what information the writer is referring to. The citation must also include the volume number and the name of the service. The date tells the reader whether the information is current.

---

[7]*The Bluebook*, Rule 14.3.1, p. 135. 2010.

Citations might appear as follows:

Correct: 14 Am. Jur. 2d *Cemeteries* § 125 (2000).

Incorrect: 14 Am. Jur. 2d § 125 (2000) (missing the topic).

Correct: 78A C.J.S. *Schools and School Districts* § 700 (2008).

Incorrect: 78A *Schools and School Districts* § 700 (2008) (missing the service).

Correct: 6 I.L.E. *Contracts* §§ 14, 16 (2008).

Incorrect: 6 I.L.E. § 14, 16 (missing the topic, a second section symbol, and the date).

Correct: 30 S.C. Jur. *Contracts* § 1 (1999).

Incorrect: S.C. Jur. *Contracts* § 1 (1999) (missing the volume number),

The short form citation for encyclopedias is *id.,* or *supra* for subsequent references (*The Bluebook* Rules 4, 15.9, & B8; *ALWD* Rule 22). When *supra* is used, the article's title is given in place of the author's name.

Treatises and Books

Treatises and books are governed by *The Bluebook* Rule 15 and *ALWD* Rule 22. These are the main elements in these types of sources:

- Author's full name (or editor or translator)
- Title in italics or underlined
- Page, sections, paragraphs, subsections
- Publisher, edition
- Date

The author's full name must be included, with the given name first. If an author has a designation, such as Jr. or Sr., it must be included as well. If multiple authors are involved, the full names of both are given, with the names separated by an ampersand (&). When more than two authors appear, there are two options: 1) give the first listed author only and follow the name with "et. al.," or 2) include all names separated by commas, with an ampersand before the last author's name. The first option is preferred unless there is some particular reason to list all authors.

Correct: Arthur L. Corbin, *Corbin on Contracts* (rev. ed. 1993).

Incorrect: Corbin, Arthur L. *Corbin on Contracts* (rev. ed. 1993) (order of name).

Correct: *Collier on Bankruptcy* 15th Ed. (Lawrence P. King, ed., 1996).

Incorrect: *Collier on Bankruptcy* (Lawrence P. King, ed., 1996) (missing edition information).

Correct: Henry J. Bailey, III & Richard B. Hagedorn, *Brady on Bank Checks: The Law of Bank Checks* (2001).

Incorrect: Henry J. Bailey, III & Richard B. Hagedorn, Brady on Bank Checks (missing the rest of the book title, title not displayed in italics, and date of publication missing)..

Correct (preferred): Dan B. Dobbs, et. al., *Prosser and Keeton's Hornbook on Torts* (5th Ed. 1988).

Correct: Dan B. Dobbs, Robert E. Keeton, W. Page Keeton, David G. Owen, & William L. Prosser, *Prosser and Keeton's Hornbook on Torts* (5th Ed. 1988).

Incorrect: *Prosser and Keeton's Hornbook on Torts* (5th Ed. 1988) (author names omitted).

Correct: Michel Foucault, *Discipline and Punish* 30-31 (Alan Sheridan trans. Vintage Books 2d ed. 1995) (1977).[8]

Incorrect: Foucault, Michael. *Discipline and Punish* 30-31 (Alan Sheridan trans. Vintage Books 1995) (1977) (author's name in reverse order with last name first and edition omitted).

The book title should be provided in full, but subtitles are omitted unless that information is particularly relevant. The title should be italicized or underlined and the first letter of every word should be capitalized, except for articles, conjunctions, and prepositions, unless those items begin the title of the material. The title should not be abbreviated.

A pinpoint page or section should take the reader to the exact location being referenced. If the writer is citing multiple pages, the inclusive page numbers should be hyphenated but repetitious digits may or may not be dropped, depending on the citator used. If the multiple pages are nonconsecutive, the pinpoint pages are separated by a comma and all repetitious pages are retained. If the material is divided into sections, the individual section number rather than the page number is provided. If the material encompasses more than one volume, the volume number is placed before the author's name.

Correct: 1 Dan B. Dobbs, *Law of Torts*, 217-18 (2005).

Incorrect: Dan B. Dobbs, *Law of Torts*, 1, 217-18 (2005) (volume number in the wrong place).

Generally, the edition number should be included with the date in parentheses if the material has more than one edition; however, if there is only one edition, the edition information is omitted. In citations to a supplement to the main volume, "Supp." should be included in the parentheses with the date.

Correct: 1 Dan B. Dobbs, *Law of Torts*, 217-18 (Supp. 2009).

Incorrect: 1 Dan B. Dobbs, *Law of Torts*, 217-18 (Supplement 2009) (failure to abbreviate "supplement").

Correct: Dan B. Dobbs, Robert E. Keeton, W. Page Keeton, David G. Owen, & William L. Prosser, *Prosser and Keeton's Hornbook on Torts* (5th Ed. 1988).

Incorrect: Dan B. Dobbs, Robert E. Keeton, W. Page Keeton, David G. Owen, & William L. Prosser, *Prosser and Keeton's Hornbook on Torts* (1988) (leaving out the edition when there is more than one edition)

The short form of this type of citation uses either *id.* or *supra* (*The Bluebook* Rules 4, 15.10, and B8.2; *ALWD* Rule 22). Generally, if a full citation is presented and there is no intervening citation to some other authority, *id.* should be used either alone or with a different pinpoint page number. If, however, there has been an intervening authority, *supra* must be used. The following elements must be incorporated when using *supra*:

- Author's last name with a comma: Brady,
- The word *supra* (underlined or italicized), followed by a comma: Brady, *supra*,
- The word "at" if citing to a page: Brady, *supra*, at
- A page or section number leading to the exact information: Brady, *supra*, at 117

---

[8]*The Bluebook* Rule 15.4. 2010

Correct: *Id.* (No intervening cite or other change)
Incorrect: Brady, *Id.*
Correct: *Id.* at 117.
Incorrect: *Id.* 117.
Correct: *Id.* at §45.
Incorrect: *Id.* §45.
Correct: Prosser, *supra,* at 117 (intervening citation).
Incorrect: Prosser, *supra,* 117 (intervening citation).
Correct: Wright, *supra,* at § 115.
Incorrect: Wright, *supra,* § 115.

Annotations

When citing to *American Law Reports* (A.L.R.) annotations,[9] the citation must include the following elements:

- Author's full name (if available) followed by a comma
- The word "Annotation" followed by a comma (*The Bluebook* only)
- Title of the annotation (underlined or italicized) followed by a comma
- Volume number
- Abbreviation "A.L.R." followed by the series number as appropriate (2d, 3d, 4th, 5th, 6th, Fed. or Fed. 2d)
- Beginning page number
- Pinpoint page number (if appropriate)
- Year of publication

Correct: Earl L. Kellett, Annotation, *Searches and Seizures,* 68 A.L.R.2d 655 (1955) (*The Bluebook).*
Incorrect: Kellett, Earl L. Annotation, *Searches and Seizures,* 68 A.L.R.2d 655 (1955) (author name reversed with last name first).
Correct: Earl L. Kellett, Annotation, *Searches and Seizures,* 68 A.L.R.2d 655, 661 (1955) (for pinpoint citation).
Incorrect: Earl L. Kellett, Annotation, *Searches and Seizures,* 68 A.L.R.2d 661 (1955) (when annotation begins on page 655).
Correct: Earl L. Kellett, *Searches and Seizures,* 68 A.L.R.2d 655 (1955) (*ALWD*).
Incorrect: Earl L. Kellett, Annotation, *Searches and Seizures,* 68 A.L.R.2d 655 (1955) (*ALWD* does not require the word "annotation").

The short form for an A.L.R. source is either *id.* or *supra.*

Restatements

Citations to Restatements (*The Bluebook* Rules 12.9.5 and B5.1.3; *ALWD* Rule 27) have the following elements:

- The word "Restatement"
- Series number placed in parentheses (if series is needed)
- The word "of"
- Subject

---

[9]*The Bluebook* Rule 16.7.6; ALWD 24

- Section symbol
- Section number
- Year of publication

If the Restatement is not divided into subtitles, the section should be cited. If the Restatement has larger sections that are divided into subtitles, the subtitle should follow the subject. If citing a comment to a Restatement section, the writer should insert the abbreviation "cmt." with the comment number or letter after the section number. If citing to an illustration of a Restatement rule, the comment number or letter, followed by the abbreviation "illus." and the illustration number, should be used.

Correct: *Restatement (Second) of Contracts* § 100 (1981).

Incorrect: *Restatement of Contracts* § 100 (1981) (edition omitted).

Correct: *Restatement (Third) of Torts*: Apportionment of Liability § 63 (2000).

Incorrect: *Restatement (Third) of Torts* § 63 (2000) (title or subject).

Correct: *Restatement (Third) of Trusts*: Trustee Powers and Duties § 29 cmt. 1 (2007).

Incorrect: *Restatement (Third) of Trusts: Trustee Powers and Duties* § 29 comment 1 (2007) (comment not abbreviated)

Correct: *Restatement (Second) of Property,* § 2.1 cmt. c, illus. 2 (1977)

Incorrect: *Restatement (Second) of Property,* § 2.1 cmt. c, illustration 2 (1977) (illustration not abbreviated)

Using *id.* is the only option for short-form citation of Restatements. If an intervening citation or authority has been introduced, and therefore, *id* cannot be used, the full citation must be presented again.

Periodicals

Citations to periodicals, such as law reviews and journals, are similar to citations to books (*The Bluebook* Rules 16 and B9; *ALWD* Rule 23). The following elements must be included:

- Author's full name
- Article title (underlined or italicized) followed by a comma
- Volume number, if available
- Name of periodical, abbreviated
- Beginning page number
- Pinpoint page number (if applicable)
- Publication year

For the author, the entire name must be used, including any designations such as Jr. or Sr. Sometimes a student-written work does not provide an author's name, but in citing the work, the writer would provide the complete information as set out. Occasionally, the student author may provide a name at the end of the material, so the entire work should be checked before one concludes that there is no author.

In the title, the first letter of each word should be capitalized, except for articles, prepositions, or conjunctions, unless one of those is the first word of the title. Comments, Notes, or Recent Developments may be included, particularly with student-written works. For these features, everything is cited in the same manner, except that the designation of the piece, such as "Note," is added after the author's name.

TIP

This discussion is focused on citing to law reviews and law journals since these are the most commonly cited periodicals. There are special rules for citing magazines, institutional publications, newspapers, and other periodicals. *The Bluebook* and *ALWD* should be checked to confirm the proper citation form.

If the volume number is available, it should be included. Sometimes the year will be the volume number. The name of the periodical is abbreviated. For example, "Law Journal" is always abbreviated as "L.J."

After the periodical abbreviation, the page number of the beginning of the article is listed. If material on other pages was discussed and a pinpoint citation is needed, that information is added according to the rule for cases. The last element of the citation is the year, which for periodicals is generally the copyright year. Some examples are set out in Example 6-8.

The short form of citations to periodicals following the full citation uses *id.* or *supra.*

Legal Dictionaries

The Bluebook Rules 15.8 and B9 and *ALWD* Rule *25* require the following elements in a citation for a legal dictionary:

- The dictionary name (underlined or italicized) with no comma after the title – *Black's Law Dictionary*
- The pinpoint page number – 523
- Editor (*ALWD* only)
- The edition number – 9th ed.
- Publisher (*ALWD* only)
- The year of publication – 2009

EXAMPLE 6-8   PERIODICALS

Correct: Nathalie Martin, Consumer Scams and the Elderly: Preserving Independence Through Shifting Default Rules, 17 Elder L.J. 3 (2009).

Incorrect: Nathalie Martin, *Consumer Scams and the Elderly: Preserving Independence Through Shifting Default Rules,* 17 Elder Law Journal 3 (2009) ("law journal" not abbreviated).

Correct: Laura Jane Durfee, Note, Anti-Horse Slaughter Legislation: Bad for Horses, Bad for Society, 84 Ind. L.J. 353 (2009).

Incorrect: Durfee, Laura Jane. Note, Anti-Horse Slaughter Legislation: Bad for Horses, Bad for Society, 84 Ind. L.J. 353 (2009). (Incorrect format of author's name).

Correct: Tiffany L. Williams, Comment, Illinois Tool Works Inc. v. Independent Ink, Inc.: The Intersection of Patent Law and Antitrust Law in the Context of Patent Tying Arrangements, 58 Mercer L. Rev. 1035 (2007).

Incorrect: Tiffany L. Williams, Illinois Tool Works Inc. v. Independent Ink, Inc.: The Intersection of Patent Law and Antitrust Law in the Context of Patent Tying Arrangements, 58 Mercer L. Rev. 1035 (2007). ("Comment" omitted).

Correct: Recent Development, Don't Act Like You Smell Pot! (At Least, Not in the Fourth Circuit): Police-Created Exigent Circumstances in Fourth Amendment Jurisprudence, 87 N.C. L. Rev. 145 (2009).

Incorrect: 87 Recent Development, Don't Act Like You Smell Pot! (At Least, Not in the Fourth Circuit): Police-Created Exigent Circumstances in Fourth Amendment Jurisprudence, N.C. L. Rev. 145 (2009). (Incorrect placement of volume number).

Correct: *Black's Law Dictionary* 523 (9th ed. 2009) (*The Bluebook*).

Incorrect: *Black's Law Dictionary* 523 (2009). (*The Bluebook*) (no edition identified).

Correct: *Black's Law Dictionary* 523 (Bryan A. Garner ed., 9th ed. West 2009) (*ALWD*).

Incorrect: *Black's Law Dictionary* 523 (9th ed. West 2009). (*ALWD*) (no editor identified).

Correct: *Oran's Dictionary of the Law* 123 (4th ed. 2007).

Incorrect: Oran's Dictionary of the Law 123 (4th ed.) (no date identified).

For the short form of the citation, *id.* or *supra* (whichever is appropriate for the situation in which the source is cited) is used. If *supra* is used, the name of the dictionary is used in place of the author's name.

Attorney General Opinions

Citations to attorney general opinions have some characteristics of cases and some characteristics of secondary materials. *The Bluebook* (Rule 14.3 and T1) and *ALWD* (Rule 19.7) vary widely on the elements needed. These elements are in *The Bluebook*:

- Title of the opinion (if required by the state, or needed for clarity)
- Volume
- Type of opinion (including the agency from which the opinion originates)
- Page on which opinion begins
- Pinpoint page if needed
- Year

Correct: Legality of Revised Phila. Plan, 42 Op. Att'y Gen. 405 (1969).[10]

Incorrect: 42 Op. Att'y Gen. 405 (1969) (title left out [if title required by state]).

Correct: 6 Op. Att'y Gen. 16 (1976) (if title not required).

Correct: 1 Op. In. Att'y Gen. 1 (1976).

Incorrect: Op. In. Att'y Gen. 1 (1976) (volume number left out).

Correct: 75 Op. Fl. Att'y Gen. 8 (1975).

Incorrect: 75 Op. Fl. Att'y Gen. (1975) (page number left out)

Correct: Tampa Bay Rapid Transit Authority, 75 Op. Fl. Att'y Gen. 8, 10-11 (1975)

Incorrect: Tampa Bay Rapid Transit Authority, 75 Op. Fl. Att'y Gen. 8 (1975) (punctuation left out).

Looseleaf Services

The citation form for looseleaf services is found in *The Bluebook* Rule 19 and *ALWD* Rule 28. These are its elements:

- Title or case name
- Volume number (number, year, descriptive subtitle from the spine, or a combination)
- Abbreviated title of looseleaf

---

[10]*The Bluebook*. T1. 2010.

- Publisher (abbreviate in parentheses and follow service's title)
- Subdivision (paragraph or section number if available; pinpoint page if needed)
- Court abbreviation and exact date or year in parentheses

If citing a source that is not yet bound but will be, a writer would add the designation of the bound form in parentheses if it is different from the looseleaf form.

> **Correct:** 37 Med. Law Rep. (BNA) 27 (2009).
>
> **Incorrect:** 37 Med. Law Rep. (BNA) (2009) (paragraph, section, or page number left out).
>
> **Correct:** 7 Lab. L. Rep. (CCH) ¶ 3847 (2006).
>
> **Incorrect:** 7 Lab. L. Rep. ¶ 3847 (2006). (publisher omitted).

The short form of looseleaf citations for cases provides the column designation from the service binder and uses section or paragraph numbers instead of the case page number, if appropriate. If the citation is the same as the immediately preceding citation, *id.* is used.

SECONDARY AUTHORITIES ON THE INTERNET

While the availability of secondary sources on the Internet is limited, some secondary sources, such as law reviews, may be available. One example is the *University of Pennsylvania Law Review*, which happens to be the oldest, continuously published law journal in the United States. It was first published in 1852 and is one of the most cited law journals in the world. It is also one of the four law reviews that assist in the publication of *The Bluebook*.

The general rule is to cite only to the print source if it is readily available to the reader. For example, an article titled "How Should Punitive Damages Work?" by Dan Markel is found on the Internet at http://www.pennumbra.com/issues /pdfs/157-5/Markel.pdf. In print form, this article is found in volume 157, number 5, starting at page 1383. Here is the proper citation:

> **Correct:** Dan Markel, *How Should Punitive Damages Work?*, 157 U. Pa. L. Rev. 1383 (2009).

Another example is the *Northwestern University Law Review*. If an article titled "Framework Originalism and the Living Constitution" by Jack M. Balkin is found on the Internet at http://www.law.northwestern.edu/lawreview/v103 /n2/549/LR103n2Balkin.pdf, the proper citation, using the same rules, would be as follows:

> **Correct:** Jack M. Balkin, *Framework Originalism and the Living Constitution,* 103 NW. U. L. Rev. 549 (2009).

A parallel citation to the Internet site may also be provided if it will significantly improve access for the reader. For example, if a researcher was in Florida and needed the above-referenced law review articles from Pennsylvania or Northwestern, it is likely that these law reviews would be difficult to find on a library shelf in Florida. Providing the Internet address would significantly improve the access for the reader. Therefore, the following citation formats would be correct, too:

Correct: Dan Markel, *How Should Punitive Damages Work?*, 157 U. Pa. L. Rev. 1383 (2009) *available at* http://www.pennumbra.com/issues /pdfs/157-5/Markel.pdf

Correct: Jack M. Balkin, *Framework Originalism and the Living Constitution,* 103 NW. U. L. Rev. 549 (2009) *available at* http://www.law.northwestern.edu /lawreview/v103/n2/549/LR103n2Balkin.pdf

In either Internet citation, the page upon which the article appears, not the home page of the volume or the home page of the law review, is the cited page. Again, the reasoning behind this rule is to provide the reader with the citation that will take the reader to the source itself. The bottom line is that using secondary materials often means finding a library!

SUMMARY

It may seem as though enough citation rules have been presented at this point to complete any research project. However, while some of the major rules have been presented, there are many more rules within the citation manuals that have not been covered here.

It is not necessary to memorize every rule. The key is knowing where to find the correct rules in the citation manuals. In the opening scenario, John had a large citation project due the next day, and while he initially panicked, he knew that if he did not know a rule, he knew where to find it.

As a paralegal gains more experience in researching and writing, the basic citation rules will eventually come naturally. It should be remembered, however, that citations must be constantly checked to ensure that all the information that the reader needs has been provided accurately.

REVIEW **QUESTIONS**

Use either *The Bluebook* or *ALWD,* or both, as required by the instructor.

1. Identify the basic parts of a case citation where a person sues another person in state court. Provide an example. Cite the appropriate rule(s).

2. How are cases organized within a case reporter?

3. What is the main rule for citing cases in both *The Bluebook* and *ALWD* formats?

4. What is the purpose of a short form of citation? When would it be used? What rules govern the short form for cases?

5. What is a parallel citation? When is it used? How is a citation presented when there is no parallel citation? Give an example.

6. What is a pinpoint citation and what is its value?

7. What are the basic parts of a citation to an A.L.R. entry?

8. If you are not sure what an abbreviation is for a law review article, where do you look and why?

9. What is the difference between citing a source and using a citation within a textual sentence?

10. What are pocket parts, and why are they important?

APPLICATION **EXERCISES**

11. Your supervisor has a case that she thinks is located on page 26 of the 110th volume of the *South Eastern Reporter.* She is sure it was a Georgia Supreme Court case from 1972. The appellant was Shirley Jones and the appellee was Partridge Family Bakeries, Co., Inc. Provide the correct citation.

12. Your supervisor has a case from volume 119 of the Indiana Court of Appeals that starts on page 263. The parties are Amoco Oil Company and Ronald S. Pettigrew. The case was decided in 1983 and was

also reported on page 419 of volume 298 of the *North Eastern Reporter.* Provide the correct citation.

13. Your supervisor is preparing an interoffice memorandum of law. In the memo, he has cited *Richardson v. Weckworth,* 509 P.2d 1113 (Kan., 1973), for the position that a landlord has a responsibility to the tenant to repair a faulty sidewalk. The Weckworths argued that, accepting the testimony of the Richardsons as true, the largest hole or pockmark in the sidewalk did not exceed an inch and one-eighth in depth, and therefore,

there was no actionable defect that could serve as a basis of liability or contributory negligence. That information appears on page 1115. Then your supervisor provided this quote: "The court held that the landlord cannot disavow liability when he admitted to knowing the problem existed." This information is on page 1116. Prepare this section of the interoffice memorandum with the appropriate citations.

CITATION **EXERCISES**

Use *The Bluebook: A Uniform System of Citation* or *ALWD* to answer these questions. Include the citation rule.

1. Give an example of a citation for a law review article.

2. Why is the month of the decision indicated in *Birl v. Estelle*, 660 F.2d 592 (5th Cir. Nov. 1981)?

3. How does one cite a telephone interview?

4. Give the correct citation for the Eighteenth Amendment to the United States Constitution, which was repealed in 1933.

5. Name, in order of preference, the unofficial reporters for the decisions of the United States Supreme Court.

6. Where are decisions of the United States Courts of Appeals, previously the United States Circuit Courts of Appeals, reported?

7. Give an example of a citation to a Federal Rule of Civil Procedure.

8. What is the official reporter for decisions of the United States Supreme Court?

9. In which reporter are federal district court decisions reported?

10. How does one cite to a work that has no named author, editor, or translator? Give an example.

11. What is the abbreviation of the official U.S. administrative publication of the decisions and orders of the National Labor Relations Board?

12. Does any Native American group have its own reported court decisions? If so, which one(s)?

13. What is the official source for American treaties?

14. What is the official abbreviation of "Department" in a case name?

15. Write the correct citation for the following:
    a. Article 2, Section 3, Clause 1 of the United States Constitution.
    b. The Fifth Amendment to the United States Constitution
    c. The preamble of the Oklahoma constitution
    d. Sections 848 and 853 of title 21 of the United States Code, published in 1988.
    e. Disciplinary Rule 5-106(c) of the Model Code of Professional Responsibility, published in 1980.
    f. The federal statute that is §1956 of title 50 of the *United States Code*, published in 2006.
    g. Section 21 of *Corpus Juris Secundum*, Volume 11, discussing bonds, which was published in 1995.
    h. Title 31 of *the* Code of Federal Regulations, published in 1999, covering section 515.329.

QUICK **CHECK**

State whether each statement is true or false.

1. A case citation includes every party in the name.

2. The typeface for law review footnotes may be used in a court document.

3. It is not important to know how to properly cite any legal authority.

4. If an official code is being cited, "Supp." is added before the year in parentheses.

5. A pin or pinpoint citation is the exact page number upon which the specific material being cited appears.

6. The only acceptable short form citation for cases is *id.*

7. Either *id.* or *supra* may be used.

8. If a brief is being prepared for a particular court, and one of its local citation rules conflicts with the analogous rule in *The Bluebook* or *ALWD*, the court's rule should be disregarded, and the citation manual should be followed.

9. Table 1 of *The Bluebook* is extremely useful because it provides the proper format for primary authority in each jurisdiction.

10. The *Statutes at Large* are the official session laws; the abbreviation for this service is "Stat."

RESEARCH

1. Find 463 F.2d 704. What reporter did you look in for traditional library research? How did you find it on the Internet? Did you locate it on a subscription service? If so, which one? What is the complete citation? What jurisdiction does it cover? Summarize the case.

2. Find 704 F.2d 1390. What reporter did you look in for traditional library research? How did you find it on the Internet? Did you locate it on a subscription service? If so, which one? What is the complete citation? What jurisdiction does it cover? Summarize the case.

3. Find 473 U.S. 935. What reporter did you look in for traditional library research? How did you find it on the Internet? Did you locate it on a subscription service? If so, which one? What is the complete citation? What jurisdiction does it cover? Summarize the case.

4. Find 473 F.2d 1090. What reporter did you look in for traditional library research? How did you find it on the Internet? Did you locate it on a subscription service? If so, which one? What is the complete citation? What jurisdiction does it cover? Summarize the case.

INTERNET **RESEARCH**

1. Take a tour of *The Bluebook* online. Identify three updates that are not in the current edition of the text.

2. Find *Amistad v. United States* and provide the complete citation for it. Are there any cross-listings? If so, provide them.

3. Does your jurisdiction have any appellate or supreme court reports that were created by editors and bear names such as Indiana's *Blackford's Reports*? If so, identify those reports and provide a citation to at least one.

4. Check the Internet site for *ALWD*. Find three items that would help students understand citation formatting. Summarize the findings.

MEDIA **RESOURCES**

Duke Law Library & Technology: Research Tutorials:	http://www.law.duke.edu/lib/tutorials/index#
In-text Citations:	http://www.youtube.com/watch?v=XQ8fy7SPotM
Law School Videos—How to look up legal citations:	http://www.youtube.com/watch?v=C56DOOncOfo
Paralegal's Guide to Understanding Legal Citations:	http://www.theparalegalresource.com/legal-citations/?affiliate=PositionTechnologies&cd=13184:0:1:4:13&gclid=CLCM8NWL760CFYe8KgodIkWXrA
Understanding Citations Tutorial:	http://www.lib.utexas.edu/services/instruction/learningmodules/citations/

INTERNET **RESOURCES**

AutoCite:	http://support.lexisnexis.com/lexiscom/record.asp?ArticleID=lexiscom_Auto-Cite
"Blue Tips":	http://www.legalbluebook.com/Public/BlueTips.aspx
Cornell Law Free Bluebook:	http://www.law.cornell.edu/citation/
LexisNexis Academic—Legal Research Guide:	http://www4.nau.edu/library/reference/LexisNexisAcademic.htm
Shepard's Citation on Lexis/Nexis:	http://wiki.lexisnexis.com/academic/index.php?title=Shepard's_Citations
The Bluebook:	http://www.legalbluebook.com/
The Bluebook online:	http://www.legalbluebook.com/Public/Tour.aspx

zimmytws/Shutterstock

chapter **seven**

TOOLS FOR MANUAL AND ONLINE RESEARCH

LEARNING OBJECTIVES

After completing this chapter, students should be able to:

1. Understand the ethical considerations surrounding legal research.

2. Understand how to use a library.

3. Understand and use a web browser and search engines to find legal information on the Internet.

4. Learn ways to distinguish "quality" websites from sites that are not reliable.

5. Access legal sources by index, table of content and topical outline, West Key Number system, and table of cases.

6. In electronic media, access legal authorities using online citations, Boolean searches, field searches, and natural language searches.

7. Become familiar with both commercial and free legal electronic sources.

8. Understand the relative benefits of print and electronic research and combine these two forms of research effectively in researching a given issue.

CHAPTER OVERVIEW

Paralegals take on many roles in the legal environment in which they operate. Performing legal research is one part of that job. While paralegals ultimately are supervised by attorneys, they may work independently or as part of a team. The main tasks in legal research are to research the issues, update the findings, and present the findings to the supervisor. The supervisor generally takes the responsibility for the research from that point forward.

OPENING SCENARIO

John was working heavily on Heather Dobbs's case as her trial date was approaching. John needed to find support for Heather's claim against Paul. Her case involved the following facts:

- Heather lives in Indiana but works in Illinois.
- On her way home from work she stopped at a four-way stop sign.
- She looked both ways and proceeded into the intersection.
- She saw a truck coming from the west but knew that the intersection was controlled by a four-way stop sign.
- Paul, the truck driver, failed to stop at his stop sign, and struck Heather's car in the passenger's side door.
- Paul lives in Illinois.
- The damage to the car was extensive and Heather was taken to the local hospital.

Now John has to find statutes and case law to support Heather's position. That means doing some research in the office but also going to the local law library at the law school. Then he must submit the results to Jami, his supervisor, in an interoffice memorandum of law.

ETHICS IN RESEARCH

Although paralegals perform much of their research independently, some of this process involves interaction with clients and supervising attorneys. During the research process, there are important ethical issues to consider, and it is important to distinguish those activities that are appropriate for the paralegal to perform from those that are inappropriate, or possibly illegal.

Unauthorized Practice of Law

Only attorneys may give legal advice to clients, and for a paralegal to do so is *unauthorized practice of law (UPL)*, an ethics violation which may also carry criminal penalties. As part of the research process, a paralegal may be asked to interview the client to gather facts. During the course of the interview, a paralegal must be careful not to give any opinions about the client's case, or make statements that could be interpreted as legal advice.

Another way for a paralegal to commit UPL is to insert a personal opinion when writing about the facts of a client's case. When a paralegal prepares the research findings, the paralegal should state the legal findings; in other words, analyze the research and report what is stated in the legal sources. Example 7-1 shows how easily such an ethical violation can happen.

John just committed UPL, because he advised Heather about her chances of winning the case and also advised her that the research is in her favor. Even though John's statement was a casual, offhand remark, his words were a legal opinion about Heather's chances of winning.

The unauthorized practice of law is prohibited in all states, and is considered a crime in most jurisdictions. Many paralegals, particularly new paralegals, can commit UPL without realizing what they are doing. Therefore, it is important to be vigilant about statements that are made in the course of a paralegal's responsibilities.[1]

Unauthorized practice of law (UPL)

Representing a client or giving legal advice without having a license to do so. Only licensed attorneys can practice law; anyone else who gives legal advice or performs other functions without authority is engaging in UPL.

---

[1] American Bar Association. *ABA Model Guidelines for the Utilization of Paralegal Services,* Guideline 3. 2004. http://apps.americanbar.org/legalservices/paralegals/downloads/modelguidelines.pdf

> **EXAMPLE 7-1 POTENTIAL ETHICAL VIOLATION**
>
> As John works on Heather's case, his goal is to find the statutes and cases that apply to her case, analyze what the court held in the cases, and apply the results in a legal memorandum. After doing some of the research, John met with Heather to obtain a few more facts, some of which would be used in the answers to interrogatories sent by Paul's attorney. After John finished asking for the information needed on the interrogatories and getting the additional facts he needed for research, Heather said, "So, John, do you think I have a pretty good case?" John replied, "You know, Heather, from the research I have done and the information you have given me, I don't think anyone would deny that it is Paul's fault."
>
> When John made this statement to Heather, he was giving legal advice to a client. This differs from analyzing the law and preparing an interoffice memorandum of law. The interoffice memo is maintained within the office; generally only legal personnel see interoffice memos.

Confidentiality

Confidentiality

An ethical principle that requires those in the legal profession to maintain the client's information in secret.

Privileged

Information given by a client that is protected from disclosure; a court cannot compel the attorney to disclose it. The client owns the privilege, and only the client can waive it.

The ethical obligation of *confidentiality* begins at the first meeting with the client. Often it is the paralegal who first meets with the client to gain information about the case. The paralegal must remember that the information the client discloses must remain confidential, whether the information is verbal or written. The obligation of confidentiality also applies to all members of the office staff.

Information disclosed by a client to an attorney, or to a paralegal working for an attorney, is also considered *privileged*, meaning that the paralegal or the attorney cannot be compelled by a court to disclose the information. Although the concept of privilege is related to confidentiality, it is important to understand the difference between these two concepts. Everything under attorney-client privilege is confidential, but not everything confidential is privileged.

Confidentiality is an ethical duty or obligation owed by the lawyer to the client. Indeed, confidentiality is a rule of ethics. An attorney and his or her staff operate under a general rule that no information that relates to the representation of the client may be revealed. This duty of confidentiality covers nearly anything the client produces or says during the client's representation. Confidentiality arises once the client has sought legal advice or representation.

Attorney-client privilege is a rule of evidence, and is a right or claim that is asserted by the client. The attorney stands in the place of the client and holds the client's "secrets" or information. Whatever the client tells the attorney or paralegal for the purposes of obtaining representation is considered "privileged." The attorney-client privilege, as a rule of evidence, prevents opposing counsel or party from forcing the attorney (or paralegal) to disclose the client's secrets.

Generally attorneys refer to keeping things confidential as a matter of only sharing information with people on a "need-to-know" basis—sharing with someone who is directly involved with the case and needs to know the information in order to perform their role in it. But not everyone else in the office "needs to know." Without the guarantees of loyalty and confidentiality, the legal team would not be able to provide the best representation to the client because the client would not want to divulge personal information. Therefore, nothing about the private client information can be disclosed to anyone who is not part of the legal team, and certainly not to anyone outside the law office. Example 7-2 is a somewhat typical scenario of how easily confidentiality can be breached.

EXAMPLE 7-2   RESEARCH OUTSIDE THE OFFICE ENVIRONMENT

John needed to do some additional research on Heather's case, so he visited the local law school law library. As he was working with the *Indiana Digest*, Kim, one of his friends, stopped to chat. John had Heather's research file on the table and Kim saw Heather's name. Kim said, "I know Heather. Are you guys involved in that wreck she was in?" John told Kim, "Yeah, we're representing her. She is suing the guy for all her damages. She was pretty messed up."

John has breached the duty of confidentiality. First, he should not have had Heather's file out in the open on a desk in a public place. Second, he should not have told Kim that his firm was representing Heather in a lawsuit against Paul. While these actions may seem harmless, John breached his ethical duty of confidentiality.

If a paralegal is not certain as to whether information should be disclosed, the best course of action is to remain quiet. If a paralegal is in doubt as to whether information can or should be disclosed, the supervisor should be consulted.[2]

Candor

Candor is the ethical obligation to be open and honest to the court. In order to fulfill this duty, the attorney needs to have all relevant authority to provide to the court. The paralegal, in turn, owes a duty to be honest in research, even when that means that the information provided does not give the supervisor the answer he or she hoped for, or does not support the client's position. In other words, the paralegal must be truthful with the attorney, and the attorney must be truthful with the client and the court. This duty of candor is set forth in MRPC Rule 3.3 (a) (2), as shown in Exhibit 7-1.

The attorney is required to supervise the paralegal, and that supervision includes checking the paralegal's research. However, there is an element of trust between the attorney and paralegal—when attorneys assign work, they expect the results to be thorough and accurate. Example 7-3 shows how a paralegal might contribute to breaching the duty of candor.

Candor
An ethical principle that requires a practitioner to be open and honest.

EXHIBIT 7-1   RULE 3.3[3]

Advocate
Rule 3.3 Candor Toward The Tribunal

(a) A lawyer shall not knowingly:

(1) make a false statement of fact or law to a tribunal or fail to correct a false statement of material fact or law previously made to the tribunal by the lawyer;

(2) fail to disclose to the tribunal legal authority in the controlling jurisdiction known to the lawyer to be directly adverse to the position of the client and not disclosed by opposing counsel; or. . .

---

[2]Model Rules of Professional Responsibility. American Bar Association. *Client-Lawyer Relationship* Rule 1.6 Confidentiality Of Information. http://www.abanet.org/cpr/mrpc/rule_1_6.html

[3]Model Rules of Professional Responsibility. American Bar Association. *Advocate* Rule 3.3 Candor Toward The Tribunal. http://www.abanet.org/cpr/mrpc/rule_3_3.html

> ### EXAMPLE 7-3   BREACHING THE DUTY OF CANDOR
>
> As John researched Heather's case, he came across a lot of research that favored Heather's position; however, there was one case that was strongly in favor of Paul's defense. John had outlined an excellent memo to Jami identifying a statute and five cases that indicated Paul would be liable. John had updated all the cases and all were still good law. However, there was one case in which the court determined that each driver is responsible for controlling his or her vehicle at an intersection, even if the intersection is controlled by a signal or stop sign. Maybe he would just not include the case in the memo to Jami; after all, it was just one case.

Counteranalysis
A portion of the interoffice memorandum that identifies the opposing side's strongest arguments.

John is not acting ethically or professionally. His duty is to include the adverse case as a ***counteranalysis*** in the memorandum. The attorney must know both the positive and negative authority in order to prepare for trial. He or she could be caught off guard if opposing counsel later presented the negative information, or, at worst, could be accused of failing to disclose the negative authority.

Each of these ethical rules is important for paralegals to remember and abide by so that the client's interests are protected at all times. If at any time there is a question as to whether a course of action may be unethical, the best course of action is to ask the supervisor.

THE TOOLS OF RESEARCH

Expertise in legal research requires diligent practice—it cannot be done quickly, and it is very difficult to do right the first time, and every time thereafter. The first research assignments of one's career will take much more time than anticipated, and a new paralegal should allow for extra time to complete them. Initially, it is important to become familiar with the law library, the books, and the materials available on the Internet. The new paralegal should learn the names of the resources, their abbreviations, their purposes, and their locations. All of this information will make the research process easier.

Often, the hardest part of research is just getting started. Today, a researcher has two primary resources to use: the traditional library and the Internet.

The Library

In order to use a library effectively, it is important to understand how it is organized, how the library's collection is selected, and how to find assistance in using that collection.

Organization   Items in libraries are organized so that all the sources for each topic can be found easily. For example, when researchers search for a book in the general library catalog, a call number directs the researcher to a specific shelf in the library containing the books about that topic. The other books nearby on that shelf generally cover the same topic.

Law books generally do not have call numbers, but the organizational concept is very similar: like materials are placed near to each other on the shelves. For example, all the statutes are likely to be together, all the reporters in another location, and all the digests in yet another.

Permanence   One of the primary functions of a library is to provide an organized storehouse of in-depth information published throughout history. In addition to current information, researchers can also find books that are no longer published, and older issues of books and magazines. Some materials are meant to circulate—to be borrowed, taken home, and then returned by a certain date. Other materials are non-circulating, and must remain in the library.

Most legal materials are part of a non-circulating, permanent collection. Users are not allowed to take most legal materials out of a law library—they are treated as reference materials, and generally libraries will have only one copy, or very few copies, of those materials.

Assistance   Sometimes, a member of a library staff may become a paralegal's best friend. Most libraries have staff members who are trained to assist people in sorting through all the sources. They can help researchers learn to use the tools and can answer many questions.

Quality or Quantity   Although libraries accumulate large collections of information on a variety of topics, these collections are often carefully selected and organized. Libraries usually select materials based on quality rather than quantity. By working efficiently, a researcher can find quality information from a variety of credible resources. However, only the largest law libraries are likely to have complete collections of every major legal publication in existence.

Academic libraries purchase resources for use by their community of students, faculty, and staff. These resources are different from most of the information that is freely available over the Internet because they have been reviewed and recommended through a systematic selection process. This process often involves a committee consisting of faculty and library staff members, who review the materials for their worthiness to the academic community or implement suggestions made by faculty or staff of the university. This selection process ensures that the library collects sources that are reliable, authoritative, and relevant. The library may purchase only one copy of each resource, which is shared by many people.

When combining conventional, library-based research with web-based research, researchers should remember that print libraries generally are characterized as having "quality" materials, while web-based materials are characterized by "quantity." When one is researching on the web, search queries may yield numerous resources, but most will not be high quality or on point. For example, if a researcher used the search terms "comparative negligence" in any search engine, the result might be similar to the page shown in Figure 7-1.

The first entry is often a reference to Wikipedia, which is not considered to be a "quality" site because it is a site that nearly anyone can contribute to merely by adding information. Wikipedia might be useful as a place to gain basic understanding of a topic or to locate references to other sites, but it is not a source that should be relied upon exclusively.

In seeking "quality," the researcher should look for web addresses ending in ".edu" for educational institutions (law school libraries) or ".gov" for government (state and federal websites). The downside to using these websites is that while they may have a great deal of information, they will probably not have the full versions of all the documents that would be available in a physical library.

The Internet

The Internet, which is separate and distinct from databases available through a library, poses other problems. It should be noted that this discussion is centered on the "free" Internet. "Free" Internet, in this context, means anything posted on the web that is not from a paid service such as Westlaw or LexisNexis.

No one individual or group dictates what information is acceptable for publication on the Internet or how it should be presented. This lack of control

TIP

Students will find that libraries generally do not allow legal materials to be checked out. The legal materials are treated as reference materials, so the students must use the materials at the library. That means students should plan on spending extra study time in the library when research projects are assigned.

FIGURE 7-1 Google Page

❏ *Comparative negligence* **- Wikipedia, the free encyclopedia**
*en.wikipedia.org/wiki/***Comparative_negligence**

Comparative negligence, or non-absolute contributory negligence outside of the United States, is a partial legal defense that reduces the amount of damages . . .

❏ **comparative+negligence - Legal Dictionary - The Free Dictionary**
*legal-dictionary.thefreedictionary.com/***comparative+negligence**

comparative negligence n. a rule of law applied in accident cases to determine responsibility and damages based on the negligence of every party directly . . .

❏ **comparative negligence - Legal Dictionary | Law.com**
*dictionary.law.com/De***fault***.aspx?selected=256*

comparative negligence. n. a rule of law applied in accident cases to determine responsibility and damages based on the negligence of every party directly . . .

❏ **Contributory Negligence vs.** *Comparative Negligence*
*www.the-injury-lawyer-directory.com/***negligence***.html*

Learn about Contributory Negligence vs. *Comparative Negligence* at The Personal Injury Lawyer Directory.

❏ **What Is** *Comparative Negligence?* **- Illinois Department of Insurance**
insurance.illinois.gov/autoinsurance/comp_Negl.asp

Comparative negligence laws dictate how the responsibility for an accident will be shared between the parties directly involved in an accident where bodily . . .

❏ **Contributory Negligence/** *Comparative Fault* **Chart - Mwl-law.com**
www.mwl-law.com/PracticeAreas/Contributory-Neglegence.asp

Contributory *Negligence* - Matthiesen, Wickert & Lehrer, S.C. Hartford, Wisconsin.

❏ **Contributory and** *Comparative Negligence* **- FindLaw**
*injury.findlaw.com/. . ./contributory-and-***comparative-negligence***.html*

Accidents take place everyday — people are injured and property is damaged. When accidents happen, one of the first questions people typically ask is Who . . .

❏ *Comparative Negligence*
www.njcounselors.com/law.htm

New Jersey is one of a number of states which have adopted a form of the *comparative negligence* rule. Under the *comparative negligence* doctrine, a plaintiff . . .

❏ **What Is** *Comparative Negligence?* **- Free Advice - Personal Injury Law**
*injury-law.freeadvice.com/injury-law/. . ./***comparative_negligence***s.ht . . .*

Comparative negligence asserts that a plaintiff's actions were negligent and directly contributed to the harm he suffered, reducing the defendant's liability.

❏ *Comparative Negligence.* **Percentage of Fault and Injury . . .**
*www.lawfirms.com/resources/. . ./***negligence***-compensation.htm*

Comparative negligence will determine who will receive compensation for their personal injury case and how much they are eligible to receive.

means that almost anyone can publish his or her opinions, ideas, and creative works on the web. Much of this information may be interesting, but most of it may not be useful or reliable for academic research.

Legal researchers will generally save time and find more quality information by beginning with library resources and then moving to the Internet if more information or points of view are needed. Sometimes, however, if a researcher already knows a citation to a particular case or statute, the Internet may be a useful resource.

Using the Internet Many people go to the Internet first when trying to find information. It is difficult to make generalizations or definitive statements about something as diverse as the Internet, but there are some concepts that must be considered when using the Internet for authority.

Anyone can publish on the web without passing the content through an editor who is unbiased or who does not have some type of agenda. Pages might be written by a recognized expert on a topic, but they may also be written by a journalist, a disgruntled consumer, a person with time on his or her hands, or even an elementary school student. Pages can refer to material from other countries that may not have any application to the particular needs of a person in this country. Many web pages do not have authors listed. Sometimes it is difficult to determine exactly who is hosting a particular site. Many web pages are free to view, but some commercial sites will charge users a fee to access their information. However, the fact that a fee is charged should be no indication that the information is reliable.

Organization Another problem with information from the Internet is that it is not always well organized. Some directory services, such as Yahoo® or Google®, collect links to sites and place them in subject lists. But there are too many Internet pages for any single directory service or search engine to organize and index. In addition, most information on the Internet is not comprehensive, and is constantly changing. There are millions of Internet pages in existence and millions more that have been removed from the servers. No easy, reliable, or comprehensive way exists to retrieve materials in this eclectic hodgepodge of information and opinion from different decades, viewpoints, and sources.

Permanence Some well-maintained sites are updated frequently with very current information, but other sites may become quickly dated or disappear altogether without much notice and then one is not using "quality" sites. A researcher should look for the date of the site's last update to determine how current its information is.

Quantity or Quality The Internet can be a good research source for some purposes, such as reading current news, gaining some background about a government or entity, surveying opinions on a topic, or gathering ideas. The Internet can be a starting point for a project, but quantity rules over quality. Thus, the Internet is a good tool for finding background information or getting ideas, but it is usually not the best place to engage in reliable academic research.[4]

The Library and the Internet

Many libraries have Internet sites that organize information and provide access to collections of quality resources. Some of the best library web pages come from the major universities such as Cornell University or Harvard University. When using

TIP

A researcher should remember that when one uses remote access to search the library's databases, one is accessing the library's collection via the web, but is still using library resources, which tend to be more reliable.

[4]Joe Barker. Regents of the University of California, Berkeley. *Evaluating the Web Pages Checklist.* 2007. http://www.lib.berkeley.edu/TeachingLib/Guides/Internet/webeval-QuestionsToAsk.pdf

a respected library on the Internet, one can be assured that the information has been evaluated, organized, and—perhaps most importantly—updated.

Much of the information on the library Internet is from governments, companies, universities, and foreign countries. Sometimes the library has digitized material from its own collections or exhibits for people around the world to use. Although there is an increasing amount of information in this "digital library" on the Internet, researchers still will not find electronic full-text versions of all of the resources that could be found in the physical library.

Manual Research Manual research is an art. Although some researchers have entirely replaced manual research with computer-assisted research, manual research continues to hold an important place in the legal field.

The organization of each library may vary, but a researcher must be able to locate the necessary books or materials regardless of the library's layout. Researchers must be able to find out where the state and federal statutes, encyclopedias, digests, and state and federal reporters are located, as well as the material that will allow them to update and validate citations.

A researcher must also acquire tools and tricks for researching well. This includes knowing what the books in the law library do, and how they can be used the most effectively. For example, the researcher should know how an encyclopedia can aid in a search, whether a digest provides a good source of law in a particular jurisdiction, what books can be used to find cases, whether there is access to official or unofficial sources, and how the materials are updated.

Most importantly, researchers must know what tools are the most useful for answering the question at hand. On one project, simply finding a statute may be all that is needed to answer the question, whereas in another, the researcher may need to find many statutes and cases, and then analyze how they fit together to evaluate the merits of a case. Exhibit 7-2 provides an outline for doing manual research.

The information in Exhibit 7-2 applies to most research. Example 7-4 shows how a research assignment might unfold.

EXHIBIT 7-2   AN OUTLINE FOR THE MANUAL RESEARCH PROCESS

1. **Make sure the assignment is understood.** If the assignment is not understood, either confirm the assignment with the assigning supervisor or consult a secondary source, such as treatises, legal encyclopedias, or ALRs for background information on the topic of the assignment.

2. **Determine the jurisdiction.** Look at the issue and determine whether it involves federal or state law.

3. **List key words and search terms.** Identify the key words of the problem and use those words to determine the search terms. Identify synonyms and antonyms that could be used as key words in the search.

4. **Decide where to begin the research.** Many researchers start with the highest primary authority that they believe will control the situation. Otherwise, it might be a waste of time to find cases, only to find that a statute has been amended or enacted that changes the value of the cases. Another reason to find the highest primary authority first is that it often provides the researcher with an outline or overview of the analysis. The elements of a statute may serve as an outline for the analysis.

5. **Locate relevant cases.** Find relevant cases through statutory annotations, digests, or other secondary resources. Most secondary resources have indices in which the key words can be used to locate relevant case law.

6. **Update the research.** Shepardize the authorities cited to confirm whether any have been superseded, amended, repealed, or overruled, and check the pocket parts, advance sheets, looseleaf services, and other current material for new, modified, or repealed laws.

EXAMPLE 7-4   MANUAL RESEARCH ASSIGNMENT

Betty Barteau from St. Louis, Missouri, was driving on Interstate 70 when she had a tire blow out, which caused her to crash into the guardrail. The tires recently had been purchased from Acme Tire Barn in St. Louis and were manufactured by Vulcan Tires, which is headquartered in Denver, Colorado. Betty thinks someone should pay for the damages she incurred. She has come to The Gumm Firm in St. Louis to pursue her claim. After Kevin, the paralegal, along with the supervisor, Mike Gumm, interviewed Betty, Kevin was asked to perform a Westlaw search to see what results he could find.

Step 1.   Kevin must determine whether he understands the problem. If not, he might need to do some reading in secondary sources such as a legal encyclopedia or a treatise on product liability law.

Step 2.   Kevin needs to know whether the issue is one for federal or state court. The answer is going to be state court, because the requirements for filing in federal court are not met. Which state's law applies?

- Missouri state law: MO-CS (Missouri cases, because Betty is domiciled there.)
- Colorado state law: CO-CS (Colorado cases, because the company is headquartered there.)

Since the firm represents Betty, Missouri state law is chosen.

Step 3.   Once Kevin is sure he understands the problem, he selects the key words. For this problem, those might be the following:

- Tire
- Blowout
- Manufacturer
- Damages (most students will select damages, but the combination of the other terms actually provides the concept of damages)
- Liability (most students will select liability, but the combination of the other terms actually provides the concept of liability)

Step 4.   Look for alternate terms:

- Tire: tread, belts, wheel, "rubber casing," "radial belts," "bias ply"
- Blowout: blew, "blow out," deflation, deflate, explode
- Manufacturer: company, producer, owner, developer, engineer, designer

Kevin combines several terms using punctuation such as hyphens and quotation marks. Those punctuation marks provide directions to the computer. If a word is written as two words, one word, or a hyphenated word, using the hyphen will retrieve all forms. Putting words in quotation marks tells the computer to search for the exact phrase.

(Continued)

Step 5.   Kevin is sure he understands the problem, but just in case, he researches the key concepts in *Corpus Juris Secundum* (C.J.S.).

Step 6.   Kevin uses the keywords and alternate words to look for the highest authority. There does not appear to be a constitutional question, so he begins looking in the index of the state statutes. He also uses the key words to look in the index of the *Missouri Digest 2d* for cases. Kevin finds a statute on point, along with several cases that have similar facts and issues, which he reads and briefs.

Step 7.   After he has completed the research, he updates the law and prepares the memorandum to his boss.

Pocket parts
Updates of a service, such as a set of statutes, to provide current information until enough new information warrants a new hardbound volume.

Advance sheets
Updates for various services, such as regional reporters and *Shepard's* Citations? which are issued in between publications of hardback volumes.

Updating the Research   A good researcher must always check for updates, such as making sure the **pocket parts** in the sets are current, or confirming that the updated sheets are placed in the binders for the looseleaf services. Pocket parts are the supplements that publishers use to update most materials between publications of new volumes. For example, Thomson West publishes the *Indiana Code Annotated*. Each year, the volumes of statutes are updated with pocket parts showing new, modified, and repealed laws and the annotations that accompany those statutes. When the updates are large enough to justify publishing a new volume, the entire volume will be republished and the pocket part method of updating will begin again. Many reference materials are updated in this way.

Updating is also done through **advance sheets**, which are used with tools such as reporters and *Shepard's* Citations to provide the most current cases and to validate the cases, statutes, and other materials. For example, when enough cases are published, a new permanent volume of the case reporter is created. The advance sheets publish the cases in advance of the publication of the permanent volume.

Looseleaf materials are updated by current pages, which are organized chronologically in the volume where the page is replaced. The pages are hole-punched, and one or more pages must come out when one or more go in the volume. The replacement pages are indicated with a date. A researcher should confirm that the updated pages are correct.

INTERNET RESEARCH

Internet research is performed using two categories of sources: non-subscription, or "free," Internet sites, and subscription services such as Westlaw, LexisNexis, Versuslaw®, Loislaw®, and CaseMaker®. Each has benefits and drawbacks.

Non-subscription

Most people have discovered that finding an answer to a question is as easy as turning on the computer, selecting the preferred Internet search engine, typing in a few words about what they want to know, and hitting "enter" or "send." This process may yield results, but one should understand how that process occurs, and whether those results may be trusted.

The Internet holds a wealth of information, and most of the information is relatively easy to find. However, the researcher needs to weigh the value of the material found, and should only utilize websites that are reliable and are designed for legal practitioners. Students should not believe that they can "Google" a legal issue and find the answer in the list that pops up. The Internet does have some value as long as users understand what that value is.

Researchers should first confirm that the site being used contains updated and reliable legal information. The best websites are those created by law schools, the U.S. government, state governments, and subscription legal databases. Table 7-1 provides some well-known free databases. This is not an exhaustive list, but it may provide a starting point.

Note that as with all web addresses, the URLs for the sites in Table 7-1 may change. Sometimes, it is useful for a user to go to the home page of the site, which often will redirect the user to the appropriate page.

TABLE 7-1 Valid Online Resources

Suggested Free Legal Research Online Resources

Library of Congress	The world's largest collection of law books and legal resources. www.loc.gov and the law library at www.loc.gov/law/. You can access Thomas for legislative materials. http://Thomas.loc.gov
U.S. Government Printing Office	The U.S. Government Printing Office supplies links to Congressional reports, Congressional bills, the *Congressional Record*, public laws, private laws, and the United States Code. www.gpo.gov
FindLaw, sponsored by Westlaw	The world's leading provider of online legal information, FindLaw is part of West Group, which also offers the Westlaw subscription service. www.findlaw.com. <ul><li>The site for legal professionals: http://lp.findlaw.com</li><li>State specific information and some forms: http://forms.lp.findlaw.com</li><li>A variety of other information, such as the document index: http://news.lp.findlaw.com/legalnews/documents/index2.html</li><li>FindLaw news: http://legalnews.findlaw.com/</li><li>FindLaw's YouTube channel: http://www.youtube.com/user/FindLaw</li><li>Court TV: www.courttv.findlaw.com/</li><li>truTV: http://www.trutv.com/newname.html</li><li>The newer option of FindLaw Answers: http://boards.answers.findlaw.com/n/forumIndex.aspx?webtag=fl-answersidx</li></ul>
LexisONE, sponsored by LEXIS	Owned by LEXIS, LexisONE is a great legal resource for small law firms. www.lexisone.com Some of the material is by subscription only. LexisONE does have a section for free case law and forms, but the coverage is limited.
Cornell University Law School	The Legal Information Institute is a research service sponsored by Cornell Law School and is probably the best free site available. www.law.cornell.edu You can access federal and state materials, uniform laws, topical information, and much more.
Indiana University School of Law	Indiana University's School of Law provides free access to the top 20 legal resources most frequently used by law students and faculty. www.law.indiana.edu/lawlibrary/index.shtml
Washburn University School of Law	Washburn University's School of Law offers free access to ATLAS, its law library search engine. http://washburnlaw.edu/library
Internet Legal Research Group	www.ilrg.com
Google (old sites)	http://www.Google.com/search?sourceid=navclient&ie=UTF-8&rlz=1T4ADBF_enUS306US306&q=old+websites
Michie's Legal Resources	www.michie.com
The American Bar Association	www.abanet.org

Spamming
Pages created deliberately to trick the search engine into offering inappropriate, redundant, or poor-quality search results.

General Tips on Using Search Engines Most web search engines have a method of looking for key words according to location and frequency within documents. The first area that a search engine looks at is the title. When creating a search query, a user should think of whether the words are likely to appear in the title.

The next location the search engine looks at is the top of the web page. The headline or introductory paragraphs of text is a logical location for relevant terms. The search engine also looks at how frequent the key words appear. The higher the frequency, the greater the relevance of key words located in the results.

Although the methods used by search engines may be similar, the same query entered into two different search engines will yield different results, or at least a different ranking of the results. This is because of differences in the way the search engines index the web pages. Some search engines look for words that are repeated numerous times on a page in an effort to place the page higher in the listings. The creators of the web pages use this *"spamming"* technique to elevate their materials. Yahoo defines spam as "pages created deliberately to trick the search engine into offering inappropriate, redundant, or poor-quality search results." This is similar to the definitions offered by Google® and MSN as well.[5] The search engines also look at how pages link to other pages to determine the importance of a page and to decide the ranking of the page. This is a method that webmasters cannot easily manipulate.

Another technique used by search engines is measuring the results that searchers actually select, as compared to those results that a searcher simply clicks through or bypasses. Google® (www.Google.com), one of the most often-used search engines, ranks results according to the links from other websites. This concept makes sense from the standpoint that the more links that a website has, the more other sites rely on or believe in the material posted.

Google, like many search engines, uses the Boolean connectors of "and," "or," and "but not." A search is generally executed as a phrase first, then as if the word "and" were between the words, and finally as if the word "or" were between the terms. For example, if the search was for "legal research," the Google system would look for it first as "legal research," then as "legal and research," and finally "legal or research." However, if the phrase were placed in quotation marks, Google would search only for the phrase.

Another tool that can make searches more effective is the plus (+) sign. A plus sign placed before a term or phrase means that Google will include the word in the search results. If a minus (−) sign is placed before the term, that term will be excluded from the results. The other Boolean connector is the asterisk (*) or "wildcard," which allows Google to use the asterisk as a placeholder for any unknown terms. Another feature of search engines is that common words, such as "the," "an," and "for," are not searched for except in limited circumstances. These are called "stop words" because these words appear too frequently.

TIP
Researchers should review those help areas even if they believe that they know how to utilize the services.[6]

Some of these aspects of searches are found in the subscription services as well. Google®, like many search engines, provides helpful reference guides or help toggles.

Other Methods of Searching for Non-Subscription Materials Google® and other search engines perform more focused tasks in addition to general searches.

[5]Hunt, Bill. *What, Exactly, Is Search Engine Spam?* Feb 16, 2005. Retrieved May 29, 2010. Available at http://searchenginewatch.com/3483601

[6]Blachman, Nancy. *Google Guide: Making Searching Even Easier.* Retrieved May 29, 2010. Available at http://www.googleguide.com/

Google Scholar[7] offers a variety of academic resources such as scholarly papers, articles and theses, books, cases, and journals from academic and professional sources. Results can be filtered by type of result needed, such as articles, judicial opinions, and patents. While this service does provide a large amount of information, it is not a complete source of academic material. Many older cases have not been included, and the sources cannot be validated. However, it does provide a free option when beginning a research project.

The other option on this website is a connection to "Internet Archive: Wayback Machine."[8] This is generally the first site on the retrieval.

There are numerous free websites that offer legal materials, from general search engines like Google to state-specific resources such as the San Diego County Public Law Library, although these websites are not useful for conducting in-depth research. These websites might provide some background material or certain specific material such as a citation result, but one should not expect to do an entire assignment on the free Internet.

Three well-known legal providers have created networking tools with somewhat different purposes than those of legal retrieval sites. LexisNexis® is the source of LexisNexis Legal Communities,[9] which allows a user to join a community based on professional interest or practice area. Information is gathered from a variety of sources and made available on this site. Paralegal students may want to join this site and participate in the paralegal community, among others.

Martindale-Hubbell is a tool for locating lawyers and law firms all over the world. It also provides various educational materials, such as articles on legal topics. Martindale-Hubbell Connected[10] is an important professional resource that goes beyond serving as a tool to locate lawyers. There are features for law students and law firm paralegals, with articles and other educational materials for students.

This is not an exhaustive list of free sites that provide valuable information. More are added every day.

Weighing the Material It seems that anyone can post almost anything on the Internet. Usually someone can publish for a small cost and with very few limitations. Some websites appear to be authoritative, but the reality is that most websites are flawed in some way. One example is Wikipedia. When Wikipedia began, it was used often and sometimes exclusively by college students and others. It had information on nearly any subject, and invited people to update the information. Unfortunately, users can update the information right on the website and often information isn't checked before it is posted.[11] Consequently, Wikipedia became and remains an unreliable site.

In addition, information on the Internet that is otherwise reliable can become unreliable if the site does not remain current, if the host network becomes corrupted, or if the website is damaged. A researcher may not find hints that there are problems on the web in the same way the researcher might receive hints in print sources.

[7]About Google Scholar. 2011. http://scholar.Google.com/intl/en/scholar/about.html (last visited February 5, 2012)

[8]Parkening, Aaron et al. *Internet Archive: Wayback Machine.* Retrieved May 29, 2010. Available at http://www.archive.org/web/web.php

[9]LexisNexis Communities. Retrieved May 29, 2010. Available at www.lexisnexis.com/communities/

[10]*Martindale-Hubbell® Connected: Professional Networking Site for Legal Professionals.* 2010. Retrieved May 29, 2010. Available at www.martindale.com/connected

[11]*Welcome to Wikipedia.* Retrieved May 2, 2010. Available at http://en.wikipedia.org/wiki/Main_Page

To decide whether a site is authentic or valid, a researcher should look at the results with a trained eye, ask some questions, and verify the results. There are many steps that can be taken to make sure the material on a website is reliable. Here are some key questions that a researcher might consider:

- Is there an author?
- Does the site have a valid sponsor?
- Is the site accurate?
- Is the site up to date?

Exhibit 7-3 provides a few ideas to consider when evaluating information on a website.

EXHIBIT 7-3   STEPS IN VERIFYING A SITE

1. Look at the URL endings.

Domain	Ending
Government	.gov
Educational	.edu
Military	.mil
Commercial	.com
Internet (Top-level domain originally for Internet service providers and web-hosting companies)	.net
Personal page	Name, tilde (~), or percent sign (%)

2. By looking at the rest of the URL, one can determine the individual or entity that has published the page. For example, if the URL has "doj" somewhere between the http:// and the first slash mark, it is the Department of Justice.

3. By looking around the home page for other information, the researcher can evaluate the site by finding the following:

   a. "About Us" or "Background"

   b. A date on which the page was last updated

   c. An author or someone who claims responsibility for the page

   d. Author credentials

4. Finding quality indicators may help a researcher determine if the site is used by others and was created to accommodate researchers. Such indicators include the following:

   a. Links to other sites

   b. Complete information with footnotes or other reputable references

   c. Original material or reproduced material

5. Look for other evaluations of the site, such as other sites that reference this site.

   a. Use Google or some other search engine to locate the author's name to see what information is available. Plugging the URL into the site http://www.alexa.com will tell about the URL posted, such as the site's *hits* (traffic details), and related links.

   b. Research the title or publisher in a specialized directory such as www.About.com.

6. Determine whether all the information adds up.

   a. Does it make sense?

   b. Is there valid support?

   c. Is the site presented in a professional manner?

   d. Does the site present the material posted in a professional manner?

Hits

A slang term for the number of times a site has been viewed.

New researchers should learn to evaluate websites in order to use the Internet appropriately for in-depth research. The site evaluation process will become individualized as more and more research is executed on the Internet. In the meantime, Checklist 7-1 provides some steps to consider in evaluating sites.

A researcher needs to evaluate the reliability of information published in any format, but particularly information found on the Internet. Compared to that information available on subscription services, the amount of legal materials available on free sites is very small, and the standards for posting this information are much less rigorous. A researcher must remember to evaluate these sources carefully for authority, objectivity, accuracy, coverage, and timeliness. An example is shown in Example 7-5.

There is no definitive method for verifying sites, but there are a few tips that can be considered.

Authority To determine the reliability of a website, the publisher's and author's expertise or credentials should be examined first. Sometimes the web page containing the author's information is part of a larger site. If it is unclear who is posting the information, a researcher should reconsider whether the site should be

Checklist 7-1 — POSSIBLE STEPS IN EVALUATING INTERNET RESEARCH

- Search for the authority.
- Understand the domain nomenclature.
- Make sure the site is current.
- Make sure the information is accurate.
- Evaluate the coverage.
- See if there are sources listed.
- Determine how objective the material is.

EXAMPLE 7-5 EVALUATING A SITE

Evaluate the San Diego County Public Law Library: www.sdcll.org. According to its home page, it has been operating since 1891. There is a history of the library on the Welcome page.

Authority:

The library is a federal depository library and a California State Document Depository Library, so it is part of two larger entities.

Objectivity:

The library information states that the library staff will "maintain a neutral stance with regard to all parties of litigation and endeavor to maintain their confidentiality as best as possible."

Coverage and Accuracy:

The collection is identified in a separate section (http://www.sdcll.org/resources/collection.htm). Whether this source has all the information needed and whether the source is accurate will depend on the issue at hand.

Timeliness:

The site does not provide information about the timeliness of the material.

Would this be a valid site to use? The answer is "probably," but some information may need to be confirmed by other sources.

used, and whether reliability can be confirmed. If the identity of the author cannot be verified, it might be best to locate a better site. If one is looking for primary legal sources, the government and the education sites will usually be authoritative sources, while commercial sites may be questionable.

Objectivity When looking at secondary sources, it is especially important to evaluate the author's and publisher's objectivity in addition to their background. A source that is biased or one-sided generally should not be used in legal research.

If the author or publisher does have a particular bias, it does not mean that the information should be rejected automatically. An organization that advocates a position will often publish information to support its point of view. Sometimes verifiable facts can be distinguished from statements that are actually opinions presented as facts. However, some organizations may not be open about their point of view. In that case, a researcher should think twice about using the information from that site.

Coverage and Accuracy A good indication of reliability is whether the source gives the citations needed to verify the information. Information on the page may be verified by checking the cited authorities, preferably if that information can be found in two or more locations. The more important the issue is, the more careful a researcher should be in determining the accuracy of the information. If the information is full of broken links or typographical errors, find another source.

Timeliness A researcher should be able to tell when the material was written and, perhaps more importantly, when it was last updated. A good website can be distinguished by when it was last updated. If the website does not state its last update, the researcher should determine whether the information is current. Some primary legal information, particularly information that is provided for free by a governmental entity, is often out of date. Some sites post warnings stating that the material is free as a public service and should not be relied upon without checking an official publication.[12]

On non-legal sites, timeliness of the information may be sufficient, depending on the purpose of the research. If searching for information on the American Red Cross and its Relay for Life, material that was published within the past year may tell about the current relays, but material that is older may be valid only as information about past events.

However, if a paralegal is performing legal research and looking for controlling law on an issue, the most current information will be found only by looking at the most current primary authority. This means searching the appropriate government statutory code for enacted law rather than searching in the session laws, and then updating the material. If researching case law, the most current information will be found only by accessing all opinions from the controlling courts. Based on precedent and the doctrine of *stare decisis*, the cases remain in effect unless they are overturned, reversed, or modified in some fashion.

There are no hard and fast rules on finding and using free sites. However, a user should perform the additional research necessary to be sure that the information acquired is authoritative, valid, current, and appropriate.

---

[12]Carol Anne Germain & Laura Horn. University Libraries, University at Albany. *Evaluating Internet Sites 101.* 2007. http://library.albany.edu/usered/webeval/

Subscription Services

There are two main online legal databases that attorneys subscribe to: Westlaw and LexisNexis. Other services are also available, such as TheLaw.net, VersusLaw, LoisLaw, Fastcase, and CASEMaker. These services provide virtual law libraries where both primary and secondary authority can be found. Because the services are by subscription, a password is needed to use the sites.

Users are charged for searches performed in these subscription services. Each service has its own fee schedule, which can vary depending on the needs of each user. The service may charge the user per search (Westlaw or LexisNexis), or access may be provided as part of the user's attorney's bar association dues (CASEMaker). Students may have access to one or more services as part of their tuition and fees.

When starting employment, a new paralegal will usually be given access to the firm's subscription, but someone will need to explain the fee arrangement before allowing the new user to log on the system. Some providers have account representatives who will come to the office to train new users, or offer free training online through **webinars**. Other services have training tutorials on their websites. Many paralegal programs offer training in one or more services. The more knowledgeable paralegals are about using a service, the more useful and effective they will be to their employer, and the more frequently they will be asked to research in that service.

Westlaw and LexisNexis have been the workhorses of online legal research for years. As competitors, these companies constantly pressure each other to become more innovative. As a result, online legal research is constantly improving—by becoming faster, more user-friendly, and more cost effective. However, the cost factor remains a downside to using these services. Each has a variety of subscription options, but by far, both exceed the cost of the other services available. Understanding the query methods used in each service is critical to reducing the fees incurred while performing legal research.

Westlaw   West products use a unique system of research aids called the **key number system**, available only for West materials. These numbers allow a researcher to quickly access specific topics in a **digest**, which contains a summary of the each topic. All West publications are linked together through this key number system.

Westlaw also provides an update or citation checking service called KeyCite. With this service, a researcher can determine whether the information found is still good (valid) law. KeyCite also provides the researcher with other sources or citations to the source being checked.

The process for research in Westlaw is similar to the process for manual research. Checklist 7-2 illustrates this basic process.

When creating a search query in Westlaw, the research may use either a natural language method or a Boolean search method with terms and connectors. Westlaw uses standard connectors that tell the computer the relationship among the terms and find those terms within its database. A **query** is the total set of instructions that a researcher gives to the computer to have the computer search for and find supporting authority that satisfies the query. A query consists of four parts:

- Terms
- Alternate terms
- Expanders
- Connectors

Webinar
A web-based seminar conducted over the Internet.

> **TIP**
> Once one learns one service, it is easy to learn other services. The key elements are very similar, so a transfer of knowledge from one to another is easy. In addition, a new researcher can work on the tutorials provided by the different providers at any time.

Key number system
An indexing system, designed by West Publishing Company, which assigns numbers to the various legal topics and to the individual headnotes within the topics.

Digest
Small paragraphs or summaries of court opinions that are arranged by subject matter.

Query
Instructions that a researcher gives to the computer to tell the computer to search for and find specific information.

> **TIP**
> Westlaw (www.westlaw.com) began in the 1970s when West Publishing Company was a standalone company. Today it is part of Thomson Reuters. New researchers can try out the Westlaw site by taking a free trial.[13]

[13]Westlaw Training. http://west.thomson.com/westlaw/campus-research/default.aspx

Checklist 7-2   WESTLAW RESEARCH

1. **Make sure the assignment is understood.** After receiving an assignment, a researcher should make sure the topic at issue is understood or be prepared to do some background research.

2. **Determine jurisdiction.** A researcher next looks at the issue and determines whether federal or state law governs.

3. **Begin with the highest authority.** Many researchers start with the highest primary authority; otherwise, it might be a waste of time to find cases, only to find that a statute that has been amended changes the value of the cases. The highest primary authority often provides the researcher with an outline of how the analysis should flow: the elements of the enacted law, for example, make an outline for the analysis.

4. **Construct a search query.** Construct a search in Westlaw using the traditional terms and connectors method of query writing.

Terms
Developed from the key words of the assignment.

TIP
Key words are those words that if different or nonexistent would affect the outcome.

Alternate terms
Synonyms, and sometimes antonyms, for key terms.

Stop words
Words that, when used in a Westlaw query, are too common for the computer to use.

Terms **Terms** may be developed from the key words of the assignment.

Alternate Terms **Alternate terms** are synonyms, and sometimes antonyms, for the key terms. It is often necessary to try a variety of synonyms, because researchers cannot be sure what words courts have used for the same idea or concept. For example, if the assignment used the key word *motor vehicle*, alternate terms might be *car, truck, automobile, motorcycle,* or simply *vehicle*. If the researcher used only *motor vehicle*, with no alternate terms in the query, the computer would return only those cases in which the judge used the term *motor vehicle*. If other judges used the terms *car, truck, motorcycle, automobile* or any other words for *motor vehicle*, the computer would not return those cases because the computer was asked to search only for *motor vehicle*.

Sometimes antonyms can also be important search terms, depending on the issue being researched. For example, if a researcher were interested in looking for an explanation of what is considered "secured property" in a bankruptcy, it might also be important to know what is considered "unsecured."

There are a few tips to keep in mind when developing terms and alternate terms for a Westlaw search. Plurals of words are automatic. If the word "term" is used, the computer will look automatically for "terms." Westlaw will also automatically search for some abbreviations. Days of the week are automatically abbreviated, so that if *Monday* is entered, the computer will automatically search for *Mon*. The same is true of the months. With state names, a researcher can enter *Indiana*, and the computer will recognize the postal abbreviation *IN* or the abbreviation *Ind*.

Searching for compound words can be problematic. The word "restroom" can be written as one word, *restroom*, as two words, *rest room*, or as a hyphenated word, *rest-room*. In order to receive all the possible results no matter how the word is written in the cases, a researcher should use the hyphenated form *rest-room*. If the hyphenated term were not used, it would be necessary to include the three variations as terms and alternate terms in order to get all results.

Some words are referred to as **stop words** because they are too common for the computer to search. Examples include *the, is, a, an,* and *that*. Stop words, except for "the," may be included in a search if a pound (#) sign is placed immediately before the stop word (for example, "#of") or if the stop word is included in a phrase search (such as "statute of limitations").

Expanders An ***expander*** is used on the root of a word to tell the computer to retrieve any source that uses the particular word in any form. Expanders come in two forms: the root expander (!) and the universal character (*). Both are available and used similarly in other Internet-based applications. For example, if a researcher had the word "manufacture" in a query, the researcher could enter "manufact!" and the computer would retrieve "manufacture," "manufacturer," "manufactured," "manufacturing," and "manufactures." Without using the root expander, the researcher would need to enter all terms to be sure that every case discussing the concept was retrieved, no matter how the court referred to the concept.

There is a caveat, however. If a researcher used the word "automobile," the root would be "auto." The results would include words such as "automatic," "automated," "automation," and so on. Another example is the word "tabbed." If the basic term with a root expander, "tab!" were used, the results would be "tab," "tabbed," "tabbing," "table," "tablet," "tableau," and so on. When a root returns results that are not appropriate in the search results, use both the root (auto or tab) and the required word (automobile or tabbed or tabbing) rather than the root with an expander (auto! or tab!).

The other expander is the ***universal character*** (*), which is used to replace a letter. One universal character is used for each letter being replaced. For example, if the term being used were "sue," the word could be presented as "sue*" and the results would be "sue," "sues," and "sued," but not "suing," because only one expander was used. The universal character does not need to be at the end. If the term being researched were "grow," the word could be presented as "gr*w" and the results would be "grow" or "grew." (*Caveat*: Universal characters cannot be used at the beginning of a word.)

The final elements of the query are the ***connectors***, which are symbols that tell the computer how the terms should appear in the retrieved documents. When a connector is used, a researcher should put a space before and after the connector such as automobile[space]/s[space]tire. See Table 7-2 for the connectors.

Expander
Query tool that tells the computer to automatically search for many forms of a certain term.

Universal character
A character, usually an asterisk (*), used to replace a letter when doing a Westlaw search.

TIP
It is a good idea to have a dictionary or thesaurus handy when doing research so that one can check the words for synonyms and antonyms as well as for the word's root.

Connectors
Words in a query that tell the computer how the terms will appear in the retrieved documents.

TABLE 7-2 Westlaw Connectors

Connector	What It Means
A space	Means "or." (Do not type the word "or"; just put a space between words.) Denotes "this word *or* that word." Used for synonyms or antonyms. Example: car automobile auto truck means car OR automobile OR auto OR truck. This could also be written as car ^ automobile ^ with the ^ representing a space.
/s	Means the word on the left should be in the same sentence as the word on the right. Example: automobile /s trunk means find the word "automobile" within the same sentence as the word "trunk."
+s	Means the word on the left should precede the word on the right in the same sentence. Example: automobile +s trunk means find the word "automobile" before the word "trunk" in the same sentence.
/p	Means the word on the left should be in the same paragraph as the word on the right. Example: automobile /p trunk means find the word "automobile" within the same paragraph as the word "trunk."
+p	Means the word on the left should precede the word on the right in the same paragraph. Example: automobile +p trunk means find the word "automobile" before the word "trunk" in the same paragraph.
/n	Means the word on the left should be within "n" terms (n equals a number) as the word on the right. Example: automobile /10 trunk means find the word "automobile" within 10 terms of the word "trunk."

(Continued)

TABLE 7-2   *(Continued)*

Connector	What It Means
+n	Means the word on the left should precede the word on the right within so many terms where "n" is a number. Example: automobile +10 trunk means find the word "automobile" within 10 words before the word "trunk."
& (ampersand)	Means the word on the left should be in the same document as the word on the right. Example: automobile & trunk means find the word "automobile" within the same document as the word "trunk."
" " (phrase search)	Means the words within the quotation marks should be located just as presented. Use this connector with caution, because the computer is very literal. If you present "child custody" in your query, the computer will find only "child custody." It will not return authority where the concept is referred to in any other way, such as "custody of the child." So the caveat is to think how the court, for example, might refer to the concept. One would not use a phrase search unless that was the only way the court would express the idea.
%	Means "find these terms on the left but not the term on the right." Example: assault /p battery % criminal tells the computer to retrieve all documents where assault is in the same paragraph as battery but is not criminal in nature. So, the results would be based in civil law.

Annotated

Enhancements, such as cross-references and case headnotes, that provide a better understanding of the material, as well as a method of research.

Headnote

A short statement from a case that describes a particular point of law, and is given a key number in the West system.

There are other formatting options in Westlaw, such as field searches, but that is for another class. Online training and guidebooks are available through Westlaw.[14] A Westlaw search might work according to the assignment shown in Example 7-6.

The key to a successful computer search is to carefully check all the results to make sure they respond to the question searched. If not, the query should be changed, but *only one entry should be changed at a time*. If multiple entries or items are changed within a query at the same time, there is no way to know which change worked, and which did not. In Example 7-6, if the computer came back with no results, the first action would be to check the terms and alternate terms and determine whether all necessary terms and alternate terms were included, or were expanded properly. Then one should determine whether the connectors should be changed. (Hint: Often if the results are zero, open the connectors, such as changing a "/s" to a "/p," to get results.)

Westlaw's newest offering is WestlawNext™,[15] which was introduced in early 2010. The service allows a user to start a search without having to choose a specific database. Through a series of checkboxes, the user selects the appropriate jurisdictions and topical databases. The search engine, WestSearch, executes the search in multiple locations. Documents are ranked by relevance, as with the conventional Westlaw search. Users can also perform citation, party name, or KeyCite searches.

LexisNexis®   Like Westlaw, LexisNexis® allows a user to enter terms and connectors into its database to retrieve research results. LexisNexis publications include editorial enhancements, such as ***annotated*** comments and ***headnotes***. Many paralegal programs and law schools may have access to an educational version, LexisNexis® Academic.[16]

[14]Westlaw Training. http://www.westelearning.com/rc2/login.asp?

[15]http://west.thomson.com/westlawnext/default.aspx

[16]LexisNexis Academic Legal Research Solutions. 2012. http://academic.lexisnexis.com/online -services/academic/academic-content-legal-research.aspx

EXAMPLE 7-6 SAMPLE ASSIGNMENT

Remember the example earlier? Betty Barteau, from St. Louis, Missouri, was driving on Interstate 70 when she had a tire blow out, which caused her to crash into the guardrail. The tires recently were purchased from Acme Tire Barn in St. Louis and were manufactured by Allstate Tires, which is headquartered in Denver, Colorado. Betty thinks someone should pay for the damages she incurred. She has come to The Gumm Firm in St. Louis to pursue her claim. After Kevin, the paralegal, along with the supervisor, Mike Gumm, interviewed Betty, Kevin was asked to perform a Westlaw search to see what results he could find.

Step 1. Kevin must ask himself whether he understands the problem. If not, he might want to do some reading in secondary sources such as a legal encyclopedia or a treatise on automobile law.

Step 2. Kevin needs to know whether the issue is one for federal or state court. The answer is going to be state court because the requirements for filing in federal court (diversity of citizenship and damages exceeding $75,000, or a federal question) are not met. What laws would apply?

- Missouri state law MO-CS (Missouri cases, because Betty is domiciled there.)
- Colorado state law CO-CS (Colorado cases, because the company is headquartered there.)

Since the firm representing Betty is located in St. Louis, Missouri, Missouri state law is chosen.

Step 3. When Kevin is sure he understands the problem, he selects the key words. For this problem, those might be the following:

- Tire
- Blow
- Manufacturer
- Damages (most students will select damages but the combination of the other terms actually provides the concept of damages)
- Liability (most students will select liability but the combination of the other terms actually provides the concept of liability)

Step 4. Look for alternate terms, which might be these:

- Tire: nothing
- Blow: blew, blow out
- Manufacturer: company, producer, owner, developer

Now add steps 5 and 6.

Step 5. Look for expanders:

- Tire: nothing
- Blew: Bl*w, Bl*w-out (notice the universal character and the hyphenated term)
- Manufacturer: manufactur! company produc! owner develop!

Step 6. Identify the connectors and put the query together. For this problem, it might look like this:

Tire /s bl*w bl*w-out /p manufactur! company produc! owner develop!

EXHIBIT 7-4 LEXISNEXIS ACADEMIC[17]

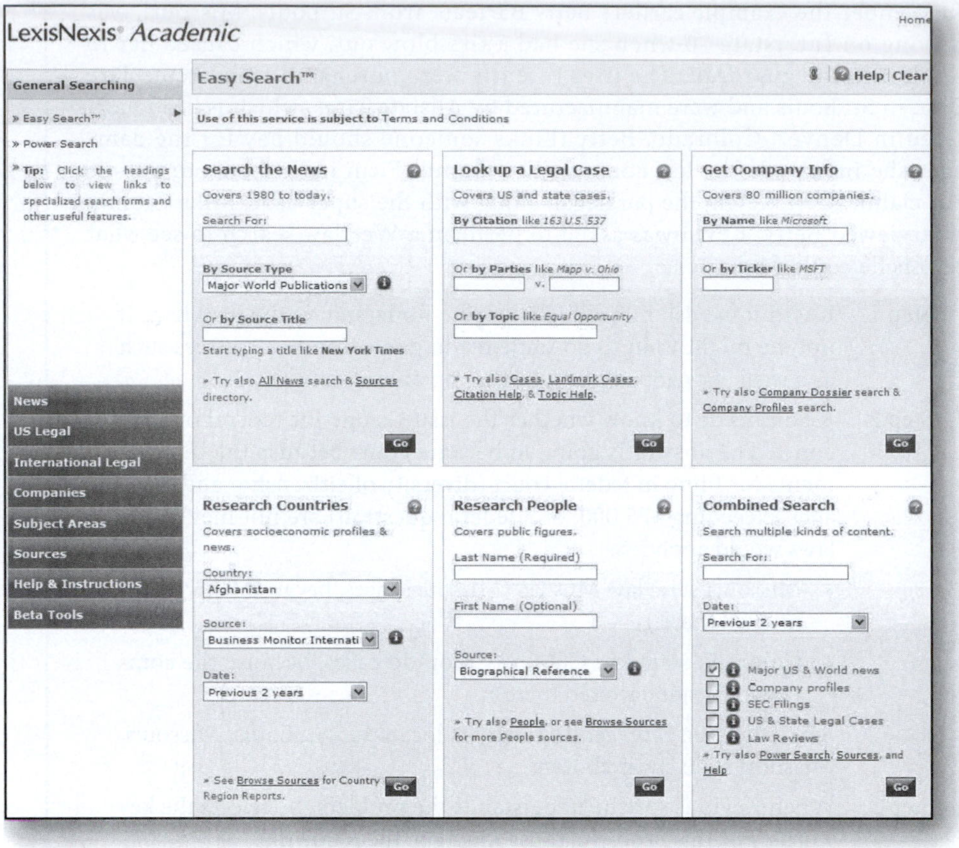

The design of a search query is very similar to that in Westlaw, but LexisNexis also has an "Easy Search" option that is similar to a fill-in-the-blank form. Exhibit 7-4 shows an "Easy Search" screen that may be used if a citation, party, or topic is known. For example, a researcher can enter the citation for a case under "Look up a Legal Case," and the case will be retrieved.

LexisNexis refers to its query form as "Terms and Connectors." The terms and connectors are similar to those used in Westlaw, shown in Table 7-2. The connectors in the LexisNexis service operate in an order of priority, as shown in Table 7-3.

As in Westlaw, in LexisNexis connectors establish the relationship between the words so the computer can find only relevant documents to satisfy the query. There are many ways to combine the connectors depending on the results desired.

Exhibit 7-5 shows the page for conducting research using LexisNexis Academic All News. On the left side are links to US Legal, International Legal, and other research options.

If a researcher looked at the various drop-down menus, he or she would see that the search boxes show a format similar to the Westlaw queries. For example, if one looked at the "Search for" box, he or she would notice a place where a key word could be entered. In the next line there is a box with "and," so that alternate words could be entered. Exhibit 7-5 shows a search for "All News." The search interface would have additional boxes for searching cases.

In 2011 LexisNexis created Lexis Advanced™, which is similar to West-lawNext. Through a process of collaboration, the company developed an approach

[17]LexisNexis Academic page 2. 2012. http://academic.lexisnexis.com/pdf/Academic_brochure.pdf

TABLE 7-3   LexisNexis Connectors

Connector	Meaning
OR	Links synonyms or alternate terms.
W/n	Links main terms or phrases where "n" is a number and no order of preference is needed (Note: 2, 3, and 4 are on the same priority level).
PRE/n	The first word comes before the second word "n" where "n" is a number and a different order would give a different meaning.
NOT W/n	The first word must appear in the document, but the second word cannot be within "n" words of the first.
W/S	The search words are in the same sentence.
W/P	The search words are in the same paragraph.
AND	Both words or phrases are within the same document.
AND NOT	Excludes documents that contain certain words or phrases.[18]

EXHIBIT 7-5 LEXISNEXIS ACADEMIC ALL NEWS[19]

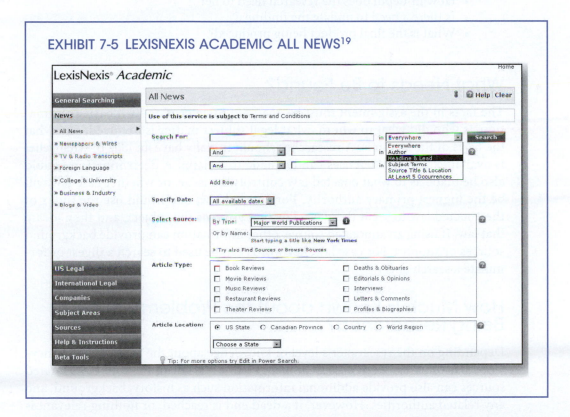

that allows access to results that are more relevant, tools that are more relevant, and an advantage in content delivery by updating, annotating, and narrowing the research so it is connected to other like documents. It also allows a user to search the web at the same time the Lexis search is performed[20]. There are a variety of tutorials available to subscribers, including free ones on YouTube. Both Westlaw and LexisNexis have created mobile applications for smartphones.

[18]LexisNexis Support Center. *Connectors.* 2012. http://support.lexisnexis.com/lawschool/record .asp?ArticleID=GS_Connectors&ALid=lawschool_basics#or

[19]*Id.* at 4.

[20]LexisNexis. *LexisNexis Launches New Release of Lexis Advance.* 2011. www.lexisnexis.com /media/press-release.aspx?id+1323111249773407

Neither Westlaw nor LexisNexis has been fully discussed here, but rather a summary of content and usage has been presented to provide an idea of the types of tools available. Once the basics of either system are learned, transferring the skills from one service to the other is relatively easy. The main concepts are similar; it is merely the way to get to the result that is a little different. No matter what service or combination of services is available, the next step is performing the research, and that has tools, too.

THE RESEARCH PROCESS

When a research assignment is first received by the paralegal, the following questions should be asked before starting the research process:

- What needs to be found?
- How much is known about the problem being researched?
- How in-depth does the research need to be?
- Is there a need to update the findings?
- What is the final product being produced?

What Needs to Be Found?

The facts in the assignment must be analyzed to determine such basic information as who did what to whom, what legal subject matter is involved, and what the basis of the action is. A researcher should initially have an idea of what relief is available, or what defenses can be made to a claim. A determination should also be made as to what enacted law controls the issue, or whether case law will be the highest primary authority. For enacted law, one would use the index of the enacted law to see if there is a law that governs the subject, and then locate that law. If using an annotated source, other information can provide background sources or support. For case law, key words can be used to search a digest or formulate a search query.

How Much Is Known about the Problem Being Researched?

Depending on the researcher's level of knowledge about the topic, subject encyclopedias often can help the researcher get an overview of the topic. Annotated sources can also provide additional information such as history, background, and any related authorities. However, if a dead end is reached, or nothing relevant is found, it may be necessary to ask the instructor, the attorney, or the supervisor additional questions. Asking follow-up questions should not be perceived as an indication of weakness or failure, and is often necessary in some projects. Time and energy should not be wasted in working on a project that is not understood.

How In-depth Should the Research Be?

Researchers need to understand that the depth of research required may vary depending on the project or case. The depth of the research may depend on who the audience is, the time available, the purpose of the research, or the type of document to be prepared. The audience may be a supervisor who wants only a short, simple, and straight-to-the-point discussion of the law. On the other hand, the supervisor may be working on a case in a new area of law, and may want broader information on what the law is, how it applies to the client's situation, and all of the steps leading to the conclusion. The final product would not be the same for each of these readers.

Do the Findings Need to Be Updated?

Updating the findings is absolutely necessary every time research is done. When an authority is used, it is critical to make sure that it is still good law. There is nothing worse than providing the supervisor with a mountain of authority, only to have a supervisor get blindsided in court by a newer case that overruled a critical case that was presented in the paralegal's memorandum. When a case is retrieved in the course of researching an issue, it is important to note the date when the law was found and when that authority was updated.

What Is the Final Product to Be Produced?

The researcher should also be aware of what product is being requested. This consideration is important at the beginning of the research process so that the researcher allows enough time to complete the project, searches for all the information required, and knows how the results of the research will be presented.

> **TIP**
> A researcher may wish to copy this page or bookmark it in some way, as it will be very useful as one learns about researching different sources.

Checklist 7-3 outlines the six steps of legal research that apply to most research projects.

Analyze the Client's Facts A researcher should understand the factual situation completely and know the client's objective. The parties involved should be identified, as well as their special standing under the law, if any, such as their position as a tenant, purchaser, or driver. The subject matter, such as real or personal property, contract, or tort, should be determined, along with the basis of the action, such as negligence, breach of contract, or strict liability. Next, the researcher should find out the type of relief available, such as a restraining order, specific performance, or compensatory damages. Then any defenses to the claim should be ascertained, such as self-defense or contributory negligence.

Recognize the Law The researcher should determine what court or agency has primary control of the situation and whether statutes, codes, or administrative

Checklist 7-3   LEGAL RESEARCH TOOLS: SIX STEPS

> I. **Analyze the client's facts:** Know the factual situation completely and know the client's objective.
>
> II. **Recognize the law:** Make determinations to start the research process.
>
> III. **Find the law:** A preliminary analysis will take the researcher to encyclopedias, treatises, and restatements for the background of the subject area, and then to the various types of primary authority.
>
> IV. **Make a research trail:** A system should be created for recording information as it is found.
>
> V. **Update the search:** Shepardize or electronically update all authorities.
>
> VI. **Report the research and comment on the adversary's position.**

rules or regulations are involved. A key question to ask is whether the issue is a substantive or a procedural problem.

Find the Law   There are many approaches to research, and the preliminary analysis will guide the researcher to encyclopedias, treatises and texts, and restatements, and then to various types of primary authority.

The function of a preliminary analysis is to identify generally the legal questions to be researched. It is important to summarize briefly any "on point" materials and record complete citations. If the problem is in an unfamiliar area of law, the researcher should read a secondary authority to become familiar with the subject area. The secondary authority generally cites cases and sometimes statutes that provide a starting point for the research. The identification of the leading case or controlling enacted law on an issue provides a key to many other sources of authority. A **general index** is available for many secondary publications.

Many researchers find the **TAPP**[21] method helpful. In this strategy, the researcher identifies the following:

Thing involved
Act or activity creating the problem
Persons involved
Place to which the problem is related

The "topic approach" can also be useful in the preliminary stages. In this method, the researcher will start with a summary of the contents, rather than the index, and then will do the following:

- Select what appears to be the appropriate fact topic.
- Select the volume that includes coverage of that topic, and turn to the beginning of the topic.
- Read the scope note to see if the topic is relevant.
- Run through the summary of contents to identify relevant sub-topics.

Make a Research Trail   Research is usually very time consuming, and yet often little time is available to complete an assignment. Setting an organized schedule may be necessary so that sufficient time is allowed for quality research. Setting up a system early on will also make the process more efficient and effective.

As research proceeds, a researcher will often be lead back to the same sources where he or she had previously been. A **research trail** is a method of tracking what documents have been reviewed so that the researcher does not waste time reviewing the same documents. Each time an authority is found, the researcher should do the following:

1. Write the title of the text, case, or other source, and give the full citation.
2. Write the court that rendered the decision.
3. Write the date the law was enacted or decided.
4. Write a brief of the relevant portion of the material. If enacted law is found, it should be broken down into its **elements**. If a case is used, a **comprehensive brief**, **thumbnail brief,** or **IRAC brief** should be prepared, including the type of action, the issues related to the problem, the significant facts for those issues, the decisions on those issues and principles, and the rules or reasoning.

General index
An index that provides a method of searching in many secondary sources; there is usually a general index for an entire collection.

TAPP
A system of research, originally developed by Lawyer's Cooperative, that suggests the researcher look for terms that describe **T**hings, **A**ctions, **P**ersons, and **P**laces.

Research trail
A listing of the places where the researcher has been with proper citations to each of the sources checked.

Elements
The parts of a legal issue or a statute that must be proven.

Comprehensive brief
A case brief that contains the citation, parties, objectives, theories of litigation, history of the case, key facts, issues, holdings, reasoning, disposition, and commentary.

Thumbnail brief
A shorter brief than a comprehensive brief; contains the citation, key facts, issues, holdings, reasoning, and disposition.

IRAC brief
A brief showing the issue, rule, analysis, and conclusion.

---

[21]The TAPP system of research was originally introduced by Lawyer's Cooperative Publishers.

5. Include the name and citation of crucial authorities provided.
6. Indicate the **key number**, **topic**, and headnote, if available.
7. List the secondary authorities checked using some symbol to indicate that supplements have been checked.
8. List all units of the search tools checked and briefly indicate the degree of relevancy.
9. Indicate with an "s" the **Shepardizing** or updating of each law or opinion.
10. If a dead end is reached, ask three basic questions:
    a. Does the fault lie in the analysis?
    b. Was the source used correctly?
    c. Is there a more useful source that might be consulted?

Key number
A number assigned to an individual description or summary of information within a topic.

Topic
Divisions in the West Key Numbering system that identify the major areas of law.

Shephardizing
A method of updating by showing all of the cases that have cited, overruled, followed, discussed, or modified the holding of a case.

Update the Search   The use of *Shepard's*® Citations[22] or some other electronic updating service, such as KeyCite, is not only necessary to make sure authority is current, but also will aid in locating additional authority. The updating process includes both finding each case and reading it to distinguish the case from or analogize the case to the fact situation at hand. The review of pocket parts and advance sheets is also an essential part of the updating process.

Report the Research and Comment on the Adversary's Position   The research results should be reported concisely but completely for both sides of an issue. The purpose of legal writing is to provide the supervisor with the authorities and a statement sufficient to enable him or her to measure the law against the facts to reach a final determination.

If the researcher has access to documents from the opposing side, he or she should check the adversary's citations, if any. Citations that are taken out of context may look good in a brief, but may have a different meaning within the whole text from which the material comes.

Analysis of case law takes experience. Researchers can gain additional experience by reading cases as often as possible to get a feel for the language. The more a researcher reads legal materials, the easier it will be to understand how legal authors think and write.

Other Services   There are several other services in addition to those described above that provide quality and reliable legal materials. Many of these subscription services provide demonstrations or tutorials that are available on the Internet.

TheLaw.net (www.thelaw.net) has various annual subscriptions that are geared to be cost-effective for an individual, or available to firms based on the number of users. Results are sorted by currency, citation frequency, search-term frequency, alphabetical order, and court hierarchy. It also has a tool to validate the sources found.

VersusLaw (www.versuslaw.com) is a subscription service that starts at about $14 per month, making it affordable to nearly anyone. As the plans increase in price, so does the database accessibility. The downside is that the coverage is not complete. For example, U.S. Supreme Court cases date from 1886; U.S. Court of Appeals cases, U.S District Court cases, and state cases range from 1930 forward. It does not have all the options that other services have, but it does provide a solid source of case law with links to state legislative websites. Some state bar associations utilize VersusLaw.

[22]*Shepard's*® Citations Service. http://law.lexisnexis.com/shepards

LoisLaw (www.loislaw.com), a service offered by Wolters Kluwer, provides access to a variety of materials such as primary law, forms, public records, and treatises. It also has an updating service called GlobalCite. The service offers subscriptions from a day to a year in duration.

CASEMaker (www.casemaker.us) was originally launched in 1998 by the Ohio State Bar Association, and is now offered by several states as part of state bar association dues. It currently has state libraries, including statutes, case law, and constitutions. The federal content dates from 1950. CaseMaker provides an online user guide with step-by-step instructions for its full-text searchable database. The CASEcheck feature does not provide instant validation, but does take the user to every case that has cited the original case. The user can then determine if the decision has been altered. CaseMaker is part of the Casemaker Consortium (www.lawriter.net), which is expanding the service. CasemakerX (www.casemakerx.com) is a legal research tool for law students and faculty and which provides free access to Casemaker libraries.

Fastcase (http://www.fastcase.com/) is similar to CaseMaker, but the interface for Fastcase works more like the Google interface because it is a web-based legal research service.[23] It claims to be one of the largest law libraries in the world, containing federal coverage from volume one of the materials, as well as legal forms and other tools. It has an automatic citation analysis feature that includes the number of times a case has been cited.

SUMMARY

No matter what research is being done, ethics are a critical consideration. The ethical rules regarding UPL, confidentiality, and candor come into play in many research projects.

Organization, permanence, assistance, and quality should be the first considerations in looking for authorities. There are a number of quality services online, but there are pitfalls of which every researcher should be aware. Physical law libraries house legal materials that can be searched by taking key words from an assignment and using indices of both secondary and primary authorities. The same key words can be used with online subscription services to locate authorities that support a client's position. It is important to remember that researchers must become familiar with the law library and law books, as well as with materials available online. Good researchers will learn the names of the legal materials, what they are used for, and where they are located. Furthermore, good researchers will use a combination of manual and online research to obtain the best research results.

REVIEW QUESTIONS

1. What are the key steps in performing manual research?

2. What are three ethical considerations with which researchers should be familiar?

3. How can a researcher commit UPL in doing research?

4. Why are users not allowed to remove legal materials from a library? Do you believe this is a good rule? Why or why not?

5. Why is it important to not only use the key words from an assignment when doing research, but also use synonyms and antonyms?

6. What should you look for when determining whether a site is valuable or not?

7. If you do not know much about the assignment you have been given, what should you do?

8. What are three things to consider when deciding how in-depth the research should be?

9. Why do you need to update the sources you have found in your research?

10. Explain the major differences between doing legal research on "free" websites and searching within a paid subscription service.

11. When doing research and locating applicable law, which is better—quality or quantity? Why?

12. Identify the meaning of the following website address endings: .com, .edu, .gov, .mil, .net

---

[23]http://www.fastcase.com/whatisfastcase/

13. What are the four parts of a Westlaw query? Explain the purposes of each.

14. What are three connectors in Westlaw? Explain the meaning of each.

15. What are three connectors in LexisNexis?

16. Why is it easier to learn a new system of paid electronic research after you have learned other systems?

17. How do the connectors of Westlaw and LexisNexis compare?

APPLICATION **EXERCISES**

1. Anastasia lives in a house that is owned by her grandmother. Her grandmother lives in a nursing home and Anastasia takes care of the home and its contents. On the property of the home, near the border of the property line, there was a very large, old shade tree. The tree was planted by Anastasia's great-grandmother and provided shade to the entire home. The tree was her grandmother's favorite tree. Her grandmother loved to sit under the shade tree all day long. Recently the next-door neighbor started renovations on his home. Anastasia returned home from work to find the large tree completely gone. The neighbor's contractor removed the tree to make room for the construction. Anastasia is your firm's new client.
   a. Anastasia wants to know if she can sue the neighbor for anything. How can you find out? What do you need to do first?
   b. Which set of laws would govern this case—federal law or state law? Why?
   c. Where would you find the laws governing the loss of property? Where will you look first?
   d. Does this law apply to Anastasia's case? Where will you look next?

2. Your firm represents Lilley Buckner, who owns a flower business and does business as Lilley & Company in your state. Recently a robber set fire to the business to cover the theft. Above the flower shop are several apartments, one of which belongs to your client. Your client leases the business property from the same person who owns the apartments. Several tenants have told the landlord that they saw someone lurking around the business after it was closed. The landlord did nothing about the complaints. The fire destroyed the business and the client's apartment. The client just discovered that she had missed her insurance payment on her apartment contents, so her insurance had lapsed. The insurance company is from another state. The landlord has insurance on the structure.
   a. What do you need to do first?
   b. What is the jurisdiction?
   c. Would this be a federal or a state case?
   d. What digest would you use and why?
   e. What key terms would you use?
   f. What alternate terms would you use?

QUICK **CHECK**

1. Examples of free search engines include
   a. Google.com, Ask.com, and SendYourQuestionstoUS.com
   b. Google.com, LexisNexis, and Escape.com
   c. Google.com, Ask.com, and Laws.com
   d. Google.com, Ask.com, and Yahoo.com

2. A program designed to take a word or set of words and look for websites on the Internet is a
   a. search engine
   b. service provider
   c. query
   d. bookmark

3. The process of using *Shepard's* to check legal citations is called
   a. Electronic filing
   b. KeyCiting
   c. Shepardizing
   d. Herding

4. A program produced and presented, usually for education, over the Internet for viewing at the user's computer is called a
   a. learning resource
   b. webinar
   c. Internet classroom
   d. Specialty Application Program

5. The American Bar Association's set of proposed ethical standards for the legal profession are the
   a. Model Rules of Ethics
   b. Model Rules of Professional Conduct
   c. Rules of Professional Responsibility
   d. Model Guidelines of Professional Ethics

6. An ethical obligation to not reveal information, which is based on a relationship of trust placed in one person by the other, is
   a. candor
   b. claim of privilege

    c. Confidentiality

    d. Self-defense exception

7. Terms, alternate terms, connectors, and expanders are all items that need to be considered when creating a
   a. Word document
   b. research plan
   c. query
   d. discovery plan

8. Stop words, connectors, and search are terms used when creating a
   a. query
   b. research plan
   c. Word document
   d. Excel spreadsheet

9. Westlaw's online citation update service is called
   a. KeyCite
   b. GlobalCite
   c. *Shepard's*
   d. Factual Research

10. What is the ethical obligation to not mislead the court or opposing counsel with false statements of law or of facts that the lawyer knows to be false?
    a. Oath of honesty
    b. Ethical oath
    c. Candor
    d. Honesty in litigation

11. Which are examples of connectors used in search queries?
    a. and, or, & not
    b. the, with, & to
    c. of, not, & the
    d. of, with, & when

RESEARCH

Consider the first Application problem. Assume that Anastasia lives in your jurisdiction. Find a statute that governs the situation. Research both manually (if you have access to books) and electronically (using either the Internet in general or a subscription service). Identify the steps you took to find the statute. Did one method prove more productive than the other? Was one method quicker than the other? Were there any drawbacks in either method?

MEDIA **RESOURCES**

LexisNexis training:	http://www.lexisnexis.com/support/training/
Tutorial on LexisNexis: Finding a Specific Legal Case	http://www.youtube.com/watch?v=17E6Q1hmciY&list=UUHdtFdh_kqhQR8mGZUYsx4Q&index=3&feature=plcp
Tutorial on LexisNexis: Finding a Specific Document	http://www.youtube.com/watch?v=O4_m9_ZqJmg&feature=related

INTERNET **RESOURCES**

American Bar Association:	www.abanet.org
CaseMaker:	www.casemaker.us
Center for Professional Responsibility. Rules of Professional Conduct:	http://www.abanet.org/cpr/mrpc/mrpc_toc.html
Cornell University Law School Legal Information Institute:	www.law.cornell.edu
	http://www.lib.berkeley.edu/TeachingLib/Guides/Internet/webeval-QuestionsToAsk.pdf
Evaluating Websites—Cornell Library:	http://olinuris.library.cornell.edu/ref/research/webeval.html
Fastcase:	http://www.fastcase.com/
FindLaw, sponsored by Westlaw:	www.findlaw.com, http://lp.findlaw.com
FindLaw answers:	http://boards.answers.findlaw.com/n/forumIndex.aspx?webtag=fl-answersidx
FindLaw Court TV:	www.courttv.findlaw.com/
FindLaw forms:	http://forms.lp.findlaw.com

FindLaw legal news:	http://news.findlaw.com/legalnews/us/sc
Google:	www.google.com
Indiana University School of Law:	www.law.indiana.edu/lawlibrary/index.shtml
Internet Legal Research Group:	www.ilrg.com
Law School 2009:	Getting Started with Online Research: http://west.thomson.com/productdetail/1-5785-5/RM157855/productdetail.aspx
Law School 2009:	Westlaw Research Guide: http://west.thomson.com/productdetail/1-5782-5/RM157825/productdetail.aspx
LexisNexis home page:	http://www.lexisnexis.com/our-solutions/us-solutions/
LexisONE, which is sponsored by LEXIS:	www.lexisone.com
LoisLaw:	www.loislaw.com
Michie's Legal Resources:	www.michie.com
San Diego County Public Law Library:	www.sdcll.org
The Library of Congress:	www.loc.gov, http://Thomas.loc.gov., www.loc.gov/law
TheLaw.net:	www.thelaw.net
U.S. Government Printing Office:	www.gpo.gov
VersusLaw:	www.versuslaw.com
Washburn University School of Law:	http://washburnlaw.edu/library
Westlaw Official Site:	http://west.thomson.com/westlaw/default.aspx?promcode=601577D29050&searchid=Reprise/
Westlaw training:	http://westlawtraining.west.thomson.com/http://westlawtraining.west.thomson.com/aw&PromType=external

zimmytws/Shutterstock

chapter **eight**

MAIN SECONDARY AUTHORITIES

LEARNING OBJECTIVES

After completing this chapter, students should be able to:

1. Differentiate between primary and secondary sources.

2. Identify appropriate uses of secondary sources.

3. Locate secondary sources relevant to a case.

4. Use secondary sources to find primary sources of law.

CHAPTER OVERVIEW

Sometimes a research question gives hints as to where an answer may be found. If these hints point to a constitutional provision or a statute, the next step is to go directly to the constitutional provision or statute and, if using an **annotated** source, look at the cases and other information annotations to find secondary sources—materials that interpret and explain the statute or provision.

There are other times, however, when very little about the subject is known, and additional information is needed before beginning research. In those situations, secondary authority may provide the background information needed to understand the issue or to find primary authority.

Instructors and supervisors disagree over whether to use primary or secondary authorities first when starting research. But whatever is used to begin the research, the final memorandum will ultimately rely on primary authority, and secondary authorities can help greatly in finding that authority. The secondary authorities that will be covered in this chapter are encyclopedias, **treatises** and books, annotations, restatements, and **periodicals**. Additional secondary authorities will be covered in the next chapter.

Annotated
Material has been added in the form of references and comments.

Treatises
Texts that legal scholars have written, focusing on a single legal subject.

Periodical
A newspaper, journal, or similar publication that is issued on a regular basis, such as a legal newspaper, bar association journal, or law review.

UNDERSTANDING SECONDARY AUTHORITY

Secondary authority is not the law itself; rather, it is material that explains, summarizes, and analyzes the law. Secondary authorities may be ordered in a hierarchy based on their strength. While there may be no absolute rule regarding the hierarchy of secondary authorities, *The Bluebook* (Rule 1.4(i)) places the secondary sources in the following hierarchical order within a signal:

> uniform and model acts
> Restatements of the Law
> **treatises** and books
> works in journals
> annotations
> magazine and newspaper articles
> working papers
> unpublished materials
> electronic sources.[1]

ALWD gives no preference. Although this hierarchy is meant to show how sources are placed within signals, it gives some insight into the weight or importance of each type of secondary authority.

Secondary authority is not written by a governmental entity such as a legislature, court, administrative agency, or county council. Rather, secondary authority is material written by scholars and legal editors that either is about the law or explains or aids in understanding the law. As such, secondary authority is never *mandatory*. It may, however, serve as a type of *persuasive authority*. Persuasive authority is any material that the court relies upon when it does not have to do so. Just as a court may cite a persuasive opinion from another jurisdiction, it may also cite a respected treatise or Restatement that it finds persuasive.

A *secondary authority* can help a researcher understand a problem, find primary authority, or provide additional secondary sources about the law. Secondary authority often sounds very authoritative and may actually quote from a primary source. However, if a researcher wants to quote the law, the researcher should find the actual law and quote directly from it instead. The strength of any authority comes from the original source, not from a source that restates an original source.

Example 8-1 shows the difference between primary and secondary authority, as well as between mandatory and persuasive authority.

Secondary authority often paraphrases or summarizes primary authority. Students are tempted to paraphrase or summarize the secondary authority in their documents and use it as primary authority, often because the paraphrased or summarized material is clearly written and the students do not have confidence in their own writing. There is also a temptation to use the words of the secondary authority in a memorandum or brief without crediting the original author. However, when someone else's materials are used without the proper citation to authority, the user is plagiarizing, which is a breach of ethics.

Secondary authority often looks appealing because primary authority is sometimes difficult to find. Secondary authority may also be more plentiful because the secondary authority provides examples or citations from the entire United States on both the state and federal levels. It is not unusual for one state to have *novel questions* or *cases of first impression*, or to have addressed an issue infrequently. But the chances are good that some state or federal court has addressed the issue. Therefore, secondary authority may exist where primary authority is scarce.

Mandatory
Any authority that the court must rely on in making its decision.

Persuasive authority
Authority a court relies on, but is not required to consider, in making a decision. An example would be the decision of an Illinois court considered persuasive by an Indiana court.

Secondary authority
Authority that summarize, paraphrase, or otherwise discuss the law, but are not the law itself.

TIP

Legal materials are divided into primary and secondary authority and mandatory and persuasive authority. The ultimate goal in research is to find primary, mandatory authority to support the client's position.

TIP

Students should understand the concepts presented in the example. Those concepts will help make them better researchers.

Novel questions
Questions which a court within a jurisdiction has not considered.

Cases of first impression
Cases that involve new issues or questions that have not been decided by the courts in a particular jurisdiction.

---

[1]*The Bluebook: A Uniform System of Citation* . Columbia Law Review Ass'n et al. eds., 19th ed. 2010.

EXAMPLE 8-1   UNDERSTANDING HOW AUTHORITY WORKS

You work for a lawyer in Indiana. Your client comes in with an issue regarding adoption of an adult. Your attorney asks you to research the question of whether one adult can adopt another. Your supervisor points you to an **Indiana statute** that is applicable and **one case in the Indiana Court of Appeals** that is on point, but there is not much other case law on the topic. You search the *Indiana Law Encyclopedia* **(I.L.E.)** covering adoption. You find the statute and case that the supervisor indicated, along with a couple of additional cases. You search *Corpus Juris Secundum* **(C.J.S.)** and find an **Illinois case** and a **Pennsylvania case** that are very similar to the client's case. How are these authorities classified?

Source	Primary	Secondary	Mandatory	Persuasive (if the court chooses to rely on the material)
Indiana statute	X		X	
Indiana Court of Appeals	X		X	
Indiana Law Encyclopedia		X		X
Corpus Juris Secundum		X		X
Illinois case	X			X
Pennsylvania case	X			X

TIP

One example of using secondary authority might be when a quote from a treatise, such as *Prosser on Torts*, supports an argument on an interpretation of some primary authority. If the secondary material is used, the researcher is effectively asking the supervisor or the court to use the secondary authority as persuasive authority. The supervisor may choose to use this as an informational source. The court may choose to use this persuasive authority provided the proper foundation has been laid for the court to do so.

Even though secondary authority may be plentiful, there are various reasons why relying on secondary authority is not appropriate and not good practice. The goal in legal writing is to use primary, mandatory authority to support the client's position. Secondary authority may state the legal concepts that apply, but it does not provide the actual source of the law upon which the court must rely. Since secondary authority collects and summarizes primary authority, the actual law is not cited.

When making their points, authors of secondary material often utilize authority from multiple jurisdictions that are not the jurisdiction within which the researcher is working. The secondary material may be based on federal law when the researcher needs state law, or the secondary authority may be based on state law when the client's situation is in a federal jurisdiction. Researchers should read each primary source that is cited in a secondary authority. If the source is important enough to cite, it is important enough to read and analyze.

Secondary authority does have value, however, when used properly. The greatest value lies in the ability to provide a researcher with a deeper understanding of the topic and to generate additional resources that lead to primary authority. But although there may be instances where a researcher can use the secondary authority in legal writing, this is the exception, not the rule. In these very limited situations, a proper foundation must be laid before a secondary authority may be used.

That proper foundation includes thorough research of the issue so that the following is known:

- All primary authority has been discussed first'
- the secondary authority is not a substitute for primary authority,
- the court will be aided in its interpretation of the law and its decision-making process,

- the secondary authority does not merely repeat the primary authority, and
- the secondary authority does not contradict what the primary authority states, unless:
  - the court being presented with the primary authority has the jurisdiction to change the law and adopt a new interpretation, and
  - there is reason to believe that the court *will* change the law.[2]

When the court is faced with a case of first impression, secondary authority is very useful in, and necessary for, the decision-making process. If there is no primary, mandatory authority on an issue, presenting an argument based on prevailing trends in other jurisdictions and scholarly writing on the topic is beneficial to the court. Courts tend to be receptive to adopting secondary authority in this type of situation. The key is to be sure that there truly is no primary, mandatory authority.

Table 8-1 shows the types of secondary authority that will be covered in this chapter.

> **TIP**
>
> It might be helpful for researchers to know what each type of authority does, to memorize the types of secondary authority, and to draft the proper citation forms.
>
> **Law reviews**
>
> Periodicals published by most law schools, similar to law journals. These secondary materials consist generally of articles that provide an analysis of new cases or legislation that has been recently implemented.

TABLE 8-1   Secondary Sources of Law

Source of Law	Purpose
Legal encyclopedias	These are multivolume sets of books on both the national and state levels that explain the law and are organized much like other forms of encyclopedias. Examples include *Corpus Juris Secundum* 11 C.J.S. *Bonds* § 21 (1995) and *West's Indiana Law Encyclopedia* 12 I.L.E. *Bonds* § 21(1995) Westlaw identifier: AMJUR or CJS
Digests (covered in a later chapter)	These sets contain small paragraphs that summarize legal issues from judicial opinions. West's key number digest is one of the largest.
Treatises	Books, often single volumes, which are published on one legal subject. Examples are *Prosser on Torts* and *Constitutional Law, 7th Ed. by John E. Nowak, Ronald D. Rotunda* Sample citation: 6A Charles Alan Wright et al., *Federal Practice and Procedure* § 1497, at 7079 (2d ed. 1990) Westlaw identifier: FPP
Form books	Form books contain forms that researchers can use as guides when they are preparing documents. Examples are *Current Legal Forms with Tax Analysis, American Jurisprudence Pleading and Practice Forms Annotated (Westlaw AMJUR –PP)*, and Vaughan's (complete) *Alabama Form Book.*
Annotations	A set of books called *American Law Reports* (1st, 2nd, 3rd, 4th, 5th, and Federal) contains court opinions with notes and commentaries, usually with a variety of references from various states to the opinions. For example, 25 ALR5th 229 Westlaw identifier: ALR
Restatements	This set of books is written by noted scholars in each field covered and is gathered by the American Law Institute (ALI). The scholars provide their opinion of the general consensus of the American courts on a particular topic or point of law. In addition, annotations supplement the main text. *Restatement (Third) of Torts: Products Liability* §14 (2009) Westlaw identifier: REST-TORT
Legal periodicals	Law-related magazines, journals, and newspapers that include law school resources, as well as resources from other legal entities, such as *ABA Journal* and *Banking Law Journal*
Law reviews	A scholarly journal focusing on legal issues, normally published by an organization of students at a law school or through a bar association; for example, *Harvard Law Review* or *University of La Verne Law Review.* Also sometimes referred to as a journal: *The Yale Law Journal* Westlaw identifier: LAWREV-PRO
Journals	Similar in many instances to **law reviews** such as *The Yale Law Journal; examples are New York Law Journal* and *Computer Law Review and Technology Journal*
Loose-leaf publications	A service that provides continually updated material that is kept in a binder. The major publishers of loose-leaf services are Bureau of National Affairs (BNA), Commerce Clearing House (CCH), Lexis Legal Publishing/Matthew Bender, and Research Institute of America (RIA).

---

[2]William P. Statsky & R. John Wernet. *Case Analysis and Fundamentals of Legal Writing*, 4th Ed.. West Legal Studies/Thomson Reuters.

TABLE 8-2 Common Features of Secondary Materials

Preface	Description of contents and brief explanation of how to use text; in the front of each volume
Table of Contents	List of topics with corresponding page numbers; in the front of each volume
Descriptive Word Index or General Index	Alphabetical list of words or phrases describing subjects discussed in the text with corresponding page numbers; usually found in a separate volume, but may also be within each volume
Table of Statutes	List of statutes and codes discussed in the text with corresponding page numbers
Table of Cases	List of cases cited in the text with corresponding page numbers
Table of Abbreviations	List of all abbreviations used in the text, including those for case reporters and other legal sources
Parallel Reference Table	Table that shows readers how to find material published in previous series or editions
Pocket Part Supplement	Supplemental material containing updates to information printed in the text; designed to be inserted in the back of the text or published as a separate pamphlet

TIP

The state materials introduced on the bottom row are only secondary materials. The goal is to find the appropriate primary sources for the problem. If this project were focused on state law, the second row would include state cases, state statutes, and state regulations.

Researchers will find that many of the secondary authorities have similar tools that help in the research process, as shown in Table 8-2.

Research may be said to occur in a definite "flow," although individual researchers will personalize their own research process based on what seems to work best for them. Sometimes a researcher will begin by checking for a statute; at other times one may start with an encyclopedia. The choice of starting points may depend on the issue or be dictated by the research tools available. The research pyramid shown in Figure 8-1 suggests one possible pattern for a research project.

FIGURE 8-1 Research Pyramid[3]

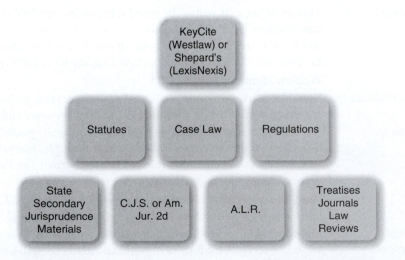

[3]Getting Started With Online Research. Thomson Reuters. 2010. http://lscontent.westlaw.com/images/content/GettingStarted10.pdf

At the bottom level are secondary materials. The middle level is primary law. The top level reminds researchers to update their sources. Other blocks could be added, such as constitutions or more specific research tools.

ENCYCLOPEDIAS

Of all the secondary sources, many paralegal students and researchers find legal encyclopedias to be the most useful place to begin a research problem. Legal encyclopedias look familiar because they resemble general encyclopedias such as *Encyclopedia Britannica* or *Encarta*. They are reference materials. Legal encyclopedias cover a broad range of subjects based on state and federal law. Generally most law libraries, and many public libraries, have legal encyclopedias.

The process for using a legal encyclopedia is very similar to that of using a general encyclopedia. *Key words* from the assignment or issue are used to search the appropriate index. For example, if a supervisor needs to know whether his client can depreciate the use of a permanent advertising sign under federal tax law, the researcher would look in the general index under "federal taxation," then look for the key words "depreciation" and "deduction." The researcher would also look around that topic area for other subtopics that may be relevant. Once the appropriate topics are found, the ***pocket parts*** of the index are checked to be sure the information has not been updated. Then the volume containing the topic "Federal Taxation" is located to read the relevant material. If the question has been answered, the pocket part of the volume is checked to confirm that the information is current.

Another option is to go directly to the volume containing federal taxation and search for the key words "deduction" and "depreciation" in the volume index or the table of contents. Again, the pocket part of that volume must be checked.

An important characteristic of encyclopedias is that they provide information about the law as it is—there is no effort to be critical or to advocate a position. In addition, there is no suggestion of changes that should be made to the law. The legal encyclopedia only provides background information and references to cases that analyze the topic of the section. One weakness of encyclopedias is that the cases cited are often old cases. However, once the researcher has cases on point, they can be updated, or used to find newer cases or cases within a particular jurisdiction.

Legal encyclopedias are divided into three types: general or national encyclopedias, local or state encyclopedias, and subject encyclopedias.

General or National Encyclopedias

The two primary national-based legal encyclopedias are *Corpus Juris Secundum (C.J.S.)*, which is published by Thomson Reuters (previously known as West), and *American Jurisprudence, Second Edition (Am. Jur. 2d)* published now by Lexis-Nexis. These encyclopedias discuss all major subjects of American law: federal and state, civil and criminal, substantive and procedural. Both of the sets in print are updated through the use of pocket parts.

While there are some important differences between the two sets, researchers should not waste time researching in both unless absolutely necessary. The encyclopedia chosen may depend on availability, training, or the researcher's preference.

Key words
Words which, if different or non-existent, would change the outcome of the issue.

Pocket parts
Paper supplements to hardbound volumes (such as *C.J.S.*) that supplement the material in the hardbound volumes.

Corpus Juris Secundum (C.J.S.) *Corpus Juris Secundum (C.J.S.)* is a reference guide to over 400 law-related topics. The title *Corpus Juris Secundum* is Latin for "body of law, second," and is named after the *Corpus Juris Civilis*, the body of Roman law codified in the sixth century by the Byzantine emperor and empress Justinian I and Theodora. *Corpus Juris Civilis* literally means "body of civil law."[4] Many scholars agree that Theodora greatly influenced the inclusion of laws protecting the rights of women.[5]

Researchers often use *C.J.S.* as a starting point for research because it provides the "***black-letter law***," or general legal principles, in the headings, which are then expanded upon in the text. *C.J.S.*'s hallmark is the presentation of an exhaustive study of each topic. When using *C.J.S.*, the researcher gains a well-rounded perspective of the law in general. *C.J.S.* is available in print, and is available online exclusively through Westlaw®.

C.J.S. comprises over 100 volumes of royal blue books (Figure 8-2) with a multivolume index. The material is arranged alphabetically and presented in a formal tone; however, some of the headings may not use the wording that a novice researcher might expect. But as researchers become more experienced in reading and analyzing legal sources, they begin to think more like lawyers or judges when doing research, and will adopt a vocabulary that more resembles formal, legal writing. Applying this vocabulary will help researchers locate the appropriate topics within *C.J.S.*

The set is updated by cumulative annual pocket parts, which update material that has been changed or supplemented. Later, replacement volumes are issued when the updates are sufficient to justify the publication of a new volume.

The West Key Number System is used throughout *C.J.S.* Other useful features include a table of cases, which can be helpful if a case title is known, and a section called "Library References" at the beginning of each topic that lists the topic and key number references included within the topic. With these topic and key number references, a researcher can continue the research for current cases within the West's *General Digests* (currently in the 12th edition, covering cases through July 7, 2010). The general digests are then compiled into the *Decennial Digests*.

The page from *C.J.S.* shown in Figure 8-2 provides an example of the type of information a researcher can expect to find in encyclopedias. The footnotes provide citations to sources discussing the narrative. A researcher using this topic would then check the pocket part at the back of the volume to be sure the material was still good law.

American Jurisprudence 2d (Am. Jur. 2d) *American Jurisprudence 2d (Am. Jur. 2d)* like *C.J.S.*, is a multivolume set of books (bound in green) that provide information on more than 400 law-related topics. *Am. Jur. 2d* and *C.J.S.* have many similar features, such as topics presented alphabetically and research references that lead to other materials. Each topic begins with a section that outlines briefly what the topic will contain as well as what might be covered elsewhere in the set. *Am. Jur. 2d* contains a general multivolume index in addition to a table of contents or index for each topic or title. The set is updated through cumulative annual

---

Black-letter law
The fundamental concepts in the law, or the basic legal principles.

---

[4]Oliver J. Thatcher, ed., *The Library of Original Sources* (Milwaukee: University Research Extension Co.)

[5]Gies, Frances and Joseph Gies. **Women in the Middle Ages**. Thomas Y. Crowell Company: (New York, 1978).

XVIII. FOREIGN CORPORATIONS

A. IN GENERAL

section number ➤ **§ S83. Definition and General Considerations**

black letter law ➤ A foreign corporation is one that derives its existence solely from the laws of another state, government, or country.

Library References

West key number ➤ Corporation § 631. 632.

narrative information on a topic ➤ A foreign corporation is one that derives its existence solely from the laws of another state, government, or country, and the term is used indiscriminately, sometimes in statutes, to designate either a corporation created by or under the laws of another state or a corporation crested by or under the laws of a foreign country.[45]

At common law a corporation may be deemed a person,[46] and statutes providing that corporations shall be deemed persons include foreign corporations.[47]

Generally, the status of a corporation as either foreign or domestic is determined solely by the place of its origin, without reference to the residence of its stockholders,[48] or incorporators,[49] or the place where its business is transacted.[50]

However, by express enactment, a corporation, a majority of whose stock is held by aliens, is, for some purposes, deemed to be a foreign corporation.[51] A domestic corporation does not become a foreign corporation merely by accepting from another state a grant of the right to own property and to transact business in such other state.[52]

Federal corporations.

A federal corporation operating within a state is considered a domestic corporation rather than a foreign corporation.[53] *The United States government is a foreign corporation with respect to a state.*[54]

§ 884. Status

A corporation exists only in contemplation, and by force, of the law, and where that law ceases to operate the corporation can have no existence.

Library References

Corporations § 631

A corporation exits only in contemplation of law and by force of the law, and where that law ceases to operate, the corporation can have no existence.[55] A state cannot impose one of its artificial creatures on another sovereignty nor confer on its corporators powers which they can lawfully exercise beyond its jurisdiction.[56] Rather, it must dwell in the place of its creation, and cannot migrate to another sovereignty.[57]

---

cases which address the points made in the article ➤

45. N.Y.—Home Owners' Loan Corp. v. Barone, 298 N.Y.S. 531, 164. Mis. 187.

Okl.—Magna Oil & Refining Co. v. Uncle Sam Oil Co. 196 P. 142, 81 Okl. 8.

46. U.S.—Magna Oil & Refining Co. v. White Star Refining Co., C.C.A.Del., 280 F. 52.

47. W.Ya.—Quesenberry v. People's Bldg. Loan & Sav. Assoc., 30. S.E. 73, 44 W.Va. 512.

48. U.S.—Philippine Sugar Estates Development Co. v. U.S., 39 Ct. Cl. 225.

Wash.—Hastings v. Anacortes Packing Co., 69 P. 776, 29 Wash. 224.

49. Ga.—Rogers v. Toccoa Electric Power Co., 137 S.E. 272, 163 Ga. 919.

50. Okl.—Magan Oil & Refining Co. v. Uncle Sam Oil Co., 196 P. 142, 81 Okl. 8.

Administrative offices

Location of corporate administrative offices in particular jurisdiction was not the same as being created or organized within that jurisdiction for purposes of establishing nationality of the corporation.

U.S.—Compagnie Financiere De Suex et de L'Union Parislenne v. U.S., 492 F 2d 798, 203 Ct. Cl. 605.

51. Wash.—Hastings v. Anacortes Packing Co. 69 P. 776, 29 Wash. 224.

52. U.S.—Philippine Sugar Estates Development Co v. U.S., 39 Ct. Cl. 225.

Ohio—Lander v. Burke, 63 N.E. 69, 65 Ohio St. 532.

53. Ala.—Ex parte First Alabama Bank of Montgomery, N.A., 461 So. 2d 1315.

Pa.—Commonwealth v. First Pennsylvania Overseas Finance Corp., 229 A.2d 896, 425 Pa. 143.

54. N.Y.—In re Merriam's Estate, 36 N.E. 505, 141 N.Y. 479, affirmed U.S. v. Perkins, 16 S.Ct. 1073, 163 U.S. 625. 41 L.Ed. 287.

55. U.S.—Magna Oil & Refining Co. v. White Star Refining Co., C.C.A.Del., 280 F. 52.

Cal.—People v. Alaska Pac. S.S. Co., 187 P. 742, 182 C. 202.

Ill.—Joseph T. Ryerson & Son v. Shaw, 115 N.E. 650, 277 Ill. 524.

56. Ala.—State v. Atlantic Coast Line R. Co., 81 So. 60, 202 Ala. 558. certiorari denied Atlantic Coast Line R. Co. v. State of Alabama, 40 S.Ct. 485, 253 U.S. 489, 64 L.Ed. 1027.

Ill.—Joseph T. Ryerson & Son v. Shaw, 115 N.E. 650, 277 Ill. 524.

Pa.—F.E. Nugent Funeral Home v. Beamish, 173 A. 177. 315 Pa. 345.

57. U.S.—Cream of Wheat Co. v. Grand Forks County, N.D., 40 S.Ct. 558, 253 U.S. 325, 64 L.Ed. 931.

Ky.—American Barge Line Co. v. Board of Sup'rs of Tax of Jefferson County, 55 S.W.2d 416, 246 Ky. 573.

FIGURE 8-2 Sample Page from *C.J.S.*

pocket parts, which provide newer cases and changes in the law, and replacement volumes when warranted. Both sets have a volume that provides a table of laws and rules for quicker access to sections discussing federal statutes, the *Code of Federal Regulations*, and other laws.

However, there are some important differences between *Am. Jur. 2d* and *C.J.S.*

> *Am. Jur. 2d* provides a summary of the best cases that support a point, rather than every case supporting it.
>
> *Am. Jur. 2d* is written in more of a conversational tone.
>
> *Am. Jur. 2d* does not have a table of cases.
>
> *Am. Jur. 2d* has two reference tools unavailable in *C.J.S.*: *Desk Book* and *New Topic Service*.
>
> *Am. Jur. 2d* and the Total Client Service Library™ service are available on both Westlaw and LexisNexis, but LexisNexis does not have *C.J.S.*

As noted, *Am. Jur. 2d* includes a *Desk Book* that provides a variety of historical and legal information, such as the U.S. Constitution and the Declaration of Independence, as well as the Monroe Doctrine and the United Nations Charter. In many ways, the *Desk Book* is similar to an almanac: it has diagrams of various governmental departments, agencies, and courts; statistics such as marriage and divorce rates and life expectancy tables; contact information of governmental agencies and departments and selected federal courts; and other miscellaneous information that a researcher may find useful. Another reference tool, *New Topic Service*, consists of various pamphlets covering emerging legal trends that may later appear as topics in the volumes.

One caveat about researching in *Am. Jur. 2d* is that because new sections may be added to an existing volume, the index may send the researcher to an outdated section in an older volume. To avoid missing updated information, the table of parallel references at the front of each volume (called the correlation table in the back of newer volumes) should be checked. This table will convert the old section number to the new section in the replacement volume.

Am. Jur. 2d is a component in the Total Client-Service Library® (TCSL), a collection of resources integrated with *Am. Jur 2d*. The TCSL includes four sets of materials: *Am. Jur. Proof of Facts* (and *Proof of Facts 2d* and *3d*); *Am. Jur. Trials*; *Am. Jur. Legal Forms 2d*; and *Am. Jur. Pleading and Practice Forms* Annotated. *Am. Jur. 2d* references the materials in the TCSL library, because those materials apply to the encyclopedia information. For example, in the discussion of evidence in *Am. Jur. 2d.*, references would be made to related information in *Am. Jur. Trials*.

The *Proof of Facts* series provides material to assist in interviewing clients, conducting discovery, preparing witnesses for trial, examining witnesses both during discover and at trial, introducing evidence at trial, and negotiating settlements. Articles on various areas of law serve as the foundation of the text. Each article gives background information on the type of case, the elements of the case that must be proven in order to win at trial, and sample questions for discovery tools such as interrogatories and depositions. Various features such as diagrams and trial exhibits are also included where appropriate. The set has a general index that can be used to search the text through descriptive words.[6]

---

[6]Legal Information Center. Guide to Using Legal Encyclopedias. 1990. http://www.law.ufl.edu/lic/ENCYCLOP06.pdf

Am. Jur. Trials focuses on trial tactics and strategies through articles authored by leading litigators. This set consists of more than 100 volumes and is divided into two parts. The first part (six volumes) is geared toward general trial matters such as case investigation, publicity management, discovery, and settlement. The rest of the set provides information on specific types of cases and provides in-depth strategies for various phases of litigation, from the initial client meeting to appeals. The volumes are updated through annual pocket parts. The set has a general index with which a descriptive word search can be used.

Am. Jur. Legal Forms 2d provides practitioners with forms for many of the documents completed by lawyers and paralegals daily. Examples of such forms are contracts, leases, minutes of corporate meetings, wills, adoptions, and name changes. Each document form is provided along with tips, checklists, advice, and a list of the required elements, as well as references to other resources. These forms are often referred to as "***boilerplate***" forms, meaning that they are drafted with general terminology, often with optional clauses to pick and choose from, and without consideration for jurisdictional requirements or the facts of a specific case. They must be adapted to the client's needs and the jurisdictional requirements. As with most secondary resources, the set is updated with cumulative pocket parts.

Boilerplate
Standard language or forms that can provide a starting point for drafting a document.

The last part of the TCSL is *Am. Jur. Pleading and Practice Forms Annotated*, which provides forms for any stage of state or federal litigation, whether civil or criminal. These boilerplate forms come with checklists of reminders such as what documents might need to accompany the form, what factors should be considered when drafting the document, and where other resources might be found. Each document has multiple examples for consideration. The set is updated with cumulative pocket parts and has a general index that can be accessed through the descriptive word method.

Specialized Encyclopedias   The general legal encyclopedias provide a wide variety of topics that researchers can use. On occasion, however, a researcher needs deeper background information on a topic. There are a few specialized encyclopedias that do just that. The most commonly known specialized encyclopedia probably is *Fletcher Cyclopedia Corporations*, a multivolume set published by West. This encyclopedia was previously published under the title *Fletcher Cyclopedia of the Law of Private Corporations* in 1931. While the title uses the term "cyclopedia," there are many who classify this as a treatise because of the comprehensive coverage of everything corporate, from the inception of a corporation to its demise. It cross-references to *Fletcher Corporation Forms*

CITING THE LAW 8-1: LEGAL ENCYCLOPEDIAS

The proper citation format for *C.J.S.* is as follows:

Volume number C.J.S. *topic name*, section number (date)
Example: 81 C.J.S. *Social Security*, § 58 (1998)
The proper citation format for *Am. Jur. 2d* is as follows
Volume number *Am. Jur. 2d topic name* section number (date)
Example: 81 *Am. Jur. 2d Social Security* § 58 (1998)

Annotated. Using the descriptive word index method is the best research option for researching in this set. An index and table of laws and rules also serve as finding tools.

State Encyclopedias

State legal encyclopedias are similar to national legal encyclopedias, providing a foundation of background information on legal topics, except that the information given is specific to one state. State encyclopedias have a variety of names, such as *Indiana Legal Encyclopedia (I.L.E.)*, West's® *Maryland Law Encyclopedia, Illinois Law & Practice (I.L.P.), Massachusetts Practice, Encyclopedia of Mississippi Law*, and *New York Jurisprudence.*

Some states have legal encyclopedias covering specialized areas of practice, such as *Georgia Jurisprudence®: Personal Injury, Business Torts, and Workers' Compensation*, and *Georgia Jurisprudence®: Criminal Law.* Approximately 20 states have state encyclopedias. However, these state services are not rigorously updated.

Using the encyclopedias, whether or not they are consistently updated, can be a starting point for research within the jurisdiction. The services will provide the researcher with background information and citations to jurisdictionally relevant authority. Therefore, the state encyclopedias, rather than national encyclopedias, may be a better starting point for state matters.

Researching with Legal Encyclopedias

There is some similarity between researching in legal encyclopedias and in general ones. Research in both legal and general encyclopedias is usually performed by either going to the relevant topic contained in a volume, or looking up key words in the index. In a legal encyclopedia, the logical first step is to either go to the volumes that contain topics related to the key words in the client's issue, or go to the index and search using the key words.

However, there are some differences when using legal encyclopedias, and working with them is not always easy. Checklist 8-1 shows the basic steps to be followed.

The facts from the research problem will determine the area of law to be researched. If the researcher is not familiar with the area of law, secondary materials, such as a legal encyclopedia, may need to be consulted. Once the decision is made to consult the encyclopedia, words should be selected from the assignment that appear to be important or could be used as a key word or phrase. The sample assignment in Example 8-2 illustrates this process. Checklist 8-2 gives some hints on using encyclopedias.

The same process can be followed when searching in state legal encyclopedias.

All legal encyclopedias serve an important function—they give the reader a foundation or starting point for further research. If a researcher does not know enough about a topic, the legal encyclopedias provide background information and a foundation upon which the researcher can build. However, it must be understood that the encyclopedias provide commentary on the law rather than providing the law itself. In addition, legal encyclopedias provide citations to a variety of resources that start the researcher on his or her way to finding the answer to a legal question.

TIP

Any time research is done, a research trail should be maintained.

Checklist 8-1

RESEARCHING IN SECONDARY SOURCES

Step	Activity
1.	Determine what the key words or phrases are from your assignment. Use a legal dictionary or thesaurus to identify alternate words that describe your key words.
2.	Use the key words to search the index of the secondary material chosen, such as the encyclopedia, or use the key words to search online. Make a research trail of the sources you view.
3.	Validate the secondary sources by checking the pocket part supplements to make sure the law is still good and is current.
4.	Read the secondary material and take notes if necessary. Identify relevant primary authority cited in the secondary sources. Add to the research trail.
5.	Locate, read, and analyze the primary authorities. Take appropriate notes.
6.	Validate the primary sources by an updating method such as Shepardizing or KeyCiting to make sure the law is still good and is current.
7.	Prepare your results for your supervisor.

EXAMPLE 8-2   SAMPLE RESEARCH ASSIGNMENT

To
Heather Rennis, Paralegal

From
Michael Kennedy, Esq.

Date: December 10, 2012
RE: *Jones v. John J. Furriers*

Mrs. Jones has come to the office because she bought a fur coat from John J. Furriers. The coat was labeled 100% sable. One day Mrs. Jones was smoking a cigarette and a hot ash accidentally fell on the coat while she was wearing it. The ash melted a hole in the coat. Mrs. Jones knew that fur burns, but acrylic melts. She wants to sue the furrier.

Heather makes the following plan:

1. Use the key words from the assignment as possible words to use to scan the encyclopedia's index or topics.

   Possible words for this scenario:
   Label
   Fur
   Product mislabeling
   Labeling requirements
   Product manufacturing

2. Brainstorm possible alternate words to use. Include all word alternatives at first; some words can be eliminated later. It is easier to eliminate later than to add later.

Term	Alternate Terms
Label	Emblem, insignia
Fur	Mink, sable, lamb, chinchilla, fox, beaver, lynx, rabbit, product
Product mislabeling	Misrepresent, fraud, misclassification,
Labeling requirement	Condition, regulation, constraint
Product manufacturing	Assemble, construct, create, produce, assemble, form, construct, develop, create

3. Search in the general index or in the table of contents using the words above. Read the applicable sections and research any appropriate references such as A.L.R. annotations, cases, or other materials such as law review articles.

4. When an appropriate section of information is found, check the pocket part for new information. Use the same title, sections, and footnotes in the pocket parts as were used in the main volumes.

TIP

One thing to remember is that the words a researcher uses may not be the same as those under which the topics are organized.

Checklist 8-2   TIPS ON USING ENCYCLOPEDIAS

Checklist—Using *Am. Jur. 2d*

A. Determine the Approach
   1. Topic Analysis
   2. Fact/Descriptive Word
   3. Table of Statutes

1. Topic Analysis Approach
   a. Consult *Desk Book* alphabetical "List of Titles" for possible applicable topics.
   b. If a topic cannot be found, follow the Fact/Descriptive Word approach in step 2.
   c. Turn to the appropriate volume(s) and examine the topic(s):
      1. Review "Scope of Topic" and "Treated Elsewhere."
      2. Consult the skeletal and expanded outlines.
      3. Read the applicable text discussion.
      4. Update with the pocket supplement, if any.
      5. Review *New Topic Service* for further material.
2. Fact/Descriptive Word Approach
   a. Compile a list of words and expressions that could lead to an applicable topic.
   b. Consult the general index and pocket supplements, if any.
   c. Turn to the encyclopedia entry and read it.
   d. Consult the pocket part again for the section information.
3. Table of Statutes
   a. Look up the law or rule in the separate volume containing the "Table of Laws and Rules."
   b. Check its pocket part.

c. Go to the appropriate volume, topic, and section and read the information.
d. Check the pocket part or supplementary pamphlets for any updated information.

Note: *Am. Jur. 2d* provides citations only to cases that are considered the most important by the editors such as federal statutory material. *Am. Jur. 2d* is on Westlaw and LexisNexis.

Checklist –Using *C.J.S.*
A. Determine the approach.
  1. Topic Analysis
  2. Fact/Descriptive Word
  3. Table of Statutes
  4. Table of Cases

1. Topic Analysis Approach
  a. Consult the list of titles in the most recently recompiled volume for possible applicable topics.
  b. If a topic cannot be found, follow the fact/descriptive word approach.
  c. Turn to the appropriate volume(s) and examine the topic:
    1. In older volumes, review the introductory scope note, which is located ahead of the analysis.
    2. In recently recompiled volumes, review the "Scope of Title," which is the first section in the discussion itself.
  d. Consult the analysis (skeletal outline) and the sub-analysis (expanded outline) to determine which sections are relevant.
  e. Read the applicable text discussion.
  f. Update with the pocket supplement, if any.
2. Fact/Descriptive Approach
  a. Compile a list of words and expressions that could lead to an appropriate topic.
  b. Consult the general index and pocket supplements, if any.
3. Table of Statutes
  a. Using the separate volume entitled *Table of Laws and Rules*, look up the law or rule.
  b. Go to the appropriate volume, topic and section.
4. Table of Cases
  a. There are separate volumes, divided alphabetically, such as A–E, where one can look up the case name.
  b. Once the case name is found, go to the volume, topic, and section that provides the information for which that case was cited.

Checklist Using Westlaw (*Am. Jur. 2d* or CJS)
  a. Use the database AMJUR or CJS.
  b. If the topic is understood, use terms and connectors or natural language.
  c. The table of contents can be browsed by clicking Expand (+) or Contract (–).
  d. To retrieve multiple sections or more, click the check boxes next to the parts wanted.
  e. Retrieved sections can be printed by clicking "Retrieve and Print" or searched by clicking "Search" and using the terms and connectors.

(Continued)

TIP

C.J.S. is more in-depth than *Am. Jur. 2d* and provides every relevant citation, but cites more to cases than to statutes. It provides topic and key number references for connection to the digests and reporters. This feature is available on Westlaw only.

Checklist Using LexisNexis (2NDARY; AMJUR)

Topic

Use the HEADING segment to search for sections that have specific terms any-where in the heading of the document. For example, take the following steps to find articles on the topic of religious freedom:

1. Click the Search tab.
2. Click the Legal source tab.
3. Click the following links in the order listed to search *American Jurisprudence 2d*: Secondary Legal / American Jurisprudence 2d

NOTE: Because the LexisNexis® services list some of the most popular sources on the main search page, you can often link to the source you want directly from the Look for a Source box.

4. Click the Terms and Connectors link if it is not already selected.
5. Click the radio button in front of Full-text of source documents.
6. Enter heading (religious freedom) in the search field.
7. Click Search.

Use the SECTION segment to retrieve sections with a specific title. For example, take the following steps to find sections titled "work product":

1. Click the Search tab.
2. Click the Legal source tab.
3. Click the following links in the order listed to search *American Jurisprudence 2d*: Secondary Legal / American Jurisprudence 2d

NOTE: Because the LexisNexis® services list some of the most popular sources on the main search page, you can often link to the source you want directly from the Look for a Source box.

5. Click the Terms and Connectors link if it is not already selected.
6. Click the radio button in front of Full-text of source documents.
7. Enter section (work product) in the search field.
8. Click Search.

Updating
Use the SUPPLEMENT segment to retrieve all text that has been added since the last printed version of *American Jurisprudence 2d*. For example, take the following steps to find all supplemental material on the topic of the Internet:

1. Click the Search tab.
2. Click the Legal source tab.
3. Click the following links in the order listed to search *American Jurisprudence 2d*: Secondary Legal / American Jurisprudence 2d

NOTE: Because the LexisNexis® services list some of the most popular sources on the main search page, one can often link to the desired source directly from the Look for a Source box.

4. Click the Terms and Connectors link if it is not already selected.
5. Click the radio button in front of Full-text of source documents.

6. Enter supplement (internet) in the search field.

7. Click Search.

Case Citations

Use the FOOTNOTES segment to retrieve all AMJUR 2d sections that cite to a case. For example, take the following steps to find all footnotes that cite *New York Times v. Sullivan*:

1. Click the Search tab.

2. Click the Legal source tab.

3. Click the following links in the order listed to search *American Jurisprudence 2d*:

4. Secondary Legal / American Jurisprudence 2d

NOTE: Because the LexisNexis® services list some of the most popular sources on the main search page, one can often link to the source one wants directly from the Look for a Source box.

5. Click the Terms and Connectors link if it is not already selected.

6. Click the radio button in front of Full-text of source documents.

7. Enter footnotes (new york times W/5 sullivan) in the search field.

8. Click Search.

NOTE: Use the W/5 connector to link concepts together. The W/5 connector finds the first word within five or fewer words of the last word.[7]

[7]Support Center. *American Jurisprudence 2d (AMJUR)*. LexisNexis. 2012. http://support.lexisnexis.com/lexiscom/record.asp?ArticleID=lexiscom_searchtip_amjur

ANNOTATIONS

1. Background

American Law Reports (A.L.R.) annotations, published since 1888, provide in-depth analysis of cases in changing, emerging, or unsettled areas of law. The annotations are sometimes referred to as "articles" and are written by legal scholars who use each identified case as the basis for the annotation. By analyzing how various courts have decided the same issue, these scholars provide an objective analysis and synthesis of the law as it currently stands from both sides of the issue.

The greatest value of the A.L.R. annotations is that they usually cover a very narrow point of law in depth. Generally, most of the cases on point are presented from all jurisdictions. The discussions are descriptive rather than critical but provide an excellent place to begin researching. There are multiple series in the A.L.R. materials, as shown in Table 8-3.

Even though each annotation is based on a case, annotations are not primary authority; rather, they are a valuable tool that allows a researcher to learn about a particular legal issue. These annotations are often used as a ***finding tool*** to locate other secondary and primary resources.

The individual articles within each annotation contain many useful features. Each article will have a page showing references to the Total Client-Service

Finding tool
Sources, such as digests, that direct a researcher to other sources.

TABLE 8-3 The *American Law Reports*

Series	Coverage
Federal	
Federal Series (A.L.R. *Fed.*)	1969–2005
Federal Series, Second (A.L.R. *Fed 2d*)	2005–
State	
First Series (A.L.R.) 175 volumes	1919–1948
Second Series (A.L.R. *2d*) 100 volumes	1048–1965
Third Series (A.L.R. *3d*) 100 volumes	1965–1980
Fourth Series (A.L.R. 4th) 90 volumes	1980–1992
Fifth Series (A.L.R. 5th)	1991-2005
Sixth Series (A.L.R. 6th)	2005–

Note: The federal issues were analyzed in A.L.R., A.L.R. *2d*, and A.L.R. *3d* along with the state issues.

Note: There were two series under the original title of Lawyers Reports Annotated (LRA) from 1888–1919.

Series	Coverage
Other Finding Aids	
A.L.R. *Table of Laws, Rules, and Regulations*	Annotations citing U.S. Code, *CFR*, federal court rules, and state statutes and constitutions
Index to Annotations	Indexes A.L.R. 2nd – 6th and A.L.R. *Fed* and A.L.R. *Fed 2d*
Word Index	A.L.R. *1st*
Quick Index	A.L.R. *1st*
A.L.R. Digests	A.L.R. *1st* (separate); A.L.R. 2nd (separate); a single digest for A.L.R. 3rd–6th, A.L.R. *Fed* and A.L.R. *Fed 2d*
Updating	
A.L.R. *1st*	Blue Book of Supplemental Decisions
A.L.R. 2nd	Later Case Service
A.L.R. 3rd, 4th, 5th, 6th, *Fed, Fed 2d*	Pocket parts
Supplemented or *Superseded*	
All *ALRs*	Annotation History Table in Index to Annotations
Electronic	
Westlaw	A.L.R.; terms and connectors or natural language; Other abbreviations are used for individual Topics or areas; Sample: ALR Fed, ALR-BKR
LexisNexis	2NDARY; LEDALR (all except ALR 1st); Sample: xx alr 3d xxx

Supersede
To replace or take the place of.

Library® and other legal references, depending on the series. Generally, each article will reference legal encyclopedias, law review articles, West Key Numbers, practice aids (forms/proof of facts), A.L.R. Digests, and electronic search queries (in the later series). Auto-Cite® allows a researcher to check citations for parallel references, treatment in prior and subsequent history, annotation references, and forms.[8] Figure 8-3 shows a page from 62 ALR 4th 16. The top of the page shows the topics covered, while the bottom of the page provides the index within the annotation.

[8]LexisNexis Support Center. What is the Auto-Cite® Service? 2012. http://support.lexisnexis.com/lexiscom/record.asp?ArticleID=Auto_Cite

---

ALR INDEX

DERIVATIVE ACTIONS—Cont'd
who is made defendant in a subsequent action as derivatively responsible, **112 ALR 404**
Welfare, personal injury recovery as affecting eligibility for, or duty to reimburse, public welfare assistance, **80 ALR3d 772, § 17**

DERIVATIVE ENTRAPMENT
Right of criminal defendant to raise entrapment defense based on having dealt with other party who was entrapped, **15 ALR5th 39**

DERIVATIVE LIABILITY
Vicarious Liability (this index)

DERMAL NITRATE TEST
Residue detection test, admissibility in criminal case of results of test to determine whether accused or victim handled or fired gun, **1 ALR4th 1072, § 3**

DERMATITIS
Cosmetics, product liability, hair straighteners and relaxants, **84 ALR4th 1090**
Federal Employers' Liability Act (FELA)
poisoning occupational disease, liability, under Federal Employers' Liability Act (FELA) (45 U.S.C.A. § 51 et seq.) for industrial or occupational disease or poisoning, **30 ALR3d 735, § 5**
statute of limitations, accrual of cause of action and tolling of limitation period of § 6 of the Federal Employers' Liability Act (FELA) (45 U.S.C.A. § 56), **16 ALR3d 637, § 23, 24**
Malpractice, treatment of skin disease, disorder, blemish or scar, **19 ALR5th 563**
Occupational disease, liability, under Federal Employers' Liability Act (FELA) (45 U.S.C.A. § 51 et seq.) for industrial or occupational disease or poisoning, **30 ALR3d 735, § 5**

DERMATITIS- Cont'd
Preexisting conditions, sufficiency of proof that condition of skin or sensory organ resulted from accident or incident in suit rather than from pre-existing condition, **2 ALR3d 446, § 2**
Products liability, hair straighteners and relaxants, **84 ALR4th 1090**
Res ipsa loquitur doctrine, applicability in action for injury to patron of beauty salon, **93 ALR3d 897**
Trade secrets, discovery of trade secret in state court action, **75 ALR4th 1009, § 5, 6, 12, 18**
Unemployment compensation, leaving or refusing employment because of allergic reaction affecting unemployment compensation, **12 ALR4th 629**
Workers' compensation
limitation of action, when limitations period begins to run as to chain for disability benefits for contracting of disease under workers' compensation or occupational diseases act, **86 ALR5th 295**
successive employers' liability for disease or condition allegedly attributable to successive employments, **34 ALR4th 958, § 3 to 5, 6(b), 9, 10, 12**

DERMATOLOGY
Employment contract, validity and construction of contractual restrictions on right of medical practitioner to practice, incident to employment agreement, **62 ALR3d 1014, § 5(a), 6, 8, 16, 19(a), 22**
Locality rule, standard of care owed to patient by medical specialist as determined by local, like community state, national, or other standards, **18 ALR4th 603, § 10**
Medical malpractice
punitive damages, allowance of punitive damages in medical malpractice action, **3 ALR5th 145**
scars, malpractice in treatment of skin disease, disorder, blemish, or scar, **19 ALR5th 563**

Consult POCKET PART for Later Annotations

FIGURE 8-3: A.L.R. Index

Each annotation lists cases that discuss every aspect of the issue in question. In addition, they also provide cases showing the split of opinion from various jurisdictions. Using this information, it is possible to gain insight into an opponent's position. Once an issue is firmly decided in a jurisdiction, A.L.R. stops providing citations to more recent cases. A.L.R.s are not exhaustive, and researchers should *supplement* their research. But the A.L.R.s are likely to be more informative on a topic than a related section of an encyclopedia. Checklist 8-3 gives an overview of how to use the A.L.R.s.

Supplement
To add to something.

FIGURE 8-4 Edward L. Raymond, Jr., J.D., Annotation, *Social host's liability for injuries incurred by third parties as a result of intoxicated guest's negligence*, 62 ALR 4th 16, 17 (1988)

[a] View that host may be held liable
[b] View that negligence action does not lie
§ 12. —Failure to supervise and control guests
§ 13. —Assisting guest to automobile and allowing to drive
§ 14. Liability based upon furnishing' liquor in violation of statute
[a] Cause of action recognized
[b] Cause of action not recognized
§ 15. Liability based upon civil liability or dram shop statute
§ 16. Liability based upon host's wanton and reckless conduct

B. PARTICULAR CIRCUMSTANCES AFFECTING LIABILITY

§ 17. Liquor not furnished by host
§ 18. Knowledge that guest intoxicated
[a] Host aware of guest's intoxication
[b] Host unaware of guest's intoxication
§ 19. Knowledge that guest would be driving
§ 20. Foreseeability of injury to third person
[a] Injury foreseeable
[b] Injury not foreseeable
§21. Host and guest as joint tortfeasors

INDEX

Abrogation of common law rule, § 3
Acquiescence, generally, § 8[a, c, d]
Adult guests, §§ 11-21
Aid or assistance, §§ 8[a, b], 13
Already intoxicated person, furnishing alcohol to, §S 14, 18[a]
Alternate transportation, § 4
Amendment of statutes §§ 6[a], 7[b], 14[a]
Assault and battery, §§ 11, 14[a], 20[a]
Assistance, §§ 8[a, b], 13
Attorney-client situation, § 15
Automobile accidents, §§ 3 et scq.
Bar, purchase of drinks for guest in, §§ 14[a], 18[a]
Barbecue, § 17
Battery, §§ 11, 14[a], 20[a]
Beach party, § 7[b]
Birthday party, § 6[a]
Broken neck, §§ 11[a], 14[a], 20[a]
BYOB events, §§ 8[b, d], 12, 15, 17

Cabin, ownership interest in, § 8[d]
Christmas party, § 6[a]
Cigareue, fire caused by, § 20[b]
Civil damage act, §§ 3[b], 6, 7, 11[b], 15
Comment and summary, § 2
Common law negligence, §§ 3-5, 11-13
Company-sponsored event; §§6[a], 7[b], 10[c], 11[b], 12, 15
Comparative negligence of guest, § 10[b]
Contribution to cost of alcohol, §§ 3[b], 6[a], 8[b], 15
Contributory negligence of guest, § 10
Control, failure to exercise, § 12 Cost of alcohol, contributions toward, §§3[b], 6[a], 8[b], 15
Crew of government vessel, § 11 [b]
Criminal statutes, § 6[b]
Death actions, §§ 6, 8[d], 11, 15, 18[b], 20[b]

The A.L.R.s have multivolume indices that include all volumes except those in the first series, which has its own index. For the first series, the resource to review is the *Blue Book of Supplemental Decisions.* A.L.R.2d is kept current with a separate set called *ALR2d Later Case Service.* Like many secondary materials, the A.L.R.s are updated with annual pocket parts. Annual supplements in the back of the volumes in A.L.R. *3d – 6th,* A.L.R. *Fed* and A.L.R. *Fed 2d* provide the means to update these sets. Additional indices for the series are the A.L.R. *Federal Quick*

Index and the A.L.R. *Quick Index (A.L.R. 3d – 6th series)*. Figure 8-6 shows an excerpt from an index page.

As is true with any printed legal material, the analysis of the articles may be changed by subsequent changes in the law. Reading material in the first and second series was confusing because the original and supplementing articles had to be read together. There is an Annotation History Table in the last volume of the A.L.R. *Index* that gives the history of all articles within the A.L.R. series. KeyCite History on Westlaw is another way to show whether the A.L.R. article has been superseded or supplemented.

An index and table of contents for the annotation, followed by a Table of Jurisdictions Represented, are also included. This page is shown in Figure 8-5. The table is very useful because it provides all of the state and federal jurisdictions cited within the annotation. The text may begin with a "Scope Note" that identifies the issue to be covered, and may also contain a "Related Matters" section that gives related annotations. The reader is also provided with a "Background and Summary" section. The annotation may or may not include a section called "Practice Pointers." In the A.L.R. *4th* pocket parts, A.L.R. *5th*, and subsequent editions, there is a section called "Research Sources" that provide helpful West digest key numbers and Westlaw queries.

It is important to note that the print and online forms of some secondary sources are different. For example, *American Law Reports (A.L.R.)* in print form contains both leading cases and articles or annotations discussing the legal issues raised in those cases. The online form, however, contains only the annotations, since the cases are available online through other sources.

A Westlaw search allows the researcher to retrieve either the A.L.R. article (from the A.L.R. database) or the case (in the appropriate state, regional, or federal database). The A.L.R. citation will be displayed as a parallel citation to the official or unofficial citations of the case. A common Westlaw search is done in the title field with the key words, generally in quotation marks. Here is an example of proper citation format:

> Jay M. Zitter, J.D. *Waiver of Right to Enforce Restrictive Covenant by Failure to Object to Other Violations*, 25 A.L.R.5th 229 (2000)

In the above citation, "25" is the volume number, "A.L.R.5th" is the fifth series of the A.L.R. set, and "229" is the page number where the annotation begins, along with the date of the source.

West's A.L.R. *Digest* divides the A.L.R. articles according to the West Key Number System containing more than 700 topics. All West materials utilize the key number system to make researching easier and more comprehensive. Under each topic, the researcher will find headnotes from cases with the ALRs, together with a listing of articles dealing with the topic in question. The later series, such as A.L.R. *Fed. 2d* and A.L.R. 4th – 6th, include instructions for using A.L.R.

Researching in A.L.R.s

The fact pattern from the client's case or the supervisor's instructions will provide a set of key words or key phrases that can be used search terms. The first place to look for these search terms is the index for each A.L.R. There is no comprehensive index for the entire set, so the index for each A.L.R. must be used. Once the relevant annotation has been found, the "Annotation History Table" should be checked to determine whether the annotation has been superseded or supplemented by a later annotation. The pocket part in the Index should always be checked, as well.

FIGURE 8-5 Table of Jurisdictions Represented

Theories of liability, §§ 3-7, 11-16
Tort Claims Act, § 11[b]
VFW hall, § 6[a]
Visibly intoxicated person, furnishing alcohol to. §§ 14, 18[a]
Wanton and reckless conduct, § 16

Wedding reception, §§ 6[a], 11[b], 12
Wife beating, §§ 11[a], 14[a], 20[a]
Wrongful death, §§ 6, 8[d], 11, 15, 18[b], 20[b]

TABLE OF JURISDICTIONS REPRESENTED

Consult POCKET PART in this volume for later cases

US: §§ 2[b], 6[a], 8[a, b],. 11[a, b], 18[a], 19
Ala: §§ 3[b], 7[a], 8[d], 11[b], 15
Cal: §§ 2[b], 4, 6[a, b], 7[b], 8[b, c], 9[b], 11[a, b], 14[a], 15, 17, 18[a], 19, 20[a]
Conn: §§ 2[b], 11[b], 16
DC: §§ 2[b], 11[b]
Fla: §§ 3[b], 6[b], 7[b]
Ca: §§ 6[a], 9[a]
Ill: §§ 3[b], 11[b], 12, 15
Ind: §§ 2[b], 6[a], 8[a], 13, 14[a], 18[a]
Iowa: §§ 7[a], 14[b], 18[a]
Mass: §§ 2[b], 5, 8[d], 11[a], 18[b]
Mich: §§ 5, 6[a], 8[b, d], 11[b]

Minn: §§ 3[b], 5, 7[b], 8[d], 15
Miss: §§ 2[b], 11[b], 14 [b]
Mo: §§ 3[b], 6[b]
Mont: §§ 3[b], 6[b], 10[a]
NJ: §§ 2[b], 3[a], 9[a], 11 [a, b], 17, 18[a], 19, 20[a, b], 21
NM: §§ 6[a], 14[a]
NY: §§ 11[b], 12, 15
Ohio: §§ 11[b], 18[a]
Or: §§ 3[a], 6[b], 8[a], 9[a], 14[a]
Pa: §§ 6[a], 8[a, b], 9[a], 10[c], ll[b], 19
SC: §§ 11[b], 14[b], 19
Tenn: § 11[b]
Wis: §§ 2[b], 3[a], 9[a], 10[b]

I. Preliminary Matters
§ 1. Introduction
[a] Scope

This annotation[1] collects and analyzes the state and federal cases which have considered the liability[2] of a social host[3] for injuries sustained by a third party[4] as a result

---

1. This annotation supersedes §§ 10-13 of the annotation at 97 ALR3d 528.

2. All theories of liability, with the exception of negligent entrustment of an automobile, are addressed in this annotation. See the annotation at 19 ALR3d 1175 for cases dealing with a host's liability for injuries suffered because of the negligent entrustment of an automobile to an intoxicated guest.

3. This annotation is concerned only with the liability of a social host

and does not include cases dealing with commercial furnishers of intoxicating liquors. Cases in which an employer-employee relationship exists incidental to the host-guest relationship are included. However, those cases in which liability is predicated on the employer-employee relationship are excluded, even where the court specifically refers to the employer as a social host. For a collection, of such cases, see the annotation at 51 ALR4th 1048.

4. This annotation is confined to

As with all research materials, it is important to update the information to make sure the most current law is presented and that it is still good law. Updating also confirms whether new cases have been decided since the annotation was first published. Updating annotations is different from updating statutes or cases in that the annotation may be replaced or revised based on changing law. To update

Checklist 8-3   HOW TO USE A.L.R. IN PRINT

Assume the research issue is based on whether evidence procured by torture or alleged torture is admissible.

1. Pull out the key words (*torture*, *admissible*, and *evidence*).

2. Determine whether there are any alternate words. **Alternate words** are synonyms, and sometimes antonyms, to the key words from the issue. Alternate words allow a researcher to think like the writers think. For example, while you may be concerned about what is "admissible", it might be useful to know what is deemed "inadmissible".

3. Use the key words within the appropriate indices. If looking for a specific federal case, look in the A.L.R *Federal* Table of Cases. If the topic is federal, look in the Quick Index at the end of A.L.R *Fed. 2d*. If it is not there, go to the combined A.L.R Index.

4. If the specific case is a state one, try A.L.R 5th and A.L.R 6th Table of Cases. If the topic is a state one, go to the combined A.L.R *Index*.

5. If looking for a specific state or federal statute or regulation, a model law, a Restatement section or code of ethics, go to the Table of Laws, Rules, and Regulations.

6. If the issue is very old, look in the Quick Index and Index to the original A.L.R.

7. Check the pocket parts.

8. If a West "key" number is available, go to the A.L.R *Digest*.

9. Once an annotation appears to be useful, read through it and note what references are made to the jurisdiction in question.

10. Use the Research References to find other legal resources.

11. Use the query (if any is available) to run a search in Westlaw or other subscriber services.

12. When cases and statutes that are on point have been found within the jurisdiction, check the primary authority in an update service such as *Shepard's* or KeyCite.

Alternate words
Synonyms and antonyms of key words that are used in a query to expand the search.

---

the articles, the supplements and pocket parts of the appropriate volume must be checked. Cases should also be updated through citator services, such as KeyCite and *Shepard's*.

The online A.L.R.*s* are updated regularly and the superseded annotations are removed from the database in most cases. The annotations are updated weekly on Westlaw and LexisNexis. In Westlaw or other subscriber services, articles may appear on the service even if they are not yet in print. Some annotations are included in the online database but are not included in the books.

The chief value of the A.L.R.*s* is that they include the full text of a court decision and annotations that analyze the point of law in the reported case. The annotations are useful because they cover extremely narrow points of law in depth, citing most of the cases decided on that point of law. A.L.R.*s* are good tools to help a researcher understand a point of law in greater detail.

EXAMPLE 8-3   QUERIES IN WESTLAW AND LEXISNEXIS

The client's issue requires research as to his liability under dram shop acts. A Westlaw query will have four parts: terms, alternate terms, expanders, and connectors.

1. The terms might be *dram shop, sale,* or *alcohol* (because dram shop acts revolve around the sale of alcohol).

2. Alternate terms might be *liquor, intoxicating,* or *purchase.*

3. Expanders are signs that tell the computer to look for variations of a word. The exclamation point (!) applied to a root of the word tells the computer to look for that root and any letters that follow that root to make a word. Expanders here might be intoxicat! and alcohol!

4. Connectors are commands to the computer to look for the terms in a certain manner. For a phrase search, the words are placed in quotation marks; this tells the computer to look for just those words in just that relationship.

5. Since this is an annotation, the logical place to look for the terms would be in the title of the annotation. A field search of the title (ti) field would be the focus of the computer search. A query for this general issue might be ti("intoxicat! liquor" alcohol! /p "dram shop")

6. This query would tell the computer that the result desired includes any variation of the of the phrase "intoxicat! liquor" or the variations of the word "alcohol" or the phrase "dram shop" in the title field of the A.L.R.s. The results would range from ordinances and statutes relating to alcohol to federal regulation of alcohol in the competitive marketplace to dram shop acts. "Dram shop" is used as an alternate phrase because the article may deal with liability under dram shop acts but not have the phrase in the title. The LexisNexis query is going to be very similar.

7. The final step is to update the search through KeyCite in Westlaw or *Shepard's* in LexisNexis.

RESTATEMENTS

Restatements are published by the American Law Institute (ALI), which was founded in the early 1920s. ALI's goal is to collect, coordinate, and clarify the common law in the United States. Each restatement covers a major area, such as torts, contracts, or property law. As the law is created, ALI collects the "rules" from the cases, organizes the material by chapters, topics, and sections, and presents those sections as the "black-letter law."[9]

In addition to the rule of law, the sections provide comments and examples to help the reader understand the rule and any major exceptions to the rule. A comprehensive index covers the entire set of restatements; additionally, each topical volume has its own index and table of contents.

Because Restatements are secondary sources, the courts are never required to utilize the Restatements in their decisions. However, courts have cited Restatements, sometimes verbatim, as the law of the jurisdiction. This makes them unlike many other secondary sources. In law school, many professors rely on the Restatements to provide the "black-letter law."

---

[9]American Law Institute. The American Law Institute 50th Anniversary. Philadelphia: American Law Institute, 1973.

Most researchers will not find the Restatements in the first series anyplace except on microfilm. While the full texts of the Restatements are not available on the ALI website, a useful discussion about the restatements and ALI can be found there.[10]

Restatements published through 1976 are supplemented by hardbound volumes called *Restatement in the Courts*. Subsequent to 1976, case annotations have been provided for each topical volume, first in hardbound volumes that are not cumulative, and later with cumulative annual pocket parts and semiannual pamphlets. ALI also publishes *Interim Case Citations to the Restatement of the Law,* which is a semiannual supplement to be used along with the other supplements. A researcher must check the coverage as listed on the spines or covers. *Shepard's* provides an updating tool in a volume called *Shepard's Restatement of the Law Citations*.[11]

All of the Restatements series are accessible via Westlaw in the REST database or in a REST-[topic name] database. When accessing Restatements on Westlaw, it is important to make sure the right series is used. The Restatements, except for the first series, are also available on LexisNexis.. To find the Restatements in LexisNexis, the "Secondary Legal" link is selected within the "Jurisprudences, Restatements and Principles of the Law" link.

Table 8-4 shows the topics covered in the Restatements. It should be noted that a later series in the Restatements does not necessarily repeal the earlier series, because some states have adopted sections from different series.

Currently, ALI has several other projects under way, such as *Principles of Government Ethics; Torts: Economic Torts and Related Wrongs; Employment Law; Principles of the Law of Nonprofit Organizations*; and *The U.S. Law of International Commercial Arbitration*.[12]

Researching in Restatements

Generally, doing research in the Restatements is similar to doing research in the other secondary sources— the topic approach and the descriptive word method are the most effective strategies. If a researcher were using the topic method, he or she would look at the table of contents in the relevant topical volume (generally in the first volume if there is more than one volume per topic), and then go to the referenced sections. If doing research in the newer volumes, the Table of Cases, located in the individual Restatement indices, would be used. When Restatements are referenced in other sources, a specific section is usually identified. As with all secondary authorities, the supplements must be checked for updates.

The Restatements are arranged by chapter, topic, title, and section, but are cited by section number only. Each section of a Restatement includes the following:

- The "black letter law" or a statement of the principle of law;
- Explanatory comments (cmts);
- Illustrations (illus.) of the law in the form of hypothetical situations; and
- Reporter's notes that provide:
  - background information on how the rule was developed
  - citations to cases used in forming the rule
  - statutes
  - treatises
  - journal articles.

[10]The American Law Institute. 2010-2011. http://www.ali.org/ali_old/thisali.htm

[11]Cohen, Morris L. and Berring, Robert C., "Restatements of the Law". In How to Find the Law 395-404. St. Paul: West Publishing Co., 1989.

[12]The American Law Institute. 2011. http://www.ali.org/

TABLE 8-4   Restatements of the Law

Coverage	Series/Notes	Citation Format (some examples)
Agency	First, Second, Third*	*Restatement (Second) of Agency § 35 (1960)*
Conflict of Laws	First, Second*	
Contracts	First, Second*	*Restatement (Second) of Contracts § 87 (1981)*
Employment Law	First, Second, Third (tentative)	
Foreign Relations Law of the United States	Second, Third*	*Restatement (Third) of Foreign Relations Law of the United States §501(1987)*
International Commercial Arbitration	Third (tentative)	
Judgments	First, Second*	
Law Governing Lawyers	Third*	
Property	First	
Property Donative Transfers	Second (supersedes Volume 4 of original Restatement	*Restatement (Third) of Property: Donative Transfers § 5 (2000)*
Property Landlord and Tenant	Second*	
Property (Mortgages)	First	
Property, Wills and Other Donative Transfers	Will eventually replace restatement Second, Property (Donative Transfers).	
Property, Servitudes	Supersedes original Restatement	
Restitution	First	
Restitution and Unjust Enrichment	Third	
Security	First (out of print but available on Westlaw and Lexis/Nexis)	*Restatement of Security § 152 (1941)*
Suretyship and Guaranty	Third* (supersedes Division II of Security)	*Restatement (Third) of Suretyship and Guaranty § 15 (1996)*
Torts	First, Second* (second supersedes first)	
Torts Apportionment of Liability	Third* (supersedes comparable parts of Torts)	
Torts Products Liability	Third (completely supersedes § 402A of Torts)	
Torts Liability for Physical and Emotional Harm	Third (Proposed final draft in two volumes; volume 1 if available. Supersedes comparable parts of Torts)	
Trusts	First, Second, Third* (Second replaced First)	
Trusts, Prudent Investor Rule	Third*	
Trusts, General Principles Trust Administration	Third (tentative draft)	
Unfair Competition	First, Second, Third*	

Note: * denotes the current volume

Example 8-4 demonstrates how a Restatement might be used in actual research.

Researching in the Restatements electronically is similar to researching them in print. On Westlaw the Restatements are in the "ALI Restatement of the Law & Principles of the Law" directory. Included are all current Restatements, as well as those followed by later Restatements, and an "archive" database that includes various drafts of the document. Up to 10 Restatement titles can be searched at once,

EXAMPLE 8-4   RESEARCH IN THE RESTATEMENTS

To
John Davis, paralegal

From
Jami Selzer

Date: December 10, 2012
RE: Malicious Prosecution

Jennifer Eckart came to the office because she instigated the arrest of her ex-husband for child neglect, even though she knew her ex-husband was not guilty. The ex-husband was released shortly after the arrest and was not prosecuted. This may be an issue of malicious prosecution but I want to know specifically if merely instigating the arrest of someone who is not prosecuted constitutes malicious prosecution. Our state does recognize the tort of malicious prosecution, but this issue of non-prosecution would be a novel question.

John would follow the following process:

He would identify the appropriate volume, which would be *Restatement of the Law Second, Torts*.

Next, John would look at the table of contents or the index to find the appropriate section pertaining to the issue of malicious prosecution. Since malicious prosecution is the main concept, he would use that phrase as the key term.

The index would send John to volume 3 of the Restatement, where he would look at its index.

That index would send him to Section 654(2)(C), dealing with arrest. If he reads the section and the comments, he would see an Illustration case that is on point with the client's situation.

He would arrive at the answer that the client may be found liable for malicious prosecution if she is responsible for the initiation of the lawful arrest of her ex-husband on a criminal charge even though ,he was released without prosecution.

However, John should not stop there; it is important to check the updates. If the state has adopted the *Restatement* as law, he will need to check all volumes of the series. If he were looking to fill a gap in the law, he would use the most recent.

In this scenario, to do a complete survey, he would review multiple volumes of the Appendix, beginning with the first volume that covers the relevant section and working through each volume in which that section is covered.

He must remember to consult pocket parts and cumulative annual supplements or pamphlets.

or each title can be searched individually. To emulate working in books where a researcher might look at sections before and after the section found, this service offers the "Full-Text Document —Table of Cases" feature on the left side of the screen, which provides the Table of Contents. KeyCite provides the updates for the findings. Figure 8-6 shows the Westlaw databases and identifiers for the Restatements and other tools from ALI.

The ⓘ can be clicked to provide the researcher with a summary of the database, a description of what it covers, how current it is, how to cite it, how to search it (terms and connectors or natural language), a list of fields that can be searched, and related references.

Restatements in LexisNexis can be found in the Restatements directory under "Secondary Legal Resources." LexisNexis includes only the most current version of each Restatement and does not include any draft documents. On the terms and connectors screen the table of contents is provided as well. Once the

---

Directory Location: My Databases > Restatements of the Law & Principles of the Law

American Law Institute: Annual Proceedings (ALI-PROCEED) ⓘ

Intellectual Property: Principles Governing Jurisdiction, Choice of Law, and Judgments in Transnational Disputes (ALI-INTPROP) ⓘ

Intellectual Property: Principles Governing Jurisdiction, Choice of Law, and Judgments in Transnational Disputes - Archive (ALI-INTPROPAR) ⓘ

Model Penal Code: Sentencing (ALI-SENTENCE) ⓘ

Principles of the Law of Aggregate Litigation (ALI-AGGLIT) ⓘ

Principles of the Law of Aggregate Litigation - Archive (ALI-AGGLITAR) ⓘ

Principles of the Law of Family Dissolution: Analysis and Recommendations (ALI-FAMDISS) ⓘ

Principles of the Law of Nonprofit Organizations (ALI-NONPROFIT) ⓘ

Principles of the Law of Software Contracts (ALI-SOFTWARE) ⓘ

Principles of the Law of Software Contracts - Archive (ALI-SOFTWAREAR) ⓘ

Restatement of the Law - Agency (REST-AGEN) ⓘ

Restatement of the Law - Agency Archive (REST-AGENAR) ⓘ

Restatement of the Law - Conflict of Laws (REST-CONFL) ⓘ

Restatement of the Law - Contracts (REST-CONTR) ⓘ

Restatement of the Law - Judgments (REST-JUDG) ⓘ

Restatement of the Law - Products Liability (REST-PL) ⓘ

Restatement of the Law - Property (REST-PROP) ⓘ

Restatement of the Law - Property Archive (REST-PROPAR) ⓘ

Restatement of the Law - Restitution (REST-RESTI) ⓘ

Restatement of the Law - Security and Suretyship and Guaranty (REST-SEC) ⓘ

Restatement of the Law - The Foreign Relations Law of the United States (REST-FOREL) ⓘ

Restatement of the Law - The Law Governing Lawyers (REST-LGOVL) ⓘ

Restatement of the Law - The Law Governing Lawyers Archive (REST-LGOVLAR) ⓘ

Restatement of the Law - Torts (REST-TORT) ⓘ

FIGURE 8-6 *(Continued)*

Restatement of the Law - Torts Archive (REST-TORTAR) ⓘ

Restatement of the Law - Trusts (REST-TRUST) ⓘ

Restatement of the Law - Trusts Archive (REST-TRUSTAR) ⓘ

Restatement of the Law - Unfair Competition (REST-UNCOM) ⓘ

Restatement of the Law Third - Employment Law (REST-EMPL) ⓘ

Restatement of the Law Third - Employment Law Archive (REST-EMPLAR) ⓘ New

Restatement of the Law Third - The U.S. Law of International Commercial Arbitration (REST-INTLARB) ⓘ New

Restatements and Principles of the Law - Combined (REST) ⓘ

Restatements and Principles of the Law - Archive (REST-ARCHIVE) ⓘ

Restatement of the Law - Archives[13]

[13]Westlaw Directory. 2012. http://web2.westlaw.com/scope/default.aspx?db=REST%2DEMPL&RP=/scope/default.wl&RS=WLW12.01&VR=2.0&SV=Split&FN=_top&MT=Westlaw&MST=

FIGURE 8-6 Restatements on Westlaw

rule is found, one should click on "Case Citations" to see subsequent cases citing that rule. LexisNexis also provides a "Book Browse" link that allows a researcher to view other rules in the Restatement volume. Shepard's is the update service in LexisNexis. Example 8-5 shows a sample search in Lexis.

When citing to Restatements, the researcher should consult rules 12.9.5 and 3.4 in *The Bluebook* and Rule 27 in *ALWD*.

For example, cite Restatement (Second) Property § 4 (1997).

Restatement (Second) Property § 4.1 cmt. a, illus. 4 (1997).

TREATISES, *HORNBOOKS*, AND BOOKS

Treatises are texts written by legal scholars that focus on a single legal subject. Typically, treatises are exhaustive, analyzing anything and everything to do with the particular area of law. Examples of some of the better-known treatises are *Prosser & Keeton on Torts* by W. Page Keeton; Corbin on *Contracts: A Comprehensive Treatise on the Rules of Contract Law* by Arthur Linton Corbin; and *Search and Seizure: A Treatise on the Fourth Amendment* by Wayne R. LaFavre. Treatises may be one- or two-volume works, or, like *Collier on Bankruptcy* by Lawrence P. King, ed, may comprise many volumes.

Hornbooks
Texts that are similar to treatises but are written by law professors for law students.

Treatises are secondary authority, but because of the reputation of the author, a treatise *can* be used as persuasive authority when cited before a court. However, as with all secondary materials, a foundation for using secondary authority must be laid first. Treatises may be cited in interoffice memoranda, although like all secondary authority, they should be cited only after all primary authority has been cited or when no primary authority exists. Treatises differ from other secondary sources in that they are often critical works. The authors may question the logic of judicial opinions or criticize the case law in general.

Most treatises have similar features. The format of most treatises is a narrative discussion of the topic with primary authority cited as support. Treatises have an

---

EXAMPLE 8-5   SEARCHING FOR RESTATEMENTS IN LEXISNEXIS

A researcher would use the "Get a Document" tab to retrieve a Restatement rule when one knows the rule number. For example, one could take the following steps to locate Restatement (Second) of Contracts § 5:

> Click the Get a Document tab.
> Click by Citation to display the Get by Citation search form.
> Click Citation Formats to display the Citation Format Assistant.
> Enter Restatement in the Option 1: Find a Citation Format field.
> Click Find.
> Click Contracts Second to display the Restatement of Contracts Second Series search form.
> Enter @ 5 in the Contracts Second field.
> Click Get.

Each document contains the text of a Restatement rule as well as official comments and illustrations. After retrieving a Restatement rule, the researcher would click "Book Browse" to view succeeding or preceding rules.

To retrieve annotations to cases that cite a Restatement rule, the researcher would do the following:

> Click the Search tab.
> Click the Legal source tab.
> Click the following links in the order listed to search case annotations from Restatement 2d, Contracts: Secondary Legal / Jurisprudences, Restatements and Principles of the Law / Contracts / Restatement of the Law 1st & 2d, Contracts—Case Citations

NOTE: Because the LexisNexis® services list some of the most popular sources on the main search page, one can often link to the desired source directly from the Look for a Source box.

> Click the Terms and Connectors link if it is not already selected.
> Enter rule (5) in the search field.

> Click Search.[14]

---

[14]LexisNexis Support Center. Restatements. 2012. http://support.lexisnexis.com/lawschool/record.asp?ArticleID=lexiscom_searchtip_restatements

---

index either as a separate volume, or in the last volume of the set. A table of contents appears in the front of each volume, along with a table of cases. Figure 8-7 shows a table of contents page from volume 15 of *Corbin on Contracts*. Some treatises will contain a table of statutes or an appendix with the relevant statutes included. Most are updated with an annual pocket part unless the treatise is a loose-leaf service, in which case it is updated by replacement pages or supplements that are placed in the binder.

Hornbooks are similar to treatises, but are generally written by law professors for law students, and are not as exhaustive as treatises. A hornbook contains an area of law in a single volume, and the authors provide a clear analysis and explanation of how the law applies to each situation. Because hornbooks are not exhaustive, they are not considered persuasive authority by the courts. However, a hornbook serves a valuable purpose by providing background information on a topic. Many of the hornbooks published by West are bound in green covers for ease in recognition. Generally such a text will be described as a "hornbook" on the cover.

Introductory Causes and Varieties of Illegality	1
1375 Public Policy as a Basis of Illegality	9
Policy I	17
Restraint of Trade Development at Common Law	25
Chapter 81	
Restraint of Trade The Sherman Antitrust Act and Later Developments	103
What Constitutes Restraint Methods of Imposing It	177
Chapter 83	193
Trade Associations Mergers Labor Unions	251
Bargains Harmful to the Administration of Justice	311
Bargains Harmful to the Public Service to Performance of Fiduciary Duty	431
Chapter 86	
Bargains to Defraud or Otherwise Injure Third Persons	461
Chapter 87	
Bargains Harmful to Marriage Family or Morality	537
Sunday Laws	551
Wagering Bargains Usury	561
Miscellaneous Illegal Bargains	623
Effects of Illegality Restitution	657
Chapter 90	691

FIGURE 8-7 Table of Contents, Corbin on Contracts, Vol. 15[15]

Researching in Treatises

As with most secondary materials, using the descriptive word approach is a good way to begin researching within a treatise. The topic approach is useful only if the researcher is already familiar with the subject matter of the search. The table of contents in each volume will indicate the coverage of the chapters and sections. For example, if the client has an issue that deals with the effect of bargains made without compliance with licensing statutes, the researcher may know little about the topic other than it is a contracts issue. But the researcher may know that *Corbin on Contracts* is a good treatise on the subject. The researcher would take a key word or phrase from the issue and look in the index or check the table of contents. That search would lead the researcher to "miscellaneous illegal bargains" and an entry showing "6a:1510." This entry means that the information is found in section 1510 of volume 6a of the treatise. The result is shown in Figure 8-8.

The table of cases should be used if a discussion on a particular case needs to be found. As in the tables of cases in other secondary sources, the cases are listed in alphabetical order. Likewise, if one is researching discussions of a particular statute, the table of statutes can be used if the treatise includes such a table.

Treatises can be found on Westlaw in the WestlawPro library. There are various databases for treatises, and finding information can be accomplished through a terms and connectors query or a natural language query. Some treatises can be found on LexisNexis by using the table of contents and terms and connectors.

[15]Arthur L. Corbin. *Corbin on Contracts, Vol. 15.* Lexis. 2002. (last visited Feb. 14, 2012) http://books.google.com/books/about/Corbin_on_contracts.html?id=SS0kAQAAMAAJ

FIGURE 8-8 6a Corbin on
Contracts § 1510 (1962)

Chapter 89

MISCELLANEOUS ILLEGAL BARGAINS

Sec.

<u>1510</u>. Licensing and Registration Statutes—Effect of Bargains Made Without Compliance.

<u>1511</u>. The Penalty of Unenforceability May Be Expressly Included or Plainly Excluded by the Terms of the Statute.

<u>1512</u>. Purpose of the Statute–For Collection of Revenue or for Protection against Wrongdoing and Incompetence.

<u>1513</u>. Various Types of Business or Profession Requiring License, Certificate, or Registration.

<u>1514</u>. Statutes as to Foreign Corporations, Trade Names, Bulk Sales, Sales of Securities.

<u>1515</u>. Power to Waive or Bargain Away Rights and Defenses Conferred by Statute.

<u>1516</u>. Effect of a Provision in a Contract That It Shall Be Incontestable for Fraud.

<u>1517</u>. Bargains With or In Aid of Alien Enemies.

§ 1510. Licensing and Registration Statutes–Effect of Bargains Made Without Compliance

Everywhere in the United States there are statutes and ordinances requiring some sort of license, certificate or registration as a prerequisite to the carrying on of various kinds of business and professional activity. These statutes vary greatly in their purposes, in their penalties and in their wording. Sometimes the payment of a license fee is required merely as an excise tax for purposes of revenue. In many cases the fee, if any, is not a tax but is an inspection, examination, or filing charge, the purpose of the license being to assure the public as to the character and competency of the persons who engage in the particular business or profession. In still others the license or registration is required as a means of limiting the number engaged in the business, or of making certain that they shall be readily available for service of process in suits brought against them, or of preventing fraud and other harms in the selling of goods and stocks.

The kind of business or profession to which such a statute applies, the name and quality of the offence committed by failure ....[16]

Law journals
Periodicals published by most law schools; similar to law reviews. These secondary materials consist generally of articles that provide an analysis of new cases or legislation that has been recently implemented.

Periodicals: Law Reviews, Law Journals, and Other Periodicals

The category of periodicals encompasses a wide variety of offerings. Law reviews and **law journals** are published several times a year by most law schools. Bar associations, both on the national and state levels, publish journals and magazines. Paralegal associations publish their own magazines. Various vendors publish magazines and journals for people who have special interests, such as *Chicago Daily Law Bulletin*, *Kentucky Bench & Bar*, and *Law Office Computing*. The general purposes

[16]Arthur L. Corbin. 6a *Corbin on Contracts*. 1962. St. Paul, MN (last visited February 14, 2012). http://www.mindserpent.com/American_History/reference/corbin/corbin_6a_89.html

> ### CITING THE LAW 8-2: TREATISES
>
> Citations to treatises will vary depending on the treatise, but all will have certain common elements, as described in Rule 15 of *The Bluebook* and Rule 21 in *ALWD*. Look at 6a Arthur L. Corbin. 6a *Corbin on Contracts*.§ 123 (1962)
>
> The volume number if the title has more than one volume.
> The author's full name, first name first.
> The book title, underlined or italicized without abbreviations.
> Use appropriate capitalization rules for titles.
> Do not punctuate between the title and the page number, section number, or paragraph number.
> Provide the pinpoint page numbers for reference.
> Provide the edition number if citing to other than the first edition. Place within the parentheses containing the year.
> Provide the year of publication or copyright year in the parentheses.
>
> Examples:
>
> Wayne R. LaFavre, *Criminal Law* 12–34 (4th ed. 2003).
> 2 Melville B. Nimmer, *Nimmer on Copyright* § 1.2(A) (1976).
> Austin W. Scott, *The Law of Trusts* § 1.2 (3rd ed. 1988).

of these materials are similar: 1) to give readers an analysis of a topic, 2) to provide practical applications and information on problems practitioners face, and 3) to help those in the field remain current in a field of knowledge. While some of these materials, such as the law reviews and journals, are well respected, these documents are secondary authority only, and therefore may only be used as persuasive authority. It is rare for courts to rely on periodicals other than law reviews.

Law Reviews and Law Journals

Law reviews and law journals consist generally of articles that provide an analysis of cases or statutes that have recently been implemented. Of all the law reviews, the *University of Pennsylvania Law Review* is the oldest, having first appeared in 1852.[17]

Some law schools use the title "law review," such as *Yale Law Review*, *Harvard Law Review*, and *St. John's Law Review*, while other schools use the title "law journal," such as *Kentucky Law Journal*, *The Georgetown Law Journal*, and *Arizona State Law Journal*. Still other schools publish both, such as *Indiana Law Review* and *Indiana Law Journal*. Some schools deviate from the law review or law journal title convention and use other names, such as *Rutgers Law Record* and *Washington University Law Quarterly*.[18] In addition to a law review of a general nature, many law schools publish law reviews devoted to specific areas of law such as environmental law, cyberlaw, criminal law, law & medicine, women's rights, or international relations.

Articles in a law review are usually written by law students or leading scholars. In any law school, it is an honor to be selected as a law review writer. The selection of writers is based on writing samples submitted to the law review's board of editors, who are typically second- and third-year law students. Each law review also has a faculty advisor.

Law reviews and law journals differ from most other secondary sources in that the law reviews and law journals offer a critical analysis and often voice strong opposition to the status quo. The articles are respected in the legal community

---

[17]About Penn Law Review. 2010. University of Pennsylvania Law Review. http://www.pennumbra.com/about/

[18]University Law Review Project. 2012. http://www.lawreviews.org/

because the law review and law journal editors set high standards that the authors must meet. Courts often cite law reviews and law journals.[19]

Law reviews and law journals have several common features. The first and foremost section is the articles, which are often quite extensive in both length and depth of coverage. The topics are diverse and the articles may be written by a variety of people, such as judges, practicing attorneys, and law school professors. The students edit the articles, confirm the proper citation format, and often offer suggestions to the author for various types of revisions. The next section usually contains comments and notes. These pieces are authored by students and are shorter than articles, but provide a deep analysis of a legal issue or problem. Comments offer a legal analysis of a recent case, statute, book, or other legal development. Notes are original treatments of legal problems, such as how the courts or legislatures should tackle problems that have not been addressed, historical or theoretical presentations, or analyses of pressing legal questions. Often, these documents start out as term papers. Each is a well-written, original treatment of an issue.[20]

The Case Comments, Recent Cases, or Recent Developments section is authored by the student editors. This section looks at recent cases or statutes and their impact. The last section is the book review section, where a critical analysis of a book related to some legal issue is presented. Usually, the publisher and price of the book are provided.

Law reviews and journals are searchable in Westlaw and LexisNexis. Westlaw can be searched by entering the identifier (JLR or Journals and Law Reviews) in the Search for a Database area, as shown in Figure 8-9.

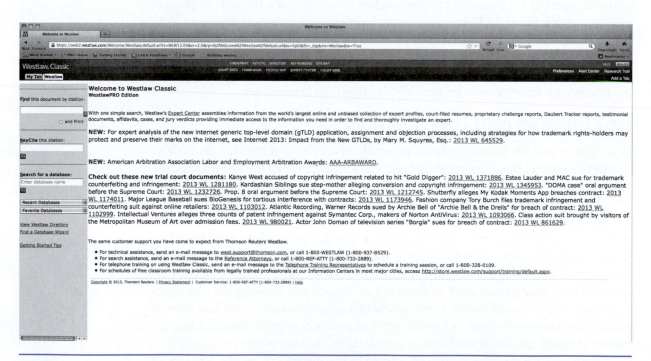

FIGURE 8-9 Westlaw[21]

[19]Harvard Law Review. About. 2009-2012. http://www.harvardlawreview.org/about.php

[20]*Id.*

[21]University of California, Hastings College of Law. *How to Search for Journals and Law Reviews.* 2011. http://www.google.com/imgres?q=law+reviews&um=1&hl=en&sa=N&biw=1280&bih=907& tbm=isch&tbnid=qzqgTB7BfB9oqM: &imgrefurl=http://www.uchastings.edu/legal-writing-research /westlaw/search-journals.html&docid=PmtSkPJEmlQF6M&imgurl=http://www.uchastings.edu /legal-writing-research/images/WestJLR1.jpg&w=347&h=423&ei=yhU8T9efBsrb0QHcwIHJCw&zo om=1&iact=rc&dur=147&sig=107897044900964918487&page=3&tbnh=165&tbnw=135&start=46& ndsp=27&ved=1t:429,r:0,s:46&tx=46&ty=141

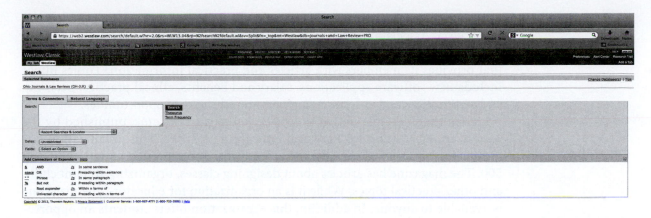

FIGURE 8-10 Westlaw Search Screen[22]

When the search screen appears, a researcher would type in the key words or use natural language as in Figure 8-10.

A similar type of search can be conducted in LexisNexis, as shown in Figure 8-11.

Bar Associations and Paralegal Associations Bar and paralegal associations also publish periodicals. In addition to the American Bar Association, all of the states plus the District of Columbia, as well as some cities or counties, have their own bar associations. There are several national paralegal associations as well as state paralegal associations. Most publish a journal, magazine, newspaper, or newsletter.

One of the benefits of being a bar association member is a subscription to the journal or magazine published by the bar association. The most prominent is the magazine of the American Bar Association, the *ABA Journal*. State journals or magazines have various titles; for example, the magazine of the Indiana State Bar Association is *Res Gestae*. These publications offer articles on practicing law, recent developments in legislation or case law, ethics, and other information of interest to attorneys, such as notices of disciplinary actions. These materials are valuable for paralegals as well because they provide information on the actual practice of law within the jurisdiction.

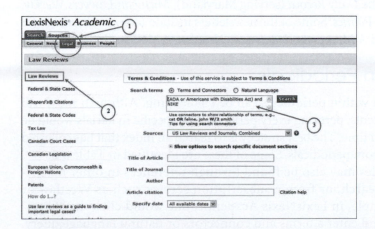

FIGURE 8-11 Searching with LexisNexis[23]

1. Law reviews are in the "Legal" tab.
2. The search is for "Law Reviews."
3. Terms are selected from the assignment, and connectors used to make a query.

---

[22]Id.

[23]California State University Northridge. *LexisNexis Searching for Law Reviews.* 2010. http://library .csun.edu/egarcia/lexisnexislawreviews.html

The National Association of Legal Assistants (NALA), the National Federation of Paralegal Associations (NPA), the American Alliance of Paralegals, Inc. (AAPI), and the National Paralegal Association (NPA) each have some type of magazine that provides its members with articles and practical information. Topics might include new software applications, salary and benefits, ethical practice, licensing and certification, and upcoming seminars and educational opportunities.

Another valuable magazine is *The Paralegal Educator*, published by the American Association for Paralegal Education (AAfPE). This organization was created for paralegal educators and currently has a membership of approximately 500. The magazine has articles about designing classes, organizing student clubs, and other practical topics. While it is an organization for educators, the magazine is available to anyone. In addition, this organization offers students an opportunity to compete for one of several scholarships if their paralegal program has a chapter of Lambda Epsilon Chi (LEX) on its campus.

Many paralegals, paralegal students, and others interested in the law subscribe to *Paralegal Today* (formerly known as *Legal Assistant Today),* which began in 1983. This magazine provides articles and information on practical topics (such as how to write a resume and discovery applications) as well as the latest news in the industry (such as certification/licensure and software).

Special Interest Publications   Practitioners who have special interests, such as trial or bankruptcy lawyers, often subscribe to additional journals and magazines that address areas of interest, such as a practice area or a lifestyle, gender, or ethnic group. The number of these journals and magazines is vast. According to a recent study, law schools do not replace their well-known law reviews and journals, but rather prefer to supplement those publications with specialized or secondary law reviews and law journals to address the needs of the specialized practitioner. In addition to the general law reviews, Harvard, Yale, and Columbia collectively publish 26 specialized law reviews, not one of which existed three decades ago.[24]

Legal Newspapers and Newsletters   Many large cities have legal newspapers that serve the city or even the state on a daily or weekly basis. Examples can be found online and include newspapers such as the *National Law Journal* (NLJ), *Akron Legal News* (serving Ohio), the *Daily Record* (serving Maryland), *Michigan Lawyers Weekly*, and *Minnesota Law & Politics*. Some of the newsletters include *Internet Newsletter for Lawyers & Law 2.0* and *A Minnesota Family Law Newsletter: MNFamilyMatters.com.*

Researching in Periodicals

Locating information within periodicals can be challenging. Although most will contain a table of contents, perusing every periodical for specific materials would be an unproductive use of time. The best strategy is to search an index that has collected articles and material from periodicals. Some of these are identified in Table 8-5.

Periodical articles may also be found through references in other materials, via an Internet search, or from a subscription service such as Westlaw or LexisNexis. For example, in LexisNexis Academic, one would click the "Legal" tab under "Search" and enter a terms and connectors or natural language query. Next, the sources to search are selected from a drop-down menu; dates may also be specified. Just like other types of research, the results will be listed alphabetically by publication. The following information is supplied:

- Source
- Date

TIP

It is never too early in a career to belong to an association or subscribe to an industry magazine. These resources provide a wealth of information.

[24]Tracey E. George and Chris Guthrie. *An Empirical Evaluation of Specialized Law Reviews.* 1999. http://www.law.fsu.edu/journals/lawreview/downloads/264/geor.pdf

TABLE 8-5 Examples of Indices for Periodicals

Title	Information
Index to Legal Periodicals & Books (I.L.P.) (1908)	Similar to the standard *The Readers' Guide to Periodical Literature* for standard research. Can be used by searching subject-author, table of contents, table of statutes, or book review. Published in monthly pamphlets, then bound. Available in print and CD-ROM. Available online as Legal Periodicals & Books[25].
	Caveats: 1) Because it is published monthly, look in all issued pamphlets. 2) It covers other countries, so pay attention to what is being viewed.
Current Law Index (C.L.I.) (1980)	Provides same searching tools as I.L.P. (configured slightly differently) except book reviews, but also indexes all articles, which I.L.P. does not do. Published in pamphlets and then collected into hardbound volumes. Electronic version is cumulative.
Current Index to Legal Periodicals (C.I.L.P.) (1948)	From the University of Washington Law School; Weekly publication with access to more than 570 legal publications with complete table of contents and citations in *Bluebook* format.[26]
Index to Periodical Articles Related to Law (1958) HeinOnline	This index was created from the Index to Periodical Articles Related to Law publication compiled and edited by Roy Mersky and Donald Dunn. Search by article title, creator or author, or journal title or subject. It searches only in this database, not in the pages of volumes. If an article is available a hyperlink will appear.[27]
Index to Foreign Legal Periodicals (I.F.L.P.) (1960)	The American Association of Law Libraries produced this multilingual index to articles and book reviews, which covers public and private international law, comparative and foreign law, and any law other than that of the U.S., U.K. Canada, or Australia, along with 80 collections of legal essays, *Festschriften*, *Mélanges*, and Congress reports. Published by the University of California, Berkeley.[28]
Jones-Chipman Index to Legal Periodicals (1791–1937 print)	Provides an index for those articles published prior to 1887, including references to various articles, papers, cases, and correspondence in a variety of legal journals from America and England, Scotland, Ireland, and the English colonies.[29]
19th Century Masterfile™	This is an "index of indexes" and the largest resource for historical research prior to 1925; covers periodicals, newspapers, books, *Congressional Record*, U.S. and U.K. government documents, and U.S. patents. (subscription)[30]
Individual law schools	Indices to the materials housed in their libraries

- Volume
- Page
- Article title
- Author
- Summary

The summary information helps the researcher decide if an article is appropriate to the specific needs of the project. Free services are also helpful in finding articles, such as the home pages of particular law school publications or the University Law Review Project.[31]

Locating articles in legal newspapers is accomplished in a similar fashion. In LexisNexis Academic, for example, a research area is accessed and "News" is

[25]H.W.Wilson. Index to Legal Periodicals & Books. 2012. http://www.ebscohost.com/academic/index-to-legal-periodicals-books

[26]Marian Gould Gallagher Law Library. Current Index to Legal Periodicals. 2011. http://lib.law.washington.edu/cilp/cilp.html

[27]HeinOnline: FAQs/Law Journal Library. 2009. http://heinonline.org/wiki/index.php/HeinOnline:FAQs/Law_Journal_Library

[28]*Index to Foreign Legal Periodicals*. 2010. http://www.law.berkeley.edu/library/iflp/

[29]Leonard A. Jones. *Jones-Chipman Index to Legal Periodicals*. AntiQbook. http://www.antiqbook.com/boox/law/44777.shtml

[30]19th Century MasterfileTM. Paratext Electronic Publishing Company. 2011. http://poolesplus.odyssi.com/cgi-bin/phtml?@landing.htm

[31]University Law Review Project. 2012. http://www.lawreview.org

clicked for law articles. On the News search screen the type of news is chosen, and a "Legal News Group File" appears. From that point, a researcher enters a basic terms and connectors query with a particular date range, if needed. The results are sorted by most recent date first. The following information is provided:

- Source title
- Date
- Article title
- Volume and issue and/or section
- Page
- Author (from byline)
- Body of article

Some useful free sites for searching newspapers are available, such as Find-Law: Legal News and Commentary and Law.com. Additional periodical materials can be located when the found source is updated. Using *Shepard's*, KeyCite, or any other citator will lead to additional materials of a similar topic.

CITING THE LAW 8-3: PERIODICALS

Citations to law reviews, journals, newspapers, newsletters, and other similar periodicals will generally include the following parts, in this order:

Author's name (Note: if written by a student, the words "Student Author" should be included after the full name has been given or as a stand-alone term if the author's name is unknown.)

- Title in italics or underlined
- Volume number or year if no volume number exists
- Periodical abbreviation
- Page number(s) including the original page the article begins on and pinpoint reference as needed
- Date in parentheses

Examples:

Julie J. Kim and John F. Bramfeld
   [Authors names]

Left Behind: The Paternalistic Treatment of Status Offenders Within the Juvenile Justice System, and *Boldly Going Where No Writer Has Gone Before … (Poor/Strange Legal Writing in Law Reviews)*
   [Title in italics or underlined]

Vol. 87 [Volume number or year if no volume number exists]
Wash. U. L. Rev. and Chi. Daily L. Bull.
   [Periodical abbreviation]

Pages 843 and 5 [Page number(s) including the original page the article begins on and pinpoint reference as needed]
   (2010) and (June 1, 1994)
   [Date in parentheses]

Examples:

Julie J. Kim, *Left Behind: The Paternalistic Treatment of Status Offenders Within the Juvenile Justice System,* 87 Wash. U. L. Rev. 843 (2010).
   John F. Bramfeld, *Boldly Going Where No Writer Has Gone Before … (Poor/Strange Legal Writing in Law Reviews).* Chi. Daily L. Bull., (June 1, 1994) at 5.

ETHICAL CONSIDERATIONS WHEN USING SECONDARY SOURCES

As with every aspect of legal work, finding and using secondary sources involves some ethical concerns. MRPC Rule 3.3, Candor toward the Tribunal, states:

a. A lawyer shall not knowingly:

1. make a false statement of fact or law to a tribunal or fail to correct a false statement of material fact or law previously made to the tribunal by the lawyer;
2. fail to disclose to the tribunal legal authority in the controlling jurisdiction known to the lawyer to be directly adverse to the position of the client and not disclosed by opposing counsel; or ... .

A researcher can ensure that this rule is followed by taking certain steps when conducting research:

Always check the date of the secondary sources to ensure current information is being reviewed.

- Do not cite secondary sources as the resource for answers; rather, use those secondary sources to better understand the issues at hand and then locate the primary source(s) of law provided within the secondary source.
- Update the secondary material being used by referring to the pocket parts.
- Use secondary sources to locate primary authority, not as the authority itself.
- Validate primary sources.

SUMMARY

Researchers can use different types of secondary sources to locate relevant primary sources of law, but secondary sources should not be used as primary sources. One of the most frequently used secondary sources for researching a broad issue may be a state or national legal encyclopedia. For an application of an issue to a case, an A.L.R. annotation may give some useful sources or an explanation of a difficult point. The *Restatements* distill case law on a particular topic into "black-letter law." Law reviews and journals are often student-run, and publish student-written articles that provide in-depth research on new or controversial topics.

Researchers should spend some time exploring how to locate and use various secondary sources relevant to a client's case, how to use secondary sources to better understand the issues of the client's case, and how to make sure those sources are current and up to date.

Above all, it must be remembered that secondary sources are not the law, but rather are discussions about the law. Therefore, the material may be cited as persuasive authority only, and the courts are not required to follow any secondary sources. The courts may *choose* to follow secondary authorities, and some secondary authorities have earned the respect of the courts, but the weight given to a secondary source is at the court's discretion. The goal of a researcher still remains to find primary authority that is mandatory for the jurisdiction in which the issue arises, to update that authority, and to validate the research by using a citator service.

REVIEW QUESTIONS

1. What is a legal encyclopedia? What is a legal encyclopedia used for in researching?
2. What is secondary authority? Provide three examples of secondary authority.
3. What is a treatise? How would you use a treatise in legal research?
4. Explain a Restatement. Why do the courts often rely on restatements?
5. What is a law review? What type of information may be found in a law review?
6. What value do legal newspapers have in research?
7. How would you use an article from a bar association journal?
8. Can secondary authority be used in an internal memorandum of law? Why or why not?
9. How do you update secondary materials?
10. What ethical concerns exist when using secondary sources?

APPLICATION **EXERCISES**

1. Your supervisor presents you with the following research problem:

   Our client wants to make improvements on his property; however, to complete some of the improvements, the client will have to enter the adjoining landowner's property. What are the rights of the client? Use a legal encyclopedia to answer the following questions:

   a. Where in the index would you look to find this information?

   b. What is the index entry?

   c. Summarize the discussion that the index entry led you to.

   d. Properly cite the entry.

   e. Does the entry provide any other resources? If so, list them (no more than five).

   f. How did you update this section, and what was listed in the update?

2. A new client, Taffy Apple, appeared at the office asking for advice on estate planning. She met with your supervisor, William Ferret. After you and Mr. Ferret interviewed Taffy, Mr. Ferrett discussed some options that she could consider. Taffy is a single mother. She has one son, Jonathan Apple, who left home 8 years ago when he was 16 and has not been in contact with Taffy more than four or five times during those 8 years. Because she was lonely, Taffy became a foster mother to Jeremy Orange, who was 11 at the time. While Jeremy was in school, Taffy attended all the school functions as his "mother" and referred to him as "son" when she spoke. During the past eight years, Jeremy has lived with her. At the time she came to the office he was attending a local community college for which Taffy helped Jeremy pay. In fact, Jeremy was with her during her initial client conference with you and Mr. Ferret. She made another appointment for the following week.

   Unfortunately, Taffy died before her next appointment. She had not completed any estate plans and she did not have a will. During her initial interview she was adamant that Jeremy was to receive part of her estate. Jeremy wants to know if he can claim any part of the extensive estate that Taffy left.

   a. List key words and phrases that you might use to search for relevant secondary sources.

   b. Determine what types of secondary sources you think might be most appropriate to research. Identify at least two different types using your key words and step b.

   c. Cite your secondary sources and explain your method of accessing them. For example, did you use a physical library? Did you use a free service on the Internet? Did you use a subscription service?

   d. Review the two secondary sources you used to identify two relevant primary sources.

   e. Find these two primary sources.

   f. Briefly review these sources for the connection to the secondary sources you used. Is there a relevant connection? Explain your answer.

3. The firm's long-standing client, Justin Case, has just been fired from his job. An interesting twist is that he owns 30% of the stock of the company from which he was fired. The majority stockholder, Timothy Trouble, owns 51% and another employee owns the rest. The majority stockholder has refused to allow the corporation to issue stock dividends. Since Timothy is also president of the corporation, he has a lot of control over the board of directors. The client has been trying to convince the board to issue dividends. Since the client's agenda is so different from Timothy's, the client believes that Justin's firing is directly related to the client's continued push to have the corporation issue dividends.

   a. Find and cite the section(s) of both *Am. Jur. 2d* and *C.J.S.* that discuss this situation.

   b. Cite the first case presented in each of those sections.

   c. What differences, if any, do you notice between the two encyclopedias?

4. The firm's clients, Fred and Wilma Flint, have two children. Penny, age 14, has been giving Fred and Wilma trouble for some time. She has been seen talking with a known member of a known religious cult. Last month, Penny did not return home after school. One of her friends told Fred that Penny got in a car with a member of the cult. Penny contacted Fred and Wilma and told them she was staying with her new friends and that she was marrying the cult leader. This was to be her last contact with her parents.

   a. Find and cite an A.L.R. annotation that discusses the activities of religious cults.

   b. Upon what case is the annotation based? Cite correctly.

   c. Does the annotation refer to any cases in your jurisdiction? If so, cite the case(s).

   d. Summarize any paragraph relating to the client's issue.

CITATION **EXERCISES**

Use *The Bluebook, ALWD,* or other appropriate validation tool. Cite the rules used.

1. A legal encyclopedia where the topic of husband and wife was found in volume 35 of Corpus Juris Secundum, section 130 and was published in 1986.

2. A treatise where the authors were Alfred C. Aman, Jr., and William T. Mayton, it was in the second edition, the title was Administrative Law and it was published in 1999.

3. A law review where the article was The Supreme Court, 1971 Term—Forward: In search of evolving doctrine on a changing court: A model for a newer equal protection and was published in 1972 in the Harvard Law Review. The author was Gerald Gunther and the article was on page 104 in volume 86.

4. An A.L.R. annotation called Liability of hospital, physician, or other individual medical practitioner for injury or death resulting from blood transfusions. It is found in the fourth series, page 136, and volume 20. The author was Jay M. Zitter, J.D.

5. Contracts, by E. Allan Farnsworth, Section 2396, published as a revision in 1961 by McNaughton.

6. Communications to Clergymen—When Are They Privileged? by Michael Kuhlmann, 1968 Valparaiso University Law Review, volume 2, p. 265.

7. Table 8-5 provided some citations for the Restatements. Find sections of the Restatements and complete the Table.

QUICK **CHECK**

For 1–6, state which resource you would use:

a. *Corpus Juris Secundum*

b. *American Jurisprudence 2d*

c. Both

1. Articles on state law

2. Articles on federal law

3. Citations to relevant cases

4. Cross-references to West key numbers

5. Cross-references to A.L.R. annotations

6. Which encyclopedia contains more detailed text?

7. The best way to locate a relevant article in an encyclopedia is to

   a. Look up search terms in the encyclopedia index to identify relevant topics and sections within topics.

   b. Browse the shelves to find a volume containing a relevant topic.

   c. Look at the table of contents for relevant topics to identify relevant sections within the topic.

   d. a and c

   e. a, b, and c

8. Which is an advantage to using a secondary source to start your legal research?

   a. It is the authority you are going to cite.

   b. It can help explain the law.

   c. You do not have to validate secondary sources.

   d. Secondary sources must be followed by judges.

9. A descriptive word index is a(n) _____ that can be found in many secondary sources.

   a. alphabetical list of words or phrases describing subjects discussed in the text with corresponding page numbers

   b. index showing all the words that are contained within a legal document

c. description of contents and brief explanation of how to use text

d. list of statutes and codes discussed in the text with corresponding page numbers

10. *American Law Reports* (A.L.R.) is an example of which type of secondary source:

    a. Law review

    b. Legal encyclopedia

    c. Collection of annotations (articles)

    d. Digest

11. Which type of secondary source does not explain or discuss the law, but simply provides a special index to case reporters?

    a. Legal encyclopedia

    b. Legal dictionary

    c. Digest

    d. Treatise

12. When your supervising attorney gives you a research assignment, what should your first step be?

    a. Head straight to primary sources of law, since those are the sources you will be citing.

    b. Ask another paralegal for help researching.

    c. Locate relevant secondary sources of law using key words or phrases.

    d. Look up your state's statute.

13. After familiarizing yourself with the topic and identifying the relevant primary sources cited within the secondary sources you found, you should _____.

    a. Sum up your research and give it to your attorney.

    b. Contact the client and tell them what you've found

    c. Locate, read, and analyze the primary sources in order to prepare your findings

    d. Locate the primary sources and tell your attorney where to find them

RESEARCH

1. Access a secondary encyclopedia such as *American Jurisprudence 2d (Am. Jur. 2d)* or *Corpus Juris Secundum (C.J.S.)*. For each of the following questions, answer the questions and properly cite to the section in *Am. Jur. 2d* or *C.J.S.* where you found the answer:
   a. Can a state impound a lost animal that is believed to have been abandoned? Cite case authority for your answer.
   b. What is the monetary liability of credit card owners for unauthorized use of their credit card? Cite statutory authority for your answer.
   c. Can a child who is born illegitimate but is later legitimized inherit from the natural father?
   d. What is the test to determine whether a game is one of chance or one of skill?
   e. Susan knowingly makes a false statement of fact under penalty of perjury. Later, she changes the story to the truth. Does this excuse the perjury? What is the controlling federal statute?
   f. Your client's grandfather just died overseas, and a family member must go to identify the body and arrange for its transport back to the United States. The client is the legal guardian of his minor brother, and both the client and the brother share one passport. May the brother travel abroad on the passport without the client? Cite authority.
   g. Would the imposition of a dress code by an employer constitute illegal sex discrimination? Cite authority.
   h. Who has the burden of proof in a prosecution for bigamy? Cite authority.

2. The topic you will be researching is whether evidence obtained by aerial surveillance is an illegal search and seizure under the Fourth Amendment. Write down relevant key words and synonyms that you could possibly use to search this topic in different indexes.
   a. Into what broad areas of the law does this question fall?
   b. Use the A.L.R. *Index* and find an A.L.R. *Fed.* annotation on the problem. Provide the citation.
   c. Examine the index at the beginning of the annotation. What section discusses the open-fields rule?
   d. Check the pocket part of the annotation. Has this annotation been superseded or supplemented?

3. Using the A.L.R. *Index*, find and properly cite the relevant annotations.
   a. Locate an annotation that discusses the tort of emotional distress that is based on the fear of contracting HIV or AIDS.
   b. Look at the Jurisdictional Table of Cited Statutes and Cases. What is the citation for the case from Maryland?
   c. Look at § 1(b) of the annotation. What is the citation of the first "related annotation"?
   d. Examine the pocket part in the back of the main volume. In what year was the pocket part issued? Locate the supplemental information in the pocket part. Examine the supplemental information for § 8(a). What is the name of the case from Mississippi that discusses exposure cases?
   e. Provide proper citations for the annotation in question 1.[32]

4. Using the General Index to *Am. Jur. 2d*, find the relevant encyclopedia topic and section. Citations need to conform to *Bluebook* or *ALWD* rules.
   a. What is the full name and citation of the topic and section number that discusses special damages for pollution?
   b. Examine the topic and section you identified in question *a*. Provide the name of the California case that discusses that deprivation of use and enjoyment of property can be considered in awarding special damages.
   c. What is the copyright date of the *Am. Jur. 2d* volume you are using?
   d. Examine the pocket part in the back of the main volume. In what year was the pocket part issued? Locate the supplemental information in the pocket part. What is the title of the *Arizona Law Review* article?[33]

5. Perform an A.L.R. search. A new client comes to the firm because his daughter is being sexually teased by another girl in her freshman class. The school policy does not say anything about same-sex teasing and the assistant principal has stated that students need to get along. The client's daughter does not want to go to school. As the days of the semester pass, the teasing increases and now, the teasing has gone to Facebook. Your assignment is to find some authority to force the school principal and board to take the matter seriously.
   a. What jurisdiction will this be in—state or federal? Why?
   b. What will be the key words?
   c. What book will you search first?
   d. What book will you search next?
   e. Did you find an annotation?
   f. Does the annotation have a topic and key number search?
   g. What is the last step you will undertake?

[32]http://www.aallnet.org/sis/ripssis/TeachIn/2007/2d_Keyrev.pdf

[33]*Id.*

INTERNET **RESEARCH**

1. In the exercises above, you were asked to use as *American Jurisprudence 2d (Am. Jur. 2d)* or *Corpus Juris Secundum (C.J.S.)* to find answers to problems. For this exercise, perform an Internet search to find the answers. Compare the findings on the Internet with the findings from the encyclopedias. Properly cite to the authority used.

   a. Can a state impound a lost animal considering it to be abandoned? Cite case authority for your answer.

   b. What is the monetary liability of credit card owners for unauthorized use of their credit cards? Cite statutory authority for your answer.

   c. Can a child who is born illegitimate but is later legitimized inherit from the natural father?

   d. What is the test to determine whether a game is one of chance or one of skill?

   e. Susan knowingly makes a false statement of fact under penalty of perjury. Later she changes the story to the truth. Does this excuse the perjury? What is the controlling federal statute?

   f. Find a law review article that Justice Ruth Bader Ginsburg authored. Cite the law review article and cite the Internet source you used. Summarize the article.

   g. Find a law review article that Justice William Rehnquist authored. Cite the law review article and cite the Internet source you used. Summarize the article.

   h. Find and cite a law review article from a law school in your state. What is the topic? When was it written? Who was the author?

MEDIA **RESOURCES**

How to Research Secondary Sources with LexisNexis.   http://www.youtube.com/watch?v=j2FpK24vsAg
Secondary Sources.   http://www.youtube.com/watch?v=oOzcqg805sQ

INTERNET **RESOURCES**

American Law Institute (restatements) at: http://www.ali.org

FindLaw for Law Students. (2010) Academic Law Journals and Law Reviews at: http://stu.findlaw.com/journals/index.html

FindLaw: Legal News and Commentary at: http://news.findlaw.com/

Internet Legal Research Group (journals) at: http://www.ilrg.com/journals.html

Law.com at: http://www.law.com

University Law Review Project at: http://www.lawreview.org

Kzenon/Shutterstock

chapter **nine**

FINDING AIDS, DRAFTING TOOLS, AND MISCELLANEOUS SECONDARY AUTHORITIES

LEARNING OBJECTIVES

After completing this chapter, students should be able to:

1. Locate appropriate secondary sources to complete research.

2. Use secondary sources as part of legal research.

3. Understand the value of finding aids.

4. Apply ethical considerations in using secondary sources.

CHAPTER OVERVIEW

This chapter will continue the discussion of secondary sources. These secondary sources are aimed at finding, understanding, and using primary authority.

This chapter will discuss the use of digests, *Words and Phrases,* and form books. Digests are used to find cases that apply to specific points of law. *Words and Phrases* is used to understand the legal meaning of a word or phrase and to find cases that show those terms in context. Form books contain samples of documents from which documents can be created to fit the client's needs. These publications, in addition to the secondary sources previously discussed, will provide the tools needed to find and understand the primary authority applicable to most legal issues.

OPENING SCENARIO

John needed to draft an injunction and complaint for Nancy Smith in her lawsuit against Norman Pardee. The law firm had filed an injunction and complaint in a similar action several years ago. John wanted to check the form books to confirm that the language of the injunction and complaint were correct and met with procedural requirements. He also needed to verify that the allegations in the complaint not only matched the precise facts of the client's case, but also stated all the elements of each cause of action according to the current law of their jurisdiction. But what would be the best tool for accomplishing this task? John had done some research on an intellectual property issue during the previous week, and had discovered that the key numbers and topics in a federal digest were very helpful for that case. Perhaps he could use the key numbers and topics in the *West Indiana Digest* to find cases on point for Nancy's injunction and complaint. Sure enough, using these library resources provided a wealth of information.

DIGESTS
The History of Digests

Digests are one of the tools used to find cases that are *on point.* They can help one determine whether the facts and issues of cases detailed in the digest are exactly the same as, or substantially similar to, the client's facts and issues. The digest system is a product of Thomson Reuters (West). The editors of the digests collect each decision; read the case; draft a *synopsis*; identify the points of law cited or explained within the case; prepare summaries of each point, called *headnotes*; and arrange the headnotes alphabetically by *topic and key number* at the beginning of the case and in the digests.

The digest system is useful when a researcher needs to answer a novel question of law, find cases on a specific legal issue or topic, or determine how different jurisdictions have decided an issue. Digests are particularly helpful when the researcher has an extensive and complex research project to complete.

American Digest System   In the early days of our legal system, when cases were first published, a lawyer was expected to read every case that was printed. As the country grew, reading every case became a daunting task. The *American Digest System* was created to collect the cases and summarize them so that finding cases on point would be an easier task. The West editors have continued to collect every published decision and organize them in federal, state, and regional groupings in the national reporter system. West publishes a variety of digests, such as the *Decennial Digests*, *Federal Practice Digest*, and individual state digests.

Some digests, such as the one that accompanies the *Lawyers' Edition Supreme Court Reporter*, are published by LexisNexis. A few states have their digests published by companies other than West. Table 9-1 provides a listing of the most frequently used digests. All of the listed digests are from West, except those that are highlighted, which are from LexisNexis.

The *American Digest System* indexes all published cases. The 10-year cumulative indices are called the *Decennial Digests*. These digests are supplemented with monthly *General Digests* that are bound yearly until it is time to publish the next *Decennial Digest*. The West editors classify the law into seven broad areas: persons, property, contracts, torts, crimes, remedies, and government. From these categories, the editors further divide the law into more than 400 topics such as contracts, insurance, negligence, and product liability, each with multiple key-numbered subdivisions called headnotes. Each headnote covers a single point of law and is given a key number for use in all West publications and on Westlaw.

Figure 9-1 shows a sample of the West Digest topics and the key numbers for those topics. A full listing of topics is available in any West digest series in print, or on Westlaw.

TIP

While reference will be made to "West," the actual company is now Thomson Reuters.

Digests
Summaries of cases divided and organized by topics and key numbers.

On point
Describes a case whose facts and issues are exactly the same or substantially similar to the facts of the client's case.

Synopsis
A summary of the case as decided in any level of court that has heard the case.

Headnote
A short description of a point of law discussed in a case.

Key Number System
A system created by West Publishing to divide the law into topics and headnotes with a specific number for each that summarizes one aspect or point of law.

TABLE 9-1 Major Digests

Digest	Coverage
Federal	
U. S. Supreme Court Digest	Supreme Court, 1790–present; West published with key numbers
U. S. Supreme Court Digest	Supreme Court, 1790–present; Lexis published with citations to the *A.L.R.*s and other aids.
Federal Digest (red books)	Federal (*Supreme Court Reporter, Federal Reporter, Federal Supplement*) prior to 1939
Modern Federal Practice Digest (green books)	Federal (*Supreme Court Reporter, Federal Reporter, Federal Supplement*) 1940–1960
Federal Practice Digest 2d (blue)	Federal (*Supreme Court Reporter, Federal Reporter, Federal Supplement*) 1961–Nov. 1975
Federal Practice Digest 3d (red)	Federal (*Supreme Court Reporter, Federal Reporter, Federal Supplement*) Dec. 1975–c. 1987 (some volumes close around 1983 so check individual volumes)
Federal Practice Digest 4th (blue)	Federal (*Supreme Court Reporter, Federal Reporter, Federal Supplement*) c. 1983–present (some volumes begin at various points until 1987, so check individual volumes)
Regional	
Atlantic Digest 1st and 2nd series	CT, DC, DE, M, MD, NH, NJ, PA, RI, VT
North Eastern Digest	Not published since 1971; covered IL, IN, MA, NY, OH
North Western Digest, 1st and 2nd series	IA, MI, MN, NE, MD, SD, WI
Pacific Digest, 1st, 2nd, 3rd, 4th series	AK, AZ, CA, CO, HI, ID, KS, MT, NM, NV, OK, OR, UT, WA, WY
South Eastern Digest, 1st and 2nd series	GA, NC, SC, VA, WV
Southern Digest,	Not published since 1988; covered AL, FL, LA, MS
South Western Digest	Not published since 1958; covered AR, KY, MO, TN, TX
States	
Title is generally *West's* [name of state] *Digest* (example *West's Indiana Digest*) various series	Available for each state except DE, NV, and UT. There is one for DC.
National	
American Digest (*Century Edition, First,* known as the *Decennial Digest,* through *Eleventh Decennial Digest* Part III)	1659–present
Century Digest	1658–1896; not part of Key Number System, but there is a conversion table in the first *Decennial Digest.*
Decennial Digest	10-year periods from 1897–2008. The *Eleventh Decennial Digest* Part III covers through 2008. After that, use the *General Digest.*
General Digest, 12th series	2008-2010; not cumulative but is currently in use
Martindale-Hubbell Law Digest	A body of statutory law updated yearly.
Specialty Digests	
Labor Relations Cumulative Digest and Index	Published by the Bureau of National Affairs, this digest provides a digest of all labor and employment cases as well as other specialty digests.
Internet	
Law Digest	Law Summaries from USLegal http://lawdigest.uslegal.com/

DIGEST TOPICS

See also Outline of the Law by Seven Main Divisions of Law, preceding this section.

The topic numbers shown below may be used in WESTLAW searches for cases within the topic and within specified key numbers.

1	Abandoned and Lost Property	43	Asylums	70	Carriers
2	Abatement and Revival	44	Attachment	79	Clerks of Courts
4	Abortion and Birth Control	45	Attorney and Client	80	Clubs
5	Absentees	46	Attorney General	81	Colleges and Universities
6	Abstracts of Title	47	Auctions and Auctioneers	82	Collision
7	Accession	48	Audita Querela	83	Commerce
8	Accord and Satisfaction	48A	Automobiles	83H	Commodity Futures Trading Regulation
9	Account	48B	Aviation	84	Common Lands
10	Account, Action on	49	Bail	85	Common Law
11	Account Stated	50	Bailment	88	Compounding Offenses
11A	Accountants	51	Bankruptcy	89	Compromise and Settlement
12	Acknowledgment	52	Banks and Banking	89A	Condominium
13	Action	54	Beneficial Associations	90	Confusion of Goods
14	Action on the Case	55	Bigamy	91	Conspiracy
15	Adjoining Landowners	56	Bills and Notes	92	Constitutional Law
15A	Administrative Law and Procedure	58	Bonds	92B	Consumer Credit
16	Admiralty	59	Boundaries	92H	Consumer Protection
17	Adoption	60	Bounties	93	Contempt
18	Adulteration	61	Breach of Marriage Promise	95	Contracts
19	Adultery	62	Breach of the Peace	96	Contribution
20	Adverse Possession	63	Bribery	97	Conversion
21	Affidavits	64	Bridges	98	Convicts
23	Agriculture	65	Brokers	99	Copyrights and Intellectual Property
24	Aliens	66	Building and Loan Associations	100	Coroners
25	Alteration of Instruments	67	Burglary	101	Corporations
26	Ambassadors and Counsuls	68	Canals	102	Costs
42	Assumpsit, Action of	69	Cancellations of Instruments	103	Counter feiting

FIGURE 9-1 West's Digest Topics[1]

[1]Charlotte School of Law. *Using the West Topic and Key Number System.* nd. https://www.charlottelaw.edu/downloads/lawlibrary/research/USING%20THE%20WEST%20TOPIC%20AND%20KEY%20NUMBER%20SYSTEM.pdf

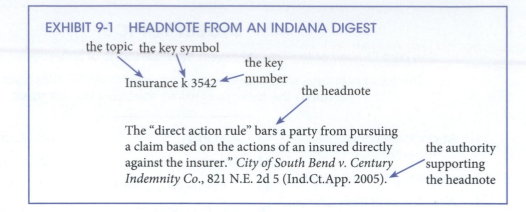

EXHIBIT 9-1 HEADNOTE FROM AN INDIANA DIGEST

the topic   the key symbol

the key number

Insurance k 3542

the headnote

The "direct action rule" bars a party from pursuing a claim based on the actions of an insured directly against the insurer." *City of South Bend v. Century Indemnity Co.*, 821 N.E. 2d 5 (Ind.Ct.App. 2005).

the authority supporting the headnote

TIP

The digest topic and Key Number System is not available in non-West materials.

Synopsis

A summary of the case as decided in any level of court that has heard the case.

TIP

The digest information is not primary authority, and because it is merely a summary of a point of law taken from a primary source, digest content cannot be cited in research memos.

Each headnote in the digest states one point of law and cites primary authority, such as cases or statutes, supporting that point of law. Unless a researcher is viewing a digest from a particular state, the digest will contain headnotes of cases from multiple jurisdictions. The researcher must pay particular attention to the jurisdiction of the headnote being read.

The editors read each case before it is published and distill the issues of law that it addressed. For each point of law, the editor prepares a headnote or short description of that point. In a case published by West, these headnotes are found near the beginning of the case, usually after the *synopsis*, or summary of the case. Researchers can peruse the headnotes to determine whether the case is pertinent to the client's situation. Exhibit 9-1 is a sample of a headnote from an Indiana digest.

The broad topic is Insurance and the key number is 3542. If this headnote appears to be useful in the research, the next step would be to find the case *City of South Bend* and read it. The Key Number System allows a researcher to use this headnote and key number to see how other courts or jurisdictions have decided this same point of law. For example, to find out how California courts have addressed the issue, the researcher would search for this topic and key number in the *Decennial* and *General Digests*, the *California Digest*, or any other digest containing California law. All digests function in a similar fashion. The digests provide a one-sentence summary of the point of, as well as the case citation, so that the researcher can find the case and read it.

Specialized Digests   Specialized digests provide links to particular courts or topical areas for specialty subjects. An example of a specialized digest is the digest on employment and labor law offered by the Bureau of National Affairs (BNA). A yearly digest on international law published by the U.S. Department of State, called *The Digest of United States Practice in International Law*, is also available. The office of the State Appellate Defender in Illinois produces a useful digest for that state, the *Illinois Criminal Law Digest*. Digests are also available for other specialties such as product liability, federal rules of evidence, and the Uniform Commercial Code. It is a good practice to determine whether there is a specialized digest for a particular subject at the beginning of the research process.

Researching in Digests

Research trail

A list of notes kept by the researcher that helps keep track of what has been found in the course of research.

Digests may be one of the most useful tools in the researcher's arsenal. When beginning research in digests, it is important to start a *research trail* to keep track of what sources one has found so that time is not wasted returning to the same material again. For example, a researcher may search the topic "husband and wife" for key numbers discussing "responsibility for child support." Multiple key numbers might relate to responsibility for child support. One key number could address payments, while another key number could deal with who must provide the support. The research trail provides a method to record which key numbers were found and reviewed. The research trail provides an outline of what has been read, thus saving valuable research time.

Periodically the West editors revise the Key Number System to accommodate major changes in the law. There are tables at the beginning of revised topics that convert old key numbers to new key numbers. A check of the pocket parts at the beginning of research may alert the researcher to changes that are not yet incorporated in the bound volumes. Another check at the end of the digest research will make sure the material is current.

To best utilize the digests in research, the first step is to determine the jurisdiction. Is it federal or state? A good rule of thumb is to consider the narrowest jurisdiction first. If a case were from Indiana, the *Indiana Digest* would be used rather than the *North Eastern Reporter Digest*. That way, fewer cases will need to be reviewed. The research goal is to locate primary authority within the jurisdiction controlling the client's issue. Table 9-2 compares the scope of coverage of the digests.

If the authority needed cannot be found in the narrowest digest, the search should be expanded into the next level and the process should be continued until the needed material is found. At each step, the pocket parts should be checked before moving to the next level of digests.

The descriptive word index is used to find key numbers that apply to the client's situation. A researcher takes the key words and alternate key words (synonyms and sometimes antonyms) from the client's case and uses those words in the index. The words in the client's issue are not always the same words that the editors use in the indices, so alternate terms should be tried. Sometimes the references in the index may seem cryptic because of the abbreviations used. A key to abbreviations in the front of the index can be used to decipher these words. For example, "Appeal and Error" appears in the index as "App & E." If relevant headnotes are not found for the key topic and number chosen, the index or outline should be reviewed again for other topics and key numbers that might be related to the topic. When relevant citations are found, they are written in the research trail. Then, the pocket parts are checked again using the same descriptive words. When the appropriate headnotes have been identified, the cited cases must be read, analyzed, and summarized. Finally, any results used must be updated.

Another method for digest research is the "one good case" method, which is probably the most expedient way to start the research. Sometimes, a researcher knows of a leading case covering the issue at hand. If so, the researcher locates the case in the digest, and uses its headnotes to find additional cases by looking up the topic and key number in the digest. If the initial case is from an ***official reporter***, it will be necessary to find the parallel citation in an unofficial West reporter to gain access to the Key Number System.

Official reporter
Official reports are published under the authority of the legislature and are usually printed by the government. Unofficial reporters are printed by private publishers (such as West) with or without authority from the legislature.

TABLE 9-2   Digests and Jurisdictional Coverage in Research

Jurisdiction	Digest	Coverage
Federal issue	*Supreme Court Digest*	narrow
	Federal Digests	broader
	American Digest System	broadest
State issue	State Digest	narrow
	Regional Digest (if available)	broader
	American Digest System	broadest

A third method of research involves finding references to leading cases in other secondary sources such as encyclopedias, treatises, *A.L.R.s*, or annotated codes. After these cases are pulled and read, the headnotes and key numbers are noted in the research trail, and used to find additional cases in the digest system.

If the topic of research has been narrowed, the topical outlines and topic index for the digest may be useful. Each topic starts with a general outline at the beginning of the topic, followed by a detailed outline, and then the relevant topics, key numbers, and headnotes. Each digest also has a words and phrases index so that if a particular word or phrase in the research is known, that word or phrase can be searched.

The table of cases can be used to find a specific case within a digest, if the name of the case is known. Each decennial digest in the *American Digest System* has a table of cases. The *General Digest* has a case table in each volume with a cumulative table at the end of the 5- or 10-year period of distribution. The cases are presented with plaintiffs' names in alphabetical order. If only one party to a case is known or it is not clear who is who in the case, the defendant/plaintiff tables can be used to identify the full title. It is important to try different spellings of the name so that a valuable case is not overlooked. For example, if the supervisor says that Myers is the name of the defendant, the first step would be to search for "Myers." However, "Myers" could be spelled many different ways, such as "Meiers," "Meijers," "Miers," and "Meyers."

Digests, like most secondary materials, are updated by pocket parts and paper supplements, as well as replacement volumes. It is a good practice to check the pocket parts or supplements before spending time reading cases that may no longer be good law.

Digests are found on Westlaw and LexisNexis, as well. In Westlaw, digest searches are called "field searches" and the user must be in a jurisdictional database. Within such a database, several field searches can be used. The first is a topic and key number search where the applicable topics and key numbers are entered as search terms in the query box. For example, if a researcher were interested in finding cases with the topic Insurance (272) and a key number of 233, the information could be entered in the query box as shown in Figure 9-2.

In Westlaw, a topic number may also be combined with a particular phrase or with descriptive terms that may appear in the headnote. For example, if a

FIGURE 9-2 Sample Query Screen from Westlaw[2]

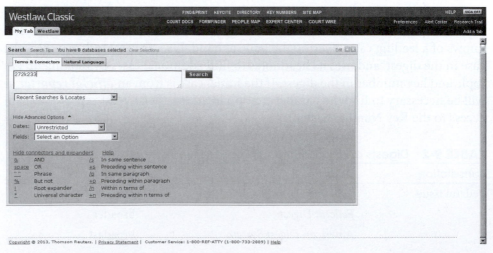

[2]Westlaw, 2012. http://web2.westlaw.com/search/default.wl?origin=Search&cfid=1&tf=0&eq=search&rlti=1&action=EditQuery&ssrc=65&vr=2.0&tc=0&method=TNC&rltdb=CLID_DB94514253010192&db=IN-CS&srch=TRUE&n=1&fn=_top&fmqv=s&service=Search&query=272K233&sskey=CLID_SSSA91476393010192&sv=Split&fcl=True&cnt=DOC&scxt=WL&cxt=RL&rs=WLW12.01&ss=CXT&rp=%2fsearch%2fdefault.wl&mt=Westlaw

researcher were interested in the topic Contracts (95) and were looking for law that applies to a particular type of clause in a contract, such as a "forum selection clause" the Westlaw query could be as follows:

> to(95) /p "forum selection clause"

OR

> to(contracts) /p "forum selection clause"

The researcher would use the second option if the topic number for Contracts were not known. In both examples, "/p" is a connector that shows that the topic Contracts with a topic (to) number 95 should be in the same paragraph (/p) as the phrase "forum selection clause."

A Westlaw search can be conducted in the headnote field, too. The headnote field is designated as "he" and could appear as follows:

> to(contracts) & he("forum selection clause")

Another field search that would include information in a digest would be a digest (di) field search. The digest includes the topic, key number, and headnote fields.

LexisNexis does not use the West topics and key numbers, but it does have a headnote system with numbers that uses "case summaries" and "LexisNexis headnotes." The case summaries give the researcher concise information regarding the case history, the facts and issues at hand, and the outcome. LexisNexis headnotes then links to the most relevant "Lexis® Search by Topic or Headnote" topic. This feature allows a researcher to search by segments, display formats, coverage, and availability.[3] Exhibit 9-2 provides an explanation.

Whether one uses a print or subscription service, the steps for researching in digests are very similar. Table 9-3 provides a guide to researching in a digest.

EXHIBIT 9-2 LEXISNEXIS SEARCHABLE SEGMENTS

Searchable Segments for Case Summaries and LexisNexis® Headnotes

You can search Case Summaries and LexisNexis Headnotes using the following segments:

- **POSTURE** (segment that describes how the case arrived before the present court)
- **OVERVIEW** (segment that contains a concise review of the case facts and holding by the court)
- **OUTCOME** (segment that provides the procedural disposition of the case)
- **LN-HEADNOTES** (segment that contains the text of LexisNexis® Headnotes)
- **LN-SUMMARY** (group segment that incorporates all of the above)

Display Formats for Case Summaries and LexisNexis® Headnotes

You can display or print search results in the following formats:

- **Cite** displays the **CITEOVERVIEW** segment
- **KWIC™** displays the **POSTURE, OVERVIEW**, and **OUTCOME** segments. If search terms appear in the **LN-HEADNOTES** segment, the KWIC™ view displays the LexisNexis® Headnotes that contain those terms.
- **Full** displays the **POSTURE, OVERVIEW, OUTCOME** , and **LN-HEADNOTES** segments

---

[3]LexisNexis Support Center. Directory of Online Resources. *Case Summaries and LexisNexis Headnotes.* 2012. http://support.lexisnexis.com/lawschool/record.asp?ArticleID=root_cs_cc#Searchable

NOTE:

If the LexisNexis Headnotes feature is turned off, the system does not show search terms that are in the **LN-HEADNOTES** segment.

Case Summaries and LexisNexis® Headnotes Coverage and Availability

Summary eligibility for all opinions on the LexisNexis service, except Federal District Court, is selected to receive Summaries and Headnotes by an online algorithm, which selects opinions that meet the following criteria:

- Contain an opinion segment of at least 5,000 characters
- Contain Core-Terms
- Contain substantive facts and legal analysis

Due to the increased volume of Federal District Court cases as a result of the E-government Public Access to Court Electronic Records (PACER) Act, not all cases can be summarized. Our attorney editors select and summarize the most important of the Federal District Court case collection. When searching for Federal District Court cases, it is important that your initial search not include segment restrictions to the **LN-SUMMARY, POSTURE, OVERVIEW, OUTCOME,** and **LN-HEADNOTES** segments.[4]

TIP

See the tutorial on using Lexis-Nexis headnotes at http://web.lexis.com/help/multimedia/detect.asp?sPage=hn2

TABLE 9-3 Steps for Researching in Digests

Step	Action
1	Start a research trail document.
2	Determine the key words and alternate words to use in the search.
3	Determine the digest needed. If it is a general question, use the *American Digest System.* If it is a federal question, use the appropriate federal digest. If the issue revolves around a state matter, use the state digest if one exists; otherwise, use the regional digest.
4	Identify a relevant topic and key number from the descriptive word index or from the topic list in the front of the volume. In electronic research, select the topic from the directory provided.
5	Choose the digest volumes that are applicable and any supplements in print. Enter the appropriate information in electronic form.
6	Read through the topic outline, read the digest paragraphs under the appropriate topic or key numbers, and locate the cases to be read. Include this information on the research trail.
7	Check the pocket parts and other updates and note this on the research trail. Electronic resources will be updated automatically.
8	If there are no cases on point, broaden the scope of the search by changing key words if necessary, or by going into a broader jurisdiction.
9	When applicable cases are found, validate the cases. Also include a date on which the research was completed so that if the research is approached again, the materials already found do not need to be validated from the beginning.

[4]*Id.*

Researchers do not cite or quote from a digest because it is a secondary authority, and should only be used as a tool to find the primary authority. If a case is found using a digest, the case itself should be cited or quoted as the authority and then updated.

WORDS AND PHRASES

Background

In many cases, the outcome depends on how the court interpreted a word or phrase. A legal dictionary can provide multiple definitions of a word, but it provides only limited information about how the word is used in context. The purpose of *Words and Phrases* (*W&P*) is to apply a word or phrase within the context of a case. This set of more than 100 volumes provides citations to cases dating back to the year 1658 that interpret words and phrases. The words and phrases are given in alphabetical order, and a small amount of information is provided about each case. *Words and Phrases* is similar to digests in that it is a tool to find cases. Like many other secondary sources, *Words and Phrases* is supplemented by cumulative annual pocket parts. When the cumulative pockets parts warrant it, a new hardbound volume is issued.

Researching in *Words and Phrases*

Look at Example 9-1.

Because it is a secondary authority, *Words and Phrases* should not be cited. Instead, the primary authority referenced in *Words and Phrases* should be located, read, analyzed, and, if appropriate, quoted.

EXAMPLE 9-1   DOING RESEARCH IN *WORDS AND PHRASES*

Terry Trubble comes to your office because he was arrested for burglary. Trubble entered a garage with an upstairs apartment that belonged to his neighbor around 7:00 in the morning on June 21.

The state statute defines burglary as "breaking and entering the dwelling of another at night with the intention to commit a crime." Based on this definition, these are the elements of burglary that must be proven:

- Breaking
- Entering
- The dwelling of another
- At night
- With the intention to commit a crime

The statutes of this jurisdiction do not define "night," and so your job is to find cases that interpret or define "night." Going to the index of *Words and Phrases*, looking for "night," and looking for cases from the client's jurisdiction would be one approach. Here, a case is found in which the court held that "night is that time period from sundown to sunrise." In that case, the court held that a person who breaks and enters after the sun has risen does not commit burglary. You check the pocket part to see if there are any newer entries, but there are none. Reading and analyzing the case to be sure it is on point with Trubble's situation is the next step. If the case is on point, it should be updated through *Shepard's*, KeyCite, or some other updating service to be sure the case is still good law. Since the case is still good law and it is on point with Trubble's situation, the client is not guilty of burglary since one of the elements is missing.

ATTORNEY GENERAL OPINIONS
Background

Attorney general (AG)
The chief law enforcement officer in each state and the federal government.

Each state, as well as the District of Columbia and the federal government, has an *attorney general* (AG). In the federal government, the AG is appointed by the president, and approved by the Senate. Once approved or confirmed, the AG becomes the head of the Department of Justice (DOJ) and a member of the president's cabinet. In many states, AGs are elected officials, while in others they are appointed.

Part of the job of the AG is to give legal advice when requested by any public officer of the state, the legislature, a county attorney, or government officials. The AG provides guidance on topics such as whether a proposed action of an agency is legal, or how a statute should be interpreted. The AG does not provide opinions or advice to private citizens. Most AGs' offices publish selected opinions, as authorized by federal or state law. The opinions of the AGs in print are found at most major law schools and online at the respective states, and on the DOJ website. The opinions published online usually do not include all the opinions that have been issued in a given jurisdiction—most start in the 1970s or later.

legality

The U.S. Attorney General derives his or her authority from the Judiciary Act of 1789, codified at 28 U.S.C. §§ 511–513. The AG is allowed to delegate responsibility for preparing formal opinions to the Office of Legal Counsel (OLC), as authorized by 28 U.S.C. § 510. The OLC's authority is outlined in 28 C.F.R. § 0.25, which states in part:

The following-described matters are assigned to, and shall be conducted, handled, or supervised by, the Assistant Attorney General, Office of Legal Counsel:

(a) Preparing the formal opinions of the Attorney General; rendering informal opinions and legal advice to the various agencies of the Government; and assisting the Attorney General in the performance of his functions as legal adviser to the President and as a member of, and legal adviser to, the Cabinet.

(b) Preparing and making necessary revisions of proposed Executive orders and proclamations, and advising as to their form and legality prior to their transmission to the President; and performing like functions with respect to regulations and other similar matters which require the approval of the President or the Attorney General.

(c) Rendering opinions to the Attorney General and to the heads of the various organizational units of the Department on questions of law arising in the administration of the Department.

(d) Approving proposed orders of the Attorney General, and orders which require the approval of the Attorney General, as to form and legality and as to consistency and conformity with existing orders and memoranda.[5]

Today, most opinions come from the OLC rather than the AG. An example of an opinion from the DOJ is shown in Case Excerpt 9-1.

State AGs' offices render similar types of opinions. For example, the Arizona AG was asked to issue an opinion on whether a school district "can provide food, beverages, or refreshments to staff or parents who assist in governing board-authorized District activities after normal school hours or on weekends." The AG determined that the district could, in fact, provide sustenance to staff or parents only where and to the extent the district is authorized to do so by the laws that cover travel, subsistence, gifts, grants, or devises. The expenditures have to comply with the Gift Clause of the Arizona Constitution.[7]

---

[5]Title 28: Judicial Administration. 2012. 28 C.F.R. § 0.25. http://ecfr.gpoaccess.gov/cgi/t/text/text-idx?c=ecfr&sid=94a1879bed443929964eab70f3cb119a&rgn=div8&view=text&node=28:1.0.1.1.9.1.1&idno=28
[7]Attorney General Opinion No. 110-003. 2010. http://www.azag.gov/opinions/2010/I10-003.pdf

CASE **EXCERPT 9-1:** *Opinion of the Attorney General*

WHETHER THE CRIMINAL PROVISIONS OF THE VIOLENCE AGAINST WOMEN ACT APPLY TO OTHERWISE COVERED CONDUCT WHEN THE OFFENDER AND VICTIM ARE THE SAME SEX

The criminal provisions of the Violence Against Women Act apply to otherwise covered conduct when the offender and victim are the same sex.

April 27, 2010
MEMORANDUM OPINION FOR THE
ACTING DEPUTY ATTORNEY GENERAL

You have asked us whether the criminal provisions of the Violence Against Women Act ("VAWA") apply to otherwise covered conduct when the offender and victim are the same sex. VAWA includes three criminal provisions: 18 U.S.C. § 2261 (2006), addressing interstate domestic violence; 18 U.S.C. § 2261A (2006), addressing interstate stalking; and 18 U.S.C. § 2262 (2006), addressing the interstate violation of a protection order. Consistent with the views we received, we conclude that each of these provisions applies when the offender and the victim are the same sex.[1]

I.

The first of VAWA's three criminal provisions, section 2261, addresses certain specified types of interstate domestic violence. Subsection (a)(1) makes it a federal crime to travel in interstate or foreign commerce, to enter or leave Indian country, or to travel within the special maritime or territorial jurisdiction of the United States "with the intent to kill, injure, harass, or intimidate a *spouse, intimate partner, or dating partner*" if, in the course of or as a result of such travel, the offender "commits or attempts to commit a crime of violence against that *spouse, intimate partner, or dating partner*." 18 U.S.C. § 2261(a)(1) (emphases added). Subsection (a)(2) makes it a federal crime to "cause[] *a spouse, intimate partner, or dating partner* to travel in interstate or foreign commerce or to enter or leave Indian country by force, coercion, duress, or fraud" and, during, as a result of, or to facilitate such conduct or travel, to "commit[] or attempt[] to commit a crime of violence against that *spouse, intimate partner, or dating partner*." *Id.* § 2261(a)(2) (emphases added). Section 2261 was part of VAWA as originally enacted in 1994, but at that time it covered only victims who were a "spouse or intimate partner" of the... .

---

[1] We received views from the Criminal and Civil Rights Divisions, the Office on Violence Against Women, and the Executive Office for United States Attorneys. See E-mail for Jeannie S. Rhee, Deputy Assistant Attorney General, Office of Legal Counsel, from Mythili Raman, Principal Deputy Assistant Attorney General, Criminal Division (Feb. 23, 2010) (attaching Memorandum for Lanny A. Breuer, Assistant Attorney General, Criminal Division, from P. Kevin Carwile, Chief, Gang Unit, and Michael S. Warbel, Trial Attorney, Criminal Division, Re: Criminal Prosecution of Same-Sex Partners Under the Violence Against Women Act (Feb. 19, 2010)); E-mail for David J. Barron, Acting Assistant Attorney General, Office of Legal Counsel, from Samuel Bagenstos, Principal Deputy Assistant Attorney General, Civil Rights Division (Apr. 8, 2010); Memorandum for Jeannie S. Rhee, Deputy Assistant Attorney General, Office of Legal Counsel, from Jennifer E. Kaplan, Attorney Advisor, Office on Violence Against Women, Re: Application of the Violence Against Women Act to Same-Sex Dating Violence (Mar. 24, 2010); E-mail for Jeannie S. Rhee, Deputy Assistant Attorney General, Office of Legal Counsel, from Margaret S. Groban, Assistant United States Attorney, EOUSA Office of Legal Programs and Policy (Feb. 10, 2010).[6]

---

[6] *Whether the Criminal Provisions of the Violence Against Women Act Apply to Otherwise Covered Conduct When the Offender and Victim are the Same Sex.* 2010. http://www.justice.gov/olc/2010/vawa-opinion-04272010.pdf

Researching with AG Opinions

The AG opinions are different from other types of secondary authority in that "[a]lthough an official interpretation of a statute by the Attorney General is not controlling, it is entitled to great respect."[8] The AG opinions are not controlling law, and as such, are persuasive authority, as stated in *Napa Valley Educators' Assn. v. Napa Valley Unified School Dist.* (1987) 194 Cal.App.3rd 243, 251 where the court held:

> Opinions of the Attorney General, while not binding, are entitled to great weight. [Citations.] In the absence of controlling authority, these opinions are persuasive 'since the legislature is presumed to be cognizant of that construction of the statute.' [Citation.].

The AG opinions have a different persuasive weight primarily because these opinions are authored by the chief legal advisor of the governmental entity and are usually followed by the governmental executive. Courts, therefore, view an AG opinion as a credible statement on enacted and case law unless the statement is superseded by a change in legislation or new court rulings.[9]

Researching AG opinions is not as easy or straightforward as researching in other secondary materials. More often than not, a citation to an AG opinion is found in another secondary authority, such as an encyclopedia, or in a primary authority, such as a statute. When enacted or case law is updated, there may be citations to AG opinions.

Generally, states provide print access to their own AG opinions, but most libraries do not carry the AG opinions of other states. More recent opinions can be found online on state or federal websites or in Westlaw and LexisNexis. A website for the National Association of Attorneys General provides sites to all AG websites.[10]

The AG opinions usually have an index that allows a researcher to use the key words from the client's case to find appropriate relevant AG opinions. The downside of these materials is that there may be few, if any, AG opinions on a topic; the indices are not updated regularly; and there is no way to tell if and when an AG opinion is no longer valid.

The opinions of the AGs may be presented in a variety of ways. In Indiana, the AG opinions are issued in the form of letters addressed to the person requesting the advisory opinion. Other states present their AG opinions very differently. In California, an AG opinion looks more like a pleading or brief for a court, with section headings and a caption.

States also use a variety of schemes for numbering and identifying each opinion. In Indiana, each is given a chronological number by year. For example, Official Opinion 2009-1 was issued June 1, 2009, and Official Opinion 2009-2 was issued June 10, 2009. This indicates that in Indiana, there are very few opinions issued, since the first was not issued until June 1. There were a total of four opinions in 2009, four in 2010, and one in 2011.[11] In Alaska, opinions are cited by their date of issuance, such as 2010 Op. Alaska Att'y Gen. (June 16). Until September 16, 2006, formal opinions issued by the Alaska AG were sequentially numbered and cited in this format: 1997 Op. Att'y Gen. No. 4 (Nov. 29). Informal opinions had the issuance date and case management number and were cited as 2001 Inf. Op. Att'y Gen. (June 16; 664-06-0111).

[8]*Thorning v. Hollister School Dist.* (1992) 11 Cal.App.4th 1598, 1604.

[9]Gregg Abbott. Attorney General of Texas. *The Attorney General Opinion Process.* https://www.oag.state.tx.us/agency/weeklyag/weekly_columns_view.php?id=208

[10]National Association of Attorneys General. 2012. http://www.naag.org/

[11]Office of the Indiana Attorney General. *Official Opinions of Attorney General Greg Zoeller.* 2012. http://www.in.gov/attorneygeneral/2355.htm

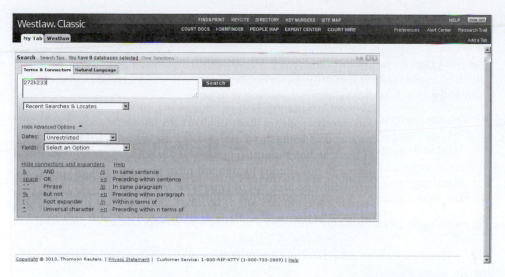

FIGURE 9-3 Alabama Attorney General Opinion Search[14]

The AG opinions are available from a variety of online sources. The Department of Justice website posts selected AG opinions.[12] The attorney general of each state posts opinions on the state government website if the opinions are available. Not all states have online AG opinions. FindLaw provides links to states' AGs' websites.[13]

Westlaw provides the opinions for the U.S. Attorney General at United States Attorney General Opinions (USAG). Most state attorney general opinions are in databases of the state, identified with the two-letter postal abbreviation, hyphen, and AG, such as IN-AG. Currently there are 17 databases for state AG opinions, and an option is provided to search all AG databases simultaneously. Figure 9-3 shows an example of a terms and connectors screen search in a state AG opinion database.

The Alabama Attorney General Opinions database is being used to search for an opinion on whether the Alabama Firefighter's Personnel Standards and Education Commission may delegate its authority to hire, promote, discipline, and terminate employees to the executive director.

The query would be the following:

"Firefighter's personnel standards and education commission" /p delegate! assign /s authority.

The results yield one opinion, 2011-001.

On LexisNexis, AG opinions are found at GENFED and USAG.

LOOSELEAF SERVICES

Foundation of Looseleaf Services

Looseleaf services provide information on a particular topic or an area of law, such as labor law. Some services are compiled in binders so that pages can be removed and updated by replacing pages rather than by inserting pocket parts in the back of a volume.

Looseleaf services
Information compiled in a ringed binder rather than a hardbound volume. These services are updated by replacing pages rather than inserting pocket parts at the end of a volume.

---

[12]The United States Department of Justice. Opinions by Date and Title. http://www.justice.gov/olc/memoranda-opinions.html

[13]FindLaw. State Resources. Attorneys General. Thomson Reuters. 2012. http://www.findlaw.com/11stategov/indexag.html

[14]Westlaw. 2012. http://web2.westlaw.com/search/default.wl?db=AL-AG&rs=WLW12.01&vr=2.0&rp=%2fsearch%2fdefault.wl&sv=Split&fn=_top&mt=Westlaw

> ### CITING THE LAW 9-1: ATTORNEY GENERAL OPINIONS
>
> For the proper citation format, consult *The Bluebook* (T1) or *ALWD* (Rule 19) or other accepted citation authority. However, most follow a similar pattern. The citation to the U.S. Attorney General's opinion is as follows:
>
> - Volume number <production use "40" or "20" as volume no.>
> - Opinion designation <production use Op. Atty. Gen or Op. Off. Leg. Counsel as opinion designation>
> - Initial page (and pinpoint cite if appropriate) <production use "100" or "17" as initial page>
> - Date <production use (1941) or (1994) as date>
>
> So an example might be 40 Op. Atty. Gen. 100 (1941) or 20 Op. Off. Leg. Counsel 17 (1994)
>
> The state citation generally consists of the following, in some combination:
>
> - Year
> - State reference
> - Chronological number, case management number, or other designation
> - Date

The best way to find a looseleaf service applicable to a research issue is to consult the annual service *Legal Looseleafs in Print,* available in most law libraries or online for a fee. This resource provides information on more than 3,500 looseleaf services. Figure 9-4 shows a sample entry.

The major looseleaf publishers are Commerce Clearing House, Incorporated (CCH), the Bureau of National Affairs (BNA), Clark Boardman Callaghan (CBC), and Matthew Bender. The CBC is now part of Thomson Reuters and Matthew Bender is now part of LexisNexis. Table 9-4 lists some of their looseleaf services.

There are three types of looseleaf services: interfiled, newsletter, or a combination of both. Newsletter looseleaf services are published as newsletters that are filed by topic. Interfiled looseleaf services provide extensive primary sources, such as opinions that may not be found in other sources such as reporters. These may include explanatory information that aids researchers in understanding the primary sources and their legal effect. The explanations give the researcher ways to integrate the material into practice. Some sets have a digest of cases that is similar to the West Key Number System; however, the topics and key numbers will not mirror the West system. Many services will also have a section on current developments, referred to as the highlights, bulletin, or report letter.

Interfiled services send updates as packets of loose pages. Filing instructions accompany updates and should be maintained for reference. The update pages are filed in the binders by page number, and the old pages are removed. Each page will have the page, paragraph (¶), or section (§) number and a date so that updating is as easy as possible. Some paragraphs or sections are further divided into subparagraphs or subsections with the decimal point being part of the reference, such as §21.003. This system is designed to accommodate new pages of information. The pages in the packet of updates are nonsequential, as only pages with new material are updated. The information in the packet only makes sense when read in the context of its proper place within the binder.

The newsletter style of looseleaf services provides each update as a single unit of information that supplements rather than replaces material in the main volume. The supplements have an index issued approximately every six months. At the end of the

When looking for looseleaf publications dealing with limited liability companies generally, for example, these are some of the entries that would be found. There are also additional entries for various state-specific looseleaf services.

The Complete Guide to Limited Liability Companies

2. Hagendorf, Wayne A.
3. Knowles Publishing
4. 1996
5. 1 vol.
6. $175 incl. 3 mos. supp.
7. annual supp.
8. 1998-$65.50; 2000-$66.50
9. OCLC 34310556; LC call # KF1380.H34

CD-ROM

Guide to Limited Liability Companies

2. Mares, Michael E., et al.
3. Practitioners Publishing
4. 1995
5. 4 vols.
6. $189
7. annual supp.
8. 2000-$135
9. LC #96-128538; OCLC 34299046;
   LC call # KF1380.G85

CD-ROM

Limited Liability Companies: Law, Practice & Forms

2. Rubenstein, Jeffrey C., et al.
3. West
4. 1994
5. 3 vols.
6. $375 incl. 3 mos. supp.
7. annual supp.
8. 1996-$280; 1997-$374.25
9. LC # 94-19489; OCLC 30623748;
   LC call # KF1380.Z95L529

Diskettes included

The Essential Limited Liability Company Handbook

2. Corporate Agent, Inc.
3. Oasis Press
4. 1995
5. 1 vol.
6. $39.95
7. periodic supp.
8. no supp. yet

Limited Liability Companies

2. -
3. CCH
4. 1995
5. 1 vol.
6. $407/yr.
7. monthly supp.
9. OCLC 33325991
On Internet: business.cch.com

CD-ROM; www

The Limited Liability Company

2. Whynott, Philip P.
3. James
4. 3rd ed. - 1999
5. 1 vol.
6. $99 incl. 3 mos. supp.
7. semiannual supp.
8. 1998- $105; 1999- $112
9. LC#95-101544; OCLC 30049424;
   LC call # KF1380.Z95B342

CD-ROM of forms included

FIGURE 9-4 Sample Entry for Legal Looseleaf Services Sample Entries[15]

year, the materials can be removed or kept for historical reference. The downside of this format is that if a regulation that is frequently discussed is being followed, it may be necessary to look in several places to get the whole picture, whereas the interfiled format puts the new information alongside the old.

Since the looseleaf services often contain full-text cases, the binders may fill up quickly. Some publishers send **transfer binders** so that an entire year's worth of cases can be removed from the main binder and placed in the transfer binder. Other

Transfer binders

Binders sent by publishers periodically to transfer or move full-text cases out of the main binders for ease in handling and reading.

[15]Infosources Publishing. *Legal Looseleafs in Print 2012*. 2012. http://www.infosourcespub.com/book5.cfm

TABLE 9-4 Sample List of Looseleaf Services

Title	Publisher	Services
The Bureau of National Affairs, Inc. (BNA)	BNA	The following is a sample of the resources available *ABA/BNA Lawyers' Manual on Professional Conduct* *Americans with Disabilities Act Manual* *Benefits Practice Center* *Collective Bargaining Negotiations and Contracts* *Corporate Governance Manual* *Corporate Practice Series* *Corporate Practice Library* *EEOC Compliance Manual* *Environment & Safety Library* *ERISA Compliance & Enforcement Library* *Export Reference Guide* *Health Care Program Compliance Guide* *Health Law & Business Series* *Health Law & Business Library* *Intellectual Property Library* *International Trade Reporter Export Reference Manual* *International Trade Reporter Import Reference Manual* *Labor and Employment Law Library* *Labor Relations Reporter®* *Media Law Reporter* *Tax Management Foreign Income Portfolios* *Tax Management Library* *Tax Management Multistate Tax Portfolios* *Tax Management Real Estate Portfolios* *Tax Management State Tax Library* *Tax Management Transfer Pricing Portfolio Series* *Tax Management U.S. Income Portfolios* *United States Patents Quarterly* For a complete list see the reference.[16]
Clark, Boardman, Callaghan (CBC)	Thomson/West	Nichols, Donald H. *Drinking /Driving Litigation: Criminal and Civil* *Advising Small Businesses* *Insider Trading: Regulations, Enforcement, and Prevention* *Lender Liability: Law, Practice and Prevention 2d* *Problem Loan Workouts*
Commerce Clearing House, Inc. (CCH)	Wolters Kluwer Law & Business	700 products in four major areas: tax and accounting, legal, health care compliance, and business compliance. Samples: *Standard Federal Tax Reporter* *U.S. Master Tax Guide* *CCH Federal Tax Guide* *Human Resources Management* *CCH Federal Securities Law Reports* *CCH Medicare and Medicaid Guide* *Employment Safety and Health Guide* *Labor and Employment Law Library*[17]
Matthew Bender	LexisNexis	*Collier Bankruptcy Cases* Erwin, Richard R. *Defense of Drunk Driving Cases: Criminal—Civil.* 3rd ed. *Federal Income, Gift and Estate Taxation* *Corporate Compliance Practice Guide: The Next Generation*
Research Institute of America	Thomson Reuters	*American Federal Tax Reports* *Federal Tax Coordinator* *Pension & Profit Sharing* *RIA's Complete Analysis of the Tax and Benefits Provisions of the 2010 Health Care Act*

[16]Using Looseleaf Services. 2012. http://subscript.bna.com/pic2/lsll.nsf/id/DTRS-5KCPRZ?OpenDocument

[17]CCH: About CCH. 2012. http://www.cch.com/About/

publishers issue a separate bound volume of cases. Most publishers have placed their materials in online libraries, on CD-ROMs, or on LexisNexis and Westlaw.

Researching in Looseleaf Services

Checklist 9-1 provides general steps for researching in looseleaf services.

Checklist 9-1   RESEARCH IN LOOSELEAF SERVICES

A researcher should take these steps:

1. Prepare a research trail document.

2. Read "How to Use This Service" to get the scope of what is covered and perhaps some examples of how to search the set.

3. Check the index to make sure everything needed is available, and determine whether the index uses paragraph or page numbering.

4. Distinguish between commentary and primary authority. Commentary may help in understanding the material better, but is not primary authority.

5. Check that the text is current according to the date of the last set of filing instructions, and determine that all supplements have been filed.

6. If pages are removed for photocopying, be careful when replacing the pages. A misfiled page can have extreme consequences for the next user, as it may be discarded in the next update.

Accessing looseleaf services is similar to accessing most secondary materials. Many have a topical index, but the index is not updated every time new material is issued. Instead, the services often use a *layered indexing system*. The main index is supplemented by a frequently revised *current index* that covers just the revision materials. It is important to check the service completely to be sure every applicable piece of the service has been reviewed. The date on each page must be checked to make sure that 1) the pages have been sequentially filed and 2) the update being referenced is the most recent.

Most services also have a table of cases, table of statutes, and table of regulations to provide multiple access points to the service. Some may have finding lists that give a quick reference for tables, charts, and summaries of major primary materials included in the set.

A looseleaf service will rarely be cited unless the material does not exist someplace else. Generally, the looseleaf service is used for background research and as a finding aid to locate primary authority.

Layered indexing system
A system for supplementing the main index of a looseleaf service with a current index that covers just the revisions issued.

Current index
In some looseleaf services, a supplemental index to the main index that is similar to advance sheets or pocket parts.

JURY INSTRUCTIONS

Basics of Jury Instructions

Jury instructions are issued by the judge and given to the jury to provide some direction to the jury during its deliberation. The judge does not tell the jury what to do. Rather, the instructions provide guidelines on the law involved in the particular case.

Most often, each attorney will draft proposed instructions and provide those instructions, in pleading format, to the judge. Some instructions may be very short, while others may be more complicated and involved. The judge may accept,

Jury instructions
Instructions given by judge to assist the jury in reaching its decision.

CITING THE LAW 9-2: CITING LOOSELEAF SERVICES

Citations to looseleaf services are discussed in *The Bluebook* Rule 19 and *ALWD* Rule 28. The following are samples of citation formats.

BNA materials:[18]

ABA/BNA Lawyers' Manual on Professional Conduct

Format: Looseleaf

Bluebook Cite Format: Law. Man. on Prof. Conduct (ABA/BNA)

Sample *Bluebook* Cite:

New York State Bar Association Opinion 574 [1986-1990 Ethics Opinions] Law. Man. on Prof. Conduct (ABA/BNA) 901:6101 (Apr. 18, 1986)

BNA's Bankruptcy Law Reporter

Format: Newsletter

Bluebook Cite Format: Bankr. L. Rep. (BNA)

Sample *Bluebook* Cite:

"Fair Debt Collection Practices Act Doesn't Exempt Lawyers in Litigation," 7 Bankr. L. Rep. (BNA) No. 17, at 502 (Apr. 27, 1995)

ALWD Rule 28 provides citation formats for CCH products:

Howerton v. Grace Hosp. Inc., 1995-2 Trade Cases (CCH) ¶ 71.208, 75.854 (W.D.N.C. July 7, 1995), *aff'd* 96 F.3d 1438 (4th Cir. 1996).

Bradley v. U.S., 91-2 U.S. Tax Cases (CCH) ¶ 50332 (2d Cir. June 24, 1991).

Dan Weber II v. Commr. [2004 Transfer Binder] Tax Ct. Rep. (CCH) Dec. 55,588, 4389 (U.S.T.C. Mar. 22, 2004).

---

reject, or modify the proposed instructions. The judge may create his or her own jury instructions, as well.

Jury Instructions have been used for only about a half-century. Prior to that, new instructions were made for each trial, and often these instructions did not state the law correctly, thereby creating the opportunity for appeal. To avoid such appealable errors, forms were created for jury instructions, which came to be known as "pattern" jury instructions. These suggested jury instructions are generally drafted by a committee that may consist of judges, legal scholars, experienced attorneys, and bar association members. The committee members study cases and then create instructions based on current law. They are written to be easily understood by the jury members, so "*legalese*" is eliminated and the law is stated in simple English. Examples of jury instructions are shown in Exhibit 9-3.

Because paralegals tend to view language from a layperson's perspective, they are often able to draft instructions in language that jury members can understand and relate to.

Jury instructions must have rigorous support from primary authority in case and statutory law. Exhibit 9-4 shows a sample from the Federal Civil Jury Instructions of the Seventh Circuit, which was prepared by the Committee on Pattern Civil Jury Instructions. These instructions were approved for publication. The comments show the type of sources that must support each instruction, and mirror the type of research that a paralegal must do when creating jury instruction. Note that they contain many references to primary authority.

Legalese
Language used in the legal profession, as distinguished from plain English used by laypersons; examples are *heretofore*, *hereunder*, and other words designed to give an air of legality to documents, verbal exchanges, and correspondence.

---

[18]How to Cite BNA Publications. 2009. http://subscript.bna.com/pic2/lsll.nsf/8e9ea8728473b3be852 569f9005d302a/2d129faf114523d985257411006181bd/$FILE/HowtoCiteBNA.pdf

EXHIBIT 9-3   SAMPLE JURY INSTRUCTIONS

INSTRUCTION NO. 1

In deciding what the facts are, you may have to decide what testimony you believe and what testimony you do not believe. You may believe all of what a witness said, or only part of it, or none of it.

In deciding what testimony to believe, consider the witness's intelligence, the opportunity the witness had to have seen or heard the things testified about, the witness's memory, any motives that witness may have for testifying a certain way, the manner of the witness while testifying, whether that witness said something different at an earlier time, the general reasonableness of the testimony, and the extent to which the testimony is consistent with any evidence that you believe.

In deciding whether or not to believe a witness, keep in mind that people sometimes hear or see things differently and sometimes forget things. You need to consider therefore whether a contradiction is an innocent misrecollection or lapse of memory or an intentional falsehood, and that may depend on whether it has to do with an important fact or only a small detail.

INSTRUCTION NO. 3

There is no burden upon a defendant to prove that he is innocent. Accordingly, the fact that a defendant did not testify must not be considered by you in any way, or even discussed, in arriving at your verdict.[19]

EXHIBIT 9-4   FEDERAL CIVIL JURY INSTRUCTIONS

1.02 NO INFERENCE FROM JUDGE'S QUESTIONS

During this trial, I have asked a witness a question myself. Do not assume that because I asked questions I hold any opinion on the matters I asked about, or on what the outcome of the case should be.

Committee Comments

A trial judge, of course, may interrogate witnesses. FED. R. EVID. 614(b); *see Ross v. Black & Decker, Inc.,* 977 F.2d 1178, 1187 (7th Cir. 1992) ("A trial judge may not advocate on behalf of a plaintiff or a defendant, nor may he betray even a hint of favoritism toward either side. This scrupulous impartiality is not inconsistent with asking a question of a witness in an effort to make the testimony crystal clear for the jury. The trial judge need not sit on the bench like a mummy when his intervention would serve to clarify an issue for the jurors. The brief, impartial questioning of the witness by the judge, as the record reflects, to make the witness' testimony clearer was entirely proper. . . ."); *Beetler v. Sales Affiliates, Inc.,* 431 F.2d 651, 654 (7th Cir. 1970)(trial judge, in aid of truth and in furtherance of justice, may question a witness in an impartial manner) (*citing United States v. Miller,* 395 F.2d 116 (7th Cir. 1968)).

An instruction reminding the jury that the judge has not intended to give any opinion or suggestion as to what the verdict should be may be helpful. *See United States v. Siegel,* 587 F.2d 721, 726 (5th Cir. 1979) (no interference with right of fair trial where questions asked by judge, for clarification, were coupled with cautionary instructions to jury); *United States v. Davis,* 89 F.3d 836 (6th Cir. 1996) (per curiam, unpublished) (no plain error where judge's statements were factually correct

---

[19]U.S. Department of Justice. United States Attorneys Kids Page: Inside the Courtroom. *Sample Jury Instructions.* n.d. http://www.justice.gov/usao/eousa/kidspage/jury.html

and jury was instructed not to consider the judge's comments, questions and rulings as evidence); Eighth Circuit Manual of Model Civil Jury Instructions 3.02 (2001), *but see United States v. Tilghman*, 134 F.3d 414, 421 (D.C. Cir. 1998) ("Although jury instructions can cure certain irregularities . . . [where] the trial judge asked questions, objected to by counsel, that could have influenced the jury's assessment of the defendant's veracity, such interference with jury fact-finding cannot be cured by standard jury instructions."); *United States v. Hoker*, 483 F.2d 359, 368 (5th Cir. 1973) ("No amount of boiler plate instructions to the jury—not to draw any inference as to the judge's feelings" can be expected to remedy extensive and prosecutorial questioning by judge.).[20]

Researching with Jury Instructions

The courts of most states, as well as many courts in the federal system, have their own pattern jury instructions. A researcher may or may not have access to the materials of a particular state, and it may be necessary to ask the law librarian where the print form of the jury instruction materials are located. If no state jury instructions exist, other pattern instructions may be found in secondary sources such as *Modern Federal Jury Instructions* or *Am. Jur. Pleading and Practice Forms, Annotated*. Many are available online, as well.

Most jury instruction manuals are indexed alphabetically by topic. Key words from the client's case may be used to find the applicable instructions. Generally, these materials are updated with pocket parts, so the pocket parts should be checked before any jury instruction is used. As research proceeds, each pattern jury instruction should be cited, and a research trail should be maintained. Once the applicable instructions are located, they may need to be modified or adapted to fit the client's case. The final set of jury instructions is then prepared according to the format specified by the supervisor and by the court's rules.

FORM BOOKS

Background

When beginning to draft a new document, most legal professionals search for pre-existing forms to provide the basic language and framework for the document. In some fields, such as bankruptcy and tax practice, the law requires the use of certain forms.

Templates

Standard form documents; also called boilerplate documents.

Boilerplate forms

Standard forms that provide a starting point for drafting documents.

Central form file

This is an office file of documents to use as forms for new documents.

Most attorneys have standard documents that they use as **templates**. These templates are sometimes called **boilerplate forms**. The first place to look for templates is in the firm's files, particularly a **central form file**, for samples of similar documents that have been used in previous cases. When using a template to create a pleading, transactional document, or any other type of writing, it is essential to adapt the form to fit the current client's situation. For example, if the client has come in to file for a divorce, the first step is to look in the central form file for a divorce petition or complaint. Then the document must be adapted so that the client's information is incorporated. Any and all references to previous clients must be removed; otherwise, the previous client's confidentiality will be breached.

If the firm does not have a central form file or does not have a form for a particular type of document, the next option is to consult one of the many form books. Table 9-5 shows some of the form books that are most often used.

[20]Federal Civil Jury Instructions Of The Seventh Circuit http://www.ca7.uscourts .gov/7thcivinstruc2005.pdf

TABLE 9-5   Form Books – Sample Offerings

Title and Publisher	Coverage
General	
American Jurisprudence Legal Forms 2d	Provides a variety of forms; alphabetically arranged; available in print and on Westlaw. Gives text, drafting guidelines, notes on using, research references, checklists, statutory references, and more.[21]
American Jurisprudence Pleading and Practice Forms Annotated	Over 43,000 litigation forms, checklists, guidelines, statutory and procedural rules, and, with annotations, provides references to primary and secondary authority.[22] Available on Westlaw.
West's Legal Forms [current edition]	Forms for general practice; alphabetically arranged by type of form such as business organizations.
Current Legal Forms with Tax Analysis (Rabkin & Johnson) Matthew Bender	Forms for general practice in looseleaf format; discussion of use of forms and of topics to which the form relates. Organized by broad topics. On Lexis/Nexis.
Cyclopedia of Legal Forms Annotated West	Forms from various jurisdictions.
Pattern Jury Instructions	Forms used to draft the instructions given to the jury
Federal	
Federal Procedural Forms, Lawyers' Edition Lawyer's Co-operative Pub. Co.	Various forms for use in federal practice.
Bender's Federal Practice Forms	Forms in both criminal and civil practice.
Moore's Manual: Federal Practice Forms Matthew Bender	Civil litigation forms. Accompanies treatise, *Moore's Manual: Federal Practice and Procedure.*
Pattern Jury Instructions West	Jury instructions for each circuit for civil and criminal cases.
State	
Pattern jury instructions for [state]	Presents instructions for each state for civil and criminal.
North Carolina Criminal Trial Practice Forms, 5th ed. West	List of forms for criminal practice; arranged to parallel the chronological order of a criminal proceeding.
Bradford Publishing	Colorado-specific legal forms.[23]
USLegal	Forms for all states.[24]
Special	
Bender's Forms of Discovery Matthew Bender	Samples of most documents needed during discovery process
Norton Bankruptcy Law and Practice. Thomson	Treatise with forms and code with practice material in appendix
Collier on Bankruptcy Matthew Bender	Currently superseding 15th edition. Available on Lexis/Nexis
Bankruptcy Code, Rules and Forms West	Contains the law from Title 11 and related provisions from Titles 18 and 28 and forms.
Form Books for Paralegals	
Paralegal Discovery: Procedures and Forms by Pat Medina Aspen	Focused on drafting discovery documents and case management.
Paralegal Litigation: Forms and Procedures by Marcy Delesandri. Aspen	Forms, checklists, and litigation procedures.
Paralegal's Litigation Handbook by Carole Bruno. Delmar Thomson Learning.	Handbook for variety of areas in litigation including forms for drafting.

[21]American Jurisprudence Legal Forms Library. 2012. http://store.westlaw.com/american-jurisprudence-legal-forms-2d/2076/14100227 /productdetail and American Jurisprudence Legal Forms Library on Westlaw. 2012. http://store.westlaw.com/american-jurisprudence-legal-forms-westlawnext-pro/164308/40980438/productdetail

[22]American Jurisprudence Pleading and Practice Forms Annotated. 2012. http://west.thomson.com/productdetail/2078/13503727 /productdetail.aspx

[23]Bradford Publishing Co. 2010. http://www.bradfordpublishing.com/Legal-Forms

[24]USLegal Forms. *Author and Publisher Forms.* 1997—2012. http://www.uslegalforms.com/authors/

General form collections are divided into legal forms, such as wills, contracts, or leases, and pleading or practice forms for documents that are filed with the court, such as complaints or motions. Attorneys often use checklists to insure that all the necessary language and client-specific material have been included.

Researching with Form Books

Generally the form book or set will have an index so that a descriptive word or topic strategy can be used to find the appropriate forms. Most form books are annotated to provide primary and secondary materials supporting each form. Very often a form book will reference cases that have approved the language used in the form, or will have or checklists and commentary explaining their use. Most form books are supplemented with pocket parts. If the form book is a looseleaf book, the supplements will be by page insert. When using that type of form book, the date on the page must be checked to confirm that the page is current. Some publishers have electronic media where their forms can be located using a key word search.

Many forms are also available online. Law schools have form banks, and some law offices, as well as federal and state government agencies, post forms on their websites. When using a form from an online source, it is usually exported to a word processing program, and then adapted to the client's case. When copying and pasting content into a form, it is very easy to make an error in adapting boilerplate language, so the final draft should be checked very carefully. Table 9-6 provides a sample of the major sources of forms online.

Exhibit 9-5 provides an example of a living will form from Indiana. This form was found in the forms archive of the Internet Legal Research Group (ILRG) website.

> **TIP**
>
> While there are many sites for forms, checking the legitimacy of the site is important. There is material in Chapter 7 that will aid researchers in determining the value of the site. Also note that many of the "free" sites are not really "free." Do not order a form without checking with a supervisor.

EXHIBIT 9-5   LIVING WILL IN INDIANA

Indiana Living Will Declaration

Declaration made this 29th day of November, 2013.

I, William E. Ferrett, being at least eighteen (18) years of age and of sound mind, willfully and voluntarily make known my desires that my dying shall not be artificially prolonged under the circumstances set forth below, and I declare:

If at any time my attending physician certifies in writing that (1) I have an incurable injury, disease, or illness; (2) my death will occur within a short time; and (3) the use of life prolonging procedures would serve only to artificially prolong the dying process, I direct that such procedures be withheld or withdrawn, and that I be permitted to die naturally with only the performance or provision of any medical procedure or medication necessary to provide me with comfort care or to alleviate pain, and, if I have so indicated below, the provision of artificially supplied nutrition and hydration. (Indicate your choice by initialing or making your mark before signing this declaration.)

_____ I wish to receive artificially supplied nutrition and hydration, even if the effort to sustain life is futile or excessively burdensome to me.

_____ I do not wish to receive artificially supplied nutrition and hydration, if the effort to sustain life is futile or excessively burdensome to me.

_____ I intentionally make no decision concerning artificially supplied nutrition and hydration, leaving the decision to my health care representative appointed under IC 16-36-1-7 or my attorney in fact with health care powers under IC 30-5-5.

In the absence of my ability to give directions regarding the use of life prolonging procedures, it is my intention that this declaration be honored by my family and physician as the final expression of my legal right to refuse medical or surgical treatment and accept the consequences of the refusal.

I understand the full import of this declaration.

Signed _____

Terre Haute, Vigo County, Indiana

City, County, and State of Residence

The declarant has been personally known to me, and I believe (him/her) to be of sound mind. I did not sign the declarant's signature above for or at the direction of the declarant. I am not a parent, spouse, or child of the declarant. I am not entitled to any part of the declarant's estate or directly financially responsible for the declarant's medical care. I am competent and at least eighteen (18) years of age.

Witness _____ Date _____

Witness _____ Date _____ [25]

EXHIBIT 9-6   RHODE ISLAND LIVING WILL

RHODE ISLAND LIVING WILL

DECLARATION

I, Betty E. Ferrett, being of sound mind, willfully and voluntarily make known my desire that my dying shall not be artificially prolonged under the circumstances set forth below, do hereby declare:

If I should have an incurable or irreversible condition that will cause my death and if I am unable to make decisions regarding my medical treatment, I direct my attending physician to withhold or withdraw procedures that merely prolong the dying process and are not necessary to my comfort, or to alleviate pain.

This authorization includes ( ) does not include ( ) the withholding or withdrawal of artificial feeding (check only one box above).

Signed this 29th day of January, 2014.

Signature

Betty E. Ferrett
1234 S. Soul St., Pawtucket, RI 026890

The declarant is personally known to me and voluntarily signed this document in my presence.

_____   _____

Norma J. Ray, Witness   Billy Boathouse, Witness
3434 S. Main St, Pawtucket, RI 02680 25 E. South St., Pawtucket, RI 02680[26]

Incorporating state requirements is another important concern when using forms. The Indiana Living Will can be compared to the Rhode Island Living Will in Exhibit 9-6. Differences in the forms result from the differing legal requirements in each state.

[25]IC 16-36-4-8
[26]http://webserver.rilin.state.ri.us/Statutes/TITLE23/23-4.11/23-4.11-3.HTM

TIP

Are there any differences between the two states' forms? What are they? Would either form work in the jurisdiction a researcher is in? Why or why not? These are some of the questions that one would ask every time a form document is used. A researcher would not leave blanks for the day, month, and year if the dates are known beforehand. Leaving blank lines can raise the question of whether the document is genuine.

TABLE 9-6   Forms Online

Subscription	
Westlaw	This site provides a variety of forms. In the directory a researcher would go to "Forms, Treatises, CLEs and Other Practice Materials." To search for all forms, go to database "Forms-All."www.westlaw.com
LexisNexis	A researcher would go to Legal>Secondary Legal>Forms & Agreements. www.academic.lexisnexis.com
Free on Internet	
Findlaw Forms	This site provides topical links to forms, with links to actual contracts produced by major corporations. http://forms.lp.findlaw.com
Various Law Schools	Example: www.washlaw.edu/legalforms
Internal Revenue Service	This site provides all tax forms and publications since 1990. www.irs.gov/formspubs
Internet Legal Research Group (ILRG)	Over 2000 forms are provided on this site. www.ilrg.comforms/index.html
AllLaw.com Legal Forms	www.alllaw.com/forms/
The 'Lectric Law Library	www.lectlaw.com/formb/htm
HG.org	http://www.hg.org/forms.html

> **TIP**
>
> On this particular website, a hint is provided that one may need to draft other forms to accompany the living will. The living will document will not be useful on its own if other documents are needed to make the living will operative.

If a paralegal were to use the living will form from Indiana, the next step would be to pull the statutes in Indiana that control a living will declaration and make sure that the form meets all requirements of the statute. Then, the paralegal would insert the client's information. The finished form should look like any other professional document that is filed with the court.

Table 9-6 provides some of the major online sources of forms.

LEGAL DICTIONARIES AND THESAURI

The Value of Dictionaries and Thesauri

Probably the first legal dictionary was *Bouvier's Law Dictionary*, originally published in 1839. The revised sixth edition was published in 1856. One of the leading legal dictionaries today is *Black's Law Dictionary (Black's)*, also available on Westlaw as *Black's Law Dictionary Digital*, and as an application for the iPhone. Other well-known legal dictionaries are *Ballentine's Law Dictionary*, *Oran's Dictionary of Law*, and *Merriam-Webster's Law Dictionary*.

Legal dictionaries are used in the same way as Webster's or any other standard English dictionary. If there is an unknown legal term that must be defined, the legal dictionary provides a definition, the proper spelling, the pronunciation, and sometimes synonyms or antonyms. The legal dictionary may also refer the user to a citation to primary or secondary authority in which the term was used. If the dictionary provides a case to define a word, the researcher should read and cite the case, not the dictionary.

Dictionaries usually are not updated with pocket parts or supplements. The editors determine when a new edition is needed. For example, the ninth edition

TABLE 9-7 Sample of Specialized Dictionaries

Topic	Title
Business	*A Dictionary of Business Law Terms*
	Glossary of Commercial Fraud
Criminal Law	*Criminal Justice Today Glossary*
	Criminal Law Glossary
Family Law	Black's Law Series: *A Dictionary of Family Law Terms*
Insurance	*Insurance Dictionary*
	Glossary of General Insurance Terms
International Law	*Dictionary of International & Comparative Law*
	International Law: A Dictionary
Labor Relations	*Dictionary of Occupational Titles*
	Labor and Legal Terminology
Medical	*Am. Jur. Proof of Facts 3d Attorney's Illustrated Medical Dictionary*
	West *Attorney's Illustrated Medical Dictionary*
	Stedman's Medical Dictionary http://www.stedmans.com/
Patent	*USPTO Patent and Trademark Glossary*
Tax	*West's Tax Law Dictionary*
	WG & L Tax Dictionary

of *Black's* (2009) contains 2,000 more terms than the eighth edition (2004), and 19,000 more terms than the seventh edition (1999). New editions sometimes provide additional enhancements.[27]

Black's and other publishers also offer specialized dictionaries, such as those shown in Table 9-7.

Black's should not be confused with *Words and Phrases*. The terms in *Words and Phrases* are defined with reference to particular primary authority. The court actually must have defined the word or phrase in a decision. *Black's* and other legal dictionaries go beyond the single case definition and provide a comprehensive look at a word or phrase.

A legal thesaurus (plural, *thesauri*) provides alternate terms, or synonyms and antonyms for legal terms and phrases. Probably the most comprehensive is *Burton's Legal Thesaurus, 4th ed.*, by William C. Burton. Another example is *Legal Thesaurus/Dictionary: A Resource for the Writer and the Computer Researcher*, by William Statsky. A third is *Ballentine's Legal Dictionary and Thesaurus*, by Jonathan S. Lynton. Legal thesauri, such as *The Free Dictionary* (http://www.thefreedictionary.com/), are also available on the Internet.

Researching with Dictionaries and Thesauri

Using *Black's Law Dictionary Digital Plus* can be made more convenient by adding its icon to the Microsoft toolbar. The researcher can click the "add-ins" tab on the Microsoft Word ribbon, type the word or phrase to be searched, and click the "Dictionary" icon, or select the word or phrase in the document being searched,

---

[27]Black's Law Dictionary, 9th Ed., http://www.blackslawdictrary.com/

> **EXAMPLE 9-2   USING BLACK'S LAW DIGITAL**
>
> 1. *Black's Law Digital (Black's)* must be installed on the toolbar of the chosen word processor or Internet browser. As an add-in to the Microsoft Word toolbar, use Microsoft Internet Explorer 6.0 or later, Firefox 1.5 or 2.0 plus Microsoft Word 2002(XP) and forward, or Corel WordPerfect X3.
> 2. Once installed, open the word processer or Internet browser. The *Black's* toolbar should appear, although the view may be different depending on the word processor.
> 3. If the *Black's* toolbar is not visible, right-click on the toolbar and select *Black's* from the list of available toolbars. Users of Internet Explorer would go to View/Toolbars/*Black's Law Dictionary Digital*.
> 4. Type a legal term, such as *habeas corpus*, in the toolbar and click the question mark icon or hit "Enter." The *Black's* window appears and the definition or list of phrases using the word will appear.
> 5. Click the *habeas corpus* link to view the definition. The terms are hyperlinked for easy use.
> 6. More tools, such as spell-checking documents, "cite as" buttons, subentries, *Words and Phrases*, and quotes are available. Using *Words and Phrases* is automatic when a term is searched in *Black's*. If there is a match, the next window appears.[29]

right-click on the word of interest, and choose *Black's* from the pop-up menu. A list of definitions is presented. The service also can be accessed from Internet Explorer.

Once in *Black's*, a researcher can link to other definitions or other sources that are hyperlinked within the first definition. *Black's* also provides a tool to access quotations that use the term, to show the term's historical significance and to provide a context.[28]

Example 9-2 shows how to find a definition using *Black's Law Digital*.

Dictionaries and legal thesauri provide an understanding of the basic concepts surrounding a word or phrase. No matter where the source is found, it must be confirmed that it is up-to-date and that it is a valid source.

DIRECTORIES

The Use of Directories

When one thinks of directories, a telephone directory or a student directory at a college may come to mind. In the legal world, a directory provides a list of lawyers, or people and entities that work with lawyers.

Probably the most well-known directory is the *Martindale-Hubbell Law Directory (Martindale-Hubbell)*. First published in 1868 as the *Martindale*

---

[28]Black's Law Dictionary Digital Plus User Guide. 2009. http://west.thomson.com/documentation/cdrom/cddoc/ldsoft/blacksug.pdf

[29]*Welcome to Black's Law Dictionary Digital Online Help.* n.d. http://www.thomsonreuterslegal.com/Black_User_Manual.pdf

Directory, Martindale-Hubbell was designed to provide the contact information of law offices, banks, and real estate offices in each city of the United States.[30] Today, the directory provides listings of attorneys, law firms, U.S. government lawyers, and corporate legal departments throughout the country. It also includes biographies of leading lawyers and law firms, firm ratings, information on more than 100 U.S. law schools, and information on international lawyers.

The directory also provides state digests, international conventions' text, uniform acts, Internet directories, specialized directories, and, in some instances, local directories.[31] Although *Martindale-Hubbell* lists every attorney licensed in each jurisdiction, it does not provide biographical information for all the attorneys listed, since firms pay to be listed in the main pages. It does, however, provide Peer Review Ratings™, an objective indicator of a lawyer's high ethical standards and professional ability. Attorneys receive Peer Review Ratings™ based on evaluations by other members of the bar and the judiciary in the United States and Canada. The first review to establish a lawyer's rating usually occurs three years after his/her first admission to the bar. After lawyers have been evaluated on their legal ability, they will receive one of three ratings:

AV Preeminent (4.5–5.0)—AV Preeminent is a significant rating accomplishment—a testament to the fact that a lawyer's peers rank him or her at the highest level of professional excellence.

BV Distinguished (3.0–4.4)—BV Distinguished is an excellent rating for a lawyer with some experience. A widely respected mark of achievement, it differentiates a lawyer from his or her competition.

Rated (1.0–2.9)—The Peer Review Rated designation demonstrates the lawyer has met the Very High criteria of General Ethical Standing.[32]

Another important directory is the *Bar Register of Preeminent Lawyers*. This 90-year-old publication lists the top lawyers and law practices as rated by their peers. Listings are given by state and by more than 70 areas of practice.[33] This service is available in print and on the Internet.

In addition, a researcher can rely on the FindLaw Lawyer Directory, which features detailed profiles of attorneys from across the United States. FindLaw provides a search box or allows a user to click on a city, state, or legal issue.[34]

Researching in Directories

While there are many reasons to use directories, the two most common are to learn about an opposing lawyer or firm, and to locate a lawyer or firm to which one might send a résumé.

---

[30] *The History of Martindale-Hubbell.* 2012. http://www.martindale.com/xp/legal/About_Martindale/Our_History/our_history.xml

[31] The Martindale-Hubbell Law Directories. 2012. http://www.martindale.com/xp/legal/About_Martindale/Products_and_Services/The_Martindale-Hubbell_Law_Directories/intro.xml#

[32] Martindale.com. Peer Review Ratings™ 2012. http://www.martindale.com/Products_and_Services/Peer_Review_Ratings.aspx

[33] The Bar Register of Preeminent Lawyers. 2012. http://www.martindale.com/xp/legal/About_Martindale/Products_and_Services/The_Bar_Register_of_Preeminent_Lawyers/the_bar_register_of_preeminent_lawyers.xml

[34] FindLaw, Find a Lawyer. 2011. http://lawyers.findlaw.com/

EXAMPLE 9-3 USING A DIRECTORY

The Allgood Law Firm picked up a new client who was injured while cleaning windows of a multi-storied building in Des Moines, Iowa. Jami, the supervising attorney, has asked John, the paralegal, to locate two or three good attorneys in the Des Moines, Iowa, area. Unless he is familiar with all the attorneys in Des Moines, he needs some help. He would do the following:

1. Find the directory that covers Iowa.
2. Search the appropriate entries for Des Moines to find firms and their contact information.
3. Read the biographical information, which includes date of birth, colleges or universities attended, honors received, and articles authored.
4. See a representative list of the clients and the areas of law in which the firm practices.

Figure 9-5 is a sample listing of a firm that might be useful to the client described in Example 9-3.

Statement of Practice Summary Civil Trial and Appellate Practice. Insurance Defense, Workers' Compensation, Insurance, Products Liability, Professional Malpractice Defense and Administrative Law. Commercial, Business, Insurance Litigation and Employment Law.

Martindale-Hubbell is also a useful tool for job hunting. If someone were looking for firms to send resumes to, he or she would search for firms in the cities of interest, and then find firms that concentrate on the kind of law the applicant is interested in. If someone gets an interview with a firm, the applicant should always research the firm before going to the interview to know some key facts about the firm, its lawyers, and its clients. The applicant should not hesitate to explain that the firm biographies were researched in *Martindale-Hubbell*. This will help create the impression that the applicant has prepared for the interview, and was interested in the position.

FIGURE 9-5 Martindale-Hubbell Usage

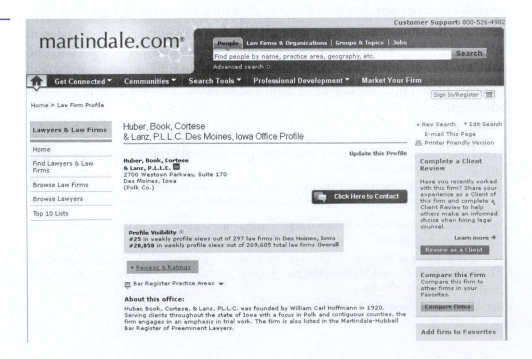

SUMMARY

A good researcher knows what tools are needed to perform quality research, and is well versed in using them. Digests provide topics and key numbers of points of law that are used to find cases on point. *Words and Phrases* is used to understand the legal meaning of a word or phrase and to find cases that provide those meanings in context. Form books provide samples of documents from which appropriate documents can be created to fit the client's needs. Dictionaries provide the definitions of words and may provide the context from primary authority.

While some secondary authorities may be cited in interoffice memoranda, the goal is still to find primary authority. The courts are not required to follow secondary authorities; the courts *may* follow these authorities if the authorities are persuasive, if a foundation has been laid, and if there is no primary authority on point. There is a process to using secondary sources as they should be used. The secondary sources are valuable for locating and explaining the primary authority and providing citations to primary authority.

REVIEW **QUESTIONS**

1. How are looseleaf services presented, and how does this differ from other legal sources?
2. What is the major difference between the BNA and CCH services?
3. Where can one find a set of looseleaf publications or topics?
4. When is it appropriate to use a looseleaf service as an initial source of legal research?
5. How is *AmJur Proof of Facts* organized?
6. The decisions of which courts are reported in the *Federal Practice Digest*?
7. Name the state digest covering the state courts of your state only. Who publishes it? How many volumes are in the set? How is it updated?
8. Why are the opinions of an attorney general given different weight than other secondary authority, such as a legal encyclopedia?
9. What value is there in consulting a legal dictionary?
10. Identify three types of information you might obtain from *Martindale-Hubbell*.
11. What process would you undertake if your supervisor asked you to draft a complaint of divorce for a new client?
12. For what type of research might you use a looseleaf service? What are two of the most prominent looseleaf services?
13. What are jury instructions? How might you, as a paralegal, assist in preparing jury instructions?
14. What is the best rating for an attorney according to *Martindale-Hubbell*? Why?

APPLICATION **EXERCISES**

15. Your supervisor has assigned you the new client who came in yesterday. Here is her story:

    Suzy Stephens has come to the law firm because she was arrested for buying large quantities of an over-the-counter drug that could be used to make an illegal drug. She had been coming to the local ZMart several times a week for the past month. ZMart's pharmacist suspected there might be a problem and informed the local sheriff's department. Without a warrant, the sheriff placed a wiretap on her phone and discovered that there was a meth lab in her house. Suzy was arrested at her house. Jami, your supervising attorney, wants to draft a motion to exclude the evidence seized as a result of the placement of the wiretap without a search warrant.

    a. Make a list of key words using this set of facts. Choose two, and search for them in two different dictionaries. Compare the definitions. How are they different?

    b. Find synonyms and antonyms for the key words you selected, using a thesaurus.

    c. Using the key words, find two digest topics and key numbers under which this scenario might fall. Write down the information.

    d. See if one of the key words you selected can be found in Words and Phrases. If so, cite the reference.

    e. Find a form for a motion to exclude evidence. Copy it for your file and provide the source.

    f. Find an attorney in your jurisdiction who would be qualified to represent your client. Cite the source you use and provide an explanation as to why you believe this person could represent your client.

16. Look at the two living will declarations in Exhibit 9-2. Compare and contrast the provisions. Create a living will for you or for a fictitious person residing in your jurisdiction.

17. Look at the jury instructions in the chapter. Is there a similar jury instruction available in your jurisdiction either at the federal or state level? Describe the information available with the instruction. Cite the source.

18. What digest or digests would contain a case decided in 2002 by the U.S. Court of Appeals for your jurisdiction based on a question of law from your jurisdiction? List each digest you would consult to find the answer.

19. Assume you know nothing about venue but your supervisor has asked you to research the issue of venue in your federal jurisdiction. What resources would you use to search, and why? Create a research trail document and list at least four sources that you would consult. Then do the same for the issue in your state jurisdiction.

20. Your firm's client, Molly Hatcher, was abused by her husband, Al Hatcher, for many years. Last week, he beat her so severely that she was hospitalized. Molly finally wants a divorce. However, her husband is still in the army and stationed at Fort Carson, an army base where the two lived and where Al still lives. Molly now lives in your state and has lived there for six months.

   a. What section(s) of the *Federal Practice Digest* covers this issue?
   b. If your state has a state digest, identify the section(s) covering the issue.
   c. Summarize the information provided.
   d. Identify the most current case cited.
   e. Did you find that information in the main volume or in the pocket part?

21. Find the digest of your state. Look for *Homicide* to answer the following questions:

   a. Identify the book that you found *Homicide* in.
   b. Identify three key numbers under *Homicide*.
   c. Properly cite the most current case under each key number you selected.
   d. Where did you find the cases?

CITATION **EXERCISES**

For these exercises, cite to *The Bluebook*, *ALWD*, or another authorized citator. Provide the citation in proper form and give the rule. Do not use any examples provided in the chapter.

1. Write a citation for an attorney general opinion from your jurisdiction.

2. Locate the rule for citing legal encyclopedias and provide a citation.

3. Write a citation for the definition of "case of first impression" from *Black's Legal Dictionary*.

4. Write a citation for a case in a looseleaf service.

5. Provide the proper citation for an attorney general opinion from your state.

6. Write a citation for a jury instruction taken from a resource in your jurisdiction.

QUICK **CHECK**

1. Using *Words and Phrases* in the initial research process is very helpful because it provides the law itself.
   a. True
   b. False

2. An article in a secondary source that has been replaced has been ___
   a. superseded
   b. supplemented
   c. suppressed
   d. surmounted

3. Which of the following is not a secondary source? ___
   a. A case reporter
   b. An encyclopedia
   c. A treatise
   d. A Restatement of Law

4. Books containing jury instructions are ___.
   a. form books
   b. pattern jury instructions
   c. required jury instructions
   d. legal thesauri

5. The editorial summaries of the legal topics addressed in a case are the ___.
   a. pocket parts
   b. key numbers
   c. headnotes
   d. page cites

6. Key words or phrases in a digest are found in the ___.
   a. prefatory material
   b. descriptive word index
   c. pocket part
   d. key numbers

7. Westlaw and LexisNexis provide full-text digests online.
   a. True
   b. False

8. Looseleaf services often contain commentary written by attorneys.
   a. True
   b. False

9. An encyclopedia is mandatory authority in your state.
   a. True
   b. False
10. Which of the following statements is incorrect?
    a. Looseleaf services contain secondary authority.
    b. Forms from formbooks should never be altered to fit your client's situation.

c. Uniform laws seek to have states use the same or similar language in the law.
d. Attorney general opinions are primary authority.

RESEARCH

1. Is there a looseleaf service that provides samples of business forms? If so, give the name of the service.
2. Identify a form for a complaint that alleges fault in a maritime collision.
3. Identify a form for a request of a trustee for copyright certification in bankruptcy.
4. In any digest volume, select a key number that has at least one case digested under it. State the key number and the citation to a case listed.
5. In the pocket part of the volume you selected for question 4, go to the key number you selected for question 4. Give the citation of one new case under this key number. (If there are none under this key number, indicate "no new cases."
6. Pick any topic. In the index, select any three key numbers under that topic. State the topic and the key numbers.
7. Go to the volume of the index that covers the letter *W*. Turn to "Wills." What is the first entry in the index under "Wills" that leads you to a key number? What is the key number?
8. Now go to the actual digest volume that covers "Wills." Find the topic you identified in question 7. What is the citation of the first case written by one of

the state courts under the key number you identified in question 7?
9. Go to the regional reporter that contains the full text of the case you identified in question 7. How many headnotes does this case have?
10. Find a jury instruction on justifiable homicide in your jurisdiction and prepare it for filing with your court. Use West's *U.S. Supreme Court Digest* or LexisNexis's *U.S. Supreme Court Reports Digest Lawyer's Edition* to answer questions a–d by providing the following:
    - An answer to the question based on the appropriate digest paragraph
    - The topic and key number (West) or topic and section number (LexisNexis) that answers the question
    - The complete and properly formatted citation to the latest case on point
    a. Is a tenant relieved of liability for rent if the rental property is accidentally destroyed by fire?
    b. Is a father's right to the custody, care, and management of his children constitutionally protected?
    c. Must an attorney, appointed by the court to represent an accused, actually represent the accused?
    d. Is a state public health law valid if it provides that any doctor who practices medicine after being convicted of a felony is guilty of a misdemeanor?

INTERNET RESEARCH

1. Find an opinion of the attorney general for your jurisdiction. What was the issue being discussed? What was the result? Identify at least two pieces of authority upon which the AG based his or her opinion.
2. Go to the website for West (www.west.thomson.com) and find the product information for any of the sources discussed in this chapter. Identify the number of volumes and any other research information available.
3. Go to the website of any two legal dictionaries. Identify all the information you can find about each dictionary, such as the manner in which you can search and the tools that the dictionary provides. Which dictionary is easier to navigate? Why? Which gave the most

information? Go back to Chapter 6 and weigh the value of each site. Is one more reliable than the other? Why?
4. Go to the website for a publisher of legal dictionaries. Identify the information available. Compare the print version of a dictionary with the Internet version. Is one better than another? Why?
5. Your client is the owner of the house who wants to rent to another person. He wants to be protected against any damage that a tenant might do. He wants the following terms in the lease:
   - a damage deposit that is twice the rent
   - rent of $650 per month due on the first day of every month

- a $25 per day late fee after two days
- all utilities are included except electricity and cable
- no pets are allowed without written permission
- a $400 damage deposit
- tenant is responsible for general maintenance such as light bulbs, cleaning, and care

- the landlord is responsible for common area maintenance
- tenant cannot have any persons living in the apartment other than those listed in the lease

Find a legal form for rental of a house. Draft a lease agreement using the form you found. Cite the source of the form.

MEDIA **RESOURCES**

Automated Legal Form Tutorial	http://law.lexisnexis.com/automated-forms/training-/-tutorials
LexisNexis Headnotes	http://web.lexis.com/help/multimedia/detect.asp?sPage=hn2
Lexis Product Tutorials	http://www.lexisnexis.com/COMMUNITY/DOWNLOADANDSUPPORTCENTER/media/p/4332.aspx
Nexis Product Tutorials	http://www.lexisnexis.com/Community/DownloadandSupportcenter/media/p/4285.aspx

INTERNET **RESOURCES**

General information at	www.lexisnexis.com
Using Secondary Sources on Westlaw. 2010:	http://lscontent.westlaw.com/images/content/UsingSSonWL10.pdf
Updating Your West Digest Search. 2010:	http://west.thomson.com/documentation/westlaw/wlawdoc/lawstu/lsdig06.pdf
Westlaw User Guide 2010:	http://store.westlaw.com/documentation/westlaw/wlawdoc/web/wlcmgd06.pdf
Westlaw Next: Using Topics and Key Numbers:	http://store.westlaw.com/documentation/westlaw/wlawdoc/web/wlntopic.pdf

chapter **ten**

RESEARCHING ENACTED LAW AND RELATED MATERIALS

Evlakhov Valeriy/Shutterstock

LEARNING OBJECTIVES

After studying this chapter, students should be able to:

1. Recognize and locate established primary authorities and utilize them for the completion of statutory research assignments.

2. Update enacted law with the most current edition.

3. Properly cite enacted law.

CHAPTER OVERVIEW

Enacted law includes constitutional provisions, statutes, administrative regulations, and ordinances. The federal, state, and local governments create and pass statutes and ordinances. In research, once the applicable enacted law is found, *legal analysis* is used to understand and explain how the enacted law applies to the facts of the client's case.

Enacted law
Law that is passed by a governmental body charged with creating law in order to set guidelines in place for future behavior.

Legal analysis
The process by which the law is applied to a set of facts in the client's case to determine what issues are important and what law is relevant to those issues.

OPENING SCENARIO

Several new cases had been opened at the Allgood Law Firm, and John had received several new assignments connected with them. One of the new cases required him to research the laws regarding search and seizure, because the police searched the client's car without a warrant. He needed to find cases that supported the client's position that the police violated her rights.

Another case was based on the state's intestate succession law. The client was a niece of the decedent and the only other relative was a first cousin. She needed to know how the estate would be distributed.

In still another assignment John needed to locate the statute on driving while intoxicated and make sure that the information in the case file was up-to-date.

John really appreciated his legal research instructor in college. She required the students to do exercise after exercise on locating and updating statutes. With all of that practice under his belt, these assignments were going to be a breeze! But first, he knew it was important to refresh his memory on exactly how to research enacted law.

WHAT IS ENACTED LAW?

Enacted law

Law that is passed by a governmental body charged with creating law in order to set guidelines in place for future behavior.

Primary authority

The law itself, consisting of enacted law and common law.

Mandatory authority

Authority that must be followed by a court in reaching a decision.

Two types of primary authority exist: case law and *enacted law*. Case law is made when an appellate court addresses a legal issue and renders a decision. Enacted law is passed by a government body in order to set rules in place for future behavior.

Enacted law is unlike case law in that it is not created as part of the resolution of a dispute. Enacted law is any law that a body proposes, considers, and votes on, and that then becomes the authority by which people must abide.

Table 10-1 provides an overview of each type of enacted law.

Any enacted law is *primary authority*. That means that any valid constitutional provision, statute, court rule, administrative regulation, or ordinance is always primary authority. A Kansas statute is primary authority. A Washington state constitutional provision is primary authority. An ordinance in Terre Haute, Indiana, is primary authority.

However, not all primary authority is *mandatory authority*. Mandatory authority is law that *must* be followed. Primary authority is mandatory authority *if* the following three conditions are met:

1. The court or geographic area in which the enacted law is being applied has authority or jurisdiction to apply the law.
2. The framers of the law intended that the law would apply to the facts at issue in the situation.
3. There is no superior law that should be applied to the facts.

This means that if a client's issue is one that would arise in a Tennessee state court, the Tennessee constitution, Tennessee statutes, Tennessee administrative

TABLE 10-1   Categories of Enacted Laws

Enacted Law	Description
Constitutions	The U.S. Constitution is the supreme law of the land.
State Constitutions	Every state has a state constitution; many of these are modeled after the U.S. Constitution.
Federal Statutes	These are federal laws created by the U.S. Congress.
State Statutes	These are laws created through a state's process in the legislature.
Federal Administrative Regulations	These regulations are made by federal administrative agencies such as the Food and Drug Administration (FDA).
State Administrative Regulations	These regulations are made by state administrative agencies, such as the Indiana Occupational Safety and Health Administration (IOSHA).
Local Codes and Ordinances	Cities or towns create local laws such as an ordinance against someone having loud mufflers on a car.
Court Rules	These are procedural rules promulgated by a court regarding practice in that court.
Uniform Laws and Model Codes	These may become law if specifically adopted and enacted; an example is the Uniform Commercial Code.

regulations, and Tennessee ordinances would be primary authority. These laws also would be mandatory authority if they applied to the client's issue. State enacted law is usually mandatory only in the state that enacted the law.

Federal enacted law is sometimes mandatory in state courts. If a U.S. Constitution provision is violated, the U.S. Constitution controls. State law cannot contravene the U.S. Constitution because the U.S. Constitution is the supreme law of the land. In addition, federal statutes may be superior to state law if the U.S. Constitution gives such authority to Congress to enact those laws. Examples are laws regarding bankruptcy, patents, and interstate commerce. Federal administrative agency regulations may be superior to state law if the issue involves a federal agency. Examples are regulations involving keeping the water of a town clean or a dispute about the safety of a worker arising under the Occupational Safety and Health Act. If the client's issue deals with one of these areas, federal statutes and regulations would be mandatory authority in the state courts because the federal laws control those situations.

CONSTITUTIONS

The U.S. Constitution

The U.S. *Constitution* is the cornerstone of our legal system. This enacted law established the federal government, described the federal government's powers, set limits on those powers, and set aside certain powers to the states. Of all the major governments in the world, this document, with its 4,400 words, is not only the oldest but also the shortest written constitution in existence today.

Constitution
A state or nation's fundamental law. The U.S. Constitution is the supreme law of the land. Each state has its own constitution.

The authority of the constitution is established in the Supremacy Clause, the common name for Article VI, Clause 2, which reads:

> This Constitution, and the Laws of the United States which shall be made in Pursuance thereof; and all Treaties made, or which shall be made, under the authority of the United States, shall be the supreme Law of the land; and the Judges in every State shall be bound thereby, any Thing in the Constitution or Laws of any State to the Contrary notwithstanding.[1]

The U.S. Constitution has three main parts: the preamble, the articles, and the amendments. The preamble has no legal effect, but describes why the Constitution was written. The opening words should be familiar to most American citizens:

> We the People of the United States, in Order to form a more perfect Union, establish Justice, insure domestic Tranquility, provide for the common defense, promote the general Welfare, and secure the Blessings of Liberty to ourselves and our Posterity, do ordain and establish this Constitution for the United States of America.[2]

The remainder of the U.S. Constitution—the articles and amendments—is the law. Each article addresses a different part of the government:

Article 1 describes the legislature, one of the three branches of government.

Article 2 establishes the executive branch, headed by the president.

[1]The Charters of Freedom. *Constitution of the United States.* http://www.archives.gov/exhibits/charters/constitution_transcript.html

[2]The U.S. Constitution. 1995–2011. http://www.usconstitution.net/const.html#Preamble

Article 3 creates the court system by establishing one Supreme Court and permitting the establishment of inferior courts as necessary.

Article 4 deals with the rights of the states.

Article 5 provides the method to amend the Constitution.

Article 6 discusses the payment of debt, makes the Constitution and all laws and treaties of the United States the supreme law of the land, and requires any officers of the United States or the states to take an oath of allegiance to the United States and the Constitution.

Article 7 delineates the ratification of the Constitution by 9 of the original 13 states.

The first 10 amendments to the U.S. Constitution, ratified in 1791, are known as the **Bill of Rights**. These amendments, as well as the 17 others that have been adopted since, guarantee many individual rights the people have in relationship to their government.

Many people know about the first 10 amendments but do not know much about the rest of the Constitution. Many of the first 10 amendments, such as those dealing with search and seizure, a fair trial by one's peers, and the prohibition against excessive fines, are directed toward the process in our criminal law system. Many important civil rights also have their basis in the Bill of Rights, such as freedom of speech, the right to due process, and the right to equal protection under the law.

Generally, constitutional arguments are based on whether an action is consistent with a constitutional provision, whether a statute violates or supports the Constitution, or how a case interprets the Constitution. The principles of constitutional interpretation are similar to those principles used to interpret the statutes or judicial decisions. Legal scholars tend to use seven methods of decision-making, summarized in Table 10-2, when interpreting the Constitution.

Bill of Rights

The first 10 amendments to the U.S. Constitution, which set forth rights, freedoms, and responsibilities, such as freedom of speech, freedom to be free from unwarranted searches and seizures, and the right to a speedy trial.

TIP

The U.S. Constitution provides that the individual rights guaranteed through the Bill of Rights and subsequent amendments may not be infringed upon by any government action.

TABLE 10-2 Types of Constitutional Interpretation

Method	Description
Textual	Examining the words of the written law and the meaning of those words at the time the law was drafted.
Functional or structural	Analyzing the structures of the law and how the law is intended to function coherently.
Historical or legislative or case history	Analyzing the history of the drafting and ratification processes and understanding the foundation of the wording, which may have changed over time.
Doctrinal	Applying the concepts of precedent and *stare decisis*, which indicate that the decisions made are normative.
Prudential	Considering external factors affecting the legal system, such as the convenience of the court or other officials or response to political pressure.
Equitable or ethical	Applying a foundational sense of justice for the parties, even if doing so contravenes what the written law says.
Natural	Applying the laws of nature to determine what is possible, and what can potentially occur.[3]

[3]Constitution Society. *Principles of Constitutional Construction.* 2011. http://www.constitution.org/cons/prin_cons.htm

The first three methods are ways to understand the written Constitution. The doctrinal, prudential, and equitable methods are ways of using external doctrines or principles when applying the Constitution to actual cases or controversies. For example, the doctrinal method is based on the concepts of precedent and *stare decisis*, which relate to the general authority of the court to hear a case or determine a legal issue. The natural method considers the "unwritten constitution of society," giving the laws of nature precedence over the laws of society and of government.

In reading and interpreting the U.S. Constitution, one can learn the following:

- It obtains authority through ratification and state admissions.
- It is based on the various provisions of the Constitution working together.
- Every word of the Constitution, except those in the preamble, is important and should be given consideration.
- The Bill of Rights gives new content to the original Constitution.
- There are three branches of government, each with certain powers that cannot be given to another branch of government (separation of powers).
- A court or forum for airing grievances must exist. [4]

These are only some of the concepts courts consider when called upon to interpret the Constitution. These principles help researchers understand the value of the Constitution and how the courts view this enacted law.

State Constitutions

Each state has its own constitution, and a state constitution may give the citizens of that state broader rights than those guaranteed by the U.S. Constitution. While constitutional issues are often thought of as questions of federal law, it is important to also research the law regarding a state's constitution when researching a constitutional law issue.

State constitutions are usually published in code books along with the statutes for that state. A state constitution also can be found on the Internet on the state's official homepage.

Researching Constitutional Law

When first analyzing a client's legal issue, it should be determined whether or not there is an issue of constitutional law. This task is not as straightforward as simply reading the U.S. Constitution and the state constitution. Constitutions are interpreted through case law. Constitutional case law is vast because the terminology used in constitutions is often inexact. Courts must interpret and define that language when writing their opinions. The ultimate decision maker in interpreting the U.S. Constitution is the U.S. Supreme Court. The final decision maker for each state's constitution is that state's highest court.

The U.S. Constitution is published in various sources, both in print and online. Two sources are the *United States Code Annotated* (published by West) and the *United States Code Service* (published by LexisNexis). These code books are helpful because they are **annotated**. Annotations are notes that follow each section of the law and summarize relevant court decisions, law review articles, and other legal authorities. The U.S. Constitution can be found at sites such as

> **TIP**
>
> A researcher should find his or her state's official homepage and bookmark that page. The website will provide access to legislative information, the state constitution, the executive branch, the judicial branch, and much more. Search engines such as http://www.usa.gov/Agencies/State_and_Territories.shtml *or* http://www.statelocalgov.net/ will provide connection to all state websites.

Annotated

A source that provides notes and commentaries that supplement the main information on the topic.

[4]*Id.*

http://www.archives.gov/exhibits/charters/constitution.html.[5] Other Internet sources of the U.S. Constitution and state constitutions are the websites of any of the law schools such as Cornell University Law School, state government websites, subscription legal services such as Westlaw or LexisNexis, and free services such as Findlaw.

Example 10-1 shows how constitutional issues are determined.

EXAMPLE 10-1 RESEARCH IN THE U.S. CONSTITUTION

Candy Chestnut came to the firm to find out what options she might have if she invested in a combination restaurant and bar. She needed to find out more about Sunday closing laws because she didn't want to lose the business that Sunday eating and drinking would bring. John and his supervising attorney, Jami, met with Candy. Jami thought this might be a First Amendment question so she told John that he needed to do some research on this area. Because the body of constitutional law is immense, John knew that an annotated version of the constitution could help guide him in where to look next. He found the following, as shown in Table 10-3.

TABLE 10-3 Annotated Constitution[6]

FIRST AMENDMENT	969
RELIGION AND EXPRESSION	969
RELIGION	969
An Overview	969
Scholarly Commentary	970
Court Tests Applied to Legislation Affecting Religion	972
Government Neutrality in Religious Disputes	974
Establishment of Religion	977
Financial Assistance to Church–Related Institutions	977
Governmental Encouragement of Religion in Public Schools: Released Time	991
Governmental Encouragement of Religion in Public Schools: Prayers and Bible Reading	993
Governmental Encouragement of Religion in Public Schools: Curriculum Restriction	996
Access of Religious Groups to School Property	997
Tax Exemptions of Religious Property	997
Exemption of Religious Organizations from Generally Applicable Laws	999
Sunday Closing Laws	999
Conscientious Objection	1000
Regulation of Religious Solicitation	1001
Religion in Governmental Observances	1002
Miscellaneous	1004

---

[5]The Charters of Freedom. *Constitution of the United States*. http://www.archives.gov/exhibits/charters/constitution.html http://www.archives.gov/exhibits/charters/constitution.html

[6]U.S. Constitution. 2010. http://topics.law.cornell.edu/constitution

Once John determined what part of the Constitution the issue involved, he went to that website and read the appropriate law and the accompanying annotations. John looked at the annotations listed on the website for the First Amendment (see the above as highlighted) and retrieved the following:

> **Sunday Closing Laws**—The history of Sunday Closing Laws goes back into United States colonial history and far back into English history. http://www.law.cornell.edu/anncon/html/amdt1afrag5_user.html **144** Commonly, the laws require the observance of the Christian Sabbath as a day of rest, although in recent years they have tended to become honeycombed with exceptions. The Supreme Court rejected an Establishment Clause challenge to Sunday Closing Laws in McGowan v. Maryland. http://www.law.cornell.edu/anncon/html/amdt1afrag5_user.html **145** The Court acknowledged [p. 1000] that historically the laws had a religious motivation and were designed to effectuate concepts of Christian theology. However, "[i]n light of the evolution of our Sunday Closing Laws through the centuries, and of their more or less recent emphasis upon secular considerations, it is not difficult to discern that as presently written and administered, most of them, at least, are of a secular rather than of a religious character, and that presently they bear no relationship to establishment of religion . . . " **146** "[T]he fact that this [prescribed day of rest] is Sunday, a day of particular significance for the dominant Christian sects, does not bar the State from achieving its secular goals. To say that the States cannot prescribe Sunday as a day of rest for these purposes solely because centuries ago such laws had their genesis in religion would give a constitutional interpretation of hostility to the public welfare rather than one of mere separation of church and State." **147** The choice of Sunday as the day of rest, while originally religious, now reflected simple legislative inertia or recognition that Sunday was a traditional day for the choice.**148** Valid secular reasons existed for not simply requiring one day of rest and leaving to each individual to choose the day, reasons of ease of enforcement and of assuring a common day in the community for rest and leisure.**149** More recently, a state statute mandating that employers honor the Sabbath day of the employee's choice was held invalid as having the primary effect of promoting religion by weighing the employee's Sabbath choice over all other interests.**150**[7]

The bold underlined numbers in this section of material are footnotes to primary authority that John could use to locate and read what he needed. Therefore, John obtained access to the U.S. Constitution, discussion, and references to sources. He remembered to make his research trail.

CITING THE LAW 10-1: CONSTITUTIONS

Constitutions are cited according to a format that includes three parts:

a. the name of the constitution as abbreviated
b. the article being cited
c. the section being cited

Here are examples of articles from the U.S. Constitution and state constitutions:

U.S. Const. art. I, § 1.
N.J Const. art. 2, ¶ 6.
Utah Const. art. VI, § 1.

---

[7]Sunday Closing Laws. http://www.law.cornell.edu/anncon/html/amdt1afrag5_user.html#amdt1a_hd19

Once the determination has been made that there is no constitutional question in the client's problem, the next step is to determine whether statutory law governs the client's issue.

STATUTES

The Making of Statutes

The U.S. Congress and all state legislative bodies pass enacted law generally called statutes. Congress has a *bicameral* body, and legislation may originate from either house in the form of *bills*. All states have a bicameral legislature except Nebraska, which has a *unicameral* legislature. The bills go through an extensive process to become law. Figure 10-1 shows how a bill becomes a law from proposal through committees, through votes in each house, and finally by action from the chief executive.

When analyzing statutes, researchers should also keep the concept of *federalism* in mind. Under the concept of federalism, states may not make laws that conflict with federal laws. Any state laws determined to be in conflict with federal laws will be declared unconstitutional.

Whether in the U.S. Congress or in a state legislature, a bill is referred to as an *engrossed bill* or an *enrolled bill*. An engrossed bill is the official legislative proposal prepared in final form for vote after being discussed and approved by appropriate committees. Engrossing generally occurs before bills receive a final voting passage in the house in which the bill originates or before a bill is sent to the opposite chamber. If one were to view an engrossed bill, it would be common to see the original language with "strike-out" provisions.

Enrolled bills are those that have been agreed to by both legislative bodies in an identical form. The enrolled bill must be exact in its deletion, amendment, substitution, or agreement by both bodies. The engrossed bill is presented to the enrolling clerk, either the enrolling clerk of the House or the secretary of the Senate, who prepares the enrolled bill for presentation to the president (or governor, if a state bill). Once the bill is certified, a slip is attached to the bill stating that the bill is truly enrolled. It is then sent to the Speaker of the House for signature. No matter which legislative body originates a bill, the enrolled bill must be signed first by the Speaker of the House, then by the vice president of the United States or the lieutenant governor in the state (who is president of the Senate). After appropriate signatures are obtained, a House bill is returned to the clerk for presentation to the president (or governor), while a Senate bill is returned to the secretary of the Senate for presentation to the president (or governor).

Federal Statutes

A proposed bill becomes law once the president signs it. If the president refuses to sign the bill (a "veto") Congress can override the president's veto by a two-thirds vote of each Congressional chamber. An enacted law is then sent to the Archivist of the United States, where the law is classified as *public* or *private*. Public laws, such as tax and bankruptcy laws, affect all citizens, while private laws, such as some immigration laws, affect only one person or a small group rather than the entire population.

Proposed bills are chronologically numbered. Whenever a law is passed, it is immediately published by the United States Government Printing Office (GPO) as a *slip law*. At the end of the legislative session, the slip laws are

Bicameral
Legislatures having two bodies or two houses, such as Congress, which has the House of Representatives and the Senate.

Bills
A proposed law that is identified by the house in which it originates, such as H.R. for House Resolution or S. for Senate.

Unicameral
A legislature that has only one body or one house, such as the Nebraska legislature.

Federalism
Federalism is a combination of bodies, such as nations or states, that exist for a common purpose.

Engrossed bill
Proposals that have been discussed and approved by appropriate committees and are prepared in a final form so that they can be voted on by legislative bodies.

Enrolled bill
The final copy of a bill or joint resolution that has passed both legislative bodies and is ready for signature by the appropriate officers, after which it will be presented to the president (or governor) for action.

Public laws
Laws, such as taxes and bankruptcy laws, that affect all citizens.

Private laws
Laws that affect only one person or a small group of people rather than the entire population.

Slip law
The bill approved and voted on by the legislature that is immediately published in a pamphlet or in single sheet form.

	House	Senate
Bill Introduced	The bill is introduced by a House member, the administration, or others, and assigned a number. It is then assigned to a committee, which usually refers it to a subcommittee. Exception: all revenue bills originate in the House.	The bill is introduced by a Senate member, the administration, or others, and assigned a number. It is then assigned to a committee, which usually refers it to a subcommittee.
Committee Action	**Subcommittee** Subcommittees perform studies, hold hearings, and make revisions. If the bill is approved here, it goes to the full committee. It is possible that a subcommittee will take no action. **Committee** Full committees may amend or rewrite the bill (mark-up) before deciding whether to send it to the House floor, recommend its approval, or kill it. If the bill is approved, the bill is reported to the full House and placed on the calendar for voice and vote. **Rules Committee** The Rules Committee issues a rule governing the debate on the House floor and sends the bill to the full House.	**Subcommittee** Subcommittees perform studies, hold hearings, and make revisions. If the bill is approved here, it goes to the full committee. It is possible that a subcommittee will take no action. **Committee** Full committees may amend or rewrite the bill (mark-up) before deciding whether to send it to the Senate floor, recommend its approval, or kill it. If the bill is approved, the bill is reported to the full Senate and placed on the calendar for voice and vote. **Rules Committee** The Rules Committee issues a rule governing the debate on the Senate floor and sends the bill to the full Senate.
Floor Action	**Full House** The bill is debated by the full House, amendments may be offered, and a vote is taken. If the bill passes in a version that is different from the version passed in the Senate, the bill is sent to a conference committee.	**Full Senate** The bill is debated by the full Senate, amendments may be offered, and a vote is taken. If the bill passes in a version that is different from the version passed in the House, the bill is sent to a conference committee.
Conference Action	**Conference Committee** Conference committees are composed of members of both the House and Senate who meet to negotiate the differences between the versions of the bills. The compromise bill is returned to both the House and Senate for a full-body vote.	
	Full House The full House votes on the conference committee version. If the joint version passes, the bill is sent to the president.	**Full Senate** The full Senate votes on the conference committee version. If the joint version passes, the bill is sent to the president.
Presidential Action	**President** The president can sign or veto the bill or do nothing. Congress may override a veto by a two-thirds (2/3) majority vote in both the House and Senate. If the bill is signed, the bill becomes law and is printed and codified.	

Note: Most states operate similarly.

FIGURE 10-1 How a Bill Becomes Law.[8] The process is of the U.S. Congress rather than of the state legislatures. U. S. Congress

collected and placed in chronological order. These are generally referred to as *session laws* because they are a compilation of the laws of a particular session of Congress or the legislature. The session laws are published in a series

[8]http://lib.lbcc.edu/handouts/images/polsci/billtolaw-sm.jpg

of hardbound volumes called *United States Statutes at Large* that contain the following:

- concurrent resolutions
- reorganization plans
- the Declaration of Independence
- the Articles of Confederation
- the Constitution
- proposed and ratified amendments to the Constitution
- proclamations by the President[9]

A similar process takes place in state legislatures.

Because the binding of the laws does not occur until the end of the legislative session, there is a significant passage of time before the laws in *Statutes at Large* are available. Several interim sources can be consulted for immediate access to the session laws, shown in Table 10-4.

TABLE 10-4   Sources of Federal Statutes before Publication of *U.S. Statutes at Large*

Publication	Coverage of Complete Text
Slip Laws	Found in libraries designated as U.S. Government Depository Libraries, generally in large cities and/or in major law school libraries. The slip laws are available generally within a week of enactment.
United States Code Congressional Administrative News Service (U.S.C.C.A.N.)	West issues this publication monthly. It contains *all* public laws, regulations, executive orders, and presidential proclamations issued during the previous month. The monthly pamphlets are bound at the end of each congressional session. Libraries and law firms can subscribe to this service.
United States Law Week (U.S.L.W.)	The Bureau of National Affairs (BNA) publishes the more significant public laws and summaries of recent cases weekly.
Government Printing Office (GPO)	Slip laws can be purchased from the GPO directly.
United States Code Service Advance Pamphlets (U.S.C.S.)	LexisNexis publishes this monthly pamphlet, which provides the text of new public laws and summaries of proposed legislation. This service also has tables that provide correlation to sections of the U.S. Code that have been affected by the new laws.
Subscription Services	Westlaw and LexisNexis provide quick access to newly enacted federal statutes, legislative history, committee reports, and debates.
Internet	Various sources on the Internet provide access to the federal statutes. One of the most comprehensive is provided through the Library of Congress on THOMAS. Another site is GPO Access at www.gpoaccess.gov/
Senator or Representative	The sponsor(s) of the legislation or the local representative(s) should be able to provide the text of the recently enacted legislation through their access to the Congressional Research Service.

[9]McKinney, Richard J. U.S. Statutes at Large: Documents and Information Included. 2004. http://www.llsdc.org/attachments/wysiwyg/544/us-statutes-contents.pdf

Once the congressional session ends, the session laws are **codified** and become **statutes**. Codifying a session law means taking a law, dividing it into parts, and organizing the parts with other "like" parts or subjects. There are 51 **titles** in the federal statutes. For example, all tax laws are placed in Title 26, the Internal Revenue Code. The **United States Code (U.S.C.),** first published in 1926, is the official version of federal statutes. The U.S.C. is not organized based on when the session law was passed—the key to codification is the subject matter.

Since 1926, the U.S.C. has been published every six years. In the interim, the publications are supplemented by pocket parts and annual cumulative supplements.[10] In addition to the U.S.C., the official publication of the code, there are two unofficial publications—**United States Code Annotated (U.S.C.A.)** and **United States Code Service (U.S.C.S.).**

Statutory language is not always clear, and a large part of the research process is reading the cases, which interpret or clarify the language of the statute. As with annotated constitutions, the annotated versions of statutes can be very helpful in legal research. The U.S.C.A. and U.S.C.S. are available in hard copy and through subscription legal databases such as Westlaw (for U.S.C.A.) and LexisNexis (for U.S.C.S.). Both databases contain the actual statutory language and are divided into the same 51 titles. The difference between the official and unofficial versions lies in the additional material that the unofficial (annotated) codes provide. Cases and other materials discuss the statute in question or provide additional information to explain or help a researcher work through a statutory issue.

Each unofficial version has its own enhancements. U.S.C.A. has the following:

- Historical Notes – the history of the statute with the Public Law number, effective date of the statute, *United States Statutes at Large* citation, and any added or deleted section information.
- Cross-References – other federal statutes that may have an impact on the statute being read.
- Federal Rules – any federal rule that may impact the statute.
- West's Federal Practice Manual references.
- Library References – other sources, such as form books or encyclopedias, that deal with the statutory topic.
- Westlaw Electronic Research – sample search queries for Westlaw.
- Code of Federal Regulations (C.F.R.) – citations to relevant regulations that may affect the statute.
- Notes to Decisions – exhaustive summaries or "blurbs" of information from cases or sample of cases that identify briefly how the statute was applied or discussed in a case and give the citation to the case in question. The case citations are grouped according to key words within the statute.
- References to texts and law review articles that comment on or explain the law.
- Statutory supplement published bimonthly that updates any public laws passed since the pocket part was published.

Codified

A formalized publication of the session laws, organized by subject.

Statutes

Laws that are enacted by the U.S. Congress and state legislatures as session laws and are codified by subject.

Titles

Divisions of the federal statutes; each title represents a topic under which the statutes are placed when codified.

United States Code (U.S.C.)

The official source of federal statutes.

United States Code Annotated (U.S.C.A.)

An unofficial source of federal statutes; published by West Publishing Company.

United States Code Service (U.S.C.S.)

An unofficial source of federal statutes originally published by Lawyer's Cooperative and currently published by LexisNexis.

[10]GPO Access United States Code: Main Page. 2009. http://www.gpoaccess.gov/uscode/.

Annotations

Notations that explain or comment upon the meaning of the information presented. When appended to statutes, the material is referred to as an annotated code or annotated statute.

Code of Federal Regulations **(C.F.R.)**

An annual publication of all executive agency regulations published in the *Federal Register* that are still in effect.

The *annotations* for U.S.C.S. are arranged similarly to those for U.S.C.A. but with a few differences. Only West publications and Westlaw (U.S.C.A.)use the West key number system. U.S.C.S. adds the following different materials:

- History – Ancillary Laws and Derivatives – (similar to Historical Notes in U.S.C.A.) the history of the statute with the Public Law number, effective date of the statute, *United States Statutes at Large* citation, and any added or deleted section information.
- **Code of Federal Regulations (*C.F.R.*)** – citations to relevant regulations that may affect the statute.
- Cross-references – other federal statutes that may have an impact on the statute.
- Research Guide – similar to Library References in U.S.C.A.; identifies other library resources that may be useful in working with the statute.
- Interpretive Notes and Decisions – Similar to U.S.C.A.'s Notes to Decisions feature; provides citations and short summaries of significant cases that have discussed or interpreted the statute, organized according to the key words in the statute.
- Cumulative Later Case and Statutory Service – issued three times a year, provides updates to the statutes. This service is cumulative.
- *Advance* – a monthly pamphlet issued after the *Cumulative Later Case and Statutory Service* that provides new laws that have not been codified, executive orders and presidential proclamations, and other executive documents.

U.S.C.S and U.S.C.A have other features in common, including the following:

A list of all 51 titles in the front of each volume.

Annotated code

A source for statutes, whether federal or state, that includes supplemental material such as citations to other primary and secondary authorities that explain or provide context for the statute.

Legislative intent

The goal or meaning that the legislature intended when it passed a law.

Legislative history

Any action that took place prior to the enactment of a statute, such as decisions or discussions in legislative committee meetings.

- The same *citation* format, with the exception of the inclusion of the publisher's annotations and other enhancements for unofficial versions.
- Conversion tables from Public Law or *U.S. Statutes at Large* citations to codified statutes and vice versa.
- Annual, cumulative pocket parts. If the pocket parts become too large, a separate soft-covered volume is created that acts as the pocket part.

Another helpful feature of an *annotated code* book is information about the *legislative intent* behind the law. Many legal issues center on the purpose of the law or the exact meaning of terms used in a law. Often, annotated codes will include references to *United States Code Congressional and Administrative News* (U.S.C.C.A.N.). This publication contains the *legislative history* of each bill, the original language of the bill, any transcripts of committee hearings, and any other available materials that might help determine the legislative intent.

State Statutes

State statutes are enacted by state legislative bodies. Each state, with the exception of Nebraska, has a bicameral legislature, meaning it has two houses. The process of enacting laws at the state level is largely the same as at the federal level, although the legislative chambers may have different names. For example, while most states have a House of Representatives, others have an Assembly or a House of Delegates.[11]

---

[11]National Conference of State Legislatures. 2010. http://www.ncsl.org

TABLE 10-5 Common Features of State Statutes

Feature	Purpose
State Constitution	Having access to the state constitution provides immediate access and readily available language.
Codification	Organized by subject so that all probate will be together, all criminal together and so on.
General Index	A general index will be either at the beginning or at the end of the set.
Title Index	Each title will be indexed within the volumes housing the title.
Pocket Parts	Statutes are updated with annual pocket parts or supplements.
Annotations	Annotations are provided in the unofficial sources of the state statutes containing cases, cross-references, and other resources.
Historical notes	These notes provide the statutory history with amendments and effective dates along with references to other library resources.
Tables	Conversion tables for finding the statute if the public law number or statutes at large citation is all that is available, as well as tables for repealed and renumbered statutes

State statutes are also first published as slip laws chronologically at the end of each legislative session, and these are usually referred to as *session laws*. Later they are codified and can be found by subject matter in state code books, just as the federal statutes are found. These laws also may be referred to as *public laws*, *statutes at large*, *codes*, *bills*, or *chaptered bills*. Most states publish the statutes by numerical title, similar to the way in which federal statutes are published, but with a slightly different appearance. For example, a federal statute would appear as 11 U.S.C. § 110 (2006). By comparison, a statute in Indiana would appear as Ind. Code. § 31-1-1-1 (2010). Some of the more heavily populated states, such as California, New York, and Texas, use topical names such as *Evidence Code*, *Civil Code*, or *Criminal Code*. Because each state is different, confirming the format through *The Bluebook*, *ALWD*, or another citation manual is important.

The state code books published by the government are the official statutes. Annotated versions or unofficial code books are frequently available. Just as with the federal statutes, official and unofficial state statutes both contain the same statutory language but the unofficial versions are annotated with additional tools to help the researcher understand and interpret the statute. All state code books are updated manually through the use of pocket parts. State statutes can be accessed through Westlaw and LexisNexis, as well as through other channels such as the state legislature's or state government's official homepage.

Most state codes have common features just as the federal statutes have. Some of the common features are found in Table 10-5.

While the federal resources refer to enhanced material as "annotations," a state's statutory code may identify the annotation section differently, such as "Notes to Decisions," "Related Topics," or "Relevant Cases."

The Elements of Statutes

Whether statutes are federal or state, they are not always clear in their language. Part of this is due to the fact that statutes are often created in a vacuum—the legislature may have enacted a statute without consulting other statutes that may be similar in substance.

Statutes may seem very confusing at first, but they are easier to understand if they are broken down into their *elements*. Elements are the major components

Session laws
Laws passed by a legislature during a session, printed chronologically by date of enactment rather than by topic.

Elements
The major components of a statute or other enacted law.

of the statute. They may be thought of as the parts that need to be proven to win or defend a case. The elements of the statute can serve as "road signs" that will guide in understanding the statute requirements. After research is concluded and the applicable law has been collected, a researcher should return to the statute and confirm that the facts of the client's situation are the same or substantially similar to the elements of the statute.

Example 10-2 involves a burglary statute. The example is set out just as it appears in the Indiana Code. A researcher needs to know the exact language because the language of the statute must be compared to the facts of the client's case to determine whether the client's situation is the same or sufficiently similar to elements of the statute.

Next, the statute must be broken down into its parts. The statute in the example seems fairly simple in its language, but other statutes may be very complex. No matter how simple or complex the statute may be, it is important to look at the entire statute and examine each of its parts. Each of the subsections of the statute is important, since each is an element that must be proven.

The highlighted words in the example are connecting language. The connecting terms are critical because they tell whether all or only some of the elements in a list must be proven. In Section 1, a person must break *and* enter. If the person breaks the glass but does not enter, that person has not committed burglary because the statute requires both elements. The client could commit some other crime, such as vandalism, but it would not be burglary. Burglary is considered a Class B felony if the person breaks and enters while armed with a deadly weapon *or* the building or structure is a dwelling *or* structure used for religious worship. If the offender breaks and enters a dwelling, it is a Class B felony, even if a deadly weapon is not used, since the word *or* connects those elements.

Uniform Laws

Governments, both federal and state, have the power to enact laws for their own entities as long as those laws do not exceed the limitations set in state or federal constitutions. Because each state has its own body of laws, confusion is created as

---

EXAMPLE 10-2   ELEMENTS OF A STATUTE

The Allworthy Law Firm had a new client, Doug Davidson, who was arrested on a charge of burglary. Jami and John had interviewed Doug and it was John's responsibility to research the state statute and identify the elements. The statute on burglary in Indiana, IC 35-43-2-1, contains this language:

Sec. 1. A person who breaks and enters the building or structure of another person, with intent to commit a felony in it, commits *burglary*, a Class C felony. However, the offense is:
(1) a Class B felony if:
   (A) it is committed while armed with a deadly weapon; or
   (B) the building or structure is a:
      (i) dwelling; or
      (ii) structure used for religious worship; and
(2) a Class A felony if it results in:
   (A) bodily injury; or
   (B) serious bodily injury;

to any person other than a defendant.

people move from state to state, engage in business with people in other states, or open offices or business operations in multiple states.

Legal experts saw a need to have greater uniformity in the laws, particularly in subjects such as business, crime, and probate. In 1892, the American Bar Association (ABA) recommended the formation of a nongovernmental body, now called the National Conference of Commissioners on Uniform State Laws (NCUSL), to promote "clarity and stability to critical areas of the law." The commissioners are qualified lawyers who have been appointed by the state executives, plus executives of the District of Columbia, Puerto Rico, and the U.S. Virgin Islands.[12] The ultimate goal is to create laws that are identical or substantially similar in all states, called **uniform laws**. This is a lofty goal, but in actuality it has not been particularly successful. In fact, approximately half of the proposals for uniform laws have not been adopted by any state.

To create a uniform law, the NCUSL drafts and approves a law, and presents it to each state legislature for consideration through the legislative process. By the time the uniform law is presented to a state legislature, the state may have laws in place that require the state to make changes to the proposed uniform law in order to pass it. Just as legislators revisit state statutes to make changes as warranted by changes in society, the commission revisits the uniform laws, which results in multiple versions. A state may adopt a uniform act as is, modify it, omit some sections, or completely reject it. A uniform law becomes primary authority only when the state adopts it. Otherwise, the proposed uniform law has no legal effect except as persuasive secondary authority.[13]

The process is not without its opponents. Exhibit 10-1 shows a portion of a letter from the Federal Trade Commission (FTC) to the chair of the NCCUSL, which expresses the FTC's objections to a proposed uniform law.

Uniform law
A prototype for a statute that has been created by the Uniform Law Commission and whose purpose is to create immediate uniformity on a particular topic among the states. Examples are the Uniform Probate Code and the Uniform Limited Partnership Act.

EXHIBIT 10-1 LETTER FROM FTC TO NCCUSL CHAIR

UNITED STATES OF AMERICA
FEDERAL TRADE COMMISSION
WASHINGTON, D.C. 20580

Bureau of Consumer Protection
Bureau of Competition
Policy Planning

July 9, 1999

Mr. John L. McClaugherty

Chair, Executive Committee
National Conference of Commissioners on Uniform State Laws
211 E. Ontario Street, Suite 1300
Chicago, Illinois 60611

Dear Mr. McClaugherty:

As the National Conference of Commissioners on Uniform State Laws (NCCUSL) prepares to consider adoption of the Uniform Computer Information Transactions Act (UCITA), the staff of the Bureaus of Consumer Protection

---

[12]Uniform Law Commission. *About the ULC.* 2012 http://www.uniformlaws.org/Narrative.aspx?title=About the ULC

[13]*Id.*

and Competition and of the Policy Planning office of the Federal Trade Commission (FTC) wishes to express the same consumer welfare concerns that it raised in its October 30, 1998 letter to Carlyle C. Ring and Professor Geoffrey Hazard, Jr. about UCITA's predecessor, Uniform Commercial Code Article 2B (August 1, 1998 draft).(1) Those concerns, with one exception, have not been addressed in any significant respect in UCITA.(2) We briefly summarize the October 30, 1998 letter and have attached a copy for your convenience.

UCITA endorses a license model for "computer information transactions."(3) For example, under UCITA a license to use software (rather than the sale of the software itself) would allow the licensor to limit or control how the licensee uses the software, even where the software has been mass-marketed to consumers. Examples of these limits or controls include restrictions on a consumer's right to sue for a product defect, to use the product, or even to publicly discuss or criticize the product.(4)

Unlike the law governing sales of goods, UCITA departs from an important principle of consumer protection that material terms must be disclosed prior to the consummation of the transaction. UCITA does not require that licensees be informed of licensing restrictions in a clear and conspicuous manner prior to the consummation of the transaction.(5)***

Respectfully submitted,

Joan Z. Bernstein, Director
Adam G. Cohn, Attorney
Division of Marketing Practices
Bureau of Consumer Protection

William J. Baer, Director
David A. Balto, Assistant Director for Policy and Evaluation
Bureau of Competition

Susan S. DeSanti, Director
Michael S. Wroblewski, Advocacy Coordinator
Policy Planning

FEDERAL TRADE COMMISSION
600 Pennsylvania Ave., NW
Washington, DC 20580

cc: NCCUSL Members

Attachment

1. This letter represents the views of the Bureaus of Consumer Protection and Competition and of the Policy Planning office and does not necessarily represent the views of the FTC or any individual Commissioner. The FTC, however, has authorized the staff to submit this letter.

***14

Here are some of the most widely adopted uniform laws:

- Uniform Commercial Code (UCC)
- Uniform Partnership Act (UPA)
- Uniform Probate Code (UPC),

14Federal Trade Commission, Bureau of Consumer Protection. 1999. http://www.ftc.gov/be /990010.shtm

- Uniform Child Custody Jurisdiction Act (UCCJA)
- Uniform Child Custody Jurisdiction and Enforcement Act (UCCJEA)
- Uniform Interstate Family Support Act (UIFSA)

The UCC is the most widely adopted set of uniform laws, and often forms the substance of commercial transactions or contracts classes in law school. Indiana's adoption of the UCC, Indiana's I.C. 26-1-1 *et seq.*, is actually called the "Uniform Commercial Code."

Closely related to uniform laws are **model acts**, which have the purpose of reforming statutes, rather than promoting uniformity. The NCUSL has proposed several model acts, as has the American Law Institute (ALI). If a uniform act fails to be adopted by a significant number of legislatures, the NCUSL may propose a model act rather than a uniform law. The Model Penal Code is probably the most frequently referenced model act, which both the NCUSL and the ALI worked on together. Model acts are sponsored by many respected entities, such as the American Bar Association (ABA). For example, the ABA supported the creation of the Model Business Corporation Act.[15]

Table 10-6 summarizes some of the better-known collections of uniform laws.

Model acts

Prototypes for statutes that may be adopted by legislatures. The purpose of model acts is to attempt to make laws uniform among the various jurisdictions. An example is the Model Business Corporation Act.

TABLE 10-6   Sample of Sources of Uniform Laws

Title and Publisher	Contents
Print Materials	
Uniform Laws Annotated West	ULA provides the text of uniform laws and model acts along with comments from commission, adopting states and date of adoption, description of modifications by states, cross references to other primary and secondary materials, access to West's key number system and other West products. No general index or table of contents. Contents are grouped by subject matter.
Uniform Laws Annotated Directory of Acts West	This directory lists all laws alphabetically and cites to the *Uniform Laws Annotated.* Also lists each state and the uniform laws that state has adopted.
Corpus Juris Secundum West	This encyclopedia has a Table of Laws and Rules that references sections within the encyclopedia where the uniform laws appear.
American Jurisprudence 2d West	This encyclopedia also has a Table of Laws and Rules to direct researchers to the appropriate sections within the service.
Martindale-Hubbell Reed Publishing	This directory contains the full text of more than 50 uniform laws and model acts in the law digest volume.
Online	
Westlaw	All uniform laws and model acts are available on Westlaw.
Lexis/Nexis	Some of the uniform laws are available.
National Conference of Commissioners on Uniform State Laws	The website for the commission, www.nccusl.org, houses the full text of all laws as well as a variety of additional information such as the adoption statistics by state and the commission comments.
Internet in general	There are numerous Internet sites where you can find the uniform laws and model acts. The following are examples: *American Law Source Online* at http://www.lawsource.com/also/usa.cgi?usm; Uniform Laws and Model Acts from Harvard Law School at http://www.law.harvard.edu/library/research/guides/united_states/uniform-laws-and-model-acts.html and Law by source: Uniform Laws from Cornell University Law School at http://www.law.cornell.edu/uniform/vol9.html.
State government websites	Various government websites have uniform laws available, such as Michigan Commission on Uniform State Laws at http://council.legislature.mi.gov/mcusl.html.

[15]American Law Sources: United States – Uniform Laws and Model Acts. 2012. http://www.lawsource.com/also/usa.cgi?usm

Any of the print materials will likely have an index that can be searched using the descriptive word approach. However, some services group the uniform laws and model acts by subject matter rather than indexing them by law alphabetically.

Researching Statutes

When researching statutes, the first step is to determine whether federal or state law applies, and if it is a question of state law, which state governs. The following issues should be considered when making this determination:

Some subjects are governed exclusively by state law, and some subjects exclusively by federal law. Some subjects are governed by both.

- While the client is subject to the jurisdiction of a state, the client may be subjected to the jurisdiction of the federal laws, too. State laws can be different from federal laws but the state laws may not be in conflict with the federal laws.
- Clients are subject to the jurisdiction of any place where they reside.
- They also may be subject to the jurisdiction of a place such as where they do business, where they visit, or where they work.
- If a client uses the benefits or services of a place, the client is subject to that place's rules and regulations. So, if the client is a resident of Georgia but is driving in Montana, the client is subject to the driving laws of Montana.

Once the jurisdiction is determined, the statutes of that jurisdiction are researched, and the relevant statutes are located.

A legal issue is easy to connect to a statute if a *citation* is provided in a problem. Once the physical book that contains the statute has been found, any supplements to that book must also be located to be sure all the information is gathered. When a statute is found online, the supplement is part of the statute. Checklist 10-1 outlines a research method for statutes.

Citation
The "address" of a source, such as 42 U.S.C.A. § 100 (West 2000. This cite means the reader should look in Title 42 of the *United States Code Annotated* under section 100 for the statute.

Checklist 10-1   RESEARCHING STATUTES

1. **Analyze your problem**
   a. Start the *research trail* that provides a method to track the sources that have been located.
   b. Use the *key words* from the assignment to research in the indices sources of enacted law being searched.
   c. Consider using alternate words—synonyms and antonyms of the key words—as search terms.
   d. Consider words that describe the parties, places, things, issue, and acts or omissions involved to expand the search.
   e. Think of various alternative subject matter entries, along with synonyms and antonyms, which might be found in the index. Think like a lawyer would think in determining these alternatives! Review client files that were based on similar issues to see how the documents, pleadings, briefs, or other writings were prepared to obtain additional hints on where to search.

Research trail
A method of tracking the sources one has looked at and making notes as one performs research for a particular assignment.

Key words
Words in a problem that if different or nonexistent would change the outcome.

2. **Find the statutes**

 a. If there is a direct citation, go to the appropriate source. Determine whether the enacted law is current by checking the **pocket part** or **supplement**, if available. If accessing online in a subscription service or government website, the law will be updated automatically.

 b. If there is no citation, begin with an index search.

 c. Use the key words from the issue to search the index in both the main volume and in the pocket part of the enacted law.

 d. Keep in mind that there is not a single set of books that provides every law for every state. Consult the state statutes for the individual states.

3. **Search the index**

 a. Using the appropriate index volumes, conduct a topic search in both the main volume and the pocket part for the appropriate citation.

 b. If the general information is located but there is not a complete citation, turn to the chapter and continue with step 4.

4. **Locate the law**

 a. Review the table of contents in both the main volume and the pocket part to locate an applicable enacted law such as a statute.

 b. If the search is thorough but nothing is found, it may be possible to conclude there is no applicable statutory law. Caveat: Be sure the supervisor or opposing counsel does not find the applicable law. Check and then check again just to make sure.

5. **Determine how current the law is**

 a. Consult the interim supplement (if any) or pocket part to determine whether the enacted law, as set down in the main volume, is still current, has been **amended**, **revised**, or possibly **repealed**.

 b. Consult any other applicable service, such as the statute legislative service, to further determine whether the law is current.

6. **Read the law**

 a. Carefully read the current text of the enacted law, as applicable, in the main volume, the pocket part, or the legislative service.

 b. If necessary, read the statute's history, amendments, or legislative history to understand the background of the law.

 c. Outline the law or break it into its elements, meaning those parts that are important in the statute. Look for **connecting language**.

7. **Read the additional references listed**

 Having determined the current text of the enacted law and broken it into its elements, read the applicable references to other materials in the main volume, the pamphlet supplements (if any), and the pocket part.

 a. Check first through the **cross-references** to determine if there is any additional relevant primary or secondary material. This information will appear at the end of the language of the law.

 b. Peruse any listed law review commentaries for possible applicable references to other sources such as law journal articles.

 c. Note any library references to the West **key number** system and encyclopedia topics for further exploration, if available.

 d. Review the "**Notes to Decisions**."

 1. Narrow the focus to particular categories by first checking out the descriptive word index in the main volume and the pocket parts.

 2. Turn to the applicable **headnotes** for useful case law if using a West product. Note the citations and look up the cases.

 (*Continued*)

Pocket part or supplement
A method that many publishers use to provide updated information that supplements the main volume of information.

Amended
Describes a preexisting law that has been corrected or changed.

Revised
A preexisting law that has been corrected or updated.

Repealed
A preexisting law that is annulled, generally by the enactment of a newer law.

Connecting language
Connecting language refers to terms such as "and" and "or" as used in a statute. If "and" is used, all elements are required. If "or" is used, a choice of elements is allowed.

Cross-references
References to other authorities that provide additional information.

Key number
A number assigned to each point of law (headnote) created by the West Publishing Company editors.

Headnote
A single point of law created by the West Publishing Company editors that appears at the beginning of cases published by West.

8. **Read the decisions**
   a. Carefully read the judicial opinion for the court's interpretation of the statute's language. Do not draw any conclusions from the headnotes; they reflect the analysis of an editor, not the court that decided the case.
   b. If the enacted law has an extensive list of decisions, use the topical headings to narrow the applicable cases.
   c. If the judicial opinion seems to apply, *brief the case*.
9. **Update the case law**
   a. Review any updating or validating service to make sure the enacted law is still "good law" and to locate additional cases that construe the enacted law.
   b. Peruse the enacted law list in front of the regional reporter bound volumes issued after the most recent legislative service pamphlet for any additional cases.
   c. Turn to the statutory tables in front of the latest reporter advance sheets for additional cases.

Brief the case
Reading an opinion and extracting the major elements in order to better understand the case.

Research in federal statutes may require searching in the *United States Statutes at Large*, which is cumbersome at best, and frustrating in general. The laws are arranged chronologically, so laws on one specific subject, such as tax law, could be located in a variety of entries within numerous volumes. If a law is subsequently amended or repealed, that information is not placed with the original law but rather will appear chronologically when it was passed. For example, a law enacted in 2000 but amended in 2002 and 2009 would require a researcher to look in all three volumes to find the complete information. If only the public law number or *Statutes at Large* reference is known, U.S.C.A. and U.S.C.S. have tables to convert those numbers to the statutory citation.

It is not necessary to consult all three versions of the United States Code (U.S.C, U.S.C.S., and U.S.C.A.). All volumes have a binding that is printed with the code sections contained within that volume. Once the researcher has located the citation for the statute, the next step is to find that statute. To find 18 USC § 121, the paralegal would look for the volume of the *United States Code* containing Title 18 and then locate section 121 within Title 18.

Good researching means checking all pocket parts and annual supplements. U.S.C. is updated with annual hardbound supplements plus slip laws in *U.S. Law Week*, U.S.C.C.A.N., and the GPO website.[16] U.S.C.A. is updated with annual pocket parts, or soft-cover pamphlets if the pocket part is too big. It is also updated with statutory supplements, slip laws, and the GPO website. U.S.C.S. is updated with annual pocket parts or soft-cover pamphlets, *Cumulative Later Case and Statutory Service, Advance,* slip laws, and the GPO website.

There are three main research techniques for finding statutes. The first is the descriptive word method, using the indices of the code books. The indices are separate, generally soft-covered volumes that are replaced each year. The key words from the client's case serve as the words to use to search these indices. The key words should be expanded by considering synonyms and antonyms. The investigative technique of the "five Ws and an H"—who, what, when, where, why, and how—can provide additional search terms covering who is involved, what is being

[16]GPO Access. 2012. http://www.gpo.gov/fdsys/browse/collectionUScode.action?collection Code=USCODE

considered, when the incident took place, where the incident took place, why the incident occurred, and how the incident occurred. Another approach is to think of the key words in terms of things, actions, persons, and places.

Like many resource publications, the indices offer some help. If one looks up a word and the publisher actually has used a different word, the publisher provides direction to the appropriate location. For example, if one used the term "bastards" but the content was under "children born out of wedlock," the publisher would provide a message such as "Children Born Out of Wedlock, this index." The researcher would then look under "Children Born Out of Wedlock." Another useful tool from the publishers is that the statutes are indexed under various terms or phrases for the same statute. Therefore, a statute can be found in numerous places within the index.

Statutes may also be researched using the topic or title approach. The statutes are divided into 51 titles. Researchers become familiar with the content under each title as they work with the titles, and going to the title may be easier than going to the index. For example, if a paralegal works in tax law, the paralegal will already know that Title 26 contains the Internal Revenue Code (I.R.C.) or tax statutes. Instead of going to the index and using "tax" or "internal revenue" to search the index, the paralegal would go directly to Title 26 and look at the table of contents. At the end of each title is an index for the statutes in that title. This method is useful for the paralegal who is very familiar with the coverage of the title and the contents within it. But if the paralegal is new to research, using the descriptive word method in the ***general index*** may be the best choice. By using the general index, the terms can be checked in a variety of places that may lead to the statute being covered by more than one title.

General index
Most research materials, particularly finding aids, have an index. The index may be a general index located in separate volumes or may be volume indexes.

Another method often used is the popular name approach. Megan's Law and the Amber Alert are two examples of statutes with popular names. These are names that were given to the statute by Congress, and are known among members of the general public. Other examples of popular names are the Death in Custody Reporting Act, the Holocaust Victim Redress Act, and the 1992 Winter Olympic Commemorative Coin Act. Popular names may also use the names of the sponsors of the legislation, such as the Sarbanes-Oxley Act, the Humphrey-Durham Drug Prescriptions Act, or the Wadsworth-Burke Bill. The U.S.C. has a table entitled "Acts Cited by Popular Name," located in the volume for Title 50. Both U.S.C.A. and U.S.C.S. have a separate volume titled *Popular Name Table*. The federal laws known by popular names are listed alphabetically, and the table directs the user to the appropriate title and section. If a researcher knows only part of the name or knows the subject the statute covered, the table often provides direction to another entry in the index. For example, if the researcher were looking for the Wage-Hour Bill, the index entry would point to the Fair Labor Standards Act of 1938. The Fair Labor Standards Act of 1938 would then state the official location: "June 25, 1939, ch. 676, 52 Stat. 1060 (29 U.S.C. 201 et. seq.) Short title, see 29 U.S.C. 201."

The search tools are similar for the electronic versions in Westlaw and LexisNexis.

For example, if one is searching in Westlaw, and has the citation, the citation can be typed into the *Find by Citation* box in the left hand corner of the Welcome page. If a citation is not known, or if a detailed search is needed, the first step is to enter the appropriate database, such as for Indiana Statutes Annotated (IN-ST-ANN). A query box would appear. Above the query box are hyperlinks to "find by citation", "table of contents", and "popular name table". To use the table of contents, a researcher could browse the table by clicking the plus (+) and minus (−) symbols next to titles that appear to relate to the statute being sought. The subparts of each section expand in a similar fashion. Using a statutes index is similar to using the table of contents with the plus and minus symbols.

In the alternative, a researcher might use one of the statute fields available. The fields are provided in a drop-down menu on the query box page. Two of the most common are the preliminary (pr) and caption (ca) fields, which are used with terms that logically might appear in the statute. The preliminary field contains terms in the title, sections, parts, and chapters of a statute. The caption field contains words and section numbers for a particular section. Another often-used field is topic (to) which contains the body or language of the statute.

Another reference tool is *Shepard's Acts and Cases by Popular Name: Federal and State* that provides citations to those federal and state statutes and cases known by popular names. The names are listed in alphabetical order for easy access. In addition, the service provides citations to *United States Statutes at Large* that give the public law number and the year of enactment.

In some cases, a case may present a "question of first impression" in a jurisdiction, meaning that the case involves a statutory provision that has not yet been interpreted by the courts. If there is no case law in that jurisdiction on the provision, outside case law may be found by researching the uniform act or model law that the statute is based on. This information can be found on the NCCUSL website. There, the researcher may find comments on the drafting of the law, as well as information on other states that have adopted the model act or uniform law. The cases from the other states may then be reviewed for their interpretations. The cases from other states, while primary authority, are only persuasive authority in the home jurisdiction. These primary persuasive authorities will be more effective than secondary materials because they interpret a statute that is similar in language to the statute in the jurisdiction in question. By contrast, the comments from the drafters of the uniform law or model act are secondary authority. These comments provide insight into the law's purpose and background, but the court can choose to disregard these comments.

TIP

No matter what service is used to research statutes, remember to check each pocket part and cumulative supplement to confirm that the material being read is current and complete. Failure to update the sources used breaches one's ethical duty to the supervisor and perhaps breaches one's duty of candor to the court.

CITING THE LAW 10-2: STATUTES AND SESSION LAWS

All citations to statutes in the U.S.C., U.S.C.A., and U.S.C.S. have the following common elements:

- Title number
- Publication
- Section symbol
- Section number
- Year of code in parentheses
- For unofficial sources, the publisher appears in the year of code

Here are some examples of a statute citation as it would be presented in all three services:

title number   publication   section symbol

section number

- 26 U.S.C. § 50 (2006)

year of code

- 26 U.S.C.A. § 50 (West 2006)
- 26 U.S.C.S § 50 (LexisNexis 2006) (*The Bluebook* style)
- 26 U.S.C.S § 50 (Lexis 2006) (*ALWD* style)
- Ind. Code § 31-1-1-1 (2003)
- Ind. Code Ann. § 31-1-1-1 (West 2003)

publisher

It is accepted practice to cite to any of the sources, whether official or unofficial, but one should not cite to any material found in the annotation itself. If material in the annotation is needed, one should go to the original source, read it, and then cite the source if it is appropriate to use.

Because statutory citations vary across the states, the citation manual should always be checked for the proper format.

Session laws contain the following:

- the official or popular name of the statute (or if not named, "Act of [full date]")
- the public law number ("Pub. L. No.") or equivalent state designation (for federal statutes enacted before 1957, use the chapter number)
- the source, consisting of a volume or year number followed by the abbreviated name of the publication ("Stat." for *Statutes at Large),* followed by the page number where the statute begins
- the year of enactment, in parentheses (omit if the year already appears in the name of the statute)
- parenthetical information indicating the current version as it appears in the codified law (or a cite to the amending act or acts)

Examples: **popular name   year of enactment   public law number**

Farm Security and Rural Investment Act of 2002, Pub. L. No. 107-171, 116 Stat. 134 ←——— **source**

Domestic Volunteer Service Act Amendments of 1984, Pub. L. No. 98-288, 98 Stat. 189 (1984)(current version at 42 U.S.C. §§ 4950-5085 (1994 & Supp. I 1995)

current version

LEGISLATIVE HISTORY

Foundational Principles for Using Legislative History

Legislative history is not enacted law. It is any action that took place prior to the statute being enacted, and any documents created from that action. These actions and documents may help a researcher in understanding a particular statute. For example, a bill is usually assigned to a committee that meets to discuss the bill and subsequently reports on the meeting. These reports of meetings are collected. By reading these reports, a researcher can gain insight into the purpose of a statute, and why particular words were chosen when the statute was drafted.

Table 10-7 shows a sample of how a bill might travel through Congress and lists the historical documents that may be created during that process.

In addition to the documents listed above, there are several services that provide information about legislative actions. Some have been mentioned previously:

- *U.S. Code Congressional & Administrative News* (U.S.C.C.A.N.)
- *Congressional Information Service Annual* (CIS)
- *Commerce Clearing House* (CCH) *Congressional Index*
- House and Senate Journals
- Digest of Public General Bills and Resolutions
- *Congressional Monitor*
- *Congressional Quarterly*[17]
- Monthly Catalog of U.S. Documents

[17]CQ Roll Call Group: Legislative Tracking. 2012. http://corporate.cqrollcall.com/wmspage .cfm?parm1=12

TABLE 10-7 How Legislative History Is Made

Action	Documents Created
Bill introduced by member of Congress	Printed bill
	Statement by Congressperson introducing bill
	Congressional Record
Hearing on bill by one house	Hearing transcripts
Recommendations by committee	Committee report
Debate on one house's floor	Congressional Record
House passes bill	Congressional Record
Hearing by other house	Hearing transcripts
House amends the bill	Printed amendment
Committee recommends to the full house	Committee report
Debate is held in second house	Congressional Record
Amendment to the bill is proposed	Printed amendment
	Congressional Record
Second house rejects amendment and passes bill	Congressional Record
A *conference committee* looks for compromise on disputed versions of the bill and reports recommendations to full Congress	Conference committee report
Debate held in each house over conference committee recommendations	Congressional report[18]

Conference committee

A joint committee consisting of members of each legislative house that seeks a compromise on disputed versions of the bill; it makes recommendations to the full Congress.

Many of these sources are available both in print and online, particularly in subscription services or on THOMAS.[19]

Although it may factor into some decisions, courts are not required to rely on legislative history, no matter how persuasive it is. In fact, many critics, such as Supreme Court Justice Antonin Scalia, argue that public laws should be interpreted strictly based on the statutory language.[20]

Bills that travel through state legislatures do not have legislative histories comparable to those of congressional bills. Often the state legislatures' materials are incomplete and difficult to acquire. Some states, however, have improved the process of tracking bills and obtaining information on them. For example, the Indiana government website has a Bills & Resolutions page for legislation in which one might find the conference committee reports and complete information on each bill. See Exhibit 10-2.

The "Action List" gives a listing of what happened, when, and where. The "Introduced Bill" gives the exact language of the proposal. The hyperlinks are

[18]Federal Legislative History. 2011. http://libguides.law.ucla.edu/federallegislativehistory

[19]The Library of Congress: THOMAS. 2010. http://thomas.loc.gov/

[20]McKinney, Richard J. and Sweet, Ellen A. Law Librarians' Society of Washington, D.C. *Federal Legislative History Research: A Practitioner's Guide to Compiling the Documents and Sifting for Legislative Intent.* 2008. http://www.llsdc.org/Fed-Leg-Hist/

EXHIBIT 10-2 INDIANA LEGISLATIVE OFFERINGS

Senate Bill 0001

2012 Second Regular Session

Latest Information

DIGEST OF SB 1 (Updated March 1, 2012 11:52 am - DI 84)

Self defense. Specifies that a person may use reasonable force against any other person in certain circumstances. Provides that a person is justified in using reasonable force against a law enforcement officer if the person reasonably believes the force is necessary to: (1) protect the person or a third person from unlawful force; (2) prevent or terminate the law enforcement officer's unlawful entry into the person's dwelling; or (3) prevent or terminate the law enforcement officer's criminal interference with property lawfully in the person's possession. Specifies that a person is not justified in using force against a law enforcement officer if: (1) the person is committing or is escaping after the commission of a crime; (2) the person provokes action by the law enforcement officer with intent to injure the law enforcement officer; (3) the person has entered into combat with the law enforcement officer or is the initial aggressor; or (4) the person reasonably believes the law enforcement officer acting lawfully or is engaged in the lawful execution of the law enforcement officer's official duties. Provides that a person is not justified in using deadly force against a law enforcement officer who the person knows or reasonably should know is a law enforcement officer unless: (1) the person reasonably believes that the law enforcement officer is acting unlawfully or is not engaged in the execution of the officer's official duties; and (2) the force is reasonably necessary to prevent serious bodily injury to the person or a third person.

Current Status:

Returned to House of Origin with Amendments

Latest Printing (PDF)

- Action List
- Introduced Bill
- Fiscal Impact Statement(s): 1(PDF), 2(PDF), 3(PDF), 4(PDF), 5(PDF), 6(PDF)
- Roll Call(s): No. 35(PDF), No. 312(PDF), No. 7377(PDF), No. 7676(PDF)
- House Committee Reports
  - Filed Committee Reports: 0001-1, 0001-1(PDF)
  - Passed Committee Reports: 0001-1, 0001-1(PDF)
- House Amendments
  - Filed: 0001-1, 0001-1(PDF), 0001-2, 0001-2(PDF)
  - Passed: 0001-2(PDF)

Senate Bill

- Senate Committee Reports
- Filed Committee Reports: 0001-1, 0001-1(PDF)
- Passed Committee Reports: 0001-1, 0001-1(PDF)
- Senate Amendments
- Conference Committee Reports[21]

---

[21]Indiana General Assembly. Senate Bill 0001. 2012 Second Regular Session. 2012. http://www.in.gov/apps/lsa/session/billwatch/billinfo?year=2012&session=1&request=getBill&doctype=SB&docno=0001

to actions taken. The bill shown in Exhibit 10-2 involved many actions, but not all bills have as much activity. Generally, if a bill will affect a large number of people, will fiscally impact the state, or is in a new area of legislation, there will be more activity. However, the information on most bills will be minimal. If searching for the legislative history of local laws, such as council or board ordinances, the availability of information can be much harder to locate, if it can be found at all.

The main reason to study legislative history is to find support for the **_legislative intent_**. Understanding what happened and why it happened can help resolve ambiguities in the language and purpose of the statute. When reading the statute and the legislative history together, the researcher can infer what the legislature intended, first by looking at the **_plain meaning_** of the language and then by finding support through the discussions of the bill. Statements may be found within the legislative history, such as why the particular bill was introduced, what impetus directed the introduction of the bill, or what problems were meant to be solved.

Researching Legislative History

Researching legislative history can be tedious and confusing. The process of reading legislative history is complex and involves multiple sources. A mountain of material can be gathered about a single piece of legislation by looking at the various versions of a bill, reading transcripts from the committee hearings, reading committee reports, and reading the remarks of speakers from debates. Table 10-7 and Exhibit 10-2 provide samples of the various locations of legislative materials. Example 10-3 illustrates how this process might unfold.

As the example shows, compiling a legislative history requires thoroughness and persistence. Although the search may not yield positive results, it is nevertheless worth the effort because occasionally the researcher will find something that will aid in interpreting a statute.[22]

Example 10-3 is only one example of the trail the researcher will follow in researching legislative history. Each time legislative history is searched, a researcher deals with different historical documents, depending on the bill. The process that is discussed above is for legislative history after 1970. The process is slightly different for pre-1970 legislative history.[23] The first place to start is to read the statute and review the historical notes. See Exhibit 10-3.

Most importantly, in Exhibit 10-3, the Public Laws and citations to _United States Statutes at Large_ are provided. Sometimes a West product will direct a researcher to U.S.C.C.A.N. and if so, the researcher should review that material right after reading the statute. U.S.C.C.A.N. provides insight into legislative intent as well as committee reports or other information. It also can provide the Public Law number if it is not already available.

The process of collecting the documents to make up the legislative history begins with the Public Law number. The first place to look is U.S.C.C.A.N., but there are several other useful tools that provide a variety of information, as shown in Table 10-8.

The information can be researched on subscription databases, such as Westlaw, as shown in Table 10-9.

---

[22]Edwards, Richard. C. _Researching Legislative History_. 2008. http://www.ilga.gov/commission/lrb/lrbres.htm

[23]McKinney, Richard J. and Sweet, Ellen A. Law Librarians' Society of Washington, D.C. _Federal Legislative Research: A Practitioner's Guide, Part II_ . 2009. http://www.llsdc.org/fed-leg-hist2/

Legislative intent
The intent or meaning that the legislature intended when it passed a law.

Plain meaning
The everyday meaning that an average person would attribute to words.

EXAMPLE 10-3   RESEARCHING LEGISLATIVE HISTORY

A new client, Stephen Jones, came to Allworthy Law Firm asking Jami to defend him on charges of perpetrating a sexual act upon a child under the age of 13. A question has arisen concerning a jury instructions regarding whether certain hearsay testimony can be admitted at trial. John researched the issue and found that these instructions are required by subsection (c) of Section 115-10 of the Illinois Code of Criminal Procedure of 1963 (725 ILCS 5/115-10(c)). However, there is a question about the reason the jury instruction is required. This requires looking at legislative history.

A search of Section 115-10 in the state's annotated statutes reveals that the requirement to give jury instructions was added to that section by P.A. 85-837.

The next step is to determine what bill became P.A. 85-837 and when the bill was passed. This is found by looking up the Public Act in the Session Laws. P.A. 85-837 was House Bill 2591 of the 85th General Assembly and was passed on June 30, 1987.

The final Legislative Synopsis and Digest for the calendar year 1987 is the next place to look. The synopses reveal that the jury instruction requirement was added to the bill by Senate Amendment No. 1. Senate Amendments Nos. 2 and 3, which did not relate to jury instructions, were also adopted. No amendments were offered and defeated; if any amendments had been offered and defeated, they might be an indication of what the legislature did not intend by House Bill 2591. Sponsors, committee assignments, total votes, and other matters are also indicated in the Digest. The bill was heard in the House Judiciary II Committee and in the Senate Judiciary Committee.

The House Journal and Senate Journal indicate the following concerning House Bill 2591:

1. Heard in the House Judiciary II Committee on May 7, 1987.
2. Passed the House on a Consent Calendar on May 22, 1987. Because the bill was on a Consent Calendar there is virtually no likelihood that there was floor debate.
3. Heard by the Senate Judiciary Committee on June 10, 1987.
4. Senate Amendment No.1 was adopted on the floor of the Senate on June 23, 1987. Senate Amendments Nos. 2 and 3 were adopted on June 25, 1987.
5. The bill, as amended, passed the Senate on June 26, 1987.
6. On June 27, 1987 the House concurred in Senate Amendments Nos. 1 and 2 and refused to concur in Senate Amendment No. 3.
7. The Senate refused to recede from Senate Amendment No. 3 on June 29, 1987, and a conference committee was requested and appointed.
8. On June 30, 1987 both the House and Senate approved the first conference committee report.

A copy of Senate Amendment No. 1, which adds the new language concerning jury instructions, is found in the Senate Journal for June 23, 1987 and may also be obtained from the State Archives.

A tape of the House Judiciary II Committee hearing on May 7, 1987 is available from the Office of the Clerk of the House. The tape, however, contains no discussion of the jury instruction requirement because that language was added later by Senate amendment. As previously noted, tapes are not available for Senate committee hearings.

Transcripts of the Senate and House floor debates may be obtained from the General Assembly website or from the Index Department. The transcripts, however, contain no debate on the jury instruction issue.

John's search of the legislative history of House Bill 2591 has so far proved fruitless. That is not necessarily the end of the story, however. Often in the legislative process, proposed language will migrate from bill to bill as the sponsor looks for a way to pass the proposal out of both houses. Therefore, he needs to search further.

The Senate sponsor of House Bill 2591 indicated in floor debate that Senate Amendment No. 1, which contained the jury instruction language, was the same as Senate Bill 1377 of the 85th General Assembly. A search of the Legislative Synopsis and Digest indices and synopses also would have indicated this. Thus, the next step is to compile a legislative history of Senate Bill 1377 because it contained language identical to that in Senate Amendment No. 1 to House Bill 2591.

If a search of Senate Bill 1377 also proves fruitless, he would look through the Digest indices for the 85th as well as one or more previous General Assemblies. As is often the case with legislative proposals, the language may have been around for several years before becoming law. Somewhere along the way someone may have said or done something significant with respect to the jury instruction issue.

Finally, bills may have been introduced in the General Assembly after the passage of House Bill 2591 (P.A. 85-837) to amend the jury instruction language. Even though these bills did not become law, they still could have a bearing on the interpretation of the jury instruction language. For example, the changes proposed by a failed bill could be an indication of what the language of P.A. 85-837 does not mean; otherwise, presumably, the changes would not have been proposed. Whatever implications may be drawn from these failed bills, it is worth the effort to search legislative history. This search begins by checking the statutes index of the Legislative Synopsis and Digest for all periods of time around and after the date when House Bill 2591 passed the General Assembly.

EXHIBIT 10-3 STATUTE AND HISTORICAL INFORMATION (FROM WESTLAW)

"20 U.S.C.A. § 1080" to "(a) Notice to Secretary and payment of loss" = the title from which the citation appears. The researcher can see the topical information of the section.

20 U.S.C.A. § 1080

United States Code Annotated Currentness

Title 20. Education

Chapter 28. Higher Education Resources and Student Assistance (Refs & Annos)

- Subchapter IV. Student Assistance (Refs & Annos)

- Part B. Federal Family Education Loan Program (Refs & Annos)

§ 1080. Default of student under Federal loan insurance program

"Upon default by the student" to "(d) … ." = the body of the statute.

(a) Notice to Secretary and payment of loss

Upon default by the student borrower on any loan covered by Federal loan insurance pursuant to this part, and prior to the commencement of suit or other enforcement proceedings upon security for that loan, the insurance beneficiary shall promptly notify the Secretary, and the Secretary shall if requested (at that time or after further collection efforts) by the beneficiary, or may on the Secretary's own motion, if the insurance is still in effect, pay to the beneficiary the amount of the loss sustained by the insured upon that loan as soon as that amount has been determined. The "amount of the loss" on any loan shall, for the purposes of this subsection and subsection (b) of this section, be deemed to be an amount equal to the unpaid balance of the principal amount and accrued interest, including interest accruing from the date of submission of a valid default claim (as determined by the Secretary) to the date on which payment is authorized by the Secretary, reduced to the extent required by section 1075(b) of this title. Such beneficiary shall be required to meet the standards of due diligence in the collection of the loan and shall be required to submit proof that the institution was contacted and other reasonable attempts were made to locate the borrower (when the location of the borrower is unknown) and proof that contact was made with the borrower (when the location is known). The Secretary shall make the determination required to carry out the provisions of this section not later than 90 days after the notification by the insurance beneficiary and shall make payment in full on the amount of the beneficiary's loss pending completion of the due diligence investigation.

(b) ... .

(c) ... .

(d) ... .

CREDIT(S)

(Pub.L. 89-329, Title IV, § 430, as added Pub.L. 99-498, Title IV, § 402(a), Oct. 17, 1986, 100 Stat. 1397, and amended Pub.L. 102-325, Title IV, § 423, July 23, 1992, 106 Stat. 543; Pub.L. 105-244, Title IV, § 426, Oct. 7, 1998, 112 Stat. 1702.

> "CREDITS" to "Pub.L. 99-498" = all prior pieces of legislation that have been passed for this statute.

HISTORICAL AND STATUTORY NOTES

Revision Notes and Legislative Reports

1986 Acts. House Report Nos. 99-383, 99-598, House Conference Report No. 99-861, and Statement by President, see 1986 U.S. Code Cong. and Adm. News, p. 2572.

1992 Acts. House Report No. 102-447 and House Conference Report No. 102-630, see 1992 U.S. Code Cong. and Adm. News, p. 334.

1998 Acts. House Conference Report No. 105-750, see 1998 U.S. Code Cong. and Adm. News, p. 417.

Amendments

1998 Amendments. Subsec. (a). Pub.L. 105-244, § 426, substituted "shall be required to submit proof that the institution was contacted and other reasonable attempts were made" for "shall be required to submit proof that reasonable attempts were made".

1992 Amendments. Subsec. (e). Pub.L. 102-325, § 423, added subsec. (e).

Effective and Applicability Provisions

1998 Acts. Amendment by Pub.L. 105-244 effective Oct. 1, 1998, except as otherwise provided, see section 3 of Pub.L. 105-244, set out as a note under section 1001 of this title.

1992 Acts. Amendment by section 423 of Pub.L. 102-325 effective July 23, 1992, see section 432(a) of Pub.L. 102-325, set out as a note under section 1078 of this title.

Prior Provisions

A prior section 1080, Pub.L. 89-329, Title IV, § 430, Nov. 8, 1965, 79 Stat. 1244; Pub.L. 90-575, Title I, § 113(b)(5), Oct. 16, 1968, 82 Stat. 1021; Pub.L. 92-318, Title I, § 132B(c), June 23, 1972, 86 Stat. 262; Pub.L. 94-482, Title I, § 127(a), Oct. 12, 1976, 90 Stat. 2125; Pub.L. 95-43, § 1(a)(33), June 15, 1977, 91 Stat. 216; Pub.L. 96-374, Title IV, §§ 416(a)(1), (b), 422, Title XIII, § 1391(a)(1), Oct. 3, 1980, 94 Stat. 1420, 1421, 1432, 1503; Pub.L. 99-272, Title XVI, §§ 16014(a)(2), 16022, Apr. 7, 1986, 100 Stat. 341, 349, related to default of student borrowers under Federal loan insurance program, prior to the general revision of this part by Pub.L. 99-498.

* * *24

TABLE 10-8   Legislative History: Using the Public Law Number

Service	Use to Find	Find
United States Code Congressional and Administrative News Service (U.S.C.C.A.N.) (West) – monthly pamphlets, then cumulative bound volumes	Table of Legislative History (Table 4) – use Public Law number	1) Original bill number (H.R. or S.) 2) Reference to committee report(s) 3) Date of passage of bill 4) Use this info to find committee and debate reports 5) Presidential signing statements 6) Discussion of background and purpose of legislation Also available on Westlaw
Congressional Information Service (C.I.S.) (Lexis) – monthly pamphlets then three cumulative bound volumes: *CIS Annual Abstracts, of Congressional Publications; CIS Annual Legislative Histories; Annual Index*	Index – subject matter, name of those testifying at hearings, bill number, popular name of statute, name of committee chairperson	*CIS Annual Abstracts* volume has summaries of 1) Bills 2) Testimony from committee hearings 3) Committee reports 4) References to days of debates to guide researchers to *Congressional Record* *CIS Annual Legislative Histories* volume: Arranged by Public Law number 1) Summary of law 2) References to appropriate documents such as *Congressional Record* 3) Documents available in CIS/Microfiche Library or provides stock numbers of Government Printing Office documents for ordering Also available on LexisNexis

[24]20 U.S.C.A. § 1080. 2012. http://web2.westlaw.com/find/default.wl?cite=20+usca+1080&rs=WLW 12.01&vr=2.0&rp=%2ffind%2fdefault.wl&sv=Split&fn=_top&mt=Westlaw

Service	Use to Find	Find

Congressional Index (Commerce Clearing House (CCH) Inc.) – weekly pamphlets with binders for each congressional session	Index for each congressional session; subject index for bill number; Status of House Bills; Status of Senate Bills	Directs to documents but does not reproduce documents. Search by:
		1) Public law number
		2) Name of law
		3) Subject matter
		4) Name of sponsor
		    Chronological record of actions taken
		    House and Senate committee and subcommittee rosters
		    Presidential vetoes
		    Voting records
		    Pending legislation
		Does not reference to *Congressional Record*

Westlaw (West) subscription service	Several databases such as 1) Billcast (BC) 2) Billcast Archives (BC-OLD) 3) BILLS 4) Congressional Record (CR)	1) Current bills 2) Public laws from previous sessions 3) Full text of pending bills 4) Legislative history for certain statutes since 1985 WestClip provides monitor for legislation See Table 10-7 for sample

LexisNexis (Lexis) subscription	"Legislation & Politics" to "U.S. Congress" or "Legislative Histories" databases
	Can go directly to document with citation
		Search by
		1) Congress session number
		2) Bill number
		3) Public law number
		4) Topic
		5) Committee report number
		    Retrieve
		1) Full text of bill
		2) Some hearing transcripts
		3) Committee reports
		4) *Congressional Record* since 1985
		5) Legislative histories for selected legislation
		    Lexis Alert provides regular updates as bill receives action
		For step-by-step instructions, visit the LexisNexis Support Center – Legislative History[25]

THOMAS (Library of Congress) – free service	"Legislation in Current Congress" "Find More Legislation" "Congressional Record"	1) Descriptions of how laws are enacted 2) Historical documents 3) Directories for House and Senate members 4) Listing of House and Senate committees 5) Calendar of committee hearings 6) Links to other legislative agencies Search by 1) Key word or phrase 2) Bill number 3) Public law number 4) Popular name Most materials are in full text from 1989[26]

(Continued)

---

[25]LexisNexis Support Center – Legislative History. 2012. http://support.lexisnexis.com/lawschool/record.asp?ArticleID=lexiscom_leghist

[26]The Library of Congress: THOMAS. 2012. http://thomas.loc.gov/home/abt_thom.html

TABLE 10-8   *(Continued)*

Service	Use to Find	Find
Government Printing Office (GPO)	GPOAccess	Available: 1) Congressional bills 2) Transcripts of hearings 3) Committee reports 4) *Congressional Record* 5) Public laws Search by: 1) Bill number 2) Public law number 3) Key words 4) Subject titles 5) *U.S.C.* citation Most materials since early 1990s are available[27]

TABLE 10-9   Westlaw Database Directory – Legislative History[28]

Westlaw Database Directory
Search for a Database

☐ Terms and Connectors	☐ Natural Language

or

Browse Databases

Main Directory

U.S. Federal Materials

Legislative History

Legislative History - U.S. Code, 1948 to present	LH
US GAO Federal Legislative Histories	FED-LH
Federal Immigration - Legislative History	FIM-LH
Federal Immigration - Congressional Record	FIM-CR
Federal Securities & Blue Sky Law - Legislative History	FSEC-LH
Federal Taxation - Legislative History	FTX-LH
Federal Taxation - Congressional Record	FTX-CR
Federal Taxation - Joint Committee on Taxation (JCS) Prints	FTX-JCS
Federal Taxation - Joint Committee on Taxation (JCX) Prints	FTX-JCX
Federal Taxation - Joint Committee on Taxation Prints (multibase)	FTX-JCTPRINT
Congressional Record	CR
Congressional Record - Health Care	FHTH-CR

[27]GPOAccess. Congressional Bills: Main Page. 2011. http://www.gpoaccess.gov/bills/index.html

[28]Westlaw Database Directory – Legislative History. 2012. http://directory.westlaw.com/default.asp?GUID=WDIR00000000000000000000000000011&RS=W&VR=2.0

U.S. Congressional Testimony	USTESTIMONY
Congressional Testimony	CONGTMY
US Political Transcripts	USPOLTRANS
Netscan Legislative History documents	NS-LH
Obama News	OBAMANEWS
Tax Reform Act of 1986 Legislative Materials	FTX-TRA86
RIA Complete Analysis of the Tax Acts	RIA-CATA
RIA Complete Analysis of the Tax Act - Historical	RIA-CATA-OLD
United States Statutes at Large 1789–1972	US-STATLRG
Arnold & Porter Collection - Legislative Histories	

While the statute itself is primary authority, legislative history is secondary authority. The courts are never required to follow legislative history and judges often criticize its use. However, legislative history serves an important purpose. By looking through the legislative history of a statute, a researcher can gain valuable insight into the meaning of and purpose behind the statute, particularly when judges have not interpreted the statute through case law. When nothing else is available, legislative history—if thoroughly documented and well argued—can provide strong support for a particular interpretation of a statute.

MUNICIPAL LAW

Charters

A *charter*, in its broad sense, is a document issuing from a sovereign power granting a group of people certain rights and liberties. An early example of a charter was the Magna Carta, issued in 1215 by King John of England to establish certain rights for the subjects of his realm. Today, charters are usually issued from a state government to incorporate municipalities, such as cities, towns, counties, villages, boroughs, and townships. These charters grant rights and establish legal procedures for the citizens of these municipal entities.

Charter
A document granted by a sovereign providing certain rights and powers for a city or town to operate. It is a city's basic source of law.

Paralegals working in municipal government need to understand what charters are and how the charters relate to ordinances and the operation of the municipality. One can think of a charter as similar to a constitution and ordinances as similar to statutes.

When a city is incorporated, the language of the incorporation document may look similar to the charter shown in Exhibit 10-4.

The charter for Las Vegas has provisions describing the territory covered, creating wards, setting up city offices, and filling vacancies in government positions. It creates a city council as the legislative body, sets terms and qualifications for office, defines the election process, describes how meetings will be held, and identifies what constitutes a quorum. The charter also creates city departments and gives them authority to act. Perhaps more importantly, a charter gives the city council the power to make resolutions, orders, and ordinances and set procedures for adopting and enacting the ordinances.[29]

[29]*Id.*

EXHIBIT 10-4 LAS VEGAS CITY CHARTER (PORTION)

LAS VEGAS CITY CHARTER
CHAPTER 517, STATUTES OF NEVADA 1983

AN ACT incorporating the City of Las Vegas in Clark County, Nevada, under a new charter; defining the boundaries thereof; and providing other matters properly relating thereto.

[Approved May 26, 1983]

ARTICLE I - Introductory and Organizational Provisions

Section 1.010 Purpose; other laws; notice.

1. In order to provide for the orderly government of the City of Las Vegas and the public health, safety, prosperity, security, comfort, convenience and general welfare of its citizens, the Legislature hereby establishes this Charter for the government of the City of Las Vegas.

2. Each power which is expressly granted by this Charter is in addition to all of the purposes, powers, rights, privileges, immunities and duties which are granted to cities by the general law of the State. Each of the provisions of NRS which apply generally to cities (not including, unless otherwise expressly mentioned in this Charter, chapter 265, 266 or 267 of NRS) and are not in conflict with the provisions of this Charter applies to the City of Las Vegas.

3. Any notice which is provided for in this Charter for any purpose is reasonably calculated to inform each interested person of any proceeding under this Charter which may directly and adversely affect his legally protected rights, if any.

(Ch. 517, Stats. 1983 p. 1391)

Sec. 1.020 Definitions. Except as otherwise provided in this Charter, unless the context otherwise requires, the definitions which are provided in sections 1.030 to 1.090, inclusive, of this Charter govern the construction of this Charter.
(Ch. 517, Stats. 1983 p. 1391)

Sec. 1.030 "City" defined. "City" means the City of Las Vegas in Clark County, Nevada.
(Ch. 517, Stats. 1983 p. 1391)

Sec. 1.040 "City Council" defined. "City Council," unless otherwise qualified, means the governing body of the City.
(Ch. 517, Stats. 1983 p. 1391)

Sec. 1.050 "Councilman" defined. "Councilman" means a member of the City Council, other than the Mayor.
(Ch. 517, Stats. 1983 p. 1392)

Sec. 1.060 "County" defined. "County" means Clark County , Nevada.
(Ch. 517, Stats. 1983 p. 1392)

Sec. 1.070 "Newspaper" defined. "Newspaper" means a newspaper which is qualified pursuant to chapter 238 of NRS, is printed and published in the City at least once each calendar week and is of general circulation in the City.
(Ch. 517, Stats. 1983 p. 1392)

Sec. 1.080 "Publication," "publish" defined. "Publication" and "publish" each means publication in at least one newspaper for the number of times which is required by the specific section of this Charter.
(Ch. 517, Stats. 1983 p. 1392)

Sec. 1.090 "State" defined. "State" means the State of Nevada.
(Ch. 517, Stats. 1983 p. 1392)[30]

[30]Las Vegas City Charter. 1983. http://www.lasvegasnevada.gov/files/CityCharter.pdf

Ordinances

Counties, cities, and townships, enact *municipal ordinances* to regulate activities that are not covered by federal or state law. These subjects include such matters as local traffic, construction zoning, building codes, noise pollution, and local taxes. The legislative body that makes ordinances may be referred to as a city council, town council, or county board of supervisors, or legislation may be a combined effort of the mayor and city council, or city and county councils. Paralegals who work in city or county government will need to be familiar with municipal ordinances. These laws may also come into play if paralegals work with firms who represent real estate developers, for example.

In local government, the city council takes on a role similar to that of the state legislature. Generally the charter gives the city council the authority to make and adopt all of the ordinances needed for the municipality to operate. It is important to note that ordinances cannot contravene the state constitution or the state statutes, or infringe upon individual rights protected in the U.S. Constitution. In the hierarchy of law, municipal law is at the bottom.

Often ordinances are published in the local newspaper, particularly in smaller communities. In addition to the text of the proposed ordinance, notice will be given of the time and place of the meeting in which the ordinance will be voted on. The meetings are public to satisfy the due process clause of the U.S. Constitution. In larger communities, the proposed ordinance as well as the text of approved ordinances is published in a separate journal. Once an ordinance has been approved, it is codified.

Municipal ordinances
Laws enacted or adopted by a local municipality that set forth rules by which the government and the citizens must conduct themselves.

Researching in Municipal Law

Researching ordinances is usually not easy because the documents relating to the ordinances are not always current and are not well organized. The best place to find a current copy of the local municipal code may be the appropriate municipal office charged with handling the code, such as the office of the county commissioners. That version of the code will likely be up-to-date. The code will probably also have a copy of the charter filed with it. While local libraries also may have copies of the local codes, often their copies are not updated.

Codes are not updated in the same way that other enacted law is—generally there are no pocket parts. Since most are maintained in looseleaf binders, the researcher should make sure any replacement pages have been properly filed.

After one finds the code, the research methods are similar to those for other enacted law: use descriptive or key words, topics, or perhaps a popular name. The codes are usually organized by topic. If the municipal code is maintained in looseleaf binders, an index may be available at the end, which can be used to find the codes that cover the issue in question.

Unfortunately, the actual municipal ordinances are usually not annotated. Cases or related materials that interpret or define the ordinance are not provided. Typically, the information provided is limited to the date of ordinance. Often the best way to obtain information about an ordinance is to go to the source—ask the city or county attorney, planning board, council, or other local government body if any cases have been decided that interpret the municipal ordinance in question. Another source of information is the commissioner's or council's minutes of the meeting where the law was discussed.

Municipal codes are often available on the state's website. For example, if a municipal ordinance were needed in Alaska, one could go to the court's portion

Shepardizing
Updating sources to be sure the sources used are still good law.

of the state government website, go to the legal research menu, and click on municipal codes. A list of all available municipal codes is hyperlinked.[31] If a source is an official government website, a researcher can be confident that the material is accurate. Another Internet source is the Municode Library. The listings of the cities or towns with available municipal codes are found by clicking on the state. The site warns that the listed codes may not be the most current.[32] However, this service does provide a good starting point for research.

Many law libraries also provide access to municipal codes. For example, the Minnesota State Law Library provides a hyperlink to local government, which in turn has a hyperlink to county and municipal ordinances. Some of the cities have complete ordinances, while others give only selected ordinances, or only particular types, such as zoning.[33]

Although most published sets of ordinances generally do not provide annotations or other information, there are some resources to fill this gap. *Ordinance Law Annotations* from Thomson West is a comprehensive digest of cases that interpret the ordinances. Ordinances are arranged in topics such as abortion, animals, buildings, elevators, ice, licenses, and massage parlors. It also includes a table of cases and an index that can be searched using the descriptive word, subject, or popular name methods. Westlaw and LexisNexis have some ordinances on their databases and there are, of course, cases interpreting these ordinances in their systems. From either system, the material can be updated by using *Shepard's* or KeyCite.

RULES OF PROCEDURE AND COURT RULES

Rules of court
Rules that govern practice and procedure before a court; generally issued by the court or by the highest court,

Laws known as **rules of court** ensure that the courts operate not only efficiently but also fairly and equally. The rules provide a wide range of practice requirements, from the time frame within which to file a document to the size of the paper on which the document must appear.

Federal Rules

Congress gives the federal courts the power to make their own rules regarding practices and procedures. The Supreme Court obtains authority to create general rules of practice from 28 U.S.C. § 2072.[34] The Federal Rules of Civil Procedure (Fed. R. Civ. P.), first promulgated in 1938, contain requirements for civil litigation in all federal district courts. These rules set out the requirements for pleadings, discovery, motions, and civil trial practice. The Federal Rules of Criminal Procedure (Fed. R. Cr. P.) became effective in 1946.[35] The Federal Rules of Appellate Procedure are the rules of practice for the circuit courts of appeals. The Federal Rules of Evidence were created in 1975 and govern any proceedings in

[31]Alaska Court System: Legal Research — Alaska Resources. 2012. http://www.courts.alaska.gov/aklegal.htm

[32]Municode.com: Municode Library. 2012. http://www.municode.com/Library/clientCodePage.aspx?clientID=12053

[33]Minnesota State Law Library. Minnesota County and Municipal Ordinances 2012. http://www.lawlibrary.state.mn.us/ordinance.html

[34]Authority for Promulgation of Rules. Title28,United States Code. 2009. http://www.uscourts.gov/uscourts/RulesAndPolicies/rules/CV2009.pdf

[35]*Id.*

the U.S. federal courts and before United States bankruptcy judges and magistrate judges. In addition, any bankruptcy case, pursuant to Title 11 of the U.S. Code, is governed by the Federal Rules of Bankruptcy Procedure.

The rules are available in several specific sets of books. The rules also can be found on court websites. The following is a list of the federal rules that paralegals will work with:

- Federal Rules of Procedure
  - Federal Rules of Civil Procedure (FRCP or Fed. R. Civ. P.)
  - Federal Rules of Criminal Procedure (FRCrP or Fed. R. Crim. P.)
  - Federal Rules of Appellate Practice
- Federal Rules of Evidence (FRE or Fed. R. Evid.)
- Federal Rules of Bankruptcy Practice
- Federal Rules of Court[36]

A **desk book**, which is a one-volume paperback book, contains all the rules without annotations.

Forms for use in various court proceedings are prescribed by the courts and presented within the rules. These boilerplate forms found in the rule books are only meant to provide formatting guidelines for documents submitted to the court. As with any boilerplate form, the user must modify the language to include the facts specific to the client. A sample form is shown in Exhibit 10-5. The information in brackets is the information that would be altered to fit the client's needs.

In Federal Bankruptcy Court, official bankruptcy forms are required in all filings. Those forms are provided by law.[37]

Each district court may also create rules for practice, called **local rules of court**, which apply only to proceedings within that court. Local court rules supplement but do not replace the Federal Rules of Civil Procedure. Paralegals filing documents in a court that they are not familiar with should consult the local rules of court to obtain instructions on the filing process required. These rules can usually be found on the website of each court. For example, the local rules for the District Court for the Southern District of Indiana covers matters such as the general format of documents presented for filing (S.D.Ind.L.R. 5.1), filing of documents electronically (S.D.Ind.L.R. 5.2), form of discovery documents (S.D.Ind.L.R. 26.1), and courtroom and courthouse decorum (S.D.Ind.L.R. 83.3).[38] Courts expect strict compliance with their rules, so it is incumbent upon the legal team to know and abide by those rules. Some courts have been known to refuse pleadings that do not meet the requirements, resulting in missed deadlines.

Desk book
A one-volume book meant to be used as a quick reference in lieu of a larger set of books.

Local rules of court
Rules for practice created by a court for proceedings within that court. These rules are based on the customs, usages, and character of the local legal community. In federal court, these rules supplement but do not replace the Federal Rules of Civil Procedure.

State Rules

State legislatures allow their state court systems to make and enforce their own sets of rules regarding practice in their court systems. Many state courts based their state court rules on the Federal Rules of Civil Procedure, which helps create uniformity among these rules. State court rules are often published in code books and are available through the state's official homepage. Local court rules are

[36]U.S. Courts. Rules and Forms in Effect. 2012. http://www.uscourts.gov/RulesAndPolicies/rules.aspx

[37]Bankruptcy Forms. 2012. http://www.uscourts.gov/FormsAndFees/Forms/BankruptcyForms.aspx

[38]U.S. District Court Southern District of Indiana. 2012. http://www.insd.uscourts.gov/

EXHIBIT 10-5 NOTICE OF APPEAL TO A FEDERAL COURT OF APPEALS

UNITED STATES DISTRICT COURT

for the

<_____> DISTRICT OF <_____>

<Name(s) of plaintiff(s)>,)	
)	Case No. <Number>
Plaintiff(s))	
v.)	
<Name(s) of defendant(s)>,)	
Defendant(s))	
)	
)	
)	
)	

NOTICE OF APPEAL

Notice is hereby given that <Name all parties taking the appeal>, [plaintiffs] [defendants] in the above named case <See Rule 3(c) for permissible ways of identifying appellants.>, hereby appeal to the United States Court of Appeals for the <_____> Circuit [from the final judgment] [from an order <describing it>] entered in this action on <Date>.

Date: <Date>   <Signature of the attorney or
                                       unrepresented party>

                                       _____
                                       <Printed name>
                                       Attorney for <party>
                                       <Address>
                                       <E-mail address>
                                       <Telephone number>[39]

always available by contacting the court, through court websites, and on the state's judicial website.

For most paralegals, the bulk of their work involves local or county courts. Many local courts have their own local rules, similar to those of the federal courts. Although most of these rules appear to be administrative in nature, such as how pleadings are accepted (in person, by facsimile, or by electronic delivery) or how material is to be cited, it is important to follow them exactly. The judges have the power to reject a pleading, which can mean delay or even dismissal if the statute of limitations or a deadline for filing passes.

Researching Rules of Court

The U.S.C.A. and U.S.C.S. both provide the rules of civil procedure for the federal courts. The Federal Rules of Civil Procedure are located after the statutes in Title 28 of U.S.C.A. The Federal Rules of Criminal Procedure are located after the statutes in Title 18. The U.S.C.S. publishes the rules in separate volumes that are not numbered. Those volumes, Federal Rules of Civil Procedure, Federal Rules of

> **TIP**
>
> Failure to timely file a complaint can lead to a claim for professional negligence or malpractice.

[39]Appellate Rules Forms. Appellate Form 1. Notice of Appeal to a Court of Appeals From a Judgment or Order of a District Court. 2011. http://www.uscourts.gov/RulesAndPolicies/FederalRulemaking /RulesAndForms/AppellateRulesForms.aspx

Criminal Procedure, Federal Rules of Appellate Practice, and the Federal Rules of Evidence, follow Title 51.

The descriptive word method, the **topic method**, or the popular name method can be used to search court rules. Each rule is followed by historical notes, notes to decisions, library references, and case references, which can assist in research.

Topic method
Researching by using the topics within a source to find information.

Several publications also provide citations to cases that interpret and discuss the rules of court. *Federal Rules Decisions* is geared toward federal district court cases that have interpreted the rules. Another West product, *Federal Rules Service, 3d*, includes the actual text of the rules and provides reference to cases interpreting the rules. *Moore's Federal Practice* and *Federal Practice and Procedure* are two treatises that provide in-depth discussions of the federal rules.

The Federal Rules of Civil Procedure and other federal rules of court are available on the Internet at the various court websites and collectively at the U.S. Courts website.[40] A variety of information related to the rules is also available, such as meetings and hearings, commentaries, and local court rules.

Once the appropriate rule is located and analyzed, the final step is to update either through *Shepard's Federal Statutes Citations* in print or on LexisNexis or by using KeyCite on Westlaw.

SUMMARY

Enacted law is any law that a governmental body proposes, considers, and votes on and which then becomes the authority by which the people must abide. It is a broad category, and includes constitutional provisions, statutes, administrative regulations, charters, court rules, and ordinances. It exists on the federal, state, and local levels.

Researching enacted law involves not only finding the enacted law, but also applying that law to a particular set of facts. Once the applicable enacted law is found, legal analysis is often required to understand and explain how the enacted law applies to the facts of the client's case. Knowing how to deconstruct a statute and determine its precise requirements or elements is one of the most valuable skills a paralegal can offer.

REVIEW QUESTIONS

1. What is a slip law, and where can it be found?
2. What does the first set of numbers stand for in the string of numbers identifying a public law? Give an example.
3. Explain the difference between an engrossed bill and an enacted bill.
4. What are *Statutes at Large*?
5. How does the U.S.C. differ from the U.S.C.A. or U.S.C.S.?
6. What are the differences among a statute, a code, and an annotated code?
7. What is the official source of federal statutes?
8. What is the difference between a session law and a codified law?
9. What is the name of the collection of your state's statutes? Does your state have an official code, unofficial code, or both?
10. What are three instances in which a client might have a constitutional issue?
11. What is legislative history and when is it used?
12. When a conflict arises between a state constitution and the U.S. Constitution, which will rule and why?
13. Explain how to use legal analysis to determine the meaning of a statute.
14. Explain what connecting language is and how it is important in understanding statutes.
15. What are the various types of rules of procedure and rules of court?
16. What is a charter and when would one be used?
17. What types of conditions do municipal laws cover?
18. Explain the concept of uniform laws. When would these laws be used in research?
19. How can statutes be updated so that you know the statutes are good law?

[40]U.S. Courts. Rules & Policies. 2012. http://www.uscourts.gov/RulesAndPolicies/rules.aspx

APPLICATION **EXERCISES**

1. Jennifer is a homeowner who hired a general contractor to install a new roof. Within 18 months of the installation, Jennifer had a leak in her second floor ceiling. The leak caused some water damage to an antique table located in the room directly below the leak. The table, but not the damage to the ceiling or roof, is covered under her homeowners' policy. Jennifer hires your law firm to sue the contractor. The supervising attorney tells you, the paralegal, that the case is a basic breach of contract complaint. What other steps should be taken?
   a. Determine whether federal or state law will apply and why.
   b. Determine what the statute of limitations is in your jurisdiction for breach of contract. Cite the authority.
   c. Are there any statutes in your jurisdiction covering contract law or general contractors that are necessary to consider? Cite the statutes and provide the elements of the statutes. (For example, with the new housing construction boomprior to the financial crisis, shoddy construction cases have dominated the courts. In response to this dilemma, some state legislatures have created Home Improvement Protection laws to protect homeowners from disreputable or inexperienced contractors).

2. Research the following scenarios and determine whether it is a federal or state law that should apply and why. Then find a statute that is applicable and outline the elements of the statute.
   a. Mary is seeking to divorce her husband of 12 years.
   b. Thomas wants to declare bankruptcy.
   c. Ann needs to probate her mother's will.
   d. Frank's company is being investigated for illegal dumping.
   e. Nancy is charged with statutory rape of her student.
   f. Robert wants to sue his employer for discrimination based on his disability.

3. Using the Popular Name Table of the U.S. Code, find the following:
   a. Act to Combat International Terrorism 1984
   b. 21st Century Nanotechnology Research and Development Act
   c. 3% Withholding Repeal and Job Creation Act

   d. 50 States Commemorative Coin Program Act
   e. 9/11 Heroes Stamp Act of 2001

4. Eliza Doolittle just became a partner in the firm where you work. When she started, she was told that she must pay her own health insurance premiums. Ms. Doolittle has asked you to determine whether those health insurance payments will be deductible on her federal tax return.
   a. What key words will you use to search?
   b. What books or database will you search?
   c. What is the applicable statute? Summarize the material you think is pertinent and properly cite the information.
   d. When was the statute effective? Does it have an expiration date?
   e. Shepardize or KeyCite the statute.

5. A client has come to the firm because he received unsolicited goods in the mail. He wants to know whether he must pay for the goods, whether he can keep the goods without paying, or whether he must return the goods. Use your state statutes to research the following.
   a. What key words will you use?
   b. Has your state adopted the Uniform Commercial Code?
   c. What information did you find?
   d. Was this in the main volume, the pocket part, or both? If you used a service, what are the applicable dates of the information?
   e. Properly cite the sources you believe apply and summarize each.

6. Using one of the Popular Name Acts in question 3, respond to the following:
   a. Which Act did you choose?
   b. What section in the U.S.C. contains the Act?
   c. What is the Public Law number of the Act?
   d. What is the legislative history of the Act?
   e. Look at the Public Law version and compare it to the codified version. Is it the same? Why or why not?
   f. Search http://cqstatetrack.com/ for any pending legislation on Megan's Law. What jurisdiction is creating or modifying legislation?

CITATION **EXERCISES**

1. What is the official citation for the Internal Revenue Code?
2. What is the U.S.C. citation for the National School Lunch Act?
3. Which title of the U.S.C. deals with war and national defense?
4. Give the correct citation for Article I, section 9, clause 2 of the U.S. Constitution.

5. Give the proper citation form for Rule 12(b) of the Federal Rules of Civil Procedure.
6. Give the proper citation for the statute in your jurisdiction that identifies the minimum age at which an individual can get a learner's permit to drive an automobile.

QUICK **CHECK**

State whether each of the following is true or false.

1. The U.S. Constitution has exactly 10 amendments.
2. Most constitutional law comes from the preamble to the U.S. Constitution.
3. State constitutions are enacted in order to limit citizen rights to a greater extent than the U.S. Constitution.
4. Annotations are helpful notes found in some publications.
5. Federalism is the principle under the U.S. Constitution that the Constitution should have more power than state laws.
6. Words such as *and* and *or* tell you whether all or just some of the elements in a statute must be met in order for the statute to apply.

RESEARCH

A. Mike Smith is your law firm's client. Mr. Smith owns a utility construction business in Indiana. He just purchased a new vehicle for his business, and he is afraid that with the extra-large tires, the vehicle may be over the maximum width limitation set by the state of Indiana.
   1. Access the relevant statute in the library, on a subscription service such as Westlaw or Lexis-Nexis, or on a free service such as the Indiana General Assembly website at http://www.in.gov/legislative/ic/code/.
   2. Review the statute to find the answers to Mr. Smith's concern. Break the statute into its elements.
   3. What is the maximum width limit? Does this limitation apply to his vehicle? Why?
B. FeelGood Hospital and insurance provider WeCoverYou are both located in your state. They sign a contract regarding health care services. The contract contains a provision requiring binding arbitration in the event of a dispute. WeCoverYou claims that the contract is void and unenforceable and files a lawsuit for declaratory relief and rescission. Feel-Good files an answer. Soon after the answer is filed, WeCoverYou petitions the court to require FeelGood to submit to binding arbitration. FeelGood claims that WeCoverYou waived the arbitration provision by (1) claiming the contract was void and unenforceable and (2) filing a lawsuit in court.
   1. Explain whether you would use enacted law for this issue and explain why or why not.
   2. Explain whether you would use federal or state law and explain why you chose one over the other.
   3. Identify the key words or phrases you would use for your research.
   4. Cite the law(s) you would use to research this topic and ensure that it is current. (Hint: Consider the state where the two companies are located.)

For the next items, assume that FeelGood Hospital is your law firm's client.

   5. Use the appropriate state's statute(s) to determine whether the insurer is correct in its claims. Be sure to cite the relevant statute(s).
   6. Analyze the statute(s) and identify the statutory elements that relate to the facts as presented.
   7. Present your conclusion as to whether your client, FeelGood Hospital, is correct.
   8. Justify your conclusion.
C. Locate the answers according to legal authority in your state. Cite your sources.
   1. Do the general obligations of a drawer apply to cashier's checks under your state's version of the Uniform Commercial Code (UCC)? Cite authority.
   2. Does your state establish a limit on its small claims courts, and if so, what is the limit? Cite the statute.
   3. Must an athletic trainer be registered in your state? Cite authority.
   4. In your state, what category of crime is the aggravated discharge of a firearm? Cite authority.
   5. Is a corporate personal representative of a decedent's estate required to furnish a bond in your state? Cite authority.
   6. In your state, what are the penalties for being convicted of the fraudulent use of a credit card?
   7. What is the minimum age to drive an automobile in your state? Cite authority.
   8. Cite the statutory law provision in your state on procuring alcoholic beverages for persons under the age of 21 years, and answer the following questions:
      a. What is the penalty for committing the offense?
      b. Is there a historical note on derivation?
   9. Identify the following based on the statutory compilation of your state.
      a. How is the set supplemented?
      b. Is there a general index? Do the separate volumes have indexes?
      c. Is there a difference between the general index and the volume index?

d. What cross-references, if any, to other non-statutory aids are provided in the compilations?

e. What kind of historical notes, if any, are given?

f. Is there a table of acts by popular names? If not, how does the compilation present the popular names?

g. Is there a reference table from the session laws of the state to the compilation? Where is the table located?

h. Is the U.S. Constitution included in the state compilation? If yes, is it annotated? Where is it located?

D. Legislation – Parallel Reference Tables: U.S.C. Use the parallel reference tables of U.S.C., U.S.C.A., or U.S.C.S. and give the U.S.C. citation for each of the public laws.

1. 106-116
17. 89-29
18. 95-127
19. 93-387
20. 90-619

E. Court Rules – Use the court rules volume of the U.S.C.A. or U.S.C.S. to answer. Cite the rule number.

1. In the Supreme Court, how much time is usually allowed for oral argument?

21. Under the Federal Rules of Appellate Procedure, is leave or consent required for a state to file an amicus curiae brief?

22. May anyone remove books from the Supreme Court Library?

INTERNET **RESEARCH**

A. Find the sources electronically. Identify where you located the answer and how you found the answer.

1. What is the effective date of 42 U.S.C. §238(d)?

2. Find and cite the United States Code Annotated (U.S.C.A.), sections 701 – 703 of title 10. Summarize the results.

3. Find and cite the United States Code Annotated (U.S.C.A.), §191 of title 50. Summarize the results.

4. Name the bill that resulted in the Vaccine and Immunization Amendments of 1990, and state its purpose.

5. When was your state's Limited Liability Companies Act enacted?

6. Research the controversy surrounding the right to bear arms and write a summary of three sources. Cite the sources.

7. What House of Congress has the power to try all impeachments?

8. What constitutional provision regulates interstate compacts?

B. For these questions, do an Internet search and write a summary of what you find for the answer. Document your sources.

1. What arguments have been presented by major cities for tighter gun control laws, such as handgun bans?

2. How has the Supreme Court, through its interpretation of the Fourth Amendment, balanced the right to privacy with the need for public safety?

C. Review the simple facts in the opening scenario. For each client's situation, find the appropriate law. Show your research trail. Find one case that might support the client. Cite your authority.

D. What is the subject matter of the proposed 28th Amendment to the Constitution?

E. How many amendments to the Constitution have not been ratified after being submitted to the states?

F. Voting qualifications designed to deny any citizen the right to vote based on the citizen's race have been prohibited by 42 U.S.C. § 1973. Has this section been given retroactive effect at any time? If so, describe.

H. Using THOMAS, locate the following, summarize the coverage, and give the sponsor:

1. H.R. 3409 of the 112th Congress.

23. The Fallen Heroes Family Act of 2011.

24. An act sponsored by Michele Bachmann regarding choice of light bulbs.

25. Patient Protection and Affordable Care Act covering more than one Congress.

MEDIA **RESOURCES**

1. *America Gets a Constitution.* 1996–2010. A&E Television Networks.

At http://www.history.com/topics/constitution/videos?paidlink=1&vid=HIS_SEM_Search&keywords=constitution&utm_source=google&utm_medium=cpc&utm_campaign=constitution&utm_term=constitution#america-gets-a-constitution

2. *Centuries of Citizenship A Constitutional Timeline.* 2004.   http://www.constitutioncenter.org/timeline/
3. *I'm Just a Bill.* School House Rock.   http://www.youtube.com/watch?v=3eeOwPoayOk

INTERNET **RESOURCES**

A. Free Sites to Find Enacted Law and help aids

1. Cases and Codes at   http://www.findlaw.com/casecode/index.html
2. Justia US Laws at   http://law.justia.com/
3. How to Find Regulations at   http://lscontent.westlaw.com/images/content/Find Regulations10.pdf
4. Law School 2010   Statute Fields on Westlaw at http://store.westlaw.com /documentation/westlaw/wlawdoc/wlres/statutef.pdf
5. The Public Library of Law at   http://www.plol.org/Pages/Search.aspx
6. Law School 2010: Administrative Law Fundamentals at Law Fundamentals at   http://lscontent.westlaw.com/images/content /AdminLaw10.pdf http://west.thomson.com /productdetail/1-6804-5/RM168045/productdetail.aspx
7. Law School 2010: Getting Started with Online Research at   http://lscontent.westlaw.com/images/content/ GettingStarted10.pdf
8. Law School 2010: How to Check Citations at   http://lscontent.westlaw.com/images/banner /SurvivalGuide/PDF08/08HowCheckCitations.pdf
9. Law School 2010: How to Find Statutes at   http://lscontent.westlaw.com/images/banner /SurvivalGuide/PDF08/08HowFindStatutes.pdf
10. Law School 2010: The Federal Legislative Process at   http://lscontent.westlaw.com/images/content/FedLegis10 .pdf http://west.thomson.com/productdetail/1-6884-5 /RM168845/productdetail.aspx
11. Law School 2010: Westlaw Research Guide at   http://west.thomson.com/documentation/westlaw /wlawdoc/lawstu/lsrsgd06.pdf
12. LexisNexis Product Tutorials at   http://www.lexisnexis.com/COMMUNITY/DOWNLOAD ANDSUPPORTCENTER/media/p/4332.aspx
13. THOMAS provided by the Library of Congress at   http://thomas.loc.gov
14. Guide to Using the United States Code Congressional and Administrative News at   http://www.law.ufl.edu /lic/guides/federal/USCCAN06.pdf
15. Edwards, Richard C. Researching Legislative History. 2008.   http://www.ilga.gov/commission/lrb/lrbres.htm
16. Morgan, Jennifer Bryan, comp. Research Tools: Research Guides: State Legislative History Research Guides on the Web. Indiana University Maurer School of Law. 2010.   http://www.law.indiana.edu/lawlibrary/research/guides /statelegislative/index.shtml
17. Zimmerman, Andrew. Zimmerman's Research Guide. 2010.   http://law.lexisnexis.com/infopro/zimmermans /disp.aspx?z=1465
18. States and Territories   http://www.usa.gov/Agencies/State_and_Territories.shtml is the official website of the federal government (www.usa .gov) and this citation links you to the states and territories individual sites.
19. State and local government   http://www.statelocalgov.net/
20. Government archives   http://www.archives.gov/exhibits/charters /constitution.html
21. U.S. Constitution. Legal Information Institute. Cornell University Law School.   http://www.law.cornell.edu/constitution/constitution .articlevi.html (last visited September 7, 2009.)

B. Subscription Services

1.	Casemaker	www.casemaker.us
2.	Fastcase	https://www.fastcase.com/
3.	Lexis/Nexis	http://www.lexisnexis.com/
4.	Loislaw	http://www.loislaw.com/
5.	TheLawNet	http://www.thelaw.net/
6.	VersusLaw	http://www.versuslaw.com/
7.	Westlaw	www.westlaw.com

chapter eleven

RESEARCHING THE COMMON LAW (CASE LAW)

lenetstan/Shutterstock

LEARNING OBJECTIVES

After completing this chapter, students should be able to:

1. Recognize established primary authorities and utilize them to complete case law research assignments.

2. Distinguish when to use each type of case law.

3. Distinguish when to use federal case law and state case law.

4. Locate case law relevant to a case.

5. Analyze case law.

6. Identify the components of a court decision.

7. Identify precedents favoring both sides of a case.

8. Understand ethical considerations when using case law.

CHAPTER OVERVIEW

Case law, common law, and judge-made law are all terms that are used interchangeably. Case law is based on court opinions from appellate level courts. An appellate court is any higher court with reviewing power over a lower court. When one party to a court case at the administrative or trial level is dissatisfied with the result, that party may ask an appellate court to review the case. When the appellate court reviews the lower court decision and makes a ruling, it becomes part of the body of case law.

OPENING SCENARIO

Several new cases had arrived at the law office, and new files were opened. John had received several new assignments on these cases. After searching the Constitution and statutes that applied to these cases, he began work on finding cases to support and interpret the enacted laws he found.

In one of the new cases, the police searched the client's car without a warrant. John needed to find cases on the law of search and seizure that supported the client's position. When he found these cases, he read them carefully to understand every part. John really appreciated having had experience locating and briefing cases during his research and writing class in college. But first, it was important to refresh his memory on exactly how to research common law.

THE FOUNDATION OF THE COMMON LAW
General Information

Common law is the system of law that originated in England and was brought to the American colonies to create a judicial system here. It consists of decisions made by courts based on established principles or custom. A court must follow prior decisions or precedent made in prior **cases** on the same or similar issues.

Court decisions are often called case law, cases, common law, or judge-made law. When the judges write **opinions** interpreting some existing law, or applying the law to a new situation, they create common law. Common law is frequently based on various authorities, legal principles, doctrines, or legal rules that courts have adopted. Common law exists on both the federal and state levels.

Court Opinions

A court opinion is the court's written explanation of its decision in a given case. In it, the court will resolve the legal dispute and provide its reasons for doing so. An opinion will generally consist of the facts, points of law, and an analysis of those points of law.

Common law comes from appellate courts only. **Trial courts** do not set precedent—they are the courts where cases are originally heard. Only after a trial court case is appealed and decided by a higher court can precedent be set. An appeal results when one party to a court case is dissatisfied with the result and asks a higher court to review the case. The **appellant** must show that the trial court made a **legal error** that affected the decision in the case. If the legal error did not affect the decision, it is known as **harmless error**. Therefore, an appellate court is any higher court with reviewing power over the lower court.

An appellate can make several types of court rulings. The court can

affirm a decision—agree with the decision of the lower court;

reverse a decision—overturn the decision of the lower court; or

remand the case—send the case back to the lower court to retry the case or enter a new decision based on the appellate court's instructions.

A decision of an appellate court may be published or unpublished. Only published cases create precedent for the lower courts.

It is important to understand the appellate process in order to know the effect of a decision made in a case. The process begins at the trial court. If the trial court resolves the dispute to the parties' satisfaction, no case law results. However, if the

---

Common law
The body of law that originated in England and that the English settlers brought to this country to guide them in disputes and help them create a judicial system here.

Cases
The collection of court decisions that comprises case law.

Opinions
The court's written explanations of its decisions in given cases.

Trial courts
The courts where cases are originally heard.

Appellant
The party who brings the appeal.

Legal error
Mistake that occurs in a lower court proceeding and may provide grounds for appeal.

Harmless error
Any error that was not prejudicial to the substantive rights of the party who alleges that the error occurred.

Affirm
Uphold the lower court's decision.

Reverse
Overturn the decision of the lower court.

Remand
Send a case back to the lower court to retry the case or to enter a new decision based on the appellate court's instructions.

TABLE 11-1   The Appellate Process

6. If the U.S. Supreme Court grants a hearing, the state court's actions are reviewed and the U.S. Supreme Court issues a written opinion

5. If the case contains a constituitional issue, losing party can request hearing in U.S. Supreme Court by filing a writ of certiorari

4. High court can grant or deny review; if review is granted the court reviews action of lower court and renders a written opinion

3. Losing party can seek additional review in highest state court (may need to file a writ of certiorari)

2. Appellate court reviews the case, may hear oral arguments, and renders a written opinion.

1. Trial ends in final order; dissatisfied party files appeal in appropriate court of appeals (Note: The right of the state to appeal in a criminal case in limited.)

parties are dissatisfied, the case may be appealed, beginning with step 1 in Table 11-1. (Note: The table reads from the bottom up.)

At step 2 in Table 11-1, when the appellate court renders a written opinion, it becomes case law if published. A researcher should check local law to determine whether unpublished decisions can be cited. For example, California Rules of Court 8.1115 provides that an opinion found in the California Court of Appeal can be cited as authority "only if it has been certified for publication or officially published." "*Depublished*" opinions, under California and Arizona rules, cannot be cited as precedent, although the rules do allow for some exceptions, such as if the case is relevant under a doctrine.[1] The federal appellate court rules do not allow for depublication, but do allow the courts to issue "*unpublished*" opinions, particularly when a decision has no precedential value. Federal Rules of Appellate Procedure Rule 32.1 now provides that unpublished opinions can be cited as precedent. However, the courts are not required to give those unpublished citations more than persuasive weight.[2] The losing party may appeal to the next highest court, shown in step 3. At step 4, this written opinion becomes case law and will affect the opinion at level 2. At level 6, the opinion becomes case law and may change the law decided at levels 2 and 4.

Appellate cases are presented to a judge or panel of judges (meaning more than one judge). The judge or panel then issues a *decision* regarding the case. When a decision is published, the case is available for attorneys and judges to study, and to apply if they have cases with similar facts and issues. If the published case is similar in facts and issues, it is *precedent*, and must be followed in later cases that have the same or similar issues of law. Precedent established by published appellate decisions is primary authority.[3]

This system of following precedent when making decisions is based on the concept of **stare decisis**, meaning "let the decision stand." The rule of *stare decisis* seems simple at first, but there are important rules that determine when case law becomes precedent. See Checklist 11-1.

Depublished
In California and Arizona, refers to a procedure allowing the states' Supreme Courts to withhold opinions from publication.

Unpublished opinions
Each system in the federal appellate court system determines its own rules to determine which opinions are published. Unpublished opinions do not set precedent.

Decision
A determination that is arrived at by a judge or a panel of judges after considering the relevant facts and the law that applies to those facts.

Precedent
A prior opinion involving the same or similar set of facts as the case presently before the court. Precedent guides the court in deciding the case at hand.

Stare Decisis
A concept meaning "let the decision stand." This principle requires judges to follow precedent.

---

[1] UCLA School of Law. *Depublication of California Court of Appeal Decisions.* 2012. http://libguides.law.ucla.edu/depublication

[2] Reagan, Robert Timothy. Citing Unpublished Federal Appellate Opinions Issued Before 2007. http://www.fjc.gov/public/pdf.nsf/lookup/citrules.pdf/$file/citrules.pdf

[3] The 'Lectric Law Library. 1995–2011. http://www.lectlaw.com/def2/p069.htm

Checklist 11-1 RULES GOVERNING PRECEDENT

In order to create precedent, a case

1. **Must come from an appellate or supreme court:** Precedent is only established by published case decisions that come from appellate or supreme courts, rather than courts that sit at the trial court level.

2. **Must be from the same jurisdiction:** A case only creates precedent for the cases within the same jurisdiction. A new appellate court case out of Arizona establishes new precedent for the trial courts of Arizona, but not for the trial courts of North Dakota and not for the supreme court of Florida. Likewise, a decision in the Ninth Circuit Court of Appeals may be precedent or are binding for U.S. District Courts in states that are in the Ninth Circuit.

3. **Must be from a higher court:** Cases only create precedent for lower courts of the same jurisdiction. A case in Illinois decided by the Court of Appeals for the Third Circuit (and intermediate appellate court) does not establish precedent for the Supreme Court of Illinois, nor does it establish precedent for the Second Circuit of Illinois, or any of the other circuit courts of appeal. An opinion from the Seventh Circuit Court of Appeals is not precedent for a case in the Third Circuit Court of Appeals.

Mandatory authority

A rule of law established in a case that is binding upon all cases heard in lower courts of the same jurisdiction that involve similar facts and issues.

Persuasive authority

Authority that a court is not required to follow, but may consider in reaching a decision.

Common law that establishes precedent in a jurisdiction where a case is filed is considered ***mandatory authority*** for that case. This means the rule of law established by that precedent is binding upon all cases heard in lower courts of the same jurisdiction when faced with similar facts and issues. See Example 11-1.

When mandatory authority exists, the doctrine of *stare decisis* dictates that a court must follow it. However, a court may also look to ***persuasive authority*** for guidance in deciding a case. Persuasive authority is often considered when mandatory authority is not available in the court's jurisdiction, as in cases of first

Binding authority

Authority that is enforceable or must be followed.

Ex post facto

"After the fact." Describes a law that is passed after the facts occurred, and changes the legal consequences of those facts.

EXAMPLE 11-1 SAMPLE

A new case holds that a search warrant affidavit must now allege that a police officer witnessed illegal weapons on the premises in order to search those premises for weapons. This new requirement replaces the old rule that a lay witness may allege the presence of illegal weapons in order to establish probable cause in the search warrant affidavit. This new precedent was issued by the Texas Court of Criminal Appeals, which is the highest criminal court in Texas.

The new requirement for search warrant affidavits will automatically apply to all *new* search warrants for illegal weapons in Texas. The new case law is ***binding authority*** on all similar cases coming after the decision, but cannot apply to any cases that occurred prior to the enactment of this new case law. To apply the new authority to previous cases would be to apply the law retroactively and to criminalize an action that was not previously criminal. This is called **ex post facto**[4] and is prohibited by the U.S. Constitution in Article I, § 9[5] and Article I, §10.[6]

---

[4]Legal Information Institute. *Ex Post Facto.* 2010. http://www.law.cornell.edu/wex/ex_post_facto

[5]Constitution of the United States. Article I, §9. http://www.archives.gov/exhibits/charters/constitution_transcript.html

[6]*Id.* at Article I, § 10.

EXAMPLE 11-2   DICTA IN THE "FAMOUS FOOTNOTE"

Dicta made by a court may not be necessary to its immediate decision, but these comments could have a far-reaching impact on future cases.

In the case of *United States v. Carolene Products Company*, 304 U.S. 144 (1938), the U.S. Supreme Court reviewed a new law regulating milk shipped in interstate commerce. The company charged with violating the law argued that the law was unconstitutional based on the Commerce Clause and Due Process Clause in the Fifth Amendment. The Court upheld the law, holding that since it was only an economic regulation, it only needed to have a "rational basis" to be constitutional.

Although the Court held that economic regulations are presumed to be constitutional if they have a "rational basis," the Court remarked in dicta that laws directed at religious or racial minorities, or those restricting the political process, might be

> *subjected to more exacting judicial scrutiny under the general prohibitions of the Fourteenth Amendment than are most other types of legislation. Id. 152, n. 4.*

Although these comments had no bearing on its decision as to the Carolene Company, this dicta was cited in later cases that held that a higher level of scrutiny should be applied to statutes that restrict the rights of certain minority groups.[7]

---

impression where the jurisdiction has not yet considered the specific legal issue, but another jurisdiction has.

A court may sometimes consider **dicta**, or *obiter dicta*, in other cases that are not controlling. *Dicta* are remarks or comments made by a court that were not necessary in rendering a decision, but may provide insight into the court's thinking or may be influential in future cases. While *dicta* are not binding, they may be persuasive. An example of *dicta* is described in Example 11-2.

Dicta

Comments made by the court that are not part of the decision at hand, and are not a necessary part of that decision.

FINDING CASE LAW

One of the most important jobs of a paralegal is to locate published cases, because these cases are the foundation of the legal profession. It is therefore critical to know where to find case law when it is needed.

Federal Reporters

Reporters are books containing published opinions from all appellate and supreme courts in the state and federal court systems. Thousands of cases are printed every year in state and federal reporters. In addition, opinions are reported in specialty reporters such as bankruptcy law reporters and federal tax law reporters. Cases can also be found on the Internet, on paid subscription services, and on CD-ROMs.

There are two different types of federal courts within the federal court system. The first type is referred to as **Article III courts**. These general jurisdiction courts are created by the authority of Article III, Section 1 of the U.S. Constitution, which states:

Reporters

Case books on both the federal and state levels that contain court opinions.

Article III courts

Courts that are created or established under Article III, Section 1, of the United States Constitution.

> The judicial power of the United States, shall be vested in one Supreme Court, and in such inferior courts as the Congress may from time to time ordain and establish.[8]

[7]See *Korematsu v. United States*, 323 U.S. 214 (1944); *Wisconsin v. Yoder*, 406 U.S. 205 (1972).

[8]The Charters Of Freedom. Constitution of the United States. The U. S. National Archives and Records Administration. 2011. http://www.archives.gov/exhibits/charters/constitution_transcript.html

FIGURE 11-1 Structure and Operation of the Federal Courts[9]

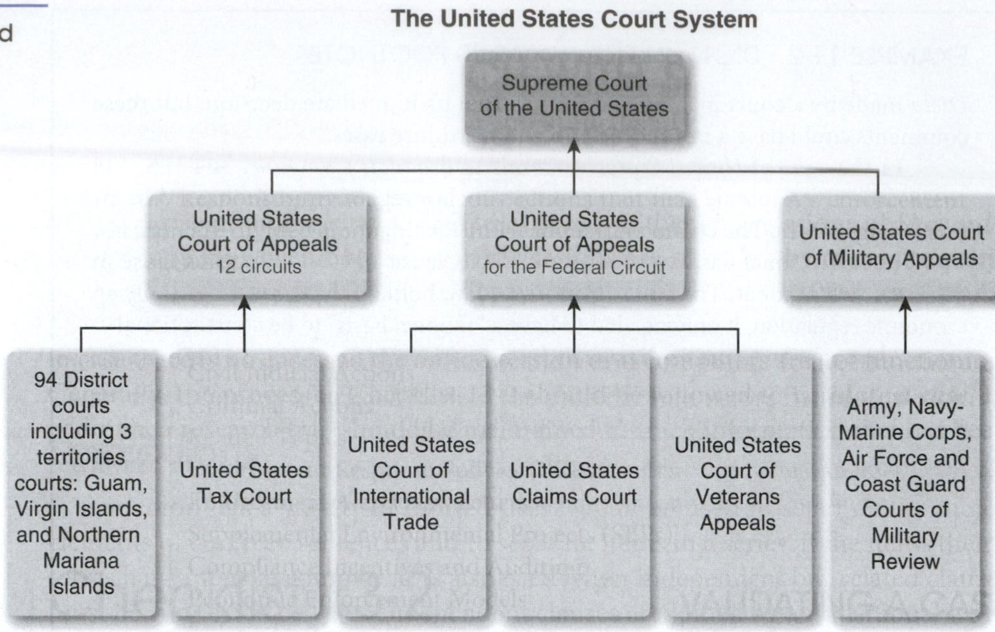

The United States Court System

Article I courts
Legislative courts created by Congress from the power given in Article I of the Constitution.

Slip opinion
The opinion sent to the printer on the day when the bench opinion is released by the Court.

Official reporter
Reporter published by a governmental entity that does not contain any enhancements or annotations.

Article III courts include the U.S. Supreme Court, the 13 U.S. Circuit Courts, the 94 U.S. District Courts, and the Court of International Trade.

Article I courts, also known as legislative courts, are limited jurisdiction courts created by Congress by the authority of Article I of the Constitution. These courts include territorial courts, such as those in the U.S. Virgin Islands; the U.S. Court of Military Appeals; and the U.S. Court of Veterans Appeals. Also included in the second type of courts are the magistrate and bankruptcy courts. Each of these courts hears a different type of case.

Figure 11-1 shows the structure of the federal court system.

United States Supreme Court The U. S. Supreme Court convenes once per year, beginning on the first Monday of October and continuing until summer.[10] The U.S. Supreme Court has more than 10,000 cases on its docket per term, and during that term, formal opinions are given in approximately 100 cases.[11] The decisions of the Supreme Court are initially published as *slip opinions*. Each slip opinion is sent to the printer following the release of the opinion from the bench, and may contain some corrections not appearing in the bench opinion. Slip opinions appear in the *United States Law Week*, published by the Bureau of National Affairs (BNA). Figure 11-2 shows the first page of a slip opinion that will appear as 564 U.S. ___ (2011).

The slip opinions are replaced within a few months with a preliminary print version that is paginated. One year after the issuance of the preliminary print version, the final version of the case is issued in a bound volume of the *United States Reports*, the *official reporter* of the Supreme Court. This reporter is published by private firms under contract with United States Government Printing Office. One of the cases in the *United States Reports* is shown in Figure 11-3.

[9]Structure of the Federal Court System. The United States Court System. http://www.4uth.gov.ua/usa/english/politics/judbranc/figure1.gif

[10]28 U. S.C. § 2.

[11]Duke Law Library and Technology. U.S. Supreme Court. 2012. http://www.law.duke.edu/lib/researchguides/ussup

FIGURE 11-2 Slip Opinion

(Slip Opinion)

OCTOBER TERM, 2010
Syllabus

NOTE: Where it is feasible, a syllabus (headnote) will be released, as is being done in connection with this case, at the time the opinion is issued. The syllabus constitutes no part of the opinion of the Court but has been prepared by the Reporter of Decisions for the convenience of the reader. See *United States* v. *Detroit Timber & Lumber Co.,* 200 U. S. 321, 337.

SUPREME COURT OF THE UNITED STATES

Syllabus

STERN, EXECUTOR OF THE ESTATE OF MARSHALL V. MARSHALL, EXECUTRIX OF THE ESTATE OF MARSHALL

CERTIORARI TO THE UNITED STATES COURT OF APPEALS FOR THE NINTH CIRCUIT

No. 10–179. Argued January 18, 2011—Decided June 23, 2011

Article III, §1, of the Constitution mandates that "[t]he judicial Power of the United States, shall be vested in one supreme Court, and in such inferior Courts as the Congress may from time to time ordain and establish," and provides that the judges of those constitutional courts "shall hold their Offices during good Behaviour" [sic] and "receive for their Services[ ] a Compensation[ ] [that] shall not be diminished" during their tenure. The questions presented in this case are whether a bankruptcy court judge who did not enjoy such tenure and salary protections had the authority under 28 U. S. C. §157 and Article III to enter final judgment on a counterclaim filed by Vickie Lynn Marshall (whose estate is the petitioner) against Pierce Marshall (whose estate is the respondent) in Vickie's bankruptcy proceedings. Vickie married J. Howard Marshall II, Pierce's father, approximately a year before his death. Shortly before J. Howard died, Vickie filed a suit against Pierce in Texas state court, asserting that J. Howard meant to provide for Vickie through a trust, and Pierce tortiously interfered with that gift. After J. Howard died, Vickie filed for bankruptcy in federal court. Pierce filed a proof of claim in that proceeding, asserting that he should be able to recover damages from Vickie's bankruptcy estate because Vickie had defamed him by inducing her lawyers to tell the press that he had engaged in fraud in controlling his father's assets. Vickie responded by filing a counterclaim for tortious interference with the gift she expected from J. Howard. The Bankruptcy Court granted Vickie summary judgment on the defamation claim and eventually awarded her hundreds of millions of dollars in damages on her counterclaim. Pierce objected that the . . . .[12]

In the early years of the Supreme Court, each volume was named after the individual responsible for publishing the volume. The first volumes have names such as Wallace, Black, Howard, Peters, Wheaton, Cranch, and Dallas. In 1875, the opinions began to be reported in the *United States Reports*. In opinions published in early volumes of the *United States Reports*, the name of the individual reporter actually appears in parentheses along with the number and volume of the *United States Reports,* for example, 68 U.S. (1 Wall.) 243 (1863).[13]

[12]Supreme Court of the United States. Sliplists 2011. 564 U. S. ___ (2011). http://www.supremecourt.gov /opinions/10pdf/10-179.pdf

[13]Columbia Law Review, Harvard Law Review, University of Pennsylvania Law Review, and Yale Law Journal, Eds. Table 1. *The Blue Book: A Uniform System Of Citation*, 18th ed. 2005.

FIGURE 11-3 *Griffins v. United States,* from the *United States Reports*

46

OCTOBER TERM, 1991
Syllabus

GRIFFIN v. UNITED STATES
CERTIORARI TO THE UNITED STATES COURT OF APPEALS FOR THE SEVENTH CIRCUIT

No. 90–6352. Argued October 7, 1991—Decided December 3, 1991

Petitioner Griffin and others were charged in a multiple-object conspiracy.

The evidence introduced at trial implicated Griffin in the first object of the conspiracy but not the second. The District Court nevertheless instructed the jury in a manner that would permit it to return a verdict against Griffin if it found her to have participated in *either one* of the two objects. The jury returned a general verdict of guilty. The Court of Appeals upheld Griffin's conviction, rejecting the argument that the verdict could not stand because it left in doubt whether the jury had convicted her as to the first or the second object.

Held: Neither the Due Process Clause of the Fifth Amendment nor this

Court's precedents require, in a federal prosecution, that a general guilty verdict on a multiple-object conspiracy be set aside if the evidence is inadequate to support conviction as to one of the objects. pp. 49–60.

(a) The historical practice fails to support Griffin's due process claim, since the rule of criminal procedure applied by the Court of Appeals was a settled feature of the common law. pp. 49–51.

(b) The precedent governing this case is not *Yates* v. *United States,* 354 U.S. 298, which invalidated a general verdict when one of the possible bases of conviction was *legally* inadequate, but *Turner* v. *United States,* 396 U.S. 398, 420, which upheld a general verdict when one of the possible bases of conviction was supported by *inadequate evidence.*

The line between *Yates* and *Turner* makes good sense: Jurors are not generally equipped to determine whether a particular theory of conviction is contrary to law, but are well equipped to determine whether the theory is supported by the facts. Although it would generally be preferable to give an instruction removing from the jury's consideration an alternative basis of liability that does not have adequate evidentiary support, the refusal to do so does not provide an independent basis for reversing an otherwise valid conviction. pp. 51–60.

913 F. 2d 337, affirmed.

Scalia, J., delivered the opinion of the Court, in which Rehnquist, C. J., and White, Stevens, O.Connor, Kennedy, and Souter, JJ., joined. Blackmun, J., filed an opinion concurring in the judgment, post, . . .[14]

Once the opinions have been bound, they are referred to as Term Opinions of the Court. It is important to note that if there are discrepancies between the print and electronic versions, the print version rules. If there are any discrepancies between the slip opinion and official published version of the opinion, it is the official version that controls.[15]

[14]*Id.* at 46.

[15]Supreme Court of the United States. 2010 Term. 2010 Term Opinions of the Court. Slip Opinions, *Per Curiams* (PC), and Original Case Decrees (D). 2012. http://www.supremecourt.gov/opinions /opinions.aspx

Later, the opinions will be published in two ***unofficial reporters***: the *Supreme Court Reporter* and *United States Supreme Court Reports, Lawyer's Edition*. The opinion is the same in all three sets of reporters. However, each unofficial reporter has its own unique enhancements and features. A law firm usually will have only one set of these cases.

The *Supreme Court Reporter* (*S.Ct.*), by West Publishing Company, reports decisions from the October 1882 term forward. In this set, West adds editorial enhancements to each opinion, including a syllabus, West's topics, key numbers, and headnotes, and references to the ALRs, C.J.S., and case annotations. West issues paper pamphlets every month, called ***advance sheets***, until a volume is ready to be bound. These advance sheets provides access to recent opinions until the bound volume is available. Beginning in 1986, West has published a paper set called an "interim edition" to pull the cases together until the bound volume is issued. Once the bound volume is issued, the advance sheets and the interim edition may be discarded.

The cases from the *Supreme Court Reporter* also can be found on Westlaw. Figure 11-4 shows the *Griffins* case.

Unofficial reporters
Reporters published by a commercial publisher; may contain annotations, enhancements, or other tools to use in the research process.

Advance sheets
Monthly pamphlets that provide decided opinions until a volume of opinions is bound.

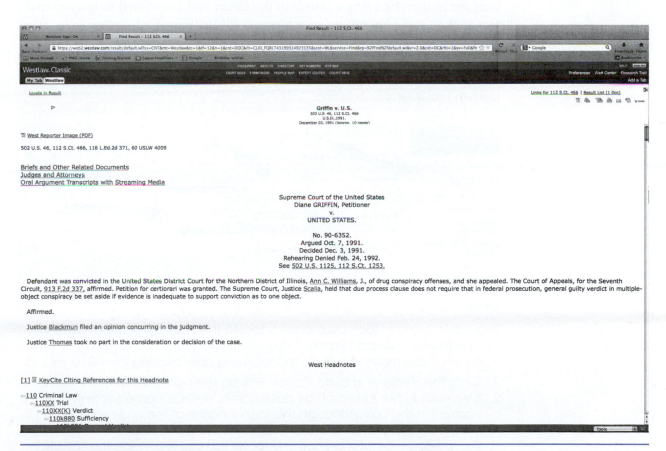

FIGURE 11-4 *Griffins v. United States,* from the *Supreme Court Reporter*[16]

[16]*Griffin v. United States,* 502 U.S. 46, 112 S.Ct. 466 (1991). Westlaw. 2012. Thomson Reuters. http://web2.westlaw.com/find/default.wl?cite=112+S.Ct.+466&rs=WLW13.01&vr=2.0&rp=%2ffind%2fdefault.wl&sv=Split&fn=_top&mt=Westlaw http://web2.westlaw.com/result/default.wl?rp=%2fsearch%2fdefault.wl&rltdb=CLID_DB26966230141310&eq=search&service=Search&action=Search&fn=_top&rs=WLW11.07&db=SCT&srch=TRUE&query=TI(GRIFFIN+%26+%22U.S.%22)&rlt=CLID_QRYRLT40628481141310&sskey=CLID_SSSA71238481141310&origin=Search&vr=2.0&method=TNC&cfid=1&mt=Westlaw&sv=Split&ssrc=599&fmqv=s

Note that Figures 11-3 and 11-4 show the same case, except that the case in Figure 11-4 has the added enhancements from the West editors. Once bound, the *Supreme Court Reporter* provides parallel citations to the *U.S. Reports* and to the other unofficial publication: *United States Supreme Court Reports, Lawyers' Edition*. This is generally referred to as *Lawyers' Edition, L.Ed., L.Ed.2d,* and *United States Law Week (U.S.L.W.)*

The *Lawyers' Edition* is currently reported by LexisNexis. The first series was published by Lawyers Cooperative and began when the Supreme Court was created. A second series, *Lawyers' Edition 2d*, began in 1956. Like the other services, *Lawyers' Edition 2d* provides advance sheets prior to the bound volume being issued. The bound volume contains any final corrections that the court issues, annotations on subjects provided by the editors, citations to and paging for the *United States Reports*, indexing to annotations, a parallel reference table, summaries of the briefs written by counsel, and information on the participating attorneys. In LexisNexis, supplements are published each year that provide additional annotations and a citator service.[17] Figure 11-5 shows how to find a case on LexisNexis.

In addition to its term opinions, there are two other types of opinions issued by the Supreme Court that the paralegal should be aware of. In-chambers opinions are written by a single justice of the Court and are related to interim matters such as stay applications or temporary injunctions. Each justice is assigned

FIGURE 11-5 Finding a Case on LexisNexis
Follow the instructions below to find a specific case in the Legal Search form in LexisNexis Academic.

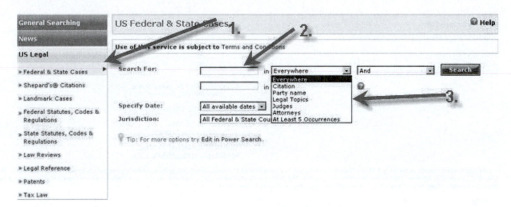

The easiest way to look up a case is to use the Look Up A Legal Case widget on the Easy Search Form.

An alternate method is to do the following after clicking the US Legal tab:

1. Click the "Federal & State Cases" link on the right side of the screen.
2. If you would like to search by case name, enter a name (or both names) in the box. Although the formal name of the case is *Roe v. Wade*, entering "Wade v. Roe" will return the same results. If you would like to search by citation number, enter the citation inside the "Citation Number" box.
3. Select Party Name or Citation from the drop-down box depending on which field you would like to search under.[18]

[17]Lexis-Nexis. The store. 2012. http://www.lexisnexis.com/store/catalog/booktemplate/productdetail.jsp?pageName=relatedProducts&prodId=7134

[18]Legal Search: Get a Case. LexisNexis 2012. http://wiki.lexisnexis.com/academic/index.php?title=Legal_Search:_Get_A_Case

to a different circuit and renders the in-chambers decisions for that circuit only.[19] Some cases are disposed of summarily, without any opinion explaining the Court's reasons for the order. Opinions Relating to Orders are opinions by individual justices commenting on such an order. Often these opinions are by justices who dissented from the decision of the court.[20]

United States Courts of Appeals The U.S. Courts of Appeals are organized into 13 circuits. Eleven of these are numbered, and cover broad regions of the country, while the other two are the D.C. Circuit, covering the District of Columbia, and the Federal Circuit, which handles specific subject areas such as customs and patents.

Each Court of Appeals hears appeals from the district courts and administrative agency decisions within its circuit. Figure 11-6 shows the breakdown for the federal circuit courts. The federal circuit court hears cases from specialized trial courts such as the patent court. [21] In addition, other federal appellate courts, such as the Court of Appeals for the Armed Forces, handle particular topical areas.

The published decisions of the United States Courts of Appeals appear in the *Federal Reporter* series. These volumes are considered to be unofficial reporters, since they are not published by the courts themselves. The U.S. Courts of Appeals cases from 1882 to 1924 are reported in the *Federal Reporter (F.)*. The *Federal Reporter, Second Series (F.2d)* covers cases from 1925 to 1988. The cases from 1989 to the present are reported in the *Federal Reporter, Third Series (F.3d)*.

> **TIP**
>
> A list of the states or areas that comprise each circuit is listed in 28 U.S.C. § 41.

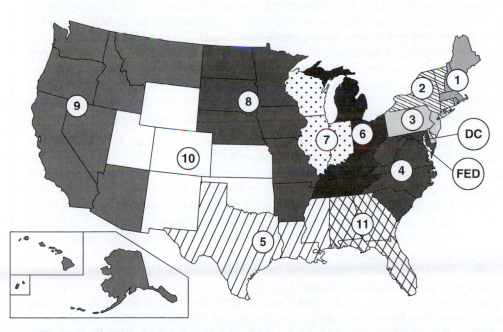

FIGURE 11-6 Geographic Boundaries of the U.S. Courts of Appeals[22]

---

[19]Supreme Court of the United States. 2010 Term. 2010 Term Opinions of the Court. 2010 Term In-Chambers Opinions http://www.supremecourt.gov/opinions/in-chambers.aspx

[20]Supreme Court of the United States. 2010 Term. 2010 Term Opinions of the Court. 2010 Term Opinions Relating to Orders. http://www.supremecourt.gov/opinions/relatingtoorders.aspx

[21]Longley, Robert. U.S. Federal Court System. About.com Guide. U.S. Government Info. 2011. http://usgovinfo.about.com/od/uscourtsystem/a/fedcourts.htm

[22]UWM Libraries. http://www.google.com/imgres?q=West%27s+federal+reporter+system&um =1&hl=en&tbm=isch&tbnid=68WSP1Xp_nTTZM:&imgrefurl=http://www4.uwm.edu/libraries /guides/legalguide.html&docid=Ey4CZRyjWFxUtM&w=559&h=344&ei=hvuFTqjqE-r30gHMurg G&zoom=1&iact=hc&vpx=688&vpy=360&dur=263&hovh=176&hovw=286&tx=88&ty=88&page= 1&tbnh=138&tbnw=225&start=0&ndsp=26&ved=1t:429,r:11,s:0&biw=1280&bih=898

2012 U.S. App. LEXIS 4161, *

RAYMOND HAYES, Plaintiff-Appellant, *v.* CITY OF CHICAGO, Defendant-Appellee.

No. 10-3750

UNITED STATES COURT OF APPEALS FOR THE SEVENTH CIRCUIT

2012 U.S. App. LEXIS 4161

January 11, 2012, Argued

March 1, 2012, Decided

PRIOR   HISTORY: [*1]

Appeal from the United States District Court for the Northern District of Illinois, Eastern Division. No. 10 C 3378—James F. Holderman, Chief Judge.

Hayes v. City of Chicago, 2010 U.S. Dist. LEXIS 117749 (N.D. Ill., Nov. 3, 2010)

COUNSEL: For RAYMOND HAYES, Plaintiff - Appellant: Kenneth N. Flaxman, Attorney, Chicago, IL.

For CITY OF CHICAGO, Defendant - Appellee: Jonathon D. Byrer, Attorney, CITY OF CHICAGO LAW DEPARTMENT, Appeals Division, Chicago, IL.

JUDGES: Before KANNE, WILLIAMS, and HAMILTON, Circuit Judges.

OPINION BY: KANNE

OPINION

Kanne, *Circuit Judge.* This case marks the fourth time Raymond Hayes has asked or could have asked a court or administrative agency to rule on whether he was unlawfully terminated by the Chicago Police Department. Namely, Hayes has litigated his claim before the Circuit Court of Cook County, the Illinois Human Rights Commission ("IHRC"), and two federal courts. Hayes brought his most recent claim to federal court in 2010. Finding that this complaint arose from the "same group of operative facts as those before the Circuit Court of Cook County," the district court dismissed Hayes's suit as barred by claim preclusion. We affirm.

I. Background

The facts here are essentially undisputed. Raymond Hayes began work as a Chicago police officer in October 1976. In 1992, the Superintendent [*2] of the Chicago Police Department charged Hayes with several counts of misconduct related to his improper arrest of a taxi driver. On March 5, 1993, after a full hearing before the Police Board, Hayes was found to have violated five departmental rules. He was subsequently fired. In April 1993, Hayes petitioned the Circuit Court of Cook County for administrative review of the Police Board's ruling. Hayes raised eleven challenges to the Police Board's decision, all of which in one way or another suggested that the Board's ruling was against the manifest weight of the evidence or that the Board had improperly considered certain evidence. Nowhere in his petition before the Circuit Court did Hayes claim that his termination was unlawfully motivated by his race. The Circuit Court of Cook County affirmed the Police Board, as did the Illinois Appellate Court. The Illinois Supreme Court denied Hayes's petition for leave to appeal. **Hayes v. Police Bd. of Chicago, 162 Ill. 2d 567, 652 N.E.2d 341, 209 Ill. Dec. 801 (Ill. 1995)** (table).[23]

FIGURE 11-7 Portion of *Hayes v. City of Chicago* on LexisNexis

[23]LexisNexis Communities Portal. Free Case Law—Full Case Display. LexisNexis, a division of Reed Elsevier Inc. 2011. http://www.lexisone.com/lx1/caselaw/freecaselaw?action=FCLRetrieveCaseDetail&caseID=1&format=FULL&resultHandle=94c307fbf6c5f92d2268e67a795dfcdb&pageLimit=10&xmlgTotalCount=17&combinedSearchTerm=age+discrimination+and+date+geq+(03%2F03%2F2011)&juriName=7th%20Circuit%20Court%20of%20Appeals&sourceFile=GENFED;7CIR

Since 2001, unpublished opinions have been printed separately in the *Federal Appendix*, also published by West. The opinions of the Fifth and Eleventh Circuits are not included in the *Federal Appendix,* because these two courts do not give unpublished opinions to the publishers.

Opinions in most Court of Appeals cases are also available on fee-based databases such as Westlaw or LexisNexis, as well as on various websites of the courts and on other Internet sites maintained by various law schools. Figure 11-7 shows a sample of a U.S. Court of Appeals case on LexisNexis.

The same case appears in Westlaw, as shown in Figure 11-8.

FIGURE 11-8 Portion of *Hayes v. City of Chicago* on Westlaw

Hayes v. City of Chicago

—F.3d—, 2012 WL 661676

C.A.7 (Ill.), 2012.

March 01, 2012 (Approx. 5 pages)

Only the Westlaw citation is currently available.

United States Court of Appeals,

Seventh Circuit.

Raymond HAYES , Plaintiff–Appellant,

v.

CITY OF CHICAGO, Defendant–Appellee.

No. 10–3750.

Argued Jan. 11, 2012.

Decided March 1, 2012.

Background: Former police officer brought action against police department, under Title VII, alleging his termination of employment was unlawfully based on his race. The United States District Court for the Northern District of Illinois, James F. Holderman, Chief Judge, 2010 WL 4627716, dismissed action as barred by claim preclusion. Officer appealed.

Holding: The Court of Appeals, Kanne, Circuit Judge, held that state court review of administrative decision sustaining discharge of police officer foreclosed officer's subsequent federal action.

Affirmed.

West Headnotes

[1] ☑ KeyCite Citing References for this Headnote

☞170B Federal Courts

Court of Appeals reviews de novo a district court's decision motions for judgment on the pleadings; in so doing, the Court reviews a judgment for defendants by employing the same standard that it applies when reviewing a motion to dismiss for failure to state a claim. Fed. Rules Civ.Pro.Rule 12(b)(6), (c).

[2] ☑ KeyCite Citing References for this Headnote

☞228 Judgment

Claim preclusion prohibits litigants from relitigating claims that were or could have been litigated during an earlier proceeding.
* * *

Appeal from the United States District Court for the Northern District of Illinois, Eastern Division. No. 10 C 3378—James F. Holderman, Chief Judge.

FIGURE 11-8 *(Continued)*

Kenneth N. Flaxman, Chicago, IL, for Plaintiff–Appellant.

Jonathon D. Byrer, City of Chicago Law Department, Chicago, IL, for Defendant–Appellee.

Before KANNE, WILLIAMS, and HAMILTON, Circuit Judges.

KANNE, Circuit Judge.

***1** This case marks the fourth time Raymond Hayes has asked or could have asked a court or administrative agency to rule on whether he was unlawfully terminated by the Chicago Police Department. Namely, Hayes has litigated his claim before the Circuit Court of Cook County, the Illinois Human Rights Commission ("IHRC"), and two federal courts. Hayes brought his most recent claim to federal court in 2010. Finding that this complaint arose from the "same group of operative facts as those before the Circuit Court of Cook County," the district court dismissed Hayes's suit as barred by claim preclusion. We affirm.

I. BACKGROUND

The facts here are essentially undisputed. Raymond Hayes began work as a Chicago police officer in October 1976. In 1992, the Superintendent of the Chicago Police Department charged Hayes with several counts of misconduct related to his improper arrest of a taxi driver. On March 5, 1993, after a full hearing before the Police Board, Hayes was found to have violated five departmental rules. He was subsequently fired. In April 1993, Hayes petitioned the Circuit Court of Cook County for administrative review of the Police Board's ruling. Hayes raised eleven challenges to the Police Board's decision, all of which in one way or another suggested that the Board's ruling was against the manifest weight of the evidence or that the Board had improperly considered certain evidence. Nowhere in his petition before the Circuit Court did Hayes claim that his termination was unlawfully motivated by his race. The Circuit Court of Cook County affirmed the Police Board, as did the Illinois Appellate Court. The Illinois Supreme Court denied Hayes's petition for leave to appeal. *Hayes v. Police Bd. of Chicago,* 162 Ill.2d 567, 209 Ill.Dec. 801, 652 N.E.2d 341 (Ill.1995) (table).[24]

Figures 11-7 and 11-8 show the same case as it appears on both LexisNexis and Westlaw, but each service provides slightly different enhancements and presentation. The case on each service has a unique identifying number (LEXIS 4161 on LexisNexis, and 2012 WL 661676 on Westlaw). The parts of each opinion are arranged differently but the language is the same. Westlaw provides the Westlaw headnotes, which are not available on LexisNexis.

United States District Courts   The trial court level of the federal system consists of 94 district courts, which are listed at 28 U.S.C. §§ 81-144. Each state has at least one federal district court. The opinions of trial courts are usually are not published, but the federal district courts are an exception. The district court judges decide which cases will be published, and only a small percentage of their opinions are submitted for publication. Their decision to publish tends to be based on the importance of the legal issues, whether the case resolves a conflict in interpretation of the law, or whether it is of great public interest.

---

[24]*Hayes v. City of Chicago,* —F.3d—, 2012 WL 661676, C.A.7 (Ill.), 2012. http://web2.westlaw.com /result/default.wl?cfid=1&mt=Westlaw&origin=Search&sskey=CLID_SSSA3644337261633&query= TI(HAYES+%26+%22CITY+OF+CHICAGO%22)&db=CTA7&rlt=CLID_QRYRLT1872437261633& method=TNC&service=Search&eq=search&rp=%2fsearch%2fdefault.wl&srch=TRUE&vr=2.0&action= Search&rltdb=CLID_DB513659251633&sv=Split&fmqv=s&fn=_top&rs=WLW12.01

The U.S. District Court cases from 1933 to 1988 are reported in the *Federal Supplement* (*F. Supp.*), and those from 1988 to the present are reported in the *Federal Supplement, Second Series* (*F. Supp. 2d*). Decisions from other bodies, such as the U.S. Court of Claims (1932–1960) and the U.S. Court of International Trade, are reported in the *Federal Supplement* as well as in their own reporters. Like the courts of appeals, the federal district courts do not publish their own opinions, so the only sources are the unofficial reporters in print, on fee-based services, and on some Internet sites.

Prior to 1880, West did not publish cases from the lower federal courts, and those that were published were printed haphazardly and in various sets of books. Beginning in 1880, West collected the lower federal court cases and published them in the set titled *Federal Cases*. Because this publication came before the *National Reporter System* was established, the cases in *Federal Cases* are reported in alphabetical order rather than in chronological order, and each case is assigned a chronological number throughout the 30 total volumes.

Federal Rules If research is focusing on the interpretation of a rule of court, the *Federal Rules Decisions* (*F.R.D.*) can be helpful. This set publishes U.S. District Court decisions interpreting the Federal Rules of Civil Procedure, Federal Rules of Criminal Procedures, Federal Rules of Evidence, Federal Rules of Appellate Procedure, Federal Rules of Sentencing Guidelines, and other federal rules.

The *Federal Rules Decisions* are also available on Westlaw. In addition to the decisions (FRD database), articles from 1938 onward may be accessed in the FRD Articles (FRD-ART) database, and rules from 1944 onward in the FRD-RULES database.

Other Federal Materials West also publishes some very specialized sets on specific subjects. In bankruptcy law practices, West's *Bankruptcy Reporter* is used routinely. It provides bankruptcy cases decided by the United States Bankruptcy Courts, the Bankruptcy Appellate Panels, and the U.S. District Courts. These cases are not found in the *Federal Supplement*. In addition, cases handed down by the U.S. Courts of Appeals and the U.S. Supreme Court regarding bankruptcy appeals will be in this reporter. Other cases can be found in *BNA's Bankruptcy Law Reporter*. These cases can be found on Westlaw under the bankruptcy court cases (FBKR-BCT) and in LexisNexis under Bankruptcy Law.

Two sets of reporters deal specifically with military cases. One is West's *Military Justice Reporter,* which provides decisions from the U.S. Court of Appeals for the Armed Forces and the Military Service Courts of Criminal Appeals. The other set is the West's *Veterans Appeals Reporter,* which provides cases from the U.S. Court of Appeals for Veterans Claims.

West's *Federal Claims Reporter* provides decisions of the U.S. Court of Federal Claims and appeals from this court decided by the U.S. Courts of Appeal and the U.S. Supreme Court. Cases in this reporter may include tax fund suits, environment and natural resource disputes, contract cases involving the government, and civilian and military pay questions.

Researching Federal Case Law Researching federal case law will be faster and more effective if the researcher is familiar with the abbreviations for the reporters and other sources. Table 11-2 shows some of the more common abbreviations used in federal reporters, regional reporters, and other law books. *Black's Law Dictionary*, *The Bluebook*, or *ALWD* should be consulted for interpretations and definitions of these terms.

This is not by any means an exhaustive list, but rather provides some of the basic abbreviations seen most frequently in locating and reading cases.

TIP

The quicker that these abbreviations become second nature to a researcher, the easier researching cases will become.

TABLE 11-2   Common Abbreviations

Word	Abbreviation	Word	Abbreviation
Atlantic, Atlantic Second series	A., A.2d	Claims	Cl.
North Eastern, North Eastern second series	N.E., N.E.2d	Chief Judge, Chief Justice	C.J.
North Western, North Western second series	N.W., N.W.2d	Judge, Justice/Judges, Justices	J./ J.J.
South Eastern, South Eastern second series	S.E., S.E.2d	District	Dist., D.
South Western, South Western second series	S.W., S.W.2d	Northern District	N.D.
Southern, Southern second series	So., So.2d	Southern District	S.D.
Pacific, Pacific second series	P., P.2d	Central District	C.D.
United States Reports	U. S.	Eastern District	E.D.
Supreme Court Reports	S.Ct.	Western District	W.D.
United States Supreme Court Reports, Lawyers' Edition, United States Supreme Court Reports, Lawyers' Edition second series	L.Ed., L.Ed.2d	Federal Rules of Civil Procedure	F.R.C.P.
United States Law Week	U.S.L.W.	Bankruptcy	Bankr.
Federal Reporter, Federal Reporter second series, *Federal Reporter* third series	F., F.2d., F.3d	Appellate	App.
Federal Supplement, Federal Supplement second series	F.Supp., F.Supp.2d	Division	Div.
Federal Rules Decisions	F.R.D.	Civil	Civ.
Circuit	Cir.	Criminal	Crim.

The National Reporter System   Starting a research project can be daunting. The West's *National Reporter System* provides several useful features that aid in the research process.

If the name, or part of the name, of the case is already known, the alphabetical table of cases provided in each volume of West's *National Reporter System* can be used to find that case within the volume. If the approximate date of the case is known, the volumes in that timeframe may be examined to locate the case. In some reporters, the cases are listed twice: first by listing all cases alphabetically, and then by listing the cases alphabetically by state (regional reporters) or by circuit (in the federal reporters).

The tables of statutes help researchers locate cases that interpret or construe any statute or constitutional provision used within the reporter. For example, cases that have interpreted Rule 12(b) of the Federal Rules of Civil Procedure may be located by looking under this table.

Words and Phrases provides cases that define the words and phrases listed. For example, if a researcher were interested in locating cases where "civil rights" was defined, one would look up "civil rights" in the table. Any cases within the volume that discussed "civil rights" would be listed.

Another feature found in the hardbound volumes of the *National Reporter System* is a listing of the judges sitting on the courts covered by a particular volume. Therefore, if a researcher were looking at a case from the Seventh Circuit Court of Appeals, the volume would list all of the justices sitting on that Seventh Circuit Court of Appeals.

Probably one of the most useful features of the *National Reporter System* is the key number system. West provides the topics, key numbers, and headnotes for each case reported in the volume. The topics are arranged alphabetically. Since this key number system is an integrated research system, all volumes and sets within the *National Reporter System* and Westlaw reference the key numbers. So, if a

TIP

This feature is not found in all volumes or in all sets.

case discussed the rule of evidence regarding "judicial notice" by the courts of the United States, it would reference the topic Evidence (157), key number Laws of the United States (34), and would appear as 157k34. A researcher could find every case in the United States that discussed this topic and key number either through the print resources (under the topic Evidence, and then Laws of the United States) or through Westlaw (157k34).

Although many state courts require that citations to cases include all parallel citations, this is not true for the cases from the United States Supreme Court; only the *United States Reports* citation is required. If the *United States Reports* citation is not yet available, the unofficial reporters may be cited.

Because the pagination of Supreme Court cases is different in each of the reporters, the unofficial reporters provide a feature called "star paging" that indicates the page breaks in the official *United States Reports* and for both unofficial reporters. The name "star paging" came from the fact that the original indicator was the asterisk or star. For example, in LexisNexis's *Supreme Court Reports, Lawyer's Edition* (L. Ed.) the page break in the official reporter is identified with a bold reference in brackets such as [**347 U.S. 485**]. In West's *Supreme Court Reporter*, an inverted "T" is inserted between the last word of one page and the first word of the next page as it would appear in the *United States Reports*. In Westlaw itself, the asterisk with the page number for the *United States Reports* is still used. Therefore, no matter which set of books is used, a researcher has the ability to properly cite to the *United States Reports*.

Digests The most comprehensive way to research federal cases is to use the digests, which contain brief summaries of points of law, organized by topics and key numbers within the West key number system. Each topic and key number will have a single point of law called the **headnote**. These headnotes are the publisher's summary of the point of law. West created this system to organize federal and state cases so that research would be easier. The headnotes may be used to find any cases that discuss the same topic and point of law.

After each headnote is a citation to the case in which the headnote appears. If a citation at the end of a headnote were *Brown v. Board of Education*, 347 U.S. 483 (1954), this case could then be located in the *United States Reports*, or at 74 S.Ct. 686 and 98 L.Ed. 873 (the unofficial reporters). It also is available at 38 A.L.R.2d 1180 as an annotation.

U.S. Supreme Court cases are covered in the *United States Supreme Court Digest*. Cases of the U.S. District Courts and U.S. Courts of Appeals are covered in the five editions of the *Federal Practice Digest*:

- *Federal Digest* covering 1754 to 1939 (the red set)
- *Modern Federal Practice Digest* covering 1939 to 1960 (the green set)
- West's *Federal Practice Digest* 2nd covering 1961 to 1975 (the blue set)
- West's *Federal Practice Digest* 3rd covering 1975 to 1992 (the burgundy set)
- West's *Federal Practice Digest* 4th covering 1992 (the navy set)

The digests are updated annually with pocket parts.

Internet and Fee-Based Services Most published and unpublished federal and state decisions are available on fee-based services such as Westlaw, LexisNexis, and CASEMaker, and on the Internet.

The fee-based services, Westlaw and LexisNexis, provide citations for all cases that are published in hard copy. The Internet version of each case indicates the page breaks in the print versions using the "star numbering" system. When

TIP
One should never quote from headnotes, because the headnotes are not the law.

Headnote
The summary of a point of law contained in West digests.

TIP
Always check the pocket part to make sure the most current information is used.

making a pinpoint citation to specific text within a case, a researcher would use the page numbers indicated with an asterisk. See Exhibit 11-1 for an example from Westlaw. If a writer wanted to quote the language, "the court did hold that there was reasonable suspicion to detain Ferguson's bags," the pinpoint citation *U.S. v. Ferguson*, 935 F2d. 1518, 1522 (7th Cir. 1991) would be made.

Although some cases are not published in the printed volumes, these unpublished cases may be available on Westlaw or LexisNexis. If the case is not published in hard copy, Westlaw and LexisNexis give the case an online designation that is different from the standard citation form. Here is an example of a Westlaw citation:

U.S. v. Salami, No. 97-6257, 1998 WL 39170 (C.A.4 (Md.) Feb. 3, 1998).

In this instance, the information includes the party names (*United States* and *Salami*), the docket number (97–6257), the year of decision (1998) followed by WL, which stands for Westlaw, and the number assigned by Westlaw (39170). At the end is the court designation and date. Another exception is the date. In a standard case citation only the year is given, but in a citation to a commercial electronic database, the full date is provided. The LexisNexis cite would appear the same except for the special LexisNexis designation.

LexisNexis has begun incorporating headnotes in its database, although the headnotes are not the same as those in the West key number system.

Many Internet sites provide cases free or for a nominal cost, but those materials are not complete and are not easily searchable. One example is the Pacer service, which provides access to many federal decisions. State courts often provide decisions as well. Other Internet sites that provide cases are maintained by law schools such as Cornell, Emory, and the University of Texas. See Exhibit 11-1 for a sample of free sites that provide cases.

EXHIBIT 11-1 SAMPLE PAGE FROM WESTLAW SHOWING STAR PAGING

U.S. v. Ferguson, 935 F.2d 1518 (CA7 (Ill.) 1991)

III. SUPPRESSION OF THE COCAINE

Ferguson moved to suppress the cocaine found in his locked bag. In arguing for suppression, the government and Ferguson dispute whether the pre-sniff meeting and discussion between Ferguson and law enforcement officers at the Chicago Union Station was consensual and whether there ***1522** was reasonable suspicion to detain Ferguson's luggage. While the trial court did not explicitly make a determination of whether the encounter between Ferguson and the officers was consensual,[FN3] the court did hold that there was reasonable suspicion to detain Ferguson's bags. In making this finding the court relied upon questions, answers and statements made between Ferguson and the law enforcement officers as well as the officers' knowledge, experience and training, Ferguson's use of an assumed name on the train ticket, Ferguson's statement that he was coming into Chicago when his ticket's destination was Detroit, the defendant's inconsistent admission and later denial that he was carrying packages for someone else, and Ferguson's furtive and nervous behavior. The court found these facts sufficient to warrant the detention of Ferguson's luggage and noted that: "Within thirty minutes the officers had made a check of the luggage and developed a basis for a warrant which was later issued."[25]

---

[25]*U.S. v. Ferguson*, 935 F.2d 1518 (CA7 (Ill.) 1991). Thomson Reuters, Inc. 2011. http://web2.westlaw .com/find/default.wl?rs=WLW11.10&rp=%2ffind%2fdefault.wl&vr=2.0&fn=_top&mt=Westlaw& cite=935+f2d+1518&sv=Split

Type of Decisions	Address
U.S. Courts	www.uscourts.gov
U.S. Supreme Court	www.supremecourtus.gov
Circuit Courts of Appeals	www.ca1.uscourts.gov
	www.ca2.uscourts.gov
	www.ca3.uscourts.gov
	www.ca4.uscourts.gov
	www.ca5.uscourts.gov
	www.ca6.uscourts.gov
	www.ca7.uscourts.gov
	www.ca8.uscourts.gov
	www.ca9.uscourts.gov
	www.ca10.uscourts.gov
	www.ca11.uscourts.gov
	www.fedcir.uscourts.gov
	www.cadc.uscourts.gov
General Search Site	www.findlaw.com
	www.lexisone.com
	http://www.oyez.org/
Legal Information Institute and law school sites	www.law.cornell.edu
	http://www.law.villanova.edu/library/law
	http://www.law.harvard.edu/library/index.html
	http://lib.law.washington.edu/research/research.html

FIGURE 11-9 Free Internet Sites Providing Federal Decisions

State Materials

State court systems may be **two-tiered** or **three-tiered** systems. Two-tiered systems have a trial-level court and one appellate-level court. Examples of two-tier systems are Montana and New York. Three-tiered systems have a trial court, an intermediate appeals court, and a final appeals court. Examples of a three-tiered system are Indiana and Washington.

A trial court is the court where the parties appear, witnesses testify, evidence is presented, and attorneys argue based on the facts of the case. A trial court may or may not have a jury. If there is a jury, the jury hears and decides the questions of fact while the judge hears and decides the questions of law. If there is no jury, the trial is referred to as a **bench trial**, meaning that the judge decides both questions of law and questions of fact. When the trial court makes its decision, the losing party may appeal to an appellate-level court.

In general, appellate-level courts decide only questions of law, not questions of fact. Appellate level courts do not hear testimony of witnesses or receive new evidence. The appellate-level court will look at the transcript of the case and briefs filed by the parties. Occasionally the appellate court may hear oral arguments by the attorneys. If the state has a three-tier system, and the party is still dissatisfied at the intermediate appellate level, the party may be able to appeal to the final appellate court, sometimes referred to as the state's supreme court.

At one time states published the opinions of their intermediate- and/or final-level appellate courts' decisions; today, very few states publish their own opinions. If a state does publish its own opinions, those opinions are bound in

Two-tiered

Court systems consisting of a trial-level court and one appeals-level court.

Three-tiered

A system consisting of a trial court, an intermediate appeals court, and a final appeals court.

Bench trial

A trial in which the judge decides questions of both law and fact.

Official Reporter

Reporters published by the governmental entity that do not contain any enhancements or annotations.

Unofficial reporters

Reporters published by a commercial publisher that may contain annotations, enhancements, or other tools to use in the research process.

Parallel Citations

Other locations of sources where the same case may be found.

TIP

Refer to Figure 11-11.

Parallel cites

Other locations of sources where the same case may be found.

official reporters under governmental scrutiny. If the opinions are not published by the government, they are published with government approval by independent publishers such as West. These publications are the *unofficial reporters*. Publishers such as West and LexisNexis publish the most well-known unofficial reporters. In these reporters, the cases themselves are published exactly as they appear in the official reporters. However, the unofficial reporters contain additional information such as headnotes and summaries of the case. Cases often appear in more than one case reporter, and the researcher may find *parallel citations* to the same case.

There are several Internet sites available for free case law research.

The most reliable and up-to-date sites are those associated with the government or with law schools. State case law can also be found using LexisNexis and Westlaw, or other Internet legal research resources, just as in researching federal case law.

Finding Parallel Cites   A parallel citation is a citation that includes references to more than one location for the same case. The *official citation* will appear first in most states' formats. The other citations will be to the unofficial publications in which the case also appears. Some courts require all parallel cites to be listed for each case, and it is proper form in some jurisdictions to give all the parallel cites for every case for the convenience of the reader. However, a researcher may only have access to one set of reporters. In those situations, there are several ways to find parallel citations.

The first step is to look at the case in a reporter. Often the reporter will provide both the official and unofficial citations. In a regional reporter, the heading of the case underneath the party names will give the official citation. If using Westlaw, all of the parallel citations are in the header. Figure 11-11 shows an example from Westlaw.

FIGURE 11-11 Parallel Citations on Westlaw

---

821 N.E.2d 95
62 Mass.App.Ct. 783, 821 N.E.2d 95
(Cite as: 62 Mass.App.Ct. 783, 821 N.E.2d 95)

Appeals Court of Massachusetts,
Suffolk.
J. Michael BOYD, administrator,[FN1]

[FN1]Of the estate of Kelly Ann Boyd.

v.

NATIONAL RAILROAD PASSENGER CORPORATION[FN2] & others.[FN3]

[FN2]Doing business as and also known as Amtrak.
[FN3]Massachusetts Bay Transportation Authority and Richard Prone.

No. 03-P-312.
Argued May 12, 2004.
Decided Jan. 20, 2005.
Further Appellate Review Granted July 6, 2005.[26]

---

[26]*Boyd v. National Railroad Passenger Corporation*, 62 Mass.App.Ct.783, 821 N.E.2d 95 (2005). 2011. Thomson Reuters.

Many state digests provide a volume that may be called "Plaintiffs/Defendants Table." The cases are presented in alphabetical order by the plaintiff and then by the defendant. So, knowing the name of one or the other will allow a researcher to find the case.

Other tools for finding parallel citations are the *National Reporter Bluebook* and the state *Blue and White* books. If a researcher had only the official citation for a case, such as 62 Mass.App.Ct. 783, the *National Reporter Blue Book* would provide the unofficial citation—821 N.E.2d 95. Since about half of the states continue to publish official reporters, those states continue to have *Blue and White Books* to find parallel cites, such as the *Ohio Blue and White Book*. The blue pages give the official citations and the white pages give the parallel citations from the regional reporters. No matter which citation is available, the parallel citation can be located by looking in either the blue or white pages.

Citation services can also be used to find parallel cites. When a researcher finds case law that is applicable to the client's situation, the material must be updated to make sure that the case is still good law. The parallel cites may also be found at that time. The two primary tools for that purpose are *Shepard's*, available on LexisNexis or in print, and KeyCite, available through Westlaw. Using either of these updating tools also provides the official and unofficial citations for the case.

Regional Reporters   Regional reporters contain the unofficial versions of cases. These unofficial reporters generally contain the same opinion information as the official reporters. However, if the official reporter and unofficial reporter differ in language, the language of the official reporter always controls.

Today, these unofficial reporters are generally the sets researchers most often use to find cases, because the unofficial reporters are published sooner than the official reporters and many states no longer publish official reporters. In addition, the editors of the unofficial reporters add additional information, which helps in the research process. In West publications, each case includes a synopsis, topics and key numbers, and headnotes. The key numbers allow a researcher to quickly access specific material in a digest. All West publications are linked together through this key number system. LexisNexis publications also include editorial enhancements, such as annotated comments and the publisher's version of headnotes.

Figure 11-12 shows the West Regional Reporter system, which covers all 50 states plus the District of Columbia. The system also divides the country into seven regional reporters: Atlantic, North Eastern, North Western, South Eastern, Southern, South Western, and Pacific. It is very helpful to learn the states that comprise each of the regions, or at least those of the region in which one works. Knowing this information makes doing research much easier when a case needs to be located quickly.

Digests   *Digests* provide points of law and citations to cases. The headnotes of each case link to information in the digests. All states have a separate digest except Delaware, Nevada, and Utah. The state digests contain tools similar to those mentioned under the federal information, such as a table of cases, allowing a researcher to find a case with either the plaintiff's or defendant's name.

Both LexisNexis and Westlaw provide access to the state and regional reporters, as well as many other legal resources, for a fee.

Digest

A set of books that provides summaries of points of law established in cases. Each summary consists of a topic, a key number, and headnote describing the point of law.

TIP

Digests are discussed further in Chapter 9.

Regional Reporters (State Cases)

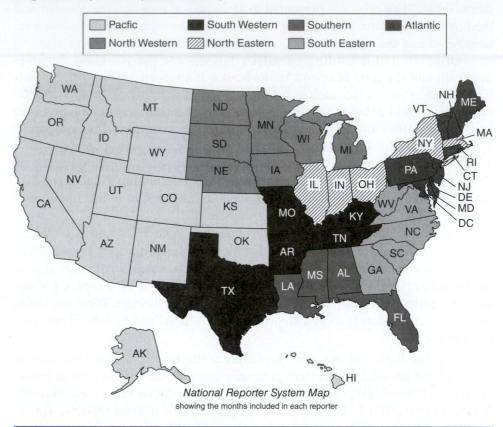

National Reporter System Map
showing the months included in each reporter

FIGURE 11-12 West's Regional Reporter System[27]

Style manual

A set of guidelines or standards created for writing, designing, and citing written works.

CITING THE LAW 11-1: CITING A CASE

A case citation tells where to find that case and can give helpful information as to whether or not the case might serve as precedent. A typical citation will include the parties, the volume of the reporter, the name of the reporter, the page the case begins on, the court, the year of the decision, and any necessary parallel cites, such as

parties   names of reporters   volumes of reporters

Smith v. Malone 317 Ill.App.3d 974, 742 N.E.2d 785 (4th Dist. 2000)

          starting page of case   court   year of decision

In a case reporter, a case citation will often be found at the top of the page for that published opinion. When reading a case opinion or other legal resource that cites to another case opinion, a case citation will be placed in a citation sentence. The citation sentence will appear immediately following the text that references that case. Be sure to consult *The Bluebook* (Rule 10), *ALWD* (Rule 12), or another *style manual* for the correct citation format when providing citations in legal writing. Further details on citing cases are discussed extensively in Chapters 5 and 6.

---

[27]West's Regional Reporter System. 2011. Thomson Reuters. http://lawschool.westlaw.com/federalcourt /NationalReporterPage.asp

PARTS OF A CASE

Once the cases are found it is important to read each case thoroughly and understand what they are about. Reading a case is easier if the researcher is familiar with the parts of a case and their purpose.

Published cases generally have similar parts. Figure 11-13 shows an Ohio case from Westlaw with the various parts identified.

It is important to take a closer look at each of the case parts identified in Figure 11-11. These first three items, the case names, the docket number, and the date of decision, along with the name of the court that decided the case, comprise the *caption* of the case. Many jurisdictions have specific rules for what should be contained in a caption and how that information should be presented.

Caption

The party names, the docket number, and the date of decision, along with the name of the court that decided the case.

FIGURE 11-13 Parts of a Case

Appellate Court of Illinois,
Fourth District.
John P. DUFFY, Petitioner-Appellant,
v.
The ILLINOIS DEPARTMENT OF HUMAN RIGHTS; The Illinois Human Rights Commission; Christie Clinic, P.C.; and Ellen E. Roney, M.D., Respondents-Appellees. [1]
No. 4-04-0204. [2]
Argued Nov. 17, 2004.
Decided Dec. 20, 2004. [3]

Background: Former patient appealed decision of Human Rights Commission dismissing patient's claim of handicap discrimination by clinic's department of internal medicine.

Holding: The Appellate Court, McCullough, J., held that medical clinic was not a place of public accommodation as defined by Human Rights Act, and thus Commission did not have jurisdiction to hear patient's claim.

Affirmed. [4]
Appleton, J., concurred in result and filed opinion.
West Headnotes

[1] Civil Rights 78 ⟋1045 [5]
78 Civil Rights
78I Rights Protected and Discrimination Prohibited in General
78k1043 Public Accommodations
78k1045 k. Medical Facilities and Services. Most Cited Cases

Medical clinic dispensing medical services to public was not a place of public accommodation as defined by Human Rights Act, even though clinic participated in Medicare and Medicaid programs, and thus Human Rights Commission did not have jurisdiction to hear former patient's claim alleging that clinic, in violation of Act, discriminated against him because of his handicap; examples of places of public accommodation listed in Act were fundamentally different from medical clinics. S.H.A. 775 ILCS 5/5-101(A)(1). [6]

[2] Statutes 361 ⟋194
361 Statutes
361VI Construction and Operation
361VI(A) General Rules of Construction
361k187 Meaning of Language
361k194 k. General and Specific Words and Provisions. Most Cited Cases

[1] The parties to the case.

[2] The docket number.

[3] The dates the cases were argued and decided.

[4] The synopsis and disposition

[5] West key number

[6] West headnote

Under the "doctrine of ejusdem generis," where a statute lists several classes of persons or things but provides that the list is not exhaustive, court interprets the class of unarticulated persons or things as those "others such like" the named persons or things.

**1187 *237 ***120 Peter Andjelkovich, Bradley Wartman (argued), Peter Andjelkovich & Associates, Chicago, for John P. Duffy.

Lisa Madigan, Attorney General, Gary S. Feinerman, Solicitor General, Mary Patricia Kerns, Assistant Attorney General, Chicago, for Department of Human Rights.

Renee L. Monfort (argued), Dobbins, Fraker, Tennant, Joy & Perlstein, P.C., Champaign, for Christie Clinic, P.C.

Max P. Lapertosa, Access Living, Chicago, for Amicus Curiae, ADAPT of Illinois.

Robert John Kane, Illinois State Medical Society, Springfield, for Amicus Curiae, Illinois State Medical Society. **[7]**

Justice McCULLOUGH delivered the opinion of the court: **[8]**

[9] Petitioner, John P. Duffy, appeals the decision of the Illinois Human Rights Commission (Commission) adopting its administrative law judge's December 1, 2003, recommended order and decision to grant the motion to dismiss of respondents, Christie Clinic, P.C., and Dr. Ellen E. Roney (collectively, the Clinic). On appeal, petitioner argues that the Commission erred in dismissing his complaint where he alleged facts sufficient to show the Clinic operated a "place of public accommodation," as defined by article five of the Human Rights Act (Act) (775 ILCS 5/5-101 through 5-103 (West 2000)). We affirm.

On December 4, 2001, petitioner filed a charge of discrimination with the Illinois Department of Human Rights (Department), alleging that the Clinic discriminated against him because of his handicap, in violation of the Act. The Director of the Department did not act on the charge within the statutorily mandated 365-day period. See 775 ILCS 5/7A-102(G)(1) (West 2000).

On December 11, 2002, petitioner filed a complaint with the Commission pursuant to section 7A-102(G)(2) of the Act (775 ILCS 5/7A-102(G)(2) (West 2002)), alleging one count of handicap discrimination ****1188 ***121** by the Clinic. The complaint alleged that on or about June 11, 2001, he received a letter from Dr. Roney advising him that the Clinic's department of internal medicine would no longer offer him treatment beginning 30 days following receipt of the letter. Petitioner claimed that the Clinic's stated reasons for termination of treatment, that it was based upon his behavior at the Clinic and his failure to follow prescribed medical treatment, were pretextual and asserted only for the purpose of concealing its discriminatory motives. Petitioner further alleged that the Clinic operated a medical facility open to the public ***238** and was a "place of public accommodation," as defined by section 5-101(A)(1) of the Act (775 ILCS 5/5-101(A)(1) (West 2002)).

On March 8, 2003, the Clinic filed a motion to dismiss, arguing that the Commission was without jurisdiction where the Clinic's internal medicine department was not a "place of public accommodation," as defined by the Act and as interpreted by case law. The administrative law judge (ALJ) recommended that the matter be dismissed, finding that a medical clinic dispensing medical services to the public is not a "business" as contemplated under section 5-101(A)(1) of the Act and thus does not qualify as a "place of public accommodation" as that term is defined under the Act (775 ILCS 5/5-101(A)(1) (West 2000)). The Commission declined review and adopted the ALJ's decision as its own, pursuant to section 8A-103(E)(1) of the Act (775 ILCS 5/8A-103(E)(1) (West 2002)). This appeal followed.

[1] Petitioner argues that the Clinic's department of internal medicine is a "place of public accommodation," as defined by the Act. Statutory construction is a question of law, and the standard of review is *de novo*. *Ferrari v. Department of Human Rights, 351 Ill. App.3d 1099, 1103, 287 Ill.Dec. 14, 815 N.E.2d 417, 422 (2004)*.

Section 5-101(A) of the Act provides as follows:

"(A) Place of Public Accommodation. (1) 'Place of public accommodation' means a business, accommodation, refreshment, entertainment, recreation, or transportation facility of any kind, whether licensed or not, whose goods, services, facilities, privileges, advantages or accommodations are extended, offered, sold, or otherwise made available to the public.

(2) By way of example, but not of limitation, 'place of public accommodation' includes facilities of the following types: inns, restaurants, eating houses, hotels, soda fountains, soft drink parlors, taverns, roadhouses, barber shops, department stores, clothing stores, hat stores, shoe stores, bathrooms, restrooms, theatres, skating rinks, public golf courses, public golf driving ranges, concerts, cafes, bicycle rinks, elevators, ice cream parlors or rooms, railroads, omnibuses, busses, stages, airplanes, street cars, boats, funeral hearses, crematories, cemeteries, and public conveyances on land, water, or air, public swimming pools and other places of public accommodation and amusement." *775 ILCS 5/5-101*(A) (West 2000).

Statutes should be construed as to render no word or phrase superfluous or meaningless. *Langendorf v. City of Urbana, 197 Ill.2d 100, 109, 257 Ill.Dec. 662, 754 N.E.2d 320, 325 (2001)*. Adopting petitioner's broad interpretation of "business * * * facility of any kind" would render the Act's definition of "place of public accommodation" and the accompanying***239** examples in section 5-101(A)(2) mere surplusage. See *Baksh v. Human Rights Comm'n, 304 Ill.App.3d 995, 1003, 238 Ill.Dec. 313, 711 N.E.2d 416, 422 (1999)*. ****1189 ***122** "Had the legislature intended such an all-encompassing definition of a 'place of public accommodation' the definition would simply read 'a "place of public accommodation" is a business facility of any kind.' " *Baksh, 304 Ill.App.3d at 1003, 238 Ill. Dec. 313, 711 N.E.2d at 422*.

[2] Under the doctrine of *ejusdem generis*, where a statute lists several classes of persons or things but provides that the list is not exhaustive, we interpret the class of unarticulated persons or things as those "others such like" the named persons or things. *Board of Trustees of Southern Illinois University v. Department of Human Rights, 159 Ill.2d 206, 211, 201 Ill.Dec. 96, 636 N.E.2d 528, 531 (1994)* (hereinafter referred to as *SIU*).

Section 5-101(A) does not contain the terms "medical facility," "medical clinic," "doctor's office," "health-care facility," or other like terms. The examples listed in section 5-101(A)(2) are also fundamentally different from medical clinics, which dispense medical care. "The cited establishments are examples of facilities for overnight accommodations, entertainment, recreation or transportation." *SIU, 159 Ill.2d at 212, 201 Ill.Dec. 96, 636 N.E.2d at 531*. "Thus, what was anticipated by the General Assembly is a restaurant, or a pub, or a bookstore." *SIU, 159 Ill.2d at 212, 201 Ill.Dec. 96, 636 N.E.2d at 531*. What was not anticipated is a private medical clinic. Because the Clinic's internal medicine department is not a "place of public accommodation" under the Act, we hold that the conduct alleged by petitioner does not fall within section 5-102(A); consequently, no jurisdiction is conferred by that section over this cause of action. See *SIU, 159 Ill.2d at 212, 201 Ill.Dec. 96, 636 N.E.2d at 531* (academic program at a state-operated university); _Baksh,_ 304 Ill.App.3d at 1006, 238 Ill.Dec. 313, 711 N.E.2d at 424 (private dental practice); _Cut 'N Dried Salon v. Department of Human Rights,_ 306 Ill.App.3d 142, 147, 239 Ill.Dec. 61, 713 N.E.2d 592, 595-96 (1999) (insurance company); _Gilbert v. Department of Human Rights,_ 343 Ill.App.3d 904, 910, 278 Ill.Dec. 747, 799 N.E.2d 465, 469 (2003) (scuba-diving school). The Commission properly dismissed petitioner's complaint.

Petitioner also argues that the Clinic's participation in Medicare and Medicaid programs brings it under the definition of "place of public accommodation." However, he cites no on-point authority for this proposition, nor does the Act create such an inference from the mere receipt of federal funds (see 775 ILCS 5/1-101 through 10-103 (West 2002)). Whether the Clinic would qualify as a "place of public accommodation" under a different definition under federal statutes, rules, or regulations is irrelevant to our analysis under the Act.

*240 Because we find that the Clinic's internal medicine department is not a "place of public accommodation" under section 5-101(A) of the Act, we need not address whether petitioner failed to exhaust his administrative remedies.

For the reasons stated, we affirm the Commission's decision dismissing petitioner's complaint.

Affirmed. [10]

TURNER, J., concurs.

APPLETON, J., specially concurs. [11]

Justice APPLETON, specially concurring: [12]

I concur with the result reached by the majority but write separately to state my belief that the provisions of the Act have no application to this situation.

Plaintiff had been a patient of the Christie Clinic department of internal medicine. Plaintiff did not attend the ****1190 ***123** physical facility of the clinic as a destination but rather to be treated by medical personnel. For whatever reason, clinic personnel decided to terminate their professional relationship with plaintiff and had the right to do so. See _Olaf v. Christie Clinic Ass'n,_ 200 Ill.App.3d 191, 195, 146 Ill.Dec. 647, 558 N.E.2d 610, 613-14 (1990) (the right to engage in a physician-patient relationship is not absolute but is instead terminable at will).

I am aware of no law that requires a regulated professional-doctor, lawyer, dentist, accountant-to treat or serve every applicant. In fact, the service at issue here is recognized by the law above to be discretionary with the provider (after taking all abandonment and malpractice issues into consideration). Christie Clinic, as a place, may be forced to be open to all persons regardless of disability, but the medical personnel who work within the clinic's walls cannot be made to treat patients against their will.

Ill.App. 4 Dist.,2004.

Duffy v. Illinois Dept. of Human Rights

354 Ill.App.3d 236, 820 N.E.2d 1186, 290 Ill.Dec. 119

END OF DOCUMENT[28]

---

[10] The disposition of the case.

[11] The positions taken by other justices of the court (concur or dissent)

[12] Separate opinion by another justice who dissented or concurred.

---

[28]_Duffy v. Ill. Dept. of Human Rights,_ 354 Ill.App.3d 236, 820 N.E.2d 1186, 290 Ill.Dec. 119 (2004). Westlaw. Thomson Reuters. 2012. http://web2.westlaw.com/find/default.wl?rs=WLW11.07&rp=%2ffind%2fdefault. wl&vr=2.0&fn=_top&mt=Westlaw&cite=820+ne2d+1186&sv=Split

Parties or Case Name

The case name will appear as part of the caption of a case. The names of the parties can provide a great deal of information about a case. The party designation and case name may indicate whether the case is criminal or civil and whether it is a trial or appellate level case. There are several types of case names that a researcher should become immediately familiar with in order to save time and to understand what is being read.

Party v. Party This type of case is one of the two most common case formats, and generally indicates that some type of civil action is involved. At the trial level, the first listed party indicates the plaintiff, the second listed party in a trial level case indicates the defendant, and the "v." in between the party names indicates that this is an adversarial proceeding.

> On the appellate level, the case names may remain the in the same order, but they will be identified as appellant and appellee, or petitioner and respondent. Courts may list the appellant first no matter who the plaintiff was at the trial level. Quite frequently, the case name will identify the standing of each party at the various levels. The following, and all examples in this section, might be the case names for cases in print:
>
> Ruth MORRISON, et al., Appellants-Plaintiffs,
>
> v.
>
> Doris Ann SADLER, et al., Appellees-Defendants.
>
> or
>
> Albert G. MARRIN, Appellant
>
> v.
>
> Mary A. MARRIN, Appellee
>
> or
>
> Mark LEWIS and Dennis Winslow; Saundra Heath and Clarita Alicia Toby; Craig Hutchison and Chris Lodewyks; Maureen Kilian and Cindy Meneghin; Sarah and Suyin Lael; Marilyn Maneely and Diane Marini; and Karen and Marcye Nicholson-McFadden, Plaintiffs-Appellants,
>
> v.
>
> Gwendolyn L. HARRIS, in her official capacity as Commissioner of the New Jersey Department of Human Services; Clifton R. Lacy, in his official capacity as the Commissioner of the New Jersey Department of Health and Senior Services; and Joseph Komosinski, in his official capacity as Acting State Registrar of Vital Statistics of the New Jersey State Department of Health and Senior Services, Defendants-Respondents.

In the first example, the names of Morrison and Sadler are in all capital letters. This signifies that when writing the case name, the words used will be *Morrison* and *Sadler* only, and those names would be in italics or would be underlined.

The case name also identifies the standing of each party in each proceeding. In the first case above, Morrison was the plaintiff in the trial court and is the appellant in the current case. Sadler was the defendant in the trial court and the appellee in the current case. The "*et al.*" indicates that other parties are involved for both the plaintiff and defendant, but only the first parties on each side are listed at this appellate level.

In the second example there is no information given as to the parties' positions in the lower-level court, so one would need to read the case in order to find out who was the plaintiff in the trial.

In the third example, while the case involves several parties on both sides, as is indicated in the case name information, only the last name of the first party on each side is written all capital letters. When discussing the case in writing or writing the citation, those are the only names that would be written: *Lewis v. Harris*.

TIP

Both The Bluebook *and* ALWD have rules indicating how the parties are identified in a case citation. It is important to understand and abide by those rules.

This case also could have been presented as LEWIS *et a*l. v. HARRIS, *et al* rather than listing each party on each side.

State v. Party or United States v. Party or Commonwealth v. Party This type of case name indicates that it is usually a criminal proceeding. When someone is prosecuted for an alleged crime, the state or the federal government prosecutes the accused on behalf of all of its citizens, not just on behalf of the victim. Some jurisdictions might use the term *People* rather than *State*. The jurisdictions of Pennsylvania, Kentucky, Virginia, Massachusetts, Puerto Rico and the North Mariana Islands are technically referred to as commonwealths rather than states, and therefore criminal cases in those jurisdictions are identified as *Commonwealth*. Here are examples of criminal case names:

UNITED STATES of America, Plaintiff-Appellee,

v.

William Roy MARTIN, Defendant-Appellant.

Or

PEOPLE of the State of California, Plaintiff and Respondent,

v.

Bashala Paul BROWN, Defendant and Appellant.

Or

COMMONWEALTH of Pennsylvania, Appellant

v.

Michael COOPER, Alias Kenny Brown, Appellee.

Or

The COMMONWEALTH OF Puerto Rico on the Relation of Carlos S. QUIROS, Secretary, Department of Labor and Human Resources, Appellants,

v.

ALFRED L. SNAPP & SONS, INC.; Alfred L. Snapp, Sr., Chief Officer; John T. Watt& Son, a corporation d/b/a Timber Ridge Fruit Farm; John T. Watt, Jr., Manager; Orchard Management Co., Inc.; Harry F. Byrd, III, President-Treasurer; D. K. Russell & Sons, Inc.; J. Robert Russell, President; Whitman Orchards, a corporation; Gordon T. Whitman, President; Robert Boyd, a corporation t/a Cloverdale Farm; Robert J. Boyd, President-Treasurer; The C. L. Robinson Corporation; Delmar Robinson, Jr., President; R & T Packing Corporation; C. Robert Solenberger, President; E. Blackburn Moore; Fred L. Glaize, Jr. & Philip B. Glaize d/b/a Cresent Orchards; Frederick Farms; James R. Robinson, Manager; George B. Whitacre; H. F. Byrd & T. B. Byrd; John E. Crumpacker, Manager; H. F. Byrd; Harvey Brumback; James Clevenger; McDonald Farms; Messick & Beaver; James Beaver; Frank L. Snapp & Elmer G. Snapp d/b/a H. T. Snapp & Son; Frank L. Snapp; Elmer G. Snapp; R. Roland Snapp; Robert E. Wyatt; Stanley Bauserman; Stewart Bell; Woodside Farm; John W. Smith; William S. Franklin; Wayne S. McInturff; James B. Swing; George Cather; Garland R. Cather; Irvin R. King; Albert W. Messick; C. H. Orchards, Appellees.

In re Party In this type of case, the case name is introduced by the phrase *in re*, which means "in the matter of" or "regarding." This type of case name tells the reader that the basis of the case is not adversarial, as between two parties, but rather is focused on the rights of one individual. Generally these cases will involve probate matters, bankruptcy proceedings, disbarment of attorneys, or a guardianship. Here are examples of this type of case name:

In re Brenda Marie JONES, Debtor,

California Franchise Tax Board, Appellant,

v.

John T. Kendall, Trustee; United States Trustee, Oakland, Appellees,
Brenda Marie Jones, Debtor–Appellee.
(cited as *In re Jones*)
Or
In the Matter of Thomas F. JONES.
[a disciplinary matter]
(cited as *In re Jones*)
Or
CONSERVATORSHIP OF the Estate of Carmen Jeanette JONES.
Terry Harris, as Conservator, etc., et al., Petitioners and Respondents,
v.
Raymond P. Harris, Objector and Appellant.
Conservatorship of the Person and Estate of Carmen J. Jones.
Terry Harris, as Conservator, etc., et al., Petitioners and Respondents,
v.
Raymond P. Harris, Objector and Appellant.
(cited as *In re Jones*)

When a case uses "*In re*" along with a party's initials, or "*In re*" and the first name and first initial of the last name, the case generally involves a minor. These cases often include adoption, child custody, or some other type of action involving a juvenile. The minor's last name is left out of published opinions in order to maintain the privacy of the minor. A case name might look like the following:

In re RAY H., Jr., et al., Persons Coming Under the Juvenile Court Law.
San Diego County Health and Human Services Agency, Plaintiff and Respondent,
v.
Carolyn N., Defendant and Appellant;
Elizabeth H. et al., Appellants.
Or
In the Matter of Elizabeth W. et al.
Erie County Department of Social Services, Respondent;
Theresa W. et al., Appellants.
(cite as *In re Elizabeth W.)*
Or
In the Interest of D.S., J.W.S., IV, C.N. and D.N., Minor Children,
J.S., III, Father of D.S. and J.W.S., Appellant.
(cite as *In re D.S.*)

Ex rel. Party (Ex rel. Bonner). *Ex rel.* is loosely translated as "on behalf of," "upon relation," or "upon information." The proceeding is instituted by some state or governmental official, such as the attorney general, on behalf of the state. However, a private party, who has an interest in the matter, has instigated the action. Examples are the following:

State ex rel. Smith
v.
Cincinnati Schools
Or
Missouri ex rel. Gaines
v.
Canada

Ex parte Party Name (Ex parte Franklin). *Ex parte* means "on (or from) one side only," and generally indicates that an action is brought by one party without notice to the other party, or the other party is absent. An *ex parte* decision is one where the judge makes a decision without having all of the parties present. The legal system generally frowns upon making decisions without proper notice to interested parties, and *ex parte* decisions are usually only made in extremely urgent matters, such as where someone seeks a temporary restraining order to prevent abuse by a spouse. Some jurisdictions have abandoned the use of *ex parte*, and instead use *Application of Party Name* or *Petition of Party Name*. The jurisdiction should be checked for the proper usage.

Docket Number

The docket number is the court's way of numbering the cases that come before it. Providing each case with an individual docket number eliminates the possibility of duplication if more than one case has the same name. Generally, the clerk will require that the docket number be provided when requesting information about the case or obtaining copies of anything in the case file.

Docket numbers are usually assigned chronologically within the year a case is filed. Many courts use certain letters to describe different types of cases, such as CV for civil or CR for criminal. The docket number may also include the year the case was filed. Another number and letter combination may appear in a docket number that refers to the judge or court to which the case has been assigned.

Date of Decision

Two dates will usually follow the docket number. The first date listed is the date the case was argued before the court. The second date listed is the date the case was decided by the court. When writing a citation, the date of decision is used.

Syllabus or Synopsis (Summary)

In unofficial reporters, the syllabus, synopsis, or case summary is a general overview of the facts of the case and the holding. In newer Westlaw cases, the syllabus may be divided into "Background" and "Holding." This paragraph will give the parties, some background on the case, the judge presiding at the lower court, the outcome in that court, the judge authoring the opinion of the current case, and the court's decision. This information can tell the reader quickly whether or not the case is on point. It should be remembered, however, that this summary is not written by the court, but by the editors at the publishing house. It is only an annotation, and should not be quoted, nor should it be relied on as authority.

Topic and Key Number

Topic
In the West key numbering system, an area of the law defined by West editors for organizing the headnotes.

The West editors have divided legal materials into more than 400 major *topics*. Each of the topics is further divided into separate, specific legal concepts, each identifying a single point of law. Each major topic has a number assigned to it, and each of the separate legal concepts has an identifying number called a *key number*.

Headnote   A headnote is a paragraph summarizing the point of law. When using Westlaw, the topic, key number, and headnote make up an entry in the digest. These editorial enhancements allow the researcher to quickly determine whether the case warrants additional analysis. Because many legal cases exceed 10 pages, this editorial enhancement saves time in the research process.

Key numbers
Numbers assigned by West Publishing Company and used in West digests and Westlaw to provide an indexing method to locate points of law.

Each headnote is consecutively numbered when reported in a case. By scanning the headnotes, a researcher can find the headnote or headnotes that apply specifically to the researcher's question. A corresponding number identifies the discussion of each headnote in the body of the case. The section of the case discussing that headnote should be read carefully to confirm that it applies to the client's situation. The next step is to read the case in full and then, if applicable, update the case to make sure it is still good law.

Like the synopsis, the headnotes are prepared by editors rather than judges and therefore should not be relied on or cited as authority. The headnotes are only used to help determine whether the case may be applicable and to find other similar cases. Only the language within the opinion itself should be used as authority.

Attorneys of Record

Following the opinion, the case lists the names of the individual attorneys and law firms who represented the parties involved. Occasionally, the list includes attorneys who appeared on behalf of *amici curiae*—organizations that are not actually parties to the case, but have filed amicus briefs in support of one side or the other because they have some interest in the outcome.

The information about the counsel involved can be useful in a number of ways. First, while you can always obtain copies of documents filed in a case from the court itself, talking with the attorneys involved may provide additional information that cannot readily be obtained from reading the documents. Second, if the firm is facing an attorney, perhaps for the first time, the information in this section can be used to locate other cases that the attorney has argued, allowing one to find out how the attorney thinks and what strategies the attorney may use.

To locate attorney information online using Westlaw, for example, the query would include an attorney field search in the jurisdictional database such as

at(William +5 Bryant)

"At" is the designator for the attorney field in Westlaw, and the information inside the parentheses tells the computer that the search should include the word "William," before the word "Bryant," within five words (allowing for middle names).

By combining the attorney field and the judge field in Westlaw, a researcher can also locate cases where the particular attorney has previously appeared before a particular judge.

Writing Judge

When a case is decided by a panel of judges or justices, only one of the judges or justices is assigned to write the opinion. The remaining judges or justices on the panel will be listed at the end of the opinion, along with their position on the case.

In some cases, the name of the judge or justice is not given, such as when an opinion is short and the issues are not controversial. In those cases, the phrase "Memorandum," "Memorandum Opinion," "Memorandum by the Court," or "*Per Curiam*" (meaning "by the court") will replace the judge's name.

Opinion

Immediately after the authoring judge's name, the opinion begins. The opinion gives the facts of the case, the legal authority upon which the court bases its decision, the decision of the court, the reasoning of the court, and the disposition of the case. It is this section that is exactly the same in both the official and unofficial versions of the case.

Opinions will begin with the presentation of the facts. It is important to pay attention to these facts because the court will generally provide the *key facts* that it considered most important in reaching its decision.

Key facts
Those facts that if different or nonexistent would change the outcome of the case.

After the facts are presented, the court will apply the law in the jurisdiction to the facts at hand. The court will cite case precedent, statutes, or other authorities to rely upon.

There are several types of opinions that may be rendered, depending largely on how the panel of judges or justices votes on the outcome of the case. The following provides an overview of the most common types of opinions.

Majority *Majority* opinions occur when more than half of the judges or justices agree on the outcome. The opinion is written by a member of the majority. When the majority opinion is issued, the holding becomes the law and is binding authority on lower courts in that particular jurisdiction that are faced with the same or similar facts and issues.

Per curiam *Per curiam* opinions are issued by the entire court, and no one specific judge is identified as the writing judge. *Per curium* opinions are usually short and frequently involve issues that are not controversial. A *per curiam* decision must be unanimous. These decisions are often considered to be weak precedent and should be used cautiously.

Concurring *Concurring opinions* are written by judges or justices who are in agreement with the result, but have other reasons for agreeing, or are relying on other authorities. The concurring judge may also give advice, such as a suggestion to the legislature that while a statute was followed, it should be revised. Sometimes a concurring judge or justice will say to the rest of the panel that the panel reached the right conclusion but perhaps for the wrong reason. Some judges or justices will merely state, "I concur" without giving any reason. A concurring opinion should not be ignored because it may provide hints on how the court may view the same or similar issue in the near future.

Dissenting *Dissenting opinions* are written by the minority of judges on a panel who disagree with the results reached by the panel. A dissenting judge or justice may write a full dissenting opinion or may merely state, "I dissent" with no explanation. As with the concurring opinion, a dissenting opinion should not be ignored. Although the dissenting view may be the minority, it may signify a potential change in the near future. In addition, a dissenting opinion may provide insight into plausible arguments against the position taken by the majority. These arguments might be useful for the client as they may provide clues as to what points the opposition may raise.

Plurality *Plurality* opinions are issued when the justices comprising the majority have all written separate concurring opinions providing separate bases for the decision. Although the plurality **opinion** will resolve the dispute at hand, it results in a weak opinion because a single position has not been articulated. Consequently, a plurality opinion is not binding in future cases. It may, however, be persuasive.

Memorandum *Memorandum* opinions render a holding but offer very little, if any, reasoning or explanation to support it. A common example in U.S. Supreme Court cases is the denial of a writ of *certiorari*.

In-chambers *In-chambers* opinions are rendered by a U.S. Supreme Court Justice deciding certain types of cases alone within an assigned circuit. An example of an in-chambers opinion is an application for interim relief such as a temporary injunction or a stay of judgment.

En banc *En banc opinions* occur at the court of appeals level, with all judges in the court participating. *En banc* literally means "in the bench." All of the judges of the court participate rather than the three- or five-member panels that usually hear a case.

Majority opinion

An opinion wherein a majority of the members joined in the decision.

Per curiam

The court's written explanations of its decisions in given cases.

Concurring opinions

Separate opinions delivered by judges in a case when the judges agree with the result of the majority but do so for different reasons.

Dissenting opinion

An opinion by a member of the panel who disagrees with the majority opinion. A dissenting opinion does not create precedent.

Plurality opinion

An opinion from a group of justices who agree as to the outcome, but have different bases for their decisions.

Memorandum opinions

Court rulings that contain little or no reasoning as to why the court decided as it did.

In-chambers opinion

An opinion rendered by an individual member of the U.S. Supreme Court.

En banc

Describes an opinion in which the entire court, rather than just a panel of the court, participates in the decision-making process.

Decision

The decision is the final disposition of the case. The words *opinion, judgment, decision, holding*, and *case* are all used interchangeably for the term *decision*. The court has the option to affirm the decision of the lower court, reverse the lower court, or remand the case to the lower court for further action. A court can also **vacate** a case or dismiss it completely.

Vacate
Dismiss a case by court action.

Other Judges/Justices

After the opinion the remaining panel members are identified. The entire panel consists of these judges along with the authoring judge.

Concurring and Dissenting Opinions

Concurring and dissenting opinions, if any, appear after the decision in the case. The concurring and dissenting opinions are not law. The legally binding portion of the opinion ends with the disposition or decision. However, the concurring and dissenting opinions may have value in research for the reasons discussed above. These opinions should not be quoted as law, but should not be discounted in evaluating a client's legal position.

SUMMARY

Case opinions are the heart of legal research. Reading and understanding case law is a slow process that requires reading, rereading, understanding the parts of the case, and taking notes. Looking at the concurring and dissenting opinions, although they are not the law, may provide valuable insight into the case or the future direction of the law.

Understanding the appellate process helps in understanding cases. Each court system has particular reporters in which to find cases. Case citations are important not only to help one find the case in the reporters, but also to provide information about the case.

Knowing the difference between mandatory and persuasive authority, official and unofficial reporters, and the elements of a case can greatly aid the research process. Although case research is a time-consuming process, with persistence and skill, the answers can be found.

REVIEW **QUESTIONS**

1. What is common law?
2. What are court opinions?
3. What is the hierarchy of your state's court system?
4. What are three actions that an appellate-level court can take regarding a decision of a lower court?
5. What is precedent?
6. What is the difference between an official and an unofficial reporter?
7. What is the difference between mandatory and persuasive authority?
8. Can *dictum* be controlling law? Why or why not?
9. What is an Article III court?
10. What is a slip opinion?
11. What is the purpose of advance sheets?
12. How many federal circuit courts of appeals are there?
13. What cases are reported in the *Federal Rules Decisions*?
14. What is the value of the *National Reporter System*?
15. What is a table of cases?
16. When do you use a digest?
17. What are parallel citations?
18. What regional reporter are your state's court decisions located in, and what other states are also covered by that regional reporter?
19. Identify the parts of a case assigned by your instructor.
20. What is a docket number?
21. Explain topic, key number, and headnote.
22. What are majority opinions?
23. What are dissenting opinions?
24. How would you find a U.S. Supreme Court slip opinion?
25. What is the difference between depublished and unpublished opinions?

APPLICATION **EXERCISES**

Use the *Bluebook* or *ALWD* to answer the following:

1. If no copy of *United States Reports* is available, which unofficial reporters should you cite instead, in order of preference?

2. Where are decisions of the U.S. Courts of Appeals, previously the U.S. Circuit Courts of Appeals, reported?

3. Federal district court decisions, like federal circuit court decisions, have no official reporters. Where are district court opinions published?

4. What is the abbreviation of the official U.S. administrative publication of the decisions and orders of the National Labor Relations Board?

5. Does any Native American group have its own reported court decisions? If so, which one?

6. What is the official source for American treaties?

7. What is the official abbreviation of "Department" in a case name?

8. If Hillary Jones is the defendant in a United States District Court case for the Eastern Division of Kentucky, Samuel Adams is the plaintiff, the case begins on page 493 of the *Federal Supplement* second series in volume 303, and it was decided in 1999, what is the citation?

9. What is the minimum amount of information needed to locate a decision from any state's highest court?

10. How can one locate a decision in a regional reporter if one only has an official citation?

11. The decisions of courts in which states appear in the *North Western Reporter*?

Citation Exercises Directions: In answering the following, you will need to read the *Uniform System of Citation (The Bluebook), ALWD,* or another citation service and find the appropriate rules that apply to the questions below. **You will need to find the case in the library or on the Internet to complete the information for questions 1–5.** Then, you will create the proper form for each question.

1. State the full citation for 400 U.S. 379.

2. State the full citation for 359 N.E.2d 1151.

3. State the full citation for 349 N.E.2d 298, assuming you are including this citation in a document submitted to an Ohio court.

4. State the full citation for 354 N.E.2d 363.

5. Identify the parts of the following citation:

Myers v. Saint Mary of the Woods College, 357 N.E.2d 57 (Ind. 1993).

6. What does the following citation signify?

Myers, 357 N.E.2d at 59.

7. Write the correct citation for the following case: Black Lake Pipe Line Company, Petitioner, v. Union Construction Company, Inc. et al., Respondents, Supreme Court of Texas, May 19, 1976. Rehearing Denied June 16, 1976.

8. Why is the month of the decision indicated in *Birl v. Estelle*, 660 F.2d 592 (5th Cir. Nov. 1981)?

QUICK **CHECK**

1. The case of *Butler v. Stevens*, decided in the Arkansas Court of Appeals, serves as precedent for
   a. Arkansas district courts
   b. The Arkansas Supreme Court
   c. The U.S. Supreme Court
   d. None of the above

2. The case of *State v. Johns*, decided in an Arkansas district court, serves as precedent for
   Arkansas district courts
   The Arkansas Supreme Court
   The U.S. Supreme Court
   None of the above

3. The case of *Bowers v. Pope*, decided by the Michigan Supreme Court, serves as precedent for
   Arkansas district courts
   The Arkansas Supreme Court
   The U.S. Supreme Court
   None of the above

4. All case law comes from:
   Trial court decisions
   Some form of appellate court
   The U.S. Supreme Court
   None of the above

5. Which party may appeal a defendant's not guilty verdict in a criminal case?
   a. Defendant
   b. Prosecutor
   c. Both

6. When an appellate court *affirms* a lower court decision, what does it do?
   It changes the decision.
   It sends the case back to the lower court.
   It agrees with the decision.

Matching

Using the information in Column A, state in Column B whether the material is mandatory or persuasive authority.

Column A	Column B
A case from the U.S. Supreme Court serves as _____ for courts in the 50 states.	
A case from the Supreme Court of Oklahoma can serve as _____ for the Kentucky Court of Appeals.	
A case from the Kansas Supreme Court will serve as _____ for the trial courts of Kansas.	
A case from the U.S. Court of Appeals, Fifth Circuit (a federal court serving Texas, Louisiana and Mississippi) can serve as _____ for the state trial courts of Ohio.	

RESEARCH

Complete by manually using the books or by using other Internet sites.

1. What is the citation for the *Duchane* case, appearing in volume 400 of the *North Eastern Reporter*, Second Series?

2. Was 20 U.S.C.A. cited by any case in volume 802 of the *Federal Reporter*, Second Series? If so, which?

3. What is the name of the court decision that appears on page 423 of volume 791 of the *Federal Reporter*, Second Series?

4. What information does the court, in its final analysis, cite in *Louisiana World Exposition*, 746 F.2d at 1039?

5. In the dissenting opinion of *Glidden Co. v. Zdanok*, 370 U.S. 530, 82 S. Ct. 1459, 8 L. Ed. 2d 671 (1962), name the justice, and describe the reference he makes to *McCardle, ExParte*, an 1868 Supreme Court decision.

6. What is the name of the Supreme Court decision that appears at 468 U.S. 288, 104 S. Ct. 3065, 82 L. Ed. 2d 221 (1984)?

   a. What other Supreme Court decision, rendered in 1964 by the Warren Court, does the case in question cite to?

7. Locate page 347 of the Federal Second Series volume 704. What is the citation of the case? Provide a summary.

8. Locate page 291 of volume 551 of the *United States Reports*. What is the citation of the case? When was it decided? Who wrote the opinion? What was the First Amendment issue? Were there any concurring or dissenting opinions?

INTERNET RESEARCH

1. John Marshall is considered one of our nation's most influential Supreme Court Chief Justices. Find three of his most important decisions and identify what impact those decisions have had on the United States.

2. Find the following cases, provide the complete citation, and summarize the opinion.

   a. 661 F.2d 319
   b. 531 U.S. 98
   c. *Stern v. Marshall*
   d. 21 U.S. 1
   e. 92 F. Supp. 2d 189

MEDIA RESOURCES

None for this chapter.

INTERNET RESOURCES

A. Free Sites for Finding Case Law
   1. Supreme Court of the United States: http://www.supremecourt.gov/
   2. Cases and Codes: http://www.findlaw.com/casecode/index.html

3. Justia.com US Federal and State Courts: http://www.justia.com/courts/

4. Justia.com US Laws: http://law.justia.com/

5. Cornell Legal Information Institute—case law: http://www.law.cornell.edu/opinions.html

6. Cornell University's Legal Information Institute—legal research   http://topics.law.cornell.edu/wex/legal_research

7. Law Library of Congress's Guide to Law Online: http://www.loc.gov/law/help/guide.html

8. Links to the websites of federal courts, some of which include court decisions, may be found on the website of the Administrative Office of the U.S. Courts: http://www.uscourts.gov/courtlinks/

9. Law by Source—Federal: http://www.law.cornell.edu/federal/opinions.html

10. The Public Library of Law—Case Law: http://www.plol.org/Pages/Search.aspx

11. Locating Legal Information on the Web, from the Minnesota Association of Law Libraries: http://www.aallnet.org/chapter/mall/handout.pdf

12. Rominger Legal: http://www.romingerlegal.com/

B. Subscription Services

1. CASEMaker: www.casemaker.us (CASEMaker is listed under subscription services because only attorneys can access the site.)

2. Fastcase: https://www.fastcase.com/

3. Lexis/Nexis: http://www.lexisnexis.com/

4. Loislaw: http://www.loislaw.com/

5. TheLawNet: http://www.thelaw.net/

6. VersusLaw: http://www.versuslaw.com/

7. Westlaw: www.westlaw.com

C. Tutorials and User Guides

1. Research Fundamentals: Getting Started with Online Research: http://lscontent.westlaw.com/images/content/GettingStarted10.pdf

2. Research Fundamentals: How to Check Citations: http://lscontent.westlaw.com/images/banner/SurvivalGuide/PDF08/08HowCheckCitations.pdf

3. Research Fundamentals: How to Find Cases: http://lscontent.westlaw.com/images/content/FindCases10.pdf

4. Research Fundamentals: Using West's National Reporter System: http://lscontent.westlaw.com/images/banner/documentation/2009/NationalReporter09.pdf

5. Research Fundamentals: Westlaw Research Guide: http://west.thomson.com/documentation/westlaw/wlawdoc/lawstu/lsrsgd06.pdf

6. Research Fundamentals: Case Law Fields on Westlaw: http://west.thomson.com/documentation/westlaw/wlawdoc/lawstu/lscasefd.pdf

7. LexisNexis Academic: Find a Specific U.S. Legal Case: http://www.youtube.com/watch?v=17E6Q1hmciY&feature=player_embedded#!

8. LexisNexis Communities Portal. Free Case Law. 2011.   http://www.lexisone.com/lx1/caselaw/freecaselaw?action=FCLDisplayCaseSearchForm&l1loc=L1ED&tcode=PORTAL

9. LexisNexis Product Tutorials: http://www.lexisnexis.com/COMMUNITY/DOWNLOADANDSUPPORTCENTER/media/p/4332.aspx

10. American Bar Association Model Rules of Professional Conduct   http://www.abanet.org/cpr/mrpc/mrpc_toc.html

chapter **twelve**

THE ADMINISTRATIVE AGENCIES AND SPECIAL LAWS

Bill Perry/Fotolia

LEARNING OBJECTIVES

After completing this chapter, students should be able to:

1. Research regulations and apply them to factual situations.

2. Understand the difference between administrative law and other bodies of law.

3. Appreciate and understand how citizens' grievances concerning administrative decisions are addressed by administrative regulations and decisions.

4. Acquire a working knowledge of the practices, procedures, principles, and remedies of the judicial review of administrative actions.

CHAPTER OVERVIEW

There are certain areas of the law that many paralegals do not often research, such as administrative rules and regulations, administrative decisions, executive orders, and international law. These areas of law require a very different approach to research than do other areas. However, although they may appear to be very different from other primary sources, it is important to remember that administrative rules and regulations, administrative decisions, international law, and executive orders are primary sources of law. The cases that interpret these laws are also primary authorities.

ADMINISTRATIVE AGENCIES

General Information

Earlier, the text described how the government is divided into three branches: executive, legislative, and judicial. These three branches of government operate under a system of checks and balances, with no one branch having complete power. *Administrative agencies* are a contradiction to that concept because they hold all three areas of responsibility. Agencies make, interpret, and enforce law. See Exhibit 12-1 for a chart of the federal government and its administrative agencies.

Administrative agencies were first created at the federal level, but now exist on both the federal and state levels. They create administrative law through rules, regulations, and decisions. Agencies may be referred to by different names, such as bureaus, commissions, administrations, boards, or even corporations. As previously discussed, *enabling statutes* give administrative agencies their existence.

Administrative agencies
Part of the government, often described unofficially as the "fourth branch," that carries out laws passed by the legislature, according to the purpose for which they were created.

Enabling statute
A statute passed by the legislature that allows an agency to exist.

EXHIBIT 12-1 FEDERAL AGENCIES

The Government of the United States
The Constitution

Legislative Branch	Executive Branch	Judicial Branch
The Congress Senate House	President Vice President	The Supreme Court of the United States

The Cabinet

Department of Agriculture	Department of Commerce	Department of Defense	Department of Education	Department of Energy	Department of Health and Human Services	Department of Homeland Security	Department of Housing and Urban Development
Department of the Interior	Department of Justice	Department of Labor	Department of State	Department of Immigration	Department of Transportation	Department of the Treasury	Department of Veterans' Affairs

The following positions have the status of Cabinet rank:

White House Chief of Staff	Environmental Protection Agency	Office of Management and Budget	United States Trade Representative	United States Ambassador to the United Nations	Council of Economic Advisors	Small Business Administration

African Development Foundation	Central Intelligence Agency (CIA)	Defense Nuclear Facilities Safety Board	Environmental Protection Agency (EPA)	Farm Credit Administration
	Commission on Civil Rights		Equal Employment Opportunity Commission (EEOC)	Federal Communications Commission (FCC)
National Railroad Passenger Corporation (Amtrak)	Commodity Futures Trading Commission		Export-Import Bank of the United States	Federal Deposit Insurance Corporation (FDIC)
	Consumer Products Safety Commission (CPSC)			Federal Election Commission
Arms Control and International Security	Corporation for National and Community Service			Federal Emergency Management Agency (FEMA)
	Census Bureau			Financial Management Service (Treasury Department)
				Federal Labor Relations Authority

				Federal Maritime Commission
				Federal Mediation & Conciliation Service
				Federal Mine Safety and Health Review Commission
				Federal Reserve System
				Federal Retirement Thrift Investment Board
				Federal Trade Commission (FTC)
General Services Administration (GSA)	Inter-American Foundation	Merit Systems Protection Board	National Aeronautics and Space Administration (NASA)	Occupational Safety & Health
	International Trade Commission		National Archives and Records Administration (NARA)	Office of Government Ethics
			National Credit Union Administration	Office of Personnel Management (OPM)
			National Endowment for the Arts	
			National Labor Relations Board (NLRB)	
			National Science Foundation	
			National Transportation Safety Board (NTSB)	
			Nuclear Regulatory Commission	
Peace Corps	Railroad Retirement Board	Securities and Exchange Commission (SEC)	Tennessee Valley Authority	
Pension Benefit Guaranty Corporation		Selective Service System	Trade and Development Agency	
Postal Regulatory Commission		Small Business Administration (SBA)		
Postal Service		Social Security Administration (SSA)		

Some administrative agencies are familiar to many Americans. Examples of federal administrative agencies are the Federal Deposit Insurance Corporation (F.D.I.C.), which governs banks, and the Central Intelligence Agency (CIA), which deals with national security. A state's department of transportation, where driver's licenses are given, is a state administrative agency. Administrative agencies actually affect quite a bit of daily life. The Federal Communications Commission

(FCC) regulates the music we listen to and the television we watch. The Food and Drug Administration (FDA) protects people from harmful food or drugs.

Agencies came about because Congress determined, early in its history, that it could not keep pace with the changes in society. Congress decided to delegate certain tasks to administrative agencies to address particular issues. Agencies were established at different times throughout our history depending upon the need of Congress for assistance in a particular area, or in response to public necessity. The first agencies were created in 1789, and included the Department of the Treasury and the Department of State.

Executive departments

Agencies organized under one of the president's cabinet posts.

The 13 *executive departments* that report to the president are administrative agencies. Any agency that falls under the direction of the president is referred to as an executive agency. For example, one cabinet-level executive department is the Department of Justice, but it actually functions as an administrative agency, addressing any legal concerns of our government or its citizens.

Independent agencies

Agencies established by enabling statutes.

Independent agencies do not fall under the direction of the president. They are established by enabling statutes. Examples of independent agencies are the Central Intelligence Agency (CIA), the Securities and Exchange Commission (SEC), and the National Labor Relations Board (NLRB).

Many agencies are established to deal with major topics of interest to citizens. The Federal Aviation Administration (FAA), established in 1958, was created to help regulate the growing aviation industry. In 1970, the Environmental Protection Agency (EPA) was established to deal with the developing crisis over the quality of our air and our water.

Regulation

A law passed by an agency; similar to a statute passed by the legislature.

In some instances, agencies are combined with other agencies to form new ones. For example, the Federal Communications Commission that we know today subsumed the Federal Radio Commission (FRC) in 1934 to coincide with the creation of the Communications Act of 1934.[1]

Agencies can be headed by one of the members of the president's cabinet or, in certain circumstances, by a staff member who is hired based on his or her expertise in the particular area of law in question. These staff members are not tied to elections and do not leave the post when a new administration takes office.

Administrative Procedures Act (APA)

A federal statute that governs all procedures before administrative agencies. The same type of statute is also found on the state level.

No matter when or how it was created, each agency must act according to the enabling statute, which is worded very broadly to allow the agency maximum flexibility to do its job. Enabling statutes enacted by Congress tend to be broad, whereas *regulations* created by agencies are very detailed. It is important to read both the enabling statute and the regulations together when doing research. If the agency exceeds its authority in making a regulation, the regulation will be invalid. Therefore, understanding the enabling statute assists a researcher in determining the validity of the regulation.

It is also important to understand that there is a difference between adjudication and rulemaking. Table 12-1 shows some key factors to consider.

The *Administrative Procedures Act (APA)*[2] provides a framework in which agencies must work. Exhibit 12-2 is a page from the APA on the rulemaking powers given to agencies.

The APA provides standards for the federal agencies to follow in carrying out their duties and making law. When an issue arises, the courts look at the records of the agency to decide whether or not the agency exceeded the parameters of the APA. Learning the terminology of the administrative agencies is important for success in this area of research.

TIP

Paralegals normally cannot represent clients in court. However, specific exemptions to the unauthorized practice of law exist in the form of statutes and regulations. One example is found in the Federal Administrative Procedures Act, 5 U.S.C. § 555 (b,) which permits anybody to represent another person if allowed by a particular agency. Some agencies that allow representation by non attorneys are the Internal Revenue Service, the Social Security Administration, the Department of Labor, the Environmental Protection Agency, and the Consumer Product Safety Commission.

---

[1] 47 U.S.C. § 151 et seq. (1934).

[2] 5 U.S.C. § 551 (1982).

TABLE 12-1   Adjudication v. Rulemaking

Factor	Adjudication	Rulemaking
Number factor	Directed at large groups of people	Directed at specific individuals or businesses
Time factor	Concerns future conduct or situations	Concerns past or present conduct or events
Goal factor	Establishes a rule to deal with future conduct on an across-the-board basis	Resolves disputes or enforcement of a rule on a case-by-case basis
Fact factor	Decisions are based on legislative facts and policy	Decisions are based on adjudicative facts that are specific to disputes
Result factor	Sets standards of conduct to be applied in a later adjudication	Applies standards of conduct to determine if a violation has occurred[3]

EXHIBIT 12-2   APA RULEMAKING

Administrative Procedure Act

UNITED STATES CODE
TITLE 5 - GOVERNMENT ORGANIZATION AND EMPLOYEES
PART I - THE AGENCIES GENERALLY
Chapter 5 - ADMINISTRATIVE PROCEDURE
SUBCHAPTER II - ADMINISTRATIVE PROCEDURE

§ 553. Rule making

(a) This section applies, according to the provisions thereof, except to the extent that there is involved -

(1) a military or foreign affairs function of the United States; or

(2) a matter relating to agency management or personnel or to public property, loans, grants, benefits, or contracts.

(b) General notice of proposed rulemaking shall be published in the Federal Register, unless persons subject thereto are named and either personally served or otherwise have actual notice thereof in accordance with law. The notice shall include -

(1) a statement of the time, place, and nature of public rule making proceedings;

(2) reference to the legal authority under which the rule is proposed; and

(3) either the terms or substance of the proposed rule or a description of the subjects and issues involved.

Except when notice or hearing is required by statute, this subsection does not apply -

(A) to interpretative rules, general statements of policy, or rules of agency organization, procedure, or practice; or

(B) when the agency for good cause finds (and incorporates the finding and a brief statement of reasons therefore in the rules issued) that notice and

---

[3]William T. Mayton. *The Legislative Resolution of the Rulemaking versus Adjudication Problem in Agency Lawmaking.* 1980 Duke L.J. 103.

public procedure thereon are impracticable, unnecessary, or contrary to the public interest.

(c) After notice required by this section, the agency shall give interested persons an opportunity to participate in the rule making through submission of written data, views, or arguments with or without opportunity for oral presentation. After consideration of the relevant matter presented, the agency shall incorporate in the rules adopted a concise general statement of their basis and purpose. When rules are required by statute to be made on the record after opportunity for an agency hearing, sections 556 and 557 of this title apply instead of this subsection.

(d) The required publication or service of a substantive rule shall be made not less than 30 days before its effective date, except -

(1) a substantive rule which grants or recognizes an exemption or relieves a restriction;

(2) interpretative rules and statements of policy; or

(3) as otherwise provided by the agency for good cause found and published with the rule.

(e) Each agency shall give an interested person the right to petition for the issuance, amendment, or repeal of a rule.[4]

MAKING FEDERAL ADMINISTRATIVE LAW

Regulation
A law passed by an agency that is similar to a statute passed by the legislature.

Decisions
A determination made by an administrative law judge.

Federal Register
A daily publication that makes agency regulations and other executive branch documents available to the public for comment before final adoption.

Code of Federal Regulations
An annual publication of agency regulations passed and codified during a current year.

Administrative decisions
The written decision of an administrative law judge, similar to case law.

Administrative law refers to all laws created by the administrative agencies, such as rules or *regulations*, *decisions*, and other related actions. While the exact process for adopting regulations varies by agency, some aspects of the process are shared across agencies. Generally, an agency requests comments from the public, presides over one or more hearings about the regulation, and then decides whether to adopt it. Agencies adopt, revise, and create regulations daily. Although these rules and regulations are primary authority, they are subject to review by both Congress and the president.

When a proposed regulation or revision is published, anyone interested can submit written comments within a specified time period. Sometimes, the agency will hold hearings at which interested parties can testify as to how the proposed regulation would affect them. After the initial comment period is over, the agency may revise the proposed regulation, publish the regulation again, and reopen the comment period. This cycle may repeat several times before the agency publishes the final regulation in the *Federal Register (Fed. Reg.)*. It is important to note that no federal regulation is effective until it is published in its final form in the *Federal Register*. Once finalized, the regulations become codified and are placed in the annual volumes of the *Code of Federal Regulations* (*C.F.R.*).

Agencies also resolve disputes regarding their regulations. When an agency holds hearings to resolve these disputes, it is exercising its enforcement power. *Administrative decisions* are the laws made in those hearings. In an agency hearing, the administrative law judge determines whether a regulation was violated. The agency usually delivers a written decision interpreting the regulation. Exhibit 12-3 shows the rulemaking process.

[4]National Archives. Federal Register. Administrative Procedures Act. 5 U.S.C. § 553. http://www.archives.gov/federal-register/laws/administrative-procedure/553.html

The Reg Map
Informal Rulemaking

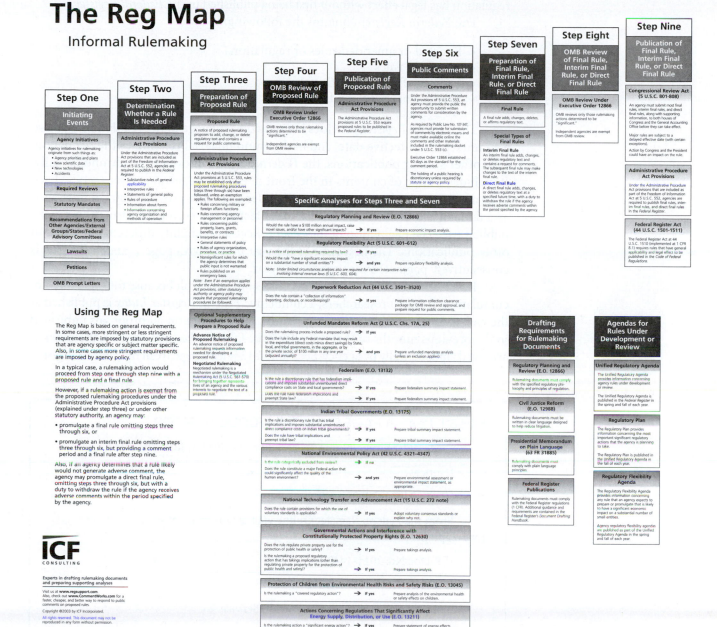

EXHIBIT 12-3 Federal Rulemaking Process[5]

Publishing Federal Administrative Law

Federal Register As federal administrative agencies adopt rules and regulations, they are published in the *Federal Register* (Fed. Reg.), as required by the Federal Register Act.[6] Because there are so many federal administrative agencies constantly making new regulations, the *Federal Register* is published every weekday, except on federal holidays. The *Federal Register* puts the public on notice that a new rule or regulation

---

[5]Office of Information and Regulatory Affairs. *Informal Rulemaking.* www.reginfo.gov

[6]Federal Register Act. 44 U.S.C. Chapter 15. http://www.archives.gov/federal-register/laws/federal-register/

is being considered, and gives the public time to respond to the proposal. No agency regulation has legal effect without first being published in the *Federal Register*.

The *Federal Register* contains the following:

- Enacted or amended rules or regulations
- Proposed rules
- Notices of administrative hearings
- Presidential proclamations

The *Federal Register* provides not only the language of the regulation, but also a summary, the effective date, and background material relating to the regulation. Like other similar publications, the *Federal Register* is organized chronologically. It includes a table of contents in the front of each issue, arranged by agency. Each issue also has an ending section called "reader aids" that provides information such as a table of the C.F.R. sections that are affected and contact information for the public's use. The pagination of the *Federal Register* is slightly different from that of other publications. The first issue of the year begins with page 1, and each issue is consecutively paginated throughout the year.

Research in the in the *Federal Register* is often difficult because the issues are not cumulative. To assist researchers, a cumulative *Federal Register Index* is published at the end of each month. The index provides information on all proposals published in the previous months of that calendar year. Like the *Federal Register*, the index is arranged alphabetically by agency. See Exhibit 12-4 for a page from the *Federal Register*.

EXHIBIT 12-4 A PAGE FROM THE FEDERAL REGISTER.

[Federal Register Volume 76, Number 112 (Friday, June 10, 2011)]

[Notices]

[Pages 34031–34032]

From the Federal Register Online via the Government Printing Office [www.gpo.gov]

[FR Doc No: 2011-14426]

DEPARTMENT OF AGRICULTURE

Animal and Plant Health Inspection Service

[Docket No. APHIS-2011-0050]

Notice of Request for Extension of Approval of an Information Collection; Animal Welfare

AGENCY: Animal and Plant Health Inspection Service, USDA.

ACTION: Extension of approval of an information collection; comment request.

SUMMARY: In accordance with the Paperwork Reduction Act of 1995, this notice announces the Animal and Plant Health Inspection Service's intention to request extension of approval of an information collection associated with Animal Welfare Act regulations for the humane handling, care, treatment, and transportation of certain animals by dealers, research facilities, exhibitors, carriers, and intermediate handlers.

DATES: We will consider all comments that we receive on or before August 9, 2011.

ADDRESSES: You may submit comments by either of the following methods:

Federal eRulemaking Portal: Go to http://www.regulations.gov/fdmspublic/component/main?main=DocketDetail&d=APHIS-2011-0050 to submit or view comments and to view supporting and related materials available electronically.

Postal Mail/Commercial Delivery: Please send one copy of your comment to Docket No. APHIS-2011-0050, Regulatory Analysis and Development, PPD, APHIS, Station 3A-03.8, 4700 River Road Unit 118, Riverdale, MD 20737-1238. Please state that your comment refers to Docket No. APHIS-2011-0050.

Reading Room: You may read any comments that we receive on this docket in our reading room. The reading room is located in room 1141 of the USDA South Building, 14th Street and Independence Avenue, SW., Washington, DC. Normal reading room hours are 8 a.m. to 4:30 p.m., Monday through Friday, except holidays. To be sure someone is there to help you, please call (202) 690-2817 before coming.

Other Information: Additional information about APHIS and its programs is available on the Internet at http://www.aphis.usda.gov.

FOR FURTHER INFORMATION CONTACT: For information on the Animal Welfare Act regulations, contact Dr. Barbara Kohn, Senior Staff Veterinarian, Animal Care, APHIS, 4700 River Road, Unit 84, Riverdale, MD 20737; (301) 734-7833. For copies of more detailed information on the information collection, contact Mrs. Celeste Sickles, APHIS's Information Collection Coordinator, at (301) 851-2908.

SUPPLEMENTARY INFORMATION:

Title: Animal Welfare.

OMB Number: 0579-0036.

Type of Request: Extension of approval of an information collection.

Abstract: Under the Animal Welfare Act (AWA or Act) (7 U.S.C. 2131 et seq.), the Secretary of Agriculture is authorized to promulgate standards and other requirements governing the humane handling, housing, care, treatment, and transportation of certain animals by dealers, research facilities, exhibitors, carriers, and intermediate handlers. The Secretary of Agriculture has delegated the authority for enforcement of the AWA to the Animal and Plant Health Inspection Service (APHIS).

The regulations in 9 CFR parts 1 through 3 were promulgated under the AWA to ensure the humane handling, care, treatment, and transportation of regulated animals under the Act. The regulations in 9 CFR part 2 require documentation of specified information by dealers, research institutions, exhibitors, carriers (including foreign air carriers), and intermediate handlers. The regulations in 9 CFR part 2 also require that facilities that use animals for regulated purposes obtain a license or register with the U.S. Department of Agriculture (USDA). Before being issued a USDA license, individuals are required to undergo prelicense inspections; once licensed, a licensee must periodically renew the license.

To help ensure compliance with the AWA regulations, APHIS performs unannounced inspections of regulated facilities. A significant component of the inspection process is review of records that must be established and maintained by regulated facilities. The information contained in these records is used by APHIS inspectors to ensure that dealers, research facilities, exhibitors, intermediate handlers, and carriers comply with the Act and regulations.

Facilities must make and maintain records that contain official identification for all dogs and cats and certification of those animals received from pounds, shelters, and private individuals. These records are used to ensure that stolen pets are not used for regulated activities. Dealers, exhibitors, and research facilities that acquire animals from nonlicensed persons are required to have the owners of the animals sign a certification statement verifying the owner's exemption from licensing under the Act. Records must also be maintained for animals other than dogs and cats when the animals are used for purposes regulated under the Act.

Research facilities must also make and maintain additional records for animals covered under the Act that are used for teaching, testing, and experimentation. This information is used by APHIS personnel to review the research facility's animal care and use program.

APHIS needs the reporting and recordkeeping requirements contained in 9 CFR part 2 to enforce the Act and regulations. APHIS also uses the collected information to provide a mandatory annual report of animal welfare activities to Congress.

We are asking the Office of Management and Budget (OMB) to approve our use of these information collection activities for an additional 3 years.

The purpose of this notice is to solicit comments from the public (as well as affected agencies) concerning our information collection.

These comments will help us:

1. Evaluate whether the collection of information is necessary for the proper performance of the functions of the Agency, including whether the information will have practical utility;
2. Evaluate the accuracy of our estimate of the burden of the collection of information, including the validity of the methodology and assumptions used;
3. Enhance the quality, utility, and clarity of the information to be collected; and
4. Minimize the burden of the collection of information on those who are to respond, through use, as appropriate, of automated, electronic, mechanical, and other collection technologies; e.g., permitting electronic submission of responses.

Estimate of burden: The public reporting burden for this collection of information is estimated to average 0.9502381 hours per response.

Respondents: Dealers, research facilities, exhibitors, carriers, and intermediate handlers; persons exempt from licensing under the AWA.

Estimated annual number of respondents: 9,985.

Estimated annual number of responses per respondent: 9.6081822.

Estimated annual number of responses: 95,937.

Estimated total annual burden on respondents: 91,163 hours. (Due to averaging, the total annual burden hours may not equal the product of the annual number of responses multiplied by the reporting burden per response.)

All responses to this notice will be summarized and included in the request for OMB approval. All comments will also become a matter of public record.

Done in Washington, DC, this 6th day of June 2011.

Kevin Shea, Acting Administrator, Animal and Plant Health Inspection Service.

[FR Doc. 2011-14426 Filed 6-9-11; 8:45 am]

BILLING CODE 3410-34-P[7]

[7]GPO Access Government Printing Office. Federal Register. Volume 76, Number 112 (Friday, June 10, 2011). (Pages 34031–34032) FR Doc No: 2011-14426. http://www.gpo.gov/fdsys/pkg/FR-2011-06-10/html/2011-14426.htm

The *Federal Register* contains many recently published rules and regulations that may not be available in the annual publication of the *Code of Federal Regulations*. To locate what is needed, the latest *Federal Register Index* may be consulted. This index is issued monthly in a cumulative format. For example, the *Federal Register Index* for March will contain all information for January, February, and March. The index is arranged alphabetically by agency, just as the C.F.R. indices are arranged. Researchers can sign up to receive the daily *Federal Register* table of contents by e-mail.[8]

The office of the *Federal Register* also publishes the *United States Government Manual*, which is sometimes referred to as the official handbook of the federal government. This manual, available in print and online, provides information on administrative agencies, as well as quasi-agencies, international organizations, and the various boards, commissions, and committees in which the United States is involved. Each entry in the manual typically gives the agency's major officials, a statement about the agency's purpose, some history of the agency, an outline of its programs, and contact information. This manual is prepared annually and is generally available in late summer.[9]

Sometimes a regulation must be located that is proposed, but not yet in force. These regulations may be found by checking the National Archives and Records on Public Inspection. This publication gives the dates on which new notices and regulations will be published in the *Federal Register*.[10]

Researching in the *Federal Register* is a difficult task because of its size and the manner in which it is published. However, an alternative source is available. The rules and regulations are codified into 50 titles and arranged by subject matter in the (C.F.R.).

Code of Federal Regulations The 50 titles of the C.F.R. are somewhat similar to the titles of the United States Code (U.S.C.). For example, Title 27 of the U.S.C. is "Intoxicating Liquors," while in the C.F.R. the title is "Alcohol, Tobacco Products and Firearms." Each of the 50 titles is divided into chapters, and the chapters are subdivided into parts. This is a similar arrangement to that of the statutes, where the titles are divided into sections, which are further divided into subsections. See Exhibit 12-5 for more information.

The C.F.R. is revised annually, with approximately one-fourth of the set issued on or around the beginning of each quarter, starting with January 1. Each year the soft-covered pamphlets are issued in a color different from the color used in the previous year. The exception is Title 3, which is always either white or black and contains the presidential materials.[11] The regulations are arranged by common words and phrases describing each topic in the index. The C.F.R. is not updated through pocket parts. Instead, the C.F.R. uses a separate, monthly publication entitled "LSA—List of C.F.R. Sections Affected." The *Federal Register*, C.F.R., and LSA are all available through the U.S. Government Printing Office's website.[12]

---

[8]Keeping America Informed. United States Government Printing Office. Welcome to GPOLIST-SERV. 2011. L

[9]GPO Access. *US Government Manual*: About. 2010. http://www.gpoaccess.gov/gmanual/about.html

[10]The Office of the Federal Register. Electronic Public Inspection Desk. 2011. http://www.ofr.gov/inspection.aspx?AspxAutoDetectCookieSupport=1

[11]GPO Access Government Printing Office. Code of Federal Regulations: About. 2012. http://www.gpoaccess.gov/cfr/about.html

[12]GPO Access Government Printing Office. 2011 http://www.gpoaccess.gov/index.html

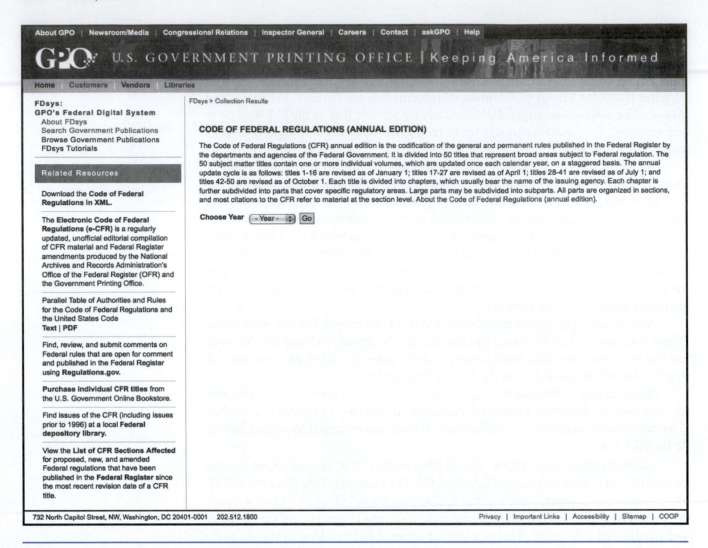

732 North Capitol Street, NW, Washington, DC 20401-0001   202.512.1800

Privacy | Important Links | Accessibility | Sitemap | COOP

EXHIBIT 12-5   Page from CFR on GPO Access[13]

ADMINISTRATIVE DECISIONS

In addition to finding regulations, research may point to administrative agency decisions that interpret the regulations in question. Issuing decisions is the judicial power of the administrative agency in action. According to the Bureau of Labor Statistics, as of May 2010 there were approximately 14,500 administrative law judges, with the largest employer of such judges being state governments.[14]

Administrative law judge

A person within an administrative agency who presides over administrative hearings.

In an administrative hearing, there is no jury. An ***administrative law judge*** (ALJ), who is generally an expert in the field, presides over the hearing and renders a decision, called an ***adjudication***. In some cases, a federal agency may also have the option of prosecuting violators in court, generally by sending the issue to the Department of Justice.

Adjudication

A formal decision rendered by an administrative agency, acting within its quasi-judicial powers.

Adjudications by an administrative law judge can be reviewed if a party is dissatisfied. In most instances, the agency will have at least two levels of review, while some agencies have three levels. A party must exhaust all administrative remedies within the agency before appealing to the courts. Exhibit 12-6 is an excerpt from an administrative hearing in the U.S. Postal Service.

[13]GPO Access. Code of Federal Regulations (CFR): Main Page. 2012. http://www.gpoaccess.gov/cfr/

[14]Bureau of Labor Statistics. Occupational employment statistics. May 2010. http://www.bls.gov/oes/current/oes231021.htm

EXHIBIT 12-6   ADMINISTRATIVE DECISION—UNITED STATES POSTAL SERVICE

August 21, 2012

In the Matter of the Petition by

ANITA Y. BELL

P.S. Docket No. DCA 11-245

APPEARANCE FOR PETITIONER

Albert E. Lum

APPEARANCE FOR RESPONDENT

Janette Barnard

FINAL DECISION ON PETITIONER'S MOTION FOR RECONSIDERATION

Petitioner, Anita Y. Bell, seeks reconsideration of a portion of the Final Decision issued in this case on March 29, 2012. Specifically, Petitioner, using newly filed evidence, argues that she did not receive $8,203 for a home-finding trip (Decision, Finding 4) but, instead, received only $7,366.30. Accordingly, Petitioner contends that the amount Respondent is entitled to collect by offset should be reduced by $836.70, the difference between those two numbers.

In support for her motion, Petitioner has submitted a copy of a statement from her credit union, which statement evidences a deposit to her account in the amount of $7,366.30 at about the time Cartus records identified a payment to her of $8,203 (see Exhibit 11 to OIG Report of Investigation (Answer, Exhibit 1)).

In opposition to Petitioner's motion for reconsideration, Respondent has submitted documentation indicating that the $836.70 in question was paid as taxes on Petitioner's behalf and argues that, as such, it is part of the amount recoverable from Petitioner. Although given the opportunity to do so, Petitioner did not reply to Respondent's opposition.

DECISION

Under the Rules of Practice that govern Debt Collection Act proceedings, reconsideration of a decision is allowed at the discretion of the Hearing Official. 39 C.F.R. §961.9. In this instance, although the evidence on which Petitioner relies was available at the time of the original hearing in this matter, I have exercised my discretion to consider the request for reconsideration in order to ensure that the original result was accurate and just. However, having considered the request, I conclude that the original decision was correct and deny the motion for reconsideration.

The documentation submitted by Respondent confirms that the $836.70 in question was paid to "taxing authorities" on Petitioner's behalf, presumably as withholding on the relocation benefit payments, which would be considered income. *See* Cartus cover letter, dated January 26, 2009; *see also* Declaration of D. Rutkowski, dated May 1, 2012. Moreover, as argued by Respondent, by signing the PS Form 178, Petitioner agreed that if she violated the Relocation Agreement "all money paid to [her] or to third parties by the USPS as benefits" would be recoverable from her as a debt due Respondent. (Answer, Exhibit 8). I agree with Respondent that, in this instance, the amount paid to taxing authorities would be considered paid to third parties on her behalf. Accordingly, as she has been found to have violated the Agreement, Petitioner remains obligated to repay that amount to Respondent.[1]

Accordingly, Petitioner's motion for reconsideration is denied and the original Final Decision is affirmed.

David I. Brochstein

Administrative Judge

[1]While having no bearing on the decision in this matter, it appears that Petitioner *may* be able to recover, or get credit for, the tax payment from the appropriate "taxing authorities" once she makes repayment to the Postal Service. *See, e.g.,* Internal Revenue Service (IRS) Publication 17, "Your Federal Income Tax", Chapter 12, "Other Income, Repayments"; IRS Publication 15, "(Circular E), Employer's Tax Guide," Section 13, last paragraph.[15]

Because the administrative hearings are the agency equivalent of a trial, the trial level in both state and federal courts is bypassed. If it is a federal matter, a party that is dissatisfied with the agency's decision often appeals to U.S. Courts of Appeals. State matters are appealed to the equivalent state court of appeal. If the party is still dissatisfied, a further appeal can be taken. On the federal level, decisions of the Courts of Appeals are appealed to the United States Supreme Court. On the state level, a party may appeal beyond the court of appeals if the state has a three-tiered court system. There are some instances, such as cases heard by the Social Security Administration, where the dissatisfied party can file a civil suit in the federal district court.

Researching Federal Administrative Law

Researching federal and state administrative law is somewhat different than researching statutes and cases. The resources used are similar, but do have some essential differences.

Regulations Because of the way the federal administrative regulations are published, the *Code of Federal Regulations* is often the most effective research tool. Several methods exist to help researchers locate the regulations in the C.F.R. In many instances the C.F.R. provision will be referenced in a federal statute if one is using an annotated version of the United States Code, such as U.S.C.A. If there is no reference to the appropriate regulation, there are other alternatives for research.

When researching regulations, it is important to check their current status for any changes or amendments. To update the C.F.R. regulation being researched, the *List of C.F.R. Sections Affected* (LSA) should be checked. This is a monthly publication that provides amendments or revisions to any regulation found in the *Code of Federal Regulations*. Updating can also be accomplished online through GPO Access, where the LSA also provides three additional services: (1) the list of C.F.R. Parts Affected Today, (2) the Current List of C.F.R. Parts Affected, and (3) Last Month's List of C.F.R. Parts Affected.[16] Exhibit 12-7 provides the home page of the LSA.

When updating research, the C.F.R. title and section should be referenced. The regulation will provide a short explanation and may indicate "amended" or "revised," along with a page reference to the *Federal Register*. The next step in

[15]United States Postal Service. 2012 Administrative Decisions. In re Bell—P.S. Docket No. DCA 11-245. 2012 http://about.usps.com/who-we-are/judicial/admin-decisions/2012/dca-11-245-fd-2012-08-21.htm

[16]GPO Access Government Printing Office. List of CFR Sections Affected (LSA): Main page. 2012. http://www.gpoaccess.gov/lsa/index.html

EXHIBIT 12-7 Home Page of the LSA

updating is to bring the regulation current to the day on which the research is being done. The researcher should look manually at the section titled "Reader Aids" at the back of the current *Federal Register*. In that section, the researcher should examine "C.F.R. Parts Affected," which covers changes since the last LSA was issued and is updated daily. The entire list should be reviewed to see if the regulation has been modified in any way.

Indexes and Tables of Contents

A one-volume print index called "C.F.R. Index and Finding Aids" allows a user to find information by agency or by subject matter. The index also has a "Parallel Table of Authorities and Rules" that provides the parallel citation for the U.S.C. title number and the C.F.R. title number. If the researched has access to the code, title, or section, the table of contents of the appropriate code volume can be scanned to locate the section needed. An index also follows each title. In addition, West's *Code of Federal Regulations* has a general index.

GPO ACCESS

Federal regulations can be accessed online through *GPO Access*.[17] On the Code of Federal Regulations main page, a user may browse the regulations, retrieve specific regulations by C.F.R. citation, or obtain search tips for using the site. If citation is known, whether current or historical, it may be entered in the boxes after identifying the revision year of interest. For example, regulations from 1997 may be found by selecting the year 1997 from the pull-down menu for revision year. Boxes are then filled in with the title, part, section, or subpart. The user may

[17]GPO Access. Code of Federal Regulations: Main Page. 2012. http://www.gpoaccess.gov/cfr/index .html

choose to receive the regulation in the form of a text file, a PDF, or a summary.[18] GPO Access has online information available from 1996 forward.

Computer-Assisted Legal Research

The C.F.R. and the *Federal Register* are available from paid legal services, such as Westlaw, LexisNexis, Loislaw, and Versuslaw. Free sites, in addition to GPO Access, include FindLaw, Cornell's Legal Information Institute, and many other law school websites. Information for a particular agency can be obtained on the agency's website. Exhibit 12-8 is a page from the Food and Drug Administration website for a regulation revised in 2010.

EXHIBIT 12-8   FOOD AND DRUG ADMINISTRATION

[Code of Federal Regulations]
[Title 21, Volume 1]
[Revised as of April 1, 2010]
[CITE: 21CFR50.27]

TITLE 21–FOOD AND DRUGS
CHAPTER I–FOOD AND DRUG ADMINISTRATION
DEPARTMENT OF HEALTH AND HUMAN SERVICES
SUBCHAPTER A–GENERAL

PART 50 – PROTECTION OF HUMAN SUBJECTS

Subpart B–Informed Consent of Human Subjects

Sec. 50.27 Documentation of informed consent.

(a) Except as provided in 56.109(c), informed consent shall be documented by the use of a written consent form approved by the IRB and signed and dated by the subject or the subject's legally authorized representative at the time of consent. A copy shall be given to the person signing the form.

(b) Except as provided in 56.109(c), the consent form may be either of the following:

(1) A written consent document that embodies the elements of informed consent required by 50.25. This form may be read to the subject or the subject's legally authorized representative, but, in any event, the investigator shall give either the subject or the representative adequate opportunity to read it before it is signed.

(2) A short form written consent document stating that the elements of informed consent required by 50.25 have been presented orally to the subject or the subject's legally authorized representative. When this method is used, there shall be a witness to the oral presentation. Also, the IRB shall approve a written summary of what is to be said to the subject or the representative. Only the short form itself is to be signed by the subject or the representative. However, the witness shall sign both the short form and a copy of the summary, and the person actually obtaining the consent shall sign a copy of the summary. A copy of the summary shall be given to the subject or the representative in addition to a copy of the short form.

[46 FR 8951, Jan. 27, 1981, as amended at 61 FR 57280, Nov. 5, 1996][19]

---

[18]GPO Access. Code of Federal Regulations: Retrieve by CFR Citation. 2012. http://www.gpoaccess .gov/cfr/retrieve.html

[19]U.S. Department of Health & Human Services. FDA U.S. Food and Drug Administration. CFR 0 Code of Federal Regulations Title 21. 21CFR50.27 2012. http://www.accessdata.fda.gov/scripts /cdrh/cfdocs/cfcfr/CFRSearch.cfm?fr=50.27

For older versions of regulations, Hein Online has historical editions covering 1938 through 1983, which are offered by subscription. In addition, Westlaw has individual C.F.R. databases from 1984, and Lexis has an archived database (CODES; CFRARC) dating back to 1981.

Administrative Decisions   Unlike cases from state and federal courts, the decisions of the administrative law judges are not filed in one set of books. The publications that contain administrative decisions are listed in *The Bluebook* in Tables T.1 (United States official administrative publications) and T.16 (Services). Some services are also provided in *ALWD*'s Appendix 8, which is available online.[20]

The Government Printing Office makes agency decisions available, as do certain commercial publishers, such as Commerce Clearing House (CCH) and the Bureau of National Affairs (BNA). For example, CCH publishes the decisions of the National Labor Relations Board. These services provide both primary and secondary materials about specific legal topics. Their format is generally looseleaf, rather than bound, and they are updated frequently by replacing old pages with new ones. The primary sources in a looseleaf service include statutes, case law, regulations, and agency decisions. Most looseleaf services now offer subscriptions to online databases. *Legal Loose-leaf in Print,* an annual publication, is an excellent tool for identifying looseleaf services by topic.

Generally, administrative decisions are located by looking at an alphabetical table of the cases, or by checking the subject matter index for the appropriate set. That information will lead to a narrative discussion, which will then give annotations to cases. From the annotations, the citation can be used to locate the actual case. Fee-based research services, such as Westlaw and LexisNexis, also provide administrative decisions.

Finding cases related to a particular section of the C.F.R. may also be accomplished by using a hard copy of *Shepherd's Citations, Shepherd's* online through LexisNexis, or KeyCite on Westlaw. *Shepherd's United States Administrative Citations* and *Shepherd's Code of Federal Regulations Citations* (print media) include citations to administrative agency and court decisions. Another print option is West's *Federal Practice Digest,* which provides head notes to federal cases and references to secondary sources that have interpreted the regulations.

Another common online option is to visit the website of the agency itself. Each agency handles violations in its own way. For example, the Environmental Protection Agency (EPA) has a page titled "Cases and Settlements" that provides references to civil and criminal enforcement cases and settlements. It includes cases resolved at the agency level and appealed to the U.S. Supreme Court.[21] Exhibit 12-9 shows the EPA's different enforcement methods.

Most civil EPA actions result in consent decrees and settlements rather than adjudications. However, consent decrees reached by settlement are filed with the appropriate federal district court and are subject to a 30-day comment period and approval by the court. Exhibit 12-10 is one of those consent decrees.

In contrast with other agencies, the National Labor Relations Board holds its own administrative adjudications and reports its own decisions. The NLRB provides manuals for case handling, guides for hearing officers, and even style manuals. It is advisable to check the agency's available practice and process information, just as one would with a court. Exhibit 12-11 provides a portion of an NLRB decision.

---

[20]ALWD. Appendix 8. Selected Official Federal Administrative Publications. P011. http://www.alwd.org/publications/pdf/CM2_Appendix8.pdf

[21]US Environmental Protection Agency. Compliance and Enforcement. Cases and Settlements. 2012. http://www.epa.gov/compliance/resources/cases/index.html

EXHIBIT 12-9   EPA ENFORCEMENT OPTIONS

Basic Information—Enforcement

EPA's enforcement offices hold persons or companies legally accountable for either civil or criminal violations of our nation's environmental laws and regulations. Responsibility for the various actions that make up EPA's enforcement program are divided among different Headquarters offices, the EPA Regions, and state agencies.

> Types of Enforcement Actions
> Civil Administrative Actions
> Civil Judicial Actions
> Criminal Actions
> Related Topics
> Enforcement Response Policies (ERPs)
> Enforcement Alerts Newsletters
> Supplemental Environmental Projects (SEPs)
> Compliance Incentives and Auditing
> Economic Enforcement Models
> Enforcement Results
> Settlements
> Civil Penalties
> Criminal Penalties
> Incarceration
> Injunctive Relief
> Supplemental Environmental Projects (SEPs)
> Superfund Penalties
> Enforcement Results Reports
> Annual Results
> OECA Accomplishments Reports
> Other Types of Activities
> Compliance Monitoring
> Compliance Incentives
> Compliance Assistance

Types of Enforcement Actions

Civil Administrative Actions—These are enforcement actions taken by EPA or a state under its own authority, without involving a judicial court process. An *Informal Administrative Action* is generally any communication from EPA or a state agency that notifies the regulated entity of a problem. A *Formal Administrative Action* by EPA or a state agency may begin with notice of violation or with the issuance of an Administrative Order (either with or without penalties) to bring about compliance. More on Civil Enforcement…

Civil Judicial Actions—These are formal lawsuits, filed in court, against persons or entities that have failed to comply with statutory or regulatory requirements or with an Administrative Order. These cases are brought to court by the U.S. Department of Justice on behalf of EPA and by the State's Attorneys General for the states. More on Civil Enforcement…

Criminal Actions—EPA or a state may also enforce against an entity or person through a criminal action, depending on the nature and severity of the violation. As opposed to civil actions, criminal actions are usually reserved for only the most serious violations, those that are willful, or knowingly committed. Court conviction can result in the imposition of fines or imprisonment. More on Criminal Enforcement

Informal Administrative Action
An action of an Administrative-agency other than adjudication, or rulemaking, such as investigation, publicity, or supervision. A majority of agency actions are done informally.

Formal Administrative Action
This is a decisional process involving an adversarial hearing mandated by a statute or rulemaking. Formal adjudication usually affects individual rights, not group. It often has a retroactive impact, rather than being prospective in impact, unlike rulemaking.

Enforcement Results

Settlements—A settlement is generally an agreed-upon resolution to an enforcement case. In an administrative action, settlements are often in the form of Consent Agreements/Final Orders (CA/FOs). In a judicial context, settlements are embodied in Consent Decrees signed by all parties to the action and filed in the appropriate court. More on Civil Settlements...

Civil Penalties—These are monetary assessments to be paid by a person or regulated entity in connection with a violation or noncompliance. Penalties act as an incentive for coming into compliance and staying in compliance with the environmental statutes and regulations. Penalties are designed to recover the economic benefit of noncompliance as well as an amount to account for the seriousness of the violation. More on Civil Enforcement...

Criminal Penalties—Federal, state or local fines imposed by a Judge at the sentencing stage of a trial. In addition to criminal penalties, an order of restitution, where a defendant is ordered to pay those affected by the violation a monetary amount, for example, a defendant may be ordered to pay a local fire department the cost of responding to and containing a hazardous waste spill. More on Criminal Enforcement...

Incarceration—When a violation is determined to be criminal in nature, "jail time" is a possibility. Incarceration is a deterrent to those who might be considering the option of violating our Nation's environmental laws to cut corners in doing business, for example. More on Criminal Enforcement...

Injunctive Relief—Injunctive relief consists of the tasks that a violator must carry out to come into compliance. More on Civil Enforcement...

Supplemental Environmental Projects (SEPs)—These are environmental improvement projects that a violator voluntarily agrees to perform, in addition to actions required to correct the violations, as part of an enforcement settlement. More on SEPs...

Superfund Penalties—The Superfund statutory penalty provisions authorize EPA to seek statutory penalties of up to $32,500 for each day of non-compliance. Stipulated penalties may be included in a settlement agreement as an incentive for the party to comply with the settlement terms. More on Superfund Penalties....[22]

EXHIBIT 12-10   CONSENT DECREE—EPA

Hecla Mining Company Settlement for the Bunker Hill Mining and Metallurgical Complex Superfund Site

Hecla Consent Decree Resources

Region 10 Press Release

Consent Decree (PDF) (66pp, / 492K, About PDF)

On June 13, 2011, a settlement agreement with the Hecla Mining Company to resolve its liabilities at the Bunker Hill Mining and Metallurgical Complex Superfund Site in northern Idaho was filed with the U.S. District Court for the District of Idaho. The agreement settles the government's claims relating to liabilities

---

[22]United States Environmental Protection Agency. Basic Information—Enforcement. 2012. http://www.epa.gov/enforcement/

under the Comprehensive Environmental Response, Compensation and Liability Act (CERCLA, commonly known as Superfund).

Under the settlement, Hecla will pay $263.4 million plus interest to the United States, the Coeur d'Alene Tribe, and the state of Idaho to resolve claims stemming from releases of wastes from its mining operations. The agreement will protect people's health, particularly young children, by ensuring the cleanup of areas heavily contaminated with lead, cadmium, arsenic, and other contaminants.

Overview of the Company

Established in 1891, Hecla Mining Company is the oldest U.S.-based precious metals mining company in North America with its U.S. operations headquartered in Coeur d'Alene, Idaho. The company has two operating mines and exploration properties in four silver mining districts in the U.S. and Mexico.

Bunker Hill Mining and Metallurgical Complex Superfund Site

The Bunker Hill Site is located in the Coeur d'Alene River Basin ("Basin") in northern Idaho and was listed on the National Priorities List (NPL) in 1983. The site includes areas contaminated with mine waste within the South Fork Coeur d'Alene River corridor and tributaries, adjacent floodplains, downstream water bodies, fill areas, and the 21-square-mile Bunker Hill "Box." The Site covers approximately 166 river miles and floodplain as well as those areas where mine wastes were relocated.

Mining activities began in the Basin over 100 years ago. The Basin was one of the leading silver, lead and zinc-producing areas in the world. The Bunker Hill Mining and Metallurgical Complex, located in Kellogg, Idaho, was the largest mineral processing facility in the Basin and included milling and smelting operations. Most of the mining and milling operations no longer operate and the Bunker Hill Mining and Metallurgical Complex was demolished. Hecla (and its predecessors) owned and operated mine and mill sites throughout the Basin and disposed of mine and mill wastes containing hazardous heavy metals including lead, cadmium, and zinc, onto the lands and waterways of the Basin since the 1880s.

Until 1968, most mine waste tailings were discharged directly into the South Fork of the Coeur d'Alene River or its tributaries; an estimated 62 million tons of tailings were discharged to streams. These tailings contained approximately 880,000 tons of lead and 720,000 tons of zinc. The area of contamination includes some 166 river miles along the South Fork and Coeur d'Alene River, Lake Coeur d'Alene and a portion of the Spokane River. The widespread contamination poses significant risks to human health and the environment. For example, a large percentage of the soil in the residential and commercial areas in the Upper Basin and Box contains lead at levels in excess of 1000 ppm, and nearly 85% of the floodplains in the lower Basin contain lead in soil at levels that is toxic to waterfowl.

More information on the Coeur d'Alene Basin and the Bunker Hill Mining and Metallurgical Complex Superfund Site is available from Region 10's website.

Summary of the consent decree

The settlement resolves a cost recovery and natural resource damage action related to the Bunker Hill Mining and Metallurgical Complex Superfund Site that was initiated by the Coeur d'Alene Tribe in 1991 and joined by the United States in 1996.

The United States, Tribe and state of Idaho will recover approximately $263.4 million pursuant to the settlement. Of this amount, approximately

$180 million will fund response actions throughout the site,

$17 million will fund response actions within Operable Unit 1 (the "Populated Areas of the Bunker Hill Box"), and

$65.85 million will be paid to the federal, tribal and state natural resource trustees

The settlement also requires Hecla to provide access to and implement proprietary controls on property they own or control within the site. The settlement includes a protocol that will govern the coordination of EPA's cleanup efforts in the Upper Basin with Hecla's mining activities in an effort to minimize potential conflicts between cleanup and mining activities.

Comment Period

The Hecla Mining Company settlement, filed with the U.S. District Court for the District of Idaho, is subject to a 30-day public comment period and approval by the federal court.

For more information, contact:

Douglas Dixon

Attorney Advisor

U.S. Environmental Protection Agency (MC2272A)

1200 Pennsylvania Avenue, NW

Washington, D.C. 20460

(202) 564-4232

dixon.douglas@epa.gov[23]

Although NLRB cases differ slightly in appearance from court cases, it should be remembered that they are law, and therefore primary authority.

State and Local Administrative Agencies

Many federal agencies are mirrored by other agencies at the state or local level. The state legislatures or governors create these agencies and empower them to make and enforce rules and regulations. Therefore, understanding how the federal administrative system works will help guide research into the decisions of state and local administrative agencies.

For example, the Department of Transportation, a federal agency, covers all transportation that crosses state boundaries, whether by road, rail, water, pipeline, or air. In addition, each state has an agency that oversees transportation within the state. Regulations promulgated by state agencies cannot conflict with regulations promulgated by federal agencies.

Some states publish administrative regulations with their state codes. Other states publish a separate ***administrative code***, which is a compilation of all rules and regulations enacted by all state agencies in that year. These codes are normally arranged by agency, and therefore by subject matter. One problem with administrative materials at the state level is that the states either do not publish an administrative compilation or do not publish materials frequently. One way to determine whether a state has administrative materials is to check table T-1 of the *Uniform System of Citation* (*The Bluebook*) or the appendix of the *ALWD Citation Manual*.

Researching state administrative law is also complicated by the fact that the administrative materials of the 50 states are not uniform in their format, scope,

Administrative code

A collection of regulations organized by subject matter.

---

[23]United States Environmental Protection Agency. Cleanup Enforcement. Hecla Mining Company Settlement for the Bunker Hill Mining and Metallurgical Complex Superfund Site. 2012. http://www .epa.gov/compliance/resources/cases/cleanup/cercla/hecla.html

EXHIBIT 12-11   NLRB DECISION (PARTIAL)[24]

Notice: This opinion is subject to formal revision before publication in the bound of NLRB decisions. Readers are requested to notify the Executive Secretary, National Labor Relations Board, Washington, D.C. 20570, of any typographical or other formal errors so that corrections can be included in the bound volumes.

Landmark Family Foods, Inc. d/b/a Church Square Supermarket *and* United Food and Commercial Workers Union Local 880. Cases 8—CA—37667 and 8—CA—38794

May 31, 2011

DECISION AND ORDER

CHAIRMAN LIEBMAN AND MEMBERS PEARCE AND HAYES

On November 2, 2010, Administrative Law Judge Jefrey D. Wedekind issued the attached decision. The Respondent filed exceptions and a supporting brief. The Acting General Counsel and the Charging Party filed answering briefs.

The National Labor Relations Board has delegated its authority in this proceeding to a three-member panel.

The Board has considered the decision and the record in light if the exceptions and briefs[1] and has decided to affirm the judge's rulings, findings,[2] and conclusions,[3] and to adopt the recommend Order.

ORDER

The National Labor Relations Board adopts the recommended Order of the administrative law judge and orders that the Respondent, Landmark Family Foods, Inc. d/b/a Church Square Supermarket, Cleveland, Ohio, its officers, agents, successors and assigns, shall take the actions set forth in the order.

Dated, Washington, D.C. May 31, 2011

Wilma B. Liebman,   Chairman

---

[1] In light of our disposition of the issues, we find no need to pass on contentions by the Acting General Counsel and the Charging Party that we should strike portions of the Respondent's brief.

[2] The Respondent has excepted to some of the judge's credibility findings. The Board's established policy is not to overrule an administrative law judge's credibility resolutions unless the clear preponderance of all the relevant evidence convinces us that they are incorrect. *Standard Dry Wall Product,* 91 NLRB *544* (1950), enfd. 188 F.2d 362 (3d Cir. 1951). We have carefully examined the record and find no basis for reversing the findings.

[3] In affirming the judge's conclusion that the Respondent violated Sec. 8(a)(5) of the Act by unilaterally ceasing benefit fund contributions for all unit employees and changing their health insurer, Member Hayes relies on the fact that the Respondent's actions were not consistent with any proposals pending in contract negotiations. He finds it unnecessary to rely on the judge's additional determination that the parties were not at impasse.

356 NLRB No. 170

Mark Gaston Pearce,   Member

Brian E. Hayes,   Member

(SEAL) NATIONAL LABOR RELATIONS BOARD

Jun S. Bang Esq., for the General Counsel.
Fred S. Papalardo Jr., Esq. and *Adam J. Davis, Esq. (Reminger Co., L.P.A.),* for the Respondent.
Daniel S. White, Esq. and *Eban O. McNair IV, Esq.,* for the Charging Party.

DECISION

Statement of the Case

Jeffery D. Wedekind, Administrative Law judge. The consolidated complaint in these cases alleges that Respondent has violated Section 8(a)(1) and (5) of the Act in various respects since its most recent collective-bargaining agreement with the Union expired in February 2007.[1] Following several prehearing conferences, the cases were tried before me on July 12-15, 2010, in Cleveland, Ohio. Thereafter, on October 7 and 8, Respondent, the General Counsel, and the Charging Party union filed posthearing briefs.[2] After considering the briefs and the entire record,[3] including my observation of the demeanor of the witnesses, I make the following

---

[1] The underlying charges and amended charges were filed by the Union between March 7, 2008 and April 29, 2010. Pursuant thereto, the General Counsel issued an Order Consolidating Cases and Second Amended Complaint on April 30, 2010. Respondent subsequently filed an answer and amended answer on May 13 and July 8, 2010, respectively.

[2] Respondent's motion to strike the Charging Party Union's brief as untimely filed is denied. The uncontroverted facts set forth in the Union's affidavit in support of accepting its brief indicate that: (1) the Union attempted to timely file the brief electronically as a Word 2010 document prior to midnight on the October 7 deadline; (2) the brief was not successfully filed at that time because the Board's e-filing system did not accept Word 2010 documents; (3) the Union eventually determined that this was the reason for the filing failure and reformatted and successfully filed the brief electronically as a Word 2003 document only 48 seconds after the deadline; and (4) the Union did not gain any advantage, or the Respondent suffer any prejudice, by the delay, as the Union did not review the briefs filed by Respondent and the General Counsel on October 7 prior to successfully filing its brief. Contrary to Respondent, and in agreement with the Union and the General Counsel, I find that these circumstances satisfy the requirements set forth in Section 102 .111(c) of the Board's Rules for accepting a late-filed brief . See *Altercare of Wadsworth, 355* NLRB No. 96, slip op. at 7 (20 10). The Union's motion to accept the late electronic filing of its brief is therefore granted.

[3] The transcript and exhibits are corrected as set forth in my September 14 Notice to Show Cause (as modified by the General Counsel's response) and the subsequent motions to correct submitted by the General Counsel and the Charging Party (ALJ Exh. 1(a)-(c)).

TABLE 12-2 Similarities and Differences in Federal and State Administrative Law

Similarities

- Both involve actions by agencies.
- Both have a wide variety of agencies, both executive and independent.
- Both have rulemaking power.
- Both have adjudication power.
- Both have investigatory powers.
- Both have similar APAs.
- Both involve the same or similar questions of judicial review of agency actions.

Differences

- Many states have some important agencies headed by elected officials rather than those officials appointed by the executive.
- Counties, cities, and other political subdivisions are not considered agencies of the state and are not governed by the state's APA.

or editing. The indexes to the state materials are difficult to use, and commercial publishers usually do not publish additional indexes. In addition, some state administrative codes overlap the federal codes.

State Administrative Agencies A number of state agencies now make their rules and regulations available online. This allows the regulations to be easily updated. Many states have a complete listing of their state agencies available through the state's official homepage on the Internet. See Exhibit 12-12, showing a sample of the agencies in the state of Illinois.

EXHIBIT 12-12 AGENCIES IN ILLINOIS

State Agencies

Aging, Department on
Agriculture, Department of
Appellate Defender, Office of
Appellate Prosecutor, Office of
Arts Council
Attorney General, Office of the
Attorney Registration & Disciplinary Commission of the Supreme Court of Illinois
Auditor General
Capital Development Board
Central Management Services, Department of
Children and Family Services, Department of
Civil Service Commission, Illinois
Commerce and Economic Opportunity, Department of
Commerce Commission, Illinois
Community College Board, Illinois
Comprehensive Health Insurance Plan, State of Illinois
Comptroller, Office of the
Corrections, Department of
Criminal Justice Information Authority
Deaf and Hard of Hearing Commission, Illinois
Developmental Disabilities, Illinois Council on
Discrimination and Hate Crimes, Commission on
Economic Recovery Commission
Education, Board of
Educational Labor Relations Board, Illinois
Elections, Board of
Emergency Management Agency

Employment Security, Department of
Environmental Protection Agency

* * *

Human Rights Commission
Human Rights, Department of
Human Services, Department of
Illinois General Assembly
Illinois House Democrats
Illinois House Republicans
Illinois Senate Democrats
Illinois Senate Republicans
Insurance, Department of
Investment, Illinois State Board of
Judicial Inquiry Board
Juvenile Justice, Department of
Labor Relations Board
Labor, Department of
Law Enforcement Training and Standards Board, Illinois
Liquor Control Commission
Lottery, Illinois
Lt. Governor, Office of the
Management and Budget, Office of

* * *

Revenue, Department of
Secretary of State, Office of the
State Fire Marshal
State Police Merit Board
State Police, Illinois
State Retirement Systems
State Treasurer, Office of the
State Universities Civil Service System
State Universities Retirement System
Student Assistance Commission, Illinois
Supreme Court, Illinois
Teachers' Retirement System
Toll Highway Authority, Illinois State
Transportation, Department of
Veterans Affairs, Department of
Volunteerism & Community Service, Governor's Commission on
Workers' Compensation Commission, Illinois[25]

From the state website, the agency's website may be accessed to see if the rules and regulations are available online. For example, Exhibit 12-13 shows the Illinois Gaming Board's Adopted Rules.

As shown in Exhibit 12-13, the Illinois Gaming Board was not current in its coverage of rules—the 2011 rules shown on the website were updated only through 2009. Therefore, the board refers researchers to the state administrative code for official sources.

Exhibit 12-14 shows a partial listing from the Administrative Code for Indiana webpage. Indiana has 930 titles in its administrative code that cover everything from air quality to veterans' affairs.

State and local administrative agencies are frequently empowered to hold hearings similar to the hearings held by federal agencies. These hearings are conducted by

[25]State of Illinois. State Agencies. 2011. http://www2.illinois.gov/pages/agencies.aspx

EXHIBIT 12-13 ILLINOIS GAMING BOARD (PARTIAL LISTING)[26]

Adopted Rules	Policy Interpretations and Action Transmittals
86 Ill. Adm. Code Part 3000 - Effective January 10, 2000	Policy Interpretations and Action Transmittals are Board approved interpretations of specific rules and regulations.

This copy of the Adopted Rules implementing the Illinois Riverboat Gambling Act, 230 ILCS 10, is prepared by staff of the Illinois Gaming Board for the convenience of the Board members and staff, licensees and other interested parties. The text is taken from the Illinois Register and official public records and maintained on a database. This text is not an official copy of the rules as published in the Illinois Administrative Code, however, and should not be relied on as official. Readers are asked to please forward comments, including notice of any errors and omissions discovered in using this document, to:

Public Information Officer

Illinois Gaming Board

801 South Seventh Street

Springfield, Illinois 62794-9474

217 524-0226 Voice

217 785-7541 Fax

800 526-0844 (Illinois Relay Center for the Hearing Impaired)

Proposed Rules

The individual rules below are the most current Illinois Gaming Board adopted rules.

Subpart A: General Provisions

Section	Name
3000.100	Definitions
3000.101	Invalidity
3000.102	Public Inquiries
3000.103	Organization of the Illinois Gaming Board
3000.104	Rulemaking Procedures
3000.105	Board Meetings
3000.110	Disciplinary Actions
3000.115	Records Retention
	Records Retention Schedule

the appropriate administrative board, which is expected to represent the public interest. The parole board for a state prison is one example of an administrative board. The parole board holds hearings to determine if prisoners should be released early from their incarceration. Like federal agency hearings, state and local agency hearings provide an informality that is not available in the court system. In addition, while courts must be impartial to the parties that appear before the court, the administrative board is accountable to the public, and must issue decisions that are in the public interest.

[26]State of Illinois. Illinois Gaming Board. Adopted Rules. 2009. http://www.igb.illinois.gov/regs/

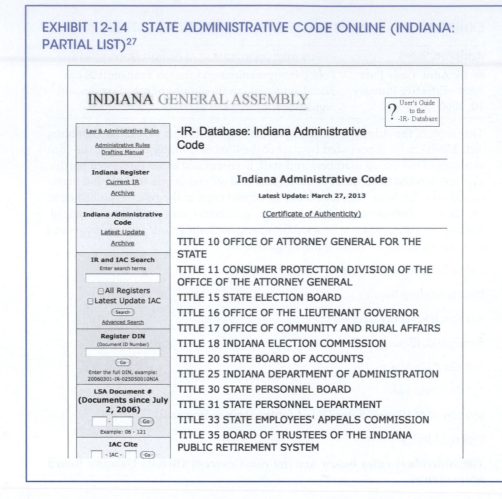

EXHIBIT 12-14 STATE ADMINISTRATIVE CODE ONLINE (INDIANA: PARTIAL LIST)[27]

EXECUTIVE MATERIALS

Executive orders

Orders or regulations that are issued by the president to interpret, begin, or give some administrative affect to a constitutional provision, statute, or treaty.

Proclamation

A formal and public declaration by the president.

Presidential memoranda

Documents issued by the president to members of the executive branch. There are three kinds of presidential memoranda: presidential determinations or findings, memoranda of disapproval, and hortatory memoranda.

The executive branch is often overlooked in legal research. Yet the executive branch issues documents that affect every American citizen in some way. There are three primary types of executive materials: *executive orders*, *proclamations*, and *presidential memoranda*. These materials have the force of law and do not require any further action by Congress.

Presidents often ask the attorney general's office for clarification on the power of these documents. The Office of Legal Counsel reviews all executive orders and other presidential materials for legality and form. See Exhibit 12-15 for a sample.

Executive materials can be found in a variety of locations. Here are some examples:

> *Federal Register*
> *Code of Federal Regulations (Title 3)*
> *Weekly Compilation of Presidential Documents*
> *Daily Compilation of Presidential Documents*
> *United States Code Service*
> *United States Statutes at Large*

[27]Indiana General Assembly. –IR- Database: Indiana Administrative Code. Indiana Administrative Code. 2012. http://www.in.gov/legislative/iac/

EXHIBIT 12-15   LEGAL EFFECTIVENESS OF PRESIDENTIAL DOCUMENTS

LEGAL EFFECTIVENESS OF A PRESIDENTIAL DIRECTIVE, AS COMPARED TO AN EXECUTIVE ORDER

A presidential directive has the same substantive legal effect as an executive order. It is the substance of the presidential action that is determinative, not the form of the document conveying that action.

Both an executive order and a presidential directive remain effective upon a change in administration, unless otherwise specified in the document, and both continue to be effective until subsequent presidential action is taken.

January 29, 2000

MEMORANDUM FOR THE COUNSEL COUNSEL [sic] TO THE PRESIDENT

You have asked our opinion whether there is any substantive legal difference between an executive order and a presidential directive. As this Office has consistently advised, it is our opinion that there is no substantive difference in the legal effectiveness of an executive order and a presidential directive that is not styled as an executive order. We are further of the opinion that a presidential directive would not automatically lapse upon a change of administration; as with an executive order, unless otherwise specified, a presidential directive would remain effective until subsequent presidential action is taken.

We are aware of no basis for drawing a distinction as to the legal effectiveness of a presidential action based on the form or caption of the written document through which that action is conveyed. *Cf.* Memorandum for Harold Judson, Assistant Solicitor General, from William H. Rose, *Re: Statement of Policy Regarding Certain Strategic Materials* (Aug. 28, 1945) (concluding that a letter from President Roosevelt stating the government's policy "constitute[d] a Presidential directive having the force and effect of law," notwithstanding its informality of form). It has been our consistent view that it is the substance of a presidential determination or directive that is controlling and not whether the document is styled in a particular manner. This principle plainly extends to the legal effectiveness of a document styled as a "presidential directive."

Moreover, as with an executive order, a presidential directive would not lose its legal effectiveness upon a change of administration. Rather, in our view, because a presidential directive issues from the Office of the Chief Executive, it would remain in force, unless otherwise specified, pending any future presidential action. *Cf.* Memorandum for Michael J. Egan, Associate Attorney General, from John M. Harmon, Acting Assistant Attorney General, Office of Legal Counsel, *Re: Proposed Amendments to 28 CFR 16, Subpart B* (Apr. 21, 1977) (raising possible concerns about a proposal to delegate to the Deputy Attorney General certain authorities to invoke executive privilege because such a delegation could potentially be inconsistent with a 1969 Memorandum from President Nixon on executive privilege). Indeed, Presidents have frequently used written forms other than executive orders to take actions that were intended to have effect during a subsequent administration. For example, delegations of presidential authority under 3 U.S.C. § 301 have been made pursuant to presidential memoranda.[1] *See also, e.g.,* Establishing a

---

[1] At various points over time, Presidents have delegated presidential functions both by executive order and by presidential memorandum. *Compare* Delegation of Authority Under Section 1401(b) of the National Defense Authorization Act for Fiscal Year 2000 (Public Law 106-65), 65 Fed. Reg. 3119 (2000), *with* Exec. Order No. 10,250 (1951) (delegation of functions to the Secretary of the Interior), *reprinted as amended in* 3 U.S.C. § 301 app. (1994).

Federal Energy Management Program, 3 Pub. Papers Gerald R. Ford 1015 (Nov. 4, 1976) (including a directive to be carried out for FY 1977).

You have also inquired whether a presidential directive could be published in the Federal Register. It is our understanding that any presidential determination or directive can be published in the Federal Register, regardless of how it is styled. At present, a range of presidential determinations and directives styled other than as executive orders are routinely published in the Federal Register. *See, e.g.*, Determination Pursuant to Section 2(c)(1) of the Migration and Refugee Assistance Act of 1962, as amended, 64 Fed. Reg. 65653 (1999); Report to Congress Regarding Conditions in Burma and U.S. Policy Toward Burma, 64 Fed. Reg. 60647 (1999) (memorandum directing the Secretary of State to transmit report to Congress). We see no reason to believe that the Federal Register would decline to publish the contemplated directive.[2]

RANDOLPH D. MOSS

Acting Assistant Attorney General

[2]Because the decision whether an item can be published is made by the Office of the Federal Register, we would suggest confirming this with that office. If you would like, we would be happy to do so on your behalf.[28]

United States Code Congressional and Administrative News
Westlaw and Lexis
GPO Access

Not all materials are found in every location, however. Of the sources listed above, one of the best sources for locating all presidential materials is the *Daily Compilation of Presidential Documents*, which began in 1965. It was called the *Weekly Compilation of Presidential Documents* until 2009. This set of materials is published by the Office of the Federal Register, and contains a variety of information, such as the following:

Executive orders

Proclamations

Speeches

Resignations

Retirements

Communications to Congress and federal agencies

Statements about bill signings and vetoes

Appointments and nominations

Reorganization plans

White House announcements

Press releases and press conferences

Acts approved by the president

Nominations submitted to the Senate[29]

[28]United States Department of Justice. Office of Legal Counsel. 2012. http://www.justice.gov/olc/predirective.htm

[29]GPO Access. Weekly Compilation of Presidential Documents: About the Weekly Comp. 2012. http://www.gpoaccess.gov/wcomp/about.html

The National Archives and Records Administration provides access to executive orders for all presidents since Franklin D. Roosevelt. It also houses the *Public Papers of the President,* containing items such as speeches, nominations, presidential papers, executive orders, and other presidential documents since the presidency of Ronald Reagan.[30]

Executive orders

Executive orders have the force of law, and are usually directives to agencies. Executive orders cover a wide range of topics such as protecting national forests from logging, or blocking access to the property of persons who have committed human rights violations. However, executive orders tend to be aimed at those inside the government. An example of an executive order is shown in Exhibit 12-16.

Executive orders can be found in all of the locations noted above, except the *United States Statutes at Large.*

EXHIBIT 12-16   EXECUTIVE ORDER

Executive Order 13575 - Establishment of the White House Rural Council

By the authority vested in me as President by the Constitution and the laws of the United States of America and in order to enhance Federal engagement with rural communities, it is hereby ordered as follows:

Section 1. Policy. Sixteen percent of the American population lives in rural counties. Strong, sustainable rural communities are essential to winning the future and ensuring American competitiveness in the years ahead. These communities supply our food, fiber, and energy, safeguard our natural resources, and are essential in the development of science and innovation. Though rural communities face numerous challenges, they also present enormous economic potential. The Federal Government has an important role to play in order to expand access to the capital necessary for economic growth, promote innovation, improve access to health care and education, and expand outdoor recreational activities on public lands.

To enhance the Federal Government's efforts to address the needs of rural America, this order establishes a council to better coordinate Federal programs and maximize the impact of Federal investment to promote economic prosperity and quality of life in our rural communities.

Sec. 2. Establishment. There is established a White House Rural Council (Council).

Sec. 3. Membership. (a) The Secretary of Agriculture shall serve as the Chair of the Council, which shall also include the heads of the following executive branch departments, agencies, and offices:

(1) the Department of the Treasury;

(2) the Department of Defense;

(3) the Department of Justice;

(4) the Department of the Interior;

(5) the Department of Commerce;

(6) the Department of Labor;

---

[30]National Archives. Presidential Libraries. Research Presidential Materials. http://www.archives.gov/presidential-libraries/research/

(7) the Department of Health and Human Services;

(8) the Department of Housing and Urban Development;

(9) the Department of Transportation;

(10) the Department of Energy;

(11) the Department of Education;

(12) the Department of Veterans Affairs;

(13) the Department of Homeland Security;

(14) the Environmental Protection Agency;

(15) the Federal Communications Commission;

(16) the Office of Management and Budget;

(17) the Office of Science and Technology Policy;

(18) the Office of National Drug Control Policy;

(19) the Council of Economic Advisers;

(20) the Domestic Policy Council;

(21) the National Economic Council;

(22) the Small Business Administration;

(23) the Council on Environmental Quality;

(24) the White House Office of Public Engagement and Intergovernmental Affairs;

(25) the White House Office of Cabinet Affairs; and such other executive branch departments, agencies, and offices as the President or the Secretary of Agriculture may, from time to time, designate.

(b) A member of the Council may designate, to perform the Council functions of the member, a senior-level official who is part of the member's department, agency, or office, and who is a full-time officer or employee of the Federal Government.

(c) The Department of Agriculture shall provide funding and administrative support for the Council to the extent permitted by law and within existing appropriations.

(d) The Council shall coordinate its policy development through the Domestic Policy Council and the National Economic Council.

Sec. 4. Mission and Function of the Council. The Council shall work across executive departments, agencies, and offices to coordinate development of policy recommendations to promote economic prosperity and quality of life in rural America, and shall coordinate my Administration's engagement with rural communities. The Council shall:

(a) make recommendations to the President, through the Director of the Domestic Policy Council and the Director of the National Economic Council, on streamlining and leveraging Federal investments in rural areas, where appropriate, to increase the impact of Federal dollars and create economic opportunities to improve the quality of life in rural America;

(b) coordinate and increase the effectiveness of Federal engagement with rural stakeholders, including agricultural organizations, small businesses, education and training institutions, health-care providers, telecommunications services providers, research and land grant institutions, law enforcement, State, local, and tribal governments, and nongovernmental organizations regarding the needs of rural America;

(c) coordinate Federal efforts directed toward the growth and development of geographic regions that encompass both urban and rural areas; and

(d) identify and facilitate rural economic opportunities associated with energy development, outdoor recreation, and other conservation related activities.

Sec. 5. General Provisions. (a) The heads of executive departments and agencies shall assist and provide information to the Council, consistent with applicable law, as may be necessary to carry out the functions of the Council. Each executive department and agency shall bear its own expense for participating in the Council.

(b) Nothing in this order shall be construed to impair or otherwise affect:

(i) authority granted by law to an executive department, agency, or the head thereof; or

(ii) functions of the Director of the Office of Management and Budget relating to budgetary, administrative, or legislative proposals.

(c) This order shall be implemented consistent with applicable law and subject to the availability of appropriations.

(d) This order is not intended to, and does not, create any right or benefit, substantive or procedural, enforceable at law or in equity by any party against the United States, its departments, agencies, or entities, its officers, employees, or agents, or any other person.

BARACK OBAMA

THE WHITE HOUSE,
June 9, 2011.[31]

State Executive Orders

State governors can also issue executive orders. These executive orders are usually found on a state government website. An example from the state of New Jersey is shown in Exhibit 12-17.

PROCLAMATIONS

A proclamation is a document that generally has no legal effect but states a condition, recognizes an event, proclaims some public awareness, provides a ceremonial decree, or triggers the effectiveness of a law. Proclamations tend to be aimed at entities outside the government. Proclamations generally have no legal effect, because they do not authorize punishment or liability if there is a violation. However, the issuance of proclamations has led to historical consequences for the American people. One of the best-known presidential proclamations is the Emancipation Proclamation issued by Abraham Lincoln in 1863. In more recent times, George W. Bush issued a proclamation in 2005 that declared the areas affected by

[31]The White House. Presidential Actions. Executive Orders. 2011. http://www.whitehouse.gov /the-press-office/2011/06/09/executive-order-establishment-white-house-rural-council

---

EXHIBIT 12-17 STATE EXECUTIVE ORDER

EXECUTIVE ORDER NO. 5

WHEREAS, the fiscal well-being of the State of New Jersey and the growth of economic opportunities for New Jersey citizens and New Jersey businesses are major priorities of this Administration; and

WHEREAS, it is in the best interest of the State of New Jersey that the Governor receive high-quality advice on an ongoing basis regarding State, regional, local and national economic conditions; and

WHEREAS, the establishment of a Governor's Council of Economic Advisors will provide an effective and efficient mechanism for the Governor to obtain advice on a broad range of economic matters;

NOW, THEREFORE, I, CHRIS CHRISTIE, Governor of the State of New Jersey, by virtue of the authority vested in me by the Constitution and by the Statutes of this State do hereby ORDER, and DIRECT:

1. There is hereby established a Governor's Council of Economic Advisors (or "Council") which shall report directly to the Governor.

2. Each member of the Council shall be appointed by and shall serve at the pleasure of the Governor.

3. The Council shall consist of a Chairperson, designated as such by the Governor, and four other members appointed by the Governor. Neither the Chair nor any member shall have a fixed term. The Chair shall establish such rules of operation as the Council may require.

4. The Council shall analyze and advise the Governor on issues related to the fiscal condition of the State of New Jersey.

5. The Council shall meet as requested by the Governor or by the Chairperson, but not less frequently than quarterly. All Department and Agency heads are directed to cooperate fully with the Council, including providing such information as the Council may determine will assist it in its duties.

6. This Order shall take effect immediately.

GIVEN, under my hand and seal this 20th day of January, Two Thousand and Ten, and of the Independence of the United States, the Two Hundred and Thirty-Fourth.

[seal]

/s/ Chris Christie

Governor

Attest:

/s/ Jeffrey S. Chiesa

Chief Counsel to the Governor[32]

Hurricane Katrina as a national disaster area. Many of the proclamations declare the recognition of a particular day, such as the one in Exhibit 12-18.

Like the president, governors of states can issue proclamations. See Exhibit 12-19 for an example from Georgia.

[32]The State of New Jersey. Executive Orders. 2012. http://www.nj.gov/infobank/circular/eocc5.pdf

EXHIBIT 12-18   PROCLAMATION

The White House
Office of the Press Secretary

For Immediate Release
June 10, 2011

Presidential Proclamation–Flag Day and National Flag Week

On June 14, 1777, the Second Constitutional Congress adopted a flag with thirteen stripes and thirteen stars to represent our Nation, one star for each of our founding colonies. The stars were set upon a blue field, in the words of the Congress's resolution, "representing a new constellation" in the night sky. What was then a fledgling democracy has flourished and expanded, as we constantly strive toward a more perfect Union.

Through the successes and struggles we have faced, the American flag has been ever present. It has flown on our ships and military bases around the world as we continue to defend liberty and democracy abroad. It has been raised in yards and on porches across America on days of celebration, and as a sign of our shared heritage. And it is lowered on days of remembrance to honor fallen service members and public servants; or when tragedy strikes and we join together in mourning. Our flag is the mark of one country, one people, uniting under one banner.

When the American flag soars, so too does our Nation and the ideals it stands for. We remain committed to defending the liberties and freedoms it represents, and we give special thanks to the members of the Armed Forces who wear our flag proudly. On Flag Day, and during National Flag Week, we celebrate the powerful beacon of hope that our flag has become for us all, and for people around the world.

To commemorate the adoption of our flag, the Congress, by joint resolution approved August 3, 1949, as amended (63 Stat. 492), designated June 14 of each year as "Flag Day" and requested that the President issue an annual proclamation calling for its observance and for the display of the flag of the United States on all Federal Government buildings. The Congress also requested, by joint resolution approved June 9, 1966, as amended (80 Stat. 194), that the President annually issue a proclamation designating the week in which June 14 occurs as "National Flag Week" and call upon citizens of the United States to display the flag during that week.

NOW, THEREFORE, I, BARACK OBAMA, President of the United States of America, do hereby proclaim June 14, 2011, as Flag Day and the week beginning June 12, 2011, as National Flag Week. I direct the appropriate officials to display the flag on all Federal Government buildings during that week, and I urge all Americans to observe Flag Day and National Flag Week by displaying the flag. I also call upon the people of the United States to observe with pride and all due ceremony those days from Flag Day through Independence Day, also set aside by the Congress (89 Stat. 211), as a time to honor America, to celebrate our heritage in public gatherings and activities, and to publicly recite the Pledge of Allegiance to the Flag of the United States of America.

IN WITNESS WHEREOF, I have hereunto set my hand this tenth day of June, in the year of our Lord two thousand eleven, and of the Independence of the United States of America the two hundred and thirty-fifth.

BARACK OBAMA[33]

[33]The White House. Presidential Actions. Proclamations. 2011. http://www.whitehouse.gov/the-press-office/2011/06/10/presidential-proclamation-flag-day-and-national-flag-week

> ### EXHIBIT 12-19 PROCLAMATION FROM THE GOVERNOR OF GEORGIA
>
> WHEREAS: During the 2010 Regular Session of the General Assembly, the Members considered House Resolution 178, a proposal to amend Article III, Section VI, Paragraph V of the Georgia Constitution by revising subparagraph (c); and
>
> WHEREAS: On May 27, 2010, the Georgia House of Representatives, by a vote of 152 yeas and 3 nays, adopted House Resolution 178 by the requisite two-thirds of the Members of the House of Representatives; and
>
> WHEREAS: On May 29, 2010, the Georgia State Senate, by a vote of 49 yeas and 0 nays, adopted House Resolution 178 by the requisite two-thirds of the Members of the Senate; and
>
> WHEREAS: Pursuant to Article X, Section I, Paragraph II of the Constitution of the State of Georgia, both houses having adopted identical versions of House Resolution 178 by the requisite constitutional majorities, the proposal was submitted to the electors of the entire State at the General Election of November 2, 2010; and
>
> WHEREAS: The proposed amendment appeared on the General Election ballot as "Constitutional Amendment 1" and stated, "Shall the Constitution of Georgia be amended so as to make Georgia more economically competitive by authorizing legislation to uphold reasonable competitive agreements?"; and
>
> WHEREAS: On November 2, 2010, the electors of the entire State voted as follows: 1,633,066 electors voted "Yes"; 783,390 electors voted "No"; and
>
> WHEREAS: The Secretary of State certified the above results and laid them before the Governor; and
>
> WHEREAS: O.C.G.A. § 21-2-502 (f) requires the Governor to issue a proclamation declaring the results of the vote of each constitutional amendment submitted to the electors of the entire State; now
>
> THEREFORE: I, Sonny Perdue, Governor of the State of Georgia, pursuant to the Constitution and statutes of this State, do hereby proclaim that a majority of the electors having voted in favor of the proposed constitutional amendment, Constitutional Amendment 1 is duly ratified.
>
> Furthermore, pursuant to Article X, Section I, Paragraph VI of the State Constitution, the resolution proposing the amendment providing no other date, Constitutional Amendment 1 shall become effective January 1, 2011.
>
> In witness whereof, I have hereunto set my hand and caused the seal of the Executive Department to be affixed this 30th day of December in the year of our Lord two thousand ten.[34]

Presidential determination or finding

Determinations or findings that must be issued, as required by statute, before certain actions can be taken.

Hortatory memoranda

Presidential memoranda, similar to proclamations, that are issued to executive agencies instead of the public.

Memorandum of disapproval

A presidential action that serves as a public veto.

PRESIDENTIAL MEMORANDA

Presidential memoranda are issued by the president and directed to members of the executive branch. There are three types of presidential memoranda: *presidential determinations* or *findings*, *memoranda of disapproval*, and *hortatory memoranda*. Some statutes require presidential determinations or findings before certain actions can be taken. One of the most common examples of a presidential determination occurs when a president must identify the status of a country

---

[34]State of Georgia. In 2010. Proclamations. 2010. http://www.georgia.gov/vgn/images/portal/cit_1210/30/18/166389164Const%20AMENDMENT%201%202010.pdf

before imposing sanctions on that country, as shown in Exhibit 12-20. A memorandum of disapproval is basically a public veto issued in a statement. A hortatory memorandum is similar to a proclamation, except that it is delivered to executive agencies rather than the public. Many of these documents can be located in the *Weekly Compilation of Presidential Documents* or the *Daily Compilation of Presidential Documents*, and the president may order publication in the *Federal Register*.[35] An example of a presidential memorandum is presented in Exhibit 12-20.

INTERNATIONAL LAW
Overview

In the most basic sense, ***international law*** deals with the way nations and international organizations work with each other. As other countries develop economically, international law increasingly affects the daily lives of U.S. citizens. Similar

International law
A body of law that governs the ways nations and international organizations work with each other.

EXHIBIT 12-20   PRESIDENTIAL MEMORANDUM

The White House
Office of the Press Secretary

For Immediate Release June 09, 2011

Presidential Memorandum–Unexpected Urgent Refugee and Migration Needs Related to Libya and Cote d'Ivoire

June 8, 2011

Presidential Determination

No. 2011-11

MEMORANDUM FOR THE SECRETARY OF STATE

SUBJECT: Unexpected Urgent Refugee and Migration Needs Related to Libya and Côte d'Ivoire

By the authority vested in me as President by the Constitution and the laws of the United States, including section 2(c)(1) of the Migration and Refugee Assistance Act of 1962 (the "Act"), as amended (22 U.S.C. 2601(c)(1)), I hereby determine, pursuant to section 2(c)(1) of the Act, that it is important to the national interest to furnish assistance under the Act, in an amount not to exceed $15 million from the United States Emergency Refugee and Migration Assistance Fund, for the purpose of meeting unexpected and urgent refugee and migration needs, including by contributions to international, governmental, and nongovernmental organizations and payment of administrative expenses of the Bureau of Population, Refugees, and Migration of the Department of State, related to the humanitarian crises resulting from the violence in Libya and Côte d'Ivoire.

You are authorized and directed to publish this memorandum in the *Federal Register*.

BARACK OBAMA[36]

---

[35]San Diego State University. SDSU Library. Memoranda, Determinations and Findings.2010. http://library.sdsu.edu/guides/tip.php?id=228&aid=65

[36]The White House. Presidential Actions. Presidential Memoranda. 2011. http://www.whitehouse.gov/the-press-office/2011/06/09/presidential-memorandum-unexpected-urgent-refugee-and-migration-needs-re

Public international law
Questions of rights among nations, or between nations and the citizens of other nations.

Private international law
Law governing issues between private persons based on circumstances that have significant relationship to multiple nations.

Customary law
Law that exists based on nations operating out of a sense of legal obligation and in the normal or usual practice.

Conventional international law
Law that comes from international agreements and accepted practice among nations.

to many other areas of law, international law has two sides: *public international law* and *private international law*.

When most people think of international law, they think of public international law. This area of the law governs how nations conduct and regulate themselves as they work with each other. Private international law involves private persons and the controversies that arise from situations that affect persons from more than one nation. Although these two areas appear to be separate and distinct, they frequently overlap.

Even if a legal professional does not work exclusively in international law, it may be useful to understand its sources. The first source is *customary law*, under which nations operate out of a sense of legal obligation. Customary law was recently codified in the Vienna Convention on the Law of Treaties (http://www .state.gov/s/l/treaty/faqs/70139.htm).

The second source of international law is referred to as *conventional international law*, which comes from international agreements. These agreements, similar to contracts, allow parties to agree upon anything as long as the agreement does not conflict with the rules of international law established under the Charter of the United Nations (http://www.un.org/en/documents/charter/).

The third source of international law comes from judicial decisions. One of the main sources of judicial decisions is the International Court of Justice, also referred to as the World Court, (http://www.icj-cij.org/homepage/), which was established by the United Nations Charter.

These three sources are considered primary sources of law. But international law also has secondary sources. One of these secondary sources revolves around general principles of law that are accepted or deemed common among nations.[37]

Researching International Law

For the practitioner who is not familiar with international law, often the best way to begin is to start with some background research on the problem at hand. It might be advantageous to read the *United Nations Documentation: Research Guide*, which provides an overview of the documents issued by the United Nations and information on actions taken by both the General Assembly and the Security Council.[38] This site also provides training tutorials on how to use the system.[39] By obtaining background information on the problem, the researcher can focus more effectively on the actual legal issue involved. Knowing the document symbols allows researchers to access large quantities of materials. If a researcher knows the document symbol, he or she can go to the documents page of the UN website (http://www.un.org/en/documents/), enter the symbol in the search box, and locate the document. So, if one entered A/63/100 in the search box and selected English, he or she would retrieve Exhibit 12-21.

The next step is to determine whether any treaties apply to the issue. If a treaty does apply, the source must be updated to make sure it is still current law, just as in any other research. Next, cases should be located that have interpreted the treaty in question.

---

[37]Cornell University Law School. Legal Information Institute. International Law. 2010. http://topics .law.cornell.edu/wex/International_law

[38]Department of Public Information (DPI), Dag Hammarskjöld Library (DHL). *United Nations Documentation: Research Guide*. 2012. http://www.un.org/Depts/dhl/resguide/.

[39]Dag Hammarskjöld Library (DHL) Training. 2012. http://www.un.org/depts/dhl/training /training.htm

---

EXHIBIT 12-21   UN DOCUMENT A/63/100

United Nations A/63/100

General Assembly Distr.: General

15 June 2008

Original: English

0838453

Sixty-third session

Annotated preliminary list of items to be included in the

provisional agenda of the sixty-third regular session of the

General Assembly*

Contents

Page

I. Introduction 14
II. Annotated list 14
1. Opening of the session by the President of the General Assembly.............. 14
2. Minute of silent prayer or meditation.. 14[40]

* * *

Research on international law can come from a wide variety of sources:

- U.S. Constitution (Article I, section 8; Article I, section 10; Article II section 2; Article III, section 2; Article IV)
- Federal statutes (22 U. S. C., Entitled Foreign Relations and Intercourse)
- Treaties and Conventions (such as UN Charter, the European Union, General Agreement on Tariffs and Trade of 1994 [GATT], North American Free Trade Agreement of 1994 [NAFTA])
- International Organizations (such as United Nations, World Health Organization, International Criminal Court, North Atlantic Treaty Organization [NATO], international Federation of Red Cross)
- Department of State
- Various international law journals (such as *Indiana Journal of Global Legal Studies*)
- Cornell University Law School—Legal Information Institute: World Law Collection
- Treaties and Other International Acts Series
- U.S. Treaties and Other International Agreements
- UN Treaty Series
- U.S. Statutes at Large
- Martindale Hubbell Law Directory (International Law Digest)
- Library of Congress—THOMAS (http://thomas.loc.gov/home/thomas. php and specifically http://thomas.loc.gov/home/treaties/treaties.html)
- GPO Access Congressional Documents (select a session and select Senate Treaty Documents from the drop down menu)

---

[40]United Nations General Assembly. *Annotated preliminary list of items to be included in the provisional agenda of the sixty-third regular session of the General Assembly.* 2008. http://daccess-dds-ny .un.org/doc/UNDOC/GEN/N08/384/53/PDF/N0838453.pdf?OpenElement

- Global Legal Information Network
- Numerous treatises on international law

A portion of a treaty to which the United States is a party is shown in Exhibit 12-22.

EXHIBIT 12-22 SINGAPORE TREATY (PORTION)

[Senate Treaty Document 110-2]

[From the U.S. Government Printing Office]

110th Congress

1st Session SENATE Treaty Doc.

110-2

SINGAPORE TREATY ON THE LAW OF TRADEMARKS

_____

MESSAGE

from

THE PRESIDENT OF THE UNITED STATES

transmitting

THE SINGAPORE TREATY ON THE LAW OF TRADEMARKS (THE "TREATY" OR "SINGAPORE TREATY") ADOPTED AND SIGNED BY THE UNITED STATES AT SINGAPORE ON MARCH 28, 2006

May 3, 2007.–The Treaty was read the first time, and together with the accompanying papers, referred to the Committee on Foreign Relations and ordered to be printed for the use of the Senate

LETTER OF TRANSMITTAL

_____

The White House, May 3, 2007.

To the Senate of the United States:

I transmit herewith for the Senate's advice and consent to ratification the Singapore Treaty on the Law of Trademarks (the ''Treaty'' or ''Singapore Treaty'') adopted and signed by the United States at Singapore on March 28, 2006. I also transmit for the information of the Senate a report of the Department of State with respect to the Treaty.

If ratified by the United States, the Treaty would offer significant benefits to U.S. trademark owners and national trademark offices, including the United States Patent and Trademark Office. The beneficial features of the Trademark Law Treaty of 1994 (the ''1994 TLT''), to which the United States is a party, are included in the Singapore Treaty, as well as the improvements to the 1994 TLT that the United States Government sought to achieve through the revision effort. Key improvements allow for national trademark offices to take advantage of electronic communication systems as an efficient and cost-saving alternative to paper communications, at such time as the office is ready to embrace the technology. The Treaty also includes trademark license recordation provisions that reduce the formalities that trademark owners face when doing business in a country that is a Contracting

Party that requires trademark license recordation. The goal of these provisions is to reduce the damaging effects that can result from failure to record a license in those jurisdictions that require recordation. These and other improvements create a more attractive treaty for World Intellectual Property Organization Member States. Consequently, once the Treaty is in force, it is expected to increase the efficiency of national trademark offices, which in turn is expected to create efficiencies and cost savings for U.S. trademark owners registering and maintaining trademarks abroad.

Ratification of the Treaty is in the best interests of the United States. I recommend, therefore, that the Senate give early and favorable consideration to the Treaty and give its advice and consent to ratification.

George W. Bush.

LETTER OF SUBMITTAL

———

Department of State,

Washington, DC, March 29, 2007.

The President,

The White House.

The President: I have the honor hereby to submit to you, with a view to its transmittal to the Senate for advice and consent to ratification, the Singapore Treaty on the Law of Trademarks (the "Treaty" or "Singapore Treaty"), adopted and signed by the United States at Singapore on March 28, 2006. This Treaty was adopted under the auspices of the World Intellectual Property Organization ("WIPO") with the objective of simplifying the process of applying for and maintaining trademark registrations and trademark license recordations in those countries or intergovernmental organizations that are parties to the Treaty ("Contracting Parties").

The Singapore Treaty revises the WIPO Trademark Law Treaty of 1994 ("1994 TLT"), to which the United States is a party along with 37 other parties.

The revisions improve upon the 1994 TLT and are intended to make the Singapore Treaty more attractive to prospective Contracting Parties, and thus expand the benefits of the Treaty, if ratified, to U.S. trademark owners filing in other countries.

* * *

Respectfully submitted.

Condoleezza Rice.

Enclosure: Key Provisions of the Singapore Treaty on the Law of Trademarks.
key provisions of the singapore treaty [sic] on the law of trademarks[41]
* * *

Once a law has been found that applies to the problem being researched, it must be checked to determine if it is still current law. For example, when applying an amendment to the United Nations Charter, the amendment must have passed all appropriate votes in order to be effective. If two-thirds of the General Assembly and all permanent members of the Security Council have not voted on the amendment, then the law is not currently in force. See Exhibit 12-23 for a sample of such controlling language.

[41]GPO Access. 110th Congress (2007–2008). Senate Treaty Documents. Treaty Doc. 110-2. 200 76. http://www.gpo.gov/fdsys/pkg/CDOC-110tdoc2/html/CDOC-110tdoc2.htm

---

EXHIBIT 12-23   TIME LIMIT IN UN CHARTER

Chapter XVIII—Amendments

Article 108

Amendments to the present Charter shall come into force for all Members of the United Nations when they have been adopted by a vote of two thirds of the members of the General Assembly and ratified in accordance with their respective constitutional processes by two thirds of the Members of the United Nations, including all the permanent members of the Security Council.[42]

A good source for researching current treaties is the annual publication from the State Department, *Treaties in Force*. This source includes treaties and international agreements that have not expired been denounced, replaced, superseded, or terminated by the participants. The first section contains bilateral treaties and international agreements. The entries are organized by country or other international entity, and then subject headings are included under each entity. The second section lists all multilateral treaties or international agreements in which the United States is a party. These are arranged by subject.[43] Again, it is important to check carefully to be sure a treaty is current. Some treaties have time limitations, or specific dates of activation.

Once the treaty has been read and it has been confirmed that it is still current, the next step is to analyze the Treaty by looking at cases that interpret the treaty. *Shepard's Federal Statute Citations* lists cases that cite particular treaties, and can be found in print or on LexisNexis.

Another important site for locating cases is the **International Court of Justice** (ICJ; often called the World Court). Established in 1946, the Court consists of 15 judges elected by an absolute majority of members of the UN General Assembly and the Security Council. These judges serve for nine-year terms, and in addition to hearing cases, provide advisory opinions by special request.[44] The decisions of the International Court of Justice first appear as separate documents and are then published in an annual compilation called *Reports of Judgments, Advisory Opinions and Orders*. A researcher can find the beginning document, written pleadings, oral arguments, correspondence, and other documents filed. All documents are public record after the court has given its final decision.[45]

The International Court of Justice is organized according to the Statute of the Court, which is part of the Charter of the United Nations. The Statute of the Court can be amended in the same way as the Charter. Exhibit 12-24 shows the table of contents of the statute.

The conduct of the International Court of Justice is also governed by its Rules of Court. These rules are similar to other rules of court discussed previously. An example is shown in Exhibit 12–25.

International Court of Justice
The judicial arm of the United Nations, which has jurisdiction to settle legal disputes and give advisory opinions on treaties and other international legal matters.

---

[42]Charter of the United Nations: Chapter XVIII: Amendments. Article 108. http://www.un.org/en/documents/charter/chapter18.shtml

[43]US Department of State. Treaties in Force. 2012. http://www.state.gov/s/l/treaty/tif/index.htm

[44]International Court of Justice. The Court. http://www.icj-cij.org/court/index.php?p1=1

[45]United Nations Documentation: Research Guide. International Court of Justice. 2012. http://www.un.org/Depts/dhl/resguide/specil.htm#icj

---

EXHIBIT 12-24   STATUTE OF THE INTERNATIONAL COURT OF JUSTICE

Statute of the International Court of Justice

Table of Contents:

Chapter I: Organization of the Court (Articles 2–33)

Chapter II: Competence of the Court (Articles 34–38)

Chapter III: Procedure (Articles 39–64)

Chapter IV: Advisory Opinions (Articles 65–68)

Chapter V: Amendment (Articles 69 & 70)[46]

In addition to the Rules of Court, the International Court of Justice has also adopted practice directions. The practice directions provide a review of the Court's working methods.[48]

One of the main roles of the International Court of Justice is to settle cases and to give advisory opinions. When a dispute comes before the Court through a unilateral application by one state against another state, the parties are stated in the caption, much like in cases in the United States. When the dispute is based on a special agreement between two states, the party names are separated by a slash rather than a "versus" symbol, such as "Brazil/Japan." Advisory proceedings, judgments, and orders are listed in chronological order.[49]

Once applicable cases have been found, the citations must be checked to ensure they are in the correct form. This form is described in rule 21.4 *et. seq.* in *The Bluebook*. For example, a citation to a treaty with three or fewer parties should begin with the name of the agreement; the abbreviated names of the parties to the agreement, separated by a hyphen; the date of signing; and one U.S. treaty source. The official United States treaty source is *United States Treaties and Other International Agreements* (U.S.T.) (T. 4). See § 21 in *ALWD*.

EXHIBIT 12-25   ARTICLE 45

Article 45

1. The pleadings in a case begun by means of an application shall consist, in the following order, of: a Memorial by the applicant; a Counter-Memorial by the respondent.

2. The Court may authorize or direct that there shall be a Reply by the applicant and a Rejoinder by the respondent if the parties are so agreed, or if the Court decides, *proprio motu* or at the request of one of the parties, that these pleadings are necessary.[47]

---

[46]International Court of Justice. Basic Documents. http://www.icj-cij.org/documents/index.php?p1=4&p2=2&p3=0

[47]International Court of Justice. Basic Documents. Rules of Court. http://www.icj-cij.org/documents/index.php?p1=4&p2=3&p3=0

[48]International Court of Justice. Basic Documents. Practice Directions. 2009. http://www.icj-cij.org/documents/index.php?p1=4&p2=4&p3=0

[49]International Court of Justice. Cases. http://www.icj-cij.org/docket/index.php?p1=3

SUMMARY

Although the materials covered in this chapter are not the most frequently researched, it is important to be familiar with them. Administrative agencies create law daily, and the executive branch produces a larger area of law than most people realize. Through the creation of administrative agencies, the issuance of executive orders, and its participation on the world stage, our government creates an important base of law, and it is important that paralegals have at least a basic understanding of these areas. As with other areas of law, it is necessary to find the primary authority that covers the issue at hand. Sometimes that means researching the background of an issue before focusing on the applicable laws.

REVIEW **QUESTIONS**

1. What is the CFR?
2. What does the *Federal Register* contain? How often is it published?
3. What are the functions of an administrative agency?
4. Is the material in the CFR primary or secondary? Why?
5. Identify whether or not an administrative agency can hold hearings, and if so, identify the procedure.
6. What is in an enabling act?
7. How do the CFR and the *Federal Register* differ?
8. How can you update regulatory research to make sure you have the most current sources?
9. How do executive orders, proclamations, and presidential memoranda differ?
10. What is a treaty?
11. What are the three main areas of research in international law?

CITATION **EXERCISES**

1. Provide the proper citation for title 21 of the Code of Federal Regulations, section 10.45 (2010).
2. Provide the proper citation for title 16 of the Code of Federal Regulations, section 1206.4. What is the effective date?
3. Provide the correct citation for Internet Research 4 below.
4. Provide the correct citation for Internet Research 5 below.
5. Provide the correct citation for Internet Research 6 below.

QUICK **CHECK**

True/False

1. A proclamation tells an administrative agency what it should do.
2. The executive branch is considered to be the unofficial fourth branch of government.
3. Executive orders have legal effect or the force of law.
4. The *Weekly Compilation of Presidential Documents* is the best place to locate current proclamations.
5. Agencies do not have lawmaking powers.
6. The *Federal Register* and the Code of Federal Regulations both contain all executive materials.
7. Administrative decisions are issued by judges who are elected to office.
8. Generally, if a party is dissatisfied with the last level of agency hearing, the party can appeal to the trial level court in either the federal system or the state court system.
9. States generally have the same or similar agencies as the federal government.
10. The North American Free Trade Agreement is an example of a treaty.

Matching

Connect the acronym in column A with the appropriate title in Column B.

1. APA
2. EEOC
3. FOIA
4. FDA
5. ALJ

A. Department of Commerce
B. Administrative Procedure Act
C. Equal Employment Opportunity Commission
D. Freedom of Information Act
E. Food and Drug Administration

6. FCC	F. Administrative law judge
7. NLRB	G. Federal Communications Commission
8. OSHA	H. National Labor Relations Board
9. FBI	I. Occupational Safety and Health Administration
10. CFR	J. Federal Bureau of Investigation
11. DOJ	K. Code of Federal Regulations
12. DOC	L. Department of Justice
13. IRS	M. Social Security Administration
14. SSA	N. Internal Revenue Service
15. SEC	O. Securities and Exchange Commission

RESEARCH

1. Locate and compare the United States Code and the Code of Federal Regulations on alimony and support payments and then look at the law for your state. Write a memo on your findings.

2. Locate 7 U.S.C. § 6b and CFR 17 Part 166 . Summarize and compare the two. Also, identify the steps you took to locate the regulation.

3. Mrs. Jones bought a fur coat from John J. Furriers. The coat was labeled 100% raccoon. One day Mrs. Jones was smoking a cigarette and a hot ash accidentally fell on the coat while she was wearing it. The ash melted a hole in the coat. Mrs. Jones knew that fur burns, but acrylic melts.
   a. Clarify legal issues being researched
   b. Determine relevant jurisdiction
   c. Determine the area of law
   d. Gather all the facts
   e. Draft a statement of the issue that you are researching
   f. Where should you look for authority?
      - State statute
      - *United States Code Annotated*
      - *United States Code Service*
      - Code of Federal Regulations
      - *American Law Reports*
   g. What key words and phrases would you search on?
      - Label
      - Fur
      - Product mislabeling
      - Labeling requirements

   Find both a statute and a regulation that would be applicable in this scenario.

INTERNET RESEARCH

1. Locate title 21 of the Code of Federal Regulations, section 10.45 (2010). What does this regulation say regarding exhaustion of administrative remedies? In which section did you find that information? What is the history of this regulation?

2. Locate title 16 of the Code of Federal Regulations, section 1206.4. Summarize what this section sets forth.

3. Locate the Code of Federal Regulations section that deals with banned toys and other products used by children. What requirements are set forth for lawn darts? What is the current *Federal Register* citation for this CFR section? Properly cite your results.

4. Find a CFR section that deals with the requirements for vehicle modifications for people with disabilities. Summarize the regulation.

5. Find the CFR section that sets the standard for making ice cream. Summarize the standard.

6. Find the CFR section that provides the standard for minimum performance required of motorcycle helmets. Summarize the section of the regulation that deals with labeling.

7. Using the current *Federal Register Index,* determine if any new regulations have been adopted in the last six months concerning the topic of regulation for clean air. Summarize the information found on at least one topic. Cite your source.

8. Locate 16 CFR § 310.4. What does this cover? Determine whether your state has a similar regulation. If your state has a similar regulation, provide the correct citation and compare the federal and state versions.

9. Go to the GPO Access website and identify how many votes were cast on Thursday, June 16, 2011 for S. No. 90 and for what were they cast?

10. While at the GPO access website, read the House Pages for H4281–H4330. Who was honored that day?

MEDIA **RESOURCES**

Global Legal Information Network:	http://www.glin.gov
GPO Access:	http://www.gpoaccess.gov
Evans, Gareth. "International Law at the Coalface: Three Decades of Learning by Doing." 2010:	http://www.gevans.org/speeches/speech414.html
THOMAS:	http://thomas.loc.gov
United Nations:	http://www.un.org
USA.Gov. Government Made Easy. A–Z Index of Government Departments and Agencies. 2011:	http://www.usa.gov/Agencies/Federal/All_Agencies/index.shtml
Washington State Office of Administrative Hearings. Unemployment insurance video demonstration:	http://www.oah.wa.gov/

chapter **thirteen**

UPDATING AND VALIDATING RESEARCH

AISPIX by Image Source/Shutterstock

LEARNING OBJECTIVES

After completing this chapter, students should be able to:

1. Validate law using an updating service.

2. Incorporate parallel citations.

3. Apply ethical considerations to legal research and writing.

CHAPTER OVERVIEW

Every day, new laws of every kind are made. Statutes are passed, amended, or repealed. Judges write new appellate decisions. And while judges do rely on older, established cases through the doctrine of *stare decisis,* courts often change the previous case law by modifying or overruling it. In addition, agencies constantly pass new regulations or make decisions on issues that come before them. A researcher must stay on top of these changes by using one of the most challenging parts of legal research—the validation process. This process is often challenging because the American legal process is constantly changing.

A **citator** is a specialized research tool that is used to update or **validate** the legal authorities that support the client's position. These tools are available either online or in print. Validation of sources using a citator is a critical step in the research phase because if the sources relied upon are not current or "good" law, the analysis will be faulty, and possibly negligent.

Citator
A research tool that is used to update or validate legal authorities so that those authorities are confirmed as "good law."

Validate
To make sure that law is valid or to affirm that the source is still "good law."

OPENING SCENARIO

Case
A single opinion written by a judge who applies the law to the facts and provides an explanation as to how a decision was reached.

John has completed the research on several of the cases that had come into the office in recent weeks. Jami was interested in two in particular but was concerned whether the cases were still good law. John knew how to answer that: he would validate the cases using Shepard's Citations or KeyCite. Once he had checked those resources, he could confirm for Jami that the cases were still good law.

VALIDATING RESEARCH AND THE APPEALS PROCESS

Validating research is crucial in the legal setting because new law is constantly being created by legislatures, judges, and administrative bodies. When new laws are created, one of two things can happen to a previous law: (1) it is changed in part, or (2) it is made entirely invalid. In order to validate cases correctly, the appeals process must be understood.

The party making the appeal must specify errors that the party alleges that the lower court made when it decided the case. The errors can be questions of law or questions of fact. When courts hear cases, the judges or justices will do one of four things, as set out in Table 13-1.

Question of fact
This question revolves around controversy over a material fact in the dispute.

If the alleged error involves a *question of fact*, the appellant must show that the lower court incorrectly weighed the strength of the evidence. However, in reviewing the facts, the reviewing court cannot substitute its own judgment for that of the lower court because the reviewing court has neither heard the witnesses nor gauged their credibility. It relies on the transcript, the documents admitted into evidence, and the briefs from the attorneys. The reviewing court may reverse the lower court's factual finding only if the record shows that a reasonable factual basis did not exist on which the lower court could base its decision, or if the record shows that the finding of fact was clearly wrong. If there is a reasonable factual basis for the result, the reviewing court will affirm the lower court's decision.

Error of law
A mistake in a court proceeding concerning an issue of law that could provide a basis for a review of the judgment in the proceeding.

If the reviewing court is presented with an *error of law*, the court will determine whether the correct law was applied by the trial court in reaching its decision. If it decides that the trial court made an error in its application of the law, the reviewing court can reverse the lower court's decision and order that the lower court retry the case and apply the correct law. Or, it can reverse the lower court's decision and render its own decision based on the evidence it has reviewed. It can also remand or return the case to the lower court with instructions to modify or reconsider an issue.

If the reviewing court is presented with an issue as to the amount of the damages, it can decrease, increase, or affirm the damage award from the lower court.

TABLE 13-1 Decision

Affirm	The reviewing court agrees with the lower court or tribunal
Reverse	The reviewing court changes the result reached in the lower court
Remand	The court sends the case back to the lower court or tribunal for further proceedings based upon the holdings in the appellate court opinion
Modify	The reviewing court partially changes the result reached in the lower court or tribunal

Ethics and Validating Research

A researcher has the responsibility to make sure that all resources being used, both primary and secondary, are both current and valid.

The validation of sources not only ensures the quality of the research but is also an ethical requirement. The ethical obligation of **candor to the court** means that the attorney is required to disclose to the court any legal authority known to the lawyer to be directly adverse to the client's position, even if the opposing attorney does not disclose the adverse authority. This duty is set forth in Rule 3.3 of the Model Rules of Professional Conduct. Although the duty of candor applies to attorneys, the paralegals working with them should know and understand the rule because they perform a substantial amount of the research. Rule 3.3 is shown in Figure 13-1.

When a paralegal validates a law, he or she is making sure that the law is still in force and has not been changed or repealed. In addition to making sure that the authority is still good law, the paralegal must **cite check** the document completely. Cite checking means that the citation format is checked for (1) accuracy of the format, (2) accuracy of the authority ("good law"), and (3) accuracy of any quotations.

Basics of the Validation Process

A **citation** is a reference to a legal authority. Each legal citation is unique and provides an "address" for a single piece of documentation. For example, a published opinion, or "reported" case, is identified by reference to the publication in which the case appears, the volume number of that publication, and the exact page upon which the case begins. All of these elements are included in the case citation.

Citations are important because the legal system depends upon the reliability of the legal authority cited by lawyers and judges. Under the doctrine of **stare decisis**, which literally means "let the decision stand," judges make decisions by looking at **precedent**, or prior cases that have a similar set of facts and issues. *Stare decisis* essentially means that judges should reach the same decision as long as the facts and issues are the same or substantially similar.

The primary purpose of validating research is to determine whether the legal authority being used is still "good law." In this process, citator services are used to identify what other legal authorities have referenced the citation or how those other legal authorities have been referenced. *Stare decisis* does not mean that the next

TIP

The goal of research is not only to find law that supports the client's position, but also to find law that is current and valid.

Candor to the court
The requirement that the attorney disclose to the court any legal authority known to the lawyer to be directly adverse to the client's position, even if the opposing attorney does not disclose any adverse authority.

Cite check
Verify accuracy of citations. This includes: 1) accuracy in format, 2) accuracy of the authority ("good law"), and 3) accuracy of any quotations.

Citation
Reference to a legal authority that provides an address that can be used to find that authority in legal publications.

Stare decisis
A doctrine that literally means "let the decision stand." This policy requires courts to follow precedent if the facts and issues are substantially similar, and if it is still good law.

Precedent
A case opinion that has been previously decided and provides guidance to a judge in a subsequent case because the facts and issues of the previous case are the same or similar to the facts and issues of the present case. Judges are required by the doctrine of *stare decisis* to decide similar cases in a similar manner for consistency.

Model Rules of Professional Conduct

Advocate Rule 3.3 Candor Toward The Tribunal

(a) A lawyer shall not knowingly:

* * *

(2) fail to disclose to the tribunal legal authority in the controlling jurisdiction known to the lawyer to be directly adverse to the position of the client and not disclosed by opposing counsel; or . . . .[1]

FIGURE 13-1 Rule 3.3 Candor toward the Tribunal

---

[1]ABA Center for Professional Responsibility: Model Rules of Professional Conduct: Advocate Rule 3.3 Candor Toward the Tribunal. 2012. http://www.abanet.org/cpr/mrpc/rule_3_3.html

Common law
A set of rules and principles that judges make in the course of writing opinions in the cases they decide. Also referred to as case law or judge-made law.

Citing case
A case that cites the authority that has been Shepardized; other case that has used the cited case in its analysis.

Cited case
A case that was found as a result of research, is on point, and is being Shepardized.

Reporter
A repository of the actual text of cases. Historically, this was a print volume; today a reporter also may be published online or in digital media.

court must always agree with or follow a prior decision. Instead of following the decision, the new court could criticize, reverse, question, distinguish, or overrule it.

If the court questions the decision, the court is *questioning* the continuing value because of intervening circumstances, new legislation, or new case law. If the court refuses to follow the opinion because the facts are significantly different from the facts before the court, the court is *distinguishing* the opinion. The court *overrules* an opinion when it refuses to follow an opinion written by the same court even if the facts are basically the same as the facts before the court.

Every time a court considers a prior decision, the decision's status, or its value as precedent, can change. The precedential value of a *cited case* can evolve for many years after it is originally decided. The validation process tracks the changing significance of law to allow lawyers and judges to see how the law's meaning has changed since it was first created.

Another benefit of the validation process is that it may lead to other resources. Additional references are provided in the authorities that cited the legal authority in question. While validating one authority, other statutes, cases, or other primary and secondary authorities may be discovered.

Validating research is easier when the terms used in the process are understood. Table 13-2 shows the meanings of some terms that are commonly used in the validation of legal research.

TABLE 13-2   Terms and Definitions Used in the Validation Process

Term	Meaning
Case	An opinion written by a judge who applies the law to the facts and provides an explanation as to how a decision was reached. Also called common law.
Citation	A reference to a legal authority that provides an address where one can find that authority in legal publications.
Citator	A publication that provides the piece of law and shows other authorities that have cited that law.
Cited case	A case that referred to in another case. It has been used by another case in its analysis.
Citing case	A case that cites the authority that has been Shepardized or KeyCited. This other case has used the cited case in its analysis.
Common law	A form of law sometimes referred to as "case law" or "judge-made law." It is a set of rules and principles that have been established by judges over the course of hearing cases and writing legal opinions about them.
KeyCite	A system created by West to update and validate a law being read. It is similar to *Shepard's Citations*.
Legal authority	Any law, such as a constitution, case, statute, regulation, or other source, that a court applies in deciding a case. It may be either mandatory (binding) or merely persuasive to the court's analysis.
Parallel citation	A citation that is the same source, but published in a different publication. For example, the same case may be published in an official reporter and an unofficial reporter.
Precedent	A case that has been previously decided and provides guidance to a judge in a subsequent case because the facts and issues are the same or similar. Judges are required by the doctrine of *stare decisis* to decide similar cases in a similar manner.
Reporter	A publication that provides a repository for the text of cases. At one time, these were only available as printed volumes. Today, reporters are also available as digital files, either online, or on CD-ROMs.
Shepardize	The process of using *Shepard's Citations* to verify the current validity of the law and to identify other sources of law that have discussed the law being applied.
Stare decisis	A doctrine that literally means "let the decision stand." This policy requires the courts to follow precedent if it the facts are substantially similar, and it is still good law.[2]

[2]Lectric Law Library. *How to Shepardize.* 2012. http://www.lectlaw.com/files/lwr17.htm

When validating sources, it is also helpful to know the abbreviations in the legal publications that are likely to be used on a regular basis. For example, "SC" or "SCt" stands for *Supreme Court Reporter*, and "US" stands for the *United States Reports*. Among the most important abbreviations a researcher should know are those for the authorities in his or her jurisdiction, followed by those for federal materials, and then some major secondary authorities. Knowing these abbreviations can make the research process quicker, easier, and more cost-effective. However, if an abbreviation is not known, it can usually be found online, in the Tables section of *The Bluebook,* or in the Appendices to *ALWD*.

There are two main providers of citator services. The original citator, *Shepard's® Citations*, is the only one that is currently in print form. One downside of using *Shepard's* in print is that there is approximately a six-month delay in printing and shipping the updated volumes. An online version of *Shepard's* is published by LexisNexis and provides updates within 24 hours. An alternative citator, *KeyCite*, is published by Thomson/West, and is available online as part of Westlaw. It, too, offers immediate updates.

There are also other citator services available. For example, LoisLaw added a citator service called GlobalCite. When the link is clicked, GlobalCite searches the LoisLaw databases and provides a list of cases that cite the case being read and gives a chronological list of citing references, a number of documents retrieved, the title and first paragraph of the document, and a hyperlink to the citing case referred to as a contextual summary. There is no complete indication of whether the case is still "good law." It does provide case treatment terms in a blue font, but every citing reference should be read to determine the case law status. It operates similarly for statutes.[3]

CaseMAKER, originally launched by the Ohio Bar Association, is a service associated with more than 25 state bar associations. CaseMAKER has a service called CaseCheck+, which provides cases that have cited the case being read and validates whether or not the case is still good law with a green "thumbs up" or a red "thumbs down" signal. This information appears at the time the case is displayed; additional information can be obtained by clicking the reference.[4]

Fastcase has a service is called Authority Check that identifies the most authoritative cases in the results, reporting how often each case in the results list has been cited. It provides a timeline view of the search results that shows the user how relevant each case is in relation to the query used.[5]

Shepard's Citators

The basic purpose of *Shepard's Citations* (*Shepard's*) is to provide information about the authority of a case, statute, or other **legal authority**. Essentially, it gives a history of the legal authority, and tells the user whether it is still "good law." Students are more likely to use the online version. However, understanding the print version will aid in understanding and using the online version. In addition, using the print version may be necessary if one's firm does not have an online service or if its computers do not function.

Legal authority
Any law such as constitution, case, statute, regulation, or other source that may be mandatory (binding) or persuasive to the court's interpretation and application of the law to the evidence presented in a case.

[3]Legal Research Tools: GlobalCite®. 2012. http://www.loislaw.com/product/information/research/tools/globalcite.htm

[4]Lawriter, LLC. Casemaker. *Casemaker+*. 2012. http://www.casemakerx.com/

[5]Fastcase. What is Fastcase. http://www.fastcase.com/whatisfastcase/

The History of *Shepard's*

In the 1800s, lawyers did not always go to school to become lawyers. In order to prepare for the practice of law, they studied or apprenticed under a lawyer who had an established practice. As an apprentice, they would "read" for the legal profession, meaning they would read every case that was decided and published. This was somewhat manageable at a time when the country was young and there were fewer cases to read. Lawyers would make notes on the cases whenever a new case used the original case as authority or when another case negatively impacted the original case. This process was an early form of research validation.

As the United States grew and the court system expanded, many more cases were being decided. Around 1873, Frank Shepard determined that the old method of validating cases was becoming too cumbersome. In response, he devised a method to index every piece of authority upon which the courts ruled. His system eventually became known as *Shepard's Citations*. The process of using this system is now referred to as "Shepardizing."[6]

Shepard's Citations offers comprehensive coverage of a majority of federal and state publications. It provides a researcher with the ability to check citations, find parallel citations, and view the history of a cited case or statute, as well as the **treatment** accorded to it by subsequent cases. A wide variety of legal authorities may be **Shepardized**:

Shepardize
Using *Shepard's Citations* to verify the current validity of the law, and to identify other sources of law that have discussed the law being used.

Treatment
When another case cites the viewed case, something is said about the viewed case, or information is given on how the case is used by a different court in a different case.

- Constitutions
- Federal and state statutes
- Federal and state case law
- Administrative regulations
- Administrative decisions
- Court rules
- Treaties
- Selected law reviews
- Selected ALRs (until 2007 in print)
- Approved jury instructions
- Restatements
- Individual U.S. patents
- Session laws

Validating Cases with *Shepard's*

The central task in validating a source is reviewing both its prior and subsequent history. The prior history includes earlier decisions leading up to the case. For example, part of the prior history of a federal circuit court case is the federal district court case leading up to it. The subsequent history of a case includes the appellate cases, or decisions in the appeals process. If a federal circuit court case was appealed to the U.S. Supreme Court, that Supreme Court case also would be part of that case's subsequent appellate history.

Shepard's can also be used as a finding tool, because it provides citations of the sources that have cited a particular case. In addition to cases, a researcher will find references to a variety of sources that mention the cited case. For example, a researcher may find references to sources such as A.L.R. annotations, law review articles, and attorneys generals' opinions.

In addition to giving the history of a case, *Shepard's* provides the treatment of the case. When the case is cited in another case, it is commented on in some way.

[6]The 'Lectric Law Library. How to Shepardize. 2012. http://www.lectlaw.com/files/lwr17.htm

This treatment affects the strength or value of the case as *precedent*. If the citing case had a negative impact, it is noted with abbreviations reflecting that impact: "o" (overruled), "r" (*reversed*), "v" (*vacated*), or "d" (*distinguished*). These abbreviations indicate that the cited case might not be "good law" any longer. For some cases, *true positive treatment* may be noted. This notation indicates that a case has been expressly followed by another decision.

All sources that have any negative impact should be read to fully understand that impact. If no negative treatment is noted, it is probably unnecessary to read every case. However, each case will have a slightly different perspective of the issue at hand and may have some useful language or information. Recent citing cases may also be useful if the cited case is old. These more recent cases could provide relevant information based on historic or societal changes affecting the cited case.

Shepard's uses a unique set of tools to identify the history and treatment of the case. Each volume has a Table of Abbreviations for quick reference. When using these abbreviations, it is important to understand the difference between "history" and "treatment." "History" refers to how that particular case was affected by the courts hearing the *same case*, as in the various levels of appeal. For example, if the cited case appears to be on point, but another court reversed the case on appeal, the cited case should not be relied on. "Treatment" refers to how a cited case is used by a different court in the context of an entirely different case. For example, another court deciding a case with a similar issue or set of facts might consider the cited case and reject its holding, instead providing a different holding on the same issue.

The treatment notations in *Shepard's* can be important guides to research. If a case is consistently being *criticized* or questioned, it may be wise to find another case to use as a foundation for research. If there is no identifying abbreviation before a citing reference, it means that the cited case was mentioned in some small way without, in most instances, an analysis of it. See Table 13-3 for the abbreviations and their meanings.

It is important to distinguish between capital and lower-case letters. Abbreviations in *Shepard's* have very different meanings depending on whether they are capital or lower case. For example, the "D" under history means "dismissed," but the "d" under treatment means "distinguished."

The citing references in *Shepard's* are listed in a certain order. The order for cases in the National Reporter System is generally the same as in the state citators:

- Citations from state and federal courts showing a case history.
- Citations from courts of the state in which the case was decided showing the treatment of the cited case.
- Citations from federal courts showing the treatment of the cited case.
- Citations from courts in states other than the state in which the cited case was decided, as reported in the particular unit of the National Reporter System. These citations are listed alphabetically and show the treatment of the cited case.
- Citations from courts of states covered by any unit of the National Reporter System other than the one that covers the cited case. For example, if the case was from Arizona, which is in the *Pacific Reporter*, this group would be any other state in any reporter other than the *Pacific Reporter*. The citations are in alphabetical order by state.
- Citations of legal periodicals, such as articles in the *American Bar Association Journal*.
- Citations to the annotations of Lawyers' Edition, United States Supreme Court Reports, and American Law Reports.
- Citations to selected legal texts.

Precedent
A case that has been previously decided and provides guidance to a judge in a subsequent case because the facts and issues of the previous case are the same or similar to the facts and issues of the present case. Judges are required by the doctrine of *stare decisis* to decide similar cases in a similar manner for consistency.

Reversed
On appeal, reconsideration, or rehearing, the citing case reversed the case being Shepardized.

Vacated
The citing case vacated or withdrew the case being Shepardized.

Distinguished
The judge in the citing case wrote that it differed from the case being Shepardized. The case may be distinguished because it involved dissimilar facts or required a different application of law.

True positive treatment
Treatment indicating that a case has been expressly followed by another case.

Same case
The citing case involves the same litigation as the case being Shepardized, but at a different stage in the proceedings.

Criticized
The citing opinion disagrees with the reasoning or result of the case being Shepardized. The citing court may not have authority to materially affect its precedential value.

Cert denied
A decision in which a higher court exercises its discretion to not accept or hear an appeal from a lower court. The decision is effected by refusing to issue a writ of certiorari, which would have required the lower court to produce a certified record of the case for purposes of appellate review. Although the higher court has refused to hear the case, the lower court's decision is still good law, and further appeal may still be possible.

Cert granted
A higher court's exercise of its discretion to accept or hear an appeal from a lower court. The decision is effected by agreeing to issue a writ of certiorari, a common-law process requiring the lower court to produce a certified record of the case for purposes of appellate review. If cert is granted, there will likely be a subsequent order or opinion by the higher court deciding the appeal.

Explained
The citing opinion interprets or clarifies the case being Shepardized in a significant way.

Affirmed
On appeal, reconsideration or rehearing, the citing case affirms or adheres to the case being Shepardized.

Modified
On appeal, reconsideration or rehearing, the citing case modified or changed in some way the case being Shepardized. This treatment includes affirming in part and reversal in part.

Dissenting opinion
The case was cited in a dissenting opinion.

Limited
Treatment indicating that the citing court refused to extend the decision of the cited case beyond precise issues involved.

Connected Case
A citing case that is related to the case being Shepardized in that it arises out of the same subject matter or involves the same parties.

Followed
The citing opinion relies on the case being Shepardized as controlling or persuasive authority.

Dismissed
History indicating the citing case dismissed an appeal from the case being Shepardized.

Overruled
The citing case expressly overrules or disapproves all or part of the case being Shepardized.

TABLE 13-3   *Shepard's* Abbreviations[7]

History		Treatment	
Abbreviation	Meaning	Abbreviation	Meaning
a		c	criticized
m		d	distinguished
r	reversed	*affirmed*	explained criticized
s	same case	*modified*	*dissenting opinion* distinguished
S	superseded	p	parallel
v	vacated	L	*limited*
cc	*Connected case*	f	*Followed*
D	*dismissed*	o	*overruled*
US cert den	Certiorari has been denied	q	questioned
US cert dis	Certiorari has been dismissed	h	*harmonized*
US cert gran	Certiorari has been granted		
US reh den	Rehearing has been denied		
US reh dis	Rehearing has been dismissed		

[7]University of New Hampshire School of Law. How to Shepardize a Case in Print. 2008 . http://library.law.unh.edu/Shepardize

Validating Statutes with *Shepard's*

Shepard's provides references to any constitutional or statutory provisions that have been cited, applied, or construed, and any situations in which a provision is affected by later legislation. *Shepard's* uses "operational letters" to note the effect of the citing reference on the constitutional provision or statute. The letters indicate whether the enacted law has been amended, repealed, or revised by later legislation. They also indicate whether the statutes has been declared valid, invalid, constitutional, or unconstitutional by the courts.

The process and coverage is very similar to that of cases. However, the abbreviations are slightly different for statutes than for cases. See Table 13-4.

Although statutes are frequently re-codified and renumbered, *Shepard's* tracks the statute section so that the researcher does not need to know the numbering of all the prior code sections.

Citations to statutes are always grouped in the following order:

- Subsequent legislative enactments, such as amendments and repeals, affecting the section
- Citations from the U.S. Supreme Court and other federal courts
- Citations of the *American Bar Association Journal*
- Citations of the annotations of Lawyers' Edition, United States Supreme Court Reports, and the American Law Reports
- Citations of selected legal texts
- Citations of specific subsections or subdivisions of the statute

Validation Using the State Editions of *Shepard's*

Shepard's publishes citators for each of the states, plus the District of Columbia and Puerto Rico. The state citators provide the means to Shepardize legal materials within each state, such as state court decisions, state and federal statutes and

TABLE 13-4 *Shepard's* Treatment of Statutes

Form of Statute

Abbreviation	Means	Abbreviation	Means
Amend	Amendment	Proc.	Proclamation
App	Appendix	Pt.	Part
Art	Article	Res.	Resolution
Ch	Chapter	§	Section
Cl	Clause	St.	Statutes at Large
Ex. Ord.	Executive Order	Subch.	Subchapter
H.C.R.	House Concurrent Resolution	Subd.	Subdivision
¶	Paragraph	Sub. ¶	Subparagraph
P.L.	Public Law	Subsec.	Subsection
Pr. L.	Private Law	Vet. Reg.	Veterans' Regulations

Operation of Statute	Definition
Legislative	
A	Amended: statute amended.
Ad	Added: New section added.
E	Extended: Provisions of an existing statute extended in its application to a later statute, or allowance of additional time for performance of duties required by a statute within a limited time.
L	Limited: Provisions of an existing statute declared not to be extended in its application to a later statute.
R	Repealed: *Abrogation* of an existing statute.
Rn	Renumbered: Renumbering of existing sections.
Rp	Repealed in part: Abrogation of part of an existing statute.
S	*Superseded*: Substitution of new legislation for an existing statute not expressly abrogated.
Va	Validated.
Judicial	
C	Constitutional: The citing case upholds the constitutionality of the statute, rule, or regulation you are Shepardizing.
U	Unconstitutional: The citing case declares unconstitutional the statute, rule or regulation you are Shepardizing.
Up	Unconstitutional in part.
V	Void or invalid.
Va	Valid.
Vp	Valid or invalid in part.

Harmonized
Treatment indicating that the citing opinion explained an apparent inconsistency and showed the inconsistency not to exist.

Abrogation
Annulling a former law by an act of legislation, usage, or constitutional authority. Abrogation may be express or implied.

Superseded
On appeal, reconsideration or rehearing, the citing case supersedes or is substituted for the case being Shepardized.

constitutions, court rules, ordinances, and other state-specific materials. The state citators provide every instance where the cited authority has been referred to by that state's courts, or where an authority from that state has been cited in any federal courts. The state citators provide citations to the *official reporters* of each state and provide the means to use the appropriate West National Reporter System citation.

Official reporters
Reporters that are published by a governmental entity rather than by a commercial publisher such as West.

It is important to note that the state reports division of a citator will include more secondary sources than the National Reporter System division. The secondary sources, such as citations to state law reviews and state bar journals, in the state report division are more regionally specific and consequently more useful to state users. Hence, the most thorough method is to Shepardize in both the state and National Reporter divisions, because some references may be found in one division, but not the other.

The citations to state cases are always arranged in the following order:

- Citations from state and federal courts showing the history of the cited case
- Citations from state courts showing the treatment accorded the cited case
- Citations from federal courts showing the treatment accorded the cited case
- Citations of legal periodicals
- Citations of the annotations of *Lawyers' Edition, United States Supreme Court Reports*, and *American Law Reports*
- Citations of selected legal texts

Thorough Shepardizing means checking a citation in every possible location that *Shepard's* offers. Failure to check all sources may result in missing authority with an important impact on the client's case.

CLOSER LOOK AT SHEPARDIZING CASES AND ENACTED LAW IN THE PRINT VERSION

Most law firms prefer to use the electronic version of *Shepard's* because it is easier and faster. However, a complete understanding of the electronic version of *Shepard's* requires an understanding of the print version.

Shepardizing Cases in the Print Version

Shepard's in print provides a separate set of citators for each court system. For example, *Shepard's United States Citations* is used to research the U.S. Supreme Court cases and *Shepard's Federal Citations* is used for the federal district court and appellate court decisions (*Federal Supplement* and *Federal Reporters*). Citators are provided for each of the regional reporters; an example is *Shepard's North Eastern Reporters Citation*. Finally, there are citators for materials in each state, such as *Shepard's California Reporter Citations*. The types of citators available are summarized in Table 13-5.

The first step in checking citations is to look at the spines of the books. The spines of the main volumes of *Shepard's Citations* provide important information to guide the user, such as the coverage of each volume.

The print version of *Shepard's* is supplemented several times each year, and the cover of each type of supplement has a different color. The quarterly supplement is issued with a red cover and the annual or semiannual supplement is issued with a gold cover. The monthly supplements (also called Advance Sheets) are white pamphlets. It is important to note that the main volumes of *Shepard's* are not cumulative. Searching the supplements will also provide information on any depublished cases—cases that in some jurisdictions, such as California, have been ordered by the state supreme court to be removed from official publication. Accurate validation requires searching in all of these supplements and advance sheets.

TABLE 13-5   *Shepard's* Materials

Source	Coverage
United States Citators	Covers citations to U.S. Supreme Court cases published in *United States Reports, Lawyer's Edition*, and *West's Supreme Court Reporter*
Federal Citators	Provides citation coverage for all U.S. lower court cases reported in the *Federal Reporter, Federal Supplement, Federal Rules Decisions, Court of Claims Reports*, and *Claims Court Reporter.*
Regional Citators	Provides citation coverage for all cases reported in the seven regional reporters: *Atlantic, North Eastern, North Western, South Eastern, South Western, Southern*, and *Pacific*. An example is *Shepard's North Eastern Reporter Citations.*
State Citators	Individual state citators including Puerto Rico and the District of Columbia. Users can Shepardize all cases, statutes, constitutions, court rules, jury instructions, and session laws for a specific state or territory. An example is *Shepard's Missouri Citations.*
Specialized Citators	Various specialized areas such as bankruptcy and the Uniform Commercial Code have individual citator services

Shepard's provides several important tools in the front pages of each volume. The table of contents provides cross-referencing page numbers showing which citing references are reported in the citator. The title page lists the specific publications in which citations appear. The citing sources list shows all the publications from which the citing references come. The preface tells about the special features of that particular citator, such as the editorial analysis, the LexisNexis number explanations, and the statute coverage. Finally, the table of abbreviations explains the abbreviations of the courts, publications, and types of analysis.[8]

In order to read the pages in *Shepard's*, it is important to understand its format. When viewing a page in *Shepard's*, the references presented will appear chronologically, with the oldest cases listed first. The citation is to the page upon which the cited case appears, not the first page of the case. In addition, the citations do not follow the same format as *The Bluebook* or *ALWD*. *Shepard's* uses its own system of shortened abbreviations in order to conserve space. These abbreviations are unique to *Shepard's*. If a citation within the pages of *Shepard's* is unfamiliar, the Table of Abbreviations may be checked for clarification.

Figure 13-2 shows a sample page from a volume of *Shepard's* for the *United States Reports*.

In this example, the researcher is interested in the case *Montieth v. Oregon*, 386 U.S. 780 (1967), which is "***on point***" because it directly addresses the client's legal issue. However, the researcher wants to make sure that it is still good law. The researcher would take the following steps in Shepardizing this case, as shown in Checklist 13-1.

The entry means that during the coverage of that particular volume of *Shepard's*, there was only one case that cited *Montieth*. The citing case is from Oregon and is located in volume 504 of the *Pacific Reporter, Second Series*, at page 1408. The researcher should locate the case at 504 P.2d 1408 and read to see if it is

TIP

A researcher should not guess at the meaning of an abbreviation, but should always check the table of authorities if there is a question. A wrong guess could have disastrous results for research. If a researcher interpreted an abbreviation to be the wrong state, for example, he or she may give the wrong weight to the reference.

On point
The cited case and the client's case are analogous or have similarities between the key facts and issues.

---

[8]LexisNexis Research Solutions. *Shepard's* Citations in Print. 2009. http://www.lexisnexis.com/shepards-citations/print/features.asp

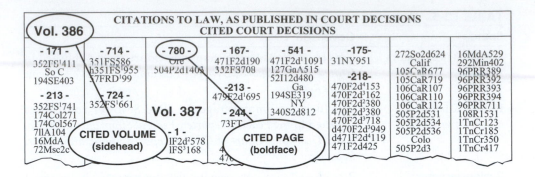

FIGURE 13-2 A Page from *Shepard's*

applicable to the research at hand. All other volumes and pamphlets of *Shepard's* containing 386 U.S. 780 should be checked in the same manner.

For other cases on the sample page in Figure 13-2, there are several citations. The citations are divided into reporters or services, which are ordered from highest to lowest authority, and in alphabetical order within regional and state

Checklist 13-1   HOW TO SHEPARDIZE

1. Examine the "What Your Library Should Contain" list on the front cover of the most current supplement of *Shepard's United States Citations*. This list provides every bound volume and supplement, allowing one to obtain all citations to date. Once the earliest volume covering the case is found, every volume and supplement thereafter must be checked.

2. Once all materials are located, start with the first hardbound volume (the oldest) that will first list the cited case. In this example, it is the one containing volume 386. Since this case was decided in 1967, it is likely that the search will require looking in several volumes of *Shepard's* to fully validate it.

3. Next, check the "Citations Included in this Volume" section of the preface to identify which citing references can be found in the citator. It will show the volume and page range for all included references.

4. The center of the bar at the top of each page identifies the set of *Shepard's* being viewed.

5. Turn to the page of *Shepard's* where the case—here, *Monteith*—is referenced. Using the headings at the top of the page, look for Vol. 386. The top left-hand side of Figure 13-2 shows "Vol. 386" in boldface type. This number identifies the list of cases in the *United States Reports* that are found in volume 386.

6. The numbers in bold print between dashes are the page numbers. These numbers are used to find 780, the starting page of the case.

7. In the third column, "Vol. 387" appears. The citations that follow "Vol. 387" are cases within that particular volume.

8. In each of the columns, the boldfaced numbers in between hash marks indicate the page numbers on which each cited case in the reporter begins. In this example, the authorities citing 386 U.S. 780 are listed under "-**780**-". There is one case listed:

Ore

504P2d1408

TIP

It's important to make sure that the correct set of books is being viewed.

TIP

If the starting page number of the case of this case is absent, it means there are no citing references to that case in that particular *Shepard's Citations* volume. However, it does not mean there are no references in other volumes or in the supplements.

TIP

Be sure to look at the correct information within the *Shepard's* pages. If a case is in volume 386, page 780, do not look at volume 387, page 780!

citations. For the case in volume 387 at page 218, there are references in the following order:

- All Federal Reporter, Second Series
- *Southern Reporter, Second Series*
- California
- Colorado

Any secondary sources citing the case would follow.

This case also has treatment indicated in the sixth and seventh entries. The "d" in front of these entries means that those particular cases were distinguished from the cited case (see Table 13-3 for treatment abbreviations).

A *Shepard's* listing also will tell the researcher that specific headnotes of the cited case were discussed in the citing case. For example, in Figure 13-2, under the case at volume 386, page 171, the citation $352FS^1411$ includes a raised "1." This means that 352FS411 discussed headnote 1 of 386 U.S. 171.

This citation in Figure 13-2, under 387 U.S. 218, illustrates the information that may be provided in a single *Shepard's* citation:

$$d471F2d^4119$$

The "d" is a treatment abbreviation for "distinguished." That means that the cited case was distinguished in this citing reference. The "471" is the volume of "F2d," which is *Federal Reporter, Second Series.* The elevated "4" is a reference to a headnote. In summary, this reference means that on page 119 of volume 471 of the *Federal Reporter, Second Series,* the point of law in headnote 4 of the cited case (386 U.S. 218) is discussed. If headnote 4 were important in the research for the client's case, the researcher could use *Shepard's* to identify the citing references that specifically discuss that headnote. It should be remembered that many of the citing references will not have headnotes. However, the lack of headnotes may also provide important information about the treatment of the case. It may indicate that the citing reference is simply listing the cited case in a string of citations or with very little discussion or analysis. Look at Figure 13-3 to work through another example.

Figure 13-3 shows a full page from the *Shepard's* citator for *Pacific Reporter, 2d Series.* Most of the citations on this page are of cases within volume 820 of the *Pacific Reporter, 2d Series.* However, the initial references on this page are from volume 819. Care must be taken to ensure that citations for different volumes are not confused.

The citations listed in *Shepard's* also include **parallel references** or **parallel citations**. These are citations to the same case or statute, but are found in different publications. For example, a case may be found in both an official reporter and an unofficial reporter. An official source is issued by a governmental entity (such as *United States Code* or U.S.C. for federal statutes and *United States Reports* or U.S. for U.S. Supreme Court cases). An unofficial source is one that has been issued by another entity, such as a publishing company (for example, *United States Code Annotated* and *Supreme Court Reporter,* issued by Thomson/West for federal statutes and U.S. Supreme Court cases, respectively). In *Shepard's,* parallel references are shown in parentheses beneath the case name. In Figure 13-3, the parallel references for 820 P2d 181 are 54 C3d 868 and 2 CaR2d 79. These are citations to the same case, but in different publications.

The order of references to a cited case is illustrated in Figure 13-3 under "**-181-**". This California case was reported in the *Pacific Reporter* as the unofficial reporter. Therefore, the first references are to the *Pacific Reporter* and the

Parallel citation
A citation that is an address to the same authority or content as the initial citation, but is printed in a different publication.

Parallel reference
Additional publications where a case can be found. If viewing an unofficial source (for example, *North Eastern Reporter, Second Series*), a parallel reference might be to *Indiana Supreme Court Reporter* or Ind.

FIGURE 13-3 Pacific Reporter, 2d Series[9]

PACIFIC REPORTER, 24 SERIES   Vol. 820

—1386—

Oregon v Ehly
1991

(109OrA456)
a 854P26421
a 826P2d6635
822P2d153

—1390—

Oregon v
Warmer
1991

(109OrA468)
s 328P24458

—1392—

Oregon v Mast
1991

(109OrA435)

| Vol.820 |

—1—

Peven v
Holladay
1991

(109OrA336)

—3—

Clark v
Schumacher
1991

(109OrA354)

—7—

SAIF Corp. v
Bement
1991

(109OrA387)

—8—

Cameron
Logging v Jones
1991

(109OrA391)

—11—

Oregon v
Cornell
1991

(109OrAJ96)
a 842P2d394
s 326P2d635

---

cc 741P2d501

—18—

Ranwick
v Olson
1991

(109OrA412)

—20—

Siegner v
Interstate
Production
Credit
Association
of Spokane
1991

(109OrA417)
333P2d¹345
352P2d964
Utah
354P2d¹⁴580
18ASJ323n

—33—

In the Matter
of the Marriage
of Goff
1991

(109OrA447)

—35—

International
Paper Co. v
Hubbard
1991

(109OrA452)
s 828P2d457

—37—

Oregon v
Freeman
1991

(109OrA472)
852P2d*280

—39—

Oregon v Hays
1991

(109OrA491)
s824P2d417

—41—

In the Matter
of Disciplinary
Proceeding
Against Niemi
1991

(117Wch2d817)
f825P2d⁴739

—47—

In re Welfare
of S.E. v
Washington
Department
of Social and
Health Services
1991

(63WAp244)
s827P2d1012

—51—

Washington
v Hughes
1991

(63WAp401)
v 852P2d1099
s 852P2d1044
s 852P2d1097

—53—

Washington v
McFadden
1991

(63WAp441)
s 832P2d487
I 830P2d*400
834P2d75
Wyo
j846P2d636

—59—

Washington
v Moore
1991

(63WAp466)
827P2d350

—62—

Judd v
Department
of Labor and
Industries
1991

(63WAp471)
829P2d204

—65—

Washington
v Warren
1991

(63WAp477)

—66—

Washington v
Olivarez
1991

(63WAp484)

—70—

Engberg
v Meyer
1991

cc 469US1077
cc 83LE516
cc 105SC577
cc 656P2d541
j 833P2d508
835P2d340
j 835P2d1093
j 837P2d1059
843P2d609
j 844P2d1074
846P2d683
847P2d*1024
850P2d601
850P2d¹603
Wash
841P2d³761
Tenn
840SW342

—176—

Berger v Tclon
Shadows Inc.
1991

—181—

Christensen v
Superior
Court of Los
Angeles County
1991

(54C38568)
(2CaR2d79)
Da01-23-1992
831P2d1200
f 831P2d¹1205
j 834P2d776
4CaR2d90
4CaR2d91
f 4CaR2d92
7CaR2d85
f 7CaR2d¹²86
f 7CaR2d²87
f 7CaR2d¹⁰87

---

f 8CaR2d¹806
f 8CaR2d²808
f 8CaR2d¹809
f 8CaR2d¹⁴810
f 9CaR26618
j 9CaR2d¹623
j 11CaR2d682
14CaR2d⁴83
16CaR2d³105
19CaR2d609
f 20CaR2d142
f 20CaR2d143
Cir. 9
f 973F2d1493
j 973F2d1495
d 984F2d1036
f 984F2d1038
Mont
c 835P2d762
Nev
855P2d¹⁰1041
Pa
625A2d672
SC
431SE561

—214—

California
v Ashmus
1991

(54C3d932)
(2CaR2d112)
De01-29-1992
f 821P2d600
822P2d¹²400
f 822P2d¹³411
822P2d¹³417
824P2d631
828P2d¹⁷118
f 828P2d¹718
f 828P2d¹⁴742
831P2d297
831P2d316
833P2d604
833P28660
833P2d¹⁴688
834P2d¹⁴¹1132
f 838P2d¹⁴741
841P2d142
841P2d926
f 842P2d¹³13
842P2d¹⁴¹1130
852P2d¹339
j 853P2d1088
855P2d1312
2CaR2d¹⁴763
f 3CaR2d96
f 3CaR2d¹⁴643
3CaR2d¹²692
f 3CaR2d¹⁴703
3CaR2d¹⁰709
4CaR3d825
f 6CaR2d¹⁴419
7CaR2d¹³216
f 7CaR2d¹577
f 7CaR2d¹⁴601

9CaR2d72
9CaR2d91
10CaR2d597
10CaR2d653
10CaR2d¹⁴681
f 10CaR2d²¹746
f 11CaR2d¹⁴218
11CaR2d¹⁶364
f 13CaR2d¹⁰13
14CaR2d157
14CaR2d406
f 14CaR2d¹⁴714
15CaR2d¹⁰370
19CaR2d¹844
j 20CaR2d633
21CaR2d740

—262—

Whitmas v
Superior Court
of Santa
Clara County
1991

(54C3d1063)
(2CaR2d160)
820P2d601
820P2d¹601
j 820P2d611
823P2d619
f 823P2d620
823P2d620
824P2d¹⁰700
j 841P2d1007
851P2d²48
2CaR2d¹377
j 2CaR2d387
4CaR2d453
f 4CaR2d454
4CaR2d454
4CaR2d¹⁰894
5CaR2d141
f 5CaR2d⁵142
5CaR2d¹483
5CaR2d726
f 5CaR2d¹¹727
6CaR2d243
6CaR2d800
f 6CaR2d¹802
f 7CaR2d48
f 7CaR2d⁵50
f 7CaR2d759
7CaR2d¹760
j 11CaR2d714
12CaR2d636
f 12CaR2d⁵651
j 16CaR2d487
16CaR2d162
c 16CaR2d⁵163
19CaR2d¹254
19CaR2d747
20CaR2d462

TIP

If the case name and parallel citations are not visible, this means there is an earlier volume of *Shepard's* with citing references to the case being researched. Find it!

next are to California sources. Following in order are all federal references (which would appear in numerical order by circuit if there were others in addition to the 9th Circuit), then state cases in alphabetical order by state.

Because this is a California case, a researcher should also Shepardize the case in the California citator to make sure that every citing reference is checked. There

[9]LawSchoolHelp.com. and Craig A. Smith. 2012. http://www.west.net/~smith/181bd4.gif

may be state-specific materials in the California citator that will not appear in the *Pacific Reporter* citator. Many California appellate courts decisions are rendered partly or completely void by the Supreme Court after they have been published in the official and unofficial reporters. This is referred to as "depublication" of a court opinion. Some jurisdictions allow a researcher to quote from depublished opinions, while others do not allow their inclusion in legal documents. Checking the advance sheets of the reporters for the publication status is the only way to tell whether part of the opinion, or the whole opinion, has been depublished. Understanding this procedure may mean the difference between being praised, chastised, or terminated from employment.

When documenting research, all citations to a source should be supplied, because some materials may not be available to the reader. In addition, when sources are cited, the correct style should be followed, depending on the jurisdiction. This style may be determined by *The Bluebook, ALWD,* or other style manuals approved in a particular jurisdiction, along with any applicable court rules. Styles and formats may vary across jurisdictions, so it is advisable to always check the rules of the court in the jurisdiction where the research will be used.

Some states also may follow very different practices in reporting cases. In the 1980s, the Indiana Court of Appeals and Indiana Supreme Court decided to abandon the publication of official reports. Indiana now relies on the regional reporters for the publication of its cases. As a result, the name of the court must be referenced in the case citation in order for the reader to identify and find the case. For example, a case citation in Indiana might appear as follows: *Datzek v. State*, 838 N.E.2d 1149, 1154 (Ind. Ct. App. 2005). This citation tells the reader that the case came from the Indiana Court of Appeals rather than from the Supreme Court. The second page number, 1154, tells the reader that the citation is for a quotation on that page.

Some entries in *Shepard's* have no citing cases listed. For example, in Figure 13-3, the entry immediately after "-1-", *Peven v. Holladay* 1991 (109 OrA336), has no references or citing cases. This simply means that no authority cited that case during the period covered by that particular volume of *Shepard's.* However, this does not mean that there are no citing references. It only means that the next volume of *Shepard's* must also be checked.

Because of the complexity of the Shepardizing process, there are many chances for error. Common errors in Shepardizing include the following:

- The first page of the citation was incorrect.
- The volume number was incorrect.
- The date was incorrect.
- The correct *Shepard's* volumes were not used.
- The complete *Shepard's* volumes were not used.
- The citation was to a first or second series of a reporter, but the researcher looked in the second or third series.
- The regional *Shepard's* was searched, rather than the state edition.
- The state *Shepard's* was searched, rather than the regional edition.

Researchers should be aware of these common errors and avoid them.

Enacted Law in Print Version of *Shepard's*

Volumes of *Shepard's* are not cumulative. The main volumes of *Shepard's Citations* for statutes are organized much the same way as those for cases. Important information on coverage can be found on the spines of the volumes. The printed version of *Shepard's* is supplemented several times a year and each type of supplement is bound by a different colored cover, just as the case supplements are. The bound volumes and supplements cover specific dates. The gold paperback supplements are annual cumulative supplements, the red paperback supplements are additional cumulative supplements, and the white paperback supplements are advance sheets. All applicable materials must be searched.

Important tools can be found in the front pages of each volume of every set. The table of contents provides cross-referencing page numbers for citing. The title page lists all of the publications in which citations appear. The preface tells about the special features of that particular citator, such as the editorial analysis, the LexisNexis number explanations, and the statute coverage. Finally, the table of abbreviations explains the abbreviations of the courts, publications, and editorial analysis letters, as well as the condensed style of the *Shepard's* service. Figure 13-4 shows the partial results of Shepardizing the statute 21 U.S.C. § 848(q)(9)(1982).

There are some notable differences in the appearance of this statutory entry and a Shepardized case. Instead of "volume," the word "title" is used to signify the citation format. Therefore, when Shepardizing a *case*, the appearance of "title" in a column would indicate that the wrong set of *Shepard's* is being used. In case volumes, boldfaced page numbers within hash marks indicate separate cases, whereas in statute volumes, the section symbol and section number appear in boldface.

The letters preceding citations provide information on the history or treatment of the statute. In Figure 13-4, the "A" in entry "A108St2146" shows that section 848(n)(11) was amended by Congress. This amendment was published in volume 108 of *United States Statutes at Large*, and appears on page 2146. The listing also shows that section 848(q)(9) has been cited in several federal cases. If there were a "C" by an entry, it would mean that the case held the statute to be constitutional. An "n" at the end of a citation means the statute was cited in an annotation, and "s" means a supplement to an annotation.

See Figure 13-5 for additional information about the citation.

The Constitution of the United States and the various state constitutions can also be Shepardized using the statute divisions of *Shepard's*. Researchers can determine whether constitutional provisions are still valid, and can locate additional references that discuss them. To use this service, a researcher would look for "Article" on the top of the *Shepard's* page along with the name of the constitution being searched. The section number appears in boldface just as in the statute service.

State statutes, or codes, are Shepardized in a manner similar to federal statutes. Citations to state statutes are grouped as follows:

- Amendments, repeals, or other state legislative action
- Citations by state courts
- Citations by federal courts
- Citations to articles in legal periodicals
- Citations to annotations of *Lawyers' Edition, United States Supreme Court Reports*, and the *American Law Reports*
- Citations to specific subdivisions

Ordinances can also be Shepardized in the statute volumes of the state citators. It should be noted, however, that the ordinances are the least complete aspect of all the services. Generally, only ordinances for large metropolitan areas are available. If ordinances are available, the county name appears in boldface type,

FIGURE 13-4 Research for *Shepard's* Statute[10]

UNITED STATES CODE			TITLE 21 § 851
§ 848(m) Cir. 1 985FS34Δ1997 985FS38Δ1997 Cir. 2 142F3d113Δ1998 Cir. 4 962FS751Δ1997 962FS808Δ1997 **§ 848(m)(1)** Cir. 4 962FS752Δ1997 **§ 848(m)(2)** Cir. 4 962FS757Δ1997 **§ 848(m)(7)** Cir. 4 962FS752Δ1997 **§ 848(m)(8)** Cir. 2 998FS173Δ1998 Cir. 4 962FS808Δ1997 **§ 848(m)(9)** Cir. 2 998FS171Δ1998 Cir. 4 962FS808Δ1997 **§ 848(m)(10)** Cir. 4 962FS752Δ1997 962FS808Δ1997 **§ 848(n)** Cir. 2 1999USDist LX2594 [Δ1999 Cir. 4 966FS1428Δ1997 968FS1083Δ1997 **§ 848(n)(1)** Cir. 4 964FS1001Δ1997 966FS1429Δ1997 968FS1081Δ1997 i) 968FS1087Δ1997 **§ 848(n) (1)(A to D)** Cir. 4 968FS1083Δ1997 **§ 848(n)(1)(A)** Cir. 4 968FS1081Δ1997 **§ 848(n)(1)(B)** Cir. 4 968FS1001Δ1997 968FS1084Δ1997 **§ 848(n)(1)(C)** Cir. 4 968FS1084Δ1997	Cir. 10 1999USDist LX5770 [Δ1999 **§ 848(n)(1)(D)** Cir. 4 968FS1081Δ1997 Cir. 10 1999USDist LX5770 [Δ1999 **§ 848(n)(2 to 12)** Cir. 4 964FS1001Δ1997 966FS1430Δ1997 **§ 848(n)(7)** Cir. 2 1999USDist LX2594 [Δ1999 **§ 848(n)(11)** A) 108St2146 **§ 848(O)(1)** Cir. 2 1999USDist LX2594 [Δ1999 998FS174Δ1998 **§ 848(q)** 512US860Δ1994 521US327Δ1997 140LE976Δ1998 118SC1697Δ1998 Cir. 4 133F3d279Δ1997 964FS1002Δ1997 971FS1007Δ1997 Cir. 5 125F3d274Δ1997 Cir. 6 2FS2d968Δ1998 Cir. 9 123F3d1204Δ1997 Cir. 10 1998USApp LX12166 [Δ1998 150F3d1263Δ1998 964FS315Δ1997 **§ 848(q)(3)** Cir. 5 162F3d353Δ1998 **§ 848(q)(4 to 8)** Cir.10 150F3d1265Δ1998 **§ 848(q)(4)** Cir. 1 985FS33Δ1997 985FS38Δ1997 Cir. 2 1998USDist LX372 [Δ1998 Cir. 7 1999USApp LX7448 [Δ1999	**§ 848(q)(4)(B)** 512US851Δ1994 512US336Δ1997 Cir. 3 3FS2d570*1997 Cir. 4 971FS1007Δ1997 977FS734Δ1997 6FS2d478Δ1998 Cir. 5 125F3d274Δ1997 127F3d414Δ1997 162F3d296Δ1998 Cir. 6 1999USApp LX10213 [Δ1999 167F3d1038Δ1999 2FS2d963[Δ1998 Cir. 7 116F3d259Δ1997 126F3d879Δ1997 130F3d784Δ1997 Cir. 9 1998USApp LX12512 [Δ1998 128F3d1287Δ1997 163F3d539Δ1998 31FS2d1189Δ1998 Cir. 10 1999USApp LX8796 [Δ1999 169F3d1254Δ1999 **§ 848(q)(5)** Cir. 1 985FS33Δ1997 985FS38Δ1997 **§ 848(q)(6)** 512US854Δ1994 Cir. 1 985FS33Δ1997 985FS38Δ1997 **§ 848(q)(7)** 512US855Δ1994 **§ 848(q)(8)** A) 108St2143 **§ 848(q)(9)** A) 110St1226 512US855Δ1994 Cir. 4 1998USApp LX10886 [Δ1998 1998USApp LX104 [Δ1998 i) 133F3d279Δ1997 151F3d163Δ1998 1998USDist LX4671 [Δ1998 964FS1030Δ1997 971FS1007Δ1997 4FS2d519Δ1998 6FS2d478Δ1998 Cir. 5 1999USDist LX6484 [Δ1999	1999USDist LX7308 [Δ1999 f) 1999USDist LX7308 [Δ1999 37FS2d816Δ1999 Cir. 7 116F3d259Δ1997 130F3d784Δ1997 Cir. 9 969FS595Δ1997 Cir. 10 150F3d1264Δ1998 **§ 848(q)(10)** A) 110St1318 Cir. 6 965FS1000Δ1997 Cir. 9 na) 150F3d1034Δ1998 Cir.10 150F3d1265Δ1998 **§ 848(q)(10)(A)** Cir. 3 146F3d201Δ1998 Cir. 10 150F3d1251Δ1998 **§ 848(q)(10)(B)** Cir. 10 150F3d1251Δ1998 **§ 848(q)(10)(C)** Cir. 10 150F3d1264Δ1998 **§ 849** Ad) 108St2046 1999US LX3640Δ1999 Cir. 7 128F3d1191Δ1997 **§ 848(e)(1)** Cir. 9 158F3d1019Δ1998 **§ 850** 1999US LX3640Δ1999 **§ 851** Cir. 1 1999USApp LX10837 [Δ1999 156F3d30Δ1998 162F3d147Δ1998 Cir. 2 1998USApp LX10182 [Δ1998 1998USApp LX23523 [Δ1998 143F3d729Δ1998 158F3d659Δ1998 167F3d105Δ1999 11FS2d458Δ1998 Cir. 3 158F3d198Δ1998 164F3d167Δ1998 1998USDist LX9493 [Δ1998

Continued

909

followed by the subject in smaller boldface type. The rest of the entries follow the same pattern as statutes and constitutions.

Court rules for every state, including rules of civil and criminal procedure, rules of evidence, and rules of appellate practice, also appear in the statute section of the state citators. The rule category appears in boldface at the top of the page,

[10]How to Shepardize: Your Guide to Complete Legal Research Through Shepard's Citations. 2003 . LexisNexis. A division of Reed Elsevier Inc. http://www.lexisnexis.com/infopro/training/reference /Shepards/shepardscompgd.pdf

FIGURE 13-5 *Shepard's* Treatment

```
                    § 848(q)(9)
         A) 110St1226
            512US855Δ1994
               Cir. 4
            1998USApp LX10886
                                [Δ1998
            1999USApp LX104
                                [Δ1998
         i) 133F3d279Δ1997
            151F3d163Δ1998
            1998USDist LX4671
                                [Δ1998
            964FS1030Δ1997
            971FS1007Δ1997
            4FS2d519Δ1998
            6FS2d478Δ1998
               Cir. 5
            1999USDist LX6484
                                [Δ1999
            1999USDist LX7308
                                [Δ1999
         f) 1999USDist LX7308
                                [Δ1999
            37FS2d816Δ1999
               Cir. 7
            116F3d259Δ1997
            130F3d784Δ1997
               Cir. 9
            969FS595Δ1997
               Cir. 10
            150F3d1264Δ1998
```

The letter "A" means that section 848(q)(9) has been amended.

The letter "i" means that this section has been interpreted by this reference.

Under Cir. 5, 1999USDistLDX6484|Δ| is a LexisNexis citation for a citing reference. The delta followed by "1999" means the court did not specify the edition of USC it cited, but Shepard's tells you the citing case was decided in 1999.[11]

and each rule appears in smaller boldface type, similar to the sections for statutes or cases. A rule may appear as in Figure 13-6.

Shepardizing in the Topical Citators in Print

Shepard's has created citators that cover specific topics, such as labor, securities, and bankruptcy law. For example, *Shepard's Bankruptcy Citations* provides coverage for cases, statutes, and regulations in the bankruptcy area. It contains citing references to U.S. Supreme Court and lower federal and state courts that have cited provisions in bankruptcy law. These citing references include the history and analysis of unrelated decisions that could have value on the cited case, such as those that have criticized or overruled the cited case. Leading law reviews and other secondary sources are retrievable, as well.[12]

FIGURE 13-6 Shepard's for Rules

Rules of
Civil
Procedure

Rule 10
475NE2d110

[11]*Id.*

[12]Shepard's Bankruptcy Citations. 2012. http://www.lexisnexis.com/store/catalog/booktemplate/productdetail.jsp?pageName=relatedProducts&catId=227&prodId=65961

VALIDATING CASES AND ENACTED LAW USING ELECTRONIC SERVICES

Shepard's Online

Shepard's is by far the most frequently used of the citator services, as well as the most complete. The most obvious difference between the print and online versions of *Shepard's* is speed. A case can be Shepardized electronically without manually searching through multiple volumes. But there are other important differences in addition to speed. Figure 13-7 shows a LexisNexis screen for using *Shepard's*.

The online service also has a few tools not available in the print version. Both negative and positive treatments of cases are highlighted in a full editorial analysis. From this analysis, a researcher is given a better idea of the validity of the cases and is alerted to potential splits in authority. At the top of the screen, summaries appear that highlight the most important results. The table of authorities lists cited cases that a case has relied upon. A researcher also can stay on top of the validity of a source through *Shepard's* Alert, which provides notification of any changes to identified cases. The online service also provides more current information. Updates of the treatment and history analyses are given within 24–48 hours of the receipt of an opinion, whereas the print version updates are given 30 days to six weeks out.[13]

Four types of alerts are available, depending on the subscription one has: the "Alert" sub-tab, "Continuous Alerts," *Shepard's* Alert, and CourtLink Alerts. The "Alert" sub-tab provides an alert that runs automatically based on the criteria selected by the user. The results are stored online or may be emailed, if this feature is included in one's subscription.

To use the alert function, a search is first run to obtain the required results. Once the results are identified, the "Save as Alert" link is clicked and the user identifies how often the alert should run and how the notification should occur. To view the results, "New" is clicked to retrieve the most current results, "By Date" to retrieve specified date retrieval, and "Focus" to search additional terms in the produced document. "Edit" is clicked to modify the alert, "Delete" to delete the alert, and "Update Now" to retrieve the results stored since the last scheduled alert was run. Alerts can also be edited to change the search terms or the sources. To make changes, the "Alerts" tab is clicked, followed by the "Edit" link to make the changes desired, such as delivery method or frequency.[14]

The "Continuous Alerts" function can send breaking news from more than 9,000 news, business, and other web sources within minutes of publication. To activate, the Alerts tab is clicked; various help buttons are provided to guide the user.[15]

Shepard's Alert allows a user to set up regular updates about any changes to a cited source. To create a new *Shepard's* Alert, the "Alerts" tab is clicked and the citation is entered. Existing alerts can be managed using edit, delete, or renew functions, or sorted by the name of each alert, the citation, the client ID, or the date of the previous or upcoming update.[16]

---

[13]Total Practice Solutions: Research Solutions. Citation Services: *Shepard's* Citations. 2012. http://law.lexisnexis.com/shepards

[14]*Shepard's* Alerts. 2012. http://web.lexis.com/help/research/gh_alerts.asp

[15]*Shepard's* Alerts. 2012. http://www.lexisnexis.com/help/continuousalerts/gh_contalert.asp

[16]*Shepard's* Alerts. 2012. http://web.lexis.com/help/research/shepalertmgrtips.asp#Create

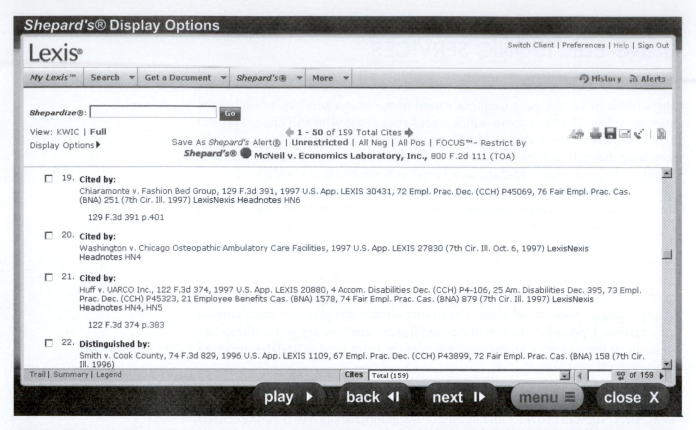

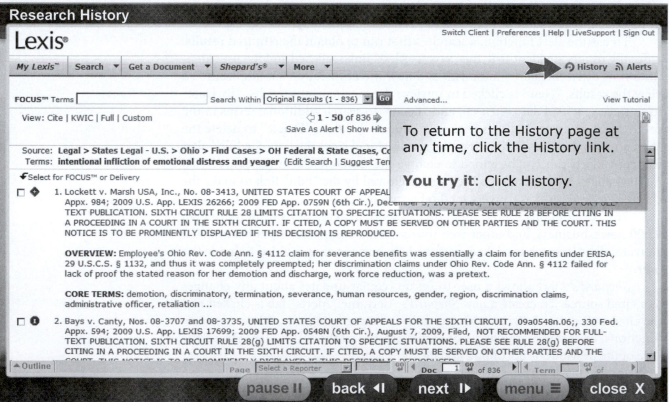

FIGURE 13-7 *Shepard's* on LexisNexis Academic[17]

[17]University of Southern California School of Law. *How to Confirm that Your Case is Good Law*. 2012. http://lawweb.usc.edu/library/research/basic/check.cfm

The CourtLink Alerts option is connected to the CourtLink system, which provides access to records from more than 1,400 court systems in the United States. Users can set up recurring searches by case number on a daily, weekly, or monthly schedule. They can also select the court, jurisdiction, or case type, in any combination, and can obtain documents online and through the public record service. CourtLink also includes eAccess, eFile, and eFM case management software.[18]

Auto-Cite

Auto-Cite is an electronic service provided by LexisNexis that validates the accuracy and precedential value of citations. Created in 1979, Auto-Cite was the first electronic citation service. It allows the user to instantly review a case's history and negative treatment and identify parallel citations. However, a major limitation is that it does not direct the user to all cases that have cited an authority in a positive manner. Auto-Cite serves three major purposes:

Identifying citations to the case, and confirming case information

Viewing subsequent history that may change a case's value as precedent

Researching the prior history of a case, identifying negative treatment, and finding additional resources related to the case[19]

Auto-Cite is used by selecting the Auto-Cite function and entering a citation. Example 13-1 shows how to review the history of *Washington v. Glucksberg*, 138 L. Ed. 2d 772, 1997 U.S. LEXIS 4039, 117 S. Ct. 2258 (1997).

The service retrieves the name of the case, the jurisdiction, the year of the decision, and any parallel cites. A response from Auto-Cite also may contain prior and subsequent history and treatment, plus a section called "makes negative reference to" that shows the cases that have been diminished in precedential value by the retrieved case.

Lexcite

The LEXCITE service in LexisNexis searches the system for all case citations, including all *Id.* and *Supra* references. If the citation for a source is known, such as a case or law review article, the service can be used to find references to the parallel citations, as well as the original citation. It also provides the citation in context. The user can locate the most current references, or indicate a date range to search within.[20]

EXAMPLE 13-1   HISTORY IN AUTO-CITE

Click the *Shepard's*® tab.
Click Auto-Cite® on the row under the *Shepard's*® tab.
Enter 138 L.Ed.2d 772 in the Enter "Citation to be Checked" field.
Click "Check." [21]

---

[18]Farlex. LexisNexis Acquires CourtLink, Inc. 2012. http://www.thefreelibrary.com/Lexisnexis +Group+acquires+Courtlink+Corp.(from+Internet+Capital . . . -a080932117

[19]Checking a Citation. 2009. http://web.lexis.com/help/research/gh_checkacitation.asp#AUTO-CITE

[20]Checking a Citation.2012. http://web.lexis.com/help/research/gh_checkacitation.asp#AUTO-CITE

[21]LexisNexis. Auto-Cite Citation Service. 2012. http://support.lexisnexis.com/lawschool/record .asp?ArticleID=lexiscom_Auto-Cite&Print=1

A CLOSER LOOK AT THE PROCESS OF VALIDATING RESEARCH WITH *SHEPARD'S*

The Process of Validating Cases in the Print Version of *Shepard's*

Validate
To make sure that law is valid or to affirm that the source is still "good law."

With the rise of online citator services, the use of the print versions of *Shepard's* is declining. However, *Shepard's* print versions are still used by many attorneys for validating sources. Although Shepardizing from the printed versions can be time-consuming and challenging, it is important to know how to use these tools in case there is no access to the online version or if computers are not functioning. Generally, the process in Checklist 13-2 should be followed to ***validate a case***. In addition, a research trail should be maintained to track information that has been retrieved.

Checklist 13-2   VALIDATING A CASE

1. Find the appropriate set of volumes for a citation. For example, for South Dakota cases, use *Shepard's South Dakota Citations, Case & Statute Edition*. A set usually consists of bound volumes and paper supplements.

2. Find the most recent pamphlet in the set. The front cover will indicate what volumes are included in the set under "What Your Library Should Contain."

3. Gather all of the volumes (including supplements) that contain the citation. Every book may not be needed. Using the citation, refer to step 2 and determine which of the materials may have references to the cited case.

4. To find the citation, turn to the page that has the applicable volume number for its reporter. Make sure the page is in the correct section—a single volume of *Shepard's* will contain citations to more than one reporter. A single page of *Shepard's* may contain references to more than one volume. The volume is identified once in the upper left corner. If the volume changes on a page, the volume will read **"Vol. xxx."**

5. Locate the page number that corresponds to the citation. The page numbers are in bold and set off by dashes in the columns. Confirm that the page number is in the correct volume.

6. Examine the information presented. Look at the parallel citations, follow the history of the case, check the treatment information, and read later sources if applicable.

7. Repeat the process for any new sources chosen.

8. Note the date of the validation in the research trail so that if time passes and an update is needed, that update can be made from the date of the last validation.

The Process of Validating Enacted Law in the Print Version of *Shepard's*

The process for validating statutes in print is similar to that process used for cases. Checklist 13-3 shows how to validate statutes.

Checklist 13-3   **VALIDATING STATUTES**

1. Locate the volumes of *Shepard's* needed by looking at the "What Your Library Should Contain" section on the front cover of the most recent supplement, the Table of Contents, and the scope pages in each volume.

2. When the appropriate volumes and supplements have been located, find the part containing title of the statute by looking at the upper corners of the pages to locate the "title" or "article" of the enacted law being researched.

3. Look for the bold-faced entry for the "section" of the enacted law being researched. In statutory research, the section numbers will not be surrounded by hash marks; rather, the section symbol (§) will appear with the section number.

4. Pay attention to all entries listed, particularly the history and treatment.

5. Conduct additional research on any of the entries that could have a negative impact on the issue being researched.

TIP

See Figure 13-4 for an example entry.

The Process of Shepardizing Research Electronically

Shepardizing electronically requires a very different procedure than *Shepard's* in print requires, but should provide similar results. This **subscription service** is located on the LexisNexis website. A source may be checked by clicking the *Shepard's* tab, entering the citation in the open field, and clicking "check" to start processing.

Shepard's Online—Cases   *Shepard's* online provides two options: "*Shepard's* for Research," and "*Shepard's* for Validation." "*Shepard's* for Research," or "Full," gives every authority for the cited case. "*Shepard's* for Validation," or "KWIC," gives the negative history only.

Shepard's online provides straightforward notation of how the cited case has been treated. The citing references are hyperlinked so that the citing case may be retrieved with a single click. Signal indicators also give visual notice of the value of the results. These indicators are shown in Figure 13-8.

A unique feature in *Shepard's* is the phrase, "Questioned By," defined in Figure 13-3. It is important to understand that "***Questioned***," as used in this notation, means that a citing court, rather than a law review editor or some other reviewer, believes the new authority has some negative impact on the case. The "Q" icon takes the user to the first reference in the citing case.[22]

Once the process begins, several research options are available on the *Shepard's* report. The user may do the following:

- Change views or display options
- See the case treatment
- Request regular *Shepard's* report updates to check a citation's status through *Shepard's* Alerts
- Customize the report by restricting the jurisdiction, treatments, headnotes, or dates
- Find vital facts or points of law within citing references

Subscription service
A service that provides information for a periodically assessed fee.

Questioned
The citing opinion questions the continuing validity or precedential value of the case being Shepardized because of intervening circumstances. A case is often questioned because it may have been overruled by statute or another case.

[22]Only on *Shepard's* 'Orange "Q" Guidance. 2008. http://law.lexisnexis.com/literature/Shepards _Orange_Q_Guide.pdf

FIGURE 13-8 *Shepard's* Signal Indicators

Source: Shepard's Citations Service at www.lexis.com. 2008. http://law.lexisnexis.com/literature /Shepards_%20Citations_Service_ Overview.pdf

Shepard's Signal™ Indicators Show Precedential Value

The *Shepard's* Signal indicators show at a glance the precedential status of a case. To review this legend while you research in *Shepard's*, click the **Legend** link at the bottom-left side of your report.

 Warning—Negative treatment indicated
Contains strong negative history of treatment of your case (for example, overruled by or reversed).

 Questioned—Validity questioned by citing references
Contains treatment that questions the continuing validity or presidential value of your case because of intervening circumstances, including judicial or legislative overruling.

 Caution—Possible negative treatment indicated
Contains history or treatment that may have a significant negative impact on your case (for example, limited or criticized by).

 Positive treatment indicated
Contains history or treatment that has a positive impact on your case (for example, affirmed or followed by). Only *Shepard's* offers this treatment.

 Cited and neutral analysis indicated
Contains treatment of your case that is neither positive nor negative.

 Citation information available
Indicates that citing references are available for your case but do not have history or treatment analysis (for example, the references are law review citations).

- View the full text of the case.
- See the table of authorities for the case.
- Refer to *Shepard's*® Summary for critical references and links.
- View the LexisNexis® headnotes of the *Shepardized*™ case.
- Hide or show prior or subsequent appellate history.
- Print, download, fax, or e-mail the reference.
- Click the underlined case name to see the case's full text.
- Display a list of all *Shepard's* Signal™ indicators and definitions.
- Move among references using the Navigation Bar.[23]

Once a researcher has found appropriate authorities to support the client's position, *Shepard's* Alert may be used to alert the user of any additional changes to the case's treatment or history. This tool saves the researcher time from having to continually update sources that have an impact on the cited authority.[24]

The table of authorities allows the user to evaluate the materials upon which the cited document relied. While the cited case itself may not have received any

---

[23]*Shepard's* Citations Service at www.lexis.com. 2008. http://law.lexisnexis.com/literature /Shepards_%20Citations_Service_Overview.pdf

[24]*Is It Still Good Law?* 2008. http://law.lexisnexis.com/literature/Shepards_Alert.pdf

negative treatment, a source within the cited case may have. If so, the cited case may no longer be "good law," since it relied on a case with negative treatment.

Another useful feature is the ability to automatically receive parallel citations through a Shepard's report.[25] See Figure 13-9 for a sample Full Format Shepard's report.

Shepard's is continually adding additional products that aid the validation process. *Shepard's* Brief Suite, formerly called CheckCite, automatically checks whether the citations being used in a brief are still "good law" without requiring the user to enter each citation in the open field of *Shepard's*. The software can also issue three different reports: *Shepard's* service for verification, or the "Get" service; QuoteCheck™ to insure that the quotes are exactly as in the case; and Check Citation Content to show differences between the content of the citations in the document and the content of the citations as verified by the *Shepard's*® Citations Service.[26]

Another useful program, particularly for California users, is *StyleCheck,* formerly called CiteRite. This software checks citations for proper format according to *The Bluebook* rules or the *California Style Manual.* In addition to statutes, cases, and administrative materials, it can check secondary sources such as model codes,

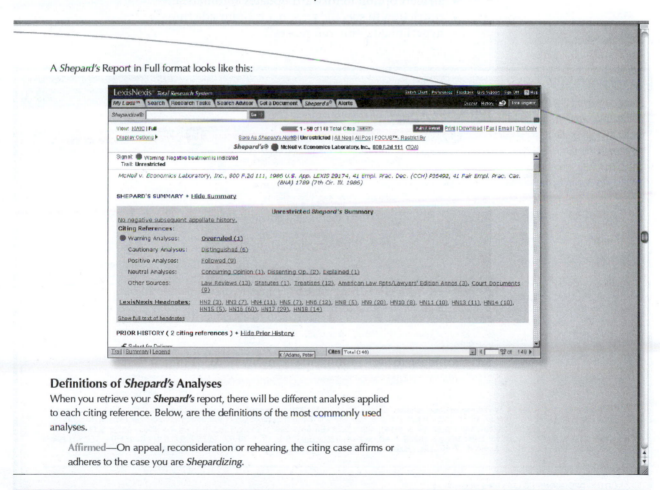

FIGURE 13-9 Full Format Shepard's Report[27]

[25]*Shepard's* Table of Authorities. 2008. http://law.lexisnexis.com/literature/Shepards_Table _Authorities.pdf

[26]*Shepard's* Brief Check Tutorial. 2007. http://w3.lexis.com/xchange/Content/HelpMultimedia /BriefCheck/briefcheck.textOnly.htm

[27]LexisNexis Paralegal User's Guide. 2007. http://www.lexisnexis.com/documents /LawSchoolTutorials/20070511013250_small.pdf

uniform codes, books, and law reviews. After checking text, the program provides an error report and gives the *Bluebook* rule for each error.[28]

Shepard's Online—Enacted Law When using *Shepard's* online to check statutes, the citation is entered just as with cases, and the researcher has two options: "*Shepard's* for Validation" or "*Shepard's* for Research." A report is generated allowing the researcher to view the negative history and treatment of the statute. Additional resources are provided in the citing references, including some treatises, briefs, motions, and law reviews. A sample report is shown in Figure 13-10.

The report provides:

- all vital affecting authority
- any strong negative treatment in a citing reference, noted by a red exclamation mark
- hyperlinked analyses
- links to recently enacted legislation, pending bills, or other activity that could affect the statute
- an alert option to forward updates automatically
- restriction to specific treatments or jurisdictions
- hyperlinked citing references[29]

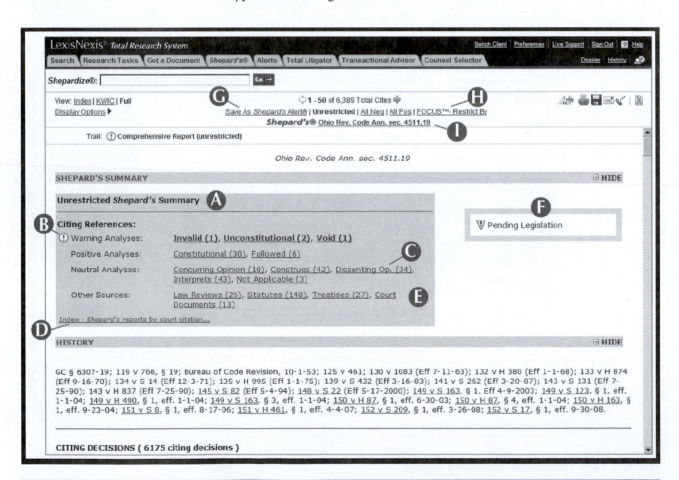

FIGURE 13-10 *Shepard's* Statutes

[28]LexisNexis InfoPro Newsletter. Information Professional Update Issue 4, April 2006. http://lexisnexis.com.ve/infopro/current/newsletter/2006/0406lnipu.asp

[29]New *Shepard's* Statute Reports: One View Shows Affecting Legislation, Pending Bills and Citing Cases. 2008. http://law.lexisnexis.com/literature/Shepard_Statutes_Overview.pdf

Although *Shepard's* is not the only source for validation of research, it is the only service that has both print and online versions. Using the print version can be challenging, but it is available in most large libraries. Moreover, understanding the print version is helpful in understanding the online version. Further, although the online version is quick, relatively easy, and complete, it requires a paid subscription.

WESTLAW AND KEYCITE
Overview of KeyCite

As an alternative to *Shepard's*, West offers KeyCite on its Westlaw online research service. KeyCite can be used with the following:

- federal and state cases, including those the West's National Reporter System and over a million unpublished cases
- federal statutes and regulations
- statutes from all 50 states
- regulations and administrative decisions from selected states
- patents issued by the U.S Patent and Trademark Office
- *American Law Reports* annotations
- articles from a variety of law reviews
- administrative decisions of certain federal agencies such as the Environmental Protection Agency (EPA), the Federal Communications Commission (FCC), and the National Labor Relations Board (NLRB)

KeyCiting Cases

KeyCite provides the user with a wide variety of validating information in the sources available on Westlaw. It is completely integrated with the West Key Number System so that a researcher can track legal issues discussed in a case, and find the same point of law discussed anywhere in the West system of reported materials. KeyCite also provides citing references to texts and treatises such as *American Jurisprudence* 2d (Am. Jur. 2d), *Norton Bankruptcy Law and Practice 3d,* and Wright and Miller's *Federal Practice and Procedure.*

A KeyCite page makes several pieces of information readily available to the researcher. The "scope" icon allows the user to view the scope of information covered in KeyCite. The Publications List provides the abbreviations that are used. KeyCite Tips directs the user to an online help center to find detailed information about using KeyCite. KeyCite Alert notifies the user if any changes occur that affect a cited document.

KeyCite also has several different features to provide a researcher with additional guidance. A symbol alerts the user that the source has a history, or that something affects the source. Although all these symbols are referred to as "flags," some depict symbols other than flags. Figure 13-11 describes the meanings of the various KeyCite status flags.

The case history is divided into three sections: direct history, negative citing references, and related references. Direct history lists decisions by the prior and subsequent authorities that have heard the cited case. For example, if the cited case is an appellate-level case that has been appealed to the supreme court, both the trial level case (if reported) and the supreme court case will appear in the history of the appellate level case both as a narrative and as a

FIGURE 13-11 KeyCite
Status Flags

Source: KeyCite Status Flags. 2002–
2010. http://www2.westlaw.com/
CustomerSupport/Knowledgebase/
Technical/WestlawCreditCard/
WebHelp/KeyCite_Status_Flags.htm

In cases and administrative decisions, a red flag warns that the case or administrative decision is no longer good law for at least one of the points of law it contains. In statutes and regulations, a red flag indicates that the statute or regulation has been amended by a recent session law or rule, repealed, superseded, or held unconstitutional or preempted in whole or in part.

In cases and administrative decisions, a yellow flag warns that the case or administrative decision has some negative history but hasn't been reversed or overruled. In statutes and regulations, a yellow flag indicates that the statute has been renumbered or transferred by a recent session law; that an uncodified session law or pending legislation affecting the statute is available (statutes merely referenced, i.e., mentioned, are not marked with a yellow flag); that the regulation has been reinstated, corrected, or confirmed; that the statute or regulation was limited on constitutional or preemption grounds or its validity was otherwise called into doubt; or that a prior version of the statute or regulation received negative treatment from a court.

In cases and administrative decisions, a blue H indicates that the case or administrative decision has some history.

In cases and administrative decisions, a green C indicates that the case or administrative decision has citing references but no direct history or negative citing references. In statutes and regulations, a green C indicates that the statute or regulation has citing references.[1]

diagram. The list of negative citing references includes all cases that have relied on, discussed, or cited the case, and that may have a negative impact on its value. Related references are cases that involve the same parties and facts as those in the cited case, whether or not the issues are the same. Case history provides links to items such as court documents and transcripts of oral arguments filed in the cited case.

KeyCite also provides a "graphical view," which helps the user visualize the direct history of the case. On this screen, the case is presented as a flow chart, with arrows showing the movement of the case through the court system. The court levels are identified on the side of the screen to clarify the hierarchy of the courts considering the case. Additional features are also provided to aid the understanding of the process. Decisions on the merits are placed in larger boxes, and lesser court orders or rulings are placed in smaller "procedural" boxes. Materials are hyperlinked for ease in accessing. To return to the cited case or the full text history, the appropriate entry above the graphic is clicked. Figure 13-12 shows an example of a graphical view.

To keep KeyCite current, direct history is added within one to four hours after the West editors receive an opinion. Nothing is added to KeyCite, however, without a rigorous editorial analysis by the Westlaw staff.

KeyCite provides a further guide to research through "treatment stars" appearing next to citing references. These stars describe the relative amount of

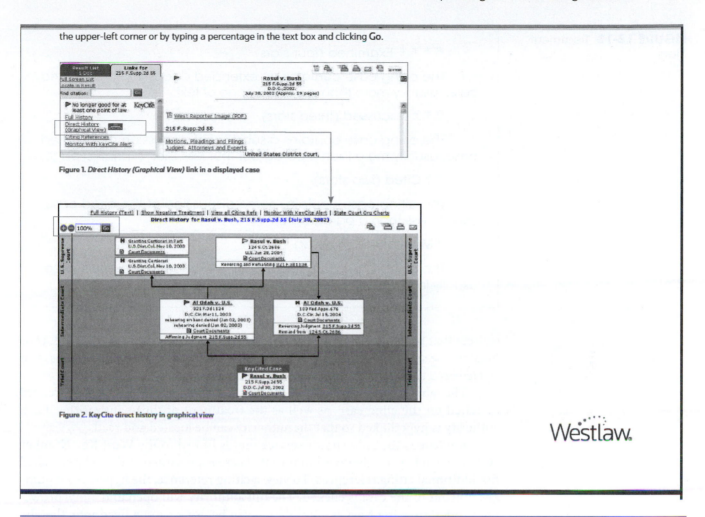

FIGURE 13-12 Graphical View of History[30]

treatment the cited case received within the citing reference, ranging from four stars to one. Figure 13-13 gives an overview of the treatment stars.

Quotation marks within a citing reference indicate that the citing reference directly quotes from the cited reference.

When using KeyCite, it is not necessary to constantly update the cited case manually. KeyCite Alert, found on the left side of the screen, notifies the researcher of any changes in the treatment of the cited case. This function can be tailored to the needs of the researcher. For example, it may be restricted to only negative treatment. The user can also select a time frame, such as daily or weekly, for notification.

Other tools on the left side of the screen include "Featured Trial Document," which gives a hyperlink to all the trial documents that referenced the cited case. In addition, a full-text case outline provides a hyperlink to the synopsis, head-notes, the opinion, and any concurring opinion. Access is also provided to petitions, briefs, and filings in the cited case. The "ResultsPlus" section gives other

[30]KeyCite Direct History in Graphical View. 2010. http://west.thomson.com/productdetail /1-6841-5/RM168415/productdetail.aspx

FIGURE 13-13 Treatment
Stars

* * * * **Examined** (four stars)

The citing case contains an extended discussion of the cited case, usually more than a printed page of text.

* * * **Discussed** (three stars)

The citing case contains a substantial discussion of the cited case, usually more than a paragraph but less than a printed page.

* * **Cited** (two stars)

The citing case contains some discussion of the cited case, usually less than a paragraph.

* **Mentioned** (one star)

The citing case contains a brief reference to the cited case, usually in a string citation.[31]

sources that have discussed the cited case or are related to the topic. For the *Armbruster* case shown in Figure 13-8, there are 19 references, including sources such as *Fletcher's Cyclopedia*, ALR, and Am. Jur. 2d.

The table of authorities allows the user to see the authorities that referenced or relied on the cited case, as well as the treatment of those authorities. Each authority is hyperlinked so that the authority can be located and read.

KeyCite is the only citator service that is linked to the West Key Number system. Each key number used in the cited case is presented and can be searched for additional citing references. To view a citing reference, the hyperlinked number in front of the case is clicked. The full authority will open and allow browsing validation using KeyCite. Validation can be done from a headnote, thereby limiting the citing references to those discussing the legal issue described in the headnote.

Figure 13-14 shows a partial KeyCite display for *Armbruster v. Quinn,* 711 F.2d 1332 (6th Cir. 1983). This is the screen that would be displayed when the "Full History" button was clicked. After the entries for the history, the citing references appear with the negative citing references listed first. The negative references are followed by other cases, administrative decisions, and other materials citing the case in question. Citing cases are categorized by the stars showing the depth of treatment given.

Users can restrict the list of citing references for greater convenience. The "Limit KeyCite Display" button at the bottom of the result page will take the user to the KeyCite Limits page. The citing references can be limited by document type, headnote, jurisdiction, date, or depth of treatment. A user can also limit by terms found within the citing references. The restrictions can be modified by clicking the "Edit Limits" button, or cancelled by clicking the "Cancel Limits" button.

The first category for limits is "document type." The menu for document types appears when KeyCite Limits is selected, as shown in Figure 13-15.

In this example, there are 4 citing references at the highest court level, 334 in other courts, 4 A.L.R.s, and 100 references in law reviews. If a type of document is

---

[31]KeyCite Help. 2010. http://text.westlaw.com/welcome/wlto/help/default.aspx?fn=_top&rs=ACC S9.11&rp=%2Fwelcome%2Fwlto%2Fhelp%2Fdefault.aspx&helpkey=KeyCite&vr=2.0&ifm=NotSet

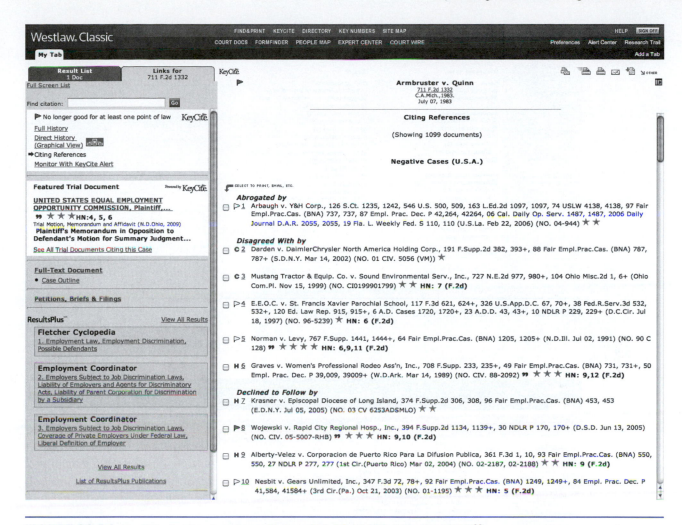

FIGURE 13-14 KeyCite for Armbruster v. Quinn, 711 F.2d 1332 (6th Cir. 1983)[32]

not highlighted, it means there are no citing references in that category. After the selections are made, the "Apply" box is clicked to retrieve the documents.

When items are limited by headnote, a similar process is followed. Each headnote is identified by topics and key numbers, and an item may be listed under more than one, as shown in Figure 13-16.

Limiting by jurisdiction, by date, and/or by depth of treatment is accomplished in the same fashion. With the date restriction, there is the choice of restricting by decision date ("Date of Document") or restricting by the date the citing references were added to Westlaw ("Date added after"). As with any restriction, "Apply" must be clicked to activate the choices.

The Limit by Locate restriction is applied differently. First, appropriate terms are selected from within the text of citing references. After selecting "Locate," the screen will appear as in Figure 13-17.

In the box, the terms are entered along with the appropriate connectors. The user also has the option to limit the search to documents that have the terms within the same paragraph as the cited reference. In Figure 13-17, the user is limiting the search to documents that include the term "establishment," but only if that

---

[32]*Armbruster v. Quinn*, 711 F.2d 1332 (6th Cir. 1983). www.westlaw.com

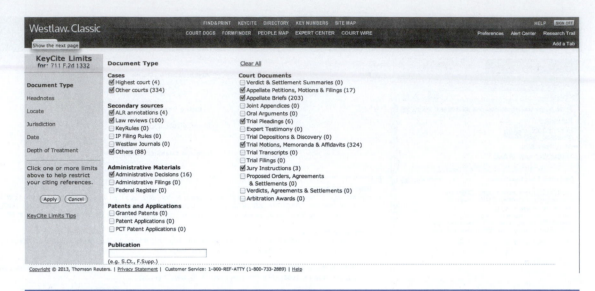

FIGURE 13-15 Limit KeyCite to Document Type[33]

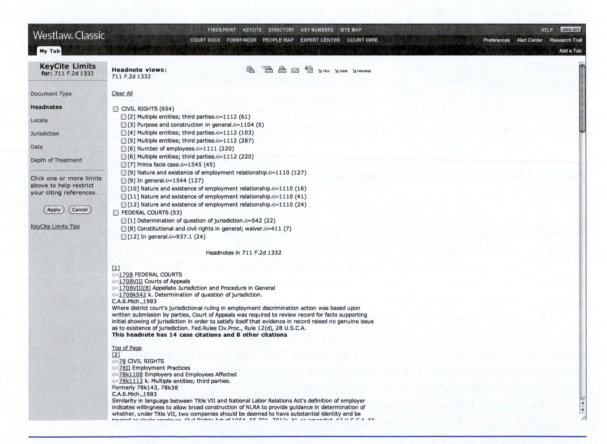

FIGURE 13-16 KeyCite Restricted by Headnotes[34]

---

[33]Using KeyCite on Westlaw. 2009. http://west.thomson.com/productdetail/1-7038-5/40888531/productdetail.aspx

[34]*Id.*

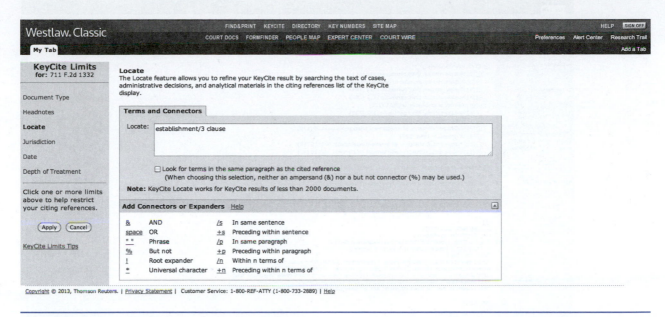

FIGURE 13-17 KeyCite and Limit by Locate[35]

term is within three words of the term "clause." Clicking "Apply" will activate the limitations. Generally, the "Locate" tool is available only if there are fewer than 2,000 citing references. If there are more than 2,000 citing references, other methods should be used to limit the references.

In every Westlaw document, the command "KeyCite Citing References for this Headnote" will appear with each headnote. Figure 13-18 shows an example from *Armbruster v. Quinn*.

This tool allows the user to focus the research on citing references that discuss the particular headnote. By clicking "KeyCite Citing References," a list of the types of citing references appears, as shown in Figure 13-19.

Each type of reference gives the total number of documents available. For example, in Figure 13-18, there are 22 cases, but no law reviews and journals. The "+" symbol by the number of documents will open the list for browsing. Clicking the "—" symbol will close the list. When the citing references have been selected, clicking "go" will display them.

The text of each headnote should always be reviewed to ensure that the correct headnote is being referenced. To illustrate, the text of the headnote in Figure 13-18 can be compared to the text of the headnote in Figure 13-18. It is the same, and therefore, these cases do address the same point of law.

KeyCiting Statutes

As with cases, the KeyCite service for statutes uses the status flags to alert the user to types of treatment. However, the meanings of these symbols are somewhat different. With statutes, there is no "H" for history. The status flags are a red flag, a yellow flag, and a green C, as shown in Figure 13-20.

The statute appears on the left-hand side of the screen, where KeyCite provides access to information on its history. For example, if the history of the statute

[35]*Id.*

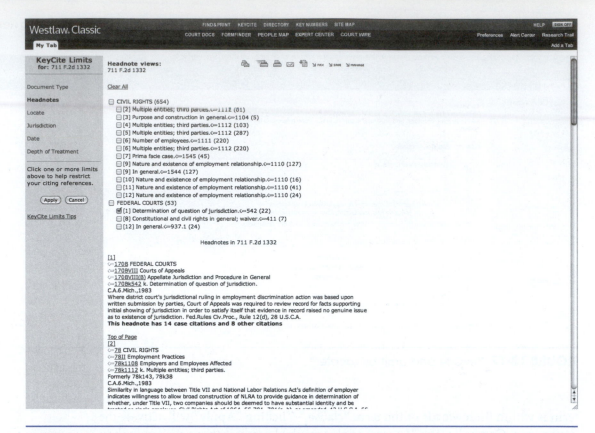

FIGURE 13-18 KeyCite Citing References for This Headnote[36]

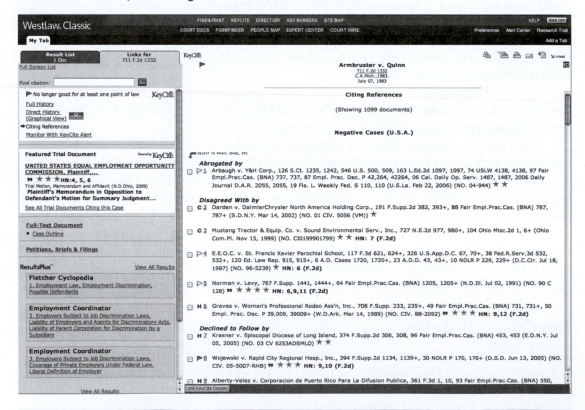

FIGURE 13-19 KeyCite Citing References[37]

[36]*Armbruster v. Quinn*, 711 F.2d 1332 (6th Cir. 1983). https://web2.westlaw.com/find/default .wl?rs=WLW10.06&ifm=NotSet&fn=_top&sv=Split&cite=711+f2d+1332&vr=2.0&rp=%2ffind%2f default.wl&mt=Westlaw

[37]*Id.*

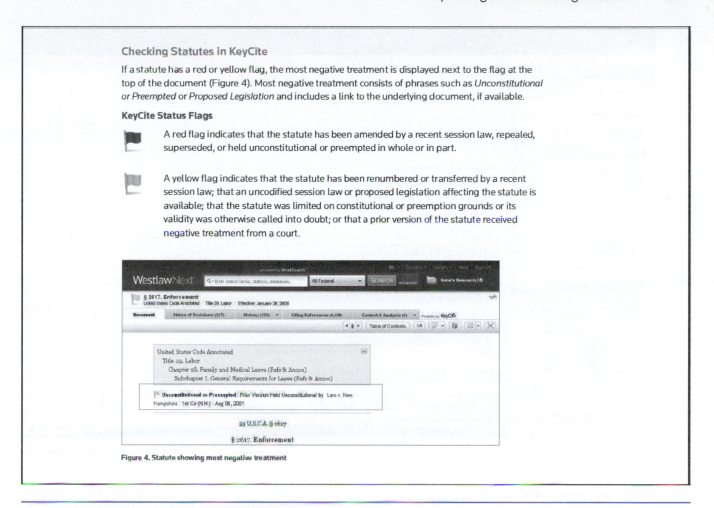

Checking Statutes in KeyCite

If a statute has a red or yellow flag, the most negative treatment is displayed next to the flag at the top of the document (Figure 4). Most negative treatment consists of phrases such as *Unconstitutional or Preempted* or *Proposed Legislation* and includes a link to the underlying document, if available.

KeyCite Status Flags

A red flag indicates that the statute has been amended by a recent session law, repealed, superseded, or held unconstitutional or preempted in whole or in part.

A yellow flag indicates that the statute has been renumbered or transferred by a recent session law; that an uncodified session law or proposed legislation affecting the statute is available; that the statute was limited on constitutional or preemption grounds or its validity was otherwise called into doubt; or that a prior version of the statute received negative treatment from a court.

Figure 4. Statute showing most negative treatment

FIGURE 13-20 Status Flags for Statutes[38]

26 U.S.C.A. § 1 (West 2008) were being researched, the left-hand side of the page would look similar to Figure 13-21.

Under the History button, all cases affecting the statute's validity will be listed, plus other legislative materials that are related to the statute. These sources are divided into six categories. Under "Updating Documents" are session laws recently passed that have affected the cited section by amendment or repeal. The "Historical and Statutory Notes" section describes the changes from the legislature that affect that section of the statute. "Bill drafts" shows all drafts of a bill that are proposed before it was enacted. The "Proposed Legislation" section provides citations to proposed bills that reference the cited statutory section. Under "Reports and Related Materials," the user can find *Congressional Record* documents, messages from the president, and reports, journals, and transcripts of testimony that are relevant to the statutory section. The last section, "Credits," provides citations to session laws that have affected the statutory section by enactment, amendment, or renumbering. These citations are listed in chronological order for ease of use.

[38]Checking Citations in KeyCite. 2010. http://west.thomson.com/documentation/westlaw/wlawdoc/web/wlnkeyci.pdf

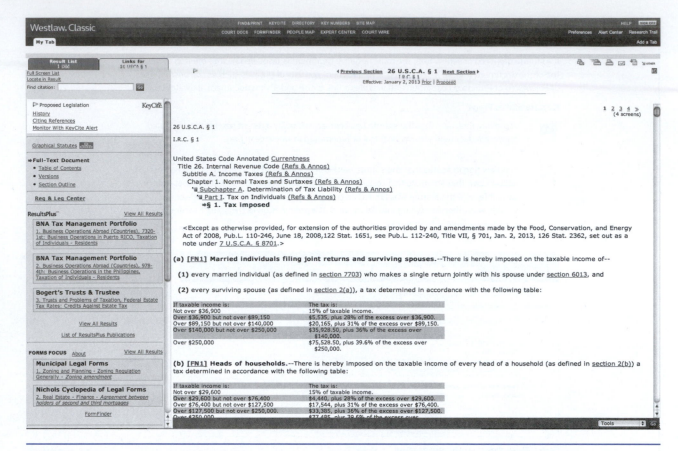

FIGURE 13-21 KeyCite Links for 26 U.S.C.A. § 1 (West 2008)

The statutes have citing references, just as cases have. Any documents that cite the statute in question are provided in the following order:

1. Cases that have an effect on the statute's validity
2. Cases from *United States Code Annotated* (U.S.C.A.), or state statutes' notes of decisions
3. Westlaw cases that are not in the notes of decisions
4. Administrative decisions
5. Federal Register documents
6. Secondary sources
7. Briefs and other court documents
8. Statutes and court rules
9. Administrative codes

Similar to KeyCite searches for cases, statutory searches may be limited using the KeyCite display at the bottom of the citing references. A search may be limited by document type, notes of decisions, jurisdiction, or date. A "Locate term" option is also available. In limiting by document type, the user has options similar to those in case searches. "Apply" must be clicked to activate the restrictions. If a different limitation is needed, "Edit Limits" at the bottom of the current view may be clicked. To remove the limitations, "Cancel Limits" can be selected.

Limiting by Notes of Decisions provides summaries of the headnotes or points of law in court decisions and attorney general opinions that have discussed the statute. These notes are topically indexed for easy reference. As with the other limitation methods, restricting is done by selecting the topics of interest and clicking "Apply." To view the text, the user selects "View Notes of Decisions Text" under the topics.

Limit by Jurisdiction is very similar. Clicking "Jurisdiction" will list the jurisdictions from which cases have been issued citing the statute in question. The user selects jurisdictions that are relevant to the research before clicking "Apply."

Limit by Date allows the user to restrict the citing document results to those within a certain time frame. The user also may obtain an update by requesting materials that were added after a certain date. Once this screen is selected by clicking "Date" on the left-hand side, a drop-down list and text boxes appear in the right-hand frame. The user has the option of using an unrestricted date, or setting a time frame "before" or "after" a certain date. The "date added after" function allows the user to select a specific date, such as the last date of research, and retrieve any materials placed on Westlaw after that date. When the selection is made, "Apply" is clicked to show the results.

Limit by Locate, while similar to Locate for cases, is slightly different in its limiting methods. Locate allows the user to search through the text of the citing references for specific terms or phrases. "Locate" is clicked on the left-hand side of the screen and terms or phrases are entered in the "Locate" box. Search terms and connectors are used just as in a Westlaw search. Clicking "Apply" will list the documents that satisfy the query. The number preceding the citation is clicked to view the full text of the citing reference. The terms or phrases from the "Locate" box will be highlighted for convenience. As with cases, "Locate" is available only if there are 2,000 or fewer results. If the citing references number more than 2000, the search can be limited in other ways, such as by date or jurisdiction.

The KeyCite Alert feature is available for statutes as well. By creating a KeyCite Alert entry, the user can specify the alert frequency. The results can be delivered to a printer, fax machine, or email address, and will be saved for 30 days. Creating the KeyCite Alert can be accomplished in two different ways. In a KeyCite result or a document, the left-hand side will show a "Monitor with KeyCite Alert" button. The KeyCite Alert wizard displays the citation and requests that the user enter a client identifier. Specific instructions are presented in a step-by-step order.

On any page of Westlaw, in the upper right-hand corner, is an "Alert Center Directory." After entering that directory, clicking "Wizard" in the KeyCite Alert section initiates a set of directions for creating an alert. Clicking "Create" and typing the citation to be monitored will bring up the "KeyCite Alert: Create Entry" page where the user can select the KeyCite Alert settings needed. Those selections can be change by clicking "Edit." Whenever an entry is made, it is important to save one's work.

The KeyCite Alert entries can be restricted as well. On the "Create Entry" page, clicking "Limit Citing Refs" reveals arrows to limit by type of restriction. Options for cases include limiting by headnote, jurisdiction, document type, or depth of treatment; options for statutes include jurisdiction, notes of decisions, and document type. Both cases and statutes have the "Locate" restriction available.

The KeyCite Alert Entry can also be deleted or modified. The entries will remain in the Alert Center directory until they are deleted. To delete, the "Alert Center" is clicked in the upper right-hand corner of any page. The arrow is clicked to locate the entry to be deleted, and the boxes next to the entries to be deleted are selected. Entries can be modified by clicking the entry's name to receive the "Alert Center Directory" page.

Other West Products

WestCheck is software that works with Westlaw and KeyCite and is similar to LexisNexis's BriefCheck. The product can be installed as an integrated application, a stand-alone application, or both. If integrated, it works with the user's word-processing program. The primary uses of WestCheck are the following:

- Creating a list of cases cited by the case the researcher has selected
- Verifying the accuracy of quotations in documents
- Retrieving documents on Westlaw[39]

WestCheck pulls citations and quotations from any word processing document and validates those citations and quotations through KeyCite and other sources. It can then prepare a printed report showing the results. When the documents are checked, the flag and star symbols are used as if the case is displayed in KeyCite. If the citation is known, the full text of the document can be retrieved on Westlaw. The QuoteRight application provides verification of citations and quotations used in the document. WestCheck also allows the user to create a table of authorities for authorities that have been cited. The primary difference between WestCheck and KeyCite is that WestCheck actually validates the citations in the created document so that user does not have to check each citation separately.[40]

The integrated and stand-alone versions of WestCheck have slightly different methods for using the service. Both systems use drop-down menus that can be followed easily. The basic premise of each system is to create or extract a citation list from a document.

The first step is verification of the citations. If a citation cannot be verified, a "question mark" symbol is displayed. This usually means that it has been typed incorrectly. The question mark will remain in place until the citation is verified by correcting the citation and running WestCheck again. If the list contains citations to services that are blocked because they are not included in the Westlaw subscription, a red symbol is displayed. Figure 13-22 shows a question mark identifying that the citation cannot be verified. The red symbol by the last entry indicates that this particular subscription to Westlaw does not include access to patent information.

After obtaining the list of citations through WestCheck, the citations can be entered in KeyCite to obtain additional citing references, or entered in other services to obtain other information. A single citation is checked by placing a check mark in the box beside the citation and under the service to be used. Clicking "Run WestCheck" brings up options for delivery. These options include delivery as separate documents, a single document, PDF images of the analogous West reporters, or a single PDF containing all case law documents in a single result. Clicking "Run Report" creates an online report that contains the KeyCite status flags in color so the status of the cited authority is immediately visible. The cases are also labeled using the star system. Offline reports are available that include a header page, a summary, a citator or document service report, a billing report, and

---

[39]Using WestCheck 5.0. 2010. http://west.thomson.com/documentation/westlaw/wlawdoc/wlsoft/wcswqref.pdf

[40]WestCheck 5.0 User Manual. 2010. http://west.thomson.com/documentation/westlaw/wlawdoc/web/wc455gd.pdf

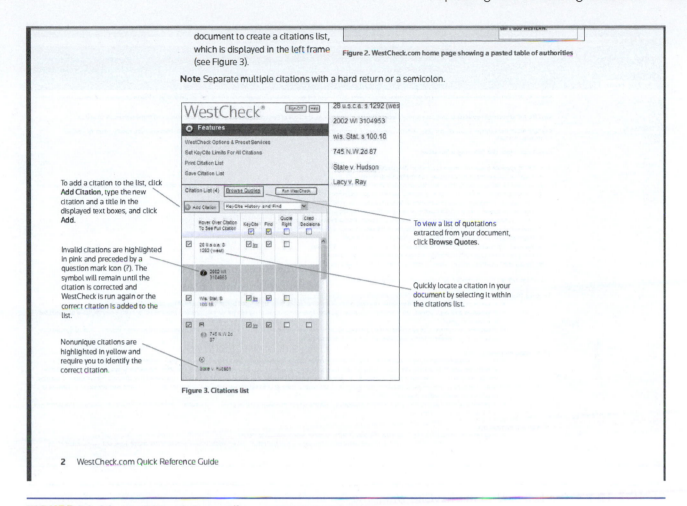

Figure 2. WestCheck.com home page showing a pasted table of authorities

document to create a citations list, which is displayed in the left frame (see Figure 3).

Note Separate multiple citations with a hard return or a semicolon.

To add a citation to the list, click **Add Citation**, type the new citation and a title in the displayed text boxes, and click **Add**.

Invalid citations are highlighted in pink and preceded by a question mark icon (?). The symbol will remain until the citation is corrected and WestCheck is run again or the correct citation is added to the list.

Nonunique citations are highlighted in yellow and require you to identify the correct citation.

To view a list of quotations extracted from your document, click **Browse Quotes**.

Quickly locate a citation in your document by selecting it within the citations list.

Figure 3. Citations list

2   WestCheck.com Quick Reference Guide

FIGURE 13-22 WestCheck Report[41]

an end page. The offline reports use the words "Red Flg," "Yel Flg," "H," and "C" in lieu of the colors and symbols.[42]

QuoteRight is a tool for validating the accuracy of quotations and creating a list of quotations found in a document. There are two viewing options: "quotations from individual citations" and "quotations from the whole list." The quotation in the user's document is compared to the quotation in the published Westlaw document, and QuoteRight will confirm or deny the accuracy of the quotation.[43]

Demonstration Using KeyCite to Perform Research

To illustrate the use of KeyCite, a demonstration may be helpful. The assignment is to locate authority to support the client's claim that there was no unlawful sexual harassment. Research uncovered a case that was on point—*Armbruster v. Quinn*, 711 F.2d 1332 (6th Cir. 1983)—presented in Figure 13-14. Now this case needs to be validated.

KeyCite information may be accessed in several ways. On the "Welcome to Westlaw" screen, a citation is typed in the "KeyCite this citation" box (second box on the left side). The search is initiated by clicking "Go." See Figure 13-23.

[41]Id. at 13.

[42]*Id.* at 18.

[43]*Id.* at 21.

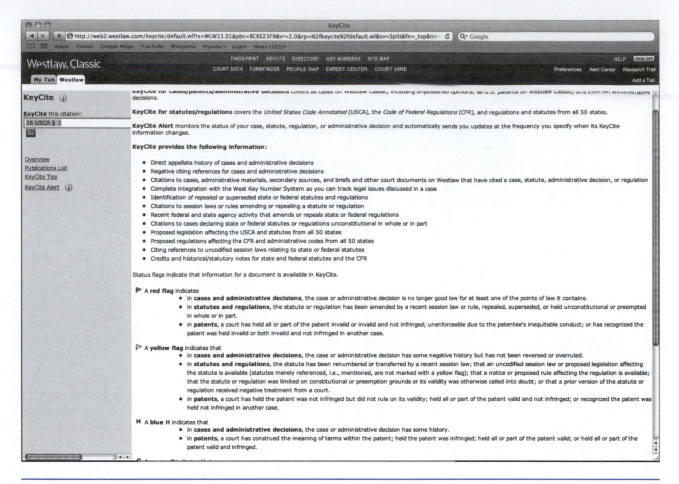

FIGURE 13-23 The Left Side of the KeyCite Welcome Screen[44]

A KeyCite button is located on the toolbar at the top of any page. Clicking "KeyCite" will display the KeyCite page. See Figure 13-24.

The user can KeyCite a document from within the document by clicking either "History" or "Citing References" on the left-hand side of the screen. If the case results are on a full-screen page, "Links for . . ." may be clicked in the top right-hand corner of the page. Figure 13-25 shows the available sources.

Status flags can also be used to access KeyCite. The flag indicates that more information is available in KeyCite. See Figure 13-26.

In summary, the procedure for researching with KeyCite is as follows:

When viewing the case in Westlaw, the KeyCite information appears on the left side of the screen. A status flag (red, yellow, or a blue "H") is displayed at the top, left-hand corner of the case. (If a statute, the word "update" will appear.) Clicking the flag will access KeyCite, or the buttons on the left-hand section of the screen may be used.

Clicking "Full History" will provide the direct history and negative citing references. Clicking "Direct History" will show a graphic display of the history of the case.

KeyCite can be entered without viewing the source first:

1. Sign in to www.westlaw.com.
2. Click on the KeyCite tab at the top of the screen.
3. Type in the citation and click "Go."

[44]Welcome to Westlaw. 2010. https://web2.westlaw.com/Welcome/Westlaw/default .wl?RS=WLW9.06&VR=2.0&FN=_top&MT=Westlaw&SV=Split

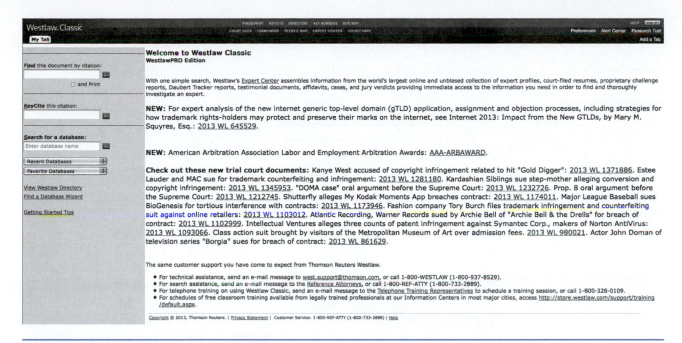

FIGURE 13-24 Westlaw Screen with Toolbar

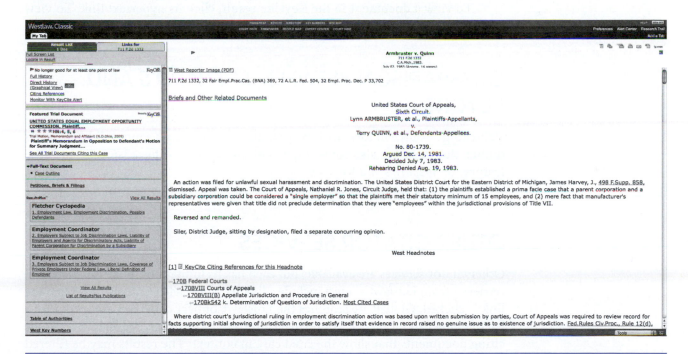

FIGURE 13-25 The Left Side of the Westlaw Screen for 711 F.2d 1332[45]

A citation can be checked by typing the citation:

1. Click the "Check a Citation in KeyCite" link at the Westlaw home page.
2. Type the citation of the source in the "Citation" box.
3. From the drop-down list under "Result," select the information to retrieve. The choices are "Full History," "Citing References," or "Negative History Only."

[45]*Armbruster v. Quinn*, 711 F.2d 1332 (6th Cir. 1983) https://web2.westlaw.com/find/default .wl?rs=WLW10.06&ifm=NotSet&fn=_top&sv=Split&cite=711+f2d+1332&vr=2.0&rp=%2ffind%2f default.wl&mt=Westlaw

Locate in Result

Links for 711 F.2d 1332 | Result List (1 Doc)

►

Armbruster v. Quinn
711 F.2d 1332
C.A.Mich.,1983.
July 07, 1983 (Approx. 14 pages)

West Reporter Image (PDF)

711 F.2d 1332, 32 Fair Empl.Prac.Cas. (BNA) 369, 72 A.L.R. Fed. 504, 32 Empl. Prac. Dec. P 33,702

Briefs and Other Related Documents

United States Court of Appeals,
Sixth Circuit.
Lynn ARMBRUSTER, et al., Plaintiffs-Appellants,
v.
Terry QUINN, et al., Defendants-Appellees.

No. 80-1739.
Argued Dec. 14, 1981.
Decided July 7, 1983.
Rehearing Denied Aug. 19, 1983.

FIGURE 13-26 Using Status Flags

Click "Go."

Click the "Citing References" link at the bottom of the page to view the list of citing references. If viewing the full history of a case, click the "Negative Only" link to view only negative history. To return to the full history, click the "Full History" link.

To view a document in the KeyCite result, click its hypertext link. To view the document's KeyCite result, click its KeyCite status flag.[46]

COMPARISON BETWEEN *SHEPARD'S* AND KEYCITE

Validating a source in KeyCite is very similar to validating a source with *Shepard's* online. But there are also some important differences. Table 13-6 compares the features of *Shepard's* and KeyCite.

Table 13-7 comparison between *Shepard's* and KeyCite signals.

OTHER CITATOR SERVICES

Other citator services are available, but each has its limitations. For example, cases retrieved from LoislawConnect include a link to a tool called GlobalCite. When the link is clicked, GlobalCite searches the LoislawConnect databases and provides a list of citing cases, called a "contextual summary." The list gives excerpts from the citing documents that show the cited case in context. The results may be filtered by negative, positive, neutral, or specific *Bluebook* treatment terms to see the precedential value of the case. The results can also be narrowed by keyword, type of law, jurisdiction, or court. The limitation to this service is that there is no clear indication of whether the case being cited is still "good law." Although some terms that indicate the treatment of the case are shown in a blue font, every citing reference

Negative treatment
Cases that have overruled or distinguished the cited case

---

[46]KeyCite Help. 2010. http://text.westlaw.com/welcome/wlto/help/default.aspx?fn=_top&rs=ACC S9.11&rp=%2Fwelcome%2Fwlto%2Fhelp%2Fdefault.aspx&helpkey=KeyCite&vr=2.0&ifm=NotSet

TABLE 13-6   A Comparison of Shepard's and KeyCite

What is being sought	KeyCite	Shepard's
Case, statute, or other authority	Can type citation in "find" box.	Can type citation in the open field.
History of found source	West attorney-editors provide the full history through the "flag" system and also provide a graphical view of the direct history. In addition, the negative citing references are listed immediately after the history.	Shepard's attorney-editors provide the full spectrum of the history. Shepard's includes an extensive analysis of cases, statutes, regulations, patents, and other primary sources.
Treatment of found source	West attorney-editors organize citing references under reasons for negative treatment, such as "abrogated by," "disagreed with by," and "declined to follow by." The neutral treatment is also provided. KeyCite does not use the term "followed." Treatment is noted with the "flag" system, and depth of treatment is represented by the "star" system.	Shepard's attorney-editors provide the full treatment analysis, including "followed" treatment and "questioned by." The term "questioned by" is unique to Shepard's. The citing references can be sorted by treatment type. Shepard's includes extensive analysis of cases, statutes, regulations, patents and other primary law sources.
Speed and ease of retrieval	A researcher cannot limit by treatment type, citing references are organized by treatment type. A researcher can limit by depth of treatment, categorized with the "star" system. To limit the KeyCite display, a button at the bottom of the citing references opens the KeyCite Limits screen. There the results can be limited by document type, headnotes, jurisdiction, date, and depth of treatment. The Locate feature allows the user to search within citing references using terms and connectors. KeyCite does not organize its answer sets by jurisdiction, making it hard to identify citations from a specific court.	Results are obtained on one screen, in one step. Shepard's Summary provides key references, editorial treatment and information on LexisNexis® headnotes from the case that match text in the citing cases. Navigation tools allow the user to go quickly to the parts of the report of greatest interest. Shepard's is organized by jurisdiction and court, so it is easy to spot citations relevant to the research. The FOCUS™ Restrict By link lets the researcher add custom restrictions by treatment, jurisdiction, date, or LexisNexis headnote, or add focus terms.
Currency	Only the obvious analysis is added right away. More subtle analysis may take longer.	Shepard's adds all history and treatment in a single step, typically within 24–48 hours.
Table of Authorities	KeyCite provides the analysis to all sources relied on in the cited case and gives the treatment of each source.	Shepard's has a similar product with the same name. The analysis follows the format for Shepard's.[47]
West's Key Numbers	Only West products have the headnotes and key number system. Specific points of law can be checked using these features.	Shepard's is not linked to West headnotes or the West key number system.
Alert System	Westlaw provides KeyCite Alert, which will automatically provide updates when additional references affect the cited authority after the date of the original research.	Shepard's Alert provides an automatic update at intervals specified by the user. Four tabs with Alert, Continuous Alerts, Shepard's Alert, and CourtLink Alert are available depending on subscription service. The CourtLink Alert is unique to LexisNexis.

[47]Shepard's and KeyCite. 2008. http://law.lexisnexis.com/literature/Shepards_vs_%20KeyCite.pdf

TABLE 13-7 *Shepard's* and KeyCite Signals

	LexisNexis (*Shepard's*)	Westlaw (KeyCite)
Negative treatment: Case is not good law for at least one of its points (overruled or reversed); statute has been amended or repealed	Red stop sign	Red status flag
Questioned by: Citing opinions question continuing validity or precedential value of case because of intervening circumstances, including judicial or legislative overruling	Orange Q	
Caution: Case has some negative history (limited, criticized); statute has section affected by pending legislation	Yellow triangle	Yellow status flag
Positive treatment: History or treatment of case has positive impact on case (affirmed, followed)	Green diamond with plus sign	
Case has some analysis which is neither positive nor negative	A in blue circle: A= analysis	
Case has some history	A in blue circle: A= analysis	Blue H
Case is cited, with no analysis	I in blue circle	Green C

<u>The cases listed in the KeyCite or *Shepard's* results may be marked as follows:</u>

	LexisNexis (*Shepard's*)	Westlaw (KeyCite)
Editorial treatment, editorial analysis	For example, followed, criticized, distinguished, harmonized, and explained.	For example, distinguished by, declined to extend, disagreement, and recognized by.
	Identifies at a glance whether a case is overruled for one point of law, but followed on another, as well as if one jurisdiction followed but another overruled.	Examined by, discussed by, cited by, mentioned by (same as depth of treatment stars); KeyCite does not uncover these splits of authority at a glance.
Citing case or decision directly quotes cited case		Quotation marks appear after the citation.
Indicates which headnotes from the case in question are discussed in the subsequent case	LexisNexis headnotes indicated after the citation.	Westlaw headnotes indicated after the citation.
Depth of treatment of cited case	Very negative treatment such as overruled, validity questioned for example questioned by, mild negative for example criticized, neutral for example explained, to the positive for example followed by.	One to four stars, from mentioned to extended examination. *Caveat:* The stars indicate how *long* the case talked about the case in question. Cases with one star may have relied heavily on the case, but did not go on at length.

<u>Search Features and other functions of KeyCite v. Shepard's:</u>

	LexisNexis (Shepard's)	Westlaw (KeyCite)
Table of authorities in cited case	Table of authorities (TOA) with editorial treatment to indicate how the case in question treated the cases it cited to.	TOA has no editorial treatment. WestlawNext does not have TOA.
	LexisAdvance uses Trail of Authorities in place of TOA. Click Activate Passages and squares will appear around the issues in the case. Click in the issue box for a list of subsequent cases dealing with that issue.	

	FOCUS	LOCATE
To search within results	LexisAdvance has narrow by options in the left bar.	WestlawNext uses Narrow by Filters.
Limiting the results	By editorial analysis (distinguished, followed, cited by, for example; focus (search for terms in the cases), date, jurisdiction, LexisNexis headnotes and Westlaw headnotes. Can also limit by positive or negative treatment and type of document using the summary table at beginning of the *Shepard's* report. LexisNexis results are arranged by jurisdiction. LexisAdvance can limit by editorial analysis (such as distinguished, followed, and cited by); jurisdiction; Lexis headnote; search terms; date.	Westlaw headnotes, locate (search for terms in the cases), jurisdiction, date, depth of treatment and document type. Filtering options are on separate pages. WestlawNext has all filtering available from the left bar. There is an additional filter for reported v. unreported.
Graphical Chart of Citing Cases	LexisAdvance has a Citing Decisions Grid showing a graphical representation of the number citing cases by court by analysis (positive, negative, etc.) and by year by analysis. *Shepard's* Graphical also shows subsequent citing cases to indicate where the case stands today.	no
Graphical History	Not in Classic Lexis, but LexisAdvance has a map, *Shepard's* Graphical, showing subsequent appellate history, both in the case itself and subsequent citing cases.	Yes—helpful in procedurally complex cases, and to identify court hierarchy in different states.[48]

must be read to determine the status of the cited case. GlobalCite operates similarly with statutes.[49] Figure 13-27 provides a screen showing the GlobalCite results.

CaseMAKER, a research service originally launched by the Ohio Bar Association, has a citator function called CASECheck+. This feature provides cases that have cited the case being read. This information appears at the time the case is displayed, validating whether the case is still good law. Once a case is located, users are provided with both positive and negative treatments. The link to negative treatments presents the citation history for federal and state cases. It also highlights the negative treatment within the case.[50] The cases are noted with the icons shown in Figure 13-28.

Fastcase includes a service called Authority Check, which identifies the most authoritative cases in the results, and reports how often each case in the results list has been cited. It also provides a timeline view of the search results that shows the user how relevant each case is in relation to the query used. Additional information is available by clicking each of the references.[51] As shown in Figure 13-29, a user would look at Authority Check and click the hyperlink "14" to generate the authority check report.

The authority check report provides links to later citing cases but does not provide treatment information, as shown in Figure 13-30.

Authority Check does not provide the user with information on whether the case is still good law.[52] A researcher must always use a citator service.

[48]Cleveland State University. Cleveland-Marshall College of Law. *Shepard's* and Keycite Compared. 2010. https://www.law.csuohio.edu/lawlibrary/guides/shepardskeycite

[49]Legal Research Tools: GlobalCite®. 2011. http://www.loislaw.com/product/information/research/tools/globalcite.htm

[50]Casemaker. Casemaker 2.2. 2012. http://www.casemaker.us/

[51]Fastcase. What is Fastcase. 2011. http://www.fastcase.com/whatisfastcase/

[52]Fastcase. *Using Authority Check*. 2012. http://www.fastcase.com/wp-content/uploads/2009/12/Introduction-to-Fastcase-2012-Handouts1.pdf

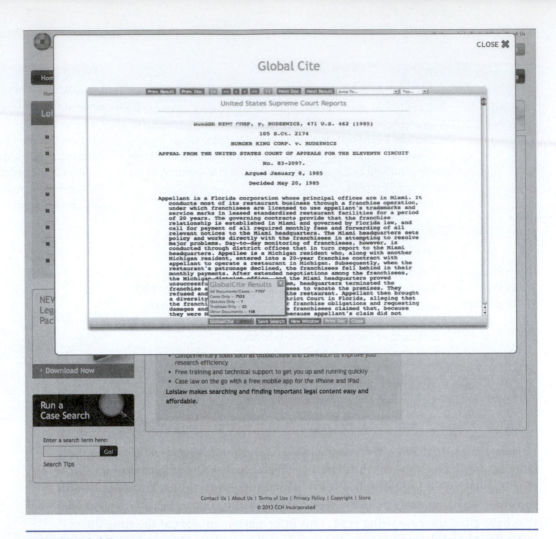

FIGURE 13-27 GlobalCite

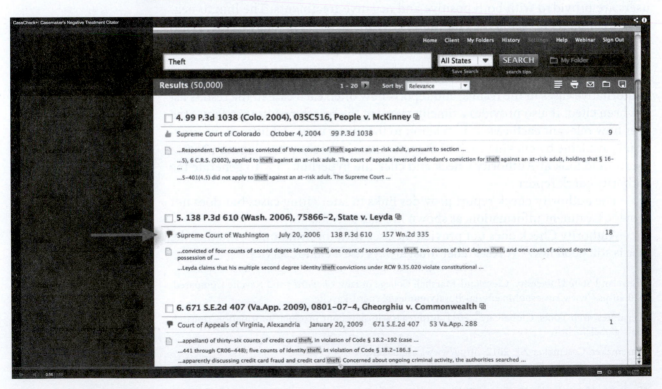

FIGURE 13-28 CASEcheck+

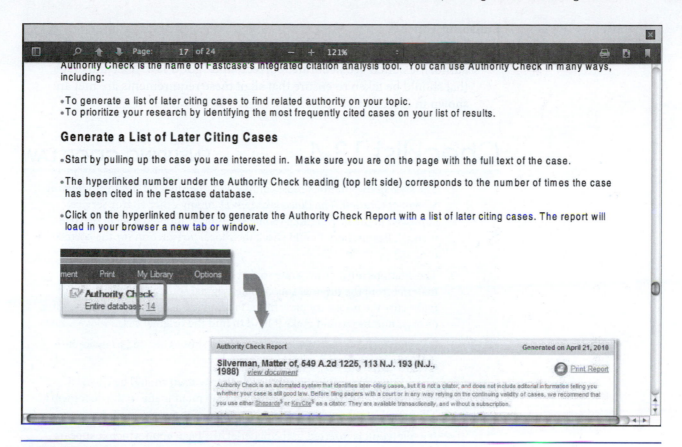

FIGURE 13-29 Authority Check in Fastcase

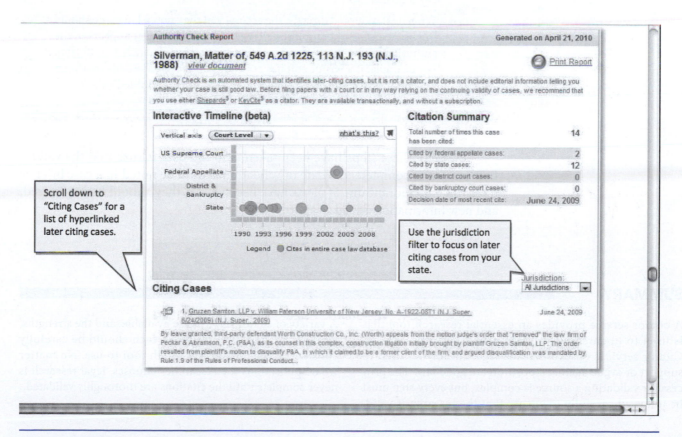

FIGURE 13-30 Authority Check Report

Finishing Touches

A researcher is not finished researching until it is confirmed that the authorities cited are accurate, correct, and "good law." Certain steps that should be taken to ensure that all of these requirements are met are shown in Checklist 13-4.

Checklist 13-4 ENSURING GOOD LAW

1. The style of the citations must comply with the rules set out in *A Uniform System of Citation: The Bluebook, ALWD,* or any other citator service approved in the jurisdiction. (Some states have adopted a separate style manual. Researchers should check their local jurisdiction for the correct format.)

2. The citations must be accurate so that the reader can find and read the material from the original source. The original source should be read to make sure the necessary parts of the citation are accurate. A wrong volume or page number would make it hard to find the original case.

3. To validate the authorities, a citator service should be used to make sure the authorities are still "good law."

4. The accuracy or applicability of the authority itself should be checked. Does the authority actually support the statement made in the document? The actual law should be read and analyzed, not merely cited.

5. If a quotation is inserted in the material, the page upon which it appears should be verified. If parallel citations are listed, those page numbers must be confirmed, too.

6. When text is quoted directly, the accuracy of the quoted language should be checked. The quotation should be written *exactly* as it appears in the authority, or else the writer must identify any changes such as with [sic]. For example, if a writer emphasizes with italics certain words that were not emphasized in the original, the note "emphasis added" should be placed in brackets at the end of the quotation.

Once all these steps have been taken, and the user is sure that the validation process is complete, the date of validation should be noted in a case brief or interoffice memorandum. If alerts have been set up, they should be monitored, and new information added as appropriate.

SUMMARY

A citator service provides an essential research tool that is used to update and validate primary sources of law. Citator services ensure that the legal authorities used to support or argue against a position are good law. The process for validating a source is complex, but every step must be followed carefully to ensure that the research is valid.

A variety of citator services are available, and the strengths, weaknesses, and capabilities of each should be carefully considered when choosing which tool to use. No matter what applications the researcher chooses, legal research is never complete until the citations are thoroughly validated.

REVIEW **QUESTIONS**

1. Explain the use of a citator service and describe its purposes.
2. Summarize the validation process and describe all the essential steps in validating a case or statute.
3. Describe three reasons *Shepard's* is used.
4. Explain three differences between *Shepard's* in print and online.
5. If you find that your cited case has been overruled, what should you do? Why? Does the overruled case have any value? Why?
6. Give three important ways KeyCite differs from *Shepard's*.
7. What are the KeyCite flags, and how do they help in the validation process?
8. What are the KeyCite stars? If you find a case with two stars, what does it mean?
9. Is there a reason to search all available citator sets when doing research? If so, what is the reason? What would be searched?
10. If you find no references under your cited case, what does it mean?
11. What is the value of BriefCheck and WestCheck?
12. What is the value of other citators such as Lexcite and Auto-Cite?

APPLICATION **EXERCISES**

Perform validation searches for the following. If you have access to both *Shepard's* and KeyCite services, use both. Otherwise, identify the service used and list any significant steps taken. Print or copy the direct history of each case. Is there any negative history? How many citing references are there? For all even-numbered citations, restrict the validation to a specific jurisdiction or a specific headnote. Identify what you did and how many citing references were listed.

1. 820 N.E.2d 1089
2. 490 U.S. 19
3. 19 U.S.C. § 160
4. 907 F.2d 707
5. 112 Cal. App. 157
6. 215 S.W.2d 701
7. 214 Az. 293
8. 372 U.S. 335
9. 248 N.Y. 339
10. 451 So. 2d 808
11. 8 U.S.C. § 1153
12. 42 U.S.C. §1982
13. 18 U.S.C. §2
14. 28 U.S.C. §2246
15. Age Discrimination in Employment Act of 1967
16. National Trails Systems Act
17. Export Apple and Pear Act
18. 28 U.S.C. § 1253

QUICK **CHECK**

1. This term means that attorneys must disclose to the court any legal authority in the controlling jurisdiction known to the lawyer to be directly adverse to the position of the client, and not disclosed by opposing counsel.
   a. citator
   b. Shepardizing
   c. candor to the court
   d. rules of court
2. You can validate case law by using_____.
   a. an online citator only
   b. a print form citatory only
   c. a secondary source
   d. both an online and printed citator
3. Which of the following is a type of citator?
   a. CiteLaw
   b. LegalCite
   c. FindLaw
   d. KeyCite
4. Which of the following is an advantage to using an online citator?
   a. Information is current and there is no need to check supplements or updates.
   b. Abbreviations and hyperlinks to citing authorities are used.
   c. Negative information is not highlighted.
   d. There are supplements you must check.
5. The _____ provide(s) the published background of the same case you are checking.
   a. signals of the case
   b. treatment of the case
   c. rules of the case
   d. history of the case

6. What is one reason to provide parallel citations?
   a. because they are required by law
   b. because they provide the history of a case
   c. because they provide the treatment of a case
   d. because they provide directions to other locations where the case may be found

7. What type of law is also known as judge-made law?
   a. common law
   b. stare decisis
   c. case
   d. Shepardized
   e. citator law

8. A case with the same or similar facts and issues as the client's case that will provide guidance to the judge when deciding your case is known as _____.
   a. Shepardized
   b. precedent
   c. *stare decisis*
   d. citator law
   e. case law

9. A red flag in a KeyCite case means the case is an important case that should be used.
   a. True
   b. False

10. In KeyCite terms, the cited case is the case being validated, and citing resources are those resources that have been used in the client's case being researched.
    a. True
    b. False

INTERNET **RESEARCH**

1. Locate the tutorial for one of the *Shepard's* products and complete it. Print out the last page of the tutorial.

2. Locate the tutorial for one of the West products and complete it. Print out the last page of the tutorial.

MEDIA **RESOURCES**

Fastcase tutorials	http://www.fastcase.com/smarter-tools/
LexisNexis product tutorials	http://www.lexisnexis.com/COMMUNITY/DOWNLOADANDSUPPORTCENTER/media/p/4332.aspx
Shepard's® tour	http://web.lexis.com/help/multimedia/detect.asp?sPage=shepards and the general site http://www.lexisnexis.com/government/solutions/research/shepards.aspx

INTERNET **RESOURCES**

Auto-Cite®:	http://support.lexisnexis.com/online/Record.asp?ARTICLEID=Auto_Cite_Components
Georgetown Law Library. *LRW Research Tutorials*:	http://www.ll.georgetown.edu/tutorials/
Law School 2009: How to Check Citations:	http://west.thomson.com/productdetail/1-5790-5/RM157905/productdetail.aspx
LexisNexis Paralegal User's Guide:	http://www.lexisnexis.com/documents/LawSchoolTutorials/20070511013250_small.pdf
LexisNexis Take a Tour:	http://web.lexis.com/help/multimedia/detect.asp?sPage=shepards
Westlaw®	http://west.thomson.com/westlaw/default.aspx?promcode=571230

chapter **fourteen**

THE FOUNDATION OF WRITING

lenetstan/Shutterstock

LEARNING OBJECTIVES

After completing this chapter, students should be able to:

1. Write clear and concise legal memoranda, briefs, letters, and documents.

2. Communicate findings in an appropriate written format.

3. Apply effective editing skills.

4. Learn accurate proofreading techniques.

5. Understand the importance of revision in legal writing.

6. Practice critical self-editing and rewriting, including evaluation for organization, clarity, and style.

7. Identify effective legal writing.

CHAPTER OVERVIEW

The aim of all writing is to communicate. In the legal setting, writing must communicate ideas logically and clearly. Legal writing also requires strong vocabulary, grammar, and punctuation skills. This chapter identifies common problems with legal writing, and guide students toward becoming more effective legal writers.

OPENING SCENARIO

Although legal writing was a major focus of his paralegal training program, John was still very surprised at how much writing was required at the law office. Drafting letters to clients, courts, insurance companies, and court reporters consumed a huge amount of time. Fortunately, John was armed with strong writing skills that he had developed in his paralegal program.

Although the firm had its own preferences for the style and format of some documents and letters, John was able to adapt. He knew the formats for all kinds of letters, and Jami, his supervising attorney, was quite impressed. His schooling paid off again!

GENERAL OVERVIEW OF LEGAL WRITING

In order to communicate effectively, writers need first to understand their subject and then to help their readers understand it, too. Most writing should answer a basic set of questions, such as

- Who is the writer?
- What is this writing about?
- What does the writer want?
- Why does it matter?

These questions must also be answered when writing in the legal setting. This holds true whether the writer is creating letters, memoranda, contracts, or briefs.

Legal writing serves many important functions in modern society. It records transactions, provides rules to follow, relays messages, and binds parties. Legal writing is the basis of everyday transactions and it can influence the future. It must be accurate, understandable, legible, organized, and complete.

The paralegal often assumes the role of a professional author. Although a paralegal is not permitted to prepare any legal document for a client without the supervision of an attorney, the paralegal is often placed in situations where he or she must draft many of the attorney's documents. When paralegals prepare legal documents, they must marshal all the skills of an effective legal writer.

To be effective, any writer must always be aware of the potential audience of a document. Although a paralegal may prepare a particular document for the client, many others may read the document as well. At some point, an opposing party and the party's counsel, or a judge, may also read it. When considering an audience, appropriate vocabulary is an important factor. Those unfamiliar with legal terminology or situations may also be part of the audience. It is incumbent upon the paralegal to communicate in a way that the audience can understand.

Lawyers and paralegals communicate with each other as part of a community that shares a common legal language. However, both lawyers and paralegals also communicate with people outside the legal community. Therefore, adapting the writing to the audience is vital.

WRITING BASICS

Some people who enter the legal field will already have strong writing backgrounds and will be comfortable with the mechanics of writing, as well as the writing process. However, others may not be as comfortable with their writing skills. Some may be skillful writers in some settings, but may be unfamiliar with the techniques and structures of legal writing. For example, in some settings, some flexibility with punctuation or grammar may be acceptable. In the legal field, however, correct grammar and punctuation is crucial. Differences in mechanics may be critical to the meaning of a sentence in a contract or a will.

The market is filled with books to assist with writing style and grammar. The following is a list of a few of the best resources. It is by no means an exhaustive list, nor is it a ranking.

1. *The Elements of Style*, by William Strunk, Jr., and E. B. White
2. *Bird by Bird: Some Instructions on Writing and Life*, by Anne Lamott
3. *The Redbook: A Manual on Legal Style*, by Bryan A. Garner
4. *Plain English for Lawyers*, by Richard C Wydick
5. *The Chicago Manual of Style*
6. *The Little Book on Legal Writing*, by Alan L. Dworsky

Various websites also provide additional information on writing effectively, such as the Purdue University Online Writing Lab, which offers writing, research, grammar, and style guides.[1] Style guides may also be found at public libraries or at a local bookstore. Having a good reference manual on hand will save time and energy during the writing process. Exhibit 14-1 shows some suggested guidelines on the basics of writing.

THE WRITING PROCESS

Many claim that they are able to sit down and immediately begin to write. But the majority of people must take the time to think and plan before beginning. The planning process provides a way to capture ideas and organize them. Usually, ideas are organized in something that resembles an outline. The legal writing process is no exception. It provides a way to organize legal research and analysis into a strong piece of writing.

Legal writing can serve a wide variety of purposes. It may simply relay results of a research project or summarize information collected to respond to discovery requests. It may be a letter to a client explaining his or her potential liability. It may be a trial brief. The purpose of the end product must be carefully considered throughout the writing process.

EXHIBIT 14-1   BASICS OF WRITING

Tell the reader everything in the first two sentences.

Do not use adjectives. An adjective equals an assertion, which equals an opinion, which equals doubt.

When in doubt, quote. Do not paraphrase unless you are totally certain that you comprehend the legal significance of every word of the paraphrased material.

Let the reader know, point by point, where confirmation of what you said can be found.

If a statute or a contract is central to the problem, quote it immediately.

Identify every document by preparer, addressee (if any), and date.

Give the full name of an entity the first time you mention it before resorting to an abbreviation.

Avoid confusion between the ordinary meaning of a certain phrase and its specialized meaning in a certain legal context by using the phrase "within the meaning of".[2]

---

[1]The Writing Lab, The OWL at Purdue, the English department, and Purdue University. *The Purdue Online Writing Lab*. 1995-2012. http://owl.english.purdue.edu/

[2]Hurd, H.T. (1986). Writing for Lawyers. Legal Assistant Today. 47.

The writing process has three stages: pre-writing, writing, and editing. In the pre-writing stage, the writer researches and analyzes the subject being written about and creates an outline. During the writing stage, all of the research and analysis comes together in a form that is tailored to its intended audience. In editing, or post-writing, the document is revised, edited, proofread, and printed as a final draft.

Many writers think that the first draft of the document will be the only or final draft, but good writing usually requires multiple revisions. Once the first draft is finished, more work is needed to revise, edit, and polish the document. Rewriting allows the writer to review all of the steps in the process to make sure that the purpose of the document has been met. Words and phrases are examined to determine if alternate terms are more effective, or more appropriate for the audience. The overall document is reviewed to confirm that it is organized, logical, and fluid. The research is also checked to make sure it is applicable and that it has been properly updated.

The Prewriting Stage

In prewriting, the writer should begin by asking basic questions about the assignment:

- Is the assignment understood?
- What is the purpose of the assignment?
- What type of document is the end product?
- Who is the audience?
- Are there any time constraints?

Understanding the Assignment The first priority of the paralegal is to make sure the assignment is understood. It is often appropriate to draft a short memo to the supervisor who assigned the task just to clarify what was asked. It may be particularly important if the assignment was given by word of mouth, because when information is given orally, key points are often left out. Restating the issue may help the writer reflect on the assignment and give the supervisor the opportunity to confirm that it is understood, or determine if more information is needed. Getting confirmation at the beginning of the assignment avoids wasting time on work that was not needed or intended.

Every product of legal writing has its own set of considerations, whether it is a client letter, an interoffice memorandum, or a pleading. For example, if a letter is written to a client, it may be transmitting information that conveys a legal opinion. If the correspondence being drafted gives any type of legal advice or an opinion, the paralegal may not sign it. A paralegal may sign the document only if the correspondence is *transmittal* or *informational* in nature, and if the firm allows paralegals to sign such correspondence.

Other considerations should be taken into account when writing for a supervisor. A supervisor may make an assignment without giving full consideration of what the outcome might be. In addition, in a workplace with more than one supervisor, each may have different expectations. In some cases, a supervisor may have access to more information than he or she provides to the paralegal when giving the assignment. This is another reason to submit a short memo back to the supervisor reiterating the assignment. It may also be useful to request sample documents that have been previously prepared for, or by, the supervisor. These may provide the best information about the supervisor's expectations.

Time constraints are also an important consideration during the prewriting stage. Time limits, deadlines, and schedules are ubiquitous in legal writing. If

Transmittal letters
Letters that generally accompany other documents and provide information about the documents transmitted. These are also generally called *cover letters*.

Informational letter
Correspondence that provides information to the reader.

there is a deadline, it's important to set aside time to complete all necessary stages of the writing process. Good research may be pointless if enough time is not left to communicate it effectively. Good writing may be pointless if it is not based on good research.

Documents may also be constrained by limitations on length. Some rules of court dictate the maximum lengths of briefs and pleadings. For example, appellate rules may specify the number of pages of an appellant's brief. Such limitations should be kept in mind during the entire writing process. While all applicable law should be gathered to support a position during the research stage, the writer may need to be more selective in the pieces of law to include in the final document because of a length limit. The document should also be organized so that all questions are adequately addressed, while staying within the length limit.

Organization   Possibly the most important step in the pre-writing process is drafting an outline. Preparing an outline allows the writer to organize ideas at the beginning of the writing process and provides the structure or framework for the document. An outline also allows the writer to break a complex writing task into manageable pieces. Just as breaking a statute into its elements aids comprehension, writing an outline breaks up a problem into its parts.

An outline can be created in a variety of ways. Some formats use complete topic sentences, while others use key words or phrases. Some use roman numerals and letters for organization, while others find these to be less important. As writers develop their skills, they often find that some formats work better than others. All that matters is that the outline can be understood by the writer.

The first step in the organizing phase of a writing project is to check with a supervisor to see if there is a standard format that is used in the office for that type of document. The office may have a standard format for a particular type of correspondence or interoffice memorandum. If the office requires a special format, then that format should be used as the basis for the outline. If documents are to be filed in court, court rules should be checked to see if they prescribe a format that must be used when submitting the documents to a particular court. Again, this format should be the basis for the outline.

It is often helpful to develop the outline around the facts and issues of the assignment. In addition, creating the outline is easier if it is broken into small pieces. Outlines are not stagnant, and often it is necessary to modify the outline as research progresses. Sections of the outline can be expanded into subtopics as the research unfolds. Sometimes an outline may need to be completely rewritten because the research has uncovered unanticipated information.

Most legal writing follows a basic formula for each point of law, often referred to as the IRAC format. With some variation, each point will include the issue or question, the rule of law that governs the issue or question, the analysis of the rule or law, and a conclusion. Each point in the outline should track this formula.

While the outline may be dependent on the requirements of office or court rules, there are some basic guidelines that can be applied to all outlines. First, the format should be consistent throughout the outline. If Roman numerals or capital letters are used for the initial major headings, then the same system should be used for all major headings. If narrative sentences, keywords, or phrases are used, that style should be used consistently throughout. Consistency will make the outline easier to use when drafting the final document. See Exhibits 14-2 and 14-3 for examples of formatting.

TIP

An outline can help a writer with time management. The outline provides stop and go points that the writer can use to pause or continue working.

EXHIBIT 14-2   FORMATTING AN OUTLINE

Heading
Statement of the assignment
Issue(s)

    I. [Issue One]
   II. [Issue Two]

Facts
Analysis

    I. [Issue One]
        A. Introduction to analysis of issue
        B. Rule of law
           1. Statement of the rule
           2. Application to client's facts
        C. Case law
           1. Facts of case
           2. Rule of law applied to the facts in the case and in the client's situation
           3. Application of the law from the case to the client's facts
        D. Counteranalysis
   II. [Issue Two]
        A. Introduction to analysis of issue
        B. Rule of law
           1. Statement of the rule
           2. Application to client's facts
        C. Case law
           1. Facts of case
           2. Rule of law applied to the facts in the case and in the client's situation
           3. Application of the law from the case to the client's facts
        D. Counteranalysis

Conclusions
Recommendations

Thesis statement
A condensed version of the main idea of the document. The thesis statement is usually no more than one or two sentences long and is presented in the first paragraph of the document.

Placement of Information The persuasive force of writing often depends on where different items of information are placed within the document. Information should be placed strategically. In general, the beginning and the ending of any writing should contain the most important information. A ***thesis statement***

EXHIBIT 14-3   FORMAT FOR SIMPLE INTEROFFICE MEMORANDUM

1. Heading
2. Statement of the assignment
3. Issue(s)
4. Facts
5. Analysis
6. Conclusions
7. Recommendations

---

is a sentence or two at the beginning that provides the reader with the essence or the main point of the document. Thus, readers can see the direction of the writing as soon as they read the beginning. The conclusion will reinforce the main points that were made, leaving those points fresh in the reader's mind. Often, readers tend to look at the end of the material to see the conclusion.

The Drafting Phase

For most people, the drafting phase may be the hardest part of the writing process. Even when it is easy to collect and research ideas, it may be very difficult to organize those ideas into a written document. This is sometimes referred to as "writer's block." One way to overcome writer's block is simply to begin putting something on paper. Whether it is good or bad doesn't really matter, because it can always be revised or rewritten.

Writers often benefit from a good working environment. Some write well early in the morning, while others prefer writing at midnight or later. Some writers adjust their schedule so that they are doing their most challenging work at the times they do their best writing. It is also important to make sure that the work location has all the resources that are needed to complete the project. Research sources, file information, and writing tools should be readily available. Having all of the resources in one place will eliminate unnecessary interruptions.

Sometimes a writer can get stuck on a particular section. If this happens, it may help to move on to a different section of the project and then come back to the problematic section later. This allows the writer to continue moving forward towards the goal instead of wasting time and becoming more frustrated with one section.

Tone   The type of end product dictates, to a large degree, the tone of the document. The tone of the document should be appropriate for its audience. If the document is an interoffice memorandum, the tone should be neutral, so that both sides of the question can be presented and the legal team can view an issue objectively. If the document is going outside the firm to an adversary or a court, the tone should be persuasive, with advocacy in mind.

If the document is to be sent to adverse counsel, the language of the document should be reasonable and measured. Although such correspondence is written as an advocate, the language should never be confrontational. In these letters, it is permissible to use technical legal terms, but it should not sound as if the writer is teaching the recipient about the law. Most documents going to someone outside the firm should be reviewed and signed by a supervisor, particularly if it is giving legal advice or a legal opinion.

Voice   The voice chosen by the writer can have a powerful effect on the message being conveyed. Active voice is strong, compelling, and persuasive. It is often more forceful and easier to understand because the actor is identified at the beginning of the sentence. Active voice immediately focuses the attention on the actor and identifies the actor's actions.

Passive voice allows a writer to deflect the attention from the actor to the object of the sentence. It is also useful when the actor is not known or is not important to the sentence. The object of the sentence that is acted upon is emphasized when passive voice is used. Exhibit 14-4 shows examples of active and passive voice.

Using Legal Language and Vocabulary   The language and vocabulary used should be tailored for the audience. If the document is going to a client, the language of the document should be clear and written in a language that the client can understand. If the client is new to the world of litigation, then he or she may not

> **TIP**
>
> Passive voice is often identified when the phrase "*by the ___*" (by the judge; by the defendant) is used. If the phrase can be changed to say, "*The judge ruled . . .*" or "*the defendant argued . . .*" and the sentence makes sense, then that phrase has an active voice.

EXHIBIT 14-4 ACTIVE AND PASSIVE VOICE

Active Voice	Passive Voice
The judge ruled against the defendant on the motion *in limine*.	The motion *in limine* was ruled on by the judge.
The defendant breached the contract when he failed to deliver the materials.	The contract was breached because the materials were not delivered. (The actor is not identified)
The defendant car dealer intentionally sold a car with defective brakes to the plaintiff.	The car with defective brakes was sold by the defendant car dealer.
The defendant car dealer intentionally sold a car with defective brakes to the plaintiff.	The car with defective brakes was sold to the plaintiff. (Here the defendant is not mentioned at all.)

TIP

The goal in writing is to communicate, not to overwhelm or frustrate the reader.

understand the legal jargon associated with the court system and the process may need to be explained in simpler terms. However, the client may be someone who is sophisticated in legal matters and may be comfortable with some of the technical terminology. Still other clients may fall somewhere in between. It is often best to use straightforward and simple language that will not overwhelm or frustrate the client.

Writing for the court requires a special style and caliber of writing. When addressing the court, it should be assumed that the judge understands the case and the law. However, most judges expect a strong argument, which should be readily apparent whether the judge reads the briefs personally, or a law clerk provides a summary of the document. However, although briefs should be persuasive, concise writing is encouraged.

Using Headings   Headings provide the reader with points of reference within the body of the writing. They are signposts to the content being discussed. If the text is long, headings help guide the reader. Depending on the audience, the headings may be used to persuade. For example, if a brief is being submitted to court, the headings could be written to advocate the client's position before the judge begins to read the text. In pleadings or briefs, headings are usually written in complete sentences. In an interoffice memorandum, the headings may be more neutral and may consist of only key words and phrases.

Writing Paragraphs   In the final document, sentences are grouped to form paragraphs. Each paragraph should relate to a single concept or idea. The first sentence of the paragraph should be a *topic sentence* that summarizes the main idea of the paragraph. The beginning and ending of every paragraph should be strong enough to attract the reader's attention. Negative information that the writer wants to minimize should be buried in the middle of the paragraph.

Legal writing is most effective when sentences are written in the active voice, with the subject placed close to the verb. The reader should be able to understand the sentence easily without having to decipher its meaning. In most instances, sentences should be short, with no more than 25 words, although they may be longer when appropriate. Complex or compound sentences may confuse the reader and should be avoided. However, every sentence should have a subject and a verb. *Sentence fragments*, or incomplete sentences, are phrases that are grammatically incorrect because they lack a subject or predicate. Many times, when a writer begins a sentence with a conjunction such as "because" or "as," a fragment will be created.

Topic sentence

The sentence in a paragraph that introduces or summarizes the main idea of the paragraph.

Sentence fragment

An incomplete sentence that does not contain both a subject and a verb, or that contains both a subject and a verb but expresses an idea incompletely. An example of a sentence fragment is "Among the reasons the defendant pled guilty."

Example

> **Sentence fragment:** As the plaintiff was walking in the crosswalk.
> **Correct:** The defendant lost control of the vehicle and hit the plaintiff as the plaintiff was walking in the crosswalk.

The sentence fragment is missing a subject and a verb. The correct sentence has a subject (the defendant) and a compound verb (lost and hit) that shows what the plaintiff was doing.

Example

> **Sentence Fragment:** Because the contract was voided.
> **Correct:** Because the contract was voided, the plaintiff was not required to pay the balance.

At first, this looks like a sentence because the word "contract" appears to be the subject, and "was voided" seems to be the verb. However, the word "because" makes this a dependent clause or phrase. The independent clause that would provide the main subject and verb is missing.

A *transition sentence* is sometimes used to connect one paragraph or section to the next. Many words can act as transition words, and choosing a variety of transition words will avoid make the writing more interesting.

All sentences and paragraphs should be parallel in construction. *Parallelism* means having all items agree. If the sentence describes a list, a compound object, or a group of activities, all items must be similar in grammatical form. If a prepositional phrase is used, all of the elements in the sentence must be in prepositional phrases. If the sentence uses gerunds, all of the items must be gerunds. See Example 14-1.

Parallelism is also needed when making a list. An article must be applied to each item in the list.

Example

> Give the documents to the chairman, the treasurer, and secretary.

This sentence is incorrect because it lacks parallelism. "The" should precede "secretary" in order to make all of the items parallel.

Parallel construction is also required in correlative expressions. These are pairs of phrases that incorporate certain words to make a comparison. Those words

Transition sentence
A sentence that provides the reader with the connection from one paragraph to the next.

Parallelism
The use of similar structure, verb tense, or number in related words, phrases, or clauses.

TIP

A thesaurus can be valuable when doing any kind of writing. It can provide alternate terms that will keep your reader interested. "For example," "therefore," and "however" are common transition words and phrases. But if they were the only transitions used, the writing would become monotonous. Instead of "for example," "specifically," "that is," or "for instance" could be used. Alternative terms for "therefore" include "as a result," "consequently," or "accordingly." Instead of using "however" one could use "although," "conversely," or "on the other hand." Spice up your writing with a thesaurus, but use alternate terms only as appropriate.

EXAMPLE 14-1 PARALLELISM

The following list is incorrect because it does not use parallel construction:
  The goals of this chapter are as follows:

- to provide a foundation for using proper grammar,
- educating users on paragraph formation,
- to improve the ability of the future paralegal to draft better documents, and
- create an ability to present arguments.

In this example, two items are prepositional phrases. "to provide" and "to improve" are prepositional phrases. "educating" is a gerund (a verb ending in "ing"), and either it must be changed to "to educate" to agree with the other items, or "to provide" and "to improve" must be changed to "providing" and "improving." "create" is a verb, and depending on how the other sentences were changed, it must be transformed into a gerund ("creating") or a prepositional phrase ("to create") to make it consistent with the other three list entries.

EXAMPLE 14-2 CORRELATIVE EXPRESSIONS

Incorrect: Either the defendant will be found guilty of first-degree murder or will accept a plea of manslaughter.

Correct: The defendant either will be found guilty of first-degree murder or will accept a plea of manslaughter.

When these correlated expressions are pairs (not only, but also), the complete pair must be used.

Incorrect: The defendant not only killed the neighbor but killed the daughter.

Correct: The defendant not only killed the neighbor but also killed the daughter.

Subject

A noun that carries out the action in the sentence.

Predicate

One of the two basic parts of a simple sentence. The predicate consists of the verb and all of the words that modify the verb or are governed by the verb, such as the direct object.

Modifier

A word or phrase that modifies something else.

Article

A word such as *a, and,* or *the* that is used as an adjective.

Adjective

A word used to describe a noun or pronoun.

Adverb

A word used to modify a verb, adjective, another adverb, or a phrase or clause, by expressing time, place, manner, degree, or cause. Adverbs often end in *–ly*.

Predicate noun

A noun or noun phrase that follows the form of the "be" verbs, and renames, or gives meaning, to the subject.

Predicate adjective

An adjective that comes after an intransitive linking verb and describes the subject.

Compound subject

Two subjects that appear in the same sentence.

Compound predicate

Two predicates that appear in the same sentence.

Direct object

A noun in a sentence that receives the action of the verb.

Indirect object

A noun that comes before the direct object, usually identifying to whom or for whom the action is being done.

include *both, and; not only, but also; either, or; neither, nor; not, but*. The comparison words must be placed in the same location in each phrase. Example 14-2 provides an example of correlative expressions.

GRAMMAR

Rules of grammar exist so that people can communicate clearly and avoid confusion in their writing. Unfortunately, many of the rules that apply to everyday writing have been forgotten. In addition, some writers tend to think in one format and write in another which often leads to errors. The rules of grammar are best understood by learning the parts of speech and how they work together to form a sentence.

The Parts of Sentences

Long ago, students learned grammar by diagramming sentences. Although this method is used less frequently now, it is still a useful tool in learning grammar. Diagramming a sentence allows a person to visualize the structure of the sentence. The reference section of this chapter contains several visual aids regarding sentence diagramming. Figure 14-1 shows how the Preamble to the U.S. Constitution would be diagramed.

A sentence has two primary parts: the ***subject*** and the ***predicate***. The subject is the person or thing that is acting. The predicate contains the main verb and everything that follows that verb. A sentence may also contain ***modifiers***, which can be a variety of word types. Modifiers may be ***articles*** (*the, a, an*); ***adjectives*** (*blue, vibrant, belligerent*); or ***adverbs*** (*quickly, belligerently, meekly*). In addition, a sentence may have ***predicate nouns*** and ***predicate adjectives***, which are nouns and adjectives that follow the verb. For example, in the sentence "The judge was a brilliant litigator," "brilliant" is the predicate adjective and "litigator" is the predicate noun. A sentence can also have ***compound subjects*** and ***predicates***. "Compound" means there are two or more in a sentence—two or more subjects or two or more predicates. A sentence also could have compound verbs—the subject could be doing two things such as "listening" and "deciding."

A ***direct object*** is the person or thing upon which the verb is acting. For example, in the sentence "The judge ordered the jury to refrain from making assumptions," "jury" is the direct object, because it received the judge's order. ***Indirect objects*** tell to whom, for whom, or what the verb is doing. In the sentence

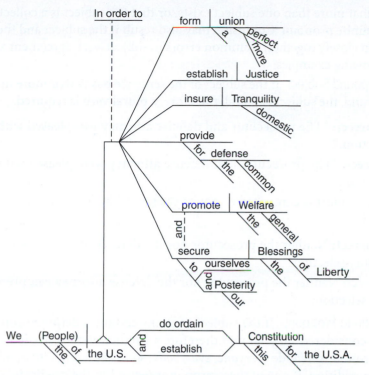

FIGURE 14-1 Diagram of the Preamble to the U.S. Constitution[3]

Legend: The main horizontal line divides the subject and predicate ("We (People)" [subject] / "do ordain and establish" [verb] / "Constitution" [direct object]. Slanted lines with single words on the line usually indicate articles ("the") or adjectives ("domestic"). Slanted lines attached to a horizontal line underneath the main line signify a prepositional phrase such as "of liberty" or "to ourselves and our posterity."

"The will left the grandson all of the real estate," "grandson" is an indirect object because it says to whom the will leaves the property. "The real estate" is a direct object because it indicates what is being left by the will.

A **preposition** is a word that describes a relationship or further defines other words in a sentence. It indicates location. Examples of prepositions are *during, in, on,* and *under.* Prepositions are combined with other words to form a prepositional phrase. **Prepositional phrases** contain, at a minimum, a preposition and a noun or pronoun that is the object of the preposition. Frequently, there also will be one or two adjectives that modify the object.

Gerunds are verbs that are used as nouns. A gerund is formed by adding *-ing* to a verb. Gerunds can be used as subjects, as objects of a verb, and as objects of a preposition. The following examples show how gerunds are used:

Subject: *Working* on the case takes up too much time.

Object of the verb: The deputy prosecutor enjoyed *working* on the case.

Object of a preposition: The prosecutor wrote a book about *working* on a case.

Subject-Verb Agreement

In every sentence, the verb must agree with the subject of the sentence in number. If the subject is singular, the verb must be singular. If the subject of the sentence is plural, the verb must be plural. Some problems occur when a subject is compound,

Preposition

A preposition links a noun, pronoun, or other parts of grammar in a sentence. These words indicate location.

Prepositional phrase

A phrase that consists of a preposition and a noun, pronoun, gerund, or clause. The phrase may also contain modifiers. The prepositional phrase functions as an adjective or an adverb depending on the question the phrase answers.

Gerund

A verb form that ends in *–ing* and serves as a noun.

[3]Separated by a Common Language. *Diagramming Sentences.* 2008. http://separatedbycommon language.blogspot.com/2008/01/diagramming-sentences.html image at http://3.bp.blogspot.com /_KniJb5dkuPY/R5JsY9LrB9I/AAAAAAAAAK4/HB6f2LA6DYA/s320/preamble.gif

meaning that more than one subject exists, or that the subject is a collective noun or an indefinite pronoun. Confusion may also result if the subject and the verb are not written closely together. Common errors in subject-verb agreement are shown in the following examples:

Compound Subject   If the subject of the sentence has two or more nouns connected by *and*, the subject is plural; therefore, a plural verb is required.

> **Incorrect:** "The prosecutor and defense attorney *was* pleased with the jury selection."
>
> **Correct:** "The prosecutor and defense attorney *were* pleased with the jury selection."

If the subject is composed of nouns connected by *or* or *nor*, a singular verb is required.

> **Incorrect:** Neither the prosecutor nor the defense attorney *were* present at the jury selection.
>
> **Correct:** Neither the prosecutor nor the defense attorney *was* present at the jury selection.

Indefinite Pronouns   If the subject contains certain indefinite pronouns, the subject is considered singular and therefore a singular verb is needed. These indefinite pronouns include *everyone*, *everybody*, *someone*, *each*, *either*, *no one*, and *neither*. In addition, if one of these pronouns is used in the predicate of the sentence, it should be a singular pronoun.

> **Incorrect:** Everybody *needs* to bring their document to the meeting.
>
> **Correct:** Everybody *needs* to bring his or her document to the meeting.

Other indefinite pronouns need a verb that matches the noun being referred to. These indefinite pronouns include *few*, *most*, *some*, *all*, *both*, and *many*.

> **Incorrect:** All of the items in the estate *has* been distributed.
>
> **Correct:** All of the items of the estate *have* been distributed.

Collective Nouns   Nouns that represent a group of people or items are called **collective nouns**. Words such as *committee*, *the court*, *jury*, *company*, and *majority* are usually singular in nature and take a singular verb, even though they represent a group of individuals.

> **Incorrect:** The majority *are* in agreement that the defendant was liable.
> The company *are* rebuilding its assets.
>
> **Correct:** The majority *is* in agreement that the defendant was liable.
> The company *is* rebuilding its assets.

Collective noun
A noun that is singular in form but identifies a group of individuals. A collective noun is treated as singular when the collection is thought of as a whole (jury) and as plural when the individual members are thought of as acting separately (jury members).

However, if one is discussing the individuals within the collective noun, a plural verb may be appropriate. If the sentence is "The company members are rebuilding their assets," the plural verb *are* would be correct because it refers to *members*.

> **Incorrect:** The members of the jury *is* in agreement that the defendant should be acquitted.
>
> **Correct:** The members of the jury *are* in agreement that the defendant should be acquitted.

Additional Problems   Some nouns, such as *politics*, *news*, and *athletics*, appear to be plural because they end with an *s*. However, these words have a singular meaning and take a singular verb.

Incorrect: "The news *are* distressing."
Correct: "The news *is* distressing."

Sometimes problems with subject–verb agreement arise because ***intervening words*** are placed between the subject and the verb. In these cases, the problem can be resolved by determining what the subject is, identifying what the verb should be, and ignoring the intervening words.

Intervening word
A word that comes between the subject and the verb.

Incorrect: "The paralegal's detailed attention to the interviews of the witnesses *deserve* praise."
Correct: "The paralegal's detailed attention to the interviews of the witnesses *deserves* praise."

The material highlighted contains the intervening words. By ignoring those words the writer and reader have a better view of the sentence. The subject is "attention" and the verb is "deserves."

Noun–Pronoun Agreement

Nouns and pronouns must agree, both in number and gender, according to the noun to which the pronoun refers. That noun is called an ***antecedent***. If the antecedent is plural, the pronoun must be plural. If multiple antecedents are joined by the word *and*, a plural pronoun also is needed. If the antecedents are joined by *or* or *nor*, the pronoun must agree in number and gender with the antecedent closest to the pronoun.

Antecedent
A word, phrase, or clause to which a pronoun refers.

Incorrect: The defendants waived *his* right to counsel.
The company issued *their* quarterly report.
James and John waived *his* right to counsel.
Either James or John must sign *their* name.
Correct: The defendants waived *their* right to counsel.
The company issued *its* quarterly report.
James and John waived *their* right to counsel.
Either James or John must sign *his* name.
Pronouns must also agree in gender:
Incorrect: James waived *their* right to counsel.
Correct: James waived *his* right to counsel.

If a pronoun refers to an unspecified person or thing, the pronoun is an ***indefinite pronoun***. Indefinite pronouns are words such as *all*, *each*, *everyone*, *somebody*, and *none*. Indefinite pronouns are usually singular.

Indefinite pronoun
A pronoun that refers in a general sense to a person, place, or thing. Examples are *anybody*, *anyone*, *each*, and *few*.

Incorrect: Everyone has the right to voice *their* opinion.
Correct: Everyone has the right to voice *his* or *her* opinion.

Personal Pronouns   ***Personal pronouns*** are *I/me*, *he/him*, *she/her*, *we/us*, and *they/them*. These pronouns change their form depending upon how the pronoun functions in a sentence. The pronouns can be subjects of the sentence, in which case the pronouns *I*, *he*, *she*, *we*, or *they* are used.

Personal pronoun
A pronoun that identifies or replaces a noun that represents a person or group of people.

Incorrect: Me and Jami are going to the court room.
Correct: Jami and I are going to the court room.

The personal pronouns *me*, *him*, *her*, *us*, and *them* function as an object of a sentence or as part of a prepositional phrase.

Incorrect: Give the brief to John and I.

Correct: Give the brief to John and me.

A good rule of thumb to help decide which personal pronoun to use is to erase or ignore the other person in the subject or object (in the example above, "John") and reread the sentence. In the example above, "Give the brief to me" sounds correct, whereas "Give the brief to I" does not.

Reflexive pronoun
A pronoun used to refer back to the subject of the sentence; usually ends in –*self* or –*selves.*

Reflexive Pronouns   ***Reflexive pronouns*** are pronouns that include the word *self,* such as *yourself, himself, herself, myself, yourselves,* and *themselves.* A reflexive pronoun reflects back on the subject so that the subject also becomes the object of the sentence. However, a reflexive pronoun is not a substitute for a personal pronoun. Each personal pronoun has its own reflexive pronoun. See Exhibit 14-5.

A reflexive pronoun may be used when the subject and the object are the same, such as "She hurt *herself.*" They are also used as the object of a preposition, such as "He performed the contract by *himself.*" Reflexive pronouns may also emphasize the subject of the sentence, such as "They performed the job *themselves.*" They generally are not used as objects or in phrases.

Incorrect: "The contract was breached by Mr. James and *myself.*"

"The judge gave *myself* a copy."

Correct: "The plaintiff injured *herself.*"

"The defendants perjured *themselves* when they lied on the stand."

"The contract was breached by Mr. James and *me.*"

Relative pronoun
A pronoun that introduces a subordinate clause. Examples of relative pronouns are *that, whose, which, who,* and *whom.*

Relative Pronouns   ***Relative pronouns*** relate groups of words to other words in the sentence. The five relative pronouns used most often in English are *who/whom, whoever/whomever, whose, that,* and *which.* Sometimes *what, when,* and *where* are relative pronouns. A relative pronoun can function as a subject, an object, or a possessive pronoun. Generally, *who* or *that* are used to refer to persons, and *that* or *which* are used to refer to non-human things or places.

When choosing between *who* or *whom, who* is used with a subject and *whom* with an object. One way to determine which form to use is to rewrite the sentence. If a writer could substitute a first-person pronoun such as *he* or *she* for the noun, then the correct relative pronoun is *who.* If *him* or *her* can be used as an object, then *whom* would be appropriate.

EXHIBIT 14-5 PERSONAL AND REFLEXIVE PRONOUNS

Personal Pronoun	Reflexive Pronoun
I	Myself
He	Himself
She	Herself
It	Itself
You (as singular)	Yourself
You (as plural)	Yourselves
We	Ourselves
They	Themselves

Incorrect: The man *whom* paid the bill was the defendant's father.
This is the woman *who* I interviewed last week.

Correct: The man *who* paid the bill was the defendant's father. (*He* paid the bill.)
This is the woman *whom* I interviewed last week. (I interviewed *her*.)

Relative pronouns are associated with a type of dependent clause called a *relative clause*. Relative clauses are either restrictive or nonrestrictive. A *restrictive clause* will define something or add information about the antecedent that is necessary to understand the sentence. Generally, a writer cannot drop the information introduced by relative clause and still retain the full meaning of the sentence. A restrictive clause usually begins with the word *that* and is not set off by a comma. For example, in the sentence "The house that had green shutters was for sale," "that had green shutters" is a relative clause and is restrictive. If the writer eliminates "that had green shutters," the sentence would refer to any house for sale.

If the clause is **nonrestrictive**, it will not define any essential terms. If the information in the relative clause were removed, the meaning of the sentence would not change. A clause beginning with *which* is a nonrestrictive clause and is set off by commas. For example, in the sentence "The house, which had green shutters, was for sale," the clause "which had green shutters" is a relative clause that is nonrestrictive. The sentence indicates that there was only one house for sale and that this particular house had green shutters.

Gender Pronouns Gender pronouns are a frequently misunderstood area and a common source of error. In law, as in many areas of business, writing must be gender neutral. The easiest way to avoid gender references is to use the plural form or eliminate pronouns altogether.

Incorrect: A paralegal must study her books to be successful.
A paralegal must study their books to be successful.

Correct: Paralegals must study their books to be successful.

When making general statements such as those in the examples above, there is a presupposition that paralegals are only female. Since there are many males in the paralegal field, this usage would be objectionable. In a similar manner, the word *chairman* has been changed to *chairperson*, *mailman* to *letter carrier*, and *committeemen* to *committeepersons*.

Verb Tense

Verb tense identifies the time when the action occurs. If an event is currently going on, the tense of the verb is the present tense. If the action has already occurred, past tense is appropriate. If the action will occur in the future, the future tense should be used. Writers use three other tenses to express time. The present perfect, past perfect, and future perfect tenses are created by adding auxiliaries such as *be*, *have*, *shall*, *may*, and *can*. Present perfect is used to indicate when an action began

Relative clause
A clause that contains a subject and a verb and begins with a relative pronoun or a relative adverb. A relative clause functions as an adjective.

Restrictive clause
A clause that defines something or adds information about the antecedent that is necessary to understand the sentence.

Nonrestrictive clause
A word or clause that identifies something about a subject but does not limit or restrict the subject; it will not define any essential terms

Verb tense
Information regarding when the action of the verb takes place. Examples are present tense, past tense, and future tense.

EXHIBIT 14-6 VERB TENSE SEQUENCE

Simple Present: They walk.
Present Perfect: They have walked.
Simple Past: They walked.
Past Perfect: They had walked.
Future: They will walk.
Future Perfect: They will have walked.

in the past but is still continuing. Future perfect is used to identify some action that will have been completed at some specific point in the future. See Exhibit 14-6 for examples of each tense.

The verb tense should remain consistent throughout a piece of writing, unless it is grammatically necessary to change tense. For example, if a document refers to a complaint that has already been filed, the past tense would be used and would continue to be used in the document every time the complaint is mentioned. Likewise, if the facts of a case are being described in a brief, the past tense would be used because the activity already occurred. However, when the position, legal analysis, or recommendation is being given, the present tense would be used. Present tense would also be used to describe laws currently in effect.

One error in verb tense usage that appears to be common is this:

Incorrect: I seen the defendant leave the plaintiff's store.

Correct: I saw the defendant leave the plaintiff's store.

A writer needs to be consistent not only in writing but also in speaking. One should be aware of the proper usage of all grammar in both written and oral formats.

Modifiers

Modifiers are words or phrases that describe either the subject, verb, or object of a sentence. If the word or phrase describes a noun or pronoun, it is an adjective. Adverbs modify adjectives, verbs, and other adverbs.

Adverbs   An adverb describes how, when, or where and is often identified by an -ly on the end. For example, in "The witness thinks slowly," the word *slowly* is an adverb because it tells how the witness thinks. On the other hand, if the sentence were "This witness is a slow thinker," *slow* would be an adjective modifying *thinker*. One would not say, "This witness is a slowly thinker."

Special rules apply when five senses— *taste*, *smell*, *look*, *sound*, and *feel*—are the verbs. If the verb is being used actively, then -ly should be attached. For example: "Roses smell sweet." A rose does not use a nose to actively smell something. Therefore, no -ly attaches to *sweet*.

Two words that tend to cause issues with many writers are *good* and *well*. If the sentence is "You did a good job," *good* describes *job* and therefore it is an adjective. If the sentence is "You did the job well," *well* tells how the job was done and it is an adverb. One exception is that any time health is referred to, the word *well* is used: "I do not feel well."

Other Common Modifier Problems   Problems with modifiers fall primarily into four categories: misplaced modifiers, squinting modifiers, dangling modifiers, and split infinitives. ***Misplaced modifiers*** are modifying words or phrases that are placed in the wrong location in a sentence. These errors cause problems by creating confusion or ambiguity in the meaning of the sentence. These problems are often solved by placing the modifiers close to the word or phrase they are modifying. *Almost*, *only*, *just*, and *not* are modifiers that are frequently misplaced. Generally, these words should be placed in front of the words they modify. Here, the writer wants to convey when parking is permitted.

Misplaced modifier
A word that is intended to modify or identify another word, but is placed in a location that makes it difficult to determine which word it modifies.

Incorrect: Parking is only permitted from 9 AM until 4 PM.

Correct: Parking is permitted only from 9 AM until 4 PM.

Placement of the modifier can change the meaning of the sentence.

A misplaced phrase or clause can make the sentence ambiguous as well as unclear:

Incorrect: In *Smith* v. *Jones*, using land thirteen feet west of their boundary, a patio was built by the claimants.

Correct: The claimants built a patio by using land thirteen feet west of their boundary.

A *squinting modifier* is located in a position where it could be construed as modifying either the word before or after it.

Incorrect: Writing the pleading clearly will improve her chances of winning the case.

Correct: Her chances of winning the case will improve if she writes the pleading clearly.

The incorrect example above could be interpreted as saying that simply writing a pleading will improve her chances, which is probably not what the writer meant. In the second example, it is understood that *clearly* describes the writing that should be done to win the case.

A *dangling modifier* is a group of words that does not refer to any noun or pronoun expressly mentioned in the sentence. The phrase may sound correct but it is grammatically incorrect because it does not express a complete thought.

Incorrect: Having filed a late response, a motion to vacate was required.

Correct: Because the attorney filed a late response, a motion to vacate was required.

The first sentence above does not say who filed the late response. The subject, *the attorney*, needs to be identified.

Split infinitives are common in spoken vernacular English, but should be avoided in professional writing. An infinitive is a form of a verb that begins with the word *to*. No modifiers or other words should be placed between the *to* and the verb:

Incorrect: He seems to *always* do it a certain way.

Correct: He *always* seems to do it a certain way.

PUNCTUATION

Some *punctuation marks* may seem insignificant, but using it correctly can be critical in legal documents. Punctuation may indicate a change in tone or in areas of emphasis. Incorrect punctuation, such as a misplaced comma, can change the entire meaning of a sentence. Errors in punctuation also may make writing appear careless and undermine the credibility of the writer.

The following is not an exhaustive list of punctuation rules. If there are any doubts about punctuation, it is wise to consult a style guide or resource manual.

The Period

The period can serve many purposes beyond simply indicating the end of a sentence. Periods are used in the following ways:

- Periods are used after an indirect question:

  Example: The students asked when the next exam would be given.
- Periods are used at the end of a polite request:

  Example: Please send your answers to the interrogatories by December 13.

Squinting modifier
A modifier that appears to identify both the words before it and those after it.

Dangling modifier
A word or phrase that modifies a word that is not expressly stated within the sentence.

Split infinitive
An infinitive (a phrase that has the word *to* and a verb) that has an adverb between *to* and the verb.

Punctuation marks
Marks that provide structure and organization to writing. Punctuation marks also signal pauses and different types of intonation.

- Periods are used with some abbreviations and initials:

Example: Bottom Dollar, Inc. has experienced a 25% growth in sales during the last year.

Example: The U.S. Postal Service is considering the closing of numerous small post offices in a cost-saving measure.

The period has some additional minor rules that must be observed. If an abbreviation is at the end of a sentence, only one period is used. If words inside quotation marks and parentheses are a complete sentence, that sentence containing the quotation will have its own period.

Commas

Commas are the most frequently used punctuation mark. They tell the reader to pause at a particular point in the sentence, and they also are used to set off numbers, dates, and introductory words or clauses and in certain other situations that require a division within a sentence. Commas can be used as shown in Example 14-3.

EXAMPLE 14-3   USING COMMAS

a. Commas are used before a ***coordinating conjunction*** (*and, but, for, or, nor, so, yet*) to separate independent clauses.

Example: The witness explained the answer, *but* the defense attorney did not understand.

b. Commas are used to set off introductory clauses, words, or phrases preceding the main clause.

Example: *Before the plaintiff's attorney could finish the question*, the witness answered.

c. Commas are used after the salutation of an informal letter and after the closing of any letter.

Example: Dear John,

Example: Very truly yours,

d. Commas are used to set off ***transitional words*** or phrases that are not necessary to the sentence's meaning.

Example: The defendant, *however*, did not stop for the police.

Example: The appropriate action, *therefore*, is to file a motion for summary judgment.

e. Commas are used to set off ***appositives*** (nouns or noun phrases that add information to other nouns or noun phrases).

Example: Professor Myers, *our legal research instructor*, assigned an interoffice memorandum of law for Wednesday.

f. Closely related one-word appositives or those comprising part of a proper name are not set off with commas.

Example: My daughter Jami received a job offer from a major law firm.

g. Commas are used to set off ***nonrestrictive clauses*** (a clause that is not needed to understand the sentence).

Example: The court denied the motion for summary judgment, determining that there was no issue to resolve.

h. Commas are used to set off phrases that contrast, limit, or are contingent expressions.

Example of a Contrasting Expression: The defendant, not the plaintiff, had the burden of proof.

Example of a Limiting Expression: The law firm purchased a table of tickets for the gala, but only for the attorneys and paralegals.

Coordinating conjunction
A simple conjunction such as *and*, *but*, or *nor* that joins parts of the sentence.

Transitional word
A word that brings two ideas together so that the information is cohesive. Examples are *consequently*, *in addition*, *also*, and *furthermore*.

Appositive
A word, phrase, or clause that is placed beside another word, phrase, or clause so that one explains the other. Both clauses must have the same grammatical construction.

Example a Contingent Expression: The sooner we receive your answer, the sooner we will be able to depose your client.

i. Commas are used to identify a quotation.

If the quotation comes in the middle of a sentence, use a comma before the quotation:

Example: The professor asked, "Does everyone have the assignment?"

If the quotation comes at the beginning of the sentence, use a comma at the end of the quotation, but inside the quotation marks:

Example: "Professor, we have the assignments," the students replied.

j. Commas are used to set off dates, time zones, and addresses.

1. If a calendar date is given without a year, or if only a month and year are given, commas are not used.

   Example: The deposition is scheduled for June 23 in our office.

   Example: The trial will begin in June 2012.

2. If the calendar date and year are given, or if both the day of the week and the calendar date are given, commas set off the date and the year from the remainder of the sentence.

   Example: The defendant was served on December 1, 2011, by the sheriff.

   Example: The deposition is scheduled for Thursday, June 23, in our office.

3. If a clock time is included in a sentence, the time zone is set off by a comma.

   Example: The deposition will take place at 9:30 a.m., EST, on June 23, 2012, in our office at 123 W. Better Drive, Springfield, Illinois. Use commas to separate parts of an address if the address is written in sentence format.

4. Use commas to separate parts of an address if the address is written in sentence format. Then please answer the interrogatories example.

   Example: Please address the interrogatories to Russell Bundt, 456 S. Capital Street, Apt. 301, Indianapolis, Indiana 46206.

5. Use commas between a city and state or city and country. Set off both with commas if the information occurs in the middle of a sentence.

   Example: The defendant was last seen in Baltimore, Maryland, on December 3.

   Example: The corporation has offices in Paris, France, and in Frankfurt, Germany.

k. Commas are used to add descriptive titles to a name.

Example: Send the letter to James A. Krocza, Esq., Iva Jean Baker, M.D., and Jami Myers, Ph.D.

l. Commas are used to indicate omitted words. However, when a comma is used, it must be clear from the context of the sentence what the omitted words are.

Example: Last week I received two envelopes of information from the client; this week, one package.

m. Commas are used to clarify sentences.

1. A comma can be used to separate identical verbs: "The candidate who wins, wins the position for two years."

2. A comma can separate words that are duplicated for emphasis: "The juvenile was warned many, many times that his behavior could result in incarceration."

3. A comma can separate an introductory phrase to avoid confusion: "The year before, the law firm expanded its operation to three cities."

Commas are always needed to separate items in a series. There is, however, some controversy over whether a comma is needed before the last item in a series. In legal writing, the comma should be placed after each item in the list as well as before the conjunction at the end of the list. Using the comma before the conjunction eliminates any possibility of misunderstanding what is being said. For example, if an estate had a provision stating: "I leave equal shares of my estate to each of my four children: Ashley, Brad, Connor, and Danielle," each would receive one-fourth of the estate. However, if the sentence read, "I leave my estate equally to Ashley, Brad, Connor and Danielle," an argument could be made that the estate was to be divided into thirds. Ashley would receive one-third, Brad would receive one-third, and Connor and Danielle would share one-third. To avoid ambiguity, always use a comma after each item in the sentence and before the conjunction.

Semicolons

A semicolon has a variety of limited uses. It can be used to separate the major elements of complex sentences and to separate items in a series, if the items themselves have internal commas. It is also used when independent but related clauses must be connected or when independent clauses are joined by a transitional word or conjunction. A semicolon may occasionally by used when a series of items is introduced by a colon.

a. A semicolon is appropriate when independent clauses in a sentence are not joined by a coordinating conjunction. An independent clause has a subject and a verb, and can stand on its own.

Example: The defense attorney delivered a forceful summation; the jury appeared mesmerized.

Conjunctive adverb
An adverb used to connect two independent clauses. A semicolon follows the first clause, then the conjunctive adverb is included, and the conjunctive adverb is followed by a comma.

b. A semicolon is used when independent clauses are joined by a ***conjunctive adverb***. Examples of conjunctive adverbs are *likewise, consequently, therefore, however,* and *moreover.*

Example: The judge ordered the attorneys to cease hostilities; therefore, the defense attorney returned to his chair.

c. If the sentence contains an extensive series of items (more than three or four) or when commas are already used within some of the items, a semicolon is appropriate to separate the groups.

Example: Witnesses were located in Denver, Colorado; Indianapolis, Indiana; and Springfield, Massachusetts.

d. If the sentence contains a list that is introduced by a colon, a semicolon is used to separate the items within the list.

Example: The elements of burglary are as follows: "breaking"; "entering"; "the house"; "of another"; and "at night."

Comma splice
A type of error that occurs when a comma is incorrectly used to forge two sentences or independent clauses together. It can be corrected by separating the two sentences into independent sentences with a period, or by using either a semicolon or a coordinating conjunction and a comma to join the two independent clauses together.

e. A semicolon is placed outside closing quotation marks or parentheses.

Example quotation: The client promised, "I will mail you a check for the retainer by Monday"; however, we have not received the check.

Example parentheses: The evidence was tainted (the chain of custody was broken); consequently, the evidence could not be used at trial.

f. It is essential to know whether a comma or semicolon should be chosen for a particular use. If a comma is used where a semicolon is necessary, it is referred to as a ***comma splice***.

Example:

Incorrect: The defense attorney was forceful, however the jury was not convinced.

Correct: The defense attorney was forceful; however, the jury was not convinced.

A semicolon should not be used when a comma is appropriate.

Example:

Incorrect: The defense attorney was forceful; but not convincing.

Correct: The defense attorney was forceful, but not convincing.

Colons

Colons are used in limited circumstances when introducing information. Colons may be used when writing the salutation of a formal letter, introducing a list, calling attention to information, or introducing a long quotation. The material that precedes the colon must be a complete sentence. Colons are always placed outside quotations and/or parentheses.

a. Use a colon in the salutation of a formal letter.

   Example: Dear Dr. Jones:

b. A colon can introduce a list and phrases with words such as "as follows" or "the following."

   Example: The plaintiff was asked to bring the following: an insurance policy, a copy of the police report, and pictures of the wrecked vehicle.

c. Colons can be used to introduce a list of bulleted items.

   Example: The organization had the option of doing one of several things:

   - Incorporating
   - Dissolving
   - Filing bankruptcy

d. Colons can be used to bring attention to information. A second complete sentence after the colon more fully explains or adds information to the preceding sentence.

   Example: The judge's remark was straight to the point: "I won't tolerate a lack of civility in my courtroom."

e. Colons can introduce long quotations.

   Example:
   In *Marbury* v. *Madison*, 5 U.S. 137, 178 (1803), the court held:

   So if a law be in opposition to the constitution; if both the law and the constitution apply to a particular case, so that the court must either decide that case conformably to the law, disregarding the constitution; or conformably to the constitution, disregarding the law; the court must determine which of these conflicting rules governs the case. This is of the very essence of judicial duty.

Apostrophes

a. An apostrophe combined with an *s* indicates possession. Whether the apostrophe comes before or after the *s* depends on whether the noun is singular or plural.

> In most instances, if the word is singular, an apostrophe is inserted before an "*s*".

Examples:

the defendant's attorney

the state's governor

James's book

b. If the word used to show possession is already plural, often an apostrophe is added after the *s.*

Examples:

the students' work (the work of more than one student)

the hospitals' cooperation (more than one hospital cooperated)

c. Apostrophes are not used in some cases when the noun has an irregular plural form. A good test for whether or not an apostrophe is needed is to substitute a possessive phrase. If one can switch "defendant's home" to "home of the defendant" and if the sentence makes sense, the possessive form should be used.

Correct: The officers served a search warrant at the defendant's home.

(The officers served a search warrant *at the home of the defendant.*)

d. "Officers" is a plural word meaning more than one officer. It does not require an apostrophe. "Defendant's" is properly shown as a possessive noun because the phrase "the home of the defendant" can be substituted for it.

If the word is plural and does not end in an *s,* add an apostrophe and an *s* to show possession.

Example:

the women's group

the jury's verdict

e. If the word requires an *es* to form the word's plural, add the *es* and then add an apostrophe after the *es.*

Example:

The Joneses' house is in foreclosure. (Mr. and Mrs. Jones own the house)

The boxes' wrapping matched.

Apostrophes are substituted for omitted letters when a contraction is formed.

Example:

they're (they are)

can't (cannot)

who's (who is)

f. Personal pronouns do not require an apostrophe to show possession. The words *yours, hers, his, hours, its,* and *whose* are possessive forms. Notice that *its* is the possessive form of *it.* "*It's*" is not a possessive; it is a contraction. *It's* means "it is."

Ellipses

a. The ellipses indicate that part of a quotation has been omitted. Generally, an ellipsis consists of three periods with a space in between each period.

   Example:

   The burglary statute required that there was a breaking, entering, . . . at night."

b. If the ellipsis occurs at the end of the sentence, add a fourth period, indicating the period at the end of the sentence.

   Example:

   The court stated that "defendant's actions indicated a lack of intent . . . ."

c. An ellipsis should not be used if the omission is at the beginning of a quotation. Instead, one should bracket the first letter of the first word used in the quotation.

   Example:

   The court held that the "[D]efendant was required to show that he did not breach the contract."

Question Marks

Question marks are usually found after a direct question that requires an answer. However, question marks have other uses.

a. Place a question mark at the end of a statement that is meant to be a question.

   Example:

   The AAfPE annual conference has been delayed until December?

b. Place a question mark in expressions of doubt.

   Example:

   The college had a retention rate of 87% (?) during 2010–11.

c. Place a question mark with a series of questions.

   Example:

   Who requested access to the evidence–the judge? the prosecutor? the defense attorney?

Quotation Marks

a. Quotation marks are used to indicate when someone else's exact words are being used. If the quotation is less than 50 words, the quotation should be placed within the same lines as the surrounding text and it should be enclosed in quotation marks.

   Example:

   The judge said, "The motion for summary judgment is hereby granted."

b. A quotation that exceeds 50 words is formatted as a ***block quotation.*** The quotation is set off from the regular text by wider margins, narrower text space, and single-line spacing. A block quotation is not enclosed in quotation marks.

Block quotation
A quotation containing 50 or more words that is identified by indenting the quotation by wider margins, narrower text space, and closer line spacing. A block quotation is not enclosed by quotation marks.

Example:

Indiana Code 36-10-3-4 identifies the manner in which members of the municipal board are appointed and the qualifications for membership. The statute provides, in part, as follows:

The members appointed under subdivisions (1), (2), and (3) shall be appointed on the basis of their interest in and knowledge of parks and recreation, but no more than one (1) member appointed under subdivisions (1) and (3) may be affiliated with the same political party. In a county having at least one (1) first or second class city, the creating ordinance must provide for one (1) ex officio board member to be appointed by the executive of that city. The member appointed by the city executive must be affiliated with a different political party than the member appointed by the county executive. However, if a county has more than one (1) such city, the executives of those cities shall agree on the member. The member serves for a term coterminous with the term of the appointing executive or executives.

c. Ex officio members have all the rights of regular members, including the right to vote. A vacancy in an ex officio position shall be filled by the appointing authority.

d. Neither a municipal executive nor a member of a county fiscal body, county executive, or municipal fiscal body may serve on a board.

e. The creating ordinance in any county may provide for:

1. the county cooperative extension coordinator;
2. the county extension educator; or
3. a member of the county extension committee selected by the committee to serve as an ex officio member of the county board, in addition to the members provided for under subsection (b).[4]

f. Quotation marks may be used to show that a particular word or phrase is an idiom, or is jargon, humor, or irony.

Example of jargon:

The defendant wanted a "divorce from bed and board."

Example of an idiom:

The city announced that "all systems are go" on the multi-million-dollar road project.

g. Quotation marks are used when the definition of a word is given after the word is listed.

Example:

The professor explained that *expungement* is a "process by which the record in a criminal conviction is destroyed or sealed."

h. Quotation marks can be used to identify titles of short works such as episodes of television shows, newspaper and magazine articles, essays, song titles, and short stories.

Example:

Did you read the article in *Time* magazine titled "Does the Constitution Still Matter" by Richard Stengel?

i. Single quotation marks indicate a quotation within a quotation.

[4]I.C. 36-10-3-4. State of Indiana. 2011. http://www.in.gov/legislative/ic/2010/title36/ar10/ch3.html

Example:

The magazine article quoted the defendant's attorney as saying, "When I asked my client, 'Did you know where your daughter was on day 28 of her disappearance?' she replied, 'No, I did not.'"

Parentheses

Parentheses typically are used to enclose words that clarify the meaning of words in the rest of the sentence. They also assist with formatting and organization.

a. Parentheses enclose words that restate or clarify words that are less important and deemphasize them.

Example:

The witness (after a brief pause) finally responded to the attorney's question.

Parentheses enclose nonessential phrases such as a references or directions.

Example:

The defendant breached his contractual duty as set forth in paragraph 6 of the contract. (See Exhibit A.)

Parentheses confirm figures that are spelled out.

Example:

The defendant has thirty (30) days to respond to the interrogatories.

Parentheses are used to enumerate items in lists.

Example:

Please bring the following to the appointment: (1) the police report, (2) the statement given to the insurance adjuster, and (3) a copy of your insurance policy.

Brackets

Brackets are used within quoted material to separate the actual words of the quote from notes or comments by the writer.

a. The term *sic* is used when there was an error in quoted material and the quote was written exactly the way it appeared in the original. The term is Latin for "so" or "this is the way it was," and is enclosed in brackets.

Example:

The court held, "While we find that the statements were inproper [*sic*], we affirm the defendant's conviction."

b. Brackets are used when inserting a comment, correction, or explanation in quoted material.

Example:

"While we find that the statements were inproper [*sic*], we affirm the defendant's convictions because, based on the overwhelming evidence of guilt, the error was harmless [the harmless error test places the burden on the state]."

c. Web addresses are enclosed in brackets called ***angle brackets***.

Example:

Mandernach, B.J. *Creating a Syllabus.* 2003. Park University Faculty Development Quick Tips. 19 September 2011. <http://www.park.edu /cetl/quicktips/syllabus.html>

Angle brackets
Brackets used to enclose web addresses.

WORD USAGE

Proper word usage is as important as correct spelling. The English language is filled with homophones—words that sound alike but have very different meanings. It may be helpful to make a list of those words that are the most troublesome to use as a reference. The following words commonly result in usage errors.

Effect (noun)	Affect (verb)
bring about, brought about, cause, or *caused; result*	to influence on or cause change in or to act in a way you do not feel like
Examples: That speech had a long-lasting effect on my thinking. Has the medicine produced any noticeable effects? He effected a commotion in the crowd.	**Example:** How do the budget cuts affect your job? He affected an air of superiority with the group.

Accept	Except
Receive willingly	Preposition - only
Give admittance or approval	Conjunction— On any other condition With the following exception only
Endure without protest	Transitive verb To take or leave out from a number or a whole Exclude omit
Make a favorable response	
Assume an obligation to pay	

	Present	Past	Participle
To recline	Lie/lying	Lay	Has/have/had lain
To put or place	Lay/laying	Laid	Has/have/had laid
To make a false statement	Lie/lying	Lied	Has/have/had lied

	Present	Past	Participle
To be seated or to be in a resting position	Sit	Sat	Have sat
To put or place	Set	Set	Has set

	Present	Past	Participle
Steady upward movement	Rise (The sun rises in the east.)	Rose	Has risen
To cause to rise	Raise (Raise your hand if you know the answer.)	Raised	Have raised

Already	All Ready
Adverb meaning "even now"	Adjective phrase meaning completely prepared

Among	Between
Refers to a group of three or more.	Refers to two people or things.
I divided the time among the three witnesses.	I divided the time between John and Fred.

Fewer	Less
Describes things that can be counted.	Refers to degree or quantity.
Example: Fewer dollars are available to consumers.	**Example:** The total number of arrests for felony murder this year was less than those arrests last year.

Good	Well
Adjective modifying a noun or pronoun	Adverb modifying a verb
Example: It was a good day to die.	**Exceptions:** When used to mean "neatly groomed" When used to mean "healthy" When used to mean "satisfactory" **Example:** I hope you are feeling well.

Lead (pronounced "leed")	Led	Lead
Means to go first	Past tense of lead	Heavy metal or the material in pencils
Example: You should lead us to the accident scene.	**Example:** He led us to the judge's chambers.	**Example:** The pencil lead was sharp.

Than	Then
Conjunction that is used when making comparisons.	Adverb indicating time.
Example: The plaintiff's argument was better than the defendant's argument.	The defendant left the scene, then proceeded to the hospital.

WORDINESS

Legal documents have a reputation for being extremely dense and wordy. And yet writing is most effective when it is accurate, clear, and concise. Wordiness refers to using unnecessary or redundant words and can be avoided by reviewing a completed document to eliminate any words that are not necessary.

EXHIBIT 14-7 WORD USAGE

Excessive/redundant usage	Alternative usage
Along the lines of	Like
At the time at which	When
During the time at which	While
In order to	To
Be of assistance to	Assist
Subsequent to	After
There can be no question but that	Unquestionably
I would like to take this opportunity to thank you	Thank you
Please be good enough to forward me the following	Please send me the following
Enclosed herewith please find	Enclosed is
There is uncontradicted evidence to support the finding	Uncontradicted evidence indicates
Enclosed is a full and complete copy	Enclosed is a full copy
Each and every witness will testify that	All witnesses will testify that
The deed is a true and correct copy	The deed is a true copy
Payment is due and owing immediately	Payment is due immediately
We demand that you cease and desist this action	We demand that you cease this action
The document is null and void because	The document is void because
Regarding the matter of	About
During the course of litigation	During litigation
In the event that	If
In the process of	During
Regardless of the fact that	Although

Exhibit 14-7 is a list of phrases that are excessive or redundant, though commonly used. Alternate words and phrases are suggested.

Very often, shorter phrases can provide the same meaning. A thesaurus can be a useful resource for finding alternatives. However, care should be taken when using a thesaurus, because some alternate words may have a unique connotation that is not applicable to the context where the word will be used. Use the word that best indicates the meaning you are trying to convey in the sentence and then determine whether it makes the sentence complete or whether it causes confusion.

THE EDITING AND PROOFREADING STAGE

Editing

Editing is the process of revising written material in order to improve the clarity and quality of the document. The editing stage of the writing process often requires more than one rewrite; if possible, the document should be rewritten as many times as necessary to achieve accuracy, brevity, and clarity.

The editing stage involves more than simply checking grammar and punctuation. The writer also should review the organization of the document, using the outline from the prewriting stage. The writer should ask whether a reader could create the same or a substantially similar outline from reading the document. The thesis statement also should be reviewed to see if it truly captures the main idea of the document.

Throughout the document, the writing should flow logically, transitioning from one idea to another or from one paragraph to the next. Each paragraph should be fully developed and include a topic sentence. The sentences within the paragraph should be cohesive.

Overall, the writing should be clear and concise. Wherever text is wordy or excessive, it should be tightened by removing redundant, vague, or misused words. Grammar, punctuation, and spelling problems should be identified, and citations checked. If math is included in the document, the calculations should be tested multiple times to be sure they are correct. If lists are used, the points in the list should match those made in the narrative.

The beginning sentences in each paragraph should also be examined. A variety of introductions and transitions should be used. The sentences in each paragraph should not be so similar in style that the material becomes boring. Most importantly, the words and structure should clearly convey the message intended.

If a document is lengthy, headings or guideposts should be considered as a way to direct the reader. These can be as simple as Roman numerals or letters, or short phrases or sentences that identify the content of each section. The guideposts can help the reader find information and know at a glance what is discussed in each part of the document.

During the editing phase, the audience again should be considered. The final document should be read to confirm that the audience will understand the message being conveyed. A document intended for an attorney may be much different than a document intended for a layperson. Plain language should be used if there is any chance that a term or the topic could be misconstrued.

Editing is a critical part of the writing process and should not be overlooked or taken lightly. It is the part of the process that ensures that the final document is a quality product.

Using a Spell-Checker

No document should ever leave a writer's hands with any misspelled words. Spelling errors tell the reader that the information was not important enough for the writer to make sure that it was correct. The authenticity, value, and reliability of the document will be diminished.

Although a spell-check feature in a word processing application can be a useful feature, it should not be the only tool the writer relies on for spelling. A computer can check spelling, but it cannot check correct usage. Many words have multiple spellings, of which one is a preferred spelling (such as *judgment* and *judgement*). Others have homophones that sound alike, but have different meanings (like *accept* and *except*). Some words have different spellings depending on usage or part of speech (for example, *mark up* is a verb, whereas *markup* is a noun). A computer spell-check feature will not make these distinctions and, therefore, will not catch them as errors. It is no substitute for consulting a good dictionary. In the legal setting, a good legal dictionary may be as valuable as a good standard dictionary.

To demonstrate the weakness of computer spell-checkers, Dr. Jerrold H. Zar, with the help of Mark Eckman, composed a poem in 1992. It contained 123 words that were correctly spelled, but incorrectly used. Over the years, the poem, ode, or song has been reprinted, usually as "author unknown" and with variations of the original language. For example, the poem shows a computer allowing "Miss steaks" for "mistakes", "it's" for "its", and "witch" for "which". The computer does not have the ability to check for logic; it is a literal machine. Therefore, it will allow words that are grammatically correct but used incorrectly.

Proofreading

Proofreading is the process of carefully examining text to find and correct typographical, formatting, and spelling errors. It is not the same process as editing, which is changing wording or content. Editing should be complete before the document is proofread. Checklist 14-1 provides proofreading guidelines.

Figure 14-2 lists some standard proofreader's marks. It includes some of the most frequently used marks, but is not an exhaustive list.

Checklist 14-1   PROOFREADING GUIDELINES

1. Make sure the material has been edited.

2. If you are the author, allow time to pass between the time the document is completed and the time of proofreading the document. Often when a document is reviewed after a passage of time, a fresh look will reveal more errors.

3. Check for consistency of style in the document. Are the margins and line spacing correct? Are there any widow or orphan lines? Is there a single line on a final page?

4. Use the spell-check feature of the word processing program. In Word, misspelled words will be shown with a red line underneath. When the word is right-clicked, a drop-down box will give spelling options. However, do not rely solely on this feature!

5. Consider printing the document for proofreading. Some writers proofread more effectively when reviewing a hard copy of the document.

6. Proofread slowly. Read the text aloud, if necessary. Proofread the document in small parts, or "chunks."

7. If proofreading is difficult, check for each type of error separately. Start with the most important errors and finish with the least important.

8. Use a variety of techniques in the proofreading process. For example, sentences can be read backwards to check for sentence fragments. Look for agreement between subjects and verbs, nouns and pronouns, and antecedents and nouns/pronouns.

9. Make sure that letters in words are not transposed or omitted, such as *from* and *form*.

10. Check for homophones, such as *there, their,* or *they're.*

11. Double-check the spelling of proper names, especially the names of clients and parties.

12. Double-check any ***boilerplate*** text to be sure that it contains no incorrect client information and that no areas are blank.

13. Check the accuracy of numbers more than once.

Boilerplate
Standard, uniform language used in a legal document that is used in all similar legal documents.

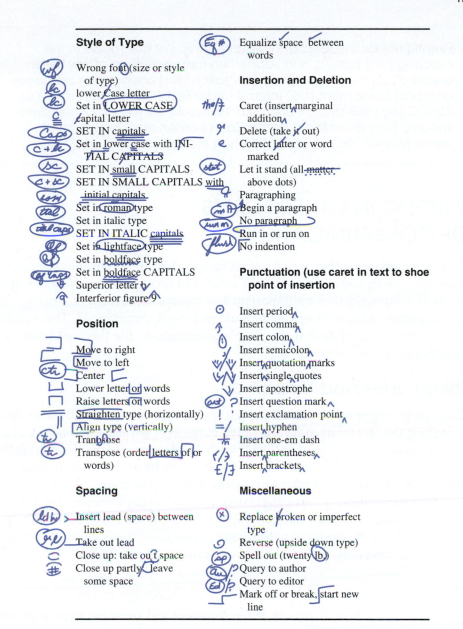

FIGURE 14-2
Proofreader's Marks[5]

Errors in written documentation can be costly, and proofreading is crucial in legal writing. For example, in *McKenna v. City of Philadelphia,* 2008 WL 4435939 (E.D. Pa. 2008) (not reported in *Federal Supplement*), the court reduced attorneys' fees by 85 hours in a civil rights case because the work done by the attorneys was "careless and confusing." The court went to great lengths to detail the spelling, grammar, math, party identification, and citation errors. Figure 14-3 shows the first paragraph of Timothy McKenna's fee petition, which is rife with errors.

Errors in legal documents can be costly. The editing and proofreading process, while seemingly mundane, is critical. When given this assignment, paralegals should excel at proofreading and editing.

[5]Author Guide. Proofreader Marks. Prentice Hall, Inc.. 2000. http://www.prenhall.com/author _guide/proofing.html

FIGURE 14-3 Errors in Fee Petition

> Plaintf [sic] for the facts and argument [sic] of law made in the mocong [sic] papers and supporting memorandum of law for an award of counsel fees, award of litgation [sic] costs, delay damages and post judgement [sic] interest under Fed. Rule of Civil Pro. 59(e), 42 USC [sic] 988 and 28 USC [sic] 1920, submits the proposed order shouold [sic] be entered as the Court's order; and in support of same, plainitff [sic] im [sic] McKenna though [sic] counsel says: . . .[6]

WRITING IN OTHER FORMS OF COMMUNICATION

When we think of writing, we do not necessarily think of electronic communications such as telephone calls, voicemail, email, and text messaging. However, these forms of communication are important and involve some form of writing, such as a voicemail reduced to writing or a telephone call summarized. These conveniences have changed the way that people communicate, but there are some basic rules that should be followed.

Telephones and Voicemail

When preparing to make a telephone call, most people do not usually write down everything they are going to say. However, in the legal setting, a telephone call can be more productive if a brief outline is made in advance. This outline serves two purposes: the caller can plan in advance what points he or she wants to cover and there is a written record of what was discussed during the conversation.

Using an outline is particularly useful when leaving voicemail messages. If an outline is followed, the voicemail will be more concise. However, when leaving a message, it is also important to be careful not to disclose any confidential information. The recording could be heard by unauthorized people.

Email

Email is now used in all aspects of our business and personal lives. However, because of its convenience and speed, the content of email tends to be more relaxed and informal than that of conventional mail. In the legal and business world, language is expected to be taken more seriously. Because of this expectation, many firms have very specific policies about how emails should be written and used. In the legal setting, the same conventions that apply to written letters should also apply to emails. Checklist 14-2 provides general guidelines that should be observed when writing an email.

In a law practice, all emails should include a confidentiality statement underneath the signature block. Many firms will have a standard confidentiality statement that may be similar to Example 14-4.

Regardless of any confidentiality statement, the sender should never assume that an email will be kept confidential. Many employers monitor the emails of their employees. Computers are sometimes shared or passwords are made available to multiple users. Email is also discoverable in litigation.

TIP

Emails are part of everyday communication. However, it is imperative that paralegals learn their employer's policies pertaining to emails as soon as they are hired. Many employers are very strict about office email being used for business purposes only. Another thing to consider revolves around security. Paralegals need to be very cognizant of what is put in an email and consider to whom the email is being sent. Many employers monitor emails in the office setting. One should never say anything in an email that one would not want a boss to read.

[6]*McKenna v. City of Philadelphia,* 2008 WL 4435939 (E.D. Pa. 2008) Thomson Reuters/West Publishing Co. 2011.

Checklist 14-2

EMAIL GUIDELINES

1. All emails should be proofread before being sent.

2. Formality should be observed, and the recipient should be addressed in the salutation.

3. All writing should be in complete sentences.

4. Tone and word choice should be appropriate for the audience and purpose.

5. Emails should be brief and concise, but not abrupt.

6. If a large amount of information needs to be sent, it should be placed in an attachment.

7. The subject line should be very specific and should refer to the body of the email.

8. Email should not be used to resolve disputes or to discuss delicate matters.

EXAMPLE 14-4   SAMPLE CONFIDENTIALITY STATEMENT

The information contained in this email or fax and any attachments thereto is sent by the firm of XYZ and is intended to be confidential and for the use of only the individual or entity designated as the recipient. The information may be protected by federal and state privacy and disclosures acts or other legal rules. If the reader of this message is not the intended recipient, you are notified that the retention, dissemination, distribution, or copying of this email (fax) is strictly prohibited. If you have received this email or fax in error, please immediately notify XYZ by email reply and immediately and permanently delete this email or fax message and any attachments thereto.

A recipient of email also should consider carefully how to reply. It is not always appropriate to hit "reply all". Once an email is sent, it cannot be retrieved. Even if a system has a button that allows a sender to recall a message, it is often too late to prevent the message from reaching its destination. Proofreading an email will often allow some time to reflect before clicking the "send" button.

Faxes

As with email, most firms may have a policy regarding the use of faxes. When a fax is sent, a cover sheet should be used that includes the sender's name, telephone, and fax number, as well as the recipient's name, telephone, and fax number, the date of the fax, and a "regarding" or subject line. A confidentiality statement also should be included similar to the statement used for emails. If there is a large volume of information to send, conventional mail or courier is usually the best way to send that material. All documents should be checked and double-checked before they are faxed.

Text Messaging

Texting continues to expand rapidly as a preferred method of sending short messages. The brevity of these messages encourages writing practices that are even more informal than those used for emails.

Many paralegals receive a personal digital assistant (PDA) device so they can remain in contact with the firm from any location. However, using a PDA to send text messages still requires formal, precise language that is appropriate for the audience. Text abbreviations should not be used if the recipient could be confused by the message.

SUMMARY

Writing effectively is an essential skill, and depends not only on the skillful planning and drafting of documents, but also on the attentive revision and proofing of those materials. The ultimate goal is to create documents that are accurate, concise, clear, and free from errors. Mastering the skill of writing is essential to becoming an important member of the legal team.

REVIEW **QUESTIONS**

1. What is active voice and when is it most effectively used?
2. What is the purpose of an outline?
3. What are the three stages of writing, and what is the purpose of each?
4. Why is it important for subjects and verbs to agree?
5. Why is punctuation important?
6. Identify three grammar weaknesses you have, and identify steps you can take to correct these problems.
7. What does it mean to write for a particular audience?
8. Why should a writer prepare an outline, particularly when drafting lengthy documents?
9. What is parallelism, and why is it important in writing?
10. What is the difference between active and passive voice?
11. What is an antecedent and how is it used?
12. How does editing differ from proofreading?
13. Why is it important to carefully draft emails and text messages?
14. Why would an outline help one prepare for telephone conversations and for leaving voicemail messages?

APPLICATION **EXERCISES**

Edit each sentence to correct any errors in grammar and punctuation. Some of the sentences contain no errors. Other sentences may need to be rewritten to fully correct the errors.

A. Parts of Speech

1. (Much/many) mail is being lost because the sender forgets to include the correct postage.
2. (Much/many) packages are also delayed.
3. (Less/fewer) criminal statistics are available for the years before 1950 than for the years since.
4. The (amount/number) of students turned away from law schools has remained constant through the years.
5. (Less/fewer) dollars are available for a greater (amount/number) of colleges.
6. The judge asked the defense attorney and I to join her in her chambers.
7. The judge is much admired, but no one admires her more than me.
8. Give the finished copies of the brief to John and myself.
9. John would have read it himself, but he is working on another case.
10. The defendant corporation argued that their rights had been abridged.
11. Legislation to (affect/effect) the rights of Americans to free legal counsel has had the (affect/effect) of increasing the staffs of public defenders' offices.
12. The (principal/principle) plaintiff in this case said she had brought the case of trial as a matter of (principal/principle).
13. (Further/farther) efforts to aid the injured person provided proved ineffective.

14. The widow of the (famous/notorious) Lindbergh kidnapper attempted to clear her husband's name.

15. I would rather write a brief (than/then) do anything else.

16. The action in battery was brought by the plaintiff to recover damages from the defendant's negligent actions. (active/passive)

17. The water rate was assessed by the county. (active/passive)

18. The verdict was given by the judge. (active)

19. After the competition the students were amazed by the results. (active)

20. David's words were at a loss to express his meaning.

21. (Jami, one other girl, and two boys are in the law library.) Jami spoke to the girl who was reading a treatise on contracts.

22. (Jami is in the law library with two other girls.) Jami spoke to the girl who was reading a treatise on contracts.

23. The man (who/whom) they saw emerge from the building fired a gun.

24. The man (who/whom) they say emerged from the building fired a gun.

25. The witness said he did not remember to (who/whom) he gave a statement.

26. The house (which/that) I made an offer on sold yesterday.

27. The automobile (that/which) was involved in the wreck has been fixed by the defendant's insurance.

28. I want to thank the person who helped me to the hospital after breaking my leg yesterday.

29. The person may feel they have to talk and then their Fifth Amendment has been violated and they could self-incriminate.

30. To potentially keep people from gaining financially from their wrong doing.

31. Because a no contest was put into place to have a plea bargain to resolve a case by removing civil consequences of a plea deal.

32. Yes, because the employer would be responsible for the employee's actions because the employee would be under the scope of the employer.

B. Punctuation

1. He was charged with assault and battery breaking and entering and rape.

2. The witness for the state failed to appear however the trial continued.

3. The Honorable John Baker former Chief Justice was in attendance.

4. Companies are like siblings the more there are of them the more they compete.

5. Please bring the following a police report your insurance policy and a picture of the wrecked vehicle.

6. The professors assignments did not include the specific assignments exceptions.

7. Ms. Myers and Mrs. Simons files are on the desk.

8. Its time for a test.

9. The defendant yelled you will not take me alive!

10. The favorite words of my child were I'll do it later mom.

11. The doctrine of res ipsa loquitur (Latin for the thing speaks for itself) is not appropriate where the plaintiff can discover the information in the possession of the defendant.

12. The court held the witness may testify as to his understanding of the contract.

13. The professor asked is everyone ready for the test?

14. The club's president was reelected by a fiftytwo percent majority.

15. The road resurfacing is right on schedule: that is, the revised uptodate, one year behind schedule.

16. John F. Kennedy, Jr., was called John John by his family members.

17. Can you imagine the look on the police officer's face when our car rear ended him?

C. Edit these phrases to remove "legalese" and jargon. Simplify them to make them easier to read. Use the smallest number of words to convey the sentence's meaning.

1. during the time at which

2. there can be no question but that

3. I would like to take this opportunity to thank you

4. Enclosed herewith please find

5. I am writing you this letter to tell you

D. Correct errors in grammar, punctuation, and spelling

Jeremiah Wallace were born in a log cabin in Polk County, Georgia in November 22, 1814. When he were seven, he moved with his family to Paducha, Kentucky. His mother dies in 1820, and his family moved to Brown County, Indiana in 1822. Unlike his family, Jeremiah learn to read.

Wallace's legal career began in 1828 when he read the law with his mentor John Billings. In 1837, Wallace passed the Indiana Bar became an lawyer (he taught himself law). He was also elected to the Indiana legislature and servd in the lower house from 1838-1842. He become partner with Billngs. In 1844 Wallace deciderd to settle up and married his long time sweetheart Rebecca Knight. And the couple has too sons and one daughter. Wallace's reputation as a skillful lawyer grew, and in 1846, he took over the law firm when Billings dies.

INTERNET **RESEARCH**

Find two articles discussing how to write a quality document. Create outlines for the articles that show how they are organized or structured. Provide the proper citations for the articles

MEDIA **RESOURCES**

SqoolTechs, LLC, 331 Fairview Drive, Union, MO 63084
Phone: 800-516-0544, Fax: 888-467-8241, Email:
admin@sqooltechs.com
School House Rock *Adverbs*:
School House Rock *Unpack Your Adjectives*:
School House Rock Grammar Rock *Pronouns*:

NeoK12 Educational Videos. *Past Participles and Present Participles*. 2010. At
NeoK12 Educational Videos. *Participial Phrases and Participles as Adjectives*:
NeoK12 Educational Videos. *Who and Whom*. 2010:

NeoK12 Educational Videos. *Active and Passive Voice*. 2010:

Strauss, Jane. *The Blue Book of Grammar and Punctuation*. 2011. "Who vs. That vs. Which Video—Part 1."

http://www.gamequarium.org/dir/SqoolTube_Videos
/Reading_and_Communication_Arts/Grammar/

http://www.schooltube.com/video/054c4aca89b412d90612/
http://www.schooltube.com/video/964198d6a8d99911f4dc/
http://www.schooltube.com/video/b107082c0278
a820f5b3/
http://www.neok12.com/php/watch.php?v=zX5501666
16d637d594d6863&t=Grammar
http://www.neok12.com/php/watch.php?v=
zX0a777b7d4e4b7c0061446b&t=Grammar
http://www.neok12.com/php/watch.php?v=zX744e0704
5f5f7f427e6559&t=Grammar.
http://www.neok12.com/php/watch.php?v=zX54557d5
b767a5a1b76657b&t=Grammar.
http://www.grammarbook.com/video/who_that
_which_1.asp

INTERNET **RESOURCES**

Darling, Charles. Professor of English and Webmaster.
Diagramming Sentences. Capital Community College,
Hartford, CT. 1999.
English Language. *Relative Pronoun*. 2007–2011.

English Grammar Revolution. 2009–2011.

Writing and Analysis

http://grammar.ccc.commnet.edu/grammar/diagrams
/diagrams.htm

http://www.englishlanguageguide.com/english
/grammar/relative-pronoun.asp
http://www.english-grammar-revolution.com
/english-grammar-exercise.html
http://legalresearch.org/docs/process13.html

chapter **fifteen**

THE CASE BRIEF

lenetstan/Shutterstock

LEARNING OBJECTIVES

After studying this chapter, students should be able to:

1. Analyze and summarize authority.

2. Draft a case brief in various formats.

3. Write a case brief accurately, precisely, concisely, and ethically.

4. Adapt the writing style and tone for the audience and purpose.

CHAPTER OVERVIEW

The goal of writing a case brief is to summarize a case by identifying the information from the case that answers or fits into the listed categories or sections. The brief is a method for reading, analyzing, and synthesizing the material presented in a case.

A case brief is simply a written summary of a reported case. It is not the researcher's personal opinion on the case; rather, it is a statement on what the court decided and why. It is objective and fact driven. Researchers use briefs of reported cases to analyze the law in relationship to a client's factual question.

All legal researchers brief cases on a regular basis. The case brief is just one of the many products of legal research, but it often forms the foundation for other types of documents. A researcher may be asked to write only a case brief, or may need to write several case briefs in preparation to write a trial brief, appellate brief, or memorandum of law.

When a paralegal is asked to prepare a case brief, the brief is often used to help an attorney save time and quickly understand what a case is about. Cases are often many pages long, and a case brief can distill a lengthy case to the most important information needed by the attorney.

OPENING SCENARIO

Jami was getting ready for trial and needed to have the issues of the client's case researched and presented in an interoffice memorandum. John had prepared many briefs in school and was very comfortable doing an "11-part brief." However, Jami wanted an "IFRAC brief." John was not familiar with that type of brief, so he asked Annie, another paralegal. Annie assured him that if he knew how to write an 11-part brief, it wouldn't be hard for him to learn how to write an IFRAC brief. It is not as detailed, but shares some parts with the 11-part brief format. She also told him that once he showed Jami he knew how to write an effective internal IFRAC brief, he might get a chance to help with preparing legal memoranda to be presented to a court, since those documents use some of the same techniques. After Annie explained the components of the IFRAC memo, John began to dig in to this new type of project.

THE CASE BRIEF PROCESS

A case brief can be organized in several different ways. The format may be dictated by the supervisor, or a researcher may be left to decide which format works best for the situation.

Four different formats are presented in this chapter. The most complex is the ***11-part brief***, which looks at every aspect of a case. An ***IRAC*** brief is simpler, and summarizes the Issues, Rule, Analysis, and Conclusion. The ***IFRAC*** brief is similar to IRAC, but includes a summary of Facts. The ***CRRACC*** stands for Conclusion, **R**ule, **R**ule Proof, **A**pplication, **C**ounterargument, and **C**onclusion. All four types of briefs share some of the same components. Once the format of the 11-part brief is understood, the IRAC, IFRAC, and CRRACC formats are easy to learn.

The primary objective of writing a case brief is to summarize the basic components of the case and to provide a better understanding of its meaning. The notes should be complete enough so that the reader does not need to refer to the case to understand the components. It must be usable long after it is drafted because it may be referred to months, or even years, after it is written. If material is important enough to cite, the complete quotation should be included. Otherwise, summarize the decision.

A variety of briefing formats may be used in the workplace, depending on what the supervisor prefers or the purpose for which the brief is prepared. A brief may be written for a single case, or to answer specific questions the supervisor will ask. On the other hand, if the assignment is to write an internal memorandum of law for a certain client based on a set of facts, multiple cases will need to be analyzed to address each of the issues in the client' situation. No matter what the purpose is, the writer not only will need to understand each case, but also will need to analyze and synthesize the cases as they apply to the client's facts.

Each paragraph of a case may contain one or more of the components of a court decision. During an analysis, components should be identified by paragraph rather than by analyzing the case as a whole. This is particularly true in paragraphs that include analysis, because different rules or laws are usually discussed within each paragraph.

The following will discuss the different types of briefs: the 11-part brief, IRAC, IFRAC, and CRRACC.

THE 11-PART BRIEF

When a paralegal has been given a research assignment to find and brief a case, the first step is to locate the case, either online or in the library. Step two is to read the case. Generally, reading a case one time is not sufficient. It should be read more than once, while making notes, highlighting, or underlining special portions. Once one has some understanding of the case, step three is to pull information from the case to complete the parts of the brief, as described in Checklist 15-1.

Writing a good case brief, and ultimately a good memorandum, requires understanding the different parts of a case. For purposes of this discussion, the case in Figure 15-1 will be used:

Margin glossary

11-part brief

A format for briefing cases that contains a citation (caption), parties, objectives and theories of the parties, procedural history, facts, issues, holdings, reasoning, the court's order (disposition), comments, and updating.

IRAC

A popular case briefing method that summarizes the Issue, Rule, Analysis, and Conclusion.

IFRAC

A case briefing method that summarizes the Issue, Facts, Rule, Analysis, and Conclusion.

CRRACC

A type of case brief; the acronym stands for **C**onclusion, **R**ule, **R**ule Proof, **A**pplication, **C**ounterargument, and **C**onclusion.

Checklist 15-1   11-PART BRIEF

1. Citation (caption)
2. Parties
3. Objectives and Theories of the Parties
4. Procedural History
5. Facts
6. Issues
7. Holdings
8. Reasoning
9. Court's Order (Disposition)
10. Comments or Commentary
11. Updating

FIGURE 15-1 *Pakalski v. CFC Pasadena Golf, LLC*

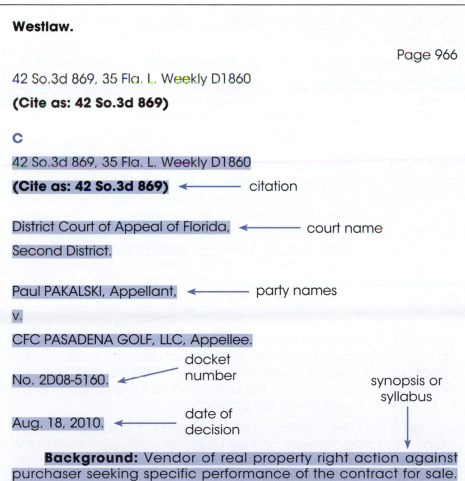

Westlaw.

Page 966

42 So.3d 869, 35 Fla. L. Weekly D1860

(Cite as: 42 So.3d 869)

c

42 So.3d 869, 35 Fla. L. Weekly D1860

(Cite as: 42 So.3d 869) ←——— citation

District Court of Appeal of Florida, ←——— court name
Second District.

Paul PAKALSKI, Appellant, ←——— party names

v.

CFC PASADENA GOLF, LLC, Appellee.

No. 2D08-5160. ←——— docket number

Aug. 18, 2010. ←——— date of decision

Background: Vendor of real property right action against purchaser seeking specific performance of the contract for sale. The Circuit Court, Pinellas County, Mark I. Shames, J., granted purchaser's motion to dismiss. Vendor appealed.

Holding: The District Court of Appeal, Kelly, J., held that vendor's acceptance and retention of purchaser's $150,000 additional deposit did not constitute an election of remedies.

Reversed and remanded.

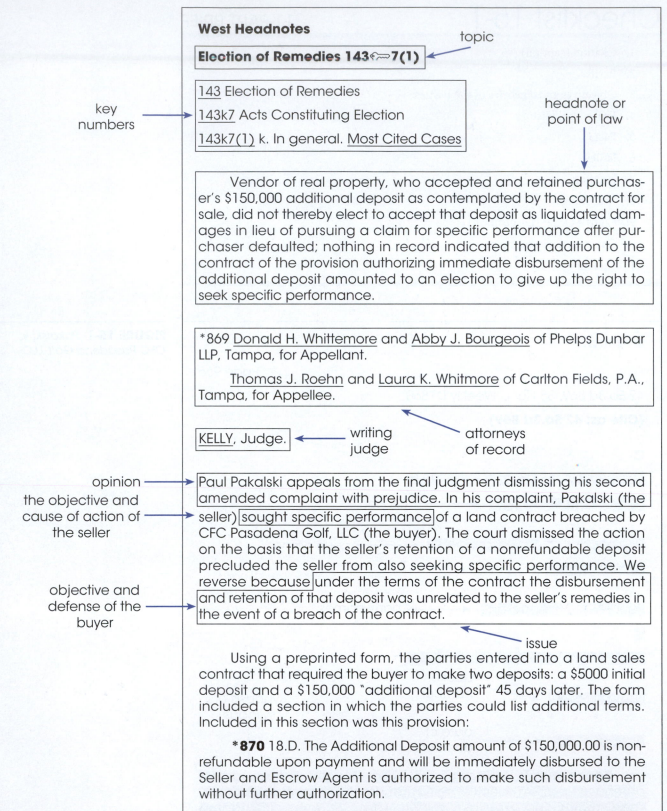

West Headnotes   topic

Election of Remedies 143⟜7(1)

key numbers

143 Election of Remedies

143k7 Acts Constituting Election

143k7(1) k. In general. Most Cited Cases

headnote or point of law

Vendor of real property, who accepted and retained purchaser's $150,000 additional deposit as contemplated by the contract for sale, did not thereby elect to accept that deposit as liquidated damages in lieu of pursuing a claim for specific performance after purchaser defaulted; nothing in record indicated that addition to the contract of the provision authorizing immediate disbursement of the additional deposit amounted to an election to give up the right to seek specific performance.

*869 Donald H. Whittemore and Abby J. Bourgeois of Phelps Dunbar LLP, Tampa, for Appellant.

Thomas J. Roehn and Laura K. Whitmore of Carlton Fields, P.A., Tampa, for Appellee.

KELLY, Judge.   writing   attorneys
                      judge   of record

opinion

the objective and cause of action of the seller

Paul Pakalski appeals from the final judgment dismissing his second amended complaint with prejudice. In his complaint, Pakalski (the seller) sought specific performance of a land contract breached by CFC Pasadena Golf, LLC (the buyer). The court dismissed the action on the basis that the seller's retention of a nonrefundable deposit precluded the seller from also seeking specific performance. We reverse because under the terms of the contract the disbursement and retention of that deposit was unrelated to the seller's remedies in the event of a breach of the contract.

objective and defense of the buyer

                                    issue

Using a preprinted form, the parties entered into a land sales contract that required the buyer to make two deposits: a $5000 initial deposit and a $150,000 "additional deposit" 45 days later. The form included a section in which the parties could list additional terms. Included in this section was this provision:

*870 18.D. The Additional Deposit amount of $150,000.00 is nonrefundable upon payment and will be immediately disbursed to the Seller and Escrow Agent is authorized to make such disbursement without further authorization.

The contract also contained a provision specifying the parties' rights in the event of a default. That provision states:

13. DEFAULT: (a) Seller Default: If . . . Seller fails, refuses or neglects to perform this Contract, Buyer may choose to receive a return of Buyer's deposit without waiving the right to seek damages or to seek specific performance . . . . (b) Buyer Default: If Buyer fails to perform this Contract

. . . Seller may choose to retain and collect all deposits paid and agreed to be paid as liquidated damages or to seek specific performance.

The buyer paid both deposits but ultimately breached the contract by failing to close the transaction and pay the balance of the purchase price. The seller left the $5,000 initial deposit in escrow and sued the buyer seeking specific performance of the contract and damages. The buyer moved to dismiss the complaint for failure to state a cause of action alleging that the seller elected his remedy by retaining the additional deposit as liquidated damages, thus precluding the seller from also seeking specific performance. The court dismissed the second amended complaint with prejudice, ruling that the seller's claims were inconsistent with the contract and that they could not be amended to state a cause of action.

— key facts and the procedural history

The facts here are similar to those before the court in *Bilow v. Benoit*, 519 So.2d 1114 (Fla. 1st DCA 1988). In *Bilow*, the parties entered into a land sales contract that provided for the buyer to pay a $5000 deposit. The parties added a handwritten clause at the end of the printed contract specifying that $1500 of that deposit would be paid to the seller immediately. The contract also provided that in the event the buyer breached, the seller could retain the deposit or alternatively seek specific performance. As is the case here, after defaulting the buyer argued that the seller, by accepting and using a portion of the deposit money, had elected to accept the deposit as liquidated damages and thus was precluded from seeking specific performance.

— internal opinion

The court rejected the buyer's argument that the seller had elected her remedy under the contract stating, "[W]e hold that Bilow's use of the monies in accordance with the contract terms is insufficient to support a finding that Bilow elected to accept the deposit as liquidated damages. The parties agreed both to an explicit use of the deposit monies and to the remedies" specified elsewhere in the contract. *Id. at 1117.* The court went on to explain that the provision in the contract giving the seller the alternative right to retain the deposit or seek specific performance in the event of a breach was "neither inconsistent with nor mutually exclusive of the handwritten provision authorizing use of the deposit monies." *Id.*

Likewise, we conclude that the seller, simply by accepting and retaining the deposit as contemplated in the provision added to section 18.D. of the parties' contract, did not elect to accept that deposit in lieu of pursuing a claim for specific performance in the event of a breach. As was the case in *Bilow*, nothing in the record indicates that adding the provision authorizing the immediate disbursement of the additional deposit amounted to an election to forego the seller's right to enforce the contract by suing for specific performance if the buyer failed to perform. Accordingly, we reverse the order dismissing the ***871** second amended complaint and remand for further proceedings.

— reasoning

Reversed and remanded. ◄——— disposition

CASANUEVA, C.J., and KHOUZAM, J., Concur. ◄——— panel

Fla. App. 2 Dist., 2010.
Pakalski v. CFC Pasadena Golf, LLC
42 So.3d 869, 35 Fla. L. Weekly D1860

Source: © 2011 Thomson Reuters. No Claim to Orig. US Gov. Works.

The parts of a case must not be confused with the parts of the brief. There are more parts of a case than there are parts of any case brief format. The information in Figure 15-2 identifies the parts of the 11-part brief.

As the name of the format implies, there are 11 separate parts of the brief, each with a different purpose and importance to the whole.

---

1. **Citation (caption)** — *Pakalski v. CFC Pasadena Golf, LLC.,* 42 So.3d 869 (Fla. 2010)

2. **Parties** —

   Pakalski: seller of land, plaintiff below, appellant here

   v.

   CFC Pasadena Golf, LLC: buyer of land, defendant below, appellee here

3. **Objectives and Theories of the Parties** —

   Objectives: Plaintiff wants the contract for the sale of land upheld.

   Defendant doesn't want to complete the contract.

   Cause of Action: Breach of contract

   Defense: No breach of contract and no specific performance required.

4. **Procedural History** —

   Prior Litigation: The lower court dismissed the plaintiff's complaint; contract not breached and no specific performance required by the defendant; plaintiff appealed to the Florida Appellate Court.

   Present Litigation: The Florida Appellate Court found that the seller's retention of the deposit did not preclude the plaintiff from a claim of specific performance in case of a breach; Result: The Florida Court of Appeals reversed the lower court's decision.

5. **Facts** —

   The parties entered into a land sales contract that required the buyer to make two deposits: a $5000 initial deposit and a $150,000 "additional deposit" 45 days later. The buyer paid both deposits but ultimately breached the contract by failing to close the transaction and pay the balance of the purchase price.

6. **Issues** — According to Florida contract law, does seller's retention of a nonrefundable deposit preclude the seller from also seeking specific performance?

7. **Holding** — No, the seller's retention of a nonrefundable deposit does not preclude the seller from also seeking specific performance.

8. **Reasoning** — Similar to *Bilow*, nothing in the record indicates that adding the provision authorizing the immediate disbursement of the additional deposit amounted to an election to forego the seller's right to enforce the contract by suing for specific performance if the buyer failed to perform.

9. **Court's Order (Disposition)** — The court reversed the order dismissing the second amended complaint and remanded the case for further proceedings.

10. **Comments** — [This section is for personal comments and other research related to the case, such as reading the *Bilow* case. (See text for further information.)]

11. **Updating** — [This section is to confirm that the case was updated in *Shepard's*, KeyCite, or another citator service, and that the case is still good law. The date when the case was briefed is indicated so that if this brief is used in the future, it will only need to be updated from the date of the brief.]

FIGURE 15-2 11-Part Brief

FIGURE 15-3

[FIG2]42 So.3d 869 (2010)

Paul PAKALSKI, Appellant,

v.

CFC PASADENA GOLF, LLC, Appellee.

No. 2D08-5160.

District Court of Appeal of Florida, Second District.

August 18, 2010

Citation or Caption

The *citation* is the address of the case. It includes the volume number, reporter abbreviation, and page number of the case. The information should be complete, providing both the official version, if it exists, and the unofficial citations. The citation should be in the proper format so that it can be used in any subsequent documents.

A citation has two primary purposes. First, a complete citation conveys valuable information about the case, including the court level, jurisdiction, date it was handed down, and case history, if included. Second, an accurate citation provides a road map for the reader to locate the law. But just like that of a roadmap, the usefulness of a citation depends on its accuracy. Inaccurate or incomplete citations will take another researcher on a detour, wasting valuable time and effort.

Some researchers treat the citation as part of the case caption. The caption is the portion of the case that provides the names of the parties, the location of the case, the court deciding the case, the docket number, and the date of the decision.

Parties The description of the parties is more than just a list of names. This section of the brief identifies some additional information about the parties that will help the reader know more about the case at a glance. In addition to the party name, the litigation status is also shown based on the level of the case. The litigation status should tell the reader not only the status of each party at the time of the decision, but also the status of each in the court below. This information can be found in the *caption*, as shown in Figure 15-3, and in the *synopsis* or *syllabus*, shown in Figure 15-4.

This case is on appeal in the District Court of Appeal of Florida; therefore, the case was in at least one other court, namely the trial court. The caption shows that Pakalski is the party who is appealing the lower court's decision.

Paul **Pakalski** appeals from the final judgment dismissing his second amended complaint with prejudice. In his complaint, **Pakalski** (the seller) sought specific performance of a land contract breached by **CFC Pasadena Golf, LLC** (the buyer). The court dismissed the action on the basis that the seller's retention of a nonrefundable deposit precluded the seller from also seeking specific performance. We reverse because under the terms of the contract the disbursement and retention of that deposit was unrelated to the seller's remedies in the event of a breach of the contract.

TIP

The official citation is the citation of the case in the reporter coming directly from the governmental body. The unofficial reporter comes from a publishing company. While both reporters provide the same case, the unofficial reporter will generally provide additional information such as in the Pakalski case.

Citation
The address of an authority. It is identifying information that enables someone to locate material.

Caption
A brief section at the beginning of a case that provides the names of the parties, the name of the court that decided the case, the docket number, and the date of decision.

Synopsis or syllabus
A brief summary of the entire court opinion, usually written by a commercial publisher.

FIGURE 15-4 Synopsis or Syllabus of the Case

FIGURE 15-5 Presentation of Party Information

> Pakalski: seller in a land contract deal/plaintiff below; appellant here.
>
> v.
>
> CFC Pasadena Golf, LLC: buyer in a land contract deal/defendant below; appellee here.

According to the synopsis or syllabus, Pakalski, the seller in a land contract, filed a complaint in the trial court alleging that CFC had breached the contract; therefore, he was the plaintiff in the lower court. CFC Pasadena Golf, LLC (CFC), the buyer in that original land contract, was sued by Pakalski; therefore, CFC was the defendant in the case below.

From reading the caption and the synopsis, the researcher has three key pieces of information: (1) the party names, (2) what the case is basically about, and (3) who sued whom for what. Using this information, the parties section of the brief would be written as shown in Figure 15-5.

By looking at just these two lines in the case brief, the reader can tell generally what the case is about.

Objectives and Theories of the Parties

Objectives
The goals each party is trying to achieve through the litigation.

Each side in a lawsuit has an **objective**: what each side wants from the other, or wants to prevent the other from doing. Sometimes the court will provide this information up front. In the synopsis, the court states that the seller "sought specific performance of a land contract." That is the seller's objective: getting the contract completed. The court also implies that the buyer does not want to conclude the contract: that is the buyer's objective. When one side wants something, the other side is likely to want the opposite (although the objectives are not always this straightforward).

In addition to objectives, the parties have legal theories that are the basis of their claims or defenses. In all litigation, each party has at least one theory. The plaintiff who is filing the complaint must show some legally recognized reason to sue, called the **cause of action**. A cause of action is based on some rule of law that allows the party who has been injured to recover either some type of **damages**, or some form of equitable relief, such as specific performance of a contract. The plaintiff must state a cause of action for every claim being made against the defendant. Each cause of action will come from a statute, regulation, constitutional provision, common law doctrine, or other law. In the *Pakalski* case, the cause of action is for specific performance of a contract.

Cause of action
The legal basis of a complaint.

Damages
A money judgment awarded in a civil action.

The cause of action is usually found within the first few paragraphs of the case. In the example case, the cause of action would be breach of contract with the remedy of specific performance. This is a common law theory.

Defense
A position that relieves the defendant of responsibility to the plaintiff.

A **defense** is a defendant's theory or a legal argument that relieves the defendant of responsibility to the plaintiff. The most common defense is a **denial**. If the denial is successful, the cause of action may be defeated for failure to establish the cause of action upon which the plaintiff relied in the complaint. In the example, the defendant denied the claim, arguing that the seller retained a nonrefundable deposit, which precluded the seller from seeking specific performance.

Denial
A defense made to a complaint that controverts an allegation in the complaint.

Internal opinions
Other case opinions the court relies on or which the court discusses within its opinion.

As a researcher reads and analyzes the case, information about the case itself should not be confused with **internal opinions**—opinions from other cases that are discussed by the court within the present opinion.

The facts here are similar to those before the court in *Bilow v. Benoit*, 519 So.2d 1114 (Fla. 1st DCA 1988). In *Bilow*, the parties entered into a land sales contract that provided for the buyer to pay a $5000 deposit. The parties added a handwritten clause at the end of the printed contract specifying that $1500 of that deposit would be paid to the seller immediately. The contract also provided that in the event the buyer breached, the seller could retain the deposit or alternatively seek specific performance. As is the case here, after defaulting the buyer argued that the seller, by accepting and using a portion of the deposit money, had elected to accept the deposit as liquidated damages and thus was precluded from seeking specific performance.

FIGURE 15-6 Internal Opinions

In the *Pakalski* case, the court discusses opinions from other cases. One example is shown in Figure 15-6.

In this excerpt, *Bilow* is an internal opinion that the court uses to compare to the facts of the case being decided. The facts in this paragraph look very similar to the facts of the case before the court. That is why a researcher must be careful that information from internal opinions is not used in any part of the case brief—except, perhaps, in the portion describing the court's reasoning.

Procedural History

Procedural history, also called judicial history or prior and present proceedings, tells where this case has been in the legal system and what has happened to it along the way. The case could have come from an administrative agency or a lower court, such as a trial court. That litigation status of the parties described in Section 2 of the brief was based on procedural history—the case had been tried in a lower court.

Not every case has procedural history. For example, if a case is brought in the U.S. District Court for the Southern District of Indiana, that is probably the only litigation at that point, because the district court is the trial court of the federal system. If the claim did not originate in an administrative proceeding at an agency, no prior proceedings would exist. However, if this case were heard at the U.S. Circuit Court of Appeals for the Seventh Circuit, there would be prior proceedings because the Seventh Circuit Court has appellate jurisdiction. Its role is to review decisions made by a lower court. Likewise, if this issue were appealed to the U.S. Supreme Court, there were probably at least two prior proceedings—in the U.S. District Court, and in the U.S. Court of Appeals. This sequence is shown in Figure 15-7.

In the procedural history, the information about the prior proceedings should be presented chronologically with the initial proceeding given first, and the most recent proceeding given last. Each proceeding in the list should provide the name of the court, the action taken by the parties, the outcome, and the basis for the decision. For example, in the *Pakalski* case, the prior proceeding was in the Florida trial court. The actual name of the court does not appear in the case, so it is necessary to check a source, such as the *Uniform System of Citation* or *ALWD*, to identify the court name. Because the attorneys are from Tampa, some additional analysis can determine that the trial court was in Tampa, in Hillsborough County, Florida, which is located in the Thirteenth Circuit. Then the history states what happened at that level, and the reason for the decision.

FIGURE 15-7 Hierarchy of Courts[1]

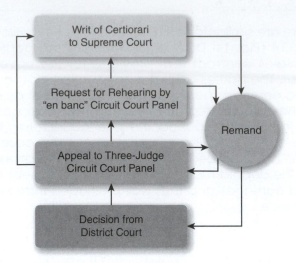

One way to clearly present the information from the prior proceedings is to consecutively number each proceeding beginning with the first, identify the court, the action taken by the parties, and the outcome. So, for the *Pakalski* case, this section might look like Figure 15-8.

Since these are the only two proceedings, using the terms "trial court" and "district court of appeal" is not confusing. However, if a case had several layers of proceedings, specifically identifying each court might help clarify what is happening in the case.

If the case being briefed is an appeal from an administrative agency, there are additional levels of review. For example, if an unemployed worker in Indiana files a claim with the Department of Workforce Development, a claims deputy makes a determination of the worker's eligibility for unemployment compensation. If the determination is not accepted by either the claimant or the employer, either may appeal by requesting a hearing before an administrative law judge (ALJ). The decision of the ALJ may then be appealed to the review board.[2] After the ***exhaustion of remedies*** at the administrative level, the decision can be appealed to the courts. Here there are four levels to the process: the claims deputy, the ALJ, the review board, and the court. With this many levels, it would be helpful to identify each forum by name.

Exhaustion of remedies

In administrative agency cases, proceeding through all levels that an agency offers to resolve a dispute until there is no further recourse at the agency level.

FIGURE 15-8 Judicial History (Prior and Present Proceedings)

1. **Trial Court:** Plaintiff sought specific performance in a land contract breached by defendant in the Thirteenth Circuit. Result: The court dismissed the action based on the plaintiff retaining a deposit.

2. **District Court of Appeal:** Plaintiff (Appellant) appeals the final judgment of the circuit court dismissing the action. Result: Appellate court reverses the judgment of the trial court.

[1]Curtis Edmonds, J.D. Federal Court Concepts. *Explaining the Structure.* Georgia Institute of Technology. 2003. http://www.catea.gatech.edu/grade/legal/structure.html

[2]Indiana Department of Workforce Development. File an Appeal. 2012. http://www.in.gov /dwd/2356.htm. (retrieved March 15, 2012)

Facts

Every case that comes before a court will present a unique set of facts. When writing a brief, the researcher must be able to identify the most important facts and connect them to the legal issues in the client's case.

In non legal settings, a *fact* may be defined as follows:

1. Something known to be true: something that can be shown to be true, to exist, or to have happened.
2. Truth or reality of something: the truth or actual existence of something, as opposed to the supposition of something or a belief about something "based on fact."
3. A piece of information: for example, a statistic or a statement of the truth
4. Actual course of events: the circumstances of an event or state of affairs, rather than an interpretation of its significance. "Matters of fact are issues for a jury, while matters of law are issues for the court."
5. Something based on evidence: something that is based on or concerned with the evidence presented in a legal case.[3]

Fact
A person, place, thing, or event that can be perceived with the senses.

In law, researchers primarily are concerned with **key facts**, which are defined as follows:

A key fact is a fact that if different or nonexistent would change the outcome.

Key fact
A fact that if different or nonexistent would change the outcome.

Researchers look at key facts when comparing a case with the client's case and determining whether it is "on point" or similar. If the key facts are similar or on point, the case is probably important. If the key facts are dissimilar, the case probably has no value to support the client.

Facts may also be referred to as explanatory facts, nonessential facts, or relevant facts.

Explanatory facts: Does this fact supplement or explain a legally relevant fact? If so, it is an explanatory fact. These facts are often referred to as *context facts*. The may be included in the brief if they help the reader understand the key facts of the case.

Nonessential facts: Does removing or changing this fact significantly change the client's situation? If not, it is likely a legally unimportant or nonessential fact. These facts would not be included in the brief.

Relevant Facts: Does removing or changing this fact significantly change the client's situation? If so, it is a legally relevant fact. These facts are also referred to as key facts, and must be included in the brief.

When writing a brief, only facts that are explanatory or relevant should be included. For example, in a case involving a drunk-driving arrest, a researcher may want to include facts about how much alcohol the person had consumed, because this fact is key or relevant to proving the violation. But the brief need not include the color of the car the person was driving, because it is nonessential.

Facts may also be categorized as substantive or procedural. **Substantive facts** are those that give rise to the plaintiff's cause of action. In other words, substantive facts are those which identify who did what to whom, and why. The **Procedural facts**, for the most part, are those describing the actions of the decision-making bodies in a proceeding such as an administrative agency hearing or a trial.

Substantive facts
Facts that pertain to the rights and obligations of the parties.

Procedural facts
Facts that pertain to the technicalities of bringing or defending in litigation.

Sometimes facts will be set out in clearly defined paragraphs, but most often, researchers will need to sift through the facts to cull the relevant facts. In the

---

[3]Encarta® World English Dictionary [North American Edition] © & (P) 2009 Microsoft Corporation. http://www.bing.com/Dictionary/Search?q=define+fact&form=DTPDIO

FIGURE 15-9 Locating
Key Facts

Facts may be "key facts" if the court

1. identifies what the parties think the facts are;
2. identifies what it believes the key facts are in the reasoning;
3. repeatedly uses the same facts or **characterizes** the facts;
4. uses adjectives such as *significant* or *crucial* when discussing facts;
5. uses the facts early in the opinion;
6. uses the same facts throughout the opinion;
7. responds to key facts acknowledged in lower tribunals; or
8. includes a discussion of similar key facts in a cited case.

Characterizing facts
Assigning alternate or different words to describe the same fact.

Elements
Essential parts of a rule of law, such as the elements of a statute.

Reasoning
Summary of the reasons why a court reached the decision it reached.

Issue
A question in the case that one is being asked to research.

TIP

Most of the cases being briefed will be appellate-level cases because most states do not publish trial court cases. At the federal level, district court cases (trial cases) are reported in the Federal Supplement.

Pakalski case, the substantive facts are interwoven with the procedural history in the first few paragraphs. In such cases, certain clues can help determine the key facts, which are listed in Figure 15-9.

In many cases, the court will identify what the parties think the issues are and then respond to those points. In some instances, the court will specifically state something like, "We believe, however, that the facts are . . . ." In most instances the court's position will not be that clear, but the court will provide hints as to what it believes the facts are and why those facts are key **elements**. A clue may be found in the court's **reasoning**, where it explains *why* it decided the way it did. The key facts will be consistent with the court's holding, so understanding the reasoning will help identify the key facts.

Another clue to finding a key fact is emphasis: the court's repeated reference to a fact in the case, use of various synonyms to describe the fact, or expansion on the application of or characterization of the term. For example, in a property case, if a court frequently refers to an existing structure on the land, or a "fixture," the presence or status of that structure may be a key fact. If the court uses certain adjectives such as "important," "little significance," or "crucial" to describe a fact, those words may indicate that it is relevant. Also, if the court uses the facts early in its opinion, those facts may be key elements.

The court may respond to references by the lower agency or court to certain facts. This could signify whether this court also considers those facts to be relevant. If the court chooses to discuss a cited opinion and provides facts from that opinion, those facts may be key facts as well.

In the fact section of the brief, some supervisors prefer key facts to be presented in a bulleted list, while other supervisors may want the facts described in a narrative. Whatever format is requested, the reader should be able to immediately determine which facts were relevant to the court's decision.

Issues

Writing the **issues** is probably the most important part of briefing a case. Properly written issues enable a researcher to focus on what is most important and avoid deviating from the objectives of the research. With the issues clearly in mind, the researcher can prepare an effective analysis of the case.

An issue is a question the court is being asked to resolve. It is rare that a case has only one issue, and a court will treat some issues with greater depth than others.

Issues are either questions of fact or questions of law. In order to write an effective legal issue, the writer must understand the *rule of law* upon which the issue is based. A rule of law can be any of the 10 types of law set out in Table 15-1.

The parties will have based the litigation on one or more rules of law. They may have disagreed over the application of the entire rule, or only one element of the rule. An **element** is one of the essential "pieces" of a law that must be proven to establish a claim. Figure 15-10 is the Indiana statute on driving on the right half of the roadway.

Negligence has four elements: a duty, a breach of duty, proximate cause, and damages. Each of these elements must be proven. In the statute above, a driver has certain duties as to the control of the vehicle. For example, "a vehicle shall be

Rule of law
A pronouncement from the government that establishes a standard of conduct for all to follow.

Element
A portion of a rule or essential component that must be present.

TABLE 15-1   Ten Types of Law

Source of Law	Purpose
Constitutions	The U.S. Constitution is the supreme law of the land. For example, Art. III, sec. 1 sets forth the creation of the U.S. Supreme Court; the First Amendment gives us the right to have free speech, religion, press, assembly, and the right to petition our grievances. Each state has its own constitution.
Statutes	These laws are enacted by the U.S. Congress and state legislatures. Statutes are enacted to prescribe conduct, define crimes, create inferior government bodies, appropriate public monies, and in general promote the public welfare. Statutes can be either procedural or substantive. For example, 26 U.S.C. § 2501 regarding taxable transfers or I.C. § 35-34-1-1 covering commencement of criminal prosecutions.
Cases, court opinions, court decisions	Cases are legal precedent, created by judges rather than legislatures, when judges can either interpret statutory law or apply the common law. For example, *Marbury v. Madison*, 5 U.S. 137 (1803) formed the basis for judicial review. In *Commonwealth v. Jones*, 880 S.W.2d 544 (Ky. 1994) the court stated that it would not substitute its decision for that of a jury regarding the occurrence of facts.
Administrative regulations	Similar to statutes but created by administrative agencies, administrative regulations generally pertain to providing benefit to someone in a specific agency situation. Examples include 20 C.F.R. 404, regarding the Social Security Act, and 18 VAC 60-20 (2008), governing the practice of dentistry and dental hygiene in Virginia.
Administrative decisions	Decisions handed down by administrative law judges. Examples are *A & W Smelters & Refiners, Inc.* (CERCLA 106(b) 94-14), involving an environmental clean-up order, and *IDEM v. Hungler*, 2008 OEA 1, which interpreted the Clean Water Act.
Rules of Court	Procedural laws governing the mechanics of litigation in a particular court. Examples include Fed.R.Civ.P. 26 (FRCP 26), involving the duty to disclose discovery, and Alaska Sup. Ct. R. 11(a)(1), concerning proper citation format.
Charters	These fundamental laws of local units of government allow the entity to function; an example is the charter for the Town of Windsor Locks, CT.
Ordinances	Laws of a local legislative branch such as a county or city council; an example is 337.20 muffler; muffler cutout; excessive smoke, gas or noise, enacted by the city of Hubbard, OH.
Executive Orders	Laws issued by a chief executive officer, such as the president or a state governor. Examples are The President: Executive Order 13508—Chesapeake Bay Protection and Restoration, and Illinois Executive Order 9 (2009), which revoked a previous order that was confusing.
Treaties	International agreements between two or more countries, such as the North American Free Trade Agreement (NAFTA).

FIGURE 15-10 Law
Excerpt: Indiana Statute
on Driving

IC 9-21-8-2

Roadways; use of right half; exceptions; traveling at reduced speeds

Sec. 2. (a) Upon all roadways of sufficienl width, a vehicle shall
be driven upon the right half of the roadway except as
follows:

(1) When overtaking and passing another vehicle proceeding in the same direction under the rules governing overtaking and passing.

(2) When the right half of a roadway is closed to traffic
under construction or repair.

(3) Upon a roadway divided into three (3) marked lanes
for traffic under the rules applicable to a roadway
divided into three (3) marked lanes.

(4) Upon a roadway designated and signposted for one-
way traffic.

(b) Upon all roadways, a vehicle proceeding at less than the
normal speed of traffic at the time and place under the
conditions then existing shall be driven:

(1) in the right-hand lane then available for traffic; or

(2) as close as practicable to the right-hand curb or edge
of the roadway;

except when overtaking and passing another vehicle proceeding in
the same direction or when preparing for a left turn at an intersection
or into a private road or driveway.

As added by P.L.2-1991, SEC.9.

driven on the right half of the roadway . . ." The element of "duty" might be in dispute if the plaintiff claimed that the defendant crossed the center line and crashed
into his vehicle. The issue might be drafted as follows.

> Under I.C. 9-21-8-2, did the defendant breach the duty to use the right
> half of the two-lane roadway when, without reason, he crossed the center
> line and proceeded for 1000 feet until impacting with plaintiff's car?

The issue has three distinct parts. The first part is the rule of law: "Under
I.C. 9-21-8-2 . . ." The second part is the question: "did the defendant breach the
duty to use the right half of the two-land roadway?" The last part consists of key
facts from the client's situation: "when, without reason, he crossed the center line
and proceeded for 1000 feet until impacting with plaintiff's car." Here is a good
formula for writing an issue:

$$issue = law + question + key\ facts$$

There are many other ways to write issues. Some writers may write a very
simple issue that contains the rule of law only, such as "Was the defendant negligent?" A writer might also add a limited number of facts or the actual law:

- Was the defendant in violation of I.C. 9-21-8-2 when he crossed the center line?
- Does crossing the center line constitute negligence?

If the reader already understands the case and the law, writing an issue in
a simple or abbreviated form, as shown above, is acceptable and is often done.

Good: Was the defendant negligent?

Better: Was the defendant negligent when he struck a child on a bicycle?

Best: According to I.C. 9-21-8-37 concerning a driver's responsibility to exercise due care when children and pedestrians are present, was the defendant negligent when he failed to keep a proper lookout for children and struck a child riding a bicycle?

FIGURE 15-11 Forms of the Same Issue

But for students, using the more extensive formula above is a valuable part of the learning experience. Having the complete issue available at all times helps the researcher remain on track. During the research process, it is easy to get off track as more research is done and more material is read. If a researcher begins to get sidetracked, the issue can be referenced to keep it in focus.

Another reason to use the complete formula for writing issues is that researchers seldom have the luxury of doing an entire research project without interruption. If a project must be set aside and then returned to later, having the complete issue written out eliminates the need to search through the file to recall the key information. Figure 15-11 shows different ways to write the same issue.

Figure 15-11 shows an example of effective issue writing. The "best" version keeps the researcher on track and helps the researcher determine the court's reasoning at a glance.

The issue section of a brief is an important element of the case-briefing process because correctly identifying and presenting the issues enables the researcher to focus the research and avoid deviating from the research objective.

Identifying the issue enables the researcher to prepare the analysis with appropriate authority and to understand the action in the case. Once the issue is defined, it needs to be analyzed. This leads the researcher to look at the court's analysis or reasoning.

The issue in the *Pakalski* contract case is not really whether the plaintiff lost the right to recover specific performance, but rather whether the lower court made an error in its decision that favored the defendant. One option for an issue would be the following.

> Under contract law, did the court commit an error when it found that the seller's retention of a nonrefundable deposit precluded the seller from seeking specific performance under section 18D of the contract?

Finding the issues in a case can be difficult. Some judges provide road signs, such as I, II, III, or A, B, C, or topical headings such as "Negligence," to identify the major issues. Other courts will identify the issues indirectly by using statements such as "we agree with the plaintiff's assessment of the issue." This information is often found in the beginning or at the end of the opinion.

Unfortunately, most courts do not expressly identify all the issues. Some courts may identify one main issue, but not the other issues in the case. In these cases, an effective strategy is to start by putting the issues into the two broad categories of substantive and procedural issues. Procedural issues are those involving the mechanics or procedures of the litigation, such as service of process or the denial of a motion for summary judgment. Substantive issues are those affecting the rights and obligations of the parties, or anything other than procedure. Examples would include the elements of a breach of contract, the rules of the road, or the definition of a hostile work environment.

TIP

There may often be more than one issue in a case.

Headnotes
Enhancements to case reports written by West Publishing Company; each headnote states a single point of law that is discussed with the case.

Concurring opinion
An opinion written by a judge who agrees with the result reached by the majority, but for different reasons.

Dissenting opinion
An opinion written by a judge who disagrees with the outcome of the case.

The *headnotes* in the unofficial reporters are a valuable tool in determining the issues of a case. Headnotes are summaries of points of law, and each headnote covers only one rule, point of law, or issue. If a case has only one or two headnotes, and both are covering the same topic, there is likely only one issue. However, if there are 14 headnotes, it is likely that a case involves multiple issues.

Reading the *concurring* and *dissenting opinions*, if any are available, can also help find the issues. The concurring opinion is written by a judge or justice who may agree with the result but perhaps not with how the result came about. A dissenting opinion is written when a judge or justice disagrees with the majority. If a judge felt strongly enough to write one of these opinions, the opinion will focus on key issues in the case. Concurring and dissenting opinions are not the law; may differ from the majority opinion, which is the law; and should not be quoted in the analysis or reasoning portion of the brief. Rather, these opinions can, and often should, be discussed in the commentary portion of the case brief.

Sometimes the court states what the parties believed the issues to be. Statements such as "appellant claims that the motion for summary judgment was erroneously ordered" or "respondent claims that the award of one-half of his personal account was unjustified" will be given. Then one would look for the court's discussion of those issues to see how the court viewed the parties' contentions.

It can be useful to read the end of the opinion first. The court may restate the issues in the holding. In the drafting of a complete issue and complete holding, the issue is written as a question as given below.

> According to I.C. 9-21-8-37 concerning a driver's responsibility to exercise due care when children and pedestrians are present, was the defendant negligent when he failed to keep a proper lookout for children and struck a child riding a bicycle?

The complete holding is then written as a statement of the issue:

> A defendant is negligent when he fails to keep a proper lookout for children and strikes a child riding a bicycle, according to I.C. 9-21-8-37.

Often minor issues are grouped at the end and are briefly discussed. When a specific issue cannot be found, it may be necessary to infer the issue before the court by looking at the court's discussion. Words such as "The issue before us is . . ." may not be present, but if the court continues discussing a particular rule or area of law, it might be important to pay particular attention, since that may point to one of the issues of the case.

Holding

Holding
The answer to the legal issue after the court applies the rules of law to the facts of the case.

The conclusion, or the *holding*, is the court's answer to the issue presented, and states the court's position on that issue. The holding states the rule of law and explains how it applies to the significant facts. If the issues in the case brief have been written correctly, the holding will provide an answer to each issue stated. The holding is usually very short. For learning purposes, students should write a complete statement of the holding. This may simply involve taking each issue and turning the question into a statement that provides the answer. In the *Pakalski* case, the holding could be stated this way:

> The court committed an error when it found that the seller's retention of a nonrefundable deposit precluded the seller from seeking specific performance under section 18D of the contract.

Figure 15-12 provides another example based on the Indiana statute discussed above.

Every issue in the case has a holding. So, if the case has three issues, there will be three holdings.

According I.C. 9-21-8-37 concerning a driver's responsibility to exercise due care when children and pedestrians are present, the defendant was negligent when he failed to keep a proper lookout for children and struck a child riding a bicycle.

FIGURE 15-12 Holding

Reasoning

The court's *reasoning* tells why the court decided as it did. It explains why the court made the decision, and what the court relied upon in making its decision. This portion of the brief may also be called the *rationale* or the *analysis*.

The court may rely on a variety of authorities when reaching its conclusion. Because of its use of authority, some refer to this as the "law" or "rule" section. When authority is cited in this section, or any place within the brief, the authority must be properly and completely cited. If a citation is given only partially, the original case will need to be revisited to obtain the whole citation, wasting time in the process.

If an issue focuses on the interpretation of a statute, the court may need to examine the language of the statute and other factors such as legislative intent. The court's interpretation of the statute will provide precedent to guide future cases when the issue arises again.

If the reasoning comes from **common law**, or judge-made law, the court looks at **precedent** or those cases with similar facts and issues that have been previously decided. In addition, the court may look at the policies behind common-law doctrines, which often come from an extensive history of case law that has been previously decided.

In the *Pakalski* case, the reasoning came from precedent.

Figure 15-13 shows a possible summary of the reasoning in *Pakalski*.

Reasoning
Summary of the reasons why a court reached the decision it reached.

Common law
Judge-made law; law created by judges in their opinions when interpreting other laws or applying laws to new situations.

Precedent
Those cases with similar facts and issues that have been previously decided, and will guide the decisions in future cases.

> **TIP**
>
> There is no "magic" wording for explaining the court's reasoning; the best approach is simply to tell what influenced the court to make its decision.

The court looked at similar facts in *Bilow v. Benoit,* 519 So.2d 1114 (Fla. 1st DCA 1988), where parties entered into a land sales contract that provided for the buyer to pay a $5000 deposit. The parties added a handwritten clause at the end of the printed contract specifying that $1500 of that deposit would be paid to the seller immediately. The contract also provided that in the event the buyer breached, the seller could retain the deposit or alternatively seek specific performance. As is the case here, after defaulting the buyer argued that the seller, by accepting and using a portion of the deposit money, had elected to accept the deposit as liquidated damages and thus was precluded from seeking specific performance. The *Bilow* court looked to the contract terms and determined Bilow accepted the deposit as liquidated damages. The parties agreed both to an explicit use of the deposit monies and to the remedies specified elsewhere in the contract Likewise, we conclude that the seller, simply by accepting and retaining the deposit as contemplated in the provision added to section 18.D of the parties' contract, did not elect to accept that deposit in lieu of pursuing a claim for specific performance in the event of a breach. Nothing in the record indicates that adding the provision authorizing the immediate disbursement of the additional deposit amounted to an election to forego the seller's right to enforce the contract by suing for specific performance if the buyer failed to perform.

Pakalski at 870–871.

FIGURE 15-13 *Pakalski* Reasoning

TABLE 15-2 Hierarchy of Law

Federal Law	State Law
U.S. Constitution	U.S. Constitution (because nothing can contravene the U.S. Constitution)
Federal statutes	State constitution
Federal common law	State statutes
Federal administrative law	State common law
	State administrative law

Sometimes the court is faced with deciding whether two different rules of law are consistent. Comparisons may help define a term, or uncover legislative intent. For example, the court may be comparing two separate state statutes, both of which use the term "majority" but which do not define "majority." The court will try to adopt a definition of "majority" that is consistent across both statutes.

The courts are generally hesitant to rule that one law is inconsistent with another; however, sometimes it is necessary. When there is an inconsistency, the courts may apply a hierarchy of law as shown in Table 15-2.

Within this hierarchy, if a law is inconsistent with a higher authority, the higher authority controls. Table 15-3 shows various outcomes that may occur when this hierarchy is applied. Note: This table presumes that there is a reason for both federal and state laws to apply.

TABLE 15-3 Rule of Law Comparison

Inconsistent Laws		What Controls?
U.S. Constitution	Any other law	U.S. Constitution
Federal statute	Federal administrative provision	Federal statute
Federal statute	Federal statute	Court attempts to decide which statute Congress intended to control in the given situation by looking at the date of implementation, specificity of language, and so on.
Federal statute	Federal common law	Federal statute
State statute	State constitution	State constitution
State statute	State common law	State statute
State statute	State administrative provision	State statute
State statute	State statute	Just as with the two federal statutes, the court attempts to decide which statute the legislature intended to control in the given situation by looking at the date of implementation, specificity of language, and so on.
Federal statute	State statute	If the federal government has supremacy over the state in the issue at hand, the federal statute controls.
Federal administrative provision	State statute	Federal administrative provision controls if the U.S. Constitution grants supremacy over the issue at hand.

Very often, a client's situation will hinge on the language of a statute that has not yet been interpreted by the courts in the jurisdiction. The researcher will not be able to find a case on point that interprets the statute. However, it may be possible to look at how courts have interpreted similar statutes with similar language. For example, a statute may require that before local government takes certain actions, such as holding tax sales or changing zoning laws, affected property owners must be given notice of the action. Statutes are sometimes ambiguous or poorly written in defining who must receive notice and how notice must be given. If a notice provision in a particular statute has not previously been considered by a court, the court may look to how a similar notice provision has been interpreted in other statutes.

In order to argue that an opinion interpreting a particular law is a precedent for a client's case interpreting a different, but similar law, the researcher must meet the following conditions:

1. There must be a similarity in the language of the two pieces of law.
2. There must be a similarity in the purposes served by the two pieces of law.
3. There must not be any direct authority on the meaning of the piece of law involved in the client's case.

The key is to be sure that there is no authority available to define the law. Another caveat is that the law must be in the same jurisdiction as the client's case. For example, where the court is comparing two separate statutes, both of which use the term "majority" but which do not define "majority," the statutes must be from the same state. If the client's case is in Michigan, the researcher would be looking for Michigan statutes and Michigan cases.

Sometimes the court makes a statement in its opinion that is about a question that it was not asked to answer or that has nothing to do with the issue at hand. These statements are called *dicta*. This term comes from the Latin expression *obiter dictum,* meaning "a remark by the way."[4] Dicta have no binding effect but can be persuasive, and may be used by researchers to predict how a court might decide a similar issue in the future. For example, if the case dealt with a civil negligence matter, the court might state, "the defendant may be prosecuted for criminal negligence as well, based on these facts." That statement is dictum because the case is not a criminal prosecution, and there was no actual charge of criminal negligence. The court did not need to offer that insight, but it could guide future decisions.

Disposition

The *disposition* is what happened to the case based on what the court decided in the holding. Whereas the holding is a statement that answers the issue, the disposition is what the court wants done as a result of its holding. An appellate court can take one of four actions:

- *Affirm* or agree with the decision of the court below.
- *Reverse* or change the results below.
- *Reverse and remand*, or change the result and return the case to the lower court for additional action.
- *Modify* or change part of the decision of the lower court.

If there are no prior proceedings, as in a case from the federal district court, the disposition would be as simple as "judgment for the defendant." If the decision

---

Dictum or dicta (plural)
Remarks made by a court that have no bearing on the decision, but may indicate how the court would decide future cases, or other matters not contained with the case. Comes from the Latin expression *obiter dictum*, meaning "a remark by the way."

Disposition
The action taken by the court to resolve the case based on the holdings that the court made.

Affirm
The court agrees with the results from the tribunal below.

Reverse
A court with review powers changes the result from the lower tribunal.

Reverse and remand
An appellate-level court changes the result from below and sends the case back to the lower tribunal for further proceedings based on the holding of the appellate court opinion.

Modify
Partially change the results from the lower tribunal.

---

[4]*Black's Law Dictionary*, 9th Ed. West Publishing Co. St. Paul 2009.

is on a dispositive motion, the disposition might be "Motion for summary judgment denied." Generally, the disposition can be found in the last paragraph of the opinion or in the synopsis of an unofficial opinion. In the *Pakalski* case, the disposition is "Reversed and remanded."

Commentary

Commentary
The section of a case brief that allows the researcher to make personal comments, presents updated information, and lists other information that may be applicable to the case being briefed.

The ***commentary*** section of a case brief will be at the end of the brief, and notes aspects of the case that drew the researcher's attention as the case was briefed, or note any action that may need to be taken. Figure 15-14 lists some types of commentary that might be made in the briefing process.

Comments may discuss concurring and dissenting opinions that are not part of the opinion itself, but that can have some value by helping the reader understand the case or indicating issues that could affect the client's case. A researcher might note why the judge wrote the concurring or dissenting opinion, what the judge focused on in the opinion, or what the judge's concerns were. When briefing a Supreme Court case with multiple judges sitting, the number of concurring or dissenting opinions might be notable. If three judges wrote dissenting opinions and one concurred but for different reasons than the majority's opinion, that means four out of nine justices were not convinced of the holding. These opinions could signal that a change might come in later cases.

While briefing the case, the writer's personal views and feelings about the case may also be noted. Sometimes a researcher will expect a certain result and be surprised to find the court decided the case differently. Or, a court may have analyzed a case in a way that was unexpected or surprising. Those impressions can be important. The researcher might also note whether the court's reasoning was particularly persuasive or whether the dissenting opinion was more powerful than the majority's.

The commentary section may also be used to describe the counteranalysis—the point of view argued by the opposition. The commentary may be the place to play "devil's advocate," identifying how the result would change if key facts were different, for example.

Information about other opinions within the case history may also be discussed in the commentary. These prior decisions leading up the present case may provide insight into the court's reasoning, or assist in understanding the current case.

The commentary may also note other cases involving the same or similar issues. If the current case has headnotes and one or more of the headnotes are particularly powerful, other cases with the same headnote, topic, or key number can be found in the West digests, on Westlaw, LexisNexis, or on some other computer-assisted legal research system.

FIGURE 15-14
Commentary

1. Discuss concurring and dissenting opinions.
2. Identify personal views and feelings.
3. View the other side of litigation.
4. Read other cases within the same litigation.
5. Use headnotes to find other cases on point.
6. Find and read *ALR* annotations covering the issue.
7. Find law review articles or legal periodicals discussing the issue.

Other cases may be found in the *American Law Reports* (ALR) by using the key words from the case's issue in the ALR index to find an annotation covering the issue or similar issue as that in the case brief. If there is an annotation, one can see how other courts have decided the question.

Many legal periodicals, such as law reviews, summarize or comment on selected opinions. If one of these summaries is found, the analysis by the author can be noted in the commentary and compared to the analysis in the brief. In order to find a law review article, a finding tool such as *Current Law Index* or *Index to Legal Periodicals* can be used.

TIP

While a topic and key number search are limited to West products, similar information can be found in other types of digests and computer research services.

Updating

Updating is a critical step in all legal research. A well-written case brief is worthless if the case has not been updated. The 11-part brief contains a separate section on updating to serve as a reminder of the importance of this step. Shorter brief formats, such as IRAC and IFRAC, do not have separate updating sections, but it is assumed that the researcher will thoroughly update the case regardless of the format of the brief.

Updating can be accomplished through a variety of sources, but the two most prominent are *Shepard's* and KeyCite. *Shepard's* is available in print, and electronically through LexisNexis. ***Shepard's*** was the original resource for updating, and for many years, it was the only available citator service (see Chapter 13). KeyCite, a comparable citator service now offered by Westlaw, provides much the same information as *Shepard's* but in a slightly different format.

When checking a case in an updating service, a researcher will find not only the history of the case (where the case has been in the court system) but also treatment of the case by courts that have mentioned it in other cases. Reading other cases that have cited the case allows the researcher to see whether other courts reached the same conclusion, reached a different conclusion in part, or completely overruled the case.

When the case is updated, any information that impacts the case should be noted, as well as the date on which the updating was done. Cases may be briefed in June in preparation for a July trial date, only to have the trial postponed until December. In December, the cases must be updated again to make sure that the cases have not received any type of negative treatment during the delay. If the cases are not updated, the attorney may risk arguing a point of law based on authorities that are no longer valid at the time of trial.

Sheparding
One method to confirm that the law is still "good law," and verify that it has not been overruled, questioned, or otherwise.

IRAC

The 11-part case brief format is valuable for students because it requires students to seriously explore the entire case and learn from that exploration. However, many supervisors will not want such a detailed brief, and may request a more streamlined format, such as the IRAC or IFRAC form.

"IRAC" stands for the brief's four key components:

1. **Issue**
2. **Rule**
3. **Analysis**
4. **Conclusion**

The IRAC method permits researchers to prepare quality case briefs that combine legal writing, analysis, and research skills. As will be discussed in

TABLE 15-4 IRAC

Element	Purpose
Issue	The question(s) for the court to resolve. In the brief the issues are written in the form of a question. One format is "law + question + key facts = issue." Another format begins with "whether," as in "Whether the actions of the police were 'arbitrary and capricious' under the . . ." If there are multiple issues, each is listed and discussed separately.
Rule	This section provides the rules of law upon which the court relies. The court will identify the elements of a statute, or cite a case with the same or similar issues.
Analysis	In this section, sometimes called the "application," the relevant facts are applied to the rules of law. This is generally the longest and perhaps most important part of the brief and is where the court's rationale is summarized.
Conclusion	This section shows the resolution of the issues, generally in one or two sentences. It usually will answer the issue.

Chapter 16, the IRAC method is used for the discussion or analysis portion of a legal memorandum. It organizes the material, provides continuity, and makes the analysis clear.

As a format for briefing cases, the IRAC method is helpful in identifying the components of a case opinion, as shown in Table 15-4. The elements of IRAC form the heart of the case.

Issue Section

Issue

A question in the case that one is being asked to research.

In this briefing format, the *issue* is exactly the same as in the 11-part brief. Each issue should be set out and discussed separately. The issue should include the law plus the question plus key or context facts. However, some supervisors may want the issue drafted using a "whether" statement, such as "whether the police officers acted 'arbitrarily and capriciously' under . . . ."

An issue may be a very simple, direct statement, or it may include details that make the issue precise and focused. For example, a case may involve a doctor who uses sedatives on a patient at that patient's request, outside a hospital setting, and the patient dies. A simple issue might be, "Did the doctor commit murder?" A complete statement of the issue might be "According to [statute or law], did the doctor commit murder when he used sedatives at the patient's request outside of the hospital setting?"

Some questions may be useful in determining the issues. See Checklist 15-2.

However the issue is phrased, the goal is for the researcher to present the issue in a way that is clear, that identifies the relevant rule of law and key facts, and sets out the question to be researched. Each issue will have its own rule, application, and conclusion. An issue should be supported by rules and answered by the conclusion of the brief.

Rule Section

Rule section

The section of a case brief where the authority upon which the court based its decision will be identified.

The *rule section* identifies the authority upon which the court based its decision. This authority may be the elements of a statute, or a synthesis of the holdings of several cases. It will be at least 1 of the 10 types of law.

The organization of this section should make sense within the brief as a whole. The rule should move from general to specific, from a general description

Checklist 15-2 — QUESTIONS TO ASK WHEN DETERMINING ISSUES

1. What authority or rule is the issue based upon?
2. What are the elements of the rule?
3. What are the exceptions to the rule?
4. What is the policy behind the rule?
5. What are the social considerations surrounding the rule?

of the authority to the specific elements that impact the case. No matter what authority is discussed, the citation for that authority should be complete and accurate.

If the rule comes from enacted law, the actual language of the law should be quoted. If the rule comes from case law, the rule may not be stated explicitly in one case. It may be necessary to synthesize the rule from the holdings in multiple cases.

Application Section

The *application section* is the place where a researcher compares the key facts of the client's situation with the key facts of the case being briefed. It looks at the way in the law is applied to those facts. This section is comparable to the reasoning section in the 11-part brief. To be complete, this section must do all of the following:

- Examine the issue raised by the facts.
- Look at which facts help prove (or disprove) the elements of a rule.
- Determine what facts apply to the rule.
- Decide whether the facts are relevant to the rule.
- Consider what the other side will say about the application of the facts to the rule (the counteranalysis or counterargument).
- Incorporate language from the case into the discussion of the facts.

Application section
The section of a brief where the key facts of the client's situation are compared with the key facts of the case being briefed.

Usually, the attorney or supervisor will not have read the case. The purpose of the brief is to help the reader understand why the court resolved the issues the way it did. The application section is a summary of how the court analyzed the facts and issues at hand. This information will be very helpful later when a legal memorandum or other document must be prepared based on the case brief. Checklist 15-3 lists some questions to ask when analyzing a case.

Checklist 15-3 — QUESTIONS REGARDING THE ANALYSIS AND APPLICATION

1. Which key facts are aligned with which elements of the rule?
2. Why are the facts relevant?
3. How do the facts satisfy the rule?
4. What types of facts are applied to the rule?
5. Is there a counteranalysis for another solution?
6. Is there a public policy associated with the , and if so, are there specific facts to apply?

Checklist 15-4

1. What is the court's holding in the case?

2. What did the court do with the case; for example, did the court overturn, uphold, or remand?

3. Did the holding modify an existing rule of law?

4. How does the holding affect the policy of the rule?

5. How do you feel about the outcome of the case? Does it seem logical?

Conclusion Section

Conclusion

The section of the brief that includes the resolution of the issues.

The *conclusion* is the court's resolution of the issues. Every part of the IRAC brief should lead the reader to the conclusion.

When writing the conclusion, one should answer each issue before going on to the next issue. The conclusion and the position taken in the conclusion should have a solid grounding in the analysis. It is also important to mention the case's weaknesses, as those can be crucial when the case brief is used in a bigger project later on.

Some questions to ask might be what is the holding of the case, what happened procedurally as a result of the holding, and whether the holding modified an existing rule. Additional questions that may be asked when determining the conclusion are listed in Checklist 15-4.

Example 15-1 provides a hypothetical showing how an IRAC analysis could be written.

EXAMPLE 15-1 HYPOTHETICAL

Client's Situation: Dan and Mike have been neighbors for years. The two did not like each other from the beginning but in the last few years the dislike has intensified. One day Dan is erecting a privacy fence between the two yards. As Mike walks by, Dan picks up a fence board and swings around, hitting Mike on the head. Mike is taken to the emergency room and sustains a concussion. Mike seeks damages from Dan for his injuries. State A has a battery statute as follows:

A person commits battery when the person touches another person in an unwarranted and impermissible way that is harmful or offensive to the person touched when there is intent to cause the harmful or offensive contact.

Issue: Under State A's tort law for battery, is existing malice between two people enough to show the intent necessary for liability when one person swings a board during construction of a fence and hits the other person on the head?

Rule: The elements of battery are as follows:

1. Unwarranted and
2. impermissible contact
3. with a person
4. That is harmful or
5. offensive
6. With the intent to cause the harmful or
7. offensive contact

Analysis: (by statutory elements)

1. Dan's hitting Mike on the head was unwarranted and impermissible contact.
2. The cut head was harmful or offensive since Mike was injured.
3. Whether Dan intended to hit Mike becomes a matter of fact to be decided by a jury. The fact that the two men did not like each other may have some bearing but it will not be the decisive factor. In order to show the intent, it will have to be proven that Dan knew Mike was in the area and purposefully swung the board so that Mike would be hit and harmed.

Conclusion:

According to the state's tort law for battery, the contact of the board with Mike's head may be battery if other facts support the statutory elements.

EXAMPLE 15-2   IRAC BRIEF

Case: *Roe v. Wade,* 410 U.S. 113 (1973)

Facts: A woman was denied an abortion by a doctor afraid to violate a Texas criminal statute prohibiting abortions except "for the purpose of saving the life of the mother." The U.S. District Court ruled the statute unconstitutional; there was a direct appeal by Texas to the U.S. Supreme Court.

Issue: Does the Texas statute violate a woman's constitutional right to have an abortion?

Rule: The State of Texas asserts its rule (a law banning all abortions) is furthered by two interests: (1) Protecting prenatal life and (2) the medical safety of woman. The court accepts these interests, but rejects Texas's absolute rule because it violates Amendments 1, 4, 5, 9, and 14.

Application: Here (in this case) Texas's law violates this framework, because it outlaws abortions not just in the third trimester, but also in the first and second trimesters of pregnancy.

Conclusion: (Vote: 7–2) Yes: The statute is unconstitutional because the constitution protects the right to an abortion.[5]

Example 15-2 is an sample of an IRAC brief.

The length and depth of each IRAC brief will vary depending on the complexity of the issues. The reader needs enough information to follow the logic of the law and the application of the legal rule to the facts. Being thorough, logical, and well organized is the key to successful brief writing.

IFRAC (also called FIRAC)

IFRAC stands for **I**ssues, **F**acts, **R**ule, **A**nalysis, and **C**onclusion. This case briefing format is similar to IRAC, but adds a brief synopsis of the facts, which are set out as a separate section. The other sections are the same as those in the IRAC format.

[5]http://www.ucs.louisiana.edu/~ras2777/adminlaw/casebrief.html

The facts section includes a summary of what the court believes the key facts to be in a case. This may be different from the way the parties see the facts. The brief should only include facts that are relevant to the court's decision. For example, in a case where a store customer slips and falls as a result of the store's failure to de-ice a sidewalk in front of the store, the case may hinge on whether the accident was foreseeable. The store's address is probably not relevant in proving this issue. However, it may be very important to include the time of day when the accident happened. If the fall happened two hours after the store opened and it had stopped sleeting an hour before the customer arrived, the customer may be correct in arguing that the accident was foreseeable.

An example of an IFRAC brief is shown in Example 15-3, which includes a fact section.

In the IFRAC brief in Example 15-3, each element is methodically proven using the facts provided. Even though "entering" seems self-evident, the fact that the defendant actually crossed the threshold has to be stated in order for the legal analysis to be complete.

EXAMPLE 15-3   CRIMINAL LAW HYPOTHETICAL—IFRAC

Issue:
According to common law, is a burglary committed when an individual opens an unlocked door to a building at dusk with the intent to commit a theft?

Facts:
Jessica was walking her dog after dinner. As she passed by Bethany's house, she noticed that the door was slightly ajar. Jessica had recently lost her job, was about to lose her apartment, and needed some ready cash. Jessica knew Bethany a little and understood that she operated a real estate office in her house. Jessica thought there was probably some computer equipment that her boyfriend could sell. Jessica knocked on the door but after receiving no response, pushed the unlocked door open, walked into the house, and stole Bethany's computer equipment and other electronic items that are valued at well over $7500.

Rule:
The common law requirements for a burglary are that there be: (1) a breaking (2) and entry (3) of a dwelling (4) of another (5) at night (6) with the intent of committing a felony therein.

Analysis:
Element 1: Although the door was ajar and unlocked, Jessica's opening of the door was sufficient minimal force to constitute a breaking, since the nearly shut door was meant to deter unwanted entry. No actual breaking of the door or lock is necessary.

Elements 2, 3 and 4: Jessica clearly entered the house, which is not her own. The house is considered a dwelling since Bethany regularly uses the house for sleeping purposes.

Element 5: Whether it would be considered night at twilight is determined by whether Jessica's face could be discerned in natural light at that hour.

Element 6: Stealing items worth $7500 is a felony in all states.

Conclusion:
Jessica is probably subject to a charge of burglary even though it was not technically nighttime and the door was unlocked.

EXAMPLE 15-4   CIVIL CASE IFRAC BRIEF

<u>Case:</u> *Roe v. Wade*, 410 U.S. 113 (1973)

<u>Issue:</u> Does the Texas statute violate a woman's constitutional right to have an abortion?

<u>Facts:</u> A woman was denied an abortion by a doctor who was afraid of violating a Texas criminal statute prohibiting abortions except "for the purpose of saving the life of the mother." The U.S. District Court ruled the statute unconstitutional; there was a direct appeal by Texas to the U.S. Supreme Court.

<u>Rule:</u> The State of Texas asserts its rule (a law banning all abortions) is furthered by two interests: (1) protecting prenatal life and (2) the medical safety of women. The court accepts these interests, but rejects Texas's absolute rule because it violates Amendments 1, 4, 5, 9, and 14.

<u>Application:</u> Here (in this case) Texas's law violates this framework, because it outlaws abortions not just in the third trimester, but also in the first and second trimesters of pregnancy.

<u>Conclusion:</u> (Vote: 7–2) Yes: The statute is unconstitutional because the constitution protects the right to an abortion.[6]

Building on the case of *Roe v Wade* from Example 15-2, Example 15-4 shows how the addition of the facts section in an IFRAC brief can enhance understanding of the application of the rule of law to the facts.

CRRACC

CRRACC stands for **C**onclusion, **R**ule, **R**ule Proof, **A**pplication, **C**ounterargument, and **C**onclusion. This type of brief is not as common as the others previously mentioned, but it is sometimes requested. The CRRACC method emphasizes the need not only to state the rule but also to support the rule with a logically organized explanation and discussion of the cited authorities upon which the rule is based (the "rule proof"). This type of brief also states the conclusion at both the end and the beginning of the brief, which helps focus the reader on the key issue of the case.

The CRRACC brief adds a counterargument (or counteranalysis), which examines the case from the other side, before the conclusion. If there are any dissenting opinions, these are typically addressed in the counterarguments section. A sample of CRRACC is shown in Example 15-5, as it might be used for briefing *Roe v. Wade*:

EXAMPLE 15-5   CRRACC BRIEF

<u>Case:</u> *Roe v. Wade,* 410 U.S. 113 (1973)

<u>Conclusion:</u> (Vote: 7–2) Yes: The statute is unconstitutional because the constitution protects the right to an abortion.

<u>Rule:</u> The State of Texas asserts that its rule (a law banning all abortions) is furthered by two interests: (1) protecting prenatal life and (2) the medical safety of women. The court accepts these interests, but rejects Texas's absolute rule.

---

[6]*Id.*

Rule Proof: There are two countervailing interests of the woman:

1. The woman has a privacy right grounded in a "penumbra" of Amendments 1, 4, 5, 9, 14, because "activities relating to marriage, procreation, family relationships, and child rearing and education" are "fundamental" and "implicit in the concept of ordered liberty."

   The woman also has an interest in avoiding possible severe physical and psychological harm if an abortion is denied.

2. A fetus is not a "person" within the meaning of the Constitution, so it doesn't get protection as a person.

3. Therefore, a proper rule balances the interests of the state v. the interests of the woman. In the early stages of pregnancy, the woman has stronger interests than the state, but as a fetus becomes more advanced, the state interests in prenatal life and a woman's health grow to be "compelling," thus overriding the woman's interests. The result is a court-announced three-part rule (trimester framework):

   First trimester of pregnancy: no/little state interest in regulating abortion, so most abortion regulations are invalid.

   Second trimester: moderate state interest (medical health of woman), so most medical regulations are okay.

   Third trimester: Compelling state interest (fetal viability), so can outlaw abortion except to save woman's life.[7]

Application: Here Texas's law violates this framework, because it outlaws abortions not just in the third trimester, but also in the first and second trimesters of pregnancy.

Counterargument:

Dissent 1: Rehnquist (joined by White):

A. A "liberty" not found in the Bill of Rights is not absolutely protected because the correct test for social and economic regulation is whether the law has "rational relation to a valid state objective."

B. The majority ignores that rule. The trimester scheme is "judicial legislation" and historical legal prohibitions show abortion is "not so rooted in the traditions and conscience of our people as to be ranked fundamental" because the drafters of the 14th Amendment did not intend to limit the states' ability to regulate abortion.

Dissent 2: White:

A. There is "[n]othing in the language or history of the Constitution to support the Court's judgment," so the majority's decision must be a "raw exercise of judicial power" that is "improvident and extravagant."

B. The decision whether to allow abortions or not should be left to the people of the states and their legislatures—in other words, the political process.

Conclusion: (Vote: 7–2) Yes: The statute is unconstitutional because the constitution protects the right to an abortion.

Whatever format is used for a case brief, the case must be presented in an organized and logical manner that provides all the information that the reader needs to understand the case and apply it to the client's situation.

---

[7]*Id.*

FIGURE 15-15 Candor toward the Tribunal

Advocate

Rule 3.3 Candor toward The Tribunal

(a) A lawyer shall not knowingly:

(1) make a false statement of fact or law to a tribunal or fail to correct a false statement of material fact or law previously made to the tribunal by the lawyer;

(2) fail to disclose to the tribunal legal authority in the controlling jurisdiction known to the lawyer to be directly adverse to the position of the client and not disclosed by opposing counsel; or . . .

FIGURE 15-15 Candor toward the Tribunal

ETHICAL CONSIDERATIONS WHEN PREPARING CASE BRIEFS

Attorneys, and therefore paralegals, are bound by the Model Rules of Professional Conduct. Rule 3.3 particularly applies to legal research. Figure 15-15 shows the pertinent language from the rule.

This rule applies to the case brief itself as well as the validation process. Case briefs are written with the aim of preparing the attorney to discuss the current law. If that law is not valid, or does not include law that is contrary to the client's position, the attorney may not meet the duty of candor when presenting the client's case to a court.

Here are some additional considerations that apply to case briefing:

(1) There is no reason to brief a case if it has been overruled. The case should be validated *before* briefing it so that time is not wasted on the whole process of preparing a case brief for a case that has since been overruled.

(2) A researcher should not insert an opinion or unintentionally put a "spin" on the facts or analysis of the case when writing the brief. Facts that are relevant should not be omitted, but the writer should avoid embellishing the facts presented, or the analysis or reasoning of the court.

SUMMARY

Case briefing is an essential part of the research and writing process. Learning to identify facts and legal issues and apply the law to those facts and issues is the crux of analyzing and briefing the case.

Being able to draft a quality case brief is an important skill for paralegals. The student should become familiar with the elements of the 11-part brief, as well as the IRAC, IFRAC, and CRRACC briefs, as any of these may be requested by a supervising attorney. The case brief is only one type of legal research, but it often forms the foundation for other documents that may be used in practice.

REVIEW **QUESTIONS**

1. What are the elements of the 11-part brief?
2. What does IRAC stand for?
3. What does IFRAC stand for?
4. Why are cases briefed?
5. What are two ethical considerations to remember when briefing cases?
6. Why is it important to compare the facts of the client's situation with the facts of the case you wish to use?
7. Why is it important to compare the issues of the client's situation with the issues of the case you wish to use?
8. Is it sufficient when analyzing a case to merely provide the legal citation without any explanation? Why?
9. What are some ethical considerations involved in writing a case brief?

APPLICATION **EXERCISES**

1. Read the scenario and complete the questions at the end.

   Jimmy Johnson is at Dirty Frank's, a bar located in Philadelphia, PA, celebrating the Pittsburgh Steelers' Super Bowl victory. The bar advertised a free buffet. Jimmy is a serious football fanatic, having played as a defensive lineman in high school and college. The bar is packed and there are five different bartenders serving drinks and food. Jimmy is drinking beer and has been served by several different bartenders. Around midnight, Jimmy leaves and begins the drive home to New Jersey, just over the bridge from Philly. He exits off the Benjamin Franklin Bridge and travels south on Route 30 in New Jersey.

   Mary Martin has been laid off from her job with a bank. She has spent the weekend in Atlantic City, New Jersey, spending her last paycheck in hopes of "hitting it big." She gambled around the clock, did not sleep, and ended up losing everything. Now, she does not have her rent money. She is feeling alone and desperate. She heads back to her basement apartment in Philadelphia, driving north on Route 30.

   In a blaze of terrifying lights and sounds, Johnson and Martin's vehicles collide head-on. Neither driver is wearing a seatbelt. Mary's car flips and rolls off the highway. The coroner concludes that she was killed instantly by blunt force trauma. Jimmy's car is pushed into a guardrail and pole. He is rushed to the hospital and dies four days later. He never regains consciousness.

   The cause of the accident is not clear, as there are no living witnesses. The New Jersey State Police Accident Reconstruction Unit is unable to conclude where the point of impact occurred—on Jimmy's side of the road or Mary's side. Toxicology reports show that Mary had Prozac in her system and Jimmy's blood alcohol level was 0.16.

   You are a paralegal employed with a law firm located in Philadelphia. Jimmy Johnson's mother, Norma Johnson, is the executrix of his estate. She has hired your firm to defend the estate in a wrongful death action initiated by the estate of Mary Martin and filed in New Jersey state court. Johnson's mother wants to remove the case to federal court and file a wrongful death action against Dirty Frank's for serving her son the alcohol that may have contributed to the accident. She also wants to include Mary Martin's estate in the lawsuit on the grounds that Mary was liable for causing the accident.

   Robert Dexter, the senior partner of the law firm, has asked you to draft an internal memorandum of law outlining the relevant facts that will help remove this case to federal court. Important in your analysis will be the jurisdiction in which Mary's estate filed her claim and what will be necessary to remove the case. He wants you to include the law on wrongful death and liability of alcohol establishments for serving customers. (*Hint:* You might include the term "dram shop" in your research.) Included in those arguments should be an analysis of why the case can be in federal court with both defendants.

   a. First, draft a summary of the facts of this scenario in outline form.

   b. Next, draft the issues that you believe exist, based on this scenario. Your focus should be on identifying the relevant issues and questions to address in your research.

2. "Grampa" Joe is near death. His niece, Maggie May, comes to see him. Grampa Joe gives her $75,000 in exchange for her promise that she will move in with him, and take care of him, the house, and the bills. She must also agree never to put him in a nursing home. Maggie May accepts the offer, expecting Grampa Joe to be dead within a year or two. Grampa Joe lives for seven years at a cost of $10,000.00 per year. Maggie May puts Grampa Joe in a nursing home as an indigent.

   a. Draft an issue for this fact pattern.

   b. What jurisdiction should this case be brought in if Maggie May is your firm's client? Why?

3. You are a paralegal at a small law firm. An attorney provides you with this summary involving a client, Malcolm Parker:

   Parker owns a tavern, the Bar None. Last Sunday evening, Davis, a customer in the bar, got into a heated discussion with Lewis, the bartender. Lewis became angry and threw a glass of whiskey at Davis, splashing him in the face with the alcohol. The alcohol caused severe burning of Davis' eyes. Lewis asked Karel, the bouncer, to eject Davis from the bar. Karel grabbed Davis' arm, dislocating it. Davis is suing Parker for $100,000 for the damage to his eyes and his arm. Bartender Lewis has worked at the Bar None for only two weeks, during which time there were no complaints. Parker did a background check on Lewis before hiring him and found nothing to suggest a violent temperament. Assume the incident took place in your state and that all parties involved are residents of the state.

   a. Identify as many legal issues as you can as well as potential legal issues that will need more follow-up.

   b. Draft the legal issue(s) for this client's situation and analyze the case law that is relevant to this fact pattern.

CITATION **EXERCISES**

Locate the case and provide the proper citation.

1. Locate the case at page 1116 of *Federal Reporter, Second Series*, in volume 477.

2. Locate the case decided in 1972, located in volume 408 of the *United States Reports,* and beginning on page 238.

3. Locate the case on page 153 of volume 428 of the *United States Reports.*

QUICK **CHECK**

1. A case brief is _____.
   a. a persuasive writing
   b. your opinion of the case
   c. objective and fact driven
   d. a brief to the court

2. Which one of the following is NOT a component of the IRAC method of briefing a case?
   a. Issue
   b. Conclusion
   c. Reasoning
   d. Analysis

3. An explanatory fact _____.
   a. is legally unimportant
   b. is legally relevant
   c. helps explain a legally relevant fact
   d. should not be included in your facts section

4. The rules section of a brief will list the _____ that the court relied on in the analysis or reasoning.
   a. primary sources of law
   b. secondary sources of law
   c. both primary and secondary sources of law
   d. rationale

5. The legal principle to be taken from the court's decision is called the _____.
   a. rationale
   b. holding
   c. primary source
   d. secondary source

6. What ethical consideration should you keep in mind before beginning to brief a case?
   a. Make sure you know the statutes the case refers to.
   b. Make sure you know whether the court relied on state or federal law.
   c. Make sure you validate the case to ensure it is good law.
   d. Make sure the date of the case was within the past five years.

RESEARCH

1. Find a case in your jurisdiction based on breach of contract (or any other topic assigned by your professor) and brief the case.

2. Brief the following cases cited in Citation Exercise 1 as assigned.
   a. After locating the case at page 1116 of *Federal Reporter, Second Series*, in volume 477, prepare an 11-part brief.
   b. After locating the case decided in 1972 located in volume 408 of the *United States Reports* where the case begins on page 238, prepare an IRAC brief.
   c. After locating the case on page 153 of volume 428 in the *United States Reports*, prepare an IFRAC brief.

3. Refer to the *U.S. v. Lopez* case on the Oyez website. Compare the facts and issues of the client's situation with the facts and issues of the authority found and determine whether the authority applies to the client's situation. The issue needs to be framed with the law and the key facts, usually with context facts to flesh out the issue. A properly drafted issue will frame the research and reduce the research time.

   a. What is the question being asked?
   b. Is the question procedural in nature? Why?
   c. Is the question substantive in nature? Why?
   d. What law is involved?
   e. What are the elements of the statute?
   f. What are the key facts and issue(s) in the case?
   g. How many issues exist?
   h. What is the primary issue?
   i. Are there sub-issues or separate issues?

4. Access *Mapp v. Ohio*, 367 U.S. 643 (1961).
   a. List the relevant (key) facts of the case. Why are these facts relevant?
   b. List some of the unessential facts of the case. Why are they unessential?
   c. State the issue(s) of the case.
   d. State the Court's holding(s).
   e. If you have access to a citator service, validate the case. Is it still good law?

5. Using an online source locate the following case: *Minnesota v. Dickerson*, 508 U.S. 366 (1993). Use the comprehensive method (11-part brief) to prepare a case brief.

MEDIA **RESOURCES**

Theodore Forrence, Esq., *Effective Brief Writing*. 2011.

American Institute for Paralegal Studies Video Lecture Series. *Paralegal Legal Writing: Using the IRAC Method*.

http://www.youtube.com/watch?v=2VbO6WIoiLs

http://www.youtube.com/watch?v=levdy6-Mfa4&feature=related

INTERNET **RESOURCES**

Glaeser, D. (n.d.). *How to Read a Judicial Opinion*:

How To Brief A Case:

John Jay College of Criminal Justice. *How to Brief a Case.* 1999:

Westlaw. *Briefing Cases.* 2011:

http://www.class.csupomona.edu/pls/brief.html

http://www.law.uh.edu/lrw/casebrief.pdf

http://www.lib.jjay.cuny.edu/research/brief.html

http://lawschool.westlaw.com/shared/marketinfodisplay.asp?code=so&id=4&mainpage=23

chapter **sixteen**

WRITING AN INTERNAL MEMORANDUM OF LAW

Kzenon/Shutterstock

LEARNING OBJECTIVES

After completing this chapter, students should be able to:

1. Understand the purpose of the internal memorandum of law.

2. Discriminate between relevant facts and nonessential facts, formulate the issues of a case, and provide a conclusion based on research.

3. Report research results in a clear and concise manner.

4. Organize written documents based on the issues in a given case.

5. Synthesize and explain a complex series of rules, including the relationship between the rules and their subparts.

6. Write a thesis paragraph that states a conclusion and summarizes the reasons for that conclusion.

7. Understand and use an organizational structure consisting of an umbrella section and subsections, or headings and subheadings, where appropriate.

8. Assess the strength of arguments and make appropriate judgments as to which arguments to include.

9. Identify weaknesses in a case, and anticipate and address counterpoints.

10. Select the strongest and most favorable precedent in support of an argument.

Memorandum of points and authorities

Also called a "Brief in support of . . . "; usually accompanies a motion.

Trial brief

An external memorandum submitted to the court or an attorney's set of notes in preparation for trial.

Appellate brief

An external memorandum written to present arguments to an appellate court.

Internal memorandum

A document intended for someone within the firm, written in neutral language to present both sides of the law that may control the client's situation.

Counteranalysis

An alternative argument or analysis of a case from the perspective of an opposing party.

Opinion letter

A letter written to the client to advise the client as to how the law applies to a given situation.

CHAPTER OVERVIEW

A memorandum of law is a written response to a legal problem where the law is researched, analyzed, and applied to a given set of facts. There are two types of memoranda: an internal or interoffice memorandum, and an external or **advocacy** memorandum. The external memorandum of law is presented to someone outside of the firm, such as a court, to support the client's position. The external memorandum can be seen in various forms such as **memorandum of points and authorities**, **trial brief**, and **appellate brief**. These documents typically try to persuade the reader (usually the judge) to interpret the law in a manner that is favorable to the client by emphasizing the strengths of the case while minimizing or ignoring any weaknesses of the client's position.

This chapter focuses on the **internal memorandum**, sometimes referred to as a file memorandum, interoffice memorandum, or "internal memo." An internal memorandum is usually written for the supervising attorney and the client file, and is not intended to be read by anyone outside of those working on the case. Because it stays in house, it is presented in objective, neutral language. The language is not meant to persuade anyone of a particular position. It presents the law as it is, from both sides of the case.

OPENING SCENARIO

Discovery had been completed in some of the major cases John had been working on. Now it was time to organize his research into interoffice memoranda and present them to Jami. He felt confident about the memorandum on Heather Dobbs's claim because he had statutes and case law to support those statutes. He had updated the law and knew that all of his research was still good law.

In Nancy Smith's case, he felt comfortable with the support he had found regarding the injunction. When John gave a verbal report to Jami, she indicated that the court should be willing to grant the injunction to order quiet time between the hours of midnight and 5 A.M.

In the case of Jack Hammer, who wanted to eject his tenant, John was a little unsure as to the outcome. While he had found quite a bit of law to support Hammer's position, he also found several cases that he felt compelled to discuss in the **counteranalysis** portion of the memorandum. He wanted to make sure that Jami had both sides of the issue. Writing the interoffice memoranda certainly made all of the research he had done much clearer.

THE PURPOSE OF THE INTERNAL MEMORANDUM

The internal memorandum predicts how a court will rule based upon a detailed analysis of the current law as it is applied to the client's case. It strives to reveal all favorable and unfavorable authority. This analysis allows the attorney to determine both the strengths and the weaknesses of the client's case.

Internal memoranda serve several functions, and may be drafted at different points in the life of a case. At the beginning, a memorandum can help an attorney determine whether a claim has merit, and how to proceed with the claim. Once that determination is made, the memorandum can help the attorney advise the client, or draft an **opinion letter** to the client explaining the attorney's interpretation of the law and how it applies to the client's situation.

Later, memoranda can serve as the foundation for more formal legal documents that might be filed with the court. A memorandum may help identify the elements of the cause of action for drafting a complaint or establishing a defense. Memoranda will also help to determine what may be required to support or oppose motions filed with the court. During the discovery phase, memoranda can address what information needs to be obtained, or what needs to be disclosed to the opponents. As trial approaches, a research memorandum may be used to analyze whether evidence is admissible. After the trial, a research memorandum may address issues that are raised on appeal.

At every phase of a case, a well-researched and well-drafted memorandum saves the attorney from having to spend time finding, reading, and analyzing statutes, cases, and other authority. If all the necessary information is available in memoranda and supporting *case briefs*, the attorney has more time available for other tasks such as advising clients, or preparing for trial.

PREPARING TO WRITE THE INTERNAL MEMORANDUM

Researching and writing the memorandum should follow a logical process, as shown in Checklist 16-1.

Checklist 16-1   STEPS TO COMPLETING A MEMORANDUM

1. Understand the instructions for the assignment.
2. Identify any constraints upon the assignment.
3. Organize the research by creating an outline.
4. Write a rough draft.
5. Review and edit.
6. Write a final draft.
7. Edit and proofread.

Understand the Assignment

Before any work is started, it is essential to make sure the assignment is clearly understood. A statement of the assignment may be sent by email to the supervisor for clarification. If it turns out that the assignment was misunderstood, the assignment can be clarified before time is wasted on the wrong task. A paralegal should not be apprehensive in asking for this confirmation. Taking a proactive approach in laying out the assignment and any parameters surrounding the assignment *before* beginning the research shows that the paralegal is dedicated to producing a quality research product. A good supervisor will recognize the paralegal's initiative and professionalism in confirming the assignment. Moreover, the process of restating the assignment will help the researcher think through the assignment and focus on the issues that need to be researched.

Note Any Constraints on the Assignment

Before beginning the project, it is also important to note any constraints upon completion of the project. If there is a deadline on the project, that date should be noted, along with the deadlines for any other projects in a researcher's workload,

TIP

It is important that the research, analysis, and writing of the memorandum be completed in a thorough and competent manner no matter what point in the case's history that research is performed. How the attorney proceeds and how the case may be resolved may depend upon the quality of the research in the written memorandum.

Case brief
A summary of a legal opinion or case.

TIP

If a memorandum is poorly researched and the drafting skills are less than acceptable, the memorandum will have little value. The attorney will have to research and read everything for him or herself or might rely on a dangerously defective document that could undermine the client's case.

so that time may be budgeted accordingly. Any limit on page length should also be noted so that the writing can be organized to meet that limitation.

The memorandum of confirmation might appear as shown in Example 16-1.

Once confirmation has been received, the research begins and culminates in an interoffice memorandum of law.

OUTLINING

Outline

A plan for writing that provides the structure and organization of a document before it is written.

The next step in the writing process is to organize the research into an *outline*. The purpose of an outline is to help the researcher think through the topic carefully and to organize it logically before writing. It will provide the organizational framework or structure for the final memorandum. For some, creating an outline is one of the hardest steps in the process. But a well-written outline will make the rest of the project easier, save time, and result in a clearer, more coherent piece of writing.

As an outline is created, the main ideas are organized and an approach to the research process is determined. As the research is performed, the research source is placed within the outline so that time is not wasted in going back to gather the sources. Most importantly, an outline breaks a complex assignment into manageable pieces.

Since an outline is a skeleton of the whole piece, it should have a consistent format. How an outline is formatted is not as important as making sure the format is consistent. Some writers will use Roman numerals (I, II, III) to introduce the headings while other writers may use capital letters (A, B, C). Brief narrative sentences, fragments of sentences, or even single words are used to identify each section and serve as a roadmap for the writer. All points within a section must relate to the same major topic that was first stated in each capital or Roman numeral heading.

In the outline, the thesis or purpose of the research is clearly stated. What is the chief reason that the memorandum is being written? The major points to be covered should be briefly stated. Just as in a non legal research paper, an introduction should tell the reader why he or she should be interested in reading the memorandum.

The body of the outline explains the arguments to support the thesis statement. A good rule of thumb is to find at least three supporting arguments for each position taken. The strongest argument should be stated first, and then supported by authority as needed.

EXAMPLE 16-1   MEMORANDUM OF CONFIRMATION

Memorandum

To: Supervisor

From: Paralegal

Date: June 23, 2013

RE: Mary Jones's illegal search and seizure

It is my understanding that Mary Jones was subjected to an illegal search and seizure when she was stopped for a minor traffic offense and the officer searched the back seat of her car without her consent. You want me to research Tennessee law and prepare an interoffice memorandum based on whether the officer acted appropriately in the situation. The project is due by June 27, 2013, and should provide an extensive discussion.

After presenting all the issues and providing the counteranalysis for each, the conclusion is given, which should restate the thesis. The conclusion should summarize the arguments and explain why this particular conclusion was reached.

Example 16-2 provides a sample outline.

Checklist 16-2 lists some basic guidelines for preparing the outline. The main focus of the outline is on the analysis section, where the law is applied to the facts of the client's situation. While drafting the outline, the facts and issues framed in the assignment should be kept in mind at all times so that the outline of the analysis actually makes sense, and responds to the assignment. Using the IRAC method will help the writer visualize the issue, rule of law, analysis, and conclusion. Most importantly, there must be an analysis portion for each issue included in the memo.

All of the information gathered should be organized using the outline as the framework. It may be helpful to devise a method for organizing notes. Notations may be used to identify topics or sections in the outline. For example, "IA3b" written next to a source may indicate that the information belongs in Issue I, section A, part 3, subpart b of the outline.

EXAMPLE 16-2   OUTLINE FORMAT

Heading
Statement of the assignment
Issues

      I. [Issue One]
     II. [Issue Two]

Facts
Analysis

      I. [Issue One]
          A. Introduction to analysis of issue
          B. Rule of law
              1. Statement of the rule
              2. Application to client's facts
          C. Case law (to be repeated for each case presented)
              1. Facts of case
              2. Rule of law applied to the facts in the case and in the client's situation
              3. Application of the law from the case to the client's facts
          D. Counteranalysis
     II. [Issue Two]
          A. Introduction to analysis of issue
          B. Rule of law
              1. Statement of the rule
              2. Application to client's facts
          C. Case law (to be repeated for each case presented)
              1. Facts of case
              2. Rule of law applied to the facts in the case and in the client's situation
              3. Application of the law from the case to the client's facts
          D. Counteranalysis

Conclusions
Recommendations

Checklist 16-2

A writer should

1. Remember constraints.
   a. Length
   b. Time
   c. Format and organization
2. Concentrate the outline on the analysis section.
3. Keep the facts and issue(s) available as the outline is developed.
4. Be flexible; as the research progresses, the outline may change.
5. Consider the IRAC format as a way to organize the analysis section.
6. Analyze each issue separately.

The research should be analyzed critically as it is gathered and assembled. Using the best available sources, the information must be checked to ensure that it is factual, up to date, and accurate. Opposing views should also be noted if those views help to support the thesis. The writing must effectively communicate thoughts, ideas, insights, and findings to others.

Information should not be included if it is not relevant to the issues or if it is not understood. Quoted should be accurately written. If sources are not quoted, the writing should, if possible, be in the researcher's own words, without plagiarism. Any ideas borrowed from others should be properly credited and cited. As notes are organized, bibliographical information for each cited paragraph should be noted so that it can be transferred to the memorandum.

The first draft of the outline should only be considered a tentative draft; as research proceeds, the outline may change, sometimes significantly. Sometimes the outline may change to the point that a complete reorganization of the outline is necessary. After it is finished, the outline should be checked to make sure that the points covered flow logically from one to the other.

DRAFTING THE MEMORANDUM

As with many legal documents, the format for internal memoranda may vary from firm to firm and even from attorney to attorney. However, it is imperative to confirm the preferred format and follow it while drafting.

Before beginning to write the memorandum, a supervisor should be asked whether there are any files containing examples of memoranda whose formats might be applicable to the client's case. If the office does keep a file of previous memoranda, these examples will show the preferred format of the office or supervisor. The supervisor should always be asked about the format he or she prefers. The most common formats will usually include, at a minimum, the sections shown in Exhibit 16-1. The names used for these sections will vary, but the content will usually be the same. Some supervisors may prefer to have a separate section that sets out the controlling law with a complete case brief giving the issue, rule, analysis, and conclusion (as in an IRAC brief); the issue, facts, rule, analysis, and conclusion (as in an IFRAC memo); or any other combination.

EXHIBIT 16-1 SIMPLE INTEROFFICE MEMORANDUM OF LAW

Heading
Statement of the assignment
Issue(s)
Facts
Analysis
Conclusions
Recommendations

Heading

The heading section should identify the author, the recipient, and other identifying information. A caption should be centered at the top of the page to identify the document as an internal memorandum of law. Following the caption is the name of the person to whom the memo is addressed ("To:"). On the next line is the name of the author of the document ("From:"). The author is followed by the date that the document is submitted ("Date:"). Although the format may vary, the next item is typically the subject line ("RE:"). This information may include the name of the case or terms and phrases describing the subject of the memorandum. Some firms prefer placing the name of the case in a separate line, along with a docket number (if the case has been filed) and an office file number. The organization of the heading will depend on the preference of the supervisor. An example is shown in Example 16-3.

Some firms will not require a statement of the assignment in an interoffice memorandum. However, it may serve two important purposes: confirming the assignment and helping the writer frame the issues being researched.

Issues

The issues section may also be called the "questions presented" section. These are the specific legal questions that are being researched. The issues section is probably the most important part of the interoffice memorandum because it sets the stage for the research. If the issues are not clear and accurate, the research results will not answer the client's questions. There are often several issues to be researched within a single project, and each should be treated separately.

EXAMPLE 16-3 HEADING FOR AN INTEROFFICE MEMORANDUM OF LAW

Memorandum of Law

To: Jami Selzer, Esq.

From: John Bonham, Paralegal

Date: June 23, 2013

RE: Constitutionality of the search and seizure

Case Name: State v. Smith

Docket Number: 12 Civ 12-1008

Office File Number: 12-103

Each issue is normally set forth in a single sentence, in the form of a question. It is important that this sentence is accurate, brief, and clear. Issues should not be broad or general; rather, each issue should relate to a specific factual problem in the client's case.

Issues may be categorized as issues of fact or issues of law. A factual issue is one that basically asks what happened. An example might be, "Did Mrs. Collins fail to stop at the intersection?" There is no supportive law identified in this type of issue because the question is only about the facts of the case.

Questions of law are answered by interpreting the law and applying the law to the facts. This is the type of question that the judge decides in an administrative hearing, a trial, or an appeal. When a judge answers a question of law, it is called a **holding**.

When the client's case goes to trial, the case may be either a jury trial or a bench trial. If the trial is a jury trial, the jury will answer the question of fact while the judge answers the questions of law. If the trial is a bench trial, the judge will answer both types of facts.

The client may have a range of objectives that will ultimately determine and define the issues. For example, the client may want to avoid going to jail, make a claim against another party, or defend against another party's claims. In reviewing the client's objectives, the writer should begin to phrase the issues in very general terms, such as "Was the client at fault?" or "Is the client entitled to compensation?" Combined with research and investigation of the client's file, the critical question becomes, "What specific facts must the client establish in order to achieve the objective sought according to the rules of law?" And then, "What, if anything, may present difficulties in achieving the result?" Looking at the issue in this manner will help narrow the legal issues.

The client's issue may be very simple. In such cases, a supervisor may prefer to have a very short statement of the issue with only the rule of law and minimal **key facts**. Examples of simple issues are listed in Example 16-4.

There is nothing inherently wrong in writing an issue stated in this brief fashion, and in practice, issues are often written in this way. However, if an issue is written as a short statement, very little information is provided. The issue is used as the springboard for the research, and if the issue is too short or vague, it is easy to get sidetracked. It is often better to write a complete statement of the issue, particularly until one becomes more confident in his or her research skills.

A complete statement of the issue generally has three parts: the law, the question, and the key facts. Here is an example:

Law: Under Indiana statute IC 26-1-4-401(c) covering bank deposits and collections,
Question: can a bank cash a postdated check before the date specified on the check
Key Facts: if the customer notifies the bank of the postdated check?

Holding
The answer to the legal issue or the result that the court reaches when it applies the law to the facts of the case.

Key facts
Those facts that, if different or nonexistent, would change the outcome of the client's situation or case.

EXAMPLE 16-4 SIMPLE ISSUES

- Did the court commit an error in granting the motion for summary judgment?
- Did the bank erroneously cash a postdated check?
- Did the attorney file the complaint within the statute of limitations?
- Did the defendant commit battery?
- Were the defendant's due process rights violated?
- Is the defendant liable for breach of contract?

EXHIBIT 16-2   IMPROVING ISSUE WRITING

OK: Was the defendant negligent?

Better: Was the defendant negligent when he struck a child on a bicycle?

Best: According to I.C. 9-21-8-37, concerning a driver's responsibility to exercise due care when children and pedestrians are present, was the defendant negligent when he failed to keep a proper lookout for children and struck a child riding a bicycle?

Here is another example:

Law: According to the Fourteenth Amendment's due process clause,
Question: were the defendant's rights violated
Key Facts: when, as an indigent defendant in a state criminal trial, he was denied assistance of counsel?

The rule of law being applied in the client's case is referenced first, using some language from the rule. The rule of law is followed by the question that needs to be answered, and then key facts from the client's case that narrow the issue to those facts. Exhibit 16-2 shows how these elements may be incorporated into the issue.

The same issue can usually be phrased in several different ways, depending on the type of writing. If a memorandum, such as a trial memorandum, were being sent to a court, advocacy language would be used, meaning that advocacy language would bolster the client's strengths and downplay or ignore the client's weaknesses. In an interoffice memorandum, however, the goal is to present the issue in a neutral, unbiased manner. That way, the supervisor will get a feel for both sides of the case.

An example of a set of issues in an internal memorandum is shown in Exhibit 16-3.

Even if a client's case is strong, the internal memorandum should be written with the assumption that the case is uncertain, or may not be won. One of the purposes of the interoffice memorandum is to prepare for alternatives or ***contingency issues***. If, for example, the firm were defending a client accused of negligence, the goal would be to find authority that says the client was not liable. However, the memorandum should also anticipate the alternative outcome, and discuss authority showing the client is responsible, as well as the amount of damages the client may be ordered to pay. If this authority is also provided, the attorney will be prepared for that contingency.

Contingency issue
An additional issue that may be raised if the case results in an outcome that was not anticipated.

EXHIBIT 16-3   STATEMENT OF THE ISSUES IN AN INTERNAL MEMORANDUM

Statement of the Issues

1. According to Colorado Const. art. II, § 7, was the search of the bag a legal search by the police officers when the initial stop of the police was an investigatory stop?

2. Did the officers have a reasonable, articulable suspicion that Jennifer committed a crime before the search?

In some instances, the attorney assigning the memorandum may actually provide the issues to be answered. For example, the attorney might ask a researcher to prepare a legal memorandum to answer the questions "Is an off-duty police officer who uses excessive force in making a traffic stop criminally responsible under the federal Civil Rights Act?" or "Is Smith criminally responsible for his actions under 18 U.S.C. § 242?" Both of these assignments have stated the issue clearly within. They also provide clues as to where to start the research. Both provide the name or citation of the applicable statute.

In other instances, the assignment will provide little guidance as to where to begin. The researcher may need to figure out what issue is involved, and whether or not it will be based on constitutional law, statutory law, case law, or some other type of law. In this situation, the facts must be reviewed to determine what the issue is. After the research begins, other issues that also need to be addressed may be uncovered.

As the research progresses, the issues should become more precise and focused. In a case involving a statute, the issue may revolve around only one or two elements of the statute. It may focus on the definition of a specific term or phrase, and whether that definition can be interpreted to fit the client's facts. It may focus on some inconsistency between one rule of law and another, or whether a law was intended to apply to some slight variation in the facts. Setting out the issues accurately and clearly is essential for the reader to fully understand the analysis of the law.

When writing the issues, a distinction should be made between procedural and substantive issues. A procedural issue will be based on some technicality or process in the litigation, such as whether service of process was properly made, or whether the complaint was filed within the statute of limitations. Substantive issues are those that address the rights and duties of the parties. Here are some examples of substantive issues:

- Did the defendant breach the contract?
- Was the defendant negligent in operating her vehicle?
- Did the defendant violate the ordinance by playing music after 2:00 A.M.?

It is sometimes appropriate to address the substantive and procedural issues separately in the memorandum.

Facts

The facts section is a critical part of the memorandum, because the legal issues revolve around how the law is applied to a specific set of facts. The facts of each case will be unique, and nuances in the factual details may affect the outcome. It is therefore important that the facts in the memorandum are stated accurately and clearly. When writing the facts section, the ABCs of Accuracy, Brevity, and Clarity should be followed.

The facts section also provides a catalyst to remind the reader of the basis of the lawsuit. It is seldom that a paralegal or attorney has the luxury of working on only one case at a time. Therefore, an accurate, brief, and clear set of facts in an interoffice memorandum serves to provide the reader with the important case information so that the reader does not need to constantly refer to the case file to know what is happening in the client's case.

Before beginning research for the internal memorandum of law, the facts of the client's case must be collected and fully documented, whether by personally interviewing the client or relying on notes and other records from the client's file. When collecting and documenting facts, it is important to keep them organized so they can be easily accessed and understood. Some researchers organize facts

> **EXHIBIT 16-4   CATEGORIES OF FACTS**
>
> - **Key Facts:** Does removing or changing this fact significantly change the client's situation? If so, it is a key/legally significant/relevant fact.
> - **Explanatory Facts:** Does this fact supplement or explain a legally relevant fact? If so, it is an explanatory fact.
> - **Unessential Facts:** Does removing or changing this fact significantly change the client's situation? If not, it is likely a legally unimportant fact.

chronologically to get a clear picture of the sequence of events. Other researchers organize the facts by party. Very often each party will have its own set of facts or its own version of the facts. In this situation it is helpful to organize each version of the facts separately.

When writing the facts section, it is important to distinguish among key facts, explanatory facts, and unessential facts. *Key facts*, also referred to as legally significant facts or relevant facts, are those facts that, if different or nonexistent, would change the outcome of the client's case. Exhibit 16-4 lists specific questions that can be asked to help determine the type of fact.

Only the key facts and explanatory facts should be included in the facts section of the memo. Key facts are essential to the issues of the case. Explanatory facts may be included if they will help the reader understand the issues. Unessential facts should be eliminated if it is certain they have no bearing on the outcome of the case.

Keep the facts section as brief as possible but, just as when writing a case brief, include all relevant and explanatory facts as necessary to enable the reader to understand the issues. Present the facts section in narrative format with complete sentences and complete paragraphs unless instructed otherwise by a supervisor.

> **TIP**
> Some supervisors prefer to have the facts set out in bulleted information.

An example of a complete facts section in an internal memorandum is shown in Exhibit 16-5.

In an interoffice memorandum, advocacy is not the aim, and therefore facts should be stated objectively and clearly. For example, if a client is threatened with eviction for having pets in his apartment, even though the prior owner of the building allowed pets in the apartment, the facts might include these items:

- the species or breeds of the pets in question
- the date ownership of the building was transferred
- any language in the lease regarding pets

A way to make sure the facts section is precise is to define any terminology for persons and things that will be referred to frequently in the memorandum, and then use those terms consistently throughout. For example, the term "lease" should be used consistently, rather than alternative terms such as "rental agreement," and the parties should be consistently referred to as "landlord" and "tenant" rather than "landlord" and "renter" or "lessor" and "lessee." The key is consistency to prevent confusion when discussing the analysis of the case.

Analysis

The analysis section, sometimes called the discussion section, is the longest and most important part of the internal memorandum. This is where each issue is discussed, and authorities are explained and applied to the facts. The analysis is the main focus of the memorandum.

> **EXHIBIT 16-5 STATEMENT OF FACTS IN AN INTERNAL MEMORANDUM**
>
> **Facts**
>
> Jennifer was arrested and charged with possession and intent to sell methamphetamine. Police officers boarded a bus to question the passengers individually. The officers did not block the door, but were standing in the aisle. Jennifer told the police she had no baggage despite having been on the bus for several days. The officers spent five minutes talking with Jennifer after they noticed she was acting suspiciously. They asked to search her bag. Jennifer consented to this search.
>
> The officers found a suspicious package in the bag and asked Jennifer to step off the bus. While standing next to the bus, the officers opened the package and discovered four pounds of methamphetamine. Jennifer denied ownership of the bag and everything inside it. The officers then arrested Jennifer. Jennifer's fingerprints were later found on the handle of the bag, but not on the package of methamphetamine.

<table>
<tr><td valign="top">

TIP

Primary authority is a law such as a statute, a case, a court rule, or any of the 10 types of law. Mandatory authority is any law that the court must rely on. That means that if the client's case is under New York's jurisdiction, the applicable New York statute would control, along with cases from New York that are on point. By contrast, cases from Illinois would not control. Secondary authority is anything that discusses the primary authority. Persuasive authority can be primary authority from another jurisdiction or secondary authority.

Primary authority

The law itself. Examples: constitutions, statutes, case law, and administrative regulations.

Mandatory authority

Any authority that a court is required to rely upon in reaching a decision.

Topic sentence

A sentence that introduces the issues or sub issues and connects them to the thesis paragraph.

Thesis

A statement of the central idea of an argument.

Elements

The essential components of a statute or other law.

</td>
<td valign="top">

The analysis section is not an exhaustive discussion of all the law that may be applicable to the client's case. Instead, the goal is to provide an analysis of the most important authorities that apply to the key facts of the client's situation. If the key facts have been identified in the facts section, the law should be applied to each of these key facts.

The analysis should distinguish between *primary* and *secondary authorities*, and between *mandatory* and *persuasive* ones. It is important to know the jurisdiction of the cases that are used in the analysis, since jurisdiction is an important factor in determining whether the case will be mandatory authority. The goal of the research is to uncover the primary, mandatory authority to answer the questions in the client's situation. Secondary authorities should be used sparingly, if needed to help explain an area of law. Persuasive authority should only be used, where no primary authority is available, to predict a direction a court may take if the client's case is a case of first impression.

The IRAC method, as described in Chapter 15, is an effective way to organize the analysis section. The discussion of each issue should include an introduction, an explanation of the applicable legal rule, an application of the rule to the legal problem, and a conclusion. Each issue should be introduced with a *topic sentence*. Where more than one issue is discussed, to avoid confusion each issue should be presented separately with its own IRAC sequence, The IRAC format, as applied to an internal memorandum, is shown in Exhibit 16-6.

For each issue, a *thesis* statement presents the central idea of an argument. The thesis statement generally appears at the beginning of the issue to provide a focus. It takes a strong position, and asserts a conclusion that frames the discussion that follows.

When a statute applies to an issue, it is helpful to break it down into its *elements*. It is much easier to work with the individual elements than it is to work with the entire statute. One way to approach this task is to make a box, as shown in Figure16-1. A separate element is written in each field within the box. In this example, the box is used to analyze the Indiana statute for burglary, shown in Exhibit 16-7.

Assume that a client broke the window of a house, entered, and stole some tools inside. The facts would be organized as shown in Figure 16-1.

Figure 16-1 is, of course, a very simplified example. Often the analysis is much more difficult because defining the elements is not as clear-cut. The courts use different

</td></tr>
</table>

EXHIBIT 16-6   IRAC

I	Issue	As stated in the text, the issue is the single most important element of this analytical process. If the issue is not properly defined, the wrong rule or incorrect analysis could result. The issue is suggested from the facts, forms the basis for the analysis, and is often stated as the thesis sentence of the discussion.
R	Rule	The rule may come from statutes, cases, regulations, or any of the 10 types of law. The rule is connected to the facts and understanding the facts helps the reader understand the rule and how the legal meaning attaches to the facts. The rule can be written, for example, by breaking the law into its elements, providing a definition of the rule, identifying the rule's limitations or exceptions, or considering an underlying social or public policy.
A	Analysis	The analysis is sometimes referred to as the discussion wherein the issue is examined as based on the facts and rule. It is in this section that pertinent law, such as cases, is presented. Rarely does a researcher rely on just one piece of authority to support the analysis. Each case or element of the law being applied is weighed and applied to the facts to make the fact–rule connection. The counteranalysis, or key position of the other side on a particular issue, generally follows the analysis, but may be part of the analysis depending on the supervisor's preference.
C	Conclusion	The conclusion may come at the end of each issue or may appear as an overall conclusion at the end of the complete analysis, depending on the supervisor's preference. The conclusion is not a place to introduce new facts, issues, or law. It is a logical outcome based on the analysis of the client's facts and issues as compared to the authority found.

EXHIBIT 16-7   INDIANA STATUTE ON BURGLARY

IC 35-43-2-1 Burglary

Sec. 1. A person who breaks and enters the building or structure of another person, with intent to commit a felony in it, commits burglary, a Class C felony. However, the offense is:

(1) a Class B felony if:
    (A) it is committed while armed with a deadly weapon; or
    (B) the building or structure is a:
        (i) dwelling; or
        (ii) structure used for religious worship; and
(2) a Class A felony if it results in:
    (A) bodily injury; or
    (B) serious bodily injury;

to any person other than a defendant.

    As added by Acts 1976, P.L.148, SEC.3. Amended by Acts 1977, P.L.340, SEC.42; Acts 1982, P.L.204, SEC.36; P.L.88-1999, SEC.2.

Elements of the Rule: Burglary	Case Facts As Applicable	Source of Proof	Proven
Breaking	Cutting the glass of a bedroom window	Pictures, police report	Yes, glass was cut.
Entering	Enters a window after cutting glass	Pictures, police report	Yes, defendant entered.
Building or structure	Of the house	Pictures, police report	Yes, it was a house.
Of another	Defendant did not own the house	Interview, police report	Yes, the defendant was not the owner.
With the intent to commit a felony	Defendant removed tools that didn't belong to him.	Tools found in his possession were the property of the victim.	Yes, he committed theft, a felony in Indiana.

The conclusion of the analysis is that a burglary did occur, since all of the elements are met.

FIGURE 16-1 Analysis of Elements

Analogous cases

Cases that are sufficiently similar in facts and in law to the case at hand.

On point

The facts and issues in a case are similar to the facts and issues of the client's case. Thus, the case is analogous to the client's case.

tools to clarify the application of the facts to the elements, and many of these tools may be used by the researcher in the analysis section. These tools include the analogy test, balancing test, the public policy argument, and other types of judicial analysis.[1]

The analogy test is probably the most common method that the courts use, and also is one that students will use. After the rule of law is presented, **analogous cases** (precedents) are compared to the client's case. To make an analogy, the key facts of the client's case are compared to the key facts of cases previously decided. If the facts have enough similarity, the doctrine of *stare decisis* should apply, and the court is bound to apply the precedent. If the key facts of the client's case and the key facts of the established case are too dissimilar, the case cannot apply.[2] "Fact gaps" may exist, which are facts in the client's situation that do not exist in the cited case, or that exist in the cited case but not in the client's case. If a case is found where the key facts in the client's case and in the cited case match completely or substantially, the case is **on point**, and will provide the strongest authority. However, the key facts do not have to match completely in order for a case to apply. If the key facts are similar in the client case and in the analogous case, the court is likely to rule in the same way as it did in previous cases. If the key facts are dissimilar in some way, it is less clear whether the court will follow the previous case.

Generally, when one applies analogous cases, one discusses each case separately and completely. The facts and issues in the client's case will be compared with the facts and issues of each analogous case individually. When a case has been completely discussed, the next case can be presented. The discussion of the analogous cases can vary in length, content, and format. In reading cases, the court does the same thing. The court may use one or two words in describing a case that it has relied on, it may use several sentences to describe that case, or it may use a paragraph or more. In writing the interoffice memorandum of law, the key is to give the supervisor everything that he or she needs to completely understand the information provided.

---

[1] *The Four Types of Analytical Tests.* LawNerds.com, Inc. 1999-2003. http://www.lawnerds.com/guide/analysis.html#TheFourTypesofAnalyticalTests

[2] *Id.*

EXAMPLE 16-5   THE USE OF TRANSITIONS TO LINK AN ANALOGOUS CASE

In the Indiana burglary statute, a client must "break and enter" in order to commit the offense of burglary. However, a defendant need not literally "break" a door or window to meet this element of the offense. In *Moore v. State,* 267 Ind.270, 369 N.E.2d 628 (1977), it was held that the element of "breaking and entering" was met when the defendant held a gun on the victim at gunpoint, and she unlocked the door and let him into the premises. This is similar to our client's case in that, like the defendant in *Moore,* our client opened an unlocked door to gain entry into the house.

When an analogous case is presented, it should be apparent from the very first sentence why the case has been included. It is also important to have transitions that show the connections between the rule, the client's facts, and the analogous case. For example, in the burglary example above, assume that the defendant didn't actually break the window, but entered through an unlocked front door. A case is located that holds that a person need not have actually broken a door or window, but entered through an unlocked door. Transitions are used to link this authority to the client's case. If multiple cases are used in the analysis, there should be similar transitional connections between the cases. An example of the use of transitions is shown in Example 16-5.

An example of an outline using the elements of a law is shown in Exhibit 16-8.

When using analogous cases, it is not sufficient to merely cite the authorities or provide one or two sentences about the authority. The key is to analyze the authorities and show the relationship between the facts and issues in the authorities and the facts and issues of your client's case. The analysis should explain why the cases apply or why they do not. Do not present a quotation from a case, give the citation, and move on without discussing how the case applies. A *crane analysis*, where authority is quoted or cited without any context, will not help the reader will understand the value of the case. An example of a thorough case analysis is shown in Exhibit 16-9.

An analogous case can be summarized, quoted directly, or used as a combination of the two. A direct quotation is used if the exact words are the best way to express the meaning of the case, and paraphrasing is inadequate. A direct quotation should also be used if the author of the quotation is well known and respected,

Crane analysis
Lifting language out of a case and placing it within a memorandum or other document without laying a proper foundation for using the quoted content.

EXHIBIT 16-8   ELEMENTS OF ANALYSIS

   I. Statement of the general rule and the list of elements involved
     A. First element
       1. Rule
       2. Analogous cases
       3. Arguments
       4. Mini conclusion
     B. Second element
       1. Rule
       2. Analogous cases
       3. Argument
       4. Mini conclusion
     C. Counteranalysis

EXHIBIT 16-9   CASE ANALYSIS IN AN INTERNAL MEMORANDUM

Analysis

According to the facts given, the encounter between the police officers and Jennifer on the bus was a consensual interview that had escalated to an investigatory stop which then escalated to an arrest. In *State v. Whitaker*, 32 P.3d 511(Colo. App. 2000) a case with facts identical to the client's case, the court found that the initial encounter was a consensual interview that had escalated into an investigatory stop. The *Whitaker* court cited *People v. Paynter*, 955 P.2d 68 (Colo. 1998) and its discussion of the three types of police interactions: consensual interviews, investigatory stops, and arrests. In a consensual interview, seizure does not occur because the contact is voluntary. But a consensual interview can turn into an investigatory stop, bringing the protections of the Fourth Amendment into the analysis. The test is whether a reasonable person would feel free to leave or to refuse to answer questions.

In *Paynter*, the court found that asking a person for his or her identification does not escalate an encounter into an investigatory stop. A consensual interview is not a search that implicates any Fourth Amendment protections. During a consensual encounter a police officer seeks the voluntary cooperation of an individual by asking non coercive questions. Also, a citizen is free to leave at any time during such an encounter or is allowed to ignore police officers questions. In *Paynter,* the court found that asking a person for identification or questions in general as well as identifying oneself as a police officer does not convert an encounter into a constitutionally protected seizure. 955 P.2d 68, 70.

Similarly, in the client's case, the police officers were asking questions and did identify themselves as police officers, but did not coerce Jennifer, nor did they search her bag before Jennifer had consented to the search. In *Paynter*, it was established that a person is free to leave and may ignore any questions a police officer asks. In *Paynter*, the officer asked for identification without a reasonably articulable suspicion that Paynter had committed a crime, thus negating any seizure thereafter. In the client's case, Jennifer consented to the officers searching her bag, where a suspicious package was found. The consensual search escalated the consensual interview into an investigatory stop. The fact that the officers found a suspicious package gave the officers a reasonably articulable suspicion that Jennifer had committed a crime.

In *Whitaker*, the consensual interview also escalated into an investigatory stop. During the consensual interview, Jennifer initially stated to the police officers that she had no luggage despite being on the bus for several days. The same set of facts occurred in *Whitaker*. In *Whitaker*, the defendant gave the same answer—that he had no luggage although he had been traveling on buses for several days. This statement led the police officers to suspect that the defendant had committed a crime. They also found that because the package was in view of passengers on a public conveyance, its appearance appeared to contradict the statement that the passenger had no luggage. There was neither a prolonged questioning nor repeated questions about the defendant's stated lack of luggage that would create an unconstitutional escalation from a consensual encounter into an investigatory stop.

To determine whether an investigatory stop has escalated into an arrest, four factors must be established. In *People v. Rodriguez*, 945 P.2d 1351, 1362 (Colo. 1997), these four factors as used by the court were (1) length of detention, (2) whether the investigation was diligently pursued, (3) whether the suspect was required to move from one place to another, and (4) whether there were alternative and less intrusive methods available which the police unreasonably failed to pursue. In *Rodriguez*, the court found that the length of the detention of Rodriguez was reasonable in that for most of the time the officer detained him, Rodriguez was trying to find the correct VIN of the vehicle, which was part of the original reasonable suspicion of the investigatory stop. However, the court found that the police officer erred when he deprived Rodriguez and his family of 90 minutes of their day and had them travel 10 miles in a direction opposite to where they were headed.

To determine if Jennifer was unreasonably moved from inside the bus to outside the bus after the police discovered the suspicious package, the court will look at those four factors. The police officers took Jennifer outside the bus and searched the rest of the bag including the suspicious package at which time they found the methamphetamine. The police officers didn't open the suspicious package until after an investigatory stop was established. They only talked to Jennifer for five minutes. They took Jennifer just outside the bus. Based on these facts, a court will likely hold that the police were acting legally and that the consensual interview that led to an investigatory stop and ultimately led to the arrest of Jennifer was legal.

---

and using his or her words would provide additional weight to the argument. Sometimes an original quotation is difficult to understand, and paraphrasing the quotation may help the reader better understand the intent of the quotation. A writer should always provide a full citation for every authority. If the quotation follows at some point after the full citation has been given, use a **pinpoint citation** at the point of quotation.

Pinpoint citation
A citation that takes the reader to the exact page where a quotation can be found.

If the quotation is less than 50 words, the quotation can appear "in line," meaning within the text. The quotation should be relevant to the material presented. See Example 16-6 for the proper presentation of an in-line quotation.

On the other hand, if the quotation exceeded 50 words, it would be indented on both sides and single spaced. No quotation marks would be used. It might look like Example 16-7.

Legal issues are also frequently analyzed using a balancing test. In this technique, the goal is to predict how a court might decide the issue by determining the most equitable result a court would reach. A set of factors is considered in weighing one decision over another. These factors are compared to the facts of the case to determine whether a preponderance of evidence favors one party over the other.[3] An outline for the balancing test is shown in Exhibit 16-10.

In applying a balancing test, courts may look at the underlying public policy of the rule being applied. Public policy is often considered in cases where, if a rule is applied in a given situation, the result would be unfair or unjust. Common public policy arguments include the following:

1. Equity is achieved by preventing harm to an affected party, and deterring bad behavior by the offending party.

EXAMPLE 16-6   IN-LINE QUOTATION OF LESS THAN 50 WORDS

Jane Roe sought to have an abortion "performed by a competent, licensed physician, under safe, clinical conditions," *Roe v. Wade,* 410 U.S.113 at 120, 93 S.Ct. 705 at 710 (1975).

---

[3]*Id.*

EXAMPLE 16-7 QUOTATION EXCEEDING 50 WORDS

The U.S. Supreme Court created a set of parameters for the permissible regulation of abortion based on the stages of pregnancy. In its leading case, the court held as follows:

> (a) For the stage prior to approximately the end of the first trimester, the abortion decision and its effectuation must be left to the medical judgment of the pregnant woman's attending physician.
>
> (b) For the stage subsequent to approximately the end of the first trimester, the State, in promoting its interest in the health of the mother, may, if it chooses, regulate the abortion procedure in ways that are reasonably related to maternal health.
>
> (c) For the stage subsequent to viability, the State in promoting its interest in the potentiality of human life may, if it chooses, regulate, and even proscribe, abortion except where it is necessary, in appropriate medical judgment, for the preservation of the life or health of the mother.

Roe v. Wade, 410 U.S.113 at 164–165 (1975). Since the client is considering an abortion within the first trimester, no state regulation may interfere with her decision.

---

2. Applying an economic or cost–benefit analysis, acceptable losses are outweighed by potentially greater economic gains.

3. Predictability and consistency in the law will be promoted by creating a "bright line" that cannot be crossed. In this analysis, the courts look at the "straw that broke the camel's back" or that line over which the party should not step.[4]

Some cases are analyzed using an "if-then" analysis: "If this occurs, then that will happen." This test allows flexibility in deciding whether the element of a rule applies when that element is particularly vague.[5]

In some cases, some of the elements to be proven may not be in dispute. Those elements that are not likely to be contested should be indicated clearly to eliminate them from the analysis. In a burglary case, for example, both sides might

---

EXHIBIT 16-10 BALANCING TEST

    I. Statement of the general rule including interests that are balanced and factors considered

      A. First Factor
        1. Identification of the factor or rule
        2. Analogous cases
        3. Arguments
        4. Mini-conclusion

      B. Second factor
        1. Identification of the factor or rule
        2. Analogous cases
        3. Argument
        4. Mini-conclusion

      C. Evaluation of factors and balancing of interest
      D. Counteranalysis

---

[4]*Id.*

[5]*Id.*

agree that there was no question that the defendant broke the glass when enter the building. This would be clarified as follows:

> In this case, the first element of breaking is not in dispute. The glass was broken as evidenced by the police report.

It could also be worded like this:

> In this case, the first element is not in dispute. The glass found on the floor at the base of the window confirmed that the window had been broken. The state will also be able to prove that the accused broke the window because he had a cut on his hand, and the blood on the window matched his blood type.

In addition to providing support for a client's position, it is also important to discuss any potential counteranalysis. For nearly every case that is cited, an opponent may apply an alternative analysis or interpretation. In the art of advocacy, subtle differences or nuances in each case may make a big difference in an outcome. Unless the authority is "*on all fours*," there is room for argument. The internal memorandum should discuss any potential counterarguments, questions, or doubts the other side may raise, so that the attorney is prepared to confront them. The counteranalysis should follow the support for the client's position, and should be stated objectively, without ignoring any weaknesses in the client's case. The counteranalysis can be presented at the conclusion of the discussion of each issue or in a separate section after the discussion is totally completed. Presenting the counteranalysis as a separate section will help ensure that the counteranalysis is not lost in the memorandum, and will not be forgotten.

"on all fours"
A case that has facts and issues that are the same, or substantially similar, to the facts and issues of the client's case.

Secondary authority may also be integrated into the analysis, as long as the secondary authority supports the primary authority, and there is reason to use the secondary authority. Secondary authority does not replace primary authority. It can only reinforce primary authority or be used as *persuasive authority*. It cannot be used to restate the primary authority or be used in place of primary authority.

Persuasive authority
Any authority that may guide the court in making a decision, but that the court does not have to rely upon.

All sources in the memorandum, both primary and secondary, must be properly cited using the correct format. The citations should be written in a format accepted in the jurisdiction in which the case appears. A state may have its own citation manual, or it may be necessary to follow the citation formats provided in a common citation book such as *The Bluebook* or *ALWD*. The attorney can also provide information on the proper citation format. Providing proper citations is important because the attorney or other supervisors may rely on the memorandum in order to prepare arguments or other documents for the court.

Once a rough draft of the analysis section is complete, it should be reread and revised to make sure it is not only clear and logical, but also interesting and readable. Paragraphs should use a variety of introductory sentences, rather than beginning with the same statement, such as "The court held in . . ." It should also have a strong opening statement and a conclusion tying together the arguments for or against the client's position.

Before writing the final draft, go through the questions in Checklist 16-3 to make sure the analysis is complete.

Even if the writer is satisfied with the draft, it should be checked one more time before going on to the next section.

Conclusion

The conclusion section states the answer to each issue discussed. It is a brief summary of the findings, and usually contains a short, concise answer to each question raised in the Issues section. It is not, however, a place to introduce new facts, law, or

Checklist 16-3

QUESTIONS TO ASK ABOUT THE ANALYSIS SECTION

1. Is the analysis section in the proper format?
2. Are authorities discussed according to a hierarchy, applying the highest authority first?
3. Is a rule of law applied to each issue?
4. Are a variety of authorities used to support each issue?
5. Is case law presented that is on point?
6. Is every reference in the proper citation format?
7. Is each issue separately researched and written with a separate analysis for each?
8. Are headings used effectively to organize the section?
9. Have all sources been validated or **Shepardized**?

Sheppardizing
Using *Shepard's Citations* to validate an authority, to locate parallel citations, or to find subsequent history.

analysis. All facts, authorities, and analyses are discussed in the analysis and counter-analysis sections. The conclusion should emphasize only the results of the research. Citations are not included in the conclusion. If there are multiple issues, the conclusion does not need to have a separate conclusion for each issue. However, using separate paragraphs for the conclusion of each issue helps the reader follow the material.

The conclusion section should avoid *equivocal language* that sounds weak or ambiguous, such as sentences that begin with the phrase "It would appear that" or "It seems that." Statements such as, "I believe . . . " should also be avoided. The reader is not interested in what the writer believes; the reader wants to know only how the law applies to the client's case. However, the conclusion should also make an honest assessment of the case. If the authorities found are not conclusive or are in conflict, it should be stated in the conclusion. The purpose here is not to predict the client's chances of winning or losing. The function of the internal memo is merely to report objectively and analyze the authorities found.

Equivocal language
Language that is ambiguous or open to more than one interpretation.

An example of a conclusion in an internal memorandum is shown in Exhibit 16-11.

Recommendations

Recommendations section
The section of the internal memorandum that provides concrete steps the could be taken based on the analysis of the client's case and the law provided.

The *recommendations* section explains concrete steps that may be taken as a result of the analysis of the client's case. They may take a variety of directions

EXHIBIT 16-11 CONCLUSION IN AN INTERNAL MEMORANDUM

Conclusion

Fourth Amendment protections are not a defense for Jennifer, because the officers didn't search her bag until Jennifer gave them consent to do so. After this consent, a suspicious package was found that escalated the consensual interview into an investigatory stop because the officers then had a reasonably articulable suspicion that Jennifer had committed a crime.

Once the investigatory stop was established, the police legally searched Jennifer's bag and found methamphetamine, which resulted in Jennifer's arrest. The police acted legally and completed the four-factor test to escalate an investigatory stop into an arrest.

depending on the client's situation and the stage of the litigation. Often, recommendations are made as to the next steps that should be taken. The researcher may also include personal views in this section on which side has the better argument, or which side is likely to prevail. For example:

> Based on my research, I would not advise the client to sue the City because the City would not likely be found liable under 42 U.S.C. § 1983.

A common recommendation may be for further investigation to take place because of new information uncovered in the research. More information may be needed from the client, or further research may be needed. If certain facts or issues were not discussed in the cases but appear in the client's situation, those facts or issues should be identified. In some circumstances, it may be useful to include copies of authorities used, tables referred to, or photographs relied upon. Those could be referenced in this section and included in an appendix. It is important to be specific in whatever recommendations are included.

The recommendations section should also include a note that the authority used in the memorandum was validated through whatever date the research was finished. This statement lets the reader know that he or she can rely on the materials used through that date. It also provides a point to start from if the research needs to updated and validated at a later time.

Ethics Alert

Ethical considerations dictate that all authority used in preparing the memorandum must be validated. Sources may be validated either online or in print from books as discussed in previous chapters. One must never provide the recipient of the memorandum with law that is not good law! Doing so violates Rule 3.3, Candor to the Court.

THE COMPLEX INTERNAL MEMORANDUM

A complex internal memorandum of law is used to address cases that involve three or more issues, and typically is written in the 11-part brief format. However, the format of the memorandum will always be dictated by the supervisor. If one is given a choice of formats to use, it is best to use the structure that makes the most sense for the project at hand.

The complex interoffice memo has four parts in addition to those parts used in the simple interoffice memo:

- Table of Contents
- Table of authorities
- Summary of issues and conclusions
- Appendix

Some practitioners may refer to this memorandum as a "10- part memo," because the summary of issues and conclusions is equivalent to the issue section in the simple interoffice memorandum.

Table of Contents

The table of contents should be placed immediately after the heading. Each section heading within the memorandum should be listed with the page numbers of each section in the right-hand column. See Exhibit 16-12.

EXHIBIT 16-12   SAMPLE TABLE OF CONTENTS

Table of Contents

Page

Table of Authorities ii

Summary of Issues and Conclusions 1

Statement of the Assignment 1

Facts 2

Analysis 3

Issue I: [State Issue] 3

Issue II: [State Issue] 9

Recommendations 14

Table of Authorities

TIP

Both Westlaw and LexisNexis have tools for making the table of authorities. Some software packages, such as Best Authority®[6] and CitationWare[7] also provide useful tools. Word includes a template for creating a table of authorities. Visit http://office.microsoft.com/en-us/word-help/create-a-table-of-authorities-HP005189300.aspx.

[6]Best Authority®. Levitt & James, Inc. http://www.levitjames.com/Products/Best-Authority.aspx
[7]CitationWare. 2008. http://www.citationware.com/

The table of authorities is a list of every primary and secondary authority used in the analysis section, along with the page numbers where each authority is discussed. The citations should follow the format accepted in the jurisdiction where the memorandum will be used. Primary authorities are listed first, followed by secondary authorities. The primary authorities should be listed in the following order:

1. Cases, in alphabetical order
2. Constitutional provisions, in numerical order
3. Federal statutes, in numerical order
4. State statutes, in numerical order
5. Court rules, in numerical order

The page numbers are given of the exact locations in the memorandum where the authorities are cited. Exhibit 16-13 shows an example of a complete table of authorities.

EXHIBIT 16-13   TABLE OF AUTHORITIES

Cases	Page
Meritor Sav. Bank v. Vinson, 477 U.S. 57 (1986) 5, 8
United States v. McDonald, 531 F.2d 196 (4th Cir. 1976) 7, 8, 10
Constitutional Provisions
U.S. Const. art. I. § 9, cl. 1 .... 4, 7
Statutes
28 U.S.C. § 1328 (2000) 5, 6, 13
28 U.S.C. § 1331 (2000) 5, 9, 13
Court Rules
Fed. R. Civ. P. 12(b)(6) 7
Other Authorities
3 Charles Alan Wright & Arthur B. Miller, *Federal Practice and Procedure* § 1000 (4th Ed. 2011) 12

Summary of Issues and Conclusions

In the complex memo, the summary of issues and conclusions allows the reader to ascertain quickly what the memo is about. It provides a complete statement of every issue discussed in the analysis section and a brief summary of the writer's conclusion as to how each issue will be resolved.

If a summary of issues and conclusions is provided, the supervisor may or may not want statements of the issues repeated within the analysis. A supervisor should be consulted to determine the format required. If statements of the issues are not repeated within the analysis, the statements should be labeled in the analysis and the summary of issues for ease of identification. If there is no preference, it is suggested that the issues be stated twice, particularly if the analysis section is long. This allows the reader to identify each issue without having to refer back to the summary.

Appendix

The appendix provides a place to include supplemental material that assists in understanding the analysis section, such as the text of significant statutes or cases, photographs, pleadings, charts, or other data. If an appendix is included, its items should be listed in the table of contents to allow the reader to quickly reference the materials as needed. It is also helpful if the appendix documents are tabbed for quick reference.

PROOFREADING AND EDITING

Although the interoffice memorandum is meant to be used within the office, the finished product will reflect upon the professionalism and integrity of the author. Any errors in punctuation, spelling, or grammar will negatively impact the credibility of the memorandum. It is therefore essential to thoroughly proofread the final draft before sending to the supervisor. The writer should not rely on the spell-checking or grammar-checking features of word processing software, since these programs are not infallible, and do not find all possible errors. It is recommended that the final draft be printed out so that the proofreading may be done on a hard copy. Many errors are missed when reading a document on-screen, and proofreading is usually more accurate when one reads the document in print.

SUMMARY

The internal memorandum is an essential form of communication within the law office. It provides a medium to document the facts, to discriminate the relevant legal facts from those that are unessential, to define the main issues, to draw conclusions, and to offer recommendations to the attorney on how to proceed. The internal memorandum places all of this information at the attorney's fingertips, so he or she can quickly evaluate a case and decide what steps to take next.

REVIEW QUESTIONS

1. What is an outline and why is it important?
2. What are the parts of a simple interoffice memorandum?
3. What additional parts are added to the simple interoffice memorandum to make it a complex interoffice memorandum?
4. What is one major ethical consideration when writing interoffice memoranda?
5. Why is this ethical consideration important?
6. Explain how the analysis portion of the memorandum should be organized.
7. Explain the difference between a shortened and complete form of an issue. Which is most import at this stage of drafting? Why?
8. Why is it important to check with the supervisor after receiving and reviewing an assignment?

9. You are drafting a table of authorities. In your research you have a state case, a state statute, a federal case, a state court rule, and a federal constitutional provision. In what order should be these authorities appear?

10. What material might be appropriate in an appendix?

11. When drafting a memorandum, why is it important to include the date that the research was completed?

APPLICATION **EXERCISES**

"Grampa" Joe is near death. His niece, Maggie May, comes to see him. "Grampa" Joe gives her $75,000.00 in exchange for her promise that she will move in with him and take care of him, the house, and the bills. She must also never put him in a home. Maggie May accepts the offer, expecting Grampa Joe to be dead within a year or two. Grampa Joe lives for seven years at a cost of $10,000 per year. Maggie May puts Grampa Joe in a nursing home as an indigent. In Chapter 15, you answered the following:

1. Apply IRAC to the fact pattern.
2. In what jurisdiction should this case be filed?
   Now add to the research and prepare an interoffice memorandum.
3. Define and identify any statute from your jurisdiction that will apply to the fact pattern.
4. Define and identify the case law from your jurisdiction that will apply to the fact pattern. Find at least two cases.
5. Update the law.
6. Write an interoffice memorandum.

CITATION **EXERCISES**

Your supervisor asked you to create a table of authorities for a brief he is filing based on your interoffice memorandum. Create a proper table of authorities, making sure that the citations are correctly presented. The following citations were included in the memorandum:

1. § 768.56, Fla. Stat. (1981)
2. Spiegel v. Williams, 545 So. 2d 1360 (Fla. 1989)
3. State Farm Fire & Cas. Co. v. CTC Development Corp., 720 So. 2d 1072 (Fla. 1998)
4. § 768.79, Fla. Stat
5. State ex rel. Royal Insurance Co. v. Barrs, 87 Fla. 168, 99 So. 668 (1924)
6. State Farm Fire and Cas. Co. v. Metropolitan Dade County, 639 So. 2d 63 (Fla. 3rd DCA 1994), rev. denied, 649 So. 2d 234
7. Fla. Const. Article V, Section 3(b)(3)

8. Steele v. Kinsey, 801 So. 2d 297, 299 (Fla. 2d DCA 2001)
9. Weldon v. All American Life Ins. Co., 605 So. 2d 911 (Fla. 2d DCA 1992)
10. Excelsior Ins. Co. v. Pomona Park Bar & Package Store, 369 So. 2d 938 (Fla. 1979)
11. Florida Patient's Compensation Fund v. Moxley, 557 So. 2d 863 (Fla. 1990)
12. Florida Ins. Guar. Ass'n, Inc. v. Johnson, 654 So. 2d 239, 250 (Fla. 4th DCA 1995)
13. Kepple v. Aetna Cas. & Sur. Co., 634 So. 2d 220 (Fla. 2d DCA 1994)
14. O'Conner v. Safeco Ins. Co. v. North America, 352 So. 2d 1244 (Fla. 1st DCA 1977)
15. Williams v. Florida, 399 U.S. 78, 90 S.Ct. 1893, 26 L.Ed.2d 446 (1970)

QUICK **CHECK**

1. The _____ section of a memorandum of law should include the date, client identification, author, recipient, and subject matter.
   a. facts
   b. discussion
   c. conclusion
   d. heading

2. Before you begin research for your memorandum of law, you should _____.
   a. Document the facts of your client's case.
   b. Prepare the conclusion section of the memorandum.

   c. Prepare the discussion section of the memorandum.
   d. Prepare the recommendations section of the memorandum.

3. To prepare the _____ section of a memorandum of law, you can use the IRAC method to help you organize the information find in your research.
   a. facts
   b. heading
   c. discussion
   d. issues

4. A _____ introduces the issues or sub issues and connects them to your discussion.
   a. heading
   b. conclusion
   c. topic sentence
   d. brief answer

5. You should avoid using _____ when preparing your memorandum of law.
   a. equivocal language
   b. topic sentences
   c. explanatory facts
   d. recommendations

6. Two ethical considerations to remember when preparing an internal memorandum of law are to _____.
   a. Validate authorities and use proper citations.
   b. Write in a persuasive tone and validate authorities.
   c. Never include a recommendation section even if requested by the attorney, and use proper citations.
   d. Include secondary sources in your authorities, and include a brief answers section in every memo.

7. The _____ section of the memorandum is the place where you find and discuss authority to support your client's position.

8. _____ is picking a quote from a case and placing it in your memorandum without explanation.

9. Your goal in research is to find the best _____ to support the client's position.

10. In addition to finding primary authority, we want to find _____, which is what the court must rely on for making decisions.

11. The first thing to do when using a statute in one's analysis is to break the statute into its _____.

For items 12–15, indicate whether each statement is true or false.

12. A memorandum of law should be written in a persuasive manner.

13. A memorandum of law is filed with the court.

14. The "discussion" section of the memorandum of law provides an analysis of legal research.

15. The best way to organize legal research before writing a memorandum of law is to prepare an outline.

RESEARCH

1. Locate a sample brief.

   Access either the ABA Organization or Oyez through the links below:

   ABA site http://www.americanbar.org/aba.html or

   Oyez site: http://www.oyez.org/cases/2000-2009/2007/2007_06_637

2. Review the brief.

   Review the brief for the petitioner and the respondent in a 2007 case before the U.S. Supreme Court, *Board of*

   Education of the City School District of the City of New York v. Tom F., Supreme Court Docket No. 06-637.

3. Draft the beginning of a predictive summary of the briefs.

   Summarize the arguments in the brief as if you were determining for an attorney how the Supreme Court would likely rule.

INTERNET RESEARCH

Draft an internal memorandum based on the law of your jurisdiction.

1. **Crops at an Intersection**

   Plaintiff's decedent was killed in an automobile collision at an intersection in the country. The plaintiff, on behalf of the decedent's estate, sued the other motorist and joined the county and the owner of farmland at the intersection, on the theory that decedent's view of the intersection was impaired by the crops on the farmland. Is a farmer under a duty to avoid creating crop conditions that may impair a motorist's view at an intersection?

2. **Parking Lot Accident**

   Michelle has come to your office for representation. She provides the following facts:

At 8:30 P.M. on October 21, 2012, I left a department store through the food doors at the north end of the store. We were parked in the row directly in line with the doors. This was a row in which vehicles were traveling west toward the building. We were parked in the second regular space east of the handicapped spots on the south side of the row.

I was driving the Rabbit and had backed out of the parking space after looking both ways for traffic. No car was parked on my right (west) side. There was a car on my east (left) side. As I was in the driving lane and putting the car into drive from reverse, I was hit in the right rear quarter panel by a Jeep. The Jeep was not damaged. When the driver emerged, he said, "I guess I couldn't see you because of my tinted windows and your black car."

The Jeep driver and I both returned to our original parking spots and got out. The police were called but they would not come since the lot is private property. The 2005 Jeep Liberty Sport was driven by Steven A. Shaw, who works at Conway. He and his wife, Judy L. Shaw, have Farm Bureau Insurance. The insurance card showed an address of 2317 N. 14th St., Whatever City, Whatever State 00000. His license plate number is 164548L exp. 2012. His policy number is M3909217 and the agent is John Lewman in the same town. The claims telephone number is 1-800-800-8000.

Who was liable in this instance? Why? What will the other side allege?

3. **Sexual Assault**

While Mrs. Bountiful was incarcerated at the county jail for solicitation, she claims that one evening, after all the inmates were locked down for the night, Deputy Doug entered her cell and sexually assaulted her. The deputy claims that he was lured into the cell by Mrs. Bountiful under false pretenses and that she then proceeded to sexually assault him.

4. **Housing Violation**

The Walterses, a young professional African American couple looking to buy their first house, saw a house for sale in a predominantly white neighborhood in Gary, IN. They contacted Carolyn McNeely, the realtor with whom it was listed. After showing the Walters the house, McNeely urged them not to make up their minds until she had shown them other properties in neighborhoods where they would be "more comfortable" and "fit in better." She then showed them houses in the same price range, but in predominantly black neighborhoods. When the Walters told McNeely that they intended to make an offer on the house they were originally interested in, McNeely informed them the owner had taken it off the market and was no longer interested in selling it. Do the Walters have a cause of action against McNeely under (A) the federal Fair Housing Act, (B) other federal civil rights laws, or (C) other state civil rights laws? Has the owner of the home violated any laws if he refused to sell his home?

5. **Work Product**

April Hall came into your office because she had been involved in an automobile accident and filed a cause of action. She was driving on U.S. 40 at 3:00 in the afternoon when a car driven by John McCabe pulled onto U.S. 40 from S.R. 46 into the path of April's car. April applied her brakes and attempted to swerve to avoid the accident but John's car hit her right rear quarter panel, spinning her around in the highway. Her car struck a telephone pole before finally coming to rest. At the accident scene, John gave the police insurance information. However, when April's insurance company attempted to contact the firm, it was discovered that John was actually uninsured. During discovery, this firm requested that John produce certain documents, among which were estimates of damage, repair orders, and drafts paying for the work. The law firm representing John refused to comply with this request, claiming that the material requested was part of attorney work product and therefore not discoverable. Your supervisor wants you to research the question of what constitutes work product and whether the material requested should be produced.

MEDIA **RESOURCES**

Chief Justice Roberts on the topic of writing:	http://www.youtube.com/watch?v=ZIjBzn7rbPE&feature=related
A Crash Course in Legal Writing by Bryan A. Garner:	http://www.youtube.com/watch?v=sR72bsOeooE&feature=related

INTERNET **RESOURCES**

Westlaw: How to Check Citations:	http://lscontent.westlaw.com/images/banner/SurvivalGuide/PDF08/08HowCheckCitations.pdf
Westlaw. Writing an Open Memo:	Thomson/West. 2005.http://lscontent.westlaw.com/pdf/OpenMemo.pdf
Sample memorandum at Statsky, William P. *Research and Writing in the Law*, 5th ed.:	http://www.whatsyourauthority.com/Memorandum.pdf
	http://www.clas.ufl.edu/users/usufruct/Law/LAWmemorandumexample.html
Cohen, Ezra H. *Writing Skills—Part II: How to Write a Brief or Memorandum of Law*. American Bankruptcy Institute. 2009:	http://www.abiworld.org/committees/newsletters/consumer/vol7num5/Writing_part_2.pdf

chapter **seventeen**

WRITING EXTERNAL BRIEFS

Kzenon/Shutterstock

LEARNING OBJECTIVES

After completing this chapter, students should be able to:

1. Write persuasively to convince a reader of a specific legal position.

2. Explain common features of persuasive writing.

3. Prepare a table of contents.

4. Prepare a table of authorities.

5. Describe the components of an external brief.

6. Modify an internal memorandum of law to develop an appellate brief.

CHAPTER OVERVIEW

Paralegals occasionally are asked to assist in writing memoranda that are presented to a court to support a client's case. Unlike internal memoranda and case briefs, which are written with an objective writing style, these external documents are written using a persuasive tone that advocates the client's legal position. They are often referred to as "advocacy documents."

    Persuasive legal documents include **memoranda of points and authorities**, **trial briefs**, and **appellate briefs**. Whereas **predictive writings** are used to inform the reader of what decision a court is likely to make, **persuasive writings** attempt to convince the reader that a particular legal position is the correct position.

    There are many different types of documents filed in court, depending on the type of case and the legal issues involved. It should be remembered that all court filings are formal legal documents that must follow a set format. The **local court rules** should be checked regarding the format and content of a particular court filing. If the document does not conform to the rules, the court may not accept the filing.

Memorandum of points and authorities
A type of brief filed with the court.

Trial brief
A written argument presented to the trial court to support the client's position.

Appellate brief
A brief submitted to an appellate court offering arguments as to why the lower court's decision was correct or incorrect, and should be affirmed, modified, or reversed.

Predictive writing
Writing that attempts to demonstrate or explain the likely outcome.

Persuasive writing
Writing that persuades or convinces another to adopt a certain point of view.

OPENING SCENARIO

Allworthy Law Firm had several clients whose cases were on appeal. John was working on a table of contents in one brief, cite-checking the legal citations in three other briefs, preparing a table of authorities, and drafting certain sections of an appellate brief in another case. For these tasks, John had to check the appellate rules and the local appellate rules to ensure that the table of contents and table of authorities were in the correct format, the margins were set at correct width, and the sources were in the proper order.

John soon realized that writing external briefs is a lot harder than writing interoffice memoranda because he knew someone outside the firm would be viewing his work. While he was always very careful, there was something a little different about having a judge or opposing counsel reviewing the documents. Proofreading and editing were essential!

ADVOCACY DOCUMENTS IN GENERAL

Although advocacy documents may be used for a variety of purposes, most contain several common features or components, as shown in Exhibit 17-1.

At the trial level, briefs may be submitted to the trial court to persuade the judge to decide a case or a motion in a certain way. The brief may stand alone, or may be accompanied by other documents, such as depositions or exhibits. In some instances, the brief is written to respond to the judge's request for a legal argument in a particular issue.

An appellate brief is much more sophisticated and generally longer than a trial brief. Appellate courts have a definite set of rules that must be consulted when drafting briefs.

No matter what type of brief is being drafted, it is important to remember who the audience is. Judges usually have heavy caseloads and cannot afford to waste time reading documents that are not clear or concise. Most external documents will also be read by opposing counsel. Although a poorly written brief will have little impact on the opposition's view of the case, a well-written brief might encourage settlement. An effective brief is clear, well organized, properly cited, and appropriately updated.

Case Caption

The case caption identifies, at a minimum, the parties of the case, the court in which the case is pending, the docket number, and the title of the document. Local

---

EXHIBIT 17-1   COMPONENTS OF EXTERNAL BRIEFS

1. Case Caption
2. Table of Contents*
3. Table of Authorities*
4. Introduction or Preliminary Statement
5. Statement of Facts
6. Statement of Issues or Questions Presented*
7. Summary of the Argument*
8. Argument
9. Conclusion
10. Signature and Date
11. Certificate of Service

[*denotes sections that may be more appropriate for the appellate brief]

EXHIBIT 17-2   LOCAL RULE ON CAPTIONS

Rule 9004-2 Caption of Pleadings

Unless additional information is required under 11 U.S.C. § 342(c), any pleading filed with the clerk in a contested matter must contain a caption substantially in compliance with L.B.F. 9004-2. Unless additional information is required under 11 U.S.C. § 342(c), any pleading filed with the clerk in an adversary proceeding must contain a caption substantially in compliance with L.B.F. 9004-3.

LOCAL BANKRUPTCY FORM 9004-2

[Contested Matter Caption]

IN THE UNITED STATES BANKRUPTCY COURT

FOR THE MIDDLE DISTRICT OF PENNSYLVANIA

IN RE: : CHAPTER _____

JOHN DOE   :

                    : CASE NO. - -bk- (judge's initials)

Debtor(s):   :

XYZ MORTGAGE CO.   :

          Movant: :

vs.   :

                    :

JOHN DOE   :

          Respondent   :

MOTION OF XYZ MORTGAGE CO. FOR RELIEF FROM THE STAY

Dated

                   Signature of Counsel/Movant

                   (Typed Name)

                   (Address)

                   Phone No.

                   List Bar I.D. and State of Admission[1]

court rules, as well as *The Bluebook* and *ALWD*, should be checked to determine what elements are required. Exhibit 17-2 shows an example of a court rule dictating the format for captions.

Table of Contents

The **table of contents** is generally required for trial briefs and appellate briefs, and sometimes for a memorandum of points and authorities. A table of contents usually includes the sections listed in Exhibit 17-3. The table of contents is paginated using lowercase Roman numerals such as i, ii, iii, and so on.

The table of contents provides an outline of the major sections of the brief, including the various headings and subheadings. Headings are often referred to as **point headings**. The table of contents identifies the page number of each section so the reader has quick access to the information needed. The table of contents, along with the table of authorities, is usually among the last parts to be written

Table of contents

A detailed listing of the sections of the brief, along with the page numbers upon which each section begins.

Point headings

Headings of the major sections of the brief, which state the main topic of each section.

[1]U.S. Bankruptcy Court, Middle District of Pennsylvania. 2012. http://www.pamb.uscourts.gov /content/rule-9004-2-caption-pleadings

---

EXHIBIT 17-3   TABLE OF CONTENTS SECTIONS

Table of Authorities

Statement of Facts

Issues

Summary of the Argument

Argument

Conclusion

Signature

---

because the page numbers must be known. The local rules of court will state whether a table of contents is required. Exhibit 17-4 is a local court rule regarding tables of contents.

EXHIBIT 17-4   LOCAL COURT RULE

2011 California Rules of Court

Rule 3.1113. Memorandum
(f) Format of longer memorandum

A memorandum that exceeds 10 pages must include a table of contents and a table of authorities. A memorandum that exceeds 15 pages must also include an opening summary of argument.

(Subd (f) amended and lettered effective January 1, 2007; adopted as part of subd (d); subd (d) previously amended and relettered as subd (e) effective January 1, 2004)[2]

Exhibit 17-5 shows an example of a table of contents for a brief.

EXHIBIT 17-5   TABLE OF CONTENTS

TABLE OF CONTENTS

Page

TABLE OF AUTHORITIES iii

INTRODUCTION 1

    I. CIPA VIOLATES THE FIRST AMENDMENT RIGHTS OF LIBRARY PATRONS AND THEREFORE CANNOT BE SUSTAINED AS A VALID EXERCISE OF CONGRESS'S SPENDING POWER 2

        A. The Provision of Internet Access in Public Libraries Lies at the Heart of the First Amendment 2

            1. Speech on the Internet Enjoys Maximum Constitutional Protection 3

            2. Public Libraries Play a Fundamental Role in the Dissemination of Ideas and Information, Including Internet Speech 4

            3. Blocking Software Does Not Mirror Traditional Collection Development in Public Libraries 7

        B. The Uncontroverted Evidence Presented at Trial Establishes that the Blocking Software Used to Comply with CIPA

---

[2]California Rules of Court. 2012. http://www.courtinfo.ca.gov/cms/rules/index.cfm?title=three&linkid=rule3_1113

Prohibits Library Patrons from Accessing a Vast Amount of Protected Speech 10

   C. CIPA's Content-Based Restriction on Speech Fails Strict Scrutiny 15

   D. CIPA Imposes an Unconstitutional Prior Restraint on Speech 27

      1. CIPA's Basic Blocking Requirements Create an Ongoing System of Unlawful Prior Restraint 27

      2. CIPA's Disabling Provisions Establish Additional Prior Restraints on Protected Expression 31

   E. CIPA's Disabling Provisions Are Unconstitutionally Vague 33

   F. CIPA Is Facially Invalid 37

II. CIPA IMPOSES UNCONSTITUTIONAL CONDITIONS ON THE RECEIPT OF FEDERAL FUNDS 39

   A. CIPA Distorts the Usual Functioning of the Public Library 40

   B. CIPA's Speech Restrictions Impermissibly Extend Beyond Federally Funded Internet Service 44

III. CIPA IS UNCONSTITUTIONAL AS TO MINORS 46

CONCLUSION ....50[3]

Table of Authorities

To create a ***table of authorities***, the primary authorities are cited first and are grouped into categories, such as cases, constitutional provisions, and statutes. Cases are listed first, with federal and state case law listed separately. Cases are organized alphabetically, and constitutions, statutes, court rules, and regulations are organized numerically. After all of the primary authorities have been listed, the secondary authorities are grouped together according to a consistent organizational scheme. For example, law review articles are listed together in numerical or alphabetical order, followed by treatises in alphabetical order by author, and then by other authorities, such as *Black's Law Dictionary*.

> **Table of authorities**
> A list of all the primary and secondary authorities cited within a memorandum or brief along with the page numbers on which the authorities appear.

The type of format used may be dictated by the local rules or the preference of the supervisor. Exhibit 17-6 is the California court rule regarding tables of authority.

EXHIBIT 17-6 CALIFORNIA RULES OF COURT

2012 California Rules of Court

Rule 8.204. Contents and form of briefs

(a) Contents

(1) Each brief must:

(A) Begin with a table of contents and a table of authorities separately listing cases, constitutions, statutes, court rules, and other authorities cited;

(B) State each point under a separate heading or subheading summarizing the point, and support each point by argument and, if possible, by citation of authority; and

(C) Support any reference to a matter in the record by a citation to the volume and page number of the record where the matter appears. If any part of the record is submitted in an electronic format, citations to that part must identify, with the same specificity required for the printed record, the place in the record where the matter appears.[4]

---

[3]American Civil Liberties Union. US v. ALA et al., Post-trial Brief Table of Contents. 2002. http://www.aclu.org/technology-and-liberty/us-v-ala-et-al-post-trial-brief-table-contents

[4]2012 California Rules of Court. Rule 8.204. *Content and Form of Briefs.* 2012. http://www.courtinfo.ca.gov/cms/rules/index.cfm?title=eight&linkid=rule8_204

Exhibit 17-7 shows a partial listing of a table of authorities. This case brief in *U.S. v. Stevens* was prepared on behalf of the United States at the time when Elena Kagan (now a U.S. Supreme Court Justice) was Solicitor General and Counsel of Record.

EXHIBIT 17-7   TABLE OF AUTHORITIES

TABLE OF AUTHORITIES

Cases   Page(s)

Abrams v. *United States*, 250 U.S. 616 (1919) 11

American Amusement Mach. Ass'n v. *Kendrick*, 244 F.3d 572 (7th Cir.), cert. denied, 534 U.S. 994 (2001) 37

Ash v. *State*, 718 S.W.2d 930 (Ark. 1986) 46

Ashcroft v. *Free Speech Coal.*, 535 U.S. 234 (2002) 16, 30

Barnes v. *Glen Theatre, Inc.*, 501 U.S. 560 (1991) 34

Board of Trs. v. *Fox*, 492 U.S. 469 (1989) 40

Bob Jones Univ. v. *United States*, 461 U.S. 574 (1983) 31

Brandenburg v. *Ohio*, 395 U.S. 444 (1969) 11, 30

Broadrick v. *Oklahoma*, 413 U.S. 601 (1973) 6, 39, 40, 49

Broadway v. *ASPCA*, 15 Abb. Pr. (n.s.) 51 (N.Y. Ct. of Common Pleas 1873) 34

Burson v. *Freeman*, 504 U.S. 191 (1992) 31

* * *

Constitution and Statutes:

U.S. Const.:

Amend. I (Free Speech Clause) ....***passim***

Amend. V (Due Process Clause) 4

Act of Mar. 3, 1873, ch. 252, 17 Stat. 584 (49 U.S.C. 80502) 24

Animal Fighting Prohibition Enforcement Act of 2007, Pub. L. No. 110-22, 121 Stat. 88 28

Animal Welfare Act Amendments of 1976, Pub. L. No. 94-279, § 17, 90 Stat. 421 (codified as amended at 7 U.S.C. 2156 (Supp. II 2008)) 27

Food, Conservation, and Energy Act of 2008, Pub. L. No. 110-246, § 14207, 122 Stat. 2223 28

7 U.S.C. 1901 24

7 U.S.C. 1902 24

7 U.S.C. 2131 24

7 U.S.C. 2142 24

7 U.S.C. 2156 (Supp. II 2008) 24

7 U.S.C. 2158 24

15 U.S.C. 1821 *et seq.* 24

16 U.S.C. 1331 *et seq.* 24

18 U.S.C. 48 ....*passim*

18 U.S.C. 48(a) 2, 15

18 U.S.C. 48(b) 2, 15, 37, 42, 47

Passim

A term indicating that the author cited a particular authority on multiple pages, generally in excess of five pages.

18 U.S.C. 48©(1) 2, 14, 15, 41

Ala. Code:

§ 3-1-29 (Michie 1996) 7

§ 13A-11-14 (LexisNexis 2005) 25, 34

§ 13A-12-4 (LexisNexis 2005) 27

§ 13A-12-6 (LexisNexis Supp. 2008) 28

Alaska Stat (2008):

§ 11.61.140 25

§ 11.61.145 ....26, 27

* * *

Miscellaneous:

Frank R. Ascione:

    Battered Women's Reports of Their Partners' and Their Children's Cruelty to Animals, 1 J. Emotional Abuse 1 (1998) 32

    Children Who Are Cruel to Animals: A Review of Research and Implications for Developmental Psychopathology, 6 Anthrozoös 226 (1993) 32

Debbi Farr Baker & Anne Krueger, *Cockfight Raid Called Nation's Largest*, San Diego Union-Tribune, Oct. 16, 2007 ....20, 33

Ron Barnett, *"Hog Dogging" Has Some Fighting Mad*, USA Today, Apr. 5, 2006 19

Ellen Barry, *7 Arrested in Hog and Dog Competitions*, L.A. Times, Dec. 21, 2004 20

Bill Burke, *Out of the South: Dogfighting on the Rise*, Chi. Tribune, July 5, 2007 .... 19, 33, 46

Black's Law Dictionary (8th ed. 2004) 15

Thomas R. Collins, *Long Odds Lead to Okeechobee "Crush" Prosecution*, Palm Beach Post, Oct. 24, 44[5]

* * *

Introduction or Preliminary Statement

The introduction or preliminary statement identifies the party's claim and the theory of the case by referring to the case facts. An effective brief has a summary of the main points at the very beginning.[6] This is true of nearly all analytical and persuasive writing.[7] Opening paragraphs that merely identify the parties and the **procedural history** have little persuasive value, and will not sway a judge. Exhibit 17-8 shows a comparison between an effective and an ineffective introductory statement.

TIP

Note that under the Constitution and Statutes sections of Exhibit 17-7, some entries use the word **passim**, which means the author cited this particular authority on multiple pages. This term is used when references are found on more than five pages.

[5]*United States v. Stevens. No. 08-769.* Brief for the United States. 2008. http://www.justice.gov/osg/briefs/2008/3mer/2mer/2008-0769.mer.aa.pdf

[6]Wayne Schiess. The Practical Litigator. How to Write for Trial Judges. 42. 2002. http://files.ali-aba.org/thumbs/datastorage/lacidoirep/articles/PLIT_PLIT0207-SCHIESS_thumb.pdf

[7]Bryan A. Garner, *Legal Writing in Plain English: A Text with Exercises.* 2001. University of Chicago Press.

Procedural history
Information identifying what has happened in the process of litigation to date.

EXHIBIT 17-8 COMPARISON OF OPENING PARAGRAPHS

A Typical, Ineffective Opener:

PLAINTIFF'S TRIAL BRIEF

Plaintiff, Reginald E. Baker ("Baker"), files his Trial Brief in his suit against the Texas Commission on Wages ("TCW") and the Texas Labor Commission ("TLC") (collectively, "Defendants"), as follows:

A Persuasive Opener with a Bold Synopsis:

PLAINTIFF'S TRIAL BRIEF

The EEOC's conclusions and factual findings should be admitted into evidence here. Its hearings involved the same parties in this suit, and its conclusions and factual findings are highly probative of discrimination.

1. Background....[8]

Statement of Facts

A statement of facts usually follows the table of contents and table of authorities. Many prominent legal writers agree that the facts section is second only to the issues section in importance because of its potentially persuasive effect. While many judges will already have a basic knowledge of the law applicable to the case, they will not know much about the facts of the case until these facts are explained to them. A brief statement of the factual dispute saves the judge, or other readers, from having to search through the files of pleadings and documents to determine the subject of the case. The statement of facts is also an opportunity to present these facts in advocacy language—in a light most favorable to the client. Checklist 17-1 provides some considerations when drafting the statement of facts.

Checklist 17-1 STATEMENT OF FACTS SECTION

Check with court or supervisor regarding format requirements.

1. Write concisely.
2. Write logically.
3. Reference the record.
4. Advocate positive facts in places of emphasis.
5. Minimize negative facts.
6. Describe the record accurately.
7. Include facts that will be used in the argument.
8. Present the theory of the case.
9. Include key facts and relevant background facts.[9]

---

[8]Schiess at 43.

[9]Drafting a Brief to a Court. CUNY School of Law. 2011. http://www.law.cuny.edu/academics /WritingCenter/students/strategies-techniques/court-brief/3.html

The facts should be stated in a way that leads the reader to a conclusion that the client should prevail.[10] Facts that support the client's position should be described using *active voice*, which focuses the action on the subject of the sentence. Facts that do not support of the client's position should be downplayed by using *passive voice*, as shown in Example 17-1.

The facts must be accurate and truthful. The actual facts cannot be changed, added to, or omitted. However, being accurate does not mean that a writer must be neutral. Although the facts section is not the appropriate place to argue the case, the facts may be presented in a way that is most favorable to the client or which places the client in the best light.

The statement of facts should avoid using proper nouns, unnecessary details, or unimportant dates. Using "Plaintiff" and "Defendant" to identify the parties is sufficient. Events may be presented in chronological order; however, the facts can be presented by topic if it is more effective. Verb tense should be consistent, and events should be stated in the past tense if they have already happened. An exception would be if the facts were still unfolding as the advocacy document was being written.

The statement of facts is usually presented in a narrative format; however, some courts do require that the facts be presented in numbered paragraphs. The rules of the jurisdiction should be consulted before writing.

The statement of facts in each document should be drafted without relying on the facts identified in previous proceedings or those facts of the opposing party. However, the differences between the parties' statements of fact should not be dramatic unless there is a misstatement that should be corrected.

Recitals of the facts are more persuasive if written in an affirmative manner. An affirmative sentence makes a stronger impact than does a defensively written sentence. The difference is shown in Example 17-2.

The facts should be focused, insightful, useful, and engaging. Writing in a focused manner means identifying the most important facts succinctly, yet strongly. Insightful writing means pointing out facts that others perhaps do not see. Writing is useful if the material is presented accurately and helps the reader understand the facts. Engaging writing invites the reader into the story and

Active voice

A style of writing in which the subject of the sentence performs the action. An example would be "Paralegal Paula drafted the table of authorities." The subject, Paula, is doing the action of drafting.

Passive voice

A writing style in which the subject of the sentence is being acted upon. For example: "The decision was made by the judge."

EXAMPLE 17-1   ACTIVE V. PASSIVE VOICE

Active voice (powerful): The police violated the defendant's Fourth Amendment rights.

Passive voice (weak): The defendant's Fourth Amendment rights were violated by the police.

Passive voice (defense): Mrs. Johnson was struck several times.

Active voice (prosecution): The defendant slapped Mrs. Johnson repeatedly.

EXAMPLE 17-2   AFFIRMATIVE V. DEFENSIVE SENTENCES

Defensive sentence: The record does not demonstrate the errors of law alleged by the appellant.

Affirmative sentence: The record supports the Court's conclusion.

---

[10]David L. Lee. Writing the Statement of Facts. 2012. http://www.davidleelaw.com/articles /statemen-fct.html

encourages the reader to look more closely at the facts. The writer must not only understand the arguments being made, but also believe in them.

The facts presented in this section must be documented in the court record or in *declarations* or *affidavits* attached to the brief or memorandum. These sources should be referenced in the statement of facts. References to the transcript from the lower proceedings are referred to as "Tr." (transcript) or "R." (record), while references to documents included in the record on appeal are referred to as "Doc." (document). The statement of facts should also include information about the procedural history of the case before it reached the current stage of litigation. Exhibit 17-9 is a sample fact statement, showing how the record is referenced within the document.

Declarations

Formal statement as to certain facts.

Affidavit

A written statement of facts confirmed under oath before a person such as a notary public who is authorized to administer an oath.

EXHIBIT 17-9   SAMPLE STATEMENT OF FACTS

On May 8, 2008, Indianapolis police officer Shannon Harmon responded in a marked police vehicle to a call regarding the possible burglary of a home on Mead Drive. The police dispatch indicated a witness had observed two persons forcing open the front door of the home and that a tan Chrysler 300 was parked in the driveway. Upon arrival at the home, Officer Harmon observed a tan Chrysler 300 in the driveway with a person wearing green surgical gloves, later identified as Michael Gaddie, in the driver's seat. Gaddie saw Officer Harmon and backed out of a driveway in an apparent attempt to escape the officer.

Gaddie fled through a residential area, and Officer Harmon, who had "activated his emergency lights and sirens," pursued him. (App.53). By the time Gaddie reached North Dearborn Avenue, he had, according to Officer Harmon's case report, "reached an extremely high rate of speed and began to pull away from Officer Harmon in an attempt to elude him." However, Officer Harmon did not stop the pursuit. Officer Harmon reported that during pursuit through the residential area, Gaddie ran through stop signs while Officer Harmon stopped at them. Officer Harmon also reported that Gaddie was traveling up to 60 miles per hour during this point of the chase, while he was traveling between 40 and 50 miles per hour. Yet, Officer Harmon reported that he lost Gaddie for only a short time.

When Gaddie reached 62nd Street, he crossed the center line into the opposite lane and began traveling westbound in the eastbound lane. Officer Harmon reported that this action "[put] many vehicles and citizens at risk." However, Officer Harmon continued the chase. Gaddie continued to travel westbound with Officer Harmon in pursuit, eventually precipitating a four-car personal injury accident when he hit Earl's car. Earl, who was making a legal turn into Glendale Mall, sustained severe injuries. Officer Harmon estimated that his vehicle's highest speed during the pursuit was between 50 and 60 miles per hour, while Gaddie reached speeds approaching 70 miles per hour. Even though Officer Harmon stated that he drove cautiously and obeyed traffic signs, he admitted that he was only 100 yards behind Gaddie when the accident occurred.

After the accident, Earl sued the City for her injuries. In her amended complaint, she alleged municipal liability based on Officer Harmon's decision to continue his pursuit "without due regard of the safety of other drivers and pedestrians in the vicinity and in a high traffic area...." (App.10). The City moved for summary judgment on the basis that it was immune from liability under the law enforcement provision of the Indiana Tort Claims Act (ITCA). After a hearing, the trial court denied the motion. The City sought certification of the denial for interlocutory appeal, which the trial court granted on January 12, 2011. On March 18, 2011, this court granted jurisdiction over the interlocutory appeal.[11]

---

[11]*City of Indianapolis v. Earl*, 960 N.E.2d 868 (Ind.App.,2012).

Statement of Issues or Questions Presented

The statement of issues, also referred to as questions presented, issues presented, or assignments of error, states in simple terms the legal questions to be answered by the court. There is general agreement among legal writers that the issues section is the most important part of an advocacy document.[12] Like the facts, the issues should be presented using persuasive language. Exhibit 17-10 compares an issue written in an internal memorandum with the same issue written in an appellate brief.

When drafting the issues, the ABCs of accuracy, brevity, and clarity should be followed. The reader must be able to understand each issue after reading it only once. Checklist 17-2 provides some guidelines for drafting legal issues in an advocacy document.

EXHIBIT 17-10   ISSUE WRITING

Internal Memo: In assessing liability for a participant-on-participant sports injury, will the defendant's duty be measured under the reckless-intentional standard of care or the inherent-risk standard of care?

Brief: In assessing liability for a participant-on-participant sports injury, was the defendant's duty properly measured under the reckless-intentional standard of care?[13]

Checklist 17-2   CONSIDERATIONS IN DRAFTING LEGAL ISSUES

Frame issues differently when writing documents for non-lawyers or in house documents, such as interoffice memoranda, than when framing issues for lawyers and judges in external writing.

1. Strive to meet the preferences of the supervisor to whom the issues are written in an interoffice memorandum. Use traditional formatting for briefs and documents going to external audiences.

2. Distinguish between questions of law and questions of fact when framing the issues.

3. Avoid rigid limits on sentences and word length unless prescribed by law or by the audience of the document.

4. Know what needs to be accomplished with the document. In a document seeking a review, such as a petition for review, make the issue law-based and not based on a set of facts.

5. For an intermediate-level brief, give the key facts and law so the reader has the story and can see the applicability of the law.

6. In a trial brief where the goal is to persuade the court to grant relief, begin with a summary rather than an issue statement.

7. In mediation statements, use a summary in a concise manner with specific questions.

8. In a client advice letter or email, begin with an issue statement couched in plain English rather than in legalese.

---

[12]Bryan A. Garner, *The Deep Issue: A New Approach to Framing Legal Questions*, 5 SCRIBES J. LEGAL WRITING 1,2 (1994–1995).

[13]Wayne Schiess and Elana Einhorn. *Issue Statements: Different Kinds for Different Documents*, 50 Wash. L. J. 341, 356.

> **EXHIBIT 17-11   U. S. SUPREME COURT REQUIREMENTS FOR ISSUE QUESTION**
>
> **Rule 24. Briefs on the Merits: In General**
>
> 1. A brief on the merits for a petitioner or an appellant shall comply in all respects with Rules 33.1 and 34 and shall contain in the order here indicated:
>
> (a) The questions presented for review under Rule 14.1(a). The questions shall be set out on the first page following the cover, and no other information may appear on that page. The phrasing of the questions presented need not be identical with that in the petition for a writ of certiorari or the jurisdictional statement, but the brief may not raise additional questions or change the substance of the questions already presented in those documents. At its option, however, the Court may consider a plain error not among the questions presented but evident from the record and otherwise within its jurisdiction to decide.[14]

It is critical to list all of the important issues and state them clearly; otherwise, it is possible that the court will refuse to consider the legal authorities or arguments that are omitted. The issues should be presented in the order in which they will be discussed in the argument section. The location, the format, and possibly the content of the statement of issues may be determined by the court rules. The U.S. Supreme Court, for example, sets requirements for this section in Rule 24, shown in Exhibit 17-11.

The issues are written as questions in a form that leads to an affirmative response that supports the client. Many instructors and attorneys prefer that an issue be framed as a single sentence beginning with the word "whether." A typical "whether" issue is this:

Whether an invitee into a residence has a legitimate expectation of privacy under the Fourth Amendment when the invitee's sole purpose for being present in the residence is to assist the resident in an illegal activity?[15]

A statement written in this way is not grammatically correct—it is not a complete sentence, and it is technically a statement rather than a question. However, it may be the preferred usage in the office, or the court. An issue may also be written in a form that makes the following equation:

(under) law + (does) question + (when) key facts

The issue presented above would be written as follows:

Under the Fourth Amendment's privacy guarantees, does an invitee into a residence have a legitimate expectation of privacy when the invitee's sole purpose for being present is to assist the resident in an illegal activity?[16]

This sentence presents a syllogism: The major premise is stated following "under," the minor premise follows "when," and the conclusion follows by listing the key facts.

As a paralegal student, a good learning strategy might be to focus on one method for writing issues and perfect it. Once a student learns how to write a legal issue in one format, writing issues in any other format will come easily.

[14]Rules of the Supreme Court of the United States. 2010. http://www.supremecourt.gov/ctrules /2010RulesoftheCourt.pdf.

[15]Mary Beth Beazley, A Practical Guide to Appellate Advocacy 170 n.2 (3d ed. 2010).

[16]Beazley, *supra* note 14, at 170.

Summary of the Argument

While not included in all briefs filed in court, a summary of the argument is required under some court rules, such as these:

Rule 24. Briefs on the Merits: In General

(h) A summary of the argument, suitably paragraphed. The summary should be a clear and concise condensation of the argument made in the body of the brief; mere repetition of the headings under which the argument is arranged is not sufficient.[17]

Rule 28 of the Federal Rules of Appellate Procedure

(8) a summary of the argument, which must contain a succinct, clear, and accurate statement of the arguments made in the body of the brief, and which must not merely repeat the argument headings…[18]

The jurisdiction in which the brief will be filed should be checked for this requirement.

In this section, an introductory paragraph should summarize what the argument section will prove. Basically, the summary should be an outline of the argument, including the issues in the order they will be presented, a brief summary or conclusion for each issue, and the authority upon which the conclusions are based. This section can be very important, particularly if the presiding judge may not have time to read the entire brief word by word. The summary of the argument section is generally required by the court when the argument itself is especially lengthy.

The summary should be appealing, and not merely a repeat of the point headings. Because it does summarize the argument, it is often written after the argument has been completed. It must address only the matters in the argument, and should not introduce new material.[19]

Argument

The argument section is the heart of the brief, where the writer discusses and analyzes the laws and facts. This section is similar to the analysis or discussion section of a case brief or internal memorandum of law. However, unlike the analysis section of an internal memorandum, which is objective, the argument section of external documents is written in advocacy language. In persuasive writing, the writer not only identifies the issues at hand, but also persuades the court to rule a certain way on the issues. The argument section should be clear and well organized, and supported by strong authorities that are properly cited.

Each issue should be discussed separately using proper phrasing or point headings to identify which issue is being discussed. A point heading is a statement of the conclusion the court is being asked to make. Unlike issues, which are written generally as questions, point headings are written as statements. Point headings should be drafted as strong, active voice statements. The point headings

[17]Supreme Court Rules. Rule 24. Briefs on the Merits: In General. Legal Information Institute. http://www.law.cornell.edu/rules/supct/rule_24

[18]Federal Rules of Appellate Procedure 28. Circuit Rules lf the U.S. Court of Appeals for the Seventh Circuit. 2011. http://www.ca7.uscourts.gov/rules/rules.htm#frap28

[19]Guide to Appellate Briefs: Introduction. Duke Law School. http://law.duke.edu/curriculum/appellateAdvocacy/guide.html

should be written in all capital letters and centered on the page. Any subheadings should be underlined or italicized. An example would be this excerpt:

I. GOLDILOCKS HAD IMPLIED CONSENT TO ENTER THE PREMISES; THEREFORE, HER ENTRY WAS LAWFUL

A. Elements of the Action.

The point headings also provide a roadmap for the reader, emphasize key elements, and bring the court's attention to the outcome desired. Checklist 17-3 lists some guidelines to consider when writing point headings.

The heading should be centered on the page and, if more than one issue exists, should be identified with Roman numerals (I, II, III). The subheadings, if any, are generally identified by capital letters (A, B, C). Subheadings should be used only if there are two or more subheadings for an issue.

Avoid point headings that are excessively wordy or convoluted. Exhibit 17-12 compares a simple, effective point heading with one that is excessive.

> **TIP**
>
> In writing, one cannot have an "I" without a "II", or an "A" without a "B". If there is only one point heading, it should not be given a letter or a number.

Checklist 17-3 — QUESTIONS TO CONSIDER IN DRAFTING POINT HEADINGS

1. Do the headings help the reader navigate the brief?
2. Are the major headings independent, complete, and freestanding grounds for relief?
3. Are the headings argumentative and case-specific?
4. Do the point heading in the table of contents give a clear outline of the brief's arguments?
5. Are the headings clear and readable?
6. Are there enough? Are there too many?
7. Are the headings in the brief comparable to those in another brief?[20]

EXHIBIT 17-12   POINT HEADING COMPARISON

Do not write the following:

A. Adverse employment actions should be limited to ultimate employment decisions because it is implied by the plain language of 42 USC § 2000e-2(a)(1) of Title VII and properly balances protection of employees from discrimination and employers' legitimate need to manage employees.

when the following will do:

A. Adverse employment actions should be limited to ultimate employment decisions. ~~because it is implied by the plain language of 42 USC § 2000e-2(a)(1) of Title VII and properly balances protection of employees from discrimination and employers' legitimate need to manage employees.~~[21]

---

[20]*Guide to Appellate Briefs: Introduction.* http://law.duke.edu/curriculum/appellateAdvocacy/guide.html#point

[21]UCLA Moot Court Honors Program. Appellate Brief Writing Workshop. 2006. orgs.law.ucla.edu/moot/Documents/BriefWritingWorkshop.ppt

The citations should be given in the body of the brief rather than as footnotes, unless footnotes are preferred or required by a specific supervisor or jurisdiction. The argument should do more than just summarize a plethora of cases. All authority should be analyzed and applied to the client's case so that the reader understands how and why the law should apply in the client's situation.

The argument may be organized in the IRAC format, or in one of a variety of the other formats, such as IFRAC, CCRAC, and others discussed in Chapters 15 and 16. A sample argument is shown in Exhibit 17-13, using the IRAC method.

Conclusion

Every memorandum and brief will contain a conclusion stating what action the writer desires from the court. Most court rules, such as Fed. R. App. P. 28(a)(10). require that the brief include a conclusion.

The conclusion is not meant to be a complete summary of the arguments, nor is it a place to introduce new facts, issues, or authority. Many authors debate what exactly should be included in the conclusion. It may consist of a brief summary of the essential points,[22] a short, hard-hitting two or three line declaration,[23] or a short one sentence statement.[24] It is only a *brief* statement of the major points of the argument and is the last opportunity for the writer to persuade the reader of the merits of the case. Whatever format is preferred by the supervisor or jurisdiction, the conclusion should remind the reader of exactly what it is that the party is requesting.

Exhibit 17-14 is an example of a one-sentence conclusion:

> **TIP**
>
> The conclusion should be brief, and certainly no longer than a paragraph or so. If the conclusion is longer, the information will likely be ignored.

EXHIBIT 17-13 SAMPLE ARGUMENT FORMAT

Rule of law

Case law (if necessary)

1. Name of case

2. Facts of case

3. Rule or legal authority from the case that applies to the issue being addressed

Discussion of opposing position (similar to the counteranalysis in an internal memorandum)

EXHIBIT 17-14 CONCLUSION

For the foregoing reasons, the petitioner requests that the judgment of the lower court be affirmed.

---

[22]Edward D. Re, *Brief Writing and Oral Argument* 164-65 (6th ed. 1987).

[23]Robert M. Tyler, Jr., *Practices and Strategies for a Successful Appeal*, 16 Am. J. Trial Advoc. 617, 675–676 (1993).

[24]Richard K. Neumann, Jr., *Legal Reasoning and Legal Writing* 343 (2d ed. 1994).

Signature and Date

Every document filed with the court must contain the signature of the submitting attorney and the date. Generally, trial courts have rules covering both manual and digital forms of the attorney's signature, as do appellate courts. Exhibits 17-15 and 17-16 are examples of rules regarding signature blocks.

EXHIBIT 17-15   RULE 11 ON SIGNATURE BLOCK

<u>Rule 11. Signing and verification of pleadings</u>

(A) Parties Represented by Attorney. Every pleading or motion of a party represented by an attorney shall be signed by at least one [1] attorney of record in his individual name, whose address, telephone number, and attorney number shall be stated, except that this provision shall not apply to pleadings and motions made and transcribed at the trial or a hearing before the judge and received by him in such form. A party who is not represented by an attorney shall sign his pleading and state his address. Except when specifically required by rule, pleadings or motions need not be verified or accompanied by affidavit. The rule in equity that the averments of an answer under oath must be overcome by the testimony of two [2] witnesses or of one [1] witness sustained by corroborating circumstances is abolished. The signature of an attorney constitutes a certificate by him that he has read the pleadings; that to the best of his knowledge, information, and belief, there is good ground to support it; and that it is not interposed for delay. If a pleading or motion is not signed or is signed with intent to defeat the purpose of the rule, it may be stricken as sham and false and the action may proceed as though the pleading had not been served. For a willful violation of this rule an attorney may be subjected to appropriate disciplinary action. Similar action may be taken if scandalous or indecent matter is inserted.[25]

Ethics Alert

Remember that a paralegal should never sign any document submitted to the court.

EXHIBIT 17-16   DIGITAL SIGNATURES

(2) Signatures

(A) Attorney Signatures—An electronic document which requires an attorney's signature may be signed with a digital signature or signed in the following manner:

s/ John Attorney
State Bar Number 12345
ABC Law Firm
123 South Fifth Avenue
Seattle, WA 98104
      Telephone: (206) 123-4567
      Fax: (206) 123-4567
      E-mail: John.Attorney@lawfirm.com[26]

---

[25]Indiana Rules of Court. Rules of Trial Procedure. 2012. http://www.in.gov/judiciary/rules/trial_proc/index.html

[26]Washington Courts. GR 30 Electronic Filing. 2011. http://www.courts.wa.gov/court_rules/?fa=court_rules.display&group=ga&set=GR&ruleid=gagr30

Certificate of Service

Whenever a pleading, brief, or other document is filed in court, all of the parties named in the lawsuit must receive a copy. To confirm this, every document must include a *certificate of service*. While each firm may have its preferences for the contents of a certificate of service, any format should include a verification that the document has been served, the identity of the parties that have been served, the method of service, and the date of service. It is then signed by someone in the office, usually the attorney of record. Exhibits 17-17 and 17-18 are examples of

Certificate of service
A certificate verifying that all parties involved in the action have received copies of the document being filed.

EXHIBIT 17-17 SAMPLE STATE COURT CERTIFICATE OF SERVICE

INSTRUCTIONS FOR FLORIDA SUPREME COURT APPROVED FAMILY LAW FORM 12.914, CERTIFICATE OF SERVICE

I certify that a copy of this document was [✓ **one** only] ( ) mailed ( ) faxed and mailed ( ) hand delivered to the person(s) listed below on *{date}* _____.

Other party or his/her attorney:

Name: _____

Address: _____

City, State, Zip: _____

Fax Number: _____

Signature of Party _____

Printed Name: _____

Address: _____

City, State, Zip: _____

Telephone Number: _____

Fax Number: _____

Florida Supreme Court Approved Family Law Form 12.914, Certificate of Service (9/00)[27]

EXHIBIT 17-18 FEDERAL COURT CERTIFICATE OF SERVICE

CERTIFICATE OF SERVICE

I, _____, hereby certify that on _____, I

        [name]   **[date]**

served copies of _____

                [name of document]

on the following parties by way of _____:

        [U.S. mail, UPS, overnight mail, email, fax, courier, etc.]

[List name and address of each attorney\party served]

_____   _____

Date   **Signature**

U.S. Court of Appeals for the First Circuit (Rev 10/03)[28]

---

[27]INSTRUCTIONS FOR FLORIDA SUPREME COURT APPROVED FAMILY LAW FORM 12.914, CERTIFICATE OF SERVICE. 2000. http://www.flcourts.org/gen_public/family/forms_rules/914.pdf

[28]U.S. Court of Appeals for the First Circuit. Certificate of Service. 2003. http://www.ca1.uscourts.gov/files/faq/certificate_of_service_sample_form.pdf

certificates of service for state and federal courts. Each jurisdiction may have its own format, and this should be checked before any documents are submitted.

The Appendix: Exhibits

The appendix is the place to attach various exhibits to the brief so that the court has easy access to the information referenced within the brief. These exhibits may be correspondence, deposition transcripts, pleadings, affidavits, or other documents. If referencing a document attached in the exhibits or appendix, the document should be fully discussed in the body of the brief and should be clearly labeled in the appendix. The exhibits should not be included within the body of the brief at the point of reference. If there are multiple exhibits, it may be necessary to make tabs for each document. The tabs should be clearly identified so that the reader can find each exhibit easily. It may also be useful to prepare a table of exhibits, organized by the order the documents were referenced within the text.

Rules of Court

Local rules of court
Rules that apply only in a particular court.

Documents filed with a court must comply with rules of court or *local rules of court* regarding form and content. These rules cover such topics as length, citation format, content requirements, and the number of copies that must be provided to the court. The rules of court must be reviewed carefully before preparing a document for filing. A court may refuse to consider the document if the rules are not complied with.

TRIAL BRIEFS

The majority of legal cases never actually go to trial. But for those that do, a trial brief can be a very useful legal document. A trial brief is a persuasive document that is filed with the trial court prior to the start of a trial. The trial brief provides legal support for

✓ Claims
✓ Defenses
✓ Anticipated evidentiary issues
✓ Jury instructions

Many jurisdictions do not require trial briefs, and it may not be necessary to write one for each trial. However, if the supervising attorney anticipates a legal question to arise at trial, the attorney may ask that a trial brief be written so that the legal team is prepared.

A trial brief assists the judge by providing a summary of the law supporting the plaintiff's claims or the responding party's defenses prior to the start of trial. It also provides a vehicle for the attorneys to address any anticipated evidentiary issues prior to trial. If an attorney is planning to introduce evidence that may draw an objection, the attorney may include legal authority in the trial brief for allowing that evidence to be admitted. An attorney may also provide authority for excluding evidence that it expects an opponent to introduce. In addition, the brief may include authority for the legal team's proposed jury instructions.

A trial brief must usually follow court rules prescribing its length, the form of the citations, the content of the brief, and the number of copies that must be filed with the court. These rules differ among jurisdictions, but a trial brief normally contains these features:

1. Case caption
2. Table of contents
3. Table of authorities
4. Statement of facts
5. Statement of issues/questions presented
6. Argument
7. Conclusion

Although a trial brief is written in an argumentative tone and advocates the client's legal position, it must be respectful to the court, and facts must never be added or changed to aid the client.

Many examples of trial briefs can be found on the Internet. If a firm has a **brief bank**, briefs from similar cases may provide a starting point. A trial brief has also been included as Exhibit A-1 in Appendix 1.[29]

Checklist 17-4 provides items to consider when preparing the trial brief.

Brief bank

A collection of various trial and appellate briefs that a law firm may have filed in previous cases.

Checklist 17-4 CHECKLIST FOR PREPARING AND DRAFTING THE TRIAL BRIEF

1. Consider the audience
   A. The judge
      1. List what is known about the judge. What does he or she expect?
      2. Identify strategies that are likely to persuade.
      3. If the judge is not known, research the judge by reading cases in which he or she heard.
      4. Cases can be found on Westlaw by using ju(name) or con(name) or dis(name) to retrieve cases where the judge was the writing judge or where the judge issued a concurring or dissenting opinion.
      5. In LexisNexis, open the Cases or International Cases search form and select the appropriate source from the Sources drop-down list. At the bottom of the Cases search form, enter the name of the judge.
   B. Opposing counsel
      1. List what you know about opposing counsel. What tactics does he or she use?
      2. Identify strategies that are likely to persuade.
      3. If the opposing counsel is unknown, research opposing counsel by reading cases he or she argued.
      4. Cases can be found on Westlaw by using at(name) to retrieve cases where the attorney represented a party.
      5. One can search in *Martindale-Hubbell* or similar attorney directory for information on counsel.
2. Review the materials of the case, which may contain any or all of the following:
   A. Initial client intake form
   B. Informal discovery such as notes from witness interviews
   C. Formal discovery such as
      1. Interrogatories
      2. Materials generated from requests for production
      3. Depositions

(Continued)

[29]In RE Bari v. Doyle. 2002. http://www.judibari.org/trial_brief.pdf

D. Evidence to be presented
E. Exhibits to be used at trial
F. Declarations
G. Pleadings
    1. Complaint and answer
    2. Motions for summary judgment or partial summary judgment
H. Medical information such as
    1. Hospital or doctors' records
    2. Doctors' reports
    3. X-rays
    4. Nurse's notes
    5. Pharmacy records

3. Analysis of case, facts, and potential contentions
    A. Cross-reference discrepancies and factual base
    B. Analyze and outline all areas of contention within the case
    C. Review supporting law
    D. Review potentially contrary law
    E. Update case law

4. Outline trial brief
    A. Statement of facts
    B. Analysis of liability
    C. Causation analysis
    D. Damages
    E. Personal profile
    F. Injuries
    G. Effects of injuries
    H. Post-collision medical progress
    I. Special damages
    J. Property damages
    K. Wage loss
    L. Other special damages
    M. Witnesses
    N. List of exhibits to be appended to trial brief
    O. Conclusion
    P. Draft, edit, and re-edit trial brief prior to publishing the document

APPELLATE BRIEFS

When a court (or tribunal) reaches a final decision in a case before it, at least one party is usually not happy with the decision. If that unhappy party believes the court made an *error of law*, the party may request that a higher court review the decision of the lower court. This review process is called an *appeal*, and the court that has the ability to review a lower court is said to have appellate jurisdiction. When a party chooses to appeal a trial court decision, both parties are required to file appellate briefs with the appropriate court of appeals. The party who appeals is called the *petitioner* or *appellant*, and the party who must respond to that appeal is called the *respondent* or *appellee*. Each side files an appellate brief with the court, arguing that position on the issues being appealed. A sample of an appellate brief is shown in Exhibit A-2 in Appendix 1.

The appellate brief is one of the most important forms of persuasive writing that an attorney will write. Although paralegals may assist in writing this type of document, it is highly unlikely that a paralegal will be asked to draft a complete appellate brief. Therefore, this chapter will not describe all the intricacies of writing the brief,

Error of law
A mistake in the interpretation or application of the law.

Appeal
Request to a higher court to review the decision of a lower court.

Petitioner
The party who appeals.

Respondent
The party who must respond to an appeal.

but will only present an overview of its structure and components so that a paralegal will understand enough to be able to assist with the project. Armed with this information, the paralegal will be able to note any places where language needs improvement, citations need correction, or additional information should be provided.

With a few exceptions, appellate courts will only consider issues that were raised by one of the parties in the lower court and preserved in the record for appeal. For example, if the plaintiff offers a photograph as evidence at trial, and the defendant does not want the photograph to be shown to the jury, the defendant must object to the evidence on the record, and the judge must rule on that objection. If the defendant does not make an objection on the record, the defendant has effectively waived its right to appeal on this issue. The issue may not be raised on appeal.

While lower courts may be empowered to consider both issues of law and issues of fact, the appellate court only decides issues of law. The appellate court will not make determinations on the facts of the case because it did not observe the witnesses during testimony, the reaction of the jury to evidence, or make any other direct observations of the evidence presented at trial. The appellate court therefore will not substitute its judgment for that of the jury on the facts of the case.

Appellate courts will also limit their decisions to **material errors** made by the trial courts. Although courts often make mistakes, not every mistake is significant enough to require a review by an appellate court. Some errors that a court makes are considered **harmless errors**—errors that are not substantial enough to affect the court's ultimate decision. For example, if a piece of testimony is clearly **hearsay**, but the judge allows it into evidence, it may be a material error if the testimony was strong enough to affect the jury's decision. However, if additional testimony substantiated the hearsay evidence, the admission of the hearsay might be deemed a harmless error, because the jury would have reached the same decision without it.

Although the appellate court judges have not heard the evidence as it was presented at trial, they will have access to the **record** from the lower tribunal in order to correct any errors that occurred. Pleadings, orders, exhibits, and the transcript of the proceedings are considered to be the record. Appellate courts will refuse to consider any evidence that is not part of the record. Likewise, the court will not accept an appeal unless the lower court has issued a final order. There are some exceptions to this rule such as an **interlocutory appeal**, in which a lower court asks the appellate court to immediately resolve a question before the trial can be completed.

Once a judgment is entered, the party who is disappointed with the result initiates the appeals process by filing a notice of appeal, usually with the trial court, and submits a filing fee.

The notice of appeal alerts the other party that an appeal has been initiated. The appellant must also order the trial transcript from the court reporter. A party is not required to order the entire transcript, and only the relevant portions need to be requested. Along with the transcript, the appellant must request the trial court record, which includes the pleadings filed in the case along with all exhibits that were submitted at trial.

The initial brief filed by the party who is appealing is called the "Brief for the Petitioner" or "Appellant's Brief." The brief filed by the opposing party is called the "Brief for the Respondent" or the "Appellee's Brief." The petitioner or appellant will also file a reply brief. Court rules dictate the time frame in which the briefs must be filed. The briefs will present arguments on why the lower court was correct (or incorrect), and why its decision should be **affirmed**, **modified**, or **reversed**. Because its objective is to persuade, every element of the appellate brief must use the language of an advocate.

The courts generally have strict time limits that govern the content, format, and filing dates of appellate briefs. It is extremely important to consult your

Material errors
Errors made by a court that may have affected the court's or jury's decision.

Harmless errors
Those types of errors that do not influence the court's ultimate decision.

Hearsay
Testimony of a statement made out of court by someone other than the person testifying. It is inadmissible because it is a statement made out of court by someone who is not available for cross-examination.

TIP

Court rules dictate the time frame in which a notice of appeal must be filed. Failure to file the notice of appeal before the deadline may result in waiver of the right to appeal.

Record
Pleadings, orders, exhibits, and the transcript of the proceedings that have been filed in the case.

Interlocutory appeal
An appeal in which the lower court asks the appellate court to immediately resolve a question before the trial can be completed.

Affirmed
A court of appellate jurisdiction declared that a judgment or order of a lower tribunal is valid and remains of record.

Modify
To make a change or amend an order or ruling.

Reversed
The judgment from the lower tribunal has been revoked or set aside.

jurisdiction's rules of court before preparing the appellate brief. Exhibit 17-19 shows Indiana's rule setting forth a 30-day requirement for filing.

The rules for filing vary among the states. For comparison, Exhibit 17-20 shows Minnesota's rule on filing and service of appellate briefs.

EXHIBIT 17-19 INDIANA'S RULE 9

Rule 9. Initiation Of The Appeal

A. Procedure for Filing the Notice of Appeal with the Clerk of the Indiana Supreme Court, Court of Appeals and Tax Court.

  (1) *Appeals from Final Judgments.* A party initiates an appeal by filing a Notice of Appeal with the Clerk (as defined in Rule 2(D)) within thirty (30) days after the entry of a Final Judgment is noted in the Chronological Case Summary. However, if any party files a timely motion to correct error, a Notice of Appeal must be filed within thirty (30) days after the court's ruling on such motion is noted in the Chronological Case Summary or thirty (30) days after the motion is deemed denied under Trial Rule 53.3, whichever occurs first.

  (2) *Interlocutory Appeals.* The initiation of interlocutory appeals is covered in Rule 14.

  (3) *Administrative Appeals.* A judicial review proceeding taken directly to the Court of Appeals from an order, ruling, or decision of an Administrative Agency is commenced by filing a Notice of Appeal with the Clerk within thirty (30) days after the date of the order, ruling or decision, notwithstanding any statute to the contrary.

  (4) *Abolition of Praecipe.* The praecipe for preparation of the Record is abolished.

  (5) *Forfeiture of Appeal.* Unless the Notice of Appeal is timely filed, the right to appeal shall be forfeited except as provided by P.C.R. 2.

> [Grace Period: Effective until January 1, 2014, if an appellant timely files the Notice of Appeal with the trial court clerk or the Administrative Agency, instead of the Clerk as required by App.R. 9(A)(1), the Notice of Appeal will be deemed timely filed and the appeal will not be forfeited.][30]

EXHIBIT 17-20 MINNESOTA'S RULE 104.01

104.01 Time for Filing and Service

Subdivision 1. Time for Appeal. Unless a different time is provided by statute, an appeal may be taken from a judgment within 60 days after its entry, and from an appealable order within 60 days after service by any party of written notice of its filing.

An appeal may be taken from a judgment entered pursuant to Minn. R. Civ. P. 54.02, within 60 days of the entry of the judgment only if the trial court makes an express determination that there is no just reason for delay and expressly directs the entry of a final judgment. The time to appeal from any other judgment entered pursuant to Rule 54.02 shall not begin to run until the entry of a judgment which adjudicates all the claims and rights and liabilities of the remaining parties.[31]

---

[30]Indiana Rules of Court. Rules of Appellate Procedure. 2012. http://www.in.gov/judiciary/rules/appellate/#_Toc251234826

[31]Minnesota Rules of Civil Appellate Procedure. 2012. https://www.revisor.leg.state.mn.us/court_rules/rule.php?name=aprcap-104

The rules for formatting may be very precise as well, and should not be overlooked. Exhibit 17-21 shows the extensive and detailed rules in Indiana:

EXHIBIT 17-21   INDIANA APPELLATE RULE 43 AND 44

Rule 43. Form of Briefs And Petitions

A. Applicability. This Rule governs the form of briefs, Petitions for Rehearing (Rule 54), Petitions to Transfer to the Supreme Court (Rule 57), and Petitions for Review of a Tax Court decision (Rule 63) by the Supreme Court.

B. Paper. The pages shall be 8 1/2 by 11 inch white paper of a weight normally used in printing and typing.

C. Production. The document shall be produced in a neat and legible manner using black print. It may be typewritten, printed or produced by a word processing system. It may be copied by any copying process that produces a distinct black image on white paper. Text shall appear on only one side of the paper.

D. Print Size. The font shall be Arial, Baskerville, Book Antigua, Bookman, Bookman Old Style, Century, Century Schoolbook, Courier, Courier New, CG Times, Garamond, Georgia, New Baskerville, New Century Schoolbook, Palatino or Times New Roman and the typeface shall be 12-point or larger in both body text and footnotes.

E. Spacing. All printing in the text shall be double-spaced except lengthy quotes and footnotes shall be single-spaced. Single-spaced lines shall be separated by at least 4-point spaces.

F. Numbering. The pages shall be numbered at the bottom.

G. Margins. All four margins for the text of the document shall be at least one (1) inch from the edge of the page.

H. Cover Colors. The document shall have a front and back cover in the following colors:

Appellant's Brief and Appendix: Blue.

Appellee's Brief and Appendix: Red.

Any reply brief (except as provided below): Gray.

Brief of intervenor or amicus curiae: Green.

Petition for Rehearing: White.

Brief in response to a Petition for Rehearing: White.

Petition to Transfer or for Review: Orange.

Brief in response to a Petition seeking Transfer or Review: Yellow.

Reply brief to brief in response to a Petition seeking Transfer or Review: Tan.

I. Cover Content. The front cover of the document shall conform substantially to Form #App.R. 43-1.

J. Binding. The document shall be bound in book or pamphlet form along the left margin. Any binding process which permits the document to lie flat when opened is preferred.

K. Copy of Document in Electronic Format. All documents may be accompanied by a copy of the document in electronic format. Any electronic format used by the word processing system to generate the document is permissible.

Rule 44. Brief And Petition Length Limitations

A. Applicability. This Rule governs the length of briefs, Petitions for Rehearing, Petitions to Transfer to the Supreme Court, and Petitions for Review of a Tax Court decision by the Supreme Court.

(Continued)

B. Oversized Brief. A motion requesting leave to file any oversized brief or Petition shall be filed at least fifteen (15) days before the brief or Petition is due. The motion shall state the total number of words requested, not pages.

C. Items Excluded from Length Limits. The text of the following shall not be included in the page or word length limits of this rule:

Cover information

Table of contents

Table of authorities

Signature block

Certificate of service

Word count certificate

Appealed judgment or order of trial court or Administrative Agency, and items identified in Rule 46(A)(10).

Headings and footnotes are included in the length limits.

D. Page Limits. Unless a word count complying with Section E is provided, a brief or Petition may not exceed the following number of pages:

Appellant's brief: thirty (30) pages

Appellee's brief: thirty (30) pages

Reply brief (except as provided below): fifteen (15) pages

Reply brief with cross-appellee's brief: thirty (30) pages

Brief of intervenor or amicus curiae: fifteen (15) pages

Petition for Rehearing: ten (10) pages

Brief in response to a Petition for Rehearing: ten (10) pages

Petition to Transfer: ten (10) pages

Brief in response to a Petition seeking Transfer: ten (10) pages

Reply brief to brief in response to a Petition seeking Transfer: three (3) pages

Brief of intervenor or amicus curiae on transfer or rehearing: ten (10) pages

Petition for Review of a Tax Court decision: thirty (30) pages

Brief in response to a Petition for Review of a Tax Court decision: thirty (30) pages

Reply brief to brief in response to a Petition for Review of a Tax Court decision: fifteen (15) pages

E. Word Limits. A brief or Petition exceeding the page limit of Section D may be filed if it does not exceed, and the attorney or the unrepresented party preparing the brief or Petition certifies that, including footnotes, it does not exceed, the following number of words:

Appellant's brief: 14,000 words

Appellee's brief: 14,000 words

Reply brief (except as provided below): 7,000 words

Reply brief with cross-appellee's brief: 14,000 words

Brief of intervenor or amicus curiae: 7,000 words

Petition for Rehearing: 4,200 words

Brief in response to a petition for Rehearing: 4,200 words

Petition to Transfer: 4,200 words

Brief in response to a Petition seeking Transfer: 4,200 words

Reply brief to brief in response to a Petition seeking Transfer: 1,000 words

Brief of intervenor or amicus curiae on transfer or rehearing: 4,200 words

Petition for Review of a Tax Court decision: 14,000 words

Brief in response to a Petition for Review of a Tax Court decision: 14,000 words

Reply brief to brief in response to a Petition for Review of a Tax Court decision: 7,000 words

F. Form of Word Count Certificate. The following are acceptable word count certifications: "I verify that this brief (or Petition) contains no more than (applicable limit) words," and "I verify that this brief (or Petition) contains (actual number) words." The certification shall appear at the end of the brief or Petition before the certificate of service. The attorney or the unrepresented party certifying a word count may rely on the word count of the word processing system used to prepare the brief or Petition.[32]

The rules in North Dakota, shown in Exhibit 17-22, are equally precise:

EXHIBIT 17-22 NORTH DAKOTA RULE 32

RULE 32. FORM OF BRIEFS, APPENDICES, AND OTHER PAPERS

(a) Form of a Brief.

(1) Reproduction.

(A) A brief must be typewritten, printed, or reproduced by any process that yields a clear black image on white paper. Only one side of a paper may be used.

(B) Photographs, illustrations, and tables may be reproduced by any method that results in a good copy of the original.

(2) Cover. The cover of the appellant's brief must be blue; the appellee's red; an intervenor's or amicus curiae's green; a cross-appellee's and any reply brief gray. Covers of petitions for rehearing must be the same color as the petitioning party's principal brief. The front cover of a brief must contain:

(A) the number of the case;

(B) the name of the court;

(C) the title of the case (see Rule 3(d);

(D) the nature of the proceeding (e. g., Appeal from Summary Judgment) and the name of the court, agency, or board below;

(E) the title of the brief, identifying the party or parties for whom the brief is filed;

(F) the name, bar identification number, office address, and telephone number of counsel representing the party for whom the brief is filed.

(3) Binding. The brief must be bound at the left in a secure manner that does not obscure the text and permits the brief to lie reasonably flat when open.

(4) Paper Size, Line Spacing, and Margins. The brief must be on 8½ by 11 inch paper. Margins must be at least one and one-half inch at the left and at least one inch on all other sides. Pages must be numbered at the bottom, either centered or at the right side.

(5) Typeface. Either a proportionally spaced or a monospaced face may be used.

(A) A proportionally spaced face must be 12 point or larger with no more than 16 characters per inch. The text must be double-spaced, except

(Continued)

---

[32]Indiana Rules of Court. Rules of Appellate Procedure. 2012. http://www.in.gov/judiciary/rules/appellate/#_Toc251234826

quotations may be single-spaced and indented. Headings and footnotes may be single-spaced and must be in the same typeface as the text.

(B) A monospaced face must be a 12-point font having ten characters per inch. The text, including quotations and footnotes, must be double-spaced with no more than 27 lines of type per page. Headings and footnotes must be in the same typeface as the text.

(6) Type Styles. A brief must be set in a plain, roman style, although italics or boldface may be used for emphasis. Case names must be italicized or underlined.

(7) Page and Type-Volume Limitations.

(A) **Word Limit for Proportional Typeface.** If proportionately spaced typeface is used, a principal brief may not exceed 10,500 words, and a reply brief may not exceed 2,500 words, excluding words in the table of contents, the table of citations, and any addendum. Footnotes must be included in the word count.

(B) **Page Limit for Monospaced Typeface.** If monospaced typeface is used, a principal brief may not exceed 40 pages, and a reply brief may not exceed ten pages, excluding the table of contents, the table of citations, and any addendum.

(C) **Word and Page Limit for N.D.R.Civ.P. 54(b) Certification.** If proportionately spaced typeface is used, an argument on the appropriateness of N.D.R.Civ.P. 54(b) certification may not exceed 1,250 words. If monospaced typeface is used, an argument may not exceed five pages. Word and page limits for Rule 54(b) certification are in addition to the limits set forth in (7)(A) and (7)(B).

(b) Form of an Appendix.

An appendix must comply with paragraphs (a) (1), (2), (3), and (4), with the following exceptions:

(1) the cover of a separately bound appendix must be white;

(2) an appendix may include a legible photocopy of any document found in the record of a printed judicial or agency decision;

(3) pages in the appendix must be consecutively numbered;

(4) an appendix may be prepared with double sided pages.

The appendix must be 8 ½ by 11 inches in size. Documents of a size other than 8½ by 11 inches may be included in the appendix but must be folded or placed in a file or folder within the 8½ by 11 inch appendix.

(c) Form of Other Papers.

(1) **Motion.** Rule 27 governs motion content. The form of all motion papers must comply with the requirements of paragraph (c) (3) below.

(2) **Petition for Rehearing.** Rule 40 governs petition for rehearing content.

(3) **Other Papers.** Any other paper must be reproduced in the manner prescribed by subdivision (a), with the following exceptions:

(A) a cover is not necessary if the caption and signature page together contain the information required by subdivision (a);

(B) Paragraph (a) (7) does not apply.

(d) Non-compliance.

Documents not in compliance with this rule will not be filed.[33]

Local court rules should also not be ignored. Not all jurisdictions have local rules for appellate briefs, but it is prudent to check. For example, Exhibit 17-23 shows an excerpt from a set of rules for an Illinois appellate district.

---

[33]North Dakota Supreme Court Rules N.D.R.App.P. Rule 32. Form of Briefs, Appendices, and Other Papers. March 1, 2010. http://www.ndcourts.gov/court/rules/appellat/rule32.htm

---

EXHIBIT 17-23 LOCAL RULES OF ILLINOIS APPELLATE COURT

RULES OF THE ILLINOIS APPELLATE COURT,
SECOND DISTRICT

April 7, 2011

FILED

APR 07 2011

Articles

I.   General Rules
II.   Building Rules
III. Personnel Rules

Explanatory Notes

ROBERT J. MANGAN, CLERK

APPELLATE COURT 2nd DISTRICT

Supreme Court Rule 22(h) authorizes this court to adopt rules that are consistent with the Illinois Supreme Court Rules and Illinois statutes. The Uniform Administrative and Procedural Rules Appellate Courts Second, Third, Fourth, and Fifth Districts (the Uniform Administrative Rules) also provide rules for this court. To facilitate the administration of justice, the Illinois Appellate Court, Second District (the Court), hereby enacts the following rules (the Local Rules) in addition to the Supreme Court Rules and the Uniform Administrative Rules. All prior rules issued by the Court are hereby rescinded.[34]

On the federal level, the content and format of briefs are controlled by the Federal Rules of Civil Procedure 28,[35] which are especially rigorous.

Components of an Appellate Brief

A typical appellate brief will contain the same sections as a case brief, with the addition of a jurisdiction statement and word count certificate, as shown in Exhibit 17-24.

TIP

Exhibits 17-19 through 17-23 are examples of why it is necessary to check the rules of the court with jurisdiction over your matter.

EXHIBIT 17-24 APPELLATE BRIEF FORMAT

1.   Cover page

2.   Table of contents

3.   Table of authorities

4.   Jurisdiction statement

5.   Questions presented (issues or statement of issues)

6.   Statement of the case

7.   Statement of the facts

8.   Summary of argument

9.   Argument

10. Conclusion

11. Word count certificate

---

[34]Rules of the Illinois Appellate Court, Second District. 2011.

[35]Federal Rules of Civil Procedure Rule 28 http://www.uscourts.gov/uscourts/RulesAndPolicies/rules/2010%20Rules/Civil%20Procedure.pdf

Jurisdiction Statement The jurisdiction statement states the legal basis for the court's jurisdiction over the case. It provides the statute or other authority and any essential facts that support its jurisdiction, including a brief procedural history of the case in the courts below. Some appellate courts require a jurisdictional statement, while many others do not. Exhibit 17-25 shows the portion of Fed. R. Civ. P. 28 requiring a jurisdictional statement for appellant's briefs.

Exhibits 17-26 and 17-27 provide examples of jurisdictional statements.

EXHIBIT 17-25   FED. R. CIV. P. 28(A)(4)

(4) a jurisdictional statement, including:
    (A) the basis for the district court's or agency's subject matter jurisdiction, with citations to applicable statutory provisions and stating relevant facts establishing jurisdiction;
    (B) the basis for the court of appeals' jurisdiction, with citations to applicable statutory provisions and stating relevant facts establishing jurisdiction;
    (C) the filing dates establishing the timeliness of the appeal or petition for review; and
    (D) an assertion that the appeal is from a final order or judgment that disposes of all parties' claims, or information establishing the court of appeals' jurisdiction on some other basis.[36]

EXHIBIT 17-26   SAMPLE JURISDICTION STATEMENT APPEALING FROM AN AGENCY JURISDICTION

Petitioner seeks review of the order of the Board of Immigration Appeals dismissing her appeal. This Court has jurisdiction to hear an appeal of a decision of the Board of Immigration Appeals pursuant to 8 U.S.C. § 1252 (2002). Petitioner filed her timely appeal of the Board's May 3, 2003, decision on May 7, 2002 [*sic*]. See 8 U.S.C. § 1252(b)(1) ("The petition for review must be filed not later than 30 days after the date of the final order of deportation.").[37]

EXHIBIT 17-27   SAMPLE JURISDICTION STATEMENT TO THE U.S. SUPREME COURT

JURISDICTION

The judgment of the court of appeals was entered on July 18, 2008. On October 4, 2008, Justice Souter extended the time within which to file a petition for a writ of certiorari to and including November 15, 2008. On November 6, 2008, Justice Souter further extended the time to and including December 15, 2008, and the petition was filed on that date, and was granted on April 20, 2009. The jurisdiction of this Court rests on 28 U.S.C. 1254(1).[38]

---

[36]United District Court of Appeals for the Second Circuit. FRAP 28. Briefs. 2009. http://www.ca2.uscourts.gov/clerk/Rules/FRAP/Rule_28.htm

[37]Sparknotes. The Appellate Brief. 2011. http://sparkcharts.sparknotes.com/legal/legalwriting/section3.php#Jurisdictional%20Statement

[38]*United States v. Stevens.* No. 08-769. Brief for the United States. 2008. http://www.justice.gov/osg/briefs/2008/3mer/2mer/2008-0769.mer.aa.pdf

Word Count Certificate

The local rules of court may dictate the maximum number of words or pages the appellate brief may contain. A word count certificate verifies that the brief is within the maximum number of words. Exhibit 17-28 shows the word limits in Indiana.

Word count limits may seem unimportant, but should not be disregarded. In *Abner v. Scott Memorial Hospital*, 632 F.3d 962 (7th Cir. 2011), the Seventh Circuit issued a warning because counsel had misrepresented the word count in the appellate brief. Federal Rule of Appellate Procedure 32(a)(7)(c) sets a maximum limit of 14,000 words. The appellants certified that their brief contained 13,877 words, well under the 14,000-word limit. However, the appellee noted in its brief that the appellants' brief actually contained 18,000 words. The appellants replied that they interpreted the rule to apply to the argument section only. The court was not impressed by this argument, saying this:

> Had appellants filed an 18,000-word brief with a truthful certificate, the brief would have been rejected; there would have been no occasion for sanctions, just as there is no occasion for sanctions when a brief is rejected for omitting

---

EXHIBIT 17-28 INDIANA RULE OF APPELLATE PROCEDURE 44

Word Limits. A brief or Petition exceeding the page limit of Section D may be filed if it does not exceed, and the attorney or the unrepresented party preparing the brief or petition certifies that, including footnotes, it does not exceed, the following number of words:

Appellant's brief: 14,000 words

Appellee's brief: 14,000 words

Reply brief (except as provided below): 7,000 words

Reply brief with cross-appellee's brief: 14,000 words

Brief of intervenor or amicus curiae: 7,000 words

Petition for Rehearing: 4,200 words

Brief in response to a petition for Rehearing: 4,200 words

Petition to Transfer: 4,200 words

Brief in response to a Petition seeking Transfer: 4,200 words

Reply brief to brief in response to a Petition seeking Transfer: 1,000 words

Brief of intervenor or amicus curiae on transfer or rehearing: 4,200 words

Petition for Review of a Tax Court decision: 14,000 words

Brief in response to a Petition for Review of a Tax Court decision: 14,000 words

Reply brief to brief in response to a Petition for Review of a Tax Court decision: 7,000 words

Form of Word Count Certificate. The following are acceptable word count certifications: "I verify that this brief (or Petition) contains no more than (applicable limit) words," and "I verify that this brief (or Petition) contains (actual number) words." The certification shall appear at the end of the brief or Petition before the certificate of service. The attorney or the unrepresented party certifying a word count may rely on the word count of the word processing system used to prepare the brief or Petition.[39]

---

[39]Indiana Rules of Court. Rules of Appellate Procedure. 2011. http://www.in.gov/judiciary/rules/appellate/#_Toc251234862

a statement of the standard of review or the date on which the judgment was entered, which is essential to determining the timeliness of the appeal. We reject many briefs for these and similar reasons. The problem here, by contrast, is a misrepresentation that was initially successful in averting rejection of the brief. The misrepresentation would have gone unnoticed had the appellee not called it to our attention. 634 F.3d at 963…

The response to the order to show cause, and the belated "Motion for Leave to Exceed Word Count" filed with it, advance no persuasive grounds for allowing an oversized brief to be filed, and so the brief is stricken. We could go further. As the Supreme Court pointed out in Chambers v. NASCO, Inc., 501 U.S. 32, 44-45 (1991), a court has the authority "to fashion an appropriate sanction for conduct which abuses the judicial process," including the "particularly severe sanction" of dismissal.…

The flagrancy of the violation in this case might well justify the dismissal of the appeal: let this be a warning. But in addition it is plain from the briefs that the appeal has no merit. To allow time for the appellants to file a complaint brief and the appellees to file a revised brief in response, and to reschedule oral argument, would merely delay the inevitable. 634 F.3d at 964[40]

A paralegal may be responsible for monitoring the word count and drafting the word count certificate, and any rules setting a word count limit should be strictly complied with.

Amicus Curiae Briefs

Amicus curiae
A "friend of the court."

Occasionally, individuals or organizations that are not parties to a suit may have an interest in the outcome of the litigation. Some cases involve issues that substantially impact a large category of people or entities, and the appellate court may allow non-litigants to file *amicus curiae* briefs on behalf of these groups. *Amicus curiae* means "friend of the court." The appellate court has the discretion to allow or disallow amicus briefs, and courts generally permit them if it appears that the additional information or insight offered in these briefs would benefit the court.

The format of *amicus curiae* briefs is similar to that of any other appellate brief, but there are separate rules that prescribe specific time frames, procedures, and content. Rule 37 of the U.S. Supreme Court, a portion of which is shown in Exhibit 17-29, governs *amicus curiae* briefs.

EXHIBIT 17-29   U. S. SUPREME COURT RULE 37 (IN PART)

Rule 37. Brief for an *Amicus Curiae*

1. An *amicus curiae* brief that brings to the attention of the Court relevant matter not already brought to its attention by the parties may be of considerable help to the Court. An *amicus curiae* brief that does not serve this

---

[40]Abner v. Scott Memorial Hospital, 634 F.3d 962 (7th Cir. 2011). http://web2.westlaw.com/result/default.wl?cfid=1&mt=Westlaw&origin=Search&sskey=CLID_SSSA56227385216295&query=TI(ABNER+%26+%22SCOTT+MEMORIAL%22)&db=CTA7&rlt=CLID_QRYRLT44524385216295&method=TNC&service=Search&eq=search&rp=%2fsearch%2fdefault.wl&srch=TRUE&vr=2.0&action=Search&rltdb=CLID_DB46571225216295&sv=Split&fmqv=s&fn=_top&rs=WLW11.01

purpose burdens the Court, and its filing is not favored. An amicus curiae brief may be filed only by an attorney admitted to practice before this Court as provided in Rule 5.

2. (a) An *amicus curiae* brief submitted before the Court's consideration of a petition for a writ of certiorari, motion for leave to file a bill of complaint, jurisdictional statement, or petition for an extraordinary writ, may be filed if accompanied by the written consent of all parties, or if the Court grants leave to file under subparagraph 2(b) of this Rule. Amicus *curiae* brief in support of a petitioner or appellant shall be filed within 30 days after the case is placed on the docket or a response is called for by the Court, whichever is later, and that time will not be extended. An *amicus curiae* brief in support of a motion of a plaintiff for leave to file a bill of complaint in an original action shall be filed within 60 days after the case is placed on the docket, and that time will not be extended. An *amicus curiae* brief in support of a respondent, an appellee, or a defendant shall be submitted within the time allowed for filing a brief in opposition or a motion to dismiss or affirm. An *amicus curiae* shall ensure that the counsel of record for all parties receive notice of its intention to file an *amicus curiae* brief at least 10 days prior to the due date for the *amicus curiae* brief, unless the *amicus curiae* brief is filed earlier than 10 days before the due date. Only one signatory to any *amicus curiae* brief filed jointly by more than one *amicus curiae* must timely notify the parties of its intent to file that brief. The *amicus curiae* brief shall indicate that counsel of record received timely notice of the intent to file the brief under this Rule and shall specify whether consent was granted, and its cover shall identify the party supported.[41]

WRITING EFFECTIVE BRIEFS

Although a paralegal is not likely to write an entire brief, knowing the features of an effective brief will make the paralegal a more valuable member of the legal team. Whether presented to a trial court or an appellate court, there are many characteristics that successful briefs have in common.

A brief is written from the client's perspective, in strong advocacy language. It is a persuasive document that should be crafted to emphasize the client's strongest points while minimizing weaknesses. While the weaknesses should not be distorted, they may be deemphasized by placing them in a less prominent place in the brief. A portion of the argument may focus on discrediting the opposition's position, but attacking the opposition should not be the main focus of the entire argument. Although the brief is written in a persuasive style, the overall tone of the writing should also be respectful.

Citations and quotes must be accurate and must actually support the client's issues. However, quotations should only be used sparingly. While quotations may be appropriate if the original words are the most eloquent or effective expression of an argument, overuse of quotations dilutes the value of what is said in the quoted text. Quotations have an impact only if they add something to the argument and directly support the client's position.

The fundamentals of writing apply particularly in briefs. If necessary, writing fundamentals should be reviewed before proofing the brief. In addition to using

[41]Rules of the Supreme Court of the United States. Rule 37. 2010. http://www.supremecourt.gov/ctrules/2010RulesoftheCourt.pdf

correct spelling, grammar, and punctuation, the paragraphs should be varied to hold the reader's interest. Starting each paragraph with a case citation can become repetitive and boring. Varying introductions and transitions will keep the reader engaged.

When proofreading the final draft, attention to detail is critical. Court rules and citation manuals should be read carefully to make sure the technical details are correct. Citations follow prescribed formats exactly, and the overall format of the brief must conform to court rules regarding length, content, and required elements.

ORAL ARGUMENT

Oral argument side note:

Oral argument
A presentation by the attorneys to explain the law and facts to the judges, who ask questions to clarify the issues in the case.

Oral argument is an opportunity for the attorneys to explain the law and facts to the judges, who ask questions in an effort to clarify the issues. Usually by the time oral arguments are held, the judges have studied the briefs and are prepared to ask questions. On occasion, however, the judges will not have prepared beforehand and will rely on the presentation by the attorneys. Generally, when the judges ask questions they want the attorneys to supply additional facts, clarify the issues, or examine the case from an angle not addressed in the briefs.

Not every appeal will include oral argument. Oral argument must be requested by at least one of the attorneys and must be approved by the appellate court panel. If the oral argument is approved, it is set for a time and date that is convenient for the court.

Although paralegals will not be directly involved in delivering an oral argument, they can help prepare the attorney and act as a sounding board for ideas. They may be responsible for making sure that the authorities the attorney will be using are still valid, taking notes, preparing outlines, organizing documents that might be needed, and tabbing the important parts of the trial record. They may also listen as the attorney practices the argument, critique the presentation, and think of questions that a judge may ask.

Oral arguments are governed by court rules that specify who can appear, how long each side has to speak, and other matters. Exhibit 17-30 shows Rule 28 of the U.S. Supreme Court regarding oral arguments.

EXHIBIT 17-30   U. S. SUPREME COURT RULE 28

Rule 28. Oral Argument

1. Oral argument should emphasize and clarify the written arguments in the briefs on the merits. Counsel should assume that all Justices have read the briefs before oral argument. Oral argument read from a prepared text is not favored.

2. The petitioner or appellant shall open and may conclude the argument. A cross-writ of certiorari or cross-appeal will be argued with the initial writ of certiorari or appeal as one case in the time allowed for that one case, and the Court will advise the parties who shall open and close.

3. Unless the Court directs otherwise, each side is allowed one-half hour for argument. Counsel is not required to use all the allotted time. Any request for additional time to argue shall be presented by motion under Rule 21 in time to be considered at a scheduled Conference prior to the date of oral argument and no later than 7 days after the respondent's or appellee's brief on the merits is filed, and shall set out specifically and concisely why the case cannot be presented within the half-hour limitation. Additional time is rarely accorded.

4. Only one attorney will be heard for each side, except by leave of the Court on motion filed in time to be considered at a scheduled Conference prior to the date of oral argument and no later than 7 days after the respondent's or appellee's brief on the merits is filed. Any request for divided argument shall be presented by motion under Rule 21 and shall set out specifically and concisely why more than one attorney should be allowed to argue. Divided argument is not favored.

5. Regardless of the number of counsel participating in oral argument, counsel making the opening argument shall present the case fairly and completely and not reserve points of substance for rebuttal.

6. Oral argument will not be allowed on behalf of any party for whom a brief has not been filed.

7. By leave of the Court, and subject to paragraph 4 of this Rule, counsel for an *amicus curiae* whose brief has been filed as provided in Rule 37 may argue orally on the side of a party, with the consent of that party. In the absence of consent, counsel for an *amicus curiae* may seek leave of the Court to argue orally by a motion setting out specifically and concisely why oral argument would provide assistance to the Court not otherwise available. Such a motion will be granted only in the most extraordinary circumstances.[42]

CONVERTING AN INTERNAL MEMORANDUM OF LAW INTO AN APPELLATE BRIEF

An internal memorandum of law can provide the foundation for preparing a number of other court documents, including the appellate brief. Some of the components of an internal memorandum directly correlate to components of the appellate brief. The information already researched and prepared for the internal memorandum can be transferred to the analogous sections of the appellate brief, as long as the information is still current.

Because the language of the internal memo is neutral and predictive, some revision will be required. After the information from the memo has been validated and updated, the text from the memo must be revised so that it uses a persuasive tone and advocacy language.

Once the facts, issues, and analysis have been revised to the language of an advocate, the additional sections required for an appellate brief must be added. Exhibit 17-31 compares the elements of an internal memo with the appellate brief.

EXHIBIT 17-31   COMPARISON BETWEEN INTEROFFICE MEMORANDUM AND APPELLATE BRIEF

Correlating Components Between an Internal Memo of Law and an Appellate Brief	
Internal Memo of Law	**Appellate Brief**
Heading	Cover Page
	Table of Contents
	Table of Authorities
	Jurisdiction Statement
	(Continued)

---

[42]Rules of the U.S. Supreme Court. Rule 28. 2010. http://www.supremecourt.gov/ctrules/2010RulesoftheCourt.pdf

Correlating Components Between an Internal Memo of Law and an Appellate Brief	
Internal Memo of Law	**Appellate Brief**
Statement of Assignment (sometimes required by supervising attorney or law firm)	
Issues	Issues or Questions Presented
	Constitutional Provisions, Statutes, Regulations Involved
Facts	Statement of the Case
	Statement of the Argument
Analysis (with Counteranalysis)	Argument
Conclusion	Conclusion
Recommendations	
	Signature
	Word Count Certificate
	Appendix

ETHICAL CONSIDERATIONS WHEN PREPARING COURT DOCUMENTS

There are several ethical considerations to keep in mind when preparing an appellate brief.

1. Only an attorney may sign documents submitted to the court.
2. A paralegal may be called upon to help research or proof the appellate brief, and may be asked to draft portions of it.
3. The brief must rely on valid facts and legal authority, without embellishment. Otherwise, the attorney may violate the duty of candor.
4. Paralegals might be asked to check citations within the brief. It is essential to provide the court with accurate citations to legal authorities used.
5. All authorities cited must be properly validated to ensure the court is being provided with good law.

SUMMARY

There are many ways a paralegal may be involved in preparing persuasive writings, including trial briefs and appellate briefs. To be a useful member of the legal team, the paralegal must be familiar with the different components in these persuasive writings. The formatting and content of these writings are governed by rules of court, which must be followed exactly.

REVIEW QUESTIONS

1. What are point headings?
2. How do point headings differ from memorandum issues?
3. Does an appellate brief have a table of contents? Why?
4. Identify the key sections of an appellate brief.
5. How does a table of authorities differ from a table of contents?
6. How are the authorities in a table of authorities listed?

7. Can a paralegal sign an appellate brief? Why or why not?

8. What are the rules in your jurisdiction for drafting and filing an appellate brief?

9. How does the tone of an interoffice memorandum differ from that of an appellate brief?

10. Would you tend to use the same cases in the interoffice memorandum and the appellate brief? Why or why not?

11. If two years passed between the time you created an interoffice memo and the time of the case's appeal, what is the first thing you would need to do with the authorities you cited in the memo? Why?

12. Explain how a paralegal can assist an attorney with preparing for an oral argument.

13. Why are local court rules important to check before filing a brief? What features of a brief might be covered?

APPLICATION **EXERCISES**

1. Using the citations corrected in the citation exercises below, create a table of authorities in proper format. Each citation appears on the page numbers corresponding to the citation number. For example, *Insurance Guaranty Ass'n v. Johnson*, 654 So. 2d 239, 240 (Fla. 4th 1995) would appear on pages 6 and 8 in the appellate brief.

   a. 6, 8
   b. 6, 7
   c. 10
   d. 7, 9
   e. 3, 4, 9
   f. 5, 8
   g. 4, 5, 7
   h. 3, 8, 10
   i. 4, 6
   j. 4

2. Read the article by Judge Mark P. Painter titled *Appellate Practice—Including Legal Writing From A Judge's Perspective* at http://www.plainlanguagenetwork.org /Resources/appellate.pdf. Outline the article with appropriate point headings.

CITATION **EXERCISES**

Identify the errors in the following citations and correct those errors. Some citations may have more than one error. Assume that each citation is being presented for the first time within the brief.

1. *Insurance Guaranty Ass'n v. Johnson*, 654 So. 2d 239, 240 (Fla. 4th 1995).

2. Steele et. al. v. Kinsey, 801 So. 2d 297, 299 (Fla. DCA 2001).

3. State on the relation of Royal Insurance Company v. Barrs, Fla , 99 So. 668 (1924)

4. Smith v. Sitomer, 550 So. 2d 461 (1989)

5. Florida Statute 768.79

6. Sparks v. Barnes, 755 So. 2d 718 (Fla. 2d DCA 1999)

7. *Florida Patient's Compensation Fund v. Moxley*, 557 So. 2d 863

8. Spiegel v. Williams, 545 So. 2d 1360 (Fla. 1989)

9. Deni Associates of Florida, Inc. v. State Farm Fire & Casualty Insurance Co., 711 So. 2d 1135 (Fla. 1998

10. *Weldon v. All American Life Ins. Company*, 605 So. 2d 911, 914 (Fla. 2d DCA 1992

QUICK **CHECK**

1. Which one of the following is NOT a type of persuasive writing?
   a. Memorandum of points and authorities
   b. Trial brief
   c. Appellate brief
   d. Case brief

2. This section of a persuasive writing lists the sections of a document with the page on which they are found in the document.
   a. Table of contents
   b. Statement of facts
   c. Table of authorities
   d. Argument

3. _____ are statements made under penalty of perjury and sworn to before a notary.
   a. Declarations
   b. Arguments
   c. Affidavits
   d. Advocates

4. This document has court rules that describe how the document is to be created.
   a. Case brief
   b. Interoffice memorandum
   c. Appellate brief
   d. External memorandum

5. This provides the statute or other authority and any essential facts that grant the court the jurisdiction to hear the case.
   a. Affidavit
   b. Statement of the facts
   c. Jurisdiction statement
   d. Table of authorities

6. Which of the following is not an ethical consideration that a paralegal must follow when preparing a persuasive writing to the court?
   a. Make sure you sign the document.
   b. Make sure an attorney signs the document.
   c. Make sure all authorities are validated.
   d. Check citation formats.

7. Which term refers to the tone used when writing a legal document that will be used only within your law office, such as a memorandum of law?

8. Which term refers to the tone used when writing legal documents that will be filed with the court?

For items 9–10, state whether each item is true or false.

9. A paralegal can sign a brief submitted to the court.

10. It is not necessary to check local court rules when filing documents with the court.

RESEARCH

In Chapter 16, you were given some fact patterns to research and write an interoffice memorandum of law. Make an outline of an appellate brief that would be based on the memorandum of law for each of these scenarios:

1. You work at a local law firm. The attorney you work for is going to be filing an appellate brief in state court on behalf of your client, the appellant. The attorney would like you to look up the local rules of court to determine what formatting requirements will need to be followed.
   a. Using an online source such as Westlaw, Lexis-Nexis Academic or Google, look up the rules of procedure for briefs.
   b. Use the rules to answer the following questions:
      (1) What color does the cover have to be?
      (2) What size does the paper have to be?
      (3) What print size is required?
      (4) What margins are required?
      (5) Do you have to provide a copy in electronic format?
      (6) How should the document be bound?

2. Using the information from exercise 1, find the same information in the federal jurisdictional rules applicable to your state.

INTERNET RESEARCH

Locate the appellant's brief at http://webcast-law.uchicago.edu/briefs/2004-1609AppellantBrief.pdf. This brief has the following 12 issues. Draft these issues from the appellee's point of view.

STATEMENT OF ISSUES PRESENTED FOR REVIEW

1. Whether the district court erred in failing to follow this Court's mandate by failing to "find the facts specially and state separately its conclusion of law thereon."

2. Whether the district court erred in finding sufficient competent evidence to prove infringement of the Patent by Peterson or any of its end users.

3. Whether the district court erred in considering plaintiff's demonstrative exhibits in the absence of competent evidence authenticating them.

4. Whether the district court erred in finding contributory and induced infringement where no Peterson end-user was shown to have actually installed a Peterson product in an infringing configuration or to have otherwise infringed the Patent.

5. Whether the district court erred in finding contributory infringement given plaintiff's judicial admission that Peterson's EMB product is capable of substantial non-infringing uses.

6. Whether the district court erred in finding induced infringement of the Patent in the absence of competent evidence of any intentional encouragement of infringement by Peterson.

7. Whether the district court erred in vacating, on August 18, 2004, certain findings of fact and conclusions of law entered on June 22, 2004, as to which plaintiff had not filed a timely and specific motion under Rule 52(b), F.R.Civ.P.

8. Whether the district court erred by entering, on September 2, 2004, new and different findings of fact and conclusions of law submitted by plaintiff after the August 18, 2004, hearing where: (i) the district

court on August 18 specifically adopted the proposed findings of fact and conclusions of law filed by plaintiff on June 10, 2004, (ii) plaintiff never filed any proper Rule 52(b) motion to amend the findings and conclusions orally adopted on August 18, (iii) the district court entered the findings and conclusions more than 10 days after the August 18 ruling, and (iv) the district court entered the findings and conclusions without providing Peterson due notice and an opportunity to be heard.

9. Whether the district court erred in awarding plaintiff lost profits damages where the plaintiff failed to prove by competent evidence even a single infringement of the Patent and plaintiff failed to establish the *Panduit* factors.

10. Whether the district court erred in awarding enhanced damages against Peterson.

11. Whether the district court's award of enhanced damages against Peterson is an unconstitutional or improper award of punitive damages.

12. Whether the district court erred in finding sufficient misconduct by Peterson to warrant declaring this to be an exceptional case and awarding attorneys' fees in plaintiff's favor.

MEDIA **RESOURCES**

Florida Supreme Court. *Gavel 2 Gavel.* Live Oral Arguments. 2011	http://www.floridasupremecourt.org/oral_argument/index.shtml
How To: Format Your Appellate Brief Part I. 2008	http://www.youtube.com/watch?v=olWyDgv2atU&feature=related
How To: Format Your Appellate Brief Part 2. 2008	http://www.youtube.com/watch?v=L7HWVjo-ceI&feature=related
How To: Format Your Appellate Brief Part 3. 2008	http://www.youtube.com/watch?v=ElQA4BkESVk&feature=related
How To: Format Your Appellate Brief Part 4. 2008:	http://www.youtube.com/watch?v=QmjSB9KBczQ&feature=related
How To: Format Your Appellate Brief Part 5. 2008	http://www.youtube.com/watch?v=nx_nfqm40gg&feature=related
Oral Arguments in the U.S. Supreme Court. 2011	http://www.supremecourt.gov/oral_arguments/oral_arguments.aspx
Strategies for Appellate Brief Writing. 2008	http://www.youtube.com/watch?v=2g0zkjcKOcA

INTERNET **RESOURCES**

Federal Trade Commission v. Whole Foods Market, Inc., No. 07-5276. 2008:	http://www.ftc.gov/os/caselist/0710114/080114ftcwholefoodsproofbrief.pdf
Guide to Appellate Briefs:	http://www.law.duke.edu/curriculum/appellateadvocacy/guide.html
Using Westlaw to Write a Brief:	http://lscontent.westlaw.com/images/content/documentation/2009/BriefWrite09.pdf
LexisNexis Product Tutorials:	http://www.lexisnexis.com/COMMUNITY/DOWNLOADANDSUPPORTCENTER/media/p/4332.aspx
Sparknotes. *The Appellate Brief.* 2011:	http://sparkcharts.sparknotes.com/legal/legalwriting/section3.php#Jurisdictional%20Statement
Montana YMCA Model Supreme Court, Sample Brief:	http://home.mcn.net/~montanabw/briefsmpl.html

Christian Kieffer/Shutterstock

chapter **eighteen**
CORRESPONDENCE

LEARNING OBJECTIVES

After completing this chapter, students should be able to:

1. Communicate effectively in correspondence.

2. Write a transmittal letter.

3. Draft a demand letter.

4. Develop an opinion letter.

CHAPTER OVERVIEW

In a law office, many different types of correspondence are received, written, and sent. Paralegals may draft some of the legal correspondence including **transmittal letters**, **demand letters**, **information letters**, **opinion letters**, and settlement offers. Some correspondence is sent in the form of email, which has a special set of concerns in the legal setting. Whatever the type, the value of well-written correspondence cannot be stated enough.

Transmittal letter

A letter that accompanies and transmits other documents.

Demand letter

Formal correspondence from an attorney to a party or other attorney demanding that action be taken or requesting a settlement of a claim or dispute.

Information letters

These information letters provide basic information such as a client's date for a trial or asking for information to be supplied.

Opinion letter

A formal letter from an attorney to a client or other attorney explaining an attorney's interpretation of the law as applied to a factual situation.

OPENING SCENARIO

John enjoyed drafting correspondence. While there were many similarities in the letters that he drafted, each letter was unique, and the content depended on the client's particular circumstances. John had a set of boilerplate letters he could work from, but he was always careful to ensure that each letter was carefully tailored for each client, and that any boilerplate language fit the client's unique situation.

He became adept at writing correspondence for many purposes, such as setting up client meetings, arranging for depositions, and requesting information from clients. Jami used the research that he did in some cases in opinion letters. He was also very good at drafting emails and preparing faxes. In fact, he often was asked to train new office members in the proper way to draft correspondence. John was glad that he had learned so much about correspondence in his paralegal program.

GENERAL FEATURES OF LEGAL CORRESPONDENCE

Throughout their careers, paralegals probably will draft many types of correspondence such as informational (transmittal, confirmation, or invoice) letters; persuasive (opinion) letters; and adversarial (settlement or demand) letters. Although these types of letters may vary in their requirements, all have certain elements in common. There are also a few important characteristics that define well-written correspondence.

All correspondence should be drafted with the legal sophistication of the reader in mind. A letter should talk *to* the reader, not *above* him or her. Legal citations and quotations should be kept to a minimum unless those items are a necessary part of the communication. If the letter discusses multiple issues, the text should be divided into separate, manageable topics, using headings if necessary. All correspondence should be carefully proofread before it leaves the office to make sure that it is accurate and free from any errors.

Formatting Legal Correspondence

Several styles may be used for formatting correspondence. The two most prevalent are **block-style formatting** and **modified block style** styles. Block styling means that the body of the letter (the content paragraphs) and everything else (such as the date, reference line, and salutation) are flush with the left margin. Paragraphs are single-spaced with a double space between paragraphs. Example 18-1 shows a sample of block formatting.

Block-style formatting
A style of formatting in which all text is flush to the left margin. Paragraphs are single-spaced with a double space between paragraphs.

Modified block style
A formatting style that places the return address, date, closing, and signature line slightly right of center. Each paragraph is indented five spaces.

EXAMPLE 18-1   BLOCK-STYLE LETTER FORMATTING

[Type every line flush with the left margin (begin at top of page)]

[**NOTE: if you use letterhead, leave sufficient spaces, approximately an inch, to accommodate printing on the letterhead.**]

[Inside Address if no letterhead][1]

December 1, 2012[2]

[Double space]

<u>Via Delivery Service</u>[3]

Ms. Gloria Brown, Clerk[4]
Vigo Circuit/Superior Courts
100 N. Main St.
Terre Haute, IN 47807

[Double space]

RE: *Theimann v. Stottler,* complaint[5]

[Double space]

Dear Ms. Brown:[6]

[Double space]

Enclosed is the original and three copies of the complaint in *Theimann v. Stottler*, along with the summons for the defendant, Stottler and a check for the filing fee. We want the summons served by certified mail, return receipt requested.

[Double space]

Please file-stamp two copies and return those copies, along with the receipt of payment, to us in the enclosed, self-addressed, stamped envelope. Please let me know if you need anything else.[7]

[Double space]

Sincerely,[8]

[Four spaces]

Daisy M. Dukes[9]
Paralegal

[Double space]

Enc.[10]
cc: Ms. Ellen Theimann[11]
Bcc: Mr. George Foreman[12]
KLM/jmm[13]

Legend:

1. Letterhead or inside address (heading)
2. Date
3. Method of service if other than regular mail
4. Recipient's address
5. Reference or regarding line
6. Greeting or salutation
7. Body of letter
8. Closing
9. Signatory's name and title , if appropriate
10. Enclosure notation
11. Carbon copy or courtesy copy notation
12. Blind carbon copy or blind courtesy copy
13. Initials of author/initials of preparer

Modified block styling sets the return address, date, complimentary closing, and signature line slightly right of center and indents each paragraph five spaces. Like in the block style, the paragraphs are single-spaced and there is a double space between paragraphs. See Example 18-2 for modified block formatting. Note that the closing is in line with the sender's address.

Writers should note that whether block or modified block formatting is used, paragraphs should be single-spaced with double spaces between paragraphs. A writer should insert four spaces between the closing—for example, "Sincerely," and the signer's name. This allows room for the signer to physically sign the document.

Ethical Considerations in Correspondence

Unauthorized practice of law (UPL)

Practicing law without a license.

Only lawyers can give legal advice. If the paralegal signs any document that contains legal advice or recommends a course of action, the paralegal commits the **unauthorized practice of law (UPL)** and violates several ethical guidelines for

---

EXAMPLE 18-2 MODIFIED BLOCK FORMATTING

[Begin at top of page. NOTE: If you use letterhead, leave sufficient spaces, approximately an extra inch, to accommodate printing on the letterhead.]

[Inside Address if no letterhead]

December 1, 2012

[Double space]

Ms. Gloria Brown, Clerk
Vigo Circuit/Superior Courts
100 N. Main St.
Terre Haute, IN 47807

[Double space]

indent five spaces → RE: *Theimann v. Stottler,* complaint for circuit court

[Double space]

Dear Ms. Brown:

[Double space]

Enclosed are the original and three copies of the complaint in *Theimann v. Stottler*, along with the summons for the defendant Stottler. We have enclosed a check for the filing fee. We want the summons served by certified mail, return receipt requested.

[Double space]

Please file-stamp two copies and return those copies, along with the receipt of payment, to us in the enclosed, self-addressed, stamped envelope. Please let me know if you need anything else.

[Double space]   Closing should be in line with inside address and date →

Sincerely,

[Four spaces]

Daisy M. Dukes

Paralegal

---

both attorneys and paralegals. Guideline 3 of the ABA's Model Guidelines for the Utilization of Paralegal Services states:

> **Guideline 3:** A lawyer may not delegate to a paralegal:
>
> a. Responsibility for establishing an attorney–client relationship.
> b. Responsibility for establishing the amount of a fee to be charged for a legal service.
> c. *Responsibility for a legal opinion rendered to a client* [emphasis added].[1]

A paralegal may draft an opinion, demand, or settlement letter, but the paralegal may not sign it. It is not uncommon for a paralegal to draft such letters, particularly when the paralegal and attorney have developed a relationship of trust and

---

[1]ABA Model Guidelines for the Utilization of Paralegal Services. 2004. http://www.abanet.org/legalservices/paralegals/downloads/modelguidelines.pdf

the paralegal has proven him- or herself capable. But such letters must be approved and signed by the attorney. When signing any correspondence, two important rules must be remembered: (1) Paralegals must identify themselves as paralegals and (2) paralegals cannot give legal advice. If there is any uncertainty as to whether a paralegal can sign correspondence, the supervisor should be consulted.

Audience

Correspondence can be powerful if written well. It often establishes the relationship between the sender and the receiver. Therefore, thinking about the recipient of the correspondence is important. If the correspondence appears stiff and formal, or brash and arrogant, the reader will receive a negative impression of the author. If the correspondence is not well thought out, or does not provide the information that the recipient needs, the correspondence may not inspire confidence in the reader of the writer's information.

Often the tone of the letter will be determined by the letter's audience. Correspondence should be tailored to the audience's level of sophistication. If the recipient is a layperson, it is important to explain any legal terms in simple language, and legalese should be avoided. If writing to someone who is familiar with the law, explanation of legal terms may not be necessary.

Content

Before drafting a letter, the sender must know exactly what information must be included. Determining the content is often more difficult than it appears.

The content is determined largely by the type of correspondence. If the purpose of the letter is to inform the client of an event, the content will be limited to disseminating information about that event. If the purpose of the letter is to transmit another document, such as filing a pleading with a court clerk, the content will be geared toward making sure the document is filed. If the letter is to recommend a course of action or give legal advice, the content will provide only that information, supported by relevant authority. Finally, if the letter is intended to make a demand to an opponent, the basis of the demand will be described in detail, along with the intended result.

Basic Components of Letters

All letters have certain components in common. The format for legal correspondence generally follows the same format as other business correspondence. Paralegals may find sample letters in the firm's files. Form letters can be located in form books in print, such as *Am. Jur. 2d Legal Forms*; *West's Legal Forms* (rev. 2d, 3d, 4th, and 5th eds.); *American Jurisprudence Pleading and Practice Forms Annotated*; or *Current Legal Forms with Tax Analysis*. Paid subscription services such as on LexisNexis and Westlaw also have form letters. On LexisNexis, they are found at AMJUR-LF, and on Westlaw they are under the directory link "Forms, Treatises, CLEs, and Other Practice Materials" (FORMS-ALL). Findlaw Forms (http://forms.lp.findlaw.com) is a free service.

Heading The heading includes the information normally found in a firm's *letterhead*: the name, address, and other contact information of the sender (the firm), along with a list of all the attorneys in the firm, and the paralegals, if the state allows. Often this information will be centered at the top of the firm's preprinted stationery, but the letterhead may be found elsewhere on the page such as along the side. Matching envelopes will also be embossed with the firm name and

Letterhead
The firm's stationery with the firm's contact information preprinted on it.

mailing address. A preprinted letterhead conveys a professional appearance and provides uniformity in the firm's correspondence.

As a practical matter, the letterhead should be measured so that space is allowed for the letterhead when preparing the letter using word processing software. At least two lines should separate the letterhead from the text that follows. Letterhead is used only for the first page of the document. If more than one page is required, blank sheets of the same color and weight of paper should be used. On subsequent pages, a **header** should appear on each page in the upper right-hand corner and contain the name of the addressee, the date of the letter, and the page number. This information identifies all of the pages as part of the same letter.

Header
Identification of a letter on the second and subsequent pages.

When writing a letter for personal use, the header should include the address and date. If block style is used, this information should appear on the left margin. If using modified block, the information should appear just right of center. Example 18-3 provides samples of a header using both formats.

Date The date can be extremely important in legal correspondence, especially in cases where it must be established exactly when information was conveyed to a party or a client. The date may be critical where the law requires that notice be given within a certain time frame. It can establish the date on which a party was given certain vital information, so that the party cannot later claim ignorance or lack of knowledge. The date may also establish the date on which a party agrees to a settlement, a contract, or some other course of action.

The date appears two lines below the heading or letterhead. It should have the month completely spelled out, along with the date and year, as set out in Example 18-4. The date should be the actual date of mailing, rather than the date

---

EXAMPLE 18-3   HEADERS IN PERSONAL CORRESPONDENCE

[Block Style]

22595 E. Smoky Hill Rd.
Aurora, CO 90015
January 13, 2013

Or

[Modified Block Style]

22595 E. Smoky Hill Rd.
Aurora, CO 90015
January 13, 2013

EXAMPLE 18-4   PROPER DATE FORMATTING

Correct: January 13, 2013

Incorrect: January 13th, 2013

Incorrect: Jan. 13th, 2013

Incorrect: 1-13-13

Incorrect: 1-13-2013

Incorrect: 1/13/13

the letter was written. If the letter is typed on August 2, 2012, but will be mailed on August 3, 2012, the date of the letter should be August 3, 2012.

Special Mailing or Delivery Instructions Occasionally, it will be necessary to make special arrangements, other than regular first-class mail, for the delivery of the correspondence. Any special directions as to delivery or service must be listed on the letter before the inside address and underlined so that attention is drawn to the instructions. The instructions are placed directly above the recipient's address. Examples of special arrangements might be a notation that the letter is to be hand delivered, sent by facsimile, or sent by overnight delivery. These notations provide evidence of the method of delivery.

In some cases, the attorney must verify that correspondence was actually received by the addressee. If correspondence is sent by certified mail, the address should include the phrase "Return Receipt Requested." In this case, a green card is attached to the correspondence that must be signed by the recipient. When the sender receives the signed card, this provides proof of service.

Figure 18-1 shows a completed certified mail card.

In some instances, a letter may need to be marked "Personal and Confidential" to advise that no one but the stated recipient should have access to the document. If the letter is to be confidential, that note should be placed on the envelope as well.

Inside Address The inside address is the address of the person receiving the correspondence. It must be in the proper format with the name (with Mr., Mrs., Ms., or other appropriate designation); title (if appropriate); and address as shown in Table 18-1. This information must be double-checked for accuracy.

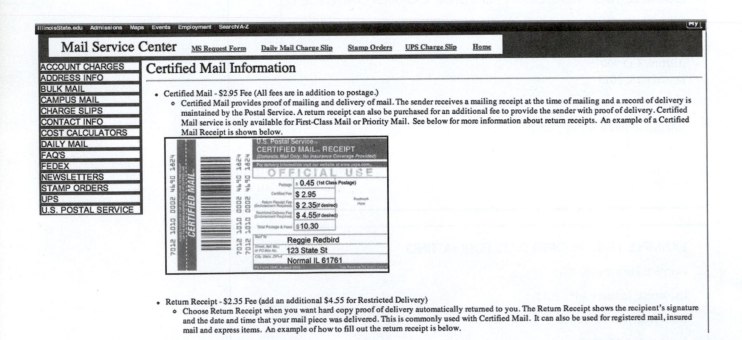

FIGURE 18-1 Certified Mail[2]

[2]Mail Service Center. Certified Mail Information. http://mailservices.illinoisstate.edu/usps/certified _mail.shtml

FIGURE 18-1 Certified Mail (*Continued*)

TABLE 18-1 Proper Formats for Inside Addresses

Correct	Incorrect
Dr. Wayne Lucas 123 S. 4th St. Atlanta, GA 30301	Wayne Lucas 123 S. 4th St. Atlanta, GA 30301
Mrs. Josephine Baker	Josephine Baker
Sister Mary Lou Dolan	Sis. Mary Lou Dolan
Professor Richard Collins	Prof. Richard Collins

Traditionally, the designation "Esq." (the abbreviation of "Esquire") is used to indicate that a person is an attorney, and is placed after the last name, separated with a comma. It is no longer considered absolutely necessary to use this term, but many attorneys still prefer to use it. If "Esq." is used, then the courtesy title such as "Mr." or "Ms." is *not* used. For example, an attorney would be referred to as "Ms. Joyce Phillips" or "Joyce Phillips, Esq.," but not as "Ms. Joyce Phillips, Esq."

Reference (Subject) Line The reference line (RE:) tells the recipient what the correspondence is about. It also ensures that the document is directed to the appropriate file, and can be returned to the correct file if it is removed. The "RE:" is set in all capital letters followed by a colon. This line generally contains the case or client name and a file designation. Each employer will have a format for the reference line. Examples might appear as follows:

RE: Cassidy v. Smith, 2010SC175
RE: Your letter of August 27, 2010

In the legal world, it is common to see the reference line follow the recipient's address. However, a few attorneys place the reference line after the salutation or, in modified block style, under the date.

The Salutation (Greeting)   The salutation should always be formal, beginning with "Dear," followed by the person's name with the proper title (such as Mr., Mrs., Ms., or Dr.), and a colon at the end. If the recipient is an attorney, the term "Esq." is not used in the salutation, but the courtesy title ("Mr." or "Ms.") is used instead.

If writing to more than one person, the salutation can be compound, such as "Dear Dr. Smith and Ms. Jones." Some titles must be spelled out, such as Professor, Dean, Sister, and Judge. If one is writing to a woman, and it is not certain if she prefers "Miss" or "Mrs.," the title "Ms." should be used. If the document is sent to an office and the name of the contact person is not known, "Dear Sir or Madam" is permissible. Job titles such as "Dear Recruiter" or "Dear Clerk:" can also be used. If possible, however, the recipient's office should be contacted to obtain the name of the person to whom the correspondence should be addressed. Do not guess at gender if it cannot be determined from the name. For example, "Chris" could be either "Christine" or "Christopher," and using the wrong title could be disastrous.

Some other variations in the salutation appear in Example 18-5.

If it is impossible to determine to whom the correspondence should be addressed, "To Whom It May Concern" may be used as the salutation. It is also proper to address a letter to "Ladies and Gentlemen" if addressing a group. However, it is always best to contact the office of the addressee before resorting to a generic salutation.

The Body   The body of the letter contains its message, and should be carefully organized. If the information is not logically organized, and the reader has to guess at information, the result could be disastrous. It might be helpful to write an outline of the letter before drafting to make sure all necessary points are covered.

EXAMPLE 18-5   SALUTATION FORMATS

Dear Dr. and Mrs. XXX: (husband and wife when husband has a professional title)
Dear Ladies and Gentlemen: (organization of both sexes)
Dear Mr. Jones and Ms. Fielder-Jones: (when wife uses hyphenated name)
Dear Drs. Pierce: (when both spouses have the same special title)
Dear Dean and Professor Spadoni: (when spouses have different titles)
Dear Judge and Mr. Myers: (when wife has special title)
Dear Messrs. Brown and Green: (old formal address)
Dear Colleagues: (members with several persons)
Dear Mr. President: or Dear Madam President:
Your Eminence: (religious dignitary)
Dear Monsignor Callen:
Dear Father Cooper:
Dear Bishop Showalter:
Dear Rabbi Goldwater:
Excellency: (governmental dignitary)
Dear (Mr. or Madam) Chief Justice:
Dear Representative Coats:
Dear Governor Daniels:
Dear Mayor Burke:

The structure and organization of the body depends on the purpose of the letter. However, whatever the letter's purpose, the body should always have an introduction, an opening paragraph, and a closing.

Each letter should have an opening paragraph that introduces the purpose of the letter. It may also contain a thesis sentence that acts as a map to tell the reader what to expect in the rest of the letter. In simple correspondence, such as a transmittal letter, this sentence will simply explain the purpose of the letter. In more complex correspondence, such as an opinion letter or a demand letter, this sentence will briefly explain the conclusion, or what the writer is trying to prove.

If quoted materials are used within the letter, the same rules apply as for quotations in other legal documents. If the quotation exceeds 50 words, separate the quotation from the paragraph, indent the quotation on both sides, and do not use quotation marks. This is illustrated in Example 18-6.

If the quotation is less than 50 words, use quotation marks and place the quotation in the flow of the sentence, as shown in Example 18-7.

There are many instances when a letter will include a list of items. For example, a list may be used to identify the steps that the recipient should take or items that should be brought to the next meeting. Lists may be set "in line" (within a paragraph), but are more emphatic if set vertically. Lists can be numbered, unnumbered, or bulleted.

If a vertical list is created to show items in a specific sequence, Arabic numerals should be used. The list should be introduced by a complete sentence that defines the list, followed by a colon. Both margins should be indented by 0.5 inch. A period should follow each number, and two spaces should separate the period and the item. Items should be double-spaced, but an item that is more than one line should be single-spaced, with a hanging indent aligning the first letter of each line. The first word of each item should be capitalized. The grammatical structure

---

EXAMPLE 18-6   SAMPLE QUOTATION 50+ WORDS

While the judge may be hesitant to find completely for you in the action, there is precedent. In *Marvin v. Marvin*, 18 Cal.3d 660, 825, 557 P.2d 106, 116 (1976) the court was faced with a woman who had lived with a man for seven years without marriage and who brought an action for enforcement of an oral contract providing her with half of the man's property. The court held that:

[Double-space between the sentence and the indented quotation.]

[Single-space the quotation, indent from both sides, and do not use quotation marks.]

> [T]he principle that adults who voluntarily live together and engage in sexual relations are nonetheless as competent as any other persons to contract respecting their earnings and property rights. Of course, they cannot lawfully contract to pay for the performance of sexual services, for such a contract is, in essence, an agreement for prostitution and unlawful for that reason. But they may agree to pool their earnings and to hold all property acquired during the relationship in accord with the law governing community property; conversely they may agree that each partner's earnings and the property acquired from those earnings remains the separate property of the earning partner.

18 Cal.3d at 685, 557 P.2d at 116. Therefore, operating on this basis, you may be entitled to a portion of those pooled assets … .

EXAMPLE 18-7   SAMPLE QUOTATION LESS THAN 50 WORDS

While the judge may be hesitant to find completely for you in the action, there is precedent. In *Marvin v. Marvin*, 18 Cal.3d 660, 825, 557 P.2d 106, 116 (1976), the court was faced with a woman who had lived with a man for seven years without marriage and who brought an action for enforcement of an oral contract providing her with half of the man's property. The court recognized the principle that "[A]dults who voluntarily live together and engage in sexual relations are nonetheless as competent as any other persons to contract respecting their earnings and property rights." 18 Cal.3d at 685, 557 P.2d at 116. Therefore, operating on this basis, you may be entitled to a portion of those pooled assets … .

---

of each item should be parallel (for example, all items must be complete sentences, or all items must be phrases). If the listing contains a complete sentence, a period should be used. An example of a correctly formatted list is shown in Example 18-8.

Horizontal listings may either be part of the sentence or be introduced by a complete thought and a colon. Each item in a horizontal list should be introduced by a number or lower-case letter in parentheses. If the horizontal list consists of words or phrases, the entries should be separated by commas. For example:

> Please bring the following items to your next appointment on December 15, 2012: (1) the insurance contract, (2) the police report, and (3) the partnership agreement.

If the horizontal listing consists of items that contain internal commas, the items are separated by a semicolon rather than a comma. For example:

> Please bring the following to your next appointment on December 15, 2012: (1) the insurance contract, if you purchased one; (2) the police report filed with the Dade Metro police department, or any other police department; and (3) any contract, employment agreement, or partnership agreement between you and John Black.

As with any writing, if a quote is taken directly from a source, the citation must be included either within the body of the writing or in footnotes, endnotes, or parenthetical text. The correct citation format must be used.

Sometimes it is necessary to insert a table, graph, or other type of graphic into the body of a letter. If possible, the table, graph, or chart should be presented

TIP

See Chapters 5 and 6 for more detailed information on citations.

EXAMPLE 18-8   NUMBERED VERTICAL LISTS

Your next meeting is scheduled for December 15, 2013, at our offices. We will be reviewing discovery requests. Please bring the following documents:

1. Your tax returns for the year 2012
2. Your books from the Shiny Auto business
3. A copy of your insurance covering the business
4. A copy of the partnership agreement
5. Copies of any witness statements, insurance claims, police reports, or other statements that pertain to the incident

We will make copies of these documents and return the originals to you.

---

on the page where it is described by the narrative. If that is not possible, a sentence should direct the reader to the page where the graphic appears.

Technically, if the format is block style, all paragraphs in the body of the letter will be flush with the left margin with double spaces between paragraphs. If the format is modified block style, the paragraphs will be indented five spaces with double spacing between the paragraphs.

The Closing The closing should be simple and professional, and should conform to the formality of the body of the letter and the salutation. Closings most commonly used in business, such as "Sincerely," "Very truly yours," or "Respectfully," may be used in legal correspondence. If the correspondence is particularly formal, "Respectfully," "Very truly yours," or "Sincerely yours" are probably the best choices. In general correspondence, "Sincerely" or "Sincerely yours" is preferred. In informal business correspondence, another option is "Cordially."

The closing should be double-spaced below the final line of the letter. Only the first word should be capitalized, and the closing should be followed by a comma. If the letter is in block style, the closing will be on the left margin. If the letter is in modified block style, the closing will be directly under the inside address and date.

The Signature Block The signature block states the name of the writer. In a legal setting, the signature block will usually provide the firm name, the name of the person sending the letter, and the sender's title. If the firm name is used, it should be in capital letters and placed below the closing with double-spacing. The writer's signature is placed four lines below the close or the firm name. The title can be on the same line as the name or it may be placed under the name. A modified block closing would appear as follows:

Very truly yours,
CLARK LAW FIRM
David N. Clark
Attorney

A block closing would appear thus:

Very truly yours,
CLARK LAW FIRM
David N. Clark
Attorney

If one is asked to sign a letter for a supervisor, the signer's initials should be placed in parentheses following the signature. If a paralegal is signing the letter, the title of paralegal must be stated. Otherwise, the reader may assume the writer is an attorney.

If more than one signature is required, the signatures should be in order of rank within the firm (for example, partner, senior associate, and junior associate). Otherwise, the signatures should be arranged in alphabetical order. In either format, vertically aligned signatures should be separated by three blank lines. In block format, the signature lines can be side by side beginning at the left margin.

Notations of Enclosures, Initials of Preparer, and Copies Sent The letter should include notations indicating those who have received copies. These notations are identified on the left margin below the signature block and separated by two blank lines.

EXAMPLE 18-9   INITIALS OF PREPARER IN SIGNATURE BLOCK

                                                    Very truly yours,

                                                    CLARK LAW FIRM

                                                    David N. Clark

        Attorney
DNC/klk or DNC: klk

The first entry is for the initials of the writer and preparer, if the two are different (for example, the paralegal who prepared the letter, and the attorney who approved and signed it). The writer's initials are in all caps, and the preparer's initials are in lower case separated by a diagonal or a colon as shown in Example 18-9.

If the sender is including documents or other enclosures with the correspondence, an enclosure notation is placed under the reference initials and generally appears as "Enc." If multiple enclosures are included, either the number of enclosures should follow in parentheses or the enclosures should be specifically listed. The word "Attachment" or "Att." may be used if the enclosure is attached to the letter. Example 18-10 shows various ways to identify enclosures and attachments.

If copies are to be forwarded to recipients other than the addressee, the distribution is noted on the left margin following the enclosure notation (if used), or after the reference initials if no enclosures accompany the correspondence. The notation "cc:" is used, which means "courtesy copies."

The notation itself might include the courtesy title, name, department, company, institution, or complete address of each recipient. The receivers are listed either in order of importance (if that can be ascertained) or alphabetically, if copies are going to multiple people. This list may be set either vertically or horizontally. Example 18-11 shows samples of copy notations.

In some instances, a copy of a letter needs to be sent to a person without other recipients knowing. A "bcc:" or "blind courtesy copy" notation indicates that the individual has received a copy, but the others do not know he or she was included in the distribution. This notation will appear flush with the left margin and *only on copies of the letter sent to the specified recipient of the blind courtesy copy and on the office copy, not on the original letter.*

EXAMPLE 18-10   ENCLOSURE NOTATIONS

<Left margin>

Enc. or

Enclosure or

Enc. 2 or

Enclosures (2) or

Enclosure: Billing Statement or

Attachment or

Attachments (2): Billing Statement

                Self-addressed Envelope

EXAMPLE 18-11   COPY NOTATION

cc: George Pringle *or*

cc: Betty Bravehart, George Pringle, Ann Summers *or*

cc: Mr. George Pringle, Insurance Adjuster, Progressive Insurance Company *or*

cc: Allan Alvarez, President

Barbara Balance, Vice President

Carole Corner, Plant Manager

Second Page Headings   If the correspondence exceeds one page, the second and succeeding pages should have a running header including the name of the addressee, the page number, and the date of the correspondence in either a vertical or horizontal format. The running head should appear flush with the left margin in block style, and aligned with the date and signature block in modified block style. It should appear one inch from the top of the page. Two spaces should separate the heading from the continuation of the correspondence.

When multiple-page letters are drafted, do not leave a single line of a paragraph on a preceding page or carry a single line of a paragraph to the next page. Similarly, the closing lines and signature should not be the only items that appear on a page. At least two lines of the correspondence should appear on the same page with the closing and signature lines. If the closing and signature appear on a page alone, someone could alter the information or add an additional page.

TYPES OF CORRESPONDENCE

Paralegals often draft letters to clients to transmit or confirm information, and sometimes do so to provide a summary of the action taken. These types of letters are also referred to as general correspondence. If the correspondence does not contain legal advice, the paralegal may have authority to sign these letters.

For other types of letters that include legal opinions and advice, such as opinion or advocacy letters, the paralegal may draft the letter, but must then submit it to a supervising attorney to approve and sign.

These letters will require appropriate components and the techniques of effective advocacy writing.

Informational Letters

Transmittal Letter   A transmittal letter, sometimes called a cover letter, is sent with documents or other items to explain the nature of the items and give directions to the recipient. A transmittal letter should state what the enclosed documents are (such as "I am enclosing a copy of the complaint"); what the recipient is expected to do with those documents (such as "please review," "please sign," "return to sender," or "please file"); and any due dates that are applicable (for example, "the complaint that is due May 7," or "these documents must be returned by December 10").

If the documents are to be filed with the clerk of a court, the transmittal letter should include a self-addressed, postage-paid envelope so that the file-stamped documents may be returned. Many courts and some law firms will not return documents

> **TIP**
> Always check with the supervisor to be sure that drafting and signing letters is allowed.

if the return envelope is not provided. Enclosing the prepaid envelope is a form of professional courtesy that should be extended as a routine business practice.

Even though a transmittal letter may seem simple, it must be drafted with great care. If the letter does not clearly convey what is expected of the recipient, problems could arise or the action might not be completed. The transmittal letter is written in a neutral tone. There is no need to influence the reader or to make a point. Example 18-12 provides a sample of a transmittal letter.

Confirming Letters   Confirming letters are used to avoid miscommunication by providing a written confirmation of an oral conversation. Attorneys and paralegals often give important instructions or reach agreements with clients, witnesses, or other attorneys over the telephone. If these oral conversations are confirmed in writing, there is no mistake as to what instructions were given or what agreements were made. Confirming letters are often used to document the following:

- An agreement that the client will bring in certain documents to his next meeting
- An agreement as to the date of the deposition that a party is to attend
- An agreement with opposing counsel as to the production of documents
- Substantive agreements that relate to the case, such as a child visitation schedule between the parents
- Agreements about the due dates of documents, particularly if an extension or delay is involved

---

EXAMPLE 18-12   TRANSMITTAL LETTER

Smith and Smith Law Firm
1000 E. Wabash
Indianapolis, IN 46240

December 21, 2012
<u>Certified Mail Return Receipt Requested</u>
Mr. Robert Jones
Clerk, Marion Circuit Court
10432 Ohio Street
Indianapolis, IN 46241

RE: *Smith v. Strong;* new filing

Dear Mr. Jones:

Enclosed please find our complaint and three copies in the above-entitled action. We are enclosing a summons directed to defendant Strong. We ask that this document be served by certified mail, return receipt requested. We have issued a check in the amount of $125 for the filing fee.

Please file-stamp the extra copies and return those in the enclosed self-addressed envelope. Thank you in advance for your help.

Sincerely,

Rebecca Easter
Paralegal

Enc: Original and three copies of complaint
Summons for defendant Strong
Check for court costs
Self-addressed envelope

- Agreements regarding setting or changing court dates, depositions, or other legal proceedings
- Any conversations that might need verification or clarification

A confirming letter might contain the following language: "This letter will confirm our conversation of September 8, 2012, in which you agreed to accept $1,500,000 in settlement of your lawsuit against the defendant, Amalgamated Corporation."

Appointment Letters Appointment letters are used by the attorney or paralegal to provide the client with notices regarding depositions, meetings, hearings, or other important dates. The letter should provide the date, time, and place (in detail) on which the client must appear. The letter should request confirmation that the client received the appointment letter and confirm the items that the client is to bring if that has been part of the request. An example is provided in Example 18-13.

Information Letters Information letters generally are used to send or obtain information, and may be issued to anyone. A request may be made, such as this:

Please bring in all medical bills incurred as a result of the accident on July 4, 2013, when you come for your appointment on September 8, 2013. We will make copies for our files.

EXAMPLE 18-13   APPOINTMENT CONFIRMATION LETTER

Smith and Smith Law Firm
1000 E. Wabash
Indianapolis, IN 46240

January 31, 2013

Mr. Pete Cornwell
123 S. 3rd St.
Greenwood, IN 46391

RE: *Cornwell v. Grayson;* deposition of Pete Cornwell

Dear Mr. Cornwell:

A deposition of you has been scheduled for Monday, February 18, 2013, at 3:00 P.M. in our offices at 1000 E. Wabash. Please arrive 30 minutes prior, or by 2:30. You should bring with you copies of your medical bills and copies of the repair bills for your camping trailer and any other items that were lost in the fire.

This deposition will be taken under oath and during this time the defendant attorney will ask you questions related to this court case. The court reporter is the person who will take down all information said while you are under oath. Mr. Smith will be present to represent you during the deposition.

Mr. Smith would like to meet you at least once before the deposition to discuss the case and to help you understand what will happen during the deposition. You should bring all of the documents identified above with you to this meeting.

Please confirm the appointment by calling the office at your convenience. You can ask for me to make the appointment. I look forward to talking with you sometime this week.

Very truly yours,

Sally Johns
Paralegal

EXAMPLE 18-14   STATUS LETTER

Smith and Smith Law Firm
1000 F. Wabash
Indianapolis, IN 46240

January 3, 2013

Ms. Megan Showalter
Red Flag Insurance Company
1234 S. Money St.
Cincinnati, OH 50155

RE: *Cornwell v. Grayson*; your claim number 0H1511 IM

Dear Ms. Showalter:

This letter is a status report regarding the progress in the above captioned matter. To date the defendant has requested that our client, Mr. Cornwell, answer a set of interrogatories and requests for admissions. We have done the same with defendant Grayson. I am enclosing copies of all documents mentioned with this letter. We are required to file answers to the interrogatories and requests within 30 days from the date of service.

We have also scheduled a deposition of the defendant for January 31, 2014. Please let us know if you have any questions to add to the deposition or if you wish to be present.

Please feel free to call if you have any questions.

Sincerely,

Frederick Jones
Paralegal

Encs. 4

Information letters may give information, such as by advising a client about the status of his or her case. A status letter may also be sent to the insurance company or other appropriate individuals or entities. Basically, the status letter provides an overview of the activities currently happening in the case, the business transaction, or other legal matter. A sample of this type of letter is shown in Example 18-14.

Invoice Letters or Billing Statements Paralegals are often asked to prepare invoice letters and billing statements for the client. The invoice letter keeps the client informed of the expenditures on behalf of the client, the ***draw*** from any retainer, and the balance that may be due. While the style of the bills is based on the format preferred by the law firm, virtually all legal billing is itemized. How often the client is billed varies from client to client and firm to firm. Some may be billed when the matter is completed, while other clients may be billed on a monthly basis. No matter how the client is billed, it is important that the client is aware of what he or she will be billed for at the beginning of the representation. This is something that the attorney will discuss at the time the attorney accepts the client's case. The billing cycle and the billing charges should be listed in the client's file.

The billing process begins with the preparation of the draft bill, which shows a compilation of time records and disbursements. The time records may come from multiple timekeepers, such as an attorney, a paralegal, and an

Draw

The amount the law firm "takes" from the client's retainer based on billing statements or agreed-to terms.

TABLE 18-2 Sample Billing Statement

Date	Personnel	Task	Time	Rate	Expense
12/20/2013	Jami Selzer	Initial conference with client	1 hour 30 minutes	$150.00 per hour	$225.00
12/20/2012	John Borders, paralegal	Initial conference with client; drafted complaint	2 hours	$75.00 per hour	$150.00
12/21/2013	Jami Selzer	Telephone conference with client; finalized complaint	30 minutes	$150.00 per hour	$75.00
1/12/2014	John Borders, paralegal	Prepared interrogatories to defendant	1 hour	$75.00 per hour	$75.00

investigator. Each timekeeper's time and hourly charge is listed, as shown in Table 18-2:

Any disbursements made by the firm on behalf of the client are itemized. The supervising attorney generally reviews the draft bill for errors or adjustments.

Once the invoice is finalized, it is sent to the client. Most law firms track bills, and if the client does not pay in a timely fashion, the law firm may consider terminating the relationship with the client or beginning collection proceedings. Checklist 18-1 provides some items to consider when drafting billing statements.

Demand Letter

A **demand letter** is used to encourage an opposing side to settle a case, or to pay a debt. It uses persuasive language to "demand" some kind of action be taken by the recipient.

The tone used in demand letters varies greatly and depends on the outcome desired. All demand letters are meant to be persuasive, but the tone of the language may vary, depending on whether the attorney wishes to establish an aggressive posture, or adopt a more *conciliatory* strategy.

Conciliatory
Willing to make concessions

Checklist 18-1   CREATING BILLING STATEMENTS

1. Never pad time. Padding time is unethical. The time billed for each task should be accurate and reflect the work performed based on the complexity of the task.

2. Include complete, accurate, and detailed descriptions of the tasks that reflect the necessity to the client's matter. Terms such as "review and revision of brief" may leave the client wondering why the task took so long. Use more descriptive terms such as "analyze," "re-draft," or "investigate."

3. Clerical and administrative tasks, as well as interoffice conferences, generally should not be included in a billing statement. Clerical tasks, while necessary to the practice of law, are generally considered part of the overhead of the firm.

4. Duplicate time entries become a red flag to clients. The client may refuse to pay for multiple charges for the same service, such as when two attorneys attend a hearing.

5. Itemize each task separately rather than listing the charges in large blocks. Itemized entries allow the client to determine the appropriateness of the time spent on the task.

6. Enclose a self-addressed, stamped envelope for the client's convenience.

FIGURE 18-2 Fair Debt
Collection Practices Act

§ 806. Harassment or abuse

A debt collector may not engage in any conduct the natural consequence of which is to harass, oppress, or abuse any person in connection with the collection of a debt. Without limiting the general application of the foregoing, the following conduct is a violation of this section:

1. The use or threat of use of violence or other criminal means to harm the physical person, reputation, or property of any person.
2. The use of obscene or profane language or language the natural consequence of which is to abuse the hearer or reader.
3. The publication of a list of consumers who allegedly refuse to pay debts, except to a consumer reporting agency or to persons meeting the requirements of section 603(f) or 604(3)1 of this Act.
4. The advertisement for sale of any debt to coerce payment of the debt.
5. Causing a telephone to ring or engaging any person in telephone conversation repeatedly or continuously with intent to annoy, abuse, or harass any person at the called number.
6. Except as provided in section 804, the placement of telephone calls without meaningful disclosure of the caller's identity.[3]

A demand letter is used for a wide variety of purposes. It may demand that a party stop a certain action (such as playing loud music at 4:00 A.M.). It might request settlement in hopes that an existing lawsuit can be resolved, or a potential lawsuit can be avoided (for example, a demand to an insurer to settle a claim resulting from a slip and fall in a grocery store). Demand letters are also used to encourage debtors to pay a past due bill or invoice (such as a late car payment or a hospital bill). Whatever the desired outcome, demand letters must comply with the requirements set forth by the Fair Debt Collection Practices Act. Figure 18-2 shows an excerpt from this statute.

States also have their own laws regarding debt collection. Figure 18-3 shows an excerpt from the fair debt collection law of Indiana.

The formatting and contents of a demand letter depend on the law firm's preferences, as well as requirements in federal and state law. In general, demand letters have the following sections and elements:

Opening The opening must identify the firm, the role of the firm, the client, and the subject of the letter. For example, the opening may state:

> This firm represents Becky Bouncer regarding the incident that occurred in the Newark Save-A-Lot grocery store on December 10, 2013.

It is not important to expand on the facts in the opening. However, it must make clear whom the letter is from and whom the firm represents.

Fact Statement The fact statement is a critical part of the demand letter. This section is where the persuasion truly begins. The key is to present the client's version of the facts in the light most favorable to the client, and also in a manner that

---

[3]Federal Trade Commission. *Fair Debt Collection Practices Act.* January 2009. Available at http://www.ftc.gov/bcp/edu/pubs/consumer/credit/cre27.pdf. Retrieved March 29, 2011.

FIGURE 18-3 Excerpt from Indiana's Fair Debt Collection Act

Debt Collection Practices That Are Prohibited

Harassment... Debt collectors may not harass, oppress, or abuse any person; they **may not:**

- use threats of violence or harm against the person, property, or reputation;
- publish a list of consumers who refuse to pay their debts, except to a credit bureau, or advertise the debt;
- use obscene or profane language;
- repeatedly use the telephone to annoy someone;
- telephone people without identifying themselves.

False statements... Debt collectors may not use any false statements when collecting a debt; they **may not:**

- use false, deceptive or misleading representations as to their identity, such as falsely implying they are attorneys or government representatives;
- falsely imply that you have committed a crime or state that you will be arrested if you do not pay your debt;
- misrepresent the amount of your debt;
- misrepresent the involvement of an attorney in collecting a debt;
- indicate that papers being sent to you are legal forms when they are not or indicate that papers being sent to you are not legal forms when they are;
- state that they will seize, garnish, attach, or sell your property or wages unless they or the creditor intends to do so and it is legal to do so;
- give false credit information about you to anyone.

Unfair Practices... Debt collectors may not engage in unfair practices such as: Debt collectors may not engage in unfair practices such as:

- collect any amount greater than your debt, unless allowed by law;
- make you accept collect calls or pay for telegrams;
- deposit a post-dated check prematurely.

If you are in Indiana and have a complaint against a Collection Agency, contact: Collection Agency Division, Secretary of State, One North Capitol, Suite 560, Indianapolis, IN 46204, 800-223-8791, 317-232-6684.[4]

is supported by witnesses, police reports, and documents. Those sources should be referenced in the fact statement.

Analysis The analysis is very similar to the analysis in other persuasive writing, such as external briefs or memoranda. The key is to provide some law that supports the client's facts and issues and explains persuasively how the law applies to those facts. It may be important to cite a statute or a portion of controlling case law in order to make a point. Citing the law helps to persuade the reader that the client stands on solid legal ground. The writer must be certain, however, that the client actually does have a claim upon which the demand can be made.

[4]Indiana Department of Financial Institutions. Fair debt collection. 2011. Available at http://www.in.gov/dfi/2588.htm. Last visited March 29, 2011.

It should be remembered that the demand letter is not the appropriate place to argue the case. The letter should not reveal too much legal or factual information that may be used by the other side to prepare its case, should litigation occur. The demand letter need only state what action is demanded, set forth the facts that support the demand, and identify the consequences that may occur if the demand is not met.

Damages and Injuries The demand letter should itemize and verify the damages and injuries. It should reference materials such as medical bills and reports, photographs, property appraisals, and any other supporting documentation that supports the credibility of the damages.

The Settlement Offer or Demand The demand or offer for settlement should be a clear, concise statement that identifies exactly what action needs to be taken or the amount that should be paid. If the recipient is to take some specific action, it should identify clearly what that action is. If written to collect a debt, the letter should specify the exact amount due. If there are several actions to take, it may be useful to set those items in a list so that it is clear exactly what is demanded.

Consequences Since the aim in a demand letter is to encourage the reader to do something on behalf of the client, whether that is to pay the client or do some activity, it is important to include a statement that explains to the reader what consequences may occur if there is no compliance with the letter. Consequences can include litigation, work stoppage, or some action that is adverse to the recipient's interests. There is a fine line between persuasion and heavy-handed threats. Persuasion is what should be done; heavy-handed threats are what should be avoided. Persuade by clearly and concisely identifying what will happen if the demand set forth in the letter is not met.

Date of Compliance The ending of the letter should be very clear as to the date that compliance is expected. The demand should give a specific date, rather than make a statement such as "You must pay the sum immediately." The term "immediately" may have different connotations depending on the reader. If a specific date is established, there is no question as to when the demand must be met.

In some instances, such as in cases where a client may be reluctant to sue, a demand letter may invite or initiate settlement discussions. This approach may be conveyed by saying, "Please contact us to discuss this matter in further detail." The supervisor will, of course, dictate the language of the demand letter. A sample demand letter is provided in Example 18-15.

To make a demand letter effective, it is important that whatever consequence is stated in the body of the demand letter is carried through in a timely fashion. If it is indicated that payment is due on January 10 or litigation will commence, a complaint should be filed on January 11. If demands are made without follow-through, the credibility of the firm may be affected.

Opinion Letter

Attorneys receive requests from clients for an explanation of the law, or a legal opinion regarding the client's rights or obligations in a particular matter. This type of letter is called an opinion letter (sometimes referred to as an advice letter), and is a type of predictive writing. A paralegal may research and draft an opinion letter, but because it contains legal advice, the paralegal may not sign it. The attorney has the responsibility to approve and sign this letter. If an opinion letter is drafted, it is critical that the attorney carefully review the letter before it leaves the office. Usually, the office will have a preferred format for the opinion letter.

EXAMPLE 18-15   DEMAND LETTER

Max and Irma Law Firm
333 Mockingbird Ln.
Flock City, IA 29101

January 8, 2014

Mr. J. R. Feathers
Feathers and Sons Builders
1414 Hummingbird Way
Flock City, IA 29101

RE: Douglas Kelly's home

Dear Mr. Feathers:

This firm represents Douglas Kelly (Kelly) regarding the home you contracted to complete for him in Flock City. Feathers and Sons Builders entered into a written contract with Kelly on November 29, 2013, regarding the building of a two-story home on lot 67 in the Williams subdivision. The total cost of the house was to be $276,000.

Our client has indicated that on January 3, 2014, you ceased working on the house. In addition, Mr. Kelly was verbally told by Milton Hanner, your site foreman, that no additional work would be done on the house. As it stands now, the house has a frame and outer walls but no finishing work has been done on the inside of the house. Our client also informed us that he has continued to make the stated payments of $30,000 twice a month. In addition, Mr. Kelly states that he has not done anything to breach the contract.

Therefore, we demand that work be completed on the house according to the written contract. That contract requires that the house be complete by February 21, 2014. If work on the house does not recommence by January 15, 2014, Mr. Kelly has asked that we initiate a lawsuit against you in Superior Court.

Please contact us upon receipt of this letter to confirm your compliance with the terms of the letter and to avoid litigation been filed.

Sincerely,
Max and Irma Law Firm

Anthony R Max, Esq.

ARM/rlt

The tone of the opinion letter should be geared toward the audience. Since this type of letter is usually written in response to a client's inquiry, the tone should be professional but clear. The letter is written for the client and his or her attorney, so legal jargon should be kept to a minimum.

Statement of the Issue   The process of writing an opinion letter is much the same as that for writing an analysis in an internal legal memorandum. The first step is to restate why the opinion letter is being written and confirm that the client requested it. Because the client will be billed for the time spent researching and drafting the letter, the client must be assured that the money was spent at his or her request. An introductory statement might state, "You have asked that I render an opinion about … ." Advice letters to clients should strive to use plain English rather than legalese. Figure 18-4 shows two examples of how legalese may be revised so that it may be understood by a layperson.

FIGURE 18-4 Issues in Client Advice Letters

> **Original:**
>
> You have requested this firm provide Loadstar Insurance Corporation (hereinafter "Loadstar") with a legal opinion regarding whether the conduct of its insured, Anthony Spencer, rose to the level of recklessness in causing injuries to the claimant, Cecelia Poole.
>
> **Revised:**
>
> You have asked for a legal opinion on the liability of Loadstar Insurance Corporation for the actions of its insured, Anthony Spencer. Specifically, when Spencer, as part of a common celebration with his soccer team, jumped on his teammate Cecilia Poole, was he behaving recklessly, subjecting him, and Loadstar, to liability?[5]

Fact Statement Next, the letter provides a brief review of the facts the letter is based upon, either in narrative or bulleted form. The fact statement is usually based on the facts delivered to the attorney by the client. Therefore, this section must accurately reflect the facts as told by the client, with the attorney emphasizing that the opinion is limited to those specific facts.

Analysis After the facts and issues are stated, the opinion letter follows a format similar to the analysis of an internal legal memorandum. The applicable law is identified and the client's facts are applied to the law. If there is more than one issue, each issue is discussed separately by identifying the issue, identifying the law that controls the issue, and applying the facts from the client's situation. Whether citations are given or not will depend on the preference of the supervisor. If a client is not familiar with legal writing, attorneys often use generic terms in lieu of legal citations, such as, "the case law provides that … ." or "legal authorities agree that … " to present the information.

Conclusion In the final paragraphs of the opinion letter, the conclusion or answer to the issue is given along with a recommendation as to how the matter should be resolved. Very often, attorneys are not overly optimistic in their recommendations because they do not want the client to have inflated expectations, or plan for events that may never happen. Thus, they phrase their recommendations in terms that describe probability rather than certainty. Attorneys will avoid language that signifies a guarantee.

The ending of the letter may provide some direction or instructions to the client as to what should be done next. For example, if the statute of limitations may be close to running out on a cause of action, the client may be instructed to contact the office within a certain number of days to decide whether or not to sue.

An opinion letter often contains an additional device, often referred to as a "protection clause." A standard clause might read as follows:

> This opinion is based upon the facts you have provided to us. Once we have taken an opportunity to review the contract entered into between you and XYZ Corporation, we will be able to provide you with a more complete opinion and analysis. Assuming the contract contains the language you have conveyed, it is my opinion that … .

Checklist 18-2 provides some guidelines for drafting an opinion letter.
A sample opinion letter is shown in Figure 18-5.

[5]*Id.* at 361

Checklist 18-2   OPINION LETTER CHECKLIST

1. Provide an introduction to lay the foundation for what is to come and why.

2. State all facts upon which the opinion is based.

3. Explain the relevant law.

4. Explain how the law applies to the given facts.

5. State an opinion or conclusion to the issue.

6. Provide recommendations.

7. Include a protection clause.

Suwyn, Siska & King
Attorneys at Law
6521 Main Street
Flushing, New York 11367
(718) 340-4200

October 23, 2012

Ms. Willi LomanLoman's Fashions
885 Seventh Avenue
New York, New York 10017

RE: Breach of Contract

Dear Ms. Loman:

I hope you have been well. Recently you wrote to us that Loman's Fashions had been sued in small claims court by a shopper for a breach of contract. As you've described it, the shopper claims that she responded to an ad for a "manufacturer's closeout" of designer leather coats; the ad stated that the "early" shopper would "catch the savings." The shopper complains that Loman's failed to have the merchandise to sell at the advertised price. Specifically, you have asked for advice on the question whether Loman's breached a contract with the shopper under the circumstances. After researching the issue, and based on the facts set out below, I believe that a court would likely conclude that Loman's did not enter into a contract with this shopper because the advertisement was not an offer to sell the coats; thus, there was no contract that Loman's could breach. I will explain this conclusion more fully below after first setting out the facts as I understand them.[1]

Loman's Fashions, a retailer of women's and men's outerwear, distributed a circular last July advertising a manufacturer's closeout of designer women's leather coats for $59.99, coats that regularly sold for $300.00. The ad announced that the store would open at 7 A.M. on Friday, July 21, and stated that the "early bird catches the savings!" After about fifteen minutes, all the advertised coats had been sold. At 7:30 A.M., a shopper inquired about the coats and was told that there were none left. She then complained that Loman's was obligated to sell her a comparably valued designer leather coat at the advertised price. The store manager declined, and the shopper filed a complaint in small claims court, claiming that Loman's had breached a contract by failing to sell the advertised leather coats at the advertised price.

You mentioned to me that the store occasionally gives rain checks when it is possible to replenish supplies of an item that Loman's can purchase at a discount. In this case, the manufacturer had discontinued the line of coats and Loman's was not willing to sell other designer leather coats at

---

[1]Opening paragraph states the client's problem, specifies the legal issue on which the client seeks advice, and states the writer's conclusion.

FIGURE 18-5 Sample Opinion Letter

such a drastic markdown. You are concerned that, if the shopper's interpretation were to be honored, Loman's would have to reconsider its marketing strategies. Although you had assumed that the advertised terms applied only while supplies lasted, your ad had not included language to that effect.[2]

You have asked for this law firm's opinion whether this shopper could succeed on her breach of contract claim.

Under these facts, a court would likely apply the well-settled law that a general advertisement that merely lists items for sale is at best an invitation to negotiate, not an offer to form a contract.[3] The courts that have considered this question focus on two related considerations.[4] The first is whether the advertisement is complete and definite in its terms. For example, where an advertisement containing terms for sale was missing the amount of goods available for sale, a court held that the seller had not made an offer that was complete and definite in all material terms. Thus, no contract was ever made between the seller and a person who submitted a purchase order.[5]

The second consideration is whether an advertisement promises to sell an item in return for something requested; for example, if a storeowner promised to sell an item for a specified price to anyone who came to the store ready to pay that amount.[6] Where such a promise was lacking, a court held that an advertisement by a department store was not an offer but an invitation to all persons that the advertiser was ready to receive offers for the goods upon the stated terms.[7] Even if a person's willingness to purchase the advertised item could be thought to turn the offer into a contract, that court ruled that a purchaser did not have the right to select the item that a seller did not have in stock or was not willing to sell at a reduced price.[8]

Applying these legal rules to Loman's advertisement supports the conclusion that the ad was not an offer to enter into a contract of sale and created no contractual duty for Loman's.[9] Here, the advertisement did not specify the amount of coats to sell, but rather described the leather coats as a "manufacturer's closeout" selling at a substantially reduced price.[10] In addition, the advertisement did not contain a promise to sell the leather coats in exchange for some requested act or promise.[11] Furthermore, the ad did not give the public the right to choose any comparably priced leather coat if the advertised coats were no longer available.[12] Although the shopper here might argue that the advertisement did not contain limiting language, for example, that the coats were for sale while supplies lasted,[13] the ad did state that the store, opening for business on the day of the sale at 7 A.M., was catering to early morning shoppers. By announcing that "the early bird catches the savings," the ad implied that the supplies would run out.[14]

---

[2]This paragraph and the preceding paragraph set out legally significant fact—facts upon which the writer will base her analysis. The factual criteria of the rule for offers under contract law, discussed in the following paragraph of the letter, are the source of the legally significant facts.

[3]The writer here restates her conclusion.

[4]The writer begins translating the law into relatively straightforward language, without naming specific cases.

[5]The writer here offers an example of how the rule would operate and then explains the implication of this analysis: that no contract was formed.

[6]The writer explains part of the rule by providing an example.

[7]The writer illustrates the point of law by discussing the facts and ruling in a similar case.

[8]The writer refers to an alternative holding in the case.

[9]The writer restates her conclusion as she moves to an analysis of her client's facts.

[10]The writer applies the first part of the rule—relating to definiteness and completeness of material terms—to Loman's facts.

[11]The writer now turns to the second part of the rule, requiring a promise in exchange for a requested act or promise, and applies it to Loman's facts.

[12]The writer points to facts (specifically, the absence of facts) in Loman's that provide an alternative basis for the writer's conclusion.

[13]The writer introduces a possible counterargument.

[14]The writer resolves the counterargument in favor of her original conclusion.

FIGURE 18-5 Sample Opinion Letter   *(Continued)*

To sum up, based on the facts as I have recited them in this letter, I believe that a court would conclude that Loman's ad did not make an offer to sell leather coats that a purchaser could accept, but that it was at best an invitation to negotiate. Thus, no contract came into existence from this transaction.[15] To avoid the possibility that Loman's will face future claims on this same point, I would recommend that, going forward, Loman's ads include language such as "while supplies last," "first come, first served," or "quantities limited–no substitutes permitted." In this way, Loman's would communicate to shoppers that there were no guarantees that they could purchase an advertised item, or a substitute. Although the additional text might increase the cost of advertising, in the long run inserting this additional language in the ads could save you time and the costs involved in defending claims such as this one.[16]

I hope this is helpful, and would be happy to discuss this matter with you further. Please feel free to call my office at (718) 340-4200 if you have questions, or would like to set up a time to meet.[17]

Very truly yours,

Madala Suwyn, Esq.

[15]The writer summarizes and restates her conclusion.
[16]The writer offers some preventive advice that addresses the possibility of future legal claims and also addresses extralegal factors—cost and time.
[17]The writer invites a follow-up conversation with the client.[6]

FIGURE 18-5 Sample Opinion Letter   *(Continued)*

EMAILS AND FAXES

Emails

Newer forms of communication, such as email, text messaging, and social networking sites, have resulted in a culture accustomed to more casual styles of writing. In electronic communication, it is common for people to communicate in sentence fragments and abbreviations, such as "brb," "ttyl," "lol," "jjk," "rotfl," or "i will c u la8r." These abbreviations may be acceptable in text messages, but in formal business communication, they are absolutely inappropriate.

Emails are an increasingly vital part of business communication, and this trend will continue to grow. Because so much business communication takes place in electronic or digital form, emails often contain information that may become valuable evidence in litigation, and are therefore discoverable. According to a substantial body of law, including both cases and court rules, a party has a duty to preserve electronic evidence once litigation is reasonably anticipated. Parties also have a duty to prevent *spoliation*—the destruction of evidence—including emails stored on computer servers and hard drives. The duties regarding the preservation of electronic information were detailed in the frequently cited opinions handed down in the *Zubulake*[7] litigation.

These cases can provide a valuable primer on the law regarding the preservation and spoliation of electronic records.

Because of their current treatment by the courts, emails must be written with the same care and seriousness as any other form of written business

TIP
A good summary of Zubulake can be found at http://www.krollontrack.co.uk/zubulake/

Spoliation
Willful destruction of evidence.

[6]CUNY School of Law. Drafting a Client Letter. 2012. http://www.law.cuny.edu/academics/WritingCenter/students/strategies-techniques/client-letter.html
[7]*Zubulake v. UBS Warburg LLC*, 216 F.R.D. 280 (S.D.N.Y. 2003)

communication. Emails should follow the same requirements as a business letter, with a salutation, introduction, body, and conclusion. If the body of the email will be long, the correspondence should be sent as an attachment. A salutation should be included in the email, with a reference to the attached document.

Faxes

While facsimiles (faxes) are not used as much as email is used today, faxes are still important. Knowing the proper way to send a fax is extremely important and usually very detailed. In general, the fax should have a cover sheet that identifies to whom the fax is addressed, the department of the recipient if appropriate, both the phone number and fax number of the recipient, and the same information from the sender. In addition, the cover sheet should indicate how many total pages, including the cover sheet, the faxed material contains so that the recipient knows that the appropriate number of pages has been received. You will also find that most attorneys will place a disclaimer on the cover sheet of the facts requesting that the fax is properly disposed of if it falls into the wrong hands.

Confidentiality
The obligation to keep the client's information private.

Confidentiality   In the field of law, faxing and emailing involves special considerations regarding confidentiality. For most types of legal communication, the U.S. postal system is preferred, largely because of the *confidentiality* it can provide. Faxes or emails do not ensure confidentiality because anyone on the receiving end may be able to read the correspondence. Faxes generally arrive at a common location in an office, which makes the fax accessible for viewing by someone other than the intended recipient. A small error in an email address may direct the message to the wrong person, and haphazardly forwarding an email potentially may result in the email being sent to thousands of persons.

An attorney's duty of confidentiality extends to electronic communication. The rule is shown in Figure 18-6.

Disclaimer
A statement that disavows or denies responsibility.

Most law firms have a *disclaimer* paragraph on all faxes and emails describing the confidential nature of the transmission. A sample disclaimer is shown in Example 18-16.

These disclaimers are of limited value, however. The disclaimer matters very little if the recipient is not an attorney, because such a receiver is not bound by ethical rules.

Email and Faxing Etiquette

Much of the etiquette applicable to any good writing is also applicable to emails and faxes. Checklist 18-3 provides some guidelines for emails and faxes.

FIGURE 18-6 Confidentiality of Information

> **Model Rules of Professional Conduct**
>
> **Client-Lawyer Relationship**
>
> *Rule 1.6 Confidentiality Of Information*
>
> (a) A lawyer shall not reveal information relating to the representation of a client unless the client gives informed consent, the disclosure is impliedly authorized in order to carry out the representation or the disclosure is permitted by paragraph (b).[8]

[8]American Bar Association Model Rules of Professional Conduct Rule 1.6 Confidentiality of Information. http://www.abanet.org/cpr/mrpc/rule_1_6.html

EXAMPLE 18-16   DISCLAIMER

The information contained in this email [fax] and any attachments hereto is sent by the firm of XYZ and is intended to be confidential and for the use of only the individual or entity designated as the recipient. The information may be protected by federal and state privacy and disclosures acts or other legal rules. If the reader of this message is not the intended recipient, you are notified that the retention, dissemination, distribution, or copying of this email [fax] is strictly prohibited. If you have received this email [fax] in error, please immediately notify XYZ by email reply and immediately and permanently delete this email [fax] message and any attachments thereto.

Checklist 18-3   EMAIL AND FAX ETIQUETTE

A. Format

1. Be concise. Emails are, by their nature, not intended to be extensive documents. If a prolonged explanation is needed, it may be better presented in an attachment to the email.

2. Provide meaningful subject line information so the recipient will know what the email is about and so the recipient can distinguish one email from another.

3. Use an appropriate structure and layout. Emails should begin "Dear XXX:" just as a letter would begin, and should be organized in paragraphs. All emails should contain a signature block.

4. Be careful with formatting. If there is a reason for special formatting, consider putting the information in an attachment. Emails are not always received in the same format as they are sent. Much depends on the computer and the software settings. Some settings, such as rich text format (rtf) and HTML, will affect the appearance. It is best to avoid HTML, as not everyone will be able to read that format.

5. Double space between paragraphs, but do not indent paragraphs.

6. Add disclaimers to the emails. Often the office will have a standard disclaimer that all employees use when transmitting business emails.

7. Use courtesy copies (cc:) sparingly.

8. Use the bcc: field or use a mail merge when the email is going to more than one person.

9. Do not overuse "Reply to All."

10. Do not ask to recall a message. Once the message has been sent, it is too late. The message should be carefully read before it is sent.

11. Do not overuse the "high priority" label. The same is true with the labels "urgent" and "important." Make sure that a document really meets these criteria before labeling them as such.

12. In faxes, use a cover sheet which identifies the sender and the sender's telephone number, and fax number, as well as the recipient's name, telephone number, extension, and fax number. Be sure to date the fax and provide any special instructions.

(Continued)

B. Grammar

1. Always use proper spelling, grammar, and punctuation. Do not take short-cuts or use abbreviations. Remember that your audience may interpret the shortcuts or abbreviations in a way that was not intended.

2. Do not write in all capital letters. In emails, the writing in all capital letters may be interpreted as yelling at the recipient. Text that is written in all capital letters is also difficult to read, and case-sensitive words, such as proper names, lose some of their meaning.

3. As with other types of writing, it is best to use active voice instead of passive voice. Make the subject of a sentence do the acting instead of being acted upon.

4. Avoid long sentences. Longer sentences are more difficult to comprehend, and are more likely to be misunderstood.

5. Keep the language gender neutral unless gender is relevant to the message.

C. Content

1. Tailor the language and tone to the intended audience.

2. Do not use email to discuss confidential information unless the office has security software, such as an encryption program, in place.

3. The content of the fax should be appropriate for people other than the recipient to see in case the fax arrives at a community or common location.

D. Answers to Emails

1. When emails are received, answer swiftly. Speed of communication is one of the values of emails. If the email is hours or days old, the purpose of the email may be lost.

2. Answer all questions posed, even if it is necessary to list the answers. It is very frustrating to send out multiple questions only to receive the answer to a couple of the questions while the rest of the questions appear to have been ignored.

3. Do not leave out the message thread. It is likely that the email is part of a conversation among a group of people. Confusion may result if the thread is not included.

4. Do not attach unnecessary files. Often people will attach a business card to every email. These attachments add to the size of the email without providing anything of importance.

E. Final Touches

1. Read the email before sending it. Check for spelling and punctuation errors, just as in any document.

2. Do not copy a message or attachment without permission.

3. Do not request delivery receipts. These tend to irritate people and clog the system.

4. Do not continue sending the same email if the recipient does not respond. After a few days, send an email inquiring whether the first email was received.

5. Do not forward chain or hoax letters.

6. Do not reply to "spam."

7. Do not send or forward emails that contain libelous, defamatory, offensive, racist, or obscene remarks. A recipient may have a frame of reference that is quite different than yours, and the message may be read out of context.

8. Do not give legal advice.

9. Be sure to identify yourself as a paralegal.

SUMMARY

Law offices use correspondence for a wide variety of purposes, such as conveying information, confirming appointments and agreements, rendering opinions, and demanding that actions be taken. Correspondence is used to communicate with clients, opposing counsel, courts, and other entities. Paralegals must be familiar with many types of correspondence, including transmittal letters, demand letters, informational letters, and opinion letters. Emails and faxes are also a vital part of legal correspondence, and should be handled with the same level of care as other communications. The two overriding rules for the paralegal in writing legal correspondence are (1) never give legal advice and (2) always write for the audience.

REVIEW **QUESTIONS**

1. Identify the basic parts of a letter.
2. What does "RE:" mean?
3. What is the purpose of a confirming letter? In what specific circumstances is it used?
4. What is the purpose of a demand letter? In what specific circumstances is it used?
5. What types of letters will probably not be signed by a paralegal? Explain why.
6. Identify three important rules in drafting email messages.
7. What type of letter has parts that are similar to the parts of an internal legal memorandum? How are those parts similar?
8. Why is it important to write with the audience in mind?
9. When would you use a blind courtesy copy, and how would you indicate in correspondence that blind courtesy copies have been sent?
10. Why should some emails have attachments rather than including all information within the body of the email?
11. To whom might you send a transmittal letter, and with what types of documents?
12. What information should be included on the cover sheet of a fax?

APPLICATION **EXERCISES**

Prepare the following letters as if you were a paralegal with a fictitious law firm. Assume that the law firm has letterhead so its address is complete. You will need to identify the recipient's address, although the names have been provided for you in most instances. Where names have not been provided you can create your own recipient or client.

1. Write a letter to the clerk of the court of your county sending a complaint for filing, along with all necessary documents. Include information or other materials necessary to get a file stamped copy returned to you. Be sure to include the appropriate notations within the letter.

2. Write a letter to Betty Spiro advising her that her deposition will be taken 30 days from today's date. Include all appropriate information that she will need in order to find your office. Betty was an eyewitness to an automobile accident in which you represent the plaintiff, Frederick Jones. The defendant, Hilary Shank, is a friend of Betty's.

3. In a continuation of the assignment in exercise 2, send the appropriate correspondence to the notary who will take the deposition.

4. You have worked for five years as a paralegal at a firm specializing in tax and intellectual property law. Previously, you worked for two years as a paralegal at a firm dealing with criminal and family law. You would like to start a blog for paralegals and other professionals to help them learn about how the law really works. To protect the clients of your current firm, you would limit the blog's topics to criminal and family law situations, using examples from actual cases but with the client's name and other details fictionalized. Would writing your blog be ethical or unethical? Why? Justify your answer.

CITATION **EXERCISES**

None. *Note*: All citations used in any correspondence should be in the proper format.

QUICK **CHECK**

1. This section of a letter contains the client or file information.
   a. Inside address
   b. Reference line
   c. Salutation
   d. Body

2. These letters that explain documents that are sent.
   a. Appointment letters
   b. Confirming letters
   c. Transmittal or cover letters
   d. Demand letters

3. In a demand letter, the _____ are itemized and verified by providing copies of support documents such as medical bills, doctor's reports, or police reports.
   a. Analysis
   b. Facts
   c. Demands
   d. Damages

4. Using a _____ tone indicates to the recipient that the writer is willing to make concessions.
   a. Persuasive
   b. Informational
   c. Conciliatory
   d. Demanding

5. Letters that put into writing an oral conversation are called _____ .
   a. Appointment letters
   b. Confirming letters

   c. Transmittal or cover letters
   d. Demand letters

6. Letters that provide the date, time, and place (completely described) of any appearance required are called _____ .
   a. Appointment letters
   b. Demand letters
   c. Confirming letters
   d. Transmittal or cover letters

7. This portion of an opinion letter includes possible courses of action or opinions about the party's rights and obligations.
   a. Conclusion
   b. Analysis
   c. Fact statement
   d. Tone

8. This portion of an opinion letter is where the attorney provides an explanation of the law and a prediction of the possible outcome.
   a. Conclusion
   b. Analysis
   c. Fact statement
   d. Topic sentence

9. Most legal correspondence is still sent by regular mail because of what concern?

10. What are the main components of a cover sheet for a fax?

RESEARCH

Use the following scenario to complete items 1–3.

Your client, Charles Deal, made an offer online to sell a lot he owns for $150,000. Mary Chesterton, who is familiar with the property and is interested in purchasing it, emailed him as follows:

> To: deal@yahoo.com
>
> From: MChesterton@gmail.com
>
> Regarding the house and wooded real estate lot as seen at www.myhouseland.com, I am interested in your lot and hereby offer to purchase the property for $145,000, all cash, with the sale to close in 30 days.
>
> Mary Chesterton

Mr. Deal replied via email:

> To: M Chesterton@Gmail.com
>
> From: deal@yahoo.com
>
> I will sell you the lot for $147,500.
>
> Charles Deal

In return, Ms. Chesterton replied:

To: deal@yahoo.com

From MChesterton@Gmail.com

I believe we have a deal!

1. Assume that Mr. Deal is your firm's client. Mr. Deal believes that he can get more than Ms. Chesterton has offered him. He has asked what risks he might face under your state's law regarding breach of contract if he turns down the offer from Ms. Chesterton and accepts a different offer.

2. Research your state's law regarding breach of contract. Compare the facts of Mr. Deal's case to your state's statute regarding breach of contract. Draft an opinion letter to Mr. Deal. Make sure to provide a recommendation to Mr. Deal on a possible course of action in the form of a conclusion.

3. Now assume now that your law firm is representing Ms. Chesterton. Ms. Chesterton believes she made a legitimate offer, and that Mr. Deal got a better offer after he had already accepted hers. She believes that a demand letter from her attorney, possibly suggesting breach of contract, will get Deal to stick to his original agreement. Using the research you performed on your state's law to draft the opinion letter, draft a demand letter to Mr. Deal. Use the sample demand letter in this chapter as a starting point.

4. Assume that the demand letter was unanswered, and the attorney wants to file a complaint in your local civil court on behalf of Ms. Chesterton against Mr. Deal.
   a. Using an online source such as Google or WhitePages.com, look up the address of your county's civil trial court. (For instance, if you live in Marion County, Indiana, look up the address for the Marion County Superior Court).
   b. Determine the cost of filing this lawsuit.
   c. Draft a transmittal letter with the intent to send a copy of the following documents to the court:
      - Appearance
      - Complaint
      - Summons
      - Check for filing fee

MEDIA **RESOURCES**

Micha Star Liberty. *California Client Communications Manual: Sample Letters and Forms*. 2012.

http://www.youtube.com/watch?v=HMr9Pil8aB4

INTERNET **RESOURCES**

The Lemon Law: Sample Demand Letter

http://www.consumeraffairs.com/lemon_law/demand_letter.html

Sample Settlement Letter

http://net.educause.edu/ir/library/pdf/CSD4832.pdf

Microsoft Trial Settlement Letter

http://www.house.gov/inslee/issues/microsoft/settlement_letter.html

Sample Settlement Letter, RIAA (Recording Industry Association of America)

http://www.haverford.edu/acc/docs/policies/copyright/riaa-2007-02-28/example-riaa-settlement-letter-2007-02-28.html

The 'Lectric Law Library

http://www.lectlaw.com/form.html

chapter nineteen

George Wada/Fotolia

DRAFTING PLEADINGS AND OTHER LITIGATION DOCUMENTS

LEARNING OBJECTIVES

After studying this chapter, students should be able to:

1. Describe the purpose and construction of pleadings, motions, and other court documents.

2. Develop checklists for the preparation of pleadings and other court documents.

3. Draft pleadings, motions, and discovery requests for use in a wide variety of litigation.

CHAPTER OVERVIEW

To draft pleadings and other litigation documents, the writer needs to have a fundamental understanding of the principles of procedural and substantive law. This chapter does not attempt to explain how to draft every type of document that may be used in litigation. Rather, it will provide instruction in how to prepare some of the key documents that will be used in court. Although the documents used in courts across the country appear very similar to one another, the rules of procedure in each jurisdiction will affect their form and content. Therefore, it is incumbent upon the writer to tailor these general forms to the specific requirements of each court.

OPENING SCENARIO

John had several assignments to complete this week. Jami asked John to draft a complaint in the Heather Dobbs automobile accident case. He knew the firm handled many auto accident cases, so he checked the sample pleadings in the form's file to see if there was a complaint from a similar case. He could use this sample as a starting point and tailor it to the facts of Heather's case. If an appropriate sample could not be located, his next step would be to find form documents in one of the many form books in the library and online.

After drafting the complaint for Heather's case, his next assignment was to prepare discovery requests for another lawsuit. Again, he knew that forms for interrogatories and requests for production could be found among the firm's many resources. Like the complaint, however, he knew he would have to look carefully at the information contained in the file and make sure those requests were modified, if necessary, for any unique circumstances in the case. Although the task seemed daunting, his colleagues told him that the process would become somewhat easier once he had a few more cases under his belt.

PLEADINGS

Pleadings are the documents used by the parties in lawsuits to formally notify the court and opposing parties of their claims, defenses, and what they intend to prove at trial. Pleadings today are similar in some ways to the writs of early English common law, but procedural statutes now define the content required for each type of pleading. Many states have patterned their procedural rules on the Federal Rules of Civil Procedure. Therefore, studying the federal rules can provide a good starting point for understanding the rules in state jurisdictions. The federal rules consist of procedural rules governing all civil actions in the federal courts. These rules were first established in 1938 by the United States Supreme Court, and can now be found in title 28 of the United States Code. Each local district court has its own procedural rules that complement the federal rules. Local rules must be consulted when preparing any federal pleading. State systems are similarly arranged. Local court rules must also be consulted before filing in state superior and circuit courts. [Note: Most of the examples in the chapter will follow the Federal Rules of Civil Procedure. Researchers will follow the rules for the court in which their case is located.] Form books that are found on the Internet and in a library are a valuable aid in drafting pleadings. Excellent form books are available for all areas of law, and some have editorial commentary to assist in drafting. The pleadings found in these books are general in nature and are sometimes referred to as *boilerplate* documents. They are to be regarded as forms only, and must be modified for the circumstances of the client. *American Jurisprudence Pleading and Practice Forms* and *West's Federal Forms* are services that provide forms for pleadings. Most states have general form books written for their jurisdictions, and subject-related form books are also available for specialized areas of the law, such as bankruptcy.

A major disadvantage of most general form books is that the forms may not be suitable for the unique circumstances of the client. It is virtually impossible to make a general pleading that is sufficient for every client who might need to use it. It is a violation of the canons of professional responsibility to use a form without properly adapting it to the client's case.

Pleadings
Documents that contain the formal allegations and defenses of the parties.

Boilerplate
A form with standardized language that must be modified for a user's circumstances.

Writing an effective pleading requires attention not only to the format of the document, but also to the language that expresses the pleading's content. When drafting a pleading, the following guidelines should be followed:

- Know what the pleading is intended to accomplish.
- Do not use language that is too broad or too narrow.
- Do not overuse legalese.
- Eliminate ambiguities in the language.
- Incorporate the unique circumstances of the client's case.
- Avoid redundancies of language such as "bequeath and bequest," "each and every," and "null and void."
- Review, revise, and redraft.

Because the pleadings define the issues in the lawsuit, great care must be taken in how they are constructed.

Formatting Pleadings

Pleadings should be presented in a way that states the facts clearly and concisely in an organized manner. Pleadings will have specific sections for different purposes, depending upon the type of pleading being prepared. However, most pleadings have certain elements in common.

Caption
The heading of a document.

All pleadings have a ***caption***, which is the part of the pleading that identifies the court and parties. Rule 10 of the Federal Rules of Civil Procedure provides that each pleading must have a caption that contains the following elements:

- The name of the court where the action is filed
- The title of the action, with the parties designated
- The name or title of the pleading
- The file number assigned by the court clerk

This format is similar to that required for captions in many state courts. In many instances the court designation in the caption must be centered on the page. It should always be capitalized. The caption must also include the names of the parties and the party designations, such as "plaintiff" or "petitioner" and "defendant" or "respondent." The names of the parties will begin on the left margin. The plaintiff is separated from the defendant by the use of the abbreviation for the word *versus*, which may be either "v." or "vs." The caption is completed by entering the case number issued by the court to the right of the names and party designations, beginning at the center of the page. For example, many states use a case number such as "No. 2012CR198," where "No." means number, "2012" indicates the year of filing, "CR" identifies a criminal matter, and "198" means that this was the 198th case filed during the year of 2012.

Heading
A heading is a catch line that describes the subject matter of a particular document.

Next, each pleading must have a ***heading,*** which is the title that indicates exactly what the pleading is. Headings are capitalized and centered two inches from the top of the first page and three spaces below the caption.

Every pleading also requires a signature of the party or attorney. Signature lines are placed at the end of the pleading, usually beginning at the center of the page. Many courts and firms will require that a solid line be provided for the actual signature, with the signer's name immediately below that signature line. If an individual is signing on behalf of a corporation or other organization, the entity's name should be placed three spaces above the signature line. The title of the individual should reflect the capacity of the individual in signing for the organization, such as "President" or "Chief Executive Officer." When the signature is that of the attorney, the signature line should show the attorney's name immediately below the line, along with the address, telephone number, and state bar association number of the attorney. The name of the attorney's law firm should appear three spaces above the signature line.

Occasionally, when pleadings are prepared, the text of the document will end at the bottom of a page, without room for the requisite signatures. No pleading or other document should ever be submitted with the final page containing only the signatures. That opens the document to the speculation that it may have been altered or that some portion of the document is missing. In order to avoid that situation, a page break may be inserted, or the bottom or right margin may be adjusted, so that some of the text runs onto the signature page.

Many pleadings and other court documents require an **acknowledgment** or certification of an authorized official, such as a notary public, that the document was actually signed by the person named in the signature block, and that the person signed the document voluntarily. This acknowledgment may also be called an **attestation** clause, a **verification**, or a **notarization**. This statement always appears at the end of the document following the signature being certified. The acknowledgment is preceded by a heading at the left margin that shows the county, state, and date of the acknowledgement; this heading is called the **jurat**. State law generally requires specific language following the jurat to certify the signature. Signatures cannot be notarized unless the notary public had the opportunity to actually observe the **signatory** signing the document. When preparing pleadings that require notification, the writer should leave the date and identity of the notary public blank so that it can be filled in at the time of the acknowledgment.

Local state and federal court rules provide specific requirements relating to paper size, margins, font, and other items the court deems important. For example, Figure 19-1 shows the requirements of the U.S. District Court for the Northern District of Indiana:

Generally, the top margin is a standard two inches on the first page, and one and one-half inches for each subsequent page. The bottom margin on each page should be at least one inch from the bottom of the paper if a full page of writing is used. The left margin on all pages should be one and one-half inches from the left side of the paper. If headings or titles are centered on the page, the margin will not be one and one-half inches from the left side. If the document uses modified block form, the beginning of each paragraph should be indented one inch or roughly 10 spaces from the left margin. If it uses block style format, all paragraphs will begin on the left margin. The width of the right margin will vary depending upon the length of the sentence and word usage. If the writer justifies the right margin, it should be one inch for all pages.

All pleadings should be double-spaced, but there are several exceptions to this rule. Triple spacing is used between the caption and the designation of the court. Triple spacing is also used before the parties and before the heading or title of the document. Single spacing is used for quotes indented within the body of a document and for addresses or telephone numbers following the name of an individual, such as the attorney.

Another important consideration is the appropriate typeface. While this may seem like an insignificant factor, the **font**, or typeface, can have a strong effect on the readability of the document. It should be no smaller than 12 points so that the reader does not miss any important information.

Capitalization is also an important consideration. Some jurisdictions require that some parts of documents be written using uppercase letters ("all caps"). Using all caps gives certain words and names emphasis. Often the caption of the pleading,

Acknowledgment
A declaration verifying that the person identified on the document is the one who signed it, and signed of his or her own free will.

Attestation
A statement certifying that a document was signed in a certain capacity.

Verification
A certificate added to pleadings to attest to the authenticity of a signature.

Notarization
A certificate added at the end of a pleading when a signature needs to be authorized.

Jurat
A certificate usually added to an affidavit, stating when, where, and before whom it was made.

Signatory
One who signs a document.

Font
The typeface used in a document.

FIGURE 19-1 Filing Rules

N.D. Ind. L.R. 5-4 Format of Papers

(a) Generally. Any pleading, motion, brief, affidavit, notice, or proposed order, whether filed electronically or by delivering it to the clerk, must:

(1) be plainly typewritten, printed, or prepared by a clearly legible copying process;

(2) use 8.5" x 11" pages;

(3) have at least 1-inch margins;

(4) use at least 12-point type in the body and at least 10-point type in footnotes;

(5) be double spaced (except for headings, footnotes, and quoted material);

(6) have consecutively numbered pages;

(7) include a title on the first page;

(8) include a separate index identifying and briefly describing each exhibit if there are more than four exhibits; and

(9) except in proposed orders and affidavits, include the filer's name, address, telephone number, fax number (where available), and e-mail address (where available).

(b) Manual Filings.

(1) *Form, Style, and Size of Papers.* Papers delivered to the clerk for filing must:

(A) be flat, unfolded, and on good-quality, white paper;

(B) not have a cover or a back; and

(C) include the filer's original signature

giving the state, court, parties, and cause number, is set in all caps. All caps are also used in the body of a pleading to emphasize certain words of importance. For example, an order of the court may say, "ORDERED AND ADJUDGED," or a notary's oath may state, "SUBSCRIBED AND SWORN TO."

Document preparers must be responsible not only for the accuracy of the information presented but also for ensuring that the documents are free of spelling and grammatical errors. An error in a legal document can detract from its professionalism, but more importantly, the error may expose the firm to legal liability. If the document preparer does not express the intent of the client in a clear and unambiguous manner, the client's interests may be adversely affected by any error or omission in the document. That can result in a loss or some other harm for which the firm would be liable. The client would need to be reimbursed for his or her loss by the law firm.

Another area where accuracy is a concern is the writing of numbers. The general rule is that when numbers are used in legal documents, they should be written in word form and then followed by the numeral in parentheses. Writing numbers in this way avoids any confusion or ambiguity. An example would be "a response is due within thirty (30) days." A similar rule applies to writing amounts of money. The specific sum of money is written in words with the numerical equivalent and parentheses, such as "Nine Hundred Fifty Dollars ($950.00)." If this amount of money included fifty cents, the decimal point would be written as "and," so it would appear as "Nine Hundred Fifty Dollars and Fifty Cents ($950.50)".

Pagination, or the process of numbering pages, should also follow a specific protocol. The first page of any pleading is not numbered. All following pages are numbered in a footer. In Microsoft Word (2010), this is done by hitting the "Insert" tab, going to "Footer," and selecting "Page Numbers." Generally, firms prefer to have the page numbers centered at the bottom of the page, and those page numbers will automatically appear one-half (1/2) inch from the bottom of the paper. However, the customs of the law firm and of the jurisdiction should be confirmed. Often a format is used that label each page as "page ___ (the current page) out of ___ (the total number of pages)," such as "Page 2 of 6." This format allows the reader to confirm that no pages are missing, and also ensures that no pages have been added. Rules for Pleadings in Federal and State Courts

The form and content of pleadings is governed by the rules of court of the jurisdiction in which they are filed. Most state rules of civil procedure set forth the requirements for pleadings, such as the caption, the complaint, counterclaims and cross-claims, service of process, the answer, and motions. Each state's court system is separate and distinct, and has its own rules of procedure enacted by the state.

In most jurisdictions, where a party is represented by an attorney, the attorney of record must sign every pleading that is filed with the court. This requirement is found in Rule 11 of the Federal Rules of Civil Procedure, which states that in signing a pleading, the attorney verifies that he or she has made a reasonable inquiry into the facts and law of the case and that there is a reasonable basis for the court's attention. This eliminates or greatly reduces the potential for frivolous lawsuits. It also indicates that the attorney is responsible for the contents of the document. If a paralegal drafts a document, the document must be submitted to the attorney for the attorney's signature. A paralegal cannot sign documents that are filed with the court.

Complaint

The initial pleading in a lawsuit that commences the action is called the ***complaint***, and is filed by the plaintiff. The purpose of the complaint is to identify the plaintiff's claims and place the defendant on notice that he or she has been sued and state the reasons why. A fundamental rule of pleading in both the state and federal systems is that the complaint must include a short, plain statement about the nature of the relief sought and the grounds upon which the relief is sought.

Statutes of Limitations   Among the most critical rules applying to the filing of complaints are the ***statutes of limitation,*** which set the time limits for filing different types of actions. These rules serve as a bar to the commencement of a lawsuit if it is not filed within the prescribed period of time. The failure to comply with the statute of limitation is an affirmative defense, and often will result in the plaintiff losing the right to bring the lawsuit.

The statutes of limitations begin to run at the time the cause of action arises, not at the time the cause of action is first pleaded in court. For example, when Heather Dobbs's vehicle was hit by the defendant's, the cause of action arose at that moment in time. The statutory timeframe began to run from that moment, and Heather must file within that set period of time. If Heather were filing the lawsuit in Indiana, that time period would be two years. If the lawsuit is filed after two years and one day, it may be dismissed on that basis. For a contract case, the statute of limitation begins at the time of the breach of contract, or when the first payment becomes overdue. The number of days constituting the statutory period begins on the day after the accrual of the cause of action. For instance, in a

Pagination
The process of numbering pages.

Complaint
The document filed by the plaintiff that identifies what has happened and that the plaintiff wants some type of compensation for damages.

Statute of limitations
The time frame within which a lawsuit may be filed.

contract action, if the payment on a promissory note was due on January 10, and payment was not received, the statute of limitation begins running on the following day, January 11. If the statutory period expires on a weekend or holiday, the statute does not expire until the next business day. In the case of a weekend, for example, the statute is said to be **tolled**, meaning that it is prevented from expiring until the next business day. There are other considerations that toll the statute of limitations such as minority, war, and so on.

All states have laws setting statutes of limitation for various actions. These deadlines will be found in the state's rules of court. As always, the jurisdictional rules should be consulted. It is imperative that paralegals understand the concept of statutes of limitation so that they can ensure that actions are properly commenced within the statutory period.

Gathering Facts   The first step in the preparation of the complaint is the gathering of facts necessary to formulate the claims. Information is gathered both from the client and from any external sources that impact the client or the issues. It is critical that the document preparer verify the information that is to be included in any pleading. A checklist helps in the information gathering process. Checklist 19-1 outlines the basic elements of an effective client interview that can be used to prepare the complaint and subsequent documents.

Tolling
Suspension of a time limit for taking action, such as a statute of limitations.

Checklist 19-1   INITIAL INTERVIEW

Personal

   Name

   Address

   Date of birth

   Social Security number

   Occupation

   Employment history

   Education

   Income

   Marital status

   Spousal information

   Children

   Assets

   Liabilities

   Medical history

Facts of the case

   Date

   Place

   Witnesses

   Addresses and telephone numbers

   Reports or statements

   Corporate officers

Insurance coverage

Narrative of incident

Damages

Personal

Property

Mitigation

Preexisting conditions

Experts

Valuation

Records

Tax

Banks

Brokerages

Insurance

Police

Medical

Corporate

Contracts

Statements

Elements of the Complaint Four elements are required in a well-drafted complaint:

- A proper identification of all parties with names and addresses
- A statement of jurisdiction
- A statement of the claim giving rise to the cause of action
- A prayer for relief

Although these four elements are basic to most complaints, the court rules may have other requirements in addition to these elements. A sample complaint is presented as Exhibit A-3 in the Appendix.

The identification of the parties and their addresses is essential to establishing the court's jurisdiction. If the party is an individual, it is sufficient to provide his or her name along with an address. If the party is a corporation, its principal place of business, along with the address of its corporate headquarters, are required. If the complaint includes a public official as a party, the official capacity of the public official must be provided.

The pleading caption states the court under which jurisdiction arises, but the complaint must also set forth the reasons establishing that court's jurisdiction. If a complaint is filed in federal district court, the complaint must include the reasons why there is federal jurisdiction over the case. If the federal question arises under a law of the United States, the appropriate statutory citation must be provided. If a United States Constitution provision is at issue, the constitutional section must be cited. If the complaint is filed in federal court based on diversity of citizenship, an appropriate allegation of that diversity must be made. The requirements for diversity of citizenship are set forth in 28 U.S.C. § 1332, as shown in Figure 19-2.

FIGURE 19-2 Federal
Jurisdiction and Diversity
of Citizenship

(a) The district courts shall have original jurisdiction of all civil actions where the matter in controversy exceeds the sum or value of $75,000, exclusive of interest and costs, and is between—

(1) citizens of different States;

(2) citizens of a State and citizens or subjects of a foreign state;

(3) citizens of different States and in which citizens or subjects of a foreign state are additional parties; and

(4) a foreign state, defined in section 1603 (a) of this title, as plaintiff and citizens of a State or of different States.

For the purposes of this section, section 1335, and section 1441, an alien admitted to the United States for permanent residence shall be deemed a citizen of the State in which such alien is domiciled.

(b) Except when express provision therefore is otherwise made in a statute of the United States, where the plaintiff who files the case originally in the Federal courts is finally adjudged to be entitled to recover less than the sum or value of $75,000, computed without regard to any setoff or counterclaim to which the defendant may be adjudged to be entitled, and exclusive of interest and costs, the district court may deny costs to the plaintiff and, in addition, may impose costs on the plaintiff.

(c) For the purposes of this section and section 1441 of this title—

(1) a corporation shall be deemed to be a citizen of any State by which it has been incorporated and of the State where it has its principal place of business, except that in any direct action against the insurer of a policy or contract of liability insurance, whether incorporated or unincorporated, to which action the insured is not joined as a party-defendant, such insurer shall be deemed a citizen of the State of which the insured is a citizen, as well as of any State by which the insurer has been incorporated and of the State where it has its principal place of business; and

(2) the legal representative of the estate of a decedent shall be deemed to be a citizen only of the same State as the decedent, and the legal representative of an infant or incompetent shall be deemed to be a citizen only of the same State as the infant or incompetent.[1]

* * *

Figure 19-3 shows an example of a jurisdiction statement in federal court based on diversity. This statement sets forth the facts that must be pleaded to establish federal diversity jurisdiction.

In its statement of the claim, the complaint must then set forth one or more *causes of action*, which demand a judicial remedy based upon some type of legal theory such as negligence, fraud, or breach of contract. Each cause of action must include all the facts that are necessary to give rise to the cause of action. If one or more material elements of the cause of action are omitted, the complaint

Cause of action

A judicial remedy based upon a law providing some form of relief against another.

[1]Cornell University Law School. Legal Information Institute. 28 U.S.C. § 1332 - Diversity of Citizenship; Amount in Controversy; Costs. 2011. http://www.law.cornell.edu/uscode/text/28/1332

Plaintiff Heather Dobbs is a resident of the state of Indiana, and defendant Paul Roberts is a resident of the state of Illinois. The matter in controversy exceeds, exclusive of interest and costs, the sum of $75,000.

FIGURE 19-3 Jurisdiction Statement

may be dismissed. For example, the material elements of a claim of negligence would be these:

- Duty
- Breach of duty
- Proximate cause
- Damage

If a cause of action is for negligence, the complaint must state facts that support each material element of this cause of action. If additional causes of action arise from the same set of facts, an additional *count* must be added to the complaint for each cause of action.

Federal Rules of Civil Procedure Rule 10 requires all allegations to be presented in the body of the complaint in numbered paragraphs. Each paragraph should contain only one set of facts and should be couched in plain language. If a complaint in federal court presents more than one theory of recovery, for example negligence and contract, each theory should be set forth in a separate numbered paragraphs that allege the particular facts that constitute each action. Each count should be sufficient to state a complete cause of action, without reliance on another count. Thus, if one count is denied by the court, the remaining counts will survive and sustain the case. Figure 19-4 shows a portion of a complaint with multiple counts.

Counts

Separate numbered paragraphs that allege the particular facts that constitute each cause of action.

COUNT I: Medical Malpractice and Wrongful Death

21. The Plaintiffs re-allege and incorporate by reference herein all of the allegations contained in paragraphs 1–19 above.
22. That on or about March 24, 2010, and thereafter, the Defendants by and through their employees/servant/agents breached the applicable standard of medical care owed to the late Kenneth Parks, which directly caused a physical injury and death of Kenneth Parks on June 4, 2010.
23. That as a direct result of the negligence and breaches of the applicable standard of medical care by the Defendant, by and through its nurses, employees, and medical staff, resulting in the death of the late Kenneth Parks, the Plaintiffs sustained those damages as outlined in the Annotated Code of Maryland, Courts and Judicial Proceedings Article, Section 3-904, to include but not limited to, mental anguish, emotional pain and suffering, and loss of companionship.

WHEREFORE: The Plaintiffs Kathleen Parks, Gary Parks, and Jodi Columbo individually, claim monetary damages against the Defendant in an amount that exceeds the jurisdiction of the District Court of Maryland, to be determined at trial, plus costs, and for any further relief that this Honorable Court determines necessary and appropriate.

FIGURE 19-4 Counts in a Negligence Action

FIGURE 19-4
(continued)

COUNT II Medical Malpractice / Negligence / Survival Action

The Plaintiffs re-allege and incorporate by reference herein all of the allegations contained in paragraphs 1–23 above.

24. That the Estate of Kenneth Parks was opened on or about June 29, 2010, in Washington County, Maryland and Jodi Columbo was appointed as Personal Representative of the Estate.
25. That Jodi Columbo as the Personal Representative of the Estate of Kenneth Parks brings this claim for the conscious pain and suffering and physical injuries, medical expenses, and other damages that the late Kenneth Parks experienced from March 26, 2010, up until the time of his death on June 4, 2010, as a direct and proximate result of the negligence and breaches of the applicable standard of medical care by the Defendant, by and through its nurses, employees, and medical staff.[2]

FIGURE 19-5 WHEREFORE Clause

WHEREFORE, plaintiff respectfully requests that this Court:

award judgment against defendant in the amount of Seven Hundred Fifty Thousand Dollars ($750,000) plus costs, interest, and attorneys' fees.

1. grant the plaintiff a trial by jury on all issues of fact.
2. grant the plaintiff such other relief as is just and equitable.

Prayer for relief
The request of the plaintiff to the court for relief based on a cause of action.

Wherefore clause
A clause requesting action by the court on the plaintiff's behalf. Also called the prayer for relief.

The **prayer for relief**, also referred to as the **wherefore clause**, is the section that concludes the complaint and asks the court for damages or judicial relief. The requirements for the prayer for relief are found in Rule 8A of the Federal Rules of Civil Procedure. The prayer for relief is often set forth separately with a title such as "Demand for Judgment," and always begins with "wherefore" in all capital letters. An example of a prayer for relief is shown in Figure 19-5.

If the plaintiff wants a jury trial, it must be specifically requested at the time the complaint is filed or shortly thereafter, if allowed by rule. If the demand for a jury trial is stated in the complaint, it can be included in the prayer for relief as a separate paragraph. Otherwise, it can be included in a separate document.

The signature is the last element of the complaint, and should not be overlooked. Rule 11 of the Federal Rules of Civil Procedure requires that an attorney, or the plaintiff if he or she is not represented, sign the complaint. The attorney's signature is required because, as an officer of the court, the attorney is held to a professional standard that prohibits him or her from filing a frivolous or fraudulent lawsuit. This signature requirement constitutes a certification by the attorney (or plaintiff) that the facts are true to the best of his or her knowledge. Figure 19-6 shows a local district court rule for signatures.

Federal courts, and many state courts, allow for electronic filing. These courts often have special rules for electronic signatures, such as the rule shown in Figure 19-7.

---

[2]The Law Office of Miller & Zois, LLC. Complaint. 2006. http://www.millerandzois.com/Sample-Negligence-Complaint.html

SIGNATURE BLOCK:

Each attorney or pro se litigant must sign the last page of the pleading. Signature name is to be typed below the signature, followed by party affiliation (CivLR 5.1(j)(4)).
Example:

Respectfully submitted

John Smith,
Attorney for plaintiff Acme
Transportation, Inc.[3]

FIGURE 19-6 United States District Court, Southern District of California

SIGNATURES:

Filing Users

The user login and password required to submit documents to the ECF system serve as the filing user's signature on all electronic documents filed with the Court. They serve as a signature for purposes of Fed.R.Civ.P. 11, all other Federal Rules of Civil Procedure, the Federal Rules of Criminal Procedure, the Local Rules of this Court, and any other purpose for which a signature is required in connection with proceedings before the Court. Therefore, it is the filing users' responsibility to safeguard their login and password.

Note: No filing user or other person may knowingly permit or cause to permit a filing user's password to be used by anyone other than an authorized agent of the filing user.

SIGNATURES:

Nine-Element Signature Block

An electronically filed document must include a nine-element signature block that contains the following typed information about the filing user:

- "/s/" typed in the space where the signature would otherwise appear,
- Name,
- Virginia bar number,
- Attorney for [party name],
- Firm name,
- Firm address,
- Telephone number,
- Fax number, and
- E-mail address.[4]

FIGURE 19-7 Electronic Signatures: United States District Court—Eastern District of Virginia: Electronic Case Filing (E-Filing) Policies and Procedures

---

[3]United States District Court, Southern District of California. Format for Filings. 2007-2012. http://www.casd.uscourts.gov/index.php?page=format-for-filings

[4]United States District Court - Eastern District of Virginia Electronic Case Filing (E-Filing) Policies and Procedures. 2010. http://www.vaed.uscourts.gov/ecf/documents/15-PoliciesandProcedures-Signatures_000.pdf

Summons

Notice to the defendant that a lawsuit has been filed and that some response is expected.

Rule 4 of the Federal Rules of Civil Procedure requires that a *summons* accompany the complaint. The summons notifies the defendant that the action has been filed and that the defendant must respond to the complaint within a certain time. The summons also indicates that should the defendant fail to answer, a judgment can be entered against him or her. The summons in federal district courts is a preprinted form that may be obtained from the clerk. The same is true for many state courts. A sample summons is shown in Appendix I, A-4.

If the defendant does not answer the complaint within the prescribed time frame, the plaintiff can have a default judgment entered against the defendant. The plaintiff's attorney must file an affidavit stating that service was made or attempted according to the requirements and that the appropriate time frame for the defendant's response has elapsed.

Responsive Pleadings

Answer

The response to the complaint, drafted in numbered paragraphs that mirror the causes of action in the complaint.

The usual response to the complaint is referred to as an *answer* but the defendant may also file a motion to dismiss the action, assert certain defenses, or admit the claim. There is a specified time, usually 20 days, from the date of the original service of process within which the defendant must respond.

The answer contains a caption that mirrors the caption on the complaint, the title of the pleading, which is usually something like "Answer" or "Defendant's Answer to Plaintiff's Complaint," and numbered paragraphs that correspond to the numbered paragraphs of the complaint.

The defendant's response to the complaint is governed by Rule 8 of the Federal Rules of Civil Procedure. [Note: State court rules provide different requirements.] Allegations that are not specifically denied in response to the complaint are deemed admitted. The defendant's answer should be set forth in a clear and plain statement that may contain the following:

- An admission or denial of the allegation
- A combination of admission in part and a denial in part
- A statement that the defendant is without sufficient knowledge or information to form a belief as to the truth of an averment, having the effect of a denial

The responses to each paragraph of the complaint must be drafted without ambiguity. It must be clear whether the allegation is admitted or denied.

The defendant may have a defense to the complaint that is based upon a matter not alleged in the complaint itself. This new matter is presented as an **affirmative defense**. There are a variety of affirmative defenses available to the defendant, and one of the most common is that the plaintiff failed to file the action within a specified time, thus violating the statute of limitations. Rule 8 of the Federal Rules of Civil Procedure provides other affirmative defenses based upon fraud, contributory negligence, release and waiver, *res judicata*, and discharge in bankruptcy. Each affirmative defense alleged in the answer must be set out as a separate matter contained in separate numbered paragraphs.

It Exhibit A-5 in Appendix I shows an answer that admits some allegations, denies some allegations, lacks information sufficient to form a belief as to the facts alleged, and on that basis denies them, alleges affirmative defenses, and requests a jury trial.

An alternative to filing an answer in response to the complaint is to ask the court dismiss the complaint based on certain defects. Rule 12 (b) of the Federal Rules of Civil Procedure provides seven possible defenses that may be raised in a motion to dismiss, as shown in Figure 19-8.

FIGURE 19-8 Rule 12(b)

b) HOW TO PRESENT DEFENSES. Every defense to a claim for relief in any pleading must be asserted in the responsive pleading if one is required. But a party may assert the following defenses by motion:

1. lack of subject-matter jurisdiction;
2. lack of personal jurisdiction;
3. improper venue;
4. insufficient process;
5. insufficient service of process;
6. failure to state a claim upon which relief can be granted; and
7. failure to join a party under Rule 19.

A motion asserting any of these defenses must be made before pleading if a responsive pleading is allowed. If a pleading sets out a claim for relief that does not require a responsive pleading, an opposing party may assert at trial any defense to that claim. No defense or objection is waived by joining it with one or more other defenses or objections in a responsive pleading or in a motion.[5]

The motion to dismiss can be part of the answer or can be filed as a separate responsive pleading. If it is filed as a separate pleading instead of an answer, the motion to dismiss must be filed within the 20 days allowed for the filing of the answer in order to avoid judgment for the plaintiff on the complaint, as stated in Rule 12(b). A sample motion to dismiss is shown in Figure 19-9.

Motion to Dismiss Defendant's Motion To Dismiss, Presenting Defenses of Failure To State a Claim, of Lack of Service of Process, of Improper Venue, and of Lack of Jurisdiction Under Rule 12(b)

The defendant moves the court as follows:

1. To dismiss the action because the complaint fails to state a claim against defendant upon which relief can be granted.
2. To dismiss the action or in lieu thereof to quash the return of service of summons on the grounds (a) that the defendant is a corporation organized under the laws of Delaware and was not and is not subject to service of process within the Southern District of New York, and (b) that the defendant has not been properly served with process in this action, all of which more clearly appears in the affidavits of M. N. and X. Y. hereto annexed as Exhibit A and Exhibit B respectively.
3. To dismiss the action on the ground that it is in the wrong district because (a) the jurisdiction of this court is invoked solely on the ground that the action arises under the Constitution and laws of the United States and (b) the defendant is a corporation incorporated under the laws of the State of Delaware and is not licensed to do or doing business in the Southern

FIGURE 19-9 A sample motion to dismiss

[5]Cornell University Law School. Legal Information Institute. Rule 12. Defenses and objections: when and how presented; motion for Judgment on the pleadings; consolidated motions; waiving defenses; pretrial hearing. . 2011. http://www.law.cornell.edu/rules/frcp/rule_12

District of New York, all of which more clearly appears in the affidavits of K. L. and V. W. hereto annexed as Exhibits C and D, respectively.

4. To dismiss the action on the ground that the court lacks jurisdiction because the amount actually in controversy is less than ten thousand dollars exclusive of interest and costs.

Signed: _____

Attorney for Defendant.

Address: _____

Notice of Motion

To: _____

Attorney for Plaintiff.

Please take notice, that the undersigned will bring the above motion on for hearing before this Court at Room ____, United States Court House, Foley Square, City of New York, on the _____ day of_____, 20__, at 10 o'clock in the forenoon of that day or as soon thereafter as counsel can be heard.

Signed: _____

Attorney for Defendant.

Address: _____ 6

FIGURE 19-9 (Continued)

Another type of responsive pleading that can be filed as part of the answer or as a separate pleading is the motion for a more definite statement. This pleading is used when a party is unable to respond to an allegation or defense because there is ambiguity or vagueness in the complaint. This is based on the principle that a party should be able to understand the nature of the claims against him or her before being required to admit or deny the claims. In a motion for a more definite statement, a party may request information sufficient enough to form a response.

Amended Pleadings

Sometimes during the course of a lawsuit it is necessary to change the pleadings because some fact has been omitted, a new fact has been discovered, or a new party has been located. An amended pleading will include additional or corrected facts, causes of action, or parties. Federal Rules of Civil Procedure Rule 15 provides a procedure for the filing of amended pleadings.

A party may freely amend the pleading when no responsive pleading has been filed. If a responsive pleading is not required and the case is still not on the trial calendar, the plaintiff may amend the complaint within the allotted time after the original service. However, once a responsive pleading has been filed, a party

---

6Justia US Law. 2005 US Code Title 28 Form 19. 2005. http://law.justia.com/codes/us/2005/title28/app/rulesofci/form19/

FIGURE 19-10 Motion to Amend

IN THE UNITED STATES DISTRICT COURT
FOR THE WESTERN DISTRICT OF TENNESSEE
EASTERN DIVISION

PAULA WEST,
Plaintiff,
v.   No. 09-CV-01234
ALFRED BENSON and
JACOB SMITH,

Defendants.

MOTION TO AMEND PLEADINGS

Comes now the plaintiff Paula West, by and through her attorney, pursuant to Rule 15 of the Federal Rules of Civil Procedure, and moves the court to allow the amendment of the complaint for the following reasons:

1. Plaintiff stated the incorrect date of the occurrence in her complaint.

2. The granting of plaintiff's motion would not surprise defendant or prejudice defendant materially.

3. Denial of plaintiff's motion would result in substantial injustice and prejudice to the plaintiff.

4. The answer is that justice would be served by granting plaintiff's motion.

WHEREFORE, plaintiff respectfully moves the court for leave to amend the complaint in this action in the manner and to the extent set forth in the amendment to complaint attached hereto.

Respectfully submitted,

Martin B. Wilson, Esq.
Address
Attorney Bar Number

Certificate of Service

* * *

must request leave of the court before filing an amended pleading. An example of a motion to amend is shown in Figure 19-10.

MOTIONS

Motions are requests for certain types of court intervention during the course of the litigation. A motion may ask the court to take some action or grant relief in favor of the moving party, such as barring evidence from being admitted, compelling the production of information during discovery, or entering judgment as to all or part of the lawsuit. A motion may be oral or written. The Federal Rules of Civil Procedure 7(b) provides:

(b) MOTIONS AND OTHER PAPERS.

(1) *In General.* A request for a court order must be made by motion. The motion must:

(A) be in writing unless made during a hearing or trial;

(B) state with particularity the grounds for seeking the order; and

(C) state the relief sought.

(2) *Form.* The rules governing captions and other matters of form in pleadings apply to motions and other papers.

As in other pleadings, motions must include a caption and title. The title of the motion should describe the type or nature of the motion, such as "motion for summary judgment." The paragraphs of the body of the motion are usually unnumbered. As with other pleadings, motions must be signed by the attorney. They must also be accompanied by a certificate of service that acknowledges that the opposing party was served a copy of the motion. Typically motions, along with all supporting documents, must be served at least five days before the scheduled hearing. Some motions, however, require a longer notice period.

It is common for a motion to be accompanied by additional documentation to support the basis of the motion. The documents may include affidavits, depositions, transcripts, or other exhibits that established the facts alleged in the motion. An affidavit is a sworn statement of facts by the signer and acknowledged by a notary. A motion may also be supported by a brief or a memorandum of law that provides the court with relevant law that supports the moving party's position.

Often the relief sought by a motion is procedural in that it corrects some defect in the pleadings. In some instances the relief may dispose of the case entirely. If the motion disposes of the lawsuit, it is called a ***dispositive motion***. Table 19-1 provides a sample of the motions and the rules governing those motions.

Typically, motions are set for a hearing allowing the moving party to argue the motion, and the opposing party to respond. However, a hearing is not required for every type of motion. Some motions may be made ***ex parte,*** which means that the court hears the motion but the hearing is attended only by the moving party.

If a hearing is required, the judge's assistant or clerk will schedule the hearing on the court's calendar. The non-moving party must be given notice of the date of the hearing. The notice must contain the nature of the motion and must provide reasonable notice of the time and place of the hearing. Figure 19-11 provides a sample notice.

Dispositive motion

A motion requesting a court order to end a cause of action.

Ex parte

A hearing attended only by the moving party.

TABLE 19-1   Motions

Motion	Federal Rule
Motion for Sanctions	Rule 11
Motion for Judgment on the Pleadings	Rule 12(c)
Motion for a More Definite Statement	Rule 12(e)
Motion to Strike	Rule 12(f)
Motion for Extension of Time	Rule 6(b)
Motion to Compel	Rule 37
Motion for Relief from Judgment	Rule 60
Motion for Summary Judgment	Rule 56
Motion to Dismiss	Rule 12(b)(6)
Motion for Judgment as a Matter of Law	Rule 50
Motion for Physical and Mental Examination	Rule 35

IN THE UNITED STATES DISTRICT COURT
FOR THE EASTERN DISTRICT OF VIRGINIA
ALEXANDRIA DIVISION

UNITED STATES OF AMERICA,
Plaintiff,

V.

MICROSEMI CORPORATION,
Defendant.

Civil Action NO. 1:08 CV 1311

Judge: Trenga, Anthony J.

Filed: February 25, 2009

Hearing Date: March 6, 2009

NOTICE OF HEARING

PLEASE TAKE NOTICE that on **March 6, 2009, at 10:00 A.M.**, or as soon thereafter as counsel may be heard, Plaintiff United States will bring on for hearing its Motion for Limited Discovery and Request for In Camera Proceeding.

RESPECTFULLY SUBMITTED,

_____/S/_____

LOWELL STERN (VA Bar #33460)

Counsel for the United States

Trial Attorney

Antitrust Division, Litigation II Section

United States Department of Justice

1401 H Street, N.W., Suite 3000

Washington, D.C. 20530

(202) 514-3676

(202) 307-6283 (fax)

Lowell.Stern@usdoj.gov

CERTIFICATE OF SERVICE

I HEREBY CERTIFY that on the 25th day of February, 2009, I will electronically file the foregoing with the Clerk of Court using the CM/ECF system, which will then send a notification of such filing (NEF) to the following:

Brian A. O'Dea

Michael Antalics

Benjamin G. Bradshaw

William T. Buffaloe

O'Melveny & Meyers LLP

1625 Eye Street, N.W.
Washington, DC 20006

FIGURE 19-11 Notice of Hearing

FIGURE 19-11
(Continued)

_____/S/_____

LOWELL STERN (VA Bar #33460)

Counsel for the United States

Trial Attorney

Antitrust Division, Litigation II Section

United States Department of Justice

1401 H Street, N.W., Suite 3000

Washington, D.C. 20530

(202) 514-3676

(202) 307-6283 (fax)

Lowell.Stern@usdoj.gov7

If there is no genuine issue as to the material facts alleged in the complaint, either party can file a motion for summary judgment under Rule 56 of the Federal Rules of Civil Procedure. The basis of this motion is that the moving party is entitled to a judgment as a matter of law because there is no material question of fact to be decided by a jury. If the motion is granted by the court, it constitutes a final adjudication on the merits, and the lawsuit is terminated. The moving party bears the burden to show by affidavit or other documents that no genuine issue of material fact exists. If any doubt exists, the motion will be denied, and the case will proceed.

A motion for summary judgment cannot be filed by the plaintiff until the appropriate time has elapsed after the service of summons and complaint. The defendant may file a motion for summary judgment at any time. The motion is generally accompanied by an affidavit regarding the lack of any factual issues and by a brief or memorandum of law in support of the motion. Exhibit A-6 in Appendix I is a sample motion for summary judgment, along with a portion of a memorandum in support of the motion.

Another motion that provides for the entry of judgment by the court based on the pleadings is the motion for judgment on the pleadings, referred to as a Rule 12(c) motion under the Federal Rules of Civil Procedure. This type of judgment is rarely granted unless the court considers the pleadings most favorable to the nonmoving party and bases its decision on the lack of disputed facts. If any question of fact exists, the motion will not be granted.

Interlocutory order

A provisional or temporary order.

A court order is required to resolve any motion. An **_interlocutory order_** is an order in which the court decides an intervening matter but not the ultimate outcome of the case. A final order is an order in which the court's ruling terminates the lawsuit. Proposed orders are generally submitted with the motion and its supporting documents. Local court rules should always be checked to determine the procedure and format in which the order must be submitted. Exhibit A-7 in Appendix I is a sample order.

DISCOVERY

Discovery

The stage of a lawsuit in which the parties obtain information and evidence.

After the initial responsive pleadings are filed in a lawsuit, the **_discovery_** period begins. During the discovery process, each party attempts to obtain as much information as possible concerning the opposing party's case. In each state, the discovery process is governed by rules of court, which are often similar to discovery rules

7http://www.justice.gov/atr/cases/f243000/243012.htm

found in the Federal Rules of Civil Procedure. The rules establish the tools available to the parties for discovery, the parameters of what may be requested, limitations on the timing of discovery, and protections for privileged and confidential information. Individual state rules vary widely so local rules and state statutes must be consulted.

The purpose of the discovery process is to allow each party to determine everything their opponent intends to present at trial, and eliminate the potential for surprise. Discovery also facilitates settlement by giving the parties the information they need to evaluate their client's and their opponent's case. To accomplish this, discovery attempts to

- Obtain facts for trial.
- Learn the opponent's position.
- Narrow the issues.
- Identify witnesses.
- Determine damages.
- Locate and preserve evidence.
- Evaluate the credibility of witnesses.

There are several different tools available for discovery, which are governed by the rules of each jurisdiction. The type of information needed generally determines what discovery tool is used. These tools include the following:

- Depositions
- Interrogatories
- Requests for production of documents
- Requests to enter land
- Requests for admissions
- Requests for physical and mental examination

Depositions

A *deposition* is the taking of a witness's testimony in question and answer format during an oral examination before an officer of the court. Depositions may be taken of parties or of witnesses who are not parties to the action. Depositions can be written or oral, but the most common practice is to take an oral deposition. During the deposition, the attorneys not only obtain information about the case, but also evaluate the demeanor and credibility of the witness.

Depositions can be taken before any judicial officer, such as a notary public, who is authorized to make an acknowledgment of the testimony. The officer may not be related to any of the parties, or be an employee of any of the parties or attorneys involved.

Depositions by oral examination are governed by Rule 30 of the Federal Rules of Civil Procedure. Depositions by written examination are governed by Rule 31 of the Federal Rules of Civil Procedure. Most state rules mirror the federal rules. In federal court and in most states, the court must give its permission before a deposition may be taken within the first 30 days after service of process. After that time, as long as the deposition is taken during the time allowed by the court rules for discovery, the deposition may be taken upon reasonable notice of the time, place, and person to be deposed.

If a deposition is of a person who is not a party, the witness must be ordered to appear at a certain time and place through the use of a *subpoena*. Occasionally an individual being deposed will be asked to bring certain documents or records or have those available for examination at the time of the deposition. If that is the case, those documents must be ordered through the use of a **subpoena** *duces tecum*, which is a command to appear at a certain time and place and to bring the documents or records required.

Deposition
Testimony given under oath that may be used in court in place of oral testimony.

Subpoena
An order requiring someone to attend such as in a hearing or court..

Subpoena *duces tecum*
An order requiring attendance and requiring one to bring or make available requested documents.

FIGURE 19-12 Notice of Taking Deposition

IN THE CIRCUIT COURT FOR BALTIMORE CITY, MARYLAND

SARAH Mulligan, Plaintiff   *

         v.   *   CASE NO. 12-C-12-07133

                *

CHARTER HOMES, Defendant   *

* *

NOTICE OF TAKING DEPOSITION

To: Frederick Farmer

Attorney for the Defendant

1234 S. Richland Hwy.

Terre Haute, IN 47807

PLEASE TAKE NOTICE that the undersigned will take the deposition upon oral examination of Steve Sams at 2:00 PM at her office, located at 111 Hulman St., Terre Haute, Indiana, on September 10, 2013, before a notary public or other person authorized by law to take depositions. This deposition is being taken for purposes of discovery, for use at trial, or for any other purpose allowed by law.

YOU ARE INVITED TO ATTEND.

Respectfully submitted,

Jami Myers Selzer

Allworthy Law Office

111 Hulman St.

Terre Haute, IN 47802

(812) 555-1234

(812) 555-1235 FAX

Bar No. 00123450

Attorney for the Plaintiff

Depositions are generally held in an office of the attorney requesting the deposition, with all parties to the lawsuit represented by counsel. A transcript of the testimony is made by a court reporter. Objections to questions are preserved in the transcript of the hearing but are not ruled upon since no judge is present. Exhibits may also be referred to and are referenced in the transcript.

It is common practice for paralegals to arrange for depositions and to draft the notice that is sent to the people involved in the deposition. Figure 19-12 provides a sample notice. Before sending the notice of the deposition, a paralegal will usually need to coordinate with the attorneys for the other parties so that a date is set on which all may be available, and to prevent scheduling conflicts.

Interrogatories

Interrogatories, governed by Rule 33 of the Federal Rules of Civil Procedure, are written questions propounded only to parties. Interrogatories are usually the first discovery tool used to obtain information from the opponent, and the information

(a) In General.

    (1) *Number.* Unless otherwise stipulated or ordered by the court, a party may serve on any other party no more than 25 written interrogatories, including all discrete subparts. Leave to serve additional interrogatories may be granted to the extent consistent with Rule 26(b)(2).

    (2) *Scope.* An interrogatory may relate to any matter that may be inquired into under Rule 26(b). An interrogatory is not objectionable merely because it asks for an opinion or contention that relates to fact or the application of law to fact, but the court may order that the interrogatory need not be answered until designated discovery is complete, or until a pretrial conference or some other time.

(b) Answers And Objections.

    (1) *Responding Party.* The interrogatories must be answered:
        (A) by the party to whom they are directed; or
        (B) if that party is a public or private corporation, a partnership, an association, or a governmental agency, by any officer or agent, who must furnish the information available to the party.

    (2) *Time to Respond.* The responding party must serve its answers and any objections within 30 days after being served with the interrogatories. A shorter or longer time may be stipulated to under Rule 29 or be ordered by the court.

    (3) *Answering Each Interrogatory.* Each interrogatory must, to the extent it is not objected to, be answered separately and fully in writing under oath.

    (4) *Objections.* The grounds for objecting to an interrogatory must be stated with specificity. Any ground not stated in a timely objection is waived unless the court, for good cause, excuses the failure.

    (5) *Signature.* The person who makes the answers must sign them, and the attorney who objects must sign any objections.

FIGURE 19-13 Federal Rules of Civil Procedure Rule 33

will often become the basis for additional discovery requests. Rule 33 limits the number of written interrogatories and also provides for the manner in which answers and objections can be given. A portion of Rule 33 is provided in Figure 19-13.

Many states also have rules that limit the length of interrogatories, and may prescribe interrogatories for various causes of action. The original of the interrogatories must be served upon the party to whom the questions are propounded and copies of both the interrogatories and the answers are delivered to all other parties. The answers must be returned to the party propounding the questions. Many courts now also allow for electronic filing of documents. In this instance, interrogatories may or may not be required to be filed with the court.

Paralegals are frequently called upon to prepare interrogatories by drafting a set of questions using clear, concise, and unambiguous language. The questions should be carefully framed so that the respondent cannot answer with a simple yes or no. The purpose of the interrogatories is to elicit a narrative response so that the person propounding the interrogatories obtains as much information as possible.

FIGURE 19-14 Sample Interrogatories

APPENDIX II. — INTERROGATORY FORMS

Form A. Uniform Interrogatories to be Answered by Plaintiff in All Personal Injury Cases (<u>Except Medical Malpractice Cases</u>): Superior Court

All questions must be answered unless the court otherwise orders or unless a claim of privilege or protective order is made in accordance with *R.* 4:17-1(b)(3).

CAPTION

1. Full name, present address and date of birth.
2. Describe in detail your version of the accident or occurrence setting forth the date, location, time and weather.
3. Detailed description of nature, extent and duration of any and all injuries.
4. Detailed description of injury or condition claimed to be permanent together with all present complaints.
5. If confined to a hospital, state its name and address, and dates of admission and discharge.
6. If any diagnostic tests were performed, state the type of test performed, name and address of place where performed, date each test was performed and what each test disclosed. Attach a copy of the test results.
7. If treated by any health care provider, state the name and present address of each health care provider, the dates and places where treatments were received and the date of last treatment. Attach true copies of all written reports provided to you by any such health care.
8. If still being treated, the name and address of each doctor or health care provider rendering treatment, where and how often treatment is received and the nature of the treatment.

* * *

CERTIFICATION

I hereby certify that the foregoing answers to interrogatories are true. I am aware that if any of the foregoing statements made by me are willfully false, I am subject to punishment.

I hereby certify that the copies of the reports annexed hereto provided by either treating physicians or proposed expert witnesses are exact copies of the entire report or reports provided by them; that the existence of other reports of said doctors or experts are unknown to me, and if such become later known or available, I shall serve them promptly on the propounding party.

The recipient of the interrogatories is required to answer each question in writing and under oath. Under oath means that the recipient must sign the answers in front of a notary public.[8]

The document should contain the caption that mirrors the caption of the complaint, must be signed by the attorney for the party propounding the interrogatories, and should be accompanied by a certificate of service. In many jurisdictions, the rules require that the interrogatories have a set of instructions that define the usage of certain words within the interrogatories. An example set of interrogatories from the New Jersey courts is available at Figure 19-14.

[8]http://www.judiciary.state.nj.us/rules/app2.pdf

Paralegals may also be asked to assist with answering interrogatories. The recipient must answer each question under oath and in writing. The answer format mirrors that of the interrogatories. Some states require that the answers be filed with the court. Some states provide for electronic filing. A paralegal should check the local and state rules governing answers to interrogatories.

If documents or records are needed to complete the answers, those documents may be attached to the answers. Many states have rules that identify how answers are to be submitted, such as Massachusetts Civil Procedure Rule 33(3), set out in Figure 19-15.

The rules of court provide a number of grounds for objecting to interrogatories. While making objections is the job of the attorney, paralegals should understand what the objections are and what purpose they serve. Generally, if an objection is not stated in the response to written discovery, that objection is waived. Sometimes there are reasons to postpone objections but it is good practice to state all applicable objections in the initial written response to interrogatories. There are exceptions to waiver, for example. If privilege is the reason for a delayed objection, courts have ruled that the reason should be clearly stated.

The primary objections are the following:

- **Argumentative:** The objection would be written as "Objection. This discovery request as phrased is argumentative. It requires the adoption of an assumption, which is improper." Another example might be, "When did you stop beating your wife?" In this statement, facts that may not be true are assumed and the question requires the answer to adopt that assumption.

---

(3) Answers; Final Request for Answers. Each interrogatory shall be answered separately and fully in writing under the penalties of perjury, unless it is objected to, in which event the reasons for objection shall be stated in lieu of the answer; each answer or objection shall be preceded by the interrogatory to which it responds. The answers are to be signed by the person making them, the objections by the person or attorney making them. The party upon whom the interrogatories have been served shall serve answers and objections, if any, within 45 days after the service of the interrogatories. The court may, on motion with or without notice, specify a shorter or longer time. Unless otherwise specified, further answers to interrogatories shall be served within 30 days of the entry of the order to answer further. The interrogating party may move for an order under Rule 37(a) with respect to any objection to or other failure to answer an interrogatory. Alternatively, for failure to serve timely answers or objections to interrogatories (or further answers, as the case may be), the interrogating party may serve a final request for answers, specifying the failure. The final request for answers shall state that the interrogating party may apply for final judgment for relief or dismissal pursuant to paragraph 4 in the event that answers or objections are not timely received. The party upon whom the interrogatories have been served shall serve the answers or objections either within 30 days from the date of service of the final request or prior to the filing of an application for a final judgment for relief or dismissal, whichever is later.[9]

FIGURE 19-15 Rule on Interrogatory Answers

---

[9]Massachusetts Civil Procedure Rule 33: Interrogatories to Parties. 2012. http://www.lawlib.state.ma.us/source/mass/rules/civil/mrcp33.html

- **Already asked, repetitive discovery:** This objection is phrased as "Objection. This discovery request has, by its substance, been previously propounded. (See Interrogatory No. ___) Continuous discovery into a matter previously asked constitutes suppression and defendant further objects on that ground."
- **Attorney-client privilege:** "Objection. This request seeks information that is subject to the attorney-client privilege." This privilege is broadly construed and extends to factual information and legal advice.
- **Attorney work product protection:** "This discovery request seeks attorney work product in violation of Rule ___ of the ___ Rules of Civil Procedure."
- **Overly broad**– "Plaintiff objects to this request as overly broad, burdensome, and vague."
- **Privileged**– "Plaintiff seeks information that is privileged as a trade secret is subject to such objections and without waiving the same, Plaintiff is not responding to the request."
- **Premature disclosure of experts:** "Objection. The interrogatory seeks the premature disclosure of expert opinion in violation of Rule ___ of the ___ Rules of Civil Procedure. The interrogatory also seeks attorney work product in violation of Rule ___ of the ___ Rules of Civil Procedure. Plaintiff has not decided on which, if any, expert witnesses may be called at trial. The attempt to ascertain the identity, writings, and opinions of plaintiff's experts who have been retained or utilized to date solely as an advisor or consultant is in violation of the work product privilege."

TIP

Here the drafter would cite the applicable law that covers attorney work product.

Requests for Production and Entry on Land

Requests for production usually follow after the submission of interrogatories in the discovery process. Answers to interrogatories may reveal the existence of documents or other tangible objects that are material and that may require inspection. Rule 34 of the Federal Rules of Civil Procedure governs requests for production of documents, electronically stored information, and tangible things, and requests to enter onto land for inspection and other purposes. The rules of court of all states have similar provisions allowing parties to request documents and other things that are relevant to the subject matter of the suit, and that are not privileged. Requests for production are not limited to documents, and may include other items such as physical objects, drawings, graphs, photographs, data compilations, and charts.

The rules permit production so that the documents and other tangible things can be inspected, examined, copied, sampled, photographed, measured, preserved, or tested. The request must be submitted to the party who has control of the material being requested. The request must also be reasonable in allowing copies or making something that is not easily transferable available for inspection. Some rules provide for reimbursement if the cost involved in the production of documents results in a substantial expense. The rule is usually specific in terms of what the request must contain, as shown in Figure 19-16.

A nonparty may be compelled to produce documents by submitting a subpoena *duces tecum* to the nonparty, under Rule 45.

It is not uncommon for paralegals to be involved in drafting requests for production. The request should list the documents without vagueness or ambiguity and with as much particularity as possible. It is common for words to be defined and specific instructions to be given., as shown in Exhibit A-8 in Appendix I.

DEFENDANT'S NAME : No. _____

Just as one can object to interrogatories, objections can be made to requests for production. A sample is provided in Exhibit A-9 in Appendix I. Objections

FIGURE 19-16 Rule 34(b)
(d)(e)

(b) Procedure.

(1) *Contents of the Request.* The request:

(A) must describe with reasonable particularity each item or category of items to be inspected;

(B) must specify a reasonable time, place, and manner for the inspection and for performing the related acts; and

(C) may specify the form or forms in which electronically stored information is to be produced.

Requests for electronically stored information are covered in sections D and E:

(D) *Responding to a Request for Production of Electronically Stored Information.* The response may state an objection to a requested form for producing electronically stored information. If the responding party objects to a requested form—or if no form was specified in the request—the party must state the form or forms it intends to use.

(E) *Producing the Documents or Electronically Stored Information.* Unless otherwise stipulated or ordered by the court, these procedures apply to producing documents or electronically stored information:

(i) A party must produce documents as they are kept in the usual course of business or must organize and label them to correspond to the categories in the request;

(ii) If a request does not specify a form for producing electronically stored information, a party must produce it in a form or forms in which it is ordinarily maintained or in a reasonably usable form or forms; and

(iii) A party need not produce the same electronically stored information in more than one form.[10]

are typically based on requests being too burdensome. The objections identified in the exhibit are in no way a complete list of available objections. The researcher should utilize objections that fit the facts of the client's situation and that comply with local court rules. If there is disagreement over the basis for the objection, and the parties fail to reach an agreement, the requesting party may file a motion to compel, asking the court to order the opposing party to comply.

Rule 34 also covers requests to enter land. In many states it is necessary to file a motion to obtain the court's permission to enter someone else's land. If good cause can be shown for the need to examine the property, the court will issue an order allowing the entry. A party may seek entry and inspection of land owned by a nonparty by serving a subpoena according to Rule 45(a)(1)(C).

Requests for Admissions

Requests for admissions serve to narrow issues in litigation, thereby eliminating those matters that are not in dispute. These requests typically follow after other discovery, such as interrogatories, requests for production, and depositions, have

[10]Legal Information Institute. Rule 34. Producing Documents, Electronically Stored Information, and Tangible Things, or Entering onto Land, for Inspection and Other Purposes. N.d. http://www.law.cornell.edu/rules/frcp/rule_34

been completed. If a party admits to any or all of the facts stated in the request for admission, those facts are deemed admitted, and need not be proven at trial. However, an admission cannot be used against a party in another lawsuit.

Rule 36 of the Federal Rules of Civil Procedure governs the request for admission process, and similar rules are found in state courts. A request for admission may ask another party to admit the truth of any matter within the scope of allowable discovery. The matter sought to be admitted can be in one of three categories:

- The application of law to facts
- The truth of statements or opinions
- The genuineness of documents

The responding party may admit a fact completely or in part. The goal of drafting the matter sought to be admitted is to make the request as clear as possible so there can be no ambiguity in an answer. The requests will have no value to the party seeking the admission if the responding party can write an answer that is evasive or vague.

Requests for admission generally follow a format similar to other discovery requests. The caption mirrors the caption of the initial pleading and the caption is followed by a title that identifies the nature of the document, such as "Plaintiff's Request for Admission of Facts." The organization of the request for admissions may have multiple parts depending upon the preferences of the supervisor or the requirements of local court rules. Some requests may include a set of instructions or a set of definitions prior to or following the actual requests. Similar to that of the complaint, the body of the request should contain the matters to be admitted in separately numbered paragraphs. The request for admissions must be signed by the attorney and must have a certificate of service showing service to the other parties involved. See Exhibit A-10 in Appendix I for a sample request.

Objections to the requests must be stated in the response. A party may not object on the ground that the request presents a genuine issue for trial. However, the rules allow the requesting party to make a motion to determine whether the answer or objection is sufficient. Unless the court finds an objection justified, the request must be answered. If the court finds that an answer does not comply with Rule 36, the court can determine that the matter is admitted or that an amended answer be served. Exhibit A-11 in Appendix I shows a typical response.

Requests for Physical and Mental Examination

Rule 35 of the Federal Rules of Civil Procedure allow a party to request an examination of a party if the party's mental or physical condition is in question. Generally this request must be ordered by the court after a motion is made based on good cause. All parties and the person being examined must be given notice. The person performing the examination must be identified along with the time, place, and scope of examination. If costs are involved, such as travel or lost wages, many jurisdictions provide for reimbursement. The findings of the physician must be served upon the opposing party.

The paralegal's role in this process depends on whether the paralegal's attorney or the opposing counsel requested the examination. Paralegals may draft the request and summarize the medical records gained from other types of discovery.

Paralegals with advanced medical training may be asked to attend the examination and take notes.

AUTHORIZATIONS

Although much of the documentary evidence to be used in litigation is secured through the discovery tools outlined above, evidence is also obtainable through the use of an *authorization* provided by either party. An authorization grants authority to someone else to turn over the information. In a lawsuit, an authorization may be used to obtain information such as the following:

Authorization
A document that gives authority to turn over documents or records, such as a medical authorization.

- Physician's records
- Hospital records
- Federal and state income tax records
- Employment records

The authorization to obtain these types of records is usually sent by mail to the custodian of the records along with a letter of explanation. The letter should identify who will pay for any costs incurred in the preparation of the records.

The medical authorization form is one of the most common authorizations. The authorization is drafted in general terms so that it is flexible enough to cover particular needs of any situation.

An authorization for the release of income tax records or employment records helps to verify certain items of damages such as lost wages incurred by a plaintiff. Similar to medical records, these records are confidential, and an authorization is required. Employment record authorizations should request an individual's employment application, payroll records, termination status, and any relevant file notes. Income tax records can be obtained from the nearest Internal Revenue Service office or from the state department of revenue.

Authorizations are generally used early in litigation, before the parties resort to other discovery tools. Obtaining the information from these authorizations helps to identify additional discovery and possibly reduce the expense of litigation. Figure 19-17 provides an example of a medical authorization.

Medical Authorization

This is to authorize you to furnish to Jami Myers-Selzer, attorney at law, any and all information and records that she may request regarding medical treatment. This authorization hereby cancels any prior authorization.

Dated this _____ day of _____, 20_____.

SUBSCRIBED AND SWORN TO before me this _____ day of _____, 20 _____.

Notary Public _____

My commission expires: _____

FIGURE 19-17 Medical Authorization

SUMMARY

Drafting pleadings is an essential skill for any paralegal in a litigation practice. Because these documents define the facts and issues in litigation, pleadings that are clear, concise, and well organized will form the backbone of the client's case. As the litigation moves forward, motions that are written effectively can streamline the issues in the case, and ensure that the client is treated fairly.

In the discovery phase, the paralegal may be indispensable for drafting discovery requests that obtain the information needed to prove the client's case. A paralegal may be equally valuable in responding to discovery requests in a way that best protects the client.

REVIEW **QUESTIONS**

1. What information should be provided in the caption to a pleading?
2. How are numbers expressed in the body of the text of any legal document?
3. What information is included in the caption of a pleading?
4. What are the purposes of a pleading?
5. What are the four basic elements that must be contained in a complaint?
6. What is the purpose of separate counts in a complaint?
7. What is the purpose of the filing of an answer by the defendant?

8. What is the discovery process?
9. What are the primary discovery tools?
10. How is a deposition different from other types of discovery?
11. What are the distinctions between depositions and interrogatories?
12. What is the effect of a request for admission on the facts contained in that document for purposes of trial?
13. Why should one obtain an authorization from a party?

APPLICATION **EXERCISES**

1. Heather Dobbs, a new client, came into the office today. Heather lives in Indiana but works in Illinois. On her way home from work last week, she was stopped at a stop sign at a four-way intersection. She looked both ways and proceeded into the intersection. She had seen a truck coming from the west on the cross street, but knew that both streets were controlled by stop signs. Unfortunately for Heather, the truck driver failed to stop at his stop sign and struck Heather's car. The damage to her 2011 Toyota Camry was extensive and Heather was taken to a local hospital. She suffered a broken pelvis, shattered nose, and sprained left wrist. She also has been under the care of a psychologist because she fears driving. Paul Roberts, the truck driver, lives in Illinois. He was driving a 2010 Dodge Ram. Sheriff Bob Bartlett arrived on the scene along with Doug Manning and Joyce Jennings of the local EMT office. Both drivers had insurance; Heather was insured by Progressive and Paul was insured by Allstate. Heather retained the Allworthy Law Firm to represent her and help her recover the losses she sustained in the collision.

   a. Draft a complaint in this matter.
   b. Draft an answer in response to this complaint.
   c. Prepare 10 interrogatories to be propounded to the defendant.
   d. Prepare a request for production.
   e. Draft a medical authorization for Heather Dobbs.

QUICK **CHECK**

Answer each of the following as true or false. If the answer is false, rewrite the question so that it is a true statement.

1. A paralegal can sign pleadings.
2. A defendant is not required to answer a complaint if the defendant is not represented by an attorney.
3. A request for production of documents is a discovery device.
4. Depositions can be taken of nonparties.
5. In order to obtain the medical records of the opposing party, the attorney merely needs to send a letter to the party's doctor.

6. Interrogatories can be served on parties and nonparties.
7. One must obtain a court order to enter the land of another.
8. The most common defense is contributory negligence.

RESEARCH

None of this Chapter.

INTERNET RESEARCH

None of this Chapter.

MEDIA RESOURCES

Little Wayne Deposition Video. 2012.   http://www.youtube.com/watch?v=bKwHSi3MG9o

What is a Deposition? Atlanta Personal Injury   http://www.youtube.com/watch?v=CPLsvnvw2uE
Lawyer Explains. 2011.

INTERNET RESOURCES

Jim Calloway. Oklahoma Bar Association.   http://www.okbar.org/members/map/articles/interview.
The Initial Client Interview. 1998–2012.   htm/

National Archives. Federal Register.   http://www.archives.gov/federal-register/write/legal-docs/
Drafting Legal Documents. Principles of Clear Writing. n.d.   clear-writing.html

About.com. Legal Careers. *Top Ten Legal Skills.* 2012.   http://legalcareers.about.com/od/legalcareerbasics/tp/
Legal-Skills.htm

Frame Legal. *Legal Document Drafting & Development.* 2010.   http://www.framelegal.com/legal-documents.aspx

Appendix I

FORMS, DOCUMENTS, BRIEFS, AND MEMORANDA

EXHIBIT A-1: TRIAL BRIEF[1]

IN THE UNITED STATES DISTRICT COURT
FOR THE MIDDLE DISTRICT OF NORTH CAROLINA

UNITED STATES OF AMERICA	)	
	)	
v.	)	NO. 1:ll-CR-161-1
	)	
JOHNNY REID EDWARDS	)	

GOVERNMENT'S TRIAL BRIEF

The United States of America, by and through the undersigned attorneys, respectfully submits its Trial Brief.

The charges against John Edwards in this case flow from his knowing and willful violation of the federal campaign finance laws during his campaign for the Democratic Party's nomination for President of the United States in 2007 and 2008. The laws at issue in this trial are straightforward: a federal candidate may only accept and receive a limited amount of money from anyone individual during an election cycle, and he must truthfully report the money he accepts and receives.

At trial, the Government will prove that John Edwards knowingly and willfully violated these bedrock laws and that he specifically did so because public revelation of his extramarital affair and the resultant pregnancy would destroy his presidential campaign.

Through the course of pre-trial litigation the Court has addressed and received briefing from both sides on a number of legal and trial-related issues, and the Government will not discuss them all again here. There are issues, however, of particular importance that the Government would like to highlight for the Court as trial begins.

What Constitutes a Contribution Under FECA

Under the Federal Election Campaign Act ("Election Act"), various types of payments constitute contributions – (1) any gift, subscription, loan, advance, or deposit of money or anything of value made by any person for the purpose of influencing any election for Federal office, is a contribution; (2) any purchase, payment, distribution, loan, advance, deposit, or gift of money or anything of value, made by any person for the purpose of influencing any election for Federal office, that is also made in cooperation, consultation, or concert, with, or at the request or suggestion of, a candidate, his authorized political committees, or their agents, is a contribution; and (3) payment of a personal expense by any person other than the candidate or the campaign committee, that would not have been made irrespective of the candidacy, is a contribution. *See* 2 U.S.C. § 431(8)(A)(i); 2 U.S.C. §441a(a)(7)(B)(i); 11 C.F.R. § 113.1(g)(6).

At trial, the Government will prove that Mellon's and Baron's payments constitute contributions in excess of the legal limit and that Edwards' knowing and willful acceptance and receipt of them was a crime. The evidence will show that Mellon and Baron each provided funds to Edwards for the purpose of influencing the 2008 election – *i.e.*, helping Edwards be elected President of the United States – and that Edwards knew it.

---

[1]http://msnbcmedia.msn.com/i/MSNBC/Sections/NEWS/120422_EdwardsTrial_GovtBrief.pdf

Edwards contends in his trial brief that Mellon's and Baron's payments are not contributions because the funds were not for personal-use expenses of Edwards that would have existed irrespective of the campaign. His argument is a recapitulation of arguments he has made in the past, and the Government will not burden the Court with a lengthy discussion of why his position is flawed. Suffice it to say that (1) whether a personal expense *exists* irrespective of the campaign (as Edwards alleges) is a separate question from a donor's *purpose* in paying the expense, *see* 11 C.F.R. § 113.1 (g)(6) (providing that third party payment of expenses for a candidate's personal use are also contributions under the Election Act "unless the payment *would have been made* (by the donor) irrespective of the candidacy") (emphasis added), and (2) the regulation is not limited to expenses that the candidate is "legally obligated to pay." In fact, the regulation's own list of examples of *per se* personal expenses includes numerous ones that carry no legal obligation, such as "admission to a sporting event," "dues… at a country club," and "vacation." 11 C.F.R. § 113.l(g)(1)(i)(F), (G), and (J). Edwards' argument lacks any support in law.

Edwards also claims that the Mellon and Baron payments cannot be contributions because they were not "unambiguously related to the campaign." Again, this is nothing new. The argument rests on a faulty legal premise and has no application to contributions or coordinated expenditures. Again, without repeating a lengthy discussion of the Supreme Court's decision in *Buckley v. Valeo*, 424 U.S. 1 (1976), the "unambiguously related to the campaign" phrase arose in the context of *independent* expenditures, and it has never been applied by the Supreme Court, much less the Fourth Circuit, as a precondition to the regulability of contributions or coordinated expenditures. *Id.* at 80.

Edwards' Proposed Legal Expert Testimony

In its ruling on the Government's motion to exclude the testimony of Scott Thomas and Robert Lenhard (Dkt. No. 106), the Court stated that "the motion is denied, but that's not a ruling on the merits." *See* Hrg. Tr., at 84:1-2 (12/1612011). The Court noted that "the cases make very clear exactly how the words are used in the question [to a putative expert at trial] can be very important[.]" *Id.* at 83:6-7. Reserving a final ruling regarding Edwards' proposed experts, the Court directed Edwards' counsel not to discuss what a particular expert might say in its opening statement. *See id.* at 83: 11-12.

At trial, the evidence will show that the specific campaign finance laws at issue – namely, whether Mellon's and Baron's payments were contributions under the law – have a straightforward application to the facts in this case that do not call for a "battle of legal experts." In fact, such a battle would only usurp the role of this Court in explaining the law and the role of the jury in applying that law to the facts of this case.

Edwards' experts' explication of "how the [Election] Act's provisions have been applied to circumstances of alleged contributions and expenditures" in other cases and matters entirely unrelated to this case lacks any relevance and would necessarily involve legal conclusions (pertaining to the Election Act or FEC enforcement actions) that are the exclusive province of this Court. Similarly, Edwards' experts' opining on what a "reasonable person" in Edwards' position "might have known" about the "prevailing interpretation" of campaign finance laws would be equally unhelpful to the jury because such testimony is precisely the sort of legal conclusion that "would merely tell the jury what result to reach, somewhat in the manner of the oath-helpers of an earlier day[.]" *United States v. Barile*, 286 F.3d 749, 759-60 (4th Cir. 2002). Edwards' belief that the Government's theory of prosecution justifies legal expert testimony flies in the face of the fundamental precept that a trial court already has its own legal expert for the application of the law: the judge. *See, e.g., United States v. Wilson*, 133 F.3d 251, 265 (4th Cir. 1997).

The law weighs in favor of exclusion of Edwards' proposed experts, and his trial brief has failed to raise any legal basis for the Court to justify the admission of such testimony. At the conclusion of the Government's case-in-chief, the Government expects that the evidence will further establish that the jury will not need expert testimony to render a true verdict.

Proposed Evidence Regarding a Government Attorney's Statement in State Court

Edwards' suggestion in his trial brief that the Government has "admitted" the novelty of its interpretation of the Federal Election Campaign Act is nonsense. To this end, his reliance on a Government attorney's statement – that this case "deals with the application of the federal campaign finance laws and how they are to be applied going forward as well as to [Edwards'] own campaign," *Hunter v. Young*, Case No. 10 CVS 149, Hrg. Tr., at 5:25-6:2 (9/12/2011) – is entirely misplaced. The Government attorney's statement reflects a fundamental truth in the common law that the disposition of a legal matter (civil or criminal) has precedential impact on subsequent legal matters going forward. *See, e.g., 14 Penn Plaza LLC v. Pyett*, 556 U.S. 247, 280 (2009) "Principles of *stare decisis* … demand respect for precedent whether judicial methods of interpretation change or stay the same.") (citation omitted). That the instant case is a significant one and will, like many cases, have a precedential impact is beyond dispute. Articulation of that basic principle is as far from an admission under Rule 80l(d)(2) as Edwards claims.

In sum, the Government was in no way conceding what Edwards alleges and in fact would have no reason to do so before the state court in the first place. Instead, as the attorney who made the statement can attest to the Court, the Government was merely attempting to persuade the state court in *Hunter v. Young* to allow this important criminal case to progress without the interference that state-case discovery matters would cause. Nothing more and nothing less. As such, to the extent the defense seeks to offer evidence of such a statement at trial it should be precluded.

Dated: April 12, 2012

Respectfully submitted,

JOHN STUART BRUCE
Attorney for the United States
Acting under authority
conferred by 28 U.S.C. § 515

JACK SMITH
Chief, Public Integrity Section
Criminal Division
U.S. Department of Justice

By: lsi Robert J. Higdon, Jr.

Robert J. Higdon, Jr.
Brian S. Meyers
Special Attorneys
U.S. Attorney's Office
310 New Bern Ave., Ste. 800
Raleigh, NC 27601-1461
Tel: (919) 856-4103
Fax: (919) 856-4887
bobby.higdon@usdoj.gov
State Bar No. 17229

By: /s/ David V. Harbach, II

David V. Harbach, II
Jeffrey E. Tsai
Trial Attorneys
Public Integrity Section
Criminal Division
U.S. Department of Justice
1400 New York Ave., N.W., Ste. 12100
Washington, DC 20005
Tel: (202) 514-1412
Fax: (202) 514-3003

CERTIFICATE OF SERVICE

This is to certify that on April 12, 2012, I filed the foregoing document on the Court's CM/ECF system, which will transmit a copy to the following counsel of record in this case:

Alan W. Duncan
Allison O. Van Laningham
Smith Moore Leatherwood LLP
P.O. Box 21927
Greensboro, NC 27420

Abbe David Lowell
Chadbourne & Parke, LLP
1200 New Hampshire Avenue, N.W.
Washington, DC 20036

/s/ Brian S. Meyers
Special Attorney
U.S. Attorney's Office
310 New Bern Ave., Suite 800
Raleigh, NC 27601-1461
Tel: (919) 856-4035
Fax: (919) 856-4887

EXHIBIT A-2: APPELLATE BRIEF[2]

ATTORNEYS FOR APPELLANT
Gene F. Price
Steven P. Langdon
Frost Brown Todd, LLC
New Albany, Indiana

ATTORNEY FOR APPELLEE
Terry Noffsinger
Noffsinger Law, P.C.
Evansville, Indiana

In the

Indiana Supreme Court

No. 31S01-0909-CV-403

CAESARS RIVERBOAT CASINO, LLC,

Appellant (Plaintiff below),

v.

GENEVIEVE M. KEPHART,

Appellee (Defendant below).

Appeal from the Harrison Circuit Court, No. 31C01-0701-CC-005
The Honorable H. Lloyd Whitis, Judge

On Petition To Transfer from the Indiana Court of Appeals, No. 31A01-0711-CV-530

September 30, 2010

Rucker, Justice.

[2]http://www.in.gov/judiciary/opinions/pdf/09301002rdr.pdf

A casino sued a patron for unpaid counter checks. The patron, a pathological gambler, countersued for damages because the casino knowingly enticed and encouraged the patron to gamble. We granted transfer to determine if casino patrons have a common law cause of action for damages stemming from the consequences of gambling losses.

BACKGROUND

Historically, Indiana has prohibited gambling. The restrictions date back to at least 1851 when the State adopted a Constitution that contained a prohibition against lotteries thereby making various forms of gambling unlawful. Ind. Const. Art. 15 § 8 (1851); Ind. Gaming Comm'n v. Moseley, 643 N.E.2d 296, 297 (Ind. 1994). The prohibition against lotteries was adopted to "minimize the harmful effects of gambling by sheltering the people from gaming enterprises promoted and operated for monetary gain … ." State v. Nixon, 384 N.E.2d 152, 161 (Ind. 1979) (declaring that pari-mutuel wagering on horse races was unconstitutional). Anti-gaming statutes were passed to "remove as far as possible the temptation for gambling and prevent the evils arising therefrom." Hatton v. Casey, 178 N.E. 303, 305 (Ind. Ct. App. 1931).

In 1988, voters approved a referendum to amend the Indiana Constitution by deleting the general prohibition against lotteries. The General Assembly then authorized lotteries conducted by the State Lottery Commission and horse race gambling in 1989. See Pub. L. No. 341-1989, 1989 Ind. Acts 2308 (special session) (codified at Ind. Code 4-30, 4-31). In 1993 riverboat gambling was authorized subject to regulation by the Indiana Gaming Commission. See Pub. L. No. 277-1993 § 124, 1993 Ind. Acts 4821 (special session) (codified at I.C. 4-33). Aside from these exceptions, gambling in this state continues to be strictly prohibited by anti-gaming laws. Schrenger v. Caesars Indiana, 825 N.E.2d 879, 883 (Ind. Ct. App. 2005), trans. denied; see I.C. §§ 35-45-5-2, 35-45-5-2 (criminalizing gambling and professional gambling such as pool-selling and bookmaking); L.E. Servs., Inc. v. State Lottery Comm'n of Ind., 646 N.E.2d 334, 340 (Ind. Ct. App. 1995), trans. denied (holding the offering of out-of-state lottery tickets for sale to the public strictly prohibited by Indiana's anti-gaming laws).

FACTS AND PROCEDURAL HISTORY

Caesars Riverboat Casino, LLC ("Caesars") operates a riverboat casino in Elizabeth, Indiana. Genevieve Kephart is a resident of Goodlettsville, Tennessee. Kephart has a pathological addiction to gambling. Caesars knew of Kephart's addiction. On March 18, 2006 Kephart travelled to Caesars after receiving an offer of free transportation, hotel room, food, and alcohol from Caesars. In a single night of gambling Kephart lost $125,000 through the use of six counter checks provided to her by Caesars.

The counter checks were returned to Caesars for insufficient funds. Caesars filed suit against Kephart on January 23, 2007 for payment of the checks, treble damages, and attorney fees as provided in Indiana Code section 34-24-3-1. Kephart counterclaimed on April 2, 2007 alleging that Caesars knew of Kephart's pathological addiction and took advantage of the addiction for gain. Kephart sought damages for the consequences resulting from the $125,000 loss, including damages for past, present, and future mental, emotional, and psychological injury; destroyed and/or strained relationships with family members and friends; doctor, hospital, pharmaceutical, or other medical expenses; loss of quality of life and enjoyment of life; and other expenses not yet known to her. Kephart contended Caesars owed her a common law duty to protect her from its enticements to gamble because it knew she was a pathological gambler.

Caesars moved to dismiss the counterclaim under Trial Rule 12(B)(6). After a hearing, the trial court denied the motion but certified its ruling for interlocutory appeal. The Court of Appeals accepted jurisdiction and in a divided opinion reversed the trial court's judgment. Caesars Riverboat Casino, LLC v. Kephart, 903 N.E.2d 117 (Ind. Ct. App. 2009). We granted transfer. See 919 N.E.2d 552 (Ind. Sept. 11, 2009) (Table).

STANDARD OF REVIEW

We review de novo the trial court's grant or denial of a motion based on Indiana Trial Rule 12(B)(6). Babes Showclub v. Lair, 918 N.E.2d 308, 310 (Ind. 2009). Such a motion tests the legal sufficiency of a claim, not the facts supporting it. Charter One Mortgage Corp. v. Condra, 865 N.E.2d 602, 604 (Ind. 2007). Viewing the complaint in the light most favorable to the non-moving party, we must determine whether the complaint states any facts on which the trial court could have granted relief. Id. at 604-05.

DISCUSSION

I.

To prevail on a claim of negligence the plaintiff must show 1) duty owed to the plaintiff by defendant, 2) breach of duty by allowing conduct to fall below the applicable standard of care, and 3) compensable injury proximately caused by defendant's breach of duty. Kroger Co. v. Plonski, 930 N.E.2d 1, 6 (Ind. 2010). Absent a duty there can be no negligence or liability based upon the breach. Id.

Where, as here, the existence of a duty has not been previously articulated, the three-part balancing test this court developed in Webb v. Jarvis, 575 N.E.2d 992, 995 (Ind. 1991) (relationship between the parties, foreseeability, and public policy) can be a useful tool in determining whether a duty exists. We say "can be" because in this case the tool has not proven to be of much assistance. Both the Court of Appeals majority as well as the dissent applied the Webb factors. And despite well-reasoned and thoughtful analysis on both sides, each reached an opposite result. Speaking for the majority, Judge Mathias concluded "[t]here is no common law duty obligating a casino operator to refrain from attempting to entice or contact gamblers that it knows or should know are compulsive gamblers." Kephart, 903 N.E.2d at 128. In dissent Judge Crone concluded, "all three [Webb] factors militate in favor of imposing a duty on Caesars to refrain from enticing to its casino known pathological gamblers who have not requested that they be removed from the casino's direct marketing list or excluded from the casino." Id. at 134 (Crone, J., dissenting).

We think it unnecessary to resolve this dispute today. Assuming without deciding that casino operators in this State might otherwise have a common law duty to refrain from attempting to entice or contact gamblers that it knows or should know are compulsive gamblers, we are of the view that the Legislature has abrogated the common law.

There is a presumption that the legislature does not intend to make any change in the common law beyond those declared in either express terms or by unmistakable implication. South Bend Cmty. Schs. Corp. v. Widawski, 622 N.E.2d 160, 162 (Ind. 1993). "An abrogation of the common law will be implied (1) where a statute is enacted which undertakes to cover the entire subject treated and was clearly designed as a substitute for the common law; or, (2) where the two laws are so repugnant that both in reason may not stand." Irvine v. Rare Feline Breeding Ctr., Inc., 685 N.E.2d 120, 123 (Ind. Ct. App. 1997), trans. denied.

When the General Assembly legalized riverboat gambling in 1993, it expressed its intent as follows:

This article is intended to benefit the people of Indiana by promoting tourism and assisting economic development. The public's confidence and trust will be maintained only through:

(1) comprehensive law enforcement supervision; and
(2) the strict regulation of facilities, persons, associations, and gambling operations under this article.

I.C. § 4-33-1-2. The Legislature established the Indiana Gaming Commission ("Commission") as the administrative agency responsible for administration, regulation and enforcement of the riverboat gaming system. See generally I.C. § 4-33-4-1. Under this statute the Commission has jurisdiction and supervision over "[a]ll persons on riverboats where gambling operations are conducted" and enjoys "[a]ll powers necessary and proper to fully and effectively execute" the statute. I.C. § 4-33-4-1(3)(B), (2). Those powers include the right to "[t]ake appropriate administrative enforcement or disciplinary action against a licensee or an operating agent." I.C. § 4-33-4-1(6). Moreover, the Commission has broad powers to "[t]ake any reasonable or appropriate action to enforce [the statue]," including the power to "[r]evoke, suspend, or renew licenses issued under [the statute]." I.C. § 4-33-4-1(16), (14). The Commission's authority also includes investigating violations, conducting hearings, adopting rules, levying and collecting penalties for noncriminal violations, and adopting a voluntary exclusion program for gamblers. I.C. §§ 4-33-4-1, 4-33-4-3. Thus it seems apparent Indiana Code 4-33 covers the entire subject of riverboat gambling. Accord Atlantic City Showboat, Inc. v. Dep't of Cmty. Affairs of State, 751 A.2d 111, 118 (N.J. Super. App. Div. 2000) (noting New Jersey's Casino Control Act is "extraordinarily pervasive and intensive" and recognizing the Act preempts well-settled areas of law (citing Hakimoglu v. Trump Taj Mahal Assocs., 70 F.3d 291, 293-94 (3rd Cir. 1995) (holding common law dram shop liability does not apply to casinos))).

In this case, not only does the statutory scheme cover the entire subject of riverboat gambling, but the statutory scheme and Kephart's common law claim are so incompatible that they cannot both occupy the same space. As the sole regulator of riverboat gambling, the Commission has adopted detailed regulations at the legislature's direction. See 68 Ind. Admin. Code §§ 1-1-1 to 19-1-5. Indiana Code sections 4-33-4-3(a)(9) and (c) require the Commission to enact a voluntary exclusion program. See 68 I.A.C. §§ 6-1-1 to 6-3-5. Under this program any person may make a request to have his or her name placed on a voluntary exclusion list by following the required procedures. 68 I.A.C. § 6-3-2. To request exclusion, applicants must provide contact information, a physical description, and desired time frame of exclusion – one year, five years, or lifetime. Id. Casinos must have procedures by which excluded individuals are not allowed to gamble, do not receive direct marketing, and are not extended check cashing or credit privileges. 68 I.A.C. § 6-3-4. A casino's failure to comply with the regulations makes it subject to disciplinary action under 68 Indiana Administrative Code article 13.

Kephart's common law claim would hold Caesars to a similar standard regarding known pathological gamblers in absence of the voluntary exclusion program. The existence of the voluntary exclusion program suggests the legislature intended pathological gamblers to take personal responsibility to prevent and protect themselves against compulsive gambling. The legislature did not require casinos to identify and refuse service to pathological gamblers who did not self-identify. Kephart's claim directly conflicts with the legislature's choice. To allow Kephart's claim to go forward under the common law would shift primary responsibility from the gambler to casino. It is apparent that the legislature intended otherwise. Therefore allowing a common law negligence claim addressing behavior essentially the same as prohibited under the statutory scheme irreconcilably conflicts with the intent of the legislature.

In sum it appears to us that by unmistakable implication the Legislature has abrogated any common law claim that casino patrons might otherwise have against casinos for damages resulting from enticing patrons to gamble and lose money at casino establishments. The trial court thus erred in denying Caesars' motion to dismiss Kephart's counter-claim under Trial Rule 12(B)(6) for failure to state a claim upon which relief can be granted.

II.

In addition to her counter claim, Kephart also raised a number of affirmative defenses.[1] An affirmative defense is a defense "upon which the proponent bears the burden of proof and which, in effect, admits the essential allegations of the complaint but asserts additional matter barring relief." Rice v. Grant County Bd. of Comm'rs, 472 N.E.2d 213, 214 (Ind. Ct. App. 1984) (emphasis omitted), trans. denied. Indiana Trial Rule 8(C) provides in relevant part, "A responsive pleading shall set forth affirmatively and carry the burden of proving: [list of defenses] and any other matter constituting an avoidance, matter of abatement, or affirmative defense." The list of affirmative defenses contained in the Rule is not exhaustive. Willis v. Westerfield, 839 N.E.2d 1179, 1185 (Ind. 2006). Instead, whether a defense is affirmative, "depends upon whether it controverts an element of a plaintiff's prima facie case or raises matters outside the scope of the prima facie case." Id. (internal citations and quotation omitted).

Although Kephart does not have a common law cause of action against Caesars for damages stemming from the consequences of her gambling losses, nothing in this opinion precludes Kephart from controverting any element of Caesars' prima facie case or from raising matters outside the scope of Caesars' prima facie case.

Conclusion

We reverse the judgment of the trial court.

Shepard, C.J., and Sullivan, J., concur.
Boehm, J., concurs in result with separate opinion.
Dickson, J., dissents with separate opinion.

Boehm, J., concurring in result.

I concur in the majority opinion with a single exception. The majority allows that the Webb v. Jarvis three factor framework may be a useful tool to analyze whether a duty exists or not. This case is, in my view, a good example of how the Webb framework generates more confusion than light, and I am pleased that the Court recognizes that Webb analysis is not always useful. But I do not share the view that it is ever helpful. As I see it, asserting the defendant has a duty to the plaintiff is nothing more than a statement that there is no legal bar to recovery on the plaintiff's claim. The majority's analysis here, which I join, is that in this case there is a reason why the plaintiff may not recover, namely, that recovery is inconsistent with a comprehensive legal scheme designed to regulate the defendant's industry.

My specific complaint about Webb is that it identifies "foreseeability" as one of the three factors the courts are to evaluate in deciding whether the defendant has a duty to the plaintiff. But whether the plaintiff's injury was reasonably foreseeable by the defendant under the facts of the case is ordinarily a component of breach because the ultimate test of negligence is typically whether the defendant acted reasonably under all the circumstances. Moreover, foreseeability

---

[1]Specifically Kephart alleges, "1. There was a lack of consideration for the checks or money claimed by Plaintiff for goods, wares, and/or services. 2. The Defendant, Mrs. Kephart, was incompetent at the time of the execution of the written instruments which are alleged in Plaintiff's complaint. 3. Any alleged contract with the Casino should be rescinded upon the following grounds: a. Breach of its implied covenant of good faith and fair dealing; b. Mrs. Kephart's capacity to contract was impaired by intoxication; c. Any checks or markers signed by Mrs. Kephart were void because they were signed under duress; d. The enforcement of any such alleged contract would be unconscionable[.] 4. By giving excessive amounts of alcohol to Mrs. Kephart, and then claiming it was injured by her actions or inactions, Caesars has waived any claim it might have for damages, pursuant to Ind. Code § 7.1-5-10-15.5(b) (1996). 5. Caesars failed to comply with Ind. Code § 34-16-1-1 (1998), which provides that any security made in consideration of money won as the result of a wager is void. 6. Caesars failed to comply with Ind. Code § 34-16-1-2 (1998), which requires that any civil action to recover any money by betting on a game be filed within one hundred eighty (180) days. 7. The prosecution of this lawsuit contravenes the Fair Debt Collection Practices Act, 15 U.S.C. §§ 1692e. 8. The Complaint fails to state a claim upon which relief can be granted." Appellant's App. at 68-69.

of injury arising from a defendant's act or omission is also relevant to the scope of liability the law will impose on the defendant. This component of ordinary tort liability is usually lumped together with causation-in-fact under the rubric of proximate cause. I have tried to spell out some of the pernicious consequences of this confusion in Theodore R. Boehm, A Tangled Webb—Reexamining the Role of Duty in Indiana Negligence Law, 37 Ind. L. Rev. 1 (2003).

I have been hoping for a case that would permit me to address this issue in a mode that would attract the attention of at least two of my colleagues, but must be content with leaving them with this small soupcon of the delights that await them in untangling this Webb.

Dickson, Justice, dissenting.

In my view, the result in this case is particularly disturbing. The Court today holds that a gambling casino may with impunity entice a person the casino knows to be a pathological gambler by offering free transportation from Tennessee to the Indiana casino, providing her with a free hotel room, food, and alcohol, and then extending her credit to gamble at the casino where she not surprisingly suffers $125,000 in casino gambling losses. These facts call for application of the well-established principle of Indiana common law that business owners must use reasonable care to protect their customers while on the business premises. Burrell v. Meads, 569 N.E.2d 637, 639 (Ind. 1991).

The rationale applied by the Court is that this common law obligation, as applied to casinos, was abrogated by implication because the Indiana Gaming Commission, pursuant to statutory directive, created a program whereby persons may voluntarily place their name on an exclusion list that would prevent their being permitted to gamble, to receive direct marketing, or to receive casino credit privileges. I disagree with this implied abrogation. "It is a well-known principle in Indiana that statutes 'in derogation of the common law [] are to be strictly construed against limitations on a claimant's right to bring suit.'" Wine-Settergren v. Lamey, 716 N.E.2d 381, 388 (Ind. 1999) (quoting Collier v. Prater, 544 N.E.2d 497, 498 (Ind. 1989)).

> This rule has special force when the statute affects a common law right or duty. When the legislature enacts a statute in derogation of the common law, the Court presumes that the legislature is aware of the common law, and does not intend to make any change therein beyond what it declares either in express terms or by unmistakable implication. In cases of doubt, a statute is construed as not changing the common law.

Bartrom v. Adjustment Bureau, Inc., 618 N.E.2d 1, 10 (Ind. 1993) (internal citations omitted). Nowhere in Indiana's statutory system of gambling regulation is there any provision that expressly or unmistakably abrogates Indiana's common law requiring business operators to exercise reasonable care for the safety of their customers and subjecting them to accountability in damages for failing to do so.[1]

The plaintiff's failure to avail herself of the Gaming Commission's voluntary program may be appropriately considered in the allocation of comparative fault between the plaintiff and the casino, but it should not prematurely preclude the plaintiff from having her day in court to seek to hold the casino accountable in damages for what appears from the allegations to be a blatant breach of duty.

This Court has often provided protection for vulnerable individuals against the unreasonable actions of others. *See, e.g.,* Livingston v. Fast Cash USA, Inc., 753 N.E.2d 572 (Ind. 2001) (holding that payday loan lenders cannot collect finance charges exceeding the statutory maximum annual percentage rate and mentioning the criminality of loansharking); Picadilly, Inc. v. Colvin, 519 N.E.2d 1217 (Ind. 1988) (holding that the common law duty to exercise reasonable care still exists for alcohol providers despite the enactment of dram shop statutes); Scott County Sch. Dist. One v. Asher, 263 Ind. 47, 324 N.E.2d 496 (1975) (recognizing the ability of minors to avoid or disaffirm contracts entered into, with the exception of contracts for necessaries). Similarly, today's case calls for upholding our common law principles rather than implying statutory repeal thereof. I therefore dissent.

Separately, I commend Justice Boehm's separate concurrence, which thoughtfully questions the Webb v. Jarvis three-factor framework and urges that we revisit our traditional but redundant application of foreseeability to analyze both duty and proximate cause, and I encourage a careful consideration of his law journal article and its recommendations.

---

[1] I also dissent today in Donovan v. Grand Victoria Casino & Resort, L.P., ___ N.E.2d ___ (Ind. 2010), urging that the comprehensive regulatory scheme controls and fails to authorize casinos to exclude patrons with card counting skills. In contrast to my dissenting views above, which emphasize the viability of a person's right to assert a common law cause of action unless expressly abrogated by statute, my dissent in Donovan is grounded on the fact that Indiana's casino gambling businesses exist only by statute and regulation and thus are governed exclusively by Indiana Gaming Commission regulation and not by common law.

EXHIBIT A-3: COMPLAINT

**IN THE UNITED STATES DISTRICT COURT
FOR THE DISTRICT OF NEBRASKA** ← caption
Omaha Division

THE UNITED STATES OF AMERICA,	)	
	)	
Plaintiff,	)	
	)	
v.	)	
	)	
QUIKTRIP CORPORATION,	)	Civil Action No. _____
	)	
Defendant.	)	
	)	
	)	
	)	
_____	)	

title →

COMPLAINT

Plaintiff United States of America alleges as follows:

INTRODUCTION

1. This is an action by the United States to enforce title III of the Americans with Disabilities Act of 1990 ("ADA"), 42 U.S.C. §§ 12181–12189, and its implementing regulation, 28 C.F.R. pt. 36. This action involves several hundred convenience stores and fuel service stations that are owned and operated by QuikTrip Corporation and that are not accessible to individuals with disabilities in violation of title III of the ADA (Title III).

Jurisdiction → ## JURISDICTION

2. The Court has jurisdiction over this action pursuant to 42 U.S.C. §§ 12188(b)(1)(B) and (b)(2) and 28 U.S.C. §§ 1331 and 1345. The Court may grant declaratory and other relief pursuant to 28 U.S.C. §§ 2201 and 2202.

3. Venue lies in this District and this Division pursuant to 28 U.S.C. § 1391 because certain discriminatory events giving rise to this action occurred at convenience stores and fuel service stations owned and operated by QuikTrip that are located in and around Omaha, Nebraska.

THE DEFENDANT

4. Defendant QuikTrip Corporation (hereinafter, QuikTrip) has its principal place of business at 4705 S. 129th E. Avenue, Tulsa, Oklahoma 74134. QuikTrip is a private entity within the meaning of Section 301 of the ADA, 42 U.S.C. § 12181.

5. QuikTrip owns and operates several hundred convenience stores and fuel service stations located in numerous states, including Arizona, Georgia, Iowa, Illinois, Kansas, Missouri, Nebraska, Oklahoma, and Texas. Several of the convenience stores and fuel service stations that QuikTrip owns and operates also have attached truck stop and travel center facilities. These convenience stores and fuel service stations, including the truck stop and travel center facilities, are places of public accommodation within the meaning of Title III of the ADA, 42 U.S.C. § 12181(7), and its implementing regulation at 28 C.F.R. § 36.104.

6. QuikTrip, and the convenience stores, fuel service stations, and truck stop and travel center facilities that QuikTrip owns and operates, are subject to the requirements of Title III of the ADA, 42 U.S.C. §§ 12181–12189, and the regulation implementing Title III of the ADA, 28 C.F.R. pt. 36.

Claim ⟶ **TITLE III OF THE ADA**

7. Title III prohibits the failure to design and construct convenience stores, fuel service stations, and truck stop and travel center facilities built for first occupancy after January 26, 1993, to be readily accessible to and usable by individuals with disabilities in accordance with the ADA Standards for Accessible Design (ADA Standards), 28 C.F.R. pt. 36, app. A. 42 U.S.C. § 12183(a)(1); 28 C.F.R. §§ 36.401, 36.406(a).

8. Title III prohibits the failure to make alterations to convenience stores, fuel service stations, and truck stop and travel center facilities in such a manner that, to the maximum extent feasible, the altered portions of the facilities are readily accessible to and usable by individuals with disabilities in accordance with the ADA Standards. 42 U.S.C. § 12183(a)(2); 28 C.F.R. §§ 36.402, 36.403, 36.406(a). It also prohibits the failure to remove architectural barriers at such facilities where such removal is readily achievable. 42 U.S.C. § 12182(a)(2)(A)(iv); 28 C.F.R. § 36.304.

9. Title III prohibits discrimination against individuals with disabilities in the full and equal enjoyment of the goods, services, facilities, privileges, advantages, or accommodations of convenience stores, fuel service stations, and truck stop and travel center facilities. 42 U.S.C. § 12182.

DEFENDANT'S DISCRIMINATORY ACTIONS

10. QuikTrip's convenience stores, fuel service stations, and truck stop and travel center facilities are constructed and altered based on prototype design plans and share common, and often identical, architectural elements and features.

11. Between early September and mid-October 2009, the United States conducted surveys of 21 QuikTrip convenience stores and fuel service stations in five states, within geographically dispersed locations in three of QuikTrip designated regional markets, including surveys of newly constructed, altered, and existing facilities. Three of the 21 facilities surveyed have truck stop and travel center facilities in addition to the convenience store and fuel service station facilities. Surveys were conducted at the following locations:

    a. QuikTrip's Des Moines Division (Nebraska and Iowa):
        (1) 715 S. Saddle Creek Road, Omaha, Nebraska 68106
        (2) 4212 S. 84th Street, Omaha, Nebraska 68127
        (3) 8727 Maple Street, Omaha, Nebraska 68134
        (4) 1704 S. 72nd Street, Omaha, Nebraska 68124
        (5) 6045 L Street, Omaha, Nebraska 68117
        (6) 1749 W. Broadway, Council Bluffs, Iowa 51501

    b. QuikTrip's St. Louis Division (Missouri and Illinois):
        (1) 10845 Lilac Drive, Bellefontaine Neighbors, Missouri 63137 (Includes Truck Stop Facilities)
        (2) 850 McNutt Street, Herculaneum, Missouri 63048 (Includes Truck Stop Facilities)
        (3) 8334 Highway N, Lake St. Louis, Missouri 63367
        (4) 608 McCambridge Ave., Madison, Illinois 62060
        (5) 1117 Camp Jackson Road, Cahokia, Illinois 62206

    c. QuikTrip's Atlanta Division (Georgia):
        (1) 5705 Fulton Industrial Blvd., S.W., Atlanta, Georgia 30336 (Includes Truck Stop Facilities)
        (2) 1836 Briarcliff Rd., N.E., Atlanta, Georgia 30324
        (3) 761 Sidney Marcus Blvd., N.E., Atlanta, Georgia 30324
        (4) 4050 Buford Highway, N.E., Atlanta, Georgia 30345
        (5) 6901 Peachtree Industrial Blvd., Atlanta, Georgia 30360
        (6) 1910 Lawrenceville Highway, Decatur, Georgia 30033
        (7) 3930 Flat Shoals Pkwy., Decatur, Georgia 30034
        (8) 5390 Riverdale Road, College Park, Georgia 30349
        (9) 3875 S. Cobb Drive, Smyrna, Georgia 30082
        (10) 7130 Mableton Pkwy., S.E., Mableton, Georgia 30126

12. Upon information and belief, including information obtained during the surveys of 21 QuikTrip facilities by the United States, Defendant has discriminated and continues to discriminate against individuals with disabilities in violation of Title III of the ADA, its regulation, and the ADA Standards by failing to provide and maintain the following accessible elements, among others, at its facilities, which are based on a prototype design:

    a. Accessible routes do not exist to connect buildings, facilities, elements, and spaces; they do not, to the maximum extent feasible, coincide with the route for the general public; they have excessive abrupt changes in level; and/or they have slopes and cross slopes that are too steep;

b. Ramps have excessive rises; they do not have appropriate landings; they do not have appropriate handrails; they have slopes and cross slopes that are too steep; and/or they do not have adequate edge protection;

c. Curb ramps have slopes and cross slopes that are too steep; they have inadequate clear passage width; their surfaces are not stable, firm, and slip-resistant; their flared sides have slopes that are too steep; they are constructed using a "built-up" design and project into vehicular traffic lanes; they lack detectable warnings; and/or they can be obstructed by parked vehicles;

d. Too few designated accessible parking spaces are provided; they are not located on the shortest accessible route of travel to an accessible entrance; they have slopes and cross slopes that are too steep; and/or they lack adequate signage reserving them for use by individuals with disabilities;

e. Fuel, water, and air dispensers have controls and operating mechanisms such as buttons and levers that are too high or otherwise beyond the reach ranges of individuals who use wheelchairs; they require tight grasping, pinching, or twisting of the wrist to operate; they lack the required clear floor space for a forward or parallel approach by a person using a wheelchair; and/or these elements are not located on accessible routes;

f. Signage is mounted too high or too low;

g. Entrance doors have excessive thresholds;

h. Interior doors have excessive thresholds; have door closers that close the doors too quickly; and/or require too much opening force;

i. Single user and multi-stall toilet rooms and elements such as toilets, urinals, lavatories, and controls and operating mechanisms are inaccessible because they lack the required clear floor space; they lack the required size and arrangement of accessible toilet stalls; toilet stalls have doors with hardware that requires grasping, twisting, or pinching; grab bars are incorrectly mounted or have the wrong dimensions; lavatories have exposed hot water pipes and other surfaces that can cause injuries; faucets and flush controls do not have accessible designs; mirrors are mounted too high; and/or controls and operating mechanisms, such as paper towel and types of dispensers, are mounted beyond the reach ranges of individuals who use wheelchairs and require tight grasping, pinching, or twisting of the wrist to operate;

j. Shelving and counters are mounted too high;

k. Food, drink, tableware, and condiment dispensers are mounted beyond the reach ranges of individuals who use wheelchairs;

l. Ground and floor surfaces have excessive abrupt changes in level, and/or they are not stable, firm, and slip-resistant; and

m. Objects, such as signs and lamps, protrude excessively from walls at locations where they are not detectable by blind individuals using a cane.

13. Upon information and belief, Defendant has discriminated against individuals with disabilities in violation of Title III of the ADA and its regulation by

a. Engaging in a policy and practice of failing to design and construct convenience stores, fuel service stations, truck stops, and travel centers to be readily accessible to and usable by individuals with disabilities in violation of 42 U.S.C. § 12183(a)(1) and 28 C.F.R. §§ 36.401, 36.406;

b. Engaging in a policy and practice of failing to make alterations to convenience stores, fuel service stations, truck stops, and travel centers so they are readily accessible to and usable by individuals with disabilities to the maximum extent feasible in violation of 42 U.S.C. § 12183(a)(2) and 28 C.F.R. §§ 36.402, 36.403, and 36.406;

c. Engaging in a policy and practice of failing to remove architectural barriers in existing facilities in accordance with 42 U.S.C. § 12182(b)(2)(A)(iv) and 28 C.F.R. § 36.304 or to otherwise make its goods, services, facilities, privileges, advantages, and accommodations available through alternative methods pursuant to 42 U.S.C. § 12182(b)(2)(A)(v) and 28 C.F.R. § 36.305; and

d. Otherwise discriminating against individuals with disabilities in violation of 42 U.S.C. § 12182 and the Title III implementing regulation.

14. The Attorney General has reasonable cause to believe that Defendant's conduct constitutes:

   a. A pattern or practice of discrimination within the meaning of 42 U.S.C. § 12188(b)(1)(B)(i) and 28 C.F.R. § 36.503(a); and

   b. Unlawful discrimination that raises an issue of general public importance within the meaning of 42 U.S.C. § 12188(b)(1)(B)(ii) and 28 C.F.R. § 36.503(b).

COMPLAINANTS

15. Thomas Ware is a Korean War Veteran who has extreme difficulty walking and ambulating and often uses a wheelchair. Mr. Ware experienced acts of discrimination by Defendant at QuikTrip locations in La Vista, Nebraska, a suburb of Omaha.

16. John K. Shannahan, also a Veteran, has difficulty walking and requires accessible elements to ambulate. Mr. Shannahan experienced acts of discrimination by QuikTrip at several QuikTrip locations in Omaha, Nebraska.

17. Messrs. Ware and Shannahan are persons with disabilities within the meaning of the ADA, as amended, 42 U.S.C. § 12102.

18. Messrs. Ware and Shannahan visited several QuikTrip locations in the Omaha region but were unable to either use, or use in a nondiscriminatory manner, QuikTrip facilities because of inaccessible elements and the failure to maintain accessible features, including parking, curb ramps, and routes.

19. QuikTrip's discriminatory actions have harmed Mr. Ware, Mr. Shannahan, and other individuals.

Prayer for Relief or WHEREFORE ⟶ PRAYER FOR RELIEF

WHEREFORE, Plaintiff United States of America prays that this Court enter an order that grants the following relief:

   a. Declares that the discriminatory practices, policies, procedures, and administrative methods of QuikTrip Corporation, as set forth above, violate Title III of the ADA, 42 U.S.C. §§ 12181-12189, and its implementing regulation at 28 C.F.R. pt. 36;

   b. Enjoins QuikTrip, its officers, agents, and employees, and all other persons and entities in active concert or participation with QuikTrip, from discriminating on the basis of disability;

   c. Orders QuikTrip to bring its convenience stores and gasoline service stations within the requirements of Title III of the ADA, its implementing regulation at 28 C.F.R. pt. 36, and the Standards for Accessible Design at Appendix A to the regulation;

   d. Orders QuikTrip to design and construct new facilities, to make alterations, and to remove barriers to access by individuals with disabilities in accordance with 42 U.S.C. §§ 12182(b)(1)(A)(i), 12183(a)(1)-(2), and the Title III implementing regulation at 28 C.F.R. pt. 36, including the Standards for Accessible Design at Appendix A to the regulation;

   e. Orders QuikTrip to provide its services, facilities, privileges, advantages, and accommodations to persons with disabilities in a nondiscriminatory manner, including providing them in the most integrated setting appropriate to the needs of the individual and to make such modifications as are necessary to prevent segregation of persons with disabilities;

   f. Awards monetary damages to Mr. Ware, Mr. Shannahan, and other persons aggrieved by QuikTrip's discriminatory actions to compensate them for the discrimination they experienced;

   g. Assesses a civil penalty against QuikTrip as authorized by 42 U.S.C. § 12188(b)(2) to vindicate the public interest;

   h. Orders such other appropriate relief as the interests of justice may require in the opinion of this Honorable Court.

The United States of America hereby requests that trial of the above and foregoing action should be held in Omaha, Nebraska, and that the case be calendared accordingly.

Date:

←Signature block.

ERIC H. HOLDER, JR.**
United States Attorney General

_____

_____
DEBORAH R. GILG
Assistant Attorney General
LAURIE KELLY
Assistant United States Attorney
District of Nebraska

THOMAS E. PEREZ**
United States Attorney
SAMUEL R. BAGENSTOS**
Deputy Assistant Attorney General
Civil Rights Division

_____
JOHN L. WODATCH**, CHIEF
PHILIP L. BREEN**, Special Legal Counsel
Disability Rights Section

_____
JEANINE M. WORDEN, Deputy Chief
Virginia Bar 29754
Disability Rights Section (NYA)
U.S. Department of Justice
950 Pennsylvania Ave., N.W.
Washington, D.C. 20530
Telephone: (202) 353-9875
Fax: (202) 514-7821
E-mail: Jeanine.Worden@usdoj.gov

_____
DOV LUTZKER, Special Counsel
California Bar 185106
Disability Rights Section (NYA) U.S.
Department of Justice
950 Pennsylvania Ave., N.W.
Washington, D.C. 20530
Telephone: (202) 514-5746
Fax: (202) 514-7821
E-mail: Dov.Lutzker@usdoj.gov

_____
WILLIAM LYNCH, Trial Attorney
Virginia Bar 71226
Disability Rights Section (NYA)
U.S. Department of Justice
950 Pennsylvania Ave., N.W.
Washington, D.C. 20530
Telephone: (202) 305-2008
Fax: (202) 514-7821
E-mail: William.Lynch@usdoj.gov
Attorneys for Plaintiff
United States of America[3]

** Thomas E. Perez and John L. Wodatch are signing in their official capacity as the Assistant Attorney General of the Civil Rights Division and Chief of the Disability Rights Section, respectively, and do not wish to receive electronic notice in this case. The same also applies to others listed with asterisks, who have not signed.

[3]U.S. v. Quicktrip Corp. 2010. http://www.ada.gov/quiktrip_complaint.htm

EXHIBIT A-4: SUMMONS

FORM 1. SUMMONS

State of Minnesota
 	
County of _____
 	
_____,
 	
                            Plaintiff,
 	
            vs.
 	
_____,
 	
Defendant.
	District Court
	
	_____ **Judicial District**
	
	Court File Number: _____
	
	Case Type: _____
	
	Summons

THIS SUMMONS IS DIRECTED TO _____.

1. **YOU ARE BEING SUED.** The Plaintiff has started a lawsuit against you. The Plaintiff's Complaint against you [is attached to this summons] [is on file in the office of the court administrator of the above-named court].* Do not throw these papers away. They are official papers that affect your rights. You must respond to this lawsuit even though it may not yet be filed with the Court and there may be no court file number on this summons.

2. **YOU MUST REPLY WITHIN 20** DAYS TO PROTECT YOUR RIGHTS.** You must give or mail to the person who signed this summons **a written response** called an Answer within 20** days of the date on which you received this Summons. You must send a copy of your Answer to the person who signed this summons located at: _____.

3. **YOU MUST RESPOND TO EACH CLAIM.** The Answer is your written response to the Plaintiff's Complaint. In your Answer you must state whether you agree or disagree with each paragraph of the Complaint. If you believe the Plaintiff should not be given everything asked for in the Complaint, you must say so in your Answer.

4. **YOU WILL LOSE YOUR CASE IF YOU DO NOT SEND A WRITTEN RESPONSE TO THE COMPLAINT TO THE PERSON WHO SIGNED THIS SUMMONS.** If you do not Answer within 20** days, you will lose this case. You will not get to tell your side of the story, and the Court may decide against you and award the Plaintiff everything asked for in the complaint. If you do not want to contest the claims stated in the complaint, you do not need to respond. A default judgment can then be entered against you for the relief requested in the complaint.

5. **LEGAL ASSISTANCE.** You may wish to get legal help from a lawyer. If you do not have a lawyer, the Court Administrator may have information about places where you can get legal assistance. **Even if you cannot get legal help, you must still provide a written Answer to protect your rights or you may lose the case.**

6. **ALTERNATIVE DISPUTE RESOLUTION.** The parties may agree to or be ordered to participate in an alternative dispute resolution process under Rule 114 of the Minnesota General Rules of Practice. You must still send your written response to the Complaint even if you expect to use alternative means of resolving this dispute.

7. **TO BE INCLUDED ONLY IF THIS LAWSUIT AFFECTS TITLE TO REAL PROPERTY:**

THIS LAWSUIT MAY AFFECT OR BRING INTO QUESTION TITLE TO REAL PROPERTY Located in _____ County, State of Minnesota, legally described as follows:

[Insert legal description of property]

The object of this action is _____.]

_____   _____
Plaintiff's attorney's signature   Dated

_____
Print or type plaintiff's attorney's name

* Use language in the first bracket when the complaint is served with the summons, language in the second bracket when the complaint is filed and the summons is served by publication.

** Use 20 days, except that in the exceptional situations where a different time is allowed by the court in which to answer, the different time should be inserted.[4]

[4]Minnesota Judicial Branch, Second District. Filing a Summons and Complaint. 2012. Http://www.mncourts.gov/district/2/?page=1123

EXHIBIT A-5: ANSWER

ROBERT TED PARKER (SBN 43024)
BERG & PARKER LLP
Four Embarcadero, Suite 1400
San Francisco, California 94111
Telephone: (415) 397-6000
Facsimile: (415) 397-9449

attorney contact information

Attorneys for Defendant
RAYMOND MAALOUF

Caption

UNITED STATES DISTRICT COURT

NORTHERN DISTRICT OF CALIFORNIA

SONY MUSIC ENTERTAINMENT INC., a Delaware corporation; ELEKTRA ENTERTAINMENT GROUP INC., a Delaware corporation; CAPITOL RECORDS, INC., a Delaware corporation; ATLANTIC RECORDING CORPORATION, a Delaware corporation; ARISTA RECORDS, INC., a Delaware corporation; UMG RECORDINGS, INC., a Delaware corporation; and VIRGIN RECORDS AMERICA, INC., a California corporation,	Case No. C 03 4085 EMC ADR **ANSWER TO COMPLAINT DENYING ALLEGATION OF COPYRIGHT INFRINGEMENT** *Pleading title* DEMAND FOR JURY TRIAL *request for jury trial*
Plaintiffs,	
vs.	
RAYMOND MAALOUF,	
Defendant.	

Defendant RAYMOND MAALOUF ("Defendant") now answers the Complaint against him alleging copyright infringement, and denies any and all such allegations, and further admits or denies the specific allegations of the Complaint and states affirmative defenses, as follows:

JURISDICTION AND VENUE

1. Defendant admits the allegations of the nature of the case in paragraph 1.   ← *response to complaint*
2. Defendant admits the allegations of subject matter jurisdiction in paragraph 2.
3. Defendant admits the allegations of personal jurisdiction of paragraph 3.

PARTIES

4. Answering paragraph 4 of the Complaint, Defendant lacks information sufficient to form a belief as to the facts alleged, and on that basis, Defendant denies them.

5. Answering paragraph 5 of the Complaint, Defendant lacks information sufficient to form a belief as to the facts alleged, and on that basis, Defendant denies them.

6. Answering paragraph 6 of the Complaint, Defendant lacks information sufficient to form a belief as to the facts alleged, and on that basis, Defendant denies them.

7. Answering paragraph 7 of the Complaint, Defendant lacks information sufficient to form a belief as to the facts alleged, and on that basis, Defendant denies them.

8. Answering paragraph 8 of the Complaint, Defendant lacks information sufficient to form a belief as to the facts alleged, and on that basis, Defendant denies them.

9.   Answering paragraph 9 of the Complaint, Defendant lacks information sufficient to form a belief as to the facts alleged, and on that basis, Defendant denies them.

10.   Answering paragraph 10 of the Complaint, Defendant lacks information sufficient to form a belief as to the facts alleged, and on that basis, Defendant denies them.

11.   Defendant admits that he resides in this District, as alleged in paragraph 11.

ALLEGED INFRINGEMENT OF COPYRIGHTS

12.   Defendant denies the allegations of paragraph 12.

13.   Answering paragraph 13 of the Complaint, Defendant lacks information sufficient to form a belief as to the facts alleged, and on that basis, Defendant denies them.

14.   Answering paragraph 14 of the Complaint, Defendant lacks information sufficient to form a belief as to the facts alleged, and on that basis, Defendant denies them.

15.   Defendant denies the allegations of paragraph 15.

16.   Defendant denies the allegations of paragraph 16.

17.   Defendant denies the allegations of paragraph 17.

18.   Defendant denies the allegations of paragraph 18.

AFFIRMATIVE DEFENSES

Defendant hereby assets the following Affirmative Defenses in this case: ⟵ **affirmative defenses**

19.   Plaintiffs fail to state a claim against Defendant on which relief can be granted.

20.   Plaintiffs have failed to join indispensable parties.

21.   Plaintiffs' claims for relief are barred by the safe harbors of 17 U.S.C. §512.

22.   Plaintiffs' claims would infringe the First, Fourth and Fifth Amendments to the U.S. Constitution.

23.   Plaintiffs' claims are barred by the First Sale doctrine.

24.   The action is barred by the doctrine of Laches, as Plaintiffs made no attempt to enjoin the file-sharing practices of which they complain, and thus have allowed the website www.KaZaA.com to continue to make songs freely available on the Internet to the network of KaZaA users, permitting the practice of music file-sharing from websites such as www.KaZaA.com to continue for a substantial time, so as to become common practice among teenage schoolchildren, freely discussed and utilized in school classes. Plaintiffs' inaction or ineffectiveness in preventing the practices of the users of the KaZaA website, allowing KaZaA's continued viability, has allowed students, including members of Defendant's household, to justifiably assume that any such file-sharing was a completely legal practice. Plaintiffs are thus guilty of laches, in that their inaction thereby lulled such students into the belief that any such file-sharing, especially as an adjunct to school activities, was acceptable to Plaintiffs. Plaintiffs' delay and inaction in allowing such file-sharing by the network of KaZaA users through www.KaZaA.com was inexcusable and prejudicial to Defendant and members of his household by reason of their change of position in reliance as a result of such delay. Plaintiffs' inaction and delay justifiably gave Defendant and members of his household the belief that any file-sharing from the KaZaA website was legitimate and authorized.

25.   Plaintiffs' action is barred by Estoppel, in that, although Plaintiffs knew the facts of any alleged file-sharing by Defendant or his household, Plaintiffs acted in such manner that said household members were entitled to, and did, believe that the continued availability of songs on the KaZaA website was intended by Plaintiffs, and any actions to download were induced by, and done in reliance on, Plaintiffs' conduct.

26.   Any file-sharing by Defendant or members of his household was done, if at all, with Innocent Intent, in that said persons believed in good faith that any such conduct did not constitute an infringement of copyright.

27.   Some or all of the purported infringements alleged by Plaintiffs are barred by the statutes of limitations set forth in section 507 of the Copyright Act, 17 U.S.C. §507, and also set forth in California Civil Code §339(1).

28.   Plaintiffs' claims are barred by the Fair Use doctrine. Any copying or usage of music by Defendant or members of his family or household was done strictly for personal use or nonprofit educational, scholarship, research, criticism or comment purposes put to productive use in studying music and performance styles as an adjunct to school music classes, or in lieu of music classes not offered in school for budgetary reasons, or for use in school classes. The method of sharing music files from the website www.KaZaA.com was freely discussed by teachers and students in schools attended by members of the Defendant's household, universally practiced by schoolmates of said household members, and resulting recordings were openly utilized in school classes attended by said household members. The practice of sharing files through the KaZaA website was thus for the sake of broadening the students' and teachers' understanding of the musical subject matter, and was thus for a socially beneficial and widely accepted purpose. Any such copying was thus without

negative connotation to students, and was indeed encouraged within the school environment. The recordings obtained by said students' file-sharing from the KaZaA website could not have been for any commercial purposes: indeed, during all relevant times, said students, including members of Defendant's household, continued to buy substantial quantities of CDs manufactured and sold by Plaintiffs at high retail prices. Thus any file-sharing by said household members had no adverse effect on the potential market for or value of its copyrighted works. Further, any file-sharing was technologically possible only in obtaining an entire song, regardless of the intended use of the work thereafter. Any file-sharing of songs through the website www.KaZaA.com by Defendant or members of Defendant's household was for nonprofit educational purposes, and thus under the protection of the Fair Use Doctrine set forth in Section 107 of the Copyright Act, 17 U.S.C.§107.

29. Plaintiffs are not entitled to equitable relief, as each of them unduly restricts access to music by assertion of rights beyond those provided in the Copyright Act. As such, Plaintiffs have misused their copyrights and have wrongfully attempted to extend the scope of the limited monopoly granted by the Copyright Act and thereby violate the antitrust laws. Defendant reserves his right to bring an action against Plaintiffs, or any of them, for antitrust violations.

30. Plaintiffs are not entitled to equitable relief, as each is guilty of conduct directly related to the merits of the controversy between the parties, sufficient to affect the equitable relations between the parties, and sufficient to invoke the doctrine of unclean hands. Defendant and his household have been personally been injured by Plaintiffs' said conduct, which continued at least through the time of filing of this action.

31. Plaintiffs' action is barred by the doctrine of Collateral Estoppel, as there has been a prior copyright infringement action that determined that file-sharing analogous to that which Plaintiffs' here assert was not unlawful.

32. Plaintiffs' claims are barred to the extent they claim copyright in works that are immoral, illegal or libelous.

33. Plaintiffs' claims are barred because of deceptive and misleading advertising in connection with distribution of the copyrighted works.

34. Plaintiffs cannot recover as Plaintiffs heretofore waived, licensed, abandoned or forfeited any rights previously held under the Copyright Act, surrendered by operation of law.

WHEREFORE, Defendant prays this Honorable Court for the following relief: ◄——— **prayer for relief**

1. For dismissal of the Plaintiffs' action with prejudice;
2. For an order that Plaintiffs' shall take no relief from their complaint herein;
3. For an award of Defendant's costs and attorneys' fees herein incurred; and
4. For such further and other relief and the Court deems fair and just.

DATED: November 6, 2003

signature block
for attorney ———►

BERG & PARKER LLP
By: _____
Robert Ted Parker

Attorneys for Defendant
RAYMOND MAALOUF

1472.001

PROOF OF SERVICE ⟵—— proof of service

The undersigned declares as follows:

I am employed in the County of San Francisco, State of California. I am over the age of eighteen years and not a party to the within action. My business address is Four Embarcadero Center, Suite 1400, San Francisco, California.

On November 6, 2003, I served the foregoing

Answer to Complaint Denying Allegations of Copyright Infringement

on the attorneys of record/interested parties in this action:

> Howard A. Slavitt
> Julie Greer
> Zuzana Svihra
> Coblentz, Patch, Duffy & Bass LLP
> One Ferry Building, Suite 200
> San Francisco, CA 94111
> (415) 391-4800
> (415) 989-1663 Fax
> Attorneys for Plaintiffs

by placing a true copy enclosed in an envelope for mailing to the following address on the date shown above following our ordinary business practices. I am readily familiar with the business practice at my place of business for collection and processing of correspondence for mailing with the United States Postal Service. Correspondence so collected and processed is deposited with the United States Postal Service that same day in the ordinary course of business.

I declare under penalty of perjury under the laws of the United States of America that the above is true and correct. Executed on November 6, 2003 at San Francisco, California.

_____

Mushen Aldridge[5]

---

[5]Electronic Frontier Foundation. *Sony v. Maalouf*, 2003. http://w2.eff.org/IP/P2P/sony_maalouf_answer.php

EXHIBIT A-6: MOTION FOR SUMMARY JUDGMENT AND MEMORANDUM IN SUPPORT OF MOTION FOR SUMMARY JUDGMENT

[EXH] IN THE UNITED STATES DISTRICT COURT
START HEREFOR THE EASTERN DISTRICT OF MICHIGAN

BARBARA GRUTTER	)
Plaintiff,	) Civil Action No. 97-75928
v.	) Hon. Bernard Friedman
LEE BOLLINGER, et al.,	)
Defendants.	) Hon. Virginia Morgan

DEFENDANT'S MOTION FOR SUMMARY JUDGMENT

Pursuant to Fed. R. Civ. P. 56 and Local Rule 7.1, and for the reasons set forth in the attached Memorandum, defendants hereby move this Court for the entry of summary judgment.

As set forth more fully in the accompanying Memorandum of Law, at the close of extensive discovery in this matter there is no genuine dispute as to any material fact. All of the record evidence confirms that the University of Michigan Law School's admissions processes fully comply with the standards set out in the Supreme Court's decision in *Regents of the University of California v. Bakke,* 438 U.S. 265 (1978). Defendants are entitled to summary judgment on all of plaintiff's claims.

In addition, a separate doctrine bars all of plaintiff's damages claims against the Board of Regents. The doctrine protecting the recipients of federal funds from being sued for money damages where it is not "obvious" that they will be liable in damages applies to the damages claim against the Board of Regents under Title VI. Accordingly, summary judgment in defendants' favor is appropriate on plaintiff's claims for damages, because there is no material dispute – indeed, there is no evidence at all – that defendants violated plaintiff's "clearly established" constitutional rights.

Pursuant to Local Rule 7.1(a), defendants state that on April 29, 1999, concurrence in this motion and the relief sought was requested from plaintiff's counsel and that such concurrence was not granted.

Respectfully submitted,

_____

Philip J. Kessler, P15921
Leonard M. Niehoff, P36695
BUTZEL LONG
350 South Main Street, Suite 300
Ann Arbor, MI 48104
(734) 213-3625
Dated: October 9, 2000

John H. Pickering
John Payton
Jane Sherburne
WILMER, CUTLER & PICKERING
2445 M Street, N.W.
Washington, D.C. 20037
(202) 663-6000

**IN THE UNITED STATES DISTRICT COURT
FOR THE EASTERN DISTRICT OF MICHIGAN**

BARBARA GRUTTER) Plaintiff,) v.) LEE BOLLINGER, *et al.,*) Defendants.) and) KIMBERLY JAMES, *et al.,*) Intervening) Defendants) _____) _____)	Civil Action No. 97-75928 Hon. Bernard Friedman Hon. Virginia Morgan

**DEFENDANTS' MEMORANDUM OF LAW IN SUPPORT OF RENEWED MOTION
FOR SUMMARY JUDGMENT**

John H. Pickering
John Payton
Jane Sherburne
WILMER, CUTLER & PICKERING
2445 M Street, N.W.
Washington, D.C. 20037
(202) 663-6000

Philip J. Kessler, P15921
Leonard M. Niehoff, P36695
BUTZEL LONG
350 South Main Street, Suite 300
Ann Arbor, MI 48104
(734) 213-3625

ATTORNEYS FOR DEFENDANTS

Dated October 9, 2000

TABLE OF CONTENTS

STATEMENT OF THE ISSUE PRESENTED	iii
CONTROLLING AUTHORITIES	iv
TABLE OF AUTHORITIES	v
INDEX OF EXHIBITS	x
INTRODUCTION	1
STATEMENT OF UNDISPUTED FACTS	3
1. The Faculty Admissions Policy	5
a. General Objectives	6
b. Grades, Test Scores, and Their Limitations	6
c. Treating Each Applicant as an Individual	8
d. The Role of Racial and Ethnic Diversity	10
2. The Admissions Process: Implementing the Admissions Policy	14
a. File-by-File Review	15
b. Race as a Single Though Important Element	17
c. The Data	18

ARGUMENT 20

  I. CONTROLLING PRECEDENT PERMITS THE COMPETITIVE CONSIDERATION
     OF RACE IN LAW SCHOOL ADMISSIONS 21

    A. A Properly Devised Admissions Program Involving the Competitive
       Consideration of Race and Ethnic Origin is Constitutional 22
    B. Diversity Is a Compelling Interest in the University Admissions Context 23
    C. *Bakke's* Limitations on the Consideration of Race in University Admissions 29
    D. *Bakke* Is Binding Precedent 32

  II. THE LAW SCHOOL COMPLIES WITH THE BAKKE STANDARD 36

  III. THE BOARD OF REGENTS OF THE UNIVERSITY OF MICHIGAN IS
      ALSO ENTITLED TO SUMMARY JUDGMENT ON PLAINTIFF'S
      DAMAGES CLAIMS UNDER TITLE VI OF THE CIVIL RIGHTS ACT 43

CONCLUSION 49

STATEMENT OF THE ISSUES PRESENTED

1. Whether the defendants are entitled to summary judgment on all of plaintiff's claims because the undisputed factual record shows that the admissions practices of the University of Michigan Law School—which involve the "competitive consideration of race" as a "single though important factor" in order to achieve the benefits of a diverse student body—comport with the standards set out in Justice Powell's controlling opinion in *Regents of the University of California v. Bakke,* 438 U.S. 265 (1978).

2. Whether the Board of Regents of the University of Michigan is entitled to summary judgment on plaintiff's damages claims brought under Title VI because it would not have been "obvious" to the Board of Regents that, by accepting federal funds, it was subjecting itself to liability in damages on account of an admissions system that complies fully with Justice Powell's controlling opinion in *Regents of the University of California v. Bakke,* 438 U.S. 265 (1978).

CONTROLLING AUTHORITIES

* * *

The Law School and the University of Michigan's Board of Regents are entitled to summary judgment on all of the claims for relief—monetary, as well as declaratory and injunctive—brought by the plaintiff in this case. Plaintiff's challenge to any use of race in admissions is foreclosed by *Bakke's* holding, in which a majority of the Court expressly permitted the "competitive consideration" of race as a factor in admissions. And plaintiff's claim that the Law School violates *Bakke* just cannot be squared with the undisputed facts in the record. The extensive record developed in this litigation confirms that the Law School fully complies with *Bakke.* Race is considered as one among many factors in the Law School's admissions process, in order to achieve a diverse student body. Summary judgment in the defendants' favor is therefore appropriate.

CONCLUSION

For the foregoing reasons, this Court should grant Defendants' motion for summary judgment.

Philip J. Kessler, P15921
Leonard M. Niehoff, P36695
BUTZEL LONG
350 South Main Street, Suite 300
Ann Arbor, MI 48104
(734) 213-3625

Respectfully submitted,

_____

John H. Pickering
John Payton
Jane Sherburne
WILMER, CUTLER & PICKERING
2445 M Street, N.W.
Washington, D.C. 20037
(202) 663-6000

ATTORNEYS FOR DEFENDANTS

Dated: October 9, 2000

Dated October 9, 2000

CERTIFICATE OF SERVICE

I hereby certify that on this 9th day of October, 2000, I caused a copy of the foregoing Renewed Motion For Summary Judgment to be served, by courier, on:

David F. Herr, Esq.
Kirk O. Kolbo, Esq.
Maslon, Edelman,
Borman & Brand
300 Norwest Center
90 South Seventh Street
Minneapolis, MN 55402

George B. Washington, Esq.
Eileen R. Scheff, Esq.
Miranda K.S. Massie, Esq.
One Kennedy Square, Suite 2137
Detroit, MI 48226

And, by Federal Express on October 10th, on:

Michael E. Rosman, Esq. Hans F. Bader, Esq. Center for Individual Rights 1233 20th Street, N.W. Washington, D.C. 20036

Kerry L. Morgan, Esq.
Pentiuk, Couvreur & Kobiljak
Suite 230, Superior Place
20300 Superior Street
Taylor, MI 48180

_____

Robin A. Lenhardt
WILMER, CUTLER & PICKERING
2445 M Street, N.W.
Washington, D.C. 20037
(202) 663-6000[6]

[6]http://www.vpcomm.umich.edu/admissions/legal/grutter/grurmsj.html

EXHIBIT A-7: COURT ORDER

IN THE UNITED STATES DISTRICT COURT
FOR THE WESTERN DISTRICT OF TENNESSEE
EASTERN DIVISION

PAULA HAYS,
Plaintiff,

v.   No. 09-01254-egb

HENDERSON COUNTY, BRIAN DUKE,
Individually and in his official capacity as Sheriff of
Henderson County, LEILANA MURPHY and
RANDALL BLANKENSHIP,
Defendants.

ORDER GRANTING SUMMARY JUDGMENT

Before the Court is Defendants' Motion to Dismiss and/or Summary Judgment pursuant to Rules 12 and 56 of the Federal Rules of Civil Procedure [D.E.13] and Plaintiff's response in opposition [D.E.15]. Because the Court finds that Plaintiff's claims are barred by the one-year statute of limitations and equitable tolling does not apply, the Court GRANTS Defendants' Motion for Summary Judgment.

FACTUAL BACKGROUND

Plaintiff Paula Hays ("Plaintiff") was employed as a correctional officer with the Henderson County Sheriff's Department during the relevant time, until she was terminated on May 9, 2008. Brian Duke ("Duke") is the Sheriff of Henderson County, Tennessee. Leilani Murphy ("Murphy") is the Henderson County Jail Administrator and Randall Blankenship ("Blankenship") is the Chief Deputy of the Henderson County Sheriff's Office. While the style of this case does not reflect it, both Murphy and Blankenship, as noted within the Complaint, are sued individually and in their official capacity.

* * *

Because Plaintiff has failed to establish that the doctrine of equitable estoppel applies, the Court finds that the statute of limitations on her claims has run and her claims are time-barred. Defendants' Motion is therefore GRANTED. Consequently, the Court need not address Defendants' remaining defenses.

IT IS SO ORDERED.

s/Edward G. Bryant
EDWARD G. BRYANT
UNITED STATES MAGISTRATE JUDGE
Date: June 9, 2010[7]

---

[7]http://www.tnwd.uscourts.gov/JudgeBryant/opinions/668.pdf

EXHIBIT A-8: REQUEST FOR PRODUCTION OF DOCUMENTS

IN THE UNITED STATES DISTRICT COURT
FOR THE DISTRICT OF DELAWARE

UNITED STATES OF AMERICA,	
Plaintiff,	Civil Action No. 99-005 (MMS)
vs.	
DENTSPLY INTERNATIONAL, INC.,	
Defendant.	

<u>PLAINTIFF'S SECOND REQUEST FOR PRODUCTION OF DOCUMENTS</u>

Pursuant to Fed. R. Civ. P. 34, the Plaintiff requests Defendant to produce and permit inspection and copying of the documents listed in this request. The inspection and performance of related acts shall be made at a site agreed upon by the parties, within 30 days of service of this request.

I.

<u>DEFINITIONS</u>

1. "Agreement" means a contract, arrangement, or understanding, formal or informal, oral or written, between two or more persons.
2. "Any" means one or more.
3. "Communication" means any disclosure, transfer, or exchange of information or opinion, however made.
4. "Dealer" means any person that distributes any products of any other person or purchases or acquires any such product for resale to any other person, such as a dental laboratory, dentist, dental school or government entity.

* * *

II.

<u>INSTRUCTIONS</u>

1. Unless otherwise specified, the documents called for by these document requests are documents in your possession, custody or control that were applicable, effective, prepared, written, generated, sent, dated, or received at any time since January 1, 1985. Documents that have been produced previously by Dentsply in response to Civil Investigative Demand ("CID") Nos. 13009 or 16446 or in response to Plaintiff's First Request for Production of Documents need not be produced again.

2. Unless otherwise specified, the documents called for by these document requests are limited in scope to those responsive documents relating to supplying, manufacturing, distributing, selling, or advertising or promoting products in the United States. For any paragraph that requests documents relating to supplying, manufacturing, distributing, selling, or advertising or promoting products in any country other than the United States, the documents called for include[*sic*] all documents in your possession, custody or control maintained in both the United States or in any other country.

3. Pursuant to Fed. R. Civ. P. 26(e), you are under a duty seasonably to supplement any response to this request for production for which you learn that the response is in some material respect incomplete or incorrect and if the additional or corrective information has not otherwise been made known to us during the discovery process or in writing.

* * *

III.

<u>DOCUMENTS DEMANDED</u>

1. For each salesperson or regional manager listed on Defendant Dentsply International Inc.'s Preliminary Witness Designations, dated March 22, 1999, as likely to be, very likely to be, or will be called as a witness for Dentsply, produce all of the following documents from that person's files and the files of Trubyte Division of Dentsply:

    a. all appointment books or logs, diaries or calendars, prepared or used in the course of employment; and
    b. for all business travel and entertainment expenses incurred on or after January 1, 1998, all statements or other documents relating to such expenses.

2. For each salesperson or regional manager listed on Defendant Dentsply International Inc.'s Preliminary Witness Designations, dated March 22, 1999, as likely to be, very likely to be, or will be called as a witness for Dentsply, produce all of the following documents from that person's files:

a. all correspondence, including electronic mail, with any individual listed on Defendant Dentsply International, Inc.'s Fed. R. Civ. P. 26(A)(1) Disclosure or Plaintiff's Rule 26(a)(1) Initial Disclosures, or with any other representative of the company, organization, or entity for whom such individual works;

b. all documents, including activity reports or notes, that relate to any meeting, telephone conversation, or other communication with any individual listed on Defendant Dentsply International, Inc.'s Fed. R. Civ. P. 26(A)(1) Disclosure or Plaintiff's Rule 26(a)(1) Initial Disclosures, or with any other representative of the company, organization, or entity for whom such individual works;

c. all documents relating to Dentsply/York Division Dealer Criteria (see e.g., DS 040148 produced in response to CID No. 13009), and any pre-existing related policies or practices now embodied in the Dealer Criteria, without regard to the time limitation specified in Instruction No. 1; and

d. all documents relating to any exclusive arrangement with a dealer or to any exclusive arrangement with a dental laboratory or dentist.

* * *

Respectfully submitted,

July 23, 1999

COUNSEL FOR PLAINTIFF
UNITED STATES OF AMERICA

CARL SCHNEE
UNITED STATES ATTORNEY

Judith M. Kinney (DSB #3643)
Assistant United States Attorney
1201 Market Street, Suite 1100
Wilmington, DE 19801
(302) 573-6277

_____/s/_____

Mark J. Botti
William E. Berlin
Frederick S. Young
Michael S. Spector
United States Department of Justice
Antitrust Division
325 Seventh Street, N.W., Suite 400
Washington, DC 20530
(202) 307-0827[8]

Certificate of Service
(properly completed)

[8]http://www.justice.gov/atr/cases/f7400/7449.htm

EXHIBIT A-9: OBJECTIONS TO REQUEST

UNITED STATES DISTRICT COURT
NORTHERN DISTRICT OF IOWA EASTERN DIVISION

UNITED STATES OF AMERICA,	
Plaintiff,	Civil Action No. C94-1023
v.	Hon. Michael J. Melloy
MERCY HEALTH SERVICES AND FINLEY TRI-STATES HEALTH GROUP, INC.,	**RESPONSE TO SECOND REQUEST FOR PRODUCTION OF DOCUMENTS TO UNITED STATES OF AMERICA**
Defendants.	

Plaintiff United States of America makes the following response to the Second Request for Production of Documents to United States of America ("the Second Request").

OBJECTIONS TO THE REQUESTS

The United States objects to the Second Request in its entirety to the extent it requests documents protected from discovery and disclosure by the attorney-client privilege, the deliberative process privilege, the work product doctrine, or any other privilege available under Federal or State statutory, constitutional, or common law.

OBJECTIONS TO DEFINITIONS AND INSTRUCTIONS

The United States objects to the Definitions and Instructions in the Second Request to the extent they attempt or purport to impose obligations greater than those authorized by the Federal Rules of Civil Procedure. The United States objects to the following paragraphs of the Definitions and Instructions of the Second Request, as follows:

A. The United States objects to paragraph A to the extent it calls for production of documents not in the possession, custody or control of the Antitrust Division of the Department of Justice, and to the extent it attempts or purports to expand the obligation of the United States to supplement its response in accordance with Fed. R. Civ. P. 26(e).

C. The United States objects to paragraph C to the extent as unduly burdensome. Without in any way waiving that or any other objection, the United States states that it is unaware of any such documents.

D. The United States objects to paragraph D to the extent it attempts or purports to expand the obligation of the United States to supplement its response in accordance with Fed. R. Civ. P. 26(b)(5).

E. The United States objects to paragraph E as unduly burdensome to the extent it attempts or purports to impose obligations to search all back up or storage systems for computer-generated material. The United States further objects to this paragraph to the extent it attempts or purports to impose on the United States the obligation to translate information in a data base or machine readable form.

* * *

OBJECTIONS AND RESPONSE TO REQUESTS

1. **Produce all declarations, affidavits, deposition transcripts, witness statements, and letters referring or relating to any merger, acquisition, partnership, consolidation, combination, joint venture or other transaction involving hospitals in or around Moline, Illinois, Davenport, Iowa, and/or Des Moines, Iowa.**

We do not understand defendants' reasons for requesting such documents. As such, the United States objects on the grounds that they are irrelevant and not calculated to lead to admissible evidence. Moreover, whatever the intendment of the request, the United States further objects to the extent that producing such documents: (i) could require the United States to disclose the existence of a fling under the Hart-Scott-Rodino Antitrust Improvements Act, 15 U.S.C. 18a, which is specifically prohibited by Section 7A(h) of the Clayton Act; (ii) could improperly invade privacy interests of private parties in violation of 15 U.S.C. 1314(f); and (iii) impair the Justice Department's law enforcement efforts. Finally, the United States objects because, even if there were some marginal relevance, that relevance would be outweighed by the undue burdensomeness of the request, compounded by its being overly broad in scope.

2. **Produce all documents relating to the safety zone for hospital mergers set forth in the Policy Statements of Antitrust Enforcement Policy in the Health Care Area, issued September 15, 1993, including, without limitation, all internal correspondence and communications and all documents and/or correspondence received, dated or effective on or after September 15, 1993.**

The United States objects to this request in part for the same reason that it objects to Request 1, namely, that defendants are targeting the exercise of prosecutorial discretion as part of discovery.

The United States further objects to this request as duplicative of Request 13 of Defendants' First Set of Interrogatories and First Request for Production of Documents and the issues presented in Defendants' Motion to Compel. As set forth in the United States' Opposition to the Motion to Compel, the documents requested are outside the scope of permissible discovery and are protected by the deliberative process privilege.

* * *

Dated: August 12, 1994

————————————————
Mary Beth McGee
Eugene D. Cohen
Jessica N. Cohen

U.S. Department of Justice
Antitrust Division
555 4th Street, N.W., Room 9901
Washington, D.C. 20001
Tel: (202) 307-1027
Fax: (202) 514-1517

VERIFICATION

I, Jessica N. Cohen, declare:

1. I am an attorney with the United States Department of Justice, Antitrust Division.
2. I verify that authorized employees and counsel for the United States assembled the facts stated herein; and that the facts herein are true and correct to the best of my knowledge, information, and belief.
3. I declare under penalty of perjury that the foregoing is true and correct.

Executed in Washington, D.C. on _____, 1994.

————————————————
Jessica N. Cohen[9]

————————————

[9]http://www.justice.gov/atr/cases/f0100/0198.htm

EXHIBIT A-10: REQUEST FOR ADMISSIONS

[EXH] STATE OF INDIANA
COUNTY OF VIGO

Heather Dobbs, Plaintiff	)	
	)	VIGO CIRCUIT COURT
v		CAUSE NO.: 12-C-12-0004
	)	
Paul Roberts, Defendant	)	
	)	

PLAINTIFF'S FIRST REQUEST FOR ADMISSIONS

Pursuant to Rule 36 of the Indiana Rules of Civil Procedure, Plaintiff, Heather Dobbs, by and through her attorneys, requests that Defendant, Paul Roberts, admit or deny the following statements of law. If objection is made, please state the reason for the objection. Please specifically deny the matter or set forth in detail the reasons why the answering party cannot truthfully admit or deny the matter. Also, please note that the term "car crash" refers to the motor vehicle collision which is the subject of this lawsuit and which occurred on or about March 17, 2012.

INSTRUCTIONS

A. Provide separate and complete sworn responses for each Request for Admission ("Request").
B. The Request will be deemed admitted unless, within ten days of service of this request, You serve a sworn written answer to the Request.
C. Your answer should specifically admit or deny the Request or set forth in detail the reasons why You cannot truthfully admit or deny it after exercising due diligence to secure the information necessary to make full and complete answers, including a description of all efforts You made to obtain the information necessary to answer the Request fully.
D. When good faith requires that You qualify Your answer or deny only a part of the matter of which an admission is requested, specify the portion that is true and qualify or deny the remainder.
E. If You consider that a matter of which an admission has been requested presents a genuine issue for trial, You may not, on that ground alone, object to the request. Instead, You must deny the matter or set forth reasons why You cannot admit or deny it.

* * *

DEFINITIONS

A. Concerning" means relating to, alluding to, referring to, constituting, describing, discussing, evidencing, or regarding.
B. "Each" means and includes "each and every," "all" means and includes "any and all," and "any" means and includes "any and all."
C. "Person" means and includes any natural person or any business, legal or governmental entity or association and the officers, directors, employees, agents, consultants and attorneys thereof.

* * *

REQUESTS FOR ADMISSION

1. Admit that you were the registered owner of a 2011 Toyota Tundra with Illinois motor vehicle tags on the date of the car crash.
2. Admit that immediately prior to impact, the vehicle operated by Plaintiff was in the oncoming lane.
3. Admit that you were controlled by a four-way stop sign.
4. Admit that you failed to stop at the four-way stop sign.
5. Admit that Plaintiff did not contribute to the cause of the car crash.
6. Admit that the vehicle that you were driving struck the Plaintiff's vehicle on the passenger's side.
7. Admit that your actions were the sole cause of the car crash.

8. Admit that no other entity contributed to cause the car crash.

9. Admit that Plaintiff was injured as a result of the car crash.

10. Admit that Plaintiff was injured as a result of the car crash caused by you.

11. Admit that you have no evidence of any kind that Heather Dobbs may have caused or contributed to the occurrence by failing to stop at the four-way stop sign.

12. The Defendant has no evidence to support the affirmative defense that the Plaintiff assumed the risk of her injuries.

13. The Defendant has no evidence to support the affirmative defense that the Plaintiff was not contributorily negligent.

14. The Defendant has no evidence to support the affirmative defense that the Plaintiff's case is barred by the Statute of Limitations.

15. The Defendant has no evidence to support the affirmative defense that the Plaintiff's case fails to state a claim upon which relief can be granted.

* * *

26. The medical bill from Pail Rehab, LLC, was reasonable regarding the treatment rendered for the car crash complained of in the Plaintiff's Complaint.

27. The medical treatment rendered by Pain Rehab, LLC was medically necessary and causally related to the car crash complained of in the Plaintiff's Complaint.

28. The medical bill from Vigo County Ambulatory Surgical Center was reasonable regarding the treatment rendered for the car crash complained of in the Plaintiff's Complaint.

29. Plaintiff continues to have pain, weakness, loss of function and loss of endurance as a result of her right leg injury.

30. Plaintiff suffered an injury to his right leg.

31. Plaintiff suffered an injury to his right leg as a result of the car crash caused by your negligence.

Allworthy Law Firm

_____

Jami Myers-Selzer
111 Hulman Street
Terre Haute, IN 47802
(812) 555-1234 telephone
(812) 555-1235 FAX
Bar No. 00123450
Attorney for the Plaintiff

Certificate of Service

I hereby certify that a copy of the foregoing First Request for Admissions was sent via U.S. Mail, first-class, postage prepaid, this 5th day of December, 2012, to:

Robert Ryan
1111 Ohio Blvd.
Terre Haute, IN 47802
Attorney for Paul Roberts

_____

Jami Myers-Selzer

EXHIBIT A-11: RESPONDENT'S RESPONSE TO REQUEST FOR ADMISSIONS

[EXH] UNITED STATES OF AMERICA FEDERAL TRADE COMMISSION

In the Matter of)	
)	Docket No. 93 15
Evanston Northwestern Healthcare)	**(Public Record Version)**
Corporation,)	
a corporation, and	
)	
ENH Medical Group, Inc.,)	
a corporation.)	

RESPONDENTS' ANSWERS AND OBJECTIONS TO
COMPLAINT COUNSEL'S NINTH REQUEST FOR ADMISSIONS
CONCERNING AUTHENTICITY AND ADMISSIBILITY

Pursuant to the Federal Trade Commission's Rules of Practice ("Rules"), 16 C.F.R. § 3.32, Respondents hereby file their answers and objections to Complaint Counsel's Ninth Request for Admissions to Respondents Evanston Northwestern Healthcare Corporation ("ENH") and ENH Medical Group, Inc. ("ENH Medical Group").

General Objections

The following general objections ("General Objections") apply to all of Complaint Counsel's Ninth Requests for Admissions ("Requests") and are incorporated by reference into each answer made herein. The assertion of the same, similar, or additional objections or the provision of partial answers in the individual responses to these Requests does not waive any of Respondents' General Objections as set forth below:

1. Respondents object to the Requests on the grounds that they have already provided Complaint Counsel with detailed reports of what they currently believe to be the "complete set" of each payor's authentic contracts with Highland Park Hospital ("HPH") and/or ENH. These detailed reports were provided to Complaint Counsel with the understanding that the reports may need to be modified and/or supplemented because discovery is ongoing, several third parties have yet to respond fully, or at all, to outstanding subpoenas and witnesses with potentially pertinent testimony to the Requests have yet to be deposed.

2. Respondents object to the Requests to the extent that they require responses greater than, beyond the requirements of, and/or at variance to the Rules. In particular, Complaint Counsel already has exceeded its limit of 50 requests for admissions. Although there is no limit on the number of requests for admission as to the authentication of documents, more than 50 of Complaint Counsel's prior Requests do not fall into this requirements of, and/or at variance to the Rules. Complaint Counsel nonetheless repeatedly asks Respondents in these Requests to admit that certain documents constitute a "complete set" of contracts with particular third party payors, thus requesting Respondents to admit that the contracts at issue were contracts at issue were not amended or superseded. These Requests for substantive admissions beyond the applicable limit are not authorized by the Rules or the scheduling orders entered in this case. Respondents' answers below are thus limited to addressing whether the documents at issue are authentic. No answer below shall be deemed to have waived this general objection.

3. Respondents object to the Requests to the extent that they seek information that is protected from disclosure by the attorney-client privilege, the work product doctrine or any other recognized privilege.

* * *

Answers and Specific Objections to Requests for Admissions
REDACTED
Highland Park Hospital

1748. The document attached to this Request for Admissions as Exhibit CX-05211 is authentic, genuine, and a true and correct copy of a contract (plus related papers) between REDACTED and Highland Park, effective REDACTED. The contract is a business record of one or both contracting parties. The contract is admissible into evidence in this matter.

ANSWER: Subject to and notwithstanding the general objections, Respondent's refer Complaint Counsel to the contract index attached hereto as Exhibit A.

1749. The document attached to this Request for Admissions as Exhibit CX-05212 is authentic, genuine, and a true and correct copy of an amendment (plus a cover letter), effective REDACTED, to CX-05211. The amendment is a business record of one or both parties to the amendment. The amendment is admissible into evidence in this matter.

* * *

VERIFICATION

I declare under penalty of perjury is true and correct to the best of my knowledge and recollection. Executed on ___ day of September, 2004.

_____

Jeffrey Hillebrand
Chief Operating Officer
Evanston Northwestern Healthcare Corporation

I declare under penalty of perjury that the foregoing is true and correct to the best of my knowledge and recollection. Executed on this _____ day of September, 2004.

_____

Dr. Joseph Golbus
President
ENH Medical Group, Inc.

Respectfully Submitted,

_____

Duane M. Kelley
WINSTON & STRAWN LLP
35 West Wacker Dr.
Chicago, IL 60601-9703
(312) 558-5764
Fax: (312) 558-5700
Email: dkelley@winston.com
Michael L. Sibarium
Charles B. Klein
WINSTON & STRAWN LLP
1400 L Street, NW
Washington, DC 20005
(202) 371-5700
Fax: (202) 371-5950
Email: msibarium@winston.com
Email: cklein@winston.com

Attorneys for Respondents

Certificate of Service[10]

---

[10]http://www.ftc.gov/os/adjpro/d9315/040907respanswertoccs9thrfac.pdf

Appendix **II**

NON LEGAL CITATIONS

Students may have some familiarity with citation format in standard bibliographies for research papers written in classes other than paralegal classes. There are two primary formats for writing formal, non legal papers: ***Modern Language Association (MLA)*** and ***American Psychological Association (APA).*** Other formats are found in the Chicago Manual of Style; American Medical Association Manual of Style (AMA); and Kate L. Turabian's *Manual for Writers of Research Papers, Theses, and Dissertations,* (popularly referred to as Turabian). Those style guides are not discussed here.

While this is not an English course, it is important to briefly talk about the two main formats, MLA and APA, before delving into legal citation. For the most part, people in social sciences—the academic field in which paralegal studies is usually classified—are more likely to use APA style than MLA. Understanding basic formatting may help with understanding legal citation formatting. In addition, writing papers in the legal world may require the use of these formats. Proper formatting will make students better writers in other classes and in various writing tasks throughout life.

MLA

The MLA, founded in 1883 by teachers and scholars, provides a writing format that is generally associated with writing in the liberal arts and humanities areas, such as English, philosophy, art history, theater, music, modern languages, religion, and history. The MLA publishes two authoritative explanations of MLA style: the *MLA Handbook for Writers of Research Papers* (currently in its seventh edition; for high school and undergraduate research papers) and the *MLA Style Manual and Guide to Scholarly Publishing* (currently in its third edition; for graduate students, professional writers, and scholars).[1] MLA is widely used in education, scholarly and literary journals, magazines, and other content published in the United States and in a number of other countries such as China, Brazil, and India.

Approach

MLA uses a two-pronged approach to citations: the signal phrases and parenthetical citations in text and the ***Works Cited page*** listing. The combination of the two reference points provides the user with a way to credit the sources used in a paper and give the reader a way to retrieve the materials cited. A ***signal phrase*** indicates that a quotation, summary, or other material taken from a source is being used. The citation in text provides information to lead the reader to the Works Cited

Modern Language Association (MLA)

A writing format founded by teachers and scholars that is generally used in the liberal arts and humanities.

American Psychological Association (APA)

A writing format developed by the American Psychological Association primarily for writers in the social sciences and the hard sciences.

> **TIP**
>
> If you are unfamiliar with MLA or APA citation rules, an excellent source that you might want to bookmark is The Owl at Purdue, http://owl.english.purdue.edu

Works Cited page

The last page of an MLA document that provides all sources used within the document.

Signal phrase

A signal phrase introduces information, such as a quotation or paraphrase, taken from a source; usually the signal phrase includes the author's name.

---

[1]Modern Language Association. *MLA Handbook for Writers of Research Papers* and the *MLA Style Manual and Guide to Scholarly Publishing.* 2010. http://www.mla.org/style_faq1

page so the signal information for a book, for example, generally would provide the author and the page (see underline):

<u>Kathryn Myers states</u> that "failure to cite the authority from which you borrow information is plagiarism and subjects a student to various forms of punishment" (93).

If the signal phrase does not identify the author, the author's name would go in the parenthetical reference after the cited material. Note that there is no punctuation between the author's name and the page reference. An example would be the following:

If you fail to cite the authority from which you borrow information, you are plagiarizing the material and you can be subject to various forms of punishment (Myers 93).

If the author were unknown, a short form of the title would appear in the parentheses. Titles of books are underlined or italicized, while titles of articles are placed in quotation marks. In addition, the page number, if known, would be added. If the source is from the Internet, it is acceptable to use a page or paragraph number provided that the material is in a stable form such as a PDF file. Some Internet sources number their paragraphs or screens, so you may be able to use those numbers, such as "par. 3" or "screen 4."

Provide the complete reference with author, title of book, place of publication, publisher, and date on the Works Cited page. The Works Cited list is in alphabetical order by author, or by work if an author is not noted. The Works Cited page provides three main parts, each followed by a period: (1) the author's or editor's name (alphabetized by last name); (2) the title of the work underlined or in italics; and (3) the publishing data, which includes the place of publication, the publisher, and the date of publication.

Tips

Remember, the goal of providing references is to provide the reader with access to the source(s) used. This allows the writer to give credence to what is presented in the document. Without the sources, a reader has no way of knowing that the writer has done anything more than give his or her own opinion. Personal opinion does not carry any weight in a requested research project. If the supervisor or instructor wants personal opinion, that will be stated. Otherwise, the supervisor or instructor is looking for authority in the material presented.

One big issue for many instructors is when students cite a reference that is a whole page long but divided into paragraphs. Many instructors will ask that a reference be provided at the end of each paragraph so that the reader will know for sure that none of the information within the paper comes from any place except the source. It also eliminates the potential for the reader to assume that no source is cited at all.

The Works Cited page always begins on a new page at the end of the paper. The title, "Works Cited," should be centered at the top of the new page. Each entry begins at the margin, but if the entry requires more than one line of information, the second and subsequent lines of an entry are indented five to seven spaces. The entries are double-spaced. Traditionally, the titles of books have been underlined, but newer versions of the MLA style guide simply require that the typeface be distinctive enough to make the title recognizable. If no author of a cited piece is available, begin the entry with the title. When citing a newspaper or magazine article that

---

TIP

MLA on the Internet

There are various sources on the Internet that students might find useful to check MLA format. In the earlier tip, students were given "The Owl at Purdue." Other sites are Long Island University, http://www2.liu.edu/cwis/cwp/library/workshop/citation.htm; MLA Citation Style at Cornell University, http://www.library.cornell.edu/newhelp/res_strategy/citing/mla.html; and Using MLA Style to Cite and Document Sources, http://bcs.bedfordstmartins.com/resdoc5e/RES5e_ch08_s1-0011.html. Remember that sites may come and go, so if the citations provided are not found, a researcher might go to the home page of a source and use any search mechanism that the website provides.

continues on subsequent pages within the issue, list the first page with a plus (+) sign after the page number. This signifies that there are additional pages to the source.

One of the most used but most confusing types of citation is a citation to a website. The citation must include the title of the web page, the name of the entire website, the identity of the organization that posted the website (if different from the website name), the full date the page was created or updated, and the date the writer visited the site. Simply citing the main page is not sufficient. Citing in MLA style is very similar to the format prescribed in *The Bluebook* or *ALWD.*

If citing an Internet newspaper or magazine, use the name of the database and the company that created the database, the library or other organization that provides access to the database, the full date of the article, and the date the site was last visited. If citing a journal, include the volume and issue number as well as the date. *If* the URL of the article is very long, which many are, only include the URL of the home page of the database; however, strive to include the exact URL to the article, if possible. The newest rules indicate that a URL is no longer required unless the reader cannot locate the source without it[2]; however, good practice requires checking with the supervisor to determine whether there is a preference for the URL. Page numbers can be cited in a variety of ways in different databases. There may be a range of pages; the starting page followed by a hyphen, blank space, and period (ex. 10- .); or the total number of pages or paragraphs for the article (7 pp. or 7 pars.). If no page information is given, which does happen on the Internet, leave the information blank so that the reader will know that the page number is absent.

The required content for a Works Cited page depends on the type of source being used. The essence of the companion citation in the Works Cited would be as follows:

Myers, Kathryn. Legal Research and Writing: The Foundational Principles. New Jersey: Pearson/Prentice Hall, 2014.

MLA provides numerous formats specific to the type of source being used. Table APP II-1 provides a few examples of some common MLA citation formatting.

TABLE APP II-1 MLA Citations

Type of Authority/ Source	Citation in Text	Works Cited Page
Book	(Myers, 111)	Myers, Kathryn. Legal Research and Writing: The Foundational Principles. New Jersey: Pearson/Prentice Hall, 2014.
Journal Article	(Castledine, 75)	Castledine, Jacqueline. "In a Solid Bond of Unity: Anticolonial Feminism in the Cold War Era." Journal of Women's History 20.2 (2008): 57–81.
Newspaper Article	(Johnson, A4)	Johnson, Reed. "Michael Jackson's Legacy Won't Be Decided in Court." Los Angeles Times 2 July 2009: A4.
Newspaper on the Web	(Johnson, 2009)	Johnson, Reed. "Michael Jackson's Legacy Won't Be Decided in Court." Los Angeles Times 2 July 2009. 7 July 2009 <http://www.latimes.com/entertainment/news/la-et-michael-legacy7-2009jul07,0,7501191.story>

[2]R-I-T Libraries. Updated by Lara Nicosia. *MLA Citation Format.* 2011. http://library.rit.edu/pubs/guides/mla.pdf

There are many additional rules that we have not touched upon here, such as sources with multiple authors, indirect sources, multivolume works, and literary works. The bottom line in using MLA style is to understand the frame of reference, become proficient in properly citing the sources, and use MLA only when required by a supervisor, instructor, or other person requesting that a document be prepared.

APA

APA style, developed around 1929, is most often seen in the social sciences, such as psychology and sociology, and in the hard sciences (chemistry and biology). Many paralegal instructors will opt for APA style if there is a research paper that is not based in legal authority, such as a research paper on the history of the paralegal profession. The APA publishes the *Publication Manual of the American Psychological Association* (*Publication Manual*) (currently in the sixth edition). Like the MLA model, APA sets forth uniform rules on manuscript format, punctuation, tables, citations, and everything in between.

Approach

In-text citations

APA requires that the author's last name and the year of publication for the source should appear in the line of text, such as "Jones, 1998, found that . . . "and a complete reference should also appear in the reference list at the end of the paper.

Reference list

The reference list provides a method for the reader to access every source used within the paper.

APA recommends that a writer use **in-text citations** that refer the reader to a list of references. An in-text citation gives the author of the source, the date of publication, and sometimes a page number in parentheses. An example of an in-text citation would be the following:

> Myers (2010) states that "failure to cite the authority from which you borrow information is plagiarism and subjects a student to various forms of punishment" (p. 93).

At the end of the paper is the **reference list**. The basic structure of a book citation in the reference list is the author's last name, then initials for first and middle names. If the work has an editor or translator, abbreviate that in parentheses and follow with a period [(Myers, K.)] or [(Myers, K. (Ed.)]. Next indicate the publication year in parentheses followed by a period (2010.). The book title is italicized, and only the first word and the word after a colon are capitalized, followed again by a period [*Legal research and writing: The foundational principles.*] The final element is the two-letter state code or the country name; however, this can be omitted for well-known cities such as London, New York, or San Francisco. The publisher's name is provided, but without "Inc.," "Books," "Publ.," or "Co." if such terms are in the publisher's name [New York: Pearson/Prentice Hall].[3] The entire reference list entry would be as follows:

> Myers, K.L. (2010). *Legal research and writing: The foundational principles.* New York: Pearson/Prentice Hall.

Tips

The basic structure of an article is the author's last name, then initials of first and middle names. Put a comma and ampersand (&) before the last author in the list and a period after the final initial [Myers, K., & Myers, J.]; then give the year of the publication in parentheses with a period [(2010.)]. The third element is the article

[3]American Psychological Association. *The Basics of APA Style.* 2012. http://www.apastyle.org/learn/tutorials/basics-tutorial.aspx

TABLE APP II-2   APA Citations

Type of Authority/ Source	Citation in Text	References
Book	(Myers, 2010)	Myers, K. L. (2010). *Legal research and writing: The foundational principles.* New York: Pearson/Prentice Hall.
Journal Article	(Castledine, 2008, p. 75)	Castledine, J. (2008). In a solid bond of unity: Anticolonial feminism in the Cold War Era. *Journal of Women's History 20*(2) 57–81.
Newspaper Article	(Johnson, 2009, p. A4)	Johnson, R. (2009, July 2). Michael Jackson's legacy won't be decided in court. *Los Angeles Times* p.A4.
Newspaper on the Web	(Johnson, 2009)	Johnson, R. (2009, July 2). Michael Jackson's legacy won't be decided in court. *Los Angeles Times* Retrieved from http://www.latimes.com/entertainment/news/la-et-michael-legacy7-2009jul07,0,7501191.story

title, which is not italicized. Capitalize only the first word and/or the first word after a colon, along with all proper nouns followed by a period [In a solid bond of unity: Anticolonial feminism in the Cold War Era.]. Next is the journal name with the volume, issue, and pages. All important words are capitalized, and the title and volume number are italicized [*Journal of Women's History 20*(2) 57–81.].[4]

The other area of particular concern is the double-spaced reference list. References should be listed alphabetically by author's last name, or alphabetically by title if there is no author; therefore, the author is presented as last name, comma, first initial of first name, period [Myers, J.]; names of multiple authors are separated by a comma and an ampersand (&) [Myers, J. & Myers, K.]. The first word of a title, any proper names, and the first word after a colon are the only words capitalized. Use the abbreviation for page (p.) or pages (pp.) to provide the page numbers from the sources being used. The first line of each reference entry is flush to the left margin. Any subsequent lines of the single entry are indented five to seven spaces to form what is called a **_hanging indent_**.[5] The questions of when to underline and when to italicize are vital, too. APA seems to prefer italics to underlining in the presentation of book or comparable titles.

With our world changing from print to Internet, rules about citing to the Internet are important. It is critical to provide an address for an Internet source that will allow the reader to find the actual source. That means that the general website address is not sufficient. If the work has a **_digital object identifier (DOI)_**, use it. A DOI is part of a system that provides identification of content-related items, such as digital files or physical objects, on digital networks.[6] If the source has no DOI, use an Internet address that is as stable as possible. If the URL is not

---

[4]*Id.*
[5]Bedford St. Martin's. Research and Documentation Online, 5th Ed. *Social Sciences: APA manuscript format.* http://bcs.bedfordstmartins.com/resdoc5e/RES5e_ch09_s1-0008.html#RES5e_ch09_s2-0008
[6]American Psychological Association. *What is a digital object identifier?* 2012. http://www.apastyle.org/learn/faqs/what-is-doi.aspx

TIP

APA on the Internet

Just as for MLA, there are several sites that provide useful information on APA formatting. Those sites comparable to the MLA sites are "The Owl at Purdue" http://owl.english.purdue.edu/owl/resource/560/01/; "APA Citation Style" at Cornell University, http://www.library.cornell.edu/resrch/citmanage/apa; and "Using Principles of APA Style to Cite and Document Sources", http://bcs.bedfordstmartins.com/resdoc5e/RES5e_ch09_o.html

Hanging indent

All lines after the first line of each entry in the reference list should be indented one-half inch from the left margin.

Digital object identifier (DOI)

A DOI attempts to provide a stable, long-lasting link for online articles. A DOI is unique to a document and consists of a long alphanumeric code. Many publishers provide an article's DOI on the first page of the document.

stable, use the home page of the site. No citation of any kind is complete without either the date of the document or the date on which the site was viewed if the document is undated or is fluid, as in the cases of newspapers or online encyclopedias.

APA style focuses on powerful and concise verbiage, which makes it well suited for legal documents that are not governed by *The Bluebook*. In working through legal citations, think of *The Bluebook* or *ALWD* as you do the style guides for non legal papers. In the citation format for non legal papers, rules and proper formats are used to convey information in the appropriate manner; the same is true for legal citations. These rules and procedures help prevent plagiarism.

COMMON ERRORS

There are some common errors that should be avoided. Remember, there are two types of citations: in-text citations and reference page or works cited pages. Make sure that the appropriate format is used in the correct location. For example, authors' names in the reference section are different between the two formats. For MLA, the last name, first name format is used, while in APA, the last name, first name initial format is used. In MLA, all important words are capitalized; in APA, only the first letter of the first word and the first word after a colon, as well as necessary capital letters, are used in the reference, but all capital letters are used in the body of the work for titles. Think of how one uses a source. When using the source in a research paper in psychology, for example, one would cite the source at its point of usage so that the reader knows the difference between the writer's personal knowledge and content that comes from a credited and credible source. Provide the content and then check with the MLA or APA style manual to make sure that the appropriate source information is provided.

Both MLA and APA provide guidelines for formatting manuscripts and using written English. When used properly, both formats help the author demonstrate credibility by accounting for the use of sources within his or her work. Both provide rules for just about every component of a citation, from punctuation to capitalization to italics and spacing, for print resources as well as online resources.

There is something else important about citations. There are numerous online sources of citation information available in addition to The Owl at Purdue. Students may have used Son of Citation Machine (http://citationmachine.net/), NoodleTools (http://www.noodletools.com/), or others. Son of Citation Machine is free, but NoodleTools is a subscription service. While there are services out there that will format citations, a researcher should be familiar with the basic rules. Just because someone puts a citation service online does not mean it is perfect or up-to-date. One should not take a chance that the method chosen by the online service is what is required for the document being prepared. Therefore, knowing the basics of citation formatting and knowing how to check the rules will aid you in a number of ways throughout college and in your career.

Appendix **III**

INTERNET SOURCES

A

A Crash Course in Legal Writing by Bryan A. Garner
   http://www.youtube.com/watch?v=sR72bsOeooE&feature=related

AAfPE
   www.aafpe.org

ABA
   www.abanet.org

About.com. Legal Careers. Top Ten Legal Skills. 2012.
   http://legalcareers.about.com/od/legalcareerbasics/tp/Legal-Skills.htm

About.com. U.S. Government Info. *The U.S. Federal Court System*. 2012.
   http://video.about.com/usgovinfo/The-US-Federal-Court-System.htmn

All Law.com
   http://www.alllaw.com

Administrative Office of the U.S. Courts
   http://www.uscourts.gov/courtlinks/

America Gets a Constitution. 1996–2010. A & E Television Networks.
   http://www.history.com/topics/constitution/videos?paidlink=1&vid=HIS
   _SEM_Search&keywords=constitution&utm_source=google&utm
   _medium=cpc&utm_campaign=constitution&utm_term=constitution
   #america-gets-a-constitution

American Bar Association Model Rules of Professional Conduct
   http://www.abanet.org/cpr/mrpc/mrpc_toc.html

American Bar Association
   www.abanet.org

American Institute for Paralegal Studies Video Lecture Series. Paralegal Legal
Writing: Using the IRAC Method.
   http://www.youtube.com/watch?v=levdy6-Mfa4&feature=related

American Law Institute (Restatements)
   http://www.ali.org

An Introduction to the U.S. Tax Court
   http://www.ustaxcourt.gov/

APA Citation Format With Microsoft Word '07—Research & Term Papers, Part 2.
   http://www.youtube.com/watch?v=w_-RB93hB10

APA style
   http://www.apastyle.org/learn/tutorials/basics-tutorial.aspx

Auto-cite®
   http://support.lexisnexis.com/online/Record.asp?ARTICLEID=Auto_Cite
   _Components

Automated legal form tutorial
http://law.lexisnexis.com/automated-forms/training-/-tutorials

B

"Blue Tips"
(http://www.legalbluebook.com/Public/BlueTips.aspx

C

Casemaker
www.casemaker.us

Cases and Codes
http://www.findlaw.com/casecode/index.html

Center for Professional Responsibility. *Rules of Professional Conduct.* 2013.
http://www.abanet.org/cpr/mrpc/mrpc_toc.html

Centuries of Citizenship: A Constitutional Timeline. 2004.
http://www.constitutioncenter.org/timeline/

Checks and balances
http://videos.howstuffworks.com/hsw/12971-our-constitution-a-system-of
-checks-and-balances-video.htm#

Chief Justice Roberts on the topic of writing
http://www.youtube.com/watch?v=ZIjBzn7rbPE&feature=related

Cohen, Ezra H. *Writing Skills—Part II. How to Write a Brief or Memorandum of
Law.* American Bankruptcy Institute. 2009.
http://www.abiworld.org/committees/newsletters/consumer/vol7num5
/Writing_part_2.pdf

Congressional Monitor
http://www.thecongressionalmonitor.com/?m=20090225

Congressional Quarterly
http://corporate.cq.com/wmspage.cfm?parm1=12

Congressional Record Index
http://www.gpo.gov/customers/cri.htm

Copyright law
http://www.copyright.gov/title17/circ92.pdf

Cornell Law Free *Bluebook*
http://www.law.cornell.edu/citation/

Cornell Legal Information Institute
http://www.law.cornell.edu/opinions.html

Cornell University Law School
www.law.cornell.edu

Cornell University's Legal Information Institute
http://topics.law.cornell.edu/wex/legal_research

Courts of Appeals
http://www.uscourts.gov/courtsofappeals.html

D

Darling, Charles. *Diagramming Sentences.* Capital Community College. 1999.
http://grammar.ccc.commnet.edu/grammar/diagrams/diagrams.htm

Duke Law Library & Technology: Research Tutorials
http://www.law.duke.edu/lib/tutorials/index#

E

eCFR

    http://ecfr.gpoaccess.gov/

Edwards, Richard C. *Researching Legislative History*. 2008.

    http://www.ilga.gov/commission/lrb/lrbres.htm

English Grammar Revolution. 2009–2011.

    http://www.english-grammar-revolution.com/english-grammar-exercise
    .html

English Language. *Relative Pronoun*. 2007–2011.

    http://www.englishlanguageguide.com/english/grammar/relative-pronoun
    .asp

    http://www.lib.berkeley.edu/TeachingLib/Guides/Internet/webeval
    -QuestionsToAsk.pdf

Evaluating Web Sites—Cornell Library

    http://olinuris.library.cornell.edu/ref/research/webeval.html

Evans, Gareth. *International Law at the Coalface: Three Decades of Learning by Doing*. 2010.

    http://www.gevans.org/speeches/speech414.html

F

Fastcase

    https://www.fastcase.com/

Federal Constitution

    http://www.gpoaccess.gov/constitution

Federal Government

    http://www.usa.gov/Agencies/State_and_Territories.shtml

Federal Judicial Center. *Impeachments of Federal Judges*

    http://www.fjc.gov/public/home.nsf/hisj

Federal Judiciary home page

    http://www.uscourts.gov/Home.aspx

Federal Trade Commission v. Whole Foods Market, Inc., No. 07-5276. 2008.

    http://www.ftc.gov/os/caselist/0710114/080114ftcwholefoodsproofbrief.pdf

FindLaw

    www.findlaw.com

FindLaw answers

    http://boards.answers.findlaw.com/n/forumIndex.aspx?webtag=fl-answersidx

FindLaw Court TV

    www.courttv.findlaw.com/

FindLaw for Law Students. *Academic Law Journals and Law Reviews*. 2010.

    http://stu.findlaw.com/journals/index.html

Findlaw for Legal Professionals

    http://lp.findlaw.com/

FindLaw forms

    http://forms.lp.findlaw.com

FindLaw: Legal News and Commentary

    http://news.findlaw.com/

Florida Supreme Court. Gavel 2 Gavel. Live Oral Arguments. 2011.
http://www.floridasupremecourt.org/oral_argument/index.shtml

Frame Legal. *Legal Document Drafting & Development.* 2010.
http://www.framelegal.com/legal-documents.aspx

G

Georgetown Law Library. LRW Research Tutorials
http://www.ll.georgetown.edu/tutorials/

Glaeser, D. *How to Read a Judicial Opinion.* n.d.
http://www.class.csupomona.edu/pls/brief.html

Global Legal Information Network
http://www.glin.gov

Google®
www.google.com

GPO Access
http://www.gpoaccess.gov

Guide to Appellate Briefs
http://www.law.duke.edu/curriculum/appellateadvocacy/guide.html

Guide to the House of Representatives
http://www.house.gov/

Guide to the Legislative Archives
http://www.archives.gov/legislative/index.html

Guide to Using the *United States Code Congressional and Administrative News.*
http://www.law.ufl.edu/lic/guides/federal/USCCAN06.pdf

H

Hieros Gamos
http://www.hg.org

International Citation Manual
http://law.wustl.edu/wugslr/index.asp?id=5512

How to Brief a Case
http://www.law.uh.edu/lrw/casebrief.pdf

How to Find Regulations
http://lscontent.westlaw.com/images/content/FindRegulations10.pdf

How to Research Secondary Sources with LexisNexis
http://www.youtube.com/watch?v=j2FpK24vsAg

How To Format Your Appellate Brief Part 1. 2008.
http://www.youtube.com/watch?v=olWyDgv2atU&feature=related

How To Format Your Appellate Brief Part 2. 2008.
http://www.youtube.com/watch?v=L7HWVjo-ceI&feature=related

How To Format Your Appellate Brief Part 3. 2008.
http://www.youtube.com/watch?v=ElQA4BkESVk&feature=related

How To Format Your Appellate Brief Part 4. 2008.
http://www.youtube.com/watch?v=QmjSB9KBczQ&feature=related

How To Format Your Appellate Brief Part 5. 2008.
http://www.youtube.com/watch?v=nx_nfqm40gg&feature=related

Howcast. *How to Understand the American Judicial System.* n.d.
   http://www.howcast.com/videos/425723-How-to-Understand-the
   -American-Judicial-System

Hamp, Bonnie. *The Unauthorized Practice of Law: A Paralegal's Duty and Responsibility.* 2005.
   http://webster.utahbar.org/barjournal/2006/01/the_unauthorized_practice
   _of_l.html

I

I'm Just a Bill. School House Rock
   http://www.youtube.com/watch?v=3eeOwPoayOk

Indiana University School of Law
   www.law.indiana.edu/lawlibrary/index.shtml

Internet Legal Research Group
   www.ilrg.com

Internet Legal Research Group (journals)
   http://www.ilrg.com/journals.html

In-text Citations
   http://www.youtube.com/watch?v=XQ8fy7SPotM

Introduction to Basic Legal Citation
   http://www.law.cornell.edu/citation/

J

Jim Calloway, Oklahoma Bar Association. *The Initial Client Interview.* 1998–2012.
   http://www.okbar.org/members/map/articles/interview.htm/

John Jay College of Criminal Justice. *How to Brief a Case.* 1999.
   http://www.lib.jjay.cuny.edu/research/brief.html.

Judith S. Kaye, C.J. *A Court System for the 21st Century.* PBS Video. 2009–2012.
   http://video.pbs.org/video/1972297584/

Jurist
   http://www.jurist.law.pitt.edu

Justia.com U.S. Laws
   http://law.justia.com/

Justia.com U.S. Federal and State Courts
   http://www.justia.com/courts/

L

Law by Source: Federal
   http://www.law.cornell.edu/federal/opinions.html

Law Library of Congress
   http://Thomas.loc.gov
   www.loc.gov/law

Law Library of Congress's Guide to Law Online
   http://www.loc.gov/law/help/guide.html

Law School 2009: Getting Started with Online Research
   http://west.thomson.com/productdetail/1-5785-5/RM157855/productdetail.aspx

Law School 2009: How to Check Citations
   http://west.thomson.com/productdetail/1-5790-5/RM157905/productdetail.aspx

Law School 2009: Westlaw Research Guide
http://west.thomson.com/productdetail/1-5782-5/RM157825/productdetail.aspx

Law School 2010: Administrative Law Fundamentals
http://lscontent.westlaw.com/images/content/AdminLaw10.pdf

Law School 2010: Getting Started with Online Research
http://lscontent.westlaw.com/images/content/GettingStarted10.pdf

Law School 2010: How to Check Citations
http://lscontent.westlaw.com/images/banner/SurvivalGuide/PDF08
/08HowCheckCitations.pdf

Law School 2010: How to Find Statutes
http://lscontent.westlaw.com/images/banner/SurvivalGuide/PDF08
/08HowFindStatutes.pdf

Law School 2010: Statute Fields on Westlaw
http://store.westlaw.com/documentation/westlaw/wlawdoc/wlres/statutef.pdf

Law School 2010: The Federal Legislative Process
http://lscontent.westlaw.com/images/content/FedLegis10.pdf

Law School 2010: Westlaw Research Guide
http://west.thomson.com/documentation/westlaw/wlawdoc/lawstu
/lsrsgd06.pdf

Law School Videos—How to look up legal citations
http://www.youtube.com/watch?v=C56DOOncOfo

Law.com
http://www.law.com

Lawsource.com
http://www.lawsource.com

'Lectric Library
http://www.lectlaw.com

Legal Documents
http://www.docstoc.com/search/memorandum-of-law-in-support-of
-motion-for-summary-disposition-or-judgment/

Legal Citation Style Guide
http://www.legalcitation.net/

LexisNexis
http://www.lexisnexis.com/

LexisNexis Academic—Legal Research Guide
http://www4.nau.edu/library/reference/LexisNexisAcademic.htm

LexisNexis Academic: Find a Specific U.S. Legal Case
http://www.youtube.com/watch?v=17E6Q1hmciY&feature=
player_embedded#!

LexisNexis Communities Portal. Free case law. 2011.
http://www.lexisone.com/lx1/caselaw/freecaselaw?action=FCLDisplayCase
SearchForm&l1loc=L1ED&tcode=PORTAL

LexisNexis Headnotes
http://web.lexis.com/help/multimedia/detect.asp?sPage=hn2

LexisNexis Home Page
  http://www.lexisnexis.com/our-solutions/us-solutions/

LexisNexis Paralegal User's Guide
  http://www.lexisnexis.com/documents/LawSchoolTutorials
  /20070511013250_small.pdf

LexisNexis Product Tutorials
  http://www.lexisnexis.com/community/downloadandsupportcenter
  /media/p/4332.aspx

LexisNexis Take a Tour
  http://web.lexis.com/help/multimedia/detect.asp?sPage=shepards

LexisNexis training
  http://www.lexisnexis.com/support/training/

LexisNexis (Free)
  www.Lexisone.com www.lexisone.com

Library of Congress
  http://www.loc.gov/index.html

List of Sections Affected via GPO Access
  http://www.gpoaccess.gov/lsa/browse.html

Little Wayne Deposition Video. 2012.
  http://www.youtube.com/watch?v=bKwHSi3MG9o

LLC
  http://www.gamequarium.org/dir/SqoolTube_Videos/Reading_and
  _Communication_Arts/Grammar/

LLRX.com
  http://www.llrx.com

LoisLaw
  www.loislaw.com

M

Micha Star Liberty. *California Client Communications Manual: Sample Letters
and Forms.* 2012.
  http://www.youtube.com/watch?v=HMr9Pil8aB4

Michie's Legal Resources
  www.michie.com

Microsoft Trial Settlement Letter
  http://www.house.gov/inslee/issues/microsoft/settlement_letter.html

Minnesota Association of Law Libraries. Locating Legal Information on the
Web
  http://www.aallnet.org/chapter/mall/handout.pdf

MLA Citation Style at Cornell University
  http://www.library.cornell.edu/newhelp/res_strategy/citing/mla.html

MLA Style
  http://www.mla.org/style

Montana YMCA Model Supreme Court, Sample Brief
  http://home.mcn.net/~montanabw/briefsmpl.html

Morgan, Jennifer Bryan, comp. *Research Tools: Research Guides: State Legislative History Research Guides on the Web.* Indiana University Maurer School of Law. 2010.

> http://www.law.indiana.edu/lawlibrary/research/guides/statelegislative/index.shtml

N

National Archives. Federal Register. *Drafting Legal Documents. Principles of Clear Writing.* n.d.

> http://www.archives.gov/federal-register/write/legal-docs/clear-writing.html

NeoK12 Educational Videos. *Active and Passive Voice.* 2010.

> http://www.neok12.com/php/watch.php?v=zX54557d5b767a5a1b76657b&t=Grammar.

NeoK12 Educational Videos. *Past Participles and Present Participles.* 2010.

> http://www.neok12.com/php/watch.php?v=zX550166616d637d594d6863&t=Grammar

NeoK12 Educational Videos. *Who and Whom.* 2010.

> http://www.neok12.com/php/watch.php?v=zX744e07045f5f7f427e6559&t=Grammar

NeoK12 Educational Videos. *Participial Phrases and Participles as Adjectives.* n.d.
> http://www.neok12.com/php/watch.php?v=zX0a777b7d4e4b7c0061446b&t=Grammar

NoodleTools
> http://www.noodletools.com/

O

Oral Arguments in the U.S. Supreme Court. 2011.
> http://www.supremecourt.gov/oral_arguments/oral_arguments.aspx

P

Paralegal's Guide to Understanding Legal Citations
> http://www.theparalegalresource.com/legal-citations/?affiliate=PositionTechnologies&cd=13184:0:1:4:13&gclid=CLCM8NWL760CFYe8KgodIkWXrA

Presidential Executive Orders
> http://www.whitehouse.gov/briefing-room/presidential-actions/executive-orders

Purpose of Legal Research
> http://topics.law.cornell.edu/wex/legal_research

R

Research Fundamentals: Case Law Fields on Westlaw
> http://west.thomson.com/documentation/westlaw/wlawdoc/lawstu/lscasefd.pdf

Research Fundamentals: Getting Started with Online Research
> http://lscontent.westlaw.com/images/content/GettingStarted10.pdf

Research Fundamentals: How to Check Citations
> http://lscontent.westlaw.com/images/banner/SurvivalGuide/PDF08/08HowCheckCitations.pdf

Research Fundamentals: How to Find Cases
> http://lscontent.westlaw.com/images/content/FindCases10.pdf

Research Fundamentals: Using West's National Reporter System
http://lscontent.westlaw.com/images/banner/documentation/2009
/NationalReporter09.pdf

Research Fundamentals: Westlaw Research Guide
http://west.thomson.com/documentation/westlaw/wlawdoc/lawstu
/lsrsgd06.pdf

Rominger Legal
http://www.romingerlegal.com/

S

Sample memorandum
http://www.whatsyourauthority.com/Memorandum.pdf

Sample settlement letter
http://net.educause.edu/ir/library/pdf/CSD4832.pdf

Sample settlement letter RIAA (Recording Industry Association of America)
http://www.haverford.edu/acc/docs/policies/copyright/riaa-2007-02-28
/example-riaa-settlement-letter-2007-02-28.html

San Diego County Public Law Library
www.sdcll.org

School House Rock Adverbs
http://www.schooltube.com/video/054c4aca89b412d90612/

School House Rock Grammar Rock Pronouns
http://www.schooltube.com/video/b107082c0278a820f5b3/

School House Rock Unlock Your Adjectives
http://www.schooltube.com/video/964198d6a8d99911f4dc/

Secondary Sources
http://www.youtube.com/watch?v=oOzcqg805sQ

Senate Journal
http://memory.loc.gov/ammem/amlaw/lwsj.html

Shepard's® Tour
http://web.lexis.com/help/multimedia/detect.asp?sPage=shepards

Shepard's Citations Service
http://www.lexisnexis.com/government/solutions/research/shepards.aspx

Shepard's Citation on Lexis/Nexis
http://wiki.lexisnexis.com/academic/index.php?title=Shepard's_Citations

Sparknotes. *The Appellate Brief.* 2011.
http://sparkcharts.sparknotes.com/legal/legalwriting/section3.php
#Jurisdictional%20Statement

Son of Citation Machine
www.citationmachine.net

State and Local Government
http://www.statelocalgov.net/

State Constitutions
http://www.constitution.org/cons/usstcons.htm

State Primary Authority
http://www.whpgs.org/f.htm

State Statutes
http://www.law.cornell.edu/statutes.html

Statsky, William P. *Research and Writing in the Law*, 5th Ed.
http://www.clas.ufl.edu/users/usufruct/Law/LAWmemorandumexample
.html

Strategies for Appellate Brief Writing. 2008.
http://www.youtube.com/watch?v=2g0zkjcKOcA

Strauss, Jane. *The Blue Book of Grammar and Punctuation. Who vs. That vs.*
Which Video—Part 1. 2011.
http://www.grammarbook.com/video/who_that_which_1.asp

Supreme Court of the United States
http://www.supremecourt.gov/

T

The Bluebook Online
http://www.legalbluebook.com/Public/Tour.aspx

The Bluebook
http://www.legalbluebook.com

TheLaw.net
www.thelaw.net

The legal memorandum
http://sparkcharts.sparknotes.com/legal/legalwriting/section2.php

The Lemon Law: Sample Demand Letter
http://www.consumeraffairs.com/lemon_law/demand_letter.html

The Library of Congress
www.loc.gov

The National Center for State Courts (Court Structure)
http://www.courtstatistics.org/Other-Pages/State_Court_Structure_Charts.aspx

The National Center for State Courts (Small Claims)
http://www.ncsc.org/Topics/Civil/Small-Claims-Courts/Resource-Guide.aspx

The Owl at Purdue
http://owl.english.purdue.edu

The Public Library of Law
http://www.plol.org/Pages/Search.aspx

The Supremacy Clause and Federal Preemption
http://www.law.umkc.edu/faculty/projects/ftrials/conlaw/preemption.htm

The University of Chicago Manual of Legal Citation (*The Maroonbook*)
http://lawreview.uchicago.edu/resources/docs/stylesheet.1009.pdf

Theodore Forrence, Esq. *Effective Brief Writing.* 2011.
http://www.youtube.com/watch?v=2VbO6WIoiLs

Thomson Reuters (West)
http://www.westpub.com
www.thomson.com

Tutorial on LexisNexis: Finding a Specific Legal Case
http://www.youtube.com/watch?v=17E6Q1hmciY&list=UUHdtFdh_kqhQR
8mGZUYsx4Q&index=3&feature=plcp

Tutorial on LexisNexis: Finding a Specific Document
http://www.youtube.com/watch?v=O4_m9_ZqJmg&feature=related

U

U.S. Constitution
http://www.archives.gov/exhibits/charters/constitution.html

U.S. Constitution
http://www.archives.gov/exhibits/charters/constitution.html

U.S. Constitution
http://www.usconstitution.net/const.html

U.S. Constitution. Legal Information Institute. Cornell University Law School.
http://www.law.cornell.edu/constitution/constitution.articlevi.html

U.S. Court of Appeals for the Armed Forces
http://www.armfor.uscourts.gov/

U.S. Court of Federal Claims
http://www.uscfc.uscourts.gov/

U.S. Courts
http://www.uscourts.gov/EducationalResources/FederalCourtBasics
/CourtStructure/ComparingFederalAndStateCourts.aspx

U.S. Customs Court
http://www.cit.uscourts.gov/

U.S. Government Printing Office
http://www.gpoaccess.gov/

Unauthorized Practice of Law by a Paralegal: What It Is and How to Avoid It
http://www.dcba.org/brief/mayissue/2002/art40502.htm

Understanding Citations Tutorial
http://www.lib.utexas.edu/services/instruction/learningmodules/citations/

United Nations
http://www.un.org

University Law Review Project
http://www.lawreview.org

Upcoming Supreme Court Cases
http://www.onthedocket.org/

Updating Your West Digest Search. 2010.
http://west.thomson.com/documentation/westlaw/wlawdoc/lawstu/lsdig06.pdf

USA.Gov. *Government Made Easy. A–Z Index of Government Departments and Agencies.* 2011.
http://www.usa.gov/Agencies/Federal/All_Agencies/index.shtml

Using Secondary Sources on Westlaw. 2010.
http://lscontent.westlaw.com/images/content/UsingSSonWL10.pdf

Using Westlaw to Write a Brief
http://lscontent.westlaw.com/images/content/documentation/2009
/BriefWrite09.pdf

V

VersusLaw
http://www.versuslaw.com/

Video: MLA Citation Format—Put Your Papers & Essays in Perfect MLA Style
http://www.youtube.com/watch?v=EK0CH6ePGgI.

Virtual Chase
http://virtualchase.justia.com/

W

Washburn University School of Law
http://washburnlaw.edu/library/

Washington State Office of Administrative Hearings. (Click on Unemployment Insurance video demonstration.)
http://www.oah.wa.gov/

Westlaw (Free)
www.Findlaw.com

Westlaw
www.westlaw.com

Westlaw. *Briefing Cases.* 2011.
http://lawschool.westlaw.com/shared/marketinfodisplay.asp?code=so&id=4&mainpage=23

Westlaw: How to Check Citations
http://lscontent.westlaw.com/images/banner/SurvivalGuide/PDF08/08HowCheckCitations.pdf

Westlaw Next: Using Topics and Key Numbers
http://store.westlaw.com/documentation/westlaw/wlawdoc/web/wlntopic.pdf

Westlaw Official Site
http://west.thomson.com/westlaw/default.aspx?promcode=601577D29050&searchid=Reprise/Google(R)/Brand/Westlaw&PromType=external

Westlaw Training
http://westlawtraining.west.thomson.com/

Westlaw. *User Guide.* 2010.
http://store.westlaw.com/documentation/westlaw/wlawdoc/web/wlcmgd06.pdf

Westlaw. *Writing an Open Memo.* 2005.
http://lscontent.westlaw.com/pdf/OpenMemo.pdf

What is a Deposition? Atlanta Personal Injury Lawyer Explains. 2011.
http://www.youtube.com/watch?v=CPLsvnvw2uE

Writing and Analysis
http://legalresearch.org/docs/process13.html

Z

Zimmerman, Andrew. *Zimmerman's Research Guide.* 2010.
http://law.lexisnexis.com/infopro/zimmermans/disp.aspx?z=1465

GLOSSARY

A

Abrogation Annulling a former law by an act of legislation, usage, or constitutional authority. Abrogation may be express or implied.

Acknowledgment A declaration verifying that the person identified on the document is the one who signed it, and signed of their own free will.

Active voice A style of writing in which the subject of the sentence performs the action. An example would be, "Paralegal Paula drafted the Table of Authorities." The subject, Paula, is doing the action of drafting.

Adjective A word used to describe a noun or pronoun.

Adjudicate The process that a court or administrative agency undertakes to resolve a dispute.

Adjudication A formal decision rendered by an administrative agency, acting within its quasi-judicial powers.

Administrative agencies Often described unofficially as the "fourth branch," these are organizations created by the executive branch of state or federal government that implement laws made by the legislative branch. Examples are the Environmental Protection Agency or the Occupational Safety and Health Administration.

Administrative code A collection of regulations organized by subject matter.

Administrative decisions Cases decided on the administrative agency level to settle disputes revolving around an agency issue, similar to case law. Written by the administrative law judge.

Administrative hearing A hearing before an administrative law judge.

Administrative law Law that defines the powers, limitations, and procedures of administrative agencies, as well as the rights of individuals who deal with these agencies.

Administrative law judges (ALJs) Also referred to as a hearing officer or hearing examiner, the ALJ is the person who conducts hearings before an administrative agency. The ALJ generally has expertise in the subject matter of the agency.

Administrative matter A hearing before a panel or administrative law judge of an administrative agency.

Administrative Procedures Act A federal statute that governs all procedures before administrative agencies. The same type of statute is also found on the state level.

Administrative regulations The rules of the administrative agencies, similar to the statutes created by the federal and state legislative bodies, which govern how the agency operates.

Advance sheets Monthly pamphlets that provide decided opinions until a volume of opinions is bound. Updates for various services, such as regional reporters and Shepard's, which are issued in the interim of the publication of hardback volumes.

Adverb A word used to modify a verb, adjective, another adverb, or a phrases or clause, by expressing time, place, manner, degree, or cause. Adverbs often end in –*ly*.

Affidavit A written statement of facts confirmed under oath before a person such as a notary public who is authorized to administer an oath.

Affirmed A court of appellate jurisdiction declared that a judgment or order of a lower tribunal is valid and remains of record. Shepard's: On appeal, reconsideration or rehearing The citing case affirms or adheres to the case being Shepardized.

Alternate terms Synonyms and antonyms of key words that are used in a query to expand the search.

Amended A pre-existing law has been corrected or changed.

American Bar Association (ABA) The country's largest voluntary professional association of attorneys. The goals of the ABA are to promote professionalism and advance the administration of justice. The ABA approves paralegal programs which voluntarily submit their materials for approval.

American Psychological Association (APA) The writing format most often used in the social sciences, such as psychology and sociology, and in the hard sciences (chemistry and biology).

Amicus Curiae A "friend of the court."

Analogous Sufficiently similar. Usually refers to a comparison of the facts and issues of a case with the facts and issues of a client's situation. Also referred to as "on point" or "on all fours."

Angle brackets Brackets used to enclose web addresses.

Annotated Enhancements, such as cross references and case headnotes, that provide a better understanding of the material, as well as a method of research.

Annotated code A source for statutes, whether federal or state, that includes supplemental material such as citations to other primary and secondary authorities that explain or provide context for the statute.

Annotations Notations that explain or comment upon the meaning of the information presented. When appended to statutes, the material is referred to as an annotated code or annotated statute.

Answer The response to the complaint, drafted in numbered paragraphs that mirror the causes of action in the complaint.

Antecedent A word, phrase, or clause to which a pronoun refers.

Appeal Asking a higher court to review the decision of a lower court.

Appellant The party who brings the appeal.

Appellate briefs Written arguments submitted to a court of appeals to support a party's position. The briefs argue for or against the lower court's decision and request that the decision be affirmed, modified, or reversed.

Appellate jurisdiction The authority of a court to review a lower tribunal's decision.

Appellee The party who must respond to an appeal.

Appositive A word, phrase, or clause that is placed beside another word, phrase, or clause so that one explains the other. Both clauses must have the same grammatical construction.

Article A word such as *a, and,* or *the* that is used as an adjective.

Article I courts Legislative courts created by Congress from the power given in Article I of the Constitution.

Article III court Courts that are created or established under article III, Section 1, of the United States Constitution.

Associate justices The Associate Justices are the eight Justices who, along with the Chief Justice, make up the U.S. Supreme Court.

Attestation A statement certifying that a document was signed in a certain capacity.

Attorney General (AG) The chief law enforcement officer in each state and the federal government.

Authorization A document that gives authority to turn over documents or records, such as a medical authorization.

B

Bench trial A trial in which the judge decides both questions of law and fact.

Bicameral Legislatures having two bodies or two houses, such as Congress, which has the House of Representatives and the Senate.

Bill of Rights The first ten amendments to the U.S. Constitution setting forth our rights, freedoms, and responsibilities, such as freedom of speech, freedom to be free from unwarranted searches and seizures, and the right to a speedy trial.

Bills A proposed law that is identified by the house in which it originates, such as H.R. for House Resolution or S. for Senate.

Binding authority Authority that is enforceable or must be followed.

Black letter law The fundamental concepts in the law, or the basic legal principles.

Block quotation A quotation containing 50 or more words that is identified by indenting the quotation by wider margins, narrower text space, and closer line spacing. A block quotation is not enclosed by quotation marks.

Block style formatting A style of formatting in which all text is flush on the left margin. Paragraphs are single spaced with a double space between paragraphs.

Bluepages The section of *The Bluebook* that contains the major rules that legal practitioners use in daily work such as in legal memoranda and court documents.

Blue tips The online reference section for frequently asked questions about citation format.

Boilerplate Standard, uniform language used in a legal documents that is used in all similar legal documents.

Boilerplate A form with standardized language that must be modified for a user's circumstances.

Boilerplate forms Standard forms that provide a starting point for drafting documents.

Brief bank A collection of various trial and appellate briefs that a law firm may have filed in previous cases.

C

Candor An ethical principle that requires a practitioner to be open and honest.

Candor to the court The requirement that the attorney disclose to the court any legal authority known to the lawyer to be directly adverse to the client's position, even if the opposing attorney does not disclose the adverse authority.

Canon law Law governing the Catholic Church during medieval times.

Caption The heading of the complaint; appears on all subsequent pleadings in a lawsuit. The heading of a document. The party names, the docket number, and the date of decision, along with the name of the court that decided the case.

Case The word *case* has different meanings depending on the context. In legal research, a case is a dispute before a court of law, or a lawsuit. It also refers to a written opinion of a judge or court that decides or comments on a lawsuit. A "case on point" is a case that may serve as precedent for a current matter. The phrase "case law" refers to the law laid down in the decisions of the courts in similar cases that have been previously decided. The phrase "case of first impression" means that the court has not previously decided a particular issue arising in the case, and the court is therefore hearing the issue for the first time without any precedent to guide it. A casebook is a book containing court decisions and other materials in a specific field of law. Generally, it is used for teaching students.

Case analysis The study of law based upon analyzing opinions written by judges and justices in actual cases. Also called "case method."

Case brief A summary of a legal opinion or case.

Case law Judicial opinions issued by courts affect how other laws are interpreted or applied. Judicial opinions in cases have the effect of modifying existing laws. In addition, the judiciary can find that certain laws are unconstitutional, which renders them invalid.

Case or controversy A requirement that courts will decide cases only when there is some actual disagreement as a reason for bringing the lawsuit.

Case reporters Books containing cases that have been decided by courts of law. They are grouped according to designations set either by the courts themselves (official reporters) or by publishing companies such as West (unofficial reporters).

Cases The collection of court decisions that comprises case law.

Cases of first impression Cases that involve new issues or questions that have not been decided by the courts in a particular jurisdiction.

Cause of action The plaintiff's reason for bringing suit. The cause of action must allege enough facts to support a claim, and provide a basis for the court to grant some kind of relief. The legal basis of a complaint.

Central form file This is an office file of documents to use as forms for new documents.

Cert denied A decision in which a higher court has exercised its discretion to not accept or hear an appeal from a lower court. The decision is effected by refusing to issue a writ of certiorari, which would have require the lower court to produce a certified record of the case for purposes of appellate review. Although the higher court refused to hear the case, the lower court's decision is still good law, and further appeal may still be possible.

Cert granted A higher court has exercised its discretion to accept or hear an appeal from a lower court. The decision is effected by agreeing to issue a writ of certiorari, a common law process requiring the lower court to produce a certified record of the case for purposes of appellate review. If cert is granted, there will likely be a subsequent order or opinion by the higher court deciding the appeal.

Certificate of service A certificate verifying that all parties involved in the action have received copies of the document being filed.

Characterizing facts Assigning alternate or different words to describe the same fact.

Charters The fundamental law of a municipality or local governmental unit which authorizes the entity to perform designated governmental functions.

Chattels Personal property, as distinguished from real property (land).

Checks and balances A system that guarantees no one branch of government will become all-powerful.

Chief Justice The Justice on the U.S. Supreme Court with the administrative authority to assign cases and preside over the Court.

Citation A combination of words, letters, and numbers that helps the user find the source of the information being quoted or referenced. The "address" of a source, such as 42 U.S.C.A. § 100 (West 2000), which means the reader should look in Title 42 of the *United States Code Annotated* under section 100 for the statute. Reference to a legal authority that provides an address that can be used to find that authority in legal publications. Information that helps the researcher locate material in a law library or online. A citation is also called a *cite*. Letters and number combinations, or other identifying information, that helps the reader find the source of the materials being used.

Citation clause Placement of a citation within the textual sentence where it is not a key part of the sentence.

Citation manual A manual providing a standard for legal citations, and acting as a depository or warehouse of accepted citation practices. The two primary resources are *Bluebook: A Uniform System of Citation, 18th Ed.*, and *ALWD* and *ALWD Citation Manual: A Professional System of Citation, 3rd Ed.*

Citation sentence Placement of a citation in a separate sentence following the textual sentence and containing only the citation.

Citator A research tool that is used to update or validate legal authorities so that those authorities are confirmed as "good law."

Cite check The citation format is checked for accuracy. This includes: 1) accuracy in format, 2) accuracy of the authority ("good law"), and 3) accuracy of any quotations.

Cited case A case that was found as a result of research, is on point, and is being Shepardized.

Citing case The case that cite the authority that has been Shepardized; other cases that have used the cited case in their analyses.

Civil case A lawsuit to enforce a right or to obtain compensation for a wrong (other than a criminal offense) done by a party to another party. These cases usually involve money damages or equitable relief (such as an injunction or specific performance).

Civil dispute A legal dispute over any matter other than a criminal matter, and involving issues that are not criminal in nature.

Civil law 1) Any law that is not criminal in nature, or 2) A legal system originating in continental Europe that emphasizes codified law, rather than case law.

Code The published statutes of a jurisdiction that are arranged in a systematic form.

Code books Books that house the statutes passed by state and federal legislatures.

Code of Federal Regulations (C.F.R.) An annual publication of all executive agency regulations published in the Federal Register that are still in effect.

Codified Collecting and arranging the laws in a systematic order with like materials (such as by subject or topic) in the same location within the statute books. The laws inform the public of acceptable and unacceptable behavior.

Collective noun A noun that is singular in form but identifies a group of individuals. A collective noun is treated as singular when the collection is thought of as a whole (jury) and as plural when the individual members are thought of as acting separately (jury members).

Comma splice A type of error that occurs when a comma is incorrectly used to forge two sentences or independent clauses together. It can be corrected by separating the two sentences into independent sentences with a period, or by using a semicolon, or a coordinating conjunction and a comma, to join the two independent clauses together.

Commentary The section of a case brief allows the researcher to make personal comments, presents update information, and lists other information that may be applicable to the case being briefed.

Commerce clause The clause in the U.S. Constitution that gives Congress the power to regulate commerce between the states and between the U.S. and foreign countries.

Common law Law that is found in the decisions of courts rather than in the statutes made by legislatures. It is also called "judge-made law." The roots of our common law come from the English law adopted by the early American colonies.

Compensatory damages Damages that compensate the injured party for some type of loss such as cost of repairing or replacing an automobile, lost wages from work, hospital and doctor bills, or property damage.

Complaint The document that initiates a civil lawsuit where the plaintiff states a cause of action against the defendant.

Compound predicate Two predicates to the sentence.

Compound subject Two subjects in a sentence.

Comprehensive brief A case brief that contains the citation, parties, objectives, theories of litigation, history of the case, key facts, issues, holdings, reasoning, disposition, and commentary.

Computer-assisted legal research or CALR Research using subscription-based services such as Westlaw® or Lexis/Nexis®, among others.

Conciliatory Willing to make concessions.

Concurrent jurisdiction Exists when two or more courts have jurisdiction over the same lawsuit.

Concurring opinion An opinion in which a judge agrees with the decision of the majority, but has different reasons for the decision.

Conference committee A joint committee consisting of members of each legislative house that seeks a compromise on disputed versions of the bill; it makes recommendations to full Congress.

Confidentiality An ethical duty requiring that private communications not be disclosed to others.

Conflicts of law Situations in which the laws of more than one jurisdiction may be applied to the case, and yet will yield a different outcome. The decision of the court depends on the jurisdictional laws that the court applies to the case.

Conjunctive adverb An adverb used to connect two independent clauses. A semicolon follows the first clause, then the conjunctive adverb is included, and the conjunctive adverb is followed by a comma.

Connected case A citing case that is related to the case being *Sheparded* in that it arises out of the same subject matter, or involves the same parties.

Connecting language Connecting language is the use of terms such as "and", and "or" in a statute. If "and" is used, all elements are required. If "or" is used, a choice of elements is allowed.

Connectors Words in a query that tell the computer how the terms will appear in the retrieved documents.

Constitution The fundamental document that the people of the United States, through their representatives, adopted at the Constitutional Convention in 1787. It is the supreme law of the land. In addition, each state has its own constitution.

Context facts Facts that add additional information to the key facts; also called explanatory facts.

Contingency Issue An additional issue that may be raised if the case results in an outcome that was not anticipated.

Conventional international law Law that comes from international agreements and accepted practice among nations.

Coordinating conjunction A simple conjunction such as *and, but*, or *nor* that joins parts of the sentence.

Counteranalysis A portion of the interoffice memorandum that identifies the opposing side's strongest arguments.

Counts Separate numbered paragraphs that allege the particular facts that constitute each cause of action.

Court of International Trade A court that reviews civil actions arising out of import transactions and federal statutes affecting international trade.

Courts of Equity Courts that determine results when the loss cannot be measured in money damages.

Crane Analysis Lifting language out of a case and placing it within a memorandum or other document without laying a proper foundation for using the quoted content.

Criminal action or case An action brought by some governmental entity (prosecutor, district attorney, state's attorney, U.S. Attorney General) involving an allegation that a crime has been committed.

Criticized The citing opinion disagrees with the reasoning or result of the case being *Shepardized*. The citing court may not have authority to materially affect its precedential value.

Cross-references References to other authorities that provide additional information.

CRRACC A type of case brief; the acronym stands for **C**onclusion, **R**ule, **R**ule Proof, **A**pplication, **C**ounterargument, and **C**onclusion.

Current index A supplemental index to the main index in some looseleaf services that is similar to advance sheets or pocket parts.

Customary law Law that exists based on nations operating out of a sense of legal obligation and in the normal or usual practice.

D

Damages A money judgment awarded in a civil action when a person has a loss as a result of injury, whether from a negligent or intentional act, or some other unlawful act or omission by another.

Dangling modifier A word or phrase that modifies a word that is not expressly stated within the sentence.

Decision A determination that is arrived at by a judge or a panel of judges after considering the relevant facts and the law that applies to those facts.

Declarations Formal statement as to certain facts.

Declaratory judgment A judgment that specifically states the rights of the parties, but does not order relief in the form of damages.

Defendant The person against whom an action is filed.

Defense A position that relieves the defendant of his or her responsibility to the plaintiff.

Demand letter Formal correspondence from an attorney to a party or other attorney demanding that action be taken or requesting a settlement of a claim or dispute.

Denial A defense made to a complaint which controverts an allegation in the complaint.

Deposition Giving testimony under oath that may be used in court in place of oral testimony.

Depublished A California and Arizona procedure allowing the states' supreme courts to withhold opinions from publication.

Desk book A one volume book meant to be used as a quick reference in lieu of a larger set of books.

Dictum or dicta (plural) Remarks made by a court that have no bearing on the decision, but may indicate how the court would decide future cases, or other matters not contained with the case. Comes from the Latin expression *obiter dictum*, meaning "a remark by the way."

Digest A set of books that provide summary paragraphs of points of law established in cases. Each summary consists of a topic, a key number, and headnote describing the point of law. West digests are organized by topics and key numbers.

Direct object A noun in a sentence that receives the action of the verb.

Disclaimer A statement that disavows or denies responsibility.

Discovery The stage of a lawsuit when the parties obtain information and evidence.

Dismissed History indicating the citing case dismissed an appeal from the case being *Shepardized*.

Disposition The action taken by the court to resolve the case based on the holdings that the court made.

Dispositive motion A motion requesting a court order to end a cause of action.

Dissenting opinion A written opinion of a judge who disagrees with the decision of the majority of judges in a case.

Distinguished The judge in the citing case wrote that it differed from the case being *Shepardized*. The case may be distinguished because it involved dissimilar facts or required a different application of law.

Diversity of citizenship The parties to the lawsuit are from different states and the amount in controversy exceeds $75,000. If those factors exist, a plaintiff may file the lawsuit in either state court where the parties live or where the incident occurred, or may file in the federal court in the state in which one of the parties lives.

Domicile A person's permanent home; the place to which he or she intends to return. Each person can have only one domicile, but can have many residences.

Draw The amount the law firm "takes" from the client's retainer based on billing statements or agreed to terms.

E

Ejectment An action for possession of land.

Elements The major components of a statute or other enacted law that must be proven.

Eleven-part brief A format for briefing cases that contains a citation (caption), parties, objectives and theories of the parties, procedural history, facts, issues, holdings, reasoning, court's order (disposition), comments, and updating.

Ellipsis points A method of indicating to a reader that material from a quotation has been omitted. Ellipsis points in a series of three periods with a space before, between, and after the periods. If the omission comes is the end of a sentence, a fourth period (the sentence period) is added.

Embedded citation A citation placed within a textual sentence, forming a key part of the sentence, without setting it off by commas.

En banc The entire court, rather than just a panel of the court, participates in the decision-making process.

Enabling statute A statute passed by the legislature that allows an agency to exist.

Enacted law Law that is passed by a governmental body charged with creating law in order to set guidelines in place for future behavior.

Engrossed bills A proposal that has been discussed and approved by appropriate committees and which is prepared in a final form so that it can be voted on by the legislative bodies.

Enrolled bills The final copy of a bill or joint resolution that has passed both legislative bodies and which is ready for signature by the appropriate officers and which then will be presented to the President (or governor) for action.

Equity Justice handed down by the chancery courts based on principles of fairness, rather than on rigid rules of common law.

Equivocal language Language that is ambiguous or open to more than one interpretation.

Error of law A mistake in the interpretation or application of the law.

Exclusive jurisdiction Power given to a court to hear a certain type of matter, which no other court has the authority to hear.

Executive branch One of the three divisions of government as set forth in the Constitution. The branch of government that is primarily responsible for enforcing the laws.

Executive departments Agencies organized under one of the president's cabinet posts.

Executive orders Orders or regulations that are issued by the president to interpret, begin, or give some administrative affect to a constitutional provision, statute, or treaty.

Exemplary damages A monetary award over and above compensatory damages, to discourage a wrongdoer and others from engaging in the same activity. Usually awarded when it is shown that an act was committed with malice or evil intent. Also called punitive damages.

Exhaustion of remedies In administrative agency cases, proceeding through all levels that an agency offers to resolve a dispute until there is no further recourse at the agency level before appealing to the appropriate state or federal court.

Expander Query tools that tell the computer to automatically search for many forms of a certain term.

Explained The citing opinion interprets or clarifies the case being *Shepardized* in a significant way.

Ex post facto "After the fact." An *ex post facto* law is a law passed after the facts occurred, but change the legal consequences of those facts.

F

Fact A person, place, thing, or event that can be perceived with the senses.

Federalism A form of government in which there is a division of power between a central body and sub-bodies. In the United States, that means that the federal government hold the primary power, but certain power is reserved to the states.

Federal Register A daily publication that makes agency regulations and other executive branch documents available to the public for comment before final adoption.

Finding tool Sources, such as digests, that direct a researcher to other sources.

Followed The citing opinion relies on the case being *Shepardized* as controlling or persuasive authority.

Full faith and credit clause Art. IV, §1 of the U.S. Constitution. This clause states, "Full Faith and Credit shall be given in each State to the public Acts, Records, and judicial Proceedings of every other state."

G

General index Most research materials, particularly finding aids, have an index. The index may be a general index located in separate volumes or may be volume indexes.

General jurisdiction Jurisdiction to hear and decide any type of case.

Gerunds A verb form that ends in *–ing* and serves as a noun is a gerund.

H

Hanging indent The second and subsequent lines of a single entry, indented five to seven spaces from the margin.

Harmless Error Any error that was not prejudicial to the substantive rights of the party who alleges that the error occurred.

Harmonized Treatment indicating that the citing opinion explained an apparent inconsistency and showed the inconsistency not to exist.

Header Identification of a letter on the second and subsequent pages.

Headnote Enhancements to case reports written by West Publishing Company; each headnote states a single point of law that is discussed with the case.

Hearsay Testimony of a statement made out of court by someone other than the person testifying. It is inadmissible because it is a statement made out of court by someone who is not available for cross-examination.

Hits A "slang" term for the number of times a site has been viewed.

Holding The answer to the legal issue or the result that the court reaches when it applies the law to the facts of the case.

Hornbooks Texts that are similar to treatises but are written by law professors for law students.

Hortatory memoranda Presidential memoranda, similar to proclamations, that are issued two executive agencies instead of the public.

I

Id. A note referring the reader to the full citation that immediately precedes the reference in the document. Its main purpose is to save space while still providing the reader with the information necessary to understand the material presented.

IFRAC A case briefing method that summarizes the issue, facts, rule, analysis, and conclusion.

In-chambers opinion An opinion that was rendered by an individual member of the U.S. Supreme Court.

Indefinite pronoun A pronoun that refers in a general sense to a person, place, or thing. Examples are *anybody, anyone, each,* and *few.*

Independent agencies Agencies established by enabling statutes.

Indirect object An object that comes before the direct object, usually identifying to whom or for whom the action is being done.

Informational letter Correspondence that provides information to the reader.

Injunction A court order that commands someone to act, or prohibits an act or conduct; usually imposed in courts of equity.

In personam jurisdiction Jurisdiction over the person.

In rem Jurisdiction that arises because the property that is the subject of the lawsuit is located within the court's geographic area of coverage.

Interlocutory appeal An appeal in which the lower court asks the appellate court to immediately resolve a question before the trial can be completed.

Interlocutory order A provisional or temporary order.

Internal memorandum A document intended for someone within the firm, written in neutral language to present both sides of the law that may control the client's situation.

Internal opinions Other case opinions the court relies on or which the court discusses within its opinion.

International Court of Justice The judicial arm of the United Nations, having jurisdiction to settle legal disputes and give advisory opinions on treaties and other international legal matters.

International Law A body of law that governs the ways nations and international organizations work with each other.

Intervening word A word that comes between the subject and the verb.

In-text citations Citations within the body of a paper that refer the reader to a list of references.

IRAC A popular case briefing method that summarizes the issue, rule, analysis, and conclusion.

IRAC brief A brief showing the issue, rule, analysis, and conclusion.

Issue A question in the case that one is being asked to research.

J

Judge A person, either elected by the people or appointed by an executive of the government, who presides over legal matters and renders a decision.

Judgment In a civil matter, the court decision as to the rights of the parties based on the pleadings filed and the evidence presented; in a criminal matter, the judgment is the determination, or lack thereof, of guilt.

Jurat A certificate usually added to an affidavit, stating when, where, and before whom it was made.

Jurisdiction The authority and power to apply specific types of law (federal, state, or local; criminal, quasi-criminal, administrative, or civil) in a specific geographic area. The power and authority of a court to hear and decide a case.

Jury Instructions Instructions are given by judge to assist the jury in reaching its decision.

K

Key facts Facts that, if different or non-existent, would change the outcome of the case; may be referred to as "relevant facts."

Key number Numbers assigned to each point of law (headnote) by West publishing Company and used in West digests and Westlaw to provide and indexing method to locate points of law.

Key number system An indexing system, designed by West Publishing Company, which assigns numbers to the various legal topics and to the individual headnotes within the topics.

Key topics A set of 400 legal topics developed by the West Publishing Company to organize key numbers and help researchers find legal authorities.

L

Law journals Periodicals published by most law schools, similar to law reviews. These secondary materials consist generally of articles that provide an analysis of new cases or legislation that has been recently implemented.

Law library A library that houses a collection of legal materials.

Law Reviews Periodicals published by most law schools, similar to law journals. These secondary materials consist generally of articles that provide an analysis of new cases or legislation that has been recently implemented.

Layered indexing system A system for supplementing the main index of a looseleaf service with a current index that covers just the revisions issued.

Legal analysis The process by which the law is applied to a client's case to determine what issues are important and what law is relevant to those issues.

Legal authority Any law such as constitution, case, statute, regulation, or other source that may be mandatory (binding) or persuasive to the court's interpretation and application of the law to the evidence presented in a case.

Legal dictionary A dictionary that is similar to a standard English dictionary, but specifically contains definitions of legal terms.

Legal Error Mistakes that occurs in a lower court proceeding which may provide grounds for appeal.

Legalese Language used in the legal profession, as distinguished from plain English used by laypersons—examples are *heretofore, hereunder,* and other words designed to give an air of legality to documents, verbal exchanges, and correspondence.

Legal interoffice memorandum A written explanation of how the law applies to a given set of facts, usually from a client's situation. Also called a "memorandum of law."

Legally unimportant facts Facts that exist in a client's situation or a case but which are not key to the outcome of the case.

Legislative history The record of everything that happened in the legislature pertaining to a statute prior to its being enacted.

Legislative intent The intent or meaning that the legislature intended when it passed a law.

Letterhead The firm's stationery with the firm's contact information pre-printed on it.

Limited Treatment indicating that the citing court refused to extend the decision of the cited case beyond precise issues involved.

Limited jurisdiction A type of jurisdiction in which a court has the power to hear only certain types of cases.

For example, family law courts cannot hear criminal matters.

Liquidated damages Money awarded based on a prior agreement signed by the parties. In a contract, it is a stated amount that parties agree will be paid should a party default on the terms of the contract.

Litigation The process by which one contests an issue in a legal proceeding.

Local Rules of Court Rules for practice created by a court for proceedings within that court. These rules are based on the customs, usages, and character of the local people. These rules supplement but do not replace the Federal Rules of Civil Procedure.

Looseleaf services Information compiled in a ringed binder rather than a hardbound volume. These services are updated by replacing pages rather than inserting pocket parts at the end of a volume.

M

Majority opinion An opinion wherein a majority of the members joined in the decision.

Mandatory authority A rule of law established in a case that is binding upon all cases heard in lower courts of the same jurisdiction when faced with similar facts and issues. The law that a particular court must rely on in making its decision. For example, an Ohio court hearing an Ohio matter must rely on Ohio constitution, statutes, and case law.

Material Errors Errors made by a court which may have affected the court's or jury's decision.

Memorandum of Points and Authorities A type of brief filed with the court. Also called a "Brief in Support of . . ." and usually accompanies a motion.

Memorandum of disapproval A presidential action that serves as a public veto.

Memorandum of law An internal document in a law firm in which a paralegal or an attorney analyzes a client's legal position without arguing for a specific interpretation of the law.

Memorandum opinions A ruling of the court which contains little or no reasoning as to why the court decided as it did.

Misplaced modifier A word that is intended to modify or identify another word, but which is placed in a location that makes it difficult to determine what word it modifies.

Model acts Prototypes for statutes that may be adopted by legislatures. The purpose of model acts is to attempt to make laws uniform among the various jurisdictions. An example is the Model Business Corporation Act.

Modern Language Association (MLA) A writing format that is generally associated with writing in the liberal arts and humanities areas, such as in English, Philosophy, Theater, Music, Modern Languages, Religion, and History.

Modified block style A formatting style that places the return address, date, closing, and signature line slightly right of center. Each paragraph is indented five spaces.

Modifier A word or phrase that modifies something else.

Modify Partially change the results from the lower tribunal.

Moot No real controversy exists.

Municipal ordinances Laws enacted or adopted by a local municipality that set forth rules by which the government and the citizens must conduct themselves.

N

Necessary and Proper Clause A clause in the Constitution giving Congress the authority to make laws: "To make all Laws which shall be necessary and proper for carrying into Execution the foregoing Powers, and all other Powers vested by this Constitution in the Government of the United States, or in any Department or Officer thereof." (U.S. Const. art. I, § 8).

Negative treatment Cases that have overruled or distinguished the cited case.

Nominal damages A small or token amount of money that is awarded when no actual loss resulted, but a wrong was committed.

Nonrestrictive clause A word or clause that identifies something about a subject but does not limit or restrict the subject; it will not define any essential terms.

Notarization A certificate added at the end of a pleading when a signature needs to be authorized.

Novel questions Questions that a court within a jurisdiction has not considered.

O

Objectives The goals each party is trying to achieve through the litigation.

Official citation The citation to the case or other primary authority published by the government.

Official reporter Reporters published by the governmental entity rather than by a commercial publisher such as West, that do not contain any enhancements or annotations.

"On all fours" A prior opinion is "on all fours" when the facts and issues are substantially the same as the facts and issues currently before the court (or in the client's case). Also referred to as "on point" or "analogous."

On point The facts and issues in a case are similar to the facts and issues of the client's case. It is analogous to the client's case.

On point The facts of the case and the facts of the client's situation are sufficiently similar; also referred to as "analogous" or "on all fours."

Opinion The written explanation of how the court reached its holding.

Opinion letter A formal letter from an attorney to a client or other attorney explaining an attorney's interpretation of the law as applied to a factual situation.

Oral argument A presentation by the attorneys to explain the law and facts to the judges, who ask questions to clarify the issues in the case.

Ordinance A law created by legislatures of local governments, such as county councils, county commissioners, or city councils.

Original jurisdiction The power of a court that is the first to hear a case.

Outline A plan for writing that provides the structure and organization of a document before it is written.

Overrule A court refuses to follow its own previous ruling even though the precedent is similar in facts and rule of law.

Overruled The citing case expressly overrules or disapproves all or part of the case being Shepardized.

P

Pagination The process of numbering pages.

Parallel citations or references Citations reported in more than one location or source. Example: a case from the *Iowa Court of Appeals* that is also reported in the *North Western Reporter*.

Parallelism Similar structure, verb tense, or number is used in related words, phrases, or clauses.

Paraphrase To state someone else's ideas in your own words.

Passive Voice A writing style in which the subject of the sentence is being acted upon. For example: "The decision was made by the judge."

Passsim A term indicating that the author cited a particular authority on multiple pages, generally in excess of five pages.

Per curiam The court's written explanations of its decisions in given cases.

Periodical A book, newspaper, journal, or similar publication that is issued on a regular basis such as a legal newspaper, bar association journal, or law review.

Personal jurisdiction The power of a court over the parties, particularly the defendant, in litigation. Also known as *in personam* jurisdiction.

Personal pronoun A pronoun that identifies or replaces a noun that represents a person or group of people.

Persuasive authority Authority that a court is not required to follow, but may consider in reaching a decision. An example would be the decision of an Illinois court considered persuasive by an Indiana court.

Persuasive writing Writing that persuades or convinces another to adopt a certain point of view.

Petitioner The party who appeals.

Pinpoint citation A citation that takes the reader to the exact page where a quotation can be found.

Plagiarism The use of someone else's material without giving credit to the source or obtaining the author's permission to use the material.

Plain meaning The everyday meaning that an average person would attribute to words.

Plaintiff The person or entity that files a complaint and commences a lawsuit.

Pleadings Formal statements by the parties to the action setting forth their claims and defenses, such as a Complaint, Answer, or Counterclaim.

Plurality opinion An opinion from a group of justices who agree as to the outcome, but each has a different basis for the decision.

Pocket parts A method of updating legal material; generally a paperback or softcover supplement or pamphlet located in the back of the main text to provide current information until enough new information warrants a new hardbound volume.

Pocket part supplement A method that many publishers use to provide updated information that supplements the main volume of information.

Point Headings Headings of the major sections of the brief, which state the main topic of each section.

Prayer for relief The request of the plaintiff to the court for relief based on a cause of action.

Precedent A prior opinion involving the facts, issues, and rule of law sufficiently similar to the facts and issues and rule of law under current consideration, which can be used to guide the court's decision in the current case.

Predicate One of the two basic parts of a simple sentence. The predicate consists of the verb and all of the words that modify the verb or are governed by the verb, such as the direct object.

Predicate adjective An adjective that comes after an intransitive linking verb and which describes the subject.

Predicate noun A noun or noun phrase that follows the form of the "be" verbs, and that renames, or gives meaning, to the subject.

Predictive writing Writing that attempts to demonstrate or explain the likely outcome.

Prepositional phrase A phrase that consists of a preposition and a noun, pronoun, gerund, or clause. The phrase may also have modifiers. The prepositional phrase functions as an adjective or an adverb depending on the question the phrase answers.

Presidential determination or finding Determinations or findings that must be issued, as required by statute, before certain actions can be taken.

Presidential memoranda Documents issued by the president to members of the executive branch. There are three kinds of presidential memoranda: presidential determinations or findings, memoranda of disapproval, and hortatory memoranda.

Primary authority The law itself. Primary types of authority include constitutions, statutes, and case law.

Private international law Law governing issues between private persons based on circumstances that have significant relationship to multiple nations.

Private laws Laws that affect only one person or a small group of people rather than the entire population.

Privilege A rule of evidence that protects from disclosure certain information given within a particular relationship. Under the attorney-client privilege, whatever a client discloses to his or her attorney cannot be used as evidence against the client. If a paralegal accidentally discloses this material, it might be used as evidence by the opposing legal team. It is very important to remember to maintain confidentiality at all times, even during casual conversations.

Privileged Information given by a client that is protected from disclosure; a court cannot compel the attorney to disclose it. The client owns the privilege, and only the client can waive it.

Procedural facts Facts that pertain to the technicalities of bringing or defending in litigation.

Procedural history Information identifying what has happened in the process of litigation to date.

Procedural law Law governing the manner in which rights are enforced or procedures are followed by courts.

Proclamations A formal and public declaration by the president.

Public international law Questions of rights among nations, or between nations and the citizens of other nations.

Public laws Law dealing with the relationship between the people and their government, the relationship between the agencies and the branches of government, and the relationship between governments themselves such as taxes and bankruptcy laws, that affect all citizens.

Punctuation marks Marks that provide structure and organization to writing. Punctuation marks also signal pauses and different types of intonation.

Punitive damages A monetary award is over and above compensatory damages, to discourage a wrongdoer and others from engaging in the same activity. Usually awarded when it can be shown that the person committed the act with malice or evil intent.

Q

Quasi in rem Jurisdiction over a person's interest in property.

Query Instructions that a researcher gives to the computer to tell the computer search for and find specific information.

Questioned The citing opinion questions the continuing validity or precedential value of the case being *Shepardized* because of intervening circumstances. A case is often questioned because it may have been overruled by statute or another case.

R

Reasoning Summary of the reasons why a court reached the decision it reached.

Record The official materials of the pretrial and trial proceedings that includes pleadings, orders, exhibits, and a transcript of the testimony.

Reference list In APA format, the listing at the end of the paper that provides complete information on the sources referenced within the paper.

Reflexive pronoun A pronoun used to refer back to the subject of the sentence and usually ends in *–self* or *–selves*.

Regulation A law passed by an agency that is similar to a statute passed by the legislature.

Relative clause A clause that contains a subject and a verb and begins with a relative pronoun or a relative adverb. A relative clause functions as an adjective.

Relative pronoun A pronoun that introduces a subordinate clause. Examples of relative pronouns are *that, whose, which, who,* and *whom.*

Relevant facts Facts that are legally and factually important to the client's case; also referred to as "key facts."

Remand The case is sent back to the lower court to re-try the case or to enter a new decision based on the appellate court's instructions.

Repealed A pre-existing law is annulled, generally by the enactment of a newer law.

Replevin An action to recover possession of chattels (personal property) that was wrongfully taken.

Reporters Case books on both the federal and state levels containing appeals court opinions. A repository of the actual text of cases. Historically, this was a print volume; today a reporter can appear online or in digital media.

Rescission The cancellation of a contract because it was based on fraud or unilateral error.

Research trail A listing of the places where the researcher has been with proper citations to each of the sources checked.

Respondent The party who must respond to an appeal.

Restitution An attempt to place a party in their previous position they would have been in had the other party not acted wrongfully.

Restrictive clause A clause that defines something or adds information about the antecedent that is necessary to understand the sentence.

Reverse and remand An appellate level court changes the result from below and sends the case back to the lower tribunal for further proceedings based on the holding of the appellate court opinion.

Reversed The judgment from the lower tribunal has been revoked or set aside on appeal, reconsideration, or rehearing. The citing case reversed the case being Shepardized.

Revised Correcting or updating a pre-existing law.

Rule of law A pronouncement from the government that establishes a standard of conduct for all to follow.

Rule section The law section of a case brief where the authority upon which the court based its decision will be identified.

Rules of court Rules, generally issued by the court or by the highest court, that govern practice and procedure before a court.

Rules of law Legal doctrines that govern conduct.

S

Same case The citing case involves the same litigation as the case being *Shepardized*, but at a different stage in the proceedings.

Search engine spamming Pages created deliberately to trick the search engine into offering inappropriate, redundant, or poor-quality search results.

Secondary authorities Authorities that summarize, paraphrase, or otherwise discuss the law, but are not the law itself.

Sentence fragment An incomplete sentence that does not contain both a subject and a verb, or that contain both the subject and a verb but the idea is incomplete. An example of a sentence fragment is "Among the reasons the defendant pled guilty."

Separation of powers The division of the power of the federal government into three separate branches: the executive, legislative, and judicial.

Service of process A method of giving notice to the defendant that a lawsuit has been filed against him or her.

Session laws Laws that are passed during a session of the legislature. The laws are presented chronologically as passed and then, at the end of the session, are codi-fied into the statutory scheme of the state or federal systems. The collected statutes that are enacted during a session of a legislature, whether state or federal.

Shepardize The Shepard's service provides information such as parallel citations, subsequent history, validity of the source, and additional leads to other law. One method to confirm that the law is still "good law," and verifies that it hasn't been overruled, questioned, or otherwise compromised.

Short form A citation form that is used if the case has been completely identified, so that the reader can easily find the full citation.

Sic A note indicating to the reader that an error originated in the source material. *Sic* is placed in brackets immediately behind the word that has the mistake.

Signal phrases Signals consisting of multiple words to direct the reader to additional information.

Signals Markers that indicate important information is to follow.

Signatory One who signs a document.

Slip law Official publication of statute shortly after it has been passed by the legislature. It is are admissible in court as evidence of the statute's passage.

Slip opinions The opinion sent to the printer on the day when the bench opinion is released by the court

Specific performance An equitable remedy in which a party is compelled to perform its obligations under a contract.

Split infinitive An infinitive (a phrase that has the word *to* and a verb) that is split by an adverb placed between *to* and the verb.

Spoliation Willful destruction of evidence.

Squinting modifier A modifier that appears to identify both the words before and after it.

Standing to Sue Having an interest in the case because the party was injured or has an interest that was adversely affected.

Stare decisis A doctrine from Latin that means "let the decision stand." Judicial decisions stand as precedent for cases that arise in the future as long as they involve similar issues or facts. In other words, if the same or similar legal issues are presented, even though by different parties, the decision of the previous court should be used as precedent.

Statute of limitation The time frame within which a lawsuit may be filed.

Statutes Laws that are enacted by the United States Congress and state legislatures as session laws and which are codified by subject.

Stop Words Words that, when used in a Westlaw query, are too common for the computer to use.

String Citations Groups of citations that together support a proposition.

Style Manual A set of guidelines or standards created for writing, designing, and citing within written works.

Subject A noun that carries out the action in the sentence.

Subject matter jurisdiction The power of a court to resolve a particular type of matter.

Subpoena A court order for someone to appear before the court.

Subpoena *duces tecum* An order requiring attendance and requiring one to bring or make available requested documents.

Subscription service A service that provides information, but has a fee attached.

Substantive facts Facts that pertain to the rights and obligations of the parties.

Substantive law The law that defines duties, rights, and responsibilities, and the conduct expected of citizens in general. For example, traffic laws that govern the operation of motor vehicles are substantive laws.

Suit A case brought in court.

Summons The document that informs the defendant that he or she has been sued and advises of a date when a response is due. A summons generally accompanies a complaint. The process by which the defendant is brought within the jurisdiction of the court.

Supersede To replace, or take the place of.

Superseded On appeal, reconsideration or rehearing, the citing case supersedes or is substituted for the case being *Shepardized*.

Supplement To add to something.

Supremacy clause Article VI of the U.S. Constitution states, "This Constitution, and the Laws of the United States which shall be made in Pursuance thereof . . . shall be the supreme Law of the Land; and the Judges in every State shall be bound thereby, any Thing in the Constitution or Laws of any State to the Contrary notwithstanding."

Syllabus or synopsis A one-paragraph summary of a court opinion, usually identifying how the case arrived at the current point within the legal system. It is usually found only in an unofficial reporter from West.

T

Table of Authorities A list of references, such as cases, statutes, and rules, in a legal document, along with the page numbers on which the references appear.

Table of Contents A detailed listing of the sections of the brief, along with the page numbers upon which each section begins.

TAPP A system of research originally developed by Lawyers' Cooperative that suggested the researcher look for terms that describe **T**hings, **A**ctions, **P**ersons, and **P**laces.

Templates Standard form documents; also called boilerplate documents.

Tenth Amendment An amendment to the U.S. Constitution that reserves to the states any powers not delegated to the federal government: "The powers not delegated to the United States by the Constitution, nor prohibited by it to the States, are reserved to the States respectively, or to the people." (U.S. Const. amend X).

Terms and connectors A type of query used by Westlaw that has four parts: terms, alternate terms, expanders, and connectors.

Thesaurus A book that provides synonyms and antonyms.

Thesis statement A condensed version of the main idea of the document. The thesis statement is usually no more than one or two sentences long and is presented in the first paragraph of the document.

Three-tiered A system consisting of a trial court, and intermediate appeals court, and a final appeals court.

Thumbnail brief A shorter brief than the comprehensive brief containing the citation, key facts, issues, holdings, reasoning, and disposition.

Titles Divisions of the federal statutes; each title represents a topic under which the statutes are placed when codified.

Tolling Suspension of the time limit for taking action, such as a statute of limitations.

Topic An area of the law defined by West editors for organizing the headnotes in the key numbering system.

Topic method Researching by using the topics within a source to find information.

Topic sentence A sentence that introduces the issues or sub-issues and connects them to the thesis paragraph.

Transfer binders Binders sent by publishers periodically to transfer or move the full text cases out of the main binders for ease in handling and reading.

Transition sentence A sentence that provides the reader with the connection from one paragraph to the next.

Transitional word A word that brings two ideas together so that the information is cohesive. Examples are *consequently, in addition, also,* and *furthermore.*

Transmittal letter Letters that generally accompany other documents and provide information about the documents transmitted. These are also generally called cover letters.

Treatises Texts that legal scholars have written, focusing on a single legal subject.

Treatment When another case cites the viewed case, something is said about the viewed case, or information is given on how the case is used by a different court in a different case.

Trial brief A type of legal writing that is presented to the court to argue in favor of a client's position or against the opposing position. The purpose of this document is advocacy.

Trial courts The courts where cases are originally heard.

True positive treatment Treatment indicating that a case has been expressly followed by another case.

Two-tiered Court systems consisting of a trial level court and one appeals level court.

U

Unauthorized practice of law (UPL) Representing a client or giving legal advice without a license to do so. Only licensed attorneys can practice law; anyone else who gives legal advice or performs other functions without authority is engaging in UPL.

Unicameral A legislature having only one body or one house, such as the Nebraska legislature.

Uniform Law A prototype for a statute that has been created by the Uniform Law Commission and whose purpose is to create immediate uniformity on a particular topic among the states. Examples are the Uniform Probate Code and the Uniform Limited Partnership Act.

United States Bankruptcy Courts Courts of exclusive jurisdiction that hear only bankruptcy matters.

United States Circuit Courts of Appeal Courts of intermediate appeal in the federal court system.

United States Code (U.S.C.) The official source of federal statutes.

United States Code Annotated (U.S.C.A.) The unofficial source of federal statutes published by West Publishing Company.

United States Code Service (U.S.C.S.) The unofficial source of federal statutes published by Lawyer's Cooperative and later by LexisNexis.

United States Court of Federal Claims A court that decides private claims against the United States where individuals seek monetary compensation.

United States District Courts The trial courts in the federal court system.

United States Supreme Court The highest court in the federal court system.

Universal character A character, usually asterisk (*), to replace a letter when doing a Westlaw search.

Unofficial The text of law published by a publishing company and not by the governmental entity from which the law originates.

Unofficial reporters Reporters published by a commercial publisher that may contain annotations, enhancements, or other tools to use in the research process.

Unpublished opinions Each system in the federal appellate court system determines its own rules to determine which opinions are published. Unpublished opinions do not set precedent.

Update To confirm that the source is still valid or still good law.

V

Vacate The court's action dismissing a case.

Vacated The citing case vacated or withdrew the case being *Shepardized.*

Validate To make sure that law is valid or to affirm that the source is still "good law."

Venue The specific geographical area over which the court has the authority to litigate and determine a case. The location where the case will be tried. Venue may be based on factors such as where the parties are domiciled, where the action took place, or where the crime was committed. Venue must not be confused with jurisdiction, which implies the inherent right of the court to legally decide a particular type of case.

Verb tense Information regarding when the action of the verb takes place. Examples are present tense, past tense, and future tense.

Verification A certificate added to pleadings to attest to the authenticity of a signature.

W

Waived A right or alternative has been given up.

Webinars A web-based seminar conducted over the Internet.

Wherefore clause A clause requesting action by the court on the plaintiff's behalf. Also called the prayer for relief.

Works Cited Page In MLA format, the page that lists the sources cited within the paper.

Writ of certiorari A formal written request to have the U.S. Supreme Court review a case; the decision to review the case is at the Court's discretion.

INDEX

A

abbreviations
in reporters, 328
Shepard's, 399–400
for validating research, 397
abrogation, 401
academic resources, 175
accept/except, 468
acknowledgment, 609
acronyms, 135
active voice, 449–450, 545
adjectives, 452
adjudicate, 41
adjudication, 352–353, 360
administrative agencies
computer-assisted legal
research for, 364–369
definition of, 350
enabling statutes, 350, 352
examples of, 350–352
executive departments as, 352
federal, 16, 28, 354–359
heading of, 352
hierarchy of, 350–351
history of, 352
independent, 352
local, 369, 372–373
overview of, 349–354
regulations created by, 352
state, 29, 369
administrative code, 90, 369
administrative decisions
classification of, 91
definition of, 354
description of, 360, 362
finding of, 365–369
online methods for
finding, 365
purpose of, 5, 82, 491
sample, 361–362
short citation forms for,
150–151
updating of, 99
administrative hearings, 91, 362

administrative law
definition of, 354
description of, 28, 88–91
federal, 354–359, 371
in *Federal Register,* 355–359
making of, 354–359
publishing of, 355–359
researching, 362–363
state, 369, 371–374
administrative law judges, 16, 74,
360, 488
administrative matter, 3
Administrative Procedures Act,
69, 74, 352
administrative regulations
in Code of Federal Regulations, 150, 354, 362–363
definition of, 150, 354
description of, 88
federal, 16, 67, 69, 88
in Federal Register, 88,
150, 354
purpose of, 5, 82, 491
short citation forms for, 150
state, 74, 90–91
administrative remedies,
exhausting of, 28
admission, requests for,
631–632
advance sheets, 172, 321, 402
adverbs
conjunctive, 462
definition of, 452, 458
advice letter. *see* opinion
letters
advisory opinions, 91
affect/effect, 468
affidavits, 546
affirm, 314
affirmative defense, 618
affirmative sentence, 545
affirmed, 400, 557
already/all ready, 469
alternate terms, 180

ALWD Citation Manual
administrative materials,
150–151
annotations, 154
Bluebook, The and, differences
between, 115–116
case citations, 132–141
description of, 7, 15, 40, 111
encyclopedias, 151–152
federal courts, 138–139
history of, 115
Internet, 140–141
local rules, 150
names of parties in case
citations, 133–136
primary authorities,
132–141
reporters, 137–138
secondary authorities,
150–159, 195
short citation forms,
141–151
signals, 123–124
state courts, 139–140
state rules, 150
structure of, 116
treatises, 152–154
typeface conventions, 132
Amber Alert, 61, 289
amended, 287
amended pleadings, 620–621
American Alliance of
Paralegals, 228
American Association for
Paralegal Education,
3, 228
American Bar Association, 18,
74, 128, 173, 227
American Digest System,
237, 240
American Jurisprudence, 6, 9,
151, 200, 202–203, 285
American Law Institute,
216, 285

American Law Reports
  background of, 209–213
  case searches from, 499
  checklist for using, 215
  citation format for, 213
  description of, 9, 100, 154
  index of, 211–213
  multivolume indices in, 212
  online, 213, 215
  in print format, 213, 215
  researching in, 213–215
  series in, 210
  table of contents for, 213
  Table of Jurisdictions, 214
  updating of, 214
  value of, 215
American Psychological
    Association, 124,
    126–127
amici curiae, 343, 566
amicus curiae briefs, 566–567
among/between, 469
analogous, 102
analogous cases, 524–525
analysis
  case, 93–96, 525–526
  counteranalysis, 166, 498, 505,
    512, 529
  crane, 525
  elements of, 525
  "if-then," 528
  legal, 269
analysis section
  of internal memorandum,
    521–530, 549
  of opinion letter, 596
angle brackets, 467
annotated, 182, 273
annotated code, 280
annotated sources, 194
annotations
  American Law Reports. see
    American Law Reports
  definition of, 280
  description of, 197
  federal codes, 64, 66
  state codes, 73
  for state statutes, 281

for United States Code
    Service, 280
  updating of, 214
answer
  to complaint, 618
  to interrogatories, 630
antecedent, 455
APA. *see* American
    Psychological Association
apostrophes, 464
appeal
  definition of, 556
  interlocutory, 557
  oral argument with, 568
appellant, 314, 556
appellate briefs
  components of, 563–564
  description of, 31, 131, 512,
    537–538
  ethical considerations in
    preparing, 570
  filing of, 558
  formatting of, 559–561, 563
  internal memorandum
    of law converted into,
    569–570
  jurisdiction statement, 564
  local rules for, 563
  as persuasive writing, 556
  rules for, 561–563
  time limits for, 557–558
  word count certificate,
    565–566
appellate court(s). see also
    specific court
  common law from, 314
  intermediate, 39–40
  issues addressed by, 557
  material errors, 557
  state, 331
appellate court judges, 557
appellate jurisdiction, 43
appellate process, 314–315
appellee, 556
appendix
  exhibits included in, 554
  external briefs, 554
  internal memorandum, 533

application section, of IRAC case
    brief, 501
appositives, 460
Archivist of the United States, 276
argument section, of external
    briefs, 549–551
Article I courts, 318
Article III courts, 317–318
articles, 452
Articles of Confederation, 59
assignment
  internal memorandum,
    513–514
  legal writing, 446–447
Associates Justice, 32
Atlantic Reporter, 9, 39
attestation, 609
attorney-client privilege,
    19, 164
attorney-client relationship, 19
attorney general, 246
attorney general opinions, 157,
    246–250
attorneys of record, 343
authority
  failure to cite, 116
  legal, 396–397
  mandatory. *see* mandatory
    authority
  persuasive. *see* Persuasive
    authority
  primary. *see* primary
    authority/authorities
  secondary. *see* secondary
    authority/authorities
Authority Check, 397, 437, 439
authorizations, 633
Auto-Cite, 210, 413

B

balancing test, 527–528
bankruptcy, 327
Bankruptcy Reporter, 327
bar associations, 228
*Bar Register of Preeminent
    Lawyers,* 263
bench trial, 331
between/among, 469

bicameral/bicameral legislature, 26, 28, 276
bill
  definition of, 276
  engrossed, 276
  enrolled, 276
  laws created from, 26–27, 84, 277
  legislative history of. *see* legislative history
billing statements, 590–591
Bill of Rights, 83, 272
binding authority, 102, 316
black-letter law, 200, 216
Black's Law Dictionary, 260–261
Black's Law Dictionary Digital Plus, 261–262
block quotation, 465–466
block-style formatting, 575, 585
Bluebook, The
  administrative materials, 150–151
  ALWD Citation Manual and, differences between, 115–116
  annotations, 154
  attorney general opinions, 157
  Bluepages, 113
  case citations, 133–136
  citation format in, 114
  description of, 7, 15, 40
  divisions of, 113–114
  encyclopedias, 151–152
  federal courts, 138–139
  history of, 111–112
  Internet, 140–141
  local rules, 150
  looseleaf services, 157–158
  names of parties in case citations, 133–136
  online, 114–115
  periodicals, 155–156
  primary authorities, 132–141
  reporters, 137–138
  Restatements, 154–155
  secondary authorities, 151–159, 195
  short citation forms, 141–151

  signals, 123–124
  state courts, 139–140
  state rules, 150
  structure of, 116
  for treatises, 152–154
  typeface conventions, 132
  updating of, 114
Blue Book of Supplemental Decisions, 212
Blue Tips, 114
body of letter, 582–585
boilerplate, 203, 256, 472, 607
books
  code, 6, 73, 281
  form. *see* form books
  short citation forms for, 152–154
  state code, 73, 281
Boolean connectors, 174
Bouvier's Law Dictionary, 260
brackets, 467
Braswell v. City of El Dorado, 55–56
brief(s)
  amicus curiae, 566–567
  appellate. *see* appellate briefs
  case. *see* case brief
  comprehensive, 188
  external. *see* external briefs
  IRAC, 188
  thumbnail, 188
  trial. *see* trial briefs
brief blank, 555
"Brief for the Petitioner," 557
brief the case, 288
Bureau of National Affairs, 240, 365
Burton's Legal Thesaurus, 261
businesses, in case citations, 136

C

cabinet, 26, 350
candor, 19, 61, 128, 165–166, 231, 395, 507
canon law, 49
caption
  of case, 335, 485–486
  definition of, 38

  of external briefs, 538–539
  of pleadings, 608, 613
case(s)
  commonwealth v. party format, 340
  definition of, 15, 314, 394, 396, 491
  ex parte party name format for, 341–342
  ex rel. party format for, 341
  LexisNexis searches, 322
  parts of. *see* case parts
  party v. party format of, 339–340
  purpose of, 491
  reading of, 74
  in re party format for, 340–341
  sample, 335–338
  short citation form for, 141–142
  state v. party format of, 340
  treatment of. *see* treatment
  United States v. party format of, 340
case analysis, 93–96, 525–526
casebook, 15
case brief
  administrative agency appeal, 488
  candor toward the tribunal application to, 507
  commentary section of, 498–499
  considerations for, 507
  CRRACC, 480, 505–507
  definition of, 513
  disposition section of, 497–498
  11-part, 480–481, 485–499
  ethical considerations, 507
  facts section of, 489–490
  format of, 480
  holding section of, 494–495
  IFRAC, 480, 503–505
  IRAC. *see* IRAC case brief
  issues section of, 490–494
  objective of, 480

case brief (*Continued*)
  objectives and theories of
    parties, 486–487
  organization of, 480
  parties section of, 485–487
  procedural history section of,
    487–488
  reasoning section of, 495–497
  sample, 481–483
  updating section of, 499
case caption, 538–539
CaseCheck+, 397, 437–438
case citations. *see also* citation(s)
  ALWD Citation Manual rules
    for, 132–141
  Bluebook, The rules for,
    133–136
  definition of, 334
  elements of, 66–67, 133
  federal courts, 138–139
  format of, 67
  Internet, 140–141
  names of parties in, 133–136
  reading of, 66–67
  state courts, 139–140
  tips for, 209
case law. *see also* common law
  creation of, 315
  definition of, 15–16, 48, 86
  enacted law versus, 270
  equitable law, 50–51
  federal, 16, 327. *see also*
    federal courts
  fee-based services for finding,
    329–330
  finding of, 317–334
  Internet services for finding,
    329–330
  judicial remedies, 51–58
  precedent created from, 2, 16,
    74, 86, 315
  reporters used to find. *see*
    reporters
  state, 331–334, 402. *see also*
    state courts
CaseMAKER, 190, 397, 437
Casemaker Consortium, 190
case name, 339–342

case of first impression,
  15, 104, 195
case or controversy, 30
case parts
  attorneys of record, 336, 343
  caption, 335, 485
  concurring opinion in, 345
  date of decision, 335, 342
  decision, 345
  description of, 68–69, 484
  disposition, 335, 338
  dissenting opinion in, 345
  docket number, 335, 342
  example of, 481–484
  headnote, 335, 342–343
  key number, 335
  opinion, 336–338, 343–344
  parties. *see* parties
  position of justices, 338, 345
  separate opinion, 338, 345
  syllabus, 335, 342, 485
  synopsis, 335, 342, 485
  topic, 342
  writing justice, 336, 343
case reporters, 6
cause of action, 42, 486, 614
central form file, 256
Central Intelligence Agency,
  351–352
cert granted, 401
certificate of service, 553–554
certified mail, 580–581
chancellors, 51
characterizing facts, 490
charter
  definition of, 49–50, 75,
    92, 301
  example of, 76, 302
  purpose of, 5, 82, 92, 491
  state law from, 75–76
  United Nations, 387–388
chattels, 54
checks and balances, 26
Chief Justice, 32
circuit courts, 35
citation(s). *see also* case citations;
  short citation forms
  constitutions, 142–143, 275

  definition of, 7, 111, 131, 286,
    334, 395–396, 485
  embedded, 118–119
  federal courts, 138–139
  federal rules, 149
  formats of, 7, 9
  goal of, 111
  indications for, 116–117
  intermediate courts of appeal,
    39–40
  Internet, 140–141
  local rules, 150
  looseleaf services,
    157–158, 254
  non-legal, 124–127
  official, 8, 332
  parallel. *see* parallel citations
  parts of, 334
  periodicals, 230
  pinpoint, 7, 138, 527
  placement of, 117–119
  punctuation used in, 8
  purposes of, 485
  questions to be answered
    by, 112
  reasons for importance, 111
  rules, 149–151
  session laws, 148
  signals in, 123–124
  spelling of, 8
  state cases, 402
  state courts, 139–140
  state rules, 150
  state statutes, 73, 144
  state supreme court cases,
    40
  state trial courts, 38
  statutes, 8, 73, 144–145,
    290–291, 400
  string. *see* string citations
  unofficial, 8
  U.S. Constitution, 60
  U.S. Courts of Appeals
    cases, 32
  U.S. Supreme Court cases, 34,
    67, 138–139
  when to use, 116–117
citation clause, 118

citation manuals
    ALWD Citation Manual. see
        ALWD Citation Manual
    Bluebook, The. see
        Bluebook, The definition
        of, 111
    purpose of, 112
    types of, 111–112
citation sentence, 118
citation services, 333
citators
    definition of, 393, 396
    federal, 403
    KeyCite. see KeyCite
    regional, 403 Shepard's. see
        Shepard's
    state, 400–403
    topical, 410
    types of, 434, 437–440
    United States, 403
cite check, 395
cited case, 396
citing case, 396
city council, 303
civil case
    definition of, 3, 36
    IFRAC brief for, 505
civil dispute, 93–94
civil judicial actions, 366
civil law, 48
civil penalties, 367
civil statutes, 15
client interview, 3, 612–613
code
    administrative, 369
    definition of, 26, 64
code books, 6
code name, 144–145
Code of Federal Regulations
    administrative regulations
        in, 150, 354, 362–363
    definition of, 71, 280
    description of, 9, 16, 70, 88,
        150, 279
    organization of, 359
    revisions to, 359
    sample page from, 71, 89, 360
    updating of, 98, 363

code year, 146
codification, 281
codified session laws, 143, 279
codified statutes, 84–85
collective nouns, 454
colon, 463
comma, 460–462
comma splice, 462
commentary, 498–499
Commerce Clause, 25
Commerce Clearing House, 365
common law. see also case law
    appellate courts as source
        of, 314
    court opinions as, 314–317
    definition of, 16, 48, 314, 396
    description of, 66, 314
    mandatory, 102–104, 316
    origins of, 48–50
    persuasive, 104–107
    reasoning from, 495
    remedies under, 51–54
    state, 74
"Commonwealth of," in case
        citations, 135–136
commonwealth v. party case
        format, 340
compensatory damages, 52
complaint
    answer to, 618
    counts included in, 615–616
    definition of, 41, 611
    electronic filing of, 616–617
    elements of, 613–618
    filing of, 616–617
    gathering facts for, 612–613
    parties identified in, 613
    prayer for relief, 616
    signature of, 616–617
    statutes of limitation,
        611–612
    summons with, 618
    wherefore clause, 616
compound predicates, 452
compound sentences, 450
compound subject, 452, 454
comprehensive brief, 188
computer-assisted legal research

administrative regulations,
        364–369
    description of, 11–12, 140
conciliatory, 591
conclusion section
    of external briefs, 551
    of internal memorandum,
        529–530, 533
    of IRAC case brief,
        502–503, 523
    of opinion letter, 596
concurrent jurisdiction, 42
concurring opinion, 34,
        344–345, 494
conference committee, 292
confidentiality, 18–19,
        164–165, 600
confidentiality statement, 474–475
confirming letters, 588–589
conflict of interest, 19
conflicts of law, 104
Congress
    agency creation by, 88
    bicameral body of, 276
    description of, 26, 60
Congressional Index, 299
Congressional Information
        Services, 298
Congressional Record, 62
conjunctive adverb, 462
connected case, 400
connecting language, 287
connectors
    LexisNexis, 185
    Westlaw, 181–182
constitution(s)
    capitalization with, 143
    citations for, 142–143, 275
    definition of, 59, 83, 271
    law creation from, 5, 15, 82
    purpose of, 491
    research in, 273–276
    short citation form for,
        142–143
    state, 72–73, 84, 98, 273, 281
    updating of, 98
    U.S. Constitution. see U.S.
        Constitution

Constitutional Convention, 98
"constitutional courts," 34
context facts, 95
contextual summary, 434
conventional international
    law, 384
coordinating conjunction,
    460
copy notations, for letters,
    586–587
Corbin on Contracts, 223–224
Corpus Juris Secundum, 6, 9, 116,
    151, 200–201, 203
Corpus Juris Secundum
    West, 285
correlative expressions,
    451–452
correspondence, legal
    audience of, 578
    block-style formatting of,
        575, 585
    content of, 578
    email, 474–475, 599–602
    ethical considerations in,
        576–578
    faxes, 475, 599–602
    features of, 575–587
    formatting of, 575–587
    letters. *see* letter(s)
    modified block style,
        575–577
    types of, 574, 587–598
counteranalysis, 166, 498, 505,
    512, 529
counterargument, 505
counts, 615–616
court(s). *see also specific court*
    federal. *see* federal courts
    hierarchy of, 29–40, 488
    litigation in, 28
    state. *see* state courts
    trial, 35–38
Court of International Trade,
    30, 35
court rules. *see* rules of court
courts of equity, 51
cover letter, 587
crane analysis, 525

criminal action, 94
criminal case
    definition of, 3, 37
    identifying of, 136
    name of, 340
criminal penalties, 367
criticized, 399
cross-references, 287
CRRACC case brief, 480,
    505–507
current index, 253
Current Law Index, 229
*Current Law to Legal
    Periodicals,* 229
customary law, 384

D

*Daily Compilation of Presidential
    Documents,* 376
damages
    compensatory, 52
    definition of, 52, 486
    exemplary, 52–53
    liquidated, 54
    nominal, 54
    punitive, 52
dangling modifier, 459
date, 146, 461, 579–580
date of decision, 335, 342
debt collection, 592–593
Decennial Digests, 237–238
decisions
    administrative. *see* administra-
        tive decisions
    affirming of, 314, 394
    date of, on case, 342
    definition of, 315
    federal law from, 72, 91
    international law from, 384
    modifying of, 394
    National Labor Relations
        Board, 370
    remanding of, 314, 394
    reversing of, 314, 394
    state law from, 74–75, 91
    U.S. Supreme Court, 318
declarations, 546
defendant, 37

defense, 486
defensive sentence, 545
demand letters, 574, 591–595
denial, 486
depositions, 625–626
depublication, 407
depublished opinion, 315
desk book, 305
dicta, 317, 497
dictionaries, legal
    description of, 2, 100
    history of, 260
    researching with, 261–262
    short citation forms for,
        156–157
    specialized, 261
    updating of, 260–261
    value of, 260–261
digests. see also specific digests
    American Digest System,
        237, 240
    definition of, 179, 237
    headnotes in, 237, 240,
        329, 333
    history of, 237, 240
    jurisdiction of, 241
    on LexisNexis, 242–244
    list of, 238
    purpose of, 197, 333
    researching in,
        240–245, 329
    sample topics in, 239
    specialized, 240
    state, 333
    synopsis in, 237, 240
    table of cases, 242
    on Westlaw, 242–243
digital signatures, 552
direct object, 452
directories, 262–264
direct quotation, 525
disclaimer, 600–601
discovery
    definition of, 624
    depositions, 625–626
    description of, 624–625
    interrogatories, 626–630
    purpose of, 625

requests for entry on land, 630–631

requests for physical and mental examination, 632–633

requests for production, 630–631

disposition, 497–498

dispositive motion, 622

dissenting opinion, 34, 344–345, 400, 494

distinguished, 399, 405

district courts, 29–31. *see also* U.S. Courts of Appeals

diversity jurisdiction, 41–42

diversity of citizenship, 103, 613–614

docket number, 335, 342

domicile, 41

draw, 590

E

eBay v. Merc-Exchange, 57

editing
  internal memorandum, 533
  legal writing, 470–471

effect/affect, 468

ejectment, 54

elements, 490–491, 522, 524

ellipses, 120–121, 465

email, 474–475, 599–602

Emancipation Proclamation, 93, 379

embedded citation, 118–119

employment record authorizations, 633

enabling statutes, 350, 352

enacted law
  administrative regulations. *see* administrative regulations
  case law versus, 270
  categories of, 270
  constitutions. *see* constitution(s)
  court rules, 270
  definition of, 269–270
  description of, 48, 59
  determination of, 186

federal, 102, 271

mandatory, 101–102

mandatory authority, 270–271

model codes, 270

naming of, 61–62

ordinances, 270

in *Shepard's* online version, 418

in *Shepard's* print version, 407–410, 414–415

statutes. *see* statutes

uniform laws, 270

en banc opinions, 344

enclosure notations, for letters, 585–586

encyclopedias, legal
  American Jurisprudence, 6, 9, 151, 200, 202–203, 206–207, 285
  characteristics of, 199
  Corpus Juris Secundum, 6, 9, 116, 151, 200–201, 203, 207
  description of, 100, 197, 199
  functions of, 204
  general, 199–203
  key words, 199
  national, 199–203
  researching with, 204–209
  short citation format for, 151–152
  specialized, 203–204
  state, 204
  tips on using, 206–208

engrossed bill, 276

enhancements, 10

enrolled bill, 276

Environmental Protection Agency
  consent decrees, 367–369
  enforcement methods, 365–367

equitable law, 50–51

equitable remedies, 54–58

equity
  courts of, 51
  definition of, 51

equivocal language, 530

error of law, 394, 556

"Esq.", 581

ethical dilemmas, 19–20

ethical violations, 164

ethics
  appellate briefs and, 570
  candor, 19, 61, 128, 165–166
  case brief preparation and, 507
  confidentiality, 18–19, 164–165
  in research, 18–20, 163–166
  secondary authorities and, 231
  unauthorized practice of law, 18–19, 163
  validating research and, 395
  in writing, 128

except/accept, 468

exclusive jurisdiction, 30, 42

executive branch
  federal, 26, 350–351
  state, 28

executive departments, 352

executive materials
  executive orders. *see* executive orders
  finding of, 374, 376
  presidential memoranda, 374, 382–383
  proclamations, 374, 379, 381–382
  sample of, 375–376

executive orders
  description of, 82, 93
  federal, 374, 377–379
  purpose of, 5, 491
  state, 379–380
  updating of, 99

exemplary damages, 52–53

exhaust administrative remedies, 28

exhaustion of remedies, 488

exhibits, 554

expanders, 181

ex parte, 622

ex parte party name case format, 341–342

explained, 401

explanatory facts, 95, 489, 521

ex post facto, 316
ex rel. party case format, 341
external briefs
  advocacy language used in,
      567
  appendix, 554
  argument section of, 549–551
  case caption, 538–539
  certificate of service, 553–554
  components of, 538
  conclusion section of, 551
  date of, 552
  introduction, 543–544
  oral argument, 568–569
  overview of, 537–538
  preliminary statement, 543
  proofreading of, 568
  signature of, 552
  statement of facts, 544–546
  statement of issues, 547–548
  summary of the argument, 549
  table of authorities,
      541–543
  table of contents, 539–541
  writing of, 567–568

F

fact gaps, 524
facts
  alternate terminology used to
      describe, 95–96
  analyzing of, 13, 94–95
  in case brief, 489–490, 504
  categories of, 521
  characterizing, 490
  context, 95
  definition of, 94, 489
  explanatory, 95, 489, 521
  gathering of, 95
  in IFRAC case brief, 504
  in internal memorandum,
      520–521
  issues and, 525
  key, 95, 489–490, 518, 521
  as key elements, 490
  legally unimportant, 95
  nonessential, 489
  procedural, 489

questions of. *see* factual
    questions
  relevant, 95, 489
  statement of, 522, 544–546
  substantive, 489–490
  unessential, 521
fact statement, 592–593, 596
factual questions
  creation of, 95
  examples of, 96
  identifying of, 3–4, 96
Fair Labor Standards Act, 14
Fastcase, 190, 397, 439
faxes, 475, 599–602
federal administrative
      agencies, 16
federal administrative law,
      354–359, 371
Federal Appendix, 325
Federal Aviation
      Administration, 352
federal case law
  description of, 16
  researching, 327
Federal Claims Reporter, 327
Federal Communications
      Commission, 351–352
federal courts. see also
        specific court
  Article I, 318
  Article III, 317–318
  citations to, 138–139
  Court of International
      Trade, 30
  description of, 28
  of general jurisdiction, 42
  governance of, 91
  hierarchy of, 30, 87, 318
  jurisdiction of, 41–42
  levels of, 86–87
  researching case law, 327
  schematic diagram of,
      30, 87, 318
  specialized, 34–35
  structure of, 30, 87, 318
Federal Deposit Insurance
      Corporation, 351
Federal Digest, 238

federal government
  administrative agencies, 16, 28
  checks and balances, 26
  executive branch of, 26,
      350–351
  judicial branch of, 27–28,
      350–351
  legislative branch of, 26,
      350–351
  overview of, 25–26
  separation of powers, 26
federalism, 14, 25, 276
federal judges, 29–31
federal jury instructions,
      255–256
federal law
  composition of, 64
  definition of, 14
  statutes. *see* statutes
  U.S. Constitution. *see* U.S.
      Constitution
Federal Practice Digest, 238, 329
Federal Register
  administrative law in, 355–359
  administrative regulations in,
      88, 150
  definition of, 354
  description of, 9, 16, 355–356
  organization of, 356
  researching in, 359
  rules and regulations in, 359
  sample page from, 70,
      357–359
  searches in, 69–70
Federal Register Index, 356, 359
federal regulations
  Code of Federal Regula-
      tions. see Code of Federal
      Regulations
  GPO Access, 363–364
Federal Reporter, 6, 9, 16, 323
federal rules
  citations to, 149
  description of, 304–305
  reporter for, 327
Federal Rules Decisions, 327
Federal Rules of Appellate
      Procedure, 92, 304

Federal Rules of Civil Procedure, 60, 92, 304–306, 607–608, 611, 615, 618, 621–622, 625, 627, 632

Federal Rules of Criminal Procedure, 92, 306

Federal Rules of Evidence, 304

Federal Rules Service, 307

federal statutes
  annotated versions of, 279
  creation of, 276–280
  description of, 15
  research in, 288
  sources of, 278

Federal Supplement, 9, 31, 66, 327

fewer/less, 469

finding tool, 209

Findlaw, 12, 140, 173

Findlaw Forms, 260

First Amendment, 82

Fletcher Cyclopedia Corporations, 203

font, 608

Food and Drug Administration, 352, 364

foreign names, in case citations, 136

formal adjudications, 91

Formal Administrative Action, 366

form books
  background on, 256, 258
  boilerplate forms, 256
  disadvantages of, 607
  list of, 257
  online access to, 260
  purpose of, 197
  researching with, 258–260
  state requirements, 259
  templates, 256

Full Faith and Credit Clause, 104

G

gender pronouns, 457

General Digest, 200, 238, 242

general index, 188, 281, 289

general jurisdiction, 42

geographic terms, in case citations, 135–136

gerunds, 453

GlobalCite, 397, 434, 438

good/well, 469

Google, 168, 173

Google Scholar, 175

government
  branches of, 25–29, 350–351
  federal. *see* federal government
  levels of, 25–29
  state, 28–29

GPO Access, 363–364

grammar
  in emails, 602
  in faxes, 602
  modifiers, 452, 458–459
  noun-pronoun agreement, 455–457
  parts of sentences, 452–453
  subject-verb agreement, 453–455
  verb tense, 457–458

H

H. Prang Trucking Co., Inc. v. Local Union No. 469, 57–58

hanging indent, 127

harmless errors, 314, 557

header, 579

heading(s)
  in legal writing, 450
  in letter, 578–579
  in pleading, 608
  point, 539, 549–550
  in table of contents, 539

headnotes
  definition of, 182, 287, 342, 494
  in digests, 237, 240, 329
  KeyCite, 424
  LexisNexis use of, 330
  numbering of, 342
  preparation of, 343
  in unofficial reporters, 494

hearing, notice of, 622–624

hearsay, 557

historical notes, 279, 281

hits, 176

holding, 94, 494–495, 518

homophones, 471

hornbooks
  definition of, 100, 221
  features of, 222

hortatory memoranda, 382–383

House of Representatives, 28, 276, 280

I

Id., 141, 148, 153

idiom, 466

IFRAC case brief, 480, 503–505

"if-then" analysis, 528

incarceration, 367

in-chambers opinions, 322–323, 344

indefinite pronouns, 454–455

independent agencies, 352

Index to Foreign Legal Periodicals, 229

Index to Legal Periodicals & Books, 229

Index to Periodical Articles Related to Law, 229

indirect objects, 452

infinitive, 459

informal adjudications, 91

Informal Administrative Action, 366

informational letters
  appointment letters, 589
  billing statements, 590–591
  confirming letters, 588–589
  description of, 574
  invoice letters, 590
  transmittal letter, 587–588

information letters, 446, 589–590
  definition of, 51
  permanent, 56
  types of, 56

Internet

international law

internal opinions, 486–487

International Court of Justice, 388–389

injunctive relief, 367
in-line quotation, 527
in personam jurisdiction, 41
in rem jurisdiction, 41, 134
in re party case format, 340–341
interfiled looseleaf services, 250
interlocutory appeal, 557
interlocutory order, 624
intermediate courts of appeal,
        39–40
internal memorandum. *see also*
        interoffice memorandum
analysis section of, 521–530, 549
injunctions
    appellate brief created
        from, 569
    appendix, 533
    assignment, 513–514
    case analysis in, 526–527
    complex, 531–533
    conclusion section of,
        529–530, 533
    definition of, 512
    drafting of, 516–531
    editing of, 533
    facts section of, 520–521
    functions of, 512
    heading section of, 517
    issues section of, 517–520
    outlining of, 514–516
    proofreading of, 533
    purpose of, 512–513
    recommendations section of,
        530–531
    steps to completing, 513–514
    summary of issues, 533
    table of authorities, 532
    table of contents, 531–532
    conventional, 384
    definition of, 383
    overview of, 383–384
    private, 384
    public, 384
    researching, 384–389
    case citations for, 140–141
    citations for books from, 117
    code of ethics for, 128
    description of, 66

federal statutes on, 278
libraries on, 169–172
MLA format evaluations, 126
organization of information
        on, 169
permanence of, 169
quantity of information on,
        169
reliability of information on,
        175–176
research uses of, 167–169
secondary authorities on,
        158–159
statutes on, 148–149, 278
uniform laws on, 285
U.S. Constitution sources
        on, 274
use of, 169
weighing of material on,
        175–177
Internet Legal Research
        Group, 173
Internet research
    case law, 329–332
    non-subscription materials
        for, 172–178
    objectivity of, 178
    resources for, 173
    search engines, 174–175
    steps in evaluating, 177
    subscription services. *see*
        subscription services
    timeliness of, 178
    verification of, 176–178
    weighing of material, 175–177
interoffice memorandum.
        see also internal
        memorandum
    definition of, 3, 96
    description of, 17
    format for, 97, 448
    string citations used in, 122
    treatises cited in, 221
interrogatories, 626–630
intervening words, 455
in-text citations, 126
introductory statement, 543–544
invoice letters, 590

IRAC case brief
    application section of, 501
    conclusion section of,
        502–503, 523
    definition of, 480, 499
    description of, 188
    issue section of, 500, 523
    overview of, 499–500
    rule section of, 500–501,
        523
    sample, 503
issues
    definition of, 490, 500
    example of, 491–492
    facts and, 525
    identifying of, 494, 500–501
    in internal memorandum,
        517–520
    in IRAC case brief, 500, 523
    procedural, 493, 520
    statement of, 518–519,
        547–548, 595
    substantive, 493, 520
    writing of, 490–494, 519, 547

J

jargon, 466
Jones-Chipman Index to Legal
        Periodicals, 229
journals, 197
judges
    administrative law, 16, 74
    appellate court, 557
    definition of, 30
    federal, 29–31
    justice versus, 32
    panel of, 315
    selection process for, 29
    state, 29
    writing, 336, 343
judgment, 94
judicial branch
    federal, 27–28, 350–351
    state, 28–29
judicial history, 487–488
judicial remedies, 51–58
Judiciary Act of 1789, 29, 31
jurat, 609

jurisdiction
  appellate, 43
  concurrent, 42
  definition of, 2, 40
  description of, 40–41
  diversity, 41–42
  exclusive, 30, 42
  general, 42
  limited, 42
  original, 43
  personal, 41, 104
  in personam, 41
  quasi in rem, 41
  in rem, 41, 134
  subject-matter, 42, 104
jurisdiction statement, 564,
  614–615
jury instructions
  basics of, 253–254
  definition of, 253
  federal, 255–256
  legalese used in, 254
  researching with, 256
  sample, 255
jury trial, 331, 616

K

KeyCite
  applications of, 419
  cases, 419–425
  demonstration of, 431–434
  description of, 189, 219,
    396–397, 499
  headnotes, 424, 426
  limiting of, 424, 428–429
  sample results of, 423
  Shepard's and, comparison
    between, 434–437
  status flags, 419–420
  statutes, 425–429
KeyCite Alert, 421
key facts, 95, 343, 489–490,
  518, 521
key number, 10, 137, 189,
  287, 342
Key Number System
  definition of, 179, 200, 237, 240
  description of, 328–329, 435

KeyCite and, 422
  revisions to, 241
key topics, 10, 137
key words, 199, 286

L

*Labor Relations Cumulative
    Digest and Index*, 238
law(s)
  administrative. *see*
    administrative law
  bills becoming, 26–27, 84, 277
  canon, 49
  case. *see* case law
  categories of, 48–64
  common. *see* common law
  Congress' role in creating, 26
  constitutional. *see*
    constitution(s)
  creation of, 26–27
  enacted. *see* enacted law
  federal. *see* federal law
  finding of, 13
  hierarchy of, 64–77, 83, 496
  international. *see*
    international law
  primary sources of. *see*
    primary sources of law
  private, 64, 276
  public, 64, 276
  recognition of, 13
  rules of, 94
  secondary, 6
  secondary sources of, 5, 100
  session. *see* session laws
  slip, 64, 84, 147–148,
    276–278, 281
  sources of, 5, 82
  state, 14
  statutory, 64, 84–86. *see also*
    statutes
  types of, 82–93
  uniform. *see* uniform laws
law journals, 100, 224–228
law libraries
  assistance at, 167
  definition of, 10
  on Internet, 169–172

municipal codes, 304
  online, 11–12
  organization of, 166, 170
  permanence of, 166–167
  physical, 10–11
  quality materials in, 167
law reviews, 100, 197, 224–228
Lawyers' Edition, 322
layered indexing system, 253
lead/led/lead, 469
legal analysis, 269
legal authority, 396–397
legal dictionaries
  description of, 2, 100
  history of, 260
  researching with, 261–262
  short citation forms for,
    156–157
  specialized, 261
  updating of, 260–261
  value of, 260–261
legal doctrine, 83
legal encyclopedias
  American Jurisprudence, 6, 9,
    151, 200, 202–203, 206–
    207, 285
  characteristics of, 199
  Corpus Juris Secundum,
    6, 9, 116, 151, 200–201,
    203, 207
  description of, 100, 197, 199
  functions of, 204
  general, 199–203
  key words, 199
  national, 199–203
  researching with, 204–209
  short citation format for,
    151–152
  specialized, 203–204
  state, 204
legal error, 314
legalese, 254, 595–596
legal language, 449–450
Legal Looseleafs in Print,
  250, 365
legally unimportant facts, 95
legal newspapers, 228–230
legal periodicals, 100

legal research. *see* research
legal writing
  assignment, 446–447
  basics of, 17, 444–445
  drafting phase of, 449–452
  editing stage of, 470–471
  email, 474–475
  ethics in, 128
  faxes, 475
  functions of, 444
  goal in, 196, 450
  grammar. *see* grammar
  headings used in, 450
  information placement,
    448–449
  IRAC format for, 447
  language used in, 449–450
  length considerations, 447
  outline for, 447–448
  overview of, 444
  paragraphs, 450–452, 542–543
  prewriting stage of, 446–449
  process of, 445–452
  proofreading stage of, 470–473
  punctuation. *see* punctuation
  purposes of, 445
  resources for, 445
  rewriting, 446
  spell-checker used with,
    471–472
  for supervisor, 446
  thesaurus use in, 451
  thesis statement, 448
  time considerations, 446–447
  tone used in, 449
  vocabulary used in, 449–450
  voice used in, 449–450
  wordiness, 468–469
  word usage, 468, 470
legislative branch
  federal, 26, 350–351
  state, 28
legislative history
  creation of, 292
  definition of, 62, 280, 291
  example of, 62–63, 292–294
  foundational principles for,
    291–294

information sources about, 291
Public Law number, 294,
  298–300
researching, 294–301
  on Westlaw, 299–301
legislative intent, 280, 294
legislature, 276
less/fewer, 469
letter(s)
  appointment, 589
  body of, 582–585
  certified mail delivery of,
    580–581
  closing of, 585
  components of, 578–587
  confirming, 588–589
  copy notations, 586–587
  date format in, 579–580
  delivery instructions for, 580
  demand, 574, 591–595
  enclosure notations, 585–586
  headers in, 579
  heading of, 578–579
  horizontal listings in, 584
  information, 446, 574,
    589–590
  inside address, 580–581
  invoice, 590
  list of items in, 583–584
  mailing of, 580
  opinion, 512, 574, 594–599
  quotations in, 583
  reference (subject) line of,
    581–582
  salutation of, 582
  second page headings, 587
  signature block of, 585–586
  special mailing of, 580
  status, 590
  transmittal, 446, 574, 587–588
letterhead, 578–579
LEXCITE, 413
lex fori, 104
Lexis Advanced, 184
LexisNexis
  annotated comments, 182
  case law searches using,
    329–330

case searches on, 322
checklist using, 208
Court of Appeals opinions,
  325–326
description of, 11–12,
  140–141, 143, 146, 175
digests on, 242–244
forms from, 260
headnotes, 182
law journals on, 226–227
law reviews on, 226–227
Lawyers' Edition, 322
legislative histories on, 299
Restatements in, 220–222
searchable segments,
  243–244
search query for, 184, 216
Shepard's on, 412
table of authorities creation
  using, 532
treatises on, 223
uniform laws on, 285
LexisNexis Legal Communities,
  175
LexisONE, 12, 173
lex loci, 104
Library of Congress, 12, 173
limited, 400
limited jurisdiction, 42
liquidated damages, 54
List of C.F.R. Sections Affected,
  362–363
litigation, 28, 36
living will, 258–259
local administrative agencies,
  369, 372–373
local government, 303
local rules, 150, 539
local rules of court
  appellate briefs, 562
  appellate brief word count,
    565
  definition of, 554
  description of, 305
LoisLaw, 190, 397, 434
looseleaf publications/services
  citations to, 157–158, 254
  current index, 253

definition of, 249
foundation of, 249–251, 253
interfiled, 250
layered indexing system used by, 253
list of, 252
newsletter, 250–251
purpose of, 100, 197
researching in, 253
sample entries, 251
short citation form for, 157–158
transfer binders, 251
types of, 250
updating of, 172

M

Magna Carta, 49–50, 301
majority opinion, 344
mandatory authority
common law, 102–104, 316
definition of, 101, 195, 270, 316, 522
enacted law, 101–102, 270–271
federal enacted law as, 271
opinion used as, 105
persuasive authority versus, 195–196
manual research, 170–172
Martindale-Hubbell, 175, 285
Martindale-Hubbell Connected, 175
Martindale-Hubbell Law Digest, 238
Martindale-Hubbell Law Directory, 262–264
material errors, 557
medical authorization, 633
Megan's Law, 61, 289
memorandum/memoranda
of confirmation, 514
of disapproval, 382–383
internal. *see* internal memorandum

interoffice. *see* interoffice memorandum
of law, 3
of points and authorities, 512, 537
memorandum opinion, 344
mental examination, request for, 632–633
Michie's Legal Resources, 173
military cases, 327
Military Justice Reporter, 327
minus (-) sign, 174
misplaced modifiers, 458–459
MLA Handbook for Writers of Research Papers, 125
MLA Style Manual and Guide to Scholarly Publishing, 125
model acts, 285
Model Penal Code, 285
Model Rules of Professional Conduct, 18, 99, 128, 395
Model State Administrative Procedures Act, 74
Modern Federal Practice, 238
Modern Language Association, 124–126
modified, 400, 557
modified block style, 575–577
modifiers, 452, 458–459
moot, 30
motions, 619–624
municipal codes, 303
municipal law
charters. *see* charter
researching in, 303–304
municipal ordinances, 303

N

National Archives and Records Administration, 377
National Association of Legal Assistants, 228
National Center for State Courts, 35
National Conference of Commissioners on Uniform State Laws, 74, 283, 285

National Federation of Paralegal Associations, 228
National Labor Relations Board, 352, 365, 370
National Paralegal Association, 228
National Reporter Blue Book, 333
National Reporter System, 7, 328–329, 399
Necessary and Proper Clause, 25
negative treatment, 434
negligence, 491–492, 615
newsletter looseleaf services, 250–251
newspapers, legal, 228–230
Nicholson v. State, 10
19th Century Masterfile, 229
nominal damages, 54
nonessential facts, 489
non-legal citations, 124–127
nonrestrictive clause, 457, 460
North American Free Trade Agreement (NAFTA), 5
North Eastern Digest, 238
North Eastern Reporter, 9, 39
North Western Digest, 238
North Western Reporter, 9, 39
notarization, 609
Notes to Decisions, 279
notice of hearing, 622–624
nouns
collective, 454
predicate, 452
pronoun agreement with, 455–457
novel questions, 195
nutshells, 100

O

obiter dicta. see dicta
objections
to interrogatories, 629–630
to requests for admission, 632
objectives, 486–487
official citations, 8, 332

official reporters, 241, 318, 332, 401
on all fours, 102, 529
online libraries, 11–12
on point, 102, 403, 524
operational letters, 400
opinion(s)
    advisory, 91
    attorney general, 157, 246–250
    in case, 343–344
    common law based on, 314–317
    concurring, 34, 344–345, 494
    definition of, 94, 314
    depublication of, 407
    depublished, 315
    dissenting, 34, 344–345, 400, 494
    en banc, 344
    in-chambers, 322–323, 344
    internal, 486–487
    issues identified after reading, 494
    majority, 344
    mandatory authority use of, 105
    memorandum, 344
    per curiam, 344
    plurality, 344
    slip, 66, 318–319
    unpublished, 315, 325
opinion letters, 512, 574, 594–599
Opinions Relating to Orders, 323
oral argument, 568–569
Ordinance Law Annotations, 304
ordinances
    definition of, 5, 64, 77, 82, 92
    municipal, 303
    purpose of, 491
    Sheperdizing of, 408–409
    updating of, 99
original jurisdiction, 43

outline
    for internal memorandum, 514–516
    for legal writing, 447–448
    for telephone messages, 474
    for voicemail messages, 474
overrule, 103

P

Pacific Digest, 238
Pacific Reporter, 9, 39, 405–406
paragraphs, 450–452, 544
paragraph symbol, 146
paralegal
    roles of, 3–4
    skills needed by, 2–3
paralegal associations, 227–228
Paralegal Educator, The, 228
Paralegal Today, 228
parallel citations
    definition of, 116, 137, 332, 396, 405
    finding of, 333
    to Internet site, 158
    Shepard's report for finding, 417
    short form for, 142
    for state cases, 329–330
parallelism, 451
parallel references, 405
paraphrasing, 117
parentheses, 467
parties
    in case brief, 485–487
    in case citations, 133–136
    in complaint, 613
    example of, 335
    objectives of, 486–487
party v. party case format, 339–340
passim, 542–543
passive voice, 449–450, 545
Peer Review Ratings, 263
"People of," in case citations, 135
per curiam opinion, 344
period, 459–460

periodicals
    from bar associations, 228
    citations to, 230
    definition of, 194
    description of, 224–225
    indices for, 229
    law journals, 100, 224–228
    law reviews, 224–228
    from paralegal associations, 227–228
    purpose of, 197
    researching in, 228–230
    short citation form for, 155–156
    special interest publications, 228
permanent injunction, 56
personal jurisdiction, 41, 104
personal pronouns, 455–456, 464
persuasive authority
    common law, 104–107
    definition of, 96, 195, 316, 522, 529
    description of, 104
    mandatory authority versus, 195–196
    secondary, 106–107
    treatises used as, 221
persuasive writing, 537, 556
petitioner, 556
physical examination, request for, 632–633
physical libraries, 10–11
pinpoint citations, 7, 138, 330, 527
plagiarism, 106, 116
plain meaning, 294
plaintiff, 36
pleadings
    acknowledgment of, 608
    amended, 620–621
    caption of, 38, 608, 613
    definition of, 17, 607
    font used in, 608
    formatting, 608–611
    heading of, 608
    number formatting in, 608

pagination of, 611
responsive, 618–620
writing of, 608
plurality opinion, 344
plus (+) sign, 174
pocket parts, 98–99, 146, 172,
199, 281, 287–288
point headings, 539, 549–550
possessive form, 464
prayer for relief, 616
preamble of U.S. Constitution,
60, 271
precedent, 2, 16, 74, 86,
102–103, 315–316,
395–396, 399, 495
predicate, 452–453
predicate adjectives, 452
predicate nouns, 452
predictive writing, 537
preliminary statement, 543
preposition, 453
prepositional phrases, 453
president, 26
presidential determinations or
findings, 382–383
presidential memoranda, 374,
382–383
primary authority/authorities
ALWD Citation Manual for,
132–141
Bluebook, The for, 132–141
case law. see case law
cases. see case citations
definition of, 270, 522
description of, 48, 97–99
enacted law. see enacted law
federal courts. see federal
courts
reporters. see reporters
secondary authorities versus,
195–196
statutes. see statutes
primary sources of law
types of, 5, 15–16, 82
updating, 98–99
prior proceedings, 487
private international law, 384
private laws, 64, 147, 276

privilege
attorney-client, 19, 164
definition of, 19, 164
privileged information, 164
procedural facts, 489
procedural history,
487–488, 543
procedural issues, 493, 520
procedural law, 60
procedural statutes, 15, 60, 84
process, service of, 41
proclamations
federal, 374, 379, 381
state, 380, 382
prong test, 102–103
pronouns
gender, 457
indefinite, 454–455
noun agreement with,
455–457
personal, 455–456, 464
reflexive, 456
relative, 456–457
Proof of Facts series, 202
proofreader's marks, 473
proofreading
external briefs, 568
internal memorandum, 533
legal writing, 470–473
protection clause, 596
public international law, 384
Public Law number, 294,
298–300
public laws, 64, 147, 276
public policy, 527
publisher, 146
punctuation
apostrophes, 464
brackets, 467
colon, 463
comma, 460–462
description of, 459
ellipses, 465
parentheses, 467
period, 459–460
question marks, 465
quotation marks, 465–467
semicolon, 462–463

punctuation marks, 459
punitive damages, 52

Q

quasi in rem jurisdiction, 41
quasi-judicial decisions, 91
query, search
in LexisNexis,
184–185, 216
in Westlaw, 179–182, 216
questioned, 415
question marks, 465
questions of fact, 394. *see also*
factual questions
questions presented, 547
quorum, 32
quotation(s)
altering of, 120–121
block, 465–466
commas with, 461
ellipsis points in,
120–121
format for, 119–120
in-line, 527
in letters, 583
punctuation for, 119–120
sic added to, 121, 467
quotation marks, 465–467
QuoteRight, 430–431

R

reasoning, 490, 495–497
recommendations section, of
internal memorandum,
530–531
record, 31, 557
reference line, 581–582
reference list, 126
reflexive pronouns, 456
reformation, 56
regional citators, 403
regional reporters, 333–334
regulations. *see* administrative regulations; *specific
regulation*
regulatory agencies, 69
relative clause, 457
relative pronouns, 456–457

relevant facts, 95, 489

remand, 314, 394

remedies
  common law, 51–54
  damages. *see* damages
  equitable, 54–58
  injunctions, 56
  judicial, 51–58

repealed, 287

replevin, 54

reporters
  abbreviations used in, 328
  bankruptcy cases, 327
  definition of, 317
  description of, 137–138
  federal rules, 327
  military cases, 327
  National Reporter System, 7,
    328–329
  official, 241, 318, 332, 401
  regional, 333–334
  Supreme Court Reporter, 6, 9,
    15, 34, 321
  United States Reports, 6, 9,
    137, 318–320
  unofficial, 321, 332–333,
    494
  U.S. Courts of Appeals
    cases, 323
  U.S. District Courts cases, 327

representatives, 278

requests for admissions, 631–632

requests for entry on land,
  630–631

requests for physical and mental
  examination, 632–633

requests for production, 630–631

rescission, 56–57

research
  depth of, 186–187
  in digests, 240–245
  directories for, 263–264
  economical approach to, 3
  ethics in, 18–20
  federal case law, 327
  in federal statutes, 288
  with form books, 258–260
  general role of, 2–3

international law, 384–389

Internet. *see* Internet
  research

introduction of, 2

with jury instructions, 256

legal dictionaries for,
  261–262

in legal encyclopedias,
  204–209

legislative history, 294–301

in looseleaf publications/
  services, 253

manual, 170–172

municipal law, 303–304

paralegal's role in, 3–4

performing of, 12–17

in periodicals, 228–230

reporting of, 14

in Restatements, 217–221

results of, 189

rewards associated with, 20

role of, 2–3

rules of court, 306–307

in statutes, 286–290

steps of, 12–13

terminology of, 5

thesaurus for, 261–262

in treatises, 223

updating of, 13, 172

in U.S. Constitution,
  273–276

validating. *see* validating
  research

research process
  adversary's position, 189
  client's facts, 187
  finding, updating, 187
  initiation of, 94–96
  persuasive authority, 96
  questions to ask before
    starting, 186–187
  selection of law, 187–188
  steps involved in, 97, 187
  updating the search, 189

research pyramid, 198

research tools
  Internet, 167–169
  library. *see* law libraries

research trail
  definition of, 188–189,
    240, 286
  example of, 296–298

respondent, 556

responsive pleadings, 618–620

Restatements
  background of, 216
  black-letter law use of, 216
  description of, 100, 197
  electronic researching in,
    218–219
  in LexisNexis, 220–222
  on microfilm, 217
  organization of, 217
  in print format, 217
  researching in, 217–221
  short citation forms for,
    154–155
  topics covered in, 218
  on Westlaw, 221
  Westlaw access to, 217

REST database, 217

restrictive clause, 457

reverse, 314

reversed, 399, 557

revised, 287

root expander, 181

rule(s)
  citations for, 149–151
  Shepardizing of, 409–410

rule 34(b)(d)(e), 631

rulemaking
  adjudication versus, 352–353
  Administrative Procedures
    Act, 353–354
  federal, 355
  steps involved in, 355

rule of law, 94, 97, 491, 496

rule section, of IRAC case brief,
  500–501, 523

rules of court
  California, 541–542
  definition of, 304
  description of, 5
  federal, 304–305
  local. *see* local rules of court
  purpose of, 5, 491

researching, 306–307
state, 305–306
updating of, 99
rules of procedure, 304–306

S

salutation, 582
same case, 399
search engines, 174–175
search query
    for LexisNexis, 184–185
    for Westlaw, 179–182
secondary authority/authorities
    ALWD Citation Manual with,
        150
    American Law Reports anno-
        tations. *see* American Law
        Reports
    in analysis section, 529
    attorney general opinions,
        157, 246–250
    Bluebook, The with, 151–158
    books, 152–154
    definition of, 195
    description of, 98, 100–101,
        194–195
    digests. see digests
    directories, 262–264
    encyclopedias. see encyclope-
        dias, legal
    ethical issues, 231
    features of, 198
    hierarchy of, 123, 195
    on Internet, 158–159
    legal dictionaries. *see* legal
        dictionaries
    looseleaf services. *see* looseleaf
        publications/services
    periodicals. see periodicals
    persuasive, 106–107
    primary authorities versus,
        195–196
    reasons for not relying on,
        196
    researching in, 205
    Restatements. *see*
        Restatements
    treatises. *see* treatises

value of, 196
Words and Phrases, 100,
    245, 261
secondary law, 6
secondary sources of law, 5, 100
sections
    multiple, 146–149
    short citation forms for,
        145–146
section symbol, 114, 146
Securities and Exchange
        Commission, 352
semicolon, 462–463
Senate, 28
senators, 278
sentence(s)
    citation, 118
    commas used to clarify, 461
    compound, 450
    parts of, 452–453
    topic, 450
    transition, 451
sentence fragments, 450–451
separation of powers, 26
series items, 462
service of process, 41
session laws
    citations to, 147–148, 290–291
    codifying of, 279
    definition of, 61, 143, 277, 281
settlement offer, 594
settlements, 367
Shepardize(d)
    definition of, 98, 396, 398
    legal authorities subject to, 398
Shepardizing
    cases, in print version of
        Shepard's, 402–407
    checklist for, 404
    constitutions, 408
    definition of, 189, 290,
        499, 530
    electronically, 415–419
    errors in, 407
    from online versions, 415–417
    ordinances, 408–409
    from print versions, 414
    rules, 409–410

state constitutions, 408
    in states, 406–407
    topical citators in print, 410
    U.S. Constitution, 408
Shepard's
    abbreviations in, 399–400
    Alert, 411
    case validation using,
        398–400, 414
    description of, 397
    enacted law, 407–410, 418
    finding tool use of, 398
    format of, 403–404
    history of, 398
    KeyCite and, comparison
        between, 434–437
    on LexisNexis, 412
    materials of, 403
    online version of, 397,
        411–413, 415–419
    Pacific Reporter, 404–405
    parallel citations in,
        405, 417
    print version of, 402–410
    purpose of, 397
    report from, 417
    sample page of, 403–404
    signal indicators, 416,
        436–437
    state editions of, 400–402
    statute validation using, 400,
        414–415
    Table of Abbreviations, 399
Shepard's Federal Statute
        Citations, 388
short citation forms
    administrative decisions,
        150–151
    administrative
        regulations, 150
    annotations, 154
    attorney general opinions,
        157, 248
    books, 152–154
    cases, 141–142
    constitutions, 142–143
    date, 146
    definition of, 133

short citation forms (*Continued*)
  encyclopedias, 151–152
  Id., 141, 148, 153
  indications for, 141
  legal dictionaries, 156–157
  publisher name, 146
  Restatements, 154–155
  sections, 145–149
  state statutes, 144–145
  statutes, 143–145, 148–149
  subsections, 145–149
  supplements, 146
  title of the code in, 144–145
  treatises, 152–154
sic, 121, 467
signal phrases, 125
signals, 123–124
signatory, 609
signature
  of complaint, 616–617
  of external brief, 552
signature block, 552,
  585–586, 617
signature line, 608
slip laws, 64, 84, 147–148,
  276–278, 281
slip opinions, 66, 318–319
South Eastern Digest, 238
South Eastern Reporter, 9, 39
Southern Reporter, 39
South Western Digest, 238
South Western Reporter, 9, 39
spamming, 174
special interest publications, 228
specific performance
  definition of, 51
  uses of, 58–59
spell-checker, 471–472
split infinitives, 459
spoliation, 599
squinting modifier, 459
standing to sue, 30
stare decisis, 16, 103, 178,
  315–316, 395–396, 524
star paging, 329–330
state administrative law, 369,
  371–374
state attorney generals, 246

state case law, 16, 331–334, 402
state citators, 400–403
state code books, 73, 281
state common law, 74
state constitutions, 72–73, 84, 98,
  281, 408
state courts
  appellate, 331
  case citation format for,
    139–140
  description of, 28, 35, 87
  governance of, 91
  intermediate courts of appeal,
    39–40
  structure of, 88, 331
  supreme court, 40
  three-tiered system of, 35–36,
    88, 331
  trial courts, 35–38
  two-tiered system of,
    35, 37, 331
state digests, 333
state executive orders, 379–380
State Farm Insurance v.
  Campbell, 53–54
state governments, 28–29
state judges, 29
state law
  administrative decisions as
    source of, 74–75
  charter as source of, 75–76
  common law as source of, 74
  definition of, 14
  ordinances as source of, 77
  state constitutions as source
    of, 72–73
  statutes as source of, 73, 286
state legal encyclopedias, 204
state legislature, 292
statement of facts, 522,
  544–546
statement of issues, 518–519,
  547–548, 595
statement of practice
  summary, 264
"State of," in case citations, 135
state proclamations, 380, 382
state rules, 150, 409–410

state statutes, 73, 144–145, 147,
  280–281, 408
state v. party case format, 340
status letter, 590
statutes
  annotated versions of, 279
  citations for, 8, 143–145, 149,
    290–291, 400
  civil, 15
  codified, 84–85
  creation of, 276
  criminal, 15
  definition of, 7, 26, 60, 84,
    276, 279
  description of, 64
  elements of, 281–282, 522
  enabling, 350, 352
  example of, 282
  federal. *see* federal statutes
  finding of, 288–289
  identification of, 86
  Internet, 148
  KeyCiting, 425–429
  key word searches for, 289
  making of, 276
  popular name approach to
    finding, 289
  procedural, 15, 60, 84
  purpose of, 5, 82, 84, 491
  researching, 286–290
  Shepard's for validating, 400,
    414–415
  short citation forms for,
    143–145, 148–149
  state, 73, 144–145, 147,
    280–281
  substantive, 15, 60, 84
  title-based approach to
    finding, 289
  topic-based approach to
    finding, 289
  treatment of, 401
  uniform laws. *see* uniform laws
  updating of, 98
  validating, 400
statutes of limitation, 611–612
statutory law, 64, 84–86. *see also*
  statutes

stop words, 180
string citations
    citation order in, 122–123
    definition of, 121
    example of, 122
    indications for, 122
    in interoffice
        memorandum, 121
    signals in, 123–124
StyleCheck, 417
subject
    compound, 454
    definition of, 452–453
subject-matter jurisdiction, 42, 104
subject-verb agreement,
        453–455
subpoena, 51, 625
subpoena *duces tecum*, 625
subscription services
    costs of, 179
    definition of, 415
    description of, 12, 179, 278
    Westlaw. *see* Westlaw
subsections
    multiple, 146–149
    short citation forms for,
        145–146
substantive facts, 489–490
substantive issues, 493, 520
substantive law, 60
substantive statutes, 15, 60, 84
suit, 36
summary judgment, motion
        for, 624
summary of the argument, 549
summons, 41, 51, 618
Superfund penalties, 367
supersede, 210
superseded, 401
supplement, 146, 211, 287, 402
supplemental environmental
        projects, 367
supra, 153
Supremacy Clause, 14, 25, 271
Supreme Court. *see* U.S.
        Supreme Court
Supreme Court Reporter, 6, 9, 15,
        34, 321

Supreme Court Reports, 329
supreme court (state), 40
syllabus, 137, 488
syllogism, 548
synopsis, 137, 237, 342, 488

T

Table of Abbreviations, 399
table of authorities, 131, 416,
        532, 541–543
table of cases, 242
table of contents
    briefs, 539–541
    definition of, 539
    example of, 540–541
    external briefs, 539–541
    internal memorandum,
        531–532
    point headings, 539
TAPP method, 188
telephone communication, 474
templates, 256
temporary restraining order, 56
Tenth Amendment, 25, 28, 60,
        72, 83
Term Opinions of the Court, 320
terms, 180
territorial courts, 86, 318
text messaging, 475–476
than/then, 469
"the," in case citations, 135
TheLaw.net, 189
then/than, 469
thesaurus
    definition of, 2
    legal writing use of, 451
    researching with, 261–262
    value of, 260–261
thesis statement, 448, 522
THOMAS, 299
three-tiered court system, 35–36,
        88, 331
thumbnail brief, 188
title index, 281
title of the code, 144–145
titles
    in case citations, 135
    commas used with, 461

tolling, 612
tone, 449
topic, 189, 237, 342
topical citators, 410
topic method, 307
topic sentence, 450, 522
Total Client-Service Library,
        202–203
transfer binders, 251
transitional words, 460
transitions, 525
transition sentence, 451
transmittal letters, 446, 574,
        587–588
treaties, 384, 386–387
Treaties in Force, 388
treatises
    definition of, 194, 221
    description of, 82, 93
    examples of, 221
    features of, 221–222
    on LexisNexis, 223
    as persuasive authority, 221
    purpose of, 5, 100, 197, 491
    researching in, 223
    short citation forms for,
        152–154
    Table of Contents, 223
    updating of, 99
    on Westlaw, 223
treatment
    of cases, 398
    definition of, 398
    negative, 434
    of statutes, 401
    true positive, 399
trial
    bench, 331
    jury, 331, 616
trial briefs
    application of, 554
    checklist for, 555
    court rules used in preparing,
        554–555
    definition of, 17, 512, 537, 554
    drafting of, 555
    function of, 554
    preparation of, 555

trial courts, 35–38, 314, 331
true positive treatment, 399
two-tiered court system,
        35, 37, 331
typeface, 132

U

unauthorized practice of law,
        18–19, 163, 576
unessential facts, 521
unicameral legislature, 276
Uniform Commercial Code,
        284–285
uniform laws
    definition of, 283
    description of, 282–283
    purpose of, 100
    sources of, 285
    types of, 284–285
*Uniform Laws Annotated
        Directory of
        Acts West,* 285
*Uniform Laws Annotated
        West,* 285
unions, in case citations, 136
United Nations Charter,
        387–388
United Nations Documentation:
        Research Guide, 384
United States Code, 8–9, 15,
        65–66, 143, 273, 279, 288
United States Code Annotated,
        8–9, 64, 66, 143, 279
*United States Code Congressio-
        nal Administrative News
        Service,* 278, 280, 298
United States Code Service, 66,
        143, 273, 279–280, 306
*United States Code Service
        Advance Pamphlets,* 278
United States Law Week,
        9, 278, 318
United States Reports, 6, 9, 137,
        318–320, 397, 405
United States Statutes at Large,
        278, 280, 294, 408
*United States Supreme Court
        Reports,* 9

United States Treaties
        and Other International
        Agreements, 389
United States v. party case
        format, 340
universal character, 181
unofficial citations, 8
unofficial reporters, 321,
        332–333, 494
unpublished opinions, 315, 325
update, 97
updating, 499
U.S. Attorney General, 246
U.S. Bankruptcy Courts, 30, 67
U.S. Circuit Courts, 139
U.S. Claims Court, 34
U.S. Constitution
    amendments to, 83, 272
    annotated versions of, 64
    articles of, 271–272
    Bill of Rights, 83, 272
    citing to, 60
    description of, 15, 59, 83,
            271–272
    federal laws from, 64
    First Amendment, 82
    Internet sources of, 274
    interpretation of, 272–273
    mandatory authority and, 102
    preamble of, 60, 271
    purpose of, 5, 491
    research in, 273–276
    Shepardizing of, 408
    Supremacy Clause,
            14, 25, 271
    Tenth Amendment, 25, 28, 60,
            72, 83
    text of, 64
    updating of, 98
U.S. Court of Appeals for the
        Armed Forces, 35, 67
U.S. Court of Federal Claims, 30,
        34, 67
U.S. Courts of Appeals
    case citation format for,
            67, 139
    description of, 16, 28–29,
            31–32, 86

geographic boundaries of, 323
    structure of, 323, 325
U.S. District Courts
    case citation format for, 67
    description of, 29–30
    jurisdiction of, 86
    reporters, 327
    structure of, 326
U.S. Federal Circuit Court, 86
U.S. Government Manual,
        88, 359
U.S. Government Printing
        Office, 12, 147, 173,
        276, 278, 300, 365
U.S. Supreme Court
    case citation format for, 67,
            138–139
    decisions of, 318
    description of, 32–33, 86, 318
    federal rules of court created
            by, 91–92
    pagination of cases, 329
    slip opinions by, 318–319
    Term Opinions of, 320
    United States Reports, 6, 9,
            137, 318–320
U.S. Supreme Court Digest,
        238, 329
U.S. Tax Court, 67
U.S.C. *see United States Code*
U.S.C.S. *see United States Code
        Service*

V

vacate(d), 345, 399
validating research
    abbreviations, 397
    basics of, 395–397
    benefits of, 396
    citators for. *see* citators
    definition of, 393, 414
    definitions used in, 396
    error of law, 394
    ethics and, 395
    final steps for, 440
    importance of, 394
    KeyCite for. *see* KeyCite
    question of fact, 394